The Why and How of Home Horticulture

The Why and How of Home Horticulture

Second Edition

D. R. Bienz
Washington State University

W. H. Freeman and Company
New York

Library of Congress Cataloging-in-Publication Data

Bienz, D. R., 1926–
The why and how of home horticulture / D. R. Bienz.
p. cm.
Includes bibliographical references and index.
ISBN 0-7167-2353-0 (cloth).—ISBN 0-7167-2286-0 (paper)
1. Gardening. 2. Horticulture. I. Title.
SB453.B49 1993
635—dc20 92-46400
CIP

Printed in the United States of America

Third printing 1997, MB

Contents

Preface

In response to requests over the years by many users of the first edition, I have updated the text to include as much as possible the latest information for the home and classroom. The second edition of *The Why and How of Home Horticulture* retains the same organization and chapter headings as the first edition; however, notable changes have been made in both the text and illustrations, primarily to include new developments in technology and perspective. A section outlining the history of gardening has been added to Chapter 1. Considerable information on mulching, composting, rotation gardening, growing without pesticides and manufactured fertilizers, and other topics of interest to organic growers has been added to the chapter on soils, the chapters on the growing of individual crops, and "The Handbook." Discussions of integrated pest management, pesticide licensing, control of soil erosion, biotechnology and genetic engineering, tissue culture, plug transplants and other advancements in plant propagation, mode of action and horticultural uses of plant growth regulators, new developments in pruning practices, and a number of other recent technologically related innovations have been included or updated in appropriate chapters. In response to suggestions from several instructors who used the first edition, "Questions for Review and Discussion" have been added at the back of the book; these refer to material covered in each chapter. Also the list of references at the end of each chapter has been completely revised and updated to include those references most appropriate and currently available. Throughout, information has been updated and many of the illustrations have been changed or replaced to reflect modern trends and developments. I hope with these additions and changes that the book will continue to offer an exciting and insightful presentation of modern home horticulture.

I have resisted adding a separate chapter on "organic gardening" because basic requirements for plant growing are the same regardless of how we label our farming and gardening techniques. The principles and most of the practices of plant growing delineated in this text apply whether or not the grower chooses to use pesticides and manufactured fertilizers.

My gratitude is extended to the many individuals who have encouraged, suggested improvements in, and otherwise assisted with the preparation of the second edition. Special thanks is due Professors Robert A. Miller and Edward G. Kirby, who reviewed the entire manuscript during its preparation and made numerous helpful suggestions. I thank the staff of W. H. Freeman and Company, including Alice Fernandes-Brown and Julia DeRosa, and especially Christine Hastings, who has had the difficult task of coordinating the manuscript and illustration review and revision process, of prodding the completion of necessary details, and of final preparation of the manuscript for publication. My son, Robert, furnished a number of photographs and has had the unenviable task of producing publishable prints from my slides and my often imperfect attempts at photography. Finally I express deep appreciation to my wife, Betty, who, as with the first edition, has reviewed the added and changed manuscript for grammar and clarity, who has helped with library research and attended to countless details that only one who has written a book can know, and who has encouraged and put up with her husband through the preparation of two editions of this text.

D. R. Bienz
May 1992

Preface to the First Edition

When, as a result of the enthusiasm for gardening that developed in the early 1970s, I was asked to teach an elective, introductory horticulture course for nonmajors, I soon discovered that no appropriate textbook existed. The excellent introductory texts available for students of commercial horticulture did not focus on the interests of home gardeners, and the numerous books written about gardening included little of the scientific horticulture necessary for understanding fundamental reasons for horticultural practices. Consequently, I developed my own syllabus, "Horticulture for the Homeowner Who Wants to Know Why."

Although this hurriedly written syllabus was far from polished and was never advertised for sale, I soon began receiving requests for copies from many parts of the country. Former students, instructors of horticulture and biological sciences at several universities and community colleges, and friends who are gardeners encouraged me to expand the syllabus into an illustrated book suitable both as a classroom text and as an informational guide for serious gardeners. What began as a minor revision eventually resulted in a rewriting of the syllabus, augmented with new information, additional chapters, and many illustrations. The outcome is this text, *The Why and How of Home Horticulture.*

The first thirteen chapters are organized in a sequence that can be used as the informational basis for a three-hour semester or a five-hour quarter course in home horticulture. The introductory chapters are concerned with reproduction, development, propagation, and planting. These are followed by chapters that deal with the relation of environmental elements to horticultural production and chapters that describe kinds of gardens and individual garden crops.

Although the chapters are sequential, each is a relatively complete unit, and they do not necessarily need to be studied in order. For example, during the fall semester I usually schedule the classes on landscaping after the material in the first four chapters has been presented, thus landscape plantings can be observed before they are covered with snow. During warm autumns the chapter on pruning may need to be assigned later so that trees and shrubs will be dormant for concurrent laboratory practice. For the same reason, when spring is early, pruning may need to be scheduled earlier than it would be if the text chapters were assigned in sequence.

The first thirteen chapters contain considerable practical information, but most of the instructions for gardening procedures are contained in "The Handbook," Chapter 14. Assembling the how-to-do-it information in one place provides a convenient garden reference and also permits, in the first thirteen chapters, a presentation of the sequential pageant of gardening that is more coherent because it is not so frequently interrupted with practical examples.

No specific section is delineated for laboratory work, but a semester or quarter of laboratory exercises, including propagating, planning, planting, storing, processing, and other activities, could be designed based on the descriptive material in "The Handbook."

It is my hope that serious gardeners not involved in academia will also find this book understandable, interesting, and useful. I would suggest they read the first thirteen chapters in sequence, relating the information in each chapter to their own experience. They should then read through "The Handbook" to become acquainted with its contents so it can be used as a reference when specific gardening needs arise.

I thank the many individuals who have contributed assistance and encouragement during my preparation of this manuscript. Naming them all would be impossible, but I would like to recognize especially F. E. Larsen and E. W. Kalin, who contributed parts of "The Handbook" and reviewed sections of the manuscript; R. L. Hausenbuiller, K. N. Nilsen, and K. A. Schekel, who also reviewed sections of the manuscript; Gunder Hefta, who reviewed the entire manuscript; and Patricia Brewer and Susan Weisberg, who spent countless hours correcting and editing.

I also thank Margaret Gurtel, who assembled most of the index and a considerable portion of the glossary and did library research for many of the tables, and my daughter, Marianne, who assisted with library research, glossary organization, preliminary typing, almost all of the final draft typing, and, perhaps most important, enthusiastic encouragement. Above all I thank my wife, Betty, who edited much of the manuscript, in several drafts, for grammar and clarity, who typed preliminary drafts, and who provided patient encouragement during the years of manuscript preparation.

I also thank the many who, over the years, have inspired me with the knowledge and appreciation of plant growing, especially my father, Rudolph Bienz, and Professors J. E. Kraus, Earl New, Leif Verner, and G. W. Woodbury.

D. R. Bienz
August 1979

CHAPTER

1

Plants and People

With much of the native flora of the world's cities replaced by concrete and brick, urban dwellers no longer live and work in intimate contact with the plant growth that provides the oxygen they breathe, the clothes they wear, the food supply they find so abundantly and conveniently displayed in their supermarkets, and even the rubber, plastic, and upholstery for the cars they drive. Yet almost without exception, people want to be near green foliage. Thriving flower and plant shops, carefully tended indoor and outdoor home gardens, trim lawns, popular natural parks and walkways, and the use of plastic foliage where live plants cannot be maintained attest to the human affection for plants. Some individuals may not be enamored of the work associated with making plants grow, but almost everyone enjoys a garden environment.

AGRICULTURE, GARDENS, AND CIVILIZATION

Our desire to be with plants may derive from ancient need. Human existence has always been dependent on food and fiber from plants or from the animals that feed on plants. Archaeological evidence suggests that in earlier times humans procured food by hunting, fishing, and gathering plant products. Obtaining enough to eat required almost every waking hour and also considerable area. For example, before Europeans came to Australia, during a season of normal climate each Australian aboriginal hunter/gatherer required six square miles to procure an adequate amount of food, and more during years of low precipitation. Distances involved in gathering food limited the size of groups living together to about ten.

Progress in human culture required the cooperative association of larger groups of people with some leisure time and thus paralleled the adoption of practices that increased the amount and availability of food. The use of fire, the art of cooking, and the invention of containers were among the more important of these practices. The most significant advances in food procurement however, and the ones that led to the development of what we term civilization, were the domestication of animals and plants and the art of cultivation. The more reliable food supply ensured by cultivation and herding and the physical security of community life provided opportunities for people to pursue occupations other than farming, as well as time to create and enjoy art and music, to develop writing, and to pursue learning and hobbies, including ornamental gardening.

Cultivation and the Progress of Human Culture

The earliest conclusive evidence of plant cultivation and domestication is dated about 7000 B.C. in Turkey and Iraq, where wheat and barley were the staple crops. The idea of cultivating plants seems to have begun in Egypt, Ethiopia, and east Asia at about the same time as or shortly after it began in the Turkey–Iraq region. Wheat and barley seeds are the oldest food products archaeologically associated with cultivation, although some agricultural historians believe that vegetatively propagated crops such as sweet potatoes and manioc—for which no direct evidence would remain—may have been cultivated earlier in more humid tropical climates. Archaeological evidence dates the first seed cultivation in the Americas fifteen hundred years later, about 5500 B.C., in southern Mexico, where a civilization arose that depended on beans, corn, and squash as its basic cultivated crops. At the same time an advanced, well-organized society whose major food crop was potatoes was developing in Peru.

In the Middle East, three cultivated river valleys were the centers of highly advanced ancient civilizations. Unique and very efficient irrigation cultures arose in the Nile, Indus, and Tigris–Euphrates valleys. The chronology of the Egyptian civilization, preserved in hieroglyphic writings, reveals that its agricultural economy was based on the annual flooding of the Nile River. Flooding provided not only irrigation water but also fertilizer in the form of a thin layer of mud. The annual flooding also leached away salts that tend to accumulate and make the soils of some arid regions unfit for cultivation (see "Crop Damage from Dissolved Chemicals" in Chapter 6). Besides wheat and barley, the staple food crops, Egyptian farmers grew dates, figs, other subtropical fruits, and most of the vegetables known in the Old World before the time of Columbus. During later periods of Egypt's cultural dominance, complex religious orders owned and farmed large tracts in cooperative arrangements akin to certain modern communal agricultural ventures. The Egyptians also prized ornamental plants, and the populace had enough leisure to establish and enjoy public and private parks and gardens (Figure 1-1). The Egyptian civilization was the center of world culture for almost four thousand years, from 6000 to 2000 B.C., and its agricultural advancements and productivity were not surpassed until the nineteenth and twentieth centuries.

There was considerable interaction among the peoples of Egypt and those of the Indus Valley and the Tigris–Euphrates area (Mesopotamia), where the Babylonian and Assyrian civilizations depended on an intricate series of canals that irrigated almost 7 million acres (2.8 million hectares) and supported a population many times that of the region today. The Hanging Gardens of Babylon, which Pliny classed as one of the seven wonders of

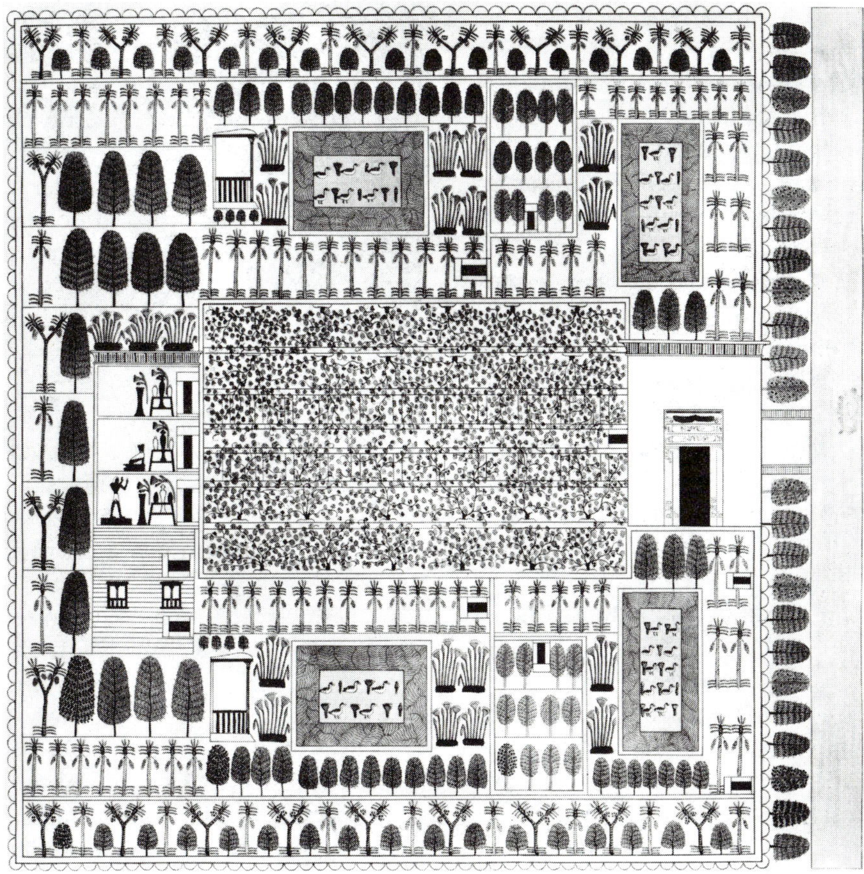

FIGURE 1-1 • Tomb painting showing the garden of a wealthy Egyptian official from the time of Amenhotep III. (From P. L. Carpenter et al., *Plants in the Landscape*, 2nd ed., W. H. Freeman and Company, New York, copyright © 1990)

the ancient world, and the detailed carvings of grains, fruits, and vegetables on public buildings and burial vaults demonstrate the importance of agriculture to Mesopotamian society.

The civilization of Mesopotamia domesticated cows between 6000 and 5000 B.C. and horses before 3000 B.C. The use of draft animals advanced farming efficiency and freed some of the workforce that had been engaged in food production to follow other pursuits. The domestication of horses also enhanced military efficiency and undoubtedly played a role in instituting slavery. Dominant societies used horses to raid less powerful neighbors and bring home captives. Although a few became concubines or household servants, most of the captives were forced to till the fields. The barbarities of a slave-based agricultural economy persisted in Europe through the Greek and Roman periods and in the "New World" until late in the nineteenth century.

The ancient civilizations of east Africa and central and southeast Asia are not so well documented as those of the Middle East, but there is evidence of early, highly developed cultures in all these areas. One of the early centers of plant culture, long neglected by Western scholars, is China. China's highly advanced civilization began five thousand years ago, domesticating such crops as rice, peaches, apricots, and many cucurbits.

It is no accident that ancient civilizations arose in the areas where they did. The successful growing of crops requires sufficient light, warm temperature, adequate irrigation water, a growing medium (usually soil), and a method of renewing the fertility of that medium. If some members of society are to be released from farming to pursue other activities, the location must also provide a means of transporting food from producers and marketing it to consumers. Egypt's desert climate supplied light and heat, and the Nile River provided irrigation water and renewed the soil's fertility. The relative ease of river transport encouraged the development of urban markets along the banks of the Nile.

The swamp on which modern Mexico City was built is another example of a location suited for the development of cultivation. Crops were grown there in ancient times on artificial islands in the shallow lake around which a city was built. Heat and light were abundant at this sunny site, and water and mud dipped from the lake supplied irrigation and renewed soil fertility. Boats carried the produce from island farms to lakefront markets (Figure 1-2).

Plant domestication and improvement continued with the Greeks, Romans, Persians, Byzantines, and in cultures in east Asia, Africa, and the Americas. Even when an empire perished, and its war machines, language, and literature were no more, the plants it had developed remained to enrich the gardens of succeeding civilizations. After Rome fell in the fifth century, its traditions of cultivation survived in the gardens of the Byzantine Empire and of Christian monasteries. From the fifth to the fifteenth century, the finest gardening and probably the most advanced agriculture could be found in China and other parts of east Asia. In the thirteenth century Marco Polo described the elegance of Chinese gardens in his remarkable account of his travels. Many gardens of that period are still maintained around Buddhist and Hindu temples in China, India, and southeast Asia.

FIGURE 1-2 • Farming on an artificial island: a farming system similar to that employed by the ancient Mexicans. Near Bangkok, Thailand, crops are currently being produced on islands created from soil from a swamp. (Courtesy of Helen Tremblay/Peter Arnold, Inc.)

Modern Technology and Agricultural Development

Spurred by the Renaissance and the European discovery of America, leadership in the development of agricultural technology moved west. The sixteenth-century explorations brought together plant heritages of Europe, Asia, and the Americas, and when these were combined the number of cultivated species almost doubled. The opening of large tracts of land in the Americas and later in Australia and New Zealand, along with the gradual evolution of the European feudal system into a free-enterprise social order, ushered in the age of the small farmer and stimulated the invention of implements that could be powered by draft animals.

Nonetheless, even by 1800 agriculture had changed little from what it had been at the peak of Egyptian civilization. In 1790, over 90 percent of American families earned their livelihood directly from farming. The hoe, the scythe, and the rake were still the principal implements of cultivation. Grain was still threshed by driving a team of oxen over sheaves spread on canvas and allowing the wind to blow away the chaff. The vegetable, fruit, and flower cultivars of the time would have been judged to be of rather poor quality by today's standards.

Then, two nineteenth-century developments and the technological progress they engendered brought more changes to agriculture than had occurred over the previous six thousand years. The first of these was the use of fossil fuels and the invention of the steam and internal combustion engines. The steamboat and steam-powered railroad helped open vast areas to farming in the Americas and Australia. Rapid and efficient transportation enabled the specialized production of crops in the areas in which they grow best. Steam engines and, later, petroleum-fueled tractors, along with the farming implements they powered, greatly increased the amount of land that one grower could farm.

The second of these developments was the Morrill Act. Signed into law by President Abraham Lincoln in 1862, the act set aside U.S. government lands to provide an endowment for the establishment of a college of agriculture and mechanical arts in each state. For the first time in human history, agriculture was recognized as a legitimate subject for advanced study. The three cooperating divisions into which land-grant universities were organized — teaching, research, and extension — permitted, to an extent hitherto impossible, the experimentation necessary for the acquisition of new information and better techniques for growing and marketing agricultural products and the dissemination of that information and those techniques to growers.

The development of fossil-fuel energy and the experimentation and education encouraged by the Morrill Act (and the agricultural research and training fostered in other countries that modeled programs on the successful American legislation) led to a virtual revolution in agriculture. The application of basic chemistry and physics to soil science helped identify the chemical elements required by plants and the mechanisms by which they are absorbed and utilized. In turn, fertilizers that have multiplied the yields of almost all crops could be synthesized. Techniques for controlling many of the most destructive crop pests were developed. With the discovery of the principles of genetics came higher-yielding, better-quality, and pest-resistant cultivars. The benefits of genetic crop improvement, initially limited primarily to agriculture in the developed world, have more recently averted widespread famine in South Asia and some other countries of the Third World as a result of the high-yielding cultivars developed at the International Wheat and Rice Institutes.

Each advance in technology — fertilizers, pesticides, improved cultivars, mechanization, new storage techniques, more rapid transportation, mass marketing — has enabled growers of crops to farm larger acreages and to produce greater quantities. Between 1790 and 1940 the percentage of the North American workforce directly dependent on farming for a living dropped from 90 to 20 percent. In 1968 about 6 percent of the workforce grew food for the United States and Canada, and in 1993 about 2.5 percent were engaged in on-the-farm production. Many others earn their living from occupations related to agriculture: the manufacture and distribution of farm machines and of the motor fuels and lubricants needed to operate them; equipment repair; the development, testing, manufacture, and distribution of pesticides and fertilizers; the storage, processing, packaging, transport, and marketing of food and fiber; the provision of services for millions of avocational growers, that is, gardeners; the planning and planting of parks, recreational areas, and indoor and outdoor home beautification projects; and the research, education, and extension needed for those engaged in farming and related activities.

One alarming trend that has continued since the immigrant settlement of North America has been the failure to recognize the finite limits of agricultural resources and the resulting destruction of farmland and pollution of water resources. Large tracts of land are irretrievably lost to crop production each year by conversion to urban and industrial uses. Much of the urban development in North America is in the areas most suitable for growing high-value horticultural crops: Orange and San Diego counties in California, north central Florida and the Florida coast, the shores of the Great Lakes, Long Island, central New Jersey, the Willamette Valley of Oregon, the lower Fraser Valley of British Columbia, and the Salt River Valley of Arizona, to name a few. Many counties with large urban populations have purchased development rights or used other means to preserve farms in suburban areas, but even more must be done if enough land to grow food and fiber for the greater populations of future generations is to be kept in production. (The ravages of erosion—frequently the result of unwise farming practices—and the loss of irrigated farmland to the accumulation of salts and alkalinity are discussed in Chapters 5 and 6.)

Modern Technology and Ornamental Horticulture

During the Renaissance, many of the European nobility enlisted the services of acclaimed architects and construction engineers to design formal gardens, some of which still survive. These gardens often encompassed vast areas of trees planted in straight rows, severely clipped hedges, and geometrically shaped flower beds, as well as numerous statues and fountains (Figure 1-3). Estate owners competed to be the first to grow exotic plants discovered in distant lands being visited for the first time by European explorers. Explorations undertaken solely or partially for the purpose of bringing new plants back to Europe were sponsored by Renaissance gardeners. When glass became available, glass conservatories were constructed so that tropical plants could be added to plant collections. These structures were called *orangeries* in recognition of the most common fruit plant grown in them.

FIGURE 1-3 • A private estate's formal garden at The Cliffs, in Oyster Bay, Long Island. (Courtesy of Michael Mathers/Peter Arnold, Inc.)

Until the middle of the nineteenth century—and in some areas much later, except for large estates—most homes in North America were not landscaped, partly because the requisite time and money were not available, partly because there was no tradition of landscaping, partly for other reasons. But as the population became more prosperous during the last half of the nineteenth century, fine parks and public and private gardens were established. The formal garden style of the European Renaissance gradually gave way to a naturalistic style in which gentle curves replaced harsh geometric designs and in which rock outcrops, rock gardens, and natural rock or wooden fences were featured instead of statuary, formal gardens, and geometric masonry walls.

Frederick Law Olmsted (1822–1903) first introduced the term *landscape architect* in conjunction with his design of Central Park in New York City. He, and other designers that he influenced, stressed that when designing parks and gardens the needs of people should be considered as well as landforms and plant materials. During the late nineteenth century, arboreta and botanical gardens were established, seed and nursery catalogs and gardening magazines first appeared, and state horticultural societies and local garden clubs were inaugurated (Figure 1-4). Both public and private breeders used exotic and native species to develop new ornamental species and cultivars.

The advent of the automobile in the twentieth century has had a tremendous impact on gardening and landscaping. Roadways and parking and garaging facilities required for the widespread use of automobiles have necessitated radical changes in urban, home, and yard design and construction. The longer commutes made possible by auto transportation led to the development of suburbs, which in turn provided the displaced agriculturists who were flocking to metropolitan areas with enough yard space to satisfy their urge to grow a few plants. That the typical American residence is an individual dwelling (with a yard planted to turf, trees, shrubs, and flowers), instead of an apartment or row house, is at least partly a result of the mobility that automobiles engender. The distances

FIGURE 1-4 • The New York Botanical Garden, the Bronx, shown in September 1910. (Courtesy of the Library of the New York Botanical Garden)

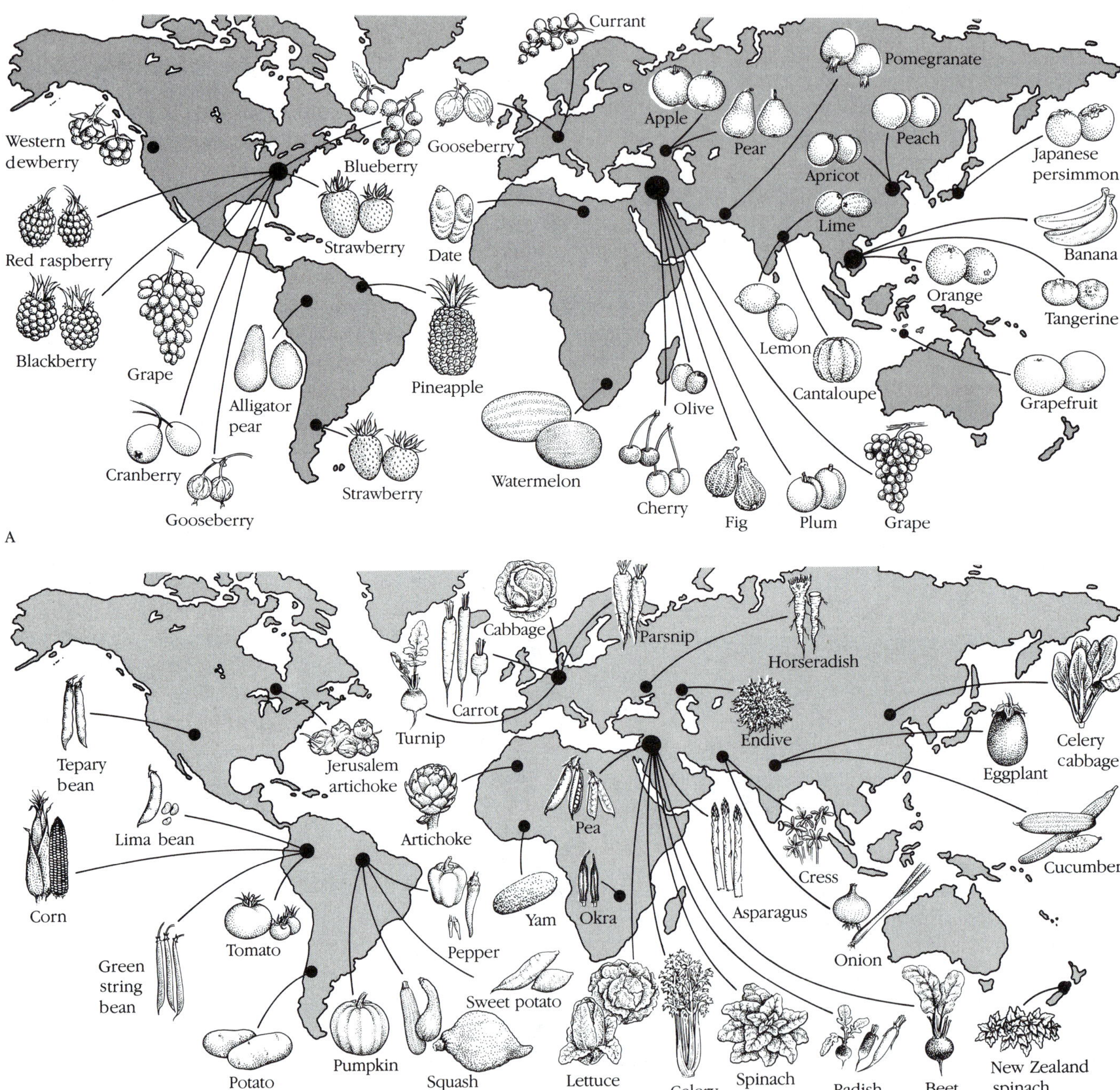

FIGURE 1-5 • Approximate geographical origin of cultivated fruits (A) and cultivated vegetables (B). (Maps reproduced by permission of Harper & Row, Publishers, Inc., from Bertha Morris Parker and Illa Podendort, *Domesticated Plants*, copyright © 1949 by Harper & Row, Publishers, Inc.)

that could be negotiated by auto made it possible for families to spend weekends at fairly distant locations and encouraged the development and landscape maintenance of public parks and public and private recreation sites away from urban centers.

One aspect of gardening that has received considerable attention in the recent past and continues to be popular is indoor beautification with plants, or *plantscaping*. To some extent this trend has resulted from the urge to "grow something" shared by an increasing number of apartment and condominium dwellers who do not have facilities for outdoor gardens. Additionally, commercial business and professional office supervisors have recognized that a few plants in a room can create a more pleasant and productive environment for customers and employees. Propagating and growing houseplants and supplying and maintaining indoor decorative plantings for commercial establishments are now important segments of the horticultural industry.

Food gardening reached what was perhaps the zenith of its popularity in the 1970s and has declined only slightly since then. In its November 1989 issue, *National Gardening,* the venerable magazine of the National Gardening Association, reported surveys showing that 31 million U.S. households grow vegetables. Between 30 and 40 percent of all vegetables consumed in North America, as well as considerable quantities of fruit, herbs, and grain legumes, are grown in home gardens. Many cities provide garden plots for apartment dwellers. *National Gardening* also reported that the amount of money spent on lawns and ornamental gardens increased by about 6 percent per year between 1979 and 1989. About 58 percent of the households surveyed had lawns, and 42 percent grew flowers. Having produce of garden-fresh quality, rather than saving money, was the main reason given by those interviewed for their food-gardening efforts. Ornamental gardeners gardened for pleasure and for the greater value that ornamentals gave their property.

The Challenge to Gardeners in an Age of Diminishing Resources

Today's gardeners have inherited a priceless heritage of plant materials developed by past generations. The tremendous diversity of domestic plants adapted to varied climates is a synthesis of the efforts of countless plant scientists, farmers, gardeners, and human observers from many cultures during the thousands of years of human civilization (Figure 1-5).

Plant domestication, mainly of ornamentals, and the improvement of food and ornamental plants continue today through the efforts of public and private commercial and amateur breeders. Averting famine, by replacing cultivars that can no longer be grown because they have become susceptible to pest attack, and by developing better-adapted, higher-yielding cultivars, is a continuing challenge for breeders of food crops. Ornamental breeders face the challenge of creating cultivars that can withstand and even help ameliorate the stresses of the modern urban environment. The genetic resources to meet both these challenges will come primarily from the wild ancestors of currently cultivated species and from wild species yet to be domesticated. This is the principal reason that the accelerating extinction of native plant species poses such a great threat to our future welfare. Gardeners should repay their plant heritage debt by supporting sensible programs that will ensure the survival of species and consequently of the plant heritage for coming generations.

HORTICULTURE IN RELATION TO OTHER DISCIPLINES

Although the production of garden crops is a horticultural activity, sooner or later most gardeners face problems that require the expertise of specialists in other fields. It seems appropriate, therefore, to devote a few paragraphs to the relationship of horticulture to other agricultural and biological sciences and related disciplines and to explain briefly what the field of horticulture encompasses.

With the very earliest domestication there was a sharp division between the occupation of the animal agriculturist, who was primarily a nomad following flocks and herds from one grassy area to another, and the more or less sedentary plant agriculturist. This division is exemplified in the biblical story of Abel, the herdsman, and Cain, the gardener. Later, as more animals became domesticated, animal agriculturists were further divided according to the kind of animal in which they specialized, as cattle, sheep, hog, or poultry producers. With the domestication of fowl and swine, the development of planted pastures, the production of hay, and the recognition of the value of manure as fertilizer, a somewhat closer relationship between some plant and animal agriculturists ensued.

As long as planting, sowing, and reaping were accomplished with hand tools and as long as farmers produced food primarily with the help of and for their families, a farmer was a farmer. With the invention of machinery that permitted each grower to produce extensive acreages of certain crops, however, plant agriculturists split into two groups: **agronomists,** who grew field crops on large acreages, and **horticulturists,** who grew garden or intensively cultivated crops. This distinction between horticultural and agronomic crops persists, even though today some horticultural crops are produced in larger fields than are agronomic crops.

The term *horticulture* is derived from two Latin words meaning "garden cultivation." Botany and related plant sciences are closely allied to horticulture, and in the past botany and horticulture were often included in the same university department. Horticulture is sometimes referred to as *applied botany.* Vocational fields related to plant pest control—**entomology** (insects), **plant pathology** (plant diseases), and weed control—as well as soils and agricultural economics, are other disciplines often studied in conjunction with horticulture.

Divisions of the Field of Horticulture

Horticulture as an educational discipline is considered both an art and a science and usually includes five different subfields. In some universities these are grouped together in a horticulture department. At other schools some of these subfields may be separate departments, or horticulture may be taught with agronomy and plant pathology in an overall plant science department. These five subfields are **pomology,** the culture of fruit; **olericulture,** the culture of vegetables; **ornamental horticulture,** the production and utilization of flowers, shrubs, and trees; **postharvest horticulture,** the processing, preservation, and storage of horticultural products; and **landscape horticulture,** the use of plant materials for beautification.

All or some of the subfield of postharvest horticulture is often part of an interdisciplinary field of food technology dealing with all aspects of storing, preserving, and processing foods. Landscape horticulture is often a part of a much larger discipline that goes by various names and may include different subfields. In the past, landscape training has been allied with either horticulture or architecture departments; now it is frequently also associated with environmental or outdoor recreation disciplines that may ally it with environmental science, forestry, or physical education. **Viticulture** and **enology,** the culture of grapes and the art of wine making, are sometimes treated as fields separate from pomology.

Horticulturists need a knowledge of various related fields, including those just mentioned as well as business, climatology, and engineering. People interested in ornamental areas of landscape architecture should have a knowledge of surveying, design, art, city and recreational facilities planning, and perhaps social science. Horticultural education and garden writing are two other rapidly growing subfields.

CLASSIFICATION OF HORTICULTURAL CROPS

◆ ◆ ◆

The human mind most easily retains a body of knowledge if its various components can be grouped in a related and orderly fashion. For example, the names of the states of the United States and the provinces of Canada are more easily remembered in groups according to geographical location or in alphabetical order than they are randomly. Analogously, garden plants can be more easily studied if they are grouped in a meaningful relationship. There are many ways of grouping and thus of classifying horticultural crops.

Horticultural Classification

One way of classifying garden crops is referred to as **horticultural classification,** which groups products according to their use:

- I. Edible crops
  - A. Fruit
    - 1. Tropical
    - 2. Subtropical
    - 3. Temperate
      - a. Tree fruit
      - b. Small fruit
  - B. Vegetables
    - 1. Cool-season
    - 2. Warm-season
  - C. Drugs, condiments, and beverages
- II. Ornamentals
  - A. Flowers and foliage plants
    - 1. Flowers for indoor use
    - 2. Flowers for outdoor use
  - B. Shrubs and trees

Obviously, not all horticultural crops can be classified neatly into one of these groups. For instance, the term **fruit** as used in a horticultural sense is somewhat different from the term used in a botanical sense. Botanically, a fruit is an enlarged ovary with attached parts, but horticulturally, a fruit is a plant part that can be consumed as a dessert or snack with little or no preparation. A **vegetable** is a plant part that may or may not require cooking but is usually consumed without much refinement and with the main course of the meal (agronomic crops usually require milling or refining before they can be consumed).

Some fruits and vegetables do not, however, readily fit this classification. For example, tomatoes, peppers, and beans, all botanically fruits, are considered vegetables because they are put to culinary uses that we ordinarily associate with vegetables. Rhubarb, usually grown as a vegetable, is normally used as a dessert, and the avocado, botanically and horticulturally a fruit, is frequently used in vegetable salads.

In addition, edible plants such as kale, hot peppers, and herbs may sometimes be used as ornamentals, but hot peppers and herbs can also be classified as **condiments,** a term that describes spices and other products used to enhance the flavor of foods (Figure 1-6). Coffee, tea, and cocoa are the most important beverage plants. Morphine

FIGURE 1-6 • *Piper nigrum*, a condiment. Both black and white pepper come from this plant. Black pepper is made by grinding both the seeds and the dried berries; white pepper is made by grinding the seeds after the berry pulp has been removed by fermentation.

from the opium poppy, caffeine from the coffee tree, and digitalis from the foxglove plant are among the useful drugs produced from horticultural crops.

Useful or Not Useful. One basis for classifying plants in the garden is their usefulness, or lack of it. Plants that are not useful are usually termed weeds. Sometimes a plant is useful in one location but may be a weed in another. Scotch broom, for example, is considered a weed on the Oregon and Washington coasts, whereas in those parts of the country where it must be planted and nurtured, it is regarded as a desirable ornamental. Indeed, it is conceivable that many plants considered weeds today may someday be found to have useful properties and may be the crop plants of tomorrow. Sunflowers and safflowers are examples of plants once considered to be weeds that have become useful in our own time.

Growth Habit. Another useful method of classifying plants is according to their habit of growth. A **herbaceous** plant has nonwoody stems (as occurs on coleus or asparagus) that usually last only one season. The contrasting **woody** plant has woody stems and generally lives for several to many years, adding new growth each year (Figure 1-7). Herbaceous plants can be classified as upright or vining, and woody plants are divided into **lianas** (woody vines), shrubs, and trees. Plants also may be classified as **deciduous** or **evergreen.** Deciduous plants shed all their leaves at one time, usually in the autumn. Evergreens, although they also shed their leaves, do so gradually during the entire year as other leaves form to replace those that are lost. Thus, evergreens are never without leaves. Evergreen plants may be further subdivided into broad-leaved and needle evergreens.

Plants are sometimes categorized on the basis of the part consumed or used by humans (Figure 1-8). Examples of this classification include the leaf (lettuce), stem (asparagus), root (carrot or sweet potato), petiole (celery or rhubarb), bud (broccoli or globe artichoke), fruit (apple or pineapple), and seed (pea or sweet corn).

FIGURE 1-7 • Conifer (woody) trees underlain by grasses and herbaceous plants. (Courtesy of Grant Heilman)

Length of Life. Plants may also be classified according to the number of seasons they survive. **Annuals** are plants that over the course of one season produce vegetative growth, flowers, and seeds and die. Biennial plants produce vegetative growth during their first season; usually their flowering is triggered by a period of cold weather. They produce flowers, fruit, and seeds in their second season and die at the end of their second year. Perennial plants are those that survive from three to many seasons.

Plants are usually classified as annual, biennial, or perennial on the basis of the part that lives the longest. Thus, even though a tree has annual leaves, it is considered to be a perennial. Rasp-

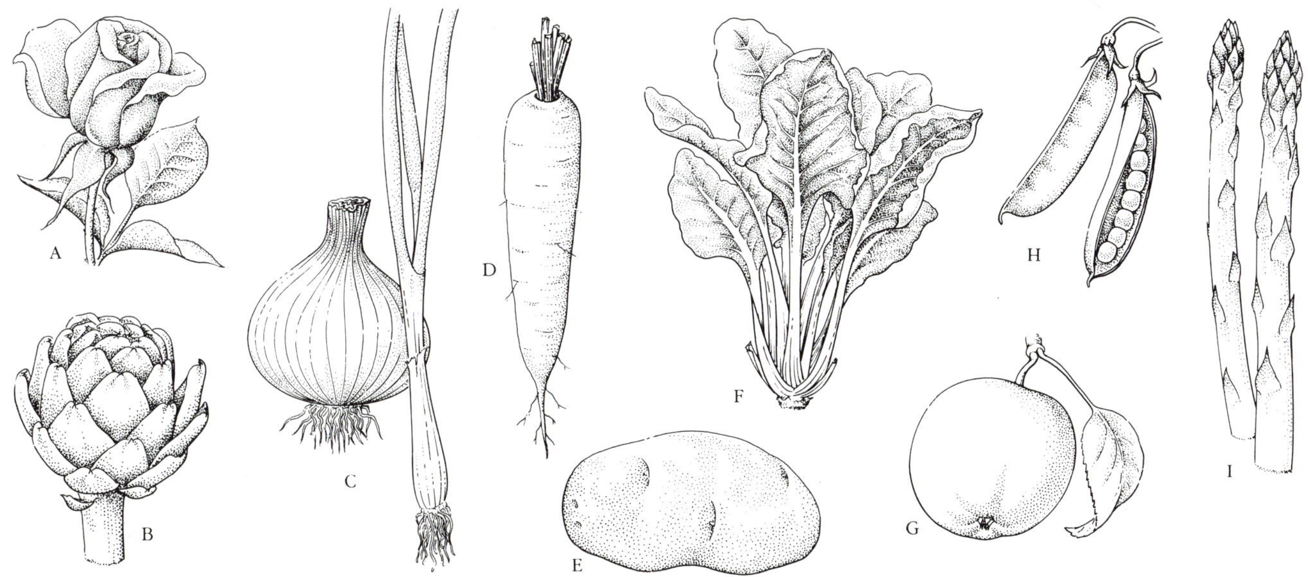

FIGURE 1-8 • Various plant parts useful to humans. (A) Rose, flower; (B) globe artichoke, flower bud; (C) onion, leaf (bulbs are morphologically platelike stems surrounded by fleshy leaves); (D) carrot, root; (E) potato, stem (tubers are the enlarged fleshy tips of underground stems); (F) chard, leaf and petiole; (G) apple, fruit; (H) pea, seed; (I) asparagus, stem and apical bud.

berries and other bramble berries have biennial canes, but because the roots are perennial, these plants are considered perennials. Most perennial flowers have tops that are annual. Carrots are considered biennials because the roots live for two seasons, even though the tops are annual.

Some crops are grown as annuals, although under certain environmental conditions they may be biennial or perennial. For example, when tomatoes are grown in the tropics, they may survive for several seasons; however, in temperate zones they are grown as annuals. Also, when biennial vegetables—celery, carrots, cabbage, beets, turnips, rutabagas—are not being produced for seed, they are grown and harvested during one season.

Temperature Tolerance. Plants are also classified according to their temperature tolerance. **Tropical** crops are those that originated in tropical areas of the earth. Plants such as bananas, pineapple, rubber, cacao, coffee, and even vegetables like watermelon and cantaloupe are of tropical origin and are subject to cold injury at temperatures considerably above the freezing point. **Subtropical** crops can tolerate some freezing temperatures but cannot survive in areas with a cold winter climate. Most **temperate-zone** plants are able to adapt so that they can survive temperatures considerably below the freezing point. Vegetables and flowers that grow in temperate-zone gardens may also be classified as cool-season or warm-season crops. **Cool-season** crops, such as radishes, peas, and pansies, are those that can withstand some degree of freezing and consequently can be planted as soon as the ground can be worked in the spring. **Warm-season** crops, such as tomatoes, muskmelons, and sweet potatoes, are mostly of tropical origin and are killed as soon as temperatures drop slightly below freezing. They should not be planted until the danger of frost is past.

Botanical (Binomial) System of Plant Classification

The **botanical system** of plant classification is based largely on the hypothesis that plants evolved from a single, less complex organism and that all plants are therefore more or less distantly related. The traditional plant categories, or **taxa,** are (in hierarchical order) kingdom, division, class, order, family, genus, and species. Subgroups are frequently used in this classification system.

Categories of Biological Classification. Although biologists have never fully agreed on the classification of living organisms, textbooks written during the first three-fourths of the twentieth century contained a relatively standardized system of higher plant classification based on, among other categories, two kingdoms, Animalia and Plantae. Largely as a result of accumulating evidence from both fossils and living organisms, groupings in the broader taxa—kingdom, division, and class—have undergone considerable reshuffling since 1965. As a consequence, most biologists now recognize five kingdoms: (1) the traditional Kingdom Animalia; (2) Kingdom Monera (bacteria and blue-green algae); (3) Kingdom Protista (algae, protozoans, and slime molds); (4) Kingdom Fungi; and (5) Kingdom Plantae. Unfortunately, there is much less agreement on how organisms of the plant kingdom should be grouped within division and class taxa and whether or not subkingdoms, subdivisions, and subclasses should be distinguished.

Fortunately, however, although they are concerned with some of the other taxa when they deal with organisms that cause disease and with microorganisms used in brewing and preserving, horticulturists work primarily with a few well-defined higher groups of the plant kingdom. The simplest grouping lists the divisions and classes of the plant kingdom as follows:

1. Division Pterophyta (ferns)
2. Division Cycadophyta (cycads)
3. Division Ginkgophyta (ginkgos)
4. Division Coniferophyta (conifers)
5. Division Anthophyta (flowering plants)
   a. Class Monocotyledonae (leaves with parallel veins, flowers with three or six parts, a single seed leaf or **cotyledon**, and vascular bundles scattered throughout the stem).
   b. Class Dicotyledonae (leaves with netted or branching veins, flowers with four or five parts, two seed leaves or cotyledons, and vascular bundles in a ring around the stem or in a vascular ring).

A few other higher-order classification terms that gardeners are likely to encounter should be mentioned. All of the above groups of plants are **tracheophytes,** plants having a vascular system. (The vascular system is discussed in "The Stem" section of Chapter 2.) The ferns, which reproduce by spores, are called **pteridophytes** in contrast to the rest of the group, **spermatophytes,** which reproduce by seed. Cycads, ginkgos, and conifers are **gymnosperms,** plants having seeds without a definite seed coat. In contrast, flowering plants are **angiosperms,** having seeds with a seed coat.

Ferns, cycads, and ginkgos are used as ornamentals (Figure 1-9). As horticultural plants, conifers are also used mainly as ornamentals, although they are of major importance to foresters for lumber, pulpwood, and recreation. Angiosperms are by far the most numerous and most important group of plants used by gardeners. Division Angiophyta is divided into the classes Monocotyledonae, or monocots, and Dicotyledonae, or dicots (Figure 1-10); these are subdivided into orders; the orders are subdivided into families; the families into genera; and the genera into species.

The botanical scheme of plant classification is called the **binomial system of nomenclature** because in it each plant is identified by two italicized Latin names, a capitalized genus name and an uncapitalized species name. These may be followed by the initial or name of the person who first assigned the botanical name. For example,

A

B

C

FIGURE 1-9 • Three evolutionary primitive plants: (A) Mexican cycad (*Divan edulis*); (B) maidenhair fern (*Adiantum pedantum*); (C) maidenhair tree (*Ginkgo biloba*). *Ginkgo biloba* is dioecious (see "The Flower" in Chapter 3). Female ginkgo trees are seldom planted as ornamentals because the fruit, shown here, is messy and has a disagreeable odor. (A, courtesy of W. H. Hodge/Peter Arnold, Inc.; B, courtesy of Grant Heilman; C, courtesy of Runk/Schoenberger, Grant Heilman)

Daucus carota L. is the botanical name of the carrot; L. stands for Linnaeus, the father of biological nomenclature, who first assigned a botanical name to the carrot. It is customary to abbreviate the generic name, using only the first letter, when it is repeated immediately following its initial use, for instance, *D. carota.*

Plants belonging to the same **genus** (subgroup of a family) have similar structure, appearance, and chromosome makeup (chromosomes are discussed

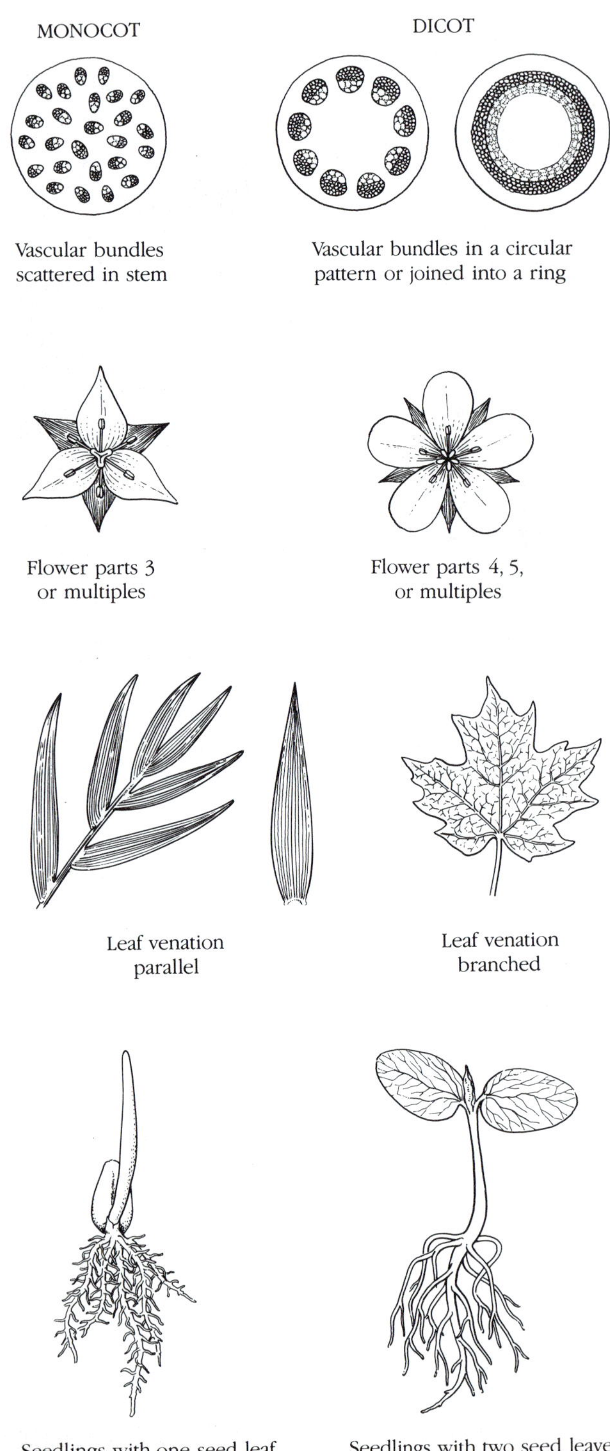

FIGURE 1-10 • A monocotyledonous plant compared with a dicotyledonous plant.

in Chapter 3). Frequently the various subgroups (species) within a genus can be intergrafted, and occasionally hybridization between species within a genus is possible.

The **species** (sp., plural spp.) is the basic unit of classification on which all botanical nomenclature is based. For horticultural plants, a species (e.g., *Spinacia oleracea, Rubus idaeus, Pinus nigra*) often, but not always, is equivalent to a horticultural kind of plant (spinach, red raspberry, Austrian pine). Plants belonging to the same species have numerous **morphological** (structural and developmental) similarities, and for plant groups that produce seed, a species usually constitutes an exclusive interbreeding population.

Subspecies (subsp.), variety (var.), and forma (f.) are three terms that designate subgroups within the traditional species. The use of these terms is sometimes confusing, and even trained taxonomists disagree on the classification into these groupings.

There is no clearly definable distinction between a botanical **variety** and a **subspecies** based on the degree of morphological variation. The term subspecies is more often used with natural than with cultivated populations and is likely to be associated with geographical distribution. Plants belonging to the same botanical variety are generally readily discernible from those of other varieties of the same species. For example, *Brassica oleracea* var. *botrytis* is cauliflower, and *B. oleracea* var. *capitata* is cabbage. Cabbage and cauliflower have the same chromosome number and similar leaves and readily intercross, but they have head characteristics that are distinctly different.

Although barriers to natural intercrossing are more frequently associated with subspecies than with varieties, there can be barriers to the natural intercrossing of two varieties of the same species. Also in the cabbage group, broccoli, *Brassica oleracea* var. *italica,* is an annual, whereas cabbage is a biennial (Figure 1-11). Although broccoli pollen can readily pollinate and cause seed to be produced on cabbage flowers, the two varieties normally do not intercross, because broccoli blooms during the fall and cabbage blooms during the spring. (The

A

B

FIGURE 1-11 • Two different kinds of crops that belong to the same species: (A) cabbage, *Brassica oleracea* var. *capitata*, and (B) sprouting broccoli, *Brassica oleracea* var. *italica*. (Photographs by Peter C. Kruithof, courtesy of Alf. Christianson Seed Co.)

botanical variety should not be confused with cultivated variety, now referred to as cultivar, which will be discussed later in this chapter.)

A **forma** is a group of individuals within a population that differs from the rest of the population in a consistent but botanically insignificant way. Usually there is less difference between two formae of a population than between two varieties or subspecies. In horticulture the term forma is often used with ornamentals to distinguish groups with different growth characteristics not reproducible with seed. For example, two important formae of Japanese yew are *Taxus cuspidata* f. *densa,* an upright form, and *T. cuspidata* f. *nana,* a spreading form. New plants are always developed by rooting cuttings of the form desired. Seedlings of either form grow into plants of various shapes and sizes but seldom produce a plant that is typically either *T. cuspidata* f. *nana* or *T. cuspidata* f. *densa.*

Advantages of the Binomial System. Using the binomial system of plant classification has a number of advantages. First, it avoids confusion: Each plant has an internationally recognized name. In fact, North Americans are probably less familiar with the Latin names of plants than are people from other countries where language localization encourages linguistic diversity. The second big advantage of the binomial system is that it reveals relationships. This is helpful because cultural practices, pesticide tolerances, and soil and climatic requirements are often similar for plants of the same group. The success of grafting one plant to another or of cross-pollinating also parallels botanical relationships.

Table 1-1 lists a few of the horticulturally more important families, and Table 1-2 provides the botanical classification of three typical crop plants.

TABLE 1-1 • *Plant families of importance to horticulture (and some common examples)*

A. Horticulturally important conifer families
1. Araucariaceae (araucaria family): Norfolk Island pine, monkey-puzzle tree
2. Cupressaceae (cypress family): cypress, juniper, eastern red cedar
3. Pinaceae (pine family): pine, spruce, fir, true cedars
4. Taxaceae (yew family): yew
5. Taxodiaceae (bald cypress family): bald cypress, redwood, giant sequoia

B. Horticulturally important monocot families
1. Amaryllidaceae (amaryllis family): amaryllis, narcissus
2. Araceae (arum family): philodendron, caladium, dieffenbachia, monstera
3. Bromeliaceae (pineapple family): pineapple, bromeliads
4. Gramineae or Poaceae (grass family): sweet corn and all grasses, including many ornamental grasses
5. Liliaceae (lily family): lily, tulip, crocus, asparagus, Joshua tree, onion
6. Orchidaceae (orchid family): 10,000 typical species; mostly ornamentals, many having aerial roots and living on live or dead organic matter
7. Iridaceae (iris family): iris
8. Palmae or Arecaceae (palm family): coconut, date, and ornamental palms

C. Horticulturally important dicot families
1. Aceraceae (maple family): maple, box elder
2. Betulaceae (birch family): birch, alder, hazelnut
3. Cactaceae (cactus family): cacti
4. Caprifoliaceae (honeysuckle family): honeysuckle, elder, viburnum, weigela
5. Caryophyllaceae (pink family): carnations and pinks
6. Chenopodiaceae (goosefoot family): beet, chard, spinach
7. Compositae or Asteraceae (sunflower family): chrysanthemum, sunflower, dahlia, calendula, marigold, zinnia, lettuce, artichoke, dandelion
8. Cruciferae or Brassicaceae (mustard family): radish, cabbage, cauliflower, broccoli, mustard, stock, and many weeds
9. Cucurbitaceae (melon family): watermelon, cantaloupe, squash, cucumber, pumpkin, gourd
10. Ericaceae (heath family): rhododendron, azalea, blueberry, cranberry
11. Fagaceae (beech family): beech, chestnut, oak
12. Juglandaceae (walnut family): walnut, pecan, hickory
13. Labiatae or Lamiaceae (mint family): mint, sage, thyme, lavender
14. Leguminosae or Fabaceae (pea family): clover, lupine, pea, bean, soybean, peanut, lima bean, wisteria, Scotch broom, sweet pea, locust, redbud, mesquite, Kentucky coffee tree
15. Moraceae (mulberry family): mulberry, fig
16. Magnoliaceae (magnolia family): magnolia, tulip tree
17. Malvaceae (mallow family): okra, hibiscus, flowering maple, rose of sharon, hollyhock, cotton
18. Oleaceae (olive family): ash, privet, lilac, forsythia, jasmine, olive
19. Papaveraceae (poppy family): poppy, bloodroot
20. Ranunculaceae (buttercup family): buttercup, larkspur, columbine, peony, anemone
21. Rosaceae (rose family): spirea, ninebark, hawthorn, rose, mountain ash, quince, apple, pear, peach, plum, cherry, apricot, raspberry, blackberry, strawberry
22. Rutaceae (rue family): lemon, orange, grapefruit, lime, citron
23. Salicaceae (willow family): poplar, cottonwood, aspen, willow
24. Saxifragaceae (saxifrage family): mock orange, currant, gooseberry, deutzia, hydrangea
25. Solanaceae (nightshade family): tobacco, petunia, potato, eggplant, pepper, tomato
26. Umbelliferae or Apiaceae (parsley family): carrot, parsley, parsnip, celery
27. Vitaceae (grape family): grape, Boston ivy

Kind, Cultivar, Strain, and Clone

Four other classification terms frequently used with horticultural crops are kind, cultivar, strain, and clone. Examples of accepted usage probably provide the best explanations.

Horticultural plants of the same **kind** usually differ from other kinds in several important aspects. For example, cherry, peach, raspberry, and apple are different kinds of fruit. Kind often, but not always, includes all members of one species. An important exception involves the crucifers mentioned earlier: Broccoli, cabbage, and cauliflower all belong to the same species but are different kinds of vegetables.

The term **cultivar** is an internationally accepted contraction of cultivated variety and is exactly equivalent to the old horticultural term vari-

TABLE 1-2 • *Botanical classification of pear, Colorado spruce, and cauliflower*

	Pear	Spruce	Cauliflower
Kingdom	Plantae	Plantae	Plantae
Division	Tracheophyta	Tracheophyta	Tracheophyta
Subdivision	Spermatophytina	Spermatophytina	Spermatophytina
Class	Angiospermae	Coniferinae	Angiospermae
Subclass	Dicotyledonae	Coniferophytae	Dicotyledonae
Order	Rosales	Coniferales	Papaverales
Family	Rosaceae	Pinaceae	Cruciferae
Genus	*Pyrus*	*Picea*	*Brassica*
Species	*communis*	*pungens*	*oleracea*
Bot. variety			*botrytis*

ety. In the *International Code of Nomenclature of Cultivated Plants—1969,* cultivar is defined as "an assemblage of cultivated plants which is clearly distinguished by any character (morphological, physiological, cytological, chemical or others), and which, when reproduced (sexually or asexually), retains its distinguishing characteristics."

"Variety" was used as a horticultural descriptor long before it became a term of botanical nomenclature, and only recently was "cultivar" adopted to replace (horticultural) variety. Thus, most older horticulturists have referred to fruit, vegetable, and ornamental "varieties" all their lives, in both their speaking and their writing. But the term cultivar should be encouraged in order to avoid confusion with botanical variety. The cultivar name is capitalized and enclosed in single quotation marks, as 'Hales Best' muskmelon or 'Red Delicious' apple.

For many years, horticulturists have designated as **strains** those groups of plants within a cultivar that have been selected and cultivated because they differ from other plants of that cultivar. The solid red sports are examples of strains of the 'Red Delicious' apple cultivar. Sometimes one strain differs from another in its resistance to a disease. For example, 'Hales Best PMR' is a powdery mildew–resistant selection of the 'Hales Best' muskmelon cultivar. Those responsible for horticultural nomenclature now recommend that groups of plants with recognizable differences from the cultivar from which they originated be classed as separate cultivars; however, the term strain is still frequently used by those long associated with the industry.

A **clone** is a genetically uniform group of plants derived from a single mother plant by asexual propagation; for example, by cuttings, crown divisions, grafts, or layering. Many clones are also designated as cultivars. Thus 'Russet Burbank' potato and 'Golden Delicious' apple are clones as well as cultivars. Clones are discussed further in Chapter 3.

WHY GROW A GARDEN?

◆ ◆ ◆

The reasons for growing gardens are as many and as diverse as are the people who grow them. Often the main purpose of a garden is to supplement the family food supply. As we have seen, 40 percent of American families now grow some type of vegetable garden. Gardens could become an even more important source of food should there be a national emergency. Although North Americans take for granted an ample supply of basic and luxury foods, production, processing, transporting, and marketing have become so complex that the continuing availability of food is extremely vulnerable to such events as strikes, natural disasters, or transportation disruptions. The two weeks' supply stocked by most supermarkets would be quickly depleted if any phase of food distribution were interrupted.

Numerous Americans garden because gardening makes them feel better. Unlike many popular sports that are primarily recreations of youth, gardening is a hobby that provides moderate to vigorous exercise for people of all ages. The benefits of gardening in treating emotional stress are becoming widely recognized, and horticulturists cooperating with medical centers at several locations have had spectacular success using gardening to alleviate mental and emotional problems. Gardening can be an especially beneficial hobby for North Americans, many of whom are engaged in indoor occupations that involve considerable stress and a minimum of physical activity.

In most localities today if a family wants to eat fresh peas from the pod, edible podded peas, kohlrabi, kale, cress, currants, dewberries, many other fruits and vegetables, or most herbs; if they want to enjoy the beauty of most kinds of annual flowers; or if they want to savor the garden-fresh flavor of fruits and vegetables, they must grow a garden. With today's mechanized harvest, only the kinds and cultivars that can be mass produced are likely to find their way to supermarket shelves. Moreover, because they must be harvested when still immature and shipped long distances, such items as tomatoes, sweet corn, peas, and strawberries purchased in a supermarket do not have the quality of those grown in a home garden. Often, too, the characteristics that enable a cultivar to withstand the necessary handling and still have eye appeal when it reaches the market (solid flesh for strawberries and tomatoes, tough skin for sweet corn kernels) do not provide the ultimate in eating quality.

Gardens also are grown to beautify the surroundings, to give sanctuary to wildlife, and to provide shade and wind protection around the home. For some people, assembling different kinds of garden plants satisfies the human urge to collect.

Recent nutritional research has resulted in considerable publicity about the effect of diet on health and longevity. Most of these studies report that public health could be improved if people consumed more fruits and vegetables.

These foods add flavor, variety, and color to meals. Dinner would be rather bland without the flavor of onions, herbs, or various fruits, the texture of a crisp salad, or the color of carrots, beets, peas, tomatoes, or peaches. Fruits and vegetables are important dietary components because many of them add bulk without calories, improving the digestion and elimination of our sedentary society. Finally, these foods are important sources — in some cases the only source — of vitamins and minerals essential to the growth and functioning of the human body. Table 14-25 lists the nutrients contained in selected fruits and vegetables.

Selected References

Bailey, L. H. *Hortus III.* New York: Macmillan, 1976. (Reprint with some revision of this earlier classic.)

———. *Manual of Cultivated Plants Most Commonly Grown in the United States and Canada.* Rev. ed. New York: Macmillan, 1949.

Better Homes and Gardens Editors. *Better Homes and Gardens Step-by-Step Successful Gardening.* Des Moines: Meredith, 1987.

Cronquist, A. *The Evolution and Classification of Flowering Plants.* 2nd ed. New York: New York Botanical Garden, 1988.

Heiser, C. B., Jr. *Seed to Civilization.* 3rd ed. Cambridge, Mass.: Harvard University Press, 1990.

International Code of Nomenclature of Cultivated Plants—1969. Vol. 64: *Regnum Vegetavile.* Utrecht: International Bureau for Plant Taxonomy and Nomenclature of the International Association for Plant Taxonomy, 1969.

Janick, J. *Horticultural Science.* 3rd ed. New York: Freeman, 1985.

Jones, S. B., and A. E. Luchsinger, *Plant Systematics.* 2nd ed. Athens: Ohio University Press, 1986.

Sauer, C. O. *Agricultural Origins and Dispersals: The Domestication of Animals and Foodstuffs.* 2nd ed. Cambridge, Mass.: MIT Press, 1969.

Sawyer, C. E. *American Gardens: A Traveller's Guide.* Brooklyn Botanic Garden Handbook 111 (A special printing of *Plants and Gardens*, vol. 42, no. 3). Brooklyn, N.Y.: Brooklyn Botanic Garden, 1986.

CHAPTER 2

Structure and Growth: The Vegetative Phase

From the day a nurse pins on our first cotton (or disposable) diaper until the day the sexton nails the pine cover on our coffin, we use, eat, and enjoy countless plant products that have characteristics of value to us. It is important to realize, however, that these products did not come into existence because a beneficent goddess of plants decreed that they should be produced to please people. Plant stems, roots, leaves, flowers, fruits, and seeds in all their forms and modifications exist because they are required for the survival, growth, and reproduction of the plant producing them. Therefore, gardeners who want to know the why and how of plant culture and plant propagation must first have some knowledge of the makeup and function of various plant structures.

Most books show the structure of plants in neatly labeled cross or longitudinal sections, with each part in its appointed place. Plant growth is likewise neatly cataloged in standardized phases. This work is no different in this regard, not because I am happy with this method but because a book does not lend itself to a more dynamic approach. The problem with such presentations is that readers often gain the impression that all plants have the same unchanging structure and growth pattern. It would be more accurate to show plant structure and growth in a three-dimensional movie, complete with sound effects, because plants are dynamic, living, changing entities. The structure at any one location will not be the same tomorrow or even in a few minutes, and no two plants are exactly alike. The discussion that follows, therefore, may not describe exactly any plant at any time, but it is useful because it represents the synthesis of knowledge gained from thousands of scientific observations of plant structure and growth.

PHASES OF PLANT GROWTH

◆ ◆ ◆

Dormancy

During their lives, most plants have both periods of active growth and periods of minimal growth. The period of inactivity is referred to as **dormancy.** In annual plants the dormant period may reside entirely within the seed. In biennial and perennial plants the dormant period normally coincides with the winter season or, in the tropics, with the period of drought when growing conditions are adverse (Figure 2-1). The dormant period of temperate-zone perennials and some biennials has two phases. During the first phase, which horticulturists refer to as the **rest period,** the plant does not grow even if environmental conditions are favorable. During the second phase the plant remains inactive because of adverse environmental conditions, but growth resumes as soon as temperature and moisture conditions become favorable.

For example, in the northern United States the fruit of an apple tree ripens in September or Oc-

FIGURE 2-1 • A dormant deciduous tree. (Courtesy of Horst Schafer/Peter Arnold, Inc.)

tober. Then the leaves turn yellow and fall from the tree. From October until sometime in January, if apple branches are cut and placed in water in a warm room, they will remain dormant. But after mid-January, if branches from the same tree are brought into a warm room, they will form buds that produce flowers and leaves (Figure 2-2). On the tree itself, however, the branches remain dormant until the temperature begins to rise in the spring. Thus the rest period of an apple tree lasts from October to January, but its dormant period lasts from October until April.

Vegetative and Reproductive Phases of Growth

Every plant goes through two general phases of active growth, a vegetative phase and a reproductive phase. During the plant's early, **vegetative** phase, its food resources are directed primarily to the growth of leaves, stems, and roots. During their early life, woody plants generally do not produce flowers or store food, regardless of care or cultural practices employed. This stage, that part of the vegetative phase when reproduction cannot be induced, is referred to as the **juvenile** stage. Some plants, English ivy and common juniper, for instance, have different foliage or growth habits during their juvenile stage of growth. In the case of long-lived plants, juvenility causes some real problems for orchardists and horticultural scientists, who must bear the expense of caring for the young orchard for four to ten years before the new trees bear fruit.

Later in the life of a plant, sugars and starches are stored, and the plant flowers and produces fruit. This later period is known as the **reproductive** phase. In many plants, especially those that

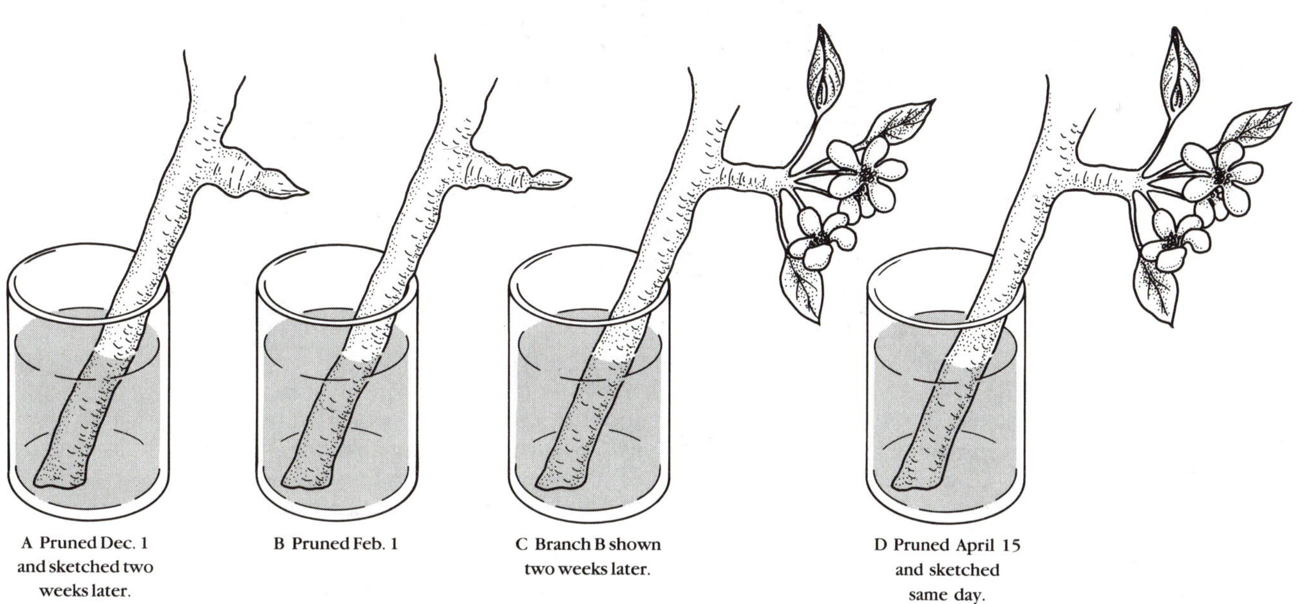
A Pruned Dec. 1 and sketched two weeks later.
B Pruned Feb. 1
C Branch B shown two weeks later.
D Pruned April 15 and sketched same day.

FIGURE 2-2 • Rest and dormancy of deciduous fruit. (A) A branch pruned from a pear tree in November or December and placed in water in a warm room remains dormant because it has not been subjected to enough cold temperature to break its rest. (B, C) The same branch brought indoors in February after several weeks of cold weather is forced into bloom. (D) By April, after a period of warm weather, the tree is blooming.

survive for only one year (annuals), reproduction marks the end of the plant's life. As the reproductive phase progresses, plant tissues begin to degenerate, and they eventually die. This degeneration and death are referred to as **senescence.** In biennial plants the vegetative phase occurs during the first year, and the reproductive phase is triggered by cool temperatures, time, a change in day length, or simply a period of dormancy. The second year is the reproductive cycle of the plant, at the end of which it becomes senescent and dies.

FIGURE 2-3 • A diagrammatic sketch showing the effects of fruit thinning. (The leaves have been left out to simplify the picture.) For a thinning experiment, a branch of plum (A) with 77 fruits remaining after the "June drop" was selected. Thirty-three of the fruits were removed, and at harvest time 41 fruits remained (B). A similar branch having 83 fruits (C) was left unthinned. At the end of the season, 69 fruits still remained on the unthinned branch (D). The fruit harvested from the thinned branch, however, weighed 20 percent more than that harvested from the unthinned branch. Results from thinning are not always so dramatic, although removing excess fruits when they are still small almost always increases the size of the fruit and improves the quality of the crop. (Experiment reported by V. R. Gardener in *Basic Horticulture*, 2nd ed., Macmillan, New York, 1951)

Usually only part of the body of a perennial plant becomes senescent with the maturation of its fruit and seeds. The above-ground structure of perennial garden flowers, for example, matures and dies, but the roots remain alive and capable of producing new shoots the following year. In regard to deciduous trees, only the fruiting body and leaves die after the seeds mature and the growing season ends.

Sometimes gardeners want vegetative growth of the leaves, stems, and roots, as with cabbage, asparagus, or carrots for food or with grass for a new lawn. At other times, reproductive growth of fruits, seeds, or flowers may be the objective, as with raspberries, sweet corn, or annual flowers. Fertilization, irrigation, planting time, and/or other cultural practices may have to be varied depending on whether vegetative or reproductive growth is desirable. For example, orchard trees old enough to bear fruit require cultural practices that maintain a balance between vegetative and reproductive growth. A tree that is overly reproductive tends to produce too many fruits, all of which will remain small because there is too little leaf area per unit of fruit to manufacture enough carbohydrates for their enlargement (Figure 2-3). The vegetative/reproductive balance is correlated with the **carbohydrate/nitrogen balance** in the plant tissue. Carbohydrates are manufactured by the plant's leaves, and nitrogen is absorbed through the root system. In orchards the carbohydrate/nitrogen balance is regulated mainly by pruning to reduce the amount of carbohydrates and by fertilizing to increase the amount of nitrogen. This use of pruning and fertilization to regulate production is detailed in later chapters.

THE CELL

◆ ◆ ◆

Whenever plant growth occurs, whether vegetative or reproductive, the process takes place within the plant's cells. Indeed, the basic unit of each living organism, plant or animal, is the **cell,** a complex factory producing the chemical reactions basic to the organism's life. Cells might be compared to the boards, bricks, and stones used as building blocks for houses. Just as building materials vary in shape, size, and function but still have common characteristics, so cells vary in shape, size, and function but still have common structural features. Although science has made considerable progress in elucidating the complexities of cell development, much remains to be learned. Only the briefest outline of cell structure and function can be included here.

Cell Structure

The basic structure of a plant cell is shown in Figure 2-4. The plant cell is encompassed by a **cell wall** made of cellulose and separated from the cell walls of neighboring cells with a cementing material, the **middle lamella.** Inside the cell wall is the **cell membrane,** which appears to regulate the flow of nutrients and other materials into and out of the cell.

The living portion of the cell, its **protoplasm,** is divided into two parts: an inner, dense-appearing portion, referred to as the **nucleus,** and an outer portion, called the **cytoplasm.** The cytoplasm contains several different kinds of bodies, called **organelles.** One group of these, the **chloroplasts,** is necessary for photosynthesis, the process of utilizing the sun's energy to manufacture sugar from inorganic elements.

Chlorophyll molecules are structures associated with membranes within the chloroplasts that help transform light energy into chemical energy. The molecular structure of chlorophyll is similar to that of hemoglobin, the oxygen-transporting molecules in the blood of animals, except that chlorophyll contains magnesium instead of the iron found in hemoglobin. It is chlorophyll that gives the leaves and stems their green color. The chlorophyll found in higher plants is usually

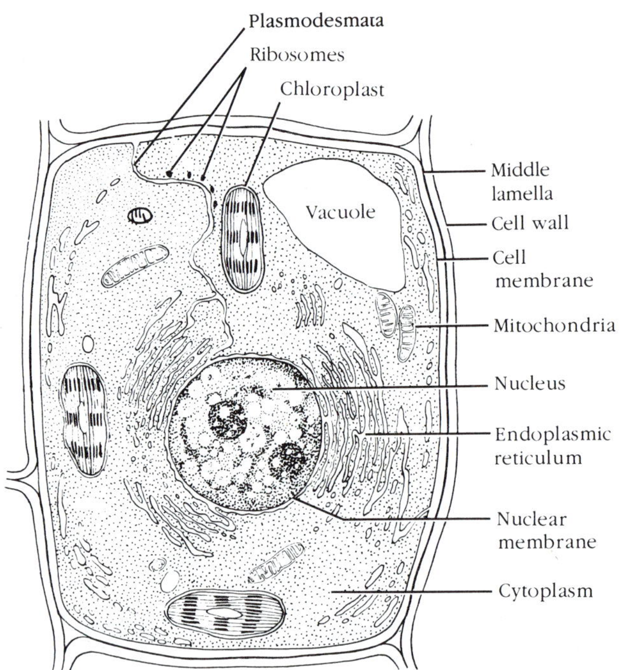

FIGURE 2-4 • Electron-microscope image of a living cell.

one of two types, known as Chlorophyll *a* and Chlorophyll *b*. Algae and other lower plants contain additional types. All chlorophylls have a similar structure and differ mainly in their ability to convert different wavelengths of the light-energy spectrum (see "Kind or Quality of Light" in Chapter 7). Chlorophyll *a* is blue-green, and Chlorophyll *b* is yellow-green. Chloroplasts usually contain about three times as many Chlorophyll *a* as Chlorophyll *b* molecules.

Also in the cytoplasm are **mitochrondria,** which provide energy for cellular activities, and organelles, which are responsible for manufacturing and storing food and other cellular activities. A large portion of the interior of many plant cells is occupied by a relatively clear liquid surrounded by a membrane called a **vacuole,** or sometimes vacuoles, as there may be more than one. Vacuoles contain dissolved carbohydrates, pigments, organic acids, and other compounds.

Running through the cytoplasm is an internal membrane, the **endoplasmic reticulum,** which is now thought to be the wall for channels that run to all areas of the cytoplasm. The endoplasmic reticulum of a cell is connected to the endoplasmic reticula of other cells and to areas outside the cell, by streams of living protoplasm, called **plasmodesmata,** that flow through openings (**pores**) in the cell wall. These intercellular channels greatly increase the opportunity for the interchange of gases and liquids. Clustered on the endoplasmic reticulum and other membranes and, to some extent, scattered throughout the cytoplasm are the **ribosomes.** These small spherical entities are associated with **ribonucleic acid (RNA)**, the substance responsible for relaying genetic information between the nucleus and the cytoplasm.

The nucleus contains regulators of most cellular activities, including reproduction. When a cell is ready to divide, long threadlike structures called **chromosomes** become visible. The electron microscope shows chromosomes to be a double strand of nucleic acid (a major component of proteins) with interconnecting chemical bonds resembling a spiral staircase. This nucleic acid is chemically known as **deoxyribonucleic acid (DNA)**. DNA, in conjunction with RNA and the ribosomes, controls the cell's function and, through the control of cells in concert, regulates the organism's structure and function.

DNA is also the hereditary bridge from one generation to the next. Segments of chromosomal DNA called **genes** pass on characteristics of parent to offspring and determine, for example, that the seed of a maple tree will produce another maple tree or that a baby will look something like its parents. Each plant and animal species has a specific number of chromosomes typical for its species. Human beings have forty-six, corn has twenty, and peas have fourteen. Usually the chromosomes of an organism are in pairs, with one of each pair, or one set, coming from the male parent and one from the female. Corn has ten pairs and humans have twenty-three pairs of chromosomes. Plants with the usual two sets are said to be **dip-**

loid and to have $2n$ number of chromosomes. Occasionally plants may have more than two sets of chromosomes. Plants with four sets ($4n$) are quite common and are called **tetraploids.** Tetraploids are usually larger but less uniform in size and shape than are diploids. This may be an advantage, as with large tetraploid snapdragons (see Figure 3-17), or a disadvantage, as with tetraploid apples, which are larger but often misshapen. Plants with an uneven number of chromosome sets (one, three, five, etc.) usually do not produce seed. Knowledge of this fact is used, for example, in developing seed for growing seedless watermelons. Tetraploid cultivars (four sets) are crossed with diploid cultivars (two sets) to produce watermelons that, because they have three sets of chromosomes (**triploid**), are seedless (see Figure 3-18).

Cell Division

Successful gardeners are those who can get plants to grow, and plants grow as a result of cell division or cell enlargement. Two different kinds of cell division occur in plants as well as in most other organisms. An increase in the number of cells in the plant body is the result of a kind of cell division called **mitosis,** in which two "daughter" cells are formed, each having the same chromosome number as the "mother" cell (Figure 2-5). (Another type of cell division, meiosis, which occurs only when an organism reproduces sexually, is described in Chapter 3.)

Mitosis, and the resulting increase in cell numbers, occurs mainly in the youngest plant tissue, just behind the rapidly growing stem or root tip, at

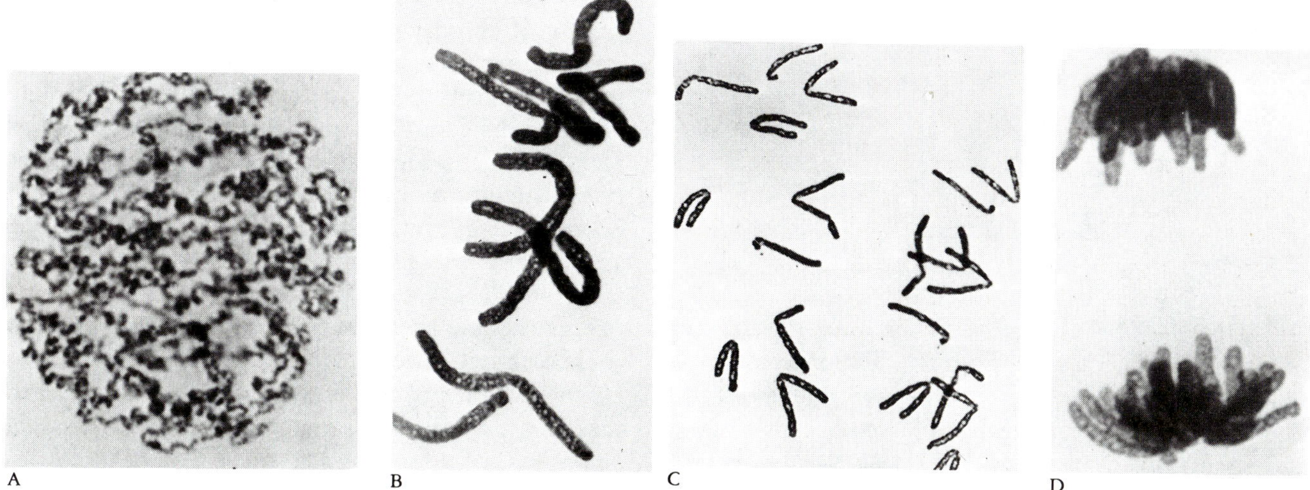

FIGURE 2-5 • Mitosis in the California coastal peony. The vegetative cells of this species have 24 chromosomes ($2n = 24$). Notice how the chromatin material becomes visible as a coiled linear structure (A), how chromosomes line up along the center of the cell (B), how they separate and pull apart toward the sides of the cell (C), and how they finally clump together (D) just prior to a wall being formed between the two groups. At mitosis two daughter cells are formed with the same number and kinds of chromosomes that existed in the original cell. (Courtesy of M. S. Walters and S. W. Brown.)

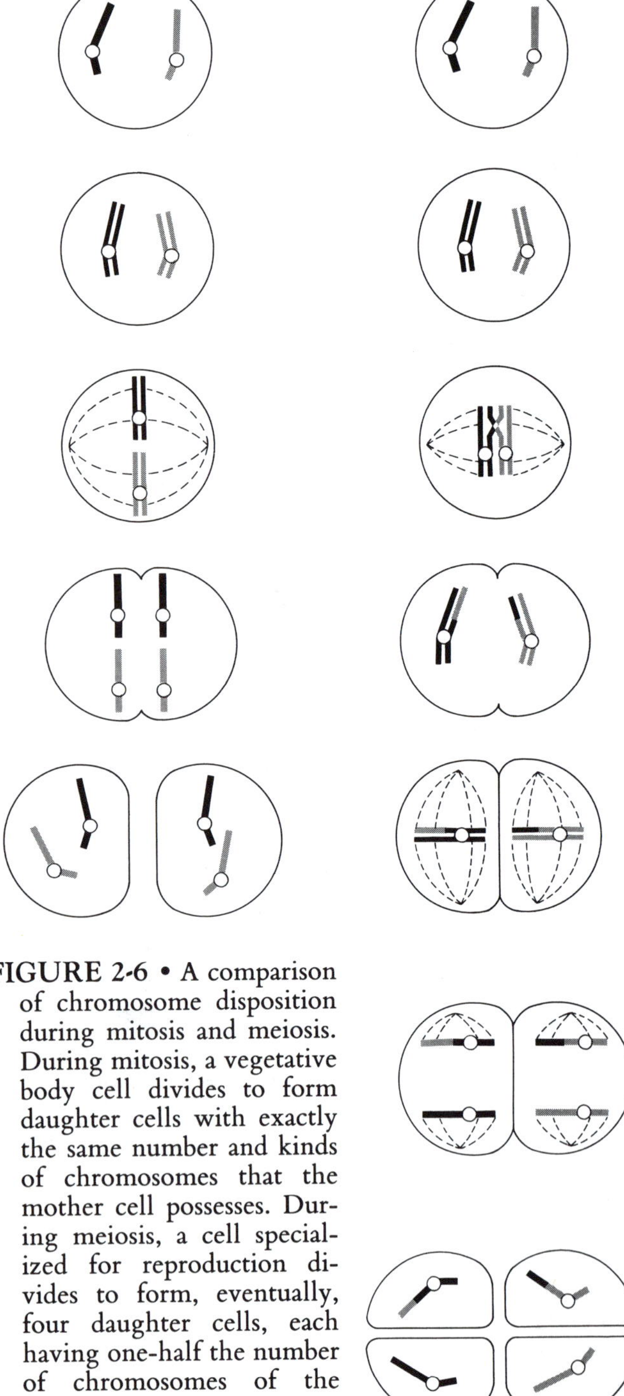

FIGURE 2-6 • A comparison of chromosome disposition during mitosis and meiosis. During mitosis, a vegetative body cell divides to form daughter cells with exactly the same number and kinds of chromosomes that the mother cell possesses. During meiosis, a cell specialized for reproduction divides to form, eventually, four daughter cells, each having one-half the number of chromosomes of the mother cell.

nodes, or in the differentiating fruit, tuber, bulb, or leaf. Because chromosomes and many organelles of newly formed cells are largely protein and because nitrogen is the major soil-borne element of protein molecules, young plants growing rapidly by means of cell division must have ample supplies of nitrogenous fertilizer.

The disposition of chromosomes during mitosis is pictured in Figure 2-6. When a cell is ready to divide, the nuclear wall disappears, and individual chromosomes become visible and arrange themselves linearly along the mid-axis of the cell. Each splits longitudinally into a pair of chromosomes. The chromosomes of each pair next move away from each other toward their respective sides of the cell, and a cell wall forms to complete the division.

Cell Enlargement

Much of what is seen as plant growth comes about as a result of cell enlargement. Just behind the region of cell division at the tip of stems or roots, or at the nodes of plants having growth in the nodal area, is the **region of cell elongation.** Cell elongation accounts for all the length growth and root spread of higher plants except for the relatively small amount that occurs as a result of cell division. Leaves, fruits, and tubers and other storage organs also expand largely through cell enlargement (Figure 2-7). In some fruits and storage tissues, cells can grow to several hundred times their original size.

Although protein is used for certain differentiating organelles in the elongating cells of stems and roots, cellulose, lignin, fiber, and other structural carbohydrates are relatively more in demand. The increase in size and in development of sweetness and flavor of fruits, bulbs, tubers, and similar storage tissue also involves the utilization and storage of carbohydrates. The visible and measurable enlargement of cells of storage tissue includes an increase of the size of the vacuole, which contains dissolved sugars and soluble carbohydrates; an increase in starch and insoluble carbohydrate

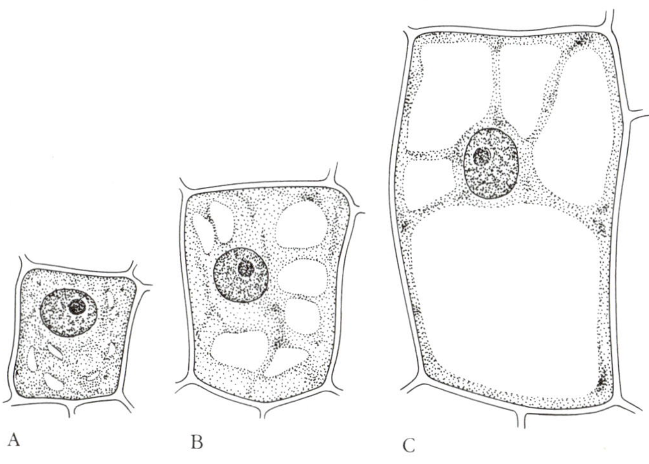

FIGURE 2-7 • A diagrammatic sketch of a newly formed meristematic cell (A), a herbaceous tissue cell of intermediate age (B), and a mature herbaceous cell (C). Although the cytoplasm may increase in size somewhat, the most dramatic change as the cells in many parts of the plant mature is their greatly enlarged vacuolar content.

granules in the cytoplasm; and an expansion of the cell wall, which is mostly lignin, cellulose, and fibrous carbohydrate material. Thus although nitrogen absorbed by the roots is the element most needed in tissue containing rapidly dividing cells, an abundant supply of carbohydrates manufactured primarily in the leaves is essential for fruit and tuber development, cell elongation, and other plant growth involving cell expansion. Carbohydrate manufacture by plants (photosynthesis and metabolism) is discussed in more detail later in this chapter.

Horticultural Significance of Cell Characteristics

Cell characteristics affect the usefulness of garden products. The juicy edible parts of most fruits and vegetables contain a large proportion of thin-walled living cells capable of growth and differentiation, called **parenchyma.** Wood and the tough fibrous plant materials used for string, paper, and clothing have large numbers of elongate thick-walled dead cells called **sclerenchyma fibers.** In the plant itself, sclerenchyma provides support.

There may be significant differences in the cells of various cultivars of the same kind of plant. For example, when the 'Russet Burbank' cultivar of potato is grown in an arid climate with irrigation, it is considered ideal for baking, mashing, and processing, because the middle lamellae break down easily when the potato is cooked but the cells remain intact, imparting a dry mealy texture. Especially when grown in areas of high rainfall, potato cultivars such as 'Katahdin' and 'Red Pontiac' contain cells in which the middle lamellae do not break down. Thus the tubers of these cultivars do not "cook to pieces," making them ideal for boiling and frying.

PLANT TISSUE AND STRUCTURE

We spoke earlier of the cell as a building block of plants and described briefly the type of cell division, called mitosis, by which plants increase their cell numbers. However, a plant is not simply a helter-skelter collection of cells dividing at random into a plant mass. Rather, each cell is part of a tissue that has a specialized function within the plant. Furthermore, tissues are organized into plant structures, each with a special purpose.

Tissue Differentiation

The differentiation of cells into specialized tissues and structures has been a subject of fascination ever since it was discovered that each living organism develops from a single cell. How is it possible for a single plant cell to multiply itself into a functioning plant, including such diverse structures as leaves, stems, roots, tubers, fruits, and seeds (Figure 2-8)?

The complete answer is not yet clear, but the mystery of tissue differentiation can now be partially explained. **Cell culture** or **tissue culture**

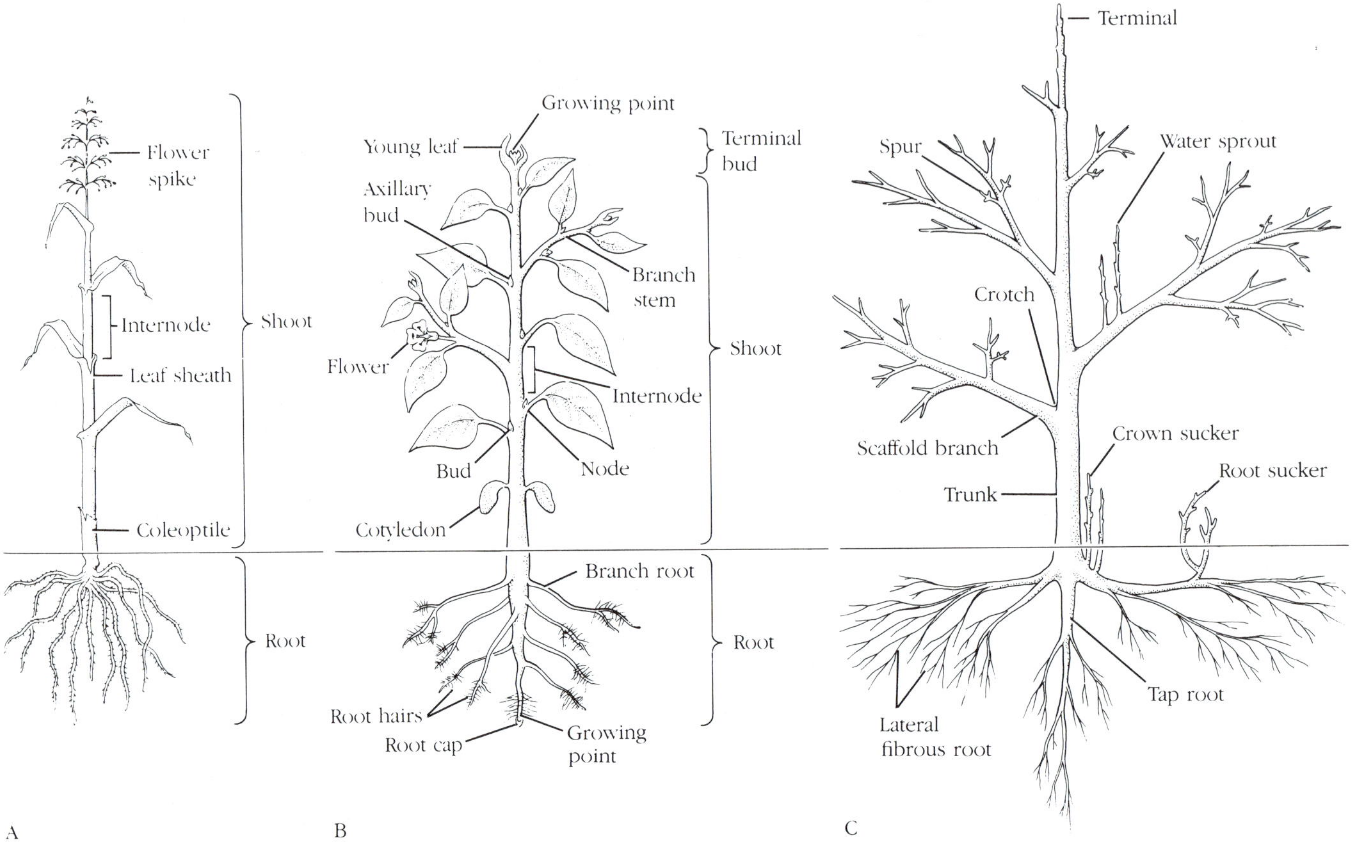

FIGURE 2-8 • Fundamental plant parts: monocot (A), herbaceous dicot (B), and woody dicot (C). Many of the structures detailed in this figure are discussed later in the text. (A and B adapted from Jules Janick et al., *Plant Science*, 3rd ed., W. H. Freeman and Company, New York, copyright © 1981)

(see the discussion in Chapter 4), by which single cells or small bits of tissue are grown on special nutrient media, has produced a few answers. For example, a single cell from a carrot root can be placed on a sterile medium containing the elements needed for plant growth, plus certain plant growth substances (growth substances are discussed in Chapter 8). If the medium containing the cell is kept circulating, often the cell will multiply to produce a mass of tissue in which all parts and all cells are alike. After the tissue mass has reached a certain critical size, which seems to be about the same, regardless of the species, the tissue develops into a hollow sphere, or **blastula,** reminiscent of certain stages of lower life forms and also one of the stages of animal embryonic development. After this point, if the tissue continues to have all the necessary growth requirements and is placed in a stationary location, roots, stems, and other structures will begin to differentiate.

Evidence from these and other experiments suggests that subtle changes in environment—perhaps differences in gravitational pressure or oxygen supply—activate or inactivate segments of DNA in the chromosome. The resulting change in the balance of chemical messages received from its DNA causes the cell to multiply into specialized tissue. For example, lower pressure at the upper surface and higher pressure at the lower surface of the cellular mass may elicit the chemical message, eventually resulting in shoot and root formation, respectively.

The major structures of the plant are the stem, the root, the leaves, and the reproductive organs—flowers, fruits, and seeds (Figure 2-8). Other plant structures such as bulbs, corms, tubers, and thorns are modifications of these major structures.

The Stem

Stems provide support for the leaves and the reproductive structures of the plant and contain the tissues that transport water, minerals, and manufactured food throughout the plant. They can also be organs of food manufacture and storage. Stems vary in appearance and structure from plant to plant, but basically there are three types among angiosperms: herbaceous dicot, woody dicot, and monocot.

Dicot Stems. The herbaceous dicot stem has the same structure as that of a first year's growth of a woody dicot; it is shown in Figure 2-9. At the tip of the stem are a series of undifferentiated cells, the **apical meristem.** Meristem is tissue capable of cell division. In a dicot, only those cells within a few millimeters of the stem tip are capable of plant elongation, by dividing or increasing in length.

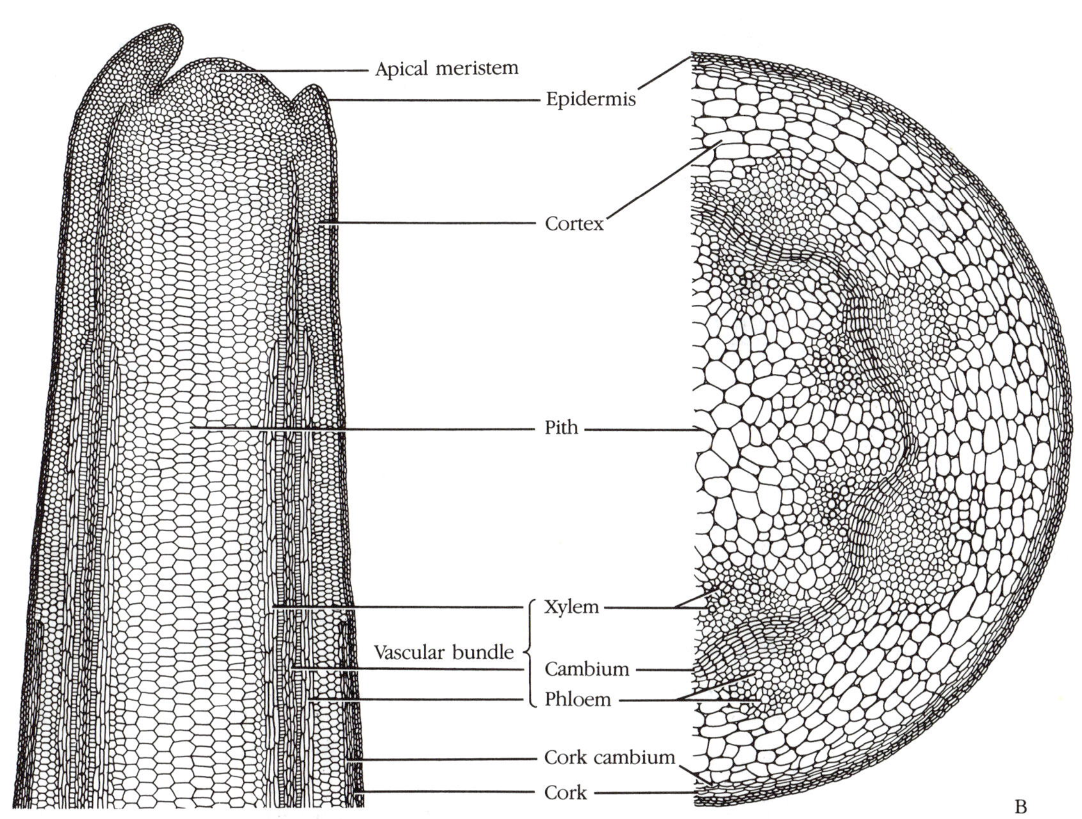

FIGURE 2-9 • Longitudinal section (A) and cross section (B) of the stem of a dicotyledonous plant. This could be either a herbaceous or a woody dicot during its initial stages of growth.

Occasionally a gardener chooses not to prune a low-growing lateral branch of a maple, oak, or other dicot tree, hoping that it will rise as the tree grows. But because elongation of a dicot occurs only at the tip of the stem, the limb will never be higher. In fact, it will grow somewhat lower as annual rings add to its girth.

Shortly after the cells in the apical meristem have formed, they begin to differentiate into various stem tissues, so that by the time a stem is a few hours to a few days old, it has a cross-sectional structure similar to the stem pictured in Figure 2-9. At the outside, providing a cover and protection is a layer of wax-coated cells known as the **epidermis.** Just inside the epidermis is the **cortex.** Cortex cells normally contain a considerable amount of chlorophyll and have an important food-manufacturing function in young stems. In the plant's early life, its cortex cells resemble the cells of the apical meristem and remain capable of some degree of differentiation into more specialized tissue.

Just inside the cortex, toward the center of the stem but outward from the pith, are the **vascular bundles.** The vascular tissue is the plant's "circulatory system" and, like the blood vessels of an animal, permeates all areas of the plant's body. A vascular bundle is made up of at least three distinct groups of cells. In its center is a single layer of meristematic tissue, the **cambium.** The cambium is constantly dividing to form phloem tissue toward the outside and xylem toward the center of the plant.

In the young dicot, the vascular bundles lie in a circular pattern between the cortex and pith. **Pith,** the tissue at the center of an herbaceous dicot plant, is made up of more undifferentiated cells. In some plant species, the pith disintegrates and a hollow-stemmed plant results. The pith is usually replaced by wood fibers from the xylem in older woody dicots. As the vascular bundles enlarge, the cambium of adjacent bundles fuses together until finally a complete ring of cambium is formed. If the plant is of a species in which the stem survives long enough to become woody, the vascular tissue in the stem will differentiate further.

Water and minerals are transported from the absorbing roots to all parts of the plant through the **xylem.** Although the xylem in a large tree may be many feet in diameter, only the youngest outer layers transport these elements. Nonfunctional xylem cells provide support in woody plants. The xylem tissue formed year by year accumulates and gradually pushes the rest of the plant tissue outward. Rapid growth—with the subsequent formation of large, thin-walled xylem cells—occurs in the spring. Much slower growth, producing small, thick-walled xylem cells, occurs in the fall; of course, growth ceases during the winter. These alternating types of growth produce the annual rings found in the trees of the temperate zone.

Unlike xylem, **phloem** cells do not accumulate from year to year. Rather, as they age and are pushed outward by the expanding xylem, they become disorganized and are gradually absorbed by surrounding tissue. Carbohydrates and other foods manufactured or elaborated in the upper parts of the plant are carried principally in the phloem.

Phloem transport of carbohydrates manufactured in the upper part of the plant is evident whenever the phloem is blocked. For example, if the wire used to tie a young tree to its supporting stake is left in place too long, the accumulating xylem expands the trunk against the wire, which cuts or girdles the bark, causing a partial blockage of the phloem. The trunk of a girdled or constricted tree will enlarge rapidly just above the constriction as a result of carbohydrates accumulating in that area of the trunk. The phloem may be blocked because of root diseases, and in such cases tuber-bearing crops such as potatoes may produce above-ground tubers as a result of the accumulation of carbohydrates in the stem. Carbohydrate accumulation stimulates reproductive growth, and sometimes phloem transport is purposely blocked by a single trunk-encircling cut through the bark. This practice increases carbohydrates in the stems and leaves, thus inducing fruiting of slow-bearing orchard trees or increasing flowering of sparse-flowering woody ornamentals (see Chapter 8 for more discussion of this practice).

In perennial-stemmed plants and occasionally in annuals and biennials, usually during the first season of growth, one layer of cortex tissue differentiates to form the **cork cambium.** This cork cambium is meristematic tissue that divides to form thick-walled cork cells toward the exterior of the plant. As the layer of cork cells widens, it pushes out to replace the epidermis with a much heavier and more permanent protective layer. The commercial cork used commonly for bottle stoppers and gaskets is the cork tissue that accumulates on the exterior of cork oak trees (*Quercus suber*).

FIGURE 2-11 • Palm trees. Because palms are monocots in which stems do not have a cambial ring, their trunks do not increase in diameter. Palms grow in height, often to 60 to 70 feet, from a terminal meristem.

Monocot Stems. Monocot stems (Figure 2-10) are made up of the same kinds of tissue as are dicot stems, but their tissue arrangement is different. The vascular bundles of monocots are scattered at random throughout the stem, and each bundle is surrounded by cortex tissue. In monocots, the vascular bundles are partially or wholly surrounded by a sheath of parenchyma cells. The older vascular bundles of monocots do not have a functioning cambium but continue active transport throughout the life of the plant. Monocots do not produce annual rings, even though some, such as palms (Figure 2-11), grow large and become quite woody. In some monocots, growth in length occurs only from a bud at the tip. In others—grasses are a prime example—growth in length occurs from nodes at the lower part of the stem. One reason grasses are better lawn plants than herbaceous dicots is that mowing does not remove the grass plant's growing point.

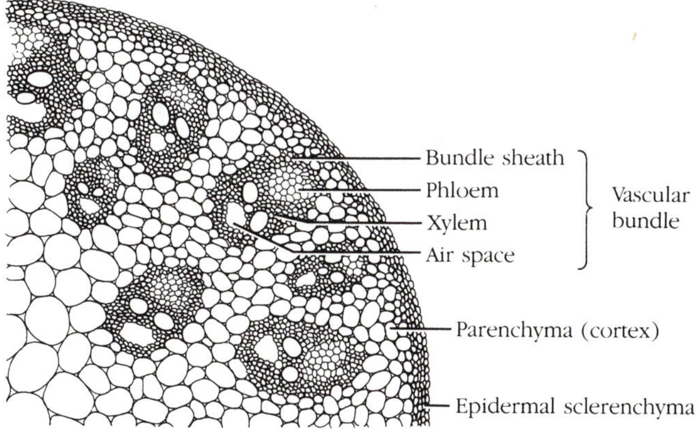

FIGURE 2-10 • Cross section of part of a monocotyledonous plant stem, showing the scattered vascular bundles.

Buds and Nodes. The elongation and branching of stems take place within structures referred to as buds. **Buds** can be described as embryonic stems surrounded by the embryonic leaf and flower tissues that will develop from them. They may be enclosed in protective sheaths that may disappear or remain as bracts or scales when the bud opens. **Nodes** are those portions of the stem where visible buds are generally located and where leaf petioles are attached. Areas of the stem be-

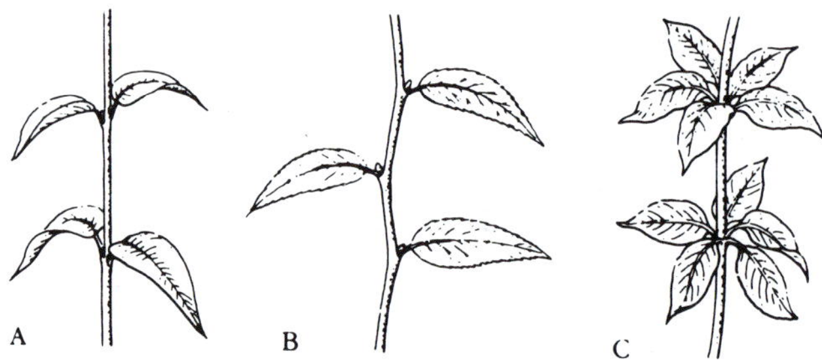

FIGURE 2-12 • Three types of leaf and bud arrangement: (A) opposite, (B) alternate, (C) whorled.

tween nodes are called **internodes** (see Figure 2-8).

Buds can be either actively growing or dormant. Growth in height of dicots commences from terminal buds, and branching commences from lateral buds lower on the stem. Occasionally buds not previously visible grow from internodal areas of stems or from roots of certain species. They are called **adventitious** buds.

Bud placement is an important diagnostic feature of woody ornamentals. Buds are **opposite** when two are located at the same node on opposite sides of the stem, **whorled** when several surround the stem at the same node, or **alternate** when each is at a different node and arranged in a spiral (Figure 2-12). Buds may produce only leaves and stems (vegetative structures), only flowers, or both vegetative structures and flowers, and so are referred to as **vegetative, flower,** or **mixed** buds, respectively.

Buds producing leaves, flowers, and fruit on temperate-zone woody plants are usually formed during the previous summer and are visible through the winter. Therefore, practices affecting flower and fruit initiation need to be completed by early summer of the year preceding the year of production.

The Root

The main functions of plant roots are to anchor the plant and to absorb the water and minerals the plant needs. The tissues of the stem are connected with those of the root, and most are duplicated in the root. At the tip of a rapidly growing root are several layers of thick-walled cells known as the **root cap.** Just behind the root cap is the region of cell division, behind that is the region of cell elongation, and behind that is the **root-hair zone.** It is principally through these few millimeters at the rapidly growing root tip that the plant is able to absorb moisture and minerals. This part of the root system is extremely delicate and subject to injury and desiccation. Almost all of these zones are destroyed with bare-root transplanting, and for this reason a transplanted plant often wilts severely, even though most of its major roots are still intact. Roots elongate almost exclusively in the regions of cell division and cell elongation. This elongation is stimulated by favorable growing conditions, which explains why roots become concentrated where moisture and mineral elements are plentiful and why tree roots can so easily grow through cracks or joints in moist, nutrient-rich sewer lines.

A cross section near the root-hair zone would show a structure similar to that in Figure 2-13. The outer cells of the root form an epidermal layer. In young root tissue this layer is quite permeable to water, and it is from cells of this layer that root hairs are produced. Just inside the epidermal layer is a layer of loosely spaced cortex cells. Water is able to pass quite rapidly through the intercellular spaces of this cortex tissue. Next to the cortex is a single layer of tissue composed of thick-walled, somewhat impermeable cells known as the **endodermis.** In the root-hair zone and younger root tissue, the endodermis is permeable enough to permit the passage of water and nutrients. Higher in the root the loss of water from the vascular system is prevented by the impervious nature of the endodermis. Next to the endodermis, toward the interior of the plant, is a layer of meristematic cells known as the **pericycle,** from which branch roots form. Adventitious buds that produce the root suckers of sumac, poplar, blackberry, raspberry, and some other plants are also initiated by cells multiplying in the pericycle. The

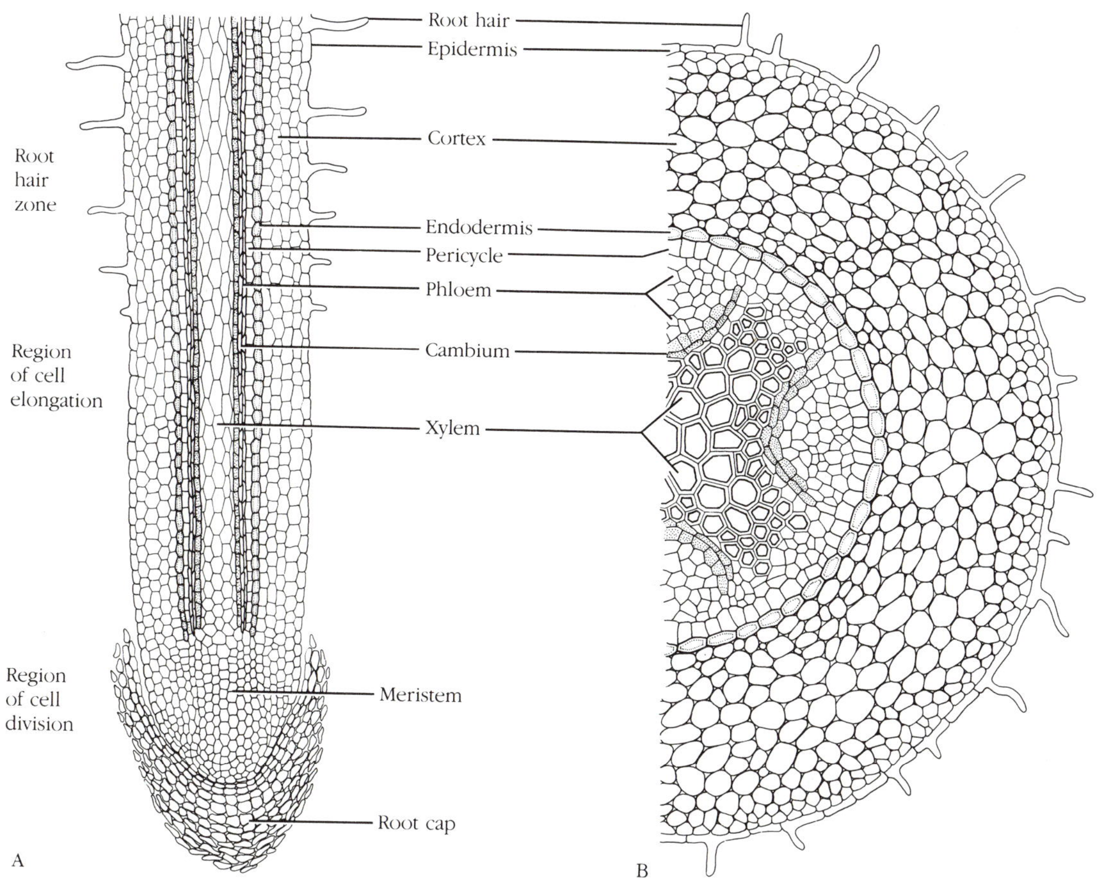

FIGURE 2-13 • Longitudinal section (A) and cross section (B) of a plant root.

fact that these suckers form from cells of the roots' inner tissue explains why some thornless blackberry cultivars produce thorny suckers (see "Gene Mutation and Bud Sports" in Chapter 3).

The vascular system is at the center of most roots. As in the stem, the xylem and phloem are formed from cells cut off by the cambium—the phloem to the outside, the xylem to the inside. The roots of most plants do not have pith.

Root systems vary in appearance and in the extent to which they penetrate the soil. The extensiveness of the root system is often associated with the environment under which the plant evolved. The extensiveness of the root system also determines, to some extent, the frequency and depth of irrigation required for the particular type of plant. Celery, for example, which originated in the swamps of the Middle East where only a small root system was needed because water was plentiful, requires frequent irrigation. Tomatoes and melons have much more extensive root systems and so are quite drought tolerant.

Plant root systems can be divided into two general groups on the basis of their growth habits (Figure 2-14). When the root system branches into a number of smaller roots near the soil line, the plants are said to have **fibrous roots.** Those plants in which the main root grows straight down from the stem and smaller side roots branch off the main root are said to be **taprooted.** The

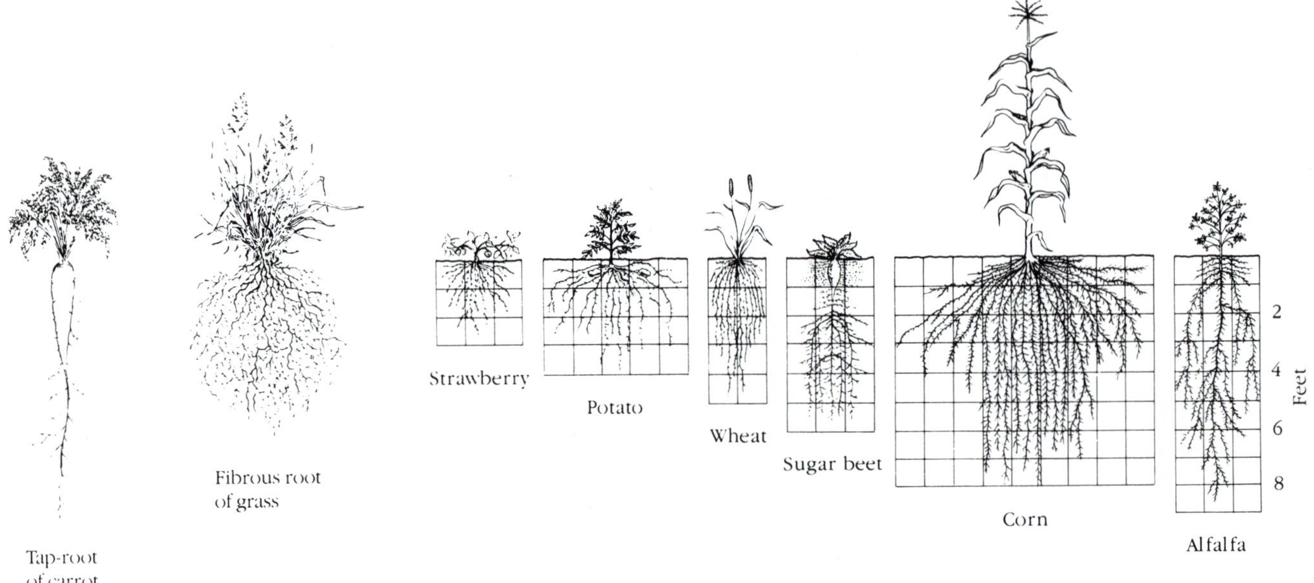

FIGURE 2-14 • (A) Root systems and (B) comparative root systems of crops grown under soil conditions that allow unrestricted root expansion. (From Jules Janick et al., *Plant Science*, 3rd ed., W. H. Freeman and Company, New York, copyright © 1981)

carrot is a well-known example of a taprooted plant. Because a widely branched root system tends to bind soil particles together, it is easier to keep a ball of earth around a fibrous-rooted plant than around a tap-rooted plant. The ball of earth prevents injury to and desiccation of the absorbing roots and allows the plant to be transplanted with less disruption of its vital functions. To create root branching, nursery workers frequently undercut taprooted plants a year or more before they are to be transplanted. Severing the lower part of the taproot six months or a year before transplanting encourages root branching and makes the plant easier to move with the root system and adhering soil particles intact (Figure 2-15).

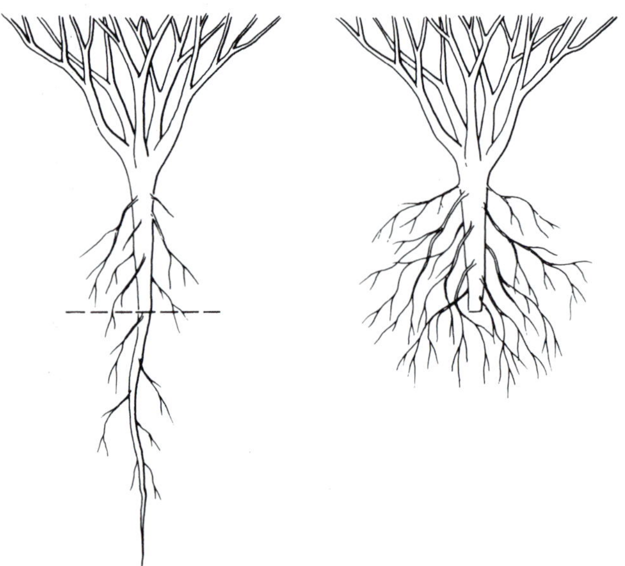

FIGURE 2-15 • The effect of undercutting a taprooted plant.

The Leaf

The main function of the leaf is the manufacture of sugar from inorganic compounds. Food for all

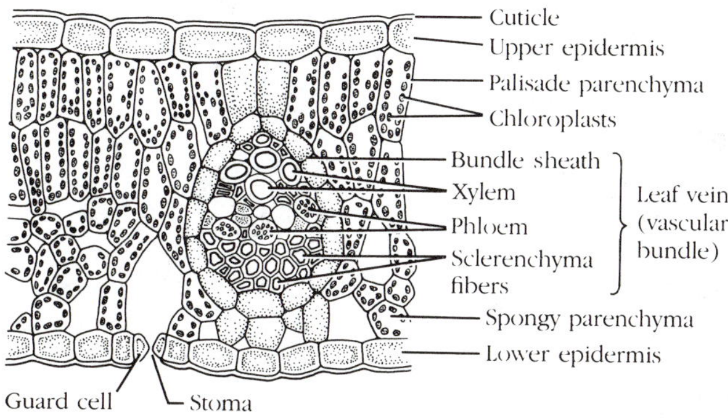

FIGURE 2-16 • Cross section of a leaf.

living creatures on this earth, plants and animals alike, is elaborated from the sugars manufactured by photosynthesis, which is carried out primarily in the leaves and herbaceous stems of green plants.

The structure of the leaf is shown in Figure 2-16. The upper surface of the leaf is a layer of epidermal cells coated with a waxy cuticle that makes it impervious to either the entry or the loss of water or other liquids. The imperviousness of the cuticle also effectively prevents solution absorption through upper leaf surfaces and explains why special treatments are usually required for foliar feeding. Just below the upper epidermis is a layer of cells arranged like the marble columns of a Greek temple or the elongated pillars of basalt sometimes found in areas of ancient volcanic activity. These cells are called the **palisade parenchyma.** Below the palisade parenchyma is an area of rather loosely packed cells called the **spongy parenchyma.** The palisade and spongy parenchyma cells contain numerous chloroplasts, in which most photosynthesis occurs.

Below the spongy parenchyma is the lower epidermis, which seldom has a thick cuticle. Scattered over the lower epidermis are several openings called **stomata.** Each stoma is bordered by two **guard cells,** which expand or contract to open or close the stoma in response to the environment and the plant's physiological condition. Droughty conditions or an excess of carbon dioxide, which is likely at night or during cool weather, causes the guard cells to collapse and close the stomata. Stomata are usually open when weather and soil moisture conditions are favorable for photosynthesis (see the section "Photosynthesis" later in this chapter and Figure 2-17).

The veins of the leaf are vascular bundles similar to those found in the stem and root. They consist of xylem and phloem separated by a cambium layer. The leaf veins are connected to the vascular system of the rest of the plant. Also associated with the bundles are supporting sclerenchyma fibers. The vascular bundles of the leaf, like those of the monocot stem mentioned earlier, are surrounded by a sheath of parenchyma cells. In addition to their vital role in the physiology of the leaf and plant, leaf veins have both diagnostic and ornamental value. As mentioned earlier, monocots

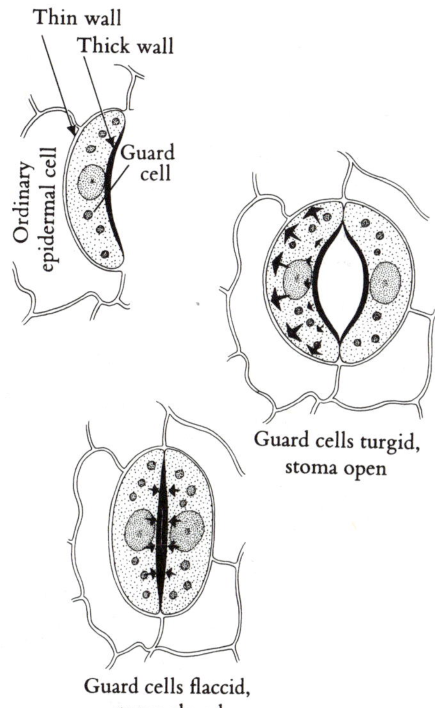

FIGURE 2-17 • Stomatal behavior. (From James Bonner and A. W. Galston, *Principles of Plant Physiology*, W. H. Freeman and Company, New York, copyright © 1952)

have more or less straight, unbranched veins arranged in the leaf in a parallel or fan-shaped configuration, whereas dicots have very crooked, branched, interconnecting veins. In addition to these generalized subclass differences, each species has its own distinctive pattern of veination, which can be useful in its identification and which influences the ornamental texture and light-reflecting qualities of the species.

Modifications of Stem, Root, and Leaf

The internal anatomy of the tubers, bulbs, and other fleshy storage organs mentioned earlier in this chapter resembles the anatomy of a stem, root, or leaf, and each is thought to have evolved from one of these three organs. These modified structures are important both as sources of food and as means of propagation for many garden crops. Some of them are shown in Figure 2-18.

Certain plants, such as the strawberry and strawberry geranium, produce horizontal aboveground stems called **stolons** or **runners.** Horizontal underground stems, such as those produced by grasses, are called **rhizomes.** Some plants, bearded iris being an example, produce large fleshy rhizomes. **Tubers** are enlarged fleshy sections of rhizomes, their "eyes" being analagous to the buds on a stem. **Corms** are solid thickened underground stems, and **bulbs** are thickened stem plates

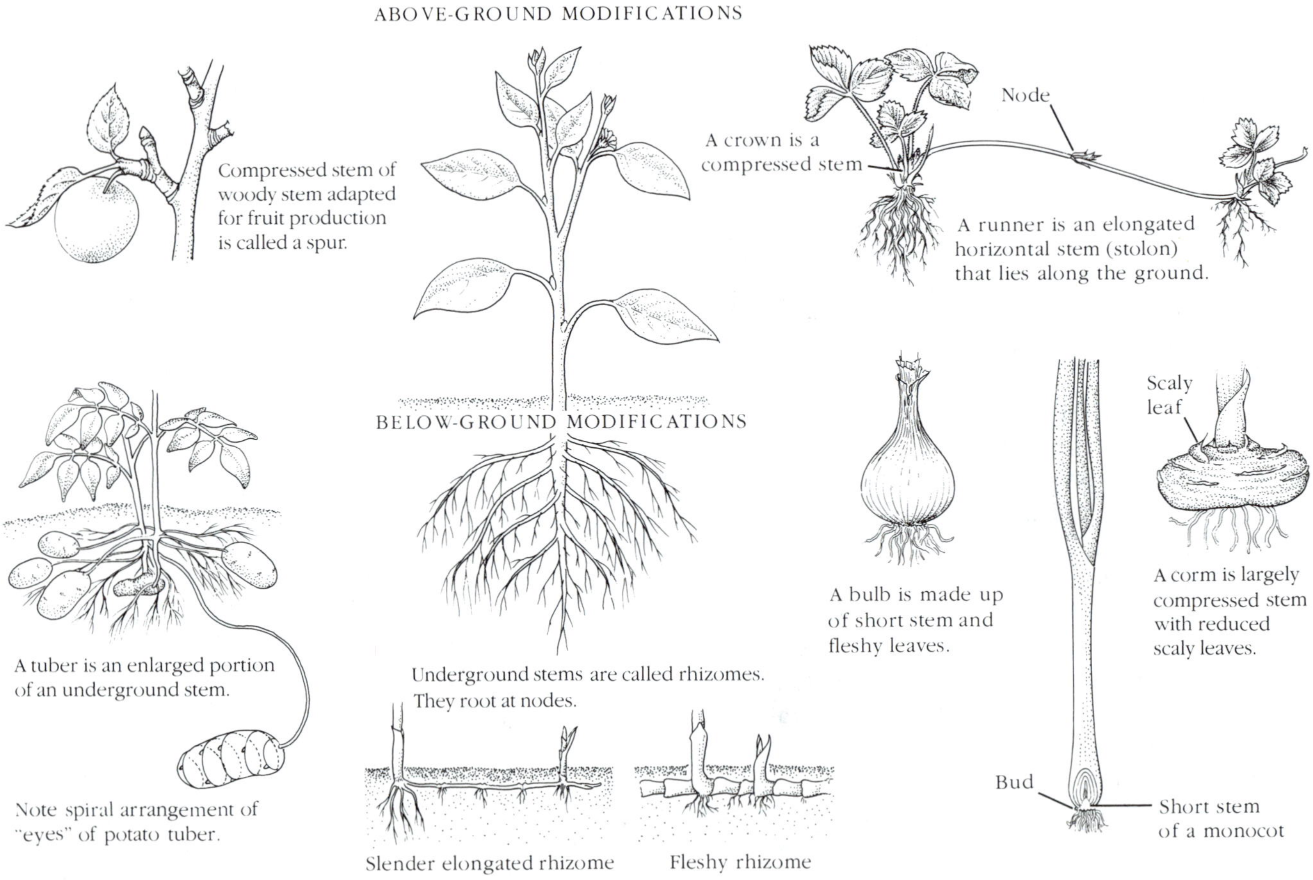

ABOVE-GROUND MODIFICATIONS

Compressed stem of woody stem adapted for fruit production is called a spur.

A crown is a compressed stem

Node

A runner is an elongated horizontal stem (stolon) that lies along the ground.

BELOW-GROUND MODIFICATIONS

A tuber is an enlarged portion of an underground stem.

Note spiral arrangement of "eyes" of potato tuber.

Underground stems are called rhizomes. They root at nodes.

Slender elongated rhizome

Fleshy rhizome

A bulb is made up of short stem and fleshy leaves.

Bud

Short stem of a monocot

Scaly leaf

A corm is largely compressed stem with reduced scaly leaves.

FIGURE 2-18 • Some modifications of stems, roots, and leaves.

FIGURE 2-19 • (A) Asparagus crown. Carbohydrates stored in the crown and fleshy roots of various herbaceous perennials provide food for early-spring growth. This one-year-old crown has already initiated several spears, and it is of the age and size usually sold by nurseries for replanting. (B) Growing asparagus. (B, courtesy of John Colwell/Grant Heilman)

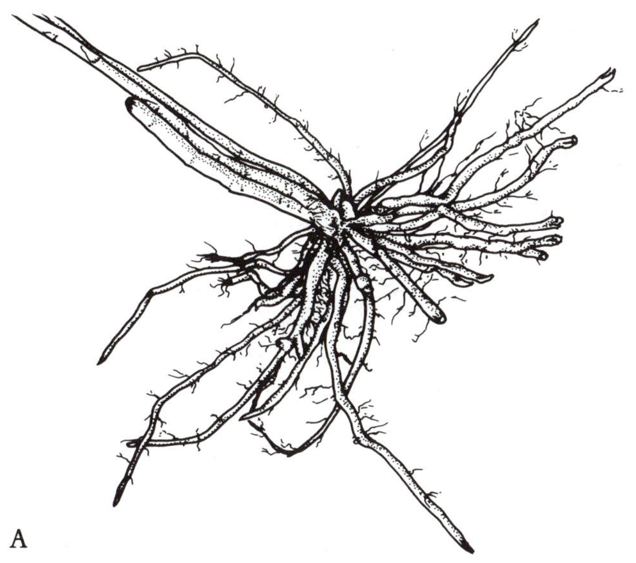

A

B

surmounted by fleshy modified leaves. Bulbs, like those of the onion and tulip, with concentric rings, the outer of which form a dry protective cover (a tunica), are called **tunicate** bulbs, and those like the lily, with fleshy overlapping leaves resembling scales, are called **scaly** bulbs (see Figures 14-30 and 14-32). The first-year stem of most biennial crop plants is a flattened platelike cluster of cells, similar to the stem portion of a nongrowing bulb. The platelike cell cluster elongates to form a typical flowering stem during the second year.

The juncture of stem and root is called the **crown.** Perennial herbaceous plants often have crowns modified into enlarged storage organs that enable the plants to survive through the winter. New shoots, including the edible portion of asparagus and rhubarb and the flower stalks of peonies and other perennial flowers, have enough energy to grow from these fleshy crowns each spring as a result of the carbohydrates stored in the crowns or in accompanying fleshy storage roots (Figure 2-19).

The roots of some species grow into enlarged **storage organs,** the function of which, like that of fleshy stems, is to enable the plant to survive periods of adverse environment. These organs are typical roots with no nodes or leaf scales. The fleshy roots of some plants are capable of initiating buds. Wild morning glory (creeping Jenny) and Canadian thistle are two well-known perennial weeds that unfortunately possess this ability. The large fleshy roots capable of forming buds are more appreciated in the sweet potato than in its relative, the morning glory. In contrast, the fleshy storage root of the dahlia does not initiate buds and must remain attached to a piece of the crown having buds if it is to grow into a new plant. Raspberries, some blackberries, and other brambles are capable of initiating buds from their widespread root system and are propagated from shoots or suckers coming from those roots. Staghorn sumac, certain poplars, and some wild roses are not so desirable as ornamentals because of their tendency to produce **root suckers** "all over the lawn" or because suckers from their roots enable them to "take over" an area. Sucker-type shoot growth can also originate from roots near the crown (as with common lilac), from the lower stem, or from **axillary buds,** which form in the protected angle between the leaf and stem, called the leaf axil (see Figure 2-8). These shoots are called **offshoots, slips, pips,** or other names, and are frequently used for propagation.

The leaves of some plants are thick and fleshy, a modification that makes them good carbohydrate and water storage organs, thus frequently enabling them to withstand drought and/or to be used for propagation. The leaves may also be modified into bud scales or spines. For example, the spines on cacti are modified leaves, and the thickened fleshy body or flattened fleshy pads are stem adaptations enabling this plant family to withstand extreme drought. The stems of woody plants may be modified to form short, thick, slow-growing **spurs** (see Figure 2-8), and the fruit and flowers of woody temperate-zone species are frequently borne on such spurs.

PLANT FUNCTIONS RESPONSIBLE FOR GROWTH

◆ ◆ ◆

Most of the functions relating to food manufacture and utilization that result in growth take place in the plant's stems, leaves, and roots.

Absorption and Translocation

Water molecules and minerals are absorbed into roots because the molecules in a liquid or gas tend to flow to those locations where they are least concentrated. Root cells contain membranes that have openings large enough to allow tiny water molecules and mineral particles to pass through but small enough to keep sugar and similar large, plant-developed molecules inside. A high concentration of sugar molecules dilutes the water molecules to a lower concentration inside the plant and permits moisture to flow from the soil into the plant root. The flow of a liquid through a semipermeable membrane from a region of higher concentration to one of lower concentration, such as occurs with water absorption into roots, is called **osmosis.** The mechanism of mineral absorption parallels water absorption, but it is not as well understood. Mineral absorption is covered in more detail in Chapter 5.

Water is absorbed into the plant only as long as the concentration outside remains higher than that inside the plant. If water concentration outside is to remain high, soil moisture must be replenished by rain or irrigation. Furthermore, the application of too much fertilizer causes the development of molecules that compete with sugar, diluting the water concentration in the soil solution and thus preventing water from entering the plant roots. Plant injury resulting from high concentrations of fertilizer is called **fertilizer burn.**

If the absorbed water remained in the root, it would eventually reach an equilibrium with the soil water. But this does not usually happen, because the concentration on the inside is reduced by **translocation** (movement within the plant) of water to other parts of the plant. Translocation occurs as a result of a "pull" created by evaporation from the leaves and by other plant activities.

A high plant-sugar concentration is also necessary for rapid water absorption, and a high sugar concentration, in turn, is dependent on a high rate of photosynthesis.

Photosynthesis

Photosynthesis is an energy-storing chemical process that takes place in the green leaves and stems of plants. In the opening paragraph of this book, food (for both humans and animals), clothes, oxygen, rubber, and plastic are mentioned as products that come from plants. Also from plants comes the wood for constructing homes and public buildings and for manufacturing paper, which in our computer age is used so extensively for storage of information; for communication via books, brochures, newspapers, and magazines; for cleaning and waste disposal as napkins, paper towels, diapers, and cleansing tissues; and for packaging fast foods, grocery store items, and durable consumer products. All of these are products of photosynthesis. In addition, the natural gas, oil, and coal that in North America supply 90 percent of our energy for heating, cooling, lighting, and powering our homes and industries come from photosynthetic energy captured from the sun by plants that grew millions of years ago. Numerous and extensive as are these goods and sources of power, their production accounts for only a fraction of the solar energy converted by photosynthesis. The major portion of that energy is utilized in the nutrition, growth, and other life processes of the plants themselves.

The chemical formula of photosynthesis is commonly written as

$$\underset{\text{carbon dioxide}}{6CO_2} + \underset{\text{water}}{6H_2O} + \underset{\text{radiant energy}}{672 \text{ calories}} \rightarrow \underset{\text{glucose}}{C_6H_{12}O_6} + \underset{\text{oxygen}}{6O_2}$$

This equation is greatly simplified. The processes that eventually result in the synthesis of sugar (and the other organic compounds now known to be produced during photosynthesis) are a complex set of stepwise reactions dependent on the healthy functioning of all plant organs interacting with a conducive environment. Vigorous roots must be absorbing in warm soil that contains water and mineral nutrients in the proper amounts; young leaves containing chlorophyll must be expanding in an uncrowded, temperate, well-lighted atmosphere that has a plentiful supply of carbon dioxide; and the countless systems that manufacture and elaborate food and supply energy to the plant, as well as the transport (vascular) system, must be healthy and functioning at near-maximum efficiency. An interruption at any point of the system halts photosynthesis.

In simplest terms, maximum production from garden or field requires maximum photosynthesis. The pages of this and succeeding chapters are devoted to plant structure and function, environmental conditions, and pest control, largely because they determine the rate of photosynthesis and, in turn, the growth of the garden.

Respiration

Solar energy that has been converted to chemical energy by means of photosynthesis is stored in the plant in various organic compounds. If plant products are burned, as in a forest fire, this energy will be released very rapidly in the form of heat and light. In living cells, such energy is released in small increments by a process referred to as **respiration,** which proceeds day and night as long as the cell continues to live. **Aerobic respiration** (i.e., oxygen-requiring), the most common and usually the only kind of respiration occurring in actively growing higher plants, can be summarized in the following equation:

$$\underset{\text{glucose}}{C_6H_{12}O_6} + \underset{\text{oxygen}}{6O_2} + \underset{\text{water}}{6H_2O} \xrightarrow[\text{ADP}]{\text{enzymes}} \underset{\text{carbon dioxide}}{6CO_2} + \underset{\text{water}}{12H_2O} + 36 \text{ ATP}$$

ATP stands for **adenosine triphosphate** and is the storage molecule from which energy can be released almost instantly in the exact quantity needed for various cell life and growth requirements. The ATP molecule releases its energy by giving up one of its three phosphorus groups to become **ADP, adenosine diphosphate.** There are millions of phosphorus-containing ATP and ADP molecules in cells, one reason that phosphorus is a major fertilizer requirement.

TABLE 2-1 • *Comparison of photosynthesis and respiration*

Photosynthesis	Respiration
1. Carbon dioxide and water are used	1. Carbon dioxide and water are released
2. Energy is stored in sugar molecules	2. Energy is released from sugar molecules
3. Occurs only during periods of light	3. Occurs during both light and dark periods
4. Occurs only in chlorophyll-containing cells	4. Occurs in all living cells
5. Increases plant weight	5. Decreases plant weight
6. Releases oxygen	6. Utilizes oxygen (aerobic respiration)

Anaerobic respiration and **fermentation** are two kinds of respiration associated with certain forms of bacteria and yeast that exist in the absence of oxygen. These kinds of respiration release much less energy than does aerobic respiration: two ATP molecules for alcohol and lactic acid fermentation, as compared with thirty-six for aerobic respiration. Fermentation is necessary for making alcoholic beverages, sauerkraut, pickles, and bread.

The effects of respiration should be considered whenever plant products are stored. The utilization of carbohydrates by respiration causes stored plant products to lose weight. Stored products also become warmer. Ideally all the energy from glucose is transformed into ATP, as shown in the aerobic respiration equation, and all ATP energy is used for plant growth – related processes. In reality some heat energy is released into the environment whenever respiration occurs. Because, as already noted, respiration occurs in every living plant cell, even cells of seemingly inert seeds, it is important that a means for heat dissipation be provided whenever living plant products are stored.

Temperature is a major environmental factor affecting both photosynthesis and respiration. Like other chemical processes, both are speeded by higher temperature but can be inhibited if the temperature rises too high. Each plant has a temperature range to which it is adapted. To grow a crop gardeners should know at least the approximate range to which it is adapted. (The effect of temperature on plant growth, product quality, and storage requirements is described in Chapter 7.) Table 2-1 compares and contrasts photosynthesis and respiration.

PHOTOSYNTHESIS, RESPIRATION, AND THE ATMOSPHERE

Photosynthesis is undoubtedly the process most important to life as we know it. At least as important as the role of photosynthesis in the production of food, fiber, and energy is its role, in conjunction with respiration, in regulating the atmosphere's gaseous content. Look again at the chemical formula for photosynthesis given earlier, and notice that carbon dioxide is consumed and oxygen is a by-product. The earth's atmosphere is approximately 79 percent nitrogen, 20 percent oxygen, and 1 percent other gases, including 0.03 percent carbon dioxide. Without its release from water molecules by photosynthesis, oxygen would be slowly depleted from the atmosphere by combustion, animal and plant respiration, and other natural forces. And without oxygen in the atmosphere, life as we know it would not exist.

Carbon dioxide is released into the atmosphere by plant and animal respiration, the breakdown of organic matter, the burning of material containing carbon, volcanic activity, and by other forces, including the buffering effect of the large carbon dioxide reservoirs in the oceans. During daylight hours, plants are constantly absorbing an enormous amount of carbon dioxide from the atmosphere. The plants on an acre of corn, for example, use 11 tons (10 metric tons) of carbon dioxide to accumulate 5,500 pounds (2,500 kg) of carbon during a growing season. Both the forces that use carbon dioxide and those that release it tend to keep the earth's supply in balance, with about 55 tons (50 metric tons) over each acre.

Note that if the atmosphere were stationary, this corn crop would use 10 percent of the carbon dioxide above it in a single growing season. That does not happen, of course, because the air is constantly being mixed and exchanged. There is speculation that the carbon dioxide around the plant canopy may become limiting when high rates of photosynthesis occur during a weather period when the air mass is stagnant. Some agriculturists suggest that the record high yields in some areas of the Pacific Coast states, British Columbia, and certain areas of western Europe may be due partly to the constant prevailing westerly winds of those regions circulating air with a high carbon dioxide content from the adjacent oceans into the air mass surrounding the crop. The excellent crops often grown on soils high in organic matter and the higher yields achieved with plastic mulch may be partly the result of higher carbon dioxide from the breakdown of organic matter (see "Modifying Temperature with Plant Covers and Mulches" in Chapter 7). Carbon dioxide is often added to the closed atmosphere of greenhouses and can be beneficial, especially in winter when air circulation from the outside has to be limited because of heating costs.

There is some evidence that human activity is causing the amount of carbon dioxide in the atmosphere to increase, a trend that has generated considerable alarm and controversy among scientists and the public. This increase results from the lowered utilization of the gas for photosynthesis because of the destruction of the plant cover by cultivation, overgrazing, and the razing of the rain forests and from the release of enormous amounts of carbon dioxide from the combustion of fossil fuels. Large gaseous molecules such as carbon dioxide cause solar energy to be retained in the atmosphere (the highly publicized "greenhouse effect"; see Figure 7-2). These greater amounts of atmospheric carbon dioxide are thought to be at least partially responsible for the higher temperatures on the earth during the age of the dinosaurs 250 millions years ago (before carbon was tied up in fossil-fuel deposits) and also for the lethally high temperatures that space probes have recently confirmed on the planet Venus. Slightly higher carbon dioxide concentrations would probably benefit plant growth if all other growing conditions were to remain as they are now; however, when all factors are considered, the higher temperatures caused by the increased amount of carbon dioxide in the atmosphere are predicted to lead to drastic climatic changes, including the creation of drought conditions over large agricultural regions of the world and the melting of ice fields, causing the oceans to flood coastal cities.

Metabolism

Just as humans need several kinds of foods, so do plants. The plant forms its proteins, complex carbohydrates, and fats by combining nitrogen and other elements with manufactured sugars. This elaboration of more complex food molecules is one form of **metabolism,** a term used to describe the chemical processes that build up and break down the various food elements in the plant body. The chemical reactions that result from photosynthesis and respiration are metabolic processes.

Transpiration and Plant Water Use

Water is used by plants for photosynthesis and for incorporation into the protoplasm and other materials of the plant body. The percentage of the total water volume absorbed by the plant that is utilized in these ways varies with the plant type (it is higher in desert plants) and climatic conditions (it is higher with moderate temperatures and high humidity), but on the average, it is probably less than 2 percent of the water absorbed. By far the greatest volume of water used by plants evaporates into the atmosphere, mostly through the stomata. When the stomata are open, carbon dioxide enters and water vapor is lost. The plants' loss of water vapor into the atmosphere is called **transpiration,** which proceeds either rapidly or slowly, depending on temperature and humidity, whenever humidity is less than 100 percent and photosynthesis is occurring. Most of the water lost from a field covered with foliage is through plant transpiration, and is much more than is lost through evaporation from the soil surface.

Transpiration will cause plants to wilt if translocation from the roots is interrupted, as happens with cut flowers, bare-root transplanting, or droughty conditions. Wilting causes the collapse of the guard cells and the closing of the stomata, which reduce, but do not eliminate, the loss of water through the leaves. Several chemical treatments have been devised to reduce transpiration; most plug or close the stomata. As a consequence, except for bare-root transplanting and a few other special situations, treatments to reduce transpiration have not been practical, mainly because closing the stomata reduces the intake of carbon dioxide and stops or drastically reduces photosynthesis.

Selected References

Esau, K. *Anatomy of Seed Plants.* New York: Wiley, 1977.

———. *Plant Anatomy.* 3rd ed. New York: Wiley, 1988.

Heyward, F. C., and C. W. Ross. *Structure of Economic Plants.* New York: Macmillan, 1967, 1938.

Salisbury, F. B., and C. W. Ross. *Plant Physiology.* 4th ed. Wadsworth, Calif.: Belmont, 1991.

CHAPTER 3

Structure and Growth: The Reproductive Phase

The processes of reproduction have long been regarded as mysterious and miraculous. No facet of biological science has received more intensive study during the past few decades, and in no area of biology has the increase in knowledge been more rapid. The new understanding has dispelled some of the mystery, but the creation of a new living organism seems as miraculous as ever. Knowledge of the principles underlying plant reproduction can enhance the enjoyment of gardening and is basic to an understanding of plant propagation (production of new plants) and plant growth. Chapter 2 described vegetative growth — stems, roots, and leaves — and this chapter discusses the organs associated with reproduction: flowers and the fruit and seeds that develop from flowers.

THE FLOWER

The typical flower (Figure 3-1) consists of four major parts, usually situated on a **receptacle**, the enlarged, terminal portion of a flower stem. Just above and attached to the receptacle is a whorl of connected or separated leaflike bracts, most often green, called **sepals**. Inward from and above the sepals are the frequently brightly colored **petals** of the flower, collectively

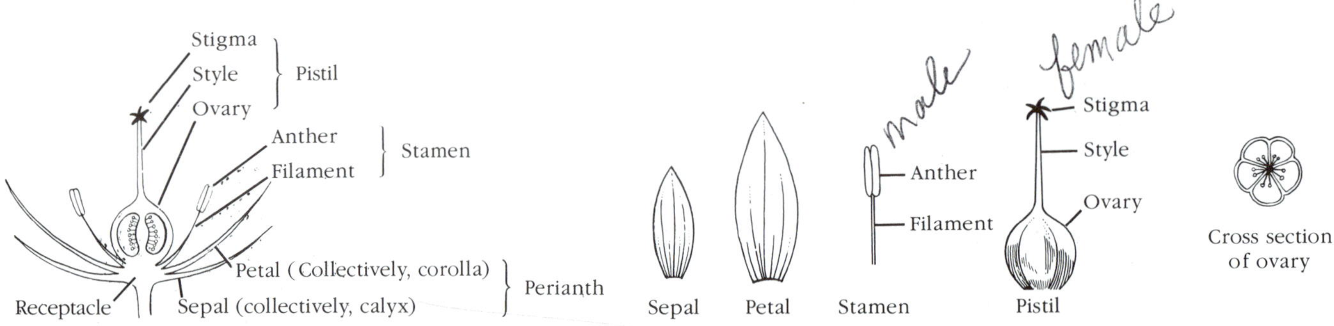

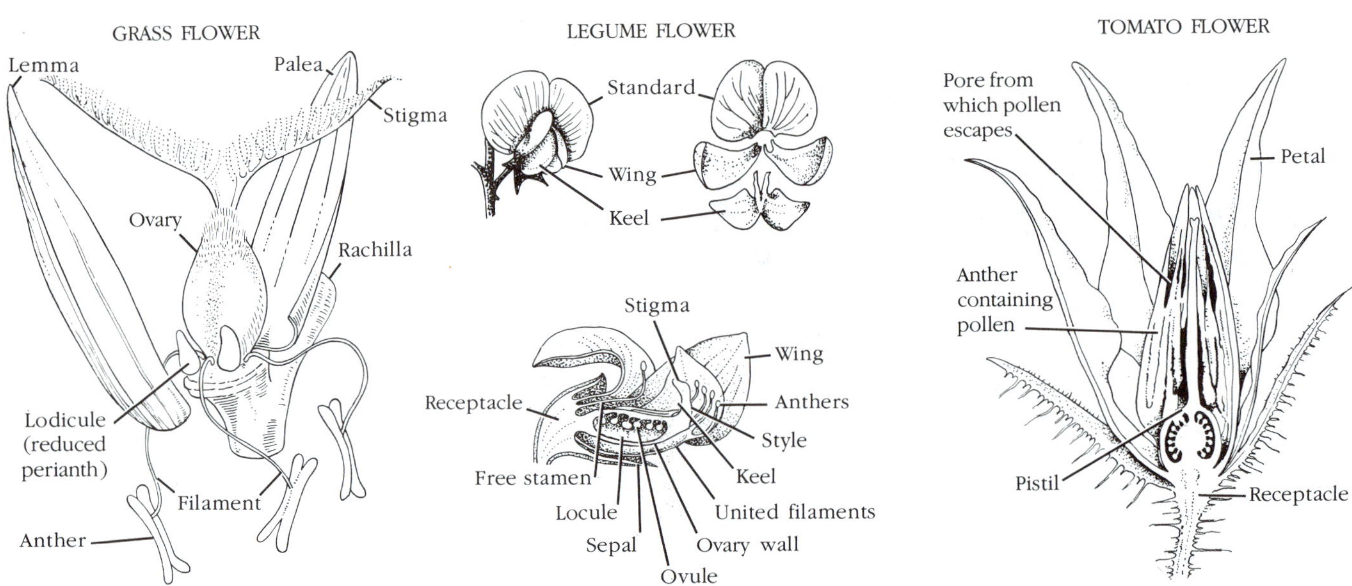

FIGURE 3-1 • Structure of the flower. (From Jules Janick et al., *Plant Science*, 3rd ed., W. H. Freeman and Company, New York, copyright © 1981)

known as the **corolla**. Insects, necessary for pollination, are attracted by the corolla. Inward from the corolla are the male organs, or **stamens**, consisting of the **anther**, in which pollen is produced, and the **filament**, the stalk that supports the anther. At the center of a typical flower is the female organ, the **pistil**. The base of the pistil is the **ovary**, which contains the **ovules**, or **embryo sacs**. Above and connected to the ovary is the **style**, topped by a usually somewhat broader, sticky **stigma**.

This description is of a **complete flower,** so named because it contains the four basic flower parts. Although the majority of horticulturally important species produce complete flowers, these flowers vary greatly in size and in the structure of the various parts (Figure 3-2). If any one of the four major flower parts is missing, the flower is **incomplete**. If the flower contains both male and female structures, it is a **perfect** flower. If either the male or female organs are missing, the flower is **imperfect**.

If each flower of a plant has both male and female organs, the plant is referred to as **hermaphroditic**. The majority of garden plants are hermaphroditic; petunias are a common example. A single plant having some flowers with only male organs and some with only female organs is

FIGURE 3-2 • Variations in flower structure. Flowers of this cultivar of the *Ranunculus* genus (*left*) have been bred to have multiple showy petals. Like most *Ranunculus* flowers they have numerous stamens and pistils arranged spirally into a cone-shaped flower center. The squash plant (*right*) is monoecious. Note the upper, open, male flower and the lower, closed, female flower with its attached ovary. If the female flower is pollinated and fertilized, its ovary will expand into a squash. (*Left*, From Philip Carpenter and Theodore Walker, *Plants in the Landscape*, copyright 1990 by W. H. Freeman and Company; *right*, courtesy of Walter Chandoha)

monoecious. Sweet corn is probably the best-known example of a monoecious horticultural crop. The tassel contains the stamens, and the silk and ear contain the pistils. Squash, cucumber, and related plants also are monoecious (see Figure 3-2). A species in which the male and female flowers are borne on separate plants is **dioecious**. Holly, asparagus, and ash are well-known examples of cultivated dioecious plants. Only the female holly plant produces berries, but it must be grown within 100 yards (100 meters) of a male plant if it is to receive sufficient pollen to produce them consistently. The male plant produces only inconspicuous male blossoms. Male asparagus plants produce smaller spears but a higher total yield than do the female plants. Male ash trees do not produce seedpods that litter lawns and sprout young trees in flower beds, and so are more popular for landscaping than are the female trees.

Modification or elimination of floral parts and flowers is common in cultivated species. Flowers of some cultivars of carnations, stocks, and petunias are "double" because their stamens, and sometimes their pistils, have been modified into petals. Selecting or breeding for higher yield has eliminated viable flowers from most cultivars of potatoes, sweet potatoes, and other crop species grown for their roots or tubers: Yields of these kinds of crops are higher when food reserves are channeled to root and tuber growth instead of to fruit and seed formation. Flowers and seeds are also undesirable on some types of coleus, foliage begonias, and other houseplants grown for their foliage, and flowering has been reduced or eliminated from these plants.

THE SEED

A **seed** can be described as a miniature plant with its own food supply and a protective cover. Seeds are basic to both the natural world and the gardener. In nature it is the seed that permits most plant species to survive periods of adverse environment. It is the seed and its attachments that disperse plant species over broad areas. From the gardener's point of view it is the seed that allows the convenient transport, storage, and propagation of many plants adapted to the garden. And it is the combination of the male and female parents' chromosomal matter (**germ plasm**) occurring as a result of seed formation that permits the wide variety of individual kinds of plants.

Seeds are useful to people other than as a means for plant reproduction: Much of the world's basic food for both humans and livestock is seed. Seeds are the portion usually consumed of wheat, barley, rice, corn, peas, beans, and many other kinds of plants. The fruits of most species do not form, or at least do not grow normally, without the concomitant formation of seeds, and the plant structure from which the seeds develop, the flowers, are an important horticultural commodity. Thus, understanding seed formation is essential to the "why" of many gardening procedures.

Pollen Formation

In angiosperms and most conifers, seeds begin their development with the differentiation of cells within the flower (Figure 3-3). In the anther, or male portion, of a flower, certain cells called **microspore mother cells** differentiate into specialized reproductive cells. These cells lose their nuclear walls, and their chromosomes form into threadlike structures that gradually shorten. The chromosomes line up in pairs (not in a single row, as in mitosis) along the center axis of the cell. If individual chromosomes of a pair touch, they may stick together and exchange equivalent parts as the two chromosomes of a pair are pulled away from each other toward opposite sides of the cell. After chromosomes are separated, a cell wall is formed through the center axis. This type of cell division by which two daughter cells are formed, each with half the chromosomes possessed by the mother cell, is called **meiosis** (see Figure 2-6).

After the microspore mother cell has undergone its first meiotic division, the chromosomes in each of the two newly formed cells line up in a single line along the center axis of the cell. This time each chromosome splits longitudinally, forming a pair of identical chromosomes. Each chromosome migrates toward its respective side of the cell, and a wall forms between the two rows. As a result of the two divisions, each microspore mother cell forms four **microspores**, each with one-half the chromosomes of the original. A heavy, waxy cover having several openings or pores forms around the microspores as they become mature **pollen** grains.

Formation of the Embryo Sac, or Ovule

Meanwhile, a somewhat similar series of events is occurring in the ovary of the pistil. A cell referred to as a **megaspore mother cell** begins to differentiate from other cells, and its chromosomes pair at its center. The megaspore mother cell divides twice to form four daughter cells, each with half the chromosome number of the original mother cell, in a process similar to the divisions that occur in the formation of pollen. However, three of the four daughter cells fail to continue to grow and are eventually absorbed back into the ovarian tissue. The fourth, the **megaspore**, enlarges to form an **embryo sac** (ovule). The megaspore's nucleus acquires a thin wall and a slight amount of cytoplasm. It then divides mitotically to form a total of eight cells as the megaspore develops into the embryo sac (see Figure 3-3). Three of these cells migrate to the **micropylar end**, the part of the embryo sac that is attached to the remainder of the ovary. This section of the embryo sac has a thin wall, and from this area there is a living cellular tissue bridge leading to the main stylar tissue of the flower. One of the three cells near the micropyle becomes the **egg cell**. The other two, which appear to serve no function, are absorbed into the ovular tissue. Three of the five other cells migrate to the other end of the embryo sac, and all three are gradually absorbed. The two remaining cells, called **polar bodies**, stay in the approximate center of the embryo sac.

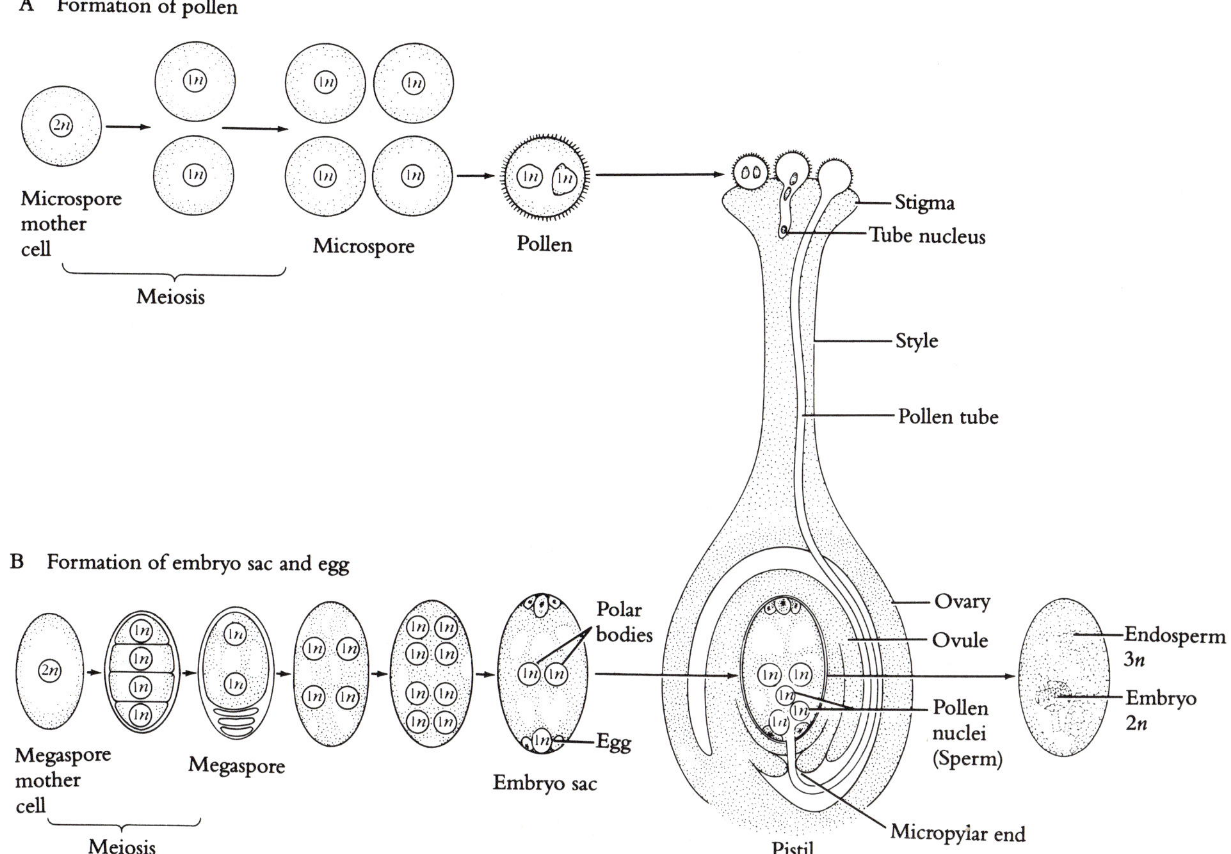

FIGURE 3-3 • Normal reproduction in flowering plants. (A) Pollen develops in the anther, beginning with a 2*n*-microspore mother cell and progressing through several divisions until the mature pollen grains, each having two 1*n* nuclei, are formed. (B) An embryo sac similarly develops in the ovary from a megaspore mother cell. When the embryo sac is fully developed, the stigma becomes sticky, and pollen grains adhere to it. One pollen nucleus becomes associated with the formation of a pollen tube, and the other divides to form two sperm, which grow down the pollen tube. One sperm nucleus fertilizes the egg, and the other joins the polar bodies to create an endosperm. (Adapted from F. C. Steward, "The Control of Growth in Plant Cells," copyright © 1963 by Scientific American, Inc., all rights reserved)

Chromosomal Behavior at Meiosis

All plants belonging to the same species normally have the same number of chromosomes, although occasionally a subspecies arises with exactly twice or three times the number typical of the species. Table 3-1 lists chromosome numbers of some representative horticultural plants. The two chromosomes that form each chromosome pair at the beginning of meiosis are essentially the same size,

TABLE 3-1 • *Chromosome numbers of representative horticultural plants*[a]

Plant	Chromosome Number	Plant	Chromosome Number
Ornamentals			
Amaryllis (*Amaryllis belladonna*)	22	Jonquil (*Narcissus jonquilla*)	14
Arborvitae (*Thuja occidentalis*)	24, 48	Juniper, creeping (*Juniperus communis*)	22
European birch (*Betula verrucosa*)	28, 42	Kentucky bluegrass (*Poa pratensis*)	62, 100
Calendula (*Calendula officinalis*)	28, 32	Lilac (*Syringa vulgaris*)	46, 47, 48
Carnation (*Dianthus* spp.)	30, 60, 90	*Magnolia* spp.	38, 76, 114
Cherry laurel (*Prunus laurocerasus*)	176	Nasturtium (*Tropaeolum majus*)	64
Chrysanthemum (*Chrysanthemum indicum*)	45, 63	Oak (*Quercus* spp.)	24
Clematis spp.	16, 32, 48	Oregon grape (*Mahonia aquifolium*)	28
Columbine (*Aquilegia vulgaris*)	14, 28	Pansy (*Viola tricolor*)	26
Cyclamen (*Cyclamen persicum*)	48, 96	Peony (*Paeonia* spp.)	10, 20
Dahlia (*Dahlia* spp.)	64	Petunia (*Petunia hybrida*)	21, 28, 35
Delphinium spp.	16, 24, 32, 48	*Philodendron* spp.	30, 32, 34
Dogwood, flowering (*Cornus florida*)	22	*Phlox* spp.	14
Easter lily (*Lilium longiflorum*)	24	Poppy, oriental (*Papaver orientale*)	28, 42
Forsythia spp.	28	*Rhododendron* spp.	26, 52, 78
Geranium (*Pelargonium hortorum*)	18	Rose (*Rosa* spp.)	14, 21, 28
Ginkgo (*Ginkgo biloba*)	24	Norway spruce (*Picea abies*)	24, 48
Gladiolus spp.	30, 45, 60, 75, 90	Sunflower (*Helianthus annuus*)	34
Hemlock (*Tsuga canadensis*)	24	Sweet pea (*Lathyrus odoratus*)	14
Hollyhock (*Althaea rosea*)	41	Tulip, garden (*Tulipa gesneriana*)	24, 36
Hyacinth (*Hyacinthus orientalis*)	16	*Wisteria* spp.	16
Impatiens (*Impatiens* spp.)	14, 16, 18, 20	Yew, Japanese (*Taxus cuspidata*)	24
India rubber tree (*Ficus elastica*)	26	Zinnia (*Zinnia elegans*)	24
Iris, bearded (*Iris* spp. and hybrids)	24, 36, 48, 60		

(*continued*)

shape, and structure and are called **homologous** chromosomes. They can be identified in all plants of a species. The ten pairs of chromosomes in corn, for example, have been given the numbers 1 through 10. By patiently observing through a microscope the length, thickness, dark and light areas, bulges, and other distinguishing features, scientists can determine which of the ten chromosomes they are viewing.

Furthermore, the segment of DNA (gene) controlling any given plant characteristic is at the same location on the same chromosome of all normal plants of a species. As a hypothetical example, if the gene that determines seed color in peas is found to be one-third of the way from the end of the long arm of chromosome 3 in a normal plant, it will be found at that same location in all normal pea plants. Genes at the same location do not always produce the same effect, however. For example, one pea seed-color gene may cause its plant to produce yellow seed; another may cause its plant to produce purple seed; another, brown; and still another, green; but the gene responsible for seed color is at the same location in all pea plants. Genes at the same location on homologous chromosomes are called **alleles**, and the total gene complement, expressed or not, is the **genotype** of the organism.

It should be emphasized that chromosomes are distributed at random during meiosis. As with the

TABLE 3-1 • *(Continued)*

Plant	Chromosome Number	Plant	Chromosome Number
Fruit			
Avocado (*Persea americana*)	24	Grapefruit (*Citrus paradisi*)	18, 27, 36
Almond (*Prunus amygdalis*)	16	Lemon (*Citrus limon*)	18, 36
Apple (*Malus sylvestris*)	34, 51, 68	Orange, sweet (*Citrus sinensis*)	18, 27, 36, 45
Apricot (*Prunus armeniaca*)	16	Peach (*Prunus persica*)	16
Blackberry (*Rubus* spp.)	28, 35, 42	Pear (*Pyrus communis*)	34, 51
Blueberry, highbush (*Vaccinium corymbosum*)	48	Plum, American (*Prunus americana*)	16
Blueberry, rabbiteye (*Vaccinium ashei*)	72	Plum, European (*Prunus domestica*)	48
Cherry, sour (*Prunus cerasus*)	32	Plum, Japanese (*Prunus salicina*)	16
Cherry, sweet (*Prunus avium*)	16, 24, 32	Quince (*Cydonia oblonga*)	34
Fig (*Ficus carica*)	26	Raspberry (*Rubus idaeus*)	14, 21, 28
Grape, American (*Vitis labrusca*)	38	Strawberry (*Fragaria* x *ananassa*)	56
Grape, European (*Vitis vinifera*)	38, 57, 76	Walnut, English (*Juglans regia*)	32
Grape, muscadine (*Vitis rotundifolia*)	40		
Vegetables			
Artichoke, Jerusalem (*Helianthus tuberosus*)	102	Muskmelon (*Cucumis melo*)	24, 48
Asparagus (*Asparagus officinalis*)	20	Onion (*Allium cepa*)	16, 32
Bean, snap and dry (*Phaseolus vulgaris*)	22	Pea (*Pisum sativum*)	14
Bean, lima (*Phaseolus lunatus*)	22	Pepper (*Capsicum annuum*)	24
Broccoli (*Brassica oleracea* var. *italica*)	18	Potato (*Solanum tuberosum*)	48
Cabbage (*Brassica oleracea* var. *capitata*)	18	Rutabaga (*Brassica napobrassica*)	38
Carrot (*Daucus carota*)	18	Squash (*Cucurbita maxima*)	24, 40
Cauliflower (*Brassica oleracea* var. *botrytis*)	18	Squash (*Cucurbita moschata*)	24, 40, 48
Celery (*Apium graveolens*)	22	Squash, summer (*Cucurbita pepo*)	40
Chives (*Allium schoenoprasum*)	16, 24, 32	Sweet potato (*Ipomoea batatas*)	16, 32
Corn (*Zea mays*)	20	Tomato (*Lycopersicon esculentum*)	24
Cucumber (*Cucumis sativus*)	24	Turnip (*Brassica rapa*)	20
Eggplant (*Solanum melongena*)	24	Watercress (*Nasturtium officinale*)	32
Leek (*Allium porrum*)	32	Watermelon (*Citrillus vulgaris*)	22
Lettuce (*Lactuca sativa*)	102		

[a]Counting chromosomes is difficult, and classification into species is not complete for some genera. Multiple unusual numbers for some species may be the result of an honest counting error, or those species may eventually have to be reclassified into two or more species.

flip of a coin, in which chance determines whether heads or tails comes up, chance determines which of each pair of chromosomes goes to a particular pollen grain or egg cell. Assume, for example, that the hypothetical pea plant has a gene for yellow seed on one of its pair of number 3 chromosomes and a gene for green seed on the other. Assume further that on one number 4 chromosome it has a gene for tall vine and on the other a gene for dwarf vine. This plant will form some pollen grains with genes for yellow seed and tall vine, others with genes for green seed and tall vine, others for yellow seed and short vine, and still others for green seed and short vine (Figure 3-4). This random distribution of genes to progeny is termed **gene segregation**.

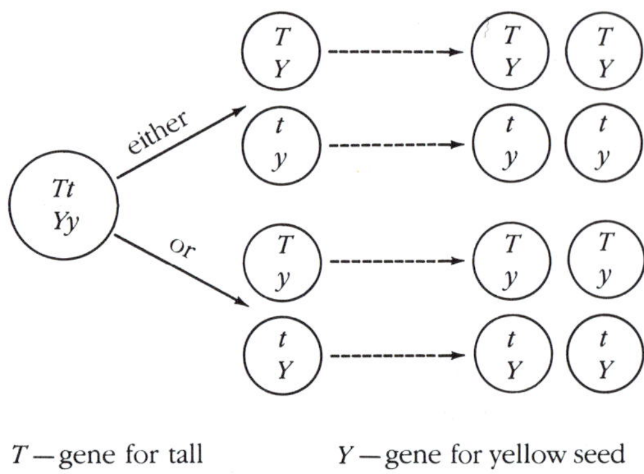

FIGURE 3-4 • The two possible ways in which genes for tall or dwarf vine and green or yellow seed color in peas can be distributed to the four pollen grains developed from a heterozygous mother cell.

POLLINATION

◆ ◆ ◆

Once a pollen grain has matured, it can be transferred to a stigma in several ways. In some species, tomatoes and peas, for example, the receptive stigma is brushed against the ripe anther to pollinate by contact. In certain conifers the pollen drops from male flowers high on the plant to receptive female flowers located lower on the same or other plants; this is pollination by gravity. Wind currents also help spread the pollen of many species, including corn and some conifers. Wind-pollinated species produce copious quantities of small, lightweight pollen. Indeed, the whole understory of a pine forest becomes coated with a layer of yellow pollen when the weather warms in the early spring. A field in which corn is being grown for seed must be at least one-quarter mile (400 meters) from the nearest field of any other corn cultivar to afford reasonable assurance that foreign pollen will not contaminate the seed. Insects, especially bees, are the most common agents of pollination for horticultural crops. Insects are necessary for pollination and the production of almost all fruits as well as for melons, squash, and cucumbers. In addition, seed production of a number of other vegetables and flowers is dependent on insects (Figure 3-5). Plant species are frequently pollinated by a combination of agents.

Plant species pollinated by contact are likely to be **self-pollinated**, that is, pollen from the plant usually fertilizes a stigma (normally the stigma of the same flower) of that plant. Although in nature self-pollination is not so common as cross-pollination, many cultivated crops, including peppers, tomatoes, eggplant, peas, beans, and most cereal grains, are self-pollinated.

Crops pollinated by wind, insects, or gravity are likely to be **cross-pollinated**, that is, pollen from one plant normally pollinates the stigma of another plant. A small percentage of the plants of many generally cross-pollinating crops are self-pollinated, and a small percentage of plants of most usually self-pollinating crops are cross-pollinated. Such variations and their consequences are discussed later in this chapter.

Aids for Pollination

For growers of crops requiring pollination the season of bloom is a critical time. Blooming usually occurs in the early spring when the weather is unstable, and the blossoms are especially susceptible to frost. Furthermore, most early-blooming crops require insects—usually active only at warmer temperatures—to transfer their pollen. Therefore, if the spring weather is cold, there may not be sufficient pollination to set a good fruit crop.

It is standard practice to place beehives in orchards at blossom time, but so far there are no good solutions for the fruit-tree grower whose orchard blooms when environmental conditions are not favorable for bee activity. Tomato growers are more fortunate, because they can use hormone sprays available at garden stores that cause tomato fruits to set when the temperature is warm enough to permit blossom formation but too cold for pollination (day temperature below 60°F [16°C] or night temperature below 45°F [7°C]). Tomatoes made to set with hormonal sprays will be seedless.

Gardeners who grow fruit-bearing crops such as tomatoes or cucumbers indoors or in a greenhouse should know that the natural agents of pol-

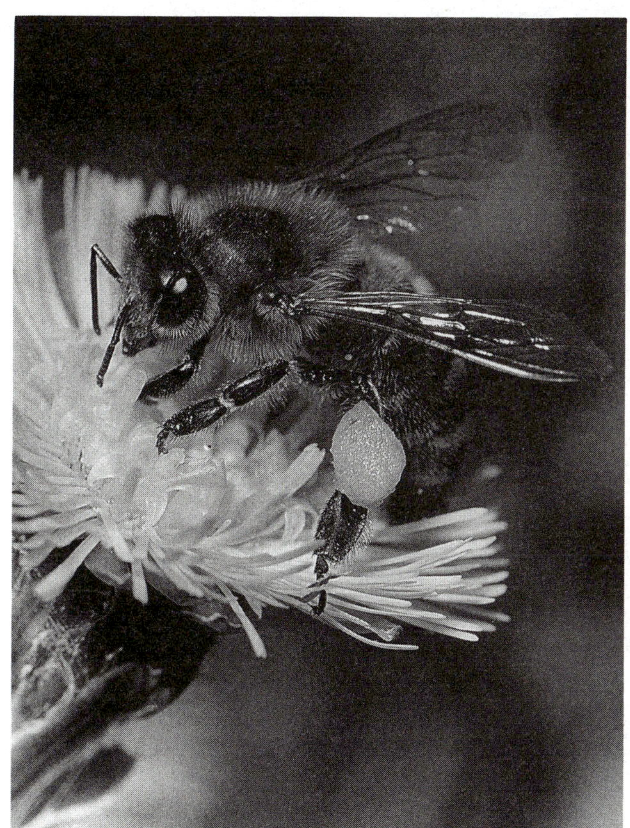

FIGURE 3-5 • Insect pollination is essential for the production of horticultural products like fruit, fruit-vegetables, vegetable seeds, and ornamental berries. Bees pollinate plants while gathering nectar, as this honeybee is doing here (*left*). Many other insects, like this moth collecting nectar with its tongue (*right*), as well as other creatures like humming-birds and bats, affect pollination. (Courtesy of Hans Pfletschinger/Peter Arnold Inc.)

lination are not present indoors. Even though tomatoes are normally self-pollinating, they require wind movement in order to pollinate effectively. To ensure good fruit set indoors, a grower must flip each open flower every day with a fingernail or "buzz" each one with a small electric pollinator designed especially for tomato flower pollination. When large numbers of cucumbers are being grown, one or more beehives may be placed in each house to pollinate the plants. If just a few plants are being grown indoors, flowers can be hand-pollinated by brushing the pollen-shedding anther of a male flower against the pistil of each open female flower (Figure 3-6).

Pollen-Tube Growth and Fertilization

As the pollen grain matures, its nucleus divides to form two nuclei. One of these, the tube nucleus, contributes to the germination of the pollen grain and the growth of the pollen tube. The other, the generative nucleus, is responsible for fertilizing the ovule. When the pollen grain alights on a receptive stigma, it is stimulated to germinate.

FIGURE 3-6 • The artificial pollination of a cucumber. The corolla has been removed from around the pollen-shedding anther cone of the male flower, and the anther cone is being brushed against the stigma of a female flower. In the foreground, the small fruit that is beginning to enlarge was pollinated a few days earlier.

Germination occurs when the **pollen tube** pushes through a pore of the pollen grain and starts growing down into the style (see Figure 3-3). Either just before or just after the pollen tube begins to grow, the generative nucleus divides to form two **sperm**.

The pollen tube grows downward into the style, pushing aside various elongate cells of the style and forcing its way to the micropylar end of the embryo sac. The two sperm follow in the pollen tube behind the tube nucleus and empty from it through the micropyle into the embryo sac. One of these sperm unites with the egg cell, and with this union, the standard (usually diploid) number of chromosomes is restored. The cell thus formed divides mitotically many times to form the **embryo** of the developing seed. After the seed has germinated, this embryo grows to develop into the new plant. The second male nucleus unites with the two polar nuclei of the embryo sac in what is referred to as **triple fusion**. The cell from this union, of course, has three sets of ($3n$) chromosomes. With repeated mitotic divisions, this cell becomes the **endosperm**, the food portion of the resulting seed (see Figure 3-3).

Gene Expression

After the egg has been fertilized, the new plant regains the gene pairs, one on each homologous

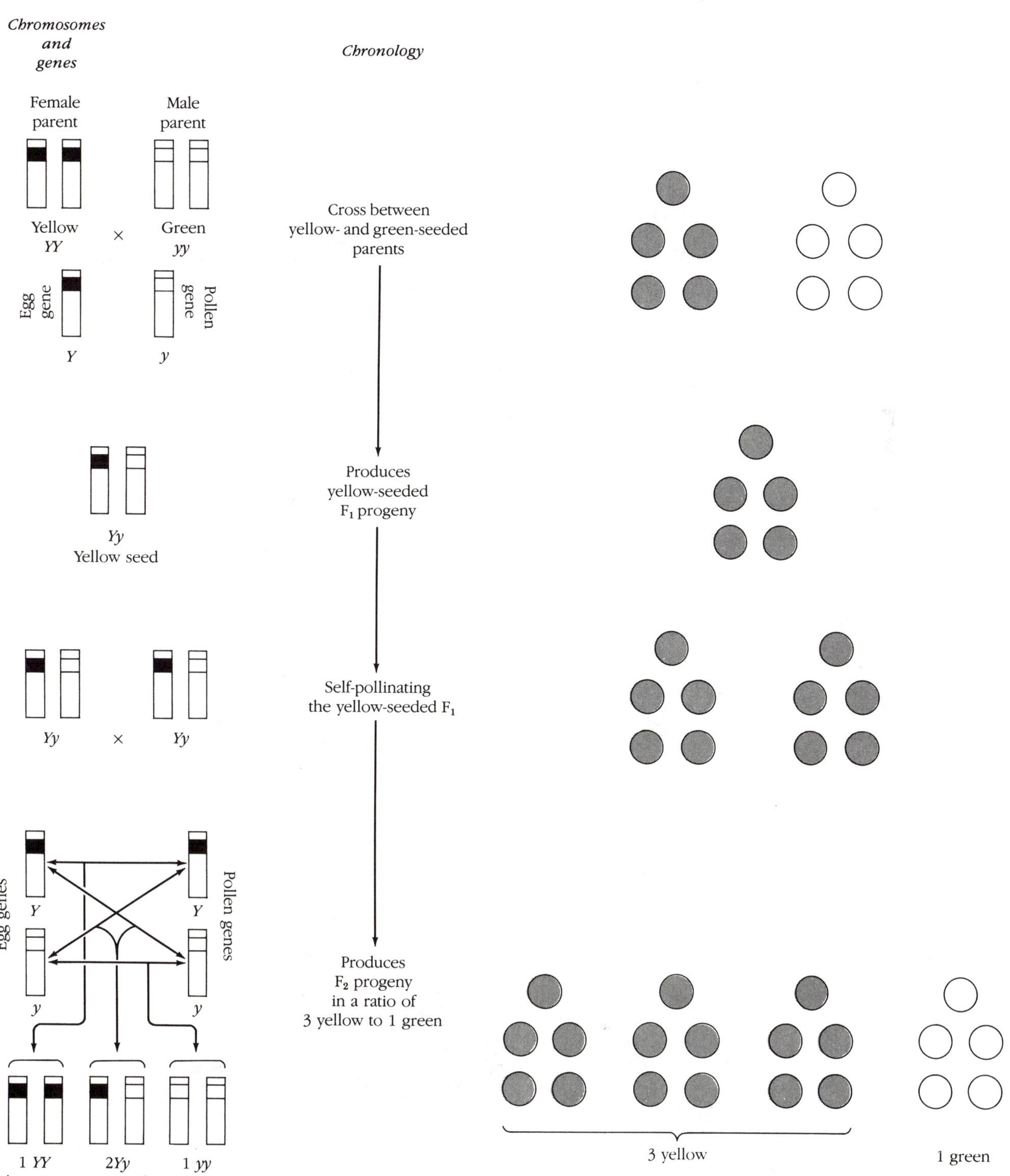

FIGURE 3-7 • Gene segregation and expression when one gene is completely dominant, through two generations.

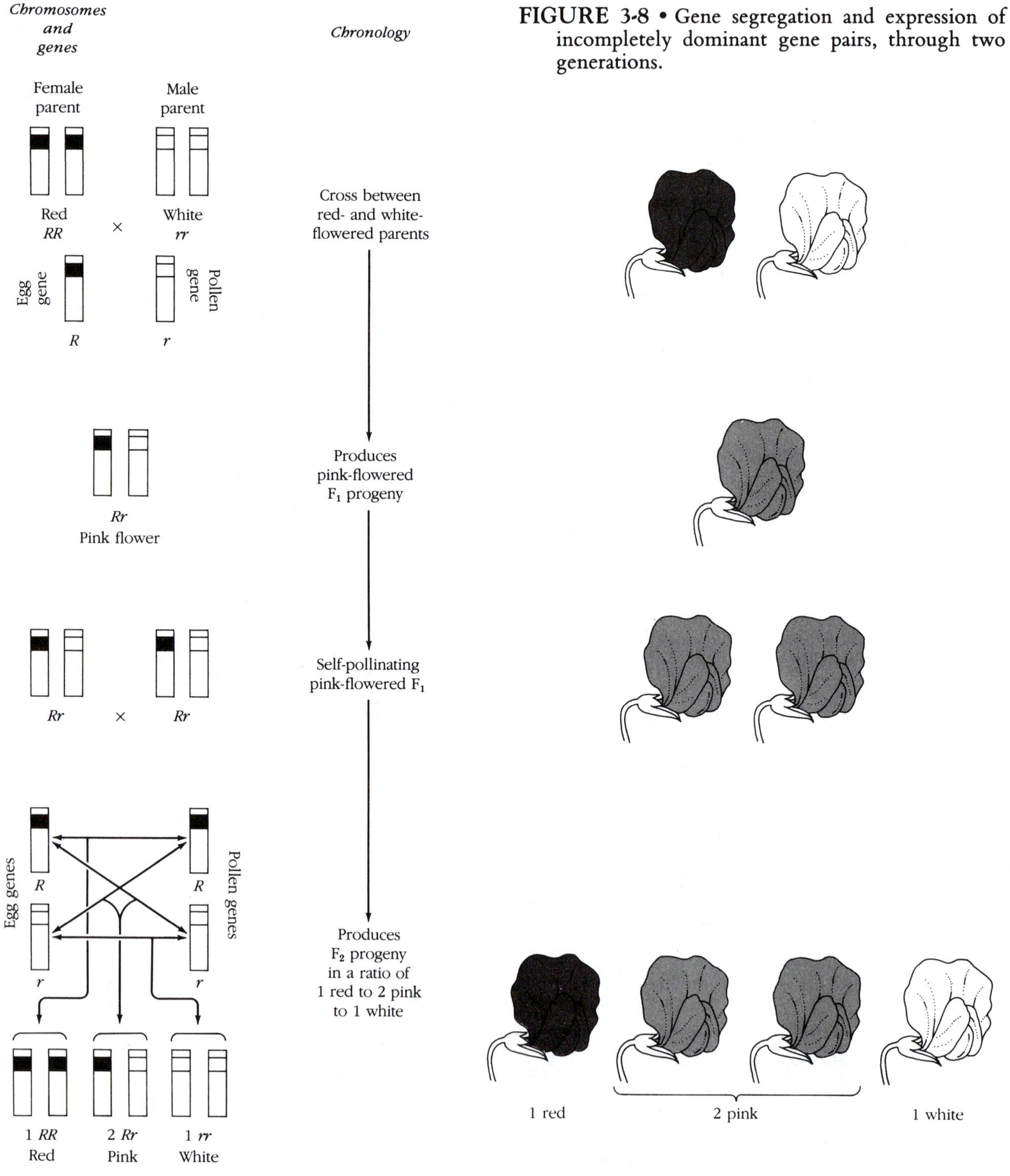

FIGURE 3-8 • Gene segregation and expression of incompletely dominant gene pairs, through two generations.

Chromosomes and genes

Chronology

Female parent

Male parent

Red
RR

×

White
rr

Egg gene

Pollen gene

R

r

Cross between red- and white-flowered parents

Rr
Pink flower

Produces pink-flowered F_1 progeny

Rr × *Rr*

Self-pollinating pink-flowered F_1

Egg genes

Pollen genes

R

R

r

r

Produces F_2 progeny in a ratio of 1 red to 2 pink to 1 white

1 *RR*
Red

2 *Rr*
Pink

1 *rr*
White

1 red

2 pink

1 white

chromosome, that are responsible for the expression, or appearance, of each characteristic. The composite of genes contained in a plant is referred to as its **genotype**, and the plant's physical appearance, resulting from its genotype, is called its **phenotype**. In Figure 3-7 the F_2 plants have a genotypic ratio for seed color of 1YY : 2Yy : 1yy and a phenotypic ratio of three yellow- to one green-seed plants. If all gene pairs on the parent plant or plants are alike, all pollen grains, all eggs, and all offspring will be alike. If, however, the gene pairs of the parent plants are not alike, random segregation and the interchange of genetic material between chromosomes will ensure that no two pollen grains, no two egg cells, or no two offspring will receive identical chromosomal material.

If the gene pairs are identical, it is easy to predict their expression. For instance, if both pea seed-color genes are for green seed color, the seed will be green. However, if the genes of a pair are different, the question of expression is more complicated. Frequently, the effect of one gene will be expressed and the other suppressed. The expressed gene is said to be **dominant** and is usually symbolized by a capital italic letter. The suppressed, or **recessive**, gene is symbolized by a lowercase italic letter. If a pea plant with one gene for yellow seed and one for green seed produces yellow seed, the yellow-seed gene is dominant and the green-seed gene is recessive. Genes for many **qualitative** characteristics—color, leaf form, presence of hairs, and so on—are either dominant or recessive. Sometimes when the genes are different, both are partially expressed. In one group of sweet peas, for example, a gene for red color paired with a gene for white color produces pink flowers (Figure 3-8). F_1, a symbol widely used in describing hybrid cultivars, is the standard abbreviation of **first filial generation**. It refers to the first generation progeny produced from a cross. F_2, F_3, and so on refer to the second, third, and later generations.

Many plant characteristics, especially those relating to size, shape, yield, and quality, are under the control of large numbers of genes, each of which adds to or modifies the characteristic. Genes that act in this way are called **quantitative** genes or factors. A grossly simplified example of the action of quantitative factors might be illustrated by plant height controlled by three pairs of genes. If three of those genes each add 2 inches (5 centimeters) to the plant, two add 4 inches (10 cm), and one adds 8 inches (20 cm), the plant will be 22 inches (56 cm) high (Figure 3-9).

The expression of genes is also affected by the environment. Russeting, the appearance of the rough corky skin that is the trademark of the 'Idaho Baking' ('Russet Burbank') potato, is reduced if the soil nitrogen content is high. The skin color of oranges is much brighter orange when the fruit is grown where the atmosphere is dry and the nights are cool. Some high-quality oranges grown in areas or during seasons unfavorable for bright orange skin color are dyed and labeled "color added." Hydrangeas are another dramatic example of the effect of environment on gene expression. Their flowers will be blue if the soil in which they are growing is highly acid and pink if it is less acid.

Gene Mutation and Bud Sports. Genes are almost always passed unchanged from generation to generation. The gene for yellow seed color in peas will continue to produce yellow seed for as many generations as it continues to be passed on to progeny. Occasionally, perhaps only once in each hundred thousand or million progeny, a pollen grain or embryo sac forms in which a gene changes. Perhaps the yellow-seed gene of a pea changes so that it produces a purple seed. Such rare changes are called **mutations**, and the mutated gene will be passed from generation to generation of offspring as faithfully as was the original gene. Many mutations produce plant characteristics already in existence and thus may not be observed. Most of the rest produce changes that cause the plant to be less desirable. Occasionally, though, a change does increase the plant's utility or beauty. Even though desirable gene changes are rare, mutation is an important tool to plant breeders, who often use chemicals and radiation to speed its rate.

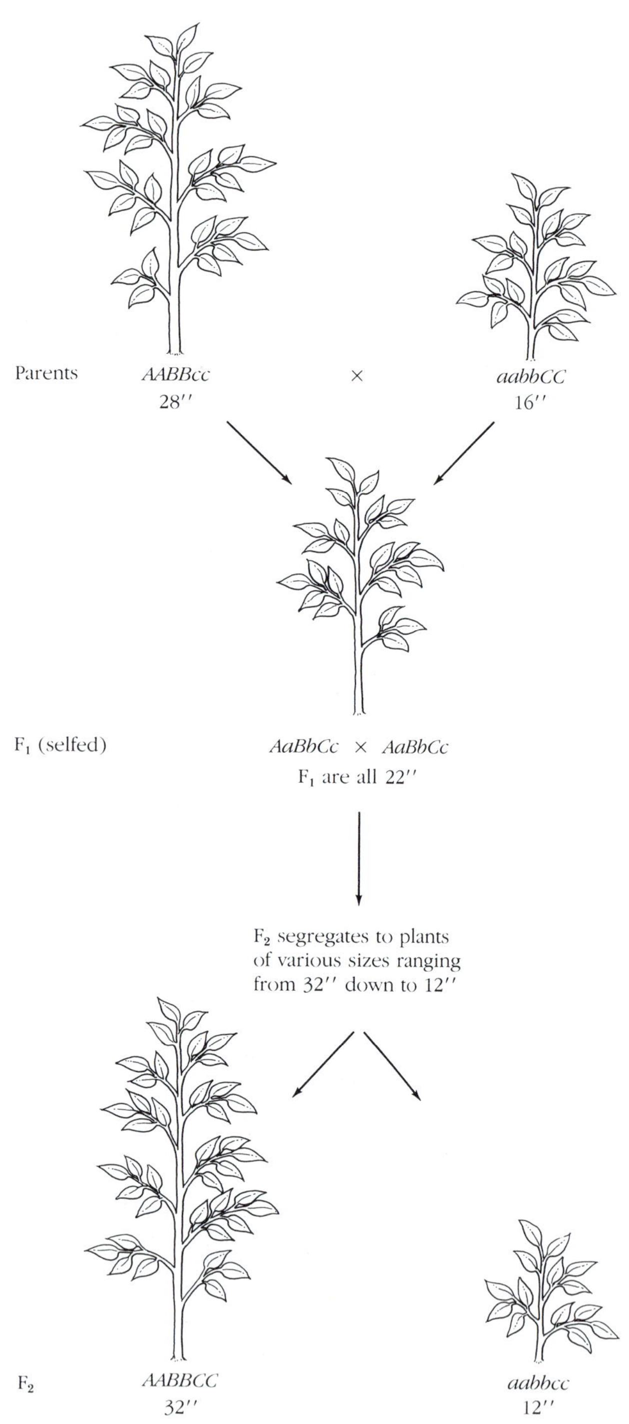

FIGURE 3-9 • The segregation of genes, illustrating quantitative inheritance. A theoretical cross is made between two plants in which plant height is controlled by three pairs of genes, each of which contributes to height as follows: $A = 4$ inches; $B = 8$ inches; $C = 4$ inches; and *a*, *b*, and *c* each contributes 2 inches. The parent plants are 28 inches and 16 inches; the F_1 progeny will be 22 inches, and the F_2 will vary from 32 inches to 12 inches, depending on genotype. Notice that some of the F_2 offspring may be taller or shorter than either parent. Traits such as size, yield, and quality are usually inherited quantitatively.

Occasionally mutations occur in a plant's body cells, but such changes cannot be easily observed unless they occur in the cells from which buds initiate and new plant parts grow. Like mutations of reproductive cells, most body-cell mutations result in undesirable characteristics, though worthwhile bud mutations have resulted in the development of a number of horticultural cultivars. Cultivars originating from bud mutation are called **bud sports** and include solid red 'Red Delicious' apples from the old striped 'Delicious' and 'Russet Burbank' potatoes from the old smooth 'Burbank' (Figure 3-10).

Bud sports can sometimes be profitable for their discoverer. A few years ago a single limb, a bud sport, from a 'Golden Delicious' apple tree sold for over $30,000. Its value was that it had nodes and spurs more closely spaced so that the trees produced from its buds were smaller in size than standard 'Golden Delicious' trees (see "Breeding to Modify Plant Growth" in Chapter 8).

New flower colors have often appeared as bud sports. Around 1910, a double red greenhouse carnation called 'Sim' was introduced. It produced a very large, double flower on a strong stem and possessed other desirable features. Over the years millions of cuttings of this carnation have been propagated. From these occasionally have come bud sports for different colors, so that now growers have white, various shades of pink, red-and-white–striped, yellow, and orange carnation

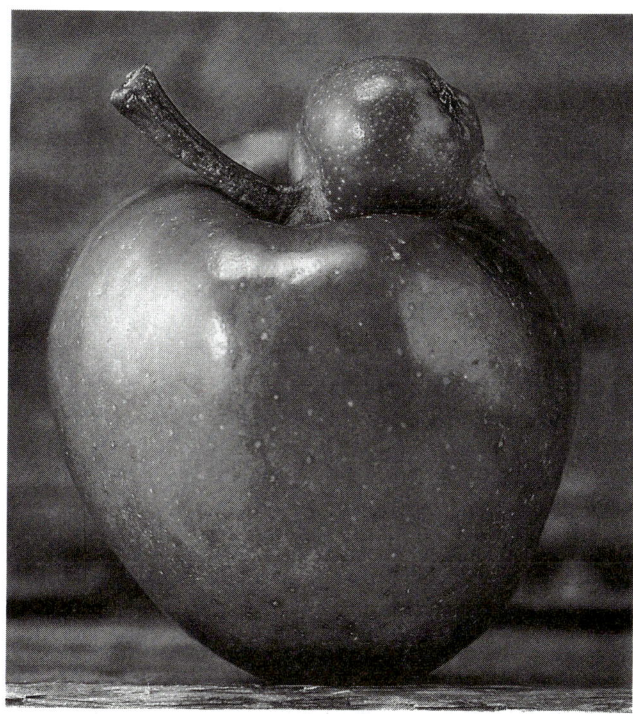

FIGURE 3-10 • Abnormal plant growth. A number of unexplained plant abnormalities are sometimes mistakenly attributed to genetic mutation and referred to as *bud sports*. "Twinning" of tree fruits is one. Occasionally two fused blossoms are initiated. If both are pollinated and develop a normal complement of seed, they will grow to equal size as connected fruits, much like Siamese twins. If one develops seed and the other does not, the one with seed grows to full size and the other remains small, as has happened with the apple in this photo. The causes of twinning are not known, but it seems to occur more frequently when blossom buds are initiated during periods of excessively cool temperature. (Courtesy of Barry L. Runk/Grant Heilman)

cultivars with the desirable features of the original 'Sim' carnation. 'Tangerine Sim' was found after patenting new plant types became legal, and its discoverer is reported to have received more than a million dollars for propagation rights.

Bud mutation is also often responsible for the green-and-white or green-and-yellow leaf variegation in certain foliage plants and ornamental shrubs. These appear when a section of a leaf mutates so that it can no longer produce **chlorophyll**. New plants must be propagated from cuttings or divisions containing both green-and-white or green-and-yellow portions. If the cutting is all green, a solid green plant will be produced. If it is all white or yellow, the new plant, lacking chlorophyll, will not be able to manufacture food and so will die.

Plants such as the variegated pothos, in which only segments of the stem have mutated, are called *chimeras*. Boysenberries and certain other trailing thornless blackberry bud sports also are chimeras. In these blackberries, only those apical meristem cells that differentiate into the epidermal and other outermost tissues have mutated to become thornless; the inner plant cells still contain the genes for producing thorns. Although new plants propagated from cuttings are thornless because they retain the mutated epidermis, the new plants that come from root suckers are thorny because they grow entirely from the inner unmutated pericycle tissue (see "The Root" in Chapter 2; "Bramble Fruits, Culture and Management" in Chapter 13).

Genetic Consequences of Self- and Cross-Pollination. It is quite possible to be an expert gardener without understanding genetic segregation. However, several interesting phenomena likely to be observed by the home gardener and several practical gardening decisions relating to the choice of cultivars and to the purchasing or growing of seed can be meaningful only to those with some knowledge of gene and chromosome distribution with self- and cross-pollination. Genetic segregation is based on the laws of chance and can be explained by using an analogy with playing cards.

Assume that the thirteen different cards in a suit are thirteen different genes scattered along the chromosomes of a species and that the four suits are four different expressions of those genes—for example, the yellow, green, brown, or purple seeds of the peas mentioned earlier. Any one diploid plant can have only two of those genes, but all four are found among the plants in the group. Let us assume that the cards are sorted so that cards of the same value are together and laid face down on the table. You are asked to choose two of each kind, that is, two aces, two kings, two queens, and so on. The cards left on the table are discarded. Next you are given other cards that exactly match in suit and value the cards in your hand. For example, if you have an ace of hearts, an ace of diamonds, a king of diamonds, and a king of clubs, these will be increased to two aces of hearts, two aces of diamonds, two kings of diamonds, and two kings of clubs. Next lay the cards in your hand

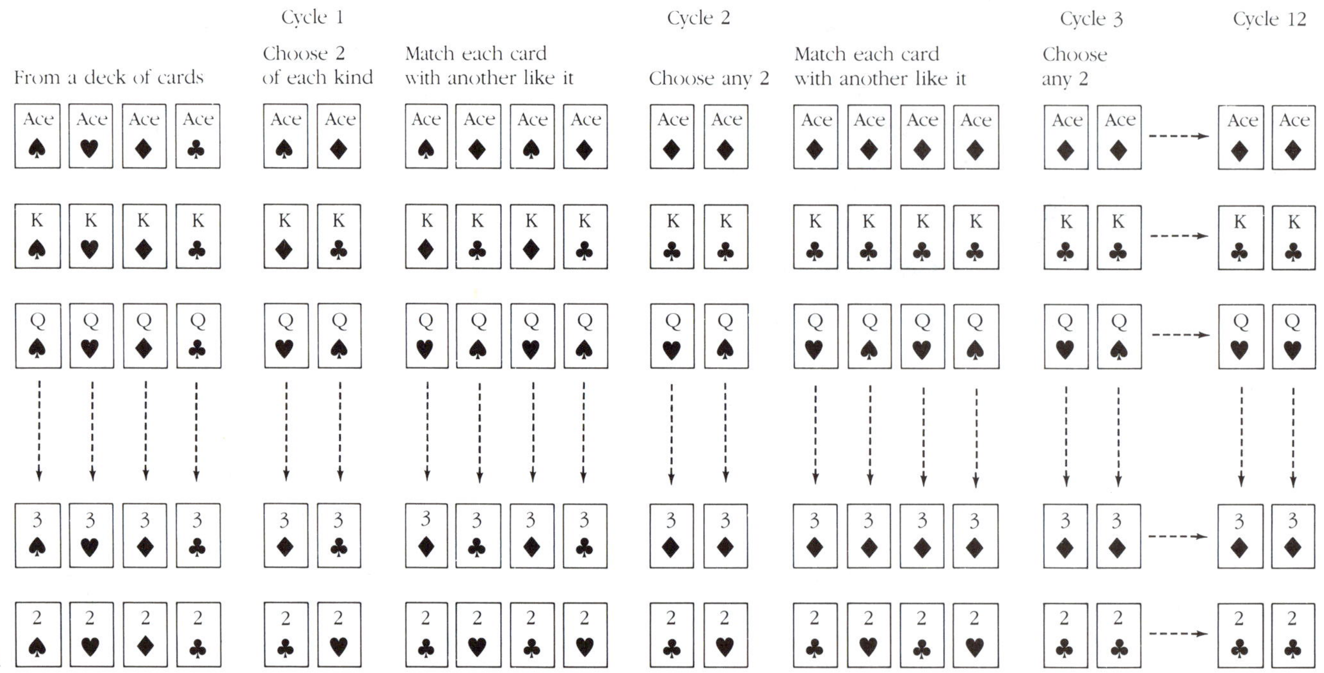

FIGURE 3-11 • Loss of genetic variability with self-pollination. (A) The loss of genetic variability resulting from self-pollination can be illustrated with a deck of cards. The doubling of the number of cards by matching suit and kind after each cycle is analogous to the doubling of chromosomes during meiosis, and the random selection of two cards at each cycle is analogous to the union of sperm and egg (each having a single set of chromosomes) to form the embryo. Approximately half of the unlike pairs of cards become alike with each cycle, just as about half of the heterozygous gene pairs become homozygous after the passage of each generation. (B) A hypothetical cross between two genetically unlike pea plants followed by self-pollination. This is the kind of program carried out by breeders attempting to improve a self-pollinated crop. It will result in essentially all gene pairs' becoming alike within ten to fourteen generations. Although the two genes of a pair in the parent plants used in such crosses are usually alike (gene pairs I–VII), the genetic diversity of F_1 and later generations will not be affected if the genes of a pair are unlike (gene pair VIII and the analogous card example in A).

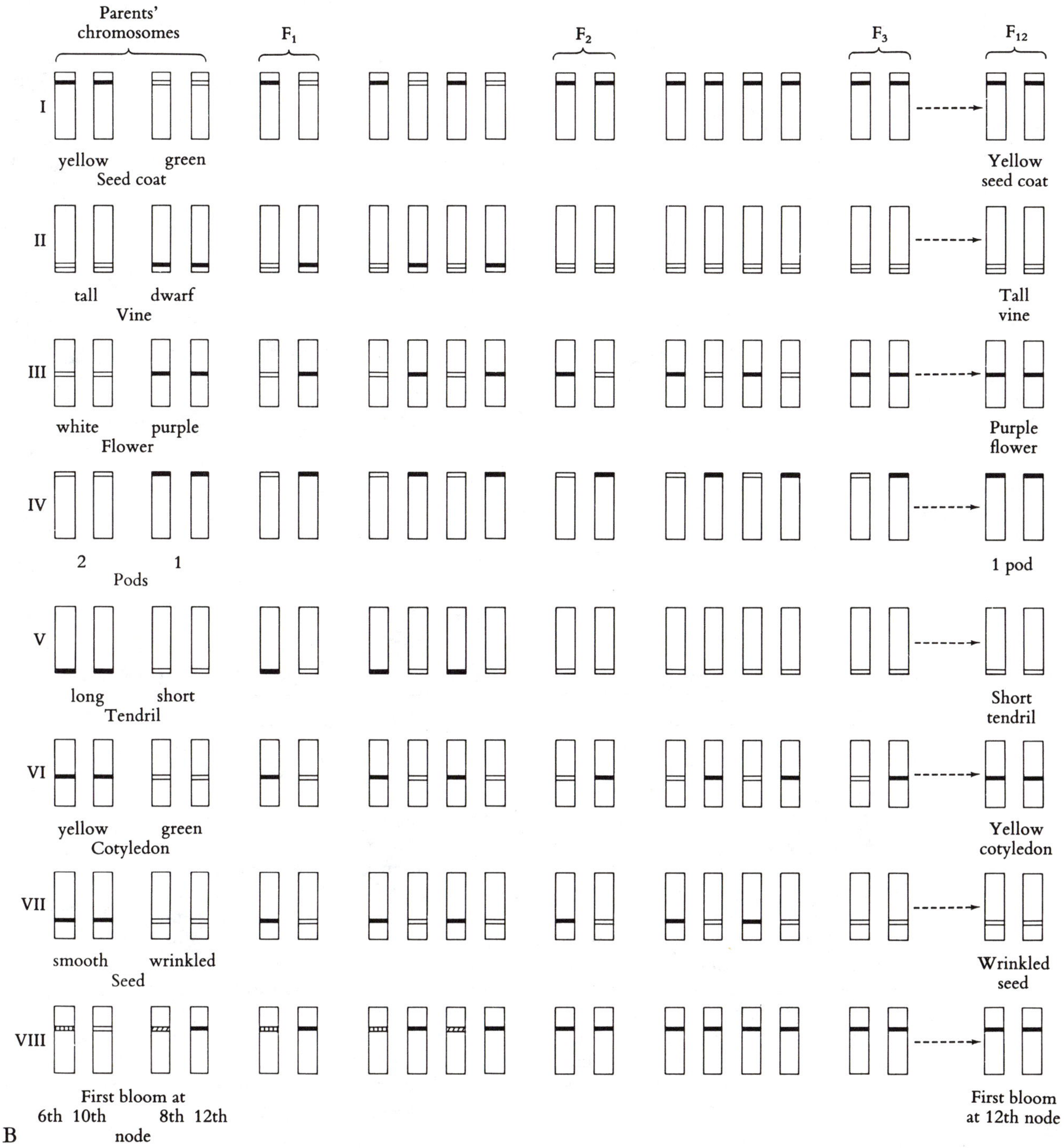

Parents' chromosomes
F_1
F_2
F_3
F_{12}
I
yellow green
Seed coat
Yellow seed coat
II
tall dwarf
Vine
Tall vine
III
white purple
Flower
Purple flower
IV
2 1
Pods
1 pod
V
long short
Tendril
Short tendril
VI
yellow green
Cotyledon
Yellow cotyledon
VII
smooth wrinkled
Seed
Wrinkled seed
VIII
First bloom at
6th 10th 8th 12th
node
First bloom at 12th node
B

face down on the table and choose from them at random two of each kind, discarding the rest. Now the new cards in your hand are duplicated as before, and the cycle of alternate discarding and duplicating is repeated. It is obvious that this procedure carried through several cycles will result in both cards of any one kind that you choose being of the same suit. This is almost exactly analogous to the loss of genetic variability that occurs with self-pollination (Figure 3-11).

Just as the pairs of cards become alike after a few cycles, so the pairs of genes on homologous chromosomes become alike after ten to fourteen generations of self-pollination. The site on a chromosome at which a gene is located is its **locus.** When both genes are alike at most loci on all chromosome pairs, the plant is said to be **homozygous.**

For a card analogy of cross-pollination, assume that a large number of players and a number of

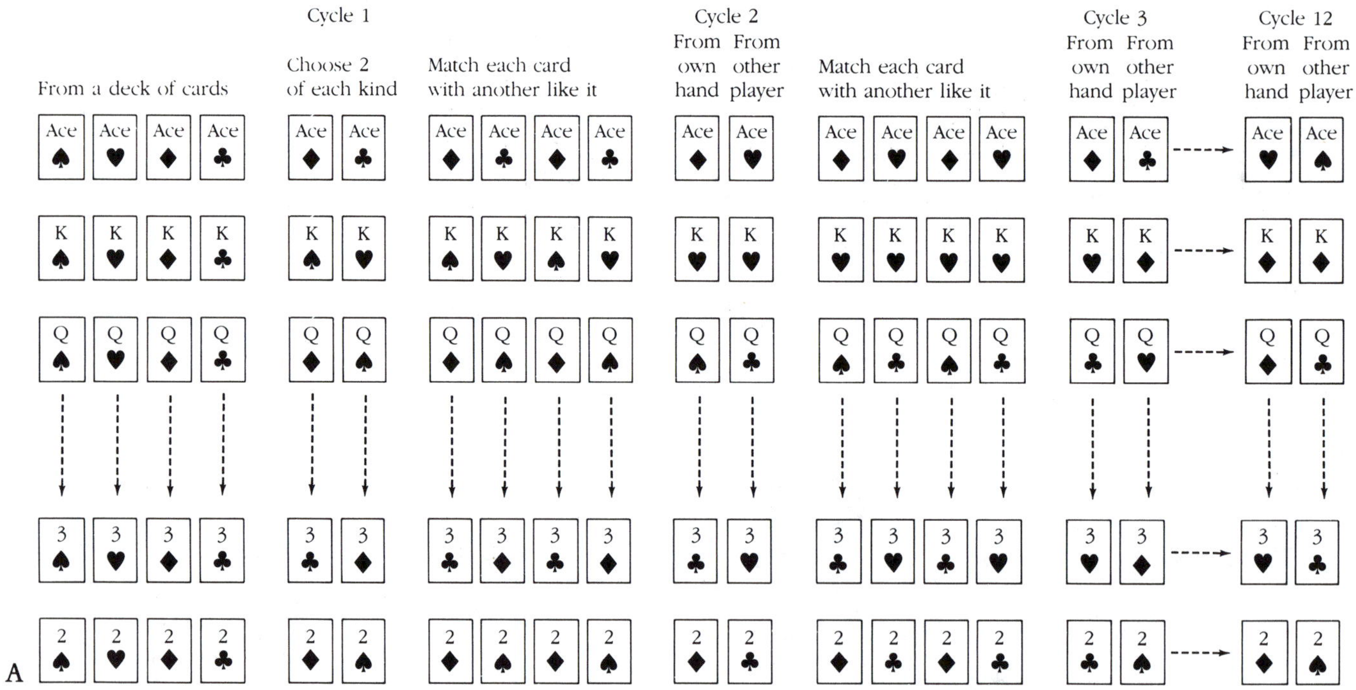

From a deck of cards | Cycle 1: Choose 2 of each kind | Match each card with another like it | Cycle 2: From own hand, From other player | Match each card with another like it | Cycle 3: From own hand, From other player | Cycle 12: From own hand, From other player

A

FIGURE 3-12 • The retention of genetic variability with cross-pollination. (A) The retention of genetic variability with cross-pollination can be demonstrated with a deck of cards. The doubling of the number of cards by matching suit and kind is analogous to the doubling of chromosomes during meiosis, and the matching of one randomly selected card from the four with one of the same kind from another player's hand is analogous to the kind of fertilization that results from cross-pollination. After twelve cycles the card pairs are as likely to be different as they were after the first cycle, just as the gene pairs of a cross-pollinated crop plant are as different after twelve generations as they were during the first. (B) When genes in a plant are unlike, the dominant one (red silk, purple pericarp, red husk, two ears per corn plant) determines the characteristic. In a breeding program involving a cross-pollinated species, similar-appearing plants must be selected in order to have a degree of cultivar uniformity after a few generations have passed.

decks of cards are involved. Each player picks at random two cards of each kind, which are exactly matched with additional cards of the same suit and kind as in the previous example. This time, however, for the second cycle a player chooses only one card of each kind from his or her own hand and one from the hand of any other player. As the cycle is repeated, cards of all suits will be in the

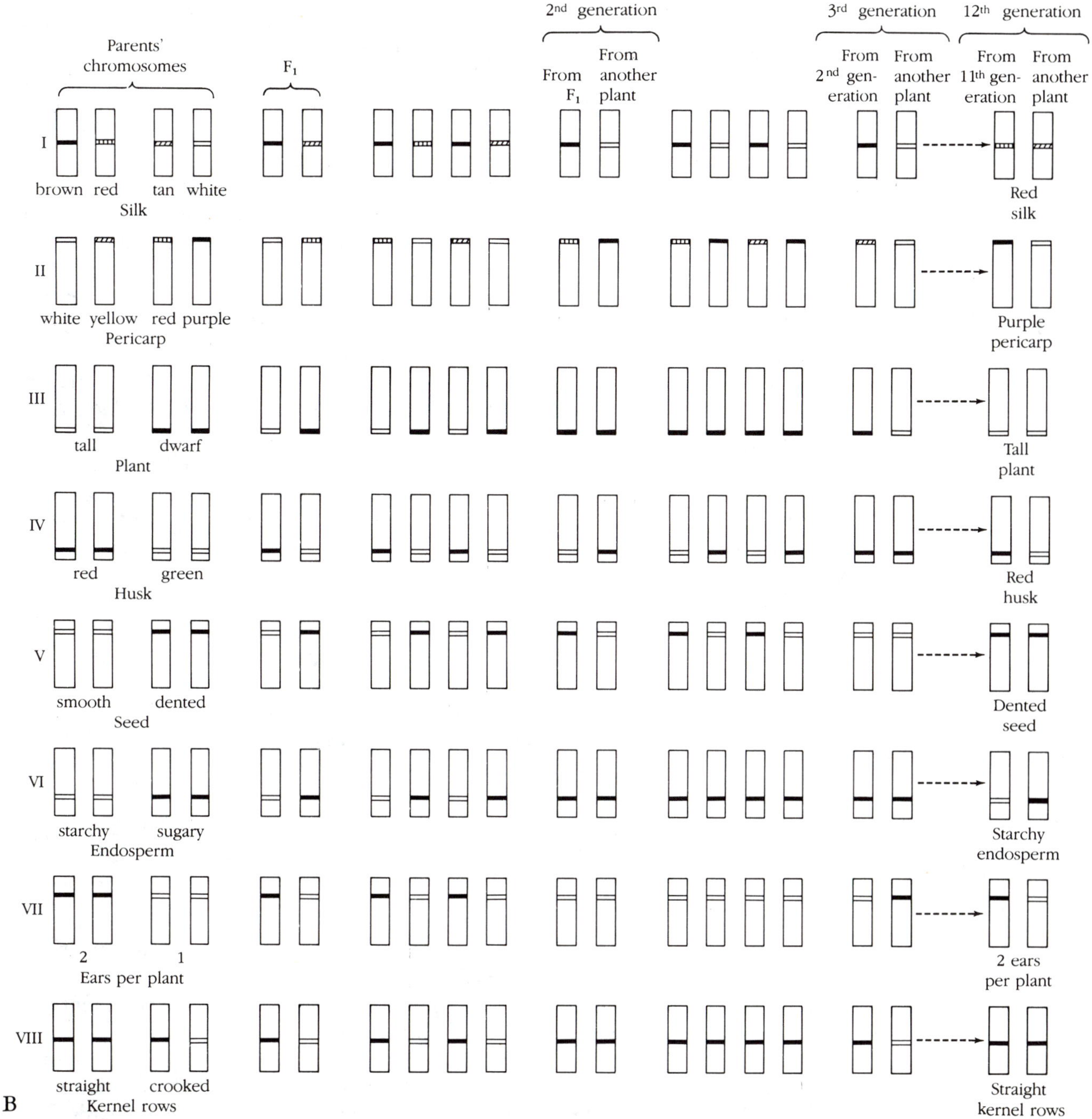

B

hands of some players and will be distributed to all players from time to time. Thus the two cards of any one kind in a player's hand are likely to be of different suits much of the time (Figure 3-12).

This is analogous to what happens with cross-pollination, in which one set of chromosomes comes from the female parent and one comes from the male parent. Just as the two cards of any one kind are likely to be of different suits, so the two genes at many loci are likely to be different. Plants with most gene pairs not alike are said to be **heterozygous**. Just as cards of all suits remain in the hands of some player and are distributed to all players from time to time, so the different kinds of genes remain in the plant population and are recombined into different combinations with each passing generation.

Seed growers find it much easier to develop uniform cultivars of self-pollinating crops than of cross-pollinating ones. By saving seeds for a few generations from single plants having the desired characteristics, they can produce a homozygous uniform cultivar of a self-pollinating crop.

Many cross-pollinating crops can be artificially self-pollinated, of course. However, self-pollinating a species that is normally cross-pollinating leads to the death and sterility of some offspring and a drastic reduction in the size, vigor, and yield of the surviving plants. Cultivars of cross-pollinated crops (except for the F_1 hybrid cultivars discussed later) are developed by selecting plants that appear similar but have considerable genetic diversity. Thus plants of a cultivar of a cross-pollinating crop like carrots are likely to be less uniform than those of a cultivar of a self-pollinating crop like snap beans.

Plant Characteristics Ensuring Cross-Pollination

Under natural conditions, plant species that cross-pollinate have an evolutionary advantage because of the genetic variation within the group of plants. If the climate changes or if seeds happen to be carried to a different location, variation in a cross-pollinated species is likely to be sufficient to enable some individuals to adapt to the new environment and survive.

In nature, a number of plant species characteristics ensure the occurrence of cross-pollination. Monoecious species, which have the male and female parts in separate flowers on the same plant, and dioecious species, which have the male and female flowers on different plants, are two such plant adaptations already mentioned. For some crop plants—for instance, the older cultivars of avocado—the stigma of a plant is never receptive at the same time that the pollen of the same plant is being shed. If the avocado tree sheds pollen in the morning, its stigmas are receptive only in the afternoon, and vice versa.

Another evolutionary adaptation to ensure cross-pollination is the development of self-incompatibility. The ovule of a self-incompatible plant is not fertilized by the pollen from that plant, even though the pollen is viable, the stigma is receptive, and the ovule can be readily fertilized with pollen from another plant. Self-incompatibility can be either structural or physiological. With structural incompatibility, the stigma and anthers of a plant are located in such a way that self-pollination does not naturally occur. For example, in some tomato flowers the style elongates far beyond the anthers so that the pollen from a flower does not reach the stigma of the same flower.

Physiological self-incompatibility is more common and causes more problems for horticulturists than does structural incompatibility. In such cases self-pollination frequently occurs, but self-fertilization does not. Pollen may fail to germinate on the stigma, or the pollen tube may grow only part way through the style (Figure 3-13).

Self-Incompatibility in Tree Fruits. If the ovary is not fertilized because of self-incompatibility or for any other reason, seeds will not form. Fertilization and, usually, seed development are essential to the development and normal growth of fruit. Thus by preventing fertilization, self-incompatibility will also prevent the formation of fruit, a fact of great importance to many gardeners.

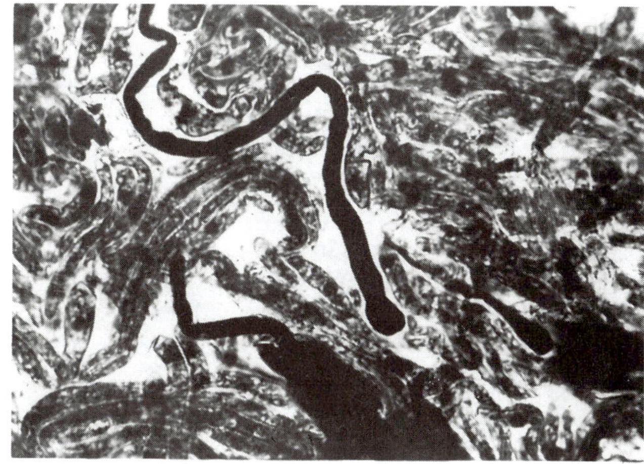

A

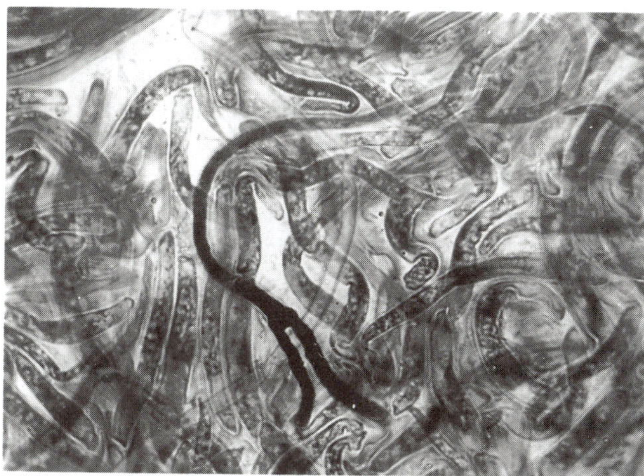

B

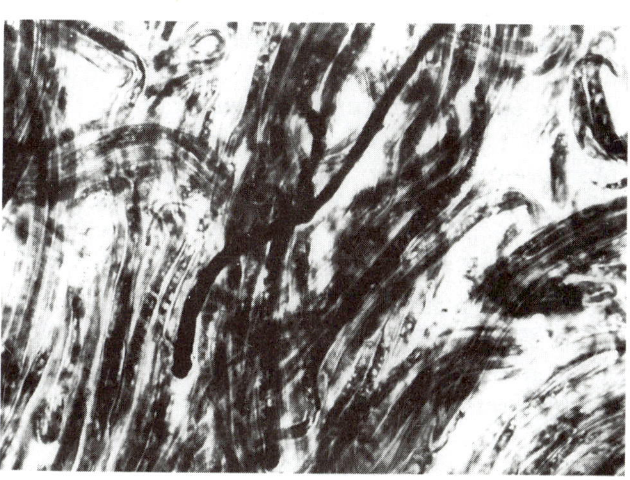

C

FIGURE 3-13 • Self-incompatibility. The tips of pollen tubes growing through styles with which they are incompatible frequently become swollen and burst (A), but occasionally they fork (B). A normal tube is shown in C.

Recall that when cells in the body of a plant divide by mitosis, the chromosomes that control their structure and function enlarge and split, providing each new cell with exactly the same genetic material as was in the original mother cell. Thus all plants propagated from the stems, roots, or leaves of a single original plant (the clones mentioned in Chapter 1) have exactly the same genetic makeup as that of the original plant from which they were propagated. If the original plant produces red flowers, all the plants of the clone will produce red flowers; if it is self-incompatible, all plants propagated from it will be self-incompatible. All temperate-zone fruit-tree cultivars are clones. If the original tree from which each cultivar developed is self-incompatible, no tree of that cultivar will pollinate any other tree of the same cultivar. Unless they receive pollen from some other source, they will not set fruit.

Self-incompatibility is probably more of a problem with sweet cherries in the western United States and Canada than with any other kind of fruit tree. Not only are sweet cherries self-incompatible, but three of the major cultivars grown in the West—'Bing', 'Lambert', and 'Royal Ann'—are sister lines that are also cross-incompatible; that is, pollen from any one cannot fertilize or produce fruit on the other two. The self- and cross-incompatibility of these three major cultivars of cherries meant, until a few years ago, that western orchardists had to plant pollinator trees of another cultivar that produced an unmarketable crop. Pollinator trees still have to be planted, of course, but plant breeders have now developed pollinator cultivars that produce marketable fruit, even though the market demand for the pollinators' fruit may not be so high as for fruit of the three standard cultivars.

Fruit trees in home gardens frequently fail to set fruit due to a lack of pollination. Because a single tree will usually produce more than enough fruit to supply one family's needs for that kind of fruit, gardeners often plant just one tree of a kind. That tree is likely to bloom profusely but never bear fruit unless a neighbor has fortuitously planted a pollinator tree nearby or unless pollination requirements are artificially supplied. Pollination requirements can be met each season by placing blooming bouquets of a pollinator cultivar in buckets of water near the nonbearing tree. A more permanent solution, when there is not enough space to plant new trees, is to graft pollinator branches into the fruitless tree. Or two trees, the desired cultivar and a pollinator, can be planted in the same hole. They can be trained to occupy the space that a single tree would normally occupy. Figure 3-14 illustrates the various methods of providing pollination.

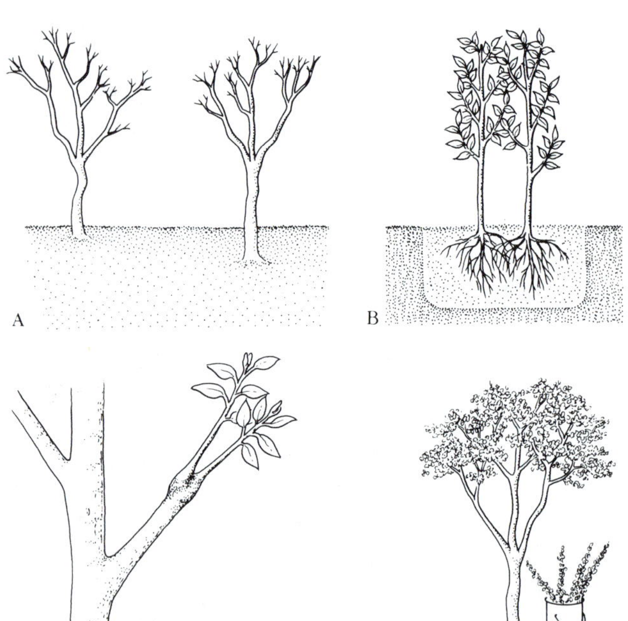

FIGURE 3-14 • Different ways of pollinating self-incompatible trees. (A) Planting two separate trees that will cross-pollinate. (B) Planting two trees that will cross-pollinate in the same hole. (C) Grafting pollinator branches onto an existing tree. (D) Placing pollinator branches in a bucket of water at the base of the tree during the bloom period.

Cultivars of apples, pears, sweet cherries, and most kinds of nuts are self-incompatible. Except for the three sweet cherries mentioned earlier, any two cultivars usually cross-pollinate. The 'J. H. Hale' cultivar of peach requires a pollinator. The common apricot and plum cultivars likely to be grown by home gardeners, sour cherries, peaches other than 'J. H. Hale', and most small fruits (except for the older cultivars of muscadine grapes; see Chapter 13) are self-compatible and do not require pollinators. Gardeners should check pollinating requirements before planting rare or unusual plum or apricot cultivars, because a few cultivars of these two fruits are self-incompatible.

Members of the cabbage family, tobacco, petunias, and some other flowers are also self-incompatible. This seldom poses a problem for growers, however, because pollination is not necessary for the formation of a head of cabbage, broccoli, or cauliflower, and annual flowers' failure to set seed is usually an advantage. Even seed growers are not greatly concerned about self-incompatibility in these crops. Because each plant of a cross-pollinated seed-reproduced cultivar has a slightly different genetic makeup (unlike the clonal plants of fruit-tree cultivars, which are genetically identical), most can pollinate one another.

Formation of the Seed

In angiosperms, both endosperm and embryo cells grow and divide a number of times. In most monocots, such as the grasses, sweet corn, daffodils, and tulips, these cells divide and subdivide until the seed is almost mature. A mature monocot seed consists of a seed coat formed from the wall of the embryo sac, an embryo formed as a result of the union of a sperm with the egg cell, and an endosperm formed as a result of the union of a sperm with two polar nuclei. The embryo that develops into the new plant is differentiated into a rudimentary root or **radicle**, a shoot or **plumule**, and a seed leaf or **coleoptile**. The endosperm, which has three sets of chromosomes, is used as food by the embryo as the seed germinates and the new plant becomes established (Figure 3-15).

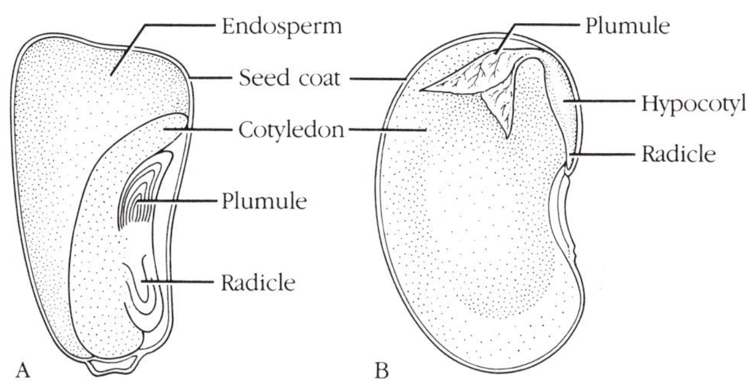

FIGURE 3-15 • A comparison of monocot (corn) seeds (A) and dicot (bean) seeds (B).

The sequence of events in the formation of seed of most dicot species is somewhat different. Sometime before the dicot seed is mature, the cells of the endosperm stop dividing. Their cell walls break down, and their contents are gradually absorbed by the expanding embryo. The mature dicot seed has a cell wall formed from the embryo sac wall and the remnants of the endosperm tissue. The remainder of the dicot seed is embryo and consists of two cotyledons or seed leaves that become the food-supplying part of the developing seedling, a plumule or shoot apex, a **hypocotyl** or lower stem, and a radicle that becomes the root (see Figure 3-15).

The seed coat of both monocot and dicot seeds consists entirely of mother plant tissue and has the characteristics of the mother plant, but the embryo and endosperm result from the union of male and female gametes and have characteristics of both the pollen and the mother plant.

F_1 Hybrid Seed

Since the general acceptance of hybrid corn in the 1930s, most growers have willingly paid high prices for hybrid seed, often without understanding the basis for hybrid superiority. The term **hybrid** refers to the progeny of unlike parents, but as generally used in the seed trade, hybrids are those cultivars that come from F_1 hybrid seed obtained by crossing two genetically diverse inbred lines (described below). Seed growers have taken advantage of hybrids' reputation by introducing and advertising hybrid cultivars of various crop and ornamental plants. Usually hybrids are superior, but sometimes they are no better than the standard or so-called **open-pollinated** cultivars of the species or kind. In a few instances very inferior lots of seed have been sold as F_1 hybrids.

During the past few years some organic and alternative agriculturists have associated hybrids with hard tomatoes, pesticides, chemical fertilizers, and corporate farming as examples of unnatural and therefore undesirable results of agricultural research. A brief discussion of the scientific bases and techniques for producing hybrid seed may clear up some of the confusion.

It was stated earlier that self-pollinating and individual plant selection for a few generations produce homozygosity, a condition in which the gene pairs of chromosomes on all plants of a line or cultivar are alike. It was also pointed out that self-pollinating a species that is naturally cross-pollinated results in the death and sterility of some offspring and reduced growth and yield of the remaining progeny. If self-pollination is continued for about ten generations, the lethality and sterility will be eliminated, and a group of plants will be developed that remain uniform generation after generation but are usually much less vigorous and lower yielding than the original cultivar from which they were developed. Such a group is called an **inbred line** or sometimes just an **inbred**.

An F_1 hybrid cultivar results from crossing two inbred lines, using one for the male parent and the other for the female parent. Because it is homozygous, the male parent contributes the same set of chromosomes to each progeny plant. The female parent does the same, although the set it contributes is quite different from the male parent's. Because each F_1 hybrid plant receives exactly the same genetic complement, collectively they comprise an extremely uniform cultivar (Figure 3-16).

When the right inbreds are crossed, a tremendous stimulation in growth results, causing the F_1 hybrid to yield considerably more and to mature

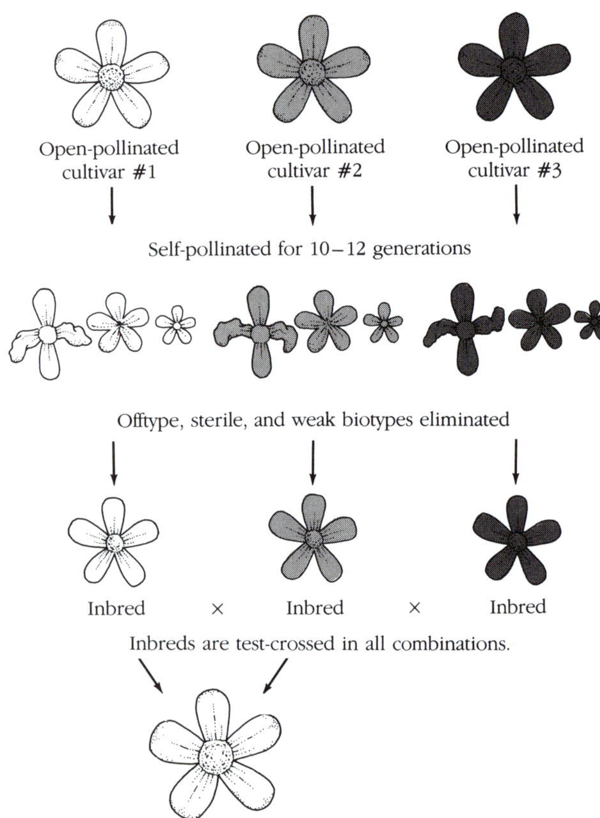
Open-pollinated cultivar #1
Open-pollinated cultivar #2
Open-pollinated cultivar #3
Self-pollinated for 10–12 generations
Offtype, sterile, and weak biotypes eliminated
Inbred
×
Inbred
×
Inbred
Inbreds are test-crossed in all combinations.
F_1 hybrid cultivar is developed by combining germ plasm of the two inbreds that produce the best progeny.

FIGURE 3-16 • The development of an F_1 hybrid cultivar.

earlier than the cultivars from which the inbreds were developed. This stimulation in growth is thought to be a consequence of the interaction of unlike gene pairs, because the most vigorous F_1 hybrids usually are produced by crossing the most different inbreds. The major advantages of F_1 hybrid cultivars, therefore, are higher yield, earlier maturity, and uniformity.

It is important to emphasize that good F_1 hybrid cultivars cannot be developed from a cross between any two inbreds. The hybrids from many inbred combinations are no better, or may even be less desirable, than existing standard cultivars. It takes years of patient research by plant breeders to determine which two inbreds produce the superior F_1 hybrid. Because the gene pairs on the two sets of chromosomes entering the hybrid are so different, their recombination as a result of either selfing or crossing produces progeny that are extremely variable in maturity, quality, and yield. For this reason, seed from F_1 hybrid cultivars should never be saved for replanting.

F_1 hybrid cultivars of self-pollinated species can easily be produced by crossing any two cultivars, because self-pollinated cultivars are, in reality, inbreds. However, F_1 hybrids of self-pollinated crops are not as likely to have a vigor, yield, or "earliness" advantage over standard cultivars, and standard cultivars of self-pollinated crops already are uniform. As a consequence, F_1 hybrids of self-pollinated crops are often not sufficiently superior to standard cultivars to warrant the extra expense of obtaining their seed.

Although F_2 hybrid seed is occasionally advertised, it should never be purchased because of the extreme variability of plants it will produce.

Each cultivar, hybrid or otherwise, must be judged by its performance in the garden. Despite the adverse publicity given them by some gardening publications, many F_1 hybrid cultivars of both annual flowers and vegetables are unsurpassed in beauty, yield, and quality and certainly deserve gardeners' consideration.

Tetraploid Cultivars

So far in this chapter discussion has been limited to those plants that have two sets of chromosomes, one acquired from the male parent and one from the female parent. As noted in Chapter 2, plants with more than two sets do exist. These include some woody ornamentals, some fruit-tree cultivars, potatoes, and certain perennial and annual flowers.

Although some plants have eight or more sets of chromosomes, home gardeners are not likely to encounter many with more than four (tetraploids). Some species produce tetraploids spontaneously, and in the past, tetraploid cultivars were selected from plants or parts of plants growing in fields or gardens. Naturally occurring tetraploids are rare, however, and difficult to discover and propagate. Today, with the use of a chemical, **colchicine**, extracted from the autumn crocus (*Colchicum autumnale*), it is not too difficult to produce tetraploid plants of most species. Colchicine prevents cell-wall formation but does not inhibit cell division, so chromosome numbers can be doubled with just enough colchicine to inhibit cell-wall formation during the time necessary for one cell division. In actual practice, chromosome doubling involves considerable trial and error to determine the right concentration and timing for a particular species.

Tetraploid cultivars of a number of annual flowers, the most notable being snapdragons, are available. Tetraploid flowers are larger than those of the diploid cultivars from which they are developed (Figure 3-17). They also are likely to produce a smaller percentage of viable pollen and fewer seeds, which is one reason that tetraploid seed is expensive. Because they are so large and spectacular, the number of tetraploid flower cultivars available on the market will undoubtedly increase.

FIGURE 3-17 • Comparison of a diploid (*left*) and a tetraploid (*right*) snapdragon. (Courtesy of W. Atlee Burpee Company)

Seedless Watermelons

In the past, seedless watermelons were sometimes mentioned as a joke, because everyone knew that watermelons could not be reproduced without seed. Like so many of the impossibilities of the past, however, seedless watermelons are now a reality, and seed for seedless watermelons is available to gardeners. Its production is possible because plants with odd sets of chromosomes do not produce seed. At meiosis the chromosomes of cells with even-numbered sets are distributed equally—one set to each pollen grain or embryo sac for diploids and two to each for tetraploids. An equal distribution of chromosomes of cells with three sets is, of course, impossible, and the imbalance of chromatin material results in infertile pollen or inviable embryo sacs or both.

To produce seed for seedless watermelon cultivars, chromosomes of the cultivar to be used for the female parent are doubled with colchicine to produce a tetraploid (Figure 3-18). This tetraploid line, which contains two chromosome sets in each egg cell, is pollinated with pollen from a diploid cultivar, producing embryos with three sets of chromosomes. This triploid seed can produce plants that flower but have no pollen. A regular diploid cultivar is planted with the triploid to produce pollen. Pollination by the diploid stimulates fruit production, but the imbalance of chromosomes in the ovules causes the seed to abort. To produce a seedless crop, a few marked plants of a diploid cultivar are planted to provide pollen. The production of seedless watermelon seed requires considerable hand labor and such seed is, therefore, expensive.

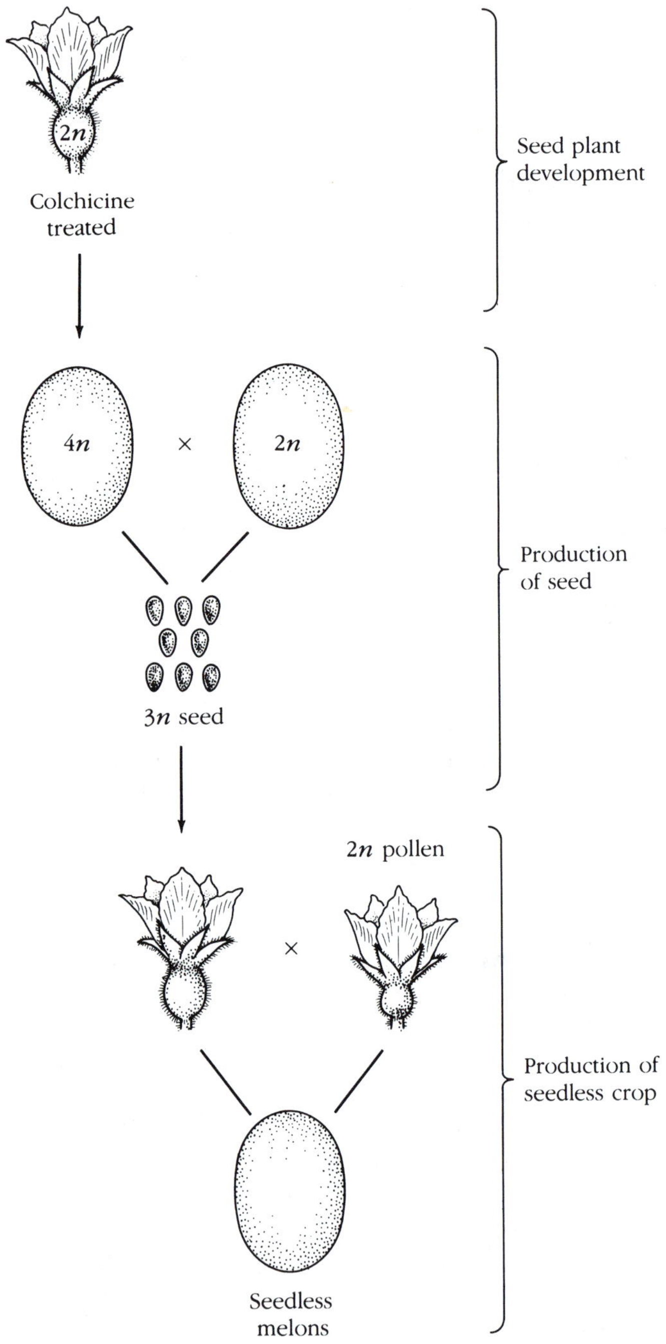

FIGURE 3-18 • The development of seedless watermelon.

THE FRUIT

In Chapter 1 it was mentioned that the horticultural definition of fruit was not the same as the botanical definition. Botanically, fruit is the mature ovary with attached parts. It may include the receptacle, remnants of the petals and sepals, pistil, and anthers, along with the seeds contained in the ovary.

Fruits can be classified botanically in several ways. One of the most common is whether they are fleshy or dry. Several of the structures normally considered to be seeds are actually dry fruits because they include part or all of the ovary as well as the ovule. For example, the so-called seed of beet or chard is actually a cluster of seeds embedded in dried ovarian tissue. This explains why these crops always emerge as a cluster of plants and why they need to be thinned, regardless of "seed" spacing at planting time. The structure we call carrot seed is also a dry fruit. Many dried seeds, such as peas and beans, are removed or remove themselves from their fruit (in this case, the pod) at maturity. Other types of dry fruits include samaras, which have wings (maple, for instance), nuts—which are one-seeded fruits with a stony wall—and a number of others (Figure 3-19).

Fruits also can be classified according to the number of ovaries incorporated into the fruiting structure, as simple, aggregate, or multiple. **Multiple** fruits develop from many separate but closely clustered flowers. Pineapples, figs, and beet seeds are examples of multiple fruits. **Aggregate** fruits, for example, raspberries and strawberries, are derived from flowers with many pistils on a common receptacle.

A majority of horticultural plants produce **simple** fruits, those derived from a single ovary. When it becomes part of a fruit, the ovary wall is called the **pericarp**, and is divided into three distinct layers—**exocarp** (outer), **mesocarp** (middle), and **endocarp** (inner). When all three layers of the pericarp are fleshy, the fruit is called a

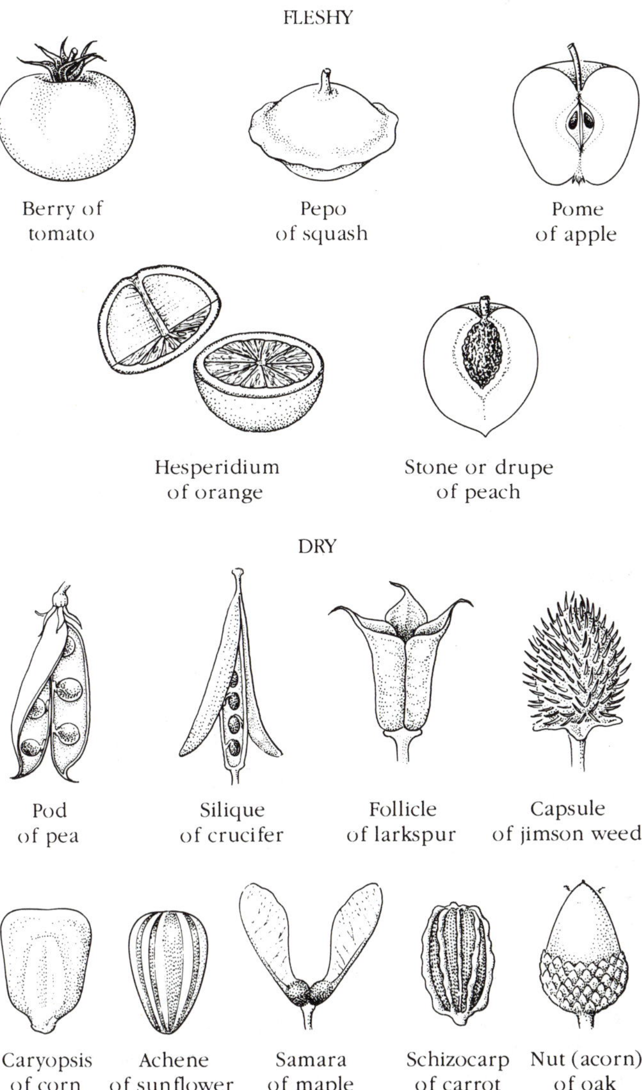

FIGURE 3-19 • Various types of simple fruits. (Adapted from R. M. Holman and W. W. Robbins, *A Textbook of General Botany*, copyright © 1939. Reprinted by permission of John Wiley & Sons, Inc.)

berry. This botanical usage of the term berry should not be confused with the edible portion of some bush fruits. Tomatoes, eggplants, and blueberries are berries, as are citrus fruits (called *hesperidiums*), in which the rind is the exocarp and mesocarp and the pulp is the endocarp. Even muskmelons (called pepos) are considered berries; their rind is the exocarp, the edible portion is the mesocarp, and the watery portion around the seeds is the endocarp.

Drupe fruits (peaches, olives, cherries, and plums, for instance) are simple fruits with a stony endocarp. **Pome** fruits (apples, pears, and quinces) are simple fruits with a papery endocarp.

Alternate Bearing

Flowers and fruits develop from either mixed buds (buds that grow both flowers and leaves) or blossom buds. Many physiological factors determine whether or not, or how many, blossom buds form on a woody plant, but perhaps the most important plant requirement is a plentiful supply of carbohydrates in its tissues. In temperate regions, blossom buds form on most fruit and spring-flowering ornamental species during June or July, remain dormant through the winter, and form blooms the following spring and ripe fruit in the autumn, fifteen or sixteen months after they are first initiated. June and July are also months for rapid growth of the current season's fruit, and the development of too much fruit may utilize most of the available carbohydrates, leaving little for the formation of blossom buds. When this occurs, the tree or shrub may enter a cycle of biennial or **alternate bearing**, in which a year of heavy fruit production alternates with a year of little or no fruit production (Figure 3-20). The alternate bearing of fruit trees often begins when an entire season's bloom is destroyed by frost. Because there is no competing crop, the set of blossom buds is extremely heavy, followed by too many fruits and no blossom buds the second season after the freeze. Biennial production is most common in older apple, pear, and large plum cultivars; it is seldom a problem with peaches, apricots, and cherries.

Trees and shrubs need high carbohydrate reserves during blossom bud formation if alternate bearing is to be avoided. Heavy nitrogen fertiliza-

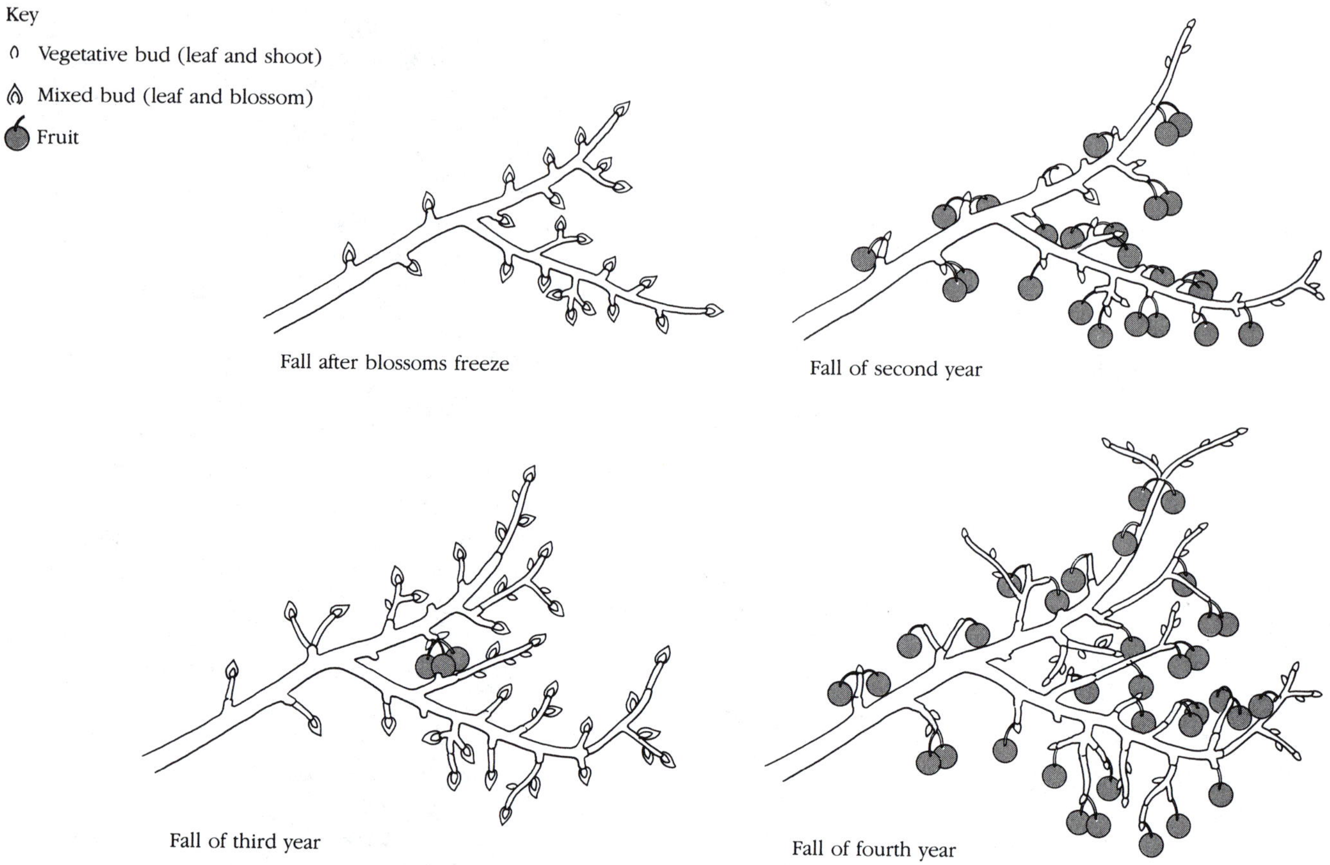

Key

Vegetative bud (leaf and shoot)

Mixed bud (leaf and blossom)

Fruit

Fall after blossoms freeze

Fall of second year

Fall of third year

Fall of fourth year

FIGURE 3-20 • The sequence of alternate bearing.

tion and heavy pruning during the spring of the season of light production and early fruit thinning during the year of heavy production (see Chapter 8) help prevent or overcome the alternate bearing of fruit trees.

Alternate-year flowering is common with some ornamentals—old-fashioned lilacs, some flowering crabapples, and mountain ash, for example—and can be prevented by removing faded blooms before seed begins to develop or some of the fruit just after petals fall.

Fruit Development

Although a few important kinds of fruits, including bananas, navel oranges, certain cucumbers, and pineapple, develop without ovule fertilization, most fruit species require pollination and fertilization to initiate the development of fruit. Moreover, the continuing development of seed is essential for and correlated with the growth of most fruit.

Only a fraction of a fruit tree's blooms normally produce mature fruit. There are two periods when small fruits are lost from the trees: (1) the postbloom drop, right after petals fall, and (2) four to six weeks later, the June drop, just as the fruit is beginning to enlarge rapidly. A lack of, or faulty, ovule fertilization and localized nutrient imbalance are thought to be the causes, but a loss of fruit at these times is normal and should not concern the gardener as more than enough to produce a crop will usually remain.

Shortly after fertilization, as the seeds begin to develop, the number of cells in the fruit rapidly increases. By the time an individual apple fruit is a month old, it has its maximum number of cells, nearly a million. During the second phase of fruit growth, the cells enlarge, and most of what is perceived as fruit growth is an increase in cell size, mainly from the enlargement of the vacuole (see Figure 2-7). As the fruit begins to mature, sugars and aromatic compounds associated with flavor accumulate.

Accompanying the ripening of many — perhaps all — fruits is a phenomenon called the **climacteric**. For most fruits, the climacteric is the time when the fruit can be harvested and possesses — or is able to develop when detached from the plant — its maximum quality. The time of the climacteric is signaled by a sharp rise in the rate of respiration. If the fruit is not harvested, its quality will gradually decline as it becomes senescent.

Most fruits will store for the longest amount of time if picked just as they reach their climacteric. Pears should be picked shortly after their climacteric, which occurs while they are still hard and immature; they will lack flavor and be grainy if left on the tree to ripen fully. The climacteric of tomatoes also occurs while the fruit still appears immature and is visually signaled by the change in color from dark green to lighter green or white as the chlorophyll breaks down. After that the fruit will mature off the vine to its full color.

Fruit and Seed Quality and Pollination

"Don't plant muskmelons next to cucumbers" is one of the more persistent warnings that have been passed down through generations of gardeners. The idea stems from the belief that fruit resulting from the fertilization of muskmelon ovaries with cucumber pollen will taste like cucumbers. Some gardeners also are reluctant to plant a golden apple tree next to a red one, fearing the effect of cross-pollination on color. There are other commonly held notions of the effect of pollination.

Let us examine the validity of these beliefs in light of the information presented in this and the previous chapters. In the first place, cucumbers and muskmelons belong to two different species, *Cucumis sativus* and *Cucumis melo*, respectively. We learned in Chapter 1 that cross-pollination between species almost never occurs, and so we must conclude that cucumber pollen cannot affect the quality of muskmelons because these two crops do not cross-pollinate.

Second, even if cross-pollination were possible, as it is with red and yellow apples, only the embryo and endosperm of the seed would be affected by the foreign pollen. The fruit is the enlarged ovary that develops entirely from tissue of the mother plant, and therefore the source of pollen cannot affect its quality. The persistence of the belief that cucumber pollen can affect muskmelon quality stems from the fact that muskmelons will taste like cucumbers if they are harvested when immature or if plant disease or unfavorable environmental conditions prevent the manufacture of sugar by the leaves as the fruit is maturing.

Experienced gardeners sometimes warn beginners that planting white iris next to colored iris will cause the colored iris to turn white or that planting different colored gladioli together will cause them all to turn one dominant color, usually peach. The assumption is that cross-pollination leads to these results. Although cross-pollination and seed production can occur in both iris and gladioli, only rarely do seedlings of either grow to maturity in a home garden. White iris do sometimes become dominant in beds of mixed colors, but because the vigorous white iris gradually crowds out other, less vigorous types. The most common peach-colored gladiolus cultivar is early and produces larger corms and more cormels — tiny corms that appear around the base of a new corm — than do other cultivars. Bulking, or massing together, the corms harvested from a mixed-cultivar planting and randomly selecting the best ones for replanting, as many gardeners do, will soon result in a preponderance of peach-colored flowers.

The effect of pollen source on the quality of horticultural products cannot be completely ignored, however. For crops like peas, beans, and corn, in which the product being grown is seed, the wrong pollen can ruin the crop. Cross-pollination between popcorn and sweet corn as a result of planting them side by side causes the popcorn not to pop and the sweet corn to be tough and starchy. The possibility of less-sweet corn as a result of cross-pollination is also the reason for seed catalogs' warning gardeners not to plant supersweet sweet corn next to standard cultivars of the same maturity. Furthermore, if seed is to be saved for planting the following year, the source of pollen becomes crucial. Growing seed at home is discussed in the next chapter.

Selected References

George, R. A. *Vegetable Seed Production.* New York: Wiley, 1985.

Glimn-Lacey, J., and P. B. Kaufman. *Botany Illustrated.* New York: Van Nostrand Reinhold, 1984.

Mauseth, J. *Botany.* New York: Holt, Rinehart and Winston, 1991.

Rogers, M. *Saving Seed: The Gardener's Guide to Growing and Saving Vegetable and Flower Seeds.* Downal, Vt.: Storey Communications, 1978.

Whealy, K., ed. *Garden Seed Inventory.* 2nd ed. Decorah, Iowa: Seed Saver Publications, 1988.

Young, J., and C. Young. *Collecting, Processing, and Germinating Seed of Wildland Plants.* Beaverton, Ore.: Timber Press, 1986.

CHAPTER 4

Propagation of Garden Plants

The production of new plants from parts of existing plants has already been defined as propagation. Some species of garden plants, including a majority of vegetables and annual flowers and many herbaceous perennial flowers and woody trees and shrubs, are propagated from seed. Seed propagation is referred to as **sexual propagation**. Other plants, including most houseplants, many popular landscape materials, most fruit trees, potatoes, sweet potatoes, and rhubarb, are propagated from stems, leaves, or roots, or from bulbs, tubers, rhizomes, fleshy roots, or other specialized structures that nature has modified from basic plant organs. This kind of propagation is referred to as **asexual** or **vegetative propagation**.

CONTAINERS AND MEDIA FOR PLANT PROPAGATION

Both sexually and asexually propagated plants are frequently started in containers, and they can grow in almost any receptacle that can accommodate the growing medium and hold together until the plant parts used for propagating (the **propagules**) are ready to be transplanted.

Commercial flats and pots of various kinds and sizes and small containers for growing individual plants are available at garden shops and stores. Flats are shallow containers designed for starting seedling transplants or small cuttings. Until a few years ago they were always made of wood and were a standard 23 × 14 × 3½ inches in length, width, and depth, respectively. Today they come in many sizes and of various materials, including wood, metal, fiberglass, pressed fiber, and, most commonly, plastic. Small flats, each containing eight to twelve transplants, are marketed every spring by the hundreds of thousands in the United States and Canada. There should be drainage holes in flats made of plastic, fiberglass, metal, or other nonporous materials. Extra nitrogen is required for plants growing in paper, new wood, and fiber flats. To provide some or all of the mineral nutrients for growing transplants, some manufacturers sell fiber flats with slow-release fertilizer incorporated in the walls and bottom.

Flats are also used to hold individual plant containers, including fiber pots, small plastic pots, plant bands, and peat pellets, all usually 1½ × 1½ inches (4 × 4 cm) or 2 × 2 inches (5 × 5 cm) in size. Plant bands are made from compressed fiber and have no bottom, so that they can be folded flat for shipping and storing. Peat pellets are dried compressed peat moss held together by coarse netting. They usually contain fertilizer and expand to several times their size when soaked in water. Various kinds of flats or trays with plugs made of peat or other inert material are the basis of various systems of transplanting that have recently revolutionized the commercial potted-plant industry. (Plug culture is being adapted for home gardeners and is described later in this chapter.)

Pots for plant growing also are available in many shapes, sizes, and materials. For propagating, clay pots, once the standard for all containerized plant growing, have been replaced by less expensive, lightweight fiber and plastic pots. Clay pots are, of course, still the most convenient and practical choice for growing houseplants when the plants will remain in the containers for extended periods of time. Empty 1-gallon (no. 10) and 5-gallon tin and plastic containers in which food is packaged for large food-preparation establishments—obtainable from restaurants, school cafeterias, and hospitals—are especially well suited for growing woody nursery stock. Like other containers, they must have drainage holes when they are used for propagation.

Emptied plastic, metal, and fiber food receptacles, such as those in which milk, cottage cheese, baked items, and eggs are purchased, can be recycled to become plant-growing containers. They need to be thoroughly washed with soap and water and be provided with drainage holes.

Like the containers used for propagating, the rooting media for transplants have changed markedly over the years. In 1940 all transplants were grown in a mix of soil, sand, and manure. Today the many materials available for growing plants are more properly called plant-growing media. The two requisites of propagating media are that they retain water and yet drain well so that oxygen can reach plant roots (see "Soil Preparation" in Chapter 14).

PROPAGATING PLANTS FROM SEED

◆ ◆ ◆

Even with increases in purchase price, the cost of garden seed represents only a small percentage of the total cost of growing a garden. Because a crop can be no better than the seed used to plant it, no gardening activity is more important than securing good seeds.

Securing Garden Seed

It is essential that gardeners plant seed that will germinate and grow vigorously; be free of disease-causing organisms, insects, and weed seed; and be the desired cultivar. Obtaining seed with these characteristics is not usually difficult in North America, but because there are so many sources for obtaining seed a few guidelines may be helpful.

Because it is impossible to distinguish, by casual observation, seed of good or poor viability or seed of different cultivars, growers must rely on the integrity of the seed dealer. Seed purchased

FIGURE 4-1 • A seed tape being planted. Lukewarm water poured along the tape will start the tape's dissolution and result in more rapid seed germination.

from a reliable local dealer or a well-known mail-order supplier will usually be satisfactory. Many seed companies label their packages with the results of a germination test, including the date and percentage of germination and the amount of foreign matter present. If the test has been made within the past six months, the results usually are a good estimate of the amount of seed that will germinate if conditions are ideal. A few firms do not include germination test results on their seed packages, relying instead on their reputation of selling only seed with good viability. It is a good idea to date packets of leftover seed that were not already dated by the company that produced them.

The garden should be planned and the seed ordered as early as possible so that the desired cultivars can be obtained before seed stocks are depleted. Seed fastened to water-soluble tape at the recommended spacing is available for some garden crops. The tape is laid in a furrow at the proper depth and covered with soil. Taped seed is expensive but convenient when conditions are good for germination (Figure 4-1). The need to field-space (**precision plant**) seeds so that commercial vegetable or flower plantings do not require expensive thinning prompted seed companies to develop a technology for encasing individual seeds of small-seeded crops in a capsule of inert, water-soluble material such as clay or talc. These **pelleted seeds** are much easier to space individually. Pelleted seed is also used in greenhouse plug culture, discussed below. Easier planting at uniform spacing may make pelleted seed (when it is available to gardeners) worth the extra cost.

Gardeners often ask whether they should grow and save their own seed. This is a difficult question, because success depends so much on the gardener's knowledge and inclinations, the time available, and the botany of the desired crops. Seed of self-pollinating crops can be saved if reasonable care is taken in harvesting and storing it (see Table 14-12, for a list of self- and cross-pollinating crops). Home-grown seeds of cross-pollinating crops will produce true to type only if the seed comes from a cultivar isolated enough so that it was not cross-pollinated by other cultivars of the same species. Seeds of F_1 hybrid cultivars should never be saved, for the reasons mentioned in Chapter 3.

For gardeners with other pursuits and limited time, gardening activities other than growing seed are probably more satisfying. Because seed represents such a small percentage of the total cost of gardening, the money saved may not be worth the bother and space required for growing, collecting, threshing, fermenting to separate the seed from pulp, drying, storing, and testing. On the other hand, some gardeners derive much satisfaction from producing their own seed; sometimes they can improve local adaptation by collecting seed from individual plants of outstanding performance; and occasionally it may be necessary to save the seeds of a cultivar for which there is no commercial seed source (see "Growing Garden Seed at Home" in Chapter 14).

Seed Dormancy

Before seeds can germinate, they must be exposed to the correct environmental conditions. For some species, this means overcoming physiological or physical seed dormancy. If seeds of native plants of cold-winter areas were to germinate immediately after they reached the soil in the late summer or fall, the newly germinated, tender young plants would not survive the winter. Consequently, nature provides various systems to delay germination until there is a longer period of favorable environment. We refer to these systems of seed-germination delay as **seed dormancy** or **seed rest.**

As explained in Chapter 2, a plant (or plant part) that is not actively growing is dormant, so technically all seed can be considered dormant until it germinates. If bud and seed physiology terminology were parallel, seed that would not germinate even if environmental conditions were favorable would be in a resting period. In reality, however, the term *seed rest* is almost never used, and the term *seed dormancy* is used to describe viable seeds that will not germinate without treatment even when all environmental conditions are favorable.

Because seed dormancy interferes with cultivation, nondormant cultivars of seed-propagated species have been selected to provide cultivated species that no longer have a dormant period. However, most woody ornamentals and asexually propagated species of garden plants still retain vestiges of either physical or physiological dormancy, and so gardeners must know how to overcome this dormancy before they can germinate seeds of these species.

Physical Dormancy. This phenomenon is common in seeds of legumes such as peas and beans, in seeds of a few other dry-seeded vegetables, and in seeds of many ornamental and perennial flowering plants. The most common manifestation of **physical dormancy** is the failure of the seed to absorb water because of an impervious seed coat. Such seed, called **hard seed,** is a problem for homemakers as well as for growers, because seeds that vary in degree of hardness cook unevenly. A pot of chili or a lentil casserole with some seeds cooked to pieces while others remain hard enough to crack teeth does nothing to encourage the consumption of beans or lentils.

Nature overcomes physical dormancy by abrading the seed coat by soil particles and water, by the action of freezing and thawing, by microorganisms, or by the chemical action of the soil solution. Hard seed can be opened by artificially abrading the seed coat (**mechanical scarification**), by treating the seeds with a strong acid (**chemical scarification**), by soaking in hot water, by burning in a fire (for a few species), or by manipulating the humidity or other environmental factors. Pea, lentil, and bean seeds grown and stored in areas of low humidity in the western United States are usually put through a mill that subjects them to a light sanding, thus ensuring the easy penetration of water through the seed coat when they are planted or cooked. Seeds of morning glory and New Zealand spinach require a long time to germinate in the garden, primarily because water penetrates the seed coat extremely slowly. To speed the action, the gardener can make a small notch with a triangular file in the coat of each seed to be planted (Figure 4-2). Nurseries frequently soak the seed of certain ornamental trees and shrubs for short periods in concentrated sulfuric

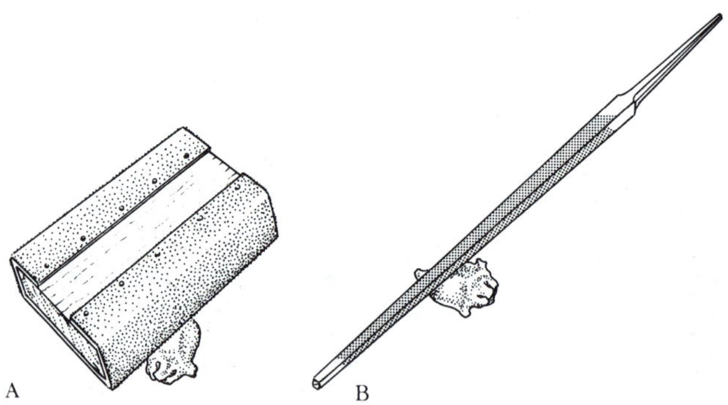

FIGURE 4-2 • Seed scarification. When only a few seeds of morning glory, New Zealand spinach, perennial sweet peas, or others with seed coats impervious to water are to be planted, germination will be speeded if the seed coat is opened slightly with a piece of sandpaper (A) or a triangular file (B).

acid to overcome physical dormancy (see Table 14-5).

Physiological Dormancy. **Physiological dormancy** is manifested in various ways. Sometimes the embryo is immature when the seed is otherwise ready for harvest, a common occurrence with early-maturing stone-fruit cultivars. The immature embryo can be made to grow if the seed is removed from its shell and placed on a special medium in a controlled environment. Even with this treatment, early seedling growth is likely to be abnormal, the leaves or roots failing to develop completely and the length of time required for the seedling to develop into a normal plant usually extending to several months.

A more satisfactory treatment is to store the seed for four to fourteen weeks, depending on the species or cultivar, in moist peat moss, sawdust, or similar material in a light plastic bag in the refrigerator. This treatment, called **stratification**, allows the embryo to mature as it would naturally if the seed were to remain in the soil over the winter. Treating with activated charcoal or thiourea is also effective with some species.

Physiological dormancy of many fruit and ornamental species is caused by chemical inhibitors within or outside the seed. The fruit itself often contains an inhibitor that prevents seeds from sprouting while they are inside it. In some crops, tomatoes being a good example, the seeds germinate as soon as they are removed from the wet, pulpy material of the fruit. For others, stratification is necessary to overcome the chemical inhibition of seed germination. The seeds of some woody plants have a combination of physical and physiological dormancy and may require both stratification and scarification before they can be germinated (see "Propagating Plants from Seed" in Chapter 14).

Seed Germination

The principal requirements for seed germination are warm temperature, moisture, and oxygen. Research by the U.S. Department of Agriculture reveals light to be much more important to inhibiting or stimulating the germination of seeds of many ornamentals than was previously supposed (see Table 14-4). Even the very low intensities of light that filter through a shallow layer of soil can affect planted seed. Whether light is stimulatory or inhibitory depends on the species. The effect is complicated by its being interrelated with the age of the seed, temperature, and perhaps other environmental factors. Light usually does not complicate the germination of garden seeds if they are planted at the recommended depth and exposed to light and dark cycles corresponding to normal day and night periods.

The temperature at which a seed germinates varies from species to species and, to some extent, from cultivar to cultivar within a species. The temperature required for any species to germinate is, however, correlated with the optimal temperature for that species to grow. Seeds of the 'Hales Best' cultivar of muskmelon, for example, cannot germinate until the soil temperature reaches approximately 72°F (22°C), and this cultivar, like all muskmelons, also requires high temperatures for normal plant growth.

If the temperature is high enough and if moisture is present, water will enter the seed, through either the seed coat or openings in it. As water combines with starch and other materials inside the seed, the seed begins to enlarge, and enzymes that control and direct the growth of the developing plant are activated. Growth-promoting substances in the seed direct the roots to grow downward and the leaves and stem to grow upward. The seed coat and endosperm of monocot seeds usually remain in the soil. In some dicot plants, such as beans, marigolds, and tomatoes, the cotyledons are pushed up through the soil and become active in photosynthesis. In others, such as peas, the cotyledons remain in the soil, and only the plumule and epicotyl emerge (Figure 4-3).

The young seedling is especially vulnerable to adverse environmental conditions while it is becoming established. Until the plumule and cotyledons reach light, begin to develop chlorophyll,

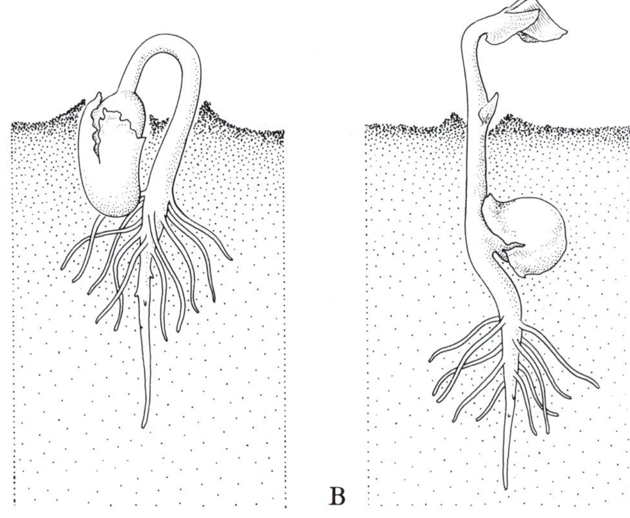

FIGURE 4-3 • Comparative germination of garden beans (A) and peas (B). The cotyledon of the bean is pushed through the surface crust, whereas the cotyledon of the pea remains in the soil.

and start manufacturing food and until the radicle elongates and develops root hairs, the young seedling is entirely dependent for its survival on the food stored in the seed and the moisture that it can soak up. If the seed is planted too deeply, its food reserves may be exhausted before the plumule reaches light. If the soil in which the seed has begun to swell becomes dry, the seedling will perish. Young seedlings are also more likely to be killed by frost, high temperature, insects, and diseases than are more mature plants.

Determining Seed Germinability. When more seed has been purchased than can be used during a single year (which frequently happens), the grower must decide whether to use the old or to purchase new seed the second or third season. Initial viability, kind of seed, and temperature and humidity of storage largely determine the length of time that seed remains viable. Tables 4-1 and 4-2 show the length of time from harvest to planting during which various kinds of vegetable and flower seed remain fit to plant in most parts of the United States. The years listed in these tables are only approximations and vary with the climate of the area. Seeds live longest when stored where temperature and humidity are low. The seed of tomato cultivars retained good viability after being stored for twenty years at the high, dry Cheyenne, Wyoming, USDA field station, whereas onion seed may lose viability in just a few months when kept in open containers in warm, humid locations. Whenever possible, seed should be stored in a cool, dry location.

A germination test should be run on seed of doubtful germinability. For this, any technique that supplies heat and moisture can be used (see "Testing Seed Germinability" in Chapter 14).

TABLE 4-1 • *The approximate length of time during which vegetable seeds of good initial germinating ability stored under proper conditions will germinate satisfactorily*

Vegetable	Years	Vegetable	Years	Vegetable	Years
Asparagus	3	Eggplant	5	Pea	3
Bean	3	Kohlrabi	5	Pepper	4
Beet	4	Leek	1	Pumpkin	4
Broccoli	4	Lettuce	5	Radish	5
Brussels sprouts	4	Muskmelon	5	Spinach	5
Cabbage	4	Mustard	4	Squash	5
Carrot	3	Okra	2	Sweet corn	1
Cauliflower	4	Onion	1	Tomato	4
Celery	5	Parsley	2	Turnip	5
Cucumber	5	Parsnip	1	Watermelon	5

TABLE 4-2 • *The approximate length of time during which flower seeds of good initial germinating ability stored under proper conditions will germinate satisfactorily*

Flower	Years	Flower	Years	Flower	Years
African daisy	3	Hollyhock	5	Shasta daisy	3
Aster	2	Marigold	3	Snapdragon	3
Calendula	5	Nasturtium	5	Stock	5
Carnation	5	Pansy	3	Sweet alyssum	4
Chrysanthemum	5	Petunia	3	Sweet pea	2
Cosmos	3	Phlox	2	Sweet sultans	5
Delphinium	1	Salpiglossis	5	Verbena	3
Dusty miller	3	Scabiosa	3	Zinnia	5

Based partially on information from California Department of Agriculture, *Bulletin*, vol. 26, no. 3, 1937.

Planting Seeds in the Garden

For direct seeding outdoors in the spring, timing is important. Generally, gardeners should plant as early as practical. For some cool-season crops, early seeding is essential so that the plants can mature before the hot days of midsummer. For other crops, especially in northern latitudes or at high altitudes, early planting is essential if they are to mature during the short growing season. On the other hand, planting before the soil is warm enough for germination only subjects the seeds and seedlings to a longer period of possible attack by soil pathogens, competition by weeds, and injury by freezing.

Different kinds of vegetables and flowers have slightly different optimal conditions for germination; however, it is possible to divide most of them into two broad groups: the cool-season and the warm-season crops. The cool-season crops include radishes, lettuce, spinach, Swiss chard, beets, carrots, onions, cauliflower, cabbage, broccoli, kohlrabi, kale, turnips, rutabagas, peas, snapdragons, pansies, and many others. These crops germinate at soil temperatures between 40° and 55°F (4.4° and 13°C) and can withstand a certain amount of freezing after they have begun to grow. Although onions, peas, spinach, radishes, and lettuce are usually planted the earliest of this group, most of them can be planted as soon as the soil has warmed and dried enough to become workable.

Warm-season crops include tomatoes, eggplant, peppers, cucumbers, squash, watermelons, cantaloupes, snap beans, lima beans, sweet corn, marigolds, zinnias, and many others. These crops require soil temperatures above 60°F (16°C) for rapid germination and are killed by temperatures slightly below freezing. Some of them are injured even when subjected to cool temperatures above the freezing point. Although sweet corn, tomatoes, and zinnias can be planted somewhat earlier than can muskmelons and watermelons, the general recommendation for planting warm-season crops is after the danger of frost, by which time the soil temperature usually has warmed sufficiently to promote rapid germination and the emergence of vigorous seedlings.

Preparing the seedbed to level the planting surface and to eliminate large clods and air pockets is important to ensure contact between moist soil and the seeds and to obtain uniform depth and spacing of the seeds. Good seedbed preparation is also necessary for the control of weeds, which are easier to eliminate before planting than after. The seedbed should be moist but not saturated with water and should never be worked when excessively wet. If irrigation is required, it should be done before planting. Irrigating after planting should be avoided, if possible, because it can cause the soil to crust, cool the soil, and encourage the growth of seed-decaying organisms. Lightly sprinkling the planted seedbed may be necessary in areas with low humidity and drying winds and with small-seeded and light-requiring flowers that must be seeded on the surface.

Each seed must be planted deeply enough to remain in contact with moisture until it has germinated. But it should not be planted so deeply that the plumule is unable to push through the soil before food reserves in the seed are exhausted. The general recommendation for depth of planting is to cover the seed by about three times its width. Small seeds like those of petunias and snapdragons should be scattered on the soil surface and raked in lightly. Seeds should be planted somewhat more shallowly during early spring when temperatures at lower soil depths are likely to be cool and somewhat more deeply during warm, dry summer periods when moisture is likely to be lacking in the upper areas of the soil (see "Propagating Plants from Seed" in Chapter 14).

Transplants

Not all plants can be seeded directly into the garden. In fact, one of the fastest-growing gardening industries is the production of **bedding plants**, which are transplants grown for flower beds and vegetable gardens. The use of transplants is economically justified when each plant occupies a fairly large area and the crop has a high economic or social value, as is true with most intensively cultivated horticultural plants. The major advantage of using transplants is, of course, earlier production. A plant started in a greenhouse six weeks before it can be seeded out-of-doors may not mature a full six weeks earlier than one directly seeded into the field, but the transplant will probably have a two- to four-week advantage in maturity, which is of real value to home gardeners. Transplanting also enables growers to germinate seeds under more controlled environmental conditions and thus ensures a more economical use of seeds. This is especially important for some double and hybrid flower cultivars, seeds of which cost several hundred dollars for a fraction of an ounce. Transplanting also permits gardeners to place each plant in its desired location in the garden.

Commonly transplanted horticultural crops include a majority of the annual and perennial flowers and muskmelons, watermelons, celery, tomatoes, eggplant, peppers, cabbage, cauliflower, broccoli, brussels sprouts, kale, collards, onions, and asparagus. Chives, parsley, catnip, caraway, sage, thyme, basil, and lavender are some of the herbs often transplanted.

Purchasing Transplants. The main consideration when purchasing transplants is obtaining vigorous plants of the proper size and desired cultivar. Transplants should be large enough to be handled easily but not so large that they have become crowded. A compact, bushy seedling is more likely to survive and produce a better mature plant than is one that has grown tall and leggy. Plants that have been stunted and those that have a gray-green or yellowish cast from a lack of fertilizer or water should be avoided. A reliable local nursery generally is the most satisfactory source of supply. Plants purchased from a supermarket, department store, or other establishment not specializing in plant production and/or sales should be carefully inspected for freedom from insects, pathogens, and physiological disorders.

Growing Transplants. Some gardeners like to grow their own transplants. Growing transplants lengthens the season of gardening enjoyment and, because the number of cultivars available for purchase as transplants is often limited, makes possible the production of cultivars not otherwise obtainable. Even considering these advantages, however, home gardeners should not attempt to grow their own transplants unless they have adequate facilities. Hobby greenhouses and other enclosed structures designed for propagation, like hotbeds and cold frames, are ideal. The factor most likely to restrict indoor plant production is light. Sufficient sunlight usually comes through an unobstructed south or west window, and good transplants can be grown at such a location if there is not a radiator under the window. High-intensity artificial lights also are satisfactory for growing some kinds of transplants (see Chapter 7 and "Propagating Plants from Seed" in Chapter 14).

Mechanization of Transplant Production and Transplanting. To reduce the cost of commercial transplanting, during the late 1970s a number of European and North American companies developed mechanized systems for growing and planting transplants. The key to the success of these systems is the tray in which the plants are produced and the constant, usually automatic, application of moisture and fertilizer to the very restricted root-growing cells in the tray. The tray cells are mechanically filled with small porous plugs made of compressed peat or other fiber. A planting device inserts a single seed into the growing medium of each cell, and the tray is moved to a greenhouse where the transplants are grown in a controlled environment. The uniformly sized plants with their tightly packed root plugs that are produced by this system are ideally adapted to planting, without the roots' being disturbed, by a machine that makes a trench, spaces and waters the transplant with nutrient solution, and covers and packs the soil around each newly placed plant. Because they can be transported without disturbing their roots, such transplants are used extensively for the machine planting of annual vegetables and flowers and herbaceous perennials. Various companies have slightly different production procedures for this kind of transplant, some of them patented, and use different tradenames for their products. These kinds of transplants are often called "speedlings," a name used for one of the early patented growing systems. They are also sometimes referred to as **plug transplants** or plugs, although the method of and time required for growing them differ somewhat from the method of and time required for growing the smaller plugs produced by what is generally known in the greenhouse and nursery industries as **plug culture**.

For production of plants from seed in the greenhouse, the most expensive procedures in space and labor are (1) providing an area with the exacting environment required for sprouting the tiny, slow-to-germinate seed and (2) digging the fragile seedlings with their intertwining roots from the pots or flats in which the seed is germinated and replanting them individually at the proper spacing. The system of growing that has become known as plug culture has greatly reduced both these expenses.

Growers who sell enough plants to afford the special facilities required grow plugs for both themselves and smaller-volume growers. The seeds are mechanically seeded into flats having many small cells, 288 to over 600 per flat. The plug seedlings are germinated in rooms with a closely monitored controlled environment. As soon as they have germinated, the seedlings are moved to greenhouses where they grow at high density for a few more weeks, just until two or three true leaves have formed, the precise length of time depending on species. Close spacing, optimal environment, and rapid turnover provide the maximal speed and percentage of germination, as well as the maximal utilization of space in the expensive controlled-environment facility and greenhouse. The uniformity and individual nature of plug seedlings permit further mechanization when they are potted. The technology of plug culture has revolutionized the bedding-plant industry and has greatly increased the efficiency of producing flowering and green pot crops grown from seed. Plug culture is also used to replace direct field seeding to obtain more nearly uniform spacing and more rapid growth of seedling trees grown by nurseries for reforestation and Christmas tree plantings.

Seed of extremely high germinability is necessary for plug culture, as it costs just as much to grow a flat in which 98 percent of the plugs produce plants as it does one in which 50 percent do. Also, the many crops that have small or oddly shaped seeds require pelleted seed (described earlier in this chapter).

Garden shops and mail-order nurseries market plug-planting systems modified for hobby greenhouses, window boxes, and artificially lighted plant-growing tables. In some locations the small nursery-plug transplants developed for commercial greenhouses are now available for purchase by home gardeners. Plugs are less expensive than are full-sized transplants, and their root system remains intact when they are planted, reducing the stress of transplanting; however they are much smaller than ordinary transplants and so need special attention. Garden centers or catalog nurseries offering them provide instructions for their planting and growing, which should be carefully followed, especially the directions for watering. The contrasting surfaces between the two kinds of growing media (in this case, the peat of the plugs and the loam of the soil) often act as a barrier to the movement of water. Thus the plug is less likely than a bare-root transplant to absorb moisture and nutrients from the soil, even though the soil may be fairly wet. Until roots have penetrated from the plug into the soil, the transplant may require watering several times each day during dry weather. At least one watering shortly after the plugs are transplanted should be a dilute nutrient solution of a concentration suitable for potbed plants (see "Fertilizing Houseplants" in Chapter 14).

PROPAGATING PLANTS ASEXUALLY

◆ ◆ ◆

For most species, propagation by seed is usually more convenient and less expensive than asexual propagation. With many cultivated crops, however, seed propagation is not feasible. Some of the reasons for propagating asexually are (1) to perpetuate plants that either never had or have lost the ability to produce seeds; (2) to reproduce plants that are heterozygous genetically and consequently will not come true from seed; (3) to control the form or size of a plant; and (4) to give the plant a stronger, more pest-resistant, or more cold-resistant root system.

Examples of plants that do not produce seed are seedless oranges, seedless grapefruits, seedless grapes, bananas, pineapple, peppermint, French tarragon, and greenhouse carnations. From the horticulturist's and consumer's point of view, the absence of seeds is highly desirable in many crops. Plants that do not come true from seeds include most temperate-zone fruits, coleus, chrysanthemums, roses, junipers, yews, and arborvitae (Figure 4-4). Seed from a 'Red Delicious' apple, for example, would produce trees having small apples, trees having large apples, and trees with fruit of various colors, shapes, textures, and flavors; but not one in 100,000 of the seeds would likely produce another 'Red Delicious' tree. The best-known example of propagation to control form or size is the use of size-controlling rootstocks for developing dwarf apple and pear trees. As another example, the top of the Camperdown elm (*Ulmus glabra* 'Camperdowni') that is so admired for its beautiful weeping growth habit is actually a liana until it is grafted onto an upright rootstock (Figure 4-5). Tree roses are another example of controlling form by grafting.

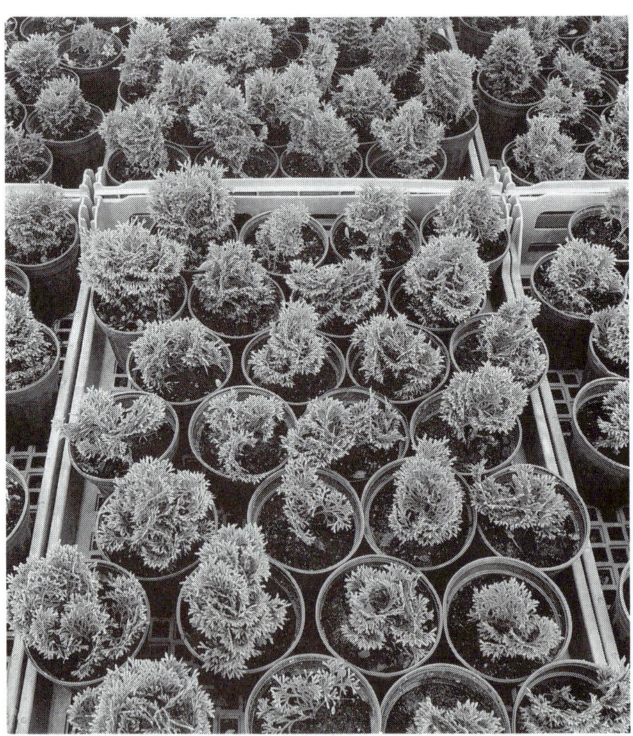

FIGURE 4-4 • A flat of dwarf arborvitae ready for transplanting. (Courtesy of Barry L. Runk/Grant Heilman)

FIGURE 4-5 • Changing growth habit by grafting. The unique growth habit of the Camperdown elm is created by grafting an *Ulmus glabra* 'Camperdowni' scion onto a normal Scotch elm (*U. glabra*) rootstock. The graft is made on an older Scotch elm trunk at the height where the tree is to head (form side branches), because the tree "weeps" from the point of the graft union.

One of the best-known examples of the use of vegetative propagation to control pests is the grafting of European grape (*Vitis vinifera*) onto American grape (*Vitis labrusca*) rootstock. Phylloxera, a grape-root aphid, was introduced into Europe along with the first American grapes taken there. Although phylloxera does not extensively injure the roots of American-type grapes, the European grapes that were propagated with cuttings had no resistance to it, and the insect soon started to spread across Europe, threatening to destroy the entire grape industry. Eventually it was found that the damage caused by phylloxera could be controlled by grafting European grapes onto American grape-root systems.

Sour oranges (*Citrus aurantium*) are used to provide a pest-resistant rootstock for plantings of sweet orange (*C. sinensis*). Peaches are sometimes used as a drought-resistant root system for plums, and the 'McIntosh' apple cultivar is sometimes used as an **interstock** in developing a cold-resistant framework for trees of such less hardy cultivars as 'Red Delicious' and 'Golden Delicious'. The use of interstocks is explained in the grafting section of this chapter.

Repairing of certain woody plants is sometimes accomplished by grafting (which is not, strictly speaking, propagation). Bridge grafting is frequently done across areas that have been damaged by freezing weather or crown girdled by rodents or accident (see Figure 14-46).

Methods of Vegetative Propagation

Vegetative propagation can be categorized into the following groupings: apomictic seed; utilization of specialized stem, leaf, and root structures; cuttage; layerage; and graftage.

Apomictic Seed. In some species, what appears to be seed may be formed without the union of male and female gametes. Such seed, referred to as **apomictic**, may form as a result of the development of a macrospore mother cell into an egg without meiosis, or it may form from a cell produced in the ovule wall. In any event, apomictic seed forms entirely from tissue of the mother plant, and cultivars propagated from such seed are clones. Bluegrasses (*Poa* spp.) are the horticultural crops most likely to be reproduced by apomictic seed. Navel oranges and several other citrus cultivars produce apomictic seed, but they are normally propagated by grafting.

Specialized Stem, Leaf, and Root Structures. Among the stem, leaf, and root modifications used for propagation are offshoots, crown divisions, stolons, rhizomes, tubers, tuberous roots, tuberous stems, bulbs, corms, and fleshy leaves (see Figure 2-18). Among the exotic species, pineapples, bananas, and sugar cane are propagated by **offshoots** (see "Modifications of Stem, Root, and Leaf" in Chapter 2). Perhaps of more interest to home gardeners are the common trees and shrubs, including lilac, flowering almond, mock orange, some of the spireas, and flowering quince, that can be propagated from offshoots.

Plants of some horticultural species can be cut or divided into a number of parts, each of which will grow into a new plant, provided it contains some stem and some root tissue. Because the area where the root meets the stem of the plant is called the **crown**, this type of propagation is referred to as **crown division**. In certain cases it is difficult to distinguish propagation by offshoots from propagation by crown division. Rhubarb and some perennial flowers, including chrysanthemums, peonies, columbine, lupine, and some perennial poppies, can be propagated by crown division. Ferns also are frequently propagated from crown divisions.

Several important horticultural crops reproduce by above-ground trailing horizontal stems called **runners** or **stolons**. Among these, strawberries (*Fragaria* spp.), strawberry geraniums (*Saxifraga sarmentosa*), and spider plants (*Chlorophytum elatum*) are three of the better known. Even more numerous are plants that reproduce and can be propagated by underground horizontal stems called **rhizomes**. Lowbush blueberries spread by rhizome-initiated shoots that surface some distance from the mother plant. Wild blueberry clones may spread in this manner to cover several hundred feet in a few years. Grasses spread by rhizomes, and several kinds are propagated from sections of rhizomes. Lily of the valley also spreads by rhizomes, as do a number of troublesome weeds, including quack grass, poison ivy, water hyacinth, and cattails.

Botanically, tubers are enlarged rhizomes. Potatoes are the best-known tuberous crop and are propagated by cutting the tubers into several pieces, each containing an eye, which is a bud cluster. The Jerusalem artichokes (*Helianthus tuberosus*) and caladium also are propagated from tubers. The "tubers" of tuberous begonias and gloxinias are really the enlarged bases of the main plant stem and are technically **stem tubers**. They differ from corms in not having scaly leaves and in enlarging rather than being renewed each year. They can be propagated by cutting them into pieces, as are tubers (see "Propagating from Fleshy Storage Organs" in Chapter 14).

A number of popular flowers, including most of the early spring–blooming ones, grow from bulbs or corms (see Table 14-10). Tulips, lilies, and narcissi are examples of bulbous crops, and gladioli, crocuses, and water chestnuts are corm forming. The growth of stems, roots, and leaves in both bulbs and corms is initiated and proceeds at the expense of the stored food material in the bulb or corm. After the above-ground portion of the plant has completed its growth cycle, the food reserves of the storage organ are replenished from the photosynthetic products manufactured primarily in the leaves. Thus it is important that the leaves of bulb and corm plants not be removed until those leaves have dried. It is also important that the leaves be left with the plant in the garden if the flowers are cut for decorating purposes.

Bulbs enlarge and form new bulbs (**offsets**) at their periphery as food reserves become available. The old corm shrivels, and a new one forms above it as upper parts of corm-producing plants senesce (see Figure 14-34). A large corm may produce two to three stems, and a new corm is produced at the base of each stem as the plant matures. Thus a single bulb or corm may multiply to form two or three new bulbs or corms during one season. Tiny corms called *cormels* also are produced around the base of the new corm. With a few years' growth these become large enough to produce flowers and are a major way of increasing corm-producing crops. Small bulbils or cormels form in the leaf axils of some bulb and corm-forming species. Lily bulbs can be separated into individual scales, each of which will produce a new tiny bulb and plant.

Some horticultural crop plants can form adventitious buds from their root systems. The sweet potato is root tissue, sometimes called a tuberous root, and is propagated from rooted shoots, called **slips**, produced when the potato is placed in a moist, sterile propagating medium (Figure 4-6). A single sweet potato can produce several crops of slips before its food reserves become exhausted. Most cane berries are capable of producing buds and shoots (suckers) from their root systems. They are propagated either by planting a section of root (root cutting) or, more frequently, by digging a shoot that has already grown from a root-produced adventitious bud. Elderberry, sumac, aspen,

FIGURE 4-6 • Sweet potato propagation. Sweet potatoes are normally propagated from pieces of stem called *slips* produced by placing the potato in a moist propagating medium. This induces sprouts to form and elongate from adventitious buds. Sweet potatoes can also be made to sprout by partially submerging the potato in water and keeping it in a warm room as shown above. New plants can be propagated by planting pieces of the stems 6 to 10 inches (15 to 25 cm) in length directly into the field or garden. (Courtesy of John D. Cunningham/Visuals Unlimited.)

poplar, wild morning glory, and many ornamental shrubs also can spread by root-initiated shoots (see "Propagating from Fleshy Storage Organs" in Chapter 14).

Cuttage. The induction of roots and/or shoots on detached plant parts is called **cuttage**. Cuttage is the most frequently used method of vegetative propagation because it is convenient and permits large numbers of plants to be produced quite rapidly from a small amount of propagating material. Most indoor foliage plants are propagated from cuttings, as are certain flowering plants, including chrysanthemums, carnations, fuschias, and geraniums. Juniper, arborvitae, false cypress, and yew are among the conifers that are propagated by cuttage. Most small-fruit species, broadleaved evergreens, and a majority of deciduous woody ornamental shrubs can be propagated by cuttage. Cuttings may be made of stems or parts of stems, leaves, or roots. Stem cuttings can be made from herbaceous plants. Softwood cuttings are made from the new succulent growth of woody plants that is produced in the spring or early summer. Hardwood cuttings are made from older wood, usually during the dormant period.

Although a cutting with a single bud can produce a new plant, as is evidenced by the successful rooting of leaf bud cuttings of several species, stem cuttings 3 to 5 inches (8 to 13 cm) long containing at least two nodes are more convenient to use. A slanting cut is made just below the lower node and a straight cut above the upper one. Because there is more meristematic tissue in the vicinity of a node, roots are more likely to form if a node is beneath the rooting medium. The slanting cut at the lower end of the cutting is traditional and is more important for identifying the lower end of the cutting than it is for permitting more surface to be in contact with the rooting medium.

As many leaves as practical should be left on the stem cutting, to provide food for root formation and growth of the new plant. Those leaves that are likely to come in contact with the rooting medium, however, should be removed, as leaves often carry microorganisms that can cause decay when they are in contact with the moist medium (see Figures 14-18, 14-19, and 14-20).

New plants can be propagated from the leaves of a few species (Figure 4-7). The leaf petioles of a number of plants, including coleus, some philodendron cultivars, and other foliage plants, can form roots but not shoots. A rooted leaf of some of these plant species may expand and grow quite large, but it will not produce new shoots unless a stem bud is attached to it.

Factors Affecting Rooting Success. Many factors affect the success of rooting. Some plants root easily, some root with difficulty, and some cannot be induced to form roots, regardless of the treatment used. The age of the plant part being rooted has an effect on its rooting success. Younger plant tissue has more meristematic tissue, which enables it to root more easily. Older tissue, however, contains more reserve carbohydrates, which are necessary for the initiation of new roots and their

FIGURE 4-7 • Propagation from leaf cuttings. The detached leaves of some houseplants, for example, the African violet (above), jade plant, and begonias, can be successfully propagated from leaves. Leaf petioles of others, including most philodendrons, pothos, and coleus, form roots but never initiate bud and stem growth unless an axillary bud is left attached to the leaf petiole. (Courtesy of Runk/Schoenberger from Grant Heilman)

growth. The optimal age of plant tissue for cuttage success varies with the species. With some, the cuttings easiest to root may be from stems not quite mature, a compromise between young tissue with abundant meristem and old tissue with ample food reserves. Obviously, the season of the year, the location of the tissue on the plant, the nutritional level, and the general vitality of the plant from which the cutting is taken all affect its ability to form roots.

The chemicals present in a cutting partly determine its ability to root. For example, it is difficult to root cuttings from apple, pear, or pine trees, but a willow twig will root if it falls on wet soil. Some chemical differences that are at least partly responsible have been identified—notably auxins (see Chapter 7), carbohydrates, certain nitrogenous compounds, and vitamins. There are probably others of which we are not yet aware.

In addition to *in vivo* plant factors, environmental conditions affect rooting. The ideal temperatures for rooting may vary from plant to plant. Relative humidity normally should be high, and adequate oxygen, moisture, and light are necessary. The rooting medium is also important.

A propagator wants to do everything possible to increase the opportunity for root formation. In large part, this means inducing a root system as quickly as possible while preventing the top of the plant from drying. Three special techniques—intermittent mist, hormones, and bottom heat—innovations in the 1940s and 1950s, are now routinely used in nurseries to increase the chance of rooting. Intermittent mist prevents the cutting from dehydrating while roots are being initiated and is supplied by a spray nozzle controlled by a solenoid valve and a time clock set to spray the propagating bench with a fine mist of water for a few seconds every few minutes. Three natural hormones used to stimulate root formation are indole-3-acetic acid (IAA), indole-3-butyric acid (IBA), and α-naphthaleneacetic acid (NAA). Commercial preparations containing one or more of these hormones are available at most garden stores. The lower end of the cutting should receive a very light dusting with the hormone compound, as too much will inhibit root formation. Bottom heat is usually supplied with heating cables in propagating benches to keep the bottom of the cutting warmer than the top. Because growth is most rapid where the temperature is highest, bottom heat encourages root growth but at the same time allows transpiration to remain low.

Only those growers who do considerable propagation will want to go to the expense and effort of setting up and maintaining a bottom-heated mist propagation bed. The average gardener who wants to start only a few plants now and then can devise a satisfactory chamber incorporating most of the innovations of the mist chamber (see "Propagating with Cuttings" in Chapter 14).

Layerage. Because **layerage** induces roots on a part of a stem attached to the mother plant, it is a method of propagation well adapted to those home gardeners who need only a few new plants of any one kind.

The cultivars most frequently propagated by layerage today are dwarf apple and pear rootstocks. Earlier in the chapter the extreme genetic variation of apple seedlings was mentioned. Because uniform rootstocks cannot be propagated from seed and, until recently, apple and pear cuttings were almost impossible to root, a method was devised to propagate them called **mound layerage** (see Figure 14-26).

Homeowners can propagate a number of species, including low-growing evergreens, currants, gooseberries, and many deciduous ornamental shrubs, by simply bending down a stem and covering it with soil. For some plants, the chance of rooting will be greater if a cut is made partway through the stem at the point where the stem is buried. Hormone treatment of the cut portion sometimes also enhances rooting.

Various large houseplants such as philodendron, ficus (see Figure 14-28), and dieffenbachia can be propagated by air layerage. Air layerage can also be used to get rid of an unsightly stem when these plants have lost their lower leaves (see "Layering to Renew or Multiply Plants" in Chapter 14).

Graftage. In propagation by **graftage**, parts of two plants are joined together in such a way that the two parts unite to form a single new plant. Graftage is used to perpetuate plant types that will not come true from seed; to adapt plants to unfavorable soil or climatic conditions; to control or prevent pest damage to roots; to control the size or shape of a plant; to change the top of a mature plant to another cultivar; and occasionally to repair rodent, machinery, or adverse weather damage to trees.

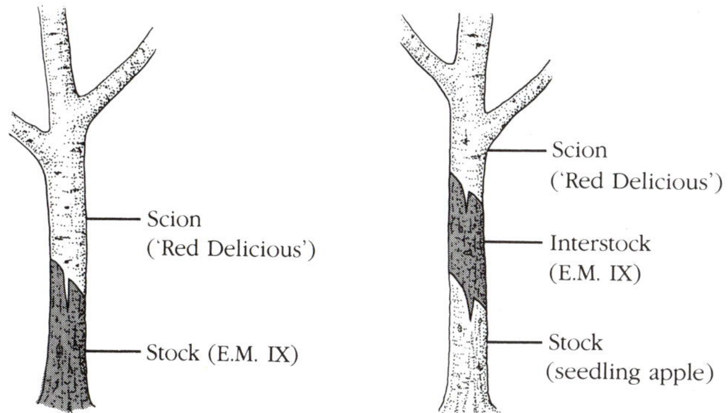

FIGURE 4-8 • Two ways of producing a dwarf apple tree. A dwarfing interstock has essentially the same effect as does a dwarfing rootstock and is sometimes used when the dwarfing stock would produce a weak or inferior root system (compare Figure 8-14).

The part of the plant that will eventually grow to be the above-ground portion is referred to as the **scion**, and the part that will be the root is called the **stock** (Figure 4-8). If the scion consists of a complete cross section of stem with one or more buds, its union with the stock is called **grafting**. If the scion is a single bud, the joining of stock and scion is called **budding**. Grafting is most likely to be successful early in the spring before winter dormancy is overcome. Most budding can be successfully done only while the bark is slipping, usually in July or August in northern states. Apples and pears were formerly propagated primarily by grafting, but with the development of vegetatively propagated rootstocks, they, as well as the stone fruits and roses, are now normally propagated by budding.

Occasionally, because of graft incompatibility or for some other reason, it is necessary to graft a piece of stem of a third cultivar between the stock and scion. This is called double working, and the inserted piece is called an **interstock**. A good example of the use of an interstock is the development of dwarf 'Bartlett' pear trees. Pear trees are made dwarf by grafting a scion of the desired cultivar onto quince rootstock. However, the most commonly grown pear cultivar, the 'Bartlett', will not unite directly with quince. To overcome this problem propagators use as an interstock a piece of stem of 'Old Home' pear cultivar, which is compatible with both 'Bartlett' pear and quince.

At least three conditions must be met if a graft is to be successful. First, the scion and stock must be graft compatible, which means that they are relatively closely related botanically. Discovering whether or not two species or two cultivars are graft compatible is mostly a matter of trial and error. For example, apples and pears are not graft compatible. However, most of the stone fruits do intergraft with another.

The second condition is that the cambium of the stock be in contact with the cambium of the scion. It is the **callus** tissue that grows from the cambium or immature xylem and phloem immediately adjacent to the cambium that permits the union of stock and scion. For the most part, grafting is limited to plants that have a definite cambium layer with associated layers of vascular tissue. Thus the dicots and the gymnosperms can be grafted, but monocots' stock and scion do not readily unite.

The third condition is that cut tissue in the graft region must be protected against drying while the graft union is being formed. Usually this is accomplished by coating the union with some type of grafting compound or wrapping it securely with plastic.

Grafting is not limited to woody plants. In some of the northern European countries, seedling stems of watermelon and cantaloupe are sometimes grafted onto roots of cold-resistant *Cucurbita* species to enable the melons to grow better and mature earlier. Coleus is a favorite for novel grafting experiments because of the many colors and leaf configurations available.

In addition to being a propagating mechanism, grafting is occasionally used for other horticultural purposes. Twisting together limbs in an approach graft across a weak crotch angle can greatly strengthen the framework of an ornamental or fruit tree. Grafting can also be used to insert pollinator branches into a tree that requires pollination by another cultivar. The use of bridge grafting for repairing bark-damaged trees has been mentioned. Another use is to change the cultivar of a mature tree, by gradually cutting off older limbs and replacing them by budding or grafting with branches of the new or desired cultivar. Changing the cultivar of an old tree by graftage is called **topworking** (see Figure 14-52).

FIGURE 4-9 • A natural graft between a branch and the trunk of a young quaking aspen (*Populus tremuloides*).

Natural grafts occur when branches cross and the pressure and abrasion of their growth bring the cambium of one into contact with the cambium of the other (Figure 4-9). Roots also intergraft naturally; wilt disease in the oak forests of the eastern and central United States is spread through the trees' vascular systems that are interconnected by natural root grafts.

Cell and Tissue Cultures

In Chapter 2, cell and tissue culture were cited as techniques for elucidating the processes of plant tissue differentiation. Cell and tissue culture have become important procedures for achieving the uniformity of asexual propagation in species for which cuttage and graftage are not feasible. The techniques of tissue culture vary depending on species. Typically, however, undifferentiated callus is created by culturing tiny bits of meristematic tissue on an agar medium fortified with inorganic and organic plant nutrients and growth regulators. Fragments of the callus are then subjected to altered nutritional and environmental conditions in order to cause roots and shoots to differentiate. In this way hundreds of plants can be obtained from a few cells of the mother plant. The procedure is time-consuming and requires costly facilities, but when uniformity is important and individual plants have high value, propagation by tissue culture is economically justifiable. Each species and sometimes each cultivar must undergo many hours of directed and trial-and-error research in order to determine the specific nutrient and environmental requirements for its successful cell or tissue culturing.

Tissue and cell culture are also being used to help solve other crop production problems, including the elimination of disease from older cultivars for which the entire planting stock has become infected with a damaging, but nonlethal, virus. During periods of rapid plant growth, cells in the apical meristem multiply more rapidly than does the virus. Trial-and-error culturing of individual cells or cell clusters isolated from fast-growing tissue often results in the formation of callus that tests free of virus.

Cell and tissue culture are used extensively in agricultural research. For example, in a promising but still experimental approach to screening for pest and stress resistance, a special type of cell culture exposes gametic or embryonic cells of diverse genetic origin to a pathogenic organism or stress factor. Millions of cells can be tested in a square foot of laboratory test tubes in much less time than it would take to screen a few plants in an acre of an outdoor field. Those cells found to be resistant can then be cultured to produce resistant clones. Cell culture also has the potential for speeding the development of F_1, hybrid cultivars. By culturing $1n$ microsporocytes and doubling the chromosomes of cells of the resulting callus with colchicine, homozygous inbreds can be produced in a few days instead of the traditional ten to fourteen generations needed with traditional plant breeding methods.

Cell culture is also the basis of genetic engineering, by which genes controlling known specific characteristics on small segments of chromosomes can be identified and changed. **Genetic mapping** (locating all the genes on each chromosome that are responsible for various characteristics of the organism) has been completed for several plant species. Currently, science is using genetic engineering to map the twenty-three pairs of human chromosomes. Using genetic engineering, cell cultures have been developed that are capable of producing more insulin at a lower cost than was possible when it had to be extracted from the pancreas of animals. Because most crop cultivars are ideal, except for one or two characteristics, genetic engineering offers the key to rapid crop improvement by providing a method for genetically changing the chromosome segments that contain the genes that control those characteristics. The myriad manipulative procedures that are being employed to develop more useful biological organisms are referred to collectively as **biotechnology**. Biotechnology is today one of the most rapidly growing fields of science, and dozens of commercial "biotech" laboratories have been established to exploit the commercial possibilities of research discoveries in this field.

Selected References

California Polytechnic State University. *Plant Propagation*. vols. I and II. San Luis Obispo: Vocational Education Productions VHS Video, California Polytechnic State University, 1989.

Cook, A. D., ed. *Propagation for the Home Gardener*. Brooklyn, N.Y.: Brooklyn Botanic Garden Handbook 103, 1984 (special printing of *Plants and Gardens*, vol. 40, no. 1).

Garner, R. J. *The Grafter's Handbook*. London: Cassell, 1989.

Hartmann, H. T., T. Hudson, et al. *Plant Propagation: Principles and Practices*, 5th ed. Englewood Cliffs, N.J.: Prentice Hall, 1990.

Seddon, G., and A. Bicknell. *Plants Plus: A Comprehensive Guide to Successful Plant Propagation*. Emmaus, Pa.: Rodale Press, 1987.

Thompson, P. *Creative Propagation: A Grower's Guide*. Beaverton, Oreg.: Timber Press, 1988.

U.S. Department of Agriculture. *Seeds* (*Yearbook of Agriculture, 1961*). Washington, D.C.: U.S. Government Printing Office, 1961.

CHAPTER

5

Soil and Soil Fertility

When natural resources are mentioned, most of us think of coal, petroleum, and mineral deposits. However, by far the most important natural resources are abundant areas of good soil and sufficient sources of fresh water. The United States is fortunate to have a larger area of good, arable soils than any other nation, as well as numerous water sources in its rivers and lakes. Until a few decades ago most citizens felt and acted as though these resources were inexhaustible, but now they have come to realize that both soil and water are limited and must be conserved.

PHYSICAL AND CHEMICAL RELATIONSHIPS OF PLANT-GROWING MEDIA

Soil is not essential for plant survival or growth. Indeed, many kinds of aquatic plants grow without soil, and if they are given some type of support, crop plants grow quite well with their roots bathed by an aerated nutrient solution in a hydroponic system. Nevertheless, most field-grown crops and gardens are produced in soil.

The main functions of soil or other growing media are to support the plant physically and to supply the necessary nutrients and water. More specifically, the medium in which a plant grows should provide the following:

1. An anchor for the roots.
2. Aeration for the roots.
3. A supply of mineral nutrients in a form available for the plant's use during periods between fertilizer applications.
4. A supply of moisture available for the plant's use during periods between irrigation.
5. An ability to maintain an acidity/alkalinity (H to OH ion) ratio in the range suitable for the plant's growth.

Soil Classification

Soil may be classified in various ways, including whether it is mineral or organic, on the basis of particle size and according to parent rock.

Organic Versus Mineral Soils. The solid particles in soil are of two general types derived from two different sources. One comes initially from the weathering of rocks; it is **inorganic** or mineral in composition and highly resistant to change. The other solid component of soils is **organic;** it comes from decaying plant and animal material. Organic matter is relatively unstable and eventually breaks down, mainly into carbon dioxide, which dissipates into the air, and water, which becomes part of the soil moisture supply. Consequently, organic matter must be constantly renewed.

When organic matter (O.M.) accumulates in swampy areas, its breakdown may be extremely slow because water excludes the oxygen necessary for decomposition of O.M. by microorganisms. Drained swamps and bogs are the main sources of **organic soils,** which by definition contain over 20 percent organic matter. These soils are called **muck** if they are well decomposed and **peat** if they are not. Organic soils are excellent for producing vegetables and small fruits, but because they are generally low lying, they tend to be frosty (see Chapter 7) and so are not used extensively to produce tree fruits. Organic soils have good water-holding capacity, aeration, permeability to water, and fertility.

If soils are composed of less than 20 percent organic matter, they are classified as **mineral soils.** The texture and structure of mineral soils determine their suitability for plant growth. Because most gardens are grown in mineral soils, most of the following discussion will pertain to them.

Soil Texture and Structure. The **texture** of a soil is determined by the proportion of each of the different-sized particles it contains. The size range of each kind of particle varies slightly depending on the classification system. The size range of sand, silt, and clay particles in two commonly accepted classification systems is shown in Table

TABLE 5-1 • *Classification of soil particles*

Particle	Diameter (mm)
USDA	
Boulders	>256
Cobbles	256–64
Pebbles	64–4
Gravel	4–2
Fine gravel	2–1
Coarse sand	1–0.5
Medium sand	0.50–0.25
Fine sand	0.25–0.10
Very fine sand	0.10–0.05
Silt	0.05–0.002
Clay	<0.002
International Classification (Atterberg) System (refers only to soil particles under 2 mm)	
Coarse sand	2.0–0.2 mm
Fine sand	0.2–0.02
Silt	0.02–0.002
Clay	<0.002

From USDA, 1957.

5-1. Virtually all soils are composed of a mixture of different-sized particles. Those having a textural mix and physical properties favorable for plant growth are called **loams.** The various textural classes are shown in Figure 5-1.

Soil **structure** refers to the way soil particles group into small clumps or **aggregates** (Figure 5-2). Aggregation in soils is dependent on the cohesive nature of the finer particles (clay and organic) and on the physical forces that organize them into structural units. Structure is important to fine-textured soils, because it affects pore space. Soil with large structural units has large pores that provide it with aeration and permit water infiltration. Soil with small structural units has small pores that give it water-holding capacity.

Soil aggregates can be of several structural forms based largely on their shape, including flat or platy, prismlike, blocklike, and spheroidal.

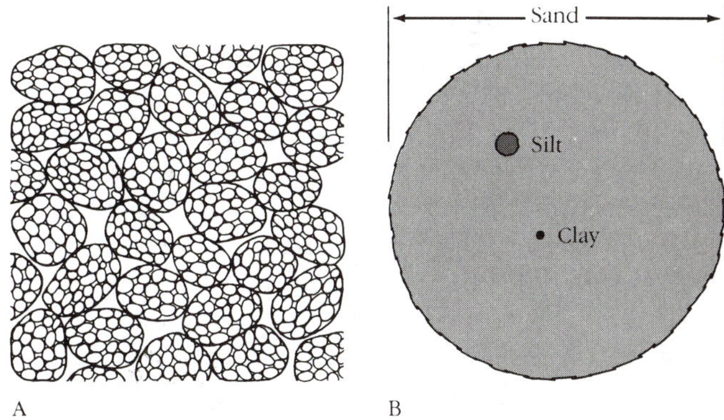

FIGURE 5-2 • Soil structure. (A) A diagrammatic sketch of well-structured soil. The aggregation of soil particles provides the fertility- and moisture-retaining advantages of fine-textured soil and the aeration and workability of coarse-textured soil. (B) Relative sizes of sand, silt, and clay soil particles. (B, courtesy of USDA)

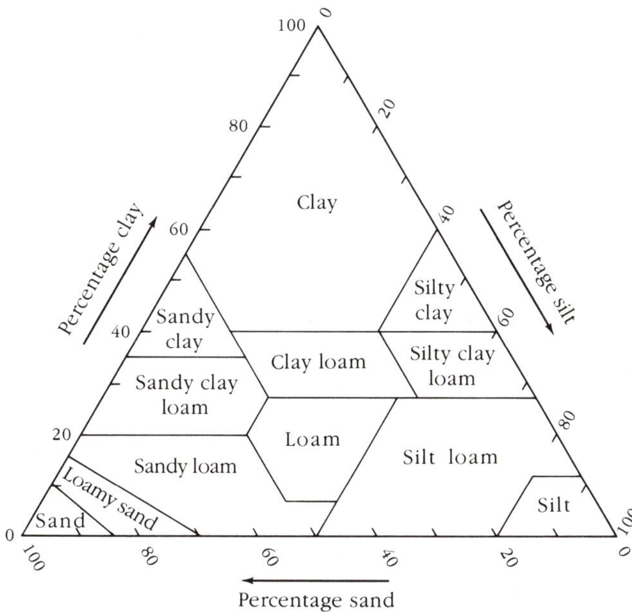

FIGURE 5-1 • Soil texture. The texture triangle shows the relative percentages of sand, silt, and clay in each textural class. In the United States the term loam refers to a soil with more or less equal proportions of sand, silt, and clay. (Courtesy of USDA)

Spheroidal aggregates are the most desirable, because they provide the best combination of pores for aeration, drainage, and water-holding capacity. The small pores in the structural units retain water, and the large pores between them provide aeration and drainage. Spheroidal aggregates are built around a central core and have rounded or irregular surfaces. They are called granules if relatively dense and crumbs if relatively porous.

Among the many physical forces that bring about aggregation are alternate freezing and thawing, alternate wetting and drying, activity of earthworms, and growth of roots. Matted roots of grasses are especially conducive to aggregation. Organic matter is important for good soil structure because it acts as a cementing agent within the structural units and because humic acid from its breakdown tends to coat the structural units and preserve their integrity, which, among other benefits, increases the proportion of spheroidal aggregates. For maximum benefit to soil structure, organic matter must be biologically active; that is, it must be in a state of being renewed by additions of manure or crop residues and of being broken down by microorganisms.

Growers who garden in fine-textured soils must be careful not to disturb them when they are wet. Pressure of any kind (cultivation, heavy rain, vehicular traffic, walking) on water-saturated soil causes the particles within an aggregate to slip past one another, thereby destroying the structure. If the soil has a high proportion of clay particles, the air spaces will be eliminated, and the soil characteristically becomes a sticky, viscous mass. When fine-textured soils that have lost their structure dry, they form large, hard clods that are difficult or impossible to work. Once the structure is destroyed, it is reestablished slowly by the physical forces mentioned earlier.

Coarse-textured soils do not have much structure. Having large pores, they have good aeration and water infiltration; however, lacking small pores, they lack good water-holding capacity.

Soil texture and structure affect many aspects of gardening. Sandy or coarse-textured soils warm rapidly in the early spring and remain friable and amenable to cultivation even when wet. Therefore, they are especially desirable for early vegetables and flowers and for root, bulb, and tuber crops. Water soaks into sandy soils readily, but such soils have low water- and nutrient-retaining capacities and are likely to be droughty and infertile. Clay or fine-textured soils warm and dry slowly and cannot be worked when wet. Although clay soils absorb water slowly, they retain nutrients and moisture well, so crops growing on them do not need irrigation or fertilizer as frequently as do those growing on sandy soils. Clay soils are best suited for main-season and late-maturing crops for which high yields are important.

Soil Profile

A vertical section through the soil, as seen in an excavation, usually shows distinct layers of varying thickness called **horizons.** The series of horizons of a soil is referred to as its **soil profile.** The

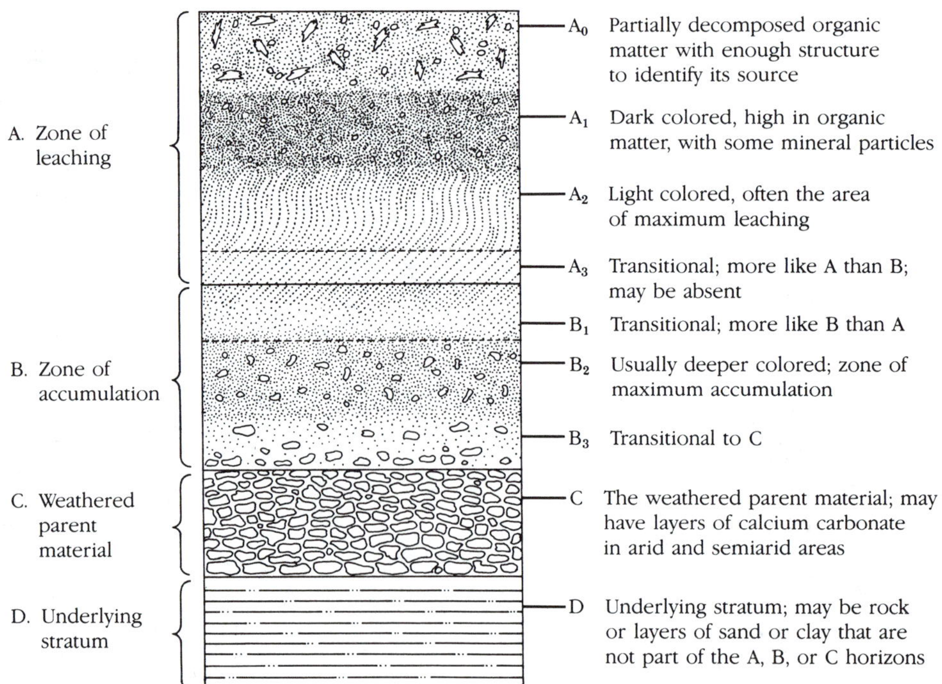
A. Zone of leaching
B. Zone of accumulation
C. Weathered parent material
D. Underlying stratum
A_0 Partially decomposed organic matter with enough structure to identify its source
A_1 Dark colored, high in organic matter, with some mineral particles
A_2 Light colored, often the area of maximum leaching
A_3 Transitional; more like A than B; may be absent
B_1 Transitional; more like B than A
B_2 Usually deeper colored; zone of maximum accumulation
B_3 Transitional to C
C The weathered parent material; may have layers of calcium carbonate in arid and semiarid areas
D Underlying stratum; may be rock or layers of sand or clay that are not part of the A, B, or C horizons

FIGURE 5-3 • A soil profile showing the principal horizons. (Adapted from USDA)

horizons in each soil vary in thickness and composition, but generally if forest or prairie soils have remained undisturbed for a long period, they will have developed three major horizons designated from top to bottom as A, B, and C. The A and B horizons are often subdivided into A_0, A_1, A_2, and A_3 and B_1, B_2, and B_3 horizons (Figure 5-3).

The A horizon is the zone from which soluble substances are dissolved and washed downward (**leached**); the B horizon is the zone in which these substances accumulate; and the C horizon is generally made up of the weathered bedrock from which the soil was formed. The bedrock itself is often referred to as the D horizon.

From the gardener's point of view, the A horizon is the one that supports most of the plant roots and from which plants extract most of their mineral nutrients and water. The B and C horizons have an important effect on water infiltration, drainage, and the growth of trees, shrubs, and other deep-rooted plants. In some soils that have been cultivated for long periods, the A horizon may have been washed away (**eroded**), and so crops are seeded and growing in the B horizon (Figure 5-4). Such soils are almost always less fertile and less easily cultivated than are those with their A horizon intact.

Some garden soils that were formed recently by water deposits or by human activity, such as excavating, filling in, and building a new home, do not have well-developed horizons. This is no great disadvantage, however, if the soil has other good plant-growing characteristics.

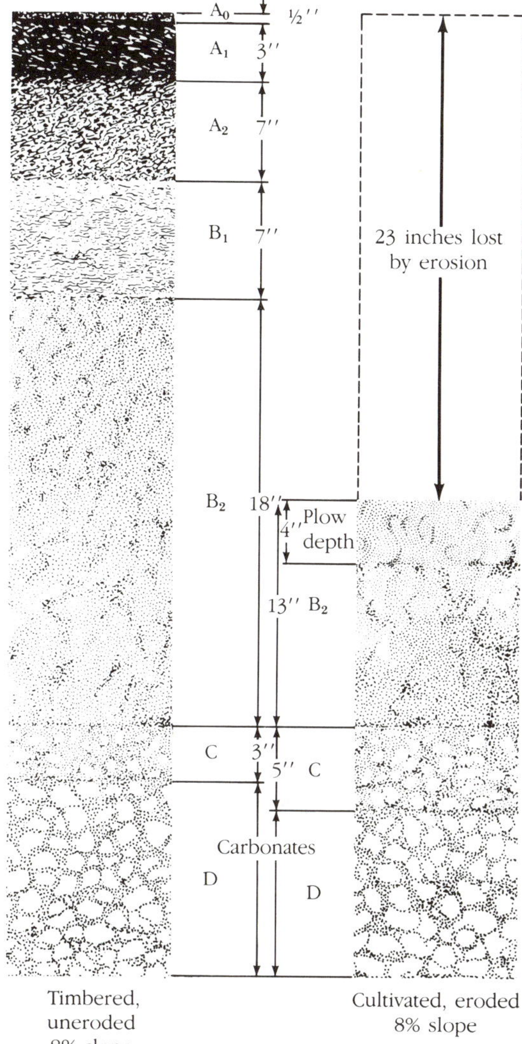

FIGURE 5-4 • Eroded soil. Uncontrolled erosion can result in the loss of productive topsoil, as shown by the profiles taken of Miami silt loam on adjoining fields. The profile on the left was taken of a field that was still covered by virgin timber, and the profile on the right was taken of a field that had been cleared and farmed for 50 to 75 years. (Adapted from USDA)

Organic Matter and Composting

The organic content of soil includes living organisms, waste products excreted by animals, and residues from the decomposition of animal and plant bodies. The extent and importance of living organisms in the soil are sometimes overlooked. An acre-foot (a volume one acre in area and one foot deep; approximately 1,200 cubic meters) of fertile soil contains up to three tons of living organisms, including worms, insects, and microorganisms (Table 5-2). Microorganisms are dependent on organic matter and contribute to the structure, formation, and maintenance of the soil. Earthworms and similar smaller worms also depend on abundant organic matter. The feeding and digestive activities of these soil inhabitants enhance the soil structure, and their downward burrowing, even through clay and hardpan, in response to tempera-

TABLE 5-2 • *Average weight of organisms in the upper foot of soil (in lb/acre) (multiply by 1.12 for kg/hectare)*

Organism	Low	High
Bacteria	500	1,000
Fungi	1,500	2,000
Actinomyces	800	1,500
Protozoa	200	400
Algae	200	300
Nematodes	25	50
Other worms and insects	800	1,000
Total	4,025	6,250

From O. N. Allen, *Experiments in Soil Bacteriology*. Minneapolis: Burgess, 1957.

ture and moisture changes, can over time greatly extend the depth of soil that is capable of sustaining the growing plants' roots (Figure 5-5).

Organic matter is important to soil productivity in many ways. It holds mineral nutrients in forms available to plants and influences soil structure and chemistry. It increases the water-holding capacity and permeability of soils. Finally, organic matter makes soils more amenable to cultivation and less susceptible to erosion.

Sources of Organic Matter. Most mineral soils benefit from added organic matter. In the past, gardeners obtained organic matter primarily from animal manures, as large amounts were readily available from barns, stables, and streets. Diversified farming was the rule then, and market gardeners usually also had a small dairy herd, a few beef animals, or a flock of sheep, as well as some chickens. Today, most manure is produced at large feedlots concentrated in certain parts of the country. Growers living near the feedlots can easily obtain manure for their crops, but for the majority of gardeners the source of manure is too distant to make it economical to spread on their land, so they must rely on other sources of organic matter.

Organic matter for today's garden comes mainly from the plowing under of crop residues and the growing of soil-improving crops, sometimes called green-manure crops. Almost any plant can be used as a soil-improving crop, although two groups are commonly used, the legumes and the grasses, including cereal crops. The legumes, plants belonging to the family Leguminosae (Fabaceae), have an advantage in being able—with the aid of nitrogen-fixing bacteria on their roots (Figure 5-6)—to change elemental nitrogen from the atmosphere into forms that plants can use. With the decay of leguminous plants, or plant parts, this nitrogen becomes available to other plants growing in the soil. Alfalfa, vetch, sweet clover, clovers, winter peas, and southern peas are some of the legumes grown as soil-improving crops. Because it is a deep-rooted perennial, alfalfa has the additional advantage of opening the subsoil to moisture and aeration. As alfalfa roots die, the channels they have formed remain to conduct water into the lower depths of the soil.

Many grasses have heavy matted root systems that provide considerable organic matter when the grass dies or is plowed under. The cereals, especially rye, are frequently used as soil-improving crops. Because these plants are cool-season annuals

FIGURE 5-5 • Through their burrowing activity, earthworms intermix soil layers to a depth of several feet. The channels they create aerate the soil and reduce erosion by allowing water to infiltrate easily. (Courtesy of Runk/Schoenberger from Grant Heilman)

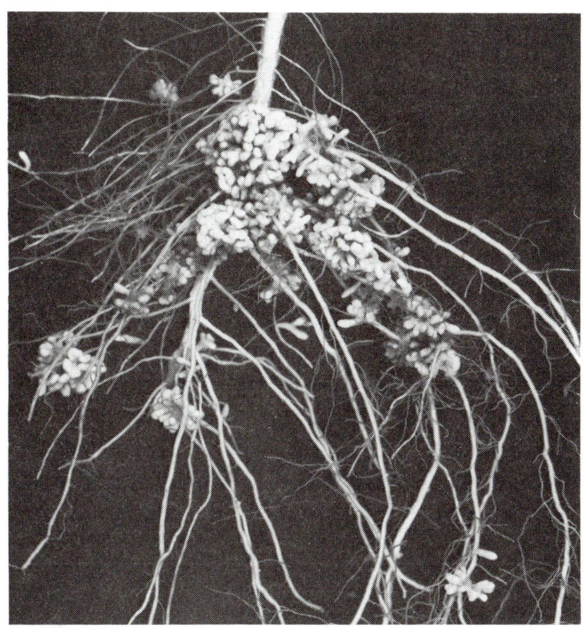

FIGURE 5-6 • Nitrogen-fixing bacteria inhabit the nodules on the root of leguminous plants. Nitrogen from the atmosphere is made available for plant growth in the symbiotic relationship between the bacteria and the higher plant. (Photo by L. J. Klebesadel, courtesy of USDA.)

or biennials, they often can be planted after the garden is harvested. Because they grow during cool weather, they produce considerable organic matter during the season when garden crops cannot be grown. In areas of intense production, organic matter is most frequently added to soil by growing cereal crops during the cooler part of the season.

Sewage sludge, the residue from sewage treatment plants, may be available to home gardeners living near large population centers. Sludge is an excellent source of organic matter and fertilizer. Growers who contemplate its use should make sure, however, that their source of supply is safe, that wastes entering the sewer system have been regulated, and that the sludge has been properly treated so that disease-causing organisms have been eliminated. In some areas, sludge may contain unacceptable quantities of heavy metals that have entered the sewer from metal conduit pipes, industrial wastes, and unused household chemicals dumped down drains. The time is fast approaching when lack of space for discarding waste and the need for organic matter in cultivated soils will mandate that all sewage sludge be used to fertilize gardens and field crops. Fulfilling that mandate, however, will necessitate more careful supervision and inspection of waste disposal facilities than is required in some communities today. For the time being, in those areas where sludge is made available as fertilizer, it can probably be safely used on ornamentals, in orchards, and as an addition to compost, where it is diluted and treated further. Small amounts of pulverized sludge can be raked into the lawn, which should be heavily watered following the application. But sludge should not be used on areas where vegetables are being grown.

Over the course of a year, the average home and yard generate thousands of pounds of waste materials that can enhance the soil's organic matter by being composted. **Composting,** a basic component of organic gardening, is a process that results in the decomposition of organic wastes into humus—a black, grainy material with a pleasant, earthy odor—that can be used for mulching, fertilizing, and soil conditioning. The process of decomposition into humus takes place whenever organic matter is in contact with soil and results from the activity of microorganisms. To decompose organic wastes rapidly, microorganisms require moisture, heat, oxygen, and a balanced supply of mineral nutrients.

Kitchen scraps that usually go into the garbage, leaves, weeds that have not yet formed seed, other garden refuse, and animal manures with litter all can be composted by placing them in a compost heap or digging them into the soil (see "Composting" in Chapter 14). Lawn clippings can be composted or used as a mulch. Early-spring prunings, as well as other organic spring-cleanup debris can be turned into mulch or compost material with a chipper-shredder rented for a few hours. Gardeners who allow these kinds of organic materials from their homes or yards to go to our overfilled municipal garbage heaps are being wasteful as well as environmentally irresponsible.

Peat moss, steer manure, and other organic soil amendments sold by garden supply outlets are also, of course, important sources of soil organic matter for yards and gardens.

Organic Matter and Nitrogen. Extra nitrogen should be added to whatever amount is required by the crop if sawdust, straw, fruit and vegetable wastes from the table, leaves, or other nonnitrogenous, undecomposed organic matter is dug directly into the soil or if soil-improving crops or crop residues are plowed or dug under. The reason is that the addition of organic matter stimulates the reproduction of microorganisms, which can extract nitrogen more easily than can plants. If soil nitrogen is not sufficient to supply both the microorganisms and the plants, it will be used by the microorganisms, leaving an insufficient amount for satisfactory plant growth. Extra nitrogen also is needed if new wooden or fiber flats are used for growing transplants; if flats are lined with newspaper to prevent the loss of soil through the cracks; or if straw, sawdust, or peat moss mulches are worked into the soil (see Table 14-14 and page 433).

Soil Chemistry

Two aspects of soil chemistry, cation exchange and pH, are important to gardeners.

Cation Exchange and Absorption. The weathering of rocks, the breakdown of organic matter, and the addition of fertilizer all add mineral salts to soil. When a salt is dissolved by the soil solution, it dissociates into its ionic form (**ions** are negatively or positively charged atoms). For example, calcium chloride, $CaCl_2$, dissociates into Ca^{2+} and two Cl^- ions. Positively charged ions (Ca^{2+}, Mg^{2+}, NH_4^+, K^+, etc.) are called **cations,** and negatively charged ions (OH^-, Cl^-, CO_3^{2-}, SO_4^{2-}) are called **anions.** It is the ions, not the salts, that the plant absorbs and that are the minerals essential for plant growth. Clay and organic matter particles, which are sometimes referred to as soil **colloids** because they are small enough to remain suspended in a solution, can attract and exchange cations, and the number of these particles present determines the soil's **cation-exchange** capacity. Organic matter particles hold one and a half to thirty times as many ions as do clay particles, another reason for the importance of organic matter in the soil.

Water molecules and acids dissociate to form H^+ ions, and an equilibrium of H^+ and other cations is maintained in the soil solution. As various cations are absorbed into the plant, their concentration in the soil solution is restored by ions displaced from organic matter and clay particles. The niches on the colloids vacated when the mineral cations move into the soil solution are in turn filled by H^+ ions. Finally, when the concentration of cations is again increased in the soil solution by the decomposition of plant residues or the addition of fertilizer, the excess of these ions displaces the H^+ ions from the colloids, thus completing the cycle. It should be emphasized that plants absorb nutrients from soil mainly in the form of ions, a point of importance in deciding the best source of fertilizer for the garden.

A soil's potential fertility depends on its cation-exchange capacity, which in turn is determined by its content of clay and organic matter particles. Soils with a low cation-exchange capacity tend to be low in fertility because cations added to such soil can easily be washed from it by excess water. Growing healthy crops on low cation-exchange soils requires light, frequent fertilization. In contrast, soils with a high cation-exchange capacity tend to retain cations in a form available for plant growth and so require less frequent application. This explains the differences in the amount and frequency of fertilizer application recommended in the two parts of Tables 14-16 and 14-17. The retention of anions like NO_3^- and SO_4^{2-} is not necessarily related to cation-exchange capacity.

Soil pH. The second aspect of soil chemistry that is important to gardeners is soil **pH,** which is the relationship of the hydrogen ions (H^+) to the

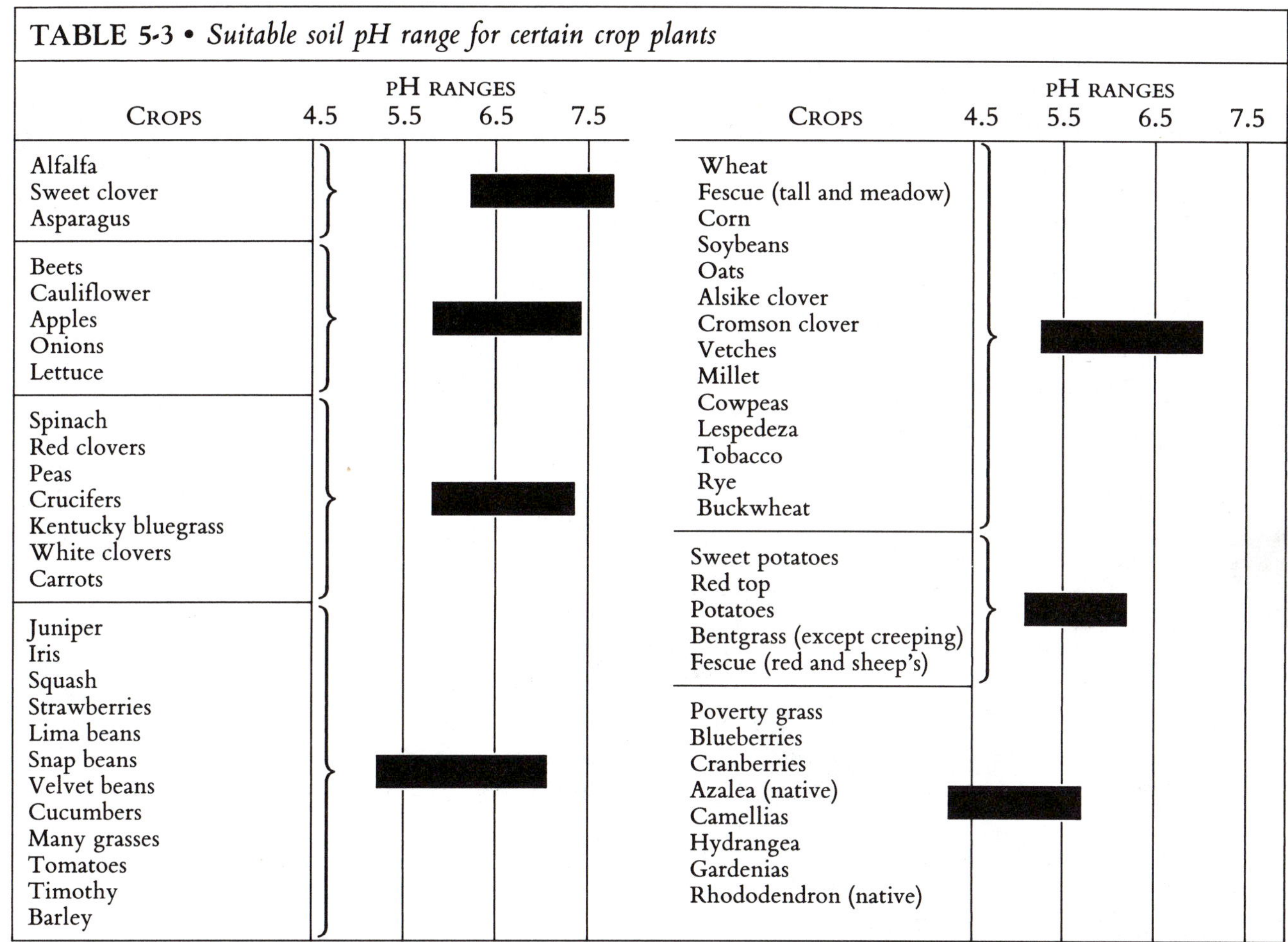

TABLE 5-3 • *Suitable soil pH range for certain crop plants*
CROPS
pH RANGES
4.5 5.5 6.5 7.5
Alfalfa
Sweet clover
Asparagus
Beets
Cauliflower
Apples
Onions
Lettuce
Spinach
Red clovers
Peas
Crucifers
Kentucky bluegrass
White clovers
Carrots
Juniper
Iris
Squash
Strawberries
Lima beans
Snap beans
Velvet beans
Cucumbers
Many grasses
Tomatoes
Timothy
Barley
CROPS
pH RANGES
4.5 5.5 6.5 7.5
Wheat
Fescue (tall and meadow)
Corn
Soybeans
Oats
Alsike clover
Cromson clover
Vetches
Millet
Cowpeas
Lespedeza
Tobacco
Rye
Buckwheat
Sweet potatoes
Red top
Potatoes
Bentgrass (except creeping)
Fescue (red and sheep's)
Poverty grass
Blueberries
Cranberries
Azalea (native)
Camellias
Hydrangea
Gardenias
Rhododendron (native)

Adapted with permission of the publisher from N. C. Brady, *The Nature and Properties of Soils,* 10th ed., copyright 1990 by the Macmillan Company.

hydroxyl ions (OH^-). These two ions determine whether a soil is acid or alkaline. When there are the same number of H^+ as OH^- ions in the soil solution, the soil is neutral and has a pH of 7; when H^+ is higher than OH^-, the pH is lower and the soil becomes acid; and when H^+ is lower than OH^-, the pH is high and the soil is alkaline.

Most exchangeable soil ions affect pH somewhat, but in most soils pH is largely determined by four cations. Two base-forming cations, calcium (Ca^{2+}) and magnesium (Mg^{2+}), are the primary contributors to alkalinity; and two acid-forming ions, hydrogen (H^+) and aluminum (Al^{3+}), largely determine acidity. Three other base-forming ions—potassium (K^+), sodium (Na^+), and ammonium (NH_4^+)—usually are not present in amounts that materially affect pH.

Because of the tendency for base-forming cations to leach away and be replaced by H^+ and Al^{3+}, soils formed in areas of high rainfall tend to become acid. Desert soils or soils formed in areas of low rainfall are likely to be neutral to alkaline, because of the accumulation of salts that release cations. Alkaline soils and the water that drains them usually have a high salt content (see "Crop Damage from Dissolved Chemicals" in Chapter 6). In North America the Great Plains, the Southwest, the high western plateaus, and many of the Rocky Mountain valleys have neutral or alkaline soils. These all are areas of low rainfall. All areas east of the Great Plains; the coastal valleys of northern California, Oregon, Washington, British Columbia, and Alaska; and a few high-altitude, high-precipitation valleys of the northern Rockies have acid soils.

Most crop plants do best in soils that are neutral or slightly acid. However, a few ornamentals, including rhododendrons, azaleas, and heathers, as well as cranberries and blueberries, all of which originated in areas of high rainfall, grow best in highly acid soils (Table 5-3). Near their southern limit of adaptability in eastern Idaho and western Wyoming, mountain blueberries grow mainly on the north slopes of high-altitude areas, most likely because of the higher soil acidity at these sites.

The pH relates to many aspects of soil important to plant growth. The physical condition of soil may be altered by changes in pH, and soil can lose structure if it becomes strongly acid or alkaline. Soil mineral nutrients are often not available to plants when the soil is strongly acid or alkaline: Iron, manganese, copper, zinc, and boron are likely to be unavailable to plants in highly alkaline soils; calcium and molybdenum may be unavailable in highly acid soils; and phosphorus may be unavailable in either highly acid or highly alkaline soils. Soil pH can also affect certain plant diseases. For example, potato scab will be less severe if the crop is grown in acid soil, and club root of crucifers can be controlled by applying lime to make the soil alkaline.

Lime, the alkaline salt of calcium, can be used quite successfully to raise the pH of soil, and so most cultivated soils in high rainfall areas are limed in order to improve crop production (Figure 5-7). Sulfur can be used to lower the pH and make the soil more acid, although the effect of sulfur is not as predictable, nor is its use as widespread as is the use of lime.

Artificial Growing Media

It is possible to grow plants in many other solid growing media besides soil. In areas of the Middle East where millennia of erosion have removed the soil, crops are occasionally produced on heavily fertilized and irrigated bales of straw arranged in

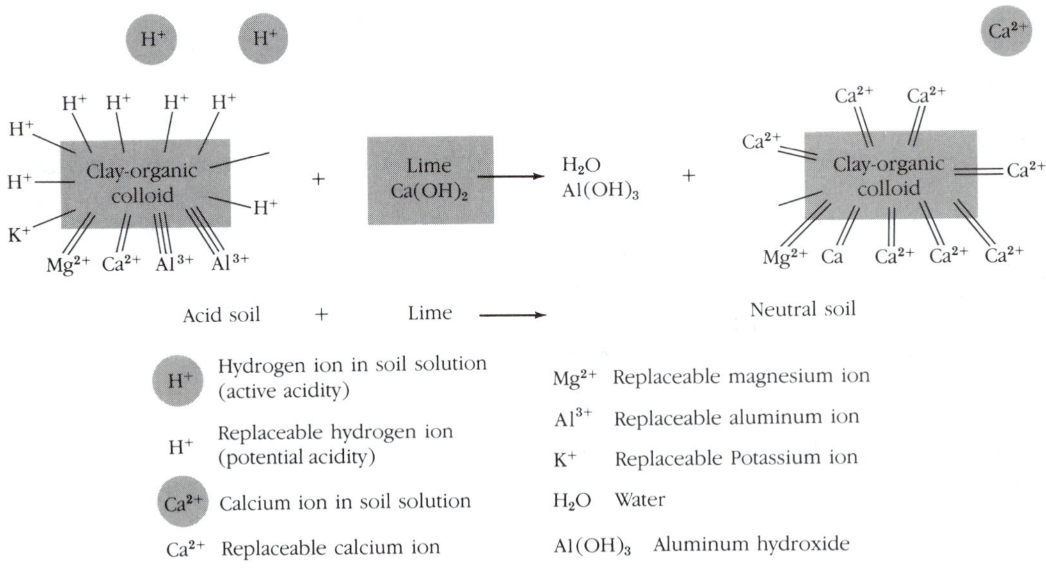

FIGURE 5-7 • Cation-exchange reactions when an acid soil is limed. (Courtesy of USDA)

rows or tightly massed on the exposed bedrock. In south Florida and on some Pacific islands, surface coral rock has been pulverized to provide a growing medium for high-value flower and vegetable crops.

Artificial growing media have replaced soil for almost all commercial potted nursery crops grown in greenhouses and outdoors, as well as for plants grown in the home. Formulating and transporting these media for commercial greenhouse, nursery, and plant-growing businesses is a multimillion-dollar industry. Supplying artificial media in small packages to retail nurseries, department stores, supermarkets, and other establishments for resale to gardeners and homeowners is also a big business. Mixes are formulated at a site near the source of one of the main ingredients, usually the inorganic base material. From that site, the growing mix is trucked to commercial growers located within a radius of several hundred miles.

Artificial plant-growing media are usually composed of a mixture of organic and inorganic components. The principal organic ingredient of mixes formulated for large commercial establishments is most often peat, and the principal inorganic ingredient is often a pulverized, usually local, lightweight rock such as perlite or volcanic pumice. Vermiculite (expanded mica) is also a common ingredient. Spaghnum moss is used in mixes in which acid-loving crops like African violets and rhododendrons are to be grown. A small amount of charcoal, which buffers the pH and absorbs toxic fumes, is another frequent addition. Other organic ingredients sometimes used, especially in mixes formulated for homeowners, include wood chips, manure, compost, forest duff, sawdust, and straw. Mica is another relatively lightweight inorganic component of some mixes. Fine gravel, crushed rock, and sand are often used in mixes that do not have to be transported far.

A major advantage of these materials, as compared with ordinary soil, is their lighter weight, a characteristic that can save thousands of dollars in transportation costs, both before and after the plants are grown. A second major reason for using artificial media is that their quality is relatively uniform, regardless of where they are formulated. This makes it possible to standardize fertilizer, irrigation, and other cultural practices, resulting in a predictable time of maturity and crop quality.

The fertilizer needed during the first few weeks of plant growth usually has been added to artificial soil mixes packaged for gardeners. Garden mixes also are usually pasteurized, which eliminates problems with disease, insects, and weeds.

SOIL FERTILITY

◆ ◆ ◆

Plants obtain the nutrients essential for their growth from the soil, but not all the nutrients in the soil are used in plant growth. Some are not required by plants, and some of those required are combined in chemical forms that plants cannot utilize. Soil fertility is usually judged by the level of available nutrients in the soil and is dependent on many complex physical and chemical interrelationships, some of which have already been discussed.

Elements Essential to Plants

Sixteen elements are known to be required by plants for proper growth. I have found that the easiest way to remember the chemical symbols for these is by means of the mnemonic device "C Hopkins Cafe managed by mine cousins Mo and Cleo." This stands for C HOPKNS CaFe Mg B Mn CuZn Mo and Cl. The first three elements, carbon (C), hydrogen (H), and oxygen (O), come from the atmosphere; the rest are obtained from the soil, absorbed into the roots as ions, and transported through the xylem to various parts of the plant. The next three elements, phosphorus (P), potassium (K), and nitrogen (N), are those most likely to be deficient and most often added to soils. These three, along with sulfur (S), calcium (Ca), and magnesium (Mg), are needed in relatively large quantities to sustain plant growth and are classified as **macronutrients.** The remaining elements, iron (Fe), boron (B), manganese (Mn), copper (Cu), zinc (Zn), molybdenum (Mo), and chlorine (Cl), although essential for the growth of plants, are used in minute quantities and are referred to as **micronutrients** (see Table 5-4).

Soil Fertilization

In nature, the abundance and growth of individual plant species and other organisms feeding from the soil tend to equilibrate relative to the soil nutrients available. If the requirements for a species are not adequate, that species will either grow at a slower rate commensurate with the food available or will be eliminated from the ecosystem. The slow growth that would result from letting nature "take its course" is usually not feasible in a garden, and so fertilizer must be applied to allow maximum growth of the desired crop (see "Fertilizing Garden Crops" in Chapter 14).

Two general types of fertilizers are available: the so-called natural or organic fertilizers and the inorganic or chemical fertilizers. The organic fertilizers are materials derived from living organisms and include manure, fishmeal, cottonseed meal, bonemeal, and sewage sludge. The chemical fertilizers are commercially prepared from inorganic minerals and include ammonium nitrate, superphosphate, and muriate of potash. Because chemical fertilizers are, on the whole, less expensive to purchase, transport, and apply, most of the fertilizers used today are chemical rather than organic.

Growers are using more commercial fertilizer today than ever before, partly because manure is scarce but primarily because they have found that adding fertilizer is the most economical way to increase the yields of most crops. Too much fertilizer, however, can be detrimental. Low color in apples, splitting of carrots, heavy vine growth and delayed ripening of tomatoes, and reduction in the flowering and fruiting of ornamentals and fruits all can be the result of heavy nitrogen application or an imbalance between nitrogen and the other elements available to the plant.

TABLE 5-4 • *The principal ionic forms of nutrients utilized by plants*

Element	Cations	Anions
	Macronutrients	
Nitrogen	NH_4^+	NO_3^-
Calcium	Ca^{2+}	
Magnesium	Mg^{2+}	
Potassium	K^+	
Phosphorus		HPO_4^{2-}, $H_2PO_4^-$
Sulfur		SO_4^{2-}
	Micronutrients	
Copper	Cu^{2+}	
Iron	Fe^{3+}	
Manganese	Mn^{2+}, Mn^{4+}	
Zinc	Zn^{2+}	
Boron		BO_3^{3-}
Molybdenum		Mo_4^{2-}
Chlorine		Cl^-

From R. L. Hausenbuiller, *Soil Science: Principles and Practices*, 3d ed. Dubuque, Iowa: Brown, 1985.

Fertilizer Analysis, Ratio, and Formula. Gardeners must understand fertilizer analysis if they are to apply fertilizer to crops in the correct amounts. Fertilizer **analysis** is the percentage by weight of the available nitrogen (as elemental nitrogen), phosphorus (as P_2O_5), and potassium (as K_2O). By law, these percentages must be listed on every bag of commercial fertilizer sold. (Soil scientists are attempting to standardize the desirable practice of using elemental phosphorus and potassium as they now use elemental nitrogen as the bases for fertilizer analyses, but most commercial companies continue to base their printed analyses on the oxide forms, as is done in this book.) The percentage of nitrogen (N) is always listed first, phosphorus (P) second, and potassium (K) third. Thus a bag of fertilizer with an analysis of 16:20:0 contains 16 percent N, 20 percent P, and no K.

Fertilizer **ratio** is the proportion of the three major elements found in the fertilizer. For example, fertilizer with an analysis of 5:10:5 has a ratio of 1:2:1, and a 16:20:0 fertilizer has a ratio of 4:5:0. A statement of fertilizer ratio is recogni-

TABLE 5-5 • *Comparison of formula, analysis, and ratio of several fertilizers*

Formula	Analysis	Ratio
Ammonium nitrate	33:0:0	1:0:0
Ammonium phosphate sulfate	16:20:0	4:5:0
Sheep manure	2:1:2	2:1:2
Fertilizers synthesized from several formulas	5:10:5	1:2:1
	16:16:16	1:1:1

tion that the balance of the various nutrient elements in the soil is as important as is the total amount of each element. Fertilizer **formula** is a statement of the materials and the amounts of each chemical that make up the fertilizer—ammonium nitrate, ammonium sulfate, superphosphate, and so on. Commercial fertilizers are formulated to fulfill varying needs and often are a mixture of fertilizers of several formulas that may or may not be listed on the bag of fertilizer (Table 5-5).

The analysis of different fertilizers varies over a wide range, from less than 1 percent available N, P, and K to more than 80 percent. Those with more than 30 lb (14 kg) total N, P, K per 100 lb (45 kg) bag are called **high analysis,** and those with less than 30 lb are **low analysis.** Because of the extra weight and consequent cost of handling, low-analysis fertilizers tend to be more expensive per unit of available nutrient. High-analysis fertilizers require more accuracy in application.

Because analyses vary so much, fertilizer recommendations are usually stated as pounds of N, P, or K, and growers must calculate the amount of fertilizers needed to supply the crop. For example, if 100 lb per acre nitrogen are required, the grower will need to apply 300 lb (140 kg) of fertilizer of an analysis of 33:0:0 or 625 lb (283 kg) of one of 16:20:0 (see "Fertilizing Garden Crops" in Chapter 14).

Determining Fertilizer Requirements. Determining which fertilizer elements are needed is frequently a dilemma for home gardeners. A deficiency of a particular element produces distinct symptoms in plants, and growers can often decide

FIGURE 5-8 • Symptoms of nitrogen deficiency. The small tomato, marigold, and cabbage seedlings on the right show the typical light color and stunted woody-growth symptoms of acute nitrogen deficiency when compared with more adequately fertilized seedlings of the same age on the left. Seedlings as badly stunted as those on the right will never produce the quality or abundance of plants that have not suffered this kind of stress.

which elements are lacking by comparing plant symptoms with pictures of nutrient deficiencies in one of the many publications printed on this subject (see Figure 5-8). However, by the time deficiency symptoms appear, it is usually too late to correct them that season, and yield and quality will have already deteriorated irreparably.

There are several ways of determining nutrient deficiencies more satisfactorily than by observing symptoms. Past experience with one's own and neighbors' successes and failures often can be helpful. Most state experiment stations and Canadian Department of Agriculture research stations publish general fertilizer recommendations for most crops in each major area of the states and provinces. In recent years gardeners have come to rely more heavily on soil testing. A number of do-it-yourself soil-testing kits are available, which generally give a rough (often extremely rough) guide to fertilizer needs. A more accurate recommendation can be obtained by sending samples of the soil to a state or reliable local commercial soil-testing laboratory (Figure 5-9). County agents have information on soil-testing services. Soil-testing laboratories analyze for available nutrients and pH and recommend fertilizer requirements for both major and minor elements.

A new commercial grower service not yet widely available for home gardeners is **foliar analysis,** in which laboratories periodically through the season monitor the nutrient content of plant leaves. A slight drop in the foliar level of a nutrient indicates a pending shortage that can be corrected by applying fertilizer to the soil or foliage.

Sources of Fertilizer. Home gardeners are often enticed into buying expensive formulations of fertilizers because they are made to believe that the brand contains something that a competitive cheaper brand does not. In general, the fertilizer that supplies the greatest amount of the element needed per unit of cost is the best buy, though there are a few exceptions. One of these is a formulation in which ammonia supplied as a gas

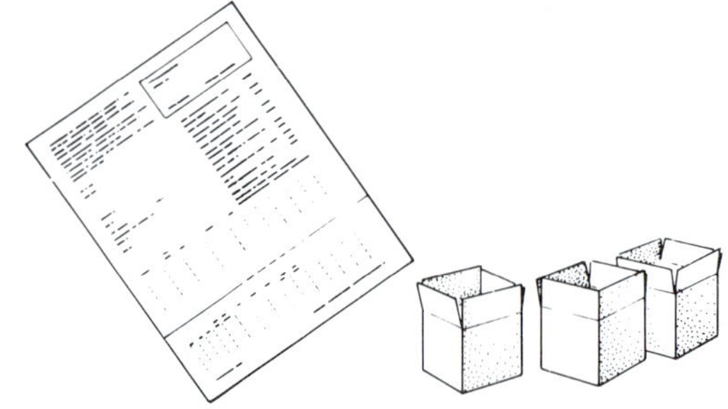

1. Obtain cartons and information sheets from your county agent, the state soil testing laboratory, or other sources.

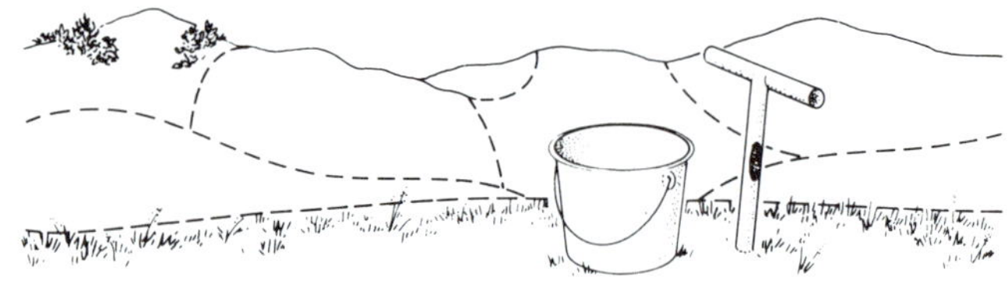

2. Map the different areas within a field—such as hilltops, mid-slopes, bottomlands, or known areas of different productivity. With a sampling tube take 10 to 15 cores, spaced an equal distance apart. Sample to tillage depth. Place cores from each sampling area in a clean bucket. Mix this composite sample well and fill the soil sample carton (about 1 pint). Repeat this process for each area in the field.

3. A field that is extremely variable, or one where little is known about the variability, requires many samples. Once a field has been intensively sampled and a soil fertility map made, select sites in representative low-, medium-, and high-fertility areas of the field that can be resampled every two to three years. Periodic resampling will show if the general soil fertility level in each area is improving or getting worse.

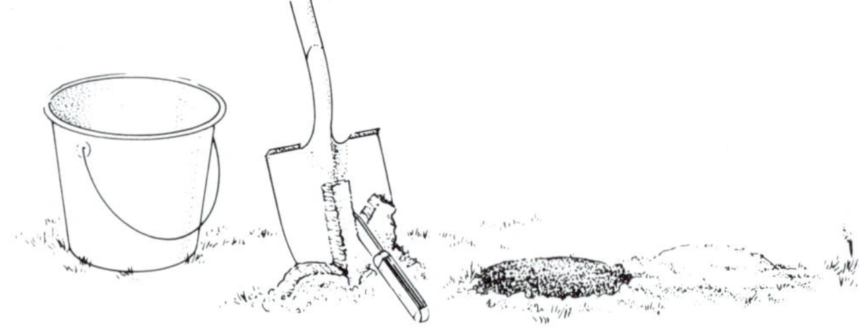

4. It is best to use a sampling tube if that is possible. If you use a spade or shovel, throw away the first shovelful. Then take a 1-inch slice from the back side of the hole (to proper sampling depth) and trim away sides of slice, leaving a 1-inch center core. Place core in a clean bucket, following procedure given in item 2. A garden trowel can be used in place of a spade or shovel.

FIGURE 5-9 • Taking routine soil samples for cultivated crops. (Adapted from A. R. Halvorsen, Washington State University Extension Circular 387) would be difficult for homeowners to apply. Another involves the use of special application equipment, for which the size or shape of the fertilizer particles makes a difference in the ease and uniformity of application. Commercial fertilizers containing N, P, and K can be bought in all areas of the United States and Canada. Other mineral elements are available for purchase at locations where soils require them.

Occasionally the effectiveness of a fertilizer compound depends on soil conditions. For example, the application of rock phosphate is recommended in some organic-gardening texts. The phosphorus in rock phosphate is soluble in acid but not in neutral-to-alkaline soils. In acid soils, rock phosphate decomposes gradually into forms that plants can use and provides some fertilizing benefit. In soils of pH 6.5 or higher, however, it never decomposes, and so its application is a waste of money and time.

Sometimes one salt of a major element produces better results than another. Lawns in some areas benefit more from nitrogen fertilization with ammonium sulfate than with ammonium nitrate. In this and other examples of differential response, the more beneficial procedure may be providing a needed element (sulfur, in the lawn example) or perhaps a change in the pH.

Correcting Minor Element Deficiencies. All of the mineral elements that plants obtain from the soil, except nitrogen, phosphorus, and potassium —that is, the micronutrients plus sulfur, calcium, and magnesium — are often referred to as minor or trace elements or nutrients. A deficiency of minor elements in plants can result either from a low concentration of the element in the soil or because the element is present in a chemical form that plants cannot utilize. Because manure and sewage sludge contain small amounts of most trace elements, gardens fertilized with these materials are seldom deficient. Rather, minor elements are deficient mainly on land where cultivation practices rely solely on chemical fertilizers and green-manure crops for mineral nutrients and organic matter. On land farmed in this way the minute amounts of trace nutrients that are removed in plant material each year are not replaced and so over many years of cropping, those nutrients are gradually depleted from the soil.

Deficiencies due to the lack of an element in the soil can usually be corrected by applying a fertilizer containing this element. For those people with small gardens it may be worth the effort or money occasionally to apply a load of fresh manure or sludge (if available in the area) or commercially bagged manure to reduce the chance of minor element deficiency. Fertilizers containing a single trace element are available; however, because it is so difficult to distinguish the symptoms of a deficiency of one minor element from those of another, garden stores usually stock fertilizers containing a mixture of all minor elements likely to be at low levels in soils of the local region.

Fertilizer elements are most likely to be "tied up" in chemical combinations unavailable to plants in soils where the pH is either excessively high (i.e., alkaline) or excessively low (i.e., acidic). When a plant deficiency is due to soil acidity, raising the pH by adding lime usually solves the problem. A nutrient tie-up in soils that are highly alkaline is not so easily corrected. Although symptoms of zinc, manganese, and boron deficiency are prevalent in some arid areas with alkaline soils, iron — which tends to bind chemically with calcium into compounds that prevent its utilization by plants — is the mineral nutrient most likely to be unavailable on soils with a high pH. Roses, fruit trees, and acid-loving shrubs like azaleas and rhododendrons are plants that on alkaline soils often develop yellow leaves with bright green veins, the typical calcium-induced iron chlorosis symptom of iron deficiency. Iron compounds — the application of which would correct deficiency symptoms in plants growing on soils of lower pH — quickly become unavailable and do not have much effect when applied to highly alkaline soils or even to the foliage of plants growing on those soils. Special organic formulations of iron that do not bind to calcium but are available for utilization by plants have been developed. These are called chelates. Zinc, manganese, and other minor elements not likely to be available in alkaline soils can also be formulated as chelates. As is true with most fertilizers, chelates are usually applied to the soil; however, when a rapid response is required, they are sometimes applied as foliar sprays, even though only a very small percentage of the material applied is absorbed through the foliage.

It is difficult to determine from symptoms whether or not a plant is deficient in a mineral element, and as mentioned, it is even more difficult to discover which element is deficient. Soil tests that reliably measure the availability of most minor elements have been devised, however, and can be very useful when a deficiency is suspected. Such tests are expensive, and so if many elements are implicated, they may not be economically feasible for a small garden. Extension personnel and agricultural consultants are usually familiar with the deficiencies common in their local area and can be helpful in diagnosing a possible nutritional problem.

Gardening Without Chemical Fertilizers. As pointed out earlier, before the advent of chemical fertilizers in the 1940s, all gardens were grown without modern fertilizers, although at that time most gardens were close to a plentiful supply of animal manure and the people then were accustomed to the odor of manure. During those earlier times, ambitious gardeners spread manure over their whole yard late in the fall and allowed the nutrients from it to leach into the soil during the winter. In the spring the residue was raked from the lawn, added to the manure already on the vegetable garden or annual flower beds, and cultivated into the soil of those areas. Manure in the orchard and on the perennial flower beds was gradually worked into the soil during the spring and early summer. Where manure is available, this is still an effective way to fertilize, provided that the family and neighbors do not object to looking at and smelling a manure-covered yard all winter. On all areas, except lawns, manure or sludge can be spread onto, and quickly cultivated into, the soil in the spring, so as to lessen its undesirable impact.

In areas where manure is not available, especially where nitrogen is the main fertilizer element needed, leguminous soil-improving crops can be used to fertilize lawns, orchards, and vegetable and cut-flower gardens (see "Growing Lawns Without Commercial Fertilizer or Pesticide" in Chapter 11, and Figure 12-2). When elements other than nitrogen are required, the compost pile or purchased forms of organic fertilizer can be used to supply them. The popularity of organic gardening has prompted garden-supply merchants to stock a number of organic fertilizers.

Growing a well-fertilized garden without chemical fertilizers is quite possible even if manure is not available. Busy gardeners, however, will find it much easier to use organic wastes and soil-improving crops if they can supplement them with high-analysis commercial fertilizers. Such supplementation may be the more environmentally responsible action because it encourages the wider utilization of organic wastes for composting and of green-manure crops for soil improvement, especially when a nonlegume is the only feasible soil-building choice.

MANAGING SOIL AND FERTILIZER FOR THE GARDEN

◆ ◆ ◆

Soil for the New Home

The easiest way for a homeowner to be certain of having usable soil is to supervise carefully the excavation and leveling at the time the house is being built. In most regions, the top 12 inches (30 cm) of soil has a relatively good structure and contains the most organic matter. The owner should make certain that this soil is scraped to one side of the lot before any excavating is begun so that it can be spread uniformly over the lot after the building is completed. This kind of careful supervision may be impossible at an already-built tract or subdivision home, where all too frequently sticky or rock-hard clay subsoil is left on the surface of the yard. From 6 to 10 inches (15 to 25 cm) of good topsoil spread over such a yard would, of course, be ideal, but topsoil is expensive, and a good lawn can be grown in subsoil improved with generous additions of organic matter. If purchased topsoil is limited, it should be reserved for flower beds and other specialized growing areas. Boards, sticks, stones, rubble, plasterboard, and other debris should, of course, be cleaned from the top 12 inches (30 cm) of soil before the area is planted to ensure successful root penetration and moisture availability. The frequent complaint of geometric dead or dying patches in a newly planted lawn can almost invariably be traced to pieces of concrete, board, or plasterboard that were buried shallowly when the yard was leveled.

FIGURE 5-10 • Managing soil on sloping sites. A ground cover like this periwinkle in front of a Michigan residence may be the most suitable management practice for a sloping site. (Courtesy of Walter Chandoha)

Managing Soil on Sloping Sites

Sloping sites offer an opportunity for interesting garden effects, but they also present a challenge in erosion prevention. Perhaps the simplest way to manage a sloping site is to plant a permanent low-growing cover crop like that shown in Figure 5-10. If the topography is not too steep and sufficient moisture is available, grass sod that can be kept mowed may be the simplest, though the least creative, solution. If the site is too steep to mow or if grass is not the preferred cover, low-growing ornamental or small fruit shrubs can be used. Trees, including fruit trees, can be planted with the grass or shrubs if these cover crops can tolerate shade and the soil is deep enough. A rock garden is another attractive way of managing a slope, although it requires a good deal of labor.

It is possible to use a sloping site for a vegetable or annual flower garden. If the slope is not too steep, erosion can be minimized by cultivating and orienting rows to the contour of the slope. In the early fall, seed of rye, Austrian winter peas, or other rapidly growing cold-tolerant crops should be scattered among the remaining garden plants and residues to protect the slope from eroding during the winter.

If the slope is too steep for ordinary cultivation, terracing may enable crops to grow on it (see Figure 5-11). Terraces can be made with soil banks kept in place by shrubs or grasses (or weeds), but upkeep of this kind of terracing is difficult, because soil banks can erode and the cover plantings must be controlled. More permanent terracing can be established with retaining walls built to create a level area, or even several levels when a moderate amount of terracing is required (see "Construction of Walks, Drives, Patios" in Chapter 14).

FIGURE 5-11 • Terracing is an art that has been practiced for thousands of years in Asia. These rice fields have been carved from steep slopes near Landruk, Nepal. (Courtesy of Bob Daemmrich with Image Works)

Cultivation

As the term is used in this text, **cultivation** includes the initial breaking up of the soil in the fall or spring with a moleboard plow, disc, rototiller, digging fork, or other machine or tool, as well as the stirring of the soil between crop plants with a disc, spike or springtooth harrow, rodweeder, rototiller, hoe, rake, or other device.

For the initial breaking up of the soil in spring or fall, a moleboard plow has the advantages of being able to reach a somewhat lower depth and of completely covering crop remains, manures, or other residues on top of the soil. Plowing, especially on the contour, produces ridges and an open soil surface, which lessens the likelihood of serious erosion. Discing tends to leave a trashy crop residue on the surface, which reduces erosion but can cause difficulty in seedbed preparation and planting. Rototillers break and mix the topsoil layer better than do the other machines, and both plows and rototillers clear the field so that an even seedbed can be prepared and later cultivations can be easily accomplished. Rototilling partially destroys the structures of certain clay soils and leaves fields more subject to erosion than does discing or plowing on the contour.

Cultivation Systems and Soil Erosion. In most of North America, cultivation has usually meant clearing away all existing plants before the crop is planted (**clean cultivation**), but complete clearing is not always necessary. In Guatemala and Mexico before Columbus arrived, numerous crops were planted together, with only enough clearing for seeds to germinate, and the garden grew as a year-round mixture of several kinds of food and fiber plants. When a plant began to age and no longer produced a useful product, it was removed, and another was planted in the spot it had occupied. Similar farming systems still exist and are being investigated as alternatives preferable to the slash-and-burn agriculture prevalent in some tropical areas. A similar system called multiple cropping, used with some success by gardeners in the United States and Canada, is discussed later in this chapter.

Clean cultivation, especially on sloping sites, often results in severe erosion. The disastrous consequences of soil erosion for the future of humanity cannot be overemphasized: The loss of an average of 1/32 inch (.8 mm) of soil each season, considered a nominal amount, will result in the loss of 30 inches (75 cm) of topsoil in a thousand years. Areas of the Middle East, North Africa, and the Indian subcontinent that once supported thriving civilizations are now rocky wastes because all the soil has washed or blown away. Abandoned farm sites in New England, the foothills of Appalachia, and the Maritime Provinces of Canada document the ravages of erosion during the short time that this kind of cultivation has been practiced in North America (Figure 5-12).

To reduce erosion, permanent cover crops of alfalfa and grass are often the best solution to soil management in commercial orchards and vineyards as well as in orchards planted primarily for home consumption. This is especially true where trees and vines are planted on hillsides. The cover crop is mowed occasionally to permit easier access through the orchard with spray and harvest equipment.

By using herbicides to control weeds, some growers produce field crops without **tillage.** In areas subject to wind and water erosion, small grains are being grown in what is known as trashy fallow. With **trashy fallow** the soil is stirred, but dried weeds, stubble, and other debris are left as a

A

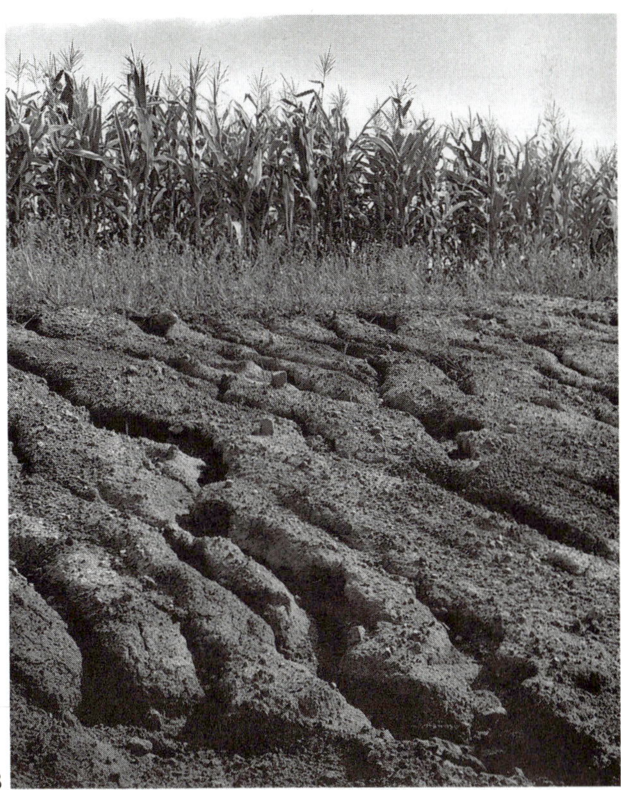

B

FIGURE 5-12 • The problem of erosion. (A) Fifteen hundred years ago, ships docked along Harbor Street in Ephesus, Asia Minor. Eventually, soil washed down from the hillsides above filled in the harbor. Mosquitoes breeding in the resulting swamps spread disease, which resulted in the abandonment of the city. Harbor Street is now almost 10 miles (19 km) from the ocean, and slopes in the mountains above Ephesus that once were cultivated now have no soil whatsoever. (B) Erosion in North America can be just as devastating and can plague homeowners as well as farmers. (B, Courtesy of Grant Heilman) mulch to protect fine soil particles from erosion. A farming system called **minitil** has resulted in better stand establishment and more rapid early growth of potatoes, sugar beets, and vegetables in areas where spring winds are severe. Crops are seeded at their usual row spacing in narrow beds rototilled from small grain stubble or a rye cover crop. Rows are oriented at right angles to the usual wind direction. A strip of stubble or cover crop is left between seeded rows to protect germinating seedlings. Later, as strips of cover crop or weeds begin to compete with the main crop, they can be removed by herbicides or cultivation. Both trashy fallow and minitil can be adapted for vegetable gardens on slopes or in areas where spring winds are detrimental to early-spring planting (see Figure 12-2).

Benefits of Cultivation. Although other systems of cultivation are sometimes used, the standard cultural practice with vegetables and flowers in the temperate zone is still clean cultivation. A number of benefits are claimed for cultivating row crops, some of which are truly beneficial and necessary. Others have been shown by modern research to be of little value or, in some instances, even detrimental to crop production. For small-seeded vegetables and flowers, a smooth, firm seedbed (which can be produced only when crop residues are turned under by cultivation) is highly desirable for uniform planting and good seed germination. However, the main benefit of cultivation has always been the control of weeds. Weeds compete with crop plants for space, moisture, light, and soil nutrients, and most horticultural crops cannot compete with the well-adapted, rapidly growing weeds that infest most fields.

One of the supposed benefits of cultivation is the conserving of water that allegedly occurs when a dust mulch seals cracks and pores, preventing the upward flow and evaporation of moisture. Research has shown that for a few heavy soils, cultivation does indeed conserve moisture by sealing cracks that penetrate deeply when these kinds of soils begin to dry. But with lighter soils, especially when only light rains have fallen, cultivation may actually lead to a more rapid loss of moisture as the wet soil is stirred to the surface.

Another benefit claimed for cultivation is increased soil aeration. Again, research has shown that with certain kinds of soils, cultivation at the proper stage may increase aeration, but if the soil has slightly more moisture than is optimal for cultivation, aeration is likely to be reduced. The passage of heavy cultivation equipment almost always reduces aeration and results in compaction in the lower depths of the soil.

Thus the major purposes of cultivation, for the home gardener as well as for the large producer, are to prepare a seedbed, to plow under various crop residues and manures, and, most importantly, to control weeds.

Cultivating Equipment. The home gardener's choice of cultivating equipment depends mainly on the area that must be cultivated. If the area is small, a spade or digging fork, a hoe, and a rake may be all that is required. If the area is larger, the grower can hire someone with equipment to do the plowing and cultivating, or the grower can rent or buy power equipment. In most regions where gardening is popular, students or other individuals do custom rototilling or tractor work on a part-time basis. It is usually possible to rent rototillers and sometimes small garden tractors with plows and/or cultivating equipment from agencies or garden and hardware stores. Unless the garden area is large or gardeners can do custom work, renting is usually cheaper, though less convenient, than buying the equipment, when all costs, including interest on the investment, are considered.

Growers contemplating buying power equipment to cultivate a garden should consider carefully the various units available. If possible, they should try out some of the units to see whether they will be satisfactory for their specific purposes, and they should at least study the literature available on such equipment and talk to dealers and owners about the advantages of various kinds of equipment. My experience has been that the least expensive units with the minimum amount of power are generally a waste of money. A unit with 4 to 6 horsepower and provision for attaching digging and cultivating equipment is the minimum with which most home gardeners will be satisfied. Often such a unit can power a lawn mower and can be used in the winter to remove snow from walks and drives. Owners of a somewhat larger acreage can buy a four-wheeled garden tractor to power several kinds of farm equipment. A few part-time farmers have bought mules or ponies broken to the harness as a power source, but anyone contemplating such a purchase needs to investigate the availability of feed and pasture and of horse-drawn hand plows and cultivating equipment as well as local ordinances regarding keeping such animals.

Rotation, Succession Planting, and Intercropping

The year-by-year cropping history of a plot of ground is referred to as its **rotation.** A proper rotation reduces pest problems and permits better utilization of nutrient elements. If sufficient area is available, garden crops should be rotated with climatically adapted field crops on which most insects and diseases of garden crops cannot survive, for instance, grasses, small grains, alfalfa, and other legumes. When the alternate crop is an annual, the plot can be planted with annual flowers or vegetables every other year. Occasionally alfalfa or other deep-rooted perennials should be planted to open the subsoil, in which case a longer rotation is required. Where space is limited, crops should be rotated within the garden. A garden map showing the location of each crop each year is essential for maintaining a beneficial rotation year after year.

Succession planting is the planting of two or more crops, one after another, during the same season; it is beneficial where garden space is limited. Succession planting is common in areas with a long growing season. In much of North America, the area planted in early-spring crops — green peas, spinach, lettuce, and radishes — which seldom occupy garden space for more than a fraction of the growing season, can be replanted with summer or fall crops of carrots, lettuce, cauliflower, cabbage, or spinach. An annual flower bed made unsightly by an early freeze can be transformed by transplanting a few clumps of hardy chrysanthemums into it. Rye, seeded after the harvest of most garden annuals, can provide organic matter and prevent soil erosion during the winter. Numerous other examples of succession cropping could be mentioned.

Intercropping (**interplanting**) or **multiple cropping** is the growing of two or more kinds of crops on the same area at the same time (Figure 5-13). It is common practice in new orchards to plant vegetables or small fruits between the rows of trees to use space unoccupied while the trees are not producing. Young orchards thus interplanted often receive better care than do those not interplanted, because the grower must care for the plot in order for the interplanted crop to produce. The intercrop should never be permitted to compete with the permanent trees, and those likely to spread pests to the orchard should be avoided. For example, the Verticillium wilt organism, which survives for many years in the soil and destroys

FIGURE 5-13 • Intercropping of lettuce and cabbage in double rows. The earlier maturing lettuce will have been harvested by the time the cabbage has expanded to occupy all of the space in the rows. (Courtesy of Walter Chandoha)

stone-fruit trees, can be spread by plantings of tomatoes, potatoes, and eggplant.

Interplanting is also possible with late-planted, widely spaced crops such as melons and squash, which can be successfully seeded or transplanted into cleared spaces among early-spring plantings of lettuce, radishes, or spinach. By the time the melons or squash plants have begun to spread, the earlier-planted crops will have been harvested. Annual flowers are often interplanted with spring bulbs to hide the unsightly dying leaves and faded blooms of the bulb plants.

Interplanting should be avoided if it results in the plants' competition for sunlight, which it often does in northern climates. For example, the intercropping of beans, sweet corn, and squash, mentioned earlier and common in Aztec gardens, is not practical in most United States and Canadian gardens. In the north the shaded beans and squash may not mature; caring for a mixed planting is inconvenient; and generally the yield is not significantly greater than it would be if the same area were planted to three separate monoculture plots. Some of the pest control and growth stimulation claims attributed to **companion cropping,** a form of intercropping in which specific kinds of plants are supposed to benefit mutually by their close association in the garden, are probably valid, but there is reason to be skeptical of others. For example, onions and garlic, both highly susceptible to many insects, are often recommended as insect-repellant companion crops. Until there is more precise information on the detrimental effects of chemical interactions among plants (sometimes called **allelopathy**) and between plants and insects, gardeners should not rely too heavily on companion cropping to solve their pest and other garden problems.

Mulching

Mulch is material spread over the surface of soil to control weeds, conserve moisture, heat or cool the soil, improve soil structure, prevent freeze damage, hasten maturity, prevent erosion, and enhance the garden's appearance. A number of different products are commonly used for mulching garden plants. Among the most popular today are landscape fabric, black and clear plastic, pebble-sized pieces of bark, gravel and river rock, sand, sawdust, leaves, straw and other organic trash, and paper.

Landscape fabric is a heavy, woven material that has the advantage of allowing moisture to penetrate down while preventing weeds from growing up. A landscape featuring shrubs and small trees planted through bark- or pebble-covered landscape fabric has become an almost universal tidy, low-maintenance planting for commercial buildings (Figure 14-61). Although the fabric is fairly expensive, it is also being used extensively by busy homeowners. Discarded carpeting made of acrylic or other weather-resistant fabric can be used as a substitute for landscape fabric if the area to be covered is small. Except for its being heavier, most carpet offers about the same benefits as does landscape fabric, although water penetration may be impeded by carpet with rubber backing still intact.

Plastics by themselves or in combination with other products are the mulching materials most widely used by commercial growers and home gardeners. Although a number of kinds of plastics are used for mulching, polyethylene is by far the most widely used because it comes in varied thicknesses, sizes, and shades and because it is relatively less expensive than most other types. Some of the advantages of polyethylene are earlier production, weed control, prevention of moisture loss, and prevention of fruit rot in crops like cucumbers and tomatoes that are frequently attacked by decay organisms when they come in contact with the soil. Polyethylene promotes earlier production of warm-season vegetables and flowers but does not seem to have much effect on the maturity of cool-season crops (Figure 5-14).

Polyethylene is especially effective in promoting the early production of muskmelons, and research in the Northwest has shown this crop to be ten to fourteen days earlier when grown on plastic

FIGURE 5-14 • Polyethylene is the least expensive of the durable sheet mulching materials. It is used extensively by commercial growers as well as by home gardeners. Almost all California fresh strawberries are grown under polyethylene row covers, as shown above, to eliminate weed growth, prevent evaporation, and increase yield. (Courtesy of Grant Heilman)

than when grown without it. For many years it was thought that the early production of warm-season crops grown with polyethylene mulch was a result of the higher soil temperature under the mulch, but it is now known that black plastic mulch raises the soil temperature only slightly and leads to early production even when the soil temperature is not increased. When a thin layer of soil is placed on top of black plastic mulch, the temperature under the soil–polyethylene layer remains exactly the same as the temperature at the same depth in unmulched soil. Yet plants growing in the soil-covered polyethylene plot are as early as those grown with exposed polyethylene. There is some evidence that the higher level of carbon dioxide in the atmosphere around very young plants growing through plastic mulch may be responsible for their earlier maturity and higher yields. The breakdown of organic matter and root respiration in the soil result in the release of CO_2, which escapes through the holes in the plastic sheet and concentrates in the atmosphere surrounding the plants growing through those holes.

The soil under clear polyethylene, unlike that under black polyethylene, is considerably warmer than unmulched soil. Consequently, plants of warm-season vegetables produce even earlier crops (muskmelons in irrigated areas of the Pacific Northwest are about seven days earlier) when grown with clear polyethylene than they do with black polyethylene mulch. Unfortunately, clear polyethylene cannot be used as a mulch in many parts of the United States because weeds can grow under the plastic. The use of clear polyethylene mulch is practical only in desert areas where the intense light day after day keeps the weeds under the plastic burned off until they are shaded out by the growing crop.

Cost is a major factor limiting the commercial use of plastic mulch. But for home gardeners who wish to mulch only a small area, its use is economically feasible (see "Mulching with Sheet Materials" in Chapter 14).

When it is exposed to light in the field, polyethylene lasts for only one season, but when it is covered with some other material, it may last for many years. Polyethylene thus is frequently used under bark, gravel, or river rock to control weeds that would otherwise come through these loose mulches.

A major disadvantage of polyethylene used as a field or garden surface mulch is the necessity of removing it after the growing season has passed. Several kinds of plastics that are biodegradable in the soil are in the developmental stage and should be available soon. The use of paper mulch has been suggested as a way of overcoming this disadvantage, although the very ease with which paper deteriorates in many situations negates its advantages as a mulching material. This is especially true in home gardens where it is likely to become ragged and unsightly long before the season is over.

A number of other materials are used as mulches around the home. As mentioned, gravel, river rock, and bark are used extensively today in combination with plastic to control weeds and retard moisture loss in ornamental plantings. Straw, sawdust, leaves, peat moss, and other organic mulches can be placed over strawberries and other herbaceous perennials and around roses and other semihardy shrubs in the fall to prevent winter damage. A 2- to 3-inch (5- to 8-cm) layer controls weeds, prevents moisture loss, and adds organic matter to plantings around the home. All loose mulches tend to keep soil temperatures uniformly cooler, an advantage in the growing of certain ornamentals.

 Selected References

Brady, N. C. *The Nature and Property of Soils.* 10th ed. New York: Macmillan, 1990.

Hausenbuiller, R. L. *Soil Science: Principles and Practices.* 3rd ed. Dubuque, Iowa: Brown, 1985.

Hunt, C. B. *Geology of Soils.* New York: Freeman, 1972.

Organic Gardening editors and J. Minnich. *The Rodale Guide to Composting.* Emmaus, Pa.: Rodale Press, 1979.

San Luis Video. *Fertilizing Landscape Plants* (videotape). San Luis Obispo, Calif.: San Luis Video Publishing, 1990.

Tate, R. L., III. *Soil Organic Matter: Biological and Ecological Effects.* New York: Wiley, 1987.

U.S. Department of Agriculture. *Soils (Yearbook of Agriculture, 1957).* Washington, D.C.: U.S. Government Printing Office, 1957.

Wild, A., ed. *Russell's Soil Conditions and Plant Growth.* 11th ed. New York: Wiley, 1988.

Water and Irrigation

Water is basic to all life, and adequate fresh water is essential to agricultural and community development. The earliest civilizations were established where rainfall or irrigation water made crop production possible. Most famines, ancient as well as modern, have been caused by too little, or occasionally too much, water, and the primary tactics in the present battle against world hunger include channeling water to arid lands and draining swampy areas.

Most crop plants require a constant supply of available moisture. Where crops and gardens are irrigated, supplying the right amount of water at the right time is a major challenge. Where rainfall is the only source of water, planting and cultivating practices need to be adapted to the supply that nature provides. Water also has aesthetic functions in many gardens where streams, waterfalls, fountains, fishponds, or swimming pools are an integral part of the landscape.

THE MOISTURE CYCLE

All water for plant growth comes initially from the ocean and is transported as atmospheric water vapor to the land, where it condenses and falls as one phase of the earth's **moisture cycle,** illustrated in Figure 6-1. Three physical principles govern the taking up and releasing of moisture by the atmosphere: (1) considerably more moisture vapor can be carried

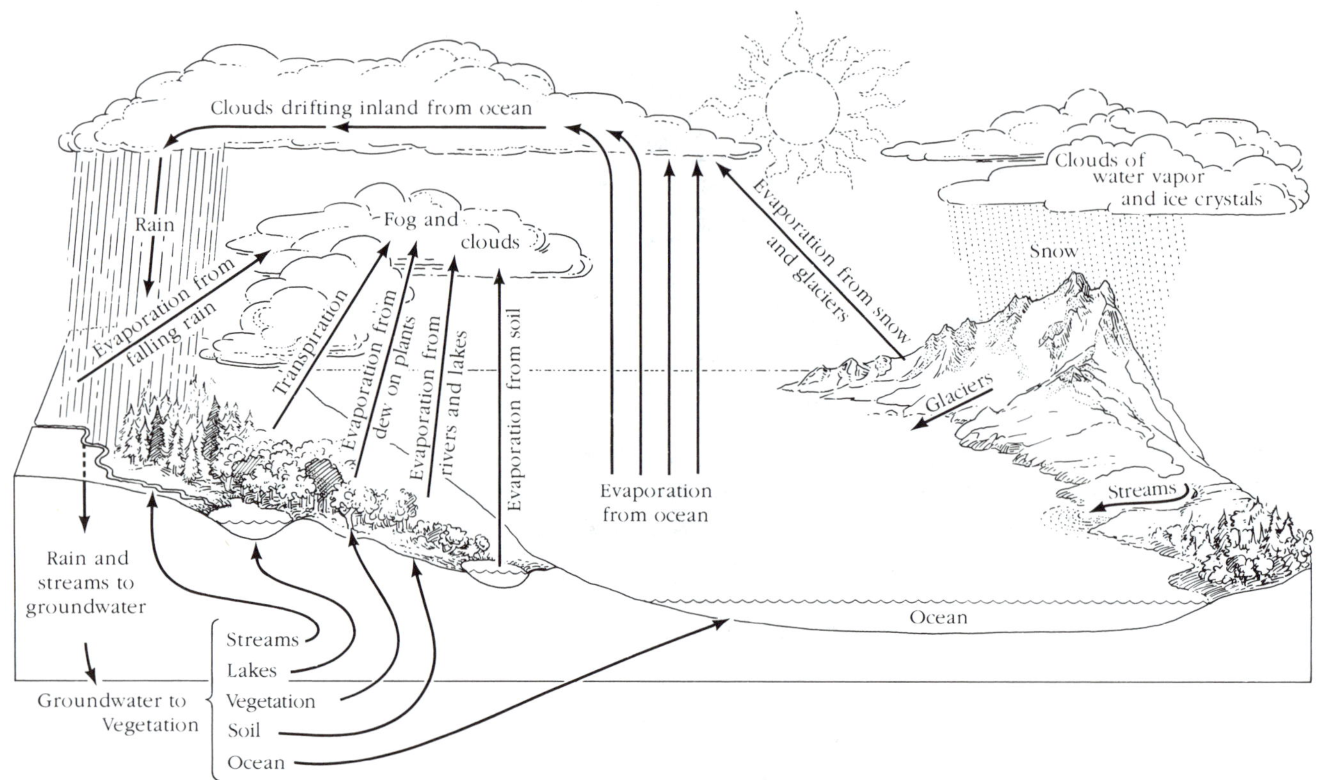

FIGURE 6-1 • The moisture cycle. (After J. Gilluly, A. C. Waters, and A. O. Woodford, *Principles of Geology*, 4th ed., W. H. Freeman and Company, New York, copyright © 1975)

by warm air than by cold air; (2) as a gas such as air is warmed, its molecules expand and move farther apart, and as a result its mass increases and its density lowers, with less weight per unit volume; and (3) the surface of the earth is subject to differential heating.

Warm air moving away from the equator picks up large quantities of vaporized moisture that is released whenever the air is cooled. When warm air meets a mass of colder air moving from the poles, widespread rains result; the cooling of warm air that is forced to rise over an area of higher elevation accounts for the heavy precipitation on the windward side of mountain ranges. Air may also be cooled by what is called a *cyclonic disturbance.* Cyclonic disturbances usually occur in the afternoon at times and in places where the humidity is high. Then the air near the surface of the earth warms, expands, and absorbs considerable moisture. This lightweight, moisture-laden air starts to rise, literally forcing openings in the cold air mass above those areas where the most surface heating has occurred. Warm air rushes upward through these openings much as warm smoke rises up a chimney. The cooling of the warm air surging through the cool air condenses moisture vapor into small droplets of water that form the cumulus clouds of a thunderstorm. The uplift of warm air may blow the falling droplets upward several times until, combining with other droplets, they reach a mass great enough that their force of gravity can overcome the force of the upward air movement and they fall to the earth's surface as raindrops. Friction of the moving air masses and differences in the electrical charge of the upward-moving small and downward-moving large water droplets are thought to be responsible for the buildup of static electricity that is discharged as lightning and thunder.

If the temperature of the upper air is below the freezing point of water, ice crystals will be formed and other water molecules will freeze to them as they move up and down through the rising air mass. This results in the very damaging hailstorms that frequently occur in some locations. The size of hailstones is directly proportional to the velocity of the upward-flowing air. Snow results when moisture condenses in and falls through air that is at a temperature below freezing. Under these conditions small ice crystals combine into loosely conglomerated snowflakes. Snow in mountainous regions is important for moisture storage, and its slow release keeps streams flowing to lowland areas through dry summers.

Some water from rain or melting snow remains on the land surface and runs off in streams or rivers, and some soaks into the soil. The amount and rapidity with which moisture enters the soil and the amount of moisture the soil can hold depend on the soil's texture and structure. The infiltration rate is slow in clay soils and rapid in sandy soils and soils high in organic matter. The retention of moisture is high in clay soils and soils high in organic matter and is low in sandy soils. Some of the moisture absorbed into the soil is pulled down through it by the force of gravity. This **gravitational water** enters the **groundwater** reservoir to become the source of springs and wells. The remainder of the water absorbed into the soil is held in the pore spaces of the soil and on the soil particles. The maximum amount of water that a soil can hold against the force of gravity is termed its **field capacity.** The moisture held in the soil is the source of water for plant growth; however, plants can absorb only part of the water contained in a soil at field capacity because some is held so tightly by soil particles that plants are unable to extract it. The stage in soil-moisture depletion at which a plant is unable to take additional moisture from the soil and, as a consequence, becomes wilted is referred to as the **wilting point.** The water held by the soil below the wilting point is **unavailable** or **hygroscopic water.** Water is available for plant growth between the field capacity of a soil and its wilting point, and the amount of water in the soil between these two points is referred to as **available** or **capillary moisture** (Figure 6-2). Clay soils hold considerable moisture at field capacity but also have a high percentage of unavailable water. Sandy soils, on the other hand, have a very low moisture percentage at field capacity but may have almost no unavailable water. Table 6-1 lists the water-holding capacity of various types of soil.

Moisture is lost from landmasses by evaporation directly from the soil surface and by absorption into plant roots. A small percentage of the water taken from the soil by plants is used in photosynthesis or is incorporated into the protoplasm of the plant body. By far the largest amount

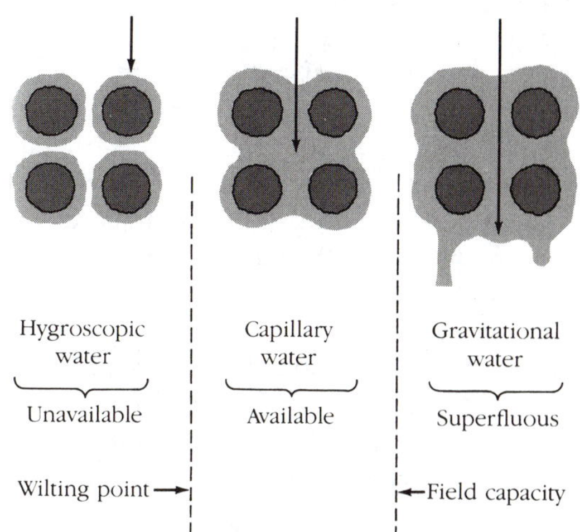

FIGURE 6-2 • The three stages of soil moisture supply. Gravitational water drains away before it can be used by plants, and hygroscopic water is bound so tightly that plants cannot absorb it. Only capillary water is available for plant use. (Adapted from J. Bonner and A. W. Galston, *Principles of Plant Physiology*, W. H. Freeman and Company, New York, copyright © 1952)

TABLE 6-1 • *Approximate water-holding capacity of various types of soil*

Soil type	Inches of water/foot (× 3.28 = cm/m)	Inches of available water/foot (× 3.28 = cm/m)
Course sand	0.40–0.75	0.20–0.40
Fine sand, loamy sand	0.75–1.25	0.40–0.70
Sandy loam, fine sandy loam	1.25–1.75	0.70–0.90
Loams and silt loams	1.50–2.30	0.75–1.10
Clay loams	1.75–2.50	0.90–1.25
Clays	1.60–2.50	0.80–1.20
Peat and muck	2.00–3.00	1.00–1.50

Data in this table are averages from several sources.

—over 99 percent for some crop plants growing in hot, arid regions—is lost by transpiration (see "Transpiration and Plant Water Use" in Chapter 2). Wherever there is a plant cover, the amount of moisture lost by transpiration is much greater than the amount lost by evaporation. The transformation of large amounts of liquid water into water vapor by transpiration consumes a lot of heat energy, partly accounting for the moist coolness of a woody garden. Without a plant cover, the loss of moisture by evaporation from the soil surface is not rapid. This minimal evaporation is the basis of a system employed by farmers in semiarid regions called **summer fallowing,** in which the land is kept completely free of plants every other year in order to store moisture for crop production during the alternate year.

The water vapor transpired by plants or, to a lesser extent, evaporated from the land surface, is an important source of precipitation for large landmasses, and the same water molecules may be involved in several precipitation–evaporation cycles as air currents move them across a continent. When a plant cover is destroyed, this recycling of precipitation is greatly reduced. The increasing length and severity of droughts that have plagued parts of Africa in recent years are thought to be caused by the destruction of plant cover by overgrazing.

WATER AND PLANT GROWTH

Water plays a vital role in plant growth and development. In some areas all of the time, and in most areas some of the time, lack of water (**water stress**) is the factor most limiting to proper plant functions. Water constitutes the greatest part of the plant body, the leaves of most trees being about 65 percent water, the roots about 70 percent, and the fruits about 85 percent; some leafy vegetables such as cabbage and spinach are about 90 percent, and melons about 95 percent, water. Water also serves as a plant nutrient, being one of the chemical constituents required in the photosynthetic process. It serves a fundamental role as the solvent for mineral elements entering the plant and facilitates the transport of minerals and manufactured foods. The normal functioning of many plants and plant parts depends on water pressure inside their cells. When plant parts are fully distended by being filled with water, they are said to be **turgid,** and most plant functions and plant growth occur only when a plant is turgid. A plant that lacks turgidity is said to be **wilted.** Water also provides the means whereby a plant can expand against external physical forces, as occurs with seed germination, seedling emergence, and most of the subsequent increases in plant size (Figure

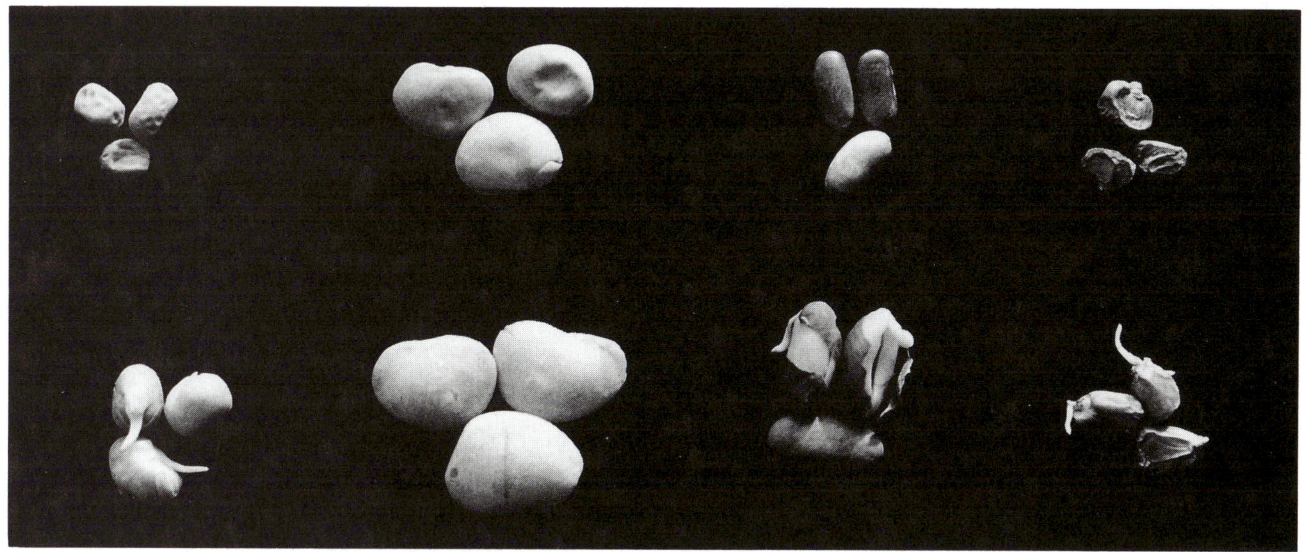

FIGURE 6-3 • Water as a means for plants to exert a force of growth. Peas, lima beans, beans, and sweet corn seeds that have absorbed water as the first stage of germination (lower) have expanded their volume to several times that of comparable dry seed (upper).

6-3). Most botanists believe that temperature control as a result of evaporative cooling by transpiration is another important function of water in plant development.

Effects of Excess Moisture

Plants growing in soil that is excessively watered appear unthrifty and may display symptoms similar to those shown by plants lacking moisture. (The term **unthrifty** is used to describe plants that are not growing as vigorously as they should but do not show symptoms of a specific problem.) An oversupply of moisture fills soil pore spaces, causing a lack of aeration that in turn restricts the growth and function of absorbing roots. With no absorbing roots, an overwatered plant may actually wilt from a lack of moisture in its stems and leaves. Wilting, yellowing, and death of the margins of leaves all can be signs that a plant is getting too much water.

Perhaps the group of plants most often overwatered are those growing in glazed pots without drainage holes. If plants are grown in these kinds of containers, care must be taken to apply just enough water to moisten the soil and then to let the soil become fairly dry before watering again. Overwatering is not as much a problem with plants in fields and gardens, but it can occur.

At planting time a lack of aeration due to excess moisture may prevent seeds from germinating. Excess moisture may also increase the activity of soil-borne disease organisms, which may lead to damping-off (Figure 6-4). **Damping-off** is the decay or death of a stem at soil level resulting from an attack by one or more of several different soil pathogens. The seedlings are literally eaten by microorganisms at the soil line and fall over and die. Often excess moisture is associated with cold soil, which also delays germination.

Excess soil moisture increases the tendency for cabbage heads to split when they are left in the garden after they mature. Splitting of cabbage can

FIGURE 6-4 • Damping-off, a disease often associated with excess moisture. In the flat in which they were growing the four cabbage seedlings on the right were beginning to fall over, wilt, and die because their stems are constricted by pathogens feeding near the soil line. The plants at the left are healthy. Once established, damping-off spreads rapidly and often destroys all the seedling plants in a container.

be delayed by grasping the mature head in both hands and twisting it partway around to sever some of the water-absorbing roots. Excess soil moisture is especially damaging to plants grown for their underground parts. With only a slight excess, potato tubers produce enlarged **lenticels,** the small corky areas that allow an interchange of gases between the interior of stems, roots, and tubers and the atmosphere. Enlarged lenticels on potato tubers are unsightly and can be the entry site for disease-causing organisms. Potatoes and root crops are more vulnerable to soft rot in overly moist soil.

Sometimes moisture falling on the above-ground portions of a plant can be detrimental. Fruits with a high sugar content—tomatoes and sweet cherries are prime examples—tend to split if moisture falls on them when they are nearly mature (Figure 6-5). Because of their high sugar content, fruits absorb water by osmosis (see Chapter 2) to the point of bursting. A light rain can destroy a nearly mature cherry crop in a few minutes. Tomatoes irrigated with sprinklers or frequently rained on are more apt to split than are those that are furrow irrigated.

Foliar diseases are more severe in areas of high rainfall and high humidity. The spores of *Phytophthora infestans,* a fungus causing late blight of potatoes, require foliar moisture for their germination. Between 1845 and 1851, late blight destroyed or damaged the potato crop over much of the world. In Ireland, where food for the impoverished population was mainly potatoes, a famine ensued. Starvation and disease (mainly typhus) killed a million and a half people, almost 20 percent of the population; another million (or about 13 percent of the population) left the country, most of them for the United States. Now in areas of high summer rainfall, potato plantings are sprayed every week with a fungicide to control this disease.

The seed-borne pathogen that causes halo blight of beans is spread by splashing water. In areas where rain is frequent, halo blight spores can spread from one or two seed-infected plants to destroy many acres of snap or dry beans. It can be

A

B

C

FIGURE 6-5 • Cracking of horticultural fruits and roots. Sweet cherries (A) and tomatoes (B) crack when rain or irrigation water falls on the ripe fruit and is absorbed by osmosis into the sugar-containing interior. In contrast, the splitting of carrot roots (C) seems to be more closely correlated with uneven spacing in the garden row and with large size than with moisture.

controlled by planting seed completely free of the causal organism. This has led to the establishment of the U.S. bean-seed industry in the arid, irrigated Twin Falls area of southern Idaho, where halo blight is rarely found.

Effects of Moisture Deficiency

Injury due to a deficiency of moisture is more common in outdoor gardens than injury due to an excess. The first plant symptom of moisture stress is a slight yellowish or grayish cast of the leaves, a symptom easily recognized by experienced growers. Growth slows, and yield may be reduced even before definite symptoms of drought become apparent. The leaves wilt, roll, and finally shed as water stress becomes more acute (Figure 6-6) and fruits wither and drop. It is important to distinguish between wilting due to a lack of soil moisture and temporary wilting that may occur during hot days when the plant is transpiring so rapidly that its roots are not able to absorb and replace the moisture being lost. With temporary wilting the plant recovers in the evening or when the weather cools.

Water stress lowers the quality of succulent vegetables by causing premature woodiness, stringiness, and toughness. Greens and salad crops, especially, require ample water, because their quality depends on their succulence and crispness. Fruit produced under droughty conditions may have a woody texture. If an edible or ornamental plant has insufficient moisture, its flowers will blast and its buds will drop before they open. Yields of beans and lima beans are greatly reduced by even moderate water stress at blossom time because of the tendency of these crops to lose their blossom buds.

FIGURE 6-6 • A tomato plant wilted because of a lack of soil moisture. The symptoms resulting from excess soil moisture can be similar. (Courtesy of Dwight R. Kuhn)

In areas of low humidity during hot weather, tomatoes sometimes develop a physiological disorder called **blossom-end rot,** the first symptom of which is a water-soaked area on the blossom end of the tomato. This area then turns brown and finally develops into a dry, shriveled, and sunken lesion that internally may involve most of the fruit. The physiology of blossom-end rot is not entirely understood, but it is known to be correlated with water stress. It is most prevalent on tomato fruits growing on vines that have been produced with optimum growing conditions during the early part of the summer and, after fruit is set, are subjected to either a lack of soil moisture or hot weather and low humidity. It is assumed that under these conditions, the leaves are able to draw moisture from the fruit, causing dehydration and death of the fruit cells farthest from the moisture source. Because blossom-end rot can also be caused by a calcium deficiency, there is probably a physiological relationship between calcium deficiency and water stress.

Potato specialists have long known that the best-quality 'Russet Burbank' (Idaho) potatoes are produced with light, frequent irrigation. A high percentage of U.S. #1 potatoes are produced in fields irrigated every three to five days. Fields irrigated more heavily every ten to fourteen days may produce a comparable total yield, but a high percentage of the potatoes will have pointed ends or restricted middles. Potatoes with restricted middles are called *bottlenecks* or *dumbbells* by the trade (Figure 6-7). Research in Idaho has shown that the benefits of frequent irrigation on 'Russet Burbank' tuber quality come from soil cooling rather than from additional water per se. Tuber growth ceases when soil temperatures rise, and the cessation and resumption of growth produce deformed tubers. Round potato cultivars are not nearly so subject to damage by a fluctuation of water supply and usually grow more satisfactorily than long-tubered cultivars in gardens where the moisture supply is uncertain.

FIGURE 6-7 • The results of faulty irrigation practices. Many types of misshapen potato tubers can be prevented by more frequent irrigation, which leads to more uniform soil temperatures.

WATER QUALITY AND WATER POLLUTION

The quality of water is lowered by pollution from sediments, nonbiodegradable trash, disease-causing microorganisms, organic wastes, dissolved chemicals, and petroleum and other liquids that do not mix with water. The pollutants come mainly from five sources — natural geological and biological phenomena, agricultural and forest industries, construction activities, municipal and home sewage, and industrial waste.

Water Pollutants

Sediments are particles of soil that become suspended in water mostly as a result of agricultural and forest activities and construction projects such as building roads, laying underground pipes and conduits, and preparing building sites. In addition to lessening the aesthetic appeal of streams and lakes, sedimentation fills in and limits the usefulness of reservoirs, blocks navigation channels, causes streams to erode and to change channels, and destroys aquatic life. The ever-greater quantities of glass, plastic, cans, foil, and other trash that foul lakes and rivers and wash onto beaches and streambanks, as well as the numerous oil spills, from small to massive, that continue to occur on waterways on which petroleum is transported, are a serious threat to the quality of water resources, a hazard to human health and recreation, and a killer of wildlife. Sediment, trash, and oil spills have a substantial, but indirect, impact on gardeners and gardening.

Microorganisms from sewage and other human waste and from animal manures contaminate drinking water and are infamous for spreading such diseases as cholera, dysentery, and typhoid. For many years municipalities and private residences discharged raw sewage into streams, lakes, and the oceans. Some still do. It was once believed that disease-causing microorganisms would be purged from a fast-flowing stream within 50 or 100 yards from where they entered and that wave action and the ocean's salt content would quickly purify larger bodies of water. This may have been true when individual discharges were occasional and scattered. But the chronicles of the ravages of waterborne diseases in both settled communities and in covered-wagon trains during the 1800s attest to the fallacy of this belief in places where more than a few people live or travel. Contamination by human and animal wastes have made many streams, lakes, and ocean beaches unsafe for recreation or other uses. Fortunately, the municipal water systems in North America are almost always free of damaging microorganisms.

Carelessly located septic tank drain-fields can contaminate drinking water. Springs or wells used for domestic water should be checked occasionally by a water-quality testing laboratory as a precaution, especially if they are located where numerous septic tanks are in use or if they are adjacent to or overlaid by farmland to which pesticides and fertilizer are applied. It is unwise to grow vegetables over a septic tank drain-field, and water from a sewage treatment facility should not be used to irrigate crops unless those crops are processed before being consumed. Because of the regulations and inspections to which our public food supply is subjected, microorganism contamination is not nearly the threat to present-day North American farmers, gardeners, or consumers that it was in the past or that it still is in other parts of the world.

Sewage and animal manures are also the source of many of the organic wastes that pollute water. Fallen or blown leaves and other plant debris, streambank weeds, and dead bodies of aquatic plants and other organisms that live and reproduce in water are additional organic water pollutants. Besides being a source of microorganisms that spread disease, organic wastes cause water to have undesirable flavors, odors, and color. Their breakdown utilizes large amounts of oxygen that can rapidly deplete this element in slow-moving streams, lakes, or ponds, resulting in the death of fish and other aquatic life. Once the oxygen is gone, a slower anaerobic type of organic matter breakdown commences that usually releases a number of foul smelling, unsavory compounds.

Dissolved chemicals are the water pollutants having the greatest direct impact on crop production and crop producers, including gardeners. Many of these chemical compounds enter water from natural sources. Small amounts of certain minerals fall with precipitation; for example, by USDA estimate 4 to 8 pounds of nitrogen per acre per year falls over agricultural lands of the United States and up to 5,000 pounds of chlorine per acre per year falls near the English coast. Minerals also are leached from rocks below the soil mantle, a process abetted by carbonic acid formed in the soil solution from the carbon dioxide generated as a consequence of organic matter breakdown. The kinds of leached minerals vary depending on the parent rock; calcium leaches from limestone and iron from basalt. Water with a high concentration of dissolved minerals is often referred to as **hard water.** Usually more minerals dissolve into groundwater than into water flowing from the surface, which is why in rural areas well water is often described as "harder" than spring water.

Many chemical compounds enter water as a result of human activity. Chemical, pharmaceutical, paper, and related industries generate and release into waterways chemical wastes including some heavy metals that are quite toxic. Large quantities of nitrogen, phosphorus, and organic compounds and smaller quantities of some other elements released from sewage and animal manures find their way into aquifers. Each year agricultural and forest industries apply fertilizer and pesticides, often more than crops can use, to millions of acres. The excess can leach into surface water or groundwater.

Damage to Farm and Garden from Dissolved Chemicals

Chemicals that dissolve in water can damage both equipment and crops. Some mineral elements separate from their soluble salts and form deposits that can plug sprinkler heads, irrigation pipes, and other conduits, especially the small tubes used for trickle irrigation described later in this chapter. The mineral residue remaining when droplets of hard water evaporate can cause unsightly spots on houseplants. Nitrogen and phosphorus encourage the growth of algae and other aquatic plants. These plants block waterways and also plug pipes and sprinklers. Perhaps more important, when water plants die their composition depletes water of its oxygen, resulting in the problems that occur with the underwater organic matter breakdown mentioned earlier. Although there is not complete agreement on all the causes of the proliferating growth of the algae that have fouled so many lakes and streams in recent years, many scientists feel that phosphorus is a major factor. Much of the phosphorus in sewage wastes comes from the household detergents used to wash clothes and dishes. Detergents containing phosphorus are now banned in some regions with lakes or streams in which the growth of algae or other aquatic plants has become an environmental hazard.

Irrigating with water that has a high mineral salt content is often a major cause of soil salt concentrations that are high enough to injure crop plants. High surface salt accumulations usually result from a combination of factors. They tend to occur in arid areas where the soluble salt content of soil is already high because of a lack of leaching. Irrigation water dissolves the salt to the depth that the soil is moistened, and evaporation tends to draw that water, with its mineral load, upward. On contact with the atmosphere, the water molecules turn to vapor, leaving the mineral compounds from both water and soil as visible red or white deposits at the soil surface. Repeated irrigations and evaporations, week after week, season after season, of water with a high salt content eventually cause phytotoxic concentrations of salt at the soil surface.

In some soils salts have accumulated in concentrations so high that crop plants can no longer be grown. The lower Tigris–Euphrates delta, once the garden spot of the Middle East, is now largely an alkali wasteland. In that delta, as has occurred more recently in many smaller irrigated tracts and as appears to be occurring in parts of the Nile delta with the cessation of the annual flooding due to the construction of the Aswan Dam, poor drainage has allowed the water table to rise, bringing to the surface soluble salts from the entire soil profile. Tile or open-ditch drainage and occasional flushing with heavy irrigation is the procedure most successfully used to leach out soil salts that have become concentrated enough to impede plant growth (Figure 6-8).

Some chemical compounds and minerals, including nitrates in high concentrations and heavy metal toxins such as chromium, lead, and selenium, can be lethal to humans and animals that ingest the water in which they are dissolved. Vertebrate poisoning by heavy metals has been a serious problem in the southwestern United States, where, after repeated use for irrigation, runoff water that has become too brackish to use has been ponded and allowed to evaporate in bird and wildlife sanctuaries. The result is dead or genetically malformed fledglings.

Some crops are more susceptible to salt damage than are others. Asparagus and beets are two crops that grow quite well where the soil salt content is high (see Table 5-3). Sometimes cultural modifications permit a crop to escape soil salt damage. For example, with furrow irrigation on alkaline soils, strawberries will grow better if planted on the edge of the bed next to the furrow than in the center of the bed, because leaching and evaporation tend to concentrate salt in the center of the bed.

We North Americans have only recently begun to recognize the serious consequences that

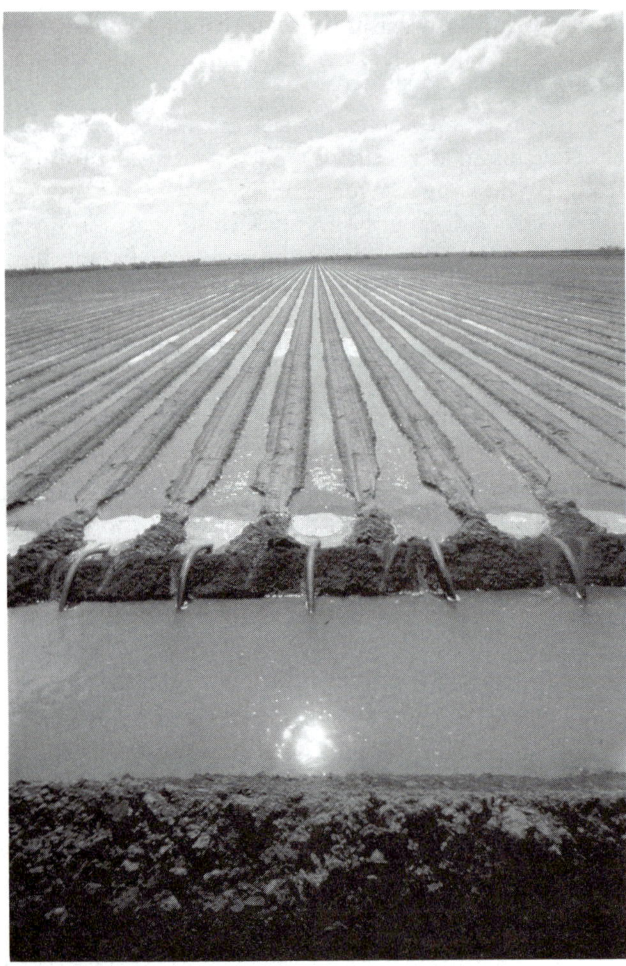

FIGURE 6-8 • Furrow irrigation. This commercial field in Colorado is being heavily irrigated to wash out high concentrations of salts that sometimes accumulate in soils of arid areas and to provide moisture for planting vegetables. Flooding of this magnitude is not desirable on land that is not almost level or where a crop is already growing. (Courtesy of Steve Kaufman with Peter Arnold, Inc.)

our careless disregard of water quality is having for our way of life as well as for the continuing productivity of our agricultural industry. Although not all kinds of water pollution have a direct impact on gardens, gardeners as citizens concerned with the environment should be at the forefront in restoring and maintaining the quality of water resources.

IRRIGATION

Until about 1940, supplemental water was almost never applied to commercially grown vegetables or vegetable gardens in the more humid areas of North America. An occasional humid-area lawn or flower bed was watered during a dry spell, but essentially irrigation was limited to arid areas. This practice has now changed, partly because of a better understanding of the benefits of supplemental watering and the introduction of more convenient sprinkler systems and partly because of the developing importance of community beautification and the provision for irrigation water from municipal water supplies. Today, supplemental irrigation is used on garden crops in most parts of North America.

In urban and suburban areas the water for irrigation usually comes from the municipal supply. A few communities located in arid areas have two piped systems, one for household use and one for irrigation. In rural areas and some suburban communities where lots are larger, water is often supplied in open ditches, or it may be pumped from a well.

Three general systems of irrigation are used in the commercial production of horticultural crops in the United States—subsurface, surface, and sprinkler. A fourth type, trickle irrigation, which was developed and is used extensively in water-short Israel, is receiving considerable attention, especially for greenhouse irrigation and for field irrigation in areas where water is in short supply or brackish.

Because it requires specialized topography and subsoil conditions usually involving large areas such as the drained Everglades of southern Florida, **subsurface irrigation** is seldom feasible for gardens. Most supplemental water applied to gardens comes from either gravity-flow surface irrigation or sprinkler systems; trickle irrigation may soon be added to this list.

Surface Irrigation

Surface irrigation is used by gardeners to (furrow-irrigate) row crops or occasionally to (flood-irrigate) lawns or other grass-covered plantings. For **furrow irrigation,** water is distributed across the garden by small ditches called **rills** or **furrows,** which are 3 to 8 inches (8 to 20 cm) deep. The furrows are usually next to the crop row; for annual crops they are 20 to 40 inches (50 to 100 cm) apart, with one or two crop rows between them (see Figure 14-12). For **flood irrigation,** ridges are established along the border of an area to permit a sheet of water to be spread over its surface. Water for surface irrigation can be brought to the garden in open ditches or by pipes or hoses.

The furrow-irrigated garden is planted on raised beds with the furrows established at planting time. The garden area must be fairly level, with just enough slope to allow water to pass slowly from the upper to the lower end, or else the rows of garden crops and furrows must be on a contour to permit the same slow, even rate of water flow.

Proper furrow irrigation requires patience and considerable skill. Enough water should be channeled into each furrow to be able to flow to the end in a few minutes, and then the amount should be diminished to the point that theoretically the last of the flow soaks in just as it reaches the end of the furrow. This achieves maximum infiltration with minimum erosion and leaching of mineral elements. In actual practice a trickle of water usually runs from the lower end of most furrows, because few irrigators are skilled enough to keep the absolute minimum in all rows. Nevertheless, the best furrow irrigator is the one who can spread the available water to irrigate the greatest number of rows simultaneously. The water should be allowed to flow in the garden until it has soaked across each bed a few inches beneath the surface (Figure 6-9).

Lawns and other planted areas to be irrigated by ridging and flooding must be absolutely level. A ridge 4 to 8 inches (10 to 20 cm) high should be established around the periphery, with the slope of the ridge gentle enough that it can be made less obtrusive by continuing the grass or cover crop planting on its surface. With care an area can

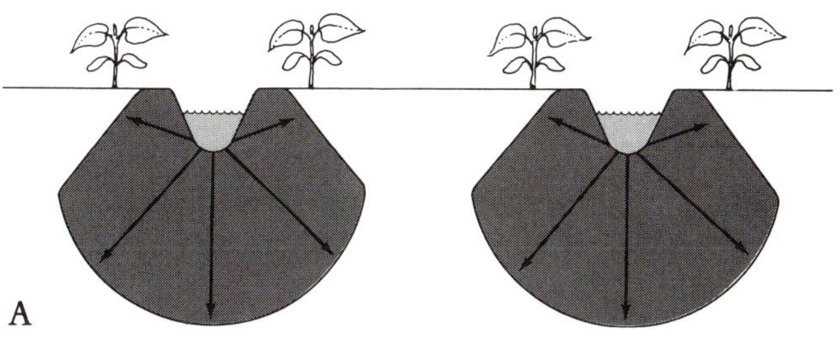

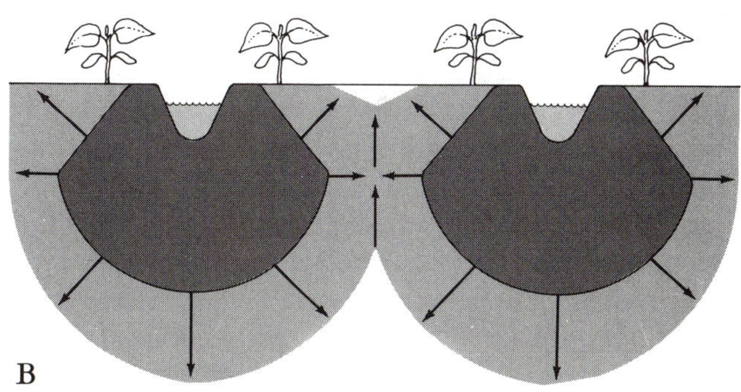

FIGURE 6-9 • Pattern of water infiltration with furrow irrigation. Arrows show the direction of water movement. The darkly shaded area (A) is the area of initial wetting. The lightly shaded area (B) becomes wet later. By the time the water has soaked across the bed to within a few inches of the surface, it will have permeated most of the area of root penetration. Although most of the movement is downward, water also moves toward the center of the furrow and then upward as a result of surface evaporation. In arid areas, toxic quantities of salts moving with the water are sometimes deposited as a crust in the center of the bed as the water evaporates.

sometimes be flood irrigated without ridging, by distributing water along the upper edge and letting it spread across a sloping area. A flood-irrigated lawn usually requires water less frequently but requires more fertilizer applications than does one that is sprinkler irrigated.

The disadvantages of surface irrigation are the leveling and contouring required, the attention necessary while the water is being applied, and the increased problems with mites and thrips, pests that are partially controlled by wetting the plants' leaves. In addition, more water is required for surface than for sprinkler irrigation. On the plus side, the investment for equipment is usually less, and foliar diseases are less likely with surface irrigation. On a small area where foliar disease is a problem, such as a rose garden, a perforated plastic soaker hose turned upside down provides the advantages of surface irrigation.

Sprinkler Irrigation

Sprinkler irrigation is the most widely used system for irrigating small yards and gardens, especially in areas of relatively high rainfall where only occasional supplemental watering during periods of drought is required. Sprinkler irrigation is convenient if the sprinkler can be attached to the pressurized home or municipal water supply. Where irrigation water comes through open canals or ditches, sprinkler irrigation is more costly, because it requires a tank and pump or some other means of providing pressure, piping or hose to deliver water to the garden, and a filter system to eliminate particulate matter and prevent clogging, as well as a sprinkler system for water distribution.

Hand-held hose sprinkling is not the best means of sprinkler irrigation. Movable sprinklers are available in a wide range of quality and price. Usually, the better-quality sprinklers are the best buy, even though they initially cost more, because they distribute water more uniformly and last longer. Sprinklers vary in their patterns of water distribution, and this should be a consideration when they are being purchased. The sprinkler or sprinkler system selected should be capable of uniformly watering the entire yard with as few moves as possible. Uniformity of application can be checked by setting flat pans at various locations under the sprinkler. Some of the newer kinds of sprinklers distribute water in a rectangular pattern, providing easier watering of garden corners. The height at which water is discharged and the height reached by the discharged water may be important considerations if tall plants are being watered or if wind is likely to affect the pattern of water distribution. The capacity of the water system determines the maximum number and size of sprinkler heads used. One medium-sized sprinkler may be the maximum if both household and irrigation water must be supplied through a ½-inch (1 ¼-cm) pipe. The pipe supplying the home from the city water main should be at least ¾ inch (2 cm) if yard irrigation is anticipated.

Permanent-set sprinkler systems with a network of underground pipes are popular with homeowners. They can be connected to a time clock to make sprinkling automatic. The permanent-set system saves considerable time and labor where extensive lawn and ornamentals must be irrigated. With the use of plastic pipe, the cost of permanent-set systems has been lowered, and with more refined sprinkler heads, their reliability has been increased.

Underground permanent-set systems are, of course, more easily installed before the yard is planted. The grounds should be thoroughly soaked and packed several times to make certain the soil has completely settled before any pipes are installed. If the soil settles after installation, the results will be either a broken pipe at the point of settling or pipes that cannot be completely drained. The installation of an underground sprinkler system requires considerable knowledge and expertise, and the homeowner should hire only well-established, experienced personnel to do the job. Complete water coverage is important and not always easy to achieve. In addition, any low spot that prevents a system from being completely drained will result in broken pipes if water freezes in them during the winter. It is possible for homeowners who are skilled to install their own systems, but before beginning, they should get the assistance and advice of an expert.

Permanent overhead sprinkler systems are being installed in commercial orchards in some areas and may be feasible for larger garden plantings. They not only supply the amount of water required whenever it is needed, but they also help control mites and small insects, provide a means of applying pesticides and fertilizers, and provide a measure of frost protection (see Chapter 7).

Some of the advantages of sprinkler irrigation are that it can be used on land that is not level, it requires less water than does surface irrigation, and it removes dust from the plant canopy. In some arid-area gardens, sprinkler irrigation may also help prevent crop injury from soil surface concentrations of salt, described earlier in the "Damage to Farm and Garden from Dissolved Chemicals" section of this chapter. Because the water from sprinkler irrigation initially soaks downward over the entire surface and, with careful monitoring, does not wet the lower soil profile, less salt is dissolved, and what is dissolved is more evenly distributed throughout the upper soil layers. This makes plant injury less likely than with furrow irrigation, in which the soaking is much deeper and the salt tends to be concentrated at the center of the planting bed.

The disadvantages of sprinkler irrigation are the cost of equipment for distributing the water, the greater chance of foliar disease, and the likelihood of uneven distribution when it is windy.

Trickle Irrigation

A relatively new system of irrigation, referred to as **drip** or **trickle irrigation,** has received considerable publicity. Increased crop growth and yield and the saving of one-half to two-thirds of the irrigation water normally used by other systems are claimed for trickle irrigation. Furthermore, because less water is required, the salt buildup is reduced and more brackish irrigation water can be used. With this system a trickle of water is discharged continuously near each plant. For fruit trees, small fruits, ornamental trees and shrubs, and greenhouse pots, a small plastic tube attached to a larger feeder line supplies each plant or pot. For row crops, perforated plastic pipes, either on the soil surface or buried, are more commonly used. Fertilizers and soil pesticides can be applied through the trickle system as they can through sprinklers. With the trickle system, however, it is possible to keep a constant dilute flow of mineral elements and even of some pesticides, a practice not possible with sprinklers because of the volume of water that a sprinkler applies.

The trickle system has proved successful in greenhouses and other plant-growing structures and shows considerable promise with grapes and tree fruits (Figure 6-10). Trickle irrigation is being used in the American Southwest, where water for irrigation is limited and what is available usually has a high salt content. Because less irrigation water is applied, this concept may become useful for irrigated areas where rising water tables are causing drainage problems.

Care of the Irrigation System

All irrigation systems require proper maintenance if water is to be distributed efficiently. Permanent-set sprinkler systems should be checked for leaks and repaired during the early spring. Hoses, sprinklers, pipes, and all other equipment should also be examined and repaired if necessary before the irrigating season begins. A drop of oil on moving parts helps ensure good sprinkler operation. Unlined ditches and canals must be kept free of weeds and trash because these materials slow water flow, allowing the loss of water by seepage through canal banks, as well as unwanted moisture in fields adjacent to the canal. Weeds along open ditches should be controlled by mowing or with chemicals, and seed screens should be installed in the stream to prevent weed seed and other debris

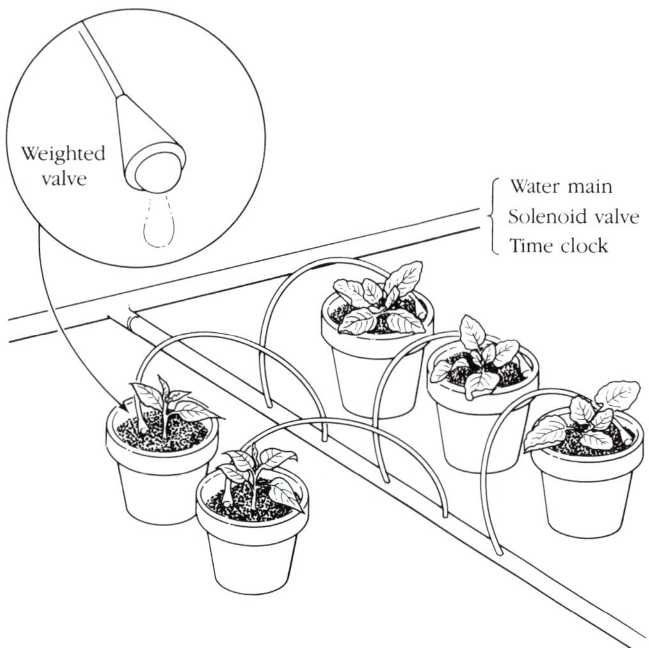

FIGURE 6-10 • Trickle irrigation system for greenhouse watering. The system is supplied from the water main of the home or greenhouse. A solenoid valve controlled by a time clock permits flexibility in timing the water application. Weighted valves connected to small plastic tubes that fit into small holes in the plastic distribution pipe are placed in the plant containers to control the amount of water each plant receives. (Adapted from Jules Janick, *Horticultural Science*, 4th ed., W. H. Freeman and Company, New York, copyright © 1985)

from contaminating the garden or plugging the distribution system.

Irrigation pipes should be moved with care so that dirt and debris do not get into them. All gaskets and moving parts of pipes, hoses, and sprinklers should be examined periodically, and worn or damaged parts replaced. Rubber and plastic hoses will last longer if they are stored out of direct sunlight, and hose fittings are less likely to be damaged by being accidently stepped on or driven over with the lawn mower or other vehicles if they are stored when not in use. Damaged fittings on rubber hoses can be easily replaced with a pocket knife and hammer. A supply of male and female replacement couplings and of hose gaskets kept with garden tools enables a quick repair of wasteful and annoying leaks. A small cut in a rubber or plastic hose can be repaired with electricians' tape, but when leaks due to weathering begin to develop, the hose is usually worn out and should be discarded. Small leaks in aluminum pipe can be repaired with "liquid aluminum," a paste material formulated for patching aluminum and available at department and hardware stores.

Before sprinkler pipes or hoses are stored for winter, they should be drained and dried completely. I usually place a drop of light oil on all moving parts of the sprinkler to prevent corrosion, although this is not always recommended by manufacturers because of the dust that sticks to oil. Permanent-set sprinkler systems should be drained completely and pumps winterized according to the manufacturer's instructions.

Frequency and Amount of Irrigation

Most frequently, the past experience of the grower determines when irrigation water should be applied. As mentioned earlier, plants that need moisture change color slightly. With experience, a grower can tell by this change in color and by the feel of the soil when water is required.

For lawns and crops covering the soil surface, pan evaporation is sometimes used to determine when to irrigate. This method is based on the fact that approximately the same amount of water evaporates from a pan as is transpired from foliage. In some irrigated areas the weather bureau informs the public via radio each morning of the amount of evaporation that has occurred during the previous twenty-four hours.

There are a number of different meters for measuring soil moisture, most based on the fact that dry soil has more electrical resistance than does moist soil. The electric current passing through the soil between two electrodes in a moisture probe or moisture block can be transposed to read directly the percentage of available moisture. Because accurate probes are expensive and difficult to calibrate and interpret, they are not used extensively by gardeners.

The amount of water required by garden plants varies depending on the plant, the plant's stage of growth, the season, humidity, wind, and other climatic factors. Despite the variation in water requirement from crop to crop, it is possible to recommend general guidelines for garden irrigation.

There is some evidence to indicate that roots are able to absorb moisture equally well from soil with a moisture content ranging from field capacity to wilting point. However, because moisture may not move rapidly within the soil, those soil particles next to the absorbing rootlets may be at the wilting point long before a soil sample shows complete available moisture depletion. Therefore, it is recommended that most horticultural crops be irrigated when 35 to 50 percent of the available moisture remains in the soil. In a medium-textured loam this is about the stage of dryness at which the soil particles are too crumbly to stick together when a handful is compressed. This squeeze test can be used also to determine the correct amount of water to add to potting soil or the range of soil moistness over which trouble-free cultivation is possible. The handful of soil should stick together in a ball when it is squeezed, but crumble readily when it is sifted through the fingers. If the compressed soil remains in a sticky ball, it is too wet for potting or cultivating.

Irrigating on a regular schedule of every five, seven, or ten days is a common practice, especially in arid parts of the country where irrigating throughout the growing season is imperative and irrigation water is usually available at fixed intervals. Irrigating on a regular schedule throughout the season is not always wise, however. Besides wasting water, overirrigation can leach nutrients, injure plants by reducing root aeration, and cause erosion. Irrigation needs to be more frequent on light sandy than on heavy clay soils. Plants use less water during the early part of the season when they are small and the weather is cool than they do during midsummer. Deep-rooted crops need to be irrigated less often than do shallow-rooted ones, and of course, deep-rooted crops should receive more water with each irrigation. As the temperature becomes cooler toward fall and as the crop matures, irrigation can be reduced.

In areas where irrigation supplements rainfall, it is important for growers to keep track of the amount of rain. Light showers often appear to supply more moisture than they actually do, and plants may suffer moisture stress even when showers are frequent. Moreover, plants on the leeward side of a building or under a roof overhang require supplemental water even during periods of heavy rain (see "Irrigating Garden Crops" in Chapter 14).

Gardening with Limited Water

For want of sufficient water, some North American gardeners who dream of growing a shady vista garden with broad green lawns bordered with exotic plants that originated in the rainy forests of Europe and east Asia find the realization of their dream impossible. Yet even in areas where rainfall is sparse and water for irrigation is unavailable, limited, or prohibitively expensive, gardening is still possible and may be even more interesting than traditional gardening because it is more of a challenge. Owing to recent widespread droughts and the growth of cities in arid regions there has developed considerable interest in using drought-tolerant plants for home and public plantings. The term **xeriscapes** has been coined to refer to these kinds of plantings.

Gardeners with limited water should, first, consider using native plants and inanimate materials. Some kind of plant cover grows almost everywhere, and the skillful use of this local flora combined with stone, driftwood, desert-bleached tree trunks, and other materials from the surrounding area can create an aesthetically appealing garden that requires no supplemental water. Cactus and succulent gardens, popular in many areas, are uniquely suitable where water is limited. **Succulents** are a group of plants belonging to several genera that can withstand periods of drought because they are capable of storing water in their greatly thickened leaves. Desert juniper, pinyon, yucca, sagebrush, potentilla, and other desert brush are interesting possibilities for desert gardens.

In regions with slightly more natural moisture, Douglas fir, ponderosa pine, Oregon grape, chokecherry, serviceberry, and other plants with localized distribution can be added to the list. These plants should be given the space in the garden that they have in nature, where they grow with little competition.

Because a thrifty lawn requires more water than most other plantings, eliminating the lawn should be considered wherever water for gardening is limited (see Figure 6-11; Chapter 11; and "Mulching with Plastic" in Chapter 14).

Fruits, vegetables, and flowers grown in arid areas require supplemental water, but they can be grown with much less water than is usually used. Because of the high rate of transpiration of weeds, complete weed control saves more water than any other practice and should be the first and foremost consideration wherever conserving water is essential. Similarly, no cover crop, weedy or otherwise,

FIGURE 6-11 • A xeriscape in Arizona. (Courtesy of Robert E. Lyons)

should be grown around tree or small fruit plantings in minimum moisture conditions. If erosion control is needed, a plastic, straw, sawdust, or bark mulch may be used to cover bare soil. Mulch also discourages weed growth and reduces evaporation.

Wide plant spacing permits the production of crops with less water. Sweet corn plants spaced at 3 × 3 or 4 × 4 feet (approximately 1 m × 1 m) produce good ears with surprisingly little moisture, especially if they are growing in clay loam soil high in organic matter. Short-season annuals, such as lettuce, radishes, spinach, peas, spring flowers produced from bulbs, pansies, bearded iris, asparagus, and rhubarb, can often be produced before moisture is depleted in the spring.

Where there is growing space for two gardens, summer fallowing — that is, growing a crop every other year and keeping the ground plant free during alternate years — may be a way to provide two years of moisture for one year of growth of some vegetables and flowers. During the year that it remains fallow, the plot can be covered with straw, peat, decomposed leaves, or other mulching material. Additional nitrogen fertilizer can be added to the mulch, which can then be plowed under to provide organic matter during the season of production.

Drainage

Getting rid of excess water is called **drainage,** and good drainage is as essential to successful gardening as is supplemental irrigation (Figure 6-12). Although tropical paddy crops, including rice and taro, thrive in water-saturated soils, most garden plants grow well only in well-aerated soil. The role of poor drainage in the development of nonproductive alkali soils in arid regions was discussed earlier in this chapter (see "Damage to Farm and Garden from Dissolved Chemicals").

Problems with excess water are most easily avoided by providing drainage at the time the home and landscape are planned. A tile drain embedded in gravel or cinders should be placed along the footing of the lowest level of the home to

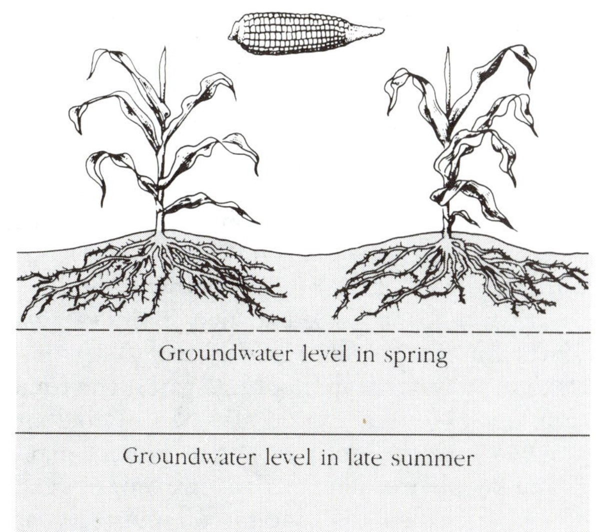

Poorly drained land

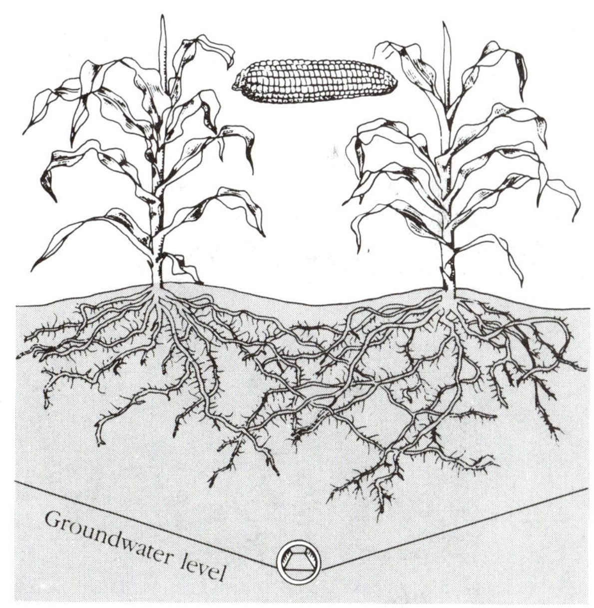

Tile-drained land

FIGURE 6-12 • The importance of good drainage. Plant roots cannot spread in a soil that is wet nearly to the surface. If the water table falls because of summer drought, the shallow-rooted crop will "burn up." (Courtesy of USDA)

prevent water from accumulating against the foundation and seeping in (Figure 6-13). The tile should drain into an open field, ditch, or storm sewer located below the level of the house footings.

For good drainage of the yard's surface, it is best if the house sits slightly above the level of the street and for the yard to be graded so that it slopes toward the street. If the house is below street level, the yard should be graded so that it slopes away from the foundation for at least 10 feet (3 m) on all sides to keep water from pooling against the foundation. Eave troughs should also be installed and channeled into the storm sewer to protect plantings and people from heavy rains streaming off the roof and to lessen the amount of moisture that might otherwise build up against foundations.

The yard should be graded so that water can drain from every part of its surface. If low spots are unavoidable, they should be tile drained, as should areas that remain damp or boggy for long periods after precipitation. Areas requiring special drainage are prevalent in the regions that have undergone glaciation in the northern United States and Canada.

If there is no way to channel drainage water into a lower-elevation storm sewer or field and if the soil strata are suitable, a dry well may get rid of

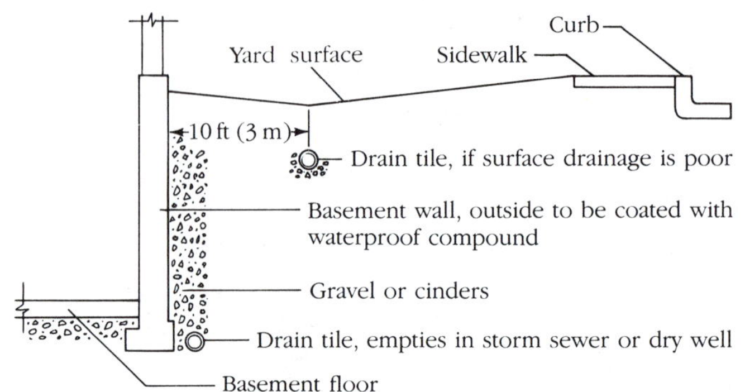

FIGURE 6-13 • Leveling a front yard where the foundation is below street level.

the unwanted water. A dry well is a hole several feet in diameter and deep enough to penetrate the impervious subsoil layer and reach at least 4 or 5 feet (about 1 to 1 ½ m) below the lowest level tile drain. Ideally, the lowest end should terminate in a sandy or gravelly soil layer through which moisture can rapidly drain away (see Figure 6-14).

Perforated fiber pipes are usually the most convenient for channeling water from the tile drains to the dry well. A few inches of gravel on the bottom of the trench in which the perforated pipes are laid further facilitate drainage. The well should be filled to within 18 to 24 inches (45 to 60

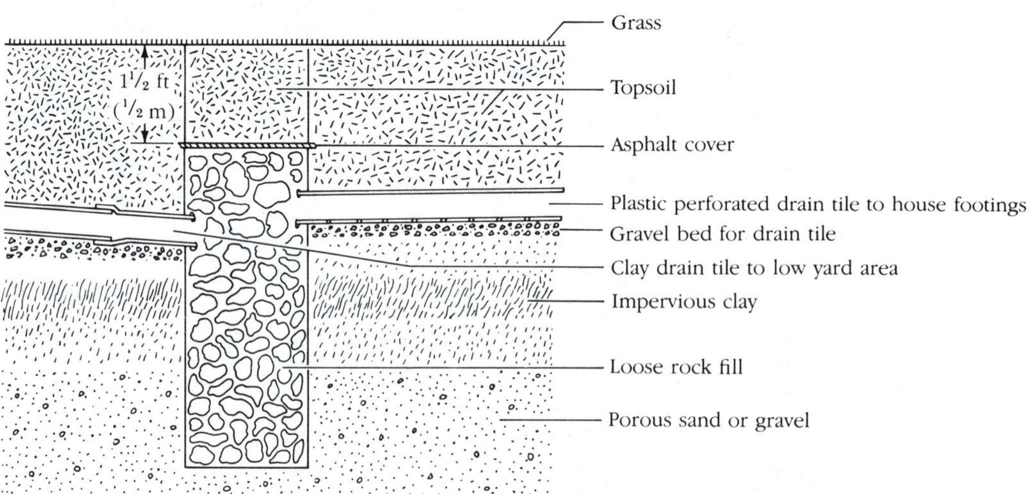

FIGURE 6-14 • Cross section of a dry well located in soil strata ideal for such a structure.

cm) of the top with rock, gravel, or other solid permanent material to provide pore space to accommodate large quantities of water. The dry well is a good place to get rid of unwanted rock, pieces of cement, or other solid nonorganic wastes that accumulate around a building site. Scraps of lumber and other organic material should not be used, as these decompose and cause the surface to settle. A heavy plastic or asphalt cover should be placed over the loose rock fill. The cover can then be topped with soil that can be used for lawn or other plantings.

 Selected References

California Polytechnic State University. *Landscape Irrigation Maintenance and Troubleshooting* and *Xeriscape—Appropriate Landscaping to Conserve Water.* San Luis Obispo: Vocational Education Productions Videos, California Polytechnic State University.

Hansen, V. E., and G. E. Stringham. *Irrigation Principles and Practices.* 4th ed. New York: Wiley, 1980.

Leopold, L. B. *Water: A Primer.* New York: Freeman, 1974.

Stern, P. H. *The Operation and Maintenance of Small Irrigation Schemes.* New York: Intermediate Tech, 1988.

Stewart, B. A., and D. R. Neilsen. *Irrigation of Agricultural Crops.* Madison, Wis.: American Society of Agronomy, 1990.

Toro Corporation. *Toro Landscape Irrigation Series—Elements of Residential Design; Residential Installation Techniques.* Minneapolis: VHS Videos, Toro Mfg. Co., 1989.

Climate, Temperature, and Light

Tomatoes and cucumbers are more likely to mature at Fort Vermilion in northern Alberta than along the coast of Washington. Summers are cooler in much of central Africa than they are in our own Midwest. Sweet corn matures in Siberia in about two-thirds the time it requires in Brazil. Both sunburn and bright red apples are more likely in the intermountain valleys of the West than they are along the East Coast. Location within the yard determines survival and earliness of many garden crops.

The importance of heat and light in photosynthesis is understood by most plant growers. Not so well understood, however, are the profound effects of moderate variations of either temperature or light on photosynthesis and on other plant growth processes. These effects, illustrated by the preceding examples, are discussed in this chapter.

CLIMATE AND HORTICULTURE

Temperature and light are two fundamental aspects of climate. Wind, clouds, rain, hail, snow, and humidity (all of which relate to the moisture cycle described in Chapter 6) are, along with elevation, latitude, and location relative to large bodies of water, some of the many factors that determine climate. The climate of a specific area in the earth's temperate zones varies from day to day, from season to season, and from year to year, and it can vary quite dramatically even in areas only a few miles apart. Nevertheless, climatologists are able to calculate statistical probabilities of certain climatic occurrences likely to affect crop and garden plant performance. Most of these statistics are compiled by and available from the national weather bureaus of the United States and Canada.

Weather Bureau Services

Because the weather affects so many industries and is so important to everyone, most governments maintain a weather-monitoring service. Weather stations are in operation in thousands of locations in every state of the United States and every province of Canada. They vary in size and complexity from a covered box housing a thermometer where someone reads daily high and low temperatures to multibuilding complexes where trained climatologists monitor space satellites, track hurricanes, make short- and long-range forecasts, and analyze long-term climatic trends.

Weather bureau information of particular interest to home gardeners includes short-term weather forecasts; frost and foul weather warnings; amount of evaporation; wind velocity; cumulative precipitation; and monthly, annual, and long-term climatic summaries.

The value of short-term forecasts and foul weather and wind warnings is apparent to North Americans. The uses of evaporation data were discussed in Chapter 6. Not so familiar are the monthly, annual, and long-term area weather summaries. These summaries, available at most large libraries and from weather bureau offices, give the average date of the last spring and first fall frost; the average date during spring and fall of other temperatures near the freezing point; high, low, and mean temperatures for each day and month; long-term average daily and monthly precipitation; record high and low temperatures and precipitation; average number of hours of sunlight; day length; evaporation; wind velocity; and much more.

Few garden sites have exactly the same weather as does a weather station; temperatures may be a few degrees colder or warmer and precipitation a little more or less. Nevertheless, these statistics can be useful when deciding what to plant, when to plant, when to irrigate, and the timing of other gardening activities. Long-term weather statistics for many locations in North America are included in Table 14-27.

Macroclimate

The term climate refers to long-term weather patterns. The climate of fairly broad geographical areas is referred to as **macroclimate,** and that of more restricted areas—community, backyard, hillside, and the like—is called **microclimate.** Macroclimate is determined by the intensity and quality of solar radiation reaching the surface of the earth; the quantity of the radiation remaining in the surface layers of the atmosphere as heat and light energy; and modifications of the impact of this energy by proximity to large bodies of water, by ocean and wind currents, and by topographical features such as mountains, forests, and irrigation projects. These factors affect not only temperature and light intensity but also precipitation patterns and moisture cycle.

Temperature is inversely correlated with latitude. The farther a particular place is from the equator, the cooler the average annual temperature becomes, because the sun's rays strike the earth more directly near the equator and, as a consequence, are filtered and scattered by less atmosphere. This concept may be easier to comprehend if one thinks of the earth as similar to a grapefruit with the atmosphere as the peel. A cut directed toward the center of the grapefruit goes through less skin than an oblique cut that slices off one corner (Figure 7-1).

The greatest amount of heat is retained at the earth's surface, where there is the greatest amount of overlying atmosphere to absorb it and to prevent its being radiated back into space. This retention of heat by the atmosphere is called the

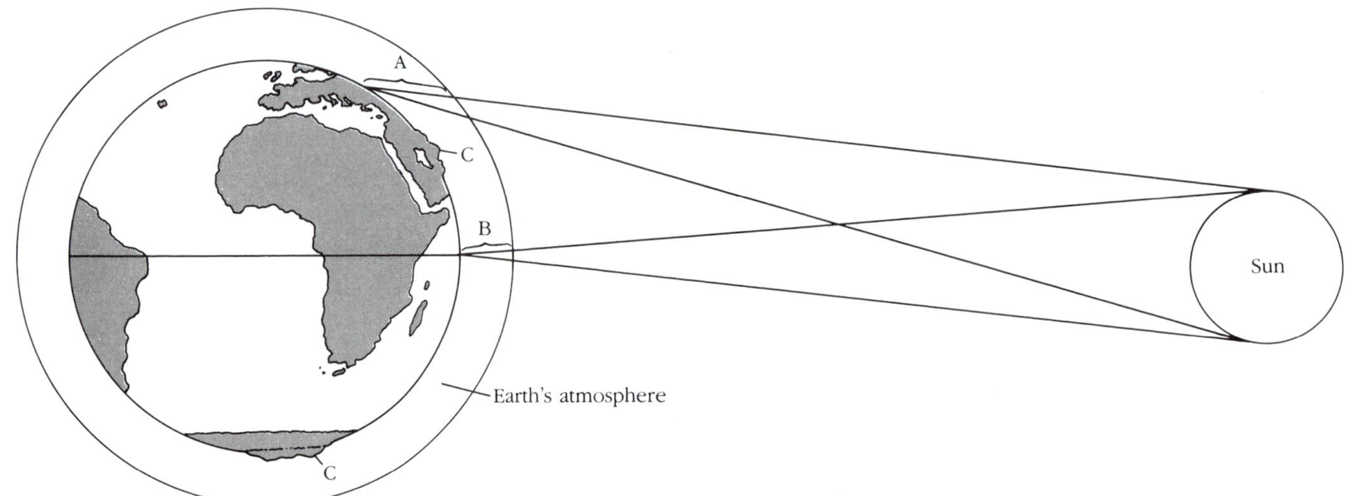

FIGURE 7-1 • The correlation of temperature and latitude. The sun's rays are filtered by more atmosphere when they strike the earth at an oblique angle (A) than when they strike it directly (B). Similarly, there is less atmosphere to filter the sun's rays above mountain ranges (C) but also less atmosphere to absorb and retain heat. Both the height of the mountain range and the thickness of the atmosphere are greatly exaggerated in this illustration.

greenhouse effect because it is the same phenomenon that warms greenhouses on sunny days (Figure 7-2). Radiant energy entering through the glass is converted to heat energy, which is prevented by the glass from escaping. The greenhouse effect of the atmosphere is greatly enhanced by certain larger gaseous molecules, notably water vapor and carbon dioxide. The accelerating release into the atmosphere of carbon dioxide from the combustion of fossil fuels is the basis of the highly publicized prediction of global warming. Because of the greenhouse effect, temperature is inversely correlated with elevation, each 300-foot rise in elevation usually meaning a 1°F drop in temperature. Differences in elevation account for the extreme temperature variations in geographically adjacent mountain-valley locations. This explains, for example, why an hour's drive from Denver or Salt Lake City with their dry, relatively mild climates can end at slopes where virtually year-round skiing is possible.

Altitude also affects the amount and quality of solar energy reaching the earth's surface. At higher elevations fewer of the ultraviolet and short rays are scattered and filtered because the sunlight passes through less atmosphere. A thinner atmosphere absorbs and retains less heat, which is why at high altitudes it is hot and bright in direct sunlight but cool in the shade, on rainy days, and during the night. This is also why at high altitudes heat is radiated out of the atmosphere so rapidly after sunset, making late spring and early fall frosts more common.

Ocean currents affect nearby landmasses. The Gulf Stream is noted mainly for warming the climate of Europe, but it also warms the southeastern United States. The Labrador Current cools eastern Canada and New England, and currents from the Gulf of Alaska cool the Pacific Coast south to Monterey, California. Climatic extremes are also moderated by large bodies of water. Summers are cooler, winters warmer, and late spring freezes less

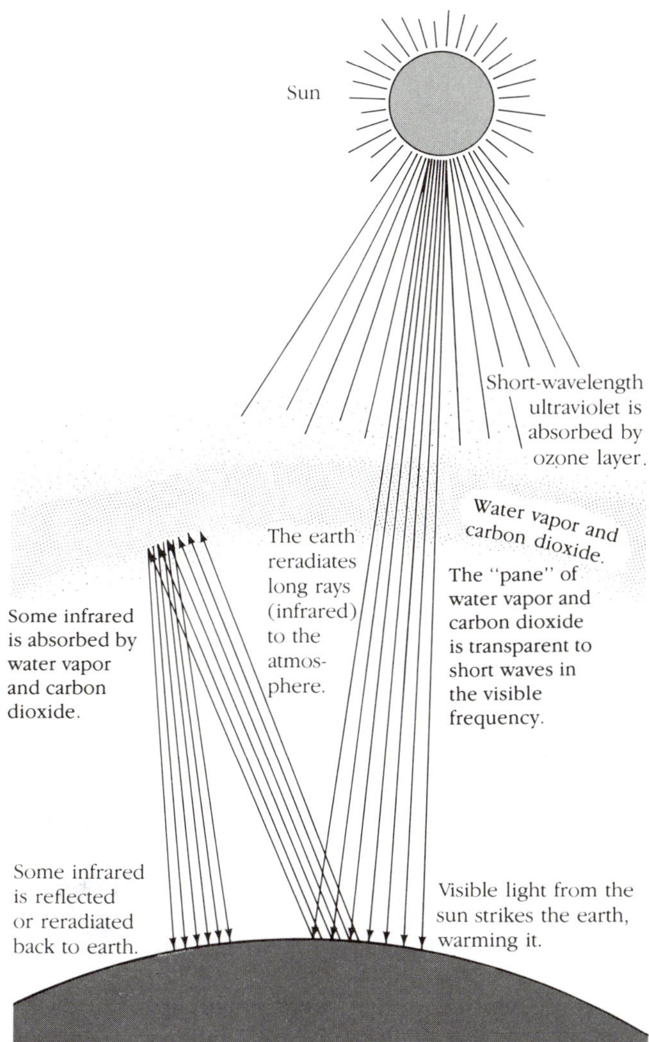

FIGURE 7-2 • The greenhouse effect.

likely near an ocean or a large lake than they are at the same latitude and altitude farther from a body of water.

Water affects freezing in two ways. Many times more heat energy is required to raise the temperature of water than to raise the temperature of air, and water releases large amounts of heat energy when it cools. Thus water acts as a heat or cold buffer, tending to moderate the rise and fall of temperatures of land areas nearby. During daylight hours in early spring, water is likely to be cooler than land, so wind blowing over a body of water cools the temperature of the land nearby, thereby delaying the bloom of fruit trees and ornamentals. During a frosty night, however, the temperature of water is likely to be considerably warmer than that of land, and plants growing near a body of water are not so likely to freeze as are those growing farther from it (Figure 7-3). This is the reason for the extensive fruit plantings on the leeward sides of the Great Lakes in Ontario, Michigan, Ohio, and New York.

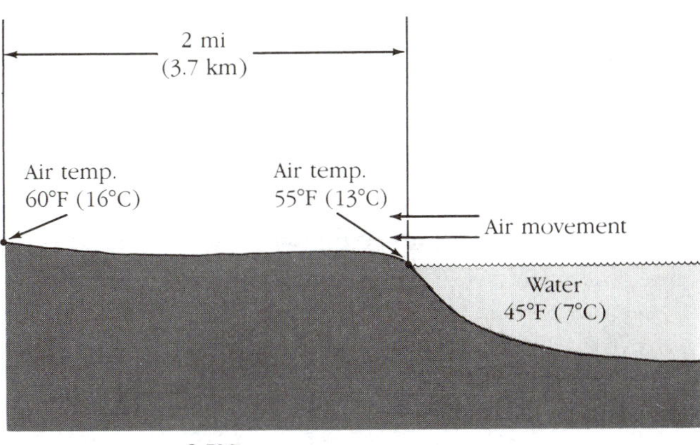

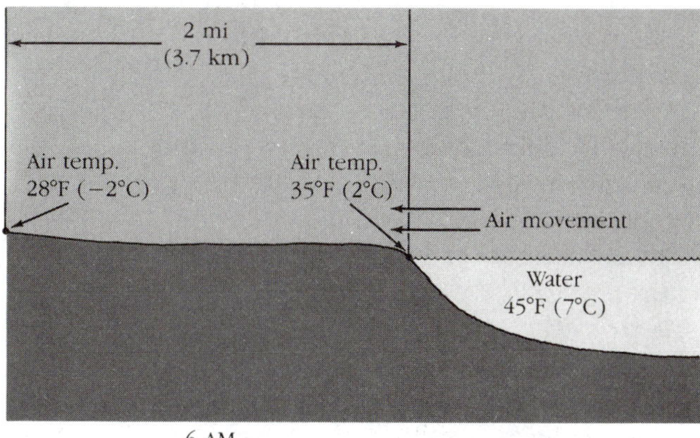

FIGURE 7-3 • Water as a temperature buffer. A body of water cools nearby areas during warm days and warms them during frosty mornings.

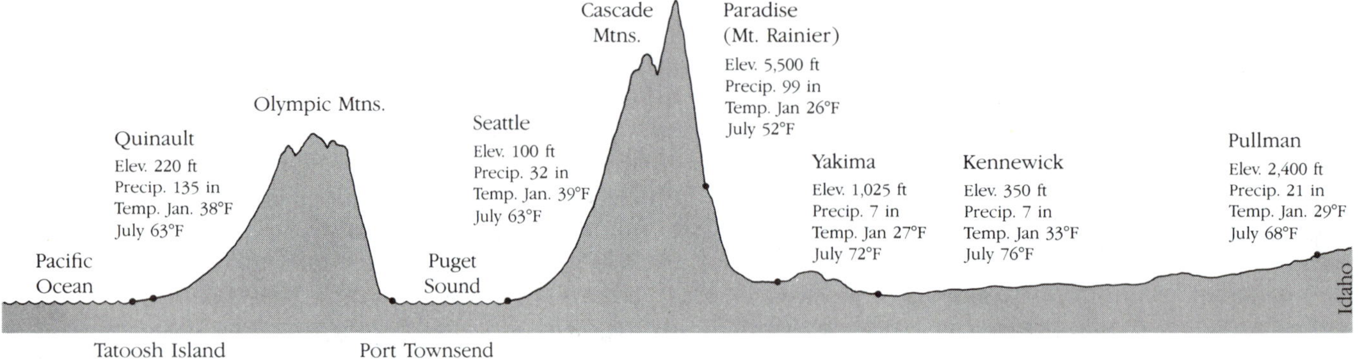

FIGURE 7-4 • Effect of the Pacific Ocean and the Olympic and Cascade mountain ranges on the climate of Washington State.

Mountain ranges have a profound effect on the moisture and temperature of nearby areas. At the latitude that includes the continental United States and southern Canada, the air of the prevailing westerly winds tends to drop its moisture as it cools when rising over the western slopes and to take up moisture as it warms when dropping down the eastern slopes. Thus some of the wettest and driest areas of the continent are found within a few miles of each other on the windward and leeward sides of the Coast and Cascade mountains that intercept moisture from Pacific storms. Mountain ranges also prevent the climate-ameliorating effect of the ocean from extending as far inland as it might otherwise, but they frequently divert winds enough to prevent Arctic fronts or severe storms from reaching protected areas (Figure 7-4). Because of the western mountains, moisture and air currents modified by the Pacific do not reach as far inland in North America as moisture and air currents modified by the Atlantic reach in Europe; however, the Sierra Nevada prevent cold air from the Great Basin from spilling into California's Central Valley, and similarly, the northern Rockies usually protect the valleys of British Columbia and the Pacific Northwest from the bitter winter winds of the Great Plains and the dry summer winds of the southwestern deserts.

Forest and brush cover also affect climate. Forested areas have a higher humidity. The recent reforestation of land denuded for thousands of years in the Mediterranean region is reported to have increased precipitation in nearby areas. Shrub and forest covers also increase water infiltration and lower runoff, which can be beneficial by preventing erosion as well as detrimental by reducing the amount of water available for irrigating nearby lowland areas.

Human activities also modify climate. Extensive reservoirs and irrigation projects increase precipitation along the paths of prevailing winds blowing over them. Metropolitan areas are warmed by combustion and other heat-producing activities, and also may have more cloudy weather and more precipitation because dust and other particulate matter released by auto exhausts and factory smokestacks provide a nucleus around which moisture can condense.

Microclimate

In contrast to macroclimate, which encompasses a fairly large geographical area, **microclimate** refers to climatic variations existing at different locations in a community or even within a single yard as the result of topographic features, direction of slope, or location of buildings or plantings. The location of a yard in relation to surrounding topographic features affects livability, especially outdoor enjoyment, and also determines to an extent what plant species can be successfully grown. A south slope, for example, warms earlier in the spring but may be hotter during the summer; the leeward side of a ridge is less subject to wind and may receive less precipitation, which may or may not be desirable; and hillside locations are less subject to frosts than are the valleys below them.

As mentioned earlier, temperature generally decreases as elevation increases. This is true during the day even for slight increases in elevation. It may not be true, however, for sloping areas during a still night when cold air, which is heavier than warm air, is likely to flow downhill and settle to the bottom of valleys and depressions. Under these conditions there occurs what is known as a **temperature inversion,** in which slopes may be several degrees warmer than depressions below them. For this reason orchards are frequently planted on hillsides and not in valleys or "frost pockets" (Figure 7-5). This also explains why home sites on hillsides are less subject to frosts than are those lower down and why planting frost-susceptible crops at the higher-elevated end of a sloping yard may afford those crops the one or two degrees of warmer temperature necessary for them to escape spring and fall freezing.

Buildings modify microclimate, making temperatures near a building warmer during cool weather. Shade-loving plants can be planted on the north side of buildings in the north temperate zone. If the climate is cool, melons and tomatoes will mature earlier, and grapevines are more likely to ripen a crop and survive if they are planted on the south side of a building. Special attention to watering should be given to plants growing under a roof overhang that shields them from rainfall.

A homeowner can also take steps to modify both the indoor and the outdoor microclimate. A wide roof overhang blocks hot rays from entering a south window when the summer sun is high in the sky but permits them to enter during the winter when the sun is lower (Figure 7-6). A deciduous tree planted on the south side of a house has a similar effect, providing shade during the summer but permitting the sun's rays to filter through during the winter when the leaves have fallen. The home and outdoor living areas can be oriented to take advantage of views, spring sunshine, and cooling breezes or to block cold winds. Planting windbreaks and constructing fences also can create a more desirable microclimate around the home.

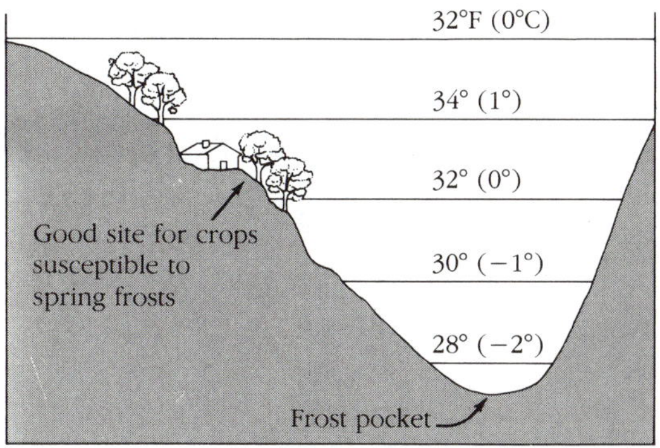

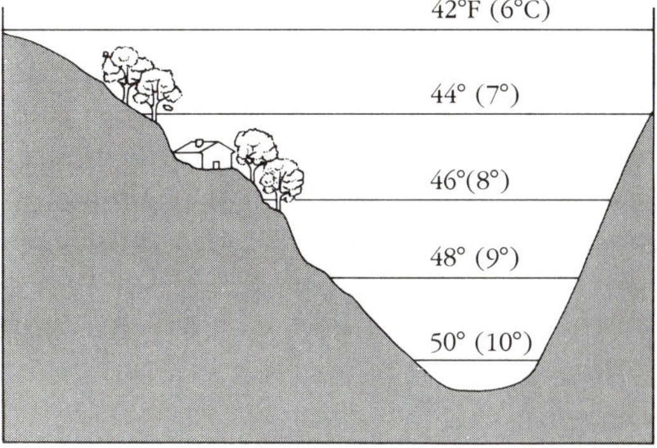

FIGURE 7-5 • Temperature differential with elevation. A homesite on a sloping area above a depression is less susceptible to damage from early spring frosts than is a site in the bottom of a valley.

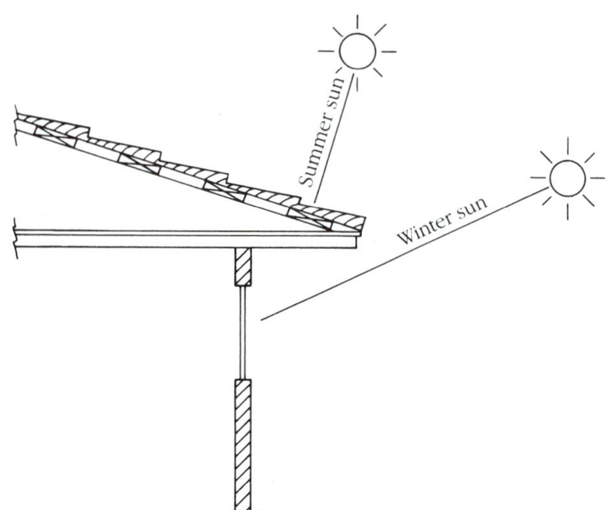

FIGURE 7-6 • Using a roof overhang to modify temperature.

PLANT ADAPTATION TO CLIMATE AND OTHER FACTORS OF THE ENVIRONMENT

Most gardeners recognize that a particular species of plant does well in either a tropical or a temperate-zone climate because that species cannot withstand frost or because it needs a cold period of dormancy to complete its life cycle. However, not even the most learned plant scientist fully understands the many factors related to the adaptation of a plant species to a particular environment. Some species are widely adapted to grow almost anywhere: Many troublesome weeds have this wide degree of adaptation. Other species have a very narrow environmental adaptation, sometimes able to grow only in a restricted valley or seacoast area.

In early June just above the Black Sea in eastern Turkey, one can observe two ribbons of color, one yellow and the other lavender, stretching along the mountains at the same elevation for as far as the eye can see. These colors are produced by two different species of blooming rhododendrons. Each of the species is the dominant vegetation for several hundred yards of mountainside, rising perhaps 50 to 100 feet of elevation. There is a line of demarcation where the two species are contiguous, but there is only a slight overlapping area in which both species are found. Also, the upper and lower limits of dominance are well defined with almost no rhododendrons above or below the vivid yellow and lavender ribbon of color.

The reasons for restricted species adaptation, as observed in the Turkish rhododendrons, are not always easy to determine. Temperature is obviously a major factor in plant adaptation. Fortunately, most crop plants grown in the temperate regions are adapted to a fairly broad range of temperatures. There are, however, many species of plants that can survive only in a very narrow temperature range. This is especially true for plants like some orchid species originating in areas near the equator where the average weekly temperature does not vary more than a degree or two during the entire year.

Moisture, including precipitation, humidity, and the annual cycle of wet/dry seasons, is a second obvious factor in plant adaptation. Cacti are adapted to survive for long periods without moisture. Some desert annuals have seeds that germinate only after enough moisture has fallen to enable them to complete their abbreviated life cycle before that moisture is depleted. Date palms pollinate when the atmosphere is very dry, so dates can be produced only where date palms flower during a dry season. Water lilies and most aroids survive only when their roots are covered with water, a condition that would be fatal to most other plants.

Plants and Other Living Organisms

The relationship of plant adaptation to the presence of pollinator insects and predator insects and diseases and the association of leguminous plant roots to rhizobium bacteria in atmospheric nitrogen fixation (Figure 5-6) have been known for many years. Only recently, however, have plant scientists begun to realize the extent and importance of the interrelationships of living organisms in plant growth and adaptation. Mycorrhizae—the fungal mycelia long known to grow in association with the roots of certain large tree species—are now thought to be necessary for most plants, enabling their host species better to exploit the surrounding soil for nutrients and moisture and, in some instances, to better resist soil-borne diseases and insects. Insect and pathogen attacks often elicit a chemical response that makes the victimized plant a less desirable food source for the attacker. Flower color is an important attractant for pollinators, as is the sweet scent of flowers pollinated by bees and the fetid scent of those pollinated by flies.

Some plants excrete volatile substances and other chemical compounds that affect other, nearby plants. The volatile substance that produces the odor of sagebrush inhibits the germination of seeds of other associated plants. Some garden plants do not grow well in fields where quackgrass (*Agropyron repens*) is present, and the aqueous solution obtained by soaking quackgrass rhizomes impedes the growth of such crop plants as sweet corn and radish. There also is accumulating evidence that the deleterious effects of other weeds on crops may come from "chemical warfare" as well as from their competition for light, moisture, and fertilizer.

Crop plants themselves can be inhibitory. Corn fodder that is not decomposed can suppress the germination and growth of several vegetables. Asparagus roots and crowns chemically reduce the growth not only of other, nearby crop plants but also of other asparagus plants growing in the vicinity. This suppression may last in a field for several years after the asparagus in that field has been destroyed. Many species of garden plants cannot grow under the canopy of black walnut (*Juglans nigra*) tree because of the phytotoxins it excretes.

A more complete understanding of the deleterious chemical interactions among plants, called allelopathy (see Chapter 5), and of other chemically related interactions among living organisms has tremendous potential for controlling diseases, insects, and weeds and for increasing production through better rotation and more compatible intercropping. An understanding of plant chemical relationships could reveal practical, science-based benefits of "companion planting," a practice endorsed by organic gardeners, which is currently of much less value than it could be if it were based on better-researched results.

TEMPERATURE

◆ ◆ ◆

Temperature is the climatic factor that, more than any other, determines the kinds of plants that can be grown in particular areas. Temperature affects the quality and maturity rate of garden products and is important to virtually all plant responses, including photosynthesis, transpiration, and respiration, all of which generally increase with a rise in temperature. Temperature also determines the kinds of pests likely to be troublesome; usually the warmer the temperature and the milder the winter, the more severe will be the plant disease and insect problems.

The optimal temperature for growth varies with different plants. Most temperate-zone vegetables and annual flowers are classified as cool-season crops, which germinate at temperatures as low as 40°F (4°C), or warm-season crops, most of which do not germinate until the soil temperature has reached about 60°F (16°C). For more detailed information on temperature and germination, see Chapter 4 and Table 14-3.

For most crop plants, both respiration and photosynthesis increase as temperature rises. But through the lower three-fourths of the growing-temperature range for any given species, the increase in photosynthesis is somewhat more rapid than is the increase in respiration. Thus the maximum growth rate occurs in the upper part of the temperature range through which the plant will grow.

Effects of Excessively High Temperature

The rate of photosynthesis continues to increase, but the rate of respiration accelerates more dramatically as the temperature rises through the upper one-fourth of the growing-temperature range, and eventually a point is reached at which the food utilized by respiration just equals the amount manufactured by photosynthesis, and growth ceases (see Figure 7-7). This upper temperature limit for growth varies from one species to another; for many crops it is about 96°F (36°C). In some locations, temperatures rise so high that there may be physiological damage to plants, which, among other things, stops photosynthesis. Thus one detrimental manifestation of excessively high temperatures is the cessation of plant growth.

Temperature and rate of respiration also have important implications for the transportation and storage of horticultural products. Once a plant is harvested, its food production via photosynthesis essentially ceases, while its food breakdown continues to be directly correlated with its rate of respiration. Thus seeds, which have a very low rate of respiration and much stored food, can remain alive for years. Potato tubers can be stored for long periods at low temperatures because their respiration rate is low, but leafy vegetables like lettuce and most floral crops, with high rates of respiration and minimal stored food, cannot be kept for long periods under even the most favorable conditions.

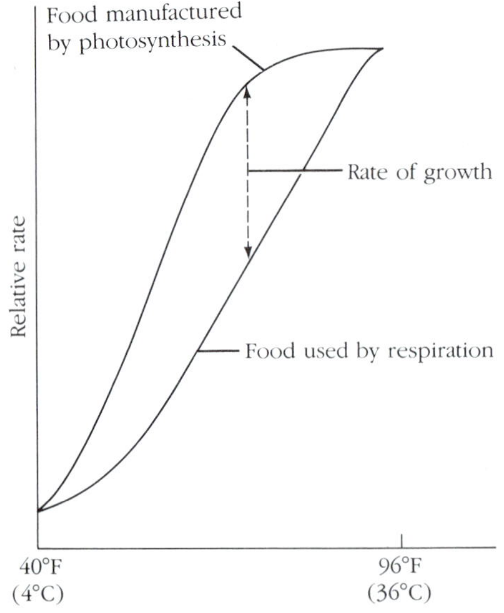

FIGURE 7-7 • Relationship of respiration, photosynthesis, and temperature to plant growth.

As with growing plants, the rate of respiration of stored products is directly correlated with temperature: Heat increases and cold decreases the respiration process. Furthermore, because heat is one of the by-products of respiration, respiration raises the temperature, and the higher temperature brings about more rapid respiration. The heat liberated by the respiration of tightly packed fruits or vegetables can have drastic consequences if refrigeration is not adequate or fails in the storage facility. Spoilage resulting from heat-induced deterioration and the rapid buildup of microorganisms can result within a few hours. Respiration also reduces stored carbohydrates. It is the sugars dissolved in cellular liquids, which provide natural sweetness and are the bases of flavor and quality of many fruits and vegetables, that are the first carbohydrates to be used. On a warm day a noticeable loss of sweetness can be detected only a few minutes after harvesting vegetables such as peas, asparagus, and sweet corn.

The relationships among temperature, respiration, loss of sugar, and storage have implications for the home gardener. Harvesting in the morning when the product is cool permits a longer retention of quality. Harvesting containers made of fibers, cloth, wood, or loosely woven materials are preferable to plastic bags or metal containers, because they permit air to circulate and the heat of respiration to dissipate. Flowers will last longer if they are cooled immediately after being gathered from the garden and if the arrangement is kept as cool as possible.

High temperatures prevent temperate-zone perennials from being grown in tropical and subtropical climates. In warm-winter areas, deciduous temperate-zone woody plants lose their leaves at the normal fall time. There is, however, too little cool weather to permit them to complete their physiological rest period. As a consequence, buds remain dormant, and leaves and blossoms form erratically or not at all during the following season. This is why apples and peaches are not grown extensively in southern Florida or in lowland areas of southern California.

Plant diseases and insect problems are likely to be more serious when temperatures are high, partly because plant pathogens and insects reproduce more rapidly during periods of high temperature and partly because a mild winter permits more than the normal carryover of insects and disease pathogens.

Effects of Low Temperature

Because so many horticultural plants are susceptible to frost and cold temperatures, most horticulturists are more concerned about temperatures too low for plant growth than they are about those too high. When temperatures are excessively cool, even though they may not be below freezing, plants do not grow, and seeds fail to germinate. Most species that originated in the tropics, including peppers, tomatoes, African violets, melons, and cucumbers, will be injured if the temperature drops much below 40°F (4°C) for any length of time.

Another problem attributable to cool temperature is the premature seed stalk formation (**bolting**) of biennial vegetables (Figure 7-8). The natural growth cycle of most biennial plants consists of vegetative growth during the first year, then winter dormancy concomitant with seed stalk initiation, followed by seed stalk formation the second summer. If for some reason temperatures are cool shortly after the crop is planted, the growth cycle will be compressed, and seed stalks are likely to be initiated during the first summer. Because biennial vegetables are grown for roots, petioles, or leaves rather than for seed, flowering and seed formation render them useless. Seed bolting often occurs when a crop such as celery is subjected to cool temperatures in order to condition it to withstand the shock of an adverse posttransplanting environment. Bolting can also occur if an unseasonably cool spring follows the planting and germination of a biennial crop.

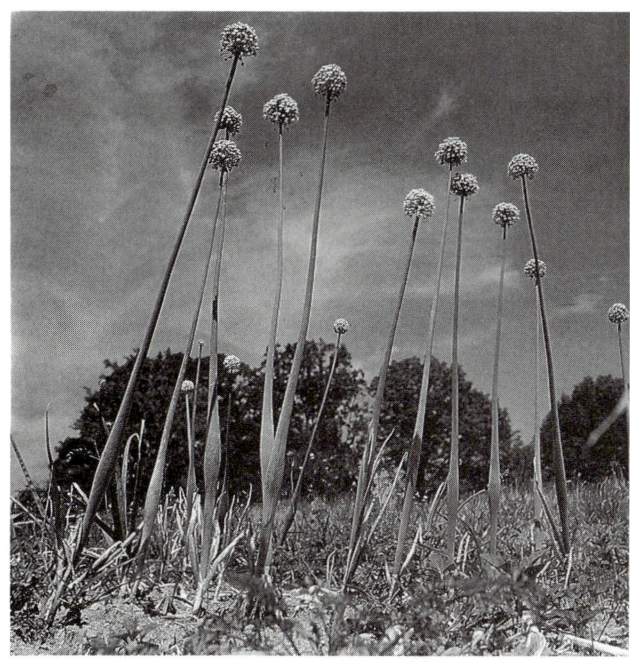

FIGURE 7-8 • Onions bolting. These year-old onions have produced seed stalks as a result of exposure to cold winter temperatures. (Courtesy of Walter Chandoha)

The temperature most significant for gardening is undoubtedly 32°F (0°C), the freezing point of water. The length of the growing season, the planting time for warm-season annual crops, and the harvest time of many garden products all are dependent on the spring and fall occurrence of this temperature.

Just as significant for the garden is the minimum temperature likely to occur during winter. Although most perennial plants that originated in cold climates can withstand some freezing during their dormant period, there is great variation in the conditioning necessary to enable them to tolerate freezing and the minimum temperature that they can be conditioned to withstand. The average minimum winter temperature determines to a large extent which perennial plants can be grown in a given area.

Tissue Freezing and Freezing Damage. The chronology of plant tissue freezing with the gradual lowering of ambient temperature typical of a frosty morning has been observed by many plant scientists. Tissue freezing begins with the formation of ice crystals in the spaces between cells. As more of the intercellular water becomes ice, water is drawn from inside the cell by osmosis, causing the membrane around the cytoplasm to shrink away from the cell wall and the intercellular ice crystals to enlarge. If the temperature becomes cold enough, the entire cell will eventually freeze. As the temperature warms after a freeze, cells of any tissue that was not killed can reabsorb water from the intercellular spaces and resume normal activity. Tissue damaged by freezing wilts because water transport (as well as all other functions) is disrupted. The death of plant tissues as a result of being frozen probably results from both the physical disruption brought about by ice formation and the physiological damage caused by the highly concentrated solution left in the shrunken protoplast.

Occasionally on an extremely still night, plants survive temperatures lower than they normally would because of a phenomenon called **supercooling.** What happens can be demonstrated by simultaneously lowering the temperature of a glass of water and keeping the water absolutely motionless. Under these conditions ice crystals do not form until the temperature falls several degrees below the freezing point. If, however, the supercooled water is moved slightly, ice will immediately form. Because of the possibility of supercooling, it is advisable to stay out of the garden after a frost until morning temperatures have risen well above the freezing point.

Freezing damage to plants occurs (1) from excessive cold during the winter, (2) from early spring or late fall frosts, or (3) from the dehydration of tissues during a time when the water supply cannot be replenished by the frozen root system (physiological drought is discussed in greater detail later in this chapter). Physical damage caused by the forces of winter also results from plants being pushed from the soil by alternate freezing and thawing (heaving) and from plants being broken by the sheer weight of ice or snow.

Damage from Winter Cold. During an occasional winter in almost every section of the United States and Canada, fruit trees and ornamentals are damaged by cold weather. It is often assumed that this damage occurs only when winter temperatures drop below the specific minimum that the plant species can tolerate. Actually, the physiological basis of cold temperature damage is complex and dependent on many variables, including the kind of plant, the part of the plant, the food and water resources in the plant tissue, the season of the year, the temperatures prior to the freeze, the rate of temperature drop, the temperature during the freeze, the temperature after the freeze, the amount of air movement, the moisture in the soil and in the plant tissue, and perhaps others.

Research has shown that most woody perennials have two distinct levels of cold tolerance: one that develops as a result of dormancy and does not depend on temperature and a second, acquired only after several days of freezing temperatures, that conditions them to withstand much colder weather. Woody plants gradually become cold tolerant in the fall after their leaves have been shed. Several weeks after leaf **abscission** (shedding) the plant achieves the maximum cold tolerance it will develop without being subjected to freezing temperatures. This innate tolerance enables it to withstand temperatures considerably below freezing even when the weather remains mild, but further cold tolerance (**temperature-induced hardiness**) will develop only if temperatures remain below freezing. The extent of this temperature-induced hardiness fluctuates with the temperature; it will be lost if temperatures rise for any length of time but will be regained if temperatures drop again before the buds start to swell.

Cold conditioning will be further discussed later in this chapter.

Plants are frequently damaged when the weather turns cold before they have achieved their maximum tolerance. In the Northwest on November 11, 1955, temperatures suddenly dropped to near 0°F (−18°C). The autumn that year had been mild, and leaves were still hanging on many fruit trees and ornamentals. About 80 percent of the orchards in the region sustained some damage, although a temperature drop to 0°F during the winter would normally cause no problem. Strawberry production was cut in half, and almost every homeowner lost some ornamentals. The injury occurred because plants were not hardened and prepared for such cold weather.

Horticultural crops are often damaged also by excessive cold during midwinter. Excessive cold may mean a few degrees below freezing in Florida and California or temperatures of −40° to −60°F (−40° to below −46°C) in the Upper Midwest, the Canadian provinces, and Alaska. During January 1969, also in the Northwest, temperatures dropped to record lows. Some thermometers in the vicinity of Pullman, Washington, recorded −50°F, which was almost 20° lower than any previously recorded minimum. Damage to orchards was extensive, and many species of ornamentals were killed outright. In native stands of ponderosa pine and grand fir, trees over one hundred years old segregated for hardiness. Some died immediately; some were damaged and remained unthrifty or died several years later; and others showed no ill effects. Although most plants were at maximum hardiness, they could not withstand this extreme cold.

The delayed appearance of damage due to cold is not unusual. During the 1950s, full-grown 'Baldwin' apple trees in some home gardens and in several commercial orchards in the Northeast began to break apart. In the Cornell University orchard in 1953 so many 'Baldwin' trees collapsed under their heavy fruit load that trees of the cultivar were considered too dangerous to harvest. A freeze in the early 1930s had killed enough tissue to permit decay fungi to become established. Although outwardly the trees grew normally, the interior supporting wood was gradually consumed by the fungi, resulting in the trees' sudden collapse twenty years later.*

Although there are some variations from cultivar to cultivar, each crop normally has a minimum temperature to which it can be hardened and below which it will be severely injured or killed. Apples, American and European plums, and sour cherries are the most hardy common tree fruits, and some cultivars will withstand temperatures of −30° to −40°F (−34° to −40°C) if conditions for maximum hardiness development have occurred. Peaches are the least hardy of the temperate-zone tree fruits, and peach buds are likely to be injured if the temperature drops below about −10° to −12°F (−23° to −24°C), and the trees will be killed if the temperature drops much below −15° to −18°F (−26° to −28°C), even when they have been subjected to ideal conditions for the development of cold tolerance. In the Washington State University orchard at Pullman during the 1969 freeze, 'Montmorency' sour cherry, 'Stanley' plum, and 'McIntosh' and 'Rome Beauty' apple trees sustained little damage. 'Delicious' and 'Golden Delicious' apple, pear, and all sweet cherry trees were injured, but most recovered. All the peach and apricot trees were completely killed. The apple and plum trees produced some fruit, but the fruit buds of sweet cherries, sour cherries, and pears were killed.

Damage from Spring and Fall Frosts. Probably more damage from cold temperatures occurs in the spring than at any other time of the year. Tender transplants planted out too early are likely to be damaged by late freezes, and even emerging seedlings are often frozen. Spring is also the time when

*These examples of cold temperature damage are from long ago because, with the exception of the freezing of the orange groves of central Florida, there have not been dramatic recent examples of cold damage to horticultural crops in North America. In fact, the 1980s was the warmest decade of the twentieth century and the warmer trend has continued into the 1990s.

the orchardist is most apt to lose a crop as a result of freeze damage because fruit buds have little resistance to cold temperature once they begin to expand and open into blooms (Figure 7-9). The fruits and blooms of woody ornamentals also are frequently damaged by spring frosts. The effects of a spring frost may last for several seasons if the destruction of blossoms results in alternate bearing. Late summer or early autumn frosts can damage tender crops before they have matured and also end the riotous color of the late-summer flower garden.

Although 32°F (0°C) is the freezing point of water, most plants do not freeze at 32°F because sugars and other soluble compounds dissolved in the cell solution, acting like antifreeze, lower the freezing point. Tomato transplants can survive temperatures of 31°F (about −1°C); blossoms of temperate-zone fruits are not damaged until temperatures fall to 28° to 24°F (−2° to −4°C), depending on kind; mature apple fruits are not seriously damaged to about 24°F; and hardened cabbage can survive a drop to about 20° to 16°F (−7° to −9°C). Remember, however, that because of temperature inversion on a still night and microclimatic differences, the temperature surrounding a low-growing plant is likely to be lower than that recorded on an eye-level thermometer and often much lower than that of a weather bureau's recording device that may be surrounded by the heat-producing paraphernalia of a city (see Figure 7-10).

Physiological Drought. If a plant is permitted to go into the winter with little moisture surrounding its roots, or if a part of the plant dehydrates because the soil or the plant's water-conducting tissue is frozen, an injury called **physiological drought** will be the result. In most northern areas one can observe this kind of water-

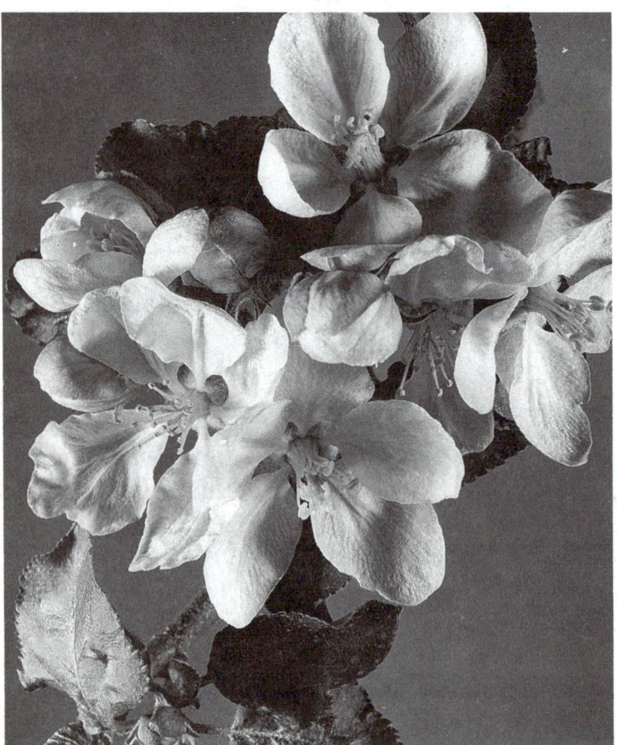

FIGURE 7-9 • Full bloom is the stage when the fruit crop is most susceptible to frost damage. (Courtesy of Runk, Schoenberger/Grant Heilman)

FIGURE 7-10 • Effect of frost on strawberry blossoms. Because they bloom early and grow close to the ground where, because of air inversion, temperature is likely to be coldest on a frosty spring morning, strawberry blossoms are especially susceptible to frost. The pistillate cone turns black (left of the pair of flowers) when the blossom freezes. With most plant species the pistil is the tissue most likely to be frost damaged.

stress injury on the windward side of exposed ornamental and fruit trees and on the southwest side of trees growing where winter sunshine is prevalent. It is much more likely to occur if the prevailing wind is also from the southwest. Bark injury that exposes the underlying wood and produces a permanent scar is called **catfacing,** and physiological drought is a major cause of catfacing of fruit and ornamental trees (Figure 7-11). Physiological drought can also occur in evergreens; it is manifest by brown needles or by the death of entire leaves or the margins of leaves of broad-leaved evergreens.

Physical Damage from Heaving, Ice, Snow, and Freezing. Another kind of cold weather damage is due to **heaving,** the alternate freezing and thawing that forces some plants completely out of the soil. Shallow-rooted perennials, including perennial flowers and strawberries, are especially subject to heaving damage.

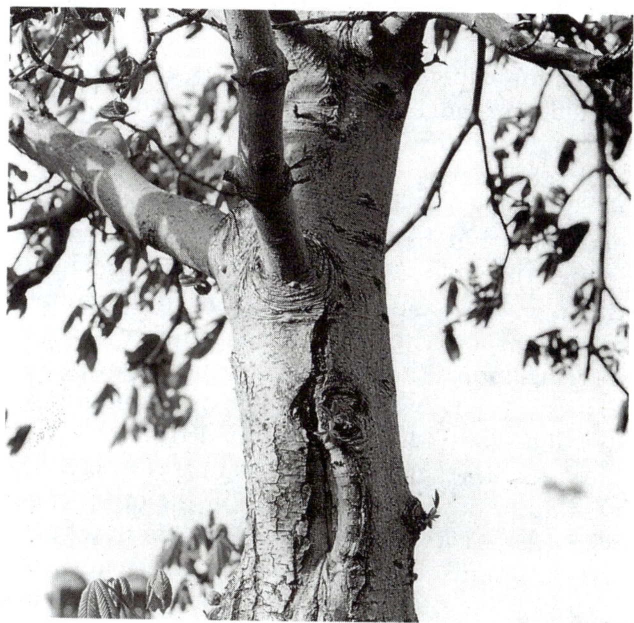

FIGURE 7-11 • Catfacing of a young 'Ruby' horse chestnut tree. This manifestation of physiological drought resulted from a drying winter wind coupled with bright sun, which dehydrated the southwest side of the unprotected trunk at a time when moisture could not be replaced because the freezing temperature had stopped translocation.

Breakage by wet snow is frequently the major winter injury to woody plants in areas with a cool, wet climate. Damage can be especially severe when there is a heavy snowfall early in the autumn before the leaves have fallen from deciduous trees and shrubs. Danger of breakage by snow discourages the growing of broad-leaved and semispreading needle evergreens at some locations. The tops of spruce, fir, and pine, especially those with a large crop of cones, are often broken by accumulations of ice and snow. Freak ice storms during which soil and plant temperatures remain below freezing but upper-air temperatures are high enough to permit rain to fall can also be physically damaging. Under these conditions ice accumulates until its weight breaks down the plant.

Although deep snow that lasts through the winter can insulate plants from freezing, it can also injure them in several ways. Some plants cannot survive being covered for long periods by the exceedingly compact layer of snow that forms as spring thawing commences. Death may result from insufficient aeration or, more commonly, because the combination of plant stress and an ideal environment for the growth of pathogens provides optimum conditions for disease. The compacting of snow as it melts is also responsible for physical damage to plants. Because thawing proceeds throughout the layer of snow rather than from the top, branches trapped in the snow can be pulled downward far beyond their breaking point as the snow settles.

The **splitting** of tree and shrub bark due to differential freezing is a common phenomenon during periods of rapidly falling temperature. The splitting, sometimes so sudden that it sounds like the crack of a rifle, can loosen the bark from the entire circumference of a tree, and it will cause the tree to die unless the damage is repaired (Figure 7-12). Not only is breakage caused by winter weather physically damaging, but it also provides pathways for the entrance of insect and disease

FIGURE 7-12 • Splitting of bark resulting from rapid freezing. When the temperature drops low enough, liquid in the woody xylem of sap-filled trees (like maple) freezes and expands, pressuring the bark which can split explosively. Trees with this kind of damage can often be saved if the bark is tacked back in place with small nails soon after the split occurs. The bark loosens at the cambium, and fastening it tightly against the wood prevents tissue dehydration and allows the cambial cells to cement the separation with new tissue similar to the union that occurs with grafting.

organisms. Injury from these pest organisms may be seen immediately, or its effects may not be noticeable for several years, as was the case with the 'Baldwin' apple trees mentioned earlier in this chapter.

Surviving Cold Temperatures

Whether a plant is able to survive a period of cold weather depends on its genetic constitution, the physiological conditioning it has undergone, and the environment to which it is subjected before, during, and after the cold. Gardeners can reduce the possibility of damage from cold by selecting hardy plants and suitable planting sites, by conditioning the plants with proper planting and cultural practices, and by using mulches and other frost-protective devices.

Plant and Site Selection. Gardeners should select plants known to be hardy in their area. An occasional choice specimen that is only half-hardy to the region can be brought through the winter with special care, but it takes dedication that most of us do not have to nurture very tender plants through winters in climates not suited for them. The U.S. Department of Agriculture has compiled a Plant Hardiness Zone Map based primarily on minimum winter temperatures (Figure 14-96). Plant lists found in gardening texts generally cite the zones from this map to which each kind of woody ornamental is adapted. Because they cover a smaller area, the plant lists published by state experimental stations and regional publishers contain more precise adaptation lists. These maps and lists are good general guides to the probable cold survival of ornamental species. However, climatic adaptation depends on many factors, and gardeners should seek advice from local authorities before making extensive plantings of materials listed as having borderline hardiness for the area.

The choice of location even within a yard may determine whether or not a particular plant will be injured by cold temperatures. The more hardy rhododendron and azalea cultivars, for example, are more subject to wind damage and fluctuations in temperature than to cold temperatures per se. Planting them on the north side of a building in a location where they are protected from the wind often enables them to grow in climates where they would not otherwise survive. On the other hand, when grapes are grown in some northern regions, they fail to manufacture and store sufficient carbohydrates. Trellising against a south wall sometimes provides them with sufficient heat to permit manufacture of the sugars needed for survival at locations where they otherwise would not be hardy. South slopes and sandy soil warm more rapidly in the spring, and crops can be planted on them earlier and will mature more quickly than if they are planted on a colder north slope or on clay soil. The importance of slope and nearness to a body of water for frost prevention have been pointed out.

Cold Conditioning and Cultural Practices. It goes without saying that gardeners will be less likely to have a garden freeze if they wait to plant until after the danger of cold injury is past. As has been mentioned, the general rule for planting vegetables and annual flowers is to plant cool-season crops as soon as the ground can be worked and to plant warm-season crops after the danger of frost is over. Where winter damage is common, lawns and woody plants should be planted during the spring rather than the fall so they can become established before winter commences.

Whether or not a plant survives a fall or winter freeze is greatly influenced by the temperature before that freeze. Plants reach their maximum tolerance only when temperatures have been fairly cold for a period of time and when there has been a gradual reduction in temperature over that period. The intensity and duration of the cold and the rate of drop or rise in temperature affect the extent of freeze injury. If the drop in temperature is gradual over a period of several days and if the cold period is not too long, the damage will be less severe than if the temperature falls rapidly or the cold period is prolonged. Air movement intensifies the injurious effect of cold temperatures. A freeze is likely to cause considerably more damage if there is a wind blowing when it occurs.

The level and type of stored food have a profound effect on how cold tolerant a plant is likely to be. Plant tissues well supplied with carbohydrates and water can withstand considerably more cold than can those that are not. Reducing the amount of nitrogen fertilizer and water supply as autumn approaches and refraining from heavy summer pruning are practices that slow vegetative growth and increase carbohydrate accumulation. Trees and shrubs that have had their carbohydrate supply depleted by heavy crops of fruit or seed become extremely susceptible to winter injury. Limiting production by removing some or all of the faded blooms or immature fruits and seeds increases the chance for woody plants to escape freeze damage the following winter.

It is important to maintain abundant soil and plant moisture throughout the winter to prevent physiological drought. Training a branch to shade the southwest exposure of trunks of fruit and ornamental trees or wrapping the trunks with commercial tree wrap to prevent drying and to reflect solar radiation often prevents the catfacing caused by physiological drought.

Conditioning a plant to withstand an adverse environment is called **hardening,** and the cold conditioning of woody perennials just described is a method of hardening. More commonly, the term hardening refers to the conditioning of transplants before they are planted in the garden or field. This has generally been done by subjecting them to cooler temperatures for a period of time. Reduced-temperature hardening is satisfactory for transplants of annual crops but should not be used for celery, cabbage, and related biennials because it can sometimes induce seed instead of petiole or head formation as it replaces winter cold (see Figure 7-8). Transplants of biennial crops should be hardened by lowering slightly the fertility of the growing media or cutting down somewhat on the amount of water supplied. Care should be taken not to overharden, however, because overhardened transplants require a long time to resume growing after they have been transplanted and never produce as high yields as do those that have not been severely hardened. Many horticulturists now recommend that transplants not be hardened at all.

Modifying Temperature with Plant Covers and Mulches. Various kinds of plastic and waxed paper covers can be used to start crops earlier than normal. Night temperatures under a plastic tent are 4° to 6°F warmer than those on the outside, and the use of plant protectors may permit planting of tomatoes and melons as much as a month earlier than without them. Daytime temperatures under a plastic tent can be as much as 20° to 25°F warmer than outside temperatures, and on warm, sunny days it may be necessary to remove the tent or at least ventilate the plants under it. Other kinds of plant-growing structures used to alter temperatures are described in Chapter 10.

The relative merits of mulching materials that can also affect time of crop maturity were discussed in Chapter 5. Most mulches do affect the growth and maturity of plants growing through them. Black and clear polyethylene have been used extensively to hasten the maturity of some warm-season vegetables. For example, muskmelons growing through a plastic mulch mature as much as ten to fourteen days earlier in certain northern areas than do similar plants growing without the benefit of mulch. A loose mulch of peat moss, straw, sawdust, shavings, or leaves is often raked over the crowns of strawberries, roses, and perennial flowers to prevent winter damage from freezing and heaving or to lessen soil temperature fluctuations (Figure 7-13). In areas where climbing roses, grapes, and trailing blackberry hybrids are not reliably winter hardy, their canes can be taken from their trellis, placed along the ground, and covered with a loose mulch for winter protection. Special pruning of grapes is necessary to produce a low branching trunk if the trunk is to be easily covered.

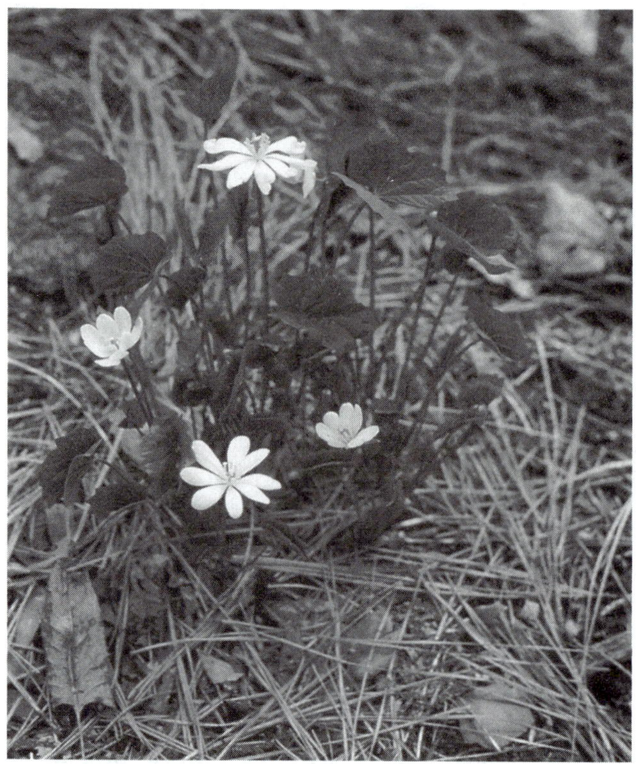

FIGURE 7-13 • Mulching for winter protection. Gardeners who protect plants with mulch are imitating nature where soil and low-growing plants are often insulated through the winter with snow, leaves, and dead plant materials as is the case with this *Jeffersonia dithylla* now pushing its blooms through a winter covering of pine needles. (Courtesy of Robert E. Lyons)

Plants should not be mulched for winter protection until after the first hard freezes; middle to late November is early enough in most areas of North America. Loose mulches should not be used around woody plants if there are rodents in the yard. Mice find straw- or shaving-mulched shrubs especially attractive for building their nests and the tasty, protected bark of such shrubs provides them with a readily available food supply. Where rodents are a problem in rose plantings, soil from between the bushes can be hilled over the crowns in the late fall to protect the lower stems from winter damage.

Snow is an excellent insulating mulch, and many semitender shrubs survive the intense cold of mountain winters under an annual protective cover of snow. Alpine flowers that routinely survive winters where temperatures reach −50°F (−46°C) in their native high mountain habitat often winterkill when transplanted to lower elevations because their new, warmer environment does not provide a protective cover of snow. In areas where snow almost always falls, it can be used to protect cold-susceptible plants by being piled over low-growing shrubs when extremely cold temperatures are forecast. Taller shrubs can be given the same protection with heavy plastic or cloth tubes constructed around them and filled with snow. Nails can be used to pin the tube around the shrub (Figure 7-14). A snow cover is especially effective in protecting blossom buds, which are usually the

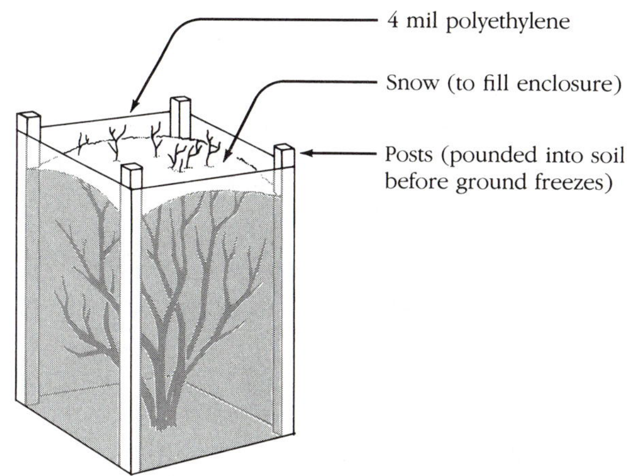

FIGURE 7-14 • Snow as protection from cold. A semihardy shrub can be protected from midwinter freezing by building a plastic tube around it and filling the tube with snow.

most cold-susceptible structures of early spring-blooming fruit and ornamental shrubs. All materials needed for protecting plants against a midwinter freeze should be assembled during the good weather of autumn; otherwise, saving the plant may not be possible or seem worth the effort when the temperature is far below freezing and the plant needs protection.

Preventing Physical Damage from Snow and Cold Weather. At locations where heavy snows accumulate, plants may require special winter attention. Securing easily broken plants with sturdy stakes, tying upright branches of evergreens together with string (or string and burlap) so that snow cannot accumulate on them, and occasionally shaking the snow from plants during heavy snowstorms help reduce breakage. Pruning should be delayed until severe winter weather is past so that the optimal number of undamaged branches can be left and winter-damaged wood can be removed. In addition, the extra branches remaining through the winter may provide some protection for the rest of the plant. Snow-covered plants should be checked frequently while the snow is melting during early spring so that branches in danger of being torn off by settling snow can be released. During extremely cold periods, trees should be examined frequently for split bark.

Preventing Spring Freezing. The fruit crop of an entire season is often destroyed by late spring frosts that occur during only a few hours on one or two nights. In most orchards petroleum-fueled heaters are used to protect the commercial crop during these occasional cold periods. Some of these heaters would be suitable for home plantings, but gardeners contemplating their use should check to make sure that the heaters comply with local antipollution ordinances. If only one or two trees near the home are to be protected, heating lamps or a kerosene heater hung in the lower branches (because hot air rises) may provide the protection required. (Do not permit heating devices to contact bark or other parts of the living plant.) A sheet of polyethylene held above the tree by long poles at each corner can be used as a canopy to keep the warm air from rising too high. Covering small plants with a long-lasting, spray-on foam and preventing air inversion by using wind machines are two additional methods commercial growers sometimes use to protect against early spring freezes.

Irrigation water also is used to prevent early spring freezing. As mentioned earlier, considerable heat energy is released as water cools, and even more (80 calories for each gram) is discharged into the environment as water freezes. To prevent crops from freezing, sprinklers should be turned on during the early morning when the temperature drops to 34°F (2°C) and left flowing until the sun has warmed the area to above the freezing point. Ice will accumulate when the temperature drops to freezing, but as long as some water remains liquid, the temperature in the vicinity will not drop below the freezing point. Frost protection with sprinklers is feasible for light freezes only, because the weight of the accumulating ice can physically damage plants.

Wind Protection. Wind damages plants by desiccating them, by physically breaking or abrading branches and leaves, and by amplifying the effects of cold temperature. In areas where wind is common, seedlings will grow better if they are planted on the leeward side of a high bed or are given some kind of artificial barrier on the windward side of the plant row (Figure 7-15). In areas of spring winds where a cereal is grown as a winter cover crop, the early growth of vegetable seedlings and transplants has been markedly improved by leaving strips of the cover crop for wind protection. Planting strips are prepared for seeding with a narrow rototiller so that each seeded row alternates with a strip of cover crop. The remaining strips of cover crop are removed by cultivation or with herbicides before they begin to crowd the seedlings.

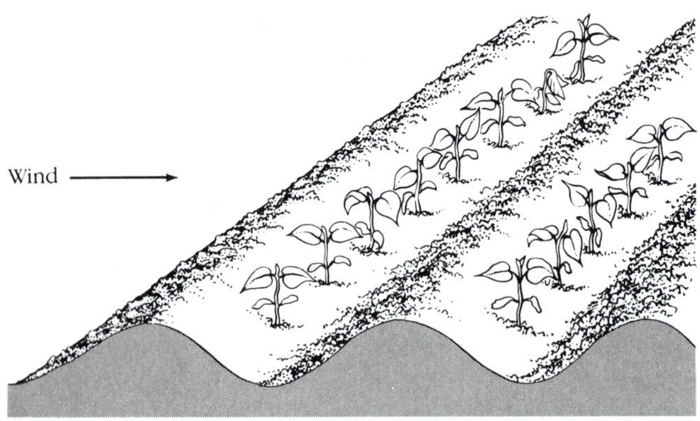

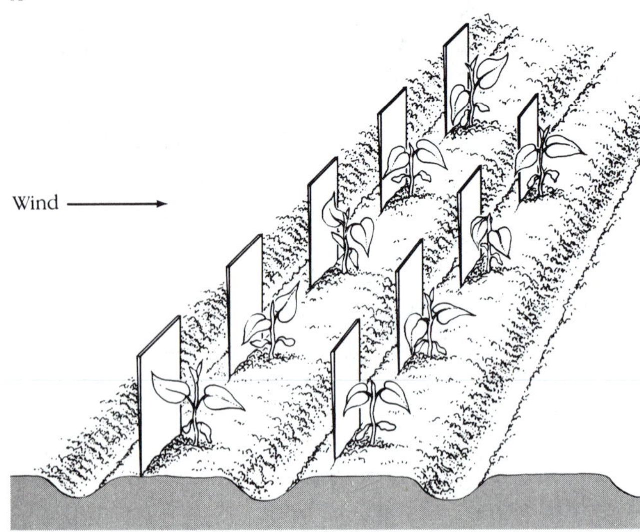

FIGURE 7-15 • Wind protection. Transplants can be partially shielded from wind by planting them on the leeward side of a raised bed (A). A shingle or other thin solid device also provides wind protection for individual plants (B).

Windbreaks and shelterbelts are the more traditional and more permanent means of wind protection for both the home and garden; these are described in Chapter 11. Where space for a windbreak is limited or nonexistent, an ornamental border, a row of bush fruits, or a row of espaliered fruit trees (see Chapter 8) along the windward side of the garden can offer some permanent wind protection. Limited temporary protection can be achieved with rows of sweet corn, sunflowers, or other tall annuals.

Heat Units

Heat units are a measure of the growing efficiency of the weather based on the fact that temperature is the climatic factor best correlated with the length of time required for a crop to mature. The heat units for any one day are calculated by subtracting a base temperature (usually 40° or 50°F, or 5° or 10°C) from the average temperature for the day. Bases of 40° or 50°F are predicated on the fact that most cool-season crops grow whenever the temperature is above 40°F, and warm-season crops do not grow when it is below 50°F. Estimating the time of maturity, the latest feasible date for fall planting, and whether long-season fruit cultivars will mature in a specific locality are common uses of accumulative heat units (see "Climate, Hardiness, and Maturity" in Chapter 14).

LIGHT AND THE GROWTH OF GARDEN PLANTS

Light is the part of the sun's energy that is visible to the human eye, but visible light is only one part of the total spectrum of solar radiation that reaches the earth. Although it is now known that the short- and long-wavelength radiation on either side of the visible spectrum is used by some plants, it is visible light that is of primary importance for plant growth.

Kind or Quality of Light

At one time or another most people have observed the use of a prism to separate light into its various wavelength components that the human eye interprets as color. The rainbow comprises the same separation. The human eye can see solar radiation from about 390 to about 760 nanometers in length (see Figure 7-16). The shortest visible rays are violet and blue; the longest are red; and green and yellow rays are intermediate in length. Some of the shorter blue and ultraviolet rays are filtered out by atmospheric gases and airborne particulate matter. The ultraviolet rays, which cause sunburn, are, along with the blue rays, important to the formation of **anthocyanin** pigments that give many plant products their red color. This is the reason that orchards in the dry, clear mountain valleys of the arid West produce highly colored apples (Figure 7-17) and also the reason that a Western suntan is likely to be darker than an Eastern suntan. The relationship between light and anthocyanin production also accounts for the faded color of coleus and other red-leaved houseplants when they are grown in low indoor light.

The bending of flower heads and some other plant parts toward the sun is a phenomenon of

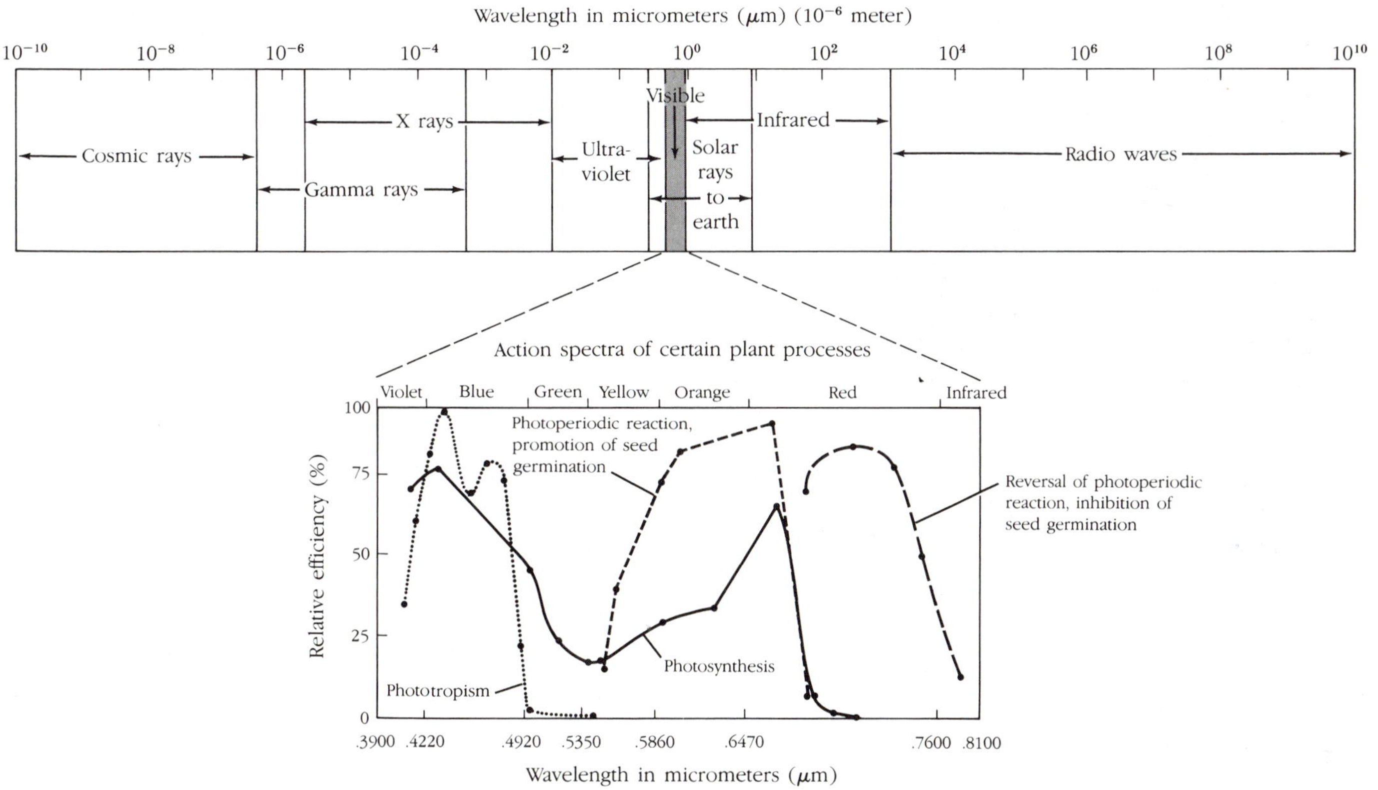

FIGURE 7-16 • The electromagnetic spectrum and the action of certain plant processes. (Adapted from L. Machlis and J. G. Torrey, *Plants in Action*, W. H. Freeman and Company, New York, copyright © 1959)

FIGURE 7-17 • The influence of light on pigmentation. Light is necessary for the formation of anthocyanin pigments, which give apples their red color. These labeled fruits were produced by sticking tapes on the fruit before the natural formation of pigment. (From Jules Janick, *Horticultural Science*, 4th ed., W. H. Freeman and Company, New York, copyright © 1985)

which most gardeners are aware. This bending of a plant part in response to light, called **phototropism,** is mediated by the blue areas of the spectrum. Although the physiological basis of phototropism is not completely understood, scientific evidence suggests that light either destroys the growth-promoting plant auxin IAA or else causes it to move from the area where light intensity is greatest. (An **auxin** is a plant growth substance that promotes cell elongation.) Regardless of the exact mechanism, more auxin accumulates on the side of the stem away from the source of light, and consequently that side grows more rapidly than does the side on which intense light rays are falling (Figure 7-18). This enables the stem to orient the flower head toward the sun or other source of light. Partly because of phototropism, potted plants growing near windows should be turned frequently to permit balanced growth.

Light energy for photosynthesis is absorbed by plants primarily from the blue-violet and orange-red parts of the spectrum. Plants appear green because they are reflecting or transmitting green light rather than absorbing it. This plant characteristic of not utilizing green light has suggested that lamps be designed for plant growth that produce light mainly in the blue and red areas of the spectrum. The earliest fluorescent lamps of this type, which gave off red and blue light almost to the exclusion of other wavelengths, were called Gro-Lux. Later, the same manufacturer introduced Gro-Lux Wide Spectrum, which emitted both a high proportion of red and blue light and some light from other areas of the spectrum. These lamps deliver light shown by recent research to be more closely correlated with the light spectra utilized in photosynthesis. The lavender glow emanating from many greenhouses each morning and evening during the winter months comes from these special plant-growing lamps.

The theoretical advantage of such specialized lamps is that they give plants more usable light in proportion to the electrical energy they consume. Gro-Lux lamps are beneficial for research and some kinds of commercial plant growing, but the higher cost and shorter life of Gro-Lux tubes usually negates any saving in energy cost that a

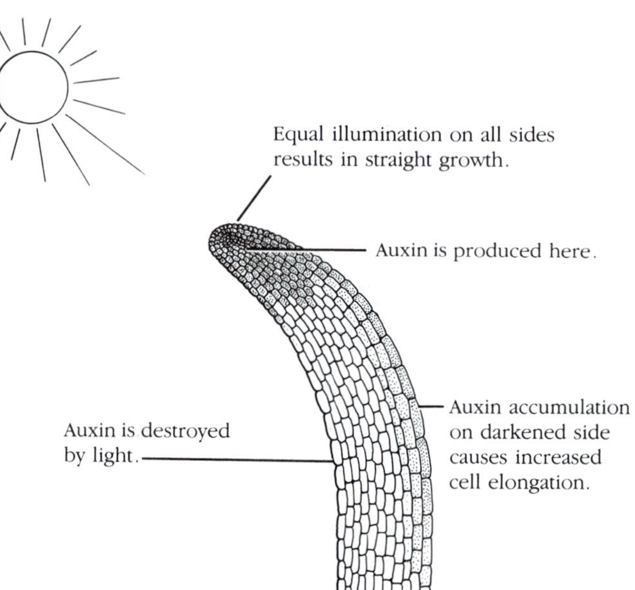

FIGURE 7-18 • Phototropism. (From Jules Janick, *Horticultural Science*, 4th ed., W. H. Freeman and Company, New York, copyright © 1985)

homeowner might realize from using them. Most hobby growers can obtain satisfactory plant growth with less expensive cool-white or warm-white fluorescent lamps or with mostly cool-white light supplemented with a minimal number of Gro-Lux lamps. Cool-white plus incandescent light bulbs (the latter to supplement the red and infrared areas of the light spectrum) are often combined to provide a light source similar in quality to sunlight. Gro-Lux lamps are sometimes added to the cool-white fluorescent and incandescent light bulbs. Mercury vapor lamps, which provide high light intensity, have also proved satisfactory for growing plants.

Light Intensity

Light intensity has traditionally been measured in units called **foot-candles** (F.C.). Although the foot-candle is no longer the universally accepted light-measuring unit to which physiologists relate plant growth, it is still the one most commonly found in gardening literature. In the eastern and midwestern United States, the light intensity in full sunlight at midday measures approximately 10,000 F.C. The intensity is much less early in the morning or later in the evening when solar rays are reaching the earth at an oblique angle and thus are being filtered by more layers of atmosphere. For the same reason, light intensity is much lower in the winter. Full sunlight in desert areas can surpass 12,000 F.C. at noon on a summer day. Light intensity is also high on clear days in the tropics. With heavy winter overcast, the light intensity outdoors at noon may be as low as 600 to 900 F.C. The interior of lighted homes measures from 50 to 300 F.C.

Plants vary in their ability to utilize light. Because philodendrons, African violets, begonias, and many other houseplants evolved under a jungle canopy, they grow well at low light intensities, making them valuable for indoor decoration. An individual leaf of most crop plants can utilize only about 1,200 F.C. of light, but because of the shading of their lower leaves, plants adapted to full sun generally respond to several times that intensity. The increased growth of most crop plants parallels increased light intensity up to about 4,000 F.C. The intensities mentioned earlier are far higher than plants are capable of using; these were maximum intensities at noon on a clear midsummer day. When lower intensities during spring and fall, morning and evening, and cloudy and overcast days are considered, the light intensity is probably not appreciably higher than the maximum that can be utilized by most crop plants during most of their growing hours at most locations.

Plants that receive less than the required amount of light respond with greater elongation. Nodes are far apart; leaves are broad and thin, and the plants have a loose, open structure (Figure 7-19). Reduced light intensity also induces succulence. Tobacco leaves used for cigar wrappers are artificially shaded so that they will produce a broad, thin leaf. Where light intensity is low, plant growth is more normal, although extremely slow, if temperatures are also kept low. Lengthening the daily period during which plants receive light can compensate somewhat for low light intensity.

Plants adapted to growing under low light intensity or plants that have been growing with low intensity will sunburn, wither, and die if they are placed where the light intensity is high. This frequently happens when potted plants are placed outdoors for the summer or when certain shade-loving plants, such as African violets, philodendrons, spurges, and ferns, are placed in direct sunlight.

There is some evidence that a variation of light intensity above the optimum for plant growth may have considerable impact on the growth of plants. Most crop plants grow somewhat taller in the East and the Midwest than do plants of the same cultivar in high-altitude areas of the West. The upper layers of cucurbit leaves often show damage when those crops are grown in the western desert, although yields do not seem to be affected. Both dwarfing and leaf damage can be

FIGURE 7-19 • Etiolated bean plant (grown in the dark) (A) and normal plant (grown in light) (B). (From J. Bonner and A. W. Galston, *Principles of Plant Physiology*, W. H. Freeman and Company, New York, copyright © 1952)

corrected by shading. The relationship of variations in light intensity and light quality to plant growth is not yet well understood, and so alert gardeners are in a position to make interesting observations in this area.

Duration of Light

In 1920 two U.S. Department of Agriculture scientists working at Beltsville, Maryland, W. W. Garner and H. A. Allard, reported that the time of flowering of a certain tobacco cultivar was determined by the length of the light period during each twenty-four-hour period. It was soon discovered that many responses in certain plants—flowering, bulbing, tuberization, and the like—are a result of the plants' exposure to a particular day length. This phenomenon is called **photoperiodism** (Figure 7-20). Some plants respond only to day lengths longer than a certain minimum; these plants are referred to as **long-day plants.** Plants responding to a day length shorter than a certain maximum are referred to as **short-day plants.** Plants that show no visible response to day length are referred to as **day neutral.**

A number of important horticultural crops respond to day length. Chrysanthemums, for example, are short-day plants; however, some cultivars can be induced to bloom by day lengths ranging from sixteen hours down to seven hours or less. Because chrysanthemums are a popular greenhouse crop, cultivars that bloom during each period between late summer and early winter at all latitudes have been developed. However, growers can induce any cultivar to bloom at just about any season of the year by covering it to shorten its day length for a period of time if they wish to have earlier blooming or by prolonging the day length with artificial light if they wish to delay bloom. The light intensity required to delay the blooming of chrysanthemums is very low, and the blooming of outdoor mums is sometimes delayed by porch or street lights. Single-crop or June-bearing strawberries are another short-day plant group that will produce excellent healthy plants but no flowers or berries if they are planted close to an all-night street or yard light. Where lights might affect strawberry flower–bud initiation, growers can plant day-neutral or ever-bearing cultivars.

Spinach is a long-day plant, and if planted late in the spring, it will produce seed stalks before it produces edible leaves. The spinach cultivars now

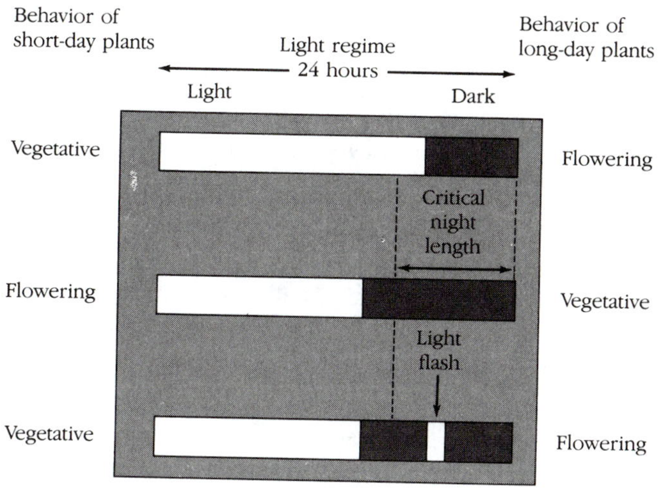

FIGURE 7-20 • Response of long-day and short-day plants to different light regimes. Interrupting the long dark period with a few minutes of light prevents flowering in short-day plants and permits flowering in long-day plants.

available require relatively long days to initiate flower buds, and just as soon as that day length arrives, the spinach plant will bloom regardless of its size. The blooming of spinach is also hastened by high temperatures, so spinach is produced either early in the spring or late in the fall when temperatures are cool and days are short.

Onion bulbing is also a long-day response, and cultivars that produce bulbs at various latitudes have been developed. For example, the Bermuda-type onion has been developed to produce during the winter in Texas; it initiates a bulb whenever the day length reaches eleven to twelve hours or more. If a cultivar of this type is planted in New York or Minnesota where climate decrees that onion planting cannot occur much before mid-March, it produces a rather interesting response. When the leaves come through the soil, the day length in those northern climates is longer than that necessary for bulbing to occur. As a consequence, the seedlings immediately initiate bulbs. However, because little food has been manufactured by the extremely small leaves, the bulbs will be about the size of a pea. Cultivars such as 'Sweet Spanish' and 'Yellow Globe' have been developed for northern areas and do not bulb until the day length has reached fifteen to sixteen hours. These cultivars germinate in March or April, producing considerable vegetative growth by mid-June, at which time bulbs are initiated. The bulbs continue to grow and are not fully developed until late August; because there is plenty of food material stored, they will be relatively large. If, on the other hand, the 'Yellow Sweet Spanish' cultivar is grown in Texas where the day length, even during midsummer, never reaches sixteen hours, growth will continue without bulbs forming, and the grower will have a crop of exceptionally large scallions.

Many other plants respond to day length. The poinsettia produces its red or white bracts under short-day conditions. Commercial poinsettia growers have to know exactly when to reduce the day length so that their plants will be in bloom for the Christmas season; poinsettias are not of much value on December 26. Poinsettias can be kept as houseplants through the summer, but they require special lighting if they are to bloom a second Christmas season. The reason is that the artificial lighting in most homes increases the day length to a point that blooms are never induced. To cause blooming, start in early November to keep the plant in a room where only natural daylight enters. All artificial lights should be removed because only a few minutes of interrupted darkness are required to delay or eliminate the flowering response. Flowering can also be induced by covering the poinsettia at sunset with a lightproof box and removing the box at sunrise. The special treatment can be stopped as soon as the bracts show color.

Like the response of spinach, the response of most plants to day length is modified by temperature and may be speeded or delayed by cold or warm weather. This fact becomes of major importance when growers are attempting to produce plants to flower on specific dates—large mums for homecoming, poinsettias for Christmas, or lilies for Easter.

Selected References

Bickford, E. D., and S. Dunn. *Lighting for Plant Growth.* Kent, Ohio: Kent State University Press, 1972.

Brooklyn Botanic Garden. *Gardening Under Light.* Handbook 93 (special printing of *Plants and Gardens,* vol. 36, no. 3). Brooklyn, N.Y.: Brooklyn Botanic Garden, 1980.

Critchfield, H. J. *General Climatology.* 4th ed. Englewood Cliffs, N.J.: Prentice-Hall, 1983.

Mooney, H. A., W. E. Winner, and E. J. Pell. *Response of Plants to Multiple Stresses.* San Diego: Academic Press, 1991.

Neiburger, M., J. G. Edingen, and W. D. Bonner. *Understanding Our Atmospheric Environment.* New York: Freeman, 1973.

Pearce, E. A., and G. Smith. *The Times Books World Weather Guide.* New York: Random House, 1990.

U.S. Environmental Service Staff. *Weather Atlas of the United States.* Detroit: Gale Research Inc., 1975.

CHAPTER 8

Regulating Plant Growth

Although not often expressed in these terms, the major goal of gardening is to utilize the finite plant growth requirements—mineral nutrients, light, and water—of the garden space in the way that will most efficiently produce the results desired. The optimal utilization of minerals, water, and light is achieved by regulating inter- and intraplant competition by spacing garden plants; by regulating plant growth by means of pruning, fruit thinning, size-controlling rootstocks, growth-regulating chemicals, phloem disruption, and plant breeding (discussed in this chapter); and by controlling garden pests (discussed in Chapter 9).

PLANT SPACING

Perhaps the most obvious way of regulating interplant competition is by the optimal spacing of each plant, but determining this is not always easy. The close spacing necessary for the maximum yield of some crop plants may reduce the size or quality of their product and increase their susceptibility to foliage diseases. Furthermore, with ornamentals the spatial organization for aesthetic effect is more important than the total utilization of the area's plant growth resources.

Considerable publicity has been given to

the plant-spacing research that started in England a few decades ago and demonstrated that optimal yield and size of vegetables usually result when plants are spaced approximately the same distance in each direction rather than in the customary wide between-row and narrow within-row planting distances. These results were achieved, however, only with complete chemical weed control, which, as will be explained later, is not usually practical in the home garden. Also essential in the home vegetable garden is space for walking between rows to weed, harvest, and perform other necessary activities. Thus except for the tiniest plots where not even a hoe is needed for maintenance and where plants can be reached from the garden borders, the garden arrangement is most convenient if vegetables are planted in rows. Extensive plantings of annual and perennial flowers and small fruits are also easier to care for when they are in rows.

Direct-seeded annuals must be thinned. Annual flowering plants produce larger blooms and blossom more profusely when the plants have room to grow to full size. Lettuce, cauliflower, and cabbage do not produce heads if they are crowded, and root vegetables will remain small and become misshapen if too many are left to grow in the row. As explained in Chapter 6, plants should be widely spaced if either water or minerals are likely to be insufficient. The recommended spacing for vegetables is listed in Table 14-2.

Size-controlling rootstocks permit growing fruit trees in a space as small as 10 × 10 feet (3 × 3 m), and the new training systems mentioned later in this chapter make it possible to produce tree fruits in even less space and to use them as dual-purpose ornamental and food plants in hedges and borders.

Planting woody ornamentals too close together, which restricts their uniform growth to full size and beauty, is the mistake most commonly made with these plants. Because trees and shrubs increase in size so tremendously as they develop, wise gardeners will draw a scale model of the yard or garden showing planting materials at full-scale size before they do any planting. This will enable them to resist the temptation to overplant. Small temporary shrubs and annual and perennial flowers can be used as filler plants to provide a pleasing effect until the more permanent plants grow to fill their allotted space. Trees and shrubs that grow to the correct size should be selected for each location. Keeping a woody plant pruned to fit a location too small for it, although possible, requires a great deal of effort. Besides, a heavily pruned plant normally is not as attractive as one permitted to grow naturally (Figure 8-1).

FIGURE 8-1 • Excessive pruning. (Courtesy of Joe Eakes/Color Advantage/Lyons)

GROWTH CONTROL BY PRUNING

◆ ◆ ◆

Pruning, the removal of parts of a plant, is the most common method of opening the plant's canopy to allow sunlight to reach leaves, flowers, and fruits and of regulating other intraplant competition. Pruning to restrict plant size is also a common method of reducing interplant competition. Roots are sometimes pruned, but when used alone, the term pruning usually means removing above-ground portions of the plant, generally stems. The main purposes of pruning are to modify plant growth and to influence the amount and character of flower and fruit production.

A term commonly used in conjunction with pruning is **training**, the modification of a plant's shape or size to suit the needs of the horticulturist. Plant training by pruning is one of the less exact, more controversial horticultural practices, perhaps because satisfactory results are possible with considerable variation in pruning techniques. There is some truth in the cliché that most plants grow relatively well in spite of the pruning they receive, and indeed, some good gardeners who have not overplanted confine their pruning to the removal of dead branches and branches that are obstructing an activity or view. For the production of fruit and for the attractive maintenance of most ornamental trees and shrubs, however, more extensive pruning is necessary.

Effects of Pruning Cuts

Because it is impossible to prescribe exact pruning procedures for each plant in each situation, intelligent pruning requires an awareness of the impact of various amounts and kinds of pruning cuts on the physiology and growth of the plant. In essence, pruning dwarfs the plant, changes its carbohydrate/nitrogen ratio, and affects its growth through auxin imbalance.

Dwarfing. The removal of branches or roots has a dwarfing effect on the entire plant, both its top and root system (Figure 8-2). The dwarfing effect is not always apparent because pruning tends to stimulate vegetative growth, especially in the vicinity of the cut. Practical use is made of this localized effect in developing the framework system of fruit trees or in directing the growth of ornamentals. Cutting the tip growth back to an outward-facing bud directs new growth outward and gives the plant a more open growth habit. Although shoot growth may be stimulated, even greatly stimulated, with excessive top pruning, the total size of pruned plants will be smaller than that of unpruned plants.

Altering Carbohydrate/Nitrogen Balance. Pruning is one of the most important tools a gardener has for regulating the carbohydrate/nitrogen balance and, concomitantly, the vegetative/reproductive growth ratio of woody plants. Pruning above-ground plant parts removes some of the stored carbohydrates and reduces the carbohydrate manufacturing organs, thus increasing the amount of nitrogen in relation to carbohydrates. This, in turn, stimulates vegetative growth relative to reproductive growth. Root pruning, on the other hand, increases the carbohydrate balance and causes the plant to become more reproductive.

Largely because it lowers the carbohydrate ratio, heavy pruning during the early life of a plant may delay flower and fruit production by several years, a delay especially disconcerting to growers of fruit trees that require many years of growing before much fruit is produced even in the best circumstances. As a general rule, if early flowering is desired, young fruit and ornamental trees and shrubs should be pruned as little as possible consistent with the development of a desirable framework and shape. Commercial apple orchards grown without pruning between their second and sixth years produce a crop one to two years earlier than do conventionally pruned trees. Few orchardists follow this practice completely, however, be-

A 

B 

FIGURE 8-2 • The dwarfing effect of pruning. Both of these two standard-sized 'Mugho' pines (*Pinus mugo*) are about twenty years old. A has been pruned each spring since it was planted, by pinching back the candles (see Figure 14-80). B was not pruned until recently when some brushy growth was trimmed from the basal branches. Note the difference in compactness. Compare their relative sizes by noting the garden tool in front of each.

cause young trees grown with no pruning are often structurally weak.

The importance of maintaining a balance between the vegetative and reproductive growth of woody plants has been stressed several times in previous chapters. To be an effective tool for regulating the amount and quality of production, pruning must be done at the right time and be correlated with mineral fertilization, thinning, and other management practices. In general, heavy pruning increases the production of stems and leaves and decreases the number of fruits and flowers. Young, vigorously vegetative trees and shrubs and those growing in fertile soils need little pruning. Older trees and shrubs and those growing on less fertile soils tend to be overly reproductive; they will produce larger flowers and fruits if they are pruned quite heavily. Excessive pruning can eliminate flower and fruit production for several years, and heavy pruning during late summer may increase freezing susceptibility because it reduces the plant's carbohydrate reserves.

Auxin and Apical Dominance. Pruning also affects the plant's growth habit and production by its effect on **apical dominance**, the tendency for the **apex** (uppermost bud) to grow more rapidly than the lower buds. Apical dominance is mediated by the natural plant auxin IAA, previously noted in connection with phototropism and the rooting of cuttings. The greatest quantities of IAA are manufactured in the apex of the plant, and the downward flow of IAA from shoot tips makes shoots grow rapidly and achieves apical dominance by stimulating cell division and inhibiting lateral bud development (see "Auxins" later in this chapter).

Plant and plant parts show varying amounts of apical dominance. Young conifer trees, for example, develop their typical Christmas tree shape because of strong apical dominance (Figure 8-3). On the other hand, spreading plants such as Pfitzer junipers show little tendency for a single apical bud to become dominant. Normally it is the uppermost branch that shows the greatest apical

FIGURE 8-3 • Apical dominance in conifers. (A) A rapidly growing apex and the reduced growth of upper laterals are typical of young trees with strong apical dominance. (B) Rounding of the crown is typical of maturity and reduced apical dominance.

dominance, but suckers—the rapidly growing, nonbranching stems that shoot from adventitious buds anywhere in a tree or shrub—are examples of extreme apical dominance lower on the tree.

Apical dominance affects plant growth in several ways besides stimulating growth of the apical meristem and inhibiting the development of lateral buds. The crotch angle at which lower side branches meet the main trunk is wider as long as the terminal bud is influencing apical dominance. If the terminal bud is removed, the shoots from buds just below the terminal will begin to grow rapidly and turn upward, causing their crotch angles to become narrow. Solid wood often fails to form in the vicinity of narrow crotch angles, resulting in a weak framework for the tree and often in breakage when the tree has to carry a heavy load of fruit or snow (see Figure 14-72).

Heavy pruning and high nitrogen fertilization enhance apical dominance, suggesting that auxin stimulation is correlated with a low carbohydrate/nitrogen ratio.

The observation that those plant parts subject to strong apical dominance do not blossom or bear fruit is further evidence of the relationship of heavy pruning, high nitrogen, auxin, and vegetative growth. Apical dominance and vegetative/reproductive growth also are affected by branch orientation. Bending a branch downward reduces its apical dominance and enables it to bloom and fruit. The vegetative/reproductive balance of trees and shrubs trained to the espaliered or pillar system (see "Pruning and Training" in Chapter 14) is maintained by orienting their branches in a horizontal or downward position. If the branches were allowed to grow in the normal upright position, the heavy pruning required for these training systems would completely inhibit flowering and fruiting.

Apical dominance is most intense in young plants and lessens as plants age. This lessening is related to the greater reproductive tendencies and open growth habit of older trees. A forester knows that a conifer is mature when it loses its Christmas tree shape and its top begins to spread (Figure 8-3).

Plant parts other than branches—potato tubers, for example—show a form of apical dominance. In late December or early January, when the tuber first becomes able to grow after its rest period, only a single sprout develops at the bud end of the tuber. As is true with trees, aging lessens tuber apical dominance, and by May several buds will germinate from each eye on the potato. Another interesting aspect of the sprouting of potato tubers is that if the tuber is cut into several pieces, apical dominance will be overcome. However, each seed piece tends to produce its first sprout from the terminal bud of the eye that was closest to the bud end of the potato (Figure 8-4).

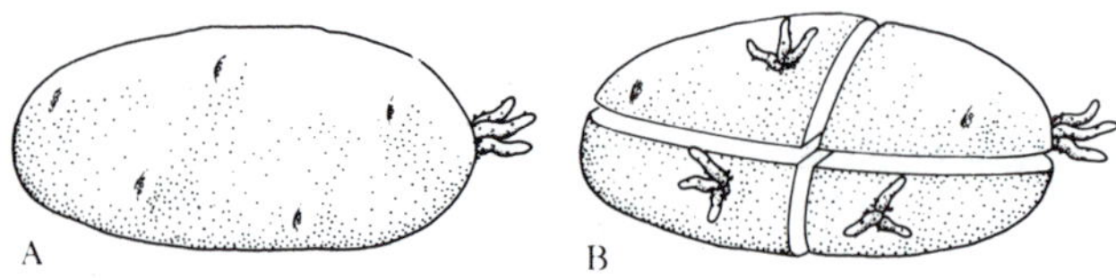

FIGURE 8-4 • Apical dominance in the potato. When tuber dormancy first begins to break (in December or January in northern areas), only the eye at the bud end initiates sprouts (A). If the tuber is cut into sections, apical dominance is overcome, and other eyes will initiate sprouts (B).

Heading Back Versus Thinning Out

The two general kinds of pruning cuts are heading back and thinning out. **Heading back** is cutting off a part of a limb or branch. When a branch is headed back, the buds nearest the cut are those most likely to be stimulated into shoot production (Figure 8-5). If only a small part of the tip of the branch has been removed, frequently only the terminal bud that remains with the plant will produce shoot growth. Therefore, pruning lightly to an outside bud is one way to force the growth of the branch in a slightly more outward direction. For many shrubs, especially when considerable portions of a branch have been removed, a number of latent buds are stimulated to produce shoots. Thus heading back generally produces a more compact or bushy plant. The extreme example of heading back is shearing plants to produce hedges or topiaries (Figure 8-6). The art of **topiary** is the shaping of woody plants to resemble objects other than plants, such as animals or geometric designs.

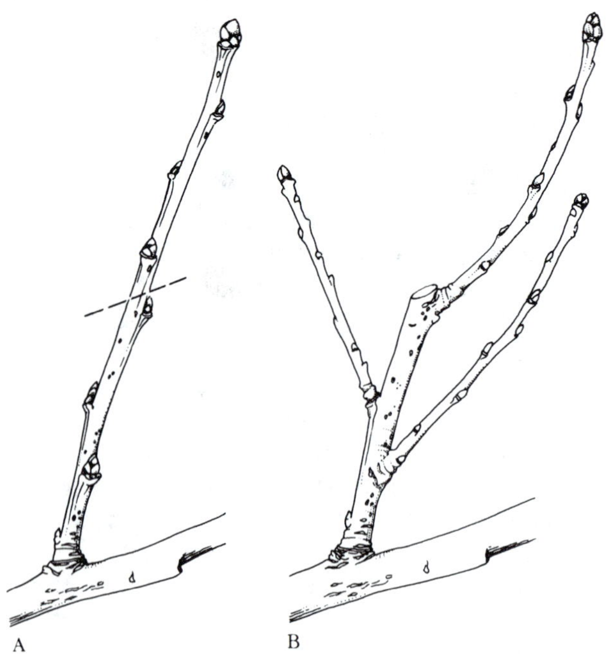

FIGURE 8-5 • Heading back redirects growth toward the highest remaining bud (A). It also frequently stimulates the growth of lower buds, resulting in a more compact growth habit (B).

Thinning out is the removal of an entire shoot or branch. Although branches near the one moved will be stimulated to grow and sometimes latent buds near the base of the removed branch will be forced to grow, thinning out generally produces a plant with a more open growth habit (Figure 8-7).

Time of Pruning

The timing of pruning depends on a number of factors, including climate, species, and the results desired. Generally, in northern latitudes, fruit trees should be pruned in the late winter or early spring. Pruning when a plant is actively growing has a more retarding effect than does pruning during the dormant season. Moreover, it is easier to see the framework of the tree when there are no leaves on it. In areas where woody plants are subject to winter damage, pruning is usually delayed until after the coldest winter weather is past because pruning somewhat increases susceptibility to winter damage. Small fruit plantings can be pruned right after harvest except in areas of extremely cold winters, where pruning is usually delayed until early spring. Pruning in the spring permits the removal of winter-damaged parts, and the extra branches left through the winter may provide some support to prevent breakage from heavy snow or strong winds.

There is an old adage that pertains to pruning ornamentals: "Prune when the knife is sharp."

A

B

FIGURE 8-6 • Hedges (A) and topiaries (B) represent the ultimate in compact growth induced by shearing. (A, Ladew Topiary Gardens, Monkton, Md., courtesy of Runk, Schoenberger/Grant Heilman; B, Disney World, courtesy of Richard Weiss/Peter Arnold, Inc.)

Because earliness of maturity and amount of production are not primary concerns of those who produce ornamentals, gardeners should prune landscape plantings when they are inclined to do so and observe that pruning is needed. There are, of course, a few precautions and guidelines for the time to prune ornamentals. One already mentioned is that heavy pruning of any woody plant late in the summer is likely to stimulate late vegetative growth and make the plant more susceptible to winter damage. Furthermore, cut surfaces are more quickly hidden by new growth if the plant is pruned just before or during its season of rapid growth. It is recommended that flowering trees and shrubs be pruned after they have bloomed. This permits the removal of dead blooms that are unsightly and also prevents a shrub or tree from forming seed or fruit that would use food reserves that otherwise could be used to produce leaves and blooms for the following season. Those shrubs that bloom in the spring and early summer are generally pruned after they have bloomed; those that bloom in late summer or autumn are usually pruned the following spring. The recommendation to prune right after blooms have faded does not apply, of course, to flowering shrubs and trees that also produce attractive fruit or seedpods. Hedges need to be pruned several times during the growing season, whenever they begin to look shaggy.

Pines and rhododendrons are normally pruned in the spring as their new shoots elongate, but most other evergreens can be pruned at any season of the year. Spring pruning of evergreens does have an advantage in that the cut ends are soon covered by new growth.

Training Systems for Trees

There are a number of training systems for trees, and the choice of which to use depends on the

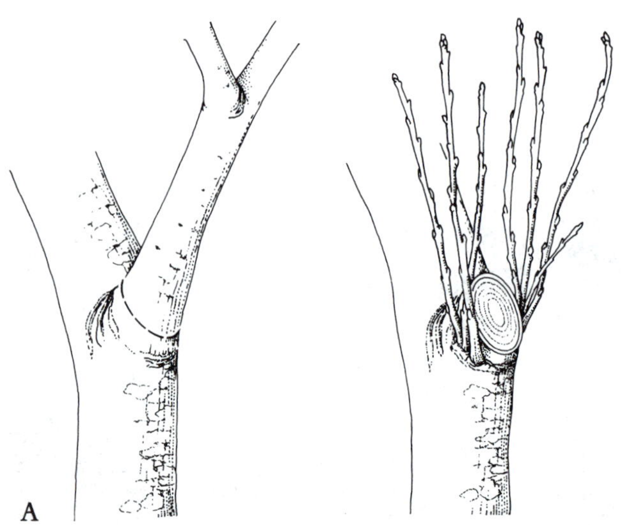

B

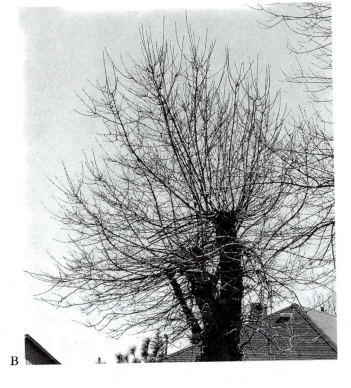

FIGURE 8-7 • Thinning out. Thinning-out cuts usually cause the plant to be more open; however, removing a large limb sometimes stimulates adventitious buds to produce sucker growth (A). Note the large number of suckers that have developed near the ends of the stubs on the excessively pruned tree skeleton (B). The cut in (A) was made at the collar, not flush with the trunk.

tree's growth habit, length of time it normally lives, and the purpose for which it is being grown. If an ornamental or shade tree has been properly selected for the location in which it is planted, it can usually be permitted to assume its natural growth habit, which is generally similar to the growth habit developed by the **central leader** system of training, best illustrated by the shape of conifer trees. With this system, the trunk is encouraged to form a central axis with the branches distributed laterally around it. Strong trees suitable for shade or timber but too tall for fruit production develop from this system.

In the open center or **vase** system of training, the central leader is cut off 18 to 30 inches (45 to 75 cm) from the ground, and two or three side branches become the scaffolds and spread to form the framework of the tree (see Figure 14-75). This system is satisfactory for peaches and a few other stone fruits; however, for plants in which tendency toward apical dominance is strong, the side branches will grow too upright if the central leader is removed.

With apples, pears, and some stone fruits, the **modified central leader**, or delayed open center, system of training is extensively used (see Figure 14-71). In this system the central leader is headed back slightly but not completely removed until after the tree is five or six years old and has borne a crop of fruit, at which time the main framework will have been established.

Several other systems of training can be used when there is limited space. When trees are trained flat in one plane so that they grow against a trellis or wall, the French term **espalier** is used to describe them (see Figure 14-73). With this type of pruning, the branches are brought out from the trunk in geometric patterns such as a U, double U, and oblique. In some sections of Europe where a lack of sufficient heat units often prevents the proper ripening of fruit, this system of pruning has been used for pears and peaches. Grown against the sunny sides of walls, the trees receive enough reflected heat to mature the fruit. This system can also be used to grow fruit along a fence or border and to grow ornamental shrubs against a wall (Figure 8-8).

Several of the many new training systems developed by orchardists could probably be used to the benefit of gardeners. With the **mold-and-hold** system trees are permitted to grow to any convenient size desired and then are kept at that size by heavy pruning. The downward orientation of side branches overcomes the inhibition of fruiting that would otherwise occur as a result of the heavy pruning. With the **pillar** system a permanent trunk is developed, and new side branches are permitted to grow each year (see Figure 14-74). The following year's crop comes from newer side branches. As with the mold-and-hold system, the side branches oriented downward are kept to encourage fruiting. The **hedgerow** system, in which dwarf trees are supported by and trained to fences and trellises, can also be adapted to small home plantings.

Recently there has been considerable publicity concerning a pruning method championed by a research forester, Alex Shigo, who argues against the practice almost universally advocated in older pruning manuals of cutting a branch flush with the larger branch from which it arose. Shigo contends that flush cuts "force the tree to sacrifice large reserves of energy and considerable quantities of wood." His research and resulting recommendations are based on his observations of the pruning that takes place naturally. At their base, where a woody plant's lateral branches connect to the trunk or to a larger branch, there is formed a distinctive ridge of tissue, or collar, that varies in width depending on the species. Shigo notes that when pruning occurs under forest conditions as a result of shading or branch crowding, unneeded branches always die back to, and break off at, the collar, regardless of how wide or narrow the collar might be. Years of observation and research have convinced him that pruning cuts made where limb abscission would naturally occur, leaving the collar intact on the tree, cause less stress to the tree and allow faster healing of the wound. Shigo's method of pruning at the collar plus other already accepted commonsense pruning practices (described in this book) have been labeled by some arboriculturists as **natural target pruning**. Although Shigo has made a major contribution by researching and formalizing this method of pruning, many observant pruners with long experience have probably always pruned at the location that resulted in the easiest and least damaging cut, the narrow base just above the collar (see Figures 8-7A and 8-9).

FIGURE 8-8 • Espalier of a pyracantha. (Courtesy of Robert E. Lyons)

General Pruning Practices

In the final analysis, pruning is an art. There are basic principles that should be followed, but once these are mastered, the pruner learns mainly by experience. Good pruners are observant people who have had considerable experience. Pruning practices for various groups of plants are briefly outlined in Chapter 14. Although each plant provides a unique pruning challenge, a few practices apply to all plants:

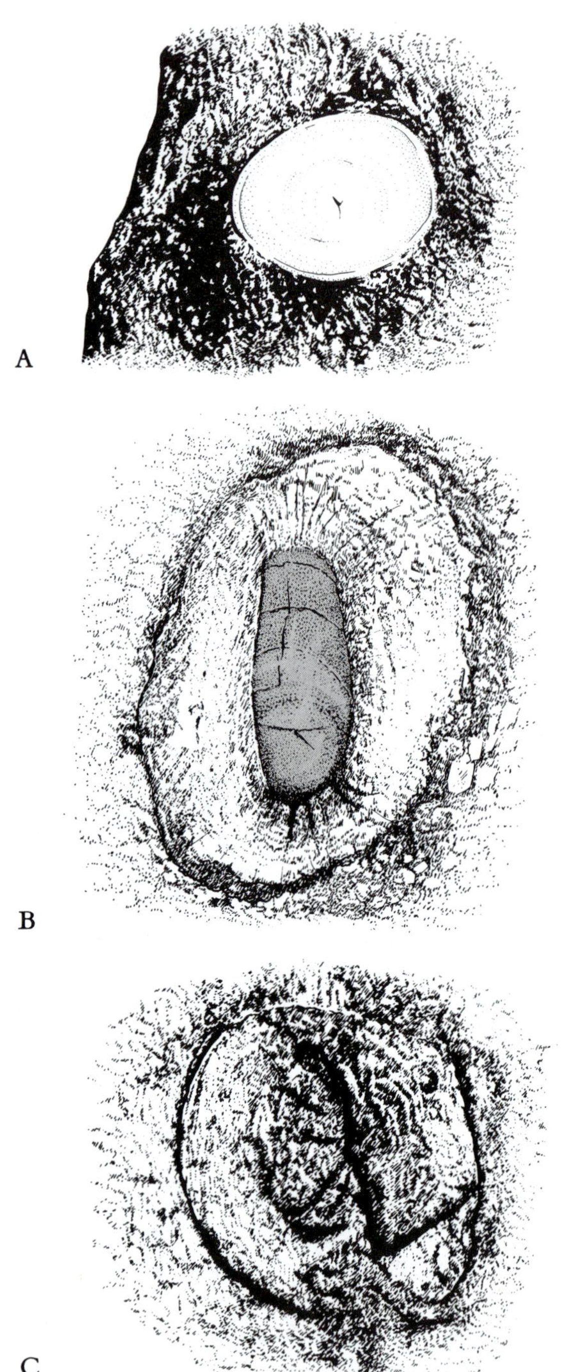

FIGURE 8-9 • A pruning wound in the process of healing. A pruning cut made smooth and flush with the collar of the remaining wood (A) will begin to callus over (B) and eventually become completely covered with bark (C).

1. Always remove dead and diseased tissue. This is important for improving the plant's appearance as well as for limiting the spread of disease. If there is the slightest suspicion that a branch is diseased, that is, if the branch has not obviously died from being overcrowded or from a lack of sunlight or if it is dying back from the tip, the pruning cut should be at least 6 inches (15 cm) behind the farthest advance of dead tissue to ensure removal of the disease-causing organisms. Where disease is present, all prunings should be burned, and with bacterial diseases, such as fireblight of apples and pears, pruning equipment should be sterilized between cuts.
2. Remove or cut back old wood, weak wood, branches that cross, and branches that form balanced crotches. A balanced crotch, which is formed by two branches growing at about the same rate from the same point on a tree, is undesirable because it tends to split (see Figure 8-10). Balanced crotches are prevented by pruning back one of the branches to keep it subordinate to the other.
3. Prune plants heavily to encourage vegetative growth and fewer and larger flowers or fruit, and prune lightly or not at all to encourage reproductive growth and numerous but smaller flowers and fruit.
4. The direction of plant growth can be regulated to some extent by the kind of pruning cut. Heading to an outward-facing bud causes the new growth to be somewhat more spreading. In general, heading back produces plants with a compact growth habit, and thinning out, by removing an entire branch, produces plants with an open growth habit.
5. Excessively heavy pruning, especially on trees, is undesirable and unnecessary. The tree or shrub should be selected to fit the location. Where pruning is necessary to keep a plant in bounds, light to moderate pruning each year is infinitely better than the excessively heavy pruning that becomes necessary when the plant has grown too large for its location.

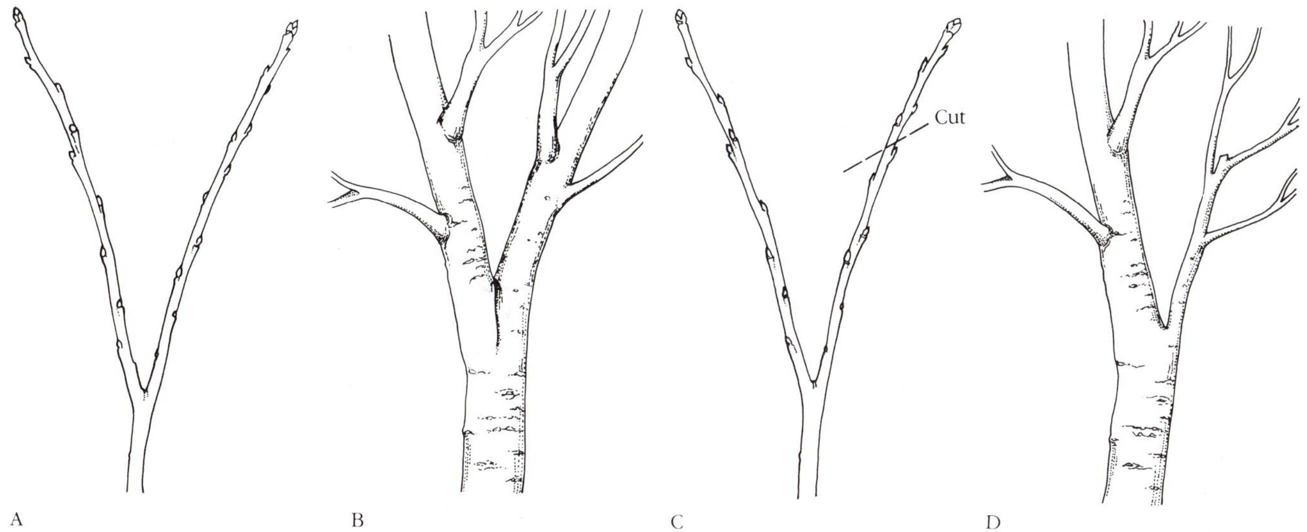

FIGURE 8-10 • Pruning a balanced crotch. If the two branches of a balanced crotch (A) are left to grow naturally, they will produce a tree with a weak framework (B) as they grow larger. If one of the branches is removed or subordinated by pruning (C), the tree will develop a much stronger framework (D) as the branches enlarge.

Flower and Fruit Thinning

Side buds are occasionally pinched from roses, peonies, chrysanthemums, and carnations to promote the development of larger terminal flowers. Although this is a thinning operation, it is called **disbudding** (see Figure 14-84). To a horticulturist, thinning generally means removing some of the small immature fruits from fruit trees (or removing excess plants from a seeded planting, described earlier). Because developing fruits compete for plant food resources, regulating the competition for mineral nutrients, light, and water by thinning the fruit is indirect but just as effective as other methods of plant growth regulation.

The main purpose of thinning is to improve fruit size and quality by providing more leaf-manufacturing area for each fruit. If thinning is done early enough, it may also increase blossoming for the following season and reduce the tendency for alternate-year bearing common in some cultivars. Thinning also allows the gardener to discard imperfect fruits — those with stings, rub damage, hail marks, and the like — thereby permitting utilization of the plant's resources by the better fruit. Thinning may also improve the winter hardening of fruit trees by lessening the drain of carbohydrates.

The timing of fruit thinning depends largely on the propensity of the tree for alternate bearing. For stone fruits and the apple and pear cultivars that normally produce a crop each year, thinning should be delayed until after the June drop (see Chapter 3), to avoid the labor of removing fruit that would fall anyway and the possibility of thinning too heavily. Normally, thinning after the June drop is too late to release carbohydrates for blossom bud formation for the following year's crop, and so some of the older apple cultivars such as 'Baldwin', 'Yellow Transparent', 'Wealthy', and 'Duchess', all of which tend toward alternate bearing, as well as other apple, pear, and plum trees that have entered an alternate-bearing cycle as a result of a spring freeze, should be thinned shortly after petals have dropped and the fruits have begun to enlarge.

Considerable fruit thinning, especially of stone fruits, is best done during the pruning operation. For peach trees, at least half the blossom buds should be removed with the wood pruned in late winter. Commercially, fruits are thinned with chemicals, but because timing is critical and application procedures vary with environment, home gardeners should not use them without local advice. The number of fruits to be left depends on the kind of tree and its vigor. A healthy, medium-sized peach tree can mature about eight hundred quality peaches. Each apple of large-fruited cultivars such as 'Delicious' requires about forty leaves to develop maximum size and quality (Figure 8-11). Only a single fruit should be left at each spur or node. Because measuring distance between fruits on a branch is usually easier than counting leaves, the following spacings are recommended, with the wider ones being for larger cultivars:

Apples and pears	6 to 8 inches (15 to 20 cm)
Peaches and nectarines	4 to 5 inches (10 to 13 cm)
Large plums and apricots	3 to 4 inches (8 to 10 cm)

Crabapples, cherries, and nuts are not usually thinned. More fruit should be left on trees thinned before their June drop. For the optimal spacing of fruit on early-thinned trees, the gardener should examine the trees and remove any surplus after the June drop.

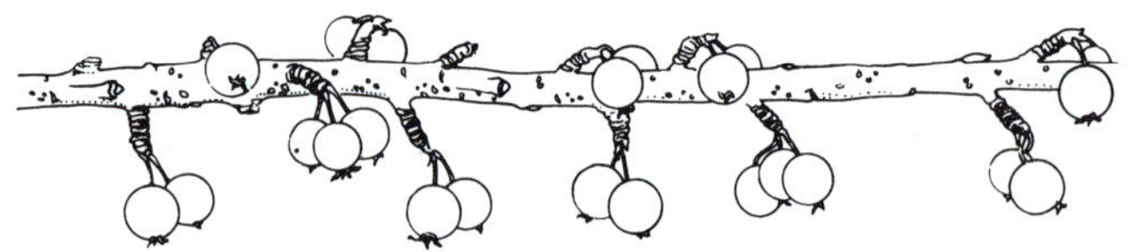

FIGURE 8-11 • Fruit thinning. The five to eight leaves produced by each spur and bud of this 15-inch (38-cm) segment of an apple tree branch can provide optimal nutrition for only two or three of the twenty-three fruits that have set. With a set this heavy, many fruits will fall during the June drop, but judicious fruit thinning still will be required.

CHEMICAL MODIFICATION OF PLANT GROWTH

Beginning during the early decades of this century and continuing to the present, plant physiologists have identified a number of chemicals that, when applied in tiny concentrations, can cause tremendous changes in the plant's growth and responses, changes far out of proportion to what would be expected from the amount applied. When first identified in plants or synthesized, these substances were often referred to as plant hormones because they have many of the characteristics of hormones found in animals. Today they are most commonly known as **plant growth substances** or **plant growth regulators**, although not all of them affect plant size. Some growth substances occur naturally in plants, and some are synthetic and have never been found in plant tissue. It is now known that in nature most plant functions are controlled by specific levels of naturally occurring growth substances interacting with one another. Synthetic substances have a molecular composition that permits them to function as substitutes for the natural ones. The synthetics are often the most useful because plants do not have mechanisms to break them down. As a result, many synthetic growth substances remain active in plants for a long time.

The basic impact of these substances is at the cellular level, where their control is primarily on the rate of cell division, cell size, and cell elongation. The effect of a specific concentration of growth regulator may be different at various times during the growing season, and one concentration may cause quite a different response than does a slightly different concentration. An example is the effect of auxin on root formation, discussed in Chapter 4. At levels below 1 ppm, auxin stimulates root formation, whereas at levels above 1 ppm it inhibits it.

Types of Plant Growth Regulators

Both natural and synthetic growth regulators can be classified into five groups based on their func-

FIGURE 8-12 • Effects of chemical growth substances. The potatoes on the left were harvested from vines that had been sprayed in early September with the sprout inhibitor maleic hydrazide. Those on the right were grown in the same location but were not treated. The photo was taken in April.

tion: (1) auxins, (2) gibberellins, (3) cytokinins, (4) ethylene and ethylene generators, and (5) growth inhibitors.

Auxins. The relationship of the principal naturally occurring auxin, indole-3-acetic acid (IAA), to various plant responses—including phototropism, the rooting of cuttings, and pruning—was described earlier. IAA is produced mainly in the apical regions of actively growing young shoots, in young leaves, and in developing embryos. It controls the rate of cell enlargement. Synthetic auxins include NAA, IBA, 2,4-D, and many other compounds. Auxins are used commercially to enhance rooting; to retard the abscission of blossoms and fruit, especially of tomatoes in cool-temperature areas and of apples and pears as they begin to ripen; to retard sprouting (Figure 8-12); and as herbicides (discussed in Chapter 9). By stimulating ethylene production, auxins hasten the ripening of fruit.

Gibberellins. Gibberellins were first recognized from the growth-stimulating effect of the corn root rot fungus, *Gibberella fujkuroi*. Dozens of gibberellins—all the natural products of higher plants or the *Gibberella* fungi, each having a slightly different chemical formula—have been isolated and identified. Gibberellins are produced in higher plants mainly in young leaves, young embryos, fruits, and roots. A major function of gibberellins in plant tissue relates to cell elongation. Commercially they are used to break the rest period of seeds and dormant buds, to prevent flower initiation, and, in combination with auxins, to prevent the abscission of fruit. They are also used to elongate and "make more typey" 'Delicious' apples and 'Bartlett' pears, to increase the berry size of seedless grapes and loosen grape clusters by lengthening the pedicel, and to lengthen the stems of sweet cherries.

Cytokinins. The word cytokinin means "cell divider," and the promotion of cell division seems to be the major function of kiniten and other natural cytokinins. Germinating seeds, roots, and young fruit are the principal sites of the synthesis of cytokinins. In addition to their role in cell division, cytokinins have been reported to contribute to apical dominance and branching; to regulate bud initiation; to enhance seed germination; to prevent abscission and the senescence of leaves, flowers, and fruits; and to inhibit root initiation.

Ethylene. For many years before ethylene was classed as a growth regulator it was known that this gas is generated by ripening fruit and that it has a role in increasing respiration and hastening the ripening process. Ethylene is synthesized in most plant organs, especially as the organs age or are subjected to stress or wounding. With the ready availability of inexpensive ethylene-generating chemicals, notably ethephon, there has been a great deal of interest in the commercial and research use of ethylene. Commercially, ethephon is used in the field to promote the uniform ripening of tomatoes and pineapple, which permits once-over mechanized harvesting. Ethephon is sometimes used to destroy the chlorophyll and develop the orange color of oranges. Bananas, which are harvested and transported when they are green, are treated with ethephon to color and ripen the bunches uniformly. Ethylene promotes the abscission of leaves, fruits, and nuts and is used to defoliate nursery stock for easier and more timely transplanting. Ethylene also stimulates floral initiation and breaks the rest in buds and seed. The ethylene generated by fruit stored in the same refrigerator as carrots, or that generated by the wounding of or fungal growth on even a single carrot root, will cause all carrots in the storage area to develop a bitter flavor. Ethylene in a carrot, onion, or potato storage area can prevent the sprouting of roots, bulbs, or tubers that are to be used after storage for seed production or propagation. Ethylene also causes flowers to wither; thus, floral arrangements are brought to an early demise if the flowers are conditioned in a refrigerator containing fruit that generates ethylene.

Growth Inhibitors. ABA, abscisic acid, abscisin II, and dormin are synonymous names for the natural plant growth regulator that contributes to the rest and dormancy of buds and seeds and to inhibiting the growth of shoots. ABA appears to inhibit growth or to induce dormancy by preventing or reducing the action of auxins, cytokinins, and gibberellins. Concomitant with its role in dormancy and winter hardiness, ABA is synthesized in the largest quantities in mature leaves when days begin to shorten in late summer and early autumn and in smaller amounts in roots, stems, and other plant tissues whenever plants are subjected to cold temperatures or to moisture stress. Immature and mature fruits also contain significant amounts. ABA and synthetic growth inhibitors are used extensively in potted-plant and other flower-growing enterprises to produce compact, free-blooming plants for retail florists and department stores. In the past, growth inhibitors were used to some extent by the fruit industry, but because of the adverse publicity concerning one of them, SADH (Alar), their use by orchardists has ceased.

Growth Regulators in the Garden

Several growth substances besides those that enhance the rooting of cuttings and assist in weed control may be useful in gardening. Compounds that cause fruit to set on tomato plants during cool periods when flowers would normally abscise (drop) are available at nurseries and are widely used by gardeners in cooler areas of the country. Also available are "stop-drop" sprays, which prevent fruit from being blown from the tree before it is fully ripe. Chemicals for blossom or fruit thinning are also available, but the timing, distribution, and concentration of their use are so precise that the home gardener who has only a few trees is wise to thin the fruit by hand. Chemicals that have a dwarfing effect on plants and encourage branching may occasionally be useful to home gardeners.

Some growth-inhibiting chemicals are being used experimentally to keep grass from growing and consequently to reduce or eliminate the need for mowing. This and countless other potential uses of growth substances promise easier and more satisfying gardening. As is true with all chemicals applied to the garden, the directions on the labels of growth substances should be followed carefully.

OTHER WAYS OF MODIFYING PLANT GROWTH

◆ ◆ ◆

In addition to being controlled by pruning and growth regulators, plant growth is modified by grafting onto size-controlling rootstocks, by scoring or girdling, and by breeding for plant size.

Grafting

Grafting (see Chapter 4) to control size is an ancient practice. With the scientific development, study, and classification of apple rootstocks by the East Malling Research Station in England, nursery workers now can produce uniform-sized apple trees ranging all the way from 8 to 10 feet (2 to 3 m) in width and height up to standard height, which may be 30 to 40 feet (9 to 12 m). Dwarfing rootstock development has been more extensive with apples than with other fruits; however, quince is usually used to dwarf pear trees, and rootstocks that slightly dwarf plum and orange trees also are available. Dwarf cultivars of peach and sour cherry are available, and dwarf sweet cherries should be available soon.

Dwarf fruit trees have been a real boon to home gardeners not only because they are small enough to grow on a city lot but also because they produce sooner after being planted and are much easier to prune, spray, harvest, and otherwise care for. Moreover, the quantity of fruit produced by a dwarf tree is more in line with the amount that one family can consume.

Dwarfing apple rootstocks are designated by the letters E.M. (East Malling) or M.M. (Malling Merton) followed by a roman numeral. The dwarf rootstock most popular with home gardeners—probably because it produces the smallest-sized tree of any widely available rootstock—is E.M. IX. Trees on E.M. IX rootstocks are not well anchored and so must be staked to prevent their being blown over or broken off by the wind. They are small, however, seldom growing over 10 feet (3 m) in height, and they often start producing fruit the second year after being planted, which accounts for their popularity. A better-anchored, fully dwarfed apple tree can be produced by using a standard seedling rootstock with E.M. IX used as an interstock, but these are more expensive, and their superiority is questioned by many authorities.

An interstock must be used for dwarfing many pear cultivars, including the popular 'Bartlett'. 'Bartlett' and some other cultivars are graft incompatible with quince (*Cydonia*), and an interstock from a cultivar such as 'Old Home', which is compatible with both 'Bartlett' pear and quince, is used as a bridge between the two (Figure 8-13).

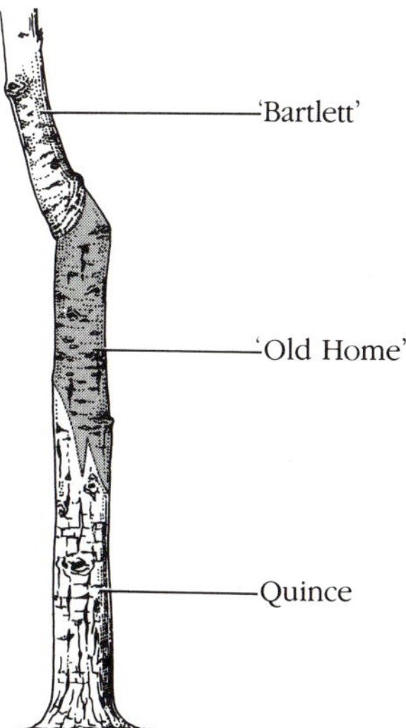

FIGURE 8-13 • Using an interstock to overcome 'Barlett'-quince graft incompatibility. During early spring an 'Old Home' scion is whip grafted onto quince (*Cydonia*), a dwarfing rootstock of pears. Later during the summer a 'Bartlett' bud is budded onto the 'Old Home' portion of the new tree. 'Old Home', a pear cultivar no longer extensively grown for its fruit, is used as a rootstock and an interstock because it is resistant to root diseases and is graft compatible with quince and also with most pear cultivars.

Homeowners often ask whether quality is affected by the rootstock. In general, dwarf fruit trees produce fruit of just as high quality as do normal-sized trees. In some instances the fruit quality of the dwarfs is higher, either because they are easier to thin out by pruning or because they usually do not produce as much shade as do normal trees, and abundant light increases color and flavor. In a few instances the quality of the scion may be affected by the root. For example, most cultivars of orange grafted to rough lemon rootstock have a lower sugar content than do the same cultivars of orange grafted to other rootstocks. This is probably due to the effect of the rootstock on the carbohydrate/nitrogen ratio of the tree.

Grafting may also be used to stimulate growth or at least provide a better root system for plants that normally produce a poor one. Hybrid tea and floribunda roses are grafted onto multiflora rose rootstocks. A multiflora root improves the vigor of the scion and also is resistant to a number of root-borne diseases. Upright junipers, *Juniperus virginiana* cultivars, produce poor root systems and are easier to propagate and better anchored if grafted to the sturdy root system of *Juniperus chinensis* 'Hertzii'.

Dwarf trees should be planted so that the graft union is above the soil surface (Figure 8-14);

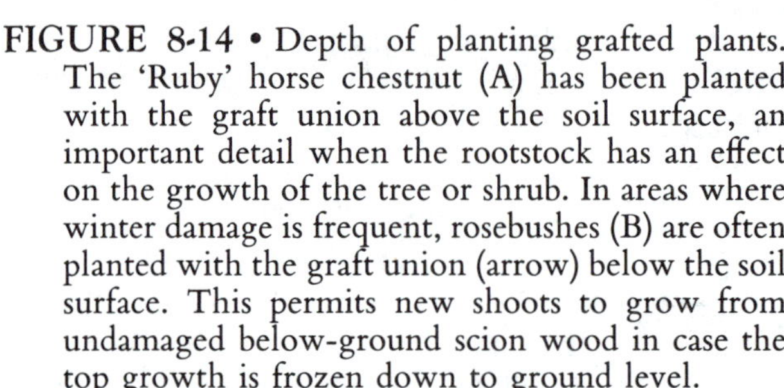

FIGURE 8-14 • Depth of planting grafted plants. The 'Ruby' horse chestnut (A) has been planted with the graft union above the soil surface, an important detail when the rootstock has an effect on the growth of the tree or shrub. In areas where winter damage is frequent, rosebushes (B) are often planted with the graft union (arrow) below the soil surface. This permits new shoots to grow from undamaged below-ground scion wood in case the top growth is frozen down to ground level.

otherwise the scion will form a root system of its own, and the effect of the rootstock will be lost. Branch growth originating below the graft union should be removed, because it will not be of the desired cultivar and because it will often outgrow the scion if allowed to remain.

Phloem Disruption

Juvenility, or the delay of fruiting, most common in apples and pears but also prevalent with plantings of other kinds of fruits, has been mentioned several times. A similar problem sometimes occurs with woody ornamentals; some cultivars of wisteria that fail to bloom year after year are a notable example. The reproduction of a nonfruiting tree or shrub can frequently be hastened by disrupting the phloem, which temporarily halts the downward transport of carbohydrates and increases the carbohydrate/nitrogen ratio in the top of the plant. It may also alter auxin and other growth-regulator relationships. The timing of **phloem disruption** is important. It must occur just before the time when blossom buds are being formed. For most temperate-zone tree fruits and spring-blooming ornamental shrubs, this is during late May of the season before blossoms and fruit are produced to affect blossom buds that are formed a month or two later in June or July.

Phloem disruption is accomplished by scoring, girdling, or bark inversion (Figure 8-15). **Scoring**, the least drastic of the three practices, consists of running a knife blade around the tree or branch in order to cut through the phloem. With scoring the effect is of short duration because the wound heals quickly. With **girdling** a strip of bark about ½ inch (1 cm) wide is removed. Generally the strip removed is not continuous; several undamaged

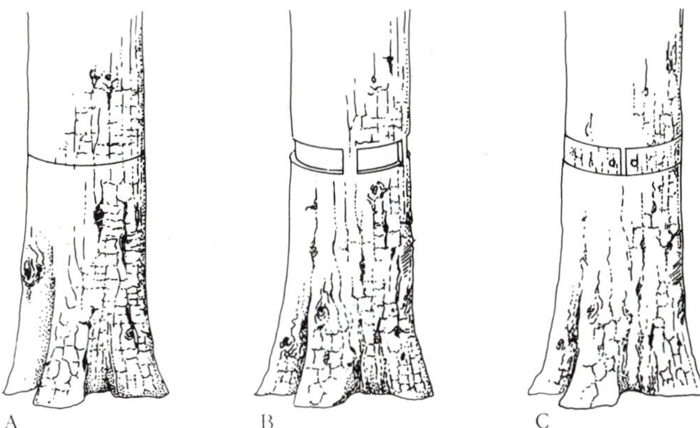

FIGURE 8-15 • Phloem disruption. Three methods of temporarily interrupting the downward flow of solutes through the phloem are scoring (A), girdling (B), and bark inversion (C).

sections of bark are left intact across the girdled area so that some phloem transport can continue. With **bark inversion** a strip of bark is removed, turned upside down, and tacked back to the area from which it was removed. Bark inversion has a less drastic but a more long-lasting effect than girdling does. The disruption of phloem by any of these methods can kill a tree or shrub if it is not done carefully, and so it is a practice of last resort when other efforts to induce reproduction have failed.

Breeding to Modify Growth

A number of years ago wheat breeders at Washington State University imported some unthrifty-appearing dwarf wheat lines from Japan. By crossing them with some of the tall wheat cultivars that had been grown for years in the Pacific Northwest, Orville Vogel and his coworkers were able to introduce short, stiff-strawed wheat cultivars that produced large heads and were adapted to that region. The major advantage of those short cultivars was that, in areas where moisture was plentiful, they could be heavily fertilized without the danger of **lodging** (falling over). Yields of wheat in the Northwest increased dramatically. The same dwarf germ plasm was used by Norman Borlaug and his coworkers to develop dwarf wheats adapted to Mexico and other subtropical regions, and a similar technology was used by plant breeders in Southeast Asia to develop dwarf rice cultivars. These introductions brought about the so-called Green Revolution and earned a Nobel Prize for Borlaug. Dwarf cereals have increased the yield potential of grains in many developing nations and are credited with saving millions of people from starvation.

Though not strictly a horticultural development, this illustrates what can be achieved by modifying plant growth by means of breeding. The development of dwarf determinant tomato plants (small-branched plants that bear fruit clusters at branch tips as well as on the stem) has made available earlier-maturing cultivars and also concentrated the maturity of this crop, in turn making mechanized harvest feasible. Bush cultivars of winter squash and pumpkins make these crops better adapted to gardens with limited space.

Plant improvement is not always a matter of cross-pollinating two varieties. Often it consists of selecting a promising individual plant that occurs in nature and propagating a new cultivar from it. For instance, orchardists have discovered occasional limbs of apples that have shortened internodes and consequently have buds and spurs much closer together. Trees propagated from scion wood from these branches, called **spur-type trees**, grow to only about two-thirds the height of normal trees and produce excellent yields. We now have spur types of many popular apple cultivars. These trees have the advantages of dwarf trees without the disadvantages of dwarf rootstocks (see "Gene Mutation and Bud Sports" in Chapter 3).

Good dwarf rootstocks of sweet cherries are not available, and naturally occurring spur-type limbs have not been found on sweet cherry trees; however, scientists in British Columbia have irradiated branches to induce a genetic mutation that caused spur-type growth in several sweet cherry cultivars, and from these they have developed spur types of several of the more popular sweet cherry cultivars.

The potential for directing plant growth by breeding has only recently been recognized. Most horticultural practices, including planting, cultivation, pest control, pruning, and especially harvest, could be facilitated by modifying the size or shape of certain plants. The most permanent and practical method of size modification of many plants is through genetic improvement.

Selected References

Brickell, C. *Pruning*. New York: Simon & Schuster, 1988.

California Polytechnic State University. *Elements of Pruning* and *Advanced Pruning*. San Luis Obispo: Vocational Education Productions VHS Video, California Polytechnic State University.

Cook, A. D., ed. *Pruning Techniques*. Brooklyn Botanic Garden Handbook 126 (special printing of *Plants and Gardens*, vol. 47, no. 1). Brooklyn, N.Y.: Brooklyn Botanic Garden, 1989.

Shigo, A. L. *Tree Pruning: A Worldwide Photo Guide*. Durham, N.H.: Shigo and Trees Assoc., 1989.

Sunset Magazine. *Pruning Handbook*. Menlo Park, Calif.: Lane, 1983.

Tukey, H. B. *Dwarfed Trees*. New York: Macmillan, 1964.

Westwood, M. N. *Temperate Zone Pomology*. 2nd ed. Beaverton, Oreg.: Timber Press, 1988.

CHAPTER 9

Garden Pests

Losses to commercial agriculture due to insects, diseases, and weeds are estimated to be between $10 billion and $15 billion annually in the United States and Canada. Birds, rats, squirrels, mice, and other animals add greatly to these extensive crop losses. Controlling plant pests is perhaps the major problem of commercial horticulture because of the ever-present yet ever-changing nature of pests. Consumers eventually pay most of the cost of agricultural pest control in higher prices for food and fiber.

Pesticide means "killer of pests" and usually refers to a chemical pest-control agent. Chemical pesticides have been researched extensively during the past five decades and currently are the most rapid and complete control measure for most controllable crop pests, especially for commercial agriculture. Because some are dangerous to animals and humans when misused, because some can pollute the environment, and because their chemistry is not understood by the general public, pest-control chemicals are a convenient source of sensational and negative publicity. Undoubtedly, chemical pest control has been overemphasized in some situations, and fortunately, other control measures are now receiving more attention. A welcome trend is the careful monitoring of pest prevalence coupled with the integration of several approaches to control each of the more devastating crop pests (see "Integrated Pest Management" later in this chapter). It should be emphasized, however, that for many pests, alternative approaches are either not available or not as reliable as chemical control. Considerably more research technology is needed before other methods can replace the chemical control of pests, especially for many kinds of large-scale commercial agriculture.

Although they are convenient, chemical pesticides are not so necessary for home gardeners as they are for large-scale growers. The small size and diversified cropping of a home garden make it less prone to pest infestation. In addition, the diversity of crops and the resulting diversity of pests make pest control with chemicals less practical in the garden because of the crop and pest specificity of many modern pesticides. Also, home gardeners can tolerate small amounts of pest damage, amounts that would not be acceptable to commercial horticulturists, whose customers demand a perfect product.

Many of the pesticides available to home gardeners today are not very effective because the high cost of developing and testing a pesticide has discouraged pesticide companies from research involving any crop not grown on a large scale. All these reasons, as well as concern about the impact of these materials on human health and the environment, have prompted many gardeners to refrain from using chemical pesticides. However, whether or not they intend to use pesticides, gardeners as citizens interested in the environment and as consumers should have some knowledge of pesticides and the regulatory control of them, if for no other reason than to be able to evaluate the conflicting and often misleading press reports concerning these agricultural tools.

Pesticide Regulations

In most countries, in recognition of the danger they can pose to human health and the environment, chemicals used in agriculture are subject to strict governmental control. In the United States the Environmental Protection Agency (EPA) is responsible for monitoring, approving, and enforcing the labeling of pesticides. The EPA can also at any time stop the sale or use of any approved pesticide it deems hazardous.

Before a pesticide is approved for release, the company producing it must show that when the chemical is applied at the recommended dosage and time, either it will leave no residue or the residue left cannot injure humans or warm-blooded animals. Testing has to be comprehensive and is expensive and time-consuming, usually continuing for several years. Each chemical must be cleared for each crop. For example, even though a company has proved that there is no residue of a particular chemical on apples when it is applied in a specified way at a specified concentration and stage of the seasonal growth cycle, it must also prove that the same amount, method, and time of application will leave no residue on peaches if it wants to recommend the chemical for peaches. The application of a pesticide can be banned in specified states, regions, or counties or at certain times of the year if its application in that location or at those times might threaten an endangered species or the general environment.

Using the information gained from its extensive testing program, a company prepares and submits to the EPA a proposed label listing those crops to which the pesticide can be applied, the concentrations, timing, and other application procedures for each formulation of the pesticide for which it is seeking approval. The label also must specify and regulate the disposal of the pesticide container and of any waste or unused pesticide, cleanup of accidental spills, protective clothing and equipment needed for application, first-aid procedures in case of accidental exposure, the time that must elapse after application before persons without protective clothing can reenter the site, possible hazards to the environment including farm animals and bees, and any other warnings and procedures deemed necessary.

When the EPA clears the chemical for use and approves the label, that label becomes a legal document. The label, which may be many pages in length, must be attached to every container in which the product is sold. Applicators who use the pesticide in any manner that does not conform to labeled directions become subject to a fine and/or arrest and can have their entire crop confiscated and destroyed.

Each formulation of each approved pesticide is classified in one of two categories, "general use" or "restricted use." Restricted-use pesticides—so classified because of their potential toxicity to the user or hazard to the environment—can be legally purchased and applied only by, or under the direction of, persons who have passed a pesticide examination and have been issued one of several classes of pesticide applicators' licenses. Persons who apply any pesticide, restricted or general use, with power equipment also must have a license.

Federal law stipulates that a state's pesticide regulations cannot be more liberal than federal regulations, but the states may impose stricter regulations, and many, especially on the West Coast, have done so. For example, in Washington state, application of the most volatile formulation of 2,4-D, the herbicide used for lawn-weed control, is banned because of the hazard that its volatility poses to the grape industry. Because they can contaminate the groundwater, a number of herbicides that the EPA has labeled for general use are classified as restricted by several western states. The more stringent state regulations do not appear on the pesticide label because labeling and packaging are required by law to be uniform throughout the United States. Instead, state regulations are promulgated by county agents and also by pesticide dealers, who face stiff penalties if they sell to unlicensed individuals any chemicals labeled as restricted by either federal or state agencies.

Pesticide Applicator Licensing

Most of the pesticides sold to the gardening public are relatively innocuous and are formulated for general use. Because these pesticides are usually applied to gardens without power equipment, most gardeners do not require a license. Growers who need to use restricted pesticides should consult their county extension agent for information on training sessions, training manuals, and examinations for pesticide applicator licenses. Pesticide training and licensing sessions are conducted periodically at several locations in each state under the direction of the EPA, usually by the state department of agriculture and the state cooperative extension service. Most states issue new pesticide application guides annually to help growers keep abreast of new materials and changing regulations.

Disposal of Pesticide Containers and Unused Pesticides

In the United States, unless the label mandates special disposal procedures, empty pesticide containers are considered nontoxic after they have been rinsed three times. The rinse water from all rinses should be emptied into the spray tank as part of the pesticide diluent and applied to the crop in accordance with labeled directions. After they have been triple rinsed, pesticide containers can be disposed of as ordinary garbage.

Growers often find themselves with a quantity of pesticide that they need to dispose of either because they bought too much and it has become outdated or because its use has been restricted and its label canceled. During the first year after a pesticide has been banned, the EPA, and presumably the pesticide-regulating agencies in other countries, often permit growers to use their remaining supply, recognizing that applying the material in the prescribed manner is the safest way to dispose of the surplus. But this is not always the case, so growers should check with a dealer or with their state extension service before using their surplus of a banned pesticide.

It is unlawful and extremely hazardous to dispose of surplus pesticides by dumping them on the ground or into a landfill or other garbage disposal site or by pouring them into a sewer or septic tank drain. Hazardous waste disposal sites are being established in many regions to accommodate pesticides, industrial wastes, and other toxic products. Disposal at these locations may require hauling for some distance and a disposal fee. To discourage the unlawful dumping of hazardous wastes, many communities designate and publicize a time during the year when homeowners can bring pesticides and other toxic surpluses to a collection site with no fee. Those who are unsure of how to dispose of questionable materials should check with local officials in charge of waste disposal or with a pesticide dealer.

WEEDS

A **weed** has been defined as a plant out of place, and almost any plant under some circumstances can be classified as out of place. However, there are some plants that are out of place under most conditions, and these are the ones that we usually categorize as weeds.

The most pestiferous weeds have certain characteristics that enable them to compete vigorously in cultivated fields. Generally, they grow more rapidly than do most crop plants. They frequently produce numerous seeds that remain viable for long periods in the soil. Usually some of the seeds display some type of dormancy and may require light, scarification, or stratification in order to germinate. In an experiment in the Midwest in which seeds of crop plants and wild species were stored underground, three wild species—curly dock (*Rumex crispus*), evening primrose (*Oenothera biennis*), and moth mullein (*Verbascum blattaria*)—still germinated after eighty years, and moth mullein still germinated after ninety years. The seeds of all crop plants had aged into inviability many years before.

The longevity and dormancy of their seeds partially explain why weeds seem to grow year after year even when they are never permitted to go to seed. Some seeds may remain physically dormant in the soil for one to twenty years or longer, until abrasion and soil chemicals eventually wear a hole in their seed coats, allowing water to reach the embryo and initiate germination. Seeds requiring light for germination remain dormant until they are brought to the surface, often by cultivating equipment, which is one good reason for only shallow cultivation of row crops. Some of the most pestiferous weeds can reproduce vegetatively as well as with seed. Bindweed (creeping Jenny, morning glory), quack grass, and Canadian thistle, three of the most notorious perennial weeds, reproduce readily from small pieces of root or rhizome (Figure 9-1).

Because weeds grow so rapidly, the damage they cause results primarily from their competition for light, water, carbon dioxide, nutrients,

FIGURE 9-1 • Perennial weeds. Quack grass, *Agropyron repens* (top), Canadian thistle, *Cirsium arvense* (bottom) are two noxious weeds that reproduce from underground rhizomes or roots. Field bindweed or wild morning glory is another garden weed that reproduces in the same way.

and space. Sometimes certain weeds inhibit the germination or prevent the growth of other species by exuding compounds selectively toxic to other plants (the allelopathy first mentioned in Chapter 5; see "Plants and Other Living Organisms" in Chapter 7).

Most weed-control methods for today's gardens can be classified as either cultural or chemical, although biological control is currently used on pastures and rangelands and may be a major control method in cultivated fields in the future.

Cultural Weed Control

Despite agricultural advances during the past one hundred years, most garden weeds are still controlled by pulling them out by hand, by using various hand tools and power equipment, and by manipulating growing procedures to reduce the weed population—all methods of **cultural** control.

Long-term weed control can be made easier by keeping weeds and weed seeds from the garden, thereby causing the reservoir of weed seeds in the garden soil to decline gradually. Perennial weeds are often introduced with a tree or shrub transplanted from the yard of a neighbor. The area around such a plant should be examined weekly for a period of time after transplanting so that any introduced weeds can be destroyed before they spread to the rest of the garden. Even those gardeners who keep their gardens free of weeds all summer often allow the weed seeds in their soil to increase by neglecting after-harvest weed control. Many kinds of annual weeds are frost hardy, short-day plants that can produce a crop of seeds when they are only a few inches high and are hardly noticeable among the frozen skeletons of the abandoned garden.

To be successful, weed control must be a community project. Even complete control will not reduce weed potential in the garden very much if seeds are blowing in or being scattered from an unmowed roadside, an abandoned yard, or a neighbor's weedy garden (Figure 9-2). Community effort is also necessary to reduce weed seed in irrigation systems, a major source of weeds spread to gardens watered from open ditches. Ditch banks should be mowed or chemically sprayed and screens installed to remove seeds before the water reaches cultivated areas. If there are no weed screens in the main canal system, growers should install their own in the waterway leading to the garden.

FIGURE 9-2 • The difficulty of weed control. Winds can blow seeds from these uncontrolled dandelions over many square blocks of lawns and gardens. (Courtesy of D. Cavagnaro/Visuals Unlimited)

Controlling weeds in annual crops is much easier if planting is delayed until the soil has warmed sufficiently to permit crop seeds to germinate and seedlings to grow rapidly. The planting bed should be cultivated lightly just before planting. If no large weeds are present, light raking with a garden rake may disturb the soil sufficiently to dry out and destroy germinating weed seeds and small seedlings.

The hoe, various kinds of cultivating equipment described in Chapter 5, and hand weeding are the most common methods of ridding the yard and growing garden of weeds. One important aspect of cultivating for weed control, whether it be tractor cultivation or hand weeding, is that weeds are much easier to kill when they are small. A few hours each week spent keeping the garden free of weeds are a much more economical use of time than several days of work once the weeds have become large.

Some weeds growing within the crop row can frequently be smothered by using a hoe or cultivator to mound enough soil onto the crop row to cover the weeds. Crop plants must not, of course, be covered. **Mounding** also helps keep irrigation furrows open in rill-irrigated fields. Later in the season cultivation should be shallow, both to prevent damage to the expanding crop roots and to avoid bringing a fresh supply of weed seeds to the surface, where they can germinate. When larger weeds are pulled from the plant row, one hand should be placed on the soil surrounding small nearby crop plants to prevent their being pulled up with the weeds.

Chemical Weed Control

With the advent of herbicides (plant killers) in the 1930s, the science of weed control began an advance that has continued at an ever-increasing pace. Although herbicides receive the same negative publicity as do other pesticides, herbicides, including all those formulated for homeowners, normally are less toxic to humans and warm-blooded animals than are insecticides. Nonetheless, a few used for commercial agriculture are quite toxic. In addition, most can destroy nontarget crops when carried to them by wind or water. In places where the water table is near the surface, the groundwater can be contaminated by certain kinds of herbicides percolating through the soil. The main long-term detrimental effect of herbicides is in altering the flora of a particular area repeatedly treated with a single herbicide over many years. An example of this result is the elimination of a number of broad-leaved species in certain wheat areas of the Great Plains and Pacific Northwest where phenoxy herbicides have been used year after year over extensive areas.

Classification of Herbicides. There are several terms with which plant growers must be acquainted if they are to apply herbicides intelligently. First, herbicides can be selective or nonselective. A **selective herbicide** is one that kills some kinds of plants with little or no injury to others; a **nonselective herbicide** is one that kills indiscriminately all plant growth to which it is applied.

Herbicides can also be classified as **contact** or **translocated,** depending on whether they injure only those parts of the plant to which they are applied or are translocated through the vascular system of the plant so that the roots and other organs to which the spray was not applied are also killed. Herbicides are classified as **residual** or **nonresidual,** depending on whether they kill only at the time of application or whether they remain active in the soil for a longer period. The period of time during which an herbicide remains active depends on many factors and may range from a few days to a number of years. I recall a neighbor who used sodium chlorate when it first became available to control wild morning glory in his garden. The morning glory was completely eradicated, but it was seven or eight years before anything else would grow on that plot of ground!

Soil texture, amount of moisture, exposure to light, and other environmental factors affect the residual life of an herbicide. Many herbicides remain active longer in sandy soils or soils low in organic matter, perhaps as a consequence of low soil microorganism activity and low moisture in these kinds of soil. For example, atrazine used on sweet corn in the Midwest always breaks down during the season in which it is applied, but in some irrigated areas of the Northwest, atrazine can be injurious to crops planted one year or even two years after it has been applied to a field. These kinds of variation in residual activity create serious problems for the commercial companies that supply these herbicides and for the growers who utilize them.

Herbicides are also classified according to the stage of growth of the crop when they are applied. A **preplant herbicide** is one that is applied before the crop is seeded; a **preemergence herbicide** is applied after the crop has been seeded but before it comes through the ground; and a **postemergence herbicide** is applied after the crop has emerged.

Use of Herbicides in Home Gardens. Because so many different kinds of plants grow around most homes and because weeding with a hoe or by hand is not completely prohibitive, herbicides are not as important for the home garden as they are for larger acreages. Nevertheless, considerable quantities of herbicides, mostly 2,4-D (2,4-dichlorophenoxyacetic acid) for weed control in lawns, are used around American homes. Although 2,4-D was one of the earliest herbicides, it is still one of the most widely used. It is one of the group of phenoxy compounds that kill broad-leaved plants but do not damage most kinds of lawn grasses unless applied at excessive rates. Homeowners who are contemplating the use of 2,4-D should make sure there are no regulations in their community prohibiting its use. This material should not be applied when there is a wind or even a slight breeze, and nearby broad-leaved plants should be protected by covering or otherwise making sure there is no drift toward them. As is true for application of any pesticide, labeled directions and local recommendations should be carefully followed. Usually an amine salt of 2,4-D is the only type supplied by nurseries and garden stores. The ester forms should never be applied around the home; they are volatile and are almost certain to drift and injure nearby susceptible plants.

Nonselective residual herbicides can be used to control unwanted weeds in a gravel pathway, along a fence row, or beneath a loose brick, cement block, or graveled patio area. Anyone contemplating the application of long-lasting residual herbicides should be certain that the area treated will not be needed for growing plants in the foreseeable future, that the herbicide chosen cannot be transported to other locations by either water or vaporization, and that there are no nearby trees with roots near the surface of the treated area.

The use of herbicide formulations available for controlling herbaceous weeds around woody plants is sometimes practical for the yard or garden. In some vegetable gardens a preplant or preemergence treatment to control annual weeds is possible. An example is the use of the herbicide trifluralin, which prevents the germination and seedling growth primarily of those plants in a single plant family, Chenopodiaceae. When the crop plants to be seeded—beans, lima beans, tomatoes, and so on—are not susceptible, and most of the weeds—redroot pigweed, lambs'-quarters, tumble pigweed, and so on—belong to the Chenopodiaceae family, the preemergence spray will control the weeds for at least half the summer. Postplant herbicides are available whenever relatively large plots of a single crop are grown.

Another herbicide that may be valuable to homeowners for controlling perennial weeds like Canadian thistle and field bindweed is glyphosphate (sold primarily under the trade name Roundup). Hoeing or pulling these weeds to control them becomes discouraging because their extensive underground root system, which can sprout new shoots from the tiniest segment, has food reserves so large that the roots can continue to sprout even when their above-ground growth has been cut off dozens of times. The most effective control for these perennial weeds is to allow them to grow in the spring without being disturbed until they have formed blossom buds. At that stage cut them off with a hoe, mower scythe, or whatever is practical; then let them resprout. When they have grown to the blossom-bud stage the second time, spray them with glyphosphate at the recommended rate. Be extremely careful to spray only the weeds. Glyphosphate is a translocated, nonselective herbicide, so it moves into and kills the underground, as well as above-ground, parts of any plants on which it falls. It is inactivated as soon as it contacts the soil, and so it poses no threat to later plantings. A small spray bottle may be used to treat individual weeds that may be growing among flowers and shrubs. The weeds may need to be oriented away from garden plants or a cardboard or plastic shield used in order to allow the spray to cover weeds without falling on desirable plantings. It may take a week or more for the weeds to show the effects of the spray. Following the initial treatment, new weed growth should be sprayed shortly after it appears during the remainder of the summer and fall. Where there is a heavy weed infestation, the treatment may need to be repeated for several years.

Garden Plant Injury from Herbicides. Herbicide damage to home plantings, often unrecognized, is common in many sections of North America, and unfortunately, very little can be done to alleviate the problem once damage has occurred. If the injury is not too severe, the affected plants may ultimately recover, but prevention is the only sure solution.

Symptoms of herbicide damage vary with the kind of herbicide, the concentration of the dosage, the species of plant, and the environment. Herbicide damage is sometimes difficult to distinguish from disease or nutrient deficiency symptoms. The type of herbicide damage most common in home gardens is caused by phenoxy compounds such as 2,4-D, mainly because phenoxys are the herbicides most commonly used in urban and suburban areas and because several garden crops are susceptible to injury by such compounds. Tomatoes and grapes are extremely sensitive; lilacs and maples are easily damaged; and most broad-leaved plants can be killed by moderate concentrations. Symptoms of phenoxy damage occur commonly on those parts of the plant that are growing rapidly. Expanding leaves become elongated, and their veins become lighter in color and contrast sharply with the remainder of the leaf (Figure 9-3). The growing point is usually abnormal and is often killed, and the plant appears generally stiff and stunted.

Herbicide mixtures containing amino triazole prevent the formation of chlorophyll, causing the growing parts of plants injured by this herbicide to be white instead of green. Nonlethal doses of several other herbicides cause severe upward cupping of leaves. **Fasciation,** the growing together of plant parts that are normally separated, is another symptom common with herbicide damage. In fact,

FIGURE 9-3 • Herbicide damage. The squash leaf on the right has been damaged by a phenoxy herbicide. Compare it with the normal leaf (left).

herbicide damage is suspected whenever there is abnormal plant growth with no other obvious cause.

Herbicide damage frequently is a result of the grower's own carelessness. Protecting susceptible plantings may require more than preventing spray materials from falling on them. Herbicides should *never* be applied when the air is moving, and label precautions concerning application at high temperature should be followed because most herbicides are volatile at high temperatures. Some nonselective translocated herbicides can enter the roots of woody plants in treated fencerows or ditchbanks and can be translocated to kill trees and shrubs some distance away. During the past few years some puzzling herbicide damage to woody plants has been traced to the use of fertilizer–herbicide mixtures formulated for spring lawn weeding and feeding. Gardeners should be cautious when using these materials around trees and shrubs.

Herbicide contamination of equipment used for application of other pesticides is a common cause of plant damage. Because some herbicides affect sensitive plants at concentrations ranging down to parts per billion and because it is almost impossible to cleanse the application equipment of every trace of a chemical, sprayers used for herbicides normally should not be used to apply insecticides or other garden sprays. Numerous instances of suspected plant damage by insecticide sprays have been traced to herbicide contamination. Growers who live in areas where weeds along roadsides and in vacant lots are controlled are fortunate, but the spraying of such waste places by inexperienced or careless public employees frequently results in herbicide damage to sensitive plants in nearby yards.

Community cooperation, zoning for home building, and regulation of pesticide application are essential to areas where gardening and extensive field monocropping exist side by side. There may sometimes be an unintentional drift of herbicides such as 2,4-D from commercial agricultural areas. Every effort is usually made to avoid such problems, but unusual weather factors can cause an unexpected drift. Herbicides are as necessary to the present-day production of some commercial crops as are light and water. Anyone contemplating the purchase of a few acres for garden crop production, or even for a landscaped home in a rural setting, should consider the herbicides being used on crops in the area. A person who decides to grow grapes in an area surrounded by wheat monoculture where phenoxy herbicides are aerially applied to every field several times each year will not be a happy neighbor. Because most herbicides are heavier than air, low-lying areas are more subject to herbicide damage than are slopes.

Damage to houseplants from herbicides or other chemicals accidently introduced in potting soil mixes is not uncommon and is difficult to trace. Soil washed from fields treated with herbicides and manure from stables where strong disinfectants have been used or from feedlots treated to prevent plant growth have occasionally been the source of chemical contaminants in potting mixes. Most of the recent instances of houseplant damage from herbicidelike chemicals to come to my attention were ultimately traced to sand purchased from sand, gravel, and cement companies. It has not yet been determined whether the contamination came from nonselective herbicides used to control weeds around the sand pit or from some material added to sand used for building purposes.

Biological Weed Control

Biological control, which has received considerable publicity in recent years, is the use of one living organism to control another. There are two major categories of biological control of weeds—crop competition and the introduction of insects or diseases to which the weed is susceptible. Weed control is much easier where a good stand of the crop is produced with plenty of light, moisture, and fertilizer. For many horticultural crops, weed control ceases to be a problem as soon as the leaves of the crop plant have spread to the point that most of the ground beneath them is shaded. Under these conditions, light and perhaps other factors necessary for plant growth are so limiting that weeds cannot become established. Crop plants may also control weeds to some extent by chemical competition. The fact that some weeds give off substances that are toxic to crop plants has already been cited. Conversely, some (perhaps all) crop plants exude substances that inhibit or prevent the germination of seeds or the growth of other competing plants in the immediate vicinity. The study of chemical "warfare" among plants is just beginning, but an understanding of this phenomenon would certainly provide ammunition for growers in their age-old struggle to control weeds.

Another facet of weed control that has received renewed interest in recent years but so far has had little impact on horticulture is the introduction of diseases to which weeds are susceptible or of insects that feed exclusively on a particular weed or weeds. This method of control has been used with some success to control certain range and pasture weeds. For example, the beetle *Chrysalina gemellata,* for which the Klamath weed, *Hypericum perforatum,* is the only known host, has been introduced into areas infested by this weed and has provided considerable control of it. This weed is a serious pest of western rangelands because it is toxic to animals. The use of pathogenic organisms and insects to control weeds is promising, and widespread research interest in biological control should result in new and interesting weed-control techniques. Unfortunately, many of these techniques may not be applicable to home gardens where the control may be too slow or where desirable plants as well as weeds may be controlled.

PLANT DISEASE AND INSECT PESTS

◆ ◆ ◆

Plant diseases and insects will be discussed together, because their control measures are similar and can be classified into the same general categories. A **disease** is often defined as any kind of injurious abnormality; it can be a physiological disorder caused by an environmental condition as well as an abnormality caused by living organisms. A **pathogen** is a biological agent that incites an injurious abnormality, and so in the broadest sense, insects and even rodents, deer, and elk can be regarded as pathogens. Generally, though, when we speak of pathogens we are referring to four different groups of organisms—viruses, bacteria, fungi, and nematodes. Several other terms used during the remainder of this chapter should be defined: A **parasite** is an organism that derives nourishment from another living organism; the **host** is the organism that provides the nourishment. An **obligate parasite** is one that can survive only on the living host. The **host range** is the group of organisms on which a pathogen or insect normally survives. A pathogen or insect with a narrow host range—that is, one able to survive on only a few plants—is generally easier to control than is one with a wide host range.

FIGURE 9-4 • Root knot lesions, a result of nematode infection. (Courtesy of John D. Cunningham/Visuals Unlimited)

Most people are aware of the different kinds of pathogens as all of them are associated with human and animal disorders as well as with plant problems. A **virus** is an infectious particle made up of a nucleic acid surrounded by a protein sheath. The known viruses are obligate parasites. **Bacteria** are one-celled plants that enter the host through wounds and most frequently rot the tissue they infect. **Fungi** are multicelled plants containing no chlorophyll. They are responsible for a majority of those disorders referred to as rusts, smuts, molds, mildews, and blights. **Nematodes** are unsegmented worms that, under optimum viewing conditions, are barely visible to the naked eye. In addition to countless diseases known to be caused directly by nematodes, many others are caused by bacteria and fungi that enter the plant through wounds made initially by nematodes (Figure 9-4). A number of root diseases occur only when both a fungus and a nematode are present in the soil.

The class of organisms that most gardeners mean when they use the term **insect** is the larger group to which insects belong—the arthropods. This group includes ticks, mites, slugs, snails, and various other similar organisms, but common usage lumps together all of these organisms as "insects" (Figure 9-5).

The variety of forms through which insects pass during their life cycles poses problems in their identification and control. Most start as an egg, pass through several **larval** stages into a **pupa**

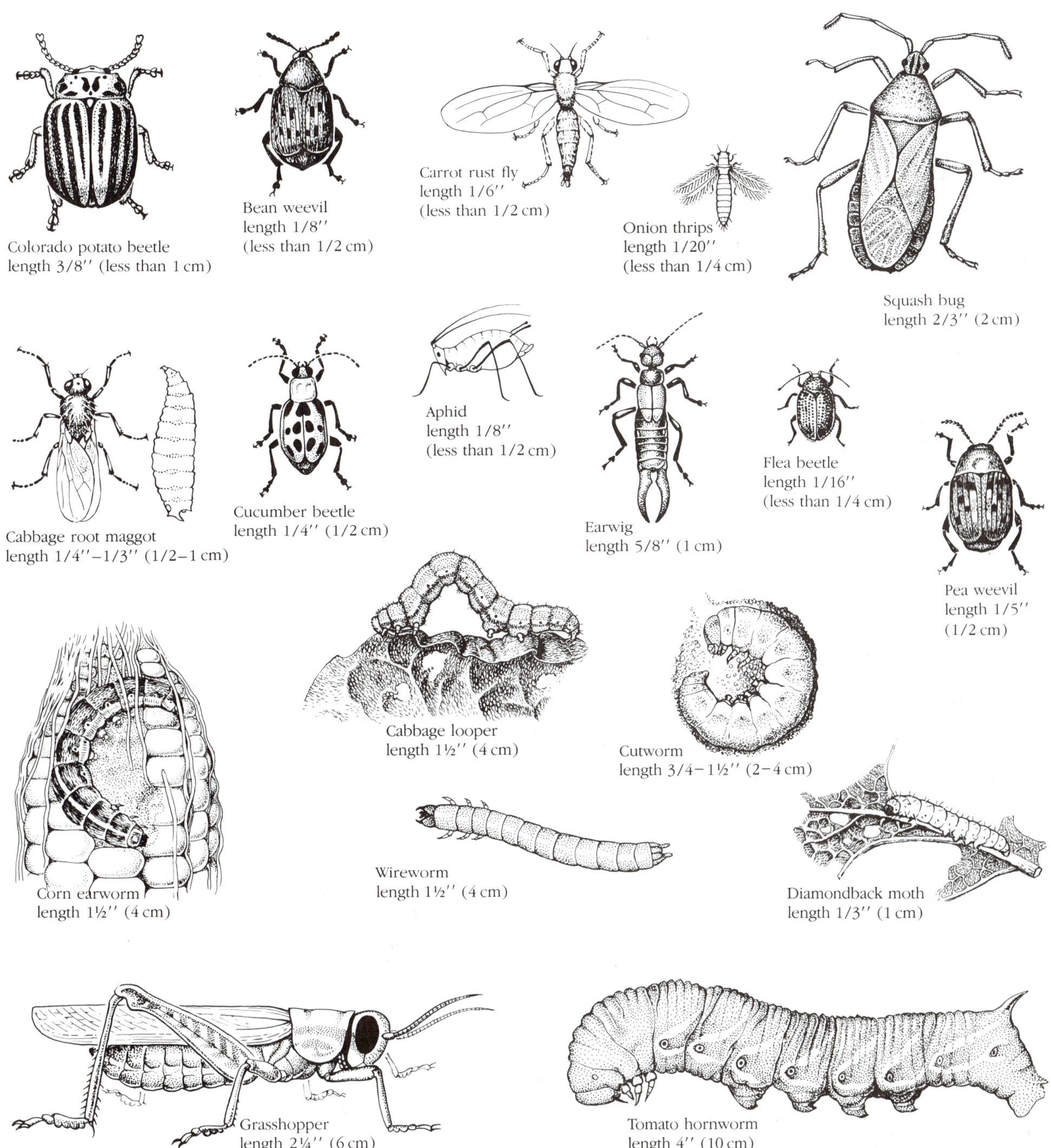

FIGURE 9-5 • Some insect pests of garden plants. (Courtesy of Washington State University)

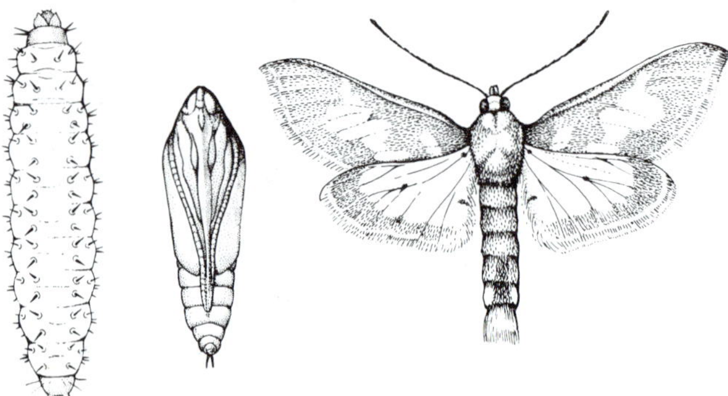

FIGURE 9-6 • The larva, pupa, and adult of a pickleworm. (Courtesy of USDA)

(resting stage), and finally emerge as an adult (Figure 9-6). Usually insects are most damaging in the larval or feeding stage. It is sometimes difficult to correlate the larvae with adult flies, moths, or butterflies because the organisms look so different at each stage.

How Pathogens and Insects Damage Plants

Crop-infesting insects and plant pathogens are troublesome mainly because they reproduce and feed. They continue to reproduce in prodigious numbers until one of three things occurs: (1) Their food supply becomes exhausted; (2) the environment becomes unfavorable for their continued multiplication; or (3) they are destroyed by a predator.

The food supply of an insect or plant pathogen becomes exhausted only when its entire host plant population is destroyed. This occurs most frequently when an entirely new pest is introduced into a region, as has occurred or is occurring with several North American species. The destruction of the American chestnut by chestnut blight introduced from the Old World is one example of a species annihilated by a newly introduced pathogen, and the relentless advance of Dutch elm disease across the continent is an example of a plant species in the process of being destroyed by a pathogen. Sometimes a host species is saved from a virulent new pathogen when genetic resistance appears in a few plants from which a new population less vulnerable to the insect or disease can be developed. This appears to be occurring with white pine in its relationship to white pine blister rust, a disease introduced from Europe that threatens the existence of all five-needled pines in North America.

In temperate climates the changing of the seasons is the most common environmental phenomenon that helps control insects and plant pathogens. Even a few degrees' drop or rise in average daily temperature or a drop or rise in humidity can mean the difference between serious pest damage and no damage at all. Pesticide action can be viewed as another example of environmental change because most pesticides control by changing the chemical environment so that it is unfavorable for the pest.

Under natural conditions, virtually all living organisms have other organisms that prey on them, keeping their population in check. This predation, coupled with genetic changes in the resistance or susceptibility of host and pest, brings about the so-called balance of nature that is nearly universal where host and pest have been associated for long periods. Because almost all garden plants were introduced into North America from elsewhere and because many popular cultivars are new developments, natural balance has not yet become established with most cultivated species. Furthermore, even when a natural balance among an insect or pathogen, its predators, and the host crop does exist, the pest control it affords is usually only partial.

Damage to a host crop by fungi, bacteria, nematodes, and insects comes about in at least three ways — (1) from direct action on the plant, usually through the loss of tissues or juices by direct feeding; (2) from toxic substances secreted into the plant; and (3) from secondary organisms that enter the plant as a result of activities by the insect or pathogen. Viruses injure plants by interfering with translocation, growth, and photosynthesis and by directly affecting the genetic mechanisms of cells.

Symptoms and Signs of Insect and Disease Infestation

Symptoms (a plant's expression of or response to an attack by an organism) and **signs** (structures produced by the causal organism) of insects and diseases are many and varied, ranging from a measurable yield decrease with no visible symptoms to the complete consumption or sudden death of the plant. Rarely, an infectious organism actually stimulates plant growth, an example being the root-rotting organism *Gibberella fujkuroi,* which also produces growth-promoting gibberellic acid. The nature of insect damage usually depends on how the insect feeds. Because chewing insects—beetles, caterpillars, and the like—eat away parts of the plant, the results of their feeding can easily be seen (Figure 9-7). Some chewing insects, such as the tent caterpillar, produce a web. Rasping insects like thrips and mites remove only the surface layers of a leaf or petal, causing affected plants to have uneven coloration or brown spots; a stunted, unthrifty appearance; abnormal growth; and sometimes (e.g., thrips on gladiolus) flower bud failure. Mites may also leave a webbing on the underside of affected leaves, which often have a dusty appearance.

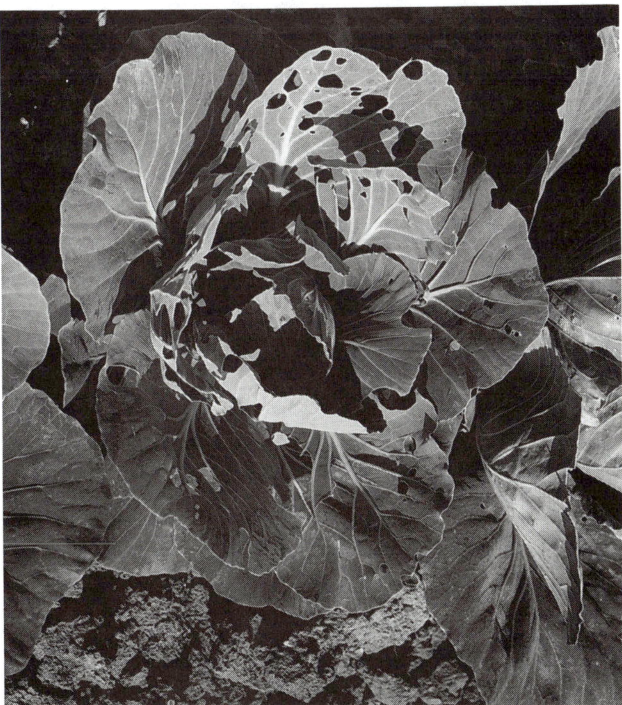

FIGURE 9-7 • Insect damage. This cabbage plant has been extensively damaged by the cabbage looper. (Courtesy of John Colwell/Grant Heilman)

Leaf miners tunnel under the surface of the leaf, causing white areas or streaks where the interior leaf cells have been destroyed. Plants infested with sucking insects such as aphids, scale, and leafhoppers grow slowly, partly because the insects are using the plants' manufactured food. Sucking insects often cause abnormal growth of meristematic tissues, either by injecting digestive toxins into the phloem or by transmitting viruses. The secretion of enzymes that affect cells in the vicinity of their feeding is common among sucking insects, but a few affect tissues quite far from where they are feeding. For example, a single squash bug feeding at the base of a squash plant can cause its entire host plant to go into shock and wilt. Like other sucking insects, scale insects cause the slow growth and unthrifty appearance of their host plant. The diagnostic feature for most scale insects, however, is the rough, scaly shell or cottonlike cover they build for their protection and for securely anchoring themselves to the host.

The most apparent signs of fungus diseases that attack above-ground plant tissues are the **mycelium** (threadlike vegetative structures) and the fruiting bodies—rust pustules, smut bodies, leaf spots, spore capsules, sclerotia, and toadstools (Figure 9-8). **Necrotic** (dead) areas on leaves, stems, or other plant parts are common symptoms of fungus diseases. The first noticeable symptoms of fungi attacking roots or the vascular system may be sudden wilting or death as a result of root destruction or xylem blockage. Phloem blockage by fungi may result in enlarged nodules on the upper part of the plant where carbohydrates are accumulating.

Bacterial diseases are characterized by their rapid spread. In herbaceous tissues they often result in soft rot and frequently are secondary invaders after the initial infection by fungi. In

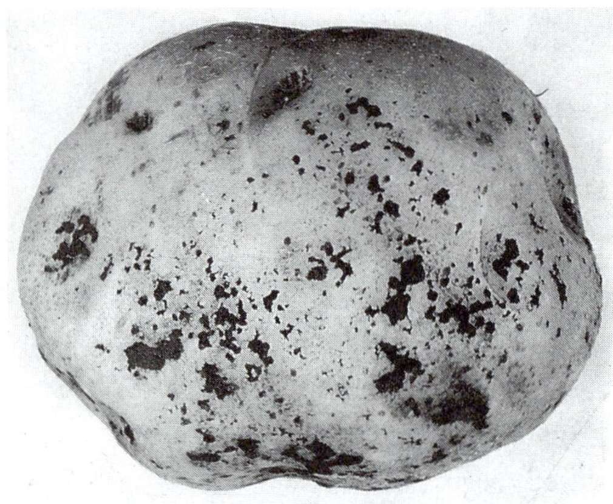

FIGURE 9-8 • *Rhizoctonia* (black scurf on potatoes). The black specks on the tuber are the hard fruiting bodies (sclerotia) of the fungus. The sclerotia send out mycelia that attack and kill the developing potato sprouts when infected tubers are planted. (From Agriculture Canada Publication 1492, "Diseases and Pests of Potatoes," revised in 1974 and reproduced by permission of the Minister of Supply and Services, Canada)

woody tissues attacked by bacteria the bark at first appears dark and water soaked and later becomes blistered and peels. Some bacteria may cause an abnormal growth of plant tissue—galls, root enlargement, and the like.

Viruses cause the death of the plant, stunting and yellowing of the plant body **mosaic** (light and dark areas) of stem and leaf (Figure 9-9), abnormal growth, or no obvious symptoms at all. The presence of a virus in a virus-infected plant showing no symptoms (a symptomless carrier) can be detected only by a complex laboratory antigenic procedure or by transmission to another plant on which it does produce symptoms. Often two viruses, neither of which produces symptoms when alone, together can severely injure infected plants.

The presence of many species of nematodes is first signaled by areas in the garden or field where susceptible plants do not grow well or sometimes do not grow at all. These areas enlarge year by year whenever susceptible crops are produced. One of the most common nematodes, the root-knot nematode, causes odd shaped, fleshy enlargements along lateral roots and raised lumps on carrots or potato tubers (see Figure 9-4).

FIGURE 9-9 • Maize dwarf mosaic virus. Many viruses cause distortion of plant tissues, lack of growth, loss of chlorophyll, and reduction of yield. (Courtesy of Grant Heilman)

Transmission of Plant-Infesting Insects and Diseases

Many, perhaps a majority of, plant pests rely wholly or partly on the movement of water and wind to disseminate. Some, for example, the corn earworm and certain rusts, survive through the winter only in mild-winter areas and spread north with the south and southwest winds as the season progresses. Others, such as the beet leafhopper, winter over on plants in desert areas or along fencerows and spread into cultivated fields during the summer. For some, including most wind-disseminated fungi, wind is the only means of long-distance spread. For others, wind merely increases the distance and rate of their travel. For example, although leafhoppers are quite capable of flying long distances, they are always more prevalent and spread greater distances in the direction of the prevailing winds. Winged aphids, too, rely on wind to speed their movement and increase their travel distance.

Several of the more serious fungus diseases, including late blight and early blight of potatoes and tomatoes, can spread only if water is present for a specified period of time, and most fungal and bacterial diseases are more severe in areas with wet climates than they are in drier areas. Water is necessary, sometimes for the growth of the pest, sometimes for its spread, and sometimes for both.

Temperature influences the spread of insects and diseases by affecting both the survival and the reproduction of the pest and the susceptibility of the host. Generally, the higher the temperature is, the more rapidly pests will multiply and spread. Freezing temperatures greatly reduce the numbers of insects and disease organisms and may eradicate some species from the area. Plants are more susceptible to pest attack when temperatures are either above or below the optimal range for plant growth.

Fungus spores, bacteria, and certain viruses can be spread by birds, animals, and people—on feathers, fur, clothes, claws, beaks, and hands. Some viruses are transmitted only by insects and often by a single species of sucking insect; for instance, aphids, leafhoppers, and white flies transmit many kinds of virus diseases and are responsible for the spread of most kinds that attack primarily the phloem.

Human carelessness is often responsible for spreading garden pests. Viruses and some diseases caused by other organisms can be spread with plant parts used for asexual propagation. To reduce the dissemination of such diseases, grower organizations have established plant certification programs for seed potatoes, small-fruit planting stock, and bulbs and corms.

Pathogens can also be spread with seed. Seeds destined for gardens are often treated with chemical dusts, partly to eliminate pathogens that might be on the exterior of the seed and partly to protect the seed from soil-borne pathogens. The seeds themselves of a few garden crops can carry virus or bacteria. Use of disease-free seed is usually the only control for these kinds of diseases, but with a few, blackleg of cabbage being one, which is discussed later in this chapter, it is possible to heat the seed to a temperature high enough to destroy the pathogen but not so high that it damages the viability of the seed. The seed packet of cabbage and related crops often carries the label "hot-water treated."

The grower who transplants from a friend's garden runs the risk not only of bringing in disease or insects on the above-ground plant parts but also of introducing nematodes and other soil-borne pathogens that are almost impossible to control. Soil-borne pests can be introduced on soil particles that adhere to equipment and tools used previously in an infested garden or even from mud tracked into the garden on dirty shoes. Some virus and bacterial diseases can be spread from plant to plant with unwashed hands. Plants that are handled frequently, such as staked tomatoes trained to a single stem or pinched chrysanthemums, are especially prone to the spread of these diseases. The transmission by smokers of tobacco mosaic virus to such relatives of tobacco as tomatoes, eggplants, peppers, petunias, and potatoes is probably not common, but because live viruses can be found in cigars and cigarettes, smokers should wash their hands as a precaution before handling any of these solanaceous garden crops.

Unsanitary garden conditions, failure to dispose of insect- or disease-infested plant material promptly by burning, use of diseased plant materials in compost piles, failure to prune away diseased plant tissue, and any practice that reduces garden plant vigor increase the likelihood of disease and insect damage.

CONTROL OF GARDEN INSECTS AND DISEASES

◆ ◆ ◆

The Pest Cycle

Although gardeners can control insects and diseases by following directions in a publication or on the label of a pesticide container, they should realize that the recommended control is based on a knowledge of the **pest cycle,** the sequential changes and interactions that occur in the host/pathogen relationship through their respective life cycles. Researchers who seek and eventually devise controls for various insects and pathogens must have a thorough knowledge of the pest cycle because control is easiest, and sometimes possible only, during one stage of the life of a crop or of insects or disease pests.

Legal Control

The most effective and least costly way to combat a pest is to keep it out of the area. Because this involves laws and their enforcement, it is referred to as **legal control,** and it is usually administered by federal or state plant quarantine offices. Travelers know that customs officials do not permit certain plant and animal products to be brought into the United States or Canada. This is an attempt to prevent the entry of insects and disease pests that are not found here but are serious problems in other parts of the world. Some of the most severe disease and insect epidemics (as well as almost all of our serious weed infestations) have resulted from the importation of a pathogen or insect (or weed seed) on products from other countries. Chestnut blight, Dutch elm disease, white pine blister rust, Japanese beetles (Figure 9-10), earwigs, fire ants, and late blight of potatoes are but a few of the unwelcome plant-pest immigrants of the past 150 years. The millions of dollars spent and the ill will generated by aerial sprays used to eradicate a few oriental fruit flies accidentally introduced into California and Florida a few years ago is an example of how costly the careless transport of plant materials can be. But the cost of eradication is only a fraction of a percent of the cost represented by the loss of yield and quality to growers and consumers had the fly been allowed to remain and spread.

Legal control cannot be effective without the cooperation of the public. The number of North American citizens traveling abroad is so great and there are so many ways of sneaking in illegal plant products that it becomes impossible for quarantine officers to control the importation of all illegal plants. Rather, it must be the responsibility of each citizen, and especially those interested in plants and gardens, to understand and educate others about the serious consequences of illegal plant and animal introduction.

Besides quarantine at the national level, there is some legal control on interstate and interprovince shipments of plant products. The grape root louse, phylloxera, and the corn borer have so far been effectively kept out of some of the western states partly as a result of inspection and control of interstate shipment of grape vines and corn seed. For many years all people driving into California have been stopped at the border and subjected to an inspection in order to prevent the importation of certain citrus fruit pests into that state. Control of the shipment of plant products to and from Hawaii and Puerto Rico is also quite stringent.

Plant quarantine officers are not trying to restrict the importation of all plant products, and importation will be allowed if there is reason for it and if the product is routed through the plant quarantine center in Washington, D.C., where it can be properly inspected. It cannot be too strongly emphasized, however, that the responsibility for legal control must rest with individual citizens and that only through education to the dangers of plant importation can legal control keep out of a country the many serious diseases and insect pests that are not presently found there.

Cultural and Physical Control of Insects and Diseases

The **cultural** and **physical** control of insects and diseases includes a broad spectrum of practices re-

A

B

FIGURE 9-10 • Japanese beetles. These common garden pests, introduced to the eastern United States and Canada from Europe, are spreading westward. (A) Adult beetle feeds on blackberry leaf. (B) Japanese beetle grubs (larvae) destroy lawn grass and other plants by feeding on their roots. (Courtesy of USDA)

lating to cultivation, the physical removal of infested or infesting entities, and barriers against infestation. **Roguing,** the removal from the garden of diseased or insect-infested plants, is quite effective with diseases or insects that spread slowly from plant to plant. Pruning provides a way of eliminating diseased plant parts or those likely to become diseased. Fireblight, a serious bacterial disease of apple and pear trees, is controlled by keeping all diseased wood pruned from the orchard and by periodic antibiotic spraying. Plowing under infested plant refuse, stirring soil to destroy insect egg masses, and other kinds of cultivation practices are effective in controlling some pests. Clubroot of crucifers and scab on potatoes can be partially controlled by regulating soil pH. Effective disease control may include various sanitation practices, such as burning diseased or insect-infested plant residues, cleaning away weeds that might harbor disease organisms or insects, washing hands frequently when garden plants are being handled, and refraining from smoking when handling tomatoes and cucurbits subject to the tobacco mosaic virus. Draining or filling low-lying land, planting windbreaks, and land leveling are effective controls for certain insect and disease problems.

Some insects and diseases can be excluded by constructing physical barriers such as the screens often placed over the openings of a greenhouse to prevent insects from entering. Rivers or large, deep, water-filled excavations sometimes act as barriers to intercept crickets and related insects before they enter cultivated areas. Hot-water treatment of seed to destroy a seed-borne pathogen is a physical method of control. During the early twentieth century seeds of cabbage and related vegetables were treated with water kept at a temperature of exactly 122°F (50°C) to destroy the fungus carried inside the seed that causes the disease called blackleg. Maintaining the exact temperature was essential because increasing it even a degree would kill some of the seed and decreasing it even one degree would allow some of the disease organisms to survive. Most seeds of these crops are now grown in locations where infection by blackleg organisms is not likely; however, the hot-water treatment is still used to control seed-borne diseases of asparagus and some other crops, and heat is used to eliminate virus from plant tissues.

Mites, thrips, and aphids can be controlled by frequent foliar sprinkling with water. If they are not too numerous, large insects, such as mealybugs on houseplants, tomato hornworms, and Colorado potato beetles, can be controlled by hand picking them from plants. Insect traps featuring such attractants as light, food, or sex-related chemicals often are used to determine the presence of damaging insects. Traps coupled with attractants and poison baits or other killing mechanisms are being used in a few places for insect control and have promising potential.

Chemical Control of Insects and Diseases

The most common method for controlling diseases and insects during the past forty years has been chemical, mainly because it is rapid and effective. Chemical pesticides designed to control insects and diseases can be classified as repellants, protectants, insecticides, miticides, fungicides, bactericides or antibiotics, and nematicides. **Ovicides** (egg killers) and **larvicides** (larva killers) are other terms sometimes used to classify chemical pesticides.

Repellants are used to protect clothing from moths and to drive away bloodsucking insects, but their possible use against plant pests has not been adequately researched. The insect repellants currently available are nontoxic to animals and humans, and they can be applied so that no residue is left on plants. These two characteristics tremendously enhance their acceptability over other forms of chemical control.

Protectants are used in largest quantities as seed treatments to prevent attacks on seedlings by soil-borne pathogens. Protective dips are used to delay the spoilage of some kinds of fresh fruits and vegetables and to lengthen the storage life of processed foods. Copper and zinc compounds, elemental sulfur, and some antibiotics are often used to protect plants from infection by fungi or bacteria.

Insecticides, fungicides, bactericides, and **nematicides** are, by definition, killers of various microorganisms. They are the compounds usually envisioned when chemical pesticides are denounced or defended and, of course, the ones most useful and available for farm or garden. The fact that viricides are not mentioned among the chemicals used for disease and insect control is indicative of the fact that viruses are not normally controlled by chemicals. Indeed, only a few of the plant bacterial diseases are subject to control by chemical means. Nematicides are relatively new.

Application of Pesticides. Chemicals can be applied as dusts, sprays, soil fumigants, or volatile granules. Dust formulations are most effective if applied in the early morning when there is some dew or residual moisture from rain on the plants that are to be dusted. Various kinds of pump dusters are available for the home gardener, and special dust formulations that come in disposable cardboard shake or pump packages are available for application on a few plants or small areas. The application of highly toxic chemicals in dust form should be avoided.

Application by spraying generally provides more complete coverage and adherence of the pesticide to the plant than does dusting. A hand-pump pressure-tank sprayer with a capacity from 2½ to 4 gallons (11 to 18 liters) is the most satisfactory application equipment for most home garden insecticide and fungicide sprays. A small trombone-type sprayer with a screened inlet hose that fits into a bucket is sometimes used; a sprayer of this sort has two handles that can be pumped back and forth to create pressure at the spray nozzle. This type of sprayer is fairly effective, but the application rate and coverage are not as uniform as they are with a tank sprayer. Another good sprayer available to home gardeners consists of a nozzle and small container in which is placed a concentrated solution of the chemical to be applied. This sprayer is designed to be connected to a garden hose and depends on water and water pressure for the correct dilution and application of the spray material. This is a good device for spraying large areas or moderate-sized trees. Some highly advertised pesticides and foliar fertilizers are formulated for this kind of application equipment. Backpack sprayers are among the more recent hand-operated pesticide application devices. They are easy to operate and maintain uniform pressure, thereby permitting even distribution and fairly rapid coverage, which makes them especially effective for applying herbicides to extensive plantings for which power equipment cannot be used.

Effective soil fumigation usually requires specialized equipment. Furthermore, many soil fumigants destroy nearby plants that happen to be rooting into the fumigated area. Consequently, fumigation is generally not very practical for the home gardener. Possible uses of soil fumigation by the amateur might be in pasteurizing potting soil for the hobby greenhouse or fumigating an area on which a plant nursery is to be established.

Pesticide Safety. Pesticide formulations packaged for sale for the home gardener or amateur horticulturist are relatively safe to use if the instructions printed on the label are carefully read and followed. Pesticide formulations packaged for the large-scale grower or commercial applicator often assume that the user has had considerable experience with pesticides and safety equipment. Even though pesticides packaged and sold in bulk by agricultural dealers are less expensive and often more effective than those sold at garden stores, they should not be used by people who are not familiar with their toxicity or who do not have the protective clothing and special equipment designed to be used when they are being applied. Even garden formulations can injure animals, humans, and plants if they are not applied as directed. All pesticides should be labeled and stored where they cannot be reached by children or others not acquainted with their dangerous nature. Pesticides should always be kept in their original containers. Small children who have taken a drink from the pesticide-filled soda-pop bottle set on a shelf or who have rolled each other around in a discarded parathion drum have been the most common victims of pesticide tragedies.

Problems Associated with Chemical Pesticides. There is not space in this text to analyze the many charges leveled against the use of chemical pesticides, but a few problems, including those already mentioned, that might affect gardeners as both potential pesticide users and food consumers should be briefly reviewed. The first is the possibility of harmful residues on edible products. Residues on food products entering market channels are strictly monitored so that they will remain well below the amount that might pose a hazard to human health. Garden produce will be safe to eat if gardeners follow directions on pesticide labels. Edible products growing along unfamiliar roadsides and cultivated fields, as well as flowers and other floral products sold primarily for decoration, should not be consumed, although the possibility of serious poisoning from such sources is remote.

The second problem is the technical difficulty of application. Whether the application is with dust or spray, by hand sprayer, by a 500-gallon mobile ground rig, or by airplane, placing the right concentration of the right chemical in the right place at the right time poses numerous problems for growers and applicators. In my experience the most common cause of faulty pesticide application is a mistake in measurement. Pesticide users should read all labels and check all measurements at least twice, be careful and accurate in applying the material, and use only clean application equipment that is in good repair.

A third problem is the possibility of injury to the host plant or to a crop plant that may be in the vicinity or may be planted at a later date. Many pesticides must be applied at specified conditions of temperature and humidity, and problems may result if there is a rapid change in the weather after application or if the grower gambles at a time when the application is necessary but environmental conditions are not ideal.

In recent years the development of genetic resistance by pests has been appearing more and more frequently. In Chapter 3 we spoke of mutation, the slight change in genetic determiners that occasionally occurs in all living species. Although mutations may happen in only a minute percentage of the population of any species, the total number of mutated individuals will be large in species for which numbers in a small area may equal trillions, as is the case with most pathogenic organisms. If a mutation permits an individual pathogenic organism to survive in the presence of a pesticide that destroys all of its sister organisms, the resistant individual can multiply astronomically because it has no competition from other organisms of its kind. In a short time the progeny of the resistant individual will number in the billions, and a new race with genetic resistance to the formerly effective pesticide will have been developed. Most readers are aware of houseflies' resistance to various materials and of the constant need for developing new pesticides to replace those that no longer control the pests against which they were once effective.

The chemical control of plant pests can disturb biological balance, sometimes to the detriment of the garden. This may result from killing beneficial organisms. Mites, for example, were not a serious problem in most orchards until DDT was introduced as an orchard spray. In addition to killing the codling moth and other apple pests, DDT was also a very effective killer of mite predators, and its use permitted the buildup of injurious mite populations. Summer spraying to rid cities of flies and mosquitoes, which was common a few years ago, frequently resulted in an almost immediate increase of thrips and aphids in the sprayed area. Apparently the fly and mosquito spray killed ladybird beetles and other predator insects but had little effect on aphids and thrips, perhaps because it did not reach them on the undersurfaces of leaves and in the other protected places where they reside.

Honeybees and other pollinating insects are often the victims of pesticide poisoning. Unfortunately, they are more susceptible to the newer insecticides than they were to some that are no longer in use. Insecticide applications for fruit trees are usually needed more after the bloom period is past, and with proper planning, gardeners should seldom need to spray a crop while it is in full bloom and is most attractive to bees. Bee losses can also be cut by waiting to apply insecticides until late evening so that their most lethal period occurs during the night when bees are not active.

How Much Insecticide and Fungicide for the Home Garden? Despite the problems that accompany their use, the benefits derived from chemical pesticides probably outweigh their disadvantages. Gardening in some areas and the growing of some crops in most areas would be difficult or impossible without them, and pesticides are essential to the abundant harvests prevalent in well-fed North America. Even so, the trend toward more natural controls that the organic movement has engendered is positive, and the increased dialogue among organic growers and traditional agriculturists can help all agriculture.

Even those growers certified as organic growers can use some pesticides, among which are the plant-derived insecticides, including pyrethrum and rotenone, insecticides containing *Bacillus thuringiensis* (see "Biological Control of Insects and Diseases" later in this chapter), and others classed as "natural." The designation natural, of necessity, is somewhat arbitrary. For example, although soap, one of the major pest-control agents of organic growers, has been around for a long time, it is as much an artificial product and, in certain situations, is as environmentally polluting as are many of the pesticides not classified as natural. If eaten, soap would also be as toxic as some other pesticides.

My advice to gardeners regarding the controversial subject of chemical pesticides would be to use them, but only when necessary. Often gardens can be grown easily with fewer pesticide treatments than are usually recommended, because gardens are more isolated than commercial fields are and because the presence of one or two insects does not prevent a garden crop from being utilized. In my own garden if a few earworms are acceptable on the latest planting of sweet corn, if hornworms and potato beetles are handpicked from tomatoes and potatoes, and if mildew-resistant rose cultivars are selected for planting, only two or three pesticide treatments on apple, pear, sweet cherry, gladiolus, and crucifers are required annually for satisfactory pest control. Not all areas are equally pest free, but with experience most gardeners can grow a variety of crops with a minimal use of pesticides.

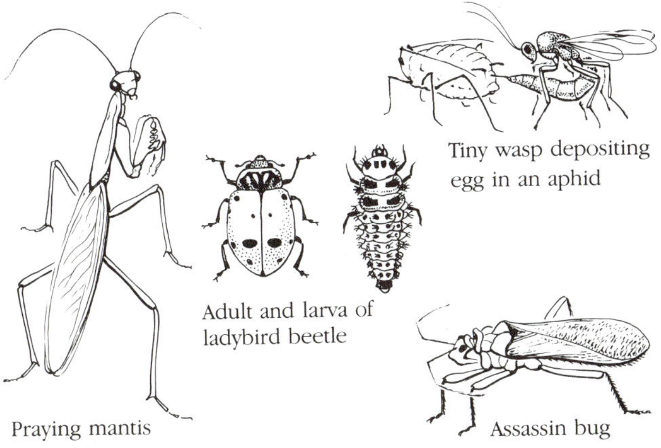

FIGURE 9-11 • Beneficial insect predators that provide biological control in the garden. (Courtesy of USDA)

Biological Control of Insects and Diseases

Biological means were first scientifically used to control pests in California in 1890 when the vedalia beetle was introduced from Australia to control the cottony cushion scale of citrus trees. With the realization of the shortcomings of chemical disease and insect control and the environmental problems sometimes arising as a result, there has been a renewed interest in biological systems of control. As advocates of biological control are quick to point out, these control methods are the ones used by nature, and fortunately for the home gardener, the natural system of checks and balances often controls plant pests when chemical control may not be feasible (Figure 9-11).

Most people are aware that birds eat many kinds of insects and that ladybird beetles, if prevalent in a garden, can control aphids and some other plant-feeding pests. Fewer are aware that yellowjackets feed on and destroy cabbage loopers and similar caterpillars and that all living organisms are subject to destruction by other living organisms. During the past fifteen years much of the pest-control research has concentrated on biocontrol. The benefits of this research are new pest-control methods based on an understanding of the relationship among crop plants, their pests, and the parasites and pathogens of those pests.

Another intriguing aspect of biological control just beginning to receive scientific recognition is the nature of evolved and evolving plant and pest chemistry, which appears to be the basis of much pest resistance and susceptibility. This area includes the inhibition of pests by plant **volatiles** (substances given off as vapors, generally aromatic). We know, for example, that a cedar closet repels moths, that some gardeners rely on marigolds and garlic to repel certain kinds of insects from their gardens, and that scientists accidently discovered insecticidal properties in a species of balsam fir when insect larvae failed to survive in cages covered with paper manufactured from that fir.

Although proved biological methods for controlling diseases and insects are limited, a few that are available to the home gardener should be mentioned. Both ladybird beetles and praying mantises are available commercially and can be purchased to spread around the home garden. The major problem with these two predators is that both are extremely mobile, and consequently the purchaser may not be the one who benefits from their activities. At least one disease organism is formulated commercially as a biocontrol for plant pests. *Ba-*

cillus thuringiensis, a natural pathogen of the cabbage looper, is sold in spore formulations under several trade names. Used in a spray within a few months of its formulation, it does a very effective job of controlling cabbage loopers and larvae of certain other moths and butterflies.

Certain pest-control measures advocated by organic gardeners probably should receive more scientific investigation. Some are very beneficial in controlling particular pests; the value of others is questionable. One recommendation that almost always limits pest damage is to do everything possible to keep plants growing vigorously.

The use of plant extracts that have pesticidal properties, although not strictly biological control, was one of the earliest methods of killing insects with a natural product. At least two, pyrethrum from a relative of chrysanthemum and rotenone from various species of the tropical genera *Derris* and *Lonchocarpus,* have been used for many years to control certain insects. Both are relatively nontoxic to humans and provide fair control for a rather broad group of plant pests. Nicotine sulfate, formulated from an extract of tobacco, was formerly a popular insecticide, but it is no longer used extensively by home gardeners because it is extremely toxic to humans.

Breeding for Control of Insects and Disease

Home gardeners should have some knowledge of the development of disease- and insect-resistant cultivars by plant breeding. Most gardeners recognize the value of disease-resistant cultivars and have had experience with at least a few. One mistake made by some home gardeners is assuming that a cultivar listed as disease resistant can resist all diseases; this is not generally true. Any one cultivar usually is resistant to only one or two diseases, and unless those diseases are prevalent in the area, that cultivar will not produce a better crop than will a nonresistant one.

Because the development of resistant cultivars has been the only reliable method of control for many virus, bacterial, and soil-borne diseases, breeding for resistance to disease has received considerable research effort. Breeding for insect resistance received only minor attention until the last ten years, perhaps because chemicals have satisfactorily controlled most insect pests. Because developing and testing a new cultivar requires from twelve to fifteen years, it will be some time before insect-resistant cultivars become generally available to the public.

Few people realize the dependence of our food supply on breeding for disease resistance. Many crops can be produced today because cultivars with improved disease resistance are introduced every few years. Pathogens and predators can mutate so that they are able to infest cultivars that formerly were resistant to them.

Wheat is an example of a major crop for which profitable production is entirely dependent on the introduction of new cultivars at frequent intervals. Because of the rapid mutation of organisms pathogenic to the wheat plant, mainly the rusts and smuts, in the past wheat cultivars have remained profitable for only about seven years. Today, thanks to a better knowledge of disease resistance, wheat cultivars may last somewhat longer, but their useful life is still relatively brief. Because the breeding and testing necessary for the introduction of a new wheat cultivar require many years, a crash program cannot develop a new resistant cultivar on demand. It is essential that wheat breeding, as well as other agricultural research, be continuing programs that can anticipate needs and count on public support and funding on a long-term basis. If funds for breeding programs were to be eliminated, it would be only a few years before this country and the world would be faced with a general famine.

Most horticultural crops are not so vulnerable to disease and insect ravages as is wheat; some cultivars have remained resistant to a particular disease or insect for twenty or thirty years. But resistance is seldom permanent, and research personnel must be ready with new cultivars if the commodity is to be produced when the old cultivar fails.

Few commercial agricultural firms are economically able to support research programs requiring the amount of time necessary for new cultivar development. Agricultural research is an infinitesimal part of our federal and state budgets, but much of the world food supply is dependent on that research budget. The public must be aware of the disaster of hunger that would result if that budget were eliminated.

Integrated Pest Management

One important development in pest-control techniques is **integrated pest management.** In the past, pest control has often meant a different pesticide for each pest, each pesticide being applied at specified intervals. For example, an apple orchard might be sprayed for codling moths each seven to fourteen days and for mites every three weeks. This kind of insurance spray program was necessary because there was no good way of determining whether or not the pest was present. As was pointed out, such frequent pesticide application destroyed predators and hastened the pest's development of resistance to the pesticide.

With integrated pest management, everything possible is done to minimize the number of chemical sprays that must be applied. Wherever they are available, resistant or partially resistant cultivars are grown. The presence of each pest likely to affect the crop is carefully monitored by sweeping with a net and counting the insects, by using food or **pheromone** attractant traps, or by other means. (Pheromones are chemical substances secreted by insects that elicit a response, most commonly a sexual response, in other insects of the same species.) Extensive research is carried out to learn the effect of temperature, day length, precipitation, and other environmental factors on the reproductivity of each problem pest, and weather patterns are carefully monitored as a portent of the multiplication of the pest to damaging numbers. The impact of various pesticides, weather patterns, and other factors on predators is also carefully researched, monitored, and, as much as possible, regulated to optimize conditions for the predators' survival and reproduction. With integrated management growers attempt to keep the number of pests below damaging levels but never to destroy its population because annihilation of the pest usually also eliminates the predator population. Plants of the crop species that may be growing along roads or fences or in abandoned fields or orchards are cataloged and either treated with control measures or destroyed so that they do not serve as a reservoir of the pest population. With these and other measures suitable for the specific crop, growers of many crops have been able to reduce drastically the number of pesticide applications. For example, many apple growers in the past sprayed their orchards almost every week but now often get by with only three or four pesticide applications during the growing season.

BIRDS AND ANIMALS

Because they are often located near uncultivated areas and usually contain only a small planting of any one crop, gardens are especially vulnerable to the feeding of birds and animals (Figure 9-12). Because birds and animals such as toads, frogs, snakes, and lizards benefit garden crops by feeding

FIGURE 9-12 • Animal damage. Landscape plantings in rural and suburban areas are frequently damaged by the feeding of deer (as above), rabbits, porcupine, and other animals. (Courtesy of Walter Chandoha)

on insects and because many people are reluctant to harm birds and mammals, their control poses special problems.

Gardens and orchards located where deer or elk are abundant should be surrounded with a fence high enough to keep them out. Rodents can be controlled by trapping or poisoning. Rodent poisons should be placed underground to lessen the likelihood that seed-eating birds, such as pheasants, doves, and grouse, or meat-consuming birds and animals, such as hawks, owls, eagles, coyotes, and weasels, will be poisoned by eating the poisons or the bodies of poisoned rodents.

Although poisoning has been used for many years to control rodents, there is little information about the impact of such control measures on the total ecology of an area. Because the burrow is sealed after the toxic compound is placed in it and the animal dies underground, poisoning is an effective method of pocket-gopher control that appears to pose little threat to nontarget organisms. But growers who scatter strychnine-treated oats above ground to control ground squirrels and field mice are probably defeating their own purpose by destroying predator animals and birds. Pellets or special dispensers that release poisonous gases are quite effective against burrowing rodents and pose little threat to other birds and animals, but they require extreme caution to prevent injury to the user. Steel traps have been designed for most kinds of rodents and are effective for small areas where animals are not numerous. Cage-type traps using bait to lure the animals are more humane.

Rodents can be discouraged by eliminating nesting sites and litter around the garden area. House cats cannot be relied on to keep rodents under control; those that are good hunters are as likely to control songbirds and game birds as they are rodents.

My own observations have led me to believe that the best way to control rodents is to encourage a good population of hawks, owls, weasels, skunks, foxes, or coyotes, even though these predators undoubtedly destroy some songbirds and their presence may necessitate special protection for farm poultry and small animals. City dwellers benefit from a predator population because controlling rodents on farmlands surrounding a community keeps them from multiplying and spreading into the urban area. Encouraging a predator population requires community or areawide education and cooperation. Reliable information on the feeding habits of various predators is also a valuable research contribution to farmers and gardeners.

Bird pests are most destructive to emerging seedlings, ripening seed crops, and ripening fruit, especially small fruit and sweet cherries. Pheasants and crows systematically dig out every germinating corn seedling from a row, pick off the sprout, and eat out the embryo and endosperm, leaving the seed coat almost intact; seed coat repellants are, therefore, relatively ineffective. Small devices such as metal discs that whirl in the wind, firecrackers, recorded bird calls of distress, and scarecrows designed to frighten birds are usually effective for a short time until the birds become used to them. State experimental stations distribute publications containing plans for cage-type traps designed to help control starlings and similar bird pests. One effective (though expensive and bothersome) bird control for the small home orchard and garden is a

FIGURE 9-13 • Netting spread over a blueberry bush to keep birds from eating the fruit. (Courtesy of Laurie L. Riley/Stock, Boston)

mesh cover. Cheesecloth can be used over a row or two of strawberries, and specially designed covers are available for small fruit trees. A narrow strip of screen or chicken wire can be bent into a convex cover over germinating seeds until the seedlings are large enough to resist bird damage (Figure 9-13). Plastic and the newer spun-polyester row covers may serve a dual purpose, protecting the seedlings from both weather and birds. Covers are, of course, impractical if more than a few rows or trees are being grown. Harvesting fruit and seed crops as soon as they are mature lessens the chance of birds' finding and damaging the crop.

Selected References

Agrios, G. N. *Plant Pathology.* 3rd ed. New York: Academic Press, 1988.

California Polytechnic State University. *Integrated Pest Management (Horticulture)* and *Integrated Pest Management in Greenhouse.* San Luis Obispo: VEP Video, California Polytechnic State University, 1990.

Carr, A. *Rodale's Color Handbook of Garden Insects.* Emmaus, Pa.: Rodale Press, 1983.

Cook, R. J., and K. F. Baker. *Nature and Practice of Biological Control of Plant Pathogens.* Text ed. Madison, Wis.: American Phytopathological Society, 1983.

Davidson, R. H., and W. F. Lyon. *Insect Pests of Farm, Garden, and Orchard.* 8th ed. New York: Wiley, 1987.

Horst, R. K. *Westcott's Plant Disease Handbook.* 5th ed. New York: Van Nostrand Reinhold, 1990.

Kite, L. P. *Controlling Lawn and Garden Insects.* San Francisco: Ortho Books, 1987.

Miller, G. R. *Weed Control in the Home Garden.* Brooklyn Botanic Garden Handbook 120 (special printing of *Plants and Gardens*, vol. 45, no. 2). Brooklyn, N.Y.: Brooklyn Botanic Garden, 1989.

Pirone, P. *Diseases and Pests of Ornamental Plants.* 5th ed. New York: Wiley, 1978.

Rice, B. *Nursery and Landscape Weed Control.* Fresno, Calif.: Thomson Publications, 1987.

Roberts, D. A. *Fundamentals of Plant Pathology.* New York: Freeman, 1978.

Sherf, A. F., and A. A. Macnab. *Vegetable Diseases and Their Control.* 2nd ed. New York: Wiley, 1986.

Smith, M., ed. *Ortho Problem Solver.* 3rd ed. San Francisco: Ortho Books, 1989. (A compilation of thousands of color photos of disease symptoms, insects, and weeds on ornamental, garden, and crop plants.)

CHAPTER

10

Indoor and Container Gardening

In our urbanized society not everyone has a plot of ground on which to grow a garden. But almost everyone does have a room with a window or an electric light, and almost everyone can find some soil or potting medium and a container, the minimal requirements for growing a potted plant indoors. The fact that container gardening is possible in apartments, dormitories, trailer houses, condominiums, offices, schoolrooms, and public buildings where outdoor gardening is not feasible probably accounts for the increasing popularity of this form of gardening (Figure 10-1). As was mentioned in Chapter 1, the care of indoor plants in commercial buildings provides part- or full-time employment for a number of horticulturists.

ENVIRONMENTAL LIMITATIONS TO GROWING PLANTS INDOORS

As anyone who has tried to grow them knows, most food-crop plants (vegetables, fruits, small grains, etc.) do not grow well indoors. The reasons are (1) too much heat, (2) too little light, (3) too low humidity, (4) atmospheric pollution, and (5) restricted rooting area. Plants designated as houseplants are able to withstand these adverse conditions to some extent because most of them were developed from ancestors native to the shade of tropical forests. Moreover, it often

FIGURE 10-1 • Houseplants used for indoor decoration. (Courtesy Cary Wolinsky/Stock Boston)

is possible to choose plants adapted to special home conditions—for example, cacti for an extremely dry atmosphere or ferns for a cool, moist corner. Even so, growth of any plant indoors is likely to be limited by one or more of these five conditions.

Temperature

Homeowners are often surprised to learn that the temperatures in their houses are too high for the optimal growing of plants. An outdoor temperature of 70° to 80°F (21° to 27°C) is certainly not detrimental to most plants; however, there is a difference between outdoor and indoor conditions. Usually outdoor temperatures are high in conjunction with high light intensity, and the combination of high light and high temperature permits a high rate of photosynthesis. Indoors, high temperatures frequently are accompanied by low light intensity, and plants suffer because all their activities except photosynthesis are speeded up. In addition, home temperatures are often kept relatively higher at night than they would be in the plant's native climate. High night temperature speeds respiration, resulting in the rapid utilization of photosynthates. Turning the thermostat down to 60°F (16°C) at bedtime benefits most houseplants.

Choosing the right location may be the secret of success with certain temperature-sensitive plants. Plants from the jungles do relatively well in the 70°+ temperatures of modern homes, but geraniums, coleus, wax-leaved begonias, impatiens, and some of the other window-box plants do poorly simply because they are adapted to cool night temperatures and relatively high light intensities. They can grow vigorously only in well-lighted, cool locations.

Light

Perhaps the major factor limiting the growth of plants indoors is the lack of light. Most foliage plants sold for indoor growing do best in light from an east or north window. Philodendron, peperomia, ficus, begonia, and other similar jungle plants can be grown fairly successfully in the interior of rooms that are well lighted with floor-to-ceiling windows, but plants should not be permanently located in the poorly lighted interiors of rooms unless supplemental light can be provided. Plants used for decoration should be left in low light locations for no longer than two weeks and then be rotated to a more favorable environment for at least a month. The amount of light required by some of the more popular houseplants is given in Table 10-1, and there is a brief discussion of artificial light sources for indoor plant growing later in this chapter.

TABLE 10-1 • *Selected easy-to-grow houseplants*

Name	Growing requirements and characteristics
Moderate-sized specimen plants	
Aglaonema (*Aglaonema* spp.)	A group of plants that tolerate fairly dark conditions; easy to root.
Aluminum plant (*Pilea cadierei*)	Shiny variegated leaves need spraying occasionally; easily damaged by overwatering.
Boston fern (*Nephrolepis exaltata*)	Rich soil; high humidity; avoid direct sunlight; fronds become almost trailing.
Dracena (*Dracaena deremensis*)	Diffused light to shade; water freely; grasslike leaves.
Dumb cane (*Dieffenbachia picta*)	Diffused light to shade; when spindly, it can be cut off and rooted in moist soil.
Philodendron (split-leaf) (*Monstera deliciosa*)	Diffused light; spray leaves; can be pinched to keep low or trained to climb.
Piggyback plant (*Tolmiea menziesii*)	Easy to grow; tolerant of gas and relatively low light intensity.
Screw pine (*Pandanus veitchii*)	Grasslike ornamental leaves; tolerant of varying environment.
Snake plant (*Sansevieria trifasciata*)	Long, straight, stiff leaves; slow-growing; tolerant of drought.
Low-growing specimen plants for moist, shaded situations	
African violet (*Saintpaulia ionantha*)	Does best in a north window; warm temperature; keep water from leaves.
Fittonia (*Fittonia verschaffeltii*)	Diffused light; good small plants for terrariums.
Maidenhair fern (*Adiantum cuneatum*)	Humid atmosphere; soil high in humus; terrariums.
Peperomias (*Peperomia* spp.)	Diffused light; easy to propagate; some appropriate for terrariums.
Polkadot plant (*Hypoestes sanguinolenta*)	Diffused light; needs pinching; easy to root.
Prayer plant (*Maranta leuconeura*)	Diffused light; leaves require occasional spraying.
Sansevieria, birdsnest (*Sansevieria trifasciata* 'Hahnii')	Will grow in a terrarium if not overwatered.
Low-growing specimen plants for dry, light situations	
Aloe (*Aloe variegata*)	Sun, sandy soil; slow-growing succulent.
Fish-hook cactus (*Mammillaria* spp.)	Group of low-growing, spiny, pot-sized cacti; useful for hot, dry locations.
Hen and chickens (house leek) (*Sempervivum* spp.)	Sandy soil; light frequent watering.
Maternity plant (*Kalanchoe daigremontiana*)	Propagated from plantlets on leaf margins; keep slightly moist.
Trailing or climbing plants	
Artillery plant (*Pilea microphylla*)	Diffused light to shade; don't overwater; terrariums or hanging baskets.
Baby's tears (*Helxine soleirolii*)	Water from bottom; likes high humidity; good for terrariums.
English ivy (*Hedera helix*)	Tolerant of a wide range of soil and light conditions; can be used in terrariums.
Grape ivy (*Cissus rhombifolia*)	Pinch tips to encourage branching; needs diffused sunlight.
Nephthytis (*Syngonium podophyllum*)	Fast-growing; diffused light to shade.
Pothos (*Scindapsus aureus*)	Variegated creepers with waxy leaves; tolerant.
Spider plant (*Chlorophytum comosum*)	Easy to grow; best where new plantlets can trail.
Swedish ivy (*Plectranthus australis*)	Ground cover or hanging basket; will grow in water or soil.
Wandering Jew (*Tradescantia* and *Zebrina* spp.)	Diffused light; humid atmosphere; will grow in water.
Wax plant (*Hoya* spp.)	A group of waxy-leaved vines tolerant of indoor conditions.
Plants that grow into small trees	
Fiddle-leaf fig (*Ficus lyrata*)	Grows to 5 ft (1½ m) or more; quite tolerant of shade.
Kentia palm (*Howeia forsteriana*)	Said to be one of the easiest palms to grow; good light but not necessarily sun.
Norfolk Island pine (*Araucaria excelsa*)	Diffused light to full sun; beautiful specimen tree.
Rubber plant (*Ficus elastica*)	Diffused light; will grow to 10 ft (3 m); broad leaves should be washed with water.
Weeping fig (*Ficus benjamina*)	Grows 2–5 ft; small leaves with graceful branches.

Humidity and Atmospheric Pollution

The humidity in homes, especially when they are being artificially heated during the winter, is likely to be lower than the humidity outdoors. The humidity around plants can be raised somewhat by placing their containers on gravel in trays containing water. The growth of ferns and other humidity-loving plants will be aided by a weekly misting. Although most other houseplants are not as adversely affected by a dry atmosphere as are ferns, many benefit from having their foliage washed off a few times a year. Besides increasing humidity, spraying washes away dust and helps control insects. Exceptions are African violet, gloxinia, and other similar hairy-leaved plants, which are damaged by being sprinkled with cold water.

Even better than gravel beds or sprinkling for increasing humidity is a home humidifier. This is good for both plants and humans, especially during the winter when the humidity is likely to be extremely low. Water boiling in a tea kettle adds to the humidity of homes heated by wood stoves.

Most houseplants are sensitive to all sorts of atmospheric pollutants. The minute quantities of propane and other manufactured gases that escape when lighting stoves and other appliances make it difficult to grow houseplants in a building where this kind of gas is used. Cooking fumes and fumes from common household cleaners are not noticeably damaging to plants in the amounts normally released in the home; however, fumes from certain adhesives and special cleaners can be injurious if they become highly concentrated.

In industrial and congested urban areas, pollution that damages outdoor plants can seep indoors and also damage houseplants. In rural areas, chemicals used for weed control on farms may injure houseplants and dust on their leaves reduces photosynthesis and encourages the buildup of a mite population. These types of pollutants are lessened by air-conditioning units that have air filters.

ADAPTING INDOOR PLANTS TO A CHANGING ENVIRONMENT

◆ ◆ ◆

It is important to choose as houseplants those that are genetically adapted to indoor growing. However, as mentioned in Chapter 7, it is possible, within limits, to acclimatize plants to the particular environment in which they are to be grown. Acclimation is especially important when plants are transferred from indoors to outdoors or vice versa, as they often are in the spring and autumn. Acclimation may also be necessary when plants are brought in from a greenhouse or when a living Christmas tree is taken from a hot, dry living room to a cold, moist winter garden.

Whenever possible, a plant should be moved from one environment to another gradually. In dim light, leaves tend to grow large and thin with little cuticle to protect them from dehydration. Therefore, moving a plant, even one that normally grows best in the full sun, from indoors directly to the sunny outdoors will cause the plant to suffer serious leaf burn or possibly death. An indoor plant relocated to the outdoors should be moved initially to a shady, protected site and for only a few hours. The time that it is outdoors can be increased each day, and when the plant can tolerate the shade for a whole day, it can be transferred for gradually longer periods to the sunny spot where it is to be permanently located. Likewise, that same plant will remain much more attractive if the move indoors in the autumn also is gradual.

During the first few days after a plant is taken to a home from a greenhouse, it should be kept in a location where the temperature, light, and humidity match as much as possible those of the greenhouse. Later, if necessary, it can be relocated, at first for a few hours and then for gradually increasing periods of time each day, to the different environment of its permanent location. Potted trees purchased as living Christmas trees (discussed later in this chapter) should also be acclimated gradually to the outdoors. After the Christmas season, they can be conditioned on a cool enclosed porch or in a garage until the soil of the garden thaws and dries enough so that they can be planted. Their roots should not be allowed to freeze, which can easily happen to a potted plant placed outdoors without root insulation.

Managing the Growing Medium

Because the amount of growing medium is so restricted for plants growing indoors, it must be specially formulated to supply them with support, water, and mineral elements. Soil and growing media are discussed in Chapters 5 and 14. Potted plants, of course, must receive adequate moisture; however, overwatering is often more of a problem than is underwatering. The grower of indoor plants must be especially careful when attempting to grow them in containers that do not have adequate drainage. Container-grown plants should be watered just enough to bring the soil to field capacity, but never so much that water stands in the container. The soil should be permitted to become rather dry before the plants are watered again. If the containers are of adequate size and if humidity is not too low, plants can often go a week between waterings. Container-grown plants should be fertilized approximately every four weeks with a commercially formulated or home-prepared fertilizer mixture (see Chapter 14). Cacti and some of the succulents do not need either as much water or as much fertilizer as do most other kinds of plants.

Insects and Diseases

The insects and insectlike pests that are most troublesome for houseplants are aphids, mealybugs, scale, spider mites, thrips, and whiteflies. The diseases most likely to infect houseplants are mildews, damping-off, nematodes, and viruses. All of these with their symptoms or the damage they are likely to cause are briefly described in Table 14-26. Ants, cutworms and other grubs, earthworms, millipedes, slugs, sowbugs, and springtails are sometimes troublesome in greenhouses but seldom require more than handpicking to remove them from houseplants. Fungus gnats—delicate, dark gray, flylike insects about ⅛ inch (¼ cm) long that are attracted to light and tend to swarm over windows—are sometimes a problem. Their larva, whitish ¼-inch (½-cm) maggots, feed on roots and burrow into the crown. Injured plants grow little, are dull colored, and may lose leaves.

The best way to control insect and disease pests of houseplants is to prevent infestation. Cut flowers and new plants should be examined to make sure that they are free of pests before they are brought into the home. New plants should be isolated for three or four weeks before they are placed next to other plants. Using sterilized soil for potting will prevent the introduction of such soil-borne problems as root rot, damping-off, nematodes, slugs, centipedes, and earthworms.

It is important to examine houseplants frequently so that insects or disease infestations can be controlled while numbers are low. A few aphids, mealybugs, thrips, spider mites, or scale can be washed from one or two infested plants by spraying them with lukewarm water or by washing the plants with a soft cloth and soapy water made with two teaspoons of mild detergent in a gallon of water (10 ml in 4 liters). The washing may need to be repeated several times as eggs hatch or nymphs mature. It is also possible to handpick and kill larger insects if only a few plants are infested. A swab dipped in alcohol can be used to eradicate a minor infestation of mealybugs or aphids. Destroying severely infested plants may be the most logical solution if the plants are not too valuable.

Mildew is most easily controlled by reducing moisture. Moving an infected plant to a less humid location and keeping water from contacting the foliage also helps.

When more than a few plants have insects or diseases or when infestations are severe, chemical control is necessary. Only formulations prepared for houseplants should be used. These contain chemicals such as malathion, rotenone, and the pyrethrins, all of which are relatively nontoxic to people and animals. The formulations contained in spray cans are convenient when only a few plants are to be treated. Concentrated solutions or wettable powders from which growers can mix their own dips or sprays are available. These more concentrated formulations are also more dangerous to both plants and the applicator, so labels should, of course, be read and followed religiously.

Systemic insecticides are widely used on potted plants in greenhouses and some are available for houseplants. These are applied to the soil in the pot, absorbed into the root system, and translocated to all parts of the plant with the water and mineral nutrients in the xylem. Such insecticides are often spectacularly effective because they control both sucking and chewing insects at all stages of growth.

KINDS OF PLANTS FOR INDOOR GARDENING

A wide selection of traditional and unusual plants are available for growing under varying indoor conditions. Growers may choose from many different groups or specialize in certain special kinds, such as ferns or cacti and succulents.

Traditional Indoor Plants

Some of the easier-to-grow indoor plants are listed in Table 10-1. This is by no means a comprehensive list, and many excellent houseplants have been omitted, but it does include plants that tolerate low light intensity and relatively warm night temperatures. Other plants, not listed, may do better if temperatures are cooler or a south window is available. For a more complete list of houseplants with photographs, descriptions, and directions for individual care, the reader should consult one of the references listed at the end of this chapter.

Unusual Indoor Plants

Cacti and Succulents. Cacti and succulents (a special group of plants with thick, drought-tolerant leaves) thrive with little care and often do well in the hot, dry interiors of homes (Figure 10-2). They should be in a sunny location, if possible, but many can survive the winter in a well-lighted room. If they cannot have a sunny location, they should be placed outside to rejuvenate during the summer. For plants growing without sun during the winter the transition should be gradual, just a few hours of sun each day until they become accustomed to the higher light intensity. They require a well-aerated, coarse growing medium and should not be watered or fertilized as often as are most houseplants.

Plants from Bulbs and Corms. Several kinds of bulbous plants can be forced indoors. Amaryllis bulbs, for example, can be potted in January with the bulb above the soil. If the planted bulb is kept at room temperature, the flower stalk will begin to elongate almost at once and will produce large pink, red, or white lilylike flowers before the leaves are fully grown. The bulb should be per-

FIGURE 10-2 • Cacti as houseplants. These planters show several interesting types of cacti and succulents suitable for dry conditions. Cacti can tolerate environmental adversities other than drought. (Courtesy Mindy Klarman/Photo Researchers)

mitted to continue growing after the flowers have faded. If the plant is kept growing through the next summer, its leaves will die down during the fall, and it will produce another flower during the next winter or early spring. The amaryllis will bloom even if kept away from a window or artificial light, but it should have full sun through the summer while its leaves are manufacturing carbohydrates.

April is the best time to plant gloxinia, although the corms of this plant are available from nurseries at other times of the year. Gloxinia corms, which produce plants having beautiful velvety leaves and trumpet-shaped flowers, do best if grown near a north or east window. Gloxinias can also be grown from seed or propagated from leaf cuttings.

Tulips, narcissi, crocus, and snowdrops — in fact most of the bulbous flowers that normally bloom in the spring — can be forced indoors during the winter. These bulbs require about three months of temperatures under 45°F (7°C) before they will begin growing. They can be stored in a container in peat moss or sawdust in the refrigerator or another cool location. Tulips and daffodils bloom about two months after they are potted and moved from cool to warm temperatures.

Garden Annuals as Indoor Plants. The bloom period of several garden annuals, including ageratum, impatiens, nicotiana, *Phlox drummondii,* and petunia, can be considerably extended if they are brought indoors just before the first fall frost. Those plants that are just beginning to bloom will remain attractive the longest; sometimes these are available from seedlings self-sown during the summer. If self-sown seedlings are not available, seeds can be planted in early August to produce potted annuals for indoor bloom during the autumn and early winter. These plants should be transplanted with a ball of soil around their roots so that the roots are not disturbed any more than necessary. As most are sun loving, they should be placed where there is ample light, near a south or west window if possible.

Fruits and Vegetables Indoors. Most vegetables require a fairly high light intensity, but if a sunny location is available, several kinds can be grown in containers. The 'Patio' cultivar of tomato, for instance, was developed especially for container growing. It produces medium-sized fruit on an upright bush and makes a very attractive addition to any south window. The 'Tiny Tim' tomato cultivar produces a profusion of cherry-type fruits on plants barely 6 inches (15 cm) high. Tomatoes will not yield well even in a south window from about December 15 to February 15 in most northern areas of the United States; thus the timing of their planting is important. Onions or scallions, butterhead and leaf lettuce, kale, and most kinds of herbs grow quite well in window containers.

Several products from the supermarket also can be grown into attractive and interesting indoor plants. Seeds from citrus fruits germinate quite easily and will grow into small trees. A sweet potato or part of a sweet potato placed in moist sand will produce slips that can be removed and planted in soil to grow into attractive and relatively long lived vines. Avocado seeds placed in moist sand often grow into small trees. An unusual plant can be grown from a fresh pineapple. The top should be cut with about 1 inch (2½ cm) of fruit attached. Trim away the soft flesh of the fruit and permit the cut surface to air dry for a few days; then plant the cutting in potting soil up to the base of the lower leaves. The plant should receive diffused light, and the soil should be permitted to dry between waterings.

Terrariums and Bottle Gardens

Terrariums and bottle gardens make interesting conversation pieces and attractive gifts. Bottle gardens can be made from any size bottles. Plants tend to grow quite well in lightly tinted bottles, but heavily tinted ones should not be used, as the colored glass blocks the rays of light from entering. Planting in narrow-necked bottles can be accomplished in one of two ways. The bottle can be

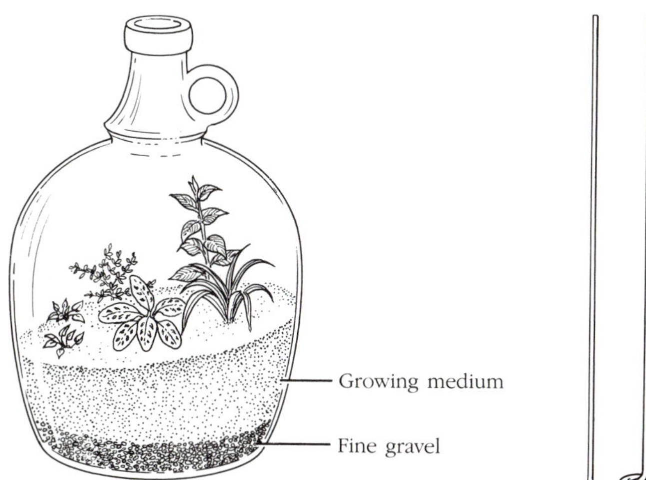

FIGURE 10-3 • Bottle garden. A bottle garden with bottle garden planting tools, a probe and a tamper made from a coat hanger.

carefully cut near its base with a glass cutter and glued together with waterproof cement after the garden has been planted. A more common method is to use plants with leaves pliant enough to force through the bottle opening without breaking.

The procedure for planting a bottle garden is not complex. Place a layer of fine gravel (about one-third of the growing medium) on the bottom of the bottle for drainage. On top of this, add enough good, properly moistened growing medium to fill the bottle about one-third full. Many growers mix a handful of charcoal into the growing medium to absorb any plant-damaging gases that may form. In order to prevent its sides from becoming soiled, the bottle should be completely dry. Using a rolled sheet of paper to direct the growing medium to the lower part of the container also helps keep the sides of the bottle clean.

Plan the arrangement of the plants on paper before beginning any planting. Carefully wash the soil from the roots of each plant. A pair of forceps long enough to reach the bottom of the container and thin enough to fit through the opening is needed to maneuver the plants and soil. Other tools can be constructed from the stiff wire of an old coat hanger. A straight piece of wire can be used as a probe to dig holes and position the plants and a piece with the end bent 90° and fashioned into a small loop makes a convenient tamper for firming the soil around plants (Figure 10-3).

After holes are scraped in the appropriate locations, gently push each plant (with its roots down) through the container opening. Tilt the bottle slightly so that the plant drops into the hole prepared for it. Tamp the growing medium firmly around the roots, and moisten it to just below field capacity. By tilting the container to allow the water to flow down its inside walls, the water both irrigates the plant and washes off any soil particles that might be clinging to the container.

Terrariums are similar to bottle gardens, except that the container has a wider opening. Both terrariums and bottle gardens can be covered with a sheet of glass or some plastic wrap. If disease-free plants are properly planted in a pasteurized growing medium and watered to just below field capacity, these kinds of container gardens should not

FIGURE 10-4 • A terrarium. (Courtesy John D. Cunningham/Visuals Unlimited)

FIGURE 10-5 • The art of bonsai is a rewarding garden hobby that requires little space but much time. (Courtesy Christine M. Douglas/Photo Researchers)

require much attention for several months (Figure 10-4).

Miniaturization of Plants

The ancient art of **bonsai,** developed in Japan, is the miniaturization of what would normally be large woody plants. The plants are dwarfed primarily by judicious root and top pruning, and the plant is shaped by pruning, staking, or tying (Figure 10-5). In Japan, bonsai plants several hundred years old and worth hundreds of dollars are prized and jealously guarded by the families who own them. Many of the Japanese bonsai were originally collected from rocky crevasses where they had been gnarled and twisted by years of adverse environment. Periodic pruning and shaping have kept them in their natural form.

Several students in one of my horticulture classes produced "instant" bonsai from small gnarled sagebrush plants transplanted from the desert. Planted in shallow containers and balanced by pieces of lichen-covered igneous rock, the twisted specimens became the centerpieces of realistic and attractive windswept landscapes. There are small shrubs native to most areas that would be just as suitable as sagebrush for bonsai.

Plants with small leaves or needles are best suited for bonsai, as small leaves or needles are more in scale with miniaturization. Most bonsai fanciers keep their plants outdoors in a protected location or in a greenhouse during most of the year and bring them in for display only on special occasions. If the bonsai is a temperate-zone plant, it must receive its usual alteration of seasons, with enough cold to overcome its rest period.

Conifers and Living Christmas Trees

Conifers can be enjoyed as temporary houseplants. Late in the autumn each year for a number of years I transplanted into a two-gallon container a surplus two- or three-foot Englemann spruce, kept it indoors through the winter into the following summer, and then moved it to another location outdoors (Figure 10-6). Because its rest period was never overcome, the tree grew little during the winter that it was indoors, but it remained green and attractive even in the dark corner where it was placed to provide a little color. A plant so treated cannot survive a second winter without cold to break its rest. Other needle evergreens would undoubtedly do as well as Englemann spruce if purchased as potted trees from a nursery.

In connection with our U-Cut Christmas tree sales we find that Douglas fir and various spruce (all of which have a compact fibrous root system) can be successfully balled and burlapped in October and November, sold as Christmas trees, and planted in the buyer's yard as soon as the ground thaws. We no longer sell pines and true fir as live Christmas trees because their survival rate when

FIGURE 10-6 • Evergreens as houseplants. This small Engelmann spruce dug from the woods during early spring will grow through the summer and provide indoor greenery throughout the following winter.

replanted has been low, perhaps because more of their widespread root system is lost in balling and burlapping.

Various kinds of potted conifers are available for purchase as live Christmas trees. While a potted tree is on display during the Christmas season, its soil should be kept moist but not too wet. The tree should be kept as cool as possible. Miniature lights, which radiate less heat than standard Christmas tree lights, can be used for decoration. At the end of the holiday season, the tree should be transferred to a cool protected site like a covered porch or garage until it can be planted outdoors in its permanent location.

In Hawaii and other areas of the tropics, Norfolk Island pines and trees of other species of the Araucariaceae family cut as Christmas trees can sometimes be rerooted and grown in the yard after Christmas. In order to grow successfully, these trees must be obtained freshly cut, have their stumps immediately placed in water, and be kept in a relatively humid room during the holidays. They should be braced against the wind and protected from humid outdoor conditions after their stump is buried in the garden soil after Christmas.

TAKING CARE OF CUT FLOWERS AND GIFT PLANTS

Flowers from the garden for an arrangement should, if possible, be gathered in the afternoon. The reason—that they will have more accumulated sugar at this time of day—may not be physiologically valid, but flowers cut in the afternoon do seem to have a slightly longer vase life than do those cut in the morning. A sharp knife should be used so that the cut is clean. The stems of most herbaceous flowering plants and roses should be placed in lukewarm (100° to 110°F; 38° to 43°C) water as soon after cutting as possible. If there is a delay in getting the cut stems into water, a second cut should be made so that the conducting tissues will not have sealed over when the stems are placed in water. The container with water and flowers should be placed in a cool location (40°F [4°C] if possible) for a few hours. Warm water is more easily taken into the vascular conducting channels than is cold, and cool temperatures reduce transpiration and respiration so that the flower becomes fully distended with water and utilizes a minimum of its stored carbohydrates. Treatments such as these that prolong the life of plants or plant materials are called **conditioning.**

Flowers that produce a milky exudate from cut surfaces—poinsettias, poppies, and dahlias, for instance—should have the end of the stem plunged into boiling water for 30 seconds before they are placed in lukewarm water. Some woody-stemmed flowers are better able to take up water if the ends of their stems are crushed with a hammer. Containers, "frogs," and other such accessories should always be washed well with soap and water and rinsed in hot water to destroy decay-causing and xylem-plugging organisms before plant materials are placed in them.

Although flowers purchased from a florist probably already have been conditioned, cutting off a few centimeters of their lower stems and placing their cut stems in lukewarm water in a cool room for a few hours may also increase their vase life somewhat. Keeping flower arrangements in a cool location when they are not being observed also extends their vase life.

Homeowners often question how they should treat potted flowering plants such as chrysanthemums, cyclamens, poinsettias, or azaleas. Most of these plants are grown by florists to be temporary bouquets. They should be placed where they can be viewed to the best advantage. They will last longer if, like cut flowers, they are placed in a cool location when not being observed. When their beauty has faded, the homeowner can, with a clear conscience, throw them on the compost heap.

Those who want to continue growing a gift plant after it has finished blooming should remove the faded blooms and move the plant to an inconspicuous corner while it undergoes its after-bloom dormancy. If the weather is favorable, mums can be planted outdoors, though they may not be hardy or programmed to bloom during the growing season. Many of the newer cultivars of poinsettia will continue to grow and produce new leaves, but they will probably not bloom again unless they are placed in a room that is dark for 14 or 15 hours through the night (see Chapter 7). These potted plants, of course, need water just as any other potted plant does.

CONTAINER PLANTING OUTDOORS

Container plants adapted to growing outdoors are popular with homeowners who have small yards and with apartment dwellers who have only a patio (Figure 10-7). Containers that can be moved to a protected location during cold periods can also be used to grow nonhardy plants in cold-winter climates. Temperature, light, and humidity are not as limiting with outdoor as with indoor container-grown plants, but close attention to growing media, water, and fertilizer is necessary because the plants' root systems are restricted. As stated in

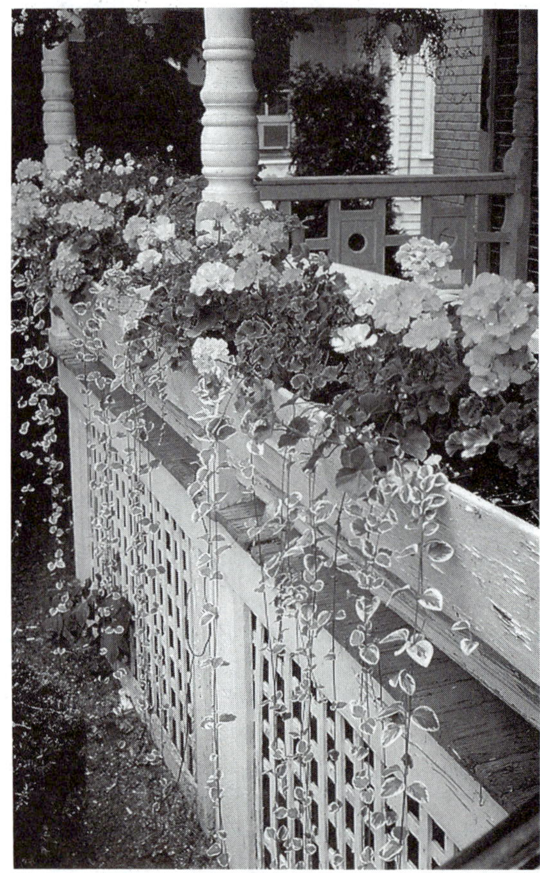

FIGURE 10-7 • Container planting outdoors. (Courtesy Walter Chandoha)

Chapter 7, roots are the plant organs most susceptible to freezing, and special insulation may be needed to protect the root system when it is no longer insulated by the earth's soil mantle.

Theoretically, any plant can be grown in a container, but from a practical standpoint, trees larger than about 10 feet (3 m) in height are too bulky for most home container plantings. A major advantage of container gardens is that the plants can be rearranged. Containers for large shrubs and small trees should be on some kind of dolly if they need to be moved for winter protection or other reasons.

In Asia, potted plants for rent are widely available from nurseries at a nominal fee for weddings, anniversary celebrations, and other special occasions. In some cities in North America as well, plants growing in containers sometimes can be rented. Renting container-growing plants, usually with maintenance included, by hotels, restaurants, and professional offices is becoming quite a common practice in many cities. As busier and more affluent North Americans move to condominiums and apartments, growing and maintaining potted plants for rent could be a promising enterprise.

SPECIALIZED STRUCTURES FOR PLANT GROWING

◆ ◆ ◆

Shortly after glass came into common use in the sixteenth and seventeenth centuries, which was about the time of the extensive explorations by European navigators, Europeans became interested in exotic plants, and collecting and growing plants introduced from Asia, Africa, and the Americas became a hobby of the European nobility. Perhaps the favorite of the many introduced exotic foods were oranges, and because oranges could not be grown outdoors in northern Europe, special glass houses were constructed in which orange trees were planted. These special buildings, known as orangeries, were the forerunner of our modern glass greenhouses.

For several centuries glass was the universal covering for greenhouses, hotbeds, and cold frames, which were the only kinds of plant-growing structures in common use. These were used primarily to produce flowers and vegetables (mostly tomatoes, cucumbers, and lettuce) on a commercial basis during the winter when they could not be grown outdoors. The introduction of fiberglass and plastic materials and the development of fluorescent lights have made possible the development of greenhouses and other plant-growing structures for hobby growers and homeowners. Such structures range from a plastic or wax paper tent that fits over a single plant to protect it from early spring frosts, to a light fixture suspended over a few plants in a corner of the living room, to plant growth chambers and greenhouses where temperature, humidity, and sometimes light can be carefully controlled.

Purposes of Plant-Growing Structures

Gardeners use plant-growing structures for a variety of reasons. One is to grow transplants for earlier crops. Because produce prices are high early in the season, home-grown early vegetables save the most money. Growing from transplants also makes a home garden more profitable by spreading production over a longer season. It is often impossible to purchase transplants of the vegetable and flower cultivars that are best adapted to a particular location, and growers can produce them early only if they grow them as transplants.

The hobby greenhouse provides the satisfaction of gardening, the beauty of flowers, and the flavor of fresh vegetables when outdoor conditions are unfavorable. The gardening season can be extended with structures other than greenhouses: Plastic and waxed paper covers are used to permit seeding or transplanting plants outdoors a month to six weeks earlier than they can be started without protection. Such an early start extends the season when vegetables, small fruits, and flowers are available from the garden.

Plant-Growing structures can shade or protect certain plants during a part of their life. Many of the most beautiful houseplants, including coleus, philodendron, and most begonias, cannot grow well in the brilliant sunlight that occurs during the summer in much of the United States. Nursery stock often needs to be protected from the sun's intense rays. Plant-growing houses covered with enough lathe to filter out one-half to three-fourths of the sun's rays can provide this protection for shade-loving plants otherwise adapted to the area. Various semiopaque compounds are sprayed on glass greenhouses to cut down the intense heat and give some shade to plants grown in conventional greenhouses during the summer. A dark, fairly heavy nylon netting is sometimes hung over shade-loving plants grown either outdoors or in a conventional greenhouse during the summer.

Plant-growing structures also protect plants from early fall frosts. Gardeners can have tomatoes from the garden into November in certain areas of the northern United States and Canada if they construct a plastic tent over the tomato vines about the time the first frost is likely. The tent should be constructed so that it can be opened on sunny days. Geraniums, coleus, and other tender perennials can be brought indoors for the winter. They can be potted and moved into a greenhouse if one is available, but many growers winter them near a window in an unheated basement.

Types of Plant-Growing Structures

Plans, do-it-yourself kits, and preassembled plant-growing structures in a wide variety of kinds, shapes, and sizes made from a wide variety of materials are available to home gardeners. They can be categorized as hotbeds and cold frames, plant protectors, indoor growing structures, and greenhouses.

Hotbeds and Cold Frames. Hotbeds and cold frames consist of four well-insulated sides and a transparent top cover that, north of the equator, slopes south in order to capture the sun's rays (Figure 10-8).

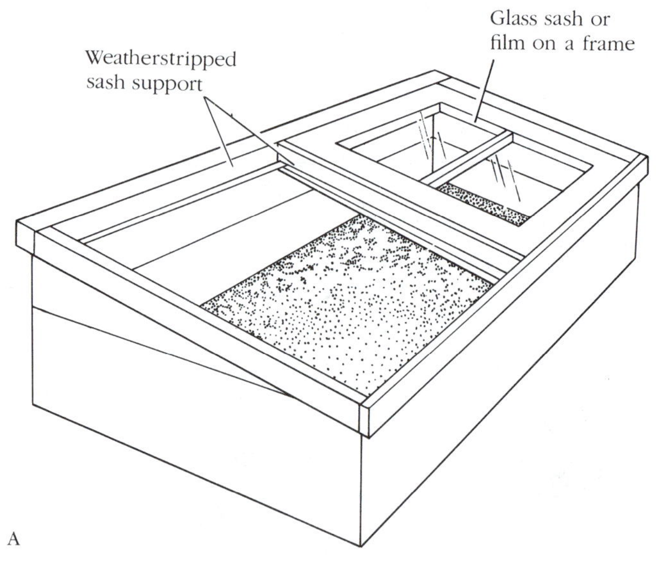

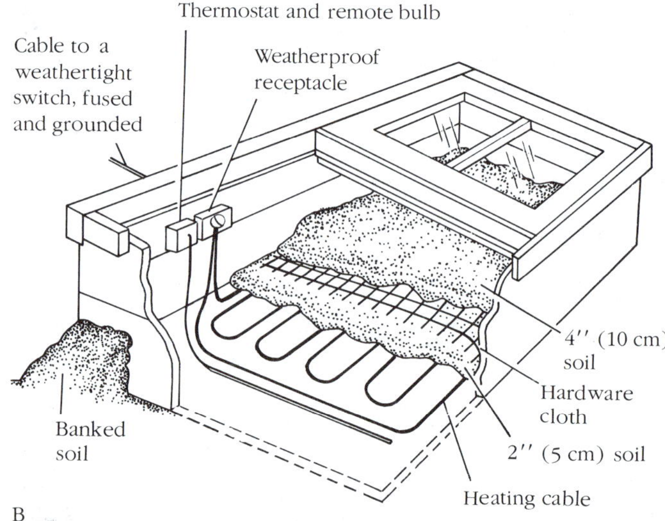

FIGURE 10-8 • Cold frame (A) and layout of heating cable for hotbed (B). (Adapted from USDA)

If no heat is added to the structure, it is called a **cold frame.** The main purpose of cold frames in cold-winter areas is to harden off transplants before they are transplanted outside. In milder climates cold frames are used for holding plants through the winter. Homeowners may wish to heat the frame, in which case it is called a **hotbed.**

The sides of the structure can be made from whatever material is available and convenient. Brick, poured concrete, and pumice blocks are sometimes used, but more commonly the structure is made of wood. If the structure is to be temporary, soil, straw, leaves, or sawdust are sometimes piled around the wooden frame to provide insulation. If fiberglass or other insulation is used in a more permanent structure, the insulation should be at least 4 inches (10 cm) thick.

Normally, the north wall of a hotbed or cold frame is built to stand 18 to 20 inches (45 to 50 cm) above ground level. The side walls should slope toward the front at least 1 inch per foot (2½ cm each 30 cm) so that the front or south side will be 10 to 14 inches (25 to 35 cm) above the soil if a standard 3 × 6 foot (1 × 2 m) sash is to be used as a cover. With the standard sash, the width of beds is 6 feet from the center of the front wall to the center of the back wall, providing approximately 5 feet 8 inches (2 m) of inside growing space. The tops of the back and front walls should have the same slope as the sides, giving the sash 2 inches (5 cm) of firm supporting surface on top of each wall. With the standard sash, the distance between cross-supports is 3 feet (1 m), and the length of the hotbed is some multiple of 3 feet.

Hotbeds and cold frames should always be located on well-drained land that is free from depressions or danger of flooding during heavy rains. The south side of a building is an ideal location because the building helps trap some of the warmth from the sun's rays. Obviously the area should not be shaded by large trees or buildings. Plants growing in hotbeds or cold frames require frequent irrigation, so a source of water should be available nearby.

Hotbeds can be heated in many different ways. Steam, hot water, or hot air can be used if available. The most convenient source of heat for small hotbeds in an area where the cost of electricity is reasonable is an electric heating cable. Heating cables come in various lengths and wattage ratings. The 60-foot (18-m), 400-watt cable is common and adapted for use with an ordinary service current of 110 to 120 volts. (A 400-watt cable uses about the same amount of current required by four 100-watt light bulbs.) USDA leaflet 445 recommends 10 to 12 watts of cable heating capacity for each square foot of bed (105–125 watts/m^2). One 60-foot cable is required for a 6 × 6 foot (4 m^2) bed and two 60-foot cables for a 6 × 12 (8 m^2) bed for late-winter and early-spring heating if warm temperatures are required. When outdoor temperatures are extremely cold, three cables may be required to heat each 6 × 12 bed. Where only moderate heat is required, as for spring growing in the South, one 60-foot cable for a four-sash 6 × 12 foot bed may be sufficient.

If electricity is to be used, the hotbed must be well insulated and the joints well fitted; the electric cables should be buried in approximately 6 inches (15 cm) of growing media; and of course, a thermostat should be installed. All electrical connections should be watertight, and all wiring should be designed for outdoor use. The major advantage of an electrically heated hotbed is that the amount of heat can be automatically controlled by the use of thermostats, and thus extremes can be avoided.

Before the advent of electricity and the development of modern heating systems, heat generated by the decomposition of manure was commonly used for hotbeds, and where manure is available, it can still be used. Temporary hotbeds can be constructed by placing a board frame on or around a flat pile of manure 12 to 24 inches (30 to 60 cm) in depth. Sash covering is placed on the frame, and about 5 to 6 inches (13 to 15 cm) of good soil is spread on top of the manure. The more usual practice for constructing a manure-heated hotbed is to dig a pit beneath the frame of the hotbed. If the temperature does not get below 12°F (−11°C) during the plant-growing period, a layer of manure 12 to 15 inches (30 to 38 cm) thick will be sufficient, provided that the bed is well banked on the outside with soil or manure and some form of covering is used over the sash during periods of low temperature. The depth of the layer should be increased 1 inch for each degree of lower temperature. Thus, about 24 to 28 inches (60 to 70 cm) of manure should be used under conditions of 0° F (−18°C) temperature. The pit should be dug deep enough so that about 5 or 6 inches of screened garden loam can be spread evenly over the manure.

Directions for preparing the manure for use in a hotbed are from *USDA Farmer's Bulletin* 1743, which recommends that only good quality straw-bedded horse or mule manure be used for hotbeds; the directions for preparation are based on this kind of manure. I know of successful hotbeds heated with cow and chicken manure, but the length of time the manure needs to be piled and turned and the time that elapses before seeds or plants can be placed in the hotbed will probably be somewhat different. The amount of straw or shavings mixed with the manure also varies the rapidity and amount of heating produced.

The manure should be placed along the side of the bed and turned occasionally for two to three days until it begins to heat. If the manure becomes dry, moisture should be added when it is turned. It is forked uniformly into the pit below the hotbed as soon as it has begun to heat uniformly. The temperature in manure-heated hotbeds is likely to rise as high as 90° or 100°F (32° or 38°C) during the first few days. Seeds should not be sown in the hotbeds until after the temperature has dropped to 85°F (30°C) or lower.

Hotbeds are inexpensive to construct, fairly easy to maintain, and quite satisfactorily produce salad greens through the winter and bedding plants for spring transplants. They deserve more attention from home gardeners.

Plant Protectors. Plant protectors are almost any kind of covering that can be placed over tender young seedlings or transplants to prevent freezing damage on cold nights during the early spring. During the early part of this century several companies manufactured plant covers of translucent reinforced paper attached to a heavy cardboard rim. The completed protector had the shape of a Mexican sombrero. These structures were known collectively by the brand name of the most widely used protector—Hot-Kap. Hot-Kaps are still available in some areas. More recently polyethylene has replaced most of the other kinds of plant protectors. A square of polyethylene and two wire hoops placed crosswise are sometimes used to protect individual plants.

Plastic can also be used to bring a nonhardy specimen shrub through a few extremely cold winter days. In many areas only the two or three subzero days each three to four winters prevent the growing of saucer magnolia, dwarf holly, pyracantha, rhododendron, or certain other choice shrubs or trees. If these plants are kept small by pruning, the homeowner can quickly erect a plastic protector around them whenever injuriously low temperatures threaten.

The potential for using polyethylene tent protectors is probably only beginning to be realized by home gardeners. In Greece, commercial strawberries are being produced 35 to 40 days earlier than normal when the plants are covered in early February with a perforated plastic tent. In the Columbia Basin of Washington, watermelons have matured 40 days earlier than normal when transplants were placed under plastic tents in mid-April. In the northern United States, Alaska, and Canada, where the accumulation of heat units is insufficient to produce such warm-season crops as melons, tomatoes, sweet potatoes, and eggplant, there seems to be real promise for using large plastic tents with some sort of variable ventilation to prevent temperatures from rising too high on extremely bright days.

Indoor Growing Structures. The requirements for plant growth are available within the walls of most homes. Temperature, oxygen, and carbon dioxide all are a part of a normal home environment; growing medium, water, and fertilizer can be easily supplied. There are some plants that do relatively well with the 250 to 400 foot-candles of light normally found in a living room. Those requiring more light can be grown next to a south window. However, many plants do require extra light, and often there is no convenient place next to a south window where plant containers can be located. Thus the growing of plants with artificial light has become popular. Artificial light sometimes is also used to supplement winter sunshine in the hobby greenhouse.

Because of homeowners' interest in artificial light for plant growing, a number of companies are manufacturing various kinds of light tables. These vary from a simple fluorescent fixture with a couple of tubes or a sunlamp with a plant holder beneath, to floor-to-ceiling light shelves with several layers of light fixtures, each fitted above a plant-growing tray. There also are fixtures with sliding glass doors, which aid in controlling humidity as well as temperature. Most of the more expensive units are fitted with a time clock. Some room dividers and other furniture are made up partly or wholly of plant-growing trays and fluorescent lights.

Homeowners can save considerable money by building their own light tables and have the benefit of a unit custom built to fit into the space available. Custom-made light tables vary from a fluorescent tube placed under an upper kitchen cabinet to light a few plants growing on the counter to very complex, carefully controlled units that may light a number of square feet.

People contemplating purchasing or building an artificial plant-growing table should keep a few facts in mind. First, the intensity of light is much higher close to the lamp than it is farther from it. Longer fluorescent tubes are more efficient in light output than are shorter tubes. A reflector placed above the tubes increases the intensity of light reaching the plants below. Furthermore, plants use about the same spectrum of irradiance as can be seen by the human eye, except that much of the light from the green area of the spectrum is reflected; thus most fixtures used for home lighting also are satisfactory for growing plants. Fluorescent tubes are used more extensively than are other light fixtures for growing indoor plants because they are relatively efficient in their use of electrical current and because they put out less heat in proportion to the intensity of light they develop (see "Kind or Quality of Light" in Chapter 7).

The question is often asked what kinds of plants are suitable for growing under artificial light. Unfortunately, if light tubes are placed too close together, the light impinging on one tube from those next to it will be converted to heat. Therefore, without special fan and cooling equipment, light tubes should be spaced no closer than 4 to 6 inches (10 to 15 cm) apart. As a consequence, most reasonably priced artificial light structures do not offer intensities high enough to be optimal for most crop plants. Most of the ornamentals grown for their foliage, as well as gloxinias, African violets, some orchids, coleus, Christmas cactus, poinsettias, and begonias, all grow well under artificial light. When seedling transplants are to be grown, the light should be placed within a foot of the container in which seedlings are being established, in order to give them the highest intensity possible.

The low intensity of artificial light-growing tables can be compensated for somewhat by having the lights on for a longer period of time. Unless short-day plants are being grown, artificial lights are kept on for sixteen hours. A time clock should be installed between the electrical outlet and the light source as a dark period is necessary for the normal growth of most plants.

The Hobby Greenhouse

Greenhouses are becoming almost as popular with American homeowners as are swimming pools. They extend the gardening season so that gardening becomes a year-round hobby, and they offer the pleasure of flowers and growing plants throughout the year (Figure 10-9).

Planning the Greenhouse. The choice of greenhouse, its size, and the material used for its construction all depend on the location available, the plants to be grown, and the finances available for its construction and maintenance. Hobby greenhouses come in a variety of shapes and sizes. Small reach-in units that attach to and replace an

FIGURE 10-9 • Various kinds of hobby greenhouses. (Upper left and lower right, courtesy of Lord & Burnham)

existing window are the simplest. When a south wall is available, the attached lean-to greenhouse may be the best choice. Most common is the even-span or standard type, which most people visualize when they think of a greenhouse. The greenhouse must be located on a well-drained site where it will receive sun throughout the day; the heating bill will be considerably lower if the location is protected from strong winds.

The width of the greenhouse should be divided into convenient work and traffic areas. Side benches should be kept 3 inches (8 cm) away from the side wall and should be no wider than the owner can reach across, 2 to 3 feet (up to 1 m). Center benches that can be serviced from both sides can be as wide as 6 feet (2 m). Walks will need to be at least 18 inches (45 cm) if one is to just squeeze between benches or wider if wheelbarrows are to be used. Normally the height at the eaves should be a minimum of 5 feet (1½ m), and the pitch of the roof should be between 25° and 30° for a glass house and somewhat steeper for one covered with fiberglass (Figure 10-10).

If a glass greenhouse is the choice, its size will often depend on the size of the units commercially available. If construction is from basic materials, size should be a multiple of the basic structural unit. Usually, however, glass greenhouses are purchased as a complete unit, either designed to be set up by the company handling them or prefabricated with do-it-yourself instructions. These are available in a variety of models and sizes.

Hobby greenhouses can also be made of fiberglass and plastics. Fiberglass does not break as easily as glass, but it has the disadvantage of being somewhat less transparent. The outer layer of some older types of fiberglass tends to weather, which makes it even less transparent. Fiberglass and glass are comparable in cost, but glass is more costly to install and more difficult for the do-it-yourself structure.

Greenhouses made of plastic are much less expensive than fiberglass or glass greenhouses, both because the plastic is less costly and because lightweight plastic requires only a minimum of framing materials. The major disadvantage of plastic greenhouses is that they must be recovered each year. Recovering a plastic greenhouse is not a difficult undertaking, but the fact that the green-

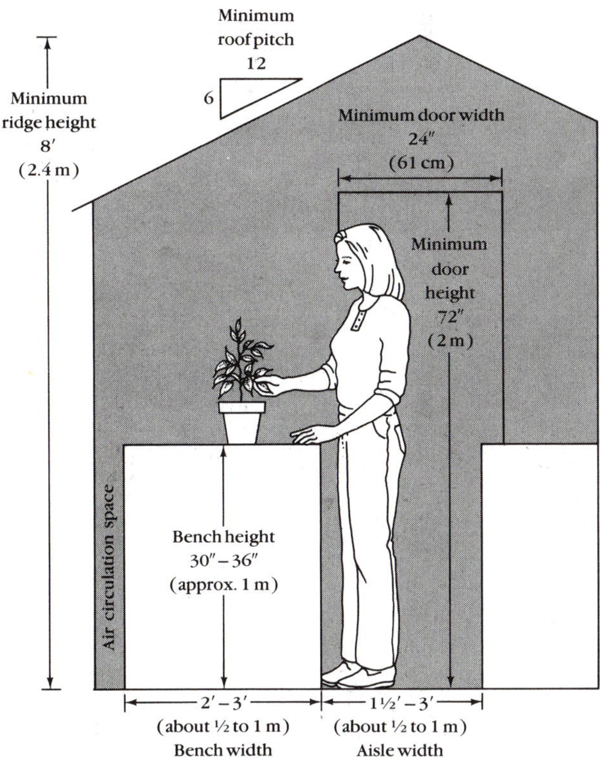

FIGURE 10-10 • Specifications for hobby greenhouses. (Courtesy of USDA)

house is likely to remain uncovered during a part of each summer precludes the growing of many kinds of plants that need a permanent greenhouse environment. Greenhouse frames are often covered with two layers of plastic to reduce the loss of heat.

Greenhouse Plant-Growing Requirements. Steam, hot water, and hot air furnaces; electric cables; and various kinds of space heaters can be used to heat greenhouses (Figure 10-11). The capacity of the heating system depends on the climate, the size of the greenhouse, and the temperature required by the plants. Often the home heating system has enough capacity to heat a small greenhouse, or perhaps the home system with an electric or a gas- or oil-fired space heater for occasional cold weather emergencies is enough to provide the needed heat. During the winter, night temperatures of 55° to 60°F (13° to 16°C) and day temperatures of 60° to 70°F (16° to 21°C) are sufficient for most plants. When space heaters are used, ample ventilation should be provided. If oxygen becomes limiting, incomplete combustion may result in the formation of carbon monoxide.

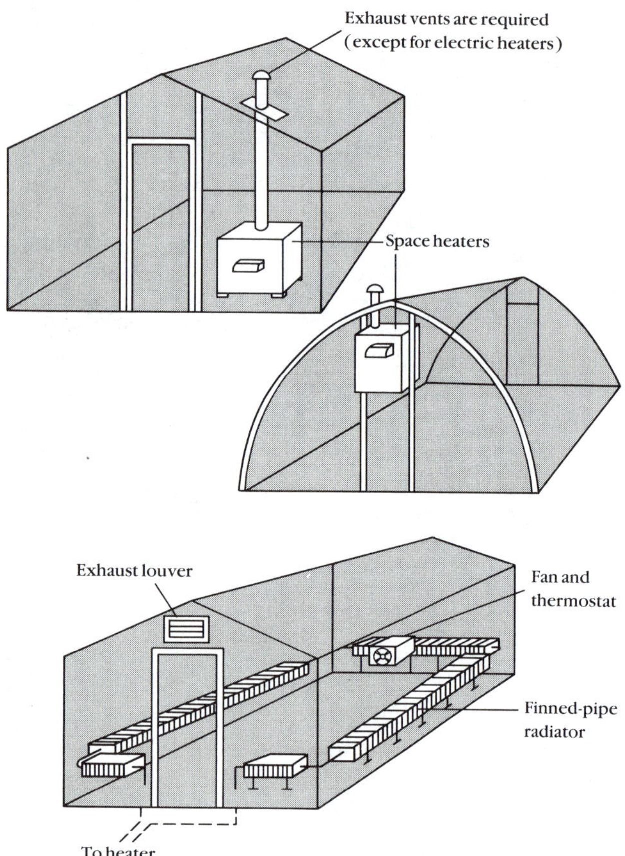

FIGURE 10-11 • Some heating systems for greenhouses. (Courtesy of USDA)

Ventilation and cooling are most often provided by vents and fans. Evaporative cooling systems, which in arid regions can lower temperatures by up to 25°F (14°C) during warm weather, are available and not too expensive. Automatic controls are available for cooling systems. Greenhouses without an air-conditioning unit are shaded during the summer by applying a special shading compound to the outside of the house. The compound is washed off by fall rains.

Supplemental light is quite expensive and not necessary for most ornamental plants likely to be grown in the greenhouse. Temperature should be kept low during the winter when light is limited to maintain a balance of plant-growing factors. In northern areas, vegetables may require supplemental light during midwinter.

The moisture supply for greenhouse crops must be carefully monitored. During cool weather, plants may not require water more often than once or twice a week, whereas during hot weather, water may be needed twice or three times a day. Soil and fertilizer recommendations for potted plants are discussed in Chapter 5.

Plants for Greenhouse Growing. Most vegetables, strawberries, and even some tropical and subtropical tree fruits can be grown in greenhouses; however, flowers and houseplants are by far the most popular hobby greenhouse products. Houseplants; specialty items such as orchids, carnivorous plants, and exotic ferns; and cuttings, seeds, corms, and bulbs of traditional greenhouse plants are available from nurseries that cater to the needs of greenhouse growers. Containers, pesticides, stakes, and supplies of various kinds can also be purchased from these dealers.

Greenhouse Pest Control. Weeds in greenhouses should be controlled even if they are under benches where they do not crowd other plants. Weeds tend to harbor and nourish insects and insect eggs and often carry diseases that can spread to other plants. Greenhouse weeds should be pulled or hoed because herbicides pose too much of a threat to other plants in a closed environment.

The major insects and diseases that are likely to be a problem in greenhouses, as well as the controls for minor infestations, are the same as those that affect houseplants discussed earlier in this chapter. Pesticides for major disease or insect problems are most often applied as sprays, and formulations for greenhouses are likely to be much more toxic to people than are formulations for houseplants. Whenever pesticides are applied in a greenhouse, it is important that signs listing the materials used and the times of application be posted and that doors be locked so that children or others do not inadvertently enter.

For greenhouses and large isolated plant-growing rooms, fumigation with smoke bombs is sometimes the most practical insect control. Smoke bombs contain an insecticide that is spewed into the room in the form of smoke when the wick is lighted. Their active ingredient is usually highly toxic, and people using them must be extremely careful. In fact, only a licensed applicator is permitted to apply many of these kinds of materials.

As with houseplants, strict sanitation and a daily examination of plants for insects and diseases will minimize pest problems and the amount of pesticide needed for the home greenhouse.

Selected References

Bowles, J. P., ed. *Indoor Gardening.* Brooklyn Botanic Garden Handbook 112 (special printing of *Plants and Gardens,* vol. 43, no. 1). Brooklyn, N.Y.: Brooklyn Botanic Garden, 1987.

Dreilinger, S., ed. *Indoor Bonsai.* Brooklyn Botanic Garden Handbook 125 (special printing of *Plants and Gardens,* vol. 46, no. 3). Brooklyn, N.Y.: Brooklyn Botanic Garden, 1990.

Faust, J. L. *The New York Times Book of Houseplants.* New York: Random House, 1983.

Herwig, R. *The Good Housekeeping Encyclopedia of Houseplants.* New York: Hearst Books, 1990.

Larson, R. A. *Introduction to Floriculture.* 2nd ed. San Diego: Academic Press, 1992.

Manaker, G. H. *Interior Plantscaping: Installation, Maintenance, and Management.* 2nd ed. Englewood Cliffs, N.J.: Prentice-Hall, 1987.

Martin, T., ed. *Greenhouses and Garden Rooms.* Brooklyn Botanic Garden Handbook 116 (special printing of *Plants and Gardens,* vol. 44, no. 2). Brooklyn, N.Y.: Brooklyn Botanic Garden, 1988.

Ortho Books Editorial Staff. *Gardening in Containers.* San Francisco: Ortho Books, 1983.

Pfahl, P. B., and E. W. Kalin. *American Style of Flower Arranging.* Englewood Cliffs, N.J.: Prentice-Hall, 1982.

Shapiro, A. M. *The Homeowner's Complete Handbook for Add-on Solar Greenhouses and Sunspaces.* Emmaus, Pa.: Rodale Press, 1985.

Smith, M. D., ed. *Ortho's Complete Guide to Successful Houseplants.* San Francisco: Ortho Books, 1984.

Sunset Magazine Editors. *House Plants.* Menlo Park, Calif.: Lane, 1983.

Time-Life Books Editors. *Flowering Houseplants.* Alexandria, Va.: Time-Life Books, 1990.

Time-Life Books Editors. *Time-Life Book of Foliage Houseplants.* Alexandria, Va.: Time-Life Books, 1986.

CHAPTER 11

The Ornamental Garden

The ornamental garden has always been an important form of artistic expression. Much has been written about the ornamental gardens of the world, which in design and purpose are as varied as are the people who created them and the landforms on which they were created. This text is concerned primarily with gardens around the home.

The use of plants and inanimate materials to enhance the utility and beauty of the area around a home is called home **landscaping**. There may be several different gardens along with nongarden utilitarian areas within the landscape (Figure 11-1). What is important is that their combinations have beauty and harmony as well as practicality.

THE HOME LANDSCAPE

Not uncommon is the house that is almost being pushed from its foundation by the "cute little sapling" that someone planted next to it twenty years ago or the living room that must be artificially lighted all day because three gorgeous rhododendrons block out light from its windows (Figure 11-2). Many homes have outdoor eating areas that are seldom used because food, table service, and all the incidentals have to be carried from the kitchen, down a flight of stairs, through the basement, or across 100 yards of back lawn. Only by careful planning can these kinds of mistakes be avoided.

FIGURE 11-1 • Lush home landscaping foundation planting. (Courtesy of Grant Heilman)

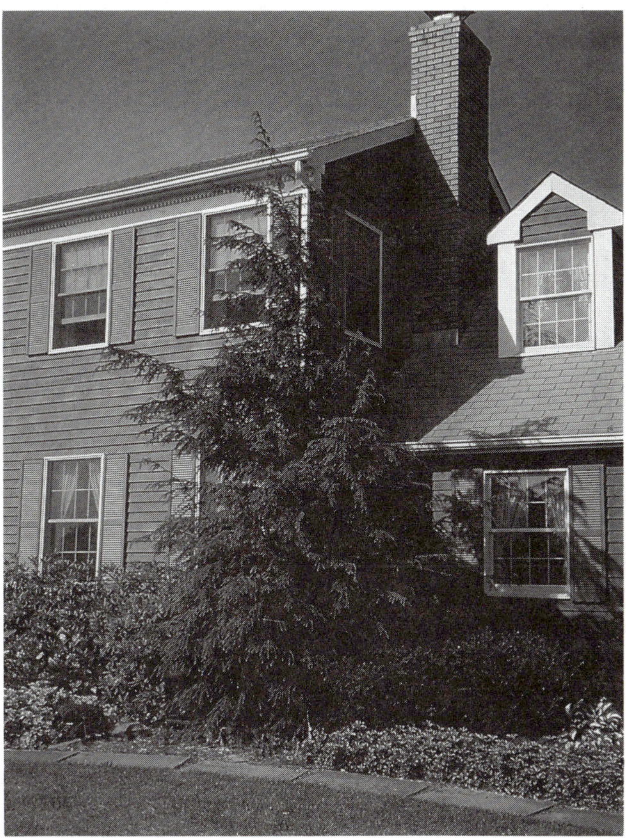

FIGURE 11-2 • Placement of trees. Trees and shrubs should not be planted in locations where they will grow to cover windows and crowd against foundations. (Courtesy of Walter Chandoha)

The outdoor area around a home, whether it is a 10-acre estate or a porch with a few planter boxes, can be just as important to the enjoyment and well-being of a family as is the indoor area; a house is not a home until it is landscaped in a manner that pleases the homeowner and provides for the outdoor needs and comforts of the family. Landscaping is a functional part of the home, and it should be planned at the time the house is planned.

Considerations During Construction

Those fortunate enough to build their own homes should plan for the use of outdoor as well as indoor areas. First and foremost, the house should be planned to fit the lot. Enjoyable views should be preserved and enhanced or created with landscaping. The house should be placed on the lot so that a maximum amount of yard space can be used for family activities (Figure 11-3). Figure 11-4 shows the standard symbols used in this and subsequent landscape plans. This usually means building as close to the street and as near to one edge of the property as city codes allow. Such placement provides maximum usable area with privacy behind the house and, with most lots, some usable space at one side. For suggestions on grading, topsoil, and drainage, see Chapter 5.

If at all possible, large trees and shrubs already on the lot should be saved (Figure 11-5). Such plants grow slowly, and the pleasure they provide is difficult to measure. From a purely economic standpoint a good, large tree can often add hundreds, sometimes thousands, of dollars to the

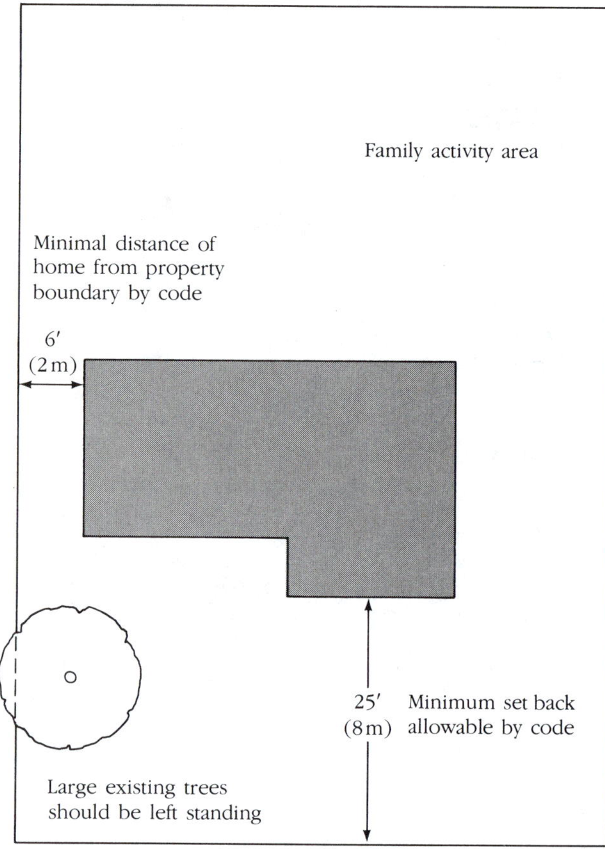

FIGURE 11-3 • Dividing up the landscape space. On a small urban or suburban lot, it is generally desirable to place the house as near to one side and the front as zoning restrictions allow, thereby permitting the maximum area for family activities.

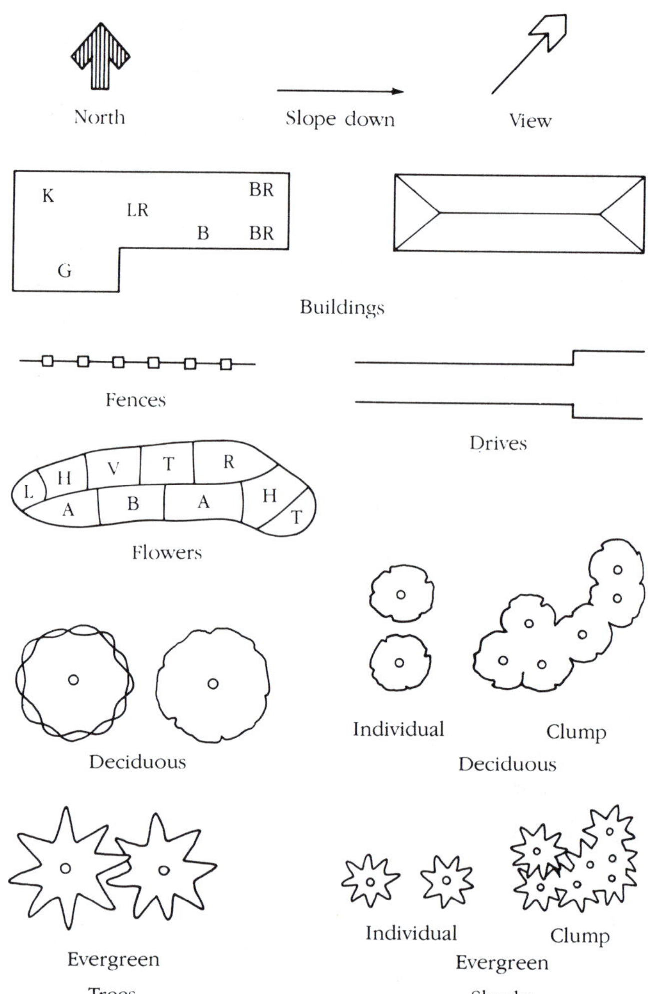

FIGURE 11-4 • Standard symbols used on the landscape plan.

value of a new home; for example, the 'Live Oak' trees growing along St. Charles Avenue in New Orleans are insured for $25,000 to $50,000 each!

Excavation and land leveling must be carefully done if existing plants are to be saved. If the soil level around a tree is to be raised, there must be provision for aerating the roots, usually by installing drain tile and leaving unfilled an area a few feet in diameter next to the trunk. If soil level is to be lowered, a wall to protect the soil around tree roots will be necessary (see "Landscape Construction" in Chapter 14).

Economic and Sequential Considerations in Landscaping

Most people want a landscape that provides maximum use and beauty at minimum cost and upkeep. It is not wise to sacrifice quality to save a little money. The cost of landscaping should be 10 to 30 percent of the cost of the home. Much of this cost is in labor, an expense that can be saved if owners are able to do the work themselves. Having professional assistance in planning the landscape is, of

FIGURE 11-5 • Using existing trees. This housing development, which was sited carefully and constructed around an existing wooded area, left as many of the existing trees as possible. (From P. L. Carpenter et al., *Plants in the Landscape*, copyright 1990 by W. H. Freeman and Company)

course, highly desirable and often not very expensive. Large landscape offices are sometimes reluctant to work on small lots, but in many communities part-time or full-time independent professionals have offices where they consult with homeowners. Large nurseries employ personnel experienced in landscaping to assist those who purchase plant materials from the nursery. In some urban areas the county extension office has one or more staff who can help with home landscape problems, and numerous government bulletins, commercially published books, and other publications are designed to help homeowners who do their own planning.

Complete landscaping immediately after a home is built is often not financially possible. However, even if there is not enough money to complete it, the landscape should be planned when the house is planned. The various elements that will make up the landscape can then be budgeted over a period of years.

The first essential is probably a front sidewalk and lawn so family and visitors are not constantly tracking mud into the house. The owner may also wish to plant a few trees. Purchasing the major trees as inexpensive, small whips the first year will bring the same results as buying much larger trees later and in the long run will save considerable money and planting effort. A few dollars' worth of annual flower seed can provide color and filler until the major shrubs and trees can be planted or grow larger. In many areas it may be necessary at least to gravel the driveway before the first winter (Figure 11-6).

In the second year the back lawn and the rest of the major trees with some foundation shrubs can be planted. Retaining walls and rock gardens may not cost very much if the homeowners can supply the labor. If money is scarce, it may be necessary to delay building benches, fountains, and pools or purchasing shrubs for specimen and border plantings until the third or fourth year.

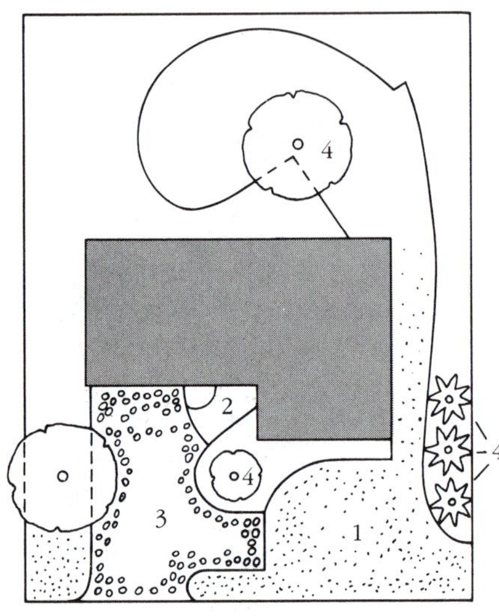

First year

1. Establish the lawn
2. Pave entrance walk
3. Gravel driveway
4. Plant major trees
5. Fill in with flowers throughout the area

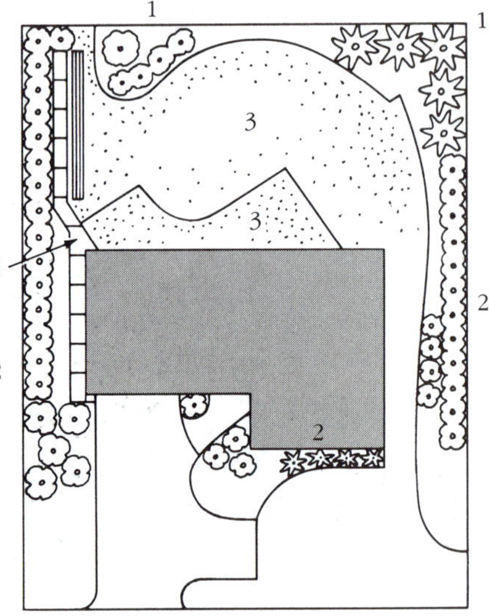

Second year

1. Plant other major trees
2. Plant foundation and border shrubs
3. Establish back lawn
4. Install other walks
5. Fill in with flowers throughout

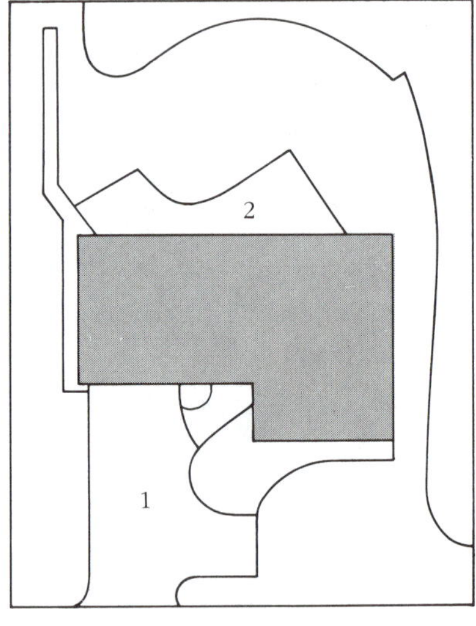

Third and fourth years

1. Pave driveway
2. Install the patio
3. Care for plantings in the entire space

FIGURE 11-6 • Sequence of landscaping spread over three years.

Many people do not have the privilege of building their own home. If they do become homeowners, they buy either a newly built tract home or an older home that already has some landscaping. A carefully planned landscape is probably even more important to a tract home than to an owner-built home because the landscape can provide uniqueness for what would otherwise be one of a monotonous row of look-alike houses. Purchasers of tract homes will not have the opportunity to coordinate outdoor–indoor areas, but they should make certain that the property can provide the outdoor amenities essential to the life-style the family desires. They may also need to amend the soil because the topsoil left around a tract home is frequently poor. For soil improvement suggestions, see Chapter 5.

Occasionally an older home has a well-planned landscape that fits the needs and delights the aesthetic senses of the purchaser, but more often minor or major renovations are necessary. Seldom is it necessary to relandscape completely. If the initial landscape plan was sound, judicious pruning and trimming and a little fertilizer can do wonders. Even if the new owners decide that the landscape is hopeless, they may find that careful planning will enable them to retain many of the existing trees and larger shrubs.

Planning the Landscape

Planning the landscaping of a home can be divided into three parts: (1) choosing design elements or materials, (2) determining limitations or considerations that make your landscape different from all others, and (3) actually planning on paper the complete landscape around the home.

Design Elements. Probably the most important design element is cubic space. All of us are familiar with the number of square feet it requires to place a chair or a kitchen cabinet or for convenient movement from area to area in our homes, but we sometimes must be reminded that the cubic space that human beings move about in and occupy as they perform the acts of daily living is as important to their emotional well-being as floor space is to furniture placement or traffic patterns. For example, the ceiling of a room is usually higher than necessary for a human to squeeze into because architectural builders know that it takes more space than that occupied by a person's body to provide adequate ventilation and the feeling of atmosphere in the room. Outdoors, ceilings are not of so much concern because the ceiling is the sky or, in some cases, the canopy of tree branches overhead. Nevertheless, the cubic space designed into the garden should fit the dimensions of the body, including the eye, and should provide for maximum utility.

Land **contour**, or the shape of the land, whether it is a hill, a valley, or a perfectly level site, is an important design element. When structures are built to accommodate a family's needs, the land around those structures must also be sculptured to fit those needs. A sloping site may be well adapted to an artistic design, but it may need considerable alteration if the family wants a level game or play area.

Plants, which some people think are the only element in landscaping, should not be considered lightly. The plants used outside the house, inside, and for the transition in between are certainly the element that gives character to the landscape scheme. But plants are a building material, and unless the landscape has been designed, even the most beautiful plants may not make the home grounds attractive or usable.

Rock adds interest and variety and often helps make the landscape appear natural. Not only are the broad surfaces of rock used for walls and patios, but rock supplies texture and color when it is used as a gravel path or drive. Rock in walls is used to retain soil and in rock gardens to simulate a natural rock outcrop. Plants that require deep, cool, moist rock pockets filled with broken stone and porous decayed vegetable matter are grown in rock gardens. Still finer particles of rock mixed with humus become the soil essential to the growth of plants.

Water as a landscaping element is used for contrast, variety, movement, and sound. Consider the beauty of the reflective surfaces of a pool or lake, the movement and sound of a fountain or a brook, or the enjoyment of swimming in a backyard pool. Water that falls as rain or that is used to irrigate or to nourish plants is a design factor that must not be overlooked. Water in the atmosphere or relative humidity may limit or enhance certain types of garden development.

A long list of manufactured building materials used as design elements, including brick, dimensioned lumber, concrete block, pipe, plastic, glass, canvas, fiberglass, and other fabrics, add much to the convenience and comfort of the landscape.

Limitations and Considerations. Most of us could not afford and would not want a "Renaissance estate." Such gardens were designed to satisfy the desires of a special class of people who had relatively large incomes and the leisure time to enjoy them. Today, gardens should be designed to satisfy the physical and emotional needs and fit the pocketbook of those using them.

An athletic family may need a volleyball court, a swimming pool, or a games area. Another family might want an area set aside for cultivating vegetables. Others may want facilities for eating outdoors or a secluded place in which to sit and read. Such needs should be seriously considered and planned for.

The major physical limitation in gardens of today is the size and shape of the property, which is often determined by the amount of money the family can spend for a building site as well as by the neighborhood they choose. A very small lot in an exclusive neighborhood may cost more than several acres in a less prestigious area. One should not, however, consider only the price quoted by the realtor when judging the relative cost of two lots. Public utilities, such as paved streets, sidewalks, storm sewers, sewer lines, and water mains, as well as cost of commuting to work, school, church, and shopping centers, all are important considerations in the expense of a homesite. A small lot with parks and playgrounds nearby may be more desirable than a larger lot so far from these amenities that a playground and picnic area must be provided in the yard. Regardless of cost, the lot—that piece of land with definite geometrical borders imposed by civilization—is what, in many cases, decides the kind of house that is built, and it always dictates landscape patterns.

The orientation of the house, which is important to comfort and convenience, is usually determined by the location, shape, and size of the lot. When possible, the house should be placed so that maximum sunlight reaches all sides and certain rooms at certain times of the day. Sunny kitchens and living areas, especially where the climate is cool, are more important than sunny bedrooms. Those areas that are always shaded are difficult to landscape because few plants thrive in perpetual shade. If the house is oriented at a 45° angle to the north, it will have the smallest amount of perpetually shaded area. Windows and glass doors in the living areas should, if possible, face the garden or a scenic view rather than a busy street. Where wind velocity is high, doorways and large windows should face away from the direction of the prevailing wind or be protected from its force by a wall or planting.

The style or type of architecture is another definite consideration. A two-story Cape Cod house requires a different landscape than does a low, ranch-style house; a box style, different from a cottage.

Climatic influence is one of the main considerations in landscaping. Prevailing winds must be controlled for pleasant living both inside and outside. The factor of most concern in regard to the survival of plants is temperature. Cold temperatures during the winter determine which plants will survive in the landscape, and spring frosts often damage early blooms or limit the early planting of annuals. High summer temperatures in some areas preclude the use of many fine cool-climate species and increase the need for shade trees. It is also important that the landscape be attractive during the entire year, not just in summer.

FIGURE 11-7 • A view enhances the economic, as well as the aesthetic, value of the property. (Courtesy Michael Mathers/Peter Arnold, Inc.)

Views are an important design element (Figure 11-7). Some people buy a lot with a view at a premium price and maintain long utility lines and roads to have that view. If your lot has a good view, take advantage of it by framing it with trees and locating outdoor living areas so that you can enjoy it. If you have a view that is undesirable, screen it with a fence or a planting. Views can be created within the confines of the property with imaginative design and placement of gardens.

Maintenance is important. An elaborate place poorly maintained is less attractive than a well-maintained place with little landscaping. Most people have limited time to devote to gardening, and hiring a gardener is expensive, so a simple, easy-to-maintain landscape is the most satisfactory solution for most of us.

The Landscape Plan

A coordinated and pleasing landscape requires a guide or plan. In fact, several rough sketches and preliminary plans generally are needed. It is easiest for most people inexperienced in drafting to use a large piece of graph paper to show to scale the yard area and the location of buildings and plants that are to be saved. The initial drawing should be constructed so that a square on the graph paper is equal to an appropriate number of square feet of yard space. The graph paper plan can be traced to provide the basic house–yard relationship for the analysis and other preliminary plans. The graph paper or a neater traced copy can be used for the finished plan.

Analysis Plan. The **analysis plan** (see Figure 11-8) should include those views to be preserved or enhanced; unsightly views or objects that need screening; the general direction of wind during various seasons; the direction of the summer and winter sun; and the locations of utility poles, overhead lines, underground cables, sewer pipes, and water pipes. It should also include the general locations of rooms within the house. The kitchen, laundry, and garage are service areas; the entrance way or room where guests first enter the home is the public area; and the family room, dining room, and living room are areas of family activity or privacy. Logically these indoor divisions should extend to the outdoors, and so the next step is to divide the yard into public, service, and family activities or private areas.

Each of these areas should be considered separately, and several trial sketches showing walks, drives, walls, plantings, and other design elements should be drawn. While making these sketches, the designer should keep in mind the analysis plan so that the effects of the sun and wind are considered, tall-growing trees are not planted under utility lines or walks placed directly over water or sewer pipes, and willows or similar trees are not planted where their wide-ranging roots will enter and plug sewer lines. Separate sketches drawn to a large scale may be necessary for detailed explanations of such elements as rock gardens, planter boxes, pools, and walls.

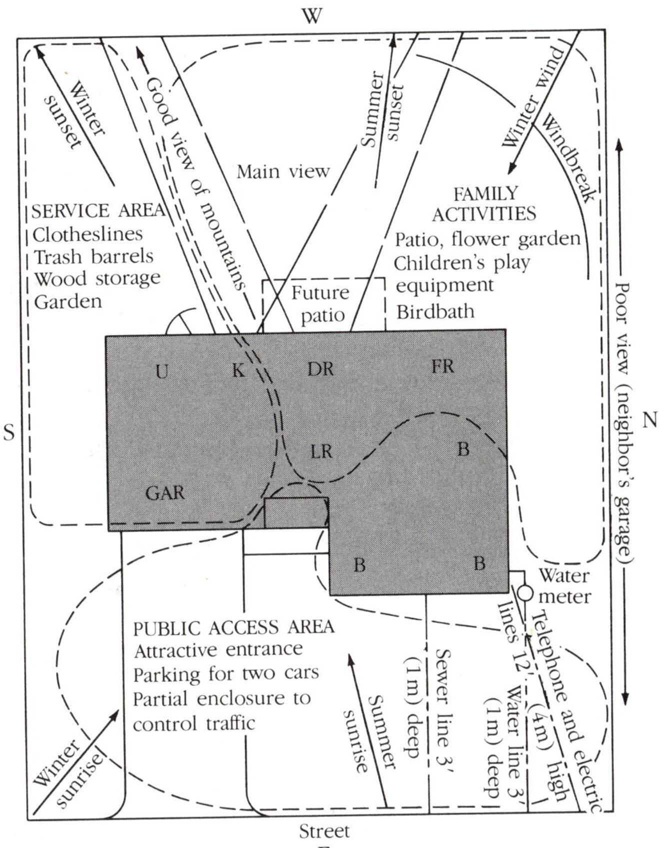

FIGURE 11-8 • A completed analysis plan. (Courtesy E. B. Adams, from *Homescaping*, Intermountain Regional Publication 4. Extension Service, University of Wyoming, Laramie, Wyo. Reprinted and/or revised periodically)

The Public Area. The public area, or front yard with its drive, walks, lawn, and trees, should be arranged to serve the purpose of attractively displaying the home to the owner and those who pass by. The public area is traditionally landscaped with a broad expanse of lawn in front of the house, a couple of trees and/or some large shrubs along the sides of the yard to frame the house, and some foundation shrubs to help tie the house to its surroundings. If the house is balanced and appears to have approximately the same weight on either side, the framing trees should be about equal in size. If the house has unequal balance, a larger tree should be planted on the smaller-appearing side. A large existing tree that heads above the home is a desirable asset even if it is directly in front. Large trees normally should not be planted in front of a home, however, because they hide so much of it for such a long period while they are growing.

Foundation shrubs should be planted at the corners of the house and on both sides of the doorway. If the house has a wide front, a cluster of shrubs at a few other strategic locations and/or a small flowering tree 10 to 12 feet (3 to 4 m) from the foundation and a few feet toward the wide side of the house from its entrance will help tie the house to its surroundings. The foundations of most modern homes are not so unattractive that they must be completely hidden with shrubbery. As a general rule, foundation shrubs look best in clusters of two or more rather than as single specimens (Figure 11-9). They should be planted far enough from the foundation so that they do not crowd against it when they are mature.

Although in North America front yards have traditionally been lawns, there are other attractive ways of landscaping the public area. In England the area in front of the home is often a flower garden. In the American Southwest, where water is scarce, cacti gardens often occupy that area. With impending energy, water, and land shortages, more and more homeowners throughout the United States and Canada are using something other than grass for the public area (Figure 11-10).

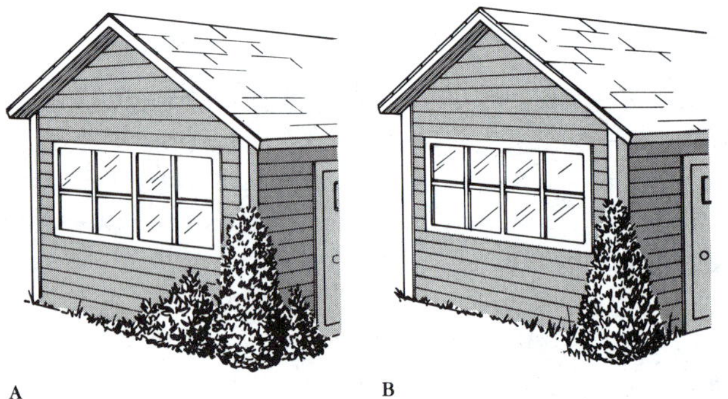

FIGURE 11-9 • Foundation shrubs. If there is room, a cluster of two or more shrubs (A) is usually more attractive than a single specimen (B) as foundation planting.

FIGURE 11-10 • An alternative to a lawn. (Courtesy of J. R. Holland/Stock, Boston)

For some homes a semicircular driveway with an island of rock and low-growing shrubs is a practical solution. Where the yard is sloping, a rock garden planted with native or drought-tolerant, slow-growing shrubs may offer a low-maintenance alternative. Low-growing shrubs planted through a mulch of black plastic covered with river rock, cedar bark, or cedar rounds is another way of keeping down maintenance labor and cost. In some situations the front yard may be covered with a masonry or asphalt paving and decorated with border plantings, raised bed plantings, and/or potted plants. Such a yard may either be left open for public view or screened with a fence, wall, or hedge to provide a family living area.

Regardless of the choice of landscaping, the public area planting should enhance the appearance of the home, should not interfere with convenience, and should be easy to maintain. Perhaps the most common mistakes in landscaping the public area are selecting foundation shrubs that grow too large, thus hiding the home and/or covering the windows, and planting too much. It is difficult to picture shrubs at their mature size when all one has to look at are small specimens from the nursery; a planting plan with shrubs and trees scaled to mature size helps overcome the temptation to overplant.

The Service Area. The service area should be located convenient to the kitchen and driveway and should be screened from the public and private areas by plantings or fences, as it is here that clotheslines, a woodpile, garbage cans, and other such objects are placed. The service area should be as compact and well planned as the modern kitchen to maximize its convenience and usefulness. Vegetable and cut-flower gardens are often included in the service area; their presence or absence and their size depend on the time and effort the owner wishes to spend in caring for them.

The Private Area. The private area, or the area for outdoor living, is usually at the rear of the lot and should be connected to the living side of the house. It should be screened from public view. Privacy can be secured with informal shrub groups or formal hedges, trellises, fences, or walls. Outdoor patios or living terraces, outdoor fireplaces, space for athletic activities, pools, saunas, fountains, flower gardens, shrub borders, and shade trees are in this area. Fences, walls, walks, statuary, and other inanimate elements can be included in the private area.

Walks and Drives. After the use areas are identified, they must be connected by a circulatory system of walks, drives, paths, patios, or terraces. Walks and drives should be direct and useful, durable, and built on good foundations, with sufficient slope for drainage. Walks should be at least 2 feet (⅔ m) wide for each person likely to walk abreast. Those surfaces that are constantly used, such as entrance walks and patios, should be surfaced with concrete, brick, flagstone, or other durable material; paths used only occasionally may be surfaced with stepping stones, cedar rounds, rolled gravel, or thick turf. Drives should be built for service. They should be easily accessible from the street, have convenient turns, include adequate off-street parking, be built at least 10 feet (3 m) wide with a crown and gutter, and be surfaced with gravel, asphalt, or concrete (see "Landscape Construction" in Chapter 14). Suggestions for landscaping sloping sites, building terraces, and constructing retaining walls can be found in Chapters 5 and 14.

Locating the Plantings. Following the designation of walks, drives, patios, retaining walls, and other hard-surfaced areas, the location of large trees should be decided. The character of the landscape picture depends on the trees. Trees can be used to frame views, for shade, for windbreaks, for background, and as specimen plants.

After the trees are located, plant walls or borders can be established. A location from which the outdoor living area will be viewed frequently is selected as the vantage point. This may be a sliding door or window opening onto the outdoor living area, or it may be the patio that serves as the transition between indoor and outdoor living areas. Next an axis line should be established between the vantage point and a focal point at the far end of the outdoor living area. The focal point may be a natural view beyond the confines of the yard, or it may be a garden house, garden statue, specimen tree or shrub, or other special object in the yard to which the eye is drawn. The most effective location for the plant walls is at about the visual periphery as one looks from the vantage point along the major axis toward the focal object. A secondary axis is naturally at a right angle to the first at the widest point of clear visual perception, which usually is about two-thirds to three-fourths of the distance from the focal point (Figure 11-11).

The outdoor wall can be a solid mass of several rows of shrubs and trees. If open space is desired, the wall can be limited to a couple of trees planted relatively close to the vantage point that serve the dual purpose of providing shade and forming the focal point. In this case a fence with a few espaliered shrubs or small trees or a formal hedge may serve as the ends of the secondary axis and the background of the focal area as well as provide privacy and conserve maximum area for athletics or other purposes.

Shrubs should be placed according to size and height before their foliage, texture, color, or flow-

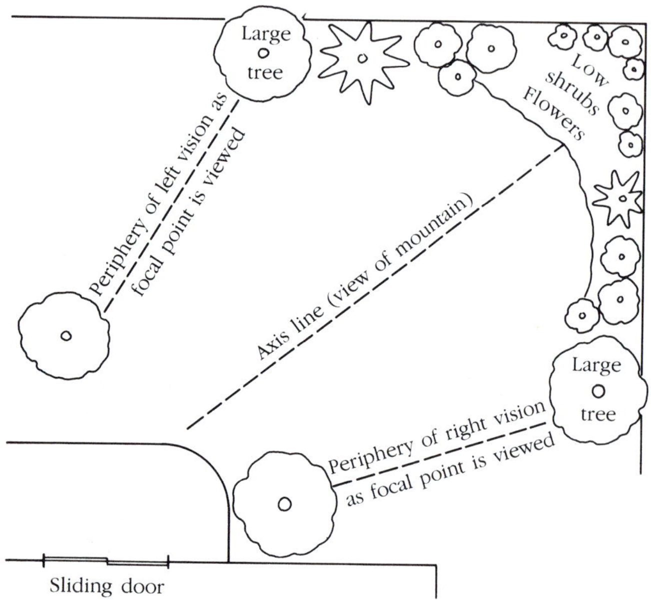

FIGURE 11-11 • Method of determining visual walls for framing and enhancing a view.

ering habit are considered. In traditional naturalistic planting, masses of shrubs and trees grown as plant walls are referred to as **border masses.** Border masses for naturalistic plantings should be planted in staggered groups and be at least two rows wide. Generally they are planted in groups of three or more of a single kind. An interesting skyline is created with rhythm and repetition in plant form.

Once the basic size and shape of plants are established, specific kinds can be selected. Nursery catalogs, garden books, local nurseries, and extension publications can help homeowners to choose the best plant for each location (see also the plants listed in tables in this chapter and in Table 14-28).

The Finished Plan. After the design elements have been located on the preliminary sketches, a finished plan should be constructed. Plants and other design elements should be numbered on the landscape plan and identified on an accompanying key (see Figure 11-12). Suggested symbols to be used in constructing the home landscape plan are shown in Figure 11-4.

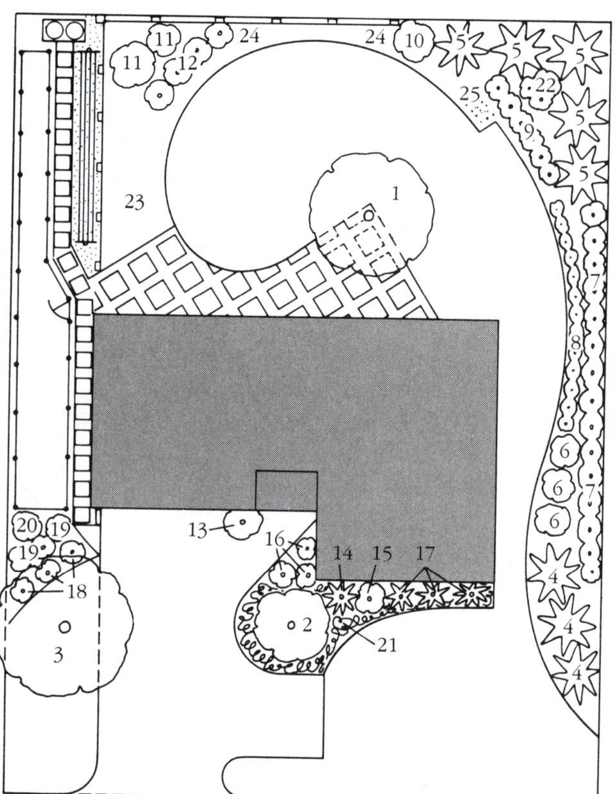

Planting key

1. Thornless honeylocust
2. Staghorn sumac
3. Cutleaf weeping birch
4. Colorado blue spruce (3)
5. Pondorosa pine (5)
6. Dwarf apple trees (3)
7. Lilac hedge (17)
8. Blue mist (Caryopteris) (16)
9. Spreading cotoneaster (6)
10. Snowball bush
11. Russian olive (2)
12. Redleaf barberry (5)
13. Mugo pine
14. Pfitzer juniper
15. Mentor barberry
16. Silver sage (3)
17. Tamarisk juniper (3)
18. Dwarf winged euonymous (3)
19. Apple serviceberry (3)
20. Caragana
21. Ground cover (Kinnikinnick)
22. Washington hawthorne
23. Salad garden
24. Annual and perennial flowers
25. Peony bed

FIGURE 11-12 • A completed planting plan keyed for plant identification. (Courtesy E. B. Adams, from *Homescaping*, Intermountain Regional Publication 4. Extension Service, University of Wyoming, Laramie, Wyo. Reprinted and/or revised periodically)

WOODY PLANTS AND PLANTINGS

◆ ◆ ◆

Much has already been said about the importance of selecting appropriate plants for each location in the landscape. There are many factors to consider when choosing plants, but perhaps the two most important are (1) whether, during most of its life span, the plant will be a size suitable for the location where it is to be planted and (2) whether the plant is adapted to grow in the climate (including microclimate) and the soil.

Woody plants, including trees, shrubs, and lianas, are the screening walls of the garden and the larger permanent fixtures that accent the landscape.

In addition to their climatic adaptation and size, woody plants should be selected for the garden on the basis of texture, color (foliage and bark as well as flower color), bloom date, rate of growth, and how well they relate to other elements of the design.

Woody plants should be attractive in the landscape during all seasons of the year. The color contrast of snow on the dark green foliage of a fir, the yellow-green branches and buds of the golden willow that are reminiscent of spring even in January and February, the velvety red fruit clusters and twisted shape of the staghorn sumac, the lacy branches and winter catkins of the birch, and the unusual branch pattern of the saucer magnolia make these plants as interesting in winter as they are in summer. Woody plants that are messy should be avoided unless the mess they make is outweighed by other desirable characteristics. For example, gardeners must determine whether the beauty, hardiness, and dense shade of the Norway maple compensate for its constant drip of honeydew caused by the difficult-to-control aphids that infest it, or whether the colorful berries and their attractiveness to birds of the European mountain ash or certain flowering crabapples are worth the mess they make when their fruit falls to the ground and rots. Trees and shrubs that constantly drop dead branches, leaves, or seedpods should be avoided.

Colors of the planting should be complementary during each season of the year. For instance, I recall a church occupying an entire block; planted alternately in the parking area around it were Dolga crabapples and scarlet maple. To me the clash of the carmine blossoms of the crabapple with the yellow blooms and unfolding maroon leaves of the maple spoiled the effect of both during the spring, when either type of tree alone would have been magnificent.

As for hardiness, it is possible for dedicated gardeners to provide winter protection for a few exotic plants, but most of us are too involved with other activities to spend cold winter evenings and mornings covering and uncovering tender shrubs, especially when there are so many good plant materials adapted to even the coldest regions.

Woody plants should be free of disease and insect pests. Often the experience of neighbors may be the best—perhaps the only—criterion on which to judge the susceptibility of a certain species to local plant pests. Certain kinds of willows and some viburnum may be impossible to grow without extensive spraying in some regions because of their susceptibility to aphids. In many areas the various kinds of ash are hardy and pest free, but in other locations they may be subject to scale or aphids or both. And it is futile to plant an American elm if Dutch elm disease has ravaged mature elms in the town in which you live.

Trees

Among their many beneficial attributes, trees offer shade and beauty, are a sanctuary for birds, control wind, and help prevent floods and erosion. Again, each tree planted should fit the location where it is to grow.

The age of family members and the length of time the family plans to live in the home should at least partially determine whether to plant a fast- or slow-growing tree. Fast-growing trees such as willow and poplar are almost always short lived; drop branches, fruit, and leaves; and frequently have suckers and shallow roots that can crack sidewalks, plug sewers, and interfere with the growing of a lawn. They do, however, provide shade

FIGURE 11-13 • Poorly placed conifer. This 'Colorado Blue Spruce', though a beautiful specimen, is crowding the porch, blocking the view from the windows behind it, and creating unwanted winter shade.

and bird sanctuaries much sooner than do oak, hickory, and other slow-growing trees. Owners must decide whether they want a tree that produces light shade or one that provides heavy shade. Grass grows much better under the canopy of trees such as birch and honey locust, which permit some sunlight to filter through, than under maple, oak, or sycamore. A number of factors determine whether a deciduous or evergreen tree should be planted in a particular location. On the south side of a home, for example, a deciduous tree provides shade during the summer and permits the sunshine to come through during the winter. It is usually a mistake to plant a conifer in front of a house. Because they are large growing, conifers can completely hide a home and create dense shade winter and summer; they belong in the border or as specimens at the side or behind the house (Figure 11-13). They also make excellent year-round windbreaks. The characteristics and adaptability of various trees are provided in Table 14-28.

Shrubs

Shrubs come in all shapes and sizes, and there is some disagreement as to whether certain plants are small trees or large shrubs. Generally, plants that grow with multiple stems at the base are considered **shrubs**; those that grow from a single stem are trees. Shrubs grow to their full size more quickly than do trees, so planting the wrong shrub is not quite so serious as is planting the wrong tree. Because they are smaller, shrubs can be more easily protected from freezes and other adverse weather conditions than can trees.

Most of the guidelines listed earlier for selecting woody plants also apply to shrubs. It is usually considered more artistically pleasing to have a mass of several of the same kind of shrubs than to have one each of a number of different kinds; however, as with other aspects of landscaping, the owner's preference takes precedence. For example, if space is limited, a gardener may wish to plant single specimens in order to enjoy as many different kinds as possible. Lists of shrubs suitable for various purposes along with their characteristics and climatic adaptability are given in Table 14-28.

Lianas

Lianas, or woody vines, serve many purposes in the modern garden. They are especially valuable for small yards where they use much less space to provide suitable plant cover for certain locations than do trees or shrubs. For example, a screen of ivy (Figure 11-14), Virginia creeper, or clematis trained to a fence or a flat wall takes up only a few inches of growing room along a property boundary, leaving the remainder of the yard for other purposes; a shrub or tree border, on the other hand, needs several feet of yard width to provide the same amount of screen.

Lianas are used to cover or soften banks or unsightly walls or fences. They can be trained to

FIGURE 11-14 • Ivy cover for walls and banks.

screen locations where screening with other plant materials would be difficult or impossible. A number of lianas such as clematis or wisteria are grown as dramatic specimens providing spectacular color to the garden during certain seasons of the year. The more popular lianas are described in Table 14-28.

Insect and Disease Control for Woody Ornamentals

It is impossible in a text with limited space to make an annotated list of the ubiquitous insect and disease pests that infest the hundreds of woody plant species. The sheer size of most shade trees, the extensiveness of woody plantings, and the numerous related wild-growing and uncared-for neighborhood specimens that become reservoirs of pest infection often make chemical control of the pests of woody ornamentals by the homeowner unfeasible or ineffective.

The best way to limit insect and disease damage to woody ornamentals is to plant kinds that are not subject to pests found in the region and to keep them growing vigorously. Proper fertilization and irrigation, along with pruning and thinning so that light can reach the branches and air can circulate through them, does much to prevent pest damage.

Cultural or chemical control of occasional infestations that occur on specific species, for example, sprinkling with water to reduce mite infestation or spraying with insecticides to control the periodic buildup of armyworms and tent caterpillars, is often necessary. A number of other pests, including bark beetles, spruce budworms, and tussock moths, may be present in large numbers only during an occasional growing season and specific environmental sequences. When these insects multiply to significant numbers, immediate control measures are essential to save the infested plants. Sometimes control of insects is necessary for reasons other than the welfare of the tree; for example, controlling aphids reduces the honeydew falling from maple trees. Occasionally other disorders are mistaken for insect damage. Stress from various sources, so common in an urban environment, results in dieback similar to the dieback sometimes caused by insect feeding (Figure 11-15). Stress also increases a tree's susceptibility to disease and insect attack. Those insects that are general feeders and the control suggestions for them are given in Table 14-26. Local pest-control experts or literature should be consulted if it becomes necessary to treat a particular species for an unusual disease or insect pest.

Windbreaks and Woody Plant Borders

Windbreaks and woody plant borders are discussed together because they have so much in common. Both are usually made up of one to several rows of woody plants of various shapes and sizes. Although the motive for planting windbreaks is generally utilitarian and the primary purpose of woody plant borders is usually ornamental, both reduce wind velocity, stop erosion, shelter birds and wildlife, and, at the same time, beautify.

Windbreaks are usually not necessary in the East and those sections of the Northwest where trees and woody shrubs are the native cover. The purposeful planting of windbreaks is also not important in most urban areas where closely spaced buildings and landscape plantings provide the protection usually afforded by windbreaks. But windbreaks are almost mandatory for rural comfort in

FIGURE 11-15 • Shade tree stress. This 'Silver' maple is showing typical dieback symptoms caused by a combination of stress factors. The area where it is located was converted from a golf course to a parking lot a few years earlier. The tree suffered bark damage (visible on the lower trunk) as a result of being gouged by heavy equipment. It is probably also suffering from a lack of root aeration as a result of soil compaction, as well as either drought or a lack of drainage in its root zone.

the plains states and provinces and the semiarid intermountain valleys. Even in newer city subdivisions and in suburban areas, a windbreak can often make the difference between a yard that can be used for family outdoor activities and one that cannot.

The right planting of trees can nearly eliminate heavy wind from around the house while still permitting light breezes to enter the yard. Because an increase in velocity of wind of 1 mile an hour (2 kph) has the same effect as dropping the temperature by 1°F (½°C), a good windbreak not only makes winter, spring, and fall outdoor living more pleasant, but it also can lower home heating bills considerably.

Specifications for a Windbreak. Windbreaks consist of from one to approximately eight rows of trees and shrubs. When space is available, several rows of shrubs and trees of various sizes and growth habits, both deciduous and evergreen, should be planted for the most effective protection against wind and snow (Figure 11-16). The planting should be at right angles to the prevailing winds and, where there is space, should extend at each end 50 feet (15 m) beyond the boundaries of the area to be protected in order to prevent winds from whipping around the windbreak. Where drifting snow is a problem, the house should be located at least 60 feet (18 m) beyond the last row of the windbreak. A five-row planting, such as that shown in Figure 11-17, gives the greatest amount of protection per row of windbreak. Plants in the windbreak should have adequate spacing (Table 11-1). Trees and shrubs for windbreak planting are available at production cost or less from the state departments of forestry or resource management in most areas. Wholesale nurseries that specialize in producing seedlings for other nurseries and for timber and Christmas tree growers often sell, for a nominal price, trees and shrubs in quantities as small as

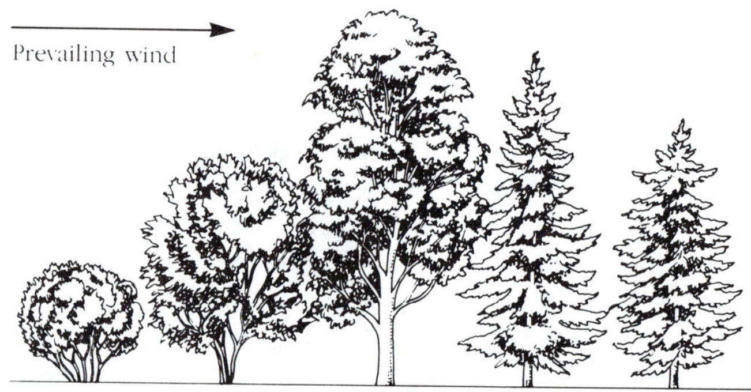

FIGURE 11-16 • Wind protection from trees and shrubs. (From *Trees Against the Wind*, Pacific Northwest Bulletin 5. Extension Service, University of Idaho, Moscow, Idaho. Revised periodically)

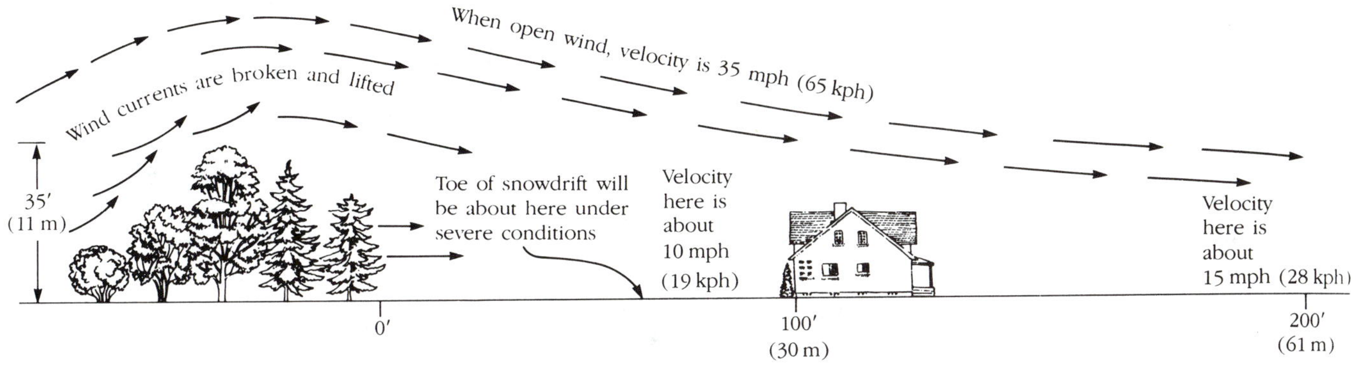

FIGURE 11-17 • Typical windbreak. (From *Trees Against the Wind*, Pacific Northwest Bulletin 5. Extension Service, University of Idaho, Moscow, Idaho. Revised periodically)

bundles of twenty-five. In most states a list of nurseries that specialize in producing seedling trees can be obtained through the local cooperative extension service.

Where wind is a problem around urban and suburban homes, space for windbreak planting may be limited. In such a situation a single row of common or upright juniper or arborvitae can make a windy backyard more livable and reduce heat loss from the home.

Windbreaks must be carefully tended if they are to be effective. They should be kept weeded and cultivated. Some pruning may be necessary, and the area should be kept free of livestock, as livestock can ruin a windbreak by chewing the lower leaves and bark and compacting the soil around the trees.

The woody plant border may have many purposes, including those mentioned for windbreaks. It can screen unsightly views, provide privacy for the family, be a sanctuary for birds and wildlife, provide beauty and shade, subdue the sound of traffic and other noise, and to some extent modify atmospheric pollutants, as well as protect from wind and drifting snow.

If the woody ornamental border is to be made up of several rows of trees and shrubs, the taller ones should be planted toward the outside and the shorter ones toward the center lawn or open area of the yard. Each row should consist of several different types of shrubs or trees to provide contrast in silhouette, in color and texture of the foliage, and in flower and leaf display through the season.

The Rose Garden

In many respects roses are in a category by themselves. Although they grow on a woody plant, they are the most popular of all garden flowers. Some kinds of roses can be grown in almost all parts of North America, including ones available for growing on arbors or trellises for borders, as hedges, as bedding plants, as specimens (e.g., tree roses), and as a source of cut flowers. Rose cultivars in many shapes, colors, and sizes are available, and new ones are being developed by plant breeders each year.

Purchasing Roses. Rosebushes are available from several sources. Older cultivars that are no longer patented may be purchased inexpensively as packaged, bare-rooted specimens from grocery and department stores. Before purchasing packaged plants, examine them carefully to make certain the stems are alive and healthy. Both patented and unpatented roses are also available from mail-order nurseries.

TABLE 11-1 • *Recommended spacings for windbreak plantings*

Situation	Tree Types	Spacings to Use: On Irrigated Land (feet)	Spacings to Use: On Dry Land (feet)
Farmstead windbreaks, main field windbreaks, and supplemental field windbreaks with more than one row:			
Between rows	All species	16	20
Between trees in the rows	Dense shrubs (row 1)[a]	3	3
	Medium-sized deciduous (row 2)	6–10	8–10
	Tall deciduous (row 3)	8–12	10–12
	Tall evergreens (row 4)	8–12	10–12
	Dense medium-height evergreens (row 5)	6–10	8–12
Single-row supplemental field windbreaks and living snow fences:			
Between trees	Tall deciduous or tall evergreen interplanted with dense shrub	6[b]	6–8
	Dense, medium-height evergreens	6	8
	Medium-sized deciduous	6–8	8–10
	Dense shrub	1.5–3	3

From *Trees Against the Wind*, Pacific Northwest Bulletin 5. Extension Service, University of Idaho, Moscow, Idaho. Revised periodically.
[a]Refer to Figure 11-16 for row number.
[b]The tall trees should be 12 feet apart with a dense shrub planted between them.

Container-grown rosebushes are available from local nurseries throughout the growing season. Although they cost considerably more than packaged rosebushes, they are the only satisfactory planting stock for late spring and summer planting. Both older standard cultivars and the newer more expensive cultivars that are still under patent are available in containers. The cultivar names are wired to each bush, and often the nursery has a catalog showing colored pictures of the cultivar in bloom. Table 11-2 lists the characteristics of selected types of roses.

Planting Roses. If winter temperatures do not go below 10°F (−12°C), bare-rooted roses can be planted any time they are fully dormant. If winter temperatures do not go below 0°F (−18°C), roses can be planted either in fall or spring; but if winter temperatures regularly drop below 0°F, roses should be planted only in the spring. Container-grown plants can, of course, be planted at any time through the summer. Bush roses should be spaced 2 to 3 feet (⅔ to 1 m) apart and climbers about 8 to 10 feet (2 to 3 m) apart.

Roses grow and bloom best where they have full sun all day, although they will grow satisfactorily if they have at least six hours of sun a day (see "Transplanting Woody Plants" in Chapter 14).

Winter Protection, Pruning, Pest Control. Hybrid tea, grandiflora, floribunda, and most ever-blooming climbing roses need winter protec-

TABLE 11-2 • *Characteristics of selected types of roses*

Type	Height and Spacing (feet)	Bloom Season	Hardiness Zone[a]	Remarks
Hybrid tea	2–6 × 3–4	All summer in cool-season areas; spring and fall in South	7	Most popular rose; flowers large, one per stem or clusters of 3 to 5; many cultivars are fragrant; wide range of colors.
Floribunda and polyantha	2–6 × 3–4	Same as hybrid tea	5	Will tolerate neglect; flowers produced in clusters, smaller but more numerous than hybrid tea; often not distinguished from hybrid tea in nursery; used for border or mass plantings.
Grandiflora	2–6 × 3–4	Same as hybrid tea	7	Flowers smaller but more numerous than hybrid tea, one per stem; flowers good for cutting.
Hybrid perpetuals	4–8 × 3–6	Late spring or early summer	3–5	June roses of our great-grandmothers' day; large flowers, somewhat coarse in appearance; hardy.
Shrub roses	Dense bushes, variable	Spring and early summer	2–3	Miscellaneous group; flowers small, single, numerous; used in borders and hedges.
Old fashioned	6–8 × 5	Spring and early summer	3–4	One of the first roses to be cultivated; flowers are less attractive than some modern types but extremely fragrant.
Tree roses	5–8 × 3	Same as hybrid tea	7	Made by grafting standard rose on an upright trunk.
Miniature roses	½ × ½	Late spring or early summer	6	Used for planter boxes, rock gardens, edging beds; flowers and plants are small.
Climbing roses	Canes 8–15	Variable	3–7	Developed from all the first five bush roses in this table; each cultivar resembles its bush counterpart in bloom season and hardiness.
Ramblers	Canes to 20	Spring and early summer	4–5	Flowers small and clustered; bloom on previous season canes; subject to mildew.
Trailing roses	Canes 8–15	Spring and early summer	4–5	Climbers with numerous single flowers; adapted to covering walls and banks.

[a]Hardiness zones are illustrated in Figure 14-96. The hardiness zone listed is for unprotected plants. With winter protection roses can be grown in zones two to three numbers lower.

TABLE 11-3 • *Insect and disease pests of roses*

Insect Pests	Symptoms and Damage	Control
Japanese beetle	The beetle consumes flowers, buds, and foliage during July and August. At present its damage is limited to the East and Midwest.	With moderate infestation insecticides can be used. In heavily infested areas, flowers may have to be protected with cheesecloth cages.
Rose chafer	Yellowish-brown beetles appear suddenly on rose petals; may destroy the entire flower.	An insecticide.
Rose leaf beetle	The small, metallic green beetle feeds on buds and flowers, often riddling them with holes. Most numerous in suburban gardens near uncultivated fields.	An insecticide into the open flower.
Rose leafhopper	The tiny greenish-yellow jumping insect sucks the contents of leaf cells from the underside, causing stippling of the leaves that resembles injury by spider mites.	An insecticide to the lower side of the rose leaf.
Rose slugs	The larvae of three species of sawflies, slugs cause the leaf to become skeletonized by feeding on them.	An insecticide as required.
Thrips	Flower petals, especially those of white varieties, become brown. The tiny yellow or brown thrip can be seen if an infested flower is shaken over a sheet of white paper.	No form of satisfactory control is available, because the opening petals cannot be completely covered with dust. Cheesecloth cages around prize blooms may protect them.
Aphids	Aphids may accumulate in large numbers on the buds, sometimes causing them to fail to open. Sticky honeydew accumulates on foliage.	Insecticide as needed.
Rose scale	Scale become encrusted on canes, where they suck the sap from plants.	Biweekly insecticide treatment will kill the young rose scale crawlers. Infested stems should be pruned away during the dormant season and the remainder of stems sprayed with a summer oil emulsion.
Rose midge	A tiny yellowish fly lays its eggs in the growing tips of rose stems. The maggots that hatch destroy the tender tissue, killing the tips and deforming the rosebuds.	Cut off and burn the infested tips daily for one month to eliminate the maggots before they complete their growth and drop to the ground. No good insecticide control is available.
Spider mites	Various species of spider mites suck juices from rose leaves, which soon become spotted, turn brown, curl, and drop off.	Avoid excessive use of insecticides, such as carbaryl, that control mites' predators but not the mites. Where mildew and blackspot are not a problem, sprinkling the underside of the leaves daily will help control mites.
Rose stem borers	Larvae burrow through the pith of the stem and sometimes cause breakage or death of the stem.	Infected parts should be trimmed off and burned.

(continued)

TABLE 11-3 • (*Continued*)

Diseases	Symptoms and Damage	Control
Black spot	Circular black spots frequently surrounded by a yellow halo appear on the leaves. Infested leaves turn yellow and die prematurely. Plant may become almost defoliated.	Black spot is spread by water, which must remain on the leaves for at least 6 hours before the infection takes place. Heavy pruning in the spring helps remove diseased branches. Spray or dust with a fungicide weekly throughout the growing season.
Powdery mildew	White powdery masses of spores appear on the young leaf shoots and buds. Buds and foliage are stunted or distorted.	The disease is spread by wind and winters over in fallen leaves. Dust with fungicide.
Rust	Yellow or orange pustules appear on the leaves. Plant may become defoliated. Rust winters over in fallen leaves and is spread by the wind. Troublesome mostly along the Pacific Coast.	Fungicide.
Cankers	Small reddish spots start on weakened plants and enlarge to girdle the stem, causing it to die.	Keep bushes growing vigorously and free of black spot. Provide winter protection. Prune all cankered canes out and disinfect pruning tools with alcohol after use on a cankered shoot.
Crown gall	Galls usually begin at ground level but sometimes higher up. They increase in size, and infected plants become stunted.	Prevent crown gall by planting roses in soil that has been free of crown gall–infected plants for at least two years. Remove any infected plants and burn them.
Virus diseases	Viruses usually are spread by propagation. They cause small angular colorless spots on the foliage. Infected plants are usually dwarfed.	Purchase plants that are free of the symptoms of viruses.

tion in areas where winter temperatures drop below 5°F (−15°C). Bush roses can be best protected by soil heaped over the crowns after the early autumn frosts but just before hard freezes are expected, mid- to late November in most areas where protection is needed (see also "Modifying Temperature with Plant Covers and Mulches" in Chapter 7). For winter protection, the canes of climbing roses should be unfastened from their trellises; held on the ground with heavy weights, notched stakes, or wire pins; and covered with several inches of soil. The soil should be removed in the early spring after the danger of severe frost is past. Tree roses can be protected from winter cold by wrapping them with straw and covering them with burlap if the temperature does not drop below −10°F. Where temperatures drop to 10° to 15°F below zero (−23° to −26°C), tree roses should also be covered with soil. This can be done by digging carefully under the roots on one side of the plant until the plant can be pulled over on the ground without breaking all root connections. In the spring after the soil thaws soil cover should be removed and the plant set upright again.

Roses also require heavy pruning (see "Pruning and Training" in Chapter 14). Suggestions for controlling the major insect and disease pests on roses are given in Table 11-3.

HERBACEOUS PLANTS AND PLANTINGS

◆ ◆ ◆

Herbaceous plants provide temporary or permanent cover and filler and add variety to the landscape. Because they are less permanent than woody plants, herbaceous plants can be changed from year to year to suit the owner's changing needs and whims.

Flowers

Flowers are enjoyed in many different ways by almost all societies. The front yard of the English cottage is planted with flowers instead of lawn; service stations and public buildings in Europe are commonly landscaped with flower beds; and vendors throughout the Middle East sell bouquets of wild and cultivated types of flowers to people who take them home once or twice a week. In Japan flower arranging is a time-honored activity. On the island of Bali no successful businessperson would think of starting the day without a floral offering to the gods.

Although in North America flowers are traditional for funerals, weddings, and other special occasions, their use in and around the home has not been as universal as in some other cultures. Nevertheless, flower growing as a hobby is becoming more popular each year.

Flowering plants come in all shapes and sizes, but the group usually classified as flowers are herbaceous flowering plants. They can be classified as spring-flowering bulbs and corms, summer-flowering bulbs and corms, annual-flowering plants, and perennial-flowering plants.

Spring-Flowering Bulbs and Corms. Some of the easiest to grow and most satisfying flowers are produced from bulbs and corms. Bulbous flowers are either large and attractive, or else they bloom early before there is much else to show in the garden. Most spring-flowering bulbs and corms should be planted in the fall to enable them to bloom in the spring, but some that originate in the tropics are not winter hardy. These nonhardy types can be forced as potted plants or stored during the winter to be planted in the early spring. Except for those noted as needing special protection, most of the genera listed in Tables 11-4 and 11-5 can survive without protection in areas along the Pacific Coast and south of the Ohio River. Farther north, bulbs and corms not definitely known to be winter hardy should be protected with a 2- to 5-inch (5- to 13-cm) mulch of straw, leaves, or shavings.

Spring-blooming bulbs must have time to develop a root system before winter and should not be planted later than late September in the North or late October in the South. Because they also are subject to injury from excess winter moisture, they should be planted only in well-drained locations. If the soil is fertile and the plants are deep green and healthy, spring fertilization is probably not necessary. It is best to fertilize in the autumn by spreading about ¼ pound (about 100 g) of ammonium nitrate or an equivalent of nitrogen from another source over each 50 square feet (4½ m^2) of bulb garden.

Faded flowers should be removed before they go to seed and rob the bulb of nutrients. However, leaves should be left on the plants until they have dried and their nutrients have moved into the bulbs. To camouflage the untidiness of dying leaves of spring-flowering bulbs, a gardener can plant fast-growing annuals such as verbena among the bulbous flowers.

Most spring-flowering bulbs can be left to multiply for several years, but when they become crowded and the flowers start to become smaller, they should be dug and separated. Tunicate bulbs (those with concentric rings, such as tulips and onions) and corms should not be dug until their plant has died and their brown protective cover has formed. After being dug, they should be kept out of direct sunlight. Daffodil and iris bulbs should be dried as quickly as possible to prevent rotting. Tunicate bulbs should be kept where the temperature is high (80°F; 27°C) for two weeks after being dug. Then, if possible, they should be stored where the temperature is about 50°F (10°C) and the humidity 75 percent. In the early fall the clumps should be separated and individual bulbs replanted into the garden.

The scaly bulbs of lily should be separated and replanted immediately after being dug because even moderate dehydration can kill them. They are usually separated and replanted as bulbs consisting of a cluster of scales. Individual scales produce new plants, but the plants thus produced are small and require several seasons of growth before they will bloom.

Summer-Flowering Bulbs. Among the summer flowers that grow from bulbs, corms, tubers, or similar underground storage organs are begonias (tuberous rooted), caladiums, callas, cannas, dahlias, gladioli, hemerocallis, and lilies. With the exception of some of the lilies, these are tropical flowers. The storage organs from which they grow are not frost hardy, and in regions where winters are cold, they must be dug and stored through the winter. Peonies and bearded iris, which are sometimes classed with summer-flowering bulb plants, are included in the section on perennial flowers.

Tuberous-rooted begonias are adapted to cool-summer climate areas with an acid soil, such as England, the U.S. Northeast, and the north Pacific Coast. They require special treatment to grow well in those parts of the country with a warmer growing season or neutral or alkaline soils. In warmer areas they can be grown during the spring or fall, or, if the temperature does not get too hot, during the summer in a location that is shaded. The soil should be kept continually moist (but not saturated) to maintain humidity around the foliage. Some gardeners successfully grow begonias by modifying soil of neutral or alkaline pH with acid peat and sulfur. In areas with this kind of soil it is better to grow begonias in planter boxes or pots containing a special acid growing medium that can be purchased at nurseries or garden stores. Another satisfactory growing medium for begonias is decomposed organic matter from coniferous forests. When this material can be conveniently obtained, it can be used to fill containers or to replace the top 8 inches (20 cm) of soil in the begonia bed.

Begonia tubers can be placed directly into the garden, but they will bloom much earlier if started indoors four to ten weeks before they are to be planted outdoors. They should be started in a friable growing medium that is at least one-third peat. They should be planted with the concave (bud) side up and can be grown relatively close together until sprouts are an inch long. Care should be taken not to damage roots when the plants are transplanted. They should not be planted into the garden until about two weeks after danger of the last frost, or about two weeks after it is safe to transplant tomatoes. They should be grown in a cool area that has light shade throughout the day. In the right location and with proper care, begonias will continue to bloom until frost, at which time they can be dug and allowed to dry for a few days with the plant left attached to the tuber. The tuber should be detached from the dried plant and stored in a cool but frost-free location with a humidity of 60 to 70 percent. In many locations it may be necessary to treat the stored tuber, the soil in which it is to be planted, and the growing plant with a fungicide in order to prevent mildew, to which begonias are extremely susceptible.

TABLE 11-4 • *Characteristics of selected types of tulips, narcissus, and bulbous iris*

Kind	Bloom Date[a]	Height (inches)	Flower Shape	Color	Remarks
Tulips (planting depth 4–7 inches; bulb spacing 2–8 inches; full sun to partial shade)					
Single early	Mid-April	6–12	Egg to cup	Various	Some, such as 'Duc van Tol', are good for early forcing.
Double early	Mid-April	8–12	Peony	Various	Forced in great quantities.
Darwin hybrids	Late April	24–28	Cup	Various	Hybrids between *T. fosteriana* and Darwin; like Darwin but flowers are larger. Mendel and Trumpet types are crosses between Darwin and Single early.
Darwin	May	24–32	Cup	Various, bright	Most popular of outdoor tulips; strong stems.
Cottage	Late April to June 1	to 36	Cup	Various, bright	Cottage, Breeder, and Darwin have been intercrossed to produce intermediate cultivars.
Breeder	May	24–32	Cup	Muted	Flower opens during day; colors bronzed; not as popular as formerly.
Lily flowered	May	20	Star	Various, bright	Flower petals pointed and folded out.
Late double	May	24	Large peony	Various	Flowers will not stay upright with rain or sprinkler irrigation.
Parrot	May	24–32	Serrated and twisted	Various	Most are sports of other types, primarily Darwin.
T. kaufmanniana	Early April	8–16	Star open	White, yellow, red, multicolor	Attractive for early bloom in rock gardens or mass plantings.
T. fosteriana	Early April	9–12	Large open	Red (mostly), yellow, white	'Red Emperor' is the most famous cultivar.
T. greigii	Early April	9–12	Bell; pointed petals	Red, yellow	Striped leaves; good for rock gardens.

(continued)

TABLE 11-4 • (*Continued*)

Kind	Bloom Date[a]	Height (inches)	Flower Shape	Color	Remarks
Rembrandt or broken	May	24–32	Cup	Multicolored	The unique coloration occurs because of virus infection; do not plant these near other tulips.
T. praestans	Late March	8	Open	Red	Good for rock gardens; multiflowered.
T. clusiana	Early April	12	Star	White with outer red stripe	Good for rock gardens.
T. tarda	April	6	Star	Yellow	Up to five flowers per stem.
Narcissus (planting depth 2–6 inches; plant spacing 3–8 inches; full sun to partial shade)					
Trumpet	April	8–19	Single	Yellow, white	Trumpet as long or longer than petals; one flower per stem.
Cupped	April	14–20	Single	Orange to white	Trumpet one-third petal length; one per stem.
Double	April	8–20	Double	Orange to white	One or more flowers per stem; fall down in rainy weather.
Triandrus hybrids	Late April	8–15	Pendant	White, yellow	Two to five flowers per stem; petals folded back.
Cyclamineus hybrids	February to March	8–15	Single	Orange, yellow	One flower per stem.
Jonquilla hybrids	Early May	11–17	Single	Orange-white	Three to five flowers per stem; strong pleasant fragrance.
Tazetta hybrids	April	15–17	Single	White, yellow, orange	Up to fifteen flowers per stem; not hardy; mostly used for forcing indoors.
Bulbous (planting depth 2–4 inches; plant spacing 3–10 inches; sun to partial shade)					
Dutch	June	20		Blue, white, yellow	After stratification can also be planted during spring to bloom in September.
Spanish	Late June	20		Various; yellow most popular	Needs winter protection.
English	July	20		Blue, purple, white	Naturalizes in milder regions.

[a]Bloom time is correct for most seasons for many locations in Hardiness zones 5, 6, and 7. Blooms come earlier in warmer regions and during seasons with above-normal temperatures and later in cooler regions and during seasons of below-normal temperatures. (Hardiness zones are illustrated in Figure 14-96.)

TABLE 11-5 • *Characteristics of selected less common spring-flowering bulbous plants*

Kind	Planting Depth (inches)	Spacing (inches)	Bloom Date[a]	Height (inches)	Flower Color	Light Exposure	Remarks
Allium	2–6	2–12	June–July	12–18	Pink, purple	Sun to part shade	Ornamental onions; many kinds.
Anemone	2–3	3–8	March–April	6–12	Various	Part shade	Many kinds and colors; wood anemones grow in heavy shade.
Brodiaea (triteleia)	3	1½	May–June	18–48	Various	Sun to part shade	Alpine gardens; many species; likes sandy soil; dig and store during summer if soil is wet.
Bulbocodium	2	3	February–March	4	Lavender	Sun	Needs well-drained soil and frequent replanting; closely related to crocus.
Camassia (spring meadow saffron)	3–4	5–9	April–May	24–30	Blue, white	Sun to part shade	Native to North America. *C. quamash* used for food by Indians of Northwest.
Chionodoxa (glory of the snow)	2	2–3	March–April	4–9	Blue, pink, white	Sun to part shade	Native to alpine meadows; short tubular open flowers in spikes.
Convallaria (lily of the valley)	1	6–12	May	9	White	Shade	Grows from rhizomes but is similar in culture to bulbous plants; grown as much for its fragrance as for its ornamentation.
Crocus	2	1–2	February–March	6–8	Yellow, purple, white	Sun to part shade	One of the first flowers of spring; some will also bloom in autumn.
Eranthis (winter aconite)	1–2	2–3	February–March	6	Yellow	Part shade	Even earlier than crocus; looks like buttercup.

(continued)

TABLE 11-5 • (*Continued*)

Kind	Planting Depth (inches)	Spacing (inches)	Bloom Date[a]	Height (inches)	Flower Color	Light Exposure	Remarks
Erythronium (adder's-tongue)	1–2	2	April	8–18	Yellow, pink, purple	Part shade	Several species; good for woodland gardens.
Fritillaria	3–6	4–15	April–May	6–12	Various	Sun to part shade	Many species of various types.
Galanthus (snowdrop)	1–2	2–3	February–March	6–12	White	Part shade	One of the harbingers of spring.
Hyacinth	2–4	3–10	April	6–12	Various	Sun to part shade	Showy spikes of very fragrant blooms; in moist climates bulbs should be lifted and stored in a cool, dry place through the summer.
Ixia (cornlily)	2–3	1–2	June	18	Various	Sun	Needs heavy mulch for winter protection north of southern states and Pacific Coast. Frequently forced in pots.
Muscari (grape hyacinth)	2–3	5	April	8	Blue spikes	Sun	Easy to grow and propagate.
Oxalis	2–3	2–4	May–July	3–12	Various	Sun to part shade	A large, varied genus; many are bulbous and hardy; good in rock gardens.
Ranunculus (buttercup)	1	3	April–May	6–8	Yellow	Sun to part shade	Tolerant.
Scilla	1	3	March–April	6–20	Blue	Part shade	Likes moderately moist soil; good for interplanting with tulips and daffodils.
Trillium	3–4	4–6	March–April	6–10	White, purple	Part shade	Needs moist soil; good for ground cover in shady places.

[a]Bloom time is correct for most seasons for many locations in hardiness zones 5, 6, and 7. Blooms come earlier in warmer regions and during seasons with above-normal temperatures and later in cooler regions and during seasons of below-normal temperatures. (Hardiness zones are illustrated in Figure 14-96.)

Because caladiums are grown for their colorful leaves, flower buds should be removed as soon as they appear. Many cultivars and types are available, ranging in size from the dwarfs that are less than 9 inches (23 cm) tall to the elephant's ear, which grow up to 6 feet (2 m) in height. Caladiums also do best in an acid soil; they cannot tolerate extreme heat and do not do well in areas where night temperatures drop below 55°F (13°C). Thus in the North they are grown mainly indoors.

Caladiums are usually started in pots in a peat–sand mix six to ten weeks before they can be planted outdoors. Frequently they are left in pots throughout the summer. In the fall, before killing frosts, the plants are allowed to become dry; the dried tops are cut off; and the tubers are stored in unwatered pots, preferably in a location where the temperature remains at about 60°F (16°C).

Callas are tall, showy plants grown as much for their attractive leaves as for their white, yellow, pink, or red blooms. The so-called flower is actually a cluster of florets on a spadix surrounded by a colorful bract or sheath. In areas where frosts seldom or never occur, callas can remain in the same location for many years without replanting. In other areas they are generally grown as potted plants.

Cannas are tall flowers with showy red or yellow blooms. They do best where the season is fairly long and the summer quite warm. Their propagation is similar to that of large dahlias.

Dahlias are grown in two ways. The small 'Unwin' hybrids are grown from seed and treated as annuals; the large, showy dahlias, which may have blooms up to 12 inches (30 cm) across, are grown from what are called tubers. Actually, the so-called dahlia tuber is a thickened root and, in order to grow, must be attached to a small piece of the lower stem containing an "eye," or bud. The root is unable to initiate buds. Dahlias do best where summer temperatures are relatively cool. Like gladioli, they should be planted in loose, friable soil late enough so that they will emerge only after the danger of frost has passed. By the end of the growing season, the single root that was planted in the spring will have developed into a clump of roots. These should be dug, dried off somewhat, and stored with the lower stem attached in a cool but above-freezing location with 60 to 70 percent humidity. As spring approaches, the clump can be divided. Exceptional plants of the dwarf type produced originally from seed can be propagated a second season by lifting the roots and storing them through the winter.

The gladiolus is a popular garden flower because it is relatively easy to grow, is extremely showy, and lasts well as a cut flower. Gladioli corms can be planted any time from a couple of weeks before the last killing frost until as late as late August in some of the warmer parts of the country. Biweekly planting of gladioli corms ensures blooms throughout most of the summer. They need full sun and well-drained soil. For longest life as cut flowers, they should be cut when one to four florets have opened. Leaves should be left on the plant to permit food production for the corm.

For winter storage, gladioli corms should be dug when plants are mature but before heavy freezes, and placed in a cool, dry location with good air circulation. The tops should be removed when they have completely dried, the scales loosened, the old corm and scales thrown away, and the new corms treated with an insecticide and a fungicide. The pest most likely to be a problem with gladiolus is the thrip. These insects feed and multiply on the flowers and foliage and, if they are numerous enough, may cause the flower buds to fail to open or to be deformed. Thrips can be controlled by dusting the corms and spraying the plants, following practices recommended locally.

Hemerocallis, or daylilies, are hardy and easy to grow throughout most of the United States and

Canada. Many types of various heights and blooming times are available, with red, pink, orange, yellow, or cream flowers. The leaves remain green and produce an attractive border even after the flowers have faded. Daylilies can be started from seeds or tubers. Seeds can be planted in late fall or early spring. The tubers, which are edible, are planted just below the surface of the soil usually during the spring, but they can be planted almost any time of year. Hemerocallis tolerates most kinds of soil and can withstand some drought. The seedpods should be removed as flowers fade. Plants need to be dug and separated when they become crowded, approximately every four to five years. In many parts of the country hemerocallis has escaped cultivation and can be found along fencerows and streambanks.

Lilies, for centuries a symbol of purity, are among the most popular, most varied, and most widely grown of all garden flowers. The native habitat of various species of lily ranges from the Arctic to the tropics. Among the dozens of popular hybrids, species, and cultivars are the following:

Lilium candidum (white madonna lily) grows 3 to 4 feet (about 1 m) in height and blooms in June.

Lilium longiflorum (Easter lily) is grown widely as a potted plant to be sold at Easter time. In climates where average January temperatures are above 35°F (2°C), potted Easter lilies can be planted outdoors after their blooms have faded. They will grow and bloom in July or August year after year in these climates.

Lilium regale blooms in July and grows 3 to 5 feet (1 to 1½ m) tall; produces white or yellow flowers.

Lilium speciosum and *L. auratum* bloom in August or September; plants grow to 4 to 6 feet (about 1 to 2 m). There are many hybrids between these two types.

Lilium testaceum is one of the oldest and best of the hybrids; produces large apricot flowers on 5- to 6-foot (1½- to 2-m) plants in June.

Lily bulbs should be planted in the fall at a depth three times the height of the bulb. They need well-drained soil and do best in full sun.

Flowering Perennials. There is a large group of flowering plants that die back each year after they have bloomed but grow each succeeding season from the crowns remaining in the ground. These plants are propagated from crown division or from seed and generally do not bloom until the second season after they are planted. Most perennials brighten the garden year after year with minimal care. Mainly they need to be kept free of weeds, be lightly fertilized and irrigated, have their faded blossoms removed, and be dug and divided whenever they become crowded. Perennials should be selected for the area where they are to be grown. Gardeners should notice what grows well in local gardens, consult nurseries, and check with the state experiment station. They should know the flowering times and plant a mixture of annuals and perennials that will provide color in the garden over a long period. In areas where winters are severe and snow cover is lacking, some perennials need a loose mulch protection. The characteristics of selected perennials are listed in Table 11-6; a more extensive listing of flowering perennials can be found in the references at the end of this chapter.

Flowering Annuals. No other group of plants adds so much color to American gardens as do annual flowers and no other group is as easy to grow (Figure 11-18). Consequently annuals are enjoying unprecedented popularity with gardeners and have received a great deal of attention from

TABLE 11-6 • *Selected perennials for the flower garden*

Kind	How Propagated	Bloom Date[a]	Height	Flower Color	Remarks
Chrysanthemum	Cuttings (crown division in spring)	July–November	½–3 ft	Various	The most popular autumn flower; blooms in response to day length; many types of flowers available; also popular as a forced flower; cultivars vary in winter hardiness.
Columbine	Seed	May–June	2–4 ft	Various	Open growth habit.
Delphinium	Seed	June	4–5 ft	Pink, blue, white	Will bloom later during season if faded blossoms are cut back; flower head is a tall spike.
Hollyhock	Seed	June–July	5–7 ft	Various	Comes in both double and single flowers; needs staking where storms or winds are severe.
Iris (bearded)	Crown division after bloom	May–June	3 ft	Various	There are also dwarf species that bloom very early in spring; needs well-drained soil and a minimum of water.
Lupine	Direct seed	May–June	3 ft	Various	Drought tolerant; large spikes; does not transplant easily.
Penstemon	Seed	June	1½–2 ft	Various	Drought tolerant; new cultivars are being developed.
Peony	Crown division	June	2–4 ft	Red, white	Can be kept in same location for many years; foliage is attractive all season.
Phlox (summer)	Crown division	July	3 ft	Various	Moss phlox blooms in early spring and is low growing; can be propagated from seed, but plants are variable.
Poppy (Iceland)	Seed	July	1½ ft	Scarlet to white	Poppies often seed themselves; can be grown as an annual in warm winter areas.
Poppy (Oriental)	Seed	July	3 ft	Scarlet to white	Brilliant flowers on rapidly growing plants. Short lived in warm climates.
Primrose	Seed	April	6–9 in	Various	Rock garden plant; seed requires freezing before it will germinate.
Violet	Seed	April	3–4 in	Purple, yellow, white	Cool climate flower; some are scented; low-growing, petite.

[a] Bloom time is correct for most seasons for many locations in hardiness zones 5, 6, and 7. Blooms come earlier in warmer regions and during seasons with above-normal temperatures and later in cooler regions and during seasons of below-normal temperatures. (Hardiness zones are illustrated in Figure 14-96.)

seed and nursery businesses as well as from amateur and professional plant breeders. As a result, plant specialists have developed hundreds of new cultivars with larger, more colorful flowers and more profuse flowering habits, and techniques that make it easier to produce annual flowers.

Frederick McGourty, editor of the Brooklyn Botanic Garden's *Plants and Gardens*, suggests in the garden's *Annuals* handbook (see Selected References at the end of this chapter) that a major advantage of annuals, especially for novice gardeners, is that "mistakes—the occasional grouping of tall plants in front of low-growing ones or the red salvia sizzling next to the pinkish-purple petunias—don't haunt forever, as does the misplacement of trees and shrubs." People with gardening experience can also find pleasure and challenge in the tremendous variety of fine annual flowering plants available today. Annuals offer gardening enjoyment for a low initial investment, an especially attractive feature for those who have invested their capital in a new house and lot and have little money left for needed plantings.

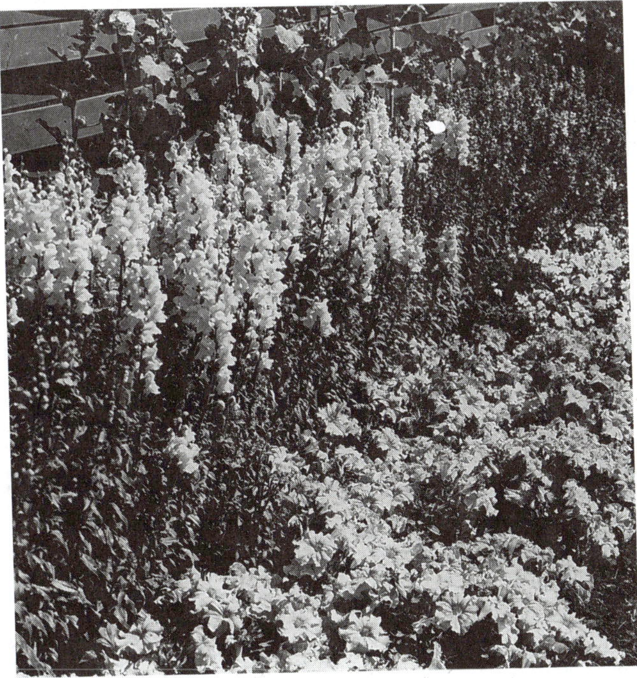

FIGURE 11-18 • A bed of annual flowers. Tall hollyhocks growing along the fence provide a background for intermediate-sized snapdragons, which, in turn, are fronted by low-growing petunias. (Courtesy of U.S. Department of Agriculture)

Annual flowers are propagated mostly from seed. The methods, advantages, and disadvantages of growing or purchasing transplants or direct seeding into the open soil were discussed in Chapter 4. I emphasize again the importance of not planting until the soil is warm enough to permit the seeds to germinate. In addition, seedling beds should be kept moist until seedlings are well established; after that annuals should be watered enough to soak the soil well, no more often than once each week. Annual flowers require enough fertilizer to keep them healthy, but they should not be overfertilized, especially with nitrogen. Heavy nitrogen fertilization will reduce or even prevent flowering. Removing dead or faded flowers not only keeps the flower bed more tidy but also directs the plant nutrient resources into blooms instead of seeds.

Most annual flowers can be grown in containers, a special advantage for city gardens, for areas where soil is poor or nonexistent, or where frost or other adverse environmental conditions preclude growing flowers in outdoor beds. Special protection is more easily provided for container-grown plants than for plants growing in the open; however, container-grown plants require more careful attention to watering and fertilization. Characteristics and suggestions for growing selected annuals are given in Table 11-7.

Rock Gardens

Rock gardens originated as an attempt to duplicate the wildflower beds of alpine regions. Because

TABLE 11-7 • *Characteristics of selected garden annuals*

Plant	Height (inches)	Exposure	Spacing (inches)	Color	Start from Seed	Transplants	Remarks
Ageratum	6–10	Sun or partial shade	10–12	Blue, violet, pink, white		X	Pinch tip of plants to encourage branching; remove dead blooms; good for edging.
Aster	6–30	Sun	10–15	Blue, white, red, pink		X	Good cut flower.
Calendula	14–18	Sun	10–15	Yellow	X	X	Good for window gardens.
Celosia (cockscomb)	16–40	Sun	10–15	Red, yellow, pink, rose	X	X	Cut flowers, plants for drying.
Cosmos	30–48	Sun	12–18	Pink, rose, white, orange	X	X	Cut flowers, background.
Dahlia ('Unwin')	18–20	Sun or partial shade	12–14	Many		X	Blooms early; good cut flower.
Dusty miller	6–12	Sun	10–15	Gray foliage		X	Good for edging.
Four o'clock	20–24	Sun	12–24	Rose, yellow, white	X	X	Temporary hedge; easy to grow.
Impatiens	6–12	Partial or deep shade	12–14	White, red, pink, orange		X	Does well in containers.
Larkspur	18–48	Sun	6–8	White, pink, blue, violet	X		Hard to transplant; grow in pots.
Lobelia	6–12	Partial shade to shade	12	Blue, white		X	Good for edging.
Marigold	6–30	Sun	4–30	Yellow, gold	X	X	Cut flowers, bedding, containers.
Nasturtium	10–12	Sun	8–12	Yellow, red, orange	X		Does well in poor soil; needs drained soil.
Pansy	6–10	Sun or shade	6–8	Various	X	X	Good cut flower; does best in cool season; pick off seed pods.

(continued)

most of the plants suitable for rock gardens originated in those regions, rock gardens grow best in areas where the growing season is relatively cool. The extent and design of the rock garden depend on the climate, the area available, the topography, the kind of stone available, and the means for transporting and placing the stone (Figure 11-19).

Rock gardens should be carefully planned and sketched on paper before any stones are moved. Areas for walking, plant materials to be used, and

TABLE 11-7 • (*Continued*)

Plant	Height (inches)	Exposure	Spacing (inches)	Color	Start from Seed	Transplants	Remarks
Petunia	8–24	Sun	12–24	Many		X	Long blooming period; does well in containers.
Pinks	6–16	Sun or partial shade	8–12	Pink, white		X	Remove dead flowers; good cut flower.
Poppy	12–16	Sun or partial shade	8–12	White, pink, red, orange	X	X	Hard to transplant.
Portulaca	6–9	Sun	10–12	Many	X		Does well in poor, dry soil; stands heat.
Snapdragon	10–36	Sun	6–10	Pink, white, yellow, red		X	Pinch tips to encourage branching; good cut flower.
Spider plant	30–36	Sun or shade	12–14	Pink, purple, white	X	X	Long blooming period; grows in dry, poor soil; good background plant.
Sweet alyssum	6–10	Sun or shade	10–12	White, purple	X	X	Long blooming period; grows in dry, poor soil but needs good drainage.
Sweet pea	8 in–6 ft	Sun	6–10	All but yellow	X		Bush or vining; needs cool temperature.
Verbena	9–12	Sun	10–15	Many	X	X	Edging, ground cover, cut flowers.
Vinca rosea	15–18	Shade or partial shade	18	White, pink, rose		X	Grow in beds; perennial grown as annual.
Zinnia	6–18	Sun	10–12	Many	X	X	Grow in rows for cutting.

Adapted from *Growing Annual Bedding Plants*, Washington State University Extension Bulletin 611. Pullman, Wash., 1973.

the general contour of the garden, as well as a rough sketch of the size and shape of stones required, should be included on the plan. Rock garden plants generally do best in soil of intermediate fertility, high in organic matter. In many areas the most successful rock gardens are grown in soil brought from a forested area and placed among the rocks. Rock gardens are most beautiful during the early spring because that is the time of year when the climate of populated areas most closely dupli-

FIGURE 11-19 • Rock gardens come in many shapes and sizes. This small, easy-to-care-for planting features a Japanese lantern and rock garden plants growing in soil pockets of this slate-covered slope. (Courtesy of Lefever, Grushow/Grant Heilman)

cates the high light intensity and cool nights of high altitude regions. Selected rock garden plants are listed in Table 11-8.

Sometimes the rock garden is built around a natural rock outcrop; more often, rocks must be brought from other locations. In some regions, sponge lava or other lightweight rock is available. In most areas, native rock is more natural and, consequently, more pleasing than exotic rock, no matter how colorful the latter may be. Using rock with moss and/or lichen already growing on it gives a newly planted rock garden an established appearance.

Flower Gardens

Flowers are grown in three types of plantings: (1) a flower border, (2) a flower bed, and (3) a cut-flower garden. Like any other planting, a flower garden is most attractive when it has been well planned. Because flowers are grown primarily for their color, color and time of bloom are two of the most important attributes to consider when planning a flower garden, though height of the plant, texture of the foliage and flowers, and climatic adaptability should also be considered. Landscape planners feel that a solid mass of one color of flower is more effective than a planting of mixed colors. Nevertheless, I often buy mixed cultivar seed packets because I enjoy the anticipation of something different with each opening bloom.

Flower beds are frequently planted in the center of large areas of lawn in parks and open public areas. Home flower plantings are easier to care for, however, if they are planted along one edge of the yard or against the foundation of the house because less labor is necessary to keep border grass from encroaching into the flower planting. Both bed and border plantings can be a mixture of annual and perennial flowers. Bulbs and other perennial flowering plants bloom during early to late spring, and annual flowers can be planted to camouflage the stems of the fading perennials and provide color in the flower garden through the summer and fall. Late-fall perennials, such as autumn crocus or chrysanthemum, can be colorful throughout the late fall and early winter.

Tall flowers in the border should be planted toward the back, shorter ones in front. The borders should be carefully planned so that there will be flowers through the entire season and so that the colors of flowers in bloom at any one time will complement one another.

A popular and simple combination succession is an early-spring mixture of tulips or daffodils and pansies, followed by a single cultivar of a long-lasting annual, such as petunias, impatiens, or geraniums, to provide a mass of color through the rest of the summer.

Because the dying remains of cut flowers may not be attractive through the late-summer months, the cut-flower garden is usually relegated to the utility area. It may be a large, separate area with several rows each of a number of flowers, or it may be a couple of rows of a favorite cut flower planted with the vegetable garden or integrated into the flower border.

Spring- and summer-flowering bulbs, such as tulips, daffodils, iris, gladioli, and lilies, and tall-growing annuals, such as snapdragons, carnations, upright zinnias, tall marigolds, and cosmos, are the kinds of flowers usually grown in the cutting garden. Perennials such as chrysanthemums, tall phlox, daisies, bearded iris, peonies, penstemon, delphiniums, and hybrid tea roses are excellent cutting flowers that must be grown in a permanent location.

Herbaceous Plants Grown for Their Vegetation

The advantage of growing plants that have attractive or unique vegetative structures is that their beauty lasts through the growing season. A few, notably ornamental kales, coleus, and some recently introduced impatiens cultivars, are grown for their colorful foliage. In Japan, ornamental kale is an important component of almost all winter gardens (Figure 11-20). Most plants in this category are noted for their picturesque form, although many do produce foliage in unusual shades of gray or green. Some, such as the cacti, provide spectacular blooms during a short season, but the blooms are a secondary bonus, not the primary purpose for which they are planted.

Unlike flowers, most of these plants are not adapted to being displayed en masse. Their location must be carefully chosen so that their unique characteristics can be viewed in an appropriate setting. Most should be planted only where there is ample space for them to expand to their natural form, and many require a specific microclimate. Certain crops usually grown as vegetables can add interesting foliage and form to the ornamental garden. These include leaf lettuce, several crucifers, globe artichoke, pepper, the cucurbits, chard, and carrots. Most herbs also can enhance ornamental plantings.

Herbaceous plants that can "climb" by either twining around or attaching to other objects are called **vines**. Vines are similar to and are used for the same purposes as are lianas. Although ivy and some other perennial vining plants are herbaceous in nature, they are usually classed with the lianas; only annual vining plants are considered to be vines. Vines are used primarily for short-term, rapid-growing screens. Selected herbaceous plants, including vines, grown for their vegetation are listed in Table 11-9.

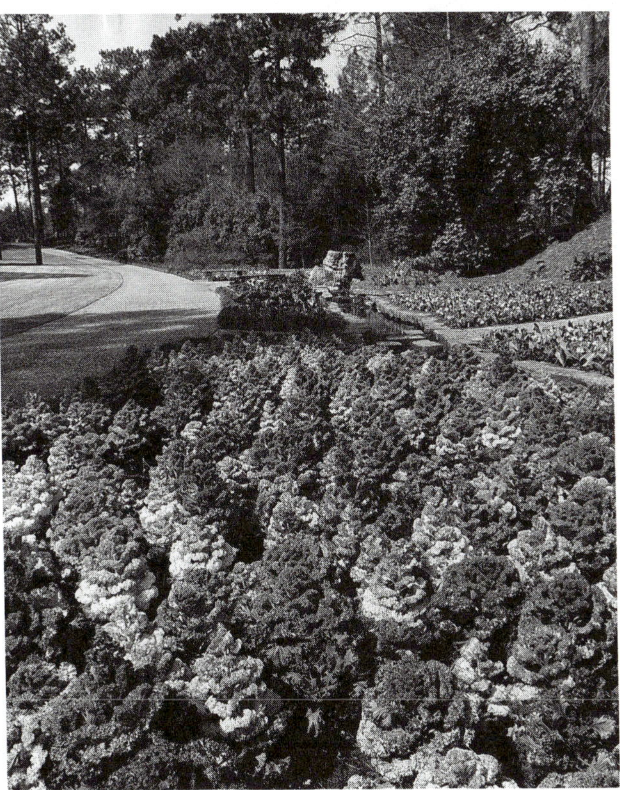

FIGURE 11-20 • Ornamental kale adds color to the garden until long after the first frost. (Courtesy of Grant Heilman)

TABLE 11-8 • *Selected easy-to-grow rock garden plants*

Name	Hardiness Zone[a]	Growth Habit	Height x Spread (inches)[b]	Soil and Exposure[c]	Remarks
Achillea Yarrow	All	Perennial	8 × 8	A	Several species of traditional herbs.
Adiantum pedatum Maidenhair fern	4–9	Fern	24 × 36	B	Good for deep shade and cool climate.
Ajuga reptans Carpet bugle	5–9	Perennial	4 × S	A	Glossy green ground cover, blue flowers.
Alyssum saxatile Golden tuft	4–9	Perennial	12 × 12	A	Cut back after bloom.
Aquilegia Columbine	All	Perennial	24 × 24	A	Blooms May and June.
Arctostaphylos uva-ursi Kinnikinnick	4–9	Liana	4 × S	A	Evergreen leaves; red berries.
Artemisia schmidtiana Silvermound	3–9	Shrub	9 × 12	D	Several cultivars of differing size.
Aubrieta deltoidea Aubrieta	3–8	Perennial	8 × 8	A	Purple flowers, May, June.
Blechnum spicant Deer fern	4–8	Fern	24 × 24	B	Evergreen for shade.
Cerastium tomentosum Snow-in-summer	All	Perennial	6 × S	A	White flower, June, July; spreads.
Convallaria majalis Lily of the valley	4–9	Perennial	8 × S	A	Dainty fragrant white flowers, April; tolerates shade.
Cotoneaster dammeri Bearberry cotoneaster	6–9	Shrub	24 × 48	A	Slow growing; red, persistent berries.
Daphne cneorum Rose daphne	6–10	Shrub	10 × S	A	Pink flowers in early spring.
Echeveria imbricata Hen and chickens	8–10	Succulent	4 × S	A	Most common hen and chickens for California.
Erica carnea 'King George' King George heath	6–9	Shrub	12 × S	B	Blooms February to April; tolerates less acid soil than most heaths.
Festuca ovina 'Glauca' Blue fescue	All	Tuft	18 × 18	A	Ground cover or edging; blue-gray grass.

(continued)

TABLE 11-8 • (*Continued*)

Name	Hardiness Zone[a]	Growth Habit	Height x Spread (inches)[b]	Soil and Exposure[c]	Remarks
Iberis sempervirens Evergreen candytuft	5–10	Tuft	8 × 8	A	Several cultivars.
Iris cristata Crested iris	All	Clump	4 × S	D	Swordlike leaves; blue flowers in May.
Juniperus spp.	All	Spreading	S	A	Several low-growing types (see Table 14-28).
Linum alpinum Alpine flax	All	Perennial herb	6 × 6	A	Blue flowers, May to September.
Nepeta mussinii Persian nepeta	4–10	Perennial herb	20 × 20	A	Violet flowers, May to September; gray foliage.
Oscularia deltoides Ice plant	9–10	Shrub	12 × 12	D	Tolerates drought; purple, fragrant flowers.
Penstemon glaber Blue penstemon	All	Perennial herb	8 × 10	A	Blue flowers, July to October.
Phlox subulata Moss phlox	2–8	Tuft	4 × 15	A	Mound of pink or blue flowers in April.
Potentilla verna Spring cinquefoil	All	Tuft	4 × 15	D	Yellow flowers, summer.
Sarcococca humilis Himalaya sarcococca	7–10	Shrub	15 × S	B	Evergreen; white flowers, October to March.
Sedum lineare	3–10	Succulent	5 × S	A	Various shapes.
Sempervivum spp. Houseleek	3–10	Succulent	4 × 10	A	Several types of interesting clustered plants.
Teucrium chamaedrys Germander	All	Shrub	12 × 18	A	Clip flower heads; good also for edging or low hedge.
Thymus Thyme	All	Ground cover	3 × S	A	Types with gray and variegated leaves.
Viola cornuta Tufted pansy	All	Perennial	3 × 5	A	Likes cool conditions.

[a]See Figure 14-96.
[b]S designates shrubs that have a spreading growth habit; spread may vary depending on age, pruning practices, and environment.

[c]A—General garden loam; sun to light shade tolerant.
B—Needs acid, well-drained soil; usually shade tolerant.
C—Tolerates wet marshy situations.
D—Needs perfect drainage, full sun; usually alkaline tolerant.

TABLE 11-9 • *Selected herbaceous plants with ornamental stems and leaves*

Name	Hardiness Zone[a]	Use	Height	Soil and Exposure[b]	Remarks
Plants Grown as Annuals					
Anethum graveolens Dill	2–9	Background	3 ft	A	Herb; airy-open growth habit.
Brassica oleraceae acephala Kale	2–9	Specimen	1 ft	A	Colorful ornamental as well as interesting vegetable types.
Capsicum spp.	5–10	Border; specimen	1–2 ft	A	Colorful fruit; ornamental and vegetable types suitable for landscape.
Coleus blumei Coleus	5–9	Color	1–2 ft	B	Many cultivars; colorful leaves; injured by cold nights.
Cucurbita pepo Bush summer squash	4–9	Specimen	3 ft	A	Bold leaf form; several cultivars.
Geranium spp.	3–10	Specimen; border	1–4 ft	A	Many types; grown for foliage form and fragrance.
Lycopersicon esculentum 'Tiny Tim' tomato	4–10	Border	1 ft	A	Attractive mound of foliage; marble-size fruit; early; other determinant cultivars also decorative.
Ricinus communis Castor bean	4–10	Specimen	8 ft	A	Grows into a huge tropical-appearing plant in a few weeks.
Senecio cineraria Dusty miller	3–9	Ground cover	6 in	A	Gray foliage; a perennial if given winter protection.
Annual Vines					
Cobaea scandens Cup and saucer vine	All	Screen	25 ft	A	2-inch purple to greenish cuplike flowers in saucerlike calyx.
Cucurbita pepo ovifera Ornamental gourd	4–10	Ground cover	12 ft	A	Multicolored ornamental fruit; picturesque leaves.
Dolichos lablab Hyacinth bean	5–10	Screen	10 ft	A	Sweetpealike flowers; velvet pods.
Ipomoea Morning glory	All	Screen	15 ft	A	Several cultivars with various flower colors.
Phaseolus coccineus Scarlet runner bean	All	Screen	8 ft	A	Clusters of scarlet flowers; pod with beans edible when young.

(continued)

TABLE 11-9 • (*Continued*)

Name	Hardiness Zone[a]	Use	Height	Soil and Exposure[b]	Remarks
			Herbaceous Perennials		
Aegopodium podagraria Bishop's weed	3–6	Ground cover	6 in	A	Prefers partial shade; can become invasive.
Allium schoenoprasum Chive	3–9	Border	1 ft	A	Herb; small grasslike mounds; evergreen if winter is mild.
Asparagus officinalis Asparagus	4–9	Background	4 ft	A	Edible, spring; airy hedge, summer; golden with red berries, fall.
Cortaderia selloana Pampas grass	8–10	Specimen	20 ft	A	May grow 8 ft in one season; fountain of sawtoothed leaves.
Cynara scolymus Globe artichoke	8–9	Specimen	3 ft	A	Cool frost-free climate; colder zones with winter protection; edible flower buds.
Festuca ovina 'Glauca' Blue fescue	3–10	Specimen	6 in	A	Tufts of blue grass; does not spread; needs drainage.
Hosta spp. Plaintain lilies	4–8	Ground cover	6 in–3 ft	A	Large heart-shaped, veined leaves; dies back in fall.
Iris spp. Bearded iris	3–9	Accent	6 in–3 ft	A	Swordlike leaves attractive all seasons; various sizes.
Lamium galeobdolon variegatum Silver nettle vine	4–9	Ground cover	6 in	B	Leaves mottled with white.
Lysimachia nummularia 'Aurea' Moneywort	3–9	Ground cover	6 in	C	Bright yellow foliage; needs shade.
Miscanthus sinensis gracilimus Eulalia grass	4–9	Specimen	6 ft	A	Tall feathery grass; attractive winter and summer.
Nepeta cataria Catnip	2–9	Specimen	2 ft	A	Mint herb; attractive to cats; gray-green leaves.
Pachysandra terminalis Japanese spurge	4–9	Ground cover	6 in	B	Leaves clustered atop evergreen herbaceous stems.
Paeonia spp. Herbaceous peony	3–9	Specimen	2 ft	A	Perennial flower; leaves shrublike all summer.
Salvia officinalis Garden sage	3–9	Ground cover	6 in	A/D	Gray-leaved herb; many other Salvia.
Thymus lanuginosus Woolly thyme	3–9	Ground cover	3 in	A	Flat, matted, gray moss; several other good Thymus.

(*continued*)

TABLE 11-9 • *Selected herbaceous plants with ornamental stems and leaves (Continued)*

Name	Hardiness Zone[a]	Use	Height	Soil and Exposure[b]	Remarks
			Selected Ferns		
Adiantum pedatum Maidenhair fern	4–8		2 ft	B	Deciduous; fine, lacy; shade loving; spreads by rootstocks.
Athyrium pycnocarpon Narrowleaf spleenwort	5–9		2–3 ft	B	Deciduous; native to rich woodland.
Blechnum brasiliense Dwarf tree fern	9–10		4 ft	B	Evergreen; nearly erect fronds; compact clusters.
Blechnum spicant Deer fern	7–9		2 ft	B	Evergreen; native to Pacific Northwest; deep shade; woodsy soil.
Botrychium virginianum Rattlesnake fern	5–9		1–2 ft	B	Deciduous; native to open woods.
Cystopteris bulbifera Bulblet fern	5–9		1–2 ft	C	Deciduous; limestone cliffs; small bulbs form on upper fronds.
Dryopteris erythrosora Oriental wood fern	4–9		2 ft	B	Deciduous; young fronds reddish, turning deep green.
Dryopteris marginalis Leather wood fern	5–9		2–3 ft	B	Evergreen; native of eastern rocky woods; adaptable.
Lygodium palmatum American climbing fern	6–10		4 ft	B	Deciduous; climbs; difficult to grow; highly acid, moist soil.
Osmunda cinnamomea Cinnamon fern	6–10		4 ft	B	Deciduous; moist, acid soil.
Osmunda regalis Royal fern	4–10		4 ft	B	Deciduous; massive; sun or shade.
Platycerium bifurcatum Staghorn fern	9–10		3 ft	B	Evergreen; the hardiest of epiphytic ferns; to 22°F.
Polystichum acrostichoides Christmas fern	4–9		1–2 ft	B	Evergreen; common eastern native; tolerant; shade.
Polystichum munitum Western sword fern	4–10		3 ft	B	Evergreen; large, coarse native from California to Alaska to Montana; shade.

(continued)

TABLE 11-9 • (*Continued*)

Name	Hardiness Zone[a]	Use	Height	Soil and Exposure[b]	Remarks
		Cacti and Succulents (see also Table 11-8)			
Cephalocereus senilis Old man cactus	10	Specimen or pot	40 ft	D	Slow growing; Mexican native; can be kept small; long white hairs.
Coryphantha vivipara (sold as *Mammillaria*)	3–10	Specimen	6 in	D	Hardy; 2-in knob-covered bodies; showy purple flowers.
Echinocactus grusonii Golden barrel cactus	9–10	Specimen	4 ft	A/D	Best-known barrel cactus; showy 3-in spines; yellow 2-in flowers, April.
Echinocerus triglochidiatus	4–9	Specimen	1 ft	A/D	Round ribbed bodies; intense profuse scarlet flowers; Great Plains native.
Ferocactus wislizenii Fishhook barrel cactus	7–10	Specimen	8 ft	D	Curves toward sun; 3-in yellow-to-red flowers, late summer.
Lemaireocereus thurberi Organ-pipe cactus	9–10	Specimen	15 ft	D	Arizona native; columnar, branching; 3-in purple blooms at night.
Opuntia compressa Eastern prickly pear	4–9	Ground cover	10 in	A	Native to eastern America; flat pads; spring bloom.
Opuntia ficus-indica Indian fig cactus	9–10	Specimen	15 ft	D	Large treelike succulent; 4-in yellow flowers, spring.
Opuntia fragilis	3–9	Ground cover	8 in	A/D	Great Plains native; hardy to central Alberta.
Opuntia polyacantha	4–9	Ground cover	8 in	D	Needs sandy soil; 3-in yellow or carmine blooms, spring.
Sedum acre Goldmoss sedum	3–9	Ground cover	4 in	A	Spreading evergreen; yellow spring flowers; can be weedy.
Sedum lineare	3–9	Ground cover	to 1 ft	A	Spreading, trailing, rooting stems; yellow flowers, late spring.
Sedum spectabile	3–9	Specimen	18 in	A	4-in rose to carmine flower clusters; 3-in blue-green leaves.

[a]See Figure 14-96.
[b]A—General garden loam; sun to light shade tolerant.
B—Needs acid, well-drained soil; usually shade tolerant.
C—Tolerates wet marshy situations.
D—Needs perfect drainage, full sun; usually alkaline tolerant.

LAWNS AND OTHER GROUND COVERS

◆ ◆ ◆

Trees, shrubs, vines, and flowers all are necessary in a garden environment; however, it is the open spaces that add depth to the vistas, accommodate movement of people and vehicles, and provide space for relaxation and recreation. Because unprotected soil turns either to dust or mud, these open areas must have some kind of cover. The cover may be hard-surface paving or mulch or a lawn or other low-growing plants.

Establishing a Lawn

Although there is reason for reducing the size of lawns or eliminating them altogether, the majority of homes still have lawns, and most homeowners at some time are concerned with growing and caring for a lawn. As a bulletin on home lawns stated, "A high quality lawn pleases the eye and increases the value of the property, but beautiful lawns don't just happen. They are the result of wise planning, hard work and proper care" (from *Home Lawns*, Washington State University Extension Bulletin 482, Pullman, Wash., revised periodically).

Perhaps the main requisite for a satisfactory lawn is the proper leveling and grading of the soil in the yard. Once the lawn is established, it is difficult to fill in holes or to change the grade. Suggestions for grading, soil, and soil preparation for lawns were given in Chapter 5. If the soil is clay or clay loam, or if deep excavations have been made in the yard, special precautions will be necessary to make certain that the soil has completely settled before the lawn is planted. If possible, the yard should be left to settle over a winter. After the lawn area is leveled and graded, it should be soaked to the depth of any excavation. The area should then be allowed to dry and any resulting depressions filled with soil. If there is considerable settling with the initial soaking, the area should be thoroughly wet and allowed to settle a second time.

Plowing, rototilling, or spading, followed by leveling with hand or power equipment, are the best methods of preparing the soil for planting. Hand raking is a desirable final leveling procedure to fill depressions where water might pool and to level high spots.

Lawns can be planted by sodding, seeding, or vegetative planting. **Sodding** is covering the soil surface with a layer of established lawn that has been grown and brought from elsewhere for that purpose (Figure 11-21). Areas around commercial buildings where an immediate cover is needed and steep banks where erosion is likely to be a problem are frequently sodded. Sodding is expensive, and the homeowner who can afford it probably can also afford to have a commercial company lay the sod.

Most kinds of grasses recommended for lawns in the central and northern parts of the United States are seeded. Generally, seeds are sold as lawn mixtures of several cultivars. Analysis tags on seed containers should be examined carefully before the seed is purchased. State and federal laws require that tags list the percentage of each kind of grass seed in the container, germination percentage, and date of germination test. Homeowners should consult their county agent or state agricultural experiment station, a seed dealer, or a nursery before

FIGURE 11-21 • Sodding. (Courtesy Walter Chandoha)

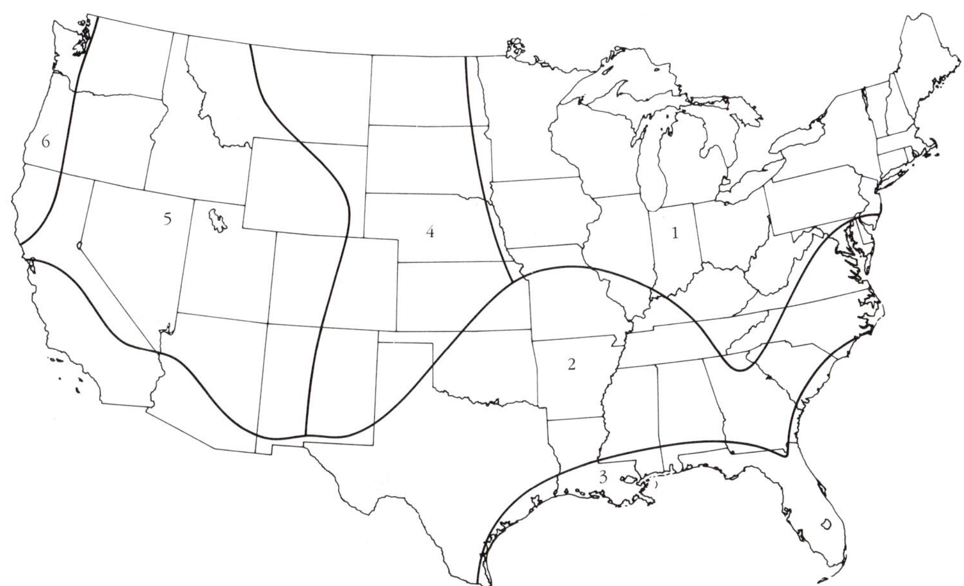

FIGURE 11-22 • Climatic regions of the United States in which the following grasses are suitable for lawns. Region 1: Common Kentucky bluegrass, Merion Kentucky bluegrass, red fescue, and colonial bent. Tall fescue, Bermuda grass, and zoysia in the southern portion of the region. Region 2: Bermuda grass and zoysia. Centipede grass, carpet grass, and St. Augustine grass in the southern portion of the region; tall fescue and Kentucky bluegrass in some northern areas. Region 3: St. Augustine grass, Bermuda grass, zoysia, carpet grass, and bahia grass. Region 4: Nonirrigated areas: Crested wheat grass, buffalo grass, and blue grama. Irrigated areas: Kentucky bluegrass and red fescue. Region 5: Nonirrigated areas: Crested wheat grass. Irrigated areas: Kentucky bluegrass and red fescue. Region 6: Colonial bent and Kentucky bluegrass. (From *Better Lawns*, USDA Home and Garden Bulletin 51. U.S. Government Printing Office, Washington, D.C. Revised periodically)

deciding on the mixture required for their lawns. Figure 11-22 illustrates regions of the United States suitable for growing various grasses. Grass seed should be bought on the basis of quality not quantity, because inexpensive mixtures often contain a high percentage of large-seeded annual grass, which is of very little value in establishing a permanent lawn.

Seed can be planted with a seeder or scattered by hand. If it is to be hand scattered, the amount required should be weighed and divided into two portions. The first portion should be scattered in one direction and the second crosswise to the first sowing. Seeds should be covered by hand raking, not more than one-fourth inch deep. The seeded area should then be firmed by rolling with a light roller or cultipacker.

Grasses that reproduce asexually can be planted by plug sodding, strip sodding, sprigging, or stolonizing. Grasses that must be planted by vegetative means include zoysia, improved strains of Bermuda grass, St. Augustine grass, centipede grass, creeping bent, and velvet bent. With **plug sodding**, small plugs generally are set 1 foot (30

TABLE 11-10 • *Characteristics of lawn plants*

	Seed, Pounds Per 1,000 Square Feet	Time of Seeding	Mowing Height (Inches)	Adaptations	Special Characteristics
Grass					
Bahia	2–3	Spring	1	Warm, humid areas.	Coarse; mostly ground cover.
Bermuda (common)	2–3	Spring	½	Warm areas.	Will grow in low fertility, highly acid soil.
Blue grama	1–1½	Spring	1½	Cool, dry areas, Great Plains.	Drought resistant; will not tolerate heavy traffic.
Buffalo	½–1	Spring	1½	Well-drained, heavy soils; Central Plains.	Drought resistant.
Canada blue	2–3	Fall	1½	Gravelly soils of low fertility.	Resists wear; thin open turf.
Carpet	3–4	Spring	1	Fertile, sandy soils, moist year-round.	Resists wear.
Centipede	2–3	Spring	1	Best low-maintenance lawn grass for the South; spreads rapidly.	Can destroy grazing value of pastures so should not be planted in farm lawns.
Chewings fescue	3–5	Fall, spring	1½	Shade-tolerant grass for cool regions.	Nonspreading, difficult to establish a good stand.
Colonial bent (Highland and Astoria)	1–2	Anytime ground isn't frozen	½	Cool, moist; New England and Oregon, Washington coast.	Forms highest-quality, fine-textured lawn; requires special care.
Crested wheat	1–2	Spring	2	Spring and fall lawn for unirrigated cool regions; dormant during midsummer.	Tough, coarse; very drought resistant.
Kentucky blue (Common, Delta)	2–3	Fall, spring	1½	Most common lawn grass in U.S.; cool humid and cool irrigated areas.	Withstands wear; drought resistant.
Kentucky blue—improved (Merion, Newport, Cougar, Windsor)	1–2	Fall, spring	¾	More heat-tolerant and leaf spot resistant than common bluegrass.	Requires more fertilizer than common bluegrass; Merion is rust susceptible.
Red fescue (Pennlawn, Rainier)	3	Fall, spring	1½	Good for cool, humid, or shady areas; tolerates acid soils.	Common in mixes with Kentucky bluegrass for cool areas.

(continued)

TABLE 11-10 • (*Continued*)

	Seed, Pounds Per 1,000 Square Feet	Time of Seeding	Mowing Height (Inches)	Adaptations	Special Characteristics
			Grass		
Red top	1–2	Fall	1½	To establish quick cover for temporary lawn or in mixtures with other grasses; overseeded with Bermuda in winter to provide year-round green.	Seldom lasts more than 2 years with heavy mowing; tolerates poorly drained acid soils.
Rye grass (annual, perennial)	4–6	Fall, spring	1½	Good for temporary cover on sloping sites and other places.	Seed is large, so rye grass is a common component of inexpensive lawn mixtures.
St. Augustine grass	(Vegetative only)	Spring, summer	1	No. 1 shade-tolerant grass for area south of Augusta, Ga., Birmingham, Ala., to coastal Texas; good for Florida muck soils.	Withstands salt spray; subject to damage by chinch bugs and several diseases.
Tall fescue (Kentucky 31, Alta)	4–6	Fall	1½	Used for playing fields and other locations where wear is more important than beauty; somewhat shade tolerant.	Extremely wear resistant; coarse textured.
Velvet bent	1–2	Fall	½	Cool humid regions; New England and Pacific Northwest coast.	Finest textured of lawn grasses; requires close mowing, regular watering, fertilizing, and disease control.
Zoysia (Japanese lawn grass, Manila grass)	1–2	Spring, summer	1	South of a line from Philadelphia to San Francisco; Manila grass is the best shade grass for the mid-South.	Turns straw yellow with first frost; resistant to wear; stands close clipping.
75% bluegrass 25% red fescue	2–4	Fall, spring	1½	Mixture for sunny locations of Canada and north and central U.S.	All-purpose mixture.
25% bluegrass 75% red fescue	2–4	Fall, spring	1½	Mixture for shady locations of Canada and north and central U.S.	All-purpose mixture.
			Other Seeded Lawn Plants		
Dichondra	Seed or vegetative plantings	Cool season	1	Central and southern California; not recommended for other areas.	Requires large amounts of water; becomes stemmy in many locations.
White clover	1–2	Fall, spring	1½	Cool areas; will not persist during hot weather.	Provides nitrogen for lawn if uniformly mixed with grass; killed out or becomes patchy if sprayed with weed killers.

Adapted from *Better Lawns*, USDA Home and Garden Bulletin 51. U.S. Government Printing Office, Washington, D.C. Revised periodically.

TABLE 11-11 • *Vegetative grasses—rate and time of planting*

Grass	Amount of Planting Material Per 1,000 Square Feet	Time of Planting
Bermuda grass	10 square feet of nursery sod or 1 bushel of stolons	Spring–summer
Buffalo grass	25–50 square feet of sod	Spring
Carpet grass	8–10 square feet of sod	Spring–summer
Centipede grass	8–10 square feet of sod	Spring–summer
Creeping bentgrass	80–100 square feet of nursery sod or 10 bushels of stolons	Fall
Velvet bentgrass	80–100 square feet of nursery sod or 10 bushels of stolons	Fall
Zoysia	30 square feet of sod when plugging; 6 square feet of sod when sprigging	Spring–summer

Adapted from *Better Lawns*, USDA Home and Garden Bulletin 51. U.S. Government Printing Office, Washington, D.C. Revised periodically.

cm) apart, but they may be set closer if more rapid coverage is desired. With **strip sodding**, strips of sod 3 to 4 inches (8 to 10 cm) wide are planted end to end in rows that are about 1 foot apart. **Sprigging** is the planting of individual plants, cuttings, or stolons obtained by tearing apart established lawns. Sprigs can be planted end to end in rows or at spaced intervals. Bermuda grass may be established by spreading shredded stolons and raking lightly to firm them into the soil.

In many climatic regions, lawns can be established at almost any season of the year if commonsense precautions are observed, but they are easiest to establish during wet periods when the temperature is moderately cool. For fall seeding in cold-weather areas, grass should be started at least 45 days before hard freezes are expected. In areas where extremely cold weather is likely, spring seeding is best. Whether a lawn is seeded, vegetatively propagated, or sodded, it must be kept moist until it becomes established. Lawns planted when the weather is hot may need to be mulched and/or sprinkled several times a day. More lawn planting information is given in Tables 11-10 and 11-11.

Renovating and Maintaining a Lawn

Whenever the decision to improve a poor lawn is made, a choice between renovating the old lawn or establishing a new one becomes necessary. If the lawn is poorly drained or there is little grass of desirable species, it is usually best to tear up the lawn with a plow or spade and establish a new one.

If there is a high percentage of desirable grasses scattered throughout the area, the lawn can usually be renovated by the following steps: (1) apply weed-control measures as necessary to rid the turf of as many weeds as possible; (2) clip the old grass close to the ground and rake away leaves, grass clippings, and any other foreign matter that has accumulated; (3) rake vigorously to loosen the surface and remove thatch; (4) cultivate and reseed bare spots; and (5) apply nitrogen fertilizer and water enough to keep the top 12 inches (30 cm) of soil moist.

Several herbicide treatments at 10- to 20-day intervals may be necessary in order to eliminate broad-leaved weeds from a long-neglected lawn area.

Timely and constant maintenance is the key to successful lawns. Suggestions for maintenance fertilization are given in Chapter 5 and in "Fertilizing Garden Crops" in Chapter 14. Suggestions for irrigation are in Chapter 6. Lawns should be mowed frequently, even though little of the top growth is removed. Reel-type mowers cut more cleanly, leaving less brown tip on the grass, but they have been largely replaced by various kinds of easier-to-adjust rotary-type mowers. With frequent mowing and good fertilizer practices, it is not usually necessary to remove the clippings. Bentgrass and Cougar and Merion bluegrass look best if cut to a height of between ¾ to 1 inch (2 to 2½ cm). Most other cool-season grasses should be kept at a height of about 1½ to 2 inches (4 to 5 cm), especially during hot weather. Crabgrass is reduced by the shading effect of taller permanent grasses.

Warm-season grasses, particularly Bermuda grass, require closer mowing than do most cool-season grasses. Bermuda grass should be cut frequently to a height of ⅝ inch (about 1½ cm) to maintain a fine-quality turf. Other warm-season grasses, such as zoysia, centipede grass, carpet grass, and St. Augustine grass, should be mowed to a height of about 1 inch. The mower should be kept sharp so the grass will be cut cleanly without bruising or tearing.

Proper mowing, irrigating, and fertilizing usually minimize the buildup of **thatch**, the accumulation of a dry layer of clippings at the soil surface, which is most likely to be a problem with fine-leaved grasses. If thatch does accumulate to a depth of ½ inch, it should be removed, as it prevents the penetration of air, water, and plant nutrients. There are several types of machines available for removing thatch that can be rented from hardware or garden stores. Early spring is generally the best time to remove thatch if removal becomes necessary.

Pest and Weed Control

The best pest control for any lawn is good management. Weeds, insects, and diseases all are likely to be less of a problem in lawns that have received a balanced fertilizer application, timely irrigation, and frequent mowing to the recommended height. Pest control in well-cared-for lawns growing in cooler regions may require only a single spring application of herbicide. In warmer regions even well-managed lawns may require more attention to keep pests from damaging or destroying them.

Even with good maintenance, however, weed seeds may become established in a lawn, having spread from a neighbor's yard or nearby weedy roadside, and herbicides may be necessary to help control them. Three different types of weeds are the usual offenders — crabgrass, other weedy grasses, and broad-leaved weeds.

Crabgrass is an annual that develops from seeds produced the previous year. New plants can continue to establish from late spring until the first fall frost. Crabgrass is most serious in the warmer parts of the Midwest, the South, and the Southwest. It does not tolerate shade, and a thick, dense turf that is cut no shorter than 1½ inches retards its growth. Raking the lawn just before mowing to raise the seed heads within reach of the mower blades helps reduce the amount of crabgrass seed in the soil. Herbicides are available that prevent the germination of crabgrass seed for several months but do not seriously damage established perennial grass. However, these materials also prevent the germination of lawn grass seed, and so a bare spot cannot be replanted for some time after a treatment to control crabgrass. There also are herbicides suitable for controlling crabgrass as it germinates and after it has begun to grow. Crabgrass killers are sold under various trade names at garden and farm stores. Directions on the label should be followed carefully to avoid damaging the lawn and nearby plants.

Coarse perennial grasses, including quack grass if it has not spread too widely, can be controlled with glyphosphate herbicide applied to the unwanted plants (see "Use of Herbicides in Home Gardens" in Chapter 9). Spray carefully only the offending plants because all grasses touched by the herbicide will be killed. Such treatment will result in a small patch of dead grass for at least part of the season until the lawn grass has spread to cover it. Single clumps of coarse perennial grass can also be dug from a lawn. All rhizomes must be removed, and the area should be immediately reseeded or resodded.

Broad-leaved weeds in lawns are generally controlled with 2,4-D (2,4-dichlorophenoxyacetic acid). The sodium salt or amine forms of 2,4-D are best for home use, as the more volatile ester forms are likely to drift onto and damage nearby shrubs and trees. It is best to apply 2,4-D in the early spring at about the time dandelions begin to bloom or in the early fall during peak periods of weed germination and growth. Herbicides should be applied when rain is not expected for at least 12 hours, and the treated lawn should not be mowed for at least 3 or 4 days. The chemical can be applied in a coarse spray from a sprayer or from a sprinkling can. Applying fertilizer just before or just after treating with 2,4-D stimulates grass growth so that it crowds into the bare spaces left by killed weeds. For further discussion of herbicides, see Chapter 9.

A number of commercial companies are formulating mixtures of herbicide and fertilizer for application to turf. These mixtures have given excellent results when large areas of turf, such as golf courses, college campuses, or parks, are to be treated. Some homeowners, however, have had problems with these materials. Accidental application to trees, shrubs, or gardens, of course, kills the treated plants, and one of the persistent herbicides sometimes used in these formulations has occasionally accumulated in concentrations high enough to damage trees and shrubs with roots in the treated turf.

Lawn grasses vary in their susceptibility to insects and diseases, but all kinds are vulnerable to some pests. Lawns are inviting to a number of soil-inhabiting insects, which can be best controlled during the spring by applying an insecticide and immediately afterward sprinkling the lawn thoroughly. One application may control the pest for several years. Control of soil insects is slow, and it may be some time before the insecticide becomes fully effective. Insecticides for above-ground insects should not be applied unless the insects are present and causing damage. When insecticides are applied, the lawn should be sprinkled very lightly to wash some of the insecticide to the base of the plants. The plants should not be watered again for several days. Some of the more troublesome lawn diseases and insect pests and controls for a few of them are described in Table 11-12.

Other Lawn Problems

Injury from other causes is occasionally mistaken for disease or insect injury. Burning with chemical fertilizer; damage from dog urine; scorching caused by placing rugs, mats, or plastic on the lawn in hot weather; injury by weed killers; and drought all may be mistaken for disease damage. Lawns are sometimes damaged by moles, pocket gophers, and field mice. Traps in mole and gopher tunnels are effective, and poison bait can control pocket gophers and field mice.

Moss growing in the lawn generally results from a lack of fertility, poor drainage, high soil acidity, excess shade, or soil compaction. Moss can be removed by hand raking, burning with ammonium sulfate, or spraying with copper sulfate.

Shade often prevents growing an attractive lawn. Under trees, grass receives insufficient light and is likely to be robbed of nutrients. The problem can be partially overcome by planting trees such as honey locust or birch that cast only light shade. Cutting away lower branches and heavy pruning to reduce the amount of shade also helps. Fertilizing trees so that their roots can feed below the level of the grass roots allows grass to use more of the surface-applied fertilizer. This can be done by placing fertilizer for trees in holes 18 inches (45 cm) deep punched with a metal rod at intervals beneath the tree canopy. Watering thoroughly through the root zone of both the grass and the trees helps keep the tree roots from concentrating on the surface. Tree roots that do protrude above the soil surface can usually be pruned off without damaging the tree. Shade-tolerant grasses, such as St. Augustine grass and Manila grass for the South and fescue for the North, should be planted in heavily shaded areas. Finally, if it is impossible to get turf grass to grow under trees, a shade-tolerant ground cover such as periwinkle, pachysandra, or ivy can be substituted.

Growing Lawns Without Commercial Fertilizer or Pesticide

Directions for growing lawns with commercial fertilizer and pesticides have become so familiar that we sometimes forget that fifty years ago bagged fertilizer and pesticides did not exist, and yet many homeowners had beautiful expanses of turf. If pesticides are not to be used, it is wise to delay planting a new lawn for one season in order to cultivate out weeds that have become established. If perennial weeds like Canadian thistle, morning glory, or quack grass are present, growers may want to compromise their "organic" principles just once, because these weeds require eight to ten years of continuous cultivation to eliminate and are almost impossible to remove from an established lawn. (They were not so universally present fifty years ago.) See "Use of Herbicides in Home Gardens" in Chapter 9 for suggestions on controlling these perennial weeds.

Years ago manure was often spread over the lawn area in late autumn or early spring. Winter and spring precipitation leached the needed fertilizer nutrients into the root zone. The fibrous residue was then raked from the turf in the early spring. Manure or sewage sludge can still be used in this way; however, composting the manure or sludge, especially if the composting is done away from urban areas, makes the operation less offensive to neighbors and reduces or eliminates the fibrous material that needs to be removed in the spring.

In areas where nitrogen is the only fertilizer recommended for lawns, planting a mixture of a recommended grass and a nitrogen-fixing legume often eliminates the need for additional fertilizer. White clover, *Trifolium repens*, is probably the best legume for most cool-area turfs, but extension personnel can supply local recommendations. Clover does stain clothes. It also tends to become patchy and bloom below the cut of the mower in places that have hot days and nights for long periods.

Earthworm castings need to be raked down in the spring, and the turf of an "organically grown" lawn should be cut no lower than 1½ inches (40 cm) so that the roughness caused by the castings remains concealed. The clippings can be left on the lawn if mowing is frequent, if the turf is not cut too short, and if there is an ample supply of earthworms to aerate the soil and help break down the organic matter. When a legume is used, a mulch of clippings removed from the lawn supplies nitrogen to a rose bed or other planting.

Plants Used as Ground Covers

Technically any plant is a ground cover; however, the term is usually reserved for low-growing spreading ornamentals. Some or most kinds of the many plant groups already discussed are classed as ground covers, including low-growing shrubs,

TABLE 11-12 • *Major insect and disease pests of home lawns*

Insect Pests	Symptoms and Damage	Control
Grubs and wireworms	Grubs are larvae of several kinds of beetles. They burrow around and kill grass roots, causing the lawn to be patchy and unthrifty. Wireworms, the larvae of the click beetle, are dark brown, hard, smooth, slender, and ½ to 1½ inches (1¼ to 4 cm) long. The grub of the Japanese beetle is probably the most destructive grub in the eastern states.	Count grubs by cutting from several places in the lawn 1 foot square (90 cm^2) strips of sod on three sides, undercutting 2 to 3 inches (5 to 8 cm) beneath the surface, and laying them back using uncut side as hinge. If there is an average of three or more grubs per square foot, an insecticide should be applied. Milky disease spores (see billbug control) are effective for some grubs. Do not apply both spores and insecticide.
Ants, wasps, and wild bees	Grass is buried by their mounds. Grass seed and roots are often damaged by their nesting.	Apply insecticide to soil in vicinity of mounds.
Mole crickets	Light brown cricketlike insects with lower surface lighter than upper. The burrowing and feeding of one mole cricket can damage several yards of newly seeded lawn in a night. Most numerous in south Atlantic and Gulf states.	When these insects are numerous, treat with a soil insecticide before planting the lawn.
Billbugs	Grubs feed on roots. Adults are tan to reddish brown beetles ⅓ to ¾ inches (less than 2 cm) long with long snouts and strong pincers. They burrow into the grass stem near soil surface and feed on leaves. Zoysia grass is especially susceptible.	Billbug grubs are susceptible to a bacterial disease, milky disease. Spore formulations can be purchased, but it may require several years for complete control. Once the disease is established, control is permanent.
Earthworms	Make mounds or castings that can interfere with mowing and give lawn an uneven surface.	Rake down castings with a fine-toothed rake. Increase mowing height to hide castings. Earthworms improve aeration and water infiltration and help decompose thatch. Can be controlled with insecticide.
Sod webworms	Light brown, hair-covered, ¾ inch (2 cm) long larvae of lawn moth. They rest in silken webs during the day and feed at night. As they grow older, they build grass and silk-lined tunnels near the surface of soil. Most damaging in areas south and east of a line from Kansas to Maryland. Irregular brown spots in lawn are first sign of damage.	Break apart drying sod. If more than three or four webworms are in a 6-inch-square (38 cm^2) section, insecticide should be applied.
Armyworms	Black-striped green larvae that usually are found in clusters of several hundred. Can eat grass down to the roots in a very short time.	Isolated groups can be destroyed by squashing them. Use insecticides for heavier infestations.

(continued)

TABLE 11-12 • (*Continued*)

Insect Pests	Symptoms and Damage	Control
Cutworms	Brown or gray caterpillars that hide in the soil during the day and cut off plants by feeding on their bases at night.	Apply insecticide.
Chinch bugs	Yellowish spots that turn rapidly into brown dead areas are the major symptoms. Young nymphs are about the size of a pinhead, bright red with a white band across their backs. Adult nymphs are black and have a white spot on back between wing pads. Adults are about ⅙ inch (less than ½ cm) long with black and white markings. Damage is most likely in the East and South.	Identify infestation by sinking a can open at both ends halfway into the turf. Fill can with water and watch for about 5 minutes for chinch bugs to float to surface. Insecticide application most effective in early spring.
Scale insects	Scale insects attach themselves to the crown or roots of grass and secrete a hard waxy or white cottony covering. They damage the plant by sucking juices from it. Plants attacked usually turn brown and die, leaving patchy, dead places in the lawn. Scale insects are most serious in the South and Southwest.	Fertilize and irrigate to keep grass growing rapidly; dispose of infested clippings. Several weekly treatments with an insecticide effective against scale during spring season may be necessary.
Leafhoppers	These ½-inch (1¼ cm) long, speckled insects suck sap from the leaves and stems of grass, killing newly seeded lawns and causing whitened patches that may be mistaken for drought damage in older lawns.	Apply insecticide when leafhoppers become numerous enough to do damage.
Insect mites	Tiny, barely visible insects that suck sap from grasses, causing leaves to be blotched and stippled and can eventually kill the plant. A fine webbing on the leaves is usually associated with mite infestation. When mites are numerous in the yard, they sometimes enter homes in large numbers.	Periodic application of miticides. Mite damage often occurs because insecticide application for other pests kills their predators.
Earwigs, ticks, chiggers, slugs, snails, fleas	These insects do not damage the lawn but often live in grass and cause annoyance or injury to people on the lawn. Some of them may enter the home from the lawn area.	Insecticides applied directly to the lawn or, in the case of ticks and fleas, insecticide treatment of animals that carry the insects onto the lawn.

(continued)

TABLE 11-12 • *Major insect and disease pests of home lawns (Continued)*

Diseases	Symptoms and Damage	Control
Brown patch	Fungus disease that attacks practically all kinds of turf grass and produces irregularly shaped brown spots 1 inch (2½ cm) to several feet in diameter. The spots have a dark, smoke green effect around the outer edges where the fungus is active. Most serious during the period of high humidity when daytime temperatures drop to develop dew or fog at night.	Avoid overstimulation with nitrogen. Apply a turf fungicide.
Dollar spot	A fungus disease most severe on Kentucky bluegrass, bentgrass, rye grass, centipede grass, and St. Augustine grass, causing straw-colored spots about the size of a silver dollar. Most serious during spring and fall periods of cool nights and warm humid days.	Turf fungicide.
Leaf spot	A disease causing reddish brown to purple black spots on the leaves of Kentucky bluegrass. It may spread to the crown, causing considerable damage.	Mow no shorter than 1¾ to 2 inches (4 to 5 cm). Use adequate but not too much fertilizer. Merion and other improved Kentucky bluegrasses have some resistance to leaf spot. Fungicide application every 7 to 10 days starting with the first symptoms also controls the disease.
Snow mold	Commonly found in the northern United States and Canada during winter and early spring, usually seen as white mold on dead brown patches of old grass as the snow melts in the spring.	Avoid nitrogenous fertilizers late in the fall. Rake away heavy matted grass and leaves before the snow comes. If severe, mercury fungicides through the winter will help control the disease.
Leaf and stem rust	Reddish-brown to black powdery spots in leaf and stems. Most serious on Merion bluegrass. Forms as a result of heavy dews during warm weather.	Increase nitrogen fertilization; water during dry periods and mow frequently.
Red thread	A fungus disease that occurs most frequently in fescues and bentgrasses during cool, wet periods. Most serious in the coastal area of the Pacific Northwest. Diseased areas vary in size and shape; appear scorched. Grass changes color from green to pink to brown and finally light tan. The fungus produces characteristic red threads or strands over the dead blades of grass.	Maintain balanced fertility and apply a cadmium fungicide in spring and fall.
Damping-off	Young seedlings in newly seeded lawns decay at the soil line and fall over. The disease is favored by cool, damp weather.	Plant the lawn when growing conditions are favorable; prepare a good seedbed and avoid overwatering. Treat the seed with a protectant fungicide.
Powdery mildew	Most severe on bluegrass; mildew appears as gray-white powdery masses on leaves and stems. Severely affected leaves may turn yellow and die.	Keep turf well fertilized and watered to maintain high vigor.
Fairy ring	These rings are caused by several fungi. Rings or circles of dark green grass appear and gradually grow larger. Just inside this ring there is often a second ring of dying or dead grass, although the grass in the center of the circle may be normal. Sometimes mushrooms grow on the ring's edge.	Keep the turf well fertilized; daily soaking of the affected area with water for a month will help control fairy ring.

lianas and vines, and herbaceous plants grown for both their flowers and their vegetation.

Ground covers are the ideal planting for banks and slopes too steep to mow; small, isolated areas that would be awkward to mow; shady areas where lawns will not grow well; and areas not designated for activities that require paving or turf and where the owner does not want the responsibility of continual maintenance of turf.

Even more than other plantings, ground covers must be ecologically adapted to their location. Unless they grow vigorously, their growing site will require constant hand weeding to eliminate competition from other species. Ground covers that grow 12 or more inches (30 cm) high will shade out the unwanted growth of weedy locations better than will fully prostrate materials. On the other hand, plants 1 to 2 feet tall may not provide the desired effect. A favorite springtime scene is a bed of daffodils that have elongated through low-growing, purple-flowered vinca. Similarly, the carpetlike effect of the ground-hugging Bar Harbor juniper (*Juniperus horizontalis* 'Bar Harbor'), kinnikinnick (*Arctostaphylos uva-ursi*), or woolly thyme (*Thymus languginosus*) may offer just the right contrast to accentuate the color and form of semidwarf evergreen shrubs or perennial flowers. The low-spreading shrubs and many of the lianas described in Tables 11-9 and 14-28, would make good ground covers.

 Selected References

Adams, E. B. *Homescaping*. Intermountain Regional Publication 4. Laramie: University of Wyoming, for the combined extension services of various Rocky Mountain, Great Plains, and Pacific Coast states. Revised and reprinted periodically.

Brickell, C., ed. *The American Horticultural Society Encyclopedia of Garden Plants*. New York: Macmillan, 1989.

California Polytechnic State University (CPSU). *Landscape Construction*. VEP Landscape Manual. San Luis Obispo: CPSU, 1989.

California Polytechnic State University. *Landscaping with Container Plants*. San Luis Obispo: VEP VHS Video, CPSU, 1989.

Carpenter, P. L., and T. D. Walker. *Plants in the Landscape*. 2nd ed. New York: Freeman, 1990.

Courtright, G. *Trees and Shrubs for Temperate Climates*. 3rd ed. Beaverton, Oreg.: Timber Press, 1988.

Daute, Horst. *The Macmillan Book of Bonzai* (Macmillan Gardening Guide Series). New York: Macmillan, 1986.

Flint, H. L. *Landscape Plants for Eastern North America Exclusive of Florida and the Immediate Gulf Coast*. New York: Wiley, 1983.

Gorkin, N. K. *Perennials: A Nursery Source Manual*. Brooklyn Botanic Garden Handbook 118 (special printing of *Plants and Gardens*, vol. 44, no. 4). Brooklyn, N.Y.: Brooklyn Botanic Garden, 1989.

Reader's Digest Editors. *Reader's Digest Guide to Creative Gardening*. New York: Random House, 1987.

Rice, G. *Handbook of Annuals and Bedding Plants*. Beaverton, Oreg.: Timber Press, 1986.

Rodale, R., ed. *The Basic Book of Organic Gardening*. New York: Ballantine, 1987.

Still, S. M. *Herbaceous Ornamental Plants*. 3rd ed. Champaign, Ill.: Stipes Publishing, 1988.

Sunset Magazine and Books Editors. *The New Sunset Western Garden Book*. 5th ed. Menlo Park, Calif.: Lane, 1990.

Time-Life Books Editors. *Gardening in Small Spaces* (Gardener's Guide Series). Alexandria, Va.: Time-Life Books, 1989.

CHAPTER

12

The Vegetable and Herb Garden

The headlines of an Associated Press news release read: "Farmers lose over $14 billion in vegetable sales." The article went on to explain that during the past year, home gardeners had grown about half the vegetables consumed in this country, valued at $14 billion, a sum that farmers supposedly would have earned had there been no home gardens. The amount of the $14 billion remaining after expenses are subtracted is a virtual tax-free savings enjoyed by the estimated 40 percent of U.S. families who grow vegetable gardens each year. The percentage of Canadians who are vegetable gardeners is about the same.

Other news releases periodically remind us of the dietary value of the high fiber, vitamin, mineral, and low fat and calorie content of vegetables in combating degenerative diseases such as obesity, hypertension, and heart disease. Carrots and cruciferous vegetables (broccoli, cauliflower, etc.) have been reported to reduce one's chances of developing certain kinds of cancer. In addition, those who grow their own vegetables benefit from the physical exercise of gardening. Research conducted by the federal government a few years ago showed that on the average gardening activities burned 220 calories per hour, about the same number as does a rapid walk.

To many, saving money and having healthier bodies may not be the most important reasons for growing vegetables.

Rather, they enjoy the thrill of watching plants grow, the primal satisfaction of directly supplying food for the body, or the gustatory pleasure derived from consuming freshly harvested vegetables and herbs.

PLANNING THE VEGETABLE GARDEN

Planning your vegetable garden is essential if you are to get optimal production from the area available. The arrival of seed catalogs in early January is often the catalyst that starts those living in cold-winter climates planning their gardens.

Like a landscape plan, a vegetable garden plan should begin with an accurate measurement of the site. The plot, with each crop row properly spaced, should be drawn to scale. Vegetables that are to be planted at the same time should be grouped together so that the areas they occupy can be weeded, cultivated, and, if feasible, replanted together. Perennials should be along one side so that they will not be disturbed when the rest of the garden is worked. The plot plan showing final location of each crop should be saved from year to year so that rotation is possible. Unless enough land is available so that a field or cover crop can be produced at least every other year, the gardener should alternate the location of individual vegetables. This permits better utilization of plant nutrient reserves and prevents the buildup of insects and soil microorganisms detrimental to a specific crop. The growth habit of each kind of plant should be considered when planning so that, for example, a sun-loving crop is not planted in the shade on the north side of a tall-growing crop such as sweet corn or so that vine crops are not located where they will spread to choke out nearby low-growing, less vigorous vegetables. Sample garden plans are shown in Figures 12-1 and 12-2.

If more than one site is available, the garden should be as near the kitchen as possible but should not be near large trees, as they will shade the site and deplete it of mineral nutrients. All problems and interesting observations that pertain to the garden should be recorded so that they will be remembered and avoided (or capitalized on) during subsequent seasons.

Size of the Garden

Don't give up the idea of a garden if you have only a small plot. A friend of mine grew so many tomatoes and beans on a 14 × 22 foot (4 × 7 m) plot that he had to give some away, and he also grew lettuce, spinach, radishes, strawberries, and cucumbers on this plot. He staked his tomatoes and trained them to a single stem. Planted 1 foot (30 cm) apart in rows 24 inches (60 cm) apart, they yielded a bushel to the picking from only a few vines. Cucumbers also can be staked and grown on a trellis or fence.

If the garden is extremely small, don't grow low-yielding kinds of vegetables such as corn, watermelon, cantaloupe, or peas. Use plenty of fertilizer and water and practice succession cropping. For instance, cabbage can be planted following spinach, or carrots can be planted in the space where radishes or lettuce were harvested.

If the garden plot is larger, of course, more can be planted. In this case it may not pay to stake plants because gardening time rather than space is likely to be limiting. Moreover, the large garden often can be arranged so that it can be cultivated by machinery. Don't overplant. A small garden well cared for will yield a great deal more than a large plot poorly managed.

Climate

The climate determines the kinds and cultivars that can be grown. In cooler areas, radishes, lettuce, beets, carrots, turnips, peas, potatoes, cauliflower, cabbage, green onions, and generally beans will grow to perfection. In warmer areas, corn, tomatoes, beans, cucumbers, and melons do well, but some of the cool-season crops cannot be grown except during early spring or late fall. At the latitude of the United States and Canada, if your garden plot is located on a south slope, you may be able to grow crops that you would be unable to

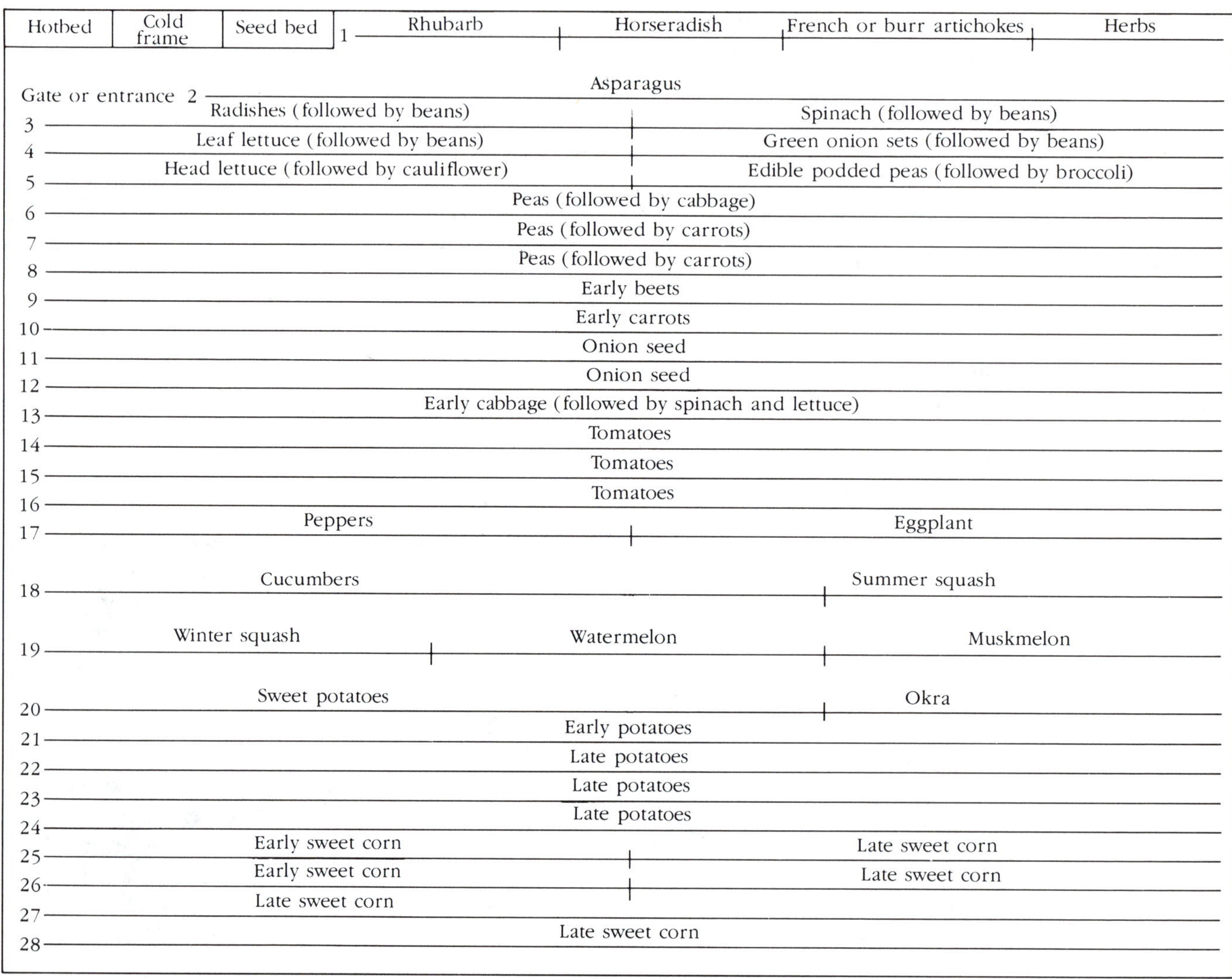

FIGURE 12-1 • The vegetable garden plan. Such a garden—length 200 feet (60 m), width 100 feet (30 m)—should produce all the vegetables a large family can use throughout the growing season and a surplus for canning, storing, and drying. (From *Suburban and Farm Vegetable Gardens*, USDA Home and Garden Bulletin 9. U.S. Government Printing Office, Washington, D.C., 1967)

grow on a north slope in the same area. Planting on the south side of a building also hastens maturity. Crops grown in a sandy soil mature earlier than those grown in a heavier clay soil, but heavy soils can be conditioned by adding humus. Growing from transplants allows crops to mature earlier and also permits the production of kinds that would not normally mature if they were direct seeded in some short-season areas. Because of their shorter growing time in the garden, transplants also free space for other crops. Short-season crops such as radishes or spinach often can be matured

I. Garden layout and first year cropping plan

Row No.		Planting Date
1A	'Sugar snap' peas (staked)	March 15*
1B	Sweet corn (early and late cultivars)	May 1
2A	Lcc	August 20*
2B	Sweet corn (early and late cultivars)	May 1
3A	Lcc	August 20*
3B	Sweet corn (early and late cultivars)	May 1
4A	Lcc	August 20*
4B	Early carrots; early beets; zucchini	April 1, May 1
5A	Lcc/late carrots; late beets	August 20*, July 1
5B	Onions (from seed and sets)	March 15
6A	Lcc	August 20*
6B	Early cabbage, broccoli, cauliflower (trnspl.)	April 10
7A	Lcc/late beans; late broccoli	August 20*, July 1
7B	Early beans	May 15
8A	Lcc	August 20*
8B	Spinach/cucumbers; radish/tomatoes; lettuce/peppers	March 15, May 15
9A	Lcc	August 20*
9B	Spinach/cucumbers; radish/tomatoes; lettuce/peppers	March 15, May 15

II. Key for Mini-til vegetable garden

Crop	Planting Date	Row Number		
		Year 1	Year 2	Year 3
Snap peas	March 15	1A	4B	7A
Sweet corn	May 1	1,2,3B	4,5,6A	7,8,9B
Carrots, beets	April 1	4B	7A	1B
Carrots, beets	July 1	5A	7B	2A
Zucchini squash	May 1	4B	7A	1B
Onions	March 15	5B	8A	2B
Cabbage, broccoli, cauliflower	April 10 (trnspl.)	6B	9A	3A
Beans	July 1	7A	1B	4A
Beans	May 15	7B	1A	4B
Spinach, radishes, leaf lettuce	March 15	8B	2A	5B
Cucumbers	May 20	8,9B	2,3A	5,6B
Tomatoes	May 10 (trnspl.)	8,9B	2,3A	5,6B
Peppers	May 20 (trnspl.)	8B	2A	5B
Spinach, head lettuce	March 15	9B	3A	6B
Eggplant	May 20 (trnspl.)	9B	3A	6B
Austrian winter pea, vetch, sweet clover*	August 20	All B rows except 4B	All A rows except 7A	All B rows except 1B

*Lcc indicates legume cover crop that supplies the nitrogen fertilizer and much of the organic matter for the garden and is planted about August 20 of the previous season. Snap peas are the cover crop for the row in which they are planted.

FIGURE 12-2 • Mini-til vegetable garden designed to have most fertilizer requirements come from winter cover crops (see "Gardening Without Chemical Fertilizers" and "Cultivation Systems and Soil Erosion" in Chapter 5). Permanent layout and first-year cropping plan is shown in Part I. Crop residues like corn stalks remain in the row and the legume cover crop is planted among them or as close as possible to them. Residues and the growing cover crop protect small seedlings and transplants from strong winds in the spring. Rows are spaced 22 inches apart (which provides 44 inches between early planted rows) so that a tiller can be used to incorporate the cover crop when it is removed about June 15 in preparation for planting the late garden vegetables. The garden is designed for a 3-year and alternate-row rotation as shown in the key (Part II). The rotation layout during years 4 through 6 is the same as during the first three years except that crops in the A and B rows are interchanged. For example, during year 4 sweet corn is planted in Row 1A and snap peas in Row 1B.

before transplants are set out, and the earlier maturity of transplanted crops may allow time to grow a succession crop.

Quantity to Plant

The amount of each vegetable planted is determined by the length of time it can be harvested from the garden, whether or not it can be stored or processed, the space available, the number of people using the garden produce and their likes and dislikes, and the yield of the vegetable. For example, a few feet of lettuce planted at one time produces all a family can consume during the time it retains good quality in the garden. Planting a small amount of this crop every two weeks provides lettuce of the right maturity throughout the season that lettuce can be grown in an area. A short row of Swiss chard or New Zealand spinach and three hills of summer squash usually provide as much of these vegetables as a family can consume. A few plants of most species of herbs supply all a family can use.

GROWING THE VEGETABLE AND HERB GARDEN

◆ ◆ ◆

The ideal soil for all-around vegetable or herb production is one that warms early, has good drainage but retains moisture, works easily, and does not pack. Sandy loam soils probably come closest to this ideal, especially if irrigation water is available. Both sandy and clay soils can be improved by the addition of manure. If manure is not available, growers must use commercial fertilizers and soil-improving crops to maintain soil structure and fertility (see Chapter 5 and "Fertilizing Garden Crops" in Chapter 14). Although clay soils may not be ideal for gardens, tomatoes, sweet corn, beans, squash, cucumbers, and most herbs produce excellent yields in them, and even root crops can be grown in carefully managed clay loams.

Vegetables are heavy users of fertilizers; however, gardens are as frequently overfertilized as underfertilized. A soil test carried out by a state or reliable commercial laboratory is the best way to determine fertilizer needs. A fertilizer program that will produce high yields depends on a number of factors. One is the type of soil in the garden. For example, acid soils frequently need phosphorus; sandy soils may be low in nitrogen and potassium; and muck and peat soils are often low in phosphorus and potassium. Another factor is the type of plant to be grown. Leafy vegetables are heavy feeders and need large and continuous supplies of nitrogen; root and tuber crops often need additional potassium; and fruit vegetables such as tomatoes and peppers respond well to phosphorus. Herbs need some fertilizer, but an overabundance of available nitrogen reduces the flavor of some kinds. Most vegetable crops and herbs grow best on soils with a pH of about 6 to 7. However, potatoes are freer of the disease known as scab when grown on soils that are either more acid or more alkaline (see Tables 14-16 and 14-17).

An adequate, uniform water supply is needed to produce quality vegetables and most herbs. Succulents and most root crops lose quality rapidly under conditions of insufficient moisture. The entire root zone of vegetables and herbs should be brought to field capacity with each irrigation. In arid areas and during periods when there is no rain, they should be watered every seven to ten days during a warm summer. If irrigation water is not available and rainfall is sparse, gardeners can grow spring and fall crops. Some compensation for a lack of moisture can also be provided by widely spacing the vegetable plants, controlling weeds, and mulching. Once established, some herbs that originated in arid areas, including sage, thyme, lavender, and tarragon, can withstand considerable drought. For determining the correct seeding time and for procedures for choosing, producing, and planting transplants, see Chapter 4 and "Propagating Plants from Seed" in Chapter 14.

Winter Vegetable Gardening

In the warmer parts of Florida, Texas, California, and Arizona, vegetable gardening can be a year-round hobby, with cool-season vegetables grown during the fall, winter, and spring and warm-season vegetables during the summer. As soon as one crop is harvested, another can be planted in its place. Because plant pests are not killed by cold temperatures in these areas, rotation among unlike vegetables or with field crops is especially important.

Slightly farther north and along the Pacific Coast where heavy freezes are infrequent, vegetables such as lettuce, broccoli, spinach, onions, and peas and most annual herbs can be planted in the fall to winter over and mature during the early spring. Some of the biennial crops can also be wintered over in these areas if they are very small during the period of cold temperatures. If biennial plants have produced a second or third set of leaves before their growth is halted by winter cold, seed stalks will be initiated and will form as soon as the weather warms in the spring.

Even farther north in many areas of the United States and Canada, such crops as spinach, lettuce, and some of the crucifers can be seeded in the fall if the small seedlings can have a snow cover or be covered with a loose mulch of straw or shavings to protect them from hard-winter freezes. The hardier perennial herbs like sage, thyme, lavender, and tarragon (with the aid of a protective mulch in the coldest areas) can be harvested from the garden during most of the winter. Also, in many areas, gardeners utilize only part of the growing season. For example, in eastern Washington State in mid-November we are still harvesting head and leaf lettuce, broccoli, carrots, beets, turnips, onions, chard, cabbage, radishes, and potatoes from the garden, even though the first light frosts occurred almost two months ago. We have often been able to keep a continuous supply of tomatoes until after Thanksgiving by harvesting them at various stages of maturity just after the first light frost and keeping them in a room where temperatures remain at 55° to 60°F (13° to 16°C). The autumn here is somewhat milder than in some other areas at our latitude (47° north), but in many sections of the northern United States and southern Canada, gardens can produce vegetables until late October and early November (see "Estimating Planting Date" in Chapter 14).

Several vegetables can be forced indoors during the winter. If there is a corner of the basement where the temperature ranges between 50° and 70°F (10° and 21°C), rhubarb can be forced. For forcing, two-year-old or older rhubarb crowns should be dug before the ground freezes. To overcome their rest period, they must be left for at least six weeks where the average daily temperature is below 40°F (4°C). In most northern areas they can be brought inside in late December or early January. They should be covered with peat moss or shavings kept moist by frequent watering. Within a few weeks they will produce light pink, delicately flavored rhubarb petioles. Witloof chicory, sometimes called French or Belgian endive, as well as the common weed dandelion can be forced in the same way. They produce tender, light-colored shoots that are excellent additions to winter salads.

In areas that have winter sunshine, a number of kinds of vegetables can be grown in containers or window boxes next to a south or west window. Some of the better vegetables for window boxes are tomatoes, leaf lettuce, and onions. 'Patio' and 'Tiny Tim', small cherry tomatoes, and 'Bibb', a butterhead lettuce, are cultivars adapted to container growing. Annual and perennial herbs also can be grown in containers.

Storing vegetables is discussed in "Storing Horticultural Products" in Chapter 14. The home gardener should store a winter's supply of carrots, beets, potatoes, onions, and squash and should also consider canning or freezing surplus vegetables for winter use (see "Home Processing" in Chapter 14).

VEGETABLES AND HERBS IN THE LANDSCAPE

◆ ◆ ◆

If there is no room or no particular desire to have a separate vegetable garden, vegetables can be produced in the form of landscape plants. Early in the season a border of 'Ruby', 'Black-seeded Simpson', 'Salad Bowl', or some other leaf lettuce is attractive. The 'Tiny Tim' cherry tomato makes an ever-changing, interesting border throughout the summer and, from July until frost, supplies salad tomatoes. Peppers and eggplants also are ornamental and make excellent garden plants. Plants of bush squash and, in areas to which they are adapted, globe artichoke become unique specimens when planted in an ornamental garden. During several years a gardener friend has had an interesting ornamental display bed made up of 'Savoy' and 'Red Rock' cabbage. Alternate plants of red- and white-stalked Swiss chard offer beauty and greens throughout the summer if only the outer leaves are harvested for table use. New Zealand spinach and kale are frequently grown for their ornamental textural appearance. Vining squash, pumpkin, and cucumber can be used as annual ground cover plants, or their vines can be grown on a trellis, arbor, or fence as a temporary screen, provided the large fruit are given some type of support.

Herb gardens have traditionally been planted for ornamental as well as culinary uses. Perennial herbs make attractive plants for a rock garden. Landscape possibilities for specific herb species are mentioned in the section on herbs at the end of this chapter. A bed of asparagus can be a welcome vegetable in the spring when greenery is abundant and fresh vegetables are scarce and a green hedge through the summer and autumn when other vegetables are abundant and green foliage is less plentiful. 'Red Emperor' tulips and daffodils can be planted with asparagus to provide color in the spring. Later the asparagus ferns will hide the dying leaves while the bulbs are maturing. These are only a few examples of the numerous possible uses for vegetables and herbs in the ornamental landscape.

GROWING HINTS FOR VARIOUS VEGETABLES

◆ ◆ ◆

In the following discussion, vegetables are divided into three groups: perennials, cool-season annuals, and warm-season annuals. Individual annual vegetables are discussed primarily in the order of their ability to withstand cold temperatures, essentially the order in which they can be planted in the spring.

Perennial Vegetables

Perennial vegetables include asparagus, rhubarb, globe artichoke, horseradish, and Jerusalem artichoke. These crops all respond to large amounts of organic matter worked into the soil before they are planted. Land that is to grow horseradish should be manured in the autumn before being planted, because fresh manure causes misshapen roots (see "Fertilizing Garden Crops" in Chapter 14).

Asparagus (*Asparagus officinalis*). Asparagus has been used as a food in the Mideast and Europe for over three thousand years, and it was grown in this country in colonial days. It is one of the first vegetable crops to reach edible maturity in the spring. It is easily grown in most temperate areas of North America and is an excellent ornamental after the cutting season. Because there is considerable labor involved in its commercial harvest, it tends to be expensive when purchased; consequently, it is an ideal crop to produce in the garden or yard. Asparagus can grow in almost any soil, including those that are relatively alkaline, but it is best adapted to well-drained sandy loams. Crowns do poorly if planted where asparagus has previously been grown, probably because of soil-borne diseases. Growth and development are retarded by excess moisture.

Asparagus is usually grown from one-year-old crowns, although it can also be produced by direct seeding. For either direct seeding or producing crowns for transplanting, seed is sown as early in the spring as the soil can be worked. Radish seed is often mixed with the asparagus seed to mark the rows for initial cultivation. Radishes can be harvested shortly after the slow-germinating asparagus emerges from the soil. Plants should be thinned to 3 to 6 inches (8 to 15 cm) in the row if crowns for transplanting are being grown and 6 to 10 inches (15 to 25 cm) if the bed is being direct seeded.

Under average conditions the crowns will be large enough to set in the field the following spring. They should be dug before they begin to grow. The smallest crowns should be discarded, as they are genetically inferior and will produce a lower total yield during the life of the planting. One-year-old asparagus crowns can also be purchased.

Asparagus is planted by placing crowns on loose soil in the bottom of a trench 8 to 10 inches (20 to 25 cm) deep, in rows 4 to 6 feet (1 to 2 m) apart with 12 to 18 inches (30 to 45 cm) between crowns within the row. The trench should be filled gradually as the spears grow up through the soil. Weeds, of course, should be controlled, and care must be exercised when hoeing so that the asparagus shoots are not cut off.

Asparagus shoots or spears are not usually cut until two full years after the crowns are set out (three years after seeding), although it may be possible to harvest a meal or two the second year. Asparagus spears begin growing in March to late April, depending on the climate. In the past it was recommended that all spears, regardless of their diameter, be cut when they reached 8 to 10 inches (20 to 25 cm) in height. Cutting all spears is still the practice of commercial growers and also the advice usually given to home gardeners because a clean-cut field makes harvest, cultivation, and weed control easier. However, the vigor and subsequent yield of the planting will be increased if all spears pencil size and smaller are allowed to grow. Small spears are a sign of low food reserves, and cutting a small spear is likely to kill the segment of crown from which it was initiated by completely exhausting its food reserves. If the garden planting is small enough to make hoeing and hand weeding feasible, it makes sense to allow small spears, whenever initiated, to produce ferns and to photosynthesize to the end of the season. Spears should not be cut for longer than six weeks during the initial cutting season or longer than eight to ten weeks or one-third the growing season for asparagus, whichever is shorter, during subsequent years (Figure 12-3).

At the end of the cutting season, if all spears have been harvested, asparagus beds should receive a thorough cultivation to eliminate weeds and loosen the soil. All subsequent spears should be allowed to produce ferns and grow through the rest of the season until the ferns become yellow and die back with the cold weather of autumn. Asparagus requires only light fertilization. Because it does not wilt from lack of water, asparagus has the reputation of being drought tolerant. But this lack of drought symptoms is misleading. Although asparagus needs good drainage, it also requires a plentiful supply of moisture throughout the growing season for good yields the following year.

An asparagus cultivar resistant to rust called 'Mary Washington' was developed in the early 1900s, and most of the open-pollinated cultivars grown today are improved selections of 'Mary Washington'. Differences in growth habit of male and female plants as well as obligatory cross-pollination (asparagus is dioecious) results in extreme plant variability in open-pollinated cultivars. Using cell and tissue culture, asparagus hybridizers have been able to develop relatively uniform hybrid cultivars. Some of the new all-male cultivars ('Jersey Giant' is currently the best known) are especially productive and uniform.

A

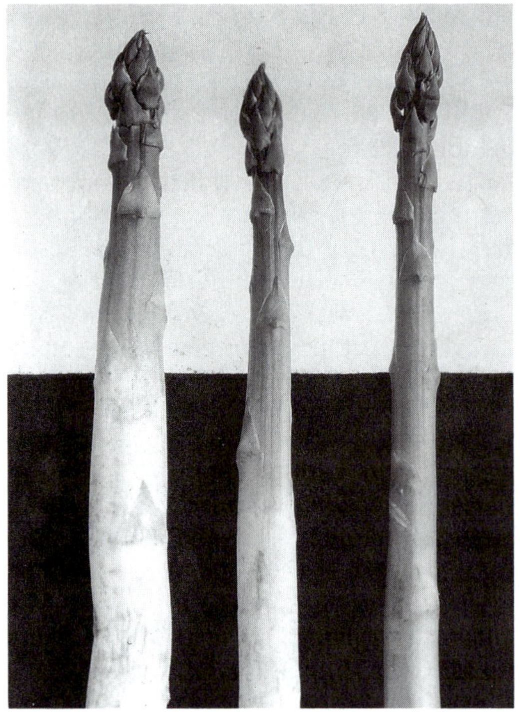

B

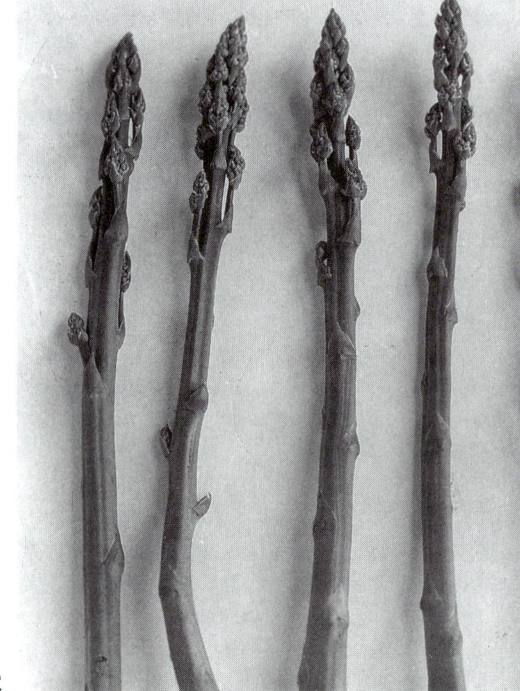

C

FIGURE 12-3 • Harvesting asparagus. An asparagus spear usually breaks off just above the section that is too tough to consume (A). Spears that have been broken off do not have the tough butts that are left on spears harvested in the usual way, by cutting below the surface. The tight asparagus spears (B) are at optimum harvest maturity. The loose, seedy spears (C) either are overmature or were formed when the temperature was high. (B and C courtesy of U.S. Department of Agriculture)

Seed and planting stock of these hybrids are expensive but, in most cases, well worth the cost, because an asparagus planting, if taken care of, should remain productive for eighteen to twenty-two years. Some plantings as old as fifty years are still being harvested. Twenty-five to thirty healthy asparagus plants should produce enough to supply fresh spears for a family of four plus some for freezing.

Rhubarb (*Rheum rhaponticum*). Rhubarb is grown for its thick leaf stalks or petioles, which are cooked into fruit sauce or made into pies. It is one of the most acidic of all vegetables, the juices having a pH of about 3.2. Like asparagus, the edible crop, which is produced early in the spring, is grown from food stored in the crown and roots during the previous growing season. Rhubarb is a hardy, easily grown, attractive plant and deserves a place in the gardens of families who live in the cooler parts of North America and who enjoy rhubarb sauce or rhubarb pie.

Rhubarb is usually propagated by crown divisions, although it can be grown from seed. Each division must have at least one bud or eye with as much root or rhizome as possible. Plants from seed take at least three years to mature, and they will not be true to the parent type.

In harvesting, which occurs over a six- to eight-week period, the stalks should be pulled, not cut. The petioles will not wilt as quickly if the broad leaves are removed from them immediately after they are pulled. Like asparagus, rhubarb needs an annual light application of fertilizer and occasional good irrigations during seasons and in areas where rainfall is limited. 'MacDonald' and 'Cherry Red' are two highly colored cultivars; 'Victoria', 'Linnaeus', and 'German Wine' are older standard sorts. Three good-sized plants will supply an average family.

Globe Artichoke (*Cynara scolymus*). Globe artichoke is another perennial grown commercially in this country in only a small area along the California coast near Monterey. It requires a cool growing season but cannot withstand freezing of the crown or roots. Its area of adaptation is relatively restricted. It grows quite well in the cooler parts of northern California and in the coastal valleys of Oregon and Washington. With some protection of the crown and roots during the winter, it can be grown in home gardens in other relatively cool areas of the country.

Globe artichoke is best propagated from crown divisions, which must contain an eye or bud and a piece of crown. The home gardener is not likely to find crown divisions for sale and so may have to produce globe artichoke plants from seed, which is entirely possible.

Plants should be spaced 3 to 4 feet (about 1 m) apart with 4 to 6 feet between rows. The artichoke plant is a thistle, and the artichokes of commerce are flower buds (Figure 12-4). To be edible they

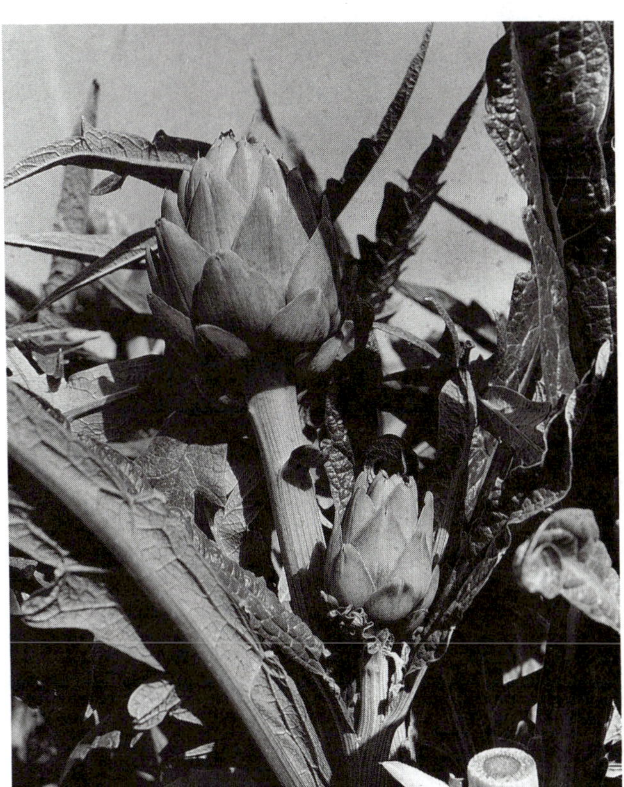

FIGURE 12-4 • The globe artichoke. (Courtesy of Grant Heilman)

must be harvested before they open. If this plant is being produced in areas with cold-winter weather, a 6- to 8-inch layer of leaves, straw, or sawdust should be placed over the crowns as soon as the first frosts come in order to protect the crowns through the winter.

Horseradish (*Armoracia rusticana*)**.** Horseradish is a perennial grown for its pungent root, which is used as a relish for meat and certain other foods. It is propagated from side roots, which can be purchased. Gardeners who wish to obtain their own planting stock can cut side roots 8 to 14 inches (20 to 35 cm) long, the diameter of a lead pencil or slightly larger, from established plants. Traditionally, the bottom of the planting stock is cut slanted and the top straight across, because otherwise the top and bottom cannot be distinguished. Root cuttings are planted 2 to 3 feet apart in the bottom of a 3- to 5-inch (8- to 13-cm) deep furrows. The basal end of the cutting should be pressed down so that it is slightly lower than the top.

For commercial production, horseradish roots are pruned twice during the season, initially when tops are 8 to 10 inches high and again six weeks later. The top of the root is carefully uncovered and lifted slightly without disturbing the lower roots. All but the main crown of leaves and all the upper branch roots are rubbed off before the root is recovered with soil. This procedure is necessary only if the main root is to be harvested each year. Commercially, the whole root is dug just before the soil freezes in late October or November. When horseradishes are grown in the home garden, enough side roots can be removed to supply the family, and the main plant left to grow for many years. The roots are hardy so can overwinter in the garden in most of North America. For convenient accessibility, roots can be dug and stored through the winter (see "Harvesting" and "Storing Horticultural Products" in Chapter 14).

Horseradish is prepared for the table by grating it into 4½ or 5 percent distilled or white wine vinegar. (It will turn dark if grated into ordinary cider vinegar.) The pickled product remains "hot" under refrigeration for a few weeks.

FIGURE 12-5 • Jerusalem artichoke. (Courtesy of Barry L. Runk/Grant Heilman)

Jerusalem Artichoke (*Helianthus tuberosus*)**.** Although the Jerusalem artichoke, a member of the sunflower family grown for its edible tuber, is propagated like the potato it is usually considered a perennial (Figure 12-5). The starch it contains is inulin, and formerly it was recommended as a food for diabetics. The tubers are relatively rough and do not store well out of the soil. It is propagated by tubers planted 18 to 20 inches (45 to 50 cm) apart in rows about 3 feet apart. Jerusalem artichokes can grow in relatively poor soil. Tubers are dug with a spade as needed, and where the soil does not freeze they can be harvested through the winter. They can be prepared for eating in the same ways that potatoes are prepared. Tubers normally do not freeze, and the Jerusalem artichoke can become a weed if small tubers are scattered through the garden with cultivating equipment.

Cool-Season Annual Vegetables

The cool-season annuals can be grown throughout the summer in the northern states and along the Pacific Coast from central California northward. Many of them are spring, fall, or winter crops in other parts of the country. A number of them are botanically biennials, but because the edible portion is produced the first year, they are grown in the garden as annuals.

Even though all of these vegetables are classified as cool-season crops, their response to temperature varies somewhat. For example, radishes, lettuce, peas, and spinach will produce an acceptable crop only if the weather is cool during their entire growing period. Onions must be planted early if a large bulb is to be produced, but they grow quite well in areas where the summer climate is relatively hot. Carrots and beets produce the best-quality crop where temperatures during the growing season average between 60° and 70°F (16° and 21°C) but can grow under a wide range of environmental conditions.

All of the cool-season crops except potatoes can withstand some frost; potatoes are vulnerable to injury by temperatures even slightly below freezing. The general recommendation is to plant cool-season crops as soon in the spring as the ground can be worked.

Peas (*Pisum sativum*). Peas are grown extensively in home gardens and are one of the more important processing crops, but few are marketed fresh anymore. They produce a quality product only when the weather is cool, but in most areas they do not grow well as a fall crop.

Pea plants are vines in growth habit. The short types grow to a height of 18 to 24 inches (40 to 60 cm), and the pole or climbing peas will reach 8 or 9 feet (2½ to 3 m) in height. The shorter vine type are the most popular today. Because in most areas peas must be planted as early in the spring as possible to mature before hot weather occurs, it is desirable to treat the seed with fungicide to protect it against decay. Peas can be grown in soil types ranging from light sandy loam to heavy clay. Pea seeds are relatively large and fairly easy to plant. In gardens they should be spaced in rows 2 to 3 feet (⅔ to 1 m) apart and 1½ to 2 inches (4 to 5 cm) apart in the row, and they should be planted 1 to 2 inches (2½ to 5 cm) deep. Peas should be harvested while green and tender and, if possible, during the cool early morning hours. They lose quality rapidly either as they become overmature on the vine or if they are left unrefrigerated for any period of time after they are harvested (Figure 12-6).

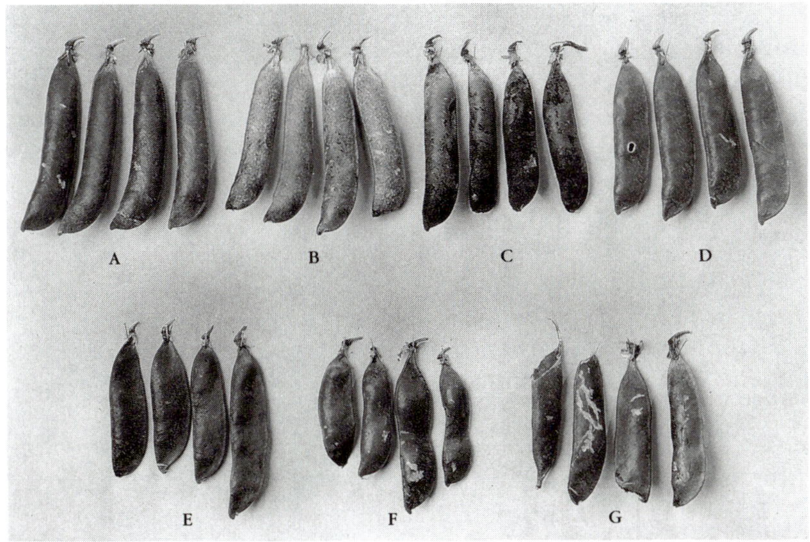

FIGURE 12-6 • Peas at various stages of maturity: (A) Well-filled pods at optimum maturity; (B) overmature pods; (C) pods damaged by pressure or friction, peas still edible; (D) undermature pods; (E) unfilled flat pods; (F) partially filled pods, two or fewer seeds; and (G) broken pods. F and G resulted from faulty fertilization.

The so-called edible-podded, sugar, or snow peas of past-generation gardens and the more recent snap or sugar snap peas do not have a tough membrane at the inner surface of the pod. Most sugar pea cultivars produce large flat pods that are harvested before the peas in them have enlarged. They were used first in this country by northern European or Asian immigrants but now are widely popular. Snap peas produce pods similar in shape to ordinary garden peas. The pods can be consumed from the time they first form until the green peas reach edible maturity, or the peas can be removed from the pods when they are at the edible stage of development. To prepare the pods of either type for cooking or for processing, both ends, along with any attached fibrous strings, are pulled from the pods.

Numerous cultivars of standard-type peas are on the market. Local garden advisers are in the best position to make recommendations. Cultivars that retain their bright green color when frozen have been developed for the processing industry, but these tend to turn a dull copper color when canned. Other cultivars listed in catalogs as canning peas will be the more preferred light green when canned. Both types have good flavor, and both are satisfactory for the home garden. 'Oregon Sugar Pod' is an excellent sugar pea. 'Sugar Snap', the original snap pea cultivar, requires a trellis for good growth. More recent cultivars do not, but most of the newer ones also do not yield as well as does the original.

Spinach (*Spinacia oleracea*). Spinach is the most important of the greens or potherb crops. There are two types, the cool-season or broad-leaf, and the warm-season or New Zealand spinach (*Tetragonia expansa*).

Broad-leaf spinach is seeded where it is to mature and is grown during the cool spring and fall months in the north and during the fall, winter, and spring in southern areas where winters are not severe. It develops seed stalks when days become long. In colder areas where winter temperatures remain above 0°F (−18°C), spinach can be seeded in the late fall to winter over and develop an earlier spring crop. The earliest harvest of spinach can be a thinning operation with well-placed plants left to grow larger. With later harvesting the plants are cut close to the surface of the ground (Figure 12-7).

New Zealand spinach may be direct seeded in place, or the plants may be transplanted. The seed tends to be impervious to water, and filing a notch in it will hasten its rapid germination. Only the tender leaves and young side shoots are used. These can be harvested and cooked like regular spinach at any time during the summer. New Zealand spinach is injured at temperatures below freezing.

Chard (*Beta vulgaris*). Chard is a leaf beet. Its planting and care are similar to those of spinach,

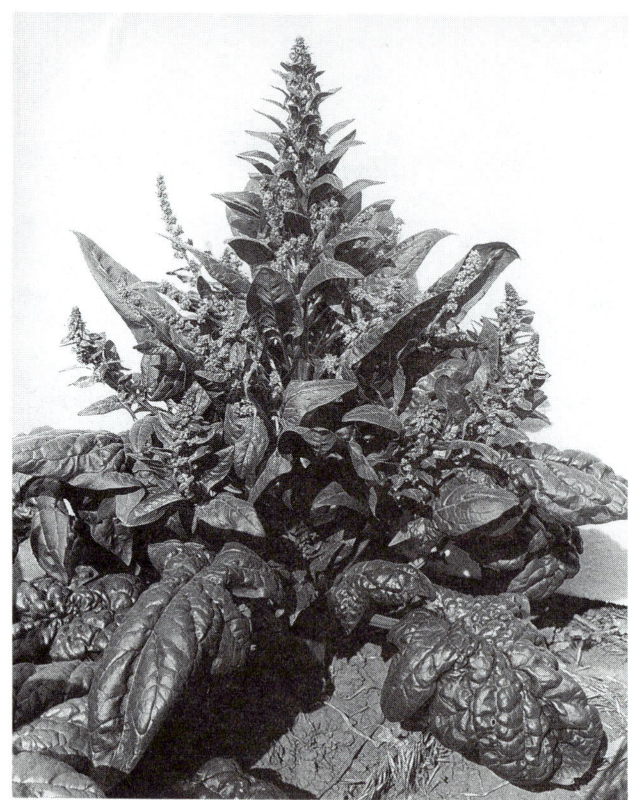

FIGURE 12-7 • Spinach. Spinach bolts to seed as a result of long days and high temperature.

and the leaves and petioles can be cooked to provide a potherb similar to spinach. It should be harvested so that the growing point is not destroyed. This allows the plant to continue producing all summer and can be done by removing the outer leaves, leaving the inner ones to expand for later harvests.

Root Crops. Root crops include radishes, turnips, rutabagas, beets, carrots, and sweet potatoes. All except sweet potatoes are cool-season crops that can be planted very early in the spring. All are herbaceous biennials except radishes, which are annuals, and sweet potatoes, which are perennials grown as annuals. Cultural practices are similar for all except for sweet potatoes, which are discussed under warm-season vegetable crops. All but sweet potatoes are grown from true seed, and all are popular home vegetable garden crops. All of the cool-season root crops can be grown in any good loamy soil but will produce better shaped roots if the soil is loose and friable. They can be planted in rows spaced as close as 12 inches (30 cm) apart. Rutabagas, turnips, beets, and carrots all will form undesirable seed stalks if they are subjected to several weeks of cool temperatures after the roots have begun to enlarge.

There are two types of radishes (*Rhaphanus sativus*). The ones universally available at grocery stores and most commonly grown by home gardeners are annuals that grow only during cool weather and mature in four to six weeks. The so-called biennial, winter, or storage radishes, including the 'Daikon' or oriental pickling radish, are planted in summer, harvested in autumn, and stored for winter use. These have long been popular in east Asia and are now being grown commercially for domestic consumption and export in the Pacific Northwest (Figure 12-8).

The short-season radishes can be planted early in the spring in the north and during the winter in the south. For successive harvests, radish seed should be planted each ten to fourteen days. Seed of fall or winter radishes can be sown from June through July. Fall-season plantings of the annual short-season cultivars can be made from August into September. The short-season types can be thinned by pulling those that are large enough to use. The larger summer and winter types should be thinned to 2 to 4 inches (5 to 10 cm) apart. Harvesting should begin as soon as the roots reach edible size. The quick-maturing cultivars must be used at once, because they soon age to become tough and pithy. The winter and fall cultivars remain edible much longer, and winter radishes can be used for several months with proper storage.

FIGURE 12-8 • Radishes. Size comparison of fall- or oriental-type ('Daikon') radish (right) with the common spring-grown ('Comet' and 'Icicle') radish (left).

Insects and diseases that attack radishes vary with locality, so local recommendations for pest control should be followed. The cabbage maggot, the larva of a small fly, is an almost universal pest of all vegetables that, like radishes, belong to the mustard family. The row in which radishes, turnips, and rutabagas are seeded usually must be caged to prevent flies from laying their eggs, or it must be treated with an insecticide if edible roots are to be grown.

Both turnips (*Brassica rapa*) and rutabagas (*Brassica napobrassica*) are essentially cool-season crops, although rutabagas can withstand some heat and drought. Because turnips are relatively quick maturing, they are grown as spring and fall crops in the north and as a winter crop in the south. Rutabagas require four to six weeks longer to mature than do turnips. Both do best in deep rich loams. Both crops are grown from seed and planted where they are to mature. After the plants are well established, they should be thinned to stand 3 to 6 inches (8 to 15 cm) apart in a row. (See the information on root maggots in the discussion of radishes.)

Turnips are used as greens or potherbs or as roots. For greens they are pulled before roots have enlarged. If their roots are to be used, young turnips are harvested when these roots reach a diameter of 2 to 3 inches (5 to 8 cm); if the roots grow too large, they become strong flavored and stringy. The best rutabagas for table use are 4 or 5 inches (10 to 13 cm) in diameter. When either of these crops is to be stored, the tops should be removed. Storage at 32°F (0°C) and about 95 percent relative humidity is best. Rutabagas can be stored through the winter.

Beets (*Beta vulgaris*) are direct seeded. Thinning is always necessary, no matter how evenly the seed has been spaced, because the so-called seeds are actually fruits or seed balls containing more than one embryo. Thinnings may be cooked as a potherb—beet greens—which many people prefer to spinach. The final spacing in the row should be from 3 to 4 inches. Final thinning can be delayed until small beets are large enough for table use.

Beets are of best quality (i.e., with uniform color and a sweet flavor) when they are grown with an average daily temperature that does not exceed 70° to 72°F (21° to 22°C). They are not normally subject to many disease or insect pests. In some irrigated areas of the West they cannot be grown because of curly top, a virus disease spread by the beet leafhopper that affects many kinds of vegetables.

The roots should be harvested when they reach a diameter of about 1½ inches. The leaves are cut off approximately a half-inch (1¼ cm) above the crown. The taproot and peeling are not removed until after the beet is cooked. Any cut or injury to the root permits excessive juicing out in the cooking water. Beets can be wrapped in foil and baked like potatoes. They are also popular as pickles.

Beets can be stored for a period of time at 32°F at 95 percent relative humidity. 'Detroit Dark-Red' and 'Crosby Egyptian' are two of the more popular cultivars. Orange-colored cultivars have recently been developed and are quite popular with home gardeners. They have a delicious flavor and do not juice out or stain as much as do red beets.

The per-capita consumption of carrots (*Daucus carota*) has increased steadily over the past fifty years since the discovery of their dietary importance. They are an especially good source of vitamin A and also contain appreciable amounts of several of the B vitamins. Of all the root crops, carrots are probably the most susceptible to misshapen roots. Heavy soils can be made more amenable for growing carrots by adding organic matter to them. An ample supply of moisture is required while the seed is germinating and the seedlings are starting their growth. It is difficult to obtain a good stand during hot weather. Because carrot seed is small, it is difficult to plant by hand, and a salt shaker makes a convenient planting tool if a regular seeder is not available.

The easiest way to thin garden carrots is to pull the largest for table use as soon as they become large enough to eat. Pulling the larger roots allows the smaller ones to enlarge to edible size. An old screwdriver is a convenient tool for digging and separating the larger roots with minimal disturbance of the smaller plants that are to remain.

Carrots have the best shape and quality when grown at temperatures between about 55° and 75°F (13° to 24°C). At lower temperatures the shape tends to be longer, and at higher temperatures it is blunt (Figure 12-9). Carrot roots develop less color and consequently less vitamin A at either high or low temperatures. Carrots can be held in storage for as long as six months if the humidity is high and the temperature is under 40°F (4°C) (see "Storing Horticultural Products" in Chapter 14).

Many cultivars of carrots are available; however, they belong mostly to four different types (Figure 12-10). The extremely long carrots are the 'Imperator' type popular in grocery stores. 'Chantenay' and 'Danvers Half Long' are pointed, half-long types of high quality. Commercially these cultivars are used for processing. 'Nantes' is one of the highest-quality cultivars. Although it is too brittle to market well and is too small for processing, it is excellent for the home garden. 'Oxheart' is a very short, stubby type, fairly low in quality. It should be grown only where soils are too heavy to produce good-quality roots of longer cultivars.

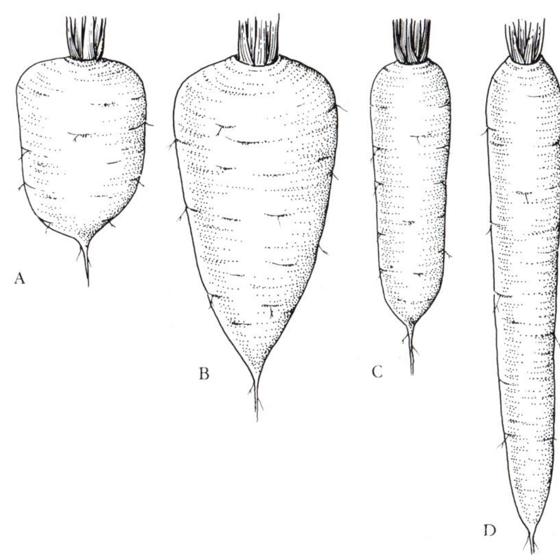

FIGURE 12-10 • Root shape of carrot cultivars: (A) 'Oxheart', (B) 'Chantenay' or 'Danvers', (C) 'Nantes', and (D) 'Imperator'.

FIGURE 12-9 • Misshapen carrot roots. Adding fresh manure to the garden was once thought to be responsible for the branching or "second growth" of carrots; however, branching seems to occur about as frequently in gardens grown without any added organic matter as in those heavily manured (see also Figure 6-5).

Salad Crops. A number of vegetable crops, grown primarily for the consumption of their uncooked leaves or petioles, are classed as salad crops. Only two, celery and lettuce, are important commercially; and only one, lettuce, is grown extensively in home gardens. Other salad crops that could have a place in the home garden are cress, endive, and Witloof chicory (also known as French or Belgian endive).

Cress (*Nasturtium officinale*), sometimes referred to as watercress, is frequently gathered from the wild in this country, but it is a common garden crop in England, where it is grown on extensive acreages. It requires a steady supply of water and probably has a place in only a few specialized home gardens.

Both endive (*Cichorium endivia*) and Witloof chicory (*Cichorium intybus*) require about the same growing conditions as does lettuce. The plants of both crops should be thinned to about 3 to 6 inches apart. Endive is sometimes covered with two boards arranged as an inverted trough over the row, which blanches the green color from it and reduces the amount of bitterness. Although Witloof chicory leaves can be used for salads, the crop is more often grown to maturity; then roots are dried and ground and can be used as a coffee substitute. More frequently, Witloof chicory is used for winter forcing (described earlier in this chapter). The roots are dug late in the fall before the ground freezes and are stored under cool, moist conditions until time for forcing.

Lettuce (*Lactuca sativa*) is the most extensively grown and most important of all salad crops. All cultivars thrive best in cool weather with an abundant supply of moisture. Most lettuce cultivars become bitter and go to seed in hot weather. Lettuce can be grown in all kinds of soil, but it requires high amounts of nitrogen. Lettuce is an excellent home garden crop because large amounts can be grown on a few square feet of ground. Plantings should be made approximately two weeks apart in the early spring for late spring and early summer harvest and starting again in July or August for autumn harvest. Summer crops of lettuce are possible in some cool coastal areas and mountain valleys of the West and in the far north.

There are two types of lettuce: leaf and head (Figure 12-11). Leaf lettuce forms a loose, open cluster of leaves; head lettuce forms a solid mass of tightly compressed leaves. Because it is easier to grow, leaf lettuce is generally preferred for home gardens, although there is no reason that gardeners cannot produce high-quality head lettuce. For earliest maturity, head lettuce can be seeded indoors about six weeks before it is to be transplanted. Later crops and leaf types are usually seeded where the plants are to mature. In the South the seed may be planted in the fall. With direct field seeding, the seeds are drilled in rows from 12 to 18 inches (30 to 45 cm) apart. Lettuce can be thinned by pulling surplus plants to use in salads. Head lettuce will not form good heads unless it is thinned to 8 to 15 inches (20 to 38 cm) apart.

Leaf lettuce may be harvested at any stage of growth before the plants send up seed stalks. Head lettuce is harvested when the heads are solid but before any sign of seed-stalk development appears. If a surplus of head lettuce is produced, it can be held in the refrigerator for as long as three weeks.

Head lettuce can be classified into three groups. The crisp types are most important commercially, and strains of the 'Great Lakes' and 'New York' cultivars are the ones most widely adapted to home gardens. Butterhead cultivars used to be available only in gourmet restaurants because the main cultivar, 'Bibb,' was best adapted to greenhouse growing and, as a consequence, was very expensive. Today butterhead cultivars such as 'Buttercrunch', 'Summer Bibb', and 'Big Boston' can be grown easily in home gardens. Cos or romaine lettuce forms loose elongated heads. It is somewhat resistant to heat. 'Paris White Cos' is a popular cultivar.

Because it requires somewhat specialized growing conditions, celery (*Apium graveolens*) has never been an important home garden crop. Celery needs a uniform moisture supply to develop good quality; hollow and stringy stalks may develop after sudden dry periods. It is best adapted to areas that have a relatively long, fairly cool, damp growing season and can withstand some freezing temperature if properly matured.

Celery seed is very small, so it is planted under glass or in specially prepared beds. The seeds should be covered lightly with sand or sandy soil. Four to five weeks after seeding the plants are transplanted or thinned to stand 1½ to 2 inches apart. Five to seven weeks later the plants can be set into the garden; thus 10 to 16 weeks are required from seeding to transplanting. Rows in the garden should be from 3 to 6 feet apart and the plants spaced 6 to 8 inches in the row.

A

B

C

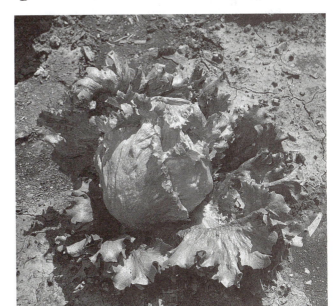

FIGURE 12-11 • Three types of lettuce. (A) 'Oakleaf' (leaf) lettuce, (B) 'Bibb' (butterhead) lettuce, and (C) 'Iceberg' (crisphead) lettuce. (Courtesy of Grant Heilman)

Because its root system is shallow, celery requires heavy fertilization and frequent irrigation. It should have a light to medium irrigation approximately each three to four days during periods of warm dry weather. Celery is subject to a deficiency of several minor elements, especially boron, which causes cracking of the petioles. This condition can be prevented or cured by soil amendments of borax or boric acid.

When it is harvested, the celery plant is cut at or just below the crown, lifted, trimmed, and washed. When necessary, celery can be held for several months in cold storage. Celery is a biennial that will initiate premature seed-stalk development if the young plants are subjected to long periods of cool temperatures.

Some cultivars of celery are grown for their roots (root celery is called celeriac), and others for the herbal qualities of their leaves and seeds. In areas where the growing season is too short or too warm to yield good-quality salad celery, celery can be grown as an herb, with its leaves and petioles used to impart a celery flavor to soups, salads, and casseroles.

Crucifer or Cole Crops. The cole crops include cabbage, cauliflower, and broccoli, which are well known in this country; and brussels sprouts, kohlrabi, kale, and collards, which are not so well known. Collards and kale are essentially leaf cabbages, and their culture is similar to that of cabbage. Both are frequently grown to add texture to an ornamental planting, and there are a number of highly colored ornamental kale cultivars.

The culture of brussels sprouts (*Brassica oleracea* var. *gemmifera*) is similar to that of cabbage except that brussels sprouts require a relatively long growing season. They are often grown from transplants. The sprouts, which resemble small cabbages, form in the leaf nodes on an elongated stem (Figure 12-12). Sprouts mature from the bottom up and can be harvested for table use or freezing whenever they become solid. 'Jade Cross' is earlier than most standard brussels sprouts cultivars and is an excellent choice for home gardens.

FIGURE 12-12 • Brussels sprouts. Sprouts at the bottom of the stem mature earliest and can be harvested whenever they become solid. (Courtesy of Ferry-Morse Seed Co.)

Of all vegetables, the cole crops are perhaps the ones most subject to attack by insects and diseases. They should not be grown in soils that have a history of nematodes or club root. Club root is a soil-borne disease characterized by extreme swelling of the roots into which the pathogen has entered. It can be controlled to some extent by raising the pH of the soil. In most sections of the country a grower of cole crops must be prepared to treat the soil for cabbage maggots and periodically to dust or spray to control cabbage loopers, cabbageworms, and aphids.

Cabbage (*Brassica oleracea* var. *capitata*) can be grown on almost any soil, but sandy loams are the most desirable for both early and late crops. This crop requires an ample but not excessive supply of moisture for maximum development; a lack of water causes premature heading. Cabbage is a cool-season crop but is not as susceptible to damage by high temperatures as are cauliflower, peas, or lettuce. It can be produced through the growing season in areas where the average July temperature is under 74°F (23°C). In the South it can be grown from late fall through the winter and early spring. For a continuous supply three crops should be grown. Seed for the first crop is planted under glass six or eight weeks before the plants are to be set in the field. The second crop is direct seeded during early spring to mature in July and August. Seed for the late crop, planted in open ground from the middle of June to early July, will produce a crop that should mature in October and can be stored. For gardeners who have difficulty getting their planting gear together more than once during the year, planting both early- and late-maturing cultivars will also extend the season during which cabbage is available from the garden.

Cabbage should not be harvested until the heads are solid. In earlier times, cabbage was stored for several months by pulling the whole plant and placing it in a pit or root cellar where the humidity was high and the temperature about 40°F. Cut heads can be stored for several weeks in an ordinary refrigerator.

Cabbage cultivars vary widely. Some have pointed heads and others have round or flat heads. Leaf color may be green to red or purple. The leaves themselves may be smooth or wrinkled. (Cultivars with wrinkled leaves are called savoy cabbage.) Cultivars mature at different seasons of the year. The most important early types are 'Golden Acre' and 'Copenhagen Market'. 'Marion Market' is a round-headed, early cultivar that is resistant to a root disease called cabbage yellows. Midseason cultivars include 'Glory of Enkhuizen', 'All Seasons', and two yellows-resistant varieties —'Wisconsin Globe' and 'Wisconsin All Seasons'. Two late cultivars are 'Danish Ballhead' and 'Wisconsin Hollander' (yellows resistant).

The culture of cauliflower (*Brassica oleracea* var. *botrytis*) is similar to that of cabbage except that cauliflower cannot withstand warm temperatures. In warm-season areas the spring crop should be transplanted or direct seeded as early as possible. The fall crop can be started in July to mature during the cool days of late fall. During hot weather the heads or curds may be discolored or fail to form. To grow them pure white, heads are blanched by tying the outside leaves over the head as it begins to form to exclude light from the curd.

Depending on weather and cultivar, the heads should be ready to harvest one or two weeks after they start to develop. The head is cut off at the juncture of the head and leaves. 'Imperial' and 'Snowball' are two of the most popular cultivars. However, there are dozens of strains, and the strain of seed used may be more important than the cultivar. Follow local recommendations in selecting cauliflower cultivars. 'Early Purple Head', a cultivar that resembles a cross between broccoli and cauliflower, produces good heads at somewhat warmer temperatures without blanching.

Broccoli (*Brassica oleracea* var. *italica*) is grown in much the same manner as is cauliflower except that the numerous heads are not blanched and that broccoli can withstand a little more summer heat than can cauliflower. Heads are formed both terminally and laterally. The first or terminal crop should be cut when the heads have reached their maximum diameter but before they begin to separate. From 4 to 6 inches of stem is included with the head. Succeeding cuts come from small individual heads that develop on shoots from leaf axils after the first head has been cut. 'Italian Green Sprouting' is a spring cultivar widely grown, and 'Waltham 29' is one of many cultivars planted in summer for fall harvest. Some recently introduced early hybrids, many of which were developed in Japan, appear to be excellent for the home garden; 'Green Comet' is one that seems widely adapted.

Kohlrabi (*Brassica oleracea* var. *caulorapa*) is a vegetable popular in Europe that deserves more attention from home gardeners in this country. The edible portion is an above-ground enlargement of the stem that resembles a very mild turnip in shape and flavor. Raw, it is an excellent addition to a relish plate, but it also can be boiled or stuffed and baked. The planting, culture, and harvest of kohlrabi are similar to those of turnips. Because the edible portion is above the ground and also because it seems to have some resistance, kohlrabi is not as susceptible to cabbage maggot damage as are the other crops of the Cruciferae family.

Bulbs. Onions are the most widely grown of the bulb crops. The others—garlic, chives, shallots, and leeks—are produced in smaller amounts. Garlic (*Allium sativum*) is grown from thickened bulb scales called cloves. In mild climate areas where it is grown commercially, it is planted in the autumn. In the home garden it should be planted as early in the spring as possible and harvested when the top has died down and the plant is completely mature. Chives (*Allium schoenoprasum*) is discussed with herbs at the end of this chapter. Leeks (*Allium porrum*) and shallots (*Allium ascalonicum*) produce succulent, thick-necked plants with a mild onionlike flavor. They are used as cooked vegetables, in salads, and as flavoring for soups and stews. Planting early in the spring enables both to be produced in most parts of the United States and Canada.

Onions (*Allium cepa*) is one of the hardiest of all vegetable crops. Commercially they are usually grown from seed sown as soon as the frost is out of the ground. In the South and Far West they can be planted in the fall. For home gardens, onions may be grown from seed, sets, or transplants. Sets are very small onions produced by thick seeding on poor ground late in the season the previous year. Crowding and late planting check the growth of the sets, so they ripen prematurely. Planted out in the spring, these sets complete their growth and develop into larger bulbs.

Onions are grown in rows spaced from 12 to 24 inches apart. If large bulbs are desired, they should be thinned to 3 to 6 inches apart in the row. The thinnings can be used to flavor salads or as scallions. Onion sets and transplants are spaced at planting time. Onion tops do not produce much shade, and onions have shallow root systems, so this vegetable cannot compete with weeds and requires heavy fertilization as well as frequent irrigation during dry periods. Onions grown to be used as green or bunch onions, also called scallions, can be pulled as soon as they are large enough for use. Onions for storage must be ripe when harvested. Maturity is indicated by softening of the neck tissues, falling over of the tops, and dying of the roots. At this time the bulbs enlarge rapidly. They are ready to harvest when the tops of about 70 percent of the plants have fallen. The onions should then be pulled and, if the weather is sunny, left in the garden until the tops and outer scales are completely dry. This procedure is called **curing.** The tops can be spread over the bulbs to prevent sunburn. After the bulbs have cured, they are topped. Ideal storage conditions are 32°F with 70 percent humidity, but onions also keep relatively well in a cool, dry basement or attic.

Onions come in three distinct colors: yellow, white, or red. They also differ in shape, some being round, some flat, and some long. Some have a very pungent flavor, and others are mild. Many of the onions grown today are hybrids. Because bulbing is initiated by day length, most onion cultivars are not widely adapted. Almost any cultivar produces satisfactory green bunch onions, but the grower who wishes to produce large bulbs should seek local cultivar recommendations.

Potato (*Solanum tuberosum*). All of the vegetable crops discussed so far can be hardened to withstand some freezing and, as a consequence, can be planted about as soon as the ground can be worked. By contrast, potatoes, although they are a cool-season crop, cannot withstand frost. Nevertheless, because the potato seed piece contains more stored food than does the seed of most crops, potatoes can regenerate their top growth in case the initial sprouts are damaged by frost or other adverse conditions. Furthermore, because potatoes require about two weeks from time of planting to emergence, they can be planted two to three weeks before the last frost is expected in the area.

Potatoes are grown as annuals and are almost always propagated vegetatively by means of whole or cut tubers called seed pieces. In regions with cool summers, some cultivars occasionally produce true seed in tomatolike fruits. In some areas of the tropics where disease-free tubers for planting stock are not available or are prohibitively expensive, true seeds harvested from cultivars carefully selected for genetic uniformity are used to produce commercial potato crops. Occasionally such seeds are advertised in North American seed catalogs; however, the potatoes grown from them mature later and are less uniform than are those grown from seed tubers (Figure 12-13).

The tuber that is the edible part of the plant is a thickened underground storage stem with scale-like leaves and buds or eyes. Potatoes are subject to numerous diseases, many of which can be carried in the seed piece. For this reason gardeners should use certified seed that has been grown in cool regions where virus disease spread is minimal and under carefully regulated conditions enforced by inspection. Potatoes sold in the spring for table use should never be used for seed. Not only are they likely to harbor disease organisms, but they also are likely to have been treated to prevent them from sprouting.

When being prepared for planting, seed tubers can be left whole or cut into two or more pieces (sets), depending on their size. Sets of 1 to 1½ ounces (30 to 40 g) produce better plants than do smaller sets, especially if growing conditions are unfavorable. Commercial growers sometimes cut their seed several weeks in advance and then permit them to **suberize** (form a protective layer resembling a new skin over the cut surface). Suberization requires high humidity, oxygen, and a temperature of 60° to 70°F. For the home garden it is probably best to cut the tubers just before they are to be planted and allow them to suberize in the soil, where conditions for suberization are usually good.

Planting depths vary. For the early crop, the seed is covered with 2 to 3 inches of soil. The late crop on heavy soils should be planted about 3 inches deep. On lighter soils the depth of planting should be increased so that the soil around the seed piece stays moist. Most potatoes are planted in rows 2½ to 4 feet (⅔ to 1¼ m) apart, with 9 to 14 inches (23 to 35 cm) between seed pieces in the rows. They may be planted with a hoe or shovel or with special planting equipment. Optimal summer growing temperatures are around 60° to 70°F. Potatoes do well in areas where the nights are relatively cool, and tuber shape and quality of long-tubered cultivars are best when soil temperatures are cool and uniform. As mentioned in Chapter 6, frequent light irrigation is recommended, especially during warm periods. Under these conditions, irrigation is more important for cooling the soil than for providing moisture. Fertilizer needs vary with different soils. Potatoes use large amounts of nitrogen and potassium (see "Fertilizing Garden Crops" in Chapter 14). Cul-

FIGURE 12-13 • Potato plants propagated sexually from true seed instead of asexually from sections of the tuber are likely to produce tubers that are extremely variable in shape, skin color, and quality, as shown above. Of the two types of potatoes available in large quantities in North America, the long russet (Idaho) type tubers are considered to have the best quality for French frying, baking, and mashing because of their mealy texture. The round red- or white-skinned types are considered best for boiling and pan frying, because they are not so likely to "cook to pieces." Differences in quality probably have as much to do with the climate under which the potatoes are grown (russets with irrigation in the low humidity of the West and round types in the more humid East and Midwest) as with cultivar differences. Recently cultivars having yellow flesh, a type that has long been popular in Europe, and cultivars having purple flesh, as well as other unusual kinds, have become available in North America. All of these can be grown easily by home gardeners. (Courtesy of David Cavagnaro/Peter Arnold, Inc.)

tivation should be shallow but sufficient to control weeds and keep the soil loose and open. Soil should be worked up around the plants when they are 6 to 8 inches high; this helps keep tubers covered and prevents their becoming exposed and sunburned.

Early potatoes are frequently dug before the tubers are mature. Sometimes home gardeners can space plants close enough so that every other plant can be removed to provide small tubers for early eating. Plants that appear diseased can also be dug for early tubers, as the tubers on these kinds of plants never grow very large anyway. For winter storage, potatoes should be dug when they are fully mature and after the vines have died and the skin no longer scuffs from the tuber. If tubers need to be harvested for storage before the vines die, they can be matured by cutting or pulling the vines 10 days to 2 weeks before tubers are dug. Potatoes should be stored at a temperature of 38° to 40°F (3° to 4°C) if possible, with a relative humidity of about 90 percent. If potatoes are stored at temperatures below 38°F, the starches in the tuber will change to sugar and the potato will become unappetizingly sweet. If the storage temperature is above 42° to 45°F (6° to 7°C), potatoes are likely to sprout as soon as their rest period is broken in early January. The long-tubered 'Russet Burbank', developed in the 1800s, is the cultivar most often grown for processing in North America. 'Red Pontiac' and 'Kennebec' are two popular round cultivars. The round cultivars are easiest to grow in home gardens because their moisture requirements are not so exacting (Figure 12-13).

Warm-Season Vegetables Grown as Annuals

The vegetables described in this section require warm temperatures for germination and grow best in areas with a relatively warm summer. Melons and sweet potatoes, especially, cannot be matured without a long, hot growing season. The introduction of new, early cultivars of most of the other warm-season vegetables permits them to mature in most parts of the United States and many areas of Canada. None of these crops should be planted until the danger of frost is past. Earlier production is possible with transplanting. Solanaceous crops transplant easily with bare roots, but the cucurbits and sweet corn will not survive if their roots are disturbed, and therefore they must be grown in some kind of transplantable container if they are to be transplanted.

Beans and Sweet Corn. Snap beans (*Phaseolus vulgaris*) and lima beans (*Phaseolus lunatus*) are among the most popular home garden vegetables. They grow well in most parts of the country and mature in 55 to 70 days. They can be planted so that they are ready to eat during most of the summer and fall and can be enjoyed fresh from the garden or as a canned or frozen product. Bean plants vary in growth habit from dwarf bush to long, viny pole types, and the pods can be green, yellow (wax), or purple. Dry beans of various kinds and most green shell beans, which are stripped from the pods like peas while still tender, belong to the same species as snap beans but require a somewhat longer growing season.

Because the seed must push large cotyledons through the soil (Figure 4-3), planting should be no deeper than necessary to get the seed to moisture. In most areas this is from 1 to 2 inches (2½ to 5 cm). Pole beans can be planted in rows and trained on wires or strings or planted in hills approximately 18 inches (45 cm) apart. Rows should be 2 to 4 feet (about ⅔ to 1½ m) apart, depending on the method of cultivation. A pole is placed in each hill for the plant to climb, and the tops of four poles are often tied together for stability. When cultivation is by hand or with a garden tractor, rows of bush beans may be spaced as close as 18 to 20 inches (45 to 50 cm), but when field equipment is used, row spacing should be at least 30 inches (75 cm). Plants should be spaced 2 to 3 inches (5 to 8 cm) in the row. In many areas only disease-resistant cultivars can be produced, and cultivars resistant to rust, mosaic, curly top, and bacterial blight are available. Although beans are legumes, their capability for nitrogen fixation is not great, therefore all types generally require fertilization. They are susceptible to moisture stress and will not form pods if moisture is deficient at the time of bloom.

Lima beans require a somewhat longer growing season than do snap beans; their seed requires slightly warmer soil for germination; and they are even more susceptible to blossom abscission if the weather becomes hot and dry when they are blooming. Otherwise, their growing requirements are similar to those of snap beans. Lima beans also grow on either bush or vining plants. Lima bean cultivars are either large seeded or small seeded.

Snap beans should be picked before the pods reach full size and when the seeds are beginning to form. Beans should not be picked when the plants have moisture on the leaves because handling the plants when they are moist tends to spread rust, a fungus disease. Green shell and lima beans should be picked as soon as the bean seeds have attained full size but before they turn white or harden. Shelling is easier if the pods are allowed to wilt for a few hours. Dry beans are harvested as soon as most of the pods are fully mature and have turned yellow. They must be harvested before the lower pods begin to shatter. Small plantings of dry beans are pulled, but bean harvesters that cut the vines just below the ground are used for large quantities. Where weather is dry, beans are allowed to dry in the field. Small quantities can be threshed in the age-old way by tromping the beans from the vines on a canvas and tossing them in the air to permit wind to blow away the chaff. Various-sized combines and threshing machines are available for larger plantings.

Sweet corn (*Zea mays*) is a warm-season crop native to the Western Hemisphere. It is a vegetable in which the highest quality can be appreciated only when it is cooked freshly harvested from the home garden. Sweet corn can succeed on any soil that is suitable for general crop production. If early maturity is wanted, a warm, sandy soil is desirable. Higher yields are produced on heavier soils more retentive of moisture and minerals. Corn needs more nitrogen that most other vegetables (see "Fertilizing Garden Crops" in Chapter 14).

Corn is planted in hills spaced 2 to 3½ feet (about ⅔ to 1 m) apart or in drills 10 to 12 inches (25 to 30 cm) apart in rows spaced 2½ to 4 feet apart. In most soils the seed should be planted 1 to 2 inches deep. Cultivation should be shallow but sufficient to control weeds. Adequate moisture is essential, especially during and shortly after silking. If either fertilizer or moisture is likely to be limiting, plants should be spaced no closer than 3×3 feet (1×1 m).

Breeders have made drastic changes in sweet corn cultivars during the past fifty years. During the 1940s and 1950s, open-pollinated cultivars were almost completely replaced by F_1 hybrids. During the past twenty years, cultivars with genes that enhance sweetness and with other genes that delay the conversion of starch to sugar have become commonplace in the sweet corn industry. Because the terminology referring to these new developments varies from company to company, deciding which cultivar to purchase can be confusing. "Normal sugary" or "(su)" and "standard hybrid" are the terms currently used to refer to the hybrid cultivars that have been grown for the past forty years. "Sugary enhanced" or "(se)," "E.H.," and "sweet gene hybrids" are some of the terms used to designate cultivars with one or more genes that increase the levels of sugars and/or delay the conversion of sugar to starch. All of the kinds described so far have normal seed weight, are relatively easy to germinate, and do not need to be isolated from other sweet corn cultivars. Cultivars designated as "supersweets," "extra sweets," "supersweet hybrid," "(sh)," and "(SH)" have the "shrunken kernel" gene, which greatly enhances their sweetness and still further delays the conversion of starch to sugar. The supersweets have a very lightweight shriveled seed that requires a higher temperature and more uniform moisture in order to germinate. The seed of the supersweets should be treated with a fungicide and should not be planted in the spring until soil temperatures have reached 65°F (18°C). Also, to produce optimum quality they need to be isolated from sweet corn cultivars that are likely to bloom at the same time and are not listed as "supersweet." "Bicolor" sweet corn cultivars produce a mixture of yellow and white kernels on each ear. They are popular because most have inherited the tender pericarp of their white-kerneled ancestors.

Sweet corn is a highly perishable crop. Even with the newer cultivars in which conversion is slower, once the sugar content reaches its maximum, it immediately begins to change to starch. Thus it is necessary that corn be picked at the right stage of maturity for highest quality. For best fresh-from-the garden eating quality or for freezing, this is the "milk" stage, when a thin milky juice exudes from kernels pressed with a thumbnail. For canning, sweet corn should be harvested at the slightly more mature "cream" stage.

Because corn loses its quality rapidly after harvest, especially when temperatures are high, it should be picked and husked as close to mealtime as possible. For home processing, it should, if possible, be harvested while temperatures are cool early in the morning and canned or frozen immediately. Sweet corn should always be refrigerated if storage is necessary.

The larvae of the corn earworm and the European corn borer are the most obvious pests of sweet corn. The corn earworm (Figure 12-14) is found almost universally in gardens and fields in North America. The female moth lays her eggs at the top of the developing ear, and the black-striped, tan, or green caterpillars that hatch from those eggs eat their way among the upper kernels, leaving feces and other debris (see Table 14-26). The European corn borer hatches in the soil and burrows its way into the interior of the stalk all the way to the tassel and ear. These burrows, usually invisible from outside, frequently break the stalk and/or damage the kernels.

FIGURE 12-14 • The corn earworm is difficult to control, and so most gardeners choose simply to clip off the damaged part of the ear tip. (Courtesy of U.S. Department of Agriculture)

Solanaceous Fruit Crops. Solanaceous fruits include tomatoes, peppers, and eggplant. Tomatoes and peppers are of tropical American origin; eggplant has been used as a food in India and Southeast Asia for millennia. All three of these vegetables are warm-season crops that should not be planted in the field until all danger of frost is past. Often the seed is planted under glass or in specially prepared beds six to eight weeks before field planting (see "Propagating Plants from Seed" in Chapter 14). In regions with short growing seasons, the seed for home gardens can be started indoors ten to twelve weeks before the plants are to be set out; these plants may be blooming before they are transplanted.

The tomato (*Lycopersicon esculentum*) ranks second among the vegetable crops grown in the United States, surpassed only by the potato. Its fruits are high in vitamins A, B_1, B_2, and C, even though they contain over 94 percent water. Tomatoes are grown by all types of vegetable gardeners on all types of soil for both fresh consumption and canning. For early maturity and in areas where the frost-free season is short, lighter, warmer soils are desirable. More fertile loam, silt loam, and clay loam soils produce greater yields.

The growth habit of tomato plants may be indeterminate or determinate. **Indeterminate** cultivars can continue growth indefinitely. Normally a blossom cluster is produced at every third node, and the terminal bud continues vegetative growth and elongation. Until recently the principal commercial cultivars were indeterminate. In contrast, the growth of **determinate** cultivars eventually terminates in a flower cluster, and shoot elongation stops. This gives a "self-pruning" or "self-topping" habit of growth. Determinate cultivars are usually earlier than indeterminate ones and are especially desirable where the growing season is cool or short. Determinate cultivars also tend to ripen their fruit more nearly at one time and are the type produced commercially for mechanized harvest. F_1 hybrid cultivars are available, but the seed is expensive, and F_1 hybrid tomatoes are usually only slightly superior to standard cultivars.

A field spacing of 2 to 4 × 4 feet is common for most indeterminate tomato cultivars when they are set out as transplants. Determinate cultivars can be transplanted as close as 12 inches in the row. Where the growing season is long, tomatoes, especially determinate cultivars, may be direct seeded. With direct seeding the plants may be spaced as close as 6 inches apart with little effect on fruit size. Direct seeding and close spacing are practiced in irrigated areas of the West where curly top (western yellow blight) prevents the growing of transplanted tomatoes. Direct-seeded tomatoes, especially if they are left closely spaced, do not seem to be as susceptible as are transplanted ones to insect-spread diseases.

Staking is practical mainly with indeterminate cultivars. With staking, plants are usually spaced 1 to 2 feet apart in the row. A stout stake 5 to 7 feet (1½ to 2 m) long is placed next to each plant, and the plant is allowed to grow to a single stem by pinching of the vegetative shoots from the axils of the leaves. The plant must be tied to the stake with string or specially purchased ties (Figure 12-15). Staked tomatoes produce mature fruit about a week earlier than do those not staked, and staking also reduces fruit rot, which frequently occurs when fruit comes in contact with wet soil. However, staking sometimes increases the amount of sunburn and cracking.

The tomato is a deep-rooted crop that can withstand considerable drought. Where irrigation is necessary, the entire root zone, which may ex-

FIGURE 12-15 • Staked tomatoes.

tend to a depth of 6 to 10 feet (2 to 3 m), should be thoroughly soaked.

Tomato fruits are tender and highly perishable, so they must be picked and handled carefully. If necessary they may be picked at the mature green stage, when cream-colored streaks show in the green ground color at the blossom end, the seeds have become firm, and the skin is still tough. The characteristic red color will develop in fruits picked at the mature green stage, and they will ripen to fairly good quality. Fruits picked after some red color is evident will color well and will develop flavor almost equal to that of tomatoes picked when fully ripe. To ripen with full color, the fruit, whether on or off the vine, must be kept at a temperature between about 55° and 85°F (13° to 30°C). For home use, tomatoes should be picked after they have started to turn red, but before they have become soft. Fruit picked at this stage has good quality and is less subject to predators, insects, and diseases than is fruit left on the vine until it is so ripe that it begins to soften.

A number of diseases and insects affect tomatoes; however, there are many areas of the country where a tomato crop can be grown with no more pest control than picking off an occasional hornworm. In humid areas and areas with high rainfall, late blight (*Phytophthora infestans*) and early blight (*Alternaria solani*) may require weekly preventive sprayings with a copper or zinc fungicide. Tomato hornworms and corn earworms occasionally may be serious enough to require spraying. Attending carefully to sanitation, washing hands frequently, and refraining from smoking when handling tomato plants help reduce the incidence of tobacco mosaic virus, which can be serious, especially with greenhouse and staked tomato plantings. Close spacing and direct seeding are necessary in some areas of the West to prevent the spread of curly top.

Several types of garden peppers (*Capsicum frutescens*) are grown. The large-fruited or bell types usually are mild and sweet; the small-fruited cultivars are pungent and distinctly hot. A small-fruited type is grown for decorative purposes. The 'Cayenne' or red pepper of commerce is the ground dried fruit of a small pungent cultivar. Paprika is made from the dried fruits of certain mild, sweet cultivars. Both sweet and hot peppers are distinct from commercial black pepper, which is made from the fruit of a tropical vine, *Piper nigrum* (Figure 1-6).

Pepper culture is similar to culture of tomatoes. Plants are spaced 1 to 2 feet in rows 3 feet apart. Peppers thrive best in warm climates with long growing seasons. They are definitely a warm-season crop and should not be planted in the open until all danger of frost is past. Peppers require at least 8 weeks from seeding for the production of optimum-sized transplants. Peppers can also be direct seeded after the soil has warmed to 65°F (18°C).

The stage of maturity at which the fruit is harvested depends on use. Sweet bell peppers usually are picked when they are of mature size but still green in color, although red fruits are in demand for some uses. Hot peppers are harvested when ripe and then are dried or pickled. Local recommendations should be followed when selecting cultivars. Curly top and other virus diseases can be serious, but in many areas peppers are free of pests. Peppers have the highest amount of ascorbic acid per pound of any common food, several times as much as do citrus fruits. New early cultivars that can grow in most sections of the country are becoming available, and they deserve a place in the garden of anyone who likes peppers.

The eggplant (*Solanum melongena*) is an important food crop in Asia and the Middle East but is not grown extensively in North America. Yet almost everyone who has tried east Asian or Middle Eastern eggplant casseroles is enthusiastic about this most delicious and versatile vegetable. It requires a warm season, and plants should not be set in the field until after the last spring frosts. The fruits of those cultivars most popular in North America are round, fairly large, and purple or white in color. The east Asian cultivars are mostly elongate (Figure 12-16). The skin is smooth and shiny, and the seeds are embedded in the flesh.

FIGURE 12-16 • Eggplant fruits. Common round (left) and long Japanese eggplant fruits.

The soil for eggplants should be fertile, and a moderate but continuous supply of moisture is essential. The Colorado potato beetle, a common pest of all solanaceous crops, is attracted from potatoes and tomatoes to eggplants when the latter are available.

The fruits are harvested as soon as the grower feels that they are large enough but before they are fully mature. They are cut with the calyx and a short piece of stem left intact. The fruit of the 'Black Beauty', the most commonly grown cultivar, can grow large, and if left on the vine too long, it will become tough and bitter. Some of the newer F_1 hybrids are of better quality and earlier maturity.

Vine Crops or Cucurbits. Included in the vine crops are watermelons, muskmelons and related melons, pumpkins, squash, and cucumbers. All of them are warm-season crops that cannot be hardened to withstand frosts. Vine crops require bees for pollination. If bees are not present because of weather or other factors, hand pollination is possible by rubbing the anthers of a male flower onto the pistil of a female one. The female flower has an enlarged ovary (small fruit) under the open flower (Figure 3-2).

Cucumber (*Cucumis sativus*) plants generally are monoecious in flowering habit; that is, the flowers are either pistillate or staminate, with both borne on the same plant. The plants are killed by even light freezes, but because their crop matures in 60 to 70 days, they can be grown in nearly all sections of the United States and southern Canada. They are adapted to most soils.

Cucumbers are planted either in hills spaced 2 to 4 feet (.6 to 1.2 m) apart or in drills with the rows 4 to 6 feet apart (1.2 to 2 m). Six or seven seeds per hill are planted, and the plants eventually are thinned to two or three per hill. When seeded in drills or rows, the plants should be thinned to stand 12 to 18 inches (30 to 45 cm) apart.

Two types of cucumbers, pickling and slicing, are grown in North America. Pickling cultivars produce large numbers of fruit that are smaller in size and more blunt in shape and generally have black spines. Slicing cultivars have fewer, larger, more elongate fruits and usually white spines. Pickling cultivars that produce only female blooms, and consequently large numbers of small fruits, have been developed. They require the interplanting of a few standard monoecious plants for pollination. Seeds of the standard cucumbers are included in the all-female cucumber seed packets. For areas where bitterness is a problem, nonbitter cultivars of slicing cucumbers are now available. They are sometimes called 'burpless', a name coined by the Burpee Seed Company for one of the earliest nonbitter cultivars.

Cucumbers are harvested on the basis of size rather than age. For slicing they are picked when 6 to 10 inches (15 to 25 cm) long; for pickling when they reach 2½ to 6 inches in length. Because healthy vines will continue to produce fruit for several months, cucumber pickers should be careful not to injure the vines. Spraying may be necessary to control striped and spotted cucumber beetles. Planting resistant cultivars is the best control for mildew.

The muskmelons, or cantaloupes, and honeydew melons (*Cucumis melo*) all are grouped under the general term melon. For satisfactory production, a frost-free season of at least 120 warm or hot days is needed. A few early cultivars such as 'Minnesota Midget' have been developed for northern gardens, but even these require bright sunlight and high temperatures to develop high sugar content and good flavor. The use of plastic mulch and transplanting considerably shorten the growing period required (see Chapter 5). Melons can be grown on a wide variety of soils. Because they are quite drought resistant and require high temperatures, they are especially well adapted to sandy loams. Melon plants are tender, and the seeds cannot germinate at soil temperatures lower than 70°F (21°C). Planting times, spacing, and seeding methods are the same as those for cucumbers.

To develop maximum quality, melons must ripen on the vine. However, for commercial handling and shipment, the stage of maturity at which they are picked depends on how they are to be marketed. Most melon cultivars form an abscission layer at maturity, and the stem loosens from the fruit. When the stem is nearly loose, the melon is said to be at the "full-slip" stage (Figure 12-17). For shipping the fruits are picked when less mature, or at the "half-slip" stage. Other indexes of maturity are softening at the blossom end, a change in color of the base of the pedicel from green to waxy, aroma, taste, and a change in ground color. Melons with a piece of stem attached were harvested when too immature and will be of inferior quality. A solid melon greenish yellow in color with a strong cantaloupe aroma usually has the best flavor.

'Hales Best' and its various strains are important shipping melons. Other good cultivars are 'Iroquois', 'Honey Rock', and 'Hearts of Gold'.

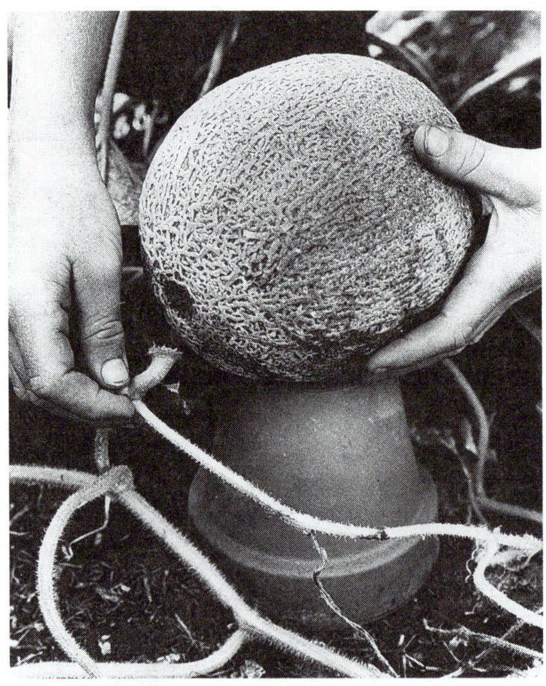

FIGURE 12-17 • Muskmelons at the "full slip" stage. (Courtesy of U.S. Department of Agriculture)

'Honey Dew', 'Honey Ball', and 'Casaba' are grown in the West. 'Minnesota Midget' and 'Chipman Lake Champlain' often ripen where the season is too cold for other cultivars. 'Burpee Early Hybrid Crenshaw' is a delicious home garden cultivar that deserves a trial in areas where standard melon cultivars mature.

Watermelons (*Citrullus vulgaris*) require a long, hot growing season and are most in demand during midsummer. For this reason they are grown mainly in the South, although short-season cultivars can be grown in many areas of the country. Soil selection, planting, and cultural methods are similar to those used for muskmelons and cucumbers. Watermelons are usually planted five or six seeds per hill and thinned to two or three plants. Each hill requires 80 to 100 square feet (7½ to 9 m²) of space.

There are no completely reliable maturity guides for watermelons. The size of the fruit and the color of the rind are not reliable indexes. Some of the more useful indications are the sound that the melon makes when rapped or thumped, the color of the spot where the melon rested on the ground, and the condition of the tendril where the fruit stem is attached. When cool, ripe melons make a dull sound when thumped; the ground spot takes on a yellowish tinge as the fruit matures; and the tendril begins to dry up.

Some of the leading cultivars are 'Tom Watson', 'Klondike', 'Dixie Queen', 'Kleckley Sweet', 'Charleston Gray', and 'Stone Mountain'. Short-season cultivars, including 'New Hampshire Midget' and 'Rhode Island Red', are usually of low quality. 'Summer Festival' is a recently developed early melon, slightly smaller than the standard size, with relatively good quality.

Pumpkins (*Cucurbita pepo*) and squash (various *Cucurbita* species), both native to the Americas, have similar cultural requirements. They are sensitive to frost but are also somewhat more tolerant of cool, moist environments than are melons or cucumbers. They need a warm, but not extremely hot, growing season. The summer types, which bear early and are eaten when immature, can be grown in about 60 days; the winter types need a long growing season. Most cultivars tolerate partial shade and are sometimes interplanted with corn.

Any fertile soil rich in humus but not excessively acid or alkaline can be used. The seeds do not germinate in cold soils but do not require as much heat as melons, so they can be planted when the soil temperature has reached 60°F. The seeds usually are planted six or seven to a hill and later are thinned to a stand of two or three plants. The flowers are monoecious. Hills of vining types should have about 60 square feet (6 m^2) of space and bush types need 30 to 40 square feet (3 to 4 m^2).

Cultivation should be shallow and frequent enough to control weeds. When plants cover the ground, they will shade out most weeds and cultivation can stop. Summer squash are harvested at any stage before the seeds begin to mature and the rind to harden—small for slicing, a little larger if they are to be stuffed. Winter types are picked when fully ripe and after the rind has hardened. Winter squash and pumpkins can be stored for 2 or 3 months at temperatures around 45° to 50°F (7° to 10°C) and a relative humidity below 75 percent. They should be harvested before they are injured by frost.

Summer squash cultivars include 'Crookneck', 'Straightneck', 'Scallop' or 'Patty Pan', 'Cocozelle', 'Zucchini', and 'Vegetable Marrow'. The leading winter squash cultivars are 'Hubbard', 'Table Queen' or 'Acorn', 'Golden Delicious', 'Buttercup', and 'Butternut'. Because squash have better cooking quality and even make better "pumpkin pie" than pumpkins do, pumpkins are grown more for fall decoration than for eating. 'Jack-O-Lantern' and 'Connecticut Field' are two decorative pumpkin cultivars; 'New England Sugar' is a small pie pumpkin. 'Jack Be Little' and 'Munchkin' are two cultivars of "miniature pumpkins" used mostly for decoration.

Okra (*Hibiscus esculentus*). Okra is a favorite vegetable of the old South, where it is cooked in many ways and is an ingredient of many southern dishes. Most northerners have tasted it only in commercially canned gumbo soups, however, and have not developed a liking for okra prepared in other ways. Okra requires about the same growing temperature as does winter squash. In northern areas the plants tend to be relatively small, but they do bloom and produce fruit. The edible portion is a fruit or pod that must be harvested while immature. Plants tend to be spiny, and gloves are needed to harvest the pods. 'Clemson Spineless' and 'Dwarf Green Long Pod' are two commonly grown cultivars.

Sweet Potatoes (*Ipomoea batatas*). Of all the vegetables commonly grown in the United States, sweet potatoes require the longest, hottest summer growing conditions. The use of plastic tents to permit the earlier setting out of plants may enable growers in a few selected northern areas to produce sweet potatoes, but gardeners ordinarily do not plant sweet potatoes unless the July/August temperature in their area averages over 77°F (25°C).

The sweet potato is related to morning glory, and the sweet potato of commerce is an enlarged fleshy storage root capable of initiating leaf and shoot buds. It is propagated by placing fleshy roots in moist sand or similar media. The sprouts that grow from the fleshy roots are removed when they reach 6 to 7 inches in height (see Figure 4-6) and are used as transplants. Several crops of sprouts can be produced by a single sweet potato if the season is long enough to permit several plantings. In the South sweet potatoes are often grown from vine cuttings secured from an early planting of slips. About half the butt end of a 15-inch (38-cm) piece of vine is buried. For planting in the garden, sprout transplants or vine cuttings are spaced at 12 to 18 inches in rows 3 to 5 feet in width.

Sweet potatoes are of two types—the moist, orange fleshed and the dry, yellow fleshed. 'Nemagold', 'Red Nancy', and 'Porto Rico' are three of the moist-fleshed cultivars; 'Big Stem Jersey' and 'Yellow Jersey' are two dry-fleshed cultivars.

Sweet potatoes should be dug when soil is dry. Slight frost will not damage the roots if they are well covered with soil, but they should not be left in the soil after frosts begin to occur frequently, as they are subject to chill damage. Bruising should be avoided. If they are to be stored, sweet potatoes should be cured for a few weeks at a relatively high temperature and humidity; 85°F (29°C) and 85 percent humidity are ideal. They should be stored in a warm, dry room.

GROWING TEMPERATE-ZONE HERBS

◆ ◆ ◆

A definitive terminology for spices and herbs is still lacking, but spices are generally considered to include flavoring compounds obtained from woody tropical plants, whereas herbs include flavoring compounds from mostly either tropical or temperate herbaceous plants. The discussion that follows includes only temperate-zone herbs.

Following a period during the early twentieth century when few herbs were used in American cooking, there is now renewed interest in these flavor ingredients. Two of undoubtedly many reasons for the increased use of herbs are that (1) international dishes calling for herbs are becoming more popular and (2) herbs are being used by health-conscious North Americans as a partial substitute for table salt.

Herbs can, of course, be purchased, but often only in the dried form. Even if fresh herbs can be bought, their flavor and aroma, like those of supermarket vegetables, cannot compare with the flavor and aroma of herbs picked directly from the garden.

Like any other horticultural planting, an herb garden needs to be planned. A few plants of any one herb will be enough for most families. The kinds that are used frequently should, of course, be included in the planting; however, a few plants of unfamiliar kinds can be grown without much time, effort, or money and may introduce the

FIGURE 12-18 • Herbs can be used to create a useful and attractive ornamental garden. (Courtesy of Grant Heilman)

grower to a new taste treat. Annual herbs are most conveniently grown in a row in the vegetable garden, but most are attractive enough to be used by themselves or mixed with annual flowers in a flower bed. Biennial herbs must be planted where they can survive the two years they need to mature. Most perennial herbs are also very attractive ornamentals and can be planted by themselves in an ornamental herb garden, mixed with other perennials in an ornamental garden, or in rows with the perennial vegetables (Figure 12-18).

The culture of herbs is similar to the culture of vegetables and flowers. Most, except for the mints and tarragon, can be grown from seed, and the familiar kinds can be purchased wherever garden seeds are sold. Seed of less familiar herbs can be obtained from farm seed suppliers or catalog seed companies. Most herbs can be seeded directly into the field; however, planting with transplants will result in earlier harvest. Perhaps more important, the use of transplants can save several weeks of hand weeding around tiny struggling seedlings; most herbs cannot compete with weeds. Transplants are especially valuable for propagating the slow-to-establish perennial and biennial species.

HARVESTING HERBS

Herbs can be harvested for immediate use any time they are of edible size and quality. For some kinds this may be for only a few weeks during the summer, but for others it may be during most of the year, both summer and winter. The method of harvesting herbs for storage depends on the part of the plant being used. Herbs grown for their seed, like caraway, dill, or anise, are subject to shattering. They are cut when nearly mature and laid on plastic or canvas to dry. If there are only a few plants, the seed can be knocked or tromped from them, and the chaff can be removed by repeatedly pouring the seed from one container to another while a light breeze is blowing. Larger quantities can be threshed in a combine adapted to vegetable or specialty crop seed harvest.

Leafy herbs to be marketed fresh or stored in the refrigerator can be cut and packed in the field or indoors. They should be tied into bundles of the size desired and kept as cool as possible until they are used. For drying, individual plants of leafy herbs should be separated and placed on paper towels or newspaper in a warm, dry, shady location where they will not get wet. Bright sun can destroy their delicate flavor as well as bleach out their color, and an unanticipated rain can greatly reduce quality.

A FEW OF THE MORE POPULAR TEMPERATE-ZONE HERBS

The following is by no means a listing of all the species used as herbs but includes mainly those used for flavoring that are relatively easy to grow in gardens. The between-row spacing is based on plant size and will need to be adjusted if the grower is using machinery to cultivate them.

Perennial Herbs (Figure 12-19)

Chives *(Allium schoenoprasum).* Tufts of chives with their grasslike leaves and purple cushion flowers are attractive ornamentals for rock or perennial herb gardens.

Uses: Young leaves add a mild onion flavor and garnish to spring salads, casseroles, soups, and omelets.

Propagation: Transplants, seed, division of old clumps.

Spacing: 8 to 12 × 24 inches (20 to 30 × 60 cm).

Time of Planting: Fall in mild climates and early spring.

A B C D

FIGURE 12-19 • Examples of perennial herbs: (A) oregano, (B) rosemary, (C) lovage, and (D) spearmint. (A, courtesy of S. Rannels/Grant Heilman; B through D, courtesy of Grant Heilman)

Culture: No special requirements; clumps should be divided each three to four years.

Harvest: Fresh leaves are cut and bunched for use. The best-quality and most popular chives are harvested before bloom during early to mid-spring.

Tarragon (*Artemesia dracunculus*). This is a vigorous pungent herb widely grown in Europe for its oil. Related to sagebrush.

Uses: The mild anise or licorice flavor adds zest to salads and other foods. Flavor component can be steeped in vinegar.

Propagation: Root or crown division.

Spacing: 1 × 3 feet (30 × 90 cm).

Time of Planting: Early spring.

Culture: Hardy; crowns should be lifted and divided every three years.

Harvest: The leaves and young shoots can be cut several times during the season to use fresh or to flavor vinegar. Drying should be rapid and away from light to prevent the leaves from turning dark.

Lavender (*Lavendula angustifolia* and other species). The various species and types of this aromatic European genus are dual-purpose herbs and low-growing ornamentals.

Uses: Dried flower spikes are used for flavoring desserts, for perfume, and sachets that repel moths. Many species and cultivars, including 'Hidcote', are popular as border-edging or ground-cover ornamentals.

Propagation: Seed, transplants, separation of established clumps.

Spacing: 15 × 30 inches (40 × 80 cm).

Time of Planting: Early spring.

Culture: Hardy, easily grown, needs good drainage.

Harvest: Blooming flower spikes are cut and dried out of the sun. Oil for perfume is extracted from the leaves and flowers.

Lemon Balm (*Melissa offinalis*). These 2-foot-high lemon-scented clumps provide contrast in an ornamental garden, in addition to their use as herbs.

Uses: Leaves are used for herbal tea, and sprigs impart a lemony flavor to drinks. Oil from the leaves is used as a perfume.

Propagation: Transplants, seed, cuttings, crown division.

Spacing: 18 × 30 inches (45 × 80 cm).

Time of Planting: Early spring.

Culture: Can grow in poor soil; spreads from seed and can become weedy.

Harvest: Young tender shoots picked in the morning can be used fresh or dried.

Spearmint (*Mentha spicata*) and peppermint (*Mentha* x *piperita*). Bright green 2-foot spreading clumps of mint give a pleasant odor to the ornamental garden.

Uses: Sprigs are used for tea and other drinks and for making mint jelly; oil is used for flavoring candies, medicines, toothpastes, chewing gums, and the like.

Propagation: Underground runners from crown divisions are set into moist soil; stem cuttings can also be rooted.

Spacing: 2 × 3 feet (60 × 90 cm).

Time of Planting: Autumn (in warm climates) or early spring.

Culture: Should not be planted where tomatoes or potatoes have been grown because of mint's susceptibility to Verticillium wilt. Otherwise mints are hardy and do not require special care.

Harvest: Sprigs can be harvested at any time during the growing season. For oil, mint is cut shortly after it blooms.

Oregano (*Origanum vulgare*). Several types are available; the flowering types are often treated as annuals.

Uses: Pizza, spaghetti, and other Italian cooking; hamburgers, veal, seafood, chicken, eggs, cabbage, tomatoes.

Propagation: Crown divisions of nonflowering kinds. Transplants of flowering kinds—the seed is extremely small and requires a temperature of 68°F (20°C) to germinate. Can become invasive.

Spacing: 12 × 30 inches (30 × 80 cm).

Time of Planting: Spring. Eight to ten weeks are required to grow transplants; plant in the garden after the soil has warmed.

Culture: No special requirements; may need to have winter protection or be grown as an annual in very cold climates.

Harvest: Leaves can be used as needed. The best flavor of flowering oreganos develops after bloom. Nonflowering types have the best flavor in late spring. Stems (or whole plants of flowering kinds) are cut and dried indoors. Leaves are stripped from stems when fully dry and stored in airtight containers. Harvest no more than 40 percent of stems if plants are to be overwintered.

Rosemary (*Rosmarinus officinalis*). This herb forms a tender shrub with light blue flowers.

Uses: Narrow-leaved aromatic silvery leaves are used to flavor meats and Italian dishes. In warmer areas, this is a somewhat drought-resistant small ornamental bush.

Propagation: Seeds, transplants, crown divisions.

Spacing: 2 × 3 feet (30 × 90 cm).

Time of Planting: Spring.

Culture: Needs heavy winter protection in northern areas or can be wintered indoors in pots.

Harvest: Leaves and tender shoots can be stripped and used at any time. New-growth shoots are cut and dried, and the leaves are stripped from them and stored in sealed containers.

Sage (*Salvia officinalis*). Sage forms a two-foot-high, sprawling shrub.

Uses: One of the most common seasoning herbs for poultry, other meats, dressings, and gravies. Its gray leaves and blue flowers make this an attractive ornamental if dead stems are pruned frequently.

Propagation: Transplants, direct seeding, cuttings, crown divisions.

Spacing: 2 × 3 feet (60 × 90 cm).

Time of Planting: Early spring.

Culture: No special care. May need winter protection in the coldest regions.

Harvest: Shoots should be cut before the plant blooms. The leaves can be harvested at any time, even through winters that are not too severe. Six to eight inches can be cut from the sage plant twice during the growing season.

Thyme (*Thymus vulgaris*). Thyme is a low-growing, wiry shrub.

Uses: Widely used fresh or dried as a flavoring for meat and egg dishes. Cultivated for a medicinal oil in Europe; it is also an attractive ornamental ground cover.

Propagation: Transplants, direct seeding, crown division.

Spacing: 18 × 36 inches (45 × 90 cm).

Time of Planting: Spring.

Culture: Requires no special care.

Harvest: When flowering, 5 to 6 inches of the top should be cut back and spread out to dry thoroughly. Dried leaves are stripped from woody stems and stored in sealed containers. Fresh leaves can be stripped from the stems for use at any time of the year.

Biennial Herbs

Celery (*Apium graveolens*). See the section of this chapter on salad vegetables.

Uses: Seeds and leaves are used to flavor pickles, soups, dressings, and other foods in which a celery flavor is desired.

Propagation: Transplants, requiring about 12 weeks from seed.

Spacing: 6 × 36 inches (15 × 90 cm).

Time of Planting: Mid- to late spring.

Culture: Celery requires special care. Its roots are shallow, so fertilizer must be adequate and available near the root system. Celery must be watered often. A straw mulch or other protection may be required when celery is overwintered for seed production.

Harvest: Leaves and stems can be harvested at any time. Umbels are cut after most of the seeds have matured and are allowed to dry, usually outdoors, on plastic or canvas sheets from which shattered seeds can be collected. Seeds should be stored in tightly closed containers.

Caraway (*Carum carvi*). Caraway is a tall spreading herb with carrotlike leaves and is grown for its aromatic seed.

Uses: Seeds are used in baked products, potato salads, chip dips, and pork roasts.

Propagation: Seed, transplants.

Spacing: 24 × 36 inches (60 × 90 cm).

Time of Planting: Spring to August.

Culture: Growth is relatively slow during the first year, and weeds can be a problem. The plant flowers early in the second growing season and matures its seed by midsummer. Can become weedy if seeds are allowed to shatter in the field.

Harvest: Same as herb celery.

Herbs Grown as Annuals (Figure 12-20)

Dill (*Anethum graveolens*). This herb is grown for both its seeds and its leaves.

Uses: The major use of seeds and seed heads is to make dill pickles; dill leaves are finely chopped to flavor meats and fish. The leaves lose their flavor when dried, although the seeds do not. Dill oil is a widely used commercial flavoring compound.

Propagation: Direct seeding is reliable; dill is reported not to transplant easily, although we have routinely transplanted volunteer plants with no difficulty.

Spacing: 3 × 30 inches (8 × 80 cm).

Time of Planting: Late fall or early spring.

Culture: No special requirements; can be weedy if seeds are allowed to scatter.

Harvest: Leaves and flower heads can be harvested throughout the season. Seed heads should be cut when seed is almost dry but before it has shattered. Seed should be dried in shade and stored in tightly closed containers.

Coriander (*Coriandum sativum*). This is a dainty herb grown in large quantities in south Asia where its seeds are used in curries. Coriander leaves (cilantro) are often used in Mexican dishes.

Uses: The ⅛-inch-diameter dried fruits are used in confections, French dressing, sausage, and cottage cheese.

Propagation: Seed.

C

B

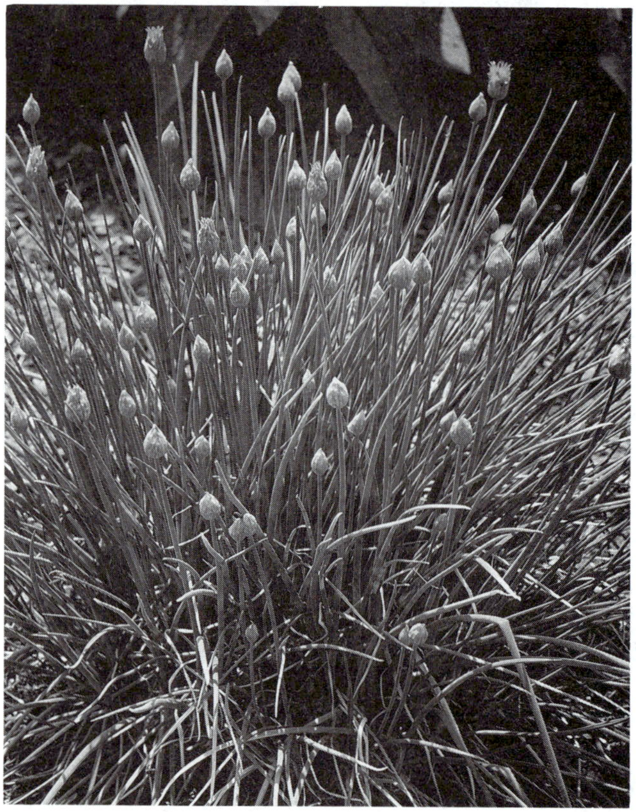

D

FIGURE 12-20 • Easy-to-grow annual herbs: (A) fennel, (B) dill, and (C) sweet basil (all annuals); and (D) chives (perennial). (A and D, courtesy S. Rannels/Grant Heilman; B and C, courtesy of Grant Heilman)

Spacing: 2 × 36 inches (5 × 60 cm).

Time of Planting: Late fall or early spring.

Culture: No special requirements.

Harvest: The plants should be cut after the fruits turn brown but before they shatter. The full flavor is not developed until the fruits are fully dry.

Florence Fennel (*Foeniculum dulce*) and Sweet Fennel (*Foeniculum officinalis*). Fennel seeds are known for their licorice flavor.

Uses: Fennel seed is used in breads, pastries, candies, and drinks; the leaves are used to flavor fish sauces and salads; and the broad stems are consumed raw or cooked as a vegetable. Cultivars developed for their fleshy roots are widely grown and used as a vegetable in the Middle East and some other parts of the world.

Propagation: Seed.

Spacing: 6 × 36 inches (15 × 90 cm).

Time of Planting: Early spring.

Culture: Very easily grown.

Harvest: The leaves and stems can be harvested whenever they are large enough. When the seeds turn brown, the plants should be cut and allowed to dry completely. The seed is threshed, cleaned, and stored in bags. Bitter fennel, *F. vulgare,* is a perennial used in much the same way as are other fennels.

Sweet Basil (*Ocimum basilicum*). This herb comes in several types and cultivars.

Uses: The leaves are used fresh or dried to flavor chicken, tomato dishes, casseroles, salads, eggs, and seafood.

Propagation: Seeds, transplants.

Spacing: 3 × 36 inches (8 × 90 cm).

Time of Planting: Spring after the danger of frost has passed.

Culture: Grows without special care.

Harvest: Basil must be harvested before the first frost, as freezing destroys the flavor compounds. The fresh leaves can be used at any time. When the plants begin to flower, they can be cut 6 to 8 inches (15 to 20 cm) above the ground and the tender shoots dried. The leaves and flowering tops are stripped from the coarse stems and stored in closed containers.

Sweet Marjoram (*Origanum marjorana*). This is one of the most popular garden herbs, a tender perennial grown as an annual.

Uses: Used in a wide variety of home cooking, including veal, liver, roast beef, egg dishes, soups, and spinach. Commercially, most is used in poultry and sausage seasonings. An oil extracted from the leaves is used in perfumes.

Propagation: Transplants, root cuttings, crown divisions.

Spacing: 8 × 24 inches (20 × 60 cm).

Time of Planting: Should be planted as early in the spring as possible so that plants will flower and produce seeds before frost.

Culture: Can be grown as a perennial in the South and along the West Coast. In cooler high-altitude areas, the season may be too short for this herb. No other special requirements.

Harvest: When they bloom, the plants should be cut back several inches and the leaves and flowering tops dried rapidly for future use. Fresh leaves can be used any time. Wild marjoram (*Origanum vulgare*) and pot marjoram (*Origanum onites*) are grown and used in the same way that sweet marjoram is, although they are not so popular with home gardeners because their flavor is not so delicate.

Parsley (*Petroselinum crispum*). Parsley is a biennial usually grown as an annual. Several types are available, including cultivars with flat and curled leaves and others with large edible roots.

Uses: Garnish for meat dishes and flavoring for salads, soups, and casseroles.

Propagation: Transplants, direct seeding; seeds slow to germinate.

Spacing: 4 × 18 inches (10 × 50 cm).

Time of Planting: Early spring.

Culture: Easily grown, hardy, widely adapted.

Harvest: Leaf quality is best during the first growing season. Parsley leaves can be harvested for table use into late fall and during the early spring of the second season. In areas where the winter is mild, harvest may be possible all winter. Commercially, the leaves are cut when they reach marketable size and are tied into bundles for marketing. Several harvests are possible. The leaves retain their flavor when dried.

Anise (*Pimpinella anisum*). Anise is a small annual herb about 2 feet high having a licorice flavor.

Uses: The leaves are used in apple and other salads and as a garnish. The seeds are used in confections such as cakes, cookies, and candies.

Propagation: Direct seeding; transplants have not grown well in our trials but have remained small and stunted.

Spacing: 4 × 24 inches (10 × 60 cm).

Time of Planting: Early spring.

Culture: Plants seem to be easily stunted by any kind of stress.

Harvest: Leaves can be harvested for fresh use throughout the summer. The fruiting umbels should be cut when seeds turn brown. The umbels should then be thoroughly dried and the seeds removed from them and stored in tightly closed containers.

Summer Savory (*Satureja hortensis*). This is a species of the mint family.

Uses: Mixes well with other herbs and spices. Leaves are used in soups, stuffings, sauces, egg dishes, potato and macaroni salad, and with snap beans.

Spacing: 4 × 30 inches (10 × 80 cm).

Propagation: Seeds, transplants, cuttings.

Time of Planting: Spring.

Culture: Grows well in a wide range of soils and climates.

Harvest: Tender leaves and stems may be used at any time. For drying, the leaves and stems are cut when the plant is in bud just before the blossoms open. They are tied in bundles and hung in a shaded place to dry. Winter savory (*Satureja montana*) is a perennial herb used in much the same way as is summer savory.

Selected References

Country Journal Editors. *The Country Journal Book of Vegetable Gardening.* Brattleboro, Vt.: Country Journal, 1983.

Crockett, J. U. *Crockett's Victory Garden.* Boston: Little, Brown, 1977.

Lorenz, O. A., and D. N. Maynard. *Knott's Handbook for Vegetable Growers.* 3rd ed. New York: Wiley, 1988.

National Gardening Association Staff. *Book of Cucumbers, Melons, and Squash; Book of Eggplant, Okra, and Peppers; Book of Lettuce and Greens; Book of Tomatoes.* New York: Random House, 1987.

Newcomb, D., and K. Newcomb. *The Complete Vegetable Gardener's Sourcebook.* Rev. ed. Englewood Cliffs, N.J.: Prentice-Hall, 1989.

Nonecke, I. L. *Vegetable Production.* New York: Van Nostrand Reinhold, 1989.

Ortho Books Editors. *All About Vegetables.* Rev. ed. San Francisco: Ortho Books, 1991.

Peirce, L. C. *Vegetables: Characteristics, Production and Marketing.* New York: Wiley, 1987.

Splittstoesser, W. E. *Vegetable Growing Handbook.* 2nd ed. Westport, Conn.: AVI, 1984.

CHAPTER

13

Growing Fruit

The appeal of high-quality fresh fruit is universal, and few foods are as popular or as nutritionally beneficial. Even so, the per-capita consumption of most kinds of fruit has been steadily declining in the United States. A major reason for this decline is that at its current price, fruit is considered by many people to be a luxury. No economical way has yet been found to mechanize the planting, the pruning, and especially the harvesting of most kinds of fruit grown for the fresh market. The packing and shipping of fruit require more hand labor than do the packing and shipping of other food products, and fruit needs special types of storage to ensure prime condition. As a consequence, fruit is costly to produce and expensive to purchase. Growing fruit as a hobby, therefore, is an excellent way to improve one's diet and at the same time lower the food bill.

Home gardeners who produce their own flowers and vegetables may not consider growing fruit because they think it requires too much space and too much specialized knowledge and equipment. Such thinking is not valid today. The many kinds of fruits that grow on herbaceous plants, lianas, and bushes take up little space. By replacing small flowering trees and ornamental shrubs with dwarf fruit trees and fruit-producing shrubs, gardeners can make their landscape provide both food and beauty. The 'Lodi' cultivar of apple on a dwarf rootstock displays almost the same show of blooms as a flowering crabapple and can produce a bonus of at least two boxes of apples in late July. Low-growing ornamentals or ground cover can be replaced by currant bushes that have attractive blooms during early spring, bright red berries and juice for jelly during summer, and, if all are not harvested, dried berries to attract birds during late fall and early winter. Brambles, such as the various kinds of raspberries and blackberries, make a pleasing hedge or, if the right types are used, an almost impenetrable fence. Grapes can be trained over an arbor to provide summer shade, and pears and other kinds of tree fruits can be espaliered along a fence line or against a wall to hide "architectural mistakes" or soften geometric patterns (Figure 13-1).

Like all garden plants, fruit trees and shrubs need timely care but not much more than ornamentals do. The pruning of fruit trees, for example, often viewed as a slightly mysterious and extremely precise operation, takes only a little more expertise than does the pruning of ornamentals. Furthermore, fruit pests, with a few exceptions, are generally easier to control than are mites on junipers, thrips on gladiolus, or the various pests of roses. In fact, at most locations strawberries, raspberries, blackberries, grapes, sour cherries, and, away from commercial orchards, even peaches and apricots require only minimal pest control. Worm-free apples, pears, and sweet cherries are difficult to produce without some use of pesticides. For these fruits pest-management measures recommending relatively innocuous materials are available from state and Canadian experiment stations, as are bulletins and pamphlets suggesting cultivars, planting procedures, and cultural practices adapted to local conditions.

FIGURE 13-1 • Dual-purpose fruit and ornamental trees. These apple espaliers trained on wires are a feature of the restored garden of Monet, the famous impressionist painter, at Giverny, France. Apples and pears trained in various space-saving configurations are a major landscape feature of small yards throughout central and southern Europe.

Fruit-producing plants are classified according to the climate in which they are produced as tropical, subtropical, or temperate-zone fruits. In the continental United States tropical fruits can be grown only at the southern tips of Florida and California, and consequently they will not be discussed in this chapter. Production of subtropical fruits will be briefly covered, and the remainder of the chapter will be devoted to temperate-zone fruits classified as **small fruits**—those produced on bushes, lianas, and herbaceous plants—or as **tree fruits.**

SMALL FRUIT PRODUCTION IN THE HOME GARDEN

◆ ◆ ◆

Small fruits are widely adapted, are relatively easy to produce, and do not require a great deal of space. With some winter protection some cultivars of raspberries, strawberries, gooseberries, and currants can be produced in even the coldest regions. Although blueberries are not adapted to the excessively high summer temperatures and alkaline soils of the inland West and Southwest, they are a profitable home garden possibility in many areas of the country. One or more cultivars of grapes are also adapted to most areas of the United States, except for the Upper Midwest and the northern Rocky Mountains, and to warmer sections of Canada.

Grapes

Commercially, grapes are by far the most important of the small fruits. On a world basis, they are listed as having the highest monetary value of all fruits, although bananas, of which many small plantings are not counted in world statistics, undoubtedly rank higher in amount produced and number of people they feed.

Types and Cultivars. The grapes produced in North America were developed primarily from three species—*Vitis vinifera, V. labruska,* and *V. rotundifolia. V. vinifera,* the European or California grape, originated in the Eastern Hemisphere and is the grape of the Middle East and Europe, having been used for thousands of years for fresh eating and for the production of raisins and wine. Most North American grape juice comes from 'Concord', a cultivar of *V. labruska,* the only one of several native American grape species extensively cultivated commercially. The muscadine grape, *V. rotundifolia,* is produced mainly in home gardens in the southeastern United States.

All grapes have a liana habit of growth, but there are differences in other characteristics. European grapes have fleshy, succulent roots, whereas the *labruska* and muscadine types have hard and woody roots. The skin of the European grape adheres tightly to the flesh, which is high in sugar content. In contrast, *labruska* grapes have a "slip skin," a watery juice, and a lower sugar content. Muscadine grapes separate easily from the cluster when mature and are usually harvested as individual berries rather than as bunches.

Until a few years ago, almost all hardy cultivars of grapes had seeds. However, as a result of fifty years of grape breeding, seedless American hybrid cultivars that combine the cold hardiness and disease resistance of *V. labruska* with the quality of *V. vinifera* have become available. Because for the first time they allow growers in the colder and wetter areas of North America to produce quality seedless table grapes, these cultivars have rapidly replaced the older seedy types. French hybrid cultivars, like the American hybrids, combine the hardiness of American grape species with the quality of European grapes to produce cultivars primarily adapted to wine production.

The characteristics of a few of the many grape cultivars are listed in Table 13-1, but gardeners should obtain recommendations locally to be certain of planting types that are climatically adapted.

Climatic Adaptation. Most cultivars of both *Vitis vinifera* and *V. rotundifolia* are injured when the temperature drops below 0°F (−18°C). *V. rotundifolia* does best in the Southeast where the summers are long, warm, and humid, and *V. vinifera* is best adapted where summers are long with hot, dry days but relatively cool nights. Consequently, the commercial production of *V. vinifera* grapes is limited to California and a few warm valleys in other western states. American-type grapes are more cold resistant. They need cool temperatures in the early part of the growing season and then warm weather and bright sunshine to mature their fruit properly. Most French and American hybrid cultivars resemble European grapes but are able to withstand temperatures as low as −15° to −17°F (−26° to −27°C).

In areas where winter damage is likely to occur, European and other less hardy grapes can be grown by keeping the permanent trunk no higher than 8 inches (20 cm) and providing winter protection by laying the vines on the ground and raking leaves, straw, or peat moss over the entire plant (Figure 13-2). In some locations certain grape cultivars may be hardy in that they will winter over without damage, but they still may not be adapted because the summer climate does not provide enough heat units for their fruit to mature. In the cool-season areas, maturity can be hastened by planting the grapes along a south or west wall. Sometimes vines can be trained to grow where there is ample sunlight even when the roots are shaded. Where summer temperatures are cool, some late-maturing cultivars cannot develop maximum resistance to winter cold, apparently because the plant cannot accumulate sufficient carbohy-

TABLE 13-1 • *Characteristics of a few grape cultivars popular in North America*

Cultivar	Seeds	Earliness[a]	Hardiness[b]	Uses[c]	Color
		American and American Hybrid			
Beta	Yes	1500	4–7	J,W	Blue
Canadice	No	1600	6–8	T,J,W	Red
Concord	Yes	2300	5–8	T,J,W	Blue
Einset	No	1600	6–8	T,J,W	Red
Glenora	No	1600	6–8	T,J,W	Blue
Himrod	No	1600	6–8	T,J,W	White
Lakemont	No	1800	6–8	T,J,W	White
Mars	No	1600	5–8	T,J,W	Blue
Niagara	Yes	2000	5–8	T,J,W	White
Reliance	No	1700	5–8	T,J,W	Red
Saturn	No	2000	6–8	T,J,W	Red
		French Hybrid			
Aurora	Yes	1900	6–8	W	White
Foch	Yes	1900	5–8	W	Blue
		European			
Blue Lake	No	1600	7–9	T,J	Blue
Casaba	Yes	1800	6–8	T,W	White
Early Muscat	Yes	1800	6–8	T,J	White
Emperor	Yes	3000	7–9	T	Red
Flame	No	2600	7–9	T,J,W	Red
Thompson	No	2300	7–9	T,J,W	White
		Muscadine			
Cowart	Yes	2800	7–9	T,J,W	Blue
Dearing	Yes	2700	7–9	T,J,W	White
Scuppernong[d]	Yes	2700	7–9	T,J,W	Red

[a]Degree-days, base 50°F (15°C) (see "Heat Units" in Chapter 7, and "Predicting Maturity" in Chapter 14).
[b]USDA hardiness zone adaptation (see Figure 14-96).
[c]T = table, J = juice, W = wine
[d]Requires a pollinator; the others listed are self-fertile.

drates. As a consequence cultivars advertised as hardy to −15°F (−26°C) may be damaged even when temperatures do not drop that low in those areas.

Grapes have an extensive root system and require deep, well-drained soil. Although they grow on both coarse- and fine-textured soils, the highest yields in both the Northeast and the Northwest are produced on sandy loams. In the South and the Southwest nematodes are sometimes a problem in sandy soils.

Propagation and Planting. Grapes are propagated by cuttage, layerage, or graftage. They do not grow true to type from seed. European-type grapes are usually grafted onto American-type rootstocks, but more often American, muscadine, and French hybrid grapes are propagated by rooting cuttings or by layering (see Chapter 14).

Grape plants can be purchased from nurseries either bare rooted or in containers as one- or two-year-old planting stock. If two-year-old plants are to be purchased, they should be examined care-

FIGURE 13-2 • Grapes, dual-purpose (food and ornamental) lianas. (Courtesy of Ronny Jaques)

fully to make certain they are not the culls that were too weak or unthrifty to be set out as one-year-old plants the previous season. (**Culls** are products that do not reach the standard of the lowest marketable grade.)

The tops of one-year-old grape transplants should be pruned to a single cane with two or three buds, and their root system should be divested of excessively long roots before the plants are planted. Two-year-old transplants should be cut back to a single stem and should have their damaged or excessively long roots removed (see "Transplanting Woody Plants" in Chapter 14).

The standard spacing for grape vines is 7 to 10 × 7 to 10 feet (2 to 3 m). If trained in two dimensions on a fence or wall, each plant should have approximately 60 square feet (6 m^2) of space. Grape plants should be placed where they will receive full sunlight for at least half of each day.

Culture and Management. Fertilizer should be applied to grapes in the early spring, two or three weeks before the plants leaf out. On sandy soils in areas with a long growing season, a split application, part in the early spring and part just after the blossoms form, is desirable. Late summer and fall applications should be avoided because they stimulate growth at a time when the plants should be storing carbohydrates in preparation for the onset of cold weather (see "Fertilizing Garden Crops" in Chapter 14).

Grapes require large quantities of potassium. A deficiency of this element is manifested by interveinal scorching along the margins of the leaves. Phosphorus deficiency is not as common as deficiencies of nitrogen and potassium, but extra amounts are needed in some areas. Magnesium deficiency is common in the East where soil pH is low, and zinc and iron deficiencies are common in vineyards growing in soils of high pH in the West.

Because of their extensive root systems, grapes do not require as much water as do many garden crops. In areas where irrigation is required, the vineyard should be soaked thoroughly and then allowed to dry before the next irrigation. Even in arid areas, permitting three weeks to elapse between irrigations generally is not harmful if the area between the vines is cultivated. Weekly irrigation during dry periods will be needed if grapes are growing in a lawn or with another heavy cover crop. Where humidity is high, sprinkler irrigation should be avoided to reduce the risk of mildew. In dry areas where mildew is not a problem, thoroughly wetting the leaves twice a week helps reduce mite and white fly infestations. Irrigation should be reduced or eliminated six to eight weeks before harvest to speed maturity and assist the onset of dormancy. The soil should again be brought to field capacity after the plants are fully dormant in November.

Vitis vinifera, V. labruska, and the hybrids are self-fruitful (able to produce fruit without another cultivar as pollinator), as are many of the newer cultivars of *V. rotundifolia.* Local nurseries or garden advisers should be consulted concerning pollinators if muscadine grapes are to be planted, however, as most older muscadine cultivars produce only male or female, not perfect, flowers.

Fruit is produced on current-season wood, and some cultivars tend to be overproductive and need to be thinned. When the initial buds are damaged, by frost or otherwise, grape vines can initiate secondary fruiting buds that will produce a partial crop.

The grape grows best and produces the best quality fruit when heavily pruned to reduce the number of fruit buds and to keep the fruiting wood near the trunk and root system. Because fruit develops primarily from shoots produced from buds on one-year-old wood, replacement canes for the following season's crop must be developed each year. Various pruning systems, each best adapted to specific areas and/or cultivars, have been devised. Regardless of whether the vines are trained on wires, on a trellis over an arbor, on a wall, or as short canes attached to a trunk, the same principles apply. After the plants have grown to maturity, they should be pruned so that only enough previous season wood to contain forty to eighty buds remains (see "Pruning and Training" in Chapter 14).

Pests and Related Problems. Grape vines are extremely susceptible to injury by 2,4-D and related phenoxy herbicides, and growers are warned never to use volatile forms of these compounds close to grape vines. If 2,4-D must be used near grapes, the home lawn formulations should be sprayed with extreme caution and only when the air is still and the temperature is lower than 85°F (29°C). Symptoms of 2,4-D damage are manifested by distorted younger leaves with light-colored raised veins and midribs along with distorted or nongrowing shoot terminals.

In many regions grapes do not require pesticides. This is true especially of American and muscadine grapes. European grapes need a weekly application of fungicide to control mildew in cool humid regions. Other pests of grapes are listed in Table 13-2.

Strawberries

Strawberries (*Fragaria* spp.) are divided into two types on the basis of their flowering and fruiting habits—the ever-bearing cultivars, which form flower buds throughout the growing season (with peak production in June and early autumn) without regard to length of day, and the single-crop or June-bearing cultivars, which form flower buds only during short days in the fall and produce fruit in early summer. The total season production for good June-bearing cultivars is about the same as for ever-bearing cultivars, so the choice of type to plant depends on whether the gardener wants production concentrated or would prefer to have fewer strawberries over the entire summer season.

Climatic Adaptation. With some winter protection, strawberries can grow in most parts of the United States and Canada where gardening is possible. However, each cultivar is generally adapted to a relatively restricted area. The highest-quality berries are produced where the temperature is relatively cool during the maturing and ripening periods. Runners do not form on strawberry plants grown in the tropics, and fruit fails to set where temperatures are excessively hot.

Strawberries require well-drained soil with the water table at least 2 feet (60 cm) below the surface at all times, and they grow best in soils of moderate fertility that contain a good supply of organic matter. Although some older cultivars of strawberries require a pollinator, all cultivars readily available today are self-fruitful and do not require planting another cultivar for cross-pollination.

Commercial plantings of strawberries are not considered profitable for more than two production seasons or three years all together. Home plantings, if they are well cared for and if the plants are thinned occasionally, may produce profitably for five or six years or even longer in some instances. Where a lack of winter cold or disease prevents the normal strawberry growth cycle, ever-bearing cultivars can be used to produce a single crop. If they are planted in the early spring and their blossoms are removed until July, they will build up sufficient carbohydrates to allow them to produce through the fall and early winter. They can be plowed out when production starts to diminish.

Propagation and Planting. New strawberry plantings are propagated from young plants produced on runners from older plantings. Because strawberries are subject to soil-borne root diseases,

TABLE 13-2 • *Major insect pests and diseases of grapes*

INSECT PESTS	SYMPTOMS AND DAMAGE	CONTROL
Phylloxera	Root mite fatal to European-type (*V. vinifera*) grapes.	Plant only plants grafted to resistant rootstocks.
Mites (various species)	Green and cream mottling of upper leaf surface and fine webbing underneath. Most serious in arid areas. Plants are weakened.	Thorough wetting of both leaf surfaces twice a week will help. Limit use of insecticides, which destroy mite predators. Miticides may be required.
Grape-berry moth	Small, brown worms that develop in fruit, causing it to ripen and drop prematurely. Not serious in most gardens.	Insecticides, if needed.
Cutworms	Damage shoots and buds by night feeding.	Cutworm baits.
Leafhoppers	Small, elongate, pale green insects with yellow and red markings; jump from leaves when disturbed. Cause rusty appearance on upper leaf surface as they suck sap from underside of leaf.	Insecticides.
Scale	Insects that cover themselves with a hard shell and remain attached to branches during the dormant season and emerge in crawler stage from May to July. Weaken plants by sucking juices.	Dormant spray.
Grapevine flea beetle	Small, steel blue jumping beetles that eat opening buds and destroy new canes and fruit. Larvae feed on leaves in summer.	Insecticides.
White flies	Fragile-appearing insects that swarm when disturbed. Their feeding reduces plant vigor and fruit sugar content and causes white stippling of leaves.	Resist most pesticides; thorough wetting of leaf surfaces as suggested for mites may reduce infestation in areas of low humidity.
DISEASES	**SYMPTOMS AND DAMAGE**	**CONTROL**
Powdery mildew	Characterized by white spots that make leaves appear as if dusted with flour; most limiting disease of *Vinifera* grapes.	Recommended fungicide, preventive sprays. Keep foliage as dry as possible.
Downy mildew	Yellow patches on upper leaf surface, followed by white cottony mildew below. Serious during cool, humid periods.	Sulfur dust as a preventive when temperatures are cool. Plants are injured by sulfur when temperature is above 85°F (29°C).
Dead arm	Caused by a fungus that enters the plant through wounds and causes loss of vigor and eventually death by girdling of a part of the plant.	Disinfect pruning equipment between cuts in vineyards where disease is present. Fungicides.
Black rot	The fruit rots, blackens, and shrivels, and is covered with tiny black pimples.	Fungicides.
Viruses	Cause various plant distortions, leaf mosaics, and stunted growth. Do not confuse with 2,4-D damage.	Plant certified virus-free plants. Prune off and burn diseased canes or destroy diseased plants.

growers usually have a more productive planting if they use plants from a reliable local or mail-order nursery rather than from a neighbor's garden. In areas where winter temperatures are relatively cold, strawberries should be planted in the early spring before the dormant plants have started to grow. In areas where the ground does not freeze through the winter, they can be planted in the late fall or during the winter. They should be spaced about 18 inches (45 cm) apart in rows ranging from 2½ to 4 feet (¾ to 1¼ m) apart. Plants are usually permitted to spread across the bed, and only the center of the furrow is cultivated clean. When the plants are planted through plastic for weed and runner control, they can be spaced as close as a foot (30 cm) apart each way.

Strawberries can also be grown around the home as a ground cover or as window-box plants. Homeowners occasionally grow strawberries in an even more novel way by planting them in holes drilled through the sides of soil-filled wooden barrels, boxes, or hollow logs.

Culture and Management. During the planting season, all strawberry blossoms should be removed so that food reserves can be used for the development of large, vigorous plants. Runners that grow into the furrows should be cut off, and weeds must be controlled.

Fertilizer requirements vary depending on soil and location. For areas of relatively high rainfall, 1 pound (500 g) of nitrogen (N) and 2 pounds (1 kg) of P_2O_5/1,000 square feet (100 m^3) should be applied at the time the plants are set into the field. An additional pound of N should be applied in July or August of that year. In drier areas about 1½ pounds of N should be applied at planting time. Other elements should be added, of course, if they are known to be required. Lime at the rate of 2 pounds/1,000 square feet applied a year before strawberries are planted is beneficial on some soils in the Atlantic Coast states. Boron is sometimes required in the Pacific Northwest and manganese in occasional plantings in the East. Other minor elements may be required in localized areas (see "Fertilizing Garden Crops" in Chapter 14).

The initial fertilization can be a split application, part worked into the soil and part placed on the soil surface in a ring surrounding each plant. After the plants have spread, fertilizer is most conveniently applied by broadcasting, followed by thorough irrigation with sprinklers to prevent burning where fertilizer is in contact with foliage.

Strawberry plants take most of their moisture from the top foot of soil, which holds from ¾ to 1½ inches (2 to 4 cm) of water, depending on texture and organic matter content. The amount of water applied with each irrigation should be proportional to the amount the soil will hold and should be just enough to bring the top foot to field capacity. The two times when water is most critical to a planting of a June-bearing strawberry cultivar are just as berries are maturing and during August when blossom buds are forming for production the following season. Where spring rains do not supply 3 inches (8 cm) of moisture per month, some irrigation in April and May will be needed. Because moisture causes ripening fruit to rot, the planting should be thoroughly soaked just before the earliest berries begin to mature. Watering during the picking season is risky, but if the planting dries, irrigation may be worth the risk. Some moisture stress immediately after harvest does not seem to be damaging, but the planting should again be well watered during blossom-bud formation in August. Irrigation should be cut back in September and early October to force the plants into dormancy, but the planting should be brought up to field capacity before it is mulched for winter.

Most strawberry cultivars are subject to winter damage if grown east of the Cascade Mountains and the Sierra Nevada and north of a line extending east from northern Arizona to northern Georgia and then northeast to the southern Chesapeake Bay. Covering the plants with a mulch of waste hay, straw, shavings, sawdust, peat moss, or leaves is the usual method of cold protection. Mulch protects from cold or fluctuating temperatures and from heaving. By delaying bloom, mulching lessens the danger of blossom damage from early spring frost, a damage to which low-growing, early-blooming strawberries are especially susceptible (see Figure 7-10). Mulch should not be placed over the plants until after the first hard autumn freeze. When growth starts in the early spring, surplus mulch should be raked from the rows into the alleyway. Where spring freezes are frequent, blossoms can be protected by temporarily raking the mulch back over the rows on the evenings when frost is anticipated. In areas where blossoms are frequently lost to spring frosts, planting ever-bearing cultivars is advisable.

Insects, Other Pests, and Diseases. Although strawberries are subject to attack by a number of pests (see Table 13-3), a satisfactory crop can be produced without pest control in home gardens in many areas, provided that disease-free planting stock is used to establish the planting. Virus, root and leaf diseases, and insect eggs and larvae can be introduced on planting stock. Considering that a healthy planting produces for several years, it is usually profitable to purchase planting stock from a reliable nursery, or, better yet, to secure plants certified pest free by the state department of agriculture. County agents, experiment stations, and state departments of agriculture can supply addresses of certified plant growers.

Birds are fond of strawberries and, during their daily feeding in a small patch, will peck holes in every berry that has started to turn red. Having a tree of ripening sweet cherries (which birds like even better than strawberries) nearby will save the strawberries but will not solve the bird-feeding problem. Deer, rabbits, and smaller rodents can destroy the strawberry plants as well as the crop by feeding on the foliage. Covering the planting with netting discourages all but the smallest vertebrate feeders (see "Controlling General Garden Pests" in Chapter 14).

Harvesting. Strawberries mature during a period of several weeks, and in order for all the berries to be harvested at the proper stage of maturity, the patch needs to be picked every two to five days, depending on the temperature. Home-grown strawberries should not be harvested until they are at least 80 percent red. Although they will continue to soften and turn red if picked sooner, they will be lower in sugar content and have less flavor. Strawberries should be picked with the caps attached unless they are to be consumed or processed immediately. They should be harvested when the temperature is cool for best storage. Commercial growers often pick only between 4:00 and 10:00 A.M. Decayed, overripe, or bird-damaged berries should be picked but discarded because decay organisms that start in a single injured berry can quickly spread both rot and a disagreeable flavor throughout an entire container. The containers used for harvesting should be dry and shallow and constructed to allow air to circulate freely. The small, thin wooden baskets, called cups or hallocks, which were the berry containers of a few years ago, have been replaced by mesh plastic and pulp paper baskets.

Bramble Fruits

The bramble fruits (*Rubus* spp.) include red, black, and purple raspberries; erect blackberries; and trailing blackberries such as dewberries, loganberries, youngberries, and boysenberries. Except for some cultivars of trailing blackberries, the production of brambles is mainly in cooler areas. The general growth habit of bramble fruits is unique, the top being biennial and the roots perennial. Except for a few ever-bearing or fall-bearing red raspberry cultivars, brambles bear a single crop of fruit on second-year canes.

Climatic Adaptation. The red raspberry is the most cold resistant of the bramble fruits, but long, hot summers, hot winds, and high soil temperatures prevent its successful culture in southern locations. Black raspberries are somewhat less winter hardy than red raspberries. Erect blackberries are slightly less cold resistant than black raspberries, and trailing blackberries are grown extensively only where winters are relatively mild. Although

TABLE 13-3 • *Major insect pests and diseases of strawberries*

Insect Pests	Symptoms and Damage	Control
White grubs (with legs), crown borers, and root weevils (legless)	White grubs infest fields recently plowed from grass. White grubs and root weevils destroy or weaken plants by feeding on roots. Crown borers feed on and hollow crown.	Soil insecticide applied at time plants are set into the garden.
Cyclamen mites	Feed on and cause stunting and crinkling of new leaves, blasting of blooms, and distortion of fruit.	Planting stock from a good nursery will have been treated to destroy mites and mite eggs. Prebloom and afterharvest miticide treatment.
Spider mites	Weaken plant by feeding on underside of older leaves. Usually most serious in arid regions during mid- and late summer.	Miticides after harvest. A jet of water strong enough to wash underside of leaves but applied so it does not splash mud on plant may help if washing is done several times after harvest.
Aphids	Cause damage mainly by spreading virus. Root aphids may require control in some locations.	Insecticides.
Slugs	Burrow into ripening fruit, leaving slimy trails.	Slug baits.
Symphylids	Centipedes that feed on feeder roots. Serious primarily in Pacific Northwest.	Soil insecticide at time of planting.
Diseases	**Symptoms and Damage**	**Control**
Virus	Reduced runner formation and decreased vigor and yield. Often nonspecific problems.	Set only certified virus-free plants. Control aphids.
Leaf spots (various fungi)	Leaves show red or purple spots with or without white or gray centers, depending on species of fungus.	Plant resistant cultivars. Fungicidal spray.
Red stele	Plants wilt and die just before or during harvest. Roots decay, with red centers. Most severe in low-lying, poorly drained areas.	Plant disease-free, resistant cultivars on land that has not produced strawberries for several years.
Verticillium wilt	Decline and collapse of plants starting with roots and lower leaves about the time berries start to ripen. Most serious in West.	Do not plant where tomatoes, peppers, eggplant, black raspberries, or other wilt-susceptible crops have grown. Rotate planting.
Fruit rot	Most serious in humid areas.	Fungicidal sprays as fruits begin to ripen. Do not harvest any damaged or partially decayed fruit.

they grow best when exposed to full sun, red raspberries are one of the very few garden fruit plants that produce a fair crop in partial shade. Brambles grow and yield better if they are given wind protection.

Brambles can be grown on a wide variety of soils if the soils are moderately fertile and have good water-holding capacity and drainage. The trailing types can be grown in somewhat unfertile, shallow soils if drainage is good. On heavier, more fertile soils, trailing blackberries may make too much vegetative growth and produce few berries.

Propagation and Planting. Like strawberries, brambles are subject to many root and virus diseases, and plants obtained from a reliable local or mail-order nursery usually produce a more successful planting than do those dug from a neighbor's garden. If they can be obtained, state-inspected certified plants will be the most satisfactory. Growers sometimes purchase a few certified plants and propagate from them.

Red raspberries and most upright blackberry cultivars are propagated from root cuttings. Roots can be dug, cut into sections, and planted in a nursery bed. They should be covered with 3 inches (8 cm) of soil. A more common method of home propagation is to plant the suckers that emerge from the lateral roots some distance from the mother plant. Suckers with woody one-year-old stems are more satisfactory than those with only soft current-season stems. Black and purple raspberries are propagated by tip layerage. Trailing blackberries can be propagated from tip cuttings or by tip or serpentine layerage. Because root cuttings of some trailing blackberry cultivars produce plants with thorny canes, root cuttings are not used to propagate thornless trailing blackberry cultivars (see "Gene Mutation and Bud Sports" in Chapter 3 and "Layering to Renew or Multiply Plants" in Chapter 14).

Both red and black raspberries and upright blackberries are planted in either a hill or hedgerow system. For the hill system, plants are spaced 3 to 3½ feet (about 1 m) and for the hedgerow system, 2½ to 3 feet (⅔ to 1 m). Trailing blackberries should be 5 to 8 feet (1½ to 2½ m) apart in the row. Rows for all brambles should be 6 to 10 feet (2 to 3 m) apart, depending on the method of cultivation and the space available. Planting is usually in the early spring, except in the mild winter areas of the South and Pacific Coast where fall or winter planting is often more practical.

Culture and Management. To facilitate cultural practices and harvest and to prevent the planting from becoming overcrowded, cultivate sucker plants from between rows and hills. After the planting becomes established, most small annual weeds are shaded out, but the common practice of forgetting about weeds in the raspberry or blackberry planting is a mistake, as competition with tall or climbing weeds can seriously retard the bramble planting and increase its susceptibility to disease.

Brambles respond well to high organic matter, and the blackberry or raspberry planting should have high priority for available manure or compost. Immature (non-seed-bearing) weeds, grass clippings, and small twigs removed from the remainder of the yard can be profitably disposed of between rows of brambles to help control weeds, prevent evaporation, and supply organic matter.

As is true with most crops, fertilizer requirements of brambles vary with location and soil. Raspberries produce highest yields when new canes grow to 6 to 8 feet in height, so fertilizer should be adjusted to stimulate this kind of growth (see "Fertilizing Garden Crops" in Chapter 14).

Because deep-rooted brambles can extract moisture from the upper 4 feet (1¼ m) of soil, they do not require as frequent irrigation as do strawberries. Moisture requirements are greatest just before and during harvest to supply the dual needs of ripening fruit and rapidly developing new canes. Brambles planted in a medium-textured soil require 2 inches (5 cm) of water every two weeks from either rain or irrigation during spring and early summer, 4 inches (10 cm) every two weeks during midsummer, and 1 to 2 inches during early fall. Watering should be tapered off after harvest to harden canes, but the soil should again be soaked to field capacity before hard freezes. Furrow irrigation is preferable to sprinkler irrigation during harvest, as water from sprinklers can knock off ripening berries.

Brambles usually produce fruit buds on current-season canes during late summer or fall of the year preceding the crop year. In addition to their usual bloom, a few so-called ever-bearing or fall-bearing cultivars of red raspberries form blossom buds during midsummer and set fruit that same fall on current-season canes.

Because brambles tend to bloom later in the spring, their blossoms are not as subject to freeze damage as are the blooms of many other fruits. All commonly produced cultivars are self-fruitful and do not require a pollinator.

The training and pruning of brambles are based on their biennial growth habit. All canes that have fruited, suckers growing in the furrow or away from the plant row, and the weakest canes should be removed from the row. The remaining strong canes should be cut back somewhat and/or tied to supporting wires or posts (see "Pruning and Training" in Chapter 14).

Insects and Diseases. Because soil-borne root diseases and virus are the pest problems most likely to destroy bramble plantings, gardeners should obtain disease-free planting stock and plant it in well-drained soil in which brambles have not previously grown. Furthermore, where virus disease is known to be a limiting factor in raspberry and blackberry production, it is usually best to grow only one kind of bramble—that is, raspberry, black raspberry, or blackberry—as each kind of bramble is often a masked carrier of viruses fatal to the other kinds. In warm, moist areas where fungus disease is a problem, old canes should be removed and destroyed as soon as they have fruited. Diseased and insect-infested canes or plants should be destroyed. Black and purple raspberries should not be planted where potatoes, tomatoes, eggplant, or peppers have recently been produced because of their susceptibility to verticillium wilt. The common insects and disease pests of brambles are described in Table 13-4.

Harvesting. Raspberries are ready to pick when they separate easily from the core that remains on the plant. Blackberries become fully colored and sweet before they are ripe. They can be picked when the depression in the tip of each drupelet or section of the berry is filled. The core of the blackberry is a part of the fruit. Boysenberries and youngberries do not develop good flavor or maximum size until they are fully ripe. Berries produced on any one plant mature during a period of several weeks, and the fruit that has ripened will need to be picked each two to four days during that period (Figure 13-3).

Raspberries and blackberries are even more fragile than strawberries. Recommendations concerning time of harvest and containers mentioned in the section on strawberries also apply to bramble fruits.

With reasonable care, plantings of bramble fruits should produce profitable harvests for six to ten years, though some have remained in production for as long as twenty years.

FIGURE 13-3 • Red raspberry maturity. In all brambleberries, fruits of a cluster do not all ripen at the same time. (Courtesy Runk, Schoenberger/Grant Heilman)

Currants and Gooseberries

Currants and gooseberries (*Ribes* spp.) are of minor commercial importance, but both are easy to grow and both produce large quantities of fruit that can be used for a variety of tasty dishes. In addition, both grow on attractive bushes, which makes them excellent crops for the home garden or dual-purpose landscape. Both are hardy, even into the prairie provinces of Canada and in southern Alaska, but do not grow well in the South or Southwest. Gooseberries are somewhat more resistant to heat than are currants.

Currants and gooseberries can be propagated with hardwood cuttings or by layerage. Cuttings of previous-season wood 8 to 10 inches (20 to 25 cm) long are rooted during late winter or early spring in a propagating bed; mist chamber; or, in humid areas, in a shaded, protected location outdoors. They are inserted so that only two buds protrude above the propagation medium. If only a few plants are needed, they can be developed by layering the lower branches of established bushes. Often branches of currants and gooseberries layer spontaneously. It is fairly safe to obtain these layered currant and gooseberry plants from a neighbor, provided that the neighbor's plants are healthy and are standard cultivars that produce large fruit. Those transplanting from an older garden, however, run the risk of introducing soil-borne pests into their own gardens. Table 13-5 lists the major pests of currants and gooseberries.

Each currant or gooseberry bush should have at least 16 square feet (2 m^2) of growing space. Bushes are best planted in the early spring and should be placed slightly deeper than they were in the nursery.

Mulching with a pest-free loose mulch is advantageous, especially in dry areas. Average fertilizer requirements are listed in Tables 14-16 and 14-17. Both commercial fertilizer and manure should be kept from touching the crowns of plants. The irrigation practices suggested for brambles should be satisfactory for currants and gooseberries.

Except for black currants, which are seldom grown in this country, planting two cultivars for pollination is not required. Pruning practices are simple. The fruit is produced on one-, two-, and three-year-old wood; older wood produces inferior fruit. In pruning, the three-year-old wood is removed after it has produced its third crop. A mature, well-pruned, fruit-bearing currant or gooseberry bush consists of three to five branches each of one-, two-, and three-year-old wood.

Both currants and gooseberries are used mainly for making jellies and jams. For jelly, currants are usually picked when some of the fruit is not fully mature. Gooseberries are usually harvested when fully sized but not yet red in color. Many people enjoy eating these fruits out of hand or with sugar and milk or cream. Gooseberries also make excellent pies. Harvesting may extend over a month or more. Any fruit that remains frequently dries on the bushes and is very attractive to birds in the late fall and early winter.

Blueberries

Berries of a number of species of *Vaccinium* are harvested from the wild for fruit, but only two, the highbush blueberry and the rabbiteye blueberry, are propagated and grown in quantity under cultivation. Where adapted, the cultivated types produce fruit that is larger, although it may be less flavorful, than fruit of the wild types. The blueberry is a good home garden crop where its specific soil and climatic requirements can be met. The highbush blueberry grows best in soil of pH between 4.3 and 4.8 and has about the same temperature and chilling requirements as do peaches. The rabbiteye blueberry is somewhat more susceptible to winter injury and requires less cold to overcome its rest period than does the highbush. Most cultivars are more flavorful when ripened where nights are cool. The highbush blueberry is adapted to the Pacific Coast valleys of Oregon, Washington, British Columbia, and northern California; the warmer parts of the Great Lakes region and Ohio Valley; and the East Coast south to

TABLE 13-4 • *Major insect pests and diseases of bramble fruits*

Insect Pests	Symptoms and Damage	Control
Aphids	Serious as vectors of virus disease.	Predators often control aphids. If virus spread is a problem, periodic insecticidal sprays may be required.
Root weevils (several species)	White or brown legless grubs that feed on roots and cause plants to be unthrifty.	Preplant soil treatment with insecticide or treatment with insecticide washed in around crown of established plantings.
Raspberry crown borer	Swelling at base of cane from larvae tunnels. Breaking of fully grown year-old canes 2 in (5 cm) below soil surface. Larvae require 2 years to mature.	Soil insecticide applied in late fall or winter 2 years in succession to kill current-season larvae just under bark near crown.
Raspberry cane maggot	Adult fly lays eggs at tip of young canes. Maggot burrows into pith, girdles cane near tip, and continues downward in pith of cane.	Wilted canes should be cut off near ground and burned.
Fruit worms (various species)	Adult beetles feed on and distort flowers and fruit. The tiny worms burrow into fruit where they may remain until harvest.	Where numerous enough to be a problem, this pest is controlled by insecticides timed to kill adults before they lay eggs.
Leaf mites (red spider and two-spotted)	These barely visible tiny mites form webs and feed on underside of leaves. Their webs and white flecking on leaves are diagnostic.	Damage is usually during a dry, postharvest period. Frequent sprinkling aids control. Except where severe defoliation occurs, pesticides should be avoided because they kill mite predators.
Fruit mites	Cause dry, mummified raspberries or hard red drupelets that "don't ripen" on blackberries.	Insecticide timed to kill wintering-over mites just before they enter the fruit bud, just before flowering.
Sawfly (northern Great Plains)	Causes brown leaf blisters each containing ⅓-in (¾ cm) or shorter flattened active larvae.	Insecticide just before blossoms open.
Tree cricket (East)	Deposits curved orange eggs in closely spaced rows 2 in long. Egg-containing punctures may cause cane to break.	Damage is usually not serious enough to require control.
Orange tortrix (Northwest)	Larvae wriggle from rolled leaf shelters and fall into picking bucket.	Requires control only if berries are to be sold.

(continued)

South Carolina. Rabbiteye blueberries are adapted to the South Atlantic states.

Propagation and Planting. A reliable nursery is the best source of plants for the gardener who wants to grow a few blueberry bushes; however, blueberries are not difficult to propagate. New plants can be developed from softwood cuttings in a mist chamber, but rooting hardwood cuttings is more popular. They should be gathered during late winter or early spring while the plants are still completely dormant. Pencil-sized hardwood cuttings 4 to 6 inches (10 to 15 cm) long from healthy shoots of the previous season's growth are cut just below a bud at the base and above a bud at the top. These are placed in a rooting medium in partial shade with one or two buds above the surface. Propagation is usually in a cold frame,

TABLE 13-4 • (*Continued*)

Diseases	Symptoms and Damage	Control
Nematodes (various)	Unthrifty growth and gradual decline of plants over a period of years. Matted roots. Root knot nematode causes enlargements, and lesion nematode causes dead spots on small roots. Nematodes intensify other root disorders.	Prevention is only control. Use nematode-free planting stock. Have soil checked for nematodes before planting. Soil fumigation before planting or long rotation with grass, corn, or small grains reduces nematodes.
Root rot	See Strawberry diseases, Table 13-3.	
Crown gall (East)	Cauliflowerlike swellings on roots, crown, or lower part of cane. Disease enters through wounds.	Avoid planting on infested sites. Disease can be spread with cultivating equipment.
Verticillium wilt (Northwest)	Most severe on black raspberries. Beginning at plant base, leaves turn yellow (often on one side). Canes turn blue and gradually die.	Do not plant where tomatoes, potatoes, or peppers have grown the previous 3 years. Plant disease-free plants and remove and burn infected plants.
Anthracnose	Most serious on black and purple raspberries in humid locations. Causes light-colored sunken spots, chiefly on canes. Canes may be girdled.	Plant on sites with good air drainage. Remove "handles" (old cane) from black raspberry at planting time. Thin planting to permit air circulation. Apply fungicide if necessary.
Cane blight (humid areas)	Enters cane through wounds, winter damage, pruning, etc. Dark brown cankers extend down from wounds to encircle cane.	Remove old canes as soon as they have fruited. Remove and burn infected canes.
Spur blight (humid North)	Brown or purple spots develop near buds on infected canes. Buds darken and shrivel, and leaves turn yellow and dry.	Thin planting to allow air circulation. Good soil drainage and weed control are important.
Viruses (mosaic, tomato ringspot, leaf curl, etc.)	Viruses produce various symptoms, including light and dark patches on leaves, distorted leaves, crumbly berries, reduced growth, sterile plants with no fruit, death of the plant. They are the agent primarily responsible for the decline of raspberry plantings in many areas.	Plant certified disease-free planting stock if available. Do not plant black and red raspberries in the same location. Do not plant healthy raspberries near diseased ones.
Fruit rot (various organisms)	Can occur on the plant or after harvest.	Pick only sound berries; pick when plants are dry and weather cool; refrigerate berries and keep them cool after harvest.
Crumbly berry	Drupelets on berries fail to stay together; generally results from failure of some drupelets to be fertilized and can be caused by a lack of bees during bloom or by plant diseases.	Do not apply insecticides near the bramble planting when it is blooming; control plant diseases.

TABLE 13-5 • *Major insect pests and diseases of currants and gooseberries*

Insect Pests	Symptoms and Damage	Control
Currant aphids	Infested leaves curl downward, protecting the aphids.	Spray before leaves curl if required.
Currant borer	Feed in the pith of canes, sometimes causing them to be stunted or to break.	Remove and burn infested branches.
Scales	Soft-bodied insects covered with a hard scaly shell.	Treat with a suitable insecticide while buds are dormant.
Mites	See Bramble insect pests, Table 13-4.	
Currant fruit fly	Causes wormy currants and is perhaps the most difficult pest to control.	Treat with suitable insecticide at intervals while fruit is enlarging. Same control should control aphids.
Imported currant worm	Blue-green ¾-in (2 cm) worm with black head. May strip currants and gooseberries of almost all foliage.	Suitable insecticide.
Diseases	**Symptoms and Damage**	**Control**
Leaf spot	Brown and, later, pale gray spots that cause defoliation.	Fungicidal treatment just before flowers open.
Anthracnose	Causes small brown spots on all above-ground parts of plants, resulting in early defoliation.	Keep plants pruned so the growth habit is open. Use fungicide if required.
White pine blister rust	Currants and gooseberries, especially black currants, are alternate hosts of this disease.	In white pine–growing areas home garden planting of some types of currants and gooseberries was often prohibited, but with the realization that not all wild currants and gooseberries can be destroyed, restrictions have been relaxed in most places.

but cuttings should root satisfactorily in a mist chamber, a home propagating bed, or even a protected location outside. For outside propagation a dampened piece of coarse burlap should be placed over the cuttings until buds start to swell. When cuttings are well rooted, they are transplanted to nursery beds, where they have more room. They should be ready to plant in their permanent location the following spring. Each highbush blueberry bush requires about 30 square feet (3 m²), and each rabbiteye should have 40 to 60 square feet (4 to 6 m²). They should be planted in their permanent location slightly deeper than they were growing in the nursery.

Culture and Management. In their native habitat, both rabbiteye and highbush blueberries grow on hummocks in and at the edges of swampy areas, so they grow quite well in wet locations. They do, however, require at least 18 inches (45 cm) of soil above the water table. In most areas they grow best in full sun, although like raspberries, they can tolerate light shade.

In regions to which blueberries are adapted, soils are usually low in all three major elements. Years ago there were numerous reports of manure's being harmful to blueberry plantings, but more recent evidence suggests that these reports were exaggerated. If manure is applied, it should be kept from direct contact with the crown. J. S. Shoemaker, in *Small Fruit Culture,* suggests that the ammonium form of nitrogen is superior to the nitrate form and that the ammonium form may be essential for blueberries. Average fertilizer requirements are listed in Tables 14-16 and 14-17. With high pH, iron deficiency (stunted growth and yellowing) or magnesium deficiency (interveinal areas turn red and yellow, beginning at the leaf tip) are likely. Iron and magnesium chelates are the formulations of these elements most likely to correct deficiencies in most areas. Follow the label directions on the purchased product. In some localities in the East, less expensive formulations of these elements may be effective.

Blueberries are not drought tolerant. A loose mulch helps retain moisture, but where rainfall does not supply enough, the planting should receive 1 to 2 inches (2½ to 5 cm) of moisture each 10 days during the harvest season and a little less, but still enough to keep the soil moist, before and after harvest.

Pests of blueberries are not numerous, and often commonsense sanitation and management practices are all the control required (see Table 13-6).

Pollinating, Training, and Pruning. There is some evidence that cultivated blueberries produce better yields with cross-pollination, so homeowners should plant at least two cultivars.

The cultivated highbush blueberry fruits on wood of the previous season's growth, and the

TABLE 13-6 • *Major insect pests and diseases of blueberries*

Insect Pests	Symptoms and Damage	Control
Blueberry maggot	Causes wormy berries. Adult is a fly about size of housefly. Most serious insect pest of commercial blueberries.	Dust or spray when adult flies appear in large numbers but before they lay eggs (early to mid-July in most northern areas).
Cranberry and cherry fruit worm	Web and filth around some fruit clusters. Feeds on fruit.	Usually not numerous enough to require control in the garden.
Blossom weevil	Feeds on blossoms. May reduce bloom 50% in some areas.	Insecticidal spray.
Scale	Reduces vigor of canes (see Grape insect pests, Table 13-2).	Dormant scale sprays.
Diseases	**Symptoms and Damage**	**Control**
Stem canker, stem blight (North Carolina)	Cankers girdle and weaken stems, prevent the growing of susceptible cultivars in the South. Blight causes dieback of stems.	Grow cultivars resistant to stem canker. Remove and destroy affected stems.
Stunt virus	Transmitted by sharp-nosed leafhopper. Internodes shortened; leaves reduced in size and chlorotic; premature red coloring.	Remove diseased plants. Do not propagate from any plant growing within ¼ mile (½ km) of diseased plants.
Necrotic ringspot virus	Spreads by nematodes. Leaves pucker, become spotted. Spots dry and crumble, leaving holes in leaves.	Plant virus-free plants on land not infested with nematodes.
Other viruses	Several viruses with various symptoms may affect plants.	Rogue diseased plants. Plant disease-free planting stock.
Mummy berry	A fungus that causes dieback of shoots, blighted blossoms, and mummified berries.	Remove and destroy mummy berries and hoe around plants to disturb sporulation on fallen berries.

largest fruit is borne on the most vigorous wood. Most cultivars tend to overbear, and some flower buds must be removed by pruning to permit the plant to develop sufficient vigorous wood for the next year's crop and to prevent the development of small berries. Heavy pruning definitely reduces the crop. Light pruning, although it may reduce the crop slightly for a given year, stimulates more vigorous wood for the next year's crop. With heavy cropping and no pruning, some of the fruit may not mature. In contrast, light pruning causes earlier maturity of the fruit as well as larger size.

When the plants are set in the field, about one-fourth of the top should be cut back along with bushy basal growth and damaged roots and shoots. During the first season all flower buds should be removed. No further pruning is needed for several years other than removal of broken or interfering branches. After the plant matures, pruning consists of removing dead, broken, and interfering branches and thinning bushy wood and old stems that are no longer vigorous. Eventually some thinning of the branches will be necessary. Erect-growing cultivars need to have some center branches removed to permit better light penetration. Branches that droop and allow the fruit to become dirty should be removed from spreading types.

Even with moderate pruning it may be desirable to rub off a few of the flower buds in each cluster to avoid overbearing and to promote larger, more uniform berries.

Harvesting. Blueberries within a cluster mature over a period of several weeks, and for the highest quality, ripe berries should be picked each four to five days. Berries are not usually mature-ripe when they turn blue, so other criteria—sweetness, ease of removal from the stem, and reduced resistance to pressure—must be considered when deciding when to harvest.

Other Small Fruits

Being a bog plant, the cranberry is suitable for home gardens only in very special situations. Some cultivars of elderberries (*Sambucus* spp.) have been domesticated and are used for jelly and wine making. A number of small fruits, including elderberries and blueberries, are sometimes transplanted from the wild. The serviceberry (*Amelanchier*), sometimes called the Juneberry and in Canada known as the Saskatoon, is frequently grown around homes in the Upper Midwest, the Rocky Mountain area, and the prairie provinces of Canada. It makes an excellent ornamental and produces delicious, although seedy, fruit. Wild currants (*Ribes* spp.), chokecherries (*Prunus virginiana*), and hawthorns (*Crategus* spp.) are among the other berry-producing plants frequently transplanted from the wild.

TREE-FRUIT PRODUCTION IN THE HOME GARDEN

◆ ◆ ◆

During the last century virtually every yard contained a few fruit trees. As yards became smaller and Americans became more mobile during this century, the number of home gardens with fruit trees declined, probably because of what might be called the four Ws: Worms, Wood, Waste, and Wait. The spread of the codling moth, the cherry fruit fly, and certain other insect pests throughout the country made it impossible to grow good fruit without using potent poisons that were the only available pest controls. Moreover, without proper pruning, standard-sized fruit trees produced too much wood and grew to enormous sizes, their crowns filled with dead and intercrossing branches. These uncared-for trees produced small wormy fruit that fell to the ground and made a wasted mess. If new trees were planted, years of waiting were required before they eventually produced a crop, and with Americans' customary mobility, more often than not the person who planted the tree had moved by the time it started to bear.

During the past few years, increasing interest in home gardening and developments in the field of **pomology** (the science of fruit growing) has led to renewed interest in the home production of tree fruits. Although it can hardly be said that tree fruits can be grown without effort, their production by amateurs is much more feasible today than it once was. The introduction of dwarf trees and newer training systems has permitted the growing of a fruit tree in an area as small as 25 square feet (2 m^2). Also, one dwarf tree produces only about as much fruit as a family is likely to consume during the season. Thus a diversity of kinds of fruit maturing at different times can be produced in the area available. Furthermore, the development of relatively safe pesticides makes the production of tree fruits much easier today than it was a few years ago.

Tree fruits grown in North America are of two types, the temperate-zone deciduous and the mostly evergreen subtropical. Of the deciduous type, two pome fruits, apples and pears, are the ones most often planted. Another pome fruit, quince, is occasionally grown for juice or jelly. Asian pears, which first gained popularity as expensive supermarket imports and are now being grown commercially in North America, are the newest kind of pome fruit for American gardens. Asian pears have the crisp texture and round shape of apples and the sweet bland flavor of pears. Peaches, nectarines, apricots, sweet and sour cherries, and plums—the stone or drupe fruits—are the other major group of deciduous fruits.

Citrus—of which oranges, grapefruit, lemons, limes, and mandarin oranges are the kinds most commonly grown in the United States—is the main group of subtropical evergreen fruits. Avocados, figs, persimmons, dates, and olives are some of the other subtropical fruits produced in this region.

The Pome Fruits

Apples (*Malus* spp.) and pears are the most widely adapted tree fruits for the home garden. Cultivars are available that can grow in all but the extreme southern parts of the continental United States and all but the coldest parts of populated Canada and Alaska. Although they have not been tested in all parts of North America, Asian pears apparently have about the same cultural and climatic requirements as do other pears. The fruits of many apple and pear cultivars store well for several months and can be used in a variety of ways.

Climatic Adaptation. Most cultivars of apples and pears can be hardened to withstand temperatures as low as −20°F (−29°C). With optimal conditions for developing cold tolerance, some of the hardier cultivars of apples can be grown where air temperatures drop as low as −40°F (−40°C). The roots are not as hardy and may be injured if soil temperatures drop to 10° to 20°F (−12° to −7°C). Spring frosts of temperatures below 28°F (−3°C) occurring at the time of bloom or shortly thereafter can seriously damage blossoms and young developing fruits. Pear blossoms are more frequently damaged by early spring frosts than are apple blossoms because pears bloom earlier. Both apples and pears must be exposed to at least six weeks of average temperature below 40°F (4°C) to break rest.

Selecting and Planting Pome Trees. Today the only apple trees that most home gardeners consider planting are those grafted to dwarfing rootstocks. Dozens of rootstocks that dwarf to varying degrees have been developed, but only a few are widely used. The most dwarfing and popular for gardens of apple rootstocks is Malling IX. Other rootstocks commonly available that dwarf to varying degrees include E.M. 26, producing trees slightly larger and better anchored; E.M. VII and M.M. 106, producing trees that average 15 to 20 feet (5 to 6 m) high; and E.M. II, producing very vigorous trees about two-thirds standard size. Trees on Malling IX rootstock can be planted as close as 10 feet (3 m) apart, and they grow to a maximum height of about 10 feet. Their size can be reduced even further by pruning. The Malling IX rootstock does not give a tree a very good anchor, and a stout steel or long-lasting wooden post should be driven next to the tree to provide support. Trees on Malling IX rootstock often produce fruit one or two years after being planted. Dwarf trees should be planted so that the graft union is above the soil line (see Figure 8-14). If the graft union is buried, the scion part of the tree is likely to root, and a standard-sized tree will result. Pear trees are dwarfed by placing them on quince rootstock, as mentioned in Chapter 8. Because quince is graft incompatible with many of the better varieties of pears, an interstock is usually necessary. Thus at least two years are required to propagate a dwarf pear tree and such a tree is likely to be fairly expensive. Better-anchored dwarf apple trees are also sometimes propagated by using a dwarfing interstock (Figure 13-4).

Pome trees are propagated by grafting or budding. Although most gardeners can easily master the art of grafting or budding, they usually buy pome trees because dwarfing rootstocks are not readily available. Those who wish to use seedling rootstocks or to change a cultivar by topworking can find a description of grafting and budding in Chapter 14.

Trees should, of course, be purchased from a reliable dealer. One-year-old trees are less expensive and easier to plant and train than are older trees. If they have scaffolds at the right location and are vigorously growing and healthy, two-year-old trees in a container may be a wise choice because they will produce earlier (see "Transplanting Woody Plants" in Chapter 14).

There are literally hundreds of cultivars of apples and almost as many pears. Probably the most popular early summer apple is still the 'Yellow Transparent' or its improved and somewhat larger fruited relative, 'Lodi'. Among the apple cultivars that mature a little later are 'Gravenstein', 'Duchess', and 'Wealthy'. 'McIntosh' is an early-fall cultivar. The more popular cultivars that can be stored for winter use are 'Red Delicious', 'Golden Delicious', 'Jonathan', 'Winesap', 'Northern Spy', 'Cortland', and 'Idared'. The trees of 'McIntosh', 'Wealthy', 'Northern Spy', and 'Winesap' are more winter hardy than are 'Red Delicious' and 'Golden Delicious'. 'Haralson' and 'Fireside' are two extra hardy cultivars developed

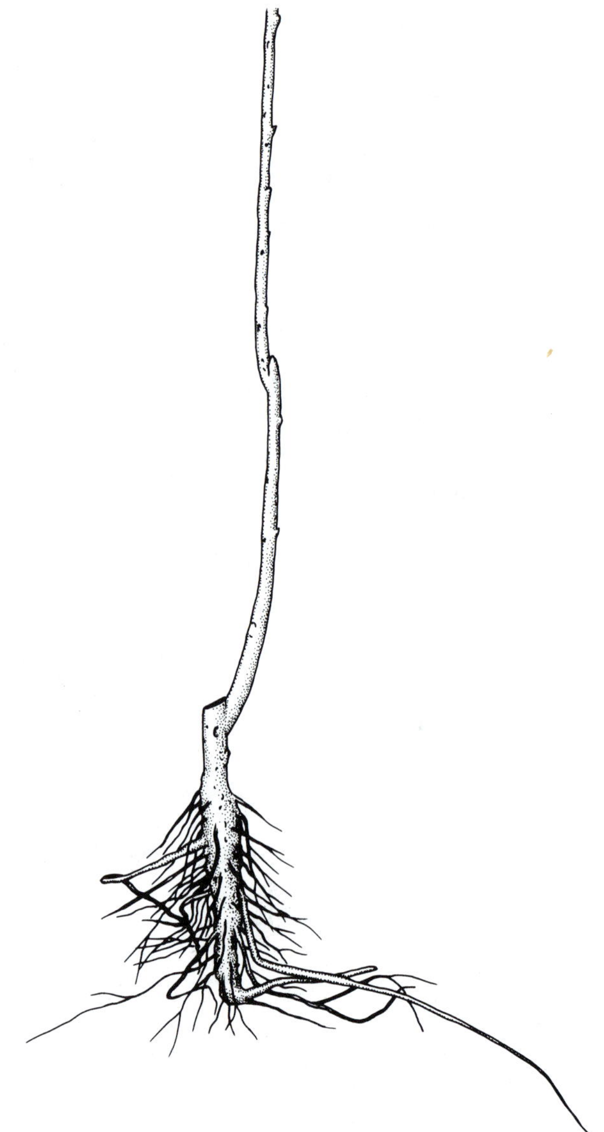

FIGURE 13-4 • Apple tree with an interstock. To produce this tree, a bud from a dwarf stock was budded to a seedling rootstock in August (lowest union). After the bud was well established by the following spring, the seedling tree was cut off just above the inserted bud. The following summer a bud of the desired cultivar ('McIntosh' in this case) was budded onto the dwarfing interstock about 10 inches above the first union. The resulting tree will be dwarfed by the interstock but will still have a sturdy seedling root system. This sketch shows an apple tree in late winter almost 30 months after the initial budding.

for the Upper Midwest prairies. 'Granny Smith', a tart, green-skinned cultivar from Australia that requires a long growing season, and 'Jonagold', the most popular apple in Europe, are two cultivars suitable for winter storage that have been added to North American nursery lists. 'Gala' is a recently introduced cultivar that matures at about the same time as does 'McIntosh'.

The most popular summer pear cultivar is 'Bartlett', even though it is not adapted to growing in some areas of eastern North America because of its susceptibility to fireblight, a bacterial disease. Later-maturing pears that can be stored into winter include 'Anjou,' 'Bosc,' 'Sekel,' and 'Winter Nellis.' 'Hosui' and 'Shinseiki' are two available cultivars of Asian pear.

Culture and Management. Apples and pears can be grown with either a cover crop or clean cultivation. More fertilizer and irrigation water are required if trees are being grown with a cover crop; however, unless water is likely to be scarce, a cover crop should be considered because of the advantages of less erosion, easier access after rain, and the possibility of using the grassy home orchard as a recreation area. Sometimes the planting is clean cultivated so as to reduce possible cover crop competition until the planting begins to produce, after which it is seeded to a cover crop. Grass that can be mowed as a lawn is the most popular cover crop for home orchards, but alfalfa, clover, or a mixture of grass and one of the legumes reduces the amount of fertilizer required for the planting. If the planting is to be cultivated during the summer, it is often desirable to plant a cold-tolerant annual cover crop such as rye or wheat that can be mowed or cultivated under the next spring. These covers will protect the soil during the months it is most likely to erode and provide organic matter for the orchard.

Many factors affect the amount of fertilizer, especially nitrogen, needed by apple and pear trees. The amount of production and quality of fruit can be regulated to some extent by the amount of nitrogen. Too much nitrogen causes the tree to be vegetative and to produce few large, poorly colored fruits; too little causes it to be highly reproductive and to produce many small, low-quality fruits. Small, light-colored leaves are usually a good indicator of too little nitrogen (see Chapter 14).

Soil tests are not completely reliable guides to orchard tree fertilization because of the difficulty of obtaining representative soil samples for a crop having roots that may reach depths of 30 feet (9 m). Although a major portion of the feeding is from the upper 2 feet (⅔ m) of soil, lower roots can pick up needed nutrients when they are deficient in the upper levels. In sandy soils in areas of high rainfall, boron may be required. Iron and zinc deficiency are common in the West. Fertilizer is most effective if applied three to four weeks before buds begin to swell in the spring.

Apple and pear trees require 32 to 36 inches (80 to 90 cm) of water annually, and irrigation is needed in areas where less than this amount falls in the form of rain or snow or where there are extensive periods of drought during the growing season. When trees are irrigated, the entire root zone should be brought to field capacity. Even in arid areas, established trees growing in soil having good water-holding capacity should not require irrigation more often than once each two or three weeks. Water can be used to reduce damage from frost (see Chapter 7).

Pruning of pome trees should be kept to a minimum, because these trees grow slowly and new growth is slow to come into production. Because the trees may bear for forty years, training must ensure a strong framework. For this reason the modified central leader system of training is recommended for orchard block plantings. Various hedgerow, fence, pillar, and espalier training systems can also be used for pome trees (see "Pruning and Training" in Chapter 14).

Fruiting Habit. Most cultivars of both apples and pears are self-unfruitful, and unless close neighbors have trees of a different cultivar, the home planting should always consist of two or more cultivars.

The fruit of apple and pear trees is borne on small twigs called **spurs,** which are produced only on wood that is at least in its second year of growth. Some of the buds on wood that was developed during the previous season grow into short spurs in the spring. Later in the season, mixed buds (buds from which both leaves and flowers will grow) develop at the tip of the spurs. The following spring these buds open to produce blossoms that grow into the fruit. Figure 13-5 shows that under ordinary circumstances the youngest wood to produce fruit is completing its third growing season as the fruit matures and also that an individual spur of the pomes produces fruit only every other year. An upset in nutritional balance or destruction of the crop is likely to cause all of the spurs to fruit during a single year and result in biennial bearing in apple or pear trees (see "Alternate Bearing" in Chapter 3).

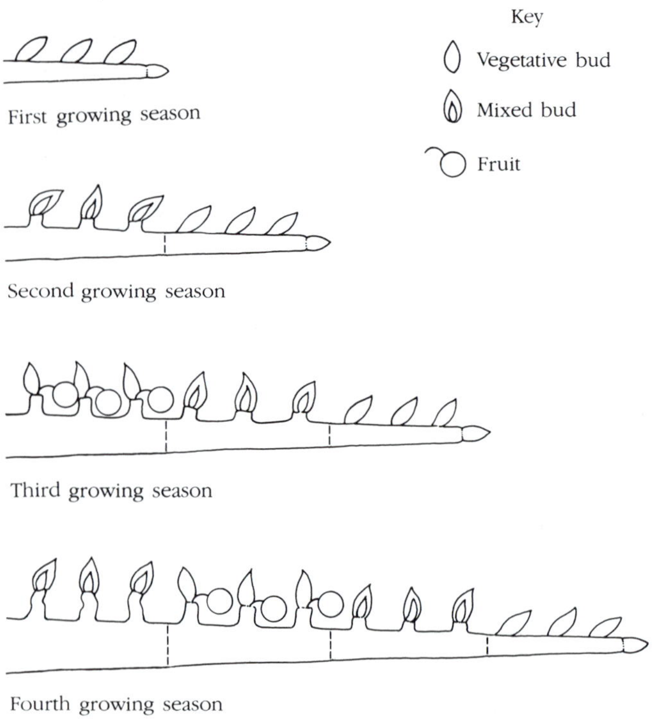

Key
Vegetative bud
Mixed bud
Fruit

First growing season

Second growing season

Third growing season

Fourth growing season

FIGURE 13-5 • Growth and fruiting habit of apple and pear trees.

Insects and Diseases. The codling moth, which is responsible for most of the worms in apples and pears, is a universal pest (Figure 13-6). Fireblight, a bacterial disease that enters wounds and open blooms, causes progressive blistering and the death of branches and eventually entire trees. Fireblight is present all over North America but is especially severe in some of the humid eastern states and provinces where it often prevents the production of 'Bartlett' pears. The major pests of pome fruits are listed in Table 13-7.

Insect control is almost always essential for apples and pears, and the gardener who grows these fruits should plan on a systematic pest-control program. Insect and disease control usually require sprays in February (dormant), just as buds are beginning to swell (delayed dormant), just before blossoms open (prepink), 10 days later, and each 16 to 21 days thereafter until just before harvest. Each application may be a single pesticide or a combination of several and may control one or several pests. Organic growers may want to experiment with *Bacillus thuringiensis,* which has controlled codling moth in some isolated orchards. County extension offices and other local governmental and private agricultural advisory agencies can help identify and recommend control measures for pome fruit pests and diseases.

Harvesting and Storage. The time of pome fruit harvest is determined by the type of fruit, variety, season, and use. Summer apples are picked for cooking when they have reached acceptable usable size. They have better flavor for eating fresh after they turn yellow or red, depending on the cultivar, and begin to soften slightly. The optimal harvest maturity of later cultivars is indicated

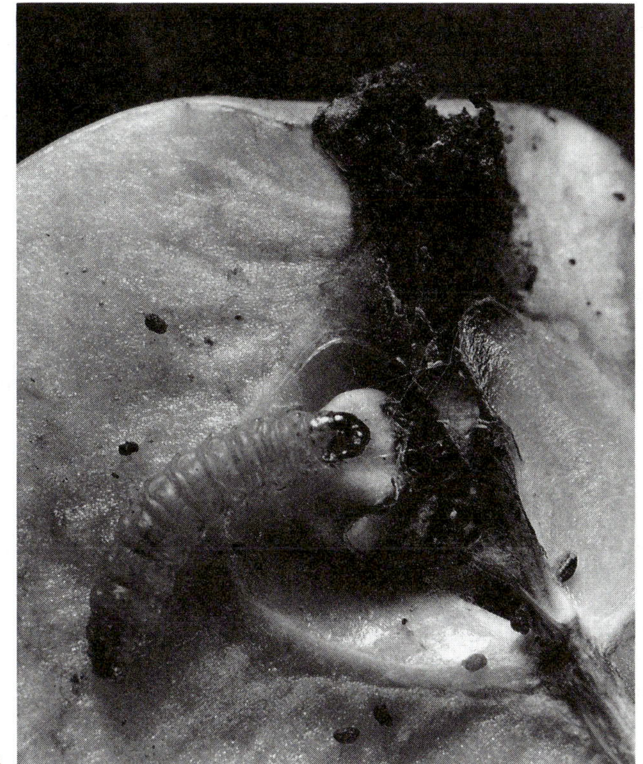
A

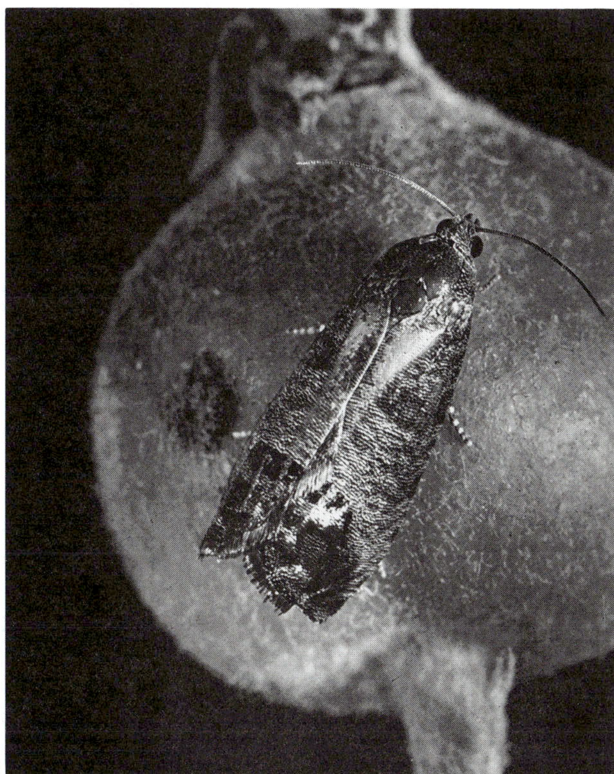
B

FIGURE 13-6 • Pests of fruit trees. The codling moth larva (A) is responsible for most wormy pome fruits; the adult moth (B). (A, courtesy Runk, Schoenberger/Grant Heilman; B, courtesy of Grant Heilman)

by a number of factors. The stem of the fruit should detach relatively easily from the spur, and the flesh should be crisp and distinctly acid with little or no starchy taste. In apples the red color is not a good indicator of maturity, but the green or yellow color is. Whenever the green area of the skin changes from a definite green to a yellowish green, the fruit is reaching maturity. The days from bloom have also been used as an index of maturity. Suggested times for a few cultivars are 'Jonathan', 135 to 145 days; 'Delicious', 145 to 150 days; 'Golden Delicious', 152 to 160 days; and 'Winesap', 165 to 175 days.

The fruit of many apple cultivars tends to fall from the tree before it is fully mature. This early drop is a serious problem when there is a heavy wind just before harvest. It can be prevented by using a stop-drop spray. Naphthalene acetic acid at 10 parts per million is the most common active ingredient of such sprays. This material becomes effective approximately 3 days after application and holds the fruit for 10 to 14 days.

TABLE 13-7 • *Major insect pests and diseases of pome fruits*

Insect Pests	Symptoms and Damage	Control
Scale (various kinds)	Several kinds cause damage by sucking juices from branches (see Grape insect pests, Table 13-2).	Dormant oil sprays before buds open.
Aphids	Several kinds of aphids infest apples and pears, including the woolly apple aphid (its name is diagnostic), which lives on all parts of the tree including roots and continues to infest aerial portions from root colonies.	Use rootstocks resistant to woolly aphid, dormant sprays to prevent eggs from hatching, and a periodic summer spray program.
Climbing cutworms	See Grape insect pests, Table 13-2.	
Tent caterpillar	Worms ½ to 1 in (1½ to 2½ cm) long emerge from eggs in early spring. Construct tentlike webs and defoliate whole limbs or entire tree.	Insecticide just before blossoms open.
Mites	Several kinds; very difficult to control (see Grape insect pests, Table 13-2).	Dormant oil spray for eggs. Periodic sprays through growing season.
Codling moth	The most serious pest of apples. Also infests pears. The white larvae usually enter fruit through calyx and leave, when mature, through a "worm hole" in the side. Moths lay eggs, which continue to hatch throughout the summer.	Insecticide spray 10 days after petal fall and each 16 to 21 days thereafter until 2 to 3 weeks before harvest. Clean up trash and scrape away loose bark to destroy adult moths.
Pear psylla	A 1/10-in (1/4 cm) reddish brown, four-winged, triangular insect found under pear bark during winter. Smaller yellow nymphs on fruit and leaves during summer. Causes leaves to turn brown and drop and fruit to be stunted and scarred, and spreads pear decline.	Dormant, delayed dormant, and prepink sprays with recommended insecticides.
Apple maggot	Most damaging east of the Great Plains and north of Arkansas and Ohio. Adult flies emerge from soil in midsummer, lay eggs in punctures in apple fruit. Eggs hatch into larvae that grow rapidly as fruit ripens.	Insecticide spray timed to kill adult flies as they emerge.
Curculios	Apple and plum curculios both damage pome fruits (see Stone fruit insect pests, Table 13-8).	Sprays used for codling moths will usually control curculios.
Diseases	**Symptoms and Damage**	**Control**
Apple scab	Brownish spots on leaves in early spring, spread to fruit. Rough pustules on fruit enlarge, even in storage, to large rough scabs.	Fungicide, during spring where summer is dry, throughout growing season where summer rains are frequent.
Powdery mildew	Fungus winters over in infected buds. As weather warms during spring, it attacks leaves, buds, and sometimes fruit with white mealy coating. Causes russeting of pear fruit.	Fungicides during spring and early summer. Pruning away affected shoots is a supplemental control effective where spread is not excessive.
Fireblight	Bacteria enter blossom during pollination period, gradually move down the branch, causing darkening of bark. Leaves and small fruits die, blacken, and remain on twigs. Most serious on pears in the East, especially 'Bartlett' cultivar. Also serious on many apple cultivars.	Prune off infected branches 12 in (30 cm) below farthest visible symptoms. Disinfect pruning equipment between cuts with a solution of 1 part household bleach to 9 parts water. Streptomycin sprays at full bloom and 7 days later. During dormant season, scrape and remove all dead bark from around cankers on larger limbs and disinfect with streptomycin.

Pears are unlike most fruits and vegetables in that they reach their highest eating quality only when they are picked at a slightly green stage. There are several commercial color and firmness tests used for pears. For the homeowner probably the best criterion is when the full size has been reached and there is a slight change in color from green to yellowish green, before fruit begins to soften. I usually harvest the bulk of my 'Bartletts' about the time the first two or three small fruits (usually wormy) become fully ripe. I leave the smaller, obviously immature fruit (about one-third of the crop) on the tree for 7 to 12 days longer.

Winter cultivars of apples and pears can be stored if they have been harvested at the proper stage of maturity and if there is a cool humid storage available, 32°F (0°C) and 95 percent humidity being ideal. In northern areas they can be stored in an insulated pit storage (see "Storing Horticultural Products" in Chapter 14).

Neither apples nor pears should be placed in the same storage facility as vegetables because the ethylene gas they emit has an adverse effect on other products. For example, it causes carrots to become bitter, inhibits sprouting, and causes an off flavor in other root, bulb, and tuber crops.

The Stone or Drupe Fruits

The stone fruits include peaches, nectarines, plums, sweet cherries, sour cherries, and apricots. Almonds are sometimes also classed with the stone fruits. All of the group are closely related, belonging to the *Prunus* genus of the family Rosaceae. Most can intergraft, and there have been interspecific crosses between some of the different kinds. All grow on medium-sized trees.

Nectarines are essentially fuzzless, somewhat fragile, peaches. Seeds from peaches sometimes grow into nectarine trees and vice versa. Both originated in China and are usually listed under the botanical name of *Prunus persica.* Apricots (*Prunus armenica*) also are thought to have been domesticated in China.

Three general groups of plums are recognized. The European plum, *Prunus domestica,* has been cultivated in Europe for many centuries and is thought to have originated from an interspecific cross between the myrobalan or cherry plum, *P. cerasifera* (now used as a rootstock for stone fruits), and the sloe plum, *P. spinosa,* of western Europe. Most cultivars of prunes, the 'Damson' plum, and the 'Green Gage' or 'Reine Claude' plum are of the *P. domestica* group. Fruit of the Japanese plum, *P. salicina,* are often larger and more tart than the European types. Trees of Japanese plum do not require as much cold to overcome their rest period, and they are less subject to disease in warm, humid climates. American plums include several *Prunus* species that are native to North America. Some have excellent cold-temperature and disease resistance, but they are not grown as extensively as are the other two types. Prunes are plum cultivars, such as 'Stanley' and 'Italian', with a sugar content high enough that they can be dried without the flesh around the pit fermenting.

Both sweet cherries, *Prunus avium,* and sour cherries, *P. cerasus,* were introduced from Europe, where there are many native related species. 'Duke' cherries are thought to have originated from a cross between sweet and sour cherries because they range somewhere between the two in hardiness, tree size, and fruit flavor.

Climatic Adaptation. Stone fruits vary somewhat in temperature requirements, especially cold tolerance. The peach is the least cold resistant; dormant peach flower buds are injured at temperatures from −5° to −10°F (−21° to −23°C). Injury occurs at higher temperatures if the plants are not well hardened. Apricots generally are more cold resistant than peaches but their early blooming habit exposes the blossoms to spring frost injury. Sweet cherries are somewhat more tolerant of low winter temperatures than are peaches, and sour cherries are at least as cold tolerant as are the more tender apple cultivars. Japanese plum cultivars vary widely in cold tolerance from those slightly less cold resistant than apples to those as tender as peaches. American-type plums are the hardiest of all stone fruits, some cultivars being as cold tolerant as the hardiest apples. European plums, including prunes, are somewhat less cold tolerant than apples but hardier than peaches or sweet cherries.

Propagation and Planting. Stone fruits are usually propagated by budding. Both sweet and sour cherries are propagated onto rootstocks of either 'Mazzard', a sweet cherry with small, black, fruits, or 'Mahaleb', a wild European *Prunus* closely related to the sour cherry. 'Mazzard' rootstock is preferred in western North America and in areas of eastern North America where moisture is sufficient and winter hardiness is not a problem. Trees with 'Mahaleb' rootstocks are usually slower growing, slightly smaller, and not as long lived, but they are less subject to injury from drought and cold temperatures.

Peaches, nectarines, apricots, and plums all can intergraft. Peaches and nectarines are usually budded to peach seedling rootstocks, although vegetatively propagated nematode-resistant peach rootstocks are used where nematodes are a problem, and 'Myrobalan' plums are used where the soil is heavy or poorly drained. Plums are mainly budded to 'Myrobalan' plum except where nematodes or droughty, sandy soils are a problem, in which case resistant peach rootstocks are used. Apricots are grafted to apricot seedling rootstocks, which have some nematode resistance, to peach rootstocks if soil is sandy or droughty, or to plum if the soil is fine textured or poorly drained. A good nursery can tell the gardener what kind of rootstock has been used.

One- or two-year-old trees can be purchased. The largest trees for their age are usually the most desirable, as stunting is often a symptom of rootstock-transmitted virus. Planting arrangements and tree spacings should be based on the ultimate size of the trees and conditions of the area where they are grown. Although dwarf trees are occasionally advertised, dwarfing rootstocks of the stone fruits are not as widely available or as reliable as those of apples and pears. Peach, sour cherry, and some plum cultivars are naturally small and can be pruned heavily enough to keep them down to a reasonable size. Apricots grow into large trees but still produce fruit while being pruned heavily enough to maintain a reasonable size. Thus, with a certain amount of pruning, all of these trees can be planted as close together as 15 feet (5 m). Standard spacing recommendations if these trees are to be grown to their ultimate size are 18 to 25 feet (6 to 8 m) for peaches, plums, and sour cherries, and 25 to 40 feet (8 to 12 m) for sweet cherries and apricots. Spur-type sweet cherry trees that have shortened internodes and grow from about one-half to two-thirds the size of standard trees have been developed but are not yet widely available.

Culture and Management. Cherries and peaches generally grow best on land where there is no sod cover crop. In home gardens, cultivating around trees is often impractical, which is perhaps one reason that apricots and plums frequently grow better than peaches or cherries in home gardens. If the section of trunk beneath the mulch can be protected from rodents, mulching may be the answer to soil management. Peach trees grow well in sod if they are heavily fertilized with nitrogen.

Excess nitrogen does not affect fruiting of stone fruits to nearly the extent it affects pomes. Enough nitrogen should be applied to produce 12 to 24 inches (30 to 60 cm) of branch growth on nonbearing peach and sour cherry trees and 6 to 15 inches (15 to 38 cm) after they begin to bear at four to six years of age. The branch growth of sweet cherries should be somewhat greater and that of plums and apricots somewhat less. This amount of growth requires, on the average, an annual application of 1½ to 2 tablespoons of nitrogen per year of age until the tree is about seven years old (see Chapter 14 for further recommendations). Zinc, manganese, and iron deficiencies are common in stone fruits in the arid West.

In regions where the annual rainfall is less than 30 inches (75 cm) or where trees are being grown with a cover crop and precipitation is less than 50 inches (127 cm), stone fruits benefit from irrigation. The frequency with which irrigation is required varies from each ten to fourteen days during midsummer in areas with no summer rainfall and sandy soil, to three to four times each growing season in areas having good winter and spring rains and soil with high moisture-retaining capacity, to only an occasional irrigation during an extremely dry summer in some regions of the East and Midwest where summer rains normally supply enough moisture. Where water stress is likely to be a problem, peaches, nectarines, plums, and apricots should be grafted to peach and cherries to 'Mahaleb' rootstocks. The soil should be soaked to field capacity to at least 4 feet (1¼ m) of depth with each irrigation and then permitted to dry before water is again applied. Deep irrigation is essential if the trees are being grown with a permanent cover crop. The relative advantages and disadvantages of sprinkler versus surface irrigation (Chapter 6) apply to stone fruits, except that cherry trees should not be sprinkled while the fruit is maturing as wetting the fruit may cause it to split. Because they usually mature their crop before the late summer drought, cherries, apricots, and early peach cultivars can be more easily grown where water is limited than can late-maturing peach or plum cultivars or most apples or pears.

Apical dominance is not as pronounced in the peach as in the apple or pear trees, so the peaches can be trained to the vase system, although in some areas the modified central leader system is preferred. Other stone fruits are usually trained to the modified central leader (see "Pruning and Training" in Chapter 14).

Flowering and Fruiting

Unlike apple trees, which produce fruit on wood that is at least two years old, peaches and nectarines produce blossom buds only on current-season wood, and blossoms and fruit only on wood that is one year old. Buds on all of the stone fruits are either blossom buds or vegetative buds, never mixed like those of apple and pear. New buds on peach trees are produced in the leaf axils starting about midsummer and continuing as long as the tree is producing new leaves so that blossoms are produced to the tips of peach branches (Figure 13-7).

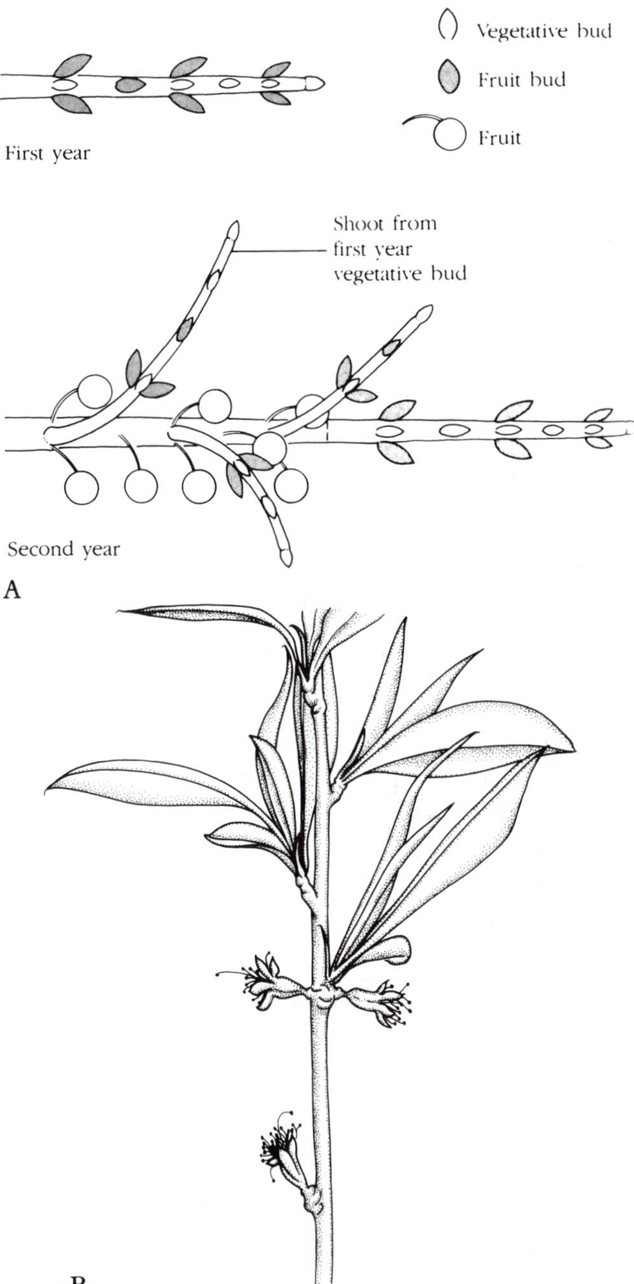

FIGURE 13-7 • The growth and fruiting habit of a peach tree. (A) A healthy peach branch produces some buds in clusters of three. The outer two are fruit buds, and the center is a vegetative bud that will develop into a new shoot. Only on an occasional node will both fruit buds develop into fruits, as is occurring in (B).

A

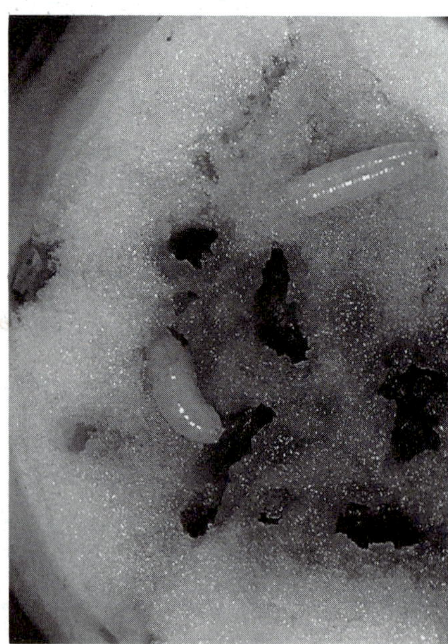

B

FIGURE 13-8 • (A) Cherry fruit fly maggot. (B) The larva of the cherry fruit fly is a serious pest of cherries in almost all sections of North America. (Courtesy of Grant Heilman)

Plums, apricots, and sour cherries produce blossom buds on the older half of current-season growth and, to a limited extent for some cultivars, on older wood. Sweet cherries produce them on older wood and in the first formed leaf axils of current-season wood. Thus blossoms and fruit are not produced as far toward the ends of the branches on cherry, apricot, or plum as they are on peach trees.

As explained in Chapter 3, most peach and apricot cultivars are self-fruitful, but some, such as the 'J. H. Hale' peach, produce poor pollen and must be cross-pollinated. Sour cherries are self-fruitful, but sweet cherries are not. The three sweet cherry cultivars popular in the West—'Bing', 'Lambert', and 'Royal Anne'—are also cross-incompatible and must have pollen from another cultivar if they are to set fruit.

Most Japanese and American plums and their hybrids require cross-pollination. Some cultivars of European plums are self-fruitful; others are not.

Insects and Diseases. Peaches, apricots, sour cherries, and plums can be produced without insect or disease control in a few areas away from commercial production of stone fruits; but in most gardens a regular spray program is necessary. As with the pome fruits, each application can be of a single or a combination of pesticides and can control one or several pests. The recommended timing of sprays for fruits in the garden or yard is early December and late January (two dormant sprays), just as buds are swelling (delayed dormant), just before blossoms open (prepink or pink), when blossom petals fall, late spring, summer, ten to fourteen days before harvest (preharvest), and postharvest. Generally it is not advisable to spray for insects unless they are present in damaging numbers (except for cherry fruit fly maggot) because the insecticide also often kills predators that may otherwise keep that insect or another in check. Insecticide applications at ten-day intervals from bloom until fruit maturity are almost always required to keep cherries free of cherry fruit fly maggots (Figure 13-8). Mite predators are frequently killed by pesticides used to control other insects, permitting a disastrous buildup of mite populations. Table 13-8 lists the major pests of stone fruits.

Cultivar Recommendations. Cultivar recommendations for stone fruits vary, of course, from one section of the country to another, and local recommendations are always best. However, a few standard cultivars that are highly adapted in many sections should be mentioned.

Peaches. Early peach cultivars of excellent quality include 'Red Haven', 'Hale Haven', and 'Golden Jubilee'; 'Early Elberta' is slightly later. 'Redskin' and 'Georgia Belle' are two later cultivars popular in the Southeast. In the West 'J. H. Hale' and 'Elberta' are standard freestone canning cultivars, but they may not mature in cooler areas where peaches can be grown. 'Reliance' is one of the hardiest peach cultivars and produces in the colder areas of Hardiness Zone 5. 'Gulf Queen' and 'Desert Gold' are two cultivars with low chilling requirements developed for the Southwest and Gulf regions.

Apricots. 'Moorpak' and 'Tilton' are two commercial varieties frequently grown in home gardens in the West. Apricots have not been regularly productive in most of the eastern part of the United States. The New York experiment station recommends 'Alfred', 'Veecot', and 'Goldcot' as three cultivars worthy of home trials in the Northeast.

Cherries. 'Bing' and 'Lambert' have long been the standard cultivars of red or black sweet cherries in the western United States. 'Royal Anne' (sometimes called 'Napoleon') is the standard white variety. All three of these, as mentioned, are self- and cross-incompatible. 'Van', a dark cultivar from Canada, or 'Rainier', a light-colored cultivar developed in Washington State, are now usually planted as pollinators. 'Emperor Francis', a white cherry, 'Ulster', and 'Windsor' are three cultivars recommended for the Northeast. 'Stella' is a self-pollinating cultivar. 'Montmorency' is a standard cultivar of sour cherries and 'North Star', developed by the University of Minnesota, is a sour cherry tree that does not grow over 8 feet (2.5 m) in height and spread. Its fruit turns dark and is semisweet when fully ripe. Sour cherry pollen will set fruit on sweet cherry trees, but sour cherry trees usually bloom too late to be reliable pollinators for sweet cherries.

Plums. 'Stanley' and 'Italian' prune are the standard prune-type plums and can be grown in most areas where plums are productive. 'Green Gage', a freestone, and 'Reine Claude' are two dessert-type plums that are excellent choices for the home gardener. 'Damson', a small, blue, tart plum, is prized for jams and preserves. Japanese plums, which are not hardy in all locations, are commonly eaten fresh. 'Santa Rosa' and 'Shiro' are two widely adapted cultivars.

Harvesting, Storing, Preserving. Time of harvesting the stone fruits depends to a large extent on their ultimate use. Peaches for canning or freezing will be a better quality if harvested before they become completely mature. Peach maturity is determined by changes in ground color. For yellow peaches this is when the green color starts to change to yellow. For home use the rest of the stone fruits should be fully mature, but not soft, when harvested.

None of the stone fruits can be stored for as long as apples, pears, and citrus, but most cultivars keep for ten to fourteen days in a refrigerator. If storage is contemplated, the fruit should be harvested when slightly immature and all damaged or imperfect fruits should be removed from the container before it is placed in storage.

All of the stone fruits can be easily processed by canning, freezing, or drying; directions are given in Chapter 14.

TABLE 13-8 • *Major insect pests and diseases of stone fruits*

<table>
<tr><th>Insect Pests</th><th>Symptoms and Damage</th><th>Control</th></tr>
<tr><td>Mites (various)</td><td>Mites hibernate under scales of bark (see Grape insect pests, Table 13-2).</td><td>Spraying before bloom, just after petals fall, and during the summer when mites are a problem.</td></tr>
<tr><td>Scale</td><td>See Grape insect pests, Table 13-2.</td><td>Dormant, delayed dormant, prebloom, petal-fall sprays. If serious a summer spray at crawler stage may be needed.</td></tr>
<tr><td>Lygus bug</td><td>Green or tan beetles that attack blossoms and fruit, causing blemish of fruit. They hide in cover crop.</td><td>Spray cover crop and trees at prebloom period.</td></tr>
<tr><td>Aphids</td><td>Several kinds attack stone fruits. They winter over as eggs and hatch in spring. They feed on young leaves, causing them to curl. Also transmit virus.</td><td>Delayed dormant and late-spring sprays as eggs are hatching and before leaves curl.</td></tr>
<tr><td>Peach tree borer</td><td>White worms with brown heads pass the winter in bark near base of tree. Worms become active in spring and feed on bark of tree. Can kill a tree in a few years. Gum, sawdust, and worm droppings exude from lower trunk area near ground level.</td><td>Fall treatment (October) with propylene dichloride emulsion in trench 2 in (5 cm) from tree trunk as follows:
<table>
<tr><th>Age of tree (years)</th><th></th><th>1</th><th>2</th><th>3</th><th>4 & up</th></tr>
<tr><td>Water (parts)</td><td></td><td>8½</td><td>7</td><td>7</td><td>6</td></tr>
<tr><td>Emulsion (parts)</td><td></td><td>1½</td><td>3</td><td>3</td><td>4</td></tr>
<tr><td rowspan="2">Amount/tree</td><td>(pints)</td><td>⅛</td><td>¼</td><td>½</td><td>½–1</td></tr>
<tr><td>(liters)</td><td>1/16</td><td>⅛</td><td>¼</td><td>¼–½</td></tr>
</table>
Also summer spray.</td></tr>
<tr><td>Peach twig borer</td><td>Larva passes winter as small brown worm that emerges about bloom time and feeds on tips of twigs, causing them to die back.</td><td>Sprays just as buds begin to swell in spring and just after the petals fall.</td></tr>
<tr><td>Oriental fruit moth</td><td>Kills twigs during spring and early summer. Bores into fruit much as codling moth does.</td><td>Early cultivars usually escape damage. Spring and summer sprays for late-maturing cultivars.</td></tr>
</table>

(continued)

Citrus Fruits

Citrus fruits are a subtropical group of evergreen fruits that include oranges, lemons, grapefruit, limes, and some lesser-known kinds and hybrids. All types are injured by freezing, with critical temperatures ranging from 26° to 18°F (−3° to −8°C). Citrus trees have fragrant blossoms, attractive shapes, and waxy green leaves, and they start to bear fruit after only two to three years, all of which make them excellent dual-purpose ornamental fruit trees in areas where they are hardy. They are also grown to some extent as potted plants and in greenhouses farther north.

Climatic Adaptation. Citrus is limited to the very warmest locations of the United States. The sweet orange (*Citrus sinensis*), one of the earliest fruits to be domesticated, is also the most popular in the United States; it is consumed in larger quantities than is any other fruit. Related to sweet oranges are a group known as "kid glove" oranges, the skin of which separates easily from the flesh. This group includes the tangerines or mandarins

Insect Pests	Symptoms and Damage	Control
Plum curculio	Long-snouted beetle feeds on leaves and fruit. Lays eggs in fruit, causing it to be wormy. Main agent for spread of brown rot.	Periodic sprays starting 10 days after petal fall.
Earwig and Japanese beetle	Both insects are general feeders on leaves and fruits. Earwigs are relatively long insects with pincers on the rear. They may enter peaches and apricots through the stem end. Japanese beetles are metallic green beetles found mainly in the East.	Control program for other insects usually controls these two.
Cherry fruit fly	Adult fly lays eggs in fruit. These hatch into small white maggots about the time the fruit matures.	Insecticide 7 to 10 days after blossom and each 10 days thereafter to harvest.
Diseases	**Symptoms and Damage**	**Control**
Brown rot	Most serious in humid areas or during wet seasons. Fruit shows soft brown areas as it ripens, becomes covered with tufts of gray mold.	Where brown rot is an annual problem, prepink, petal-fall, and preharvest fungicide sprays are required.
Powdery mildew	See Pome fruit diseases, Table 13-7.	Keep tree leaves dry if possible. Sulfur spray late spring and again 3 weeks later.
Peach leaf curl	Appears in early spring as leaves unfold. Leaves become thickened, puckered, and brittle. Fungus is carried from season to season in buds and on bark.	Spray trees with fungicide in November and again during late winter.
Coryneum blight	Causes gumming and death of buds and twigs; gumming and split bark on branches and trunk; and brown, red-bordered spots on leaves. Can cause heavy fruit losses.	Fungicide during October plus prebloom spray.
Bacterial canker	Enlarging lesions on trunks and larger limbs. Great amounts of gum are associated with active phase.	Scrape and disinfect cankers as described for fireblight of pome fruits (Table 13-7). Copper sprays.

(*C. reticulata*) and some recently developed hybrids among various citrus types, including citranges and tangelos.

Critical low temperatures are about 24°F (−4°C) for sweet orange cultivars and as low as 18°F for the satsuma. If temperatures fall lower, the crop will be destroyed and the trees badly injured.

Grapefruit (*Citrus paradisi*) grows especially well in desert conditions. Critical temperatures are between 24° and 26°F (−4° to −3°C). Lemons (*C. limon*) and limes (*C. aurantifolia*) are among the most tender of the citrus fruits, with severe injury occurring when temperatures drop to about 26°F.

Propagation and Planting. Although citrus trees can be easily rooted from cuttings, they are usually propagated by budding or grafting to rootstocks that are resistant to root diseases. Rootstocks that have been selected for specific conditions such as soil adaptation and disease resistance are available.

Most seed of citrus is produced without fertilization (apomictic), so unlike most other kinds of fruit trees, seedling citrus trees usually produce fruit like that of the parent tree. Therefore, it is possible for gardeners to produce citrus trees from seed. However, seedling trees have more thorns than do those propagated by grafting or from cuttings. Sour orange (*Citrus aurantium*), sweet orange (various cultivars), and 'Rough Lemon' are frequently used as rootstocks. Orange trees growing on 'Rough Lemon' rootstocks are reported to produce fruit of lower quality. Virus diseases create serious problems of graft incompatibility with some of the other rootstocks.

Nursery trees are available in containers, balled and burlapped, or, in some locations, bare rooted. (Those sold bare rooted usually have had their leaves removed.) They are most easily planted during the cooler, more rainy season of the year. Each orange tree needs about 400 square feet (36 m^2) of space; grapefruit need a little less, lemons a little more.

Culture and Management. Citrus trees do not require soil as deep as most deciduous fruit trees, 3 feet (1 m) of depth being enough for maximum yield. Recommendations for fertilizing with the major elements are in Tables 14-16 and 14-17. In many Florida soils, magnesium, zinc, copper, manganese, and calcium are needed for citrus. These compounds can be most easily added, with the general trace element package available at garden stores of that state. Zinc is often needed for citrus in the West. Nitrogen deficiency symptoms are light-green leaves, stunted growth, and excessive blossom production. Phosphorus deficiency causes excessively thick peeling on the fruit. Potassium deficiency causes reduced leaf size, reduced growth in the top of the tree, and small fruit with a low acid content. Magnesium deficiency causes pale-colored leaves and increased leaf abscission, especially during heavy crop production.

Because they grow continuously, citrus trees use water throughout the year. About 3 to 4 feet (about 1 m) annually or 1½ to 2½ inches (4 to 6 cm) each two to three weeks from rainfall or irrigation are required for a normal crop. It is essential that citrus not be subjected to water stress during periods of fruit set, development, and maturity. For most kinds of citrus, fruiting occurs during winter and early spring.

Citrus trees, vegetatively propagated, tend to bear some fruit two or three years after planting. Almost all kinds are self-fruitful. Blooms are not produced all at one time, as on deciduous fruit trees (Figure 13-9); however, where growth is slowed because of cool weather—as it is in much of the citrus-growing area of the United States—oranges and grapefruit tend to produce most of their blossoms in the early spring.

Citrus are pruned very little except to thin out older trees to some extent and to remove crossing and dead branches (see "Pruning and Training" in Chapter 14).

Disorders and Pests. Among the disorders that plague citrus fruit are (1) an extremely thick skin, sometimes caused by phosphorus deficiency but probably also by other factors; (2) dry, juiceless sections often caused by freezing temperatures

FIGURE 13-9 • The fruiting habit of a lemon tree. Unlike temperate-zone fruit trees, citrus trees do not necessarily produce all of their blooms at the same time.

during the ripening period; and (3) lack of color (especially in oranges) caused by warm night temperatures and a lack of sunlight while ripening.

Citrus is subject to attack by a great many diseases. Among the most serious is gummosis disease, caused by phytophthora and other fungi, which kills the bark around the graft union. It is controlled by using resistant rootstocks, by keeping the environment around the trunk as dry as possible, by pruning low-growing branches and controlling weeds, and by cutting out the infected bark and disinfecting the area around wounds. Scab limits or prevents the growing of lemons in the Southeast, but this disease can be controlled with fungicides on oranges, grapefruit, and other kinds of citrus that are less susceptible to it. Virus diseases and many unidentified disorders that may be caused by virus are controlled by using virus-free rootstock for propagation and by obtaining virus-resistant planting stock. Fruit mold, a serious postharvest disorder, can be controlled by a fungicidal dip.

A number of scale insects attack citrus, one of the most damaging being red scale. In Florida, scale can be controlled with oil sprays during the rainy season; in California, oil sprays damage citrus trees and do not offer good control. Nematodes of several species also attack citrus.

Harvesting and Storage. Citrus fruits should not be harvested until they are fully ripe, which may be ten to thirteen months after bloom, depending on the kind and cultivar. Unlike the temperate-zone fruits, citrus can be "stored" by allowing the fruit to remain on the tree. The color of oranges stored on the tree sometimes changes from orange back to green, but this does not materially affect their quality. Thus, citrus fruits can be picked from the tree as needed over a considerable period of time — a decided advantage for the backyard gardener. Lemons are harvested over the entire year, with the heaviest pickings between December and March.

Cultivars. 'Washington Navel' and 'Valencia' are the two most popular sweet orange cultivars in the West, and 'Valencia' is probably the most important one in Florida. Both are relatively seedless. 'Texas Navel', a bud mutation of 'Washington Navel', is somewhat better adapted than its parent for growing in Texas. The navel oranges are very early, maturing before Christmas in the warmer areas, and the Valencias are late, maturing in the spring and summer. 'Pineapple', an old cultivar that produces fruit with numerous seeds, is grown in Florida; 'Jaffa' is a cultivar from Israel that is gaining in popularity. 'Temple', an important cultivar in Florida, is probably a hybrid between the sweet orange and the mandarin. It peels easily and the segments separate more easily than do those of other sweet oranges but not as easily as those of mandarins.

'Marsh Seedless' (yellow flesh) and its bud sports 'Thompson' (pink flesh), 'Ruby' (red flesh), and 'Webb' (red flesh) are the most important cultivars of grapefruit. 'Eureka', 'Lisbon', and 'Villa Franca' are important lemon cultivars.

Other Subtropical Fruits

Many kinds of fruits can be produced in subtropical areas, but only a few of the more popular kinds will be described in this chapter.

Figs. Although the commercial production of figs (*Ficus* spp.) has been limited mainly to California and the adjacent southwestern states, figs are also grown for home use in the Gulf and southeastern states. Fig trees are grown mainly as ornamentals in warmer areas as far north as Trenton, New Jersey; Lewiston, Idaho; and Yakima, Washington. However, even the more cold-resistant sorts are injured by temperatures below 16°F (−9°C), and trees will be killed if temperatures drop below 5°F (−15°C). For satisfactory development, figs require long, warm, growing seasons; cool summers prevent normal growth. Water requirements are not high, but at least 24 inches (60 cm) are needed. Fig plants generally are grown from cuttings, but they can be propagated by suckers, layers, buds, grafts, and seeds as well.

Flowers of edible figs produce no pollen, and, if none is brought into the orchard, common cultivars—'Adriatic', 'Turkey', 'Kadota', 'Mission', and 'Brunswick'—will set seedless fruits parthenocarpically (without pollination). Trees of the Smyrna type ('Calmyrna' is the main U.S. cultivar of this type) cannot set fruit without pollination. When flowers are pollinated, pollen must be supplied from an almost inedible kind of fig known as caprifig. Insect pollination is required. Mature June-crop caprifigs in perforated bags are placed in Smyrna fig trees. The small fig wasps in the caprifigs become covered with pollen and seek another fig in which to lay their eggs. While moving about within the fruit, they brush pollen onto the pistils of the Smyrna fig. Because this type of pollination, called caprification, is expensive, growth substances may be used to set fruit parthenocarpically.

Persimmons. There are two types of persimmons, the native American species (*Diospyros virginiana*) and the Japanese (oriental or kaki) persimmon (*D. kaki*); only the latter type is grown commercially. It is found as far north as New Jersey and southwestern Missouri and Utah. Some cultivars are quite cold resistant and have been known to withstand 0°F temperatures, but generally kaki is classed as a subtropical fruit. It thrives wherever figs can be grown successfully. It is adapted to semiarid conditions but is also grown in regions of heavy rainfall. It thrives on rich, deep, friable soils. The trees are propagated by budding or grafting on native or kaki seedlings.

Persimmon production in this country is limited, partly because people are not aware of the necessity of ripening this fruit. Just one bite of a puckery, astringent, hard persimmon will discourage even the most dedicated connoisseur. Persimmons are harvested while still hard, but most cultivars do not become sweet and edible until they have softened.

The three main cultivars, 'Hachiya', 'Tanenashi', and 'Tamopan', set fruit without pollination when grown in California. When these cultivars are grown in the East or when other cultivars are planted, it is advisable to include a pollinator in the planting. The cultivar 'Gailey' is usually recommended as the pollinator.

Dates. The date palm (*Phoenix* spp.), a native of North Africa, is grown both for its fruit and as an ornamental in tropical and subtropical areas. In the United States commercial production is limited to the Imperial and Coachella valleys in California and to southwestern Arizona. Date palms thrive in a hot, dry climate; rain prevents fruit from maturing properly. Though some cultivars can withstand temperatures as low as 15° to 20°F (−9° to −7°C), commercial culture is limited to frost-free areas.

Because the date palm is dioecious, both a male and a female tree are needed if fruit is to be produced. For commercial production, one staminate tree is planted for every twenty-five pistillate trees. Dates are propagated from suckers that develop from the base of the palm or on its trunk. The 'Deglet Noor' and 'Maktoon' cultivars are grown extensively in California. For cooler areas, especially for ornamental purposes, the 'Hallaway' and 'Khodrawy' are used.

Olives. Olives (*Olea europea*) are native to the Mediterranean and are grown widely in that region. Olive trees can withstand temperatures of 15° to 16°F (about −9°C) but may be severely injured if the temperature drops as low as 13°F (−11°C). The tree can grow in both dry gravelly and poorly aerated soils and is very tolerant of drought, so it is a valuable ornamental in parts of the arid Southwest where water for irrigation is limited or nonexistent.

Olives are usually propagated from hardwood cuttings treated with a rooting hormone. Trees can also be budded or grafted on seedling rootstocks. Young trees for planting should have a trunk diameter of from ⅝ to ¾ inch (about 2 cm). If pruned heavily, trees can be spaced 20 × 20 feet (6 × 6 m), but they will need to be spaced 35 × 35 feet (11 × 11 m) if they are permitted to grow to full size. They are planted as far as 70 feet (21 m) apart where water is likely to be very limited.

Olive trees require little pruning. Flowers are wind pollinated, and commonly grown cultivars do not require a pollinator. Olive trees continue to produce for many years after they are planted; some in the Middle East are said to be two thousand years old.

Fruits develop their maximum oil content six to eight months after bloom, but they can be harvested a little earlier (for green olives) or can be left on the tree until later. For home consumption they are usually harvested when they turn from green to straw color or a little later, when they become reddish. (They turn black when processed.)

The bitter glucoside can be extracted by placing the olives in a solution made with 2 ounces sodium hydroxide in 1 gallon (60 g in 4 l) of water and leaving them for a few days until a color change shows that the lye has penetrated the pit (or nearly to the pit if a slightly bitter flavor is desired). The olives must then be soaked for three days in water that is changed daily or more often to remove the lye. For table use, the olives are then soaked for a day or two in a solution of 3 ounces of salt in 1 gallon (90 g in 4 l) of water. 'Mission', a late small olive, 'Mansanillo', a slightly larger olive excellent for canning, and 'Serillano', a large-sized olive for fresh consumption or canning are three popular cultivars.

Avocado. Avocados (*Persea americana*) are tropical evergreen fruits indigenous to Central and South America. In the continental United States they are grown in southern Florida, along the Gulf Coast, and in southern California. The trees may be large, reaching a height of 25 to 40 feet (8 to 12 m). They grow rapidly and come into bearing in three or four years.

Depending on the cultivar, the trees can withstand temperatures from 27° or 28°F (−2°C) down to 20°F (−7°C); however they cannot withstand extreme heat. The trees grow well on a wide range of deep, well-drained soils. They are propagated by budding or grafting on seedling stocks.

There are three types or races of avocado. The West Indian can withstand the least cold. The Guatemalan is moderately resistant to cold and is the type grown most extensively in California. The more cold resistant Mexican avocados are grown commercially in both Florida and California. 'Fuerte', a Mexican-Guatemalan hybrid and 'Hass', a Guatemalan type, are the most popular cultivars in the West. 'Winter Mexican' and 'Lula', Mexican-Guatemalan hybrids, and 'Nabal', a Guatemalan type, are three cultivars popular in Florida.

Nut Trees

In popular terminology a **nut** is a hard vegetable product, usually a fruit, enclosing an edible or usable portion within a shell. There are, geographically or climatically, two types of nut trees—the nonhardy tropical evergreen and the hardy to semihardy deciduous. Nuts that grow on nonhardy evergreen trees—for example, coconuts, Brazil nuts, and cashews—are not produced to any extent in the United States.

Vegetative propagation is necessary for all types of deciduous nut trees if high-quality, uniform nuts are to be produced. Budding and grafting are the methods used for all common nut trees except filberts (hazelnuts), which are propagated from cuttings or suckers.

Trees of deciduous nuts, except for almonds, are wind pollinated. There is a wide range of self- and cross-fruitfulness. Almonds are self-unfruitful and require outside sources of pollen. Walnut cultivars appear to be both self- and cross-fruitful, and pollen from one species may function on the pistils of another. Self-unfruitfulness, common in pecan cultivars, may be due to differences in the time when the pistils are receptive and the staminate catkins shed pollen.

Nut trees usually are trained to the modified leader form and do not require severe pruning. Pruning consists of removing superfluous and unsymmetrical branches and dead limbs. Lower branches of nut trees are removed up to 4 to 6 feet

(1¼ to 2 m) from the ground to make cultivation and other operations easier. Where they can be grown, most kinds of nut trees make excellent shade and specimen trees and often are more valuable as ornamentals than as food-producing plants.

Walnuts. Two types of walnuts are commonly grown—the American or native black walnut (*Juglans nigra*) and the Persian or English walnut (*J. regia*). The butternut (*J. cineria*), native to eastern North America, and the California black walnut (*J. hindsii*) are occasionally grown.

The black walnut is widely distributed, being found from north of the Canadian border to the Gulf of Mexico and from the Atlantic to the Pacific Ocean. It produces large crops of high-quality nuts and is a valuable timber tree as well. A number of selected cultivars with thinner shells and larger, more highly flavored kernels have been developed, including 'Thomas', 'Ohio', 'Stabler', and 'Rohwer'.

The Persian or English walnut does not have a very wide range of distribution, and commercial production is mainly in California, western Oregon, and southwestern Washington. Temperatures from 0° to −5°F (−18° to −21°C) are critical to most cultivars of these nuts, so production is limited to warmer areas. In addition, disease problems in humid climates are severe, so a moderately dry, cool growing season is desirable. 'Hartley' is the leading cultivar in California. 'Placentia' is popular in southern California, and 'Fanguette', because of its late bloom, escapes spring frost and is popular in northern California and Oregon. In the Northeast and protected valleys of the Rocky Mountains, Carpathian types from Poland, including 'Broadview', 'Schafer', 'Little Page', and 'Colby', can sometimes be produced in gardens.

Pecans. Pecans (*Carya illinoensis*) belong to the hickory group of trees. In volume of nuts produced, the pecan is surpassed only by the Persian walnut. The pecan tree is native to the southeastern and south-central United States as far west as New Mexico and as far north as southern Iowa and Indiana. Commercial plantings are confined largely to the Gulf Coast and adjacent states. Because pecans bloom late, their blossoms are not often damaged by spring frost.

The "paper shell" cultivars require a frost-free growing season of 240 to 250 days, whereas the northern types, which produce smaller nuts with harder shells, mature in 180 to 200 days. Improved hickory nuts hardy in all but the coldest regions are now available. Both pecan and hickory are good shade trees for the higher rainfall areas of the East, and because they are native to North America, there are dozens of cultivars. Many are adapted to a limited area, so local cultivar recommendations should be followed.

Filberts. Primarily because of its unusual flowering habit, the filbert (*Corylus maximus*), or hazelnut, is grown on a commercial scale mainly in mild-winter areas of Oregon and southwestern Washington. Its bloom period comes during the winter. Ordinary frosts have no effect on either pistil or pollen, but the pistils may be killed by temperatures lower than 10° to 12°F (−12° to −11°C). Most cultivars are self-unfruitful, so two should be planted. The filbert is an interesting ornamental that can survive in many areas of the country, but it does not produce consistently where winter temperatures drop to 5°F (−15°C) or lower. In Oregon and Washington 'Barcelona', with 'Dariana' as its pollinator, are the important cultivars. 'Cosford', 'Medium Long', 'Italian Red', and 'Royal' are cultivars also recommended for the Northwest.

Almonds. In many ways the almond (*Prunus amygdalus*) is similar to the peach, although its seeds or nuts have only a thin, hard layer of flesh over them. Almond flowers resemble peach blossoms, and the almond nut is the pit of the peach-like fruit. There are two types of almonds, bitter and sweet. Bitter almonds, which are grown mainly in Mediterranean countries, are used in the manufacture of flavoring extracts and prussic or hydrocyanic acid. Sweet almonds are grown commercially mainly in central California.

Sweet almond flower buds start growing earlier in the spring than do peach buds, so almonds are even more subject to late-spring frost injury. They can be grown only in areas where late frosts are rare. Both trees and nuts are subject to rot where the weather is cool or humid. Cultural practices are similar to those used in growing peaches. Almonds are insect pollinated and self-unfruitful, so a pollinator is required. 'Nonpareil', 'Mission', 'Ne Plus Ultra', 'Peerless', and 'Eureka' are important cultivars.

Selected References

Bilderback, D. E., and D. H. Patent. *Backyard Fruits and Berries.* Emmaus, Pa.: Rodale Press, 1984.

Childers, N. B. *Modern Fruit Science.* 9th ed. Mount Vernon, Va.: Horticulture Publications, 1983.

Garden Way Publishing Editors. *Fruits and Vegetables: One Thousand and One Questions Answered.* Downal, Vt.: Storey, 1990.

Ortho Books Editorial Staff. *All About Growing Fruits, Berries, and Nuts.* Rev. ed. San Francisco: Ortho Books, 1987.

Shoemaker, J. S. *Small Fruit Culture.* 4th ed. New York: McGraw-Hill, 1975.

Sunset Magazine and Books Editors. *Fruits, Nuts, and Berries: How to Grow.* Menlo Park, Calif.: Lane, 1984.

Westwood, M. N. *Temperate Zone Pomology.* Rev. ed. Beaverton, Oreg.: Timber Press, 1988.

The Handbook

PURPOSE AND ORGANIZATION

◆ ◆ ◆

To a large extent the preceding thirteen chapters tell the story of horticulture from a scientific viewpoint. Although they do include some practical information, they do not present many of the how-to-do-it directions needed by gardeners.

This chapter, therefore, has been prepared to give illustrated instructions for gardening practices. It is organized as much as possible in chronological sequence. Those tasks related to planting and propagating come first, followed by those that will need to be done while the garden is growing, followed, finally, by those concerned with harvesting and storing.

Those who wish to gain maximum benefit from this handbook should first read the entire chapter in order to find out what it contains and the ideas that can be applied to situations already encountered. After that the handbook can be used as a reference for specific information.

SOURCES OF GARDENING INFORMATION

◆ ◆ ◆

Most readers are aware that a book on gardening can cover the subject in only a general way. From time to time all gardeners will have questions that relate to their particular situation, location, or type of planting. For most of these questions there are several local sources from which answers might come.

Government Offices

Perhaps the most ready source of information and the one most likely to have the right answers for local gardening problems is the county extension staff. Counties where horticulture is important or where gardening is popular usually have a horticultural specialist on the county extension staff.

In some urban areas, experienced gardeners, often retired, act as volunteers to supply information and assistance to those less experienced in horticultural practice. In some metropolitan areas, experienced gardeners who have an interest and some free time are trained by extension horticultural specialists. When the extension staff is satisfied that the trainee has adequate knowledge, they may award him or her the title of "Master Gardener" or something similar. The trainees speak at garden club meetings, answer garden questions by telephone, and dispense information from booths at fairs and garden centers. They are able to answer most of the questions directed to them, and they can call on the county extension staff whenever more specialized information is needed.

County extension offices also maintain a supply of information pamphlets compiled by state and federal specialists that are distributed free of charge or for a nominal fee. These publications, along with many not stocked by the county extension office, are available from state and provincial agricultural information offices, which are usually a part of the agricultural college at the land-grant university of the state. Addresses of these offices are listed in Table 14-1. Federal publications are available from the Superintendent of Documents, U.S. Government Printing Office, Washington, D.C. 20402, and from the Information Division, Canada Department of Agriculture, Ottawa K1A 0C7. Pamphlets listing both federal and state bulletins available usually can be found at the county extension office.

Garden Clubs, Botanic Gardens, Commercial Garden Suppliers

Local garden clubs frequently can supply garden information. Nurseries and garden stores are also sources of up-to-date information relating to horticultural problems. Larger nurseries often hire a landscape architect to give advice on home landscaping problems. Local libraries maintain collections of garden publications, especially if gardeners let the librarians know of their interest in such information.

TABLE 14-1 • *Obtaining gardening information*

State Agricultural Colleges and Experiment Stations			
State	**University or Experiment Station**	**Post Office**	**Zip code**
Alabama	Auburn University	Auburn	36830
Alaska	University of Alaska	Fairbanks	99701
Arizona	University of Arizona	Tucson	85721
Arkansas	University of Arkansas	Fayetteville	72701
California	University of California	Berkeley	94720
	University of California	Davis	95616
	University of California	Riverside	92502
Colorado	Colorado State University	Fort Collins	80523
Connecticut	University of Connecticut	Storrs	06268
	University of Connecticut	New Haven	06504
Delaware	University of Delaware	Newark	19711
Florida	University of Florida	Gainesville	32611
Georgia	University of Georgia	Athens	30601
Hawaii	University of Hawaii	Honolulu	96822
Idaho	University of Idaho	Moscow	83843
Illinois	University of Illinois	Urbana	61801
Indiana	Purdue University	West Lafayette	47907
Iowa	Iowa State University	Ames	50010
Kansas	Kansas State University	Manhattan	66506
Kentucky	University of Kentucky	Lexington	40506
Louisiana	Louisiana State University	Baton Rouge	70893
Maine	University of Maine	Orono	04473
Maryland	University of Maryland	College Park	20742
Massachusetts	University of Massachusetts	Amherst	01002
Michigan	Michigan State University	East Lansing	48824
Minnesota	University of Minnesota	St. Paul	55101
Mississippi	Mississippi State University	Mississippi State	39762
Missouri	University of Missouri	Columbia	65201
Montana	Montana State University	Bozeman	59715
Nebraska	University of Nebraska	Lincoln	68503
Nevada	University of Nevada	Reno	89507
New Hampshire	University of New Hampshire	Durham	03824
New Jersey	Rutgers University	New Brunswick	08903
New Mexico	New Mexico State University	Las Cruces	88003

(*continued*)

Some of the larger public and private gardens disseminate gardening information. One of these, the Brooklyn Botanic Garden, distributes a quarterly publication, *Plants and Gardens*. Three of its annual quarterly issues are handbooks covering in depth specialized horticultural topics. Several dozen handbooks are available on such diverse topics as plant dyeing, plant pests, flowering shrubs, nursery sources, pruning techniques, and terrariums. A list of publications and prices can be obtained from Brooklyn Botanic Gardens, 1000 Washington Avenue, Brooklyn, N.Y. 11225.

Collectively, gardeners spend millions of dollars each year for equipment, supplies, and information, and the various companies catering to the needs and desires of gardeners dispense a great deal of useful information, ranging from advertising brochures and seed, nursery, and equipment catalogs to the gardening column or section in the local newspaper. Some of the better known periodicals catering wholly or partially to the gardening public are *Better Homes and Gardens*, *Sunset*, *National Gardening*, and *Organic Gardening and Farming*. The publisher of *Organic Gardening and*

TABLE 14-1 • *(Continued)*

STATE AGRICULTURAL COLLEGES AND EXPERIMENT STATIONS			
State	**University or Experiment Station**	**Post Office**	**Zip code**
New York	Cornell University	Ithaca	14853
	Cornell University	Geneva	14456
North Carolina	North Carolina State University	Raleigh	27607
North Dakota	North Dakota State University	Fargo	58102
Ohio	Ohio State University	Columbus	43210
Oklahoma	Oklahoma State University	Stillwater	74074
Oregon	Oregon State University	Corvallis	97331
Pennsylvania	Pennsylvania State University	University Park	16802
Puerto Rico	University of Puerto Rico	Mayaguez	00708
Rhode Island	University of Rhode Island	Kingston	02881
South Carolina	Clemson University	Clemson	29631
South Dakota	South Dakota State University	Brookings	57006
Tennessee	University of Tennessee	Knoxville	37901
Texas	Texas A & M University	College Station	77843
Utah	Utah State University	Logan	84322
Vermont	University of Vermont	Burlington	05401
Virginia	Virginia Polytechnic Institute	Blacksburg	24061
Washington	Washington State University	Pullman	99163
West Virginia	West Virginia University	Morgantown	26506
Wisconsin	University of Wisconsin	Madison	53706
Wyoming	University of Wyoming	Laramie	82071
CANADIAN AGRICULTURAL COLLEGES AND EXPERIMENT STATIONS			
Province	**University**	**Post office**	**Postal Code**
Alberta	University of Alberta	Edmonton	T6G 2E1
British Columbia	University of British Columbia	Vancouver	V6T 1W5
Ontario	University of Guelph	Guelph	N1G 2W1
Quebec	Université Labal	Cité Universitaire Quebec, Quebec	G1K 7P4
Quebec	McGill University	P.O.B. 6070 Montreal	H3C 3G1
Manitoba	University of Manitoba	Winnipeg	R3T 2N2
Nova Scotia	Nova Scotia Agricultural College	Truro	B2N 5E3
Saskatchewan	University of Saskatchewan	Saskatoon	S7N 0W0

Farming, Rodale Press, has a series of publications dealing with the "natural" or "organic" way of gardening. *Good Housekeeping*, *The New York Botanic Garden*, and *Greystone Press* each has published in *Illustrated Encyclopedia of Gardening* with ten or more profusely colored volumes on garden topics from A to Z. Time-Life has a series of books on gardening, and *Sunset*'s Lane Publishers has produced an extensive how-to-do-it series on various aspects of gardening. Several companies that supply pesticides and fertilizers have published gardening literature, for example, the extensive series of books by the Ortho Division of the Chevron Chemical Company.

The Yellow Pages of the local telephone directory list various local businesses offering supplies and services, such as seed, nursery stock, turf, pesticides, fertilizer, tools and equipment for sale or rent, rototilling, landscape services, soil testing, and even medical care for sick plants.

Scientific and Trade Publications

Although most readers of this book are probably not vitally interested in the professional aspects of horticulture, they should be aware that there is a professional organization called the American Society for Horticultural Science that sponsors a national meeting each year at which scientists interested in horticulture meet, discuss new developments and problems, and generally exchange ideas on many aspects of horticulture. This society also sponsors two bimonthly publications, *HortScience* and the *Journal of the American Society for Horticultural Science*, both of which publish papers reporting their members' research findings. *HortScience* also publishes news of horticulture and horticulturists. Another organization, the American Horticultural Society (AHS), and its journal, *American Horticulturist*, cater to a national membership who are more interested in ornamental and hobby horticulture. Besides an annual three- or four-day meeting, AHS sponsors tours to locations worldwide that have interest for gardeners.

Trade publications such as *American Vegetable Grower*, *Western Fruit Grower*, *Florists' Review*, and countless others supply information primarily for commercial growers.

SOIL PREPARATION

Sequential Preparation of Small Areas for Planting

1. Spread manure, compost, peat, and/or fertilizer evenly over the area to be dug. Determine that the soil has a moisture level suitable for working by pressing a quantity of soil in your hands. If it forms a ball that breaks easily when dropped, it is all right for working. If it forms a ball that does not break, it is too wet to work. Sometimes the soil may be so dry and hard that it is physically impossible to work. Such soil needs to be irrigated. If the area is covered with sod, it may be necessary or desirable to remove it before the soil is dug (Figure 14-1).
2. Begin spading at the side of the garden that most needs to have the soil level raised. This may be the low corner or a side that needs to be raised for appearances or for irrigation and drainage.
3. Spading down 6 to 8 inches (15 to 20 cm), directly turn over each shovelful of the first row.
4. Pile the soil from the second row upside down on the first row, leaving a trench where the soil from the second row was removed.
5. Rake plant residue and added organic matter from the third row into the furrow and then dig the soil from the third row, turning it upside down into the empty furrow.
6. Repeat Step 5 until the bed is completely worked.
7. Rake immediately to break up clods, remove trash from the surface, and prepare a uniform seedbed.

Sequential Preparation of Larger Areas for Planting

1. Broadcast organic matter and/or fertilizer and determine that the soil moisture level is suitable, as in the previous Step 1.
2. Work the soil to a depth of at least 6 inches with a moleboard plow, disc, or rototiller.
3. Break up clods and level with a harrow or other equipment.

Growing Media for Container-Grown Plants

When growing medium for only a few potted plants is needed, growers usually find it most efficient to buy commercially formulated and pasteurized potting mixes (discussed in Chapter 5) from a nursery or department store garden center. Growers who contemplate home propagation or need relatively large quantities of soil media may find it necessary, or at least much less expensive, to put together their own potting mix.

A

FIGURE 14-1 • Lifting sod. Using a sharp spade, carefully cut around a square chunk of sod. An area about 18 inches (46 cm) × 18 inches can be conveniently lifted (A). With a long-nosed shovel, "clam gun," or a straight-handled spade, dig under the sod at a depth of about 2 inches (5 cm) until the square of sod is loosened (B). Next, turn the square upside down, and scrape away surplus soil until the bottom surface is smooth and the square has a uniform thickness (C). The square of sod can now be used for patching an old lawn or sodding a new one.

B

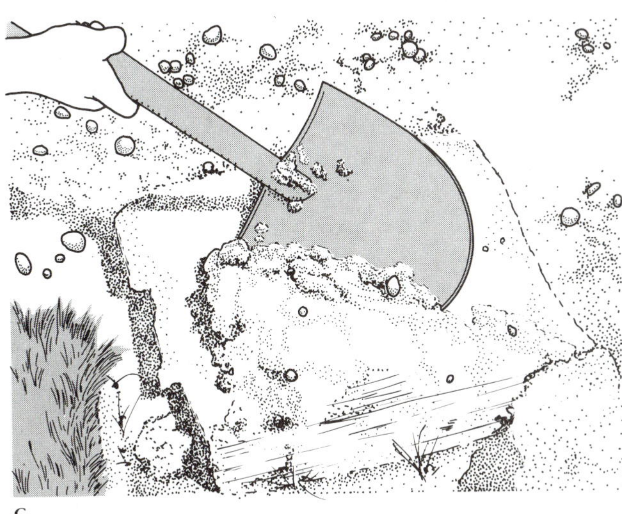

C

Media for Rooting Cuttings. Sand, perlite, a mixture of sand and peat, and a mixture of sand and vermiculite all are used as rooting media. I prefer perlite when it is easily obtained and can be kept moist. The medium for rooting cuttings should not be fertilized.

Media for Starting Transplant Seedlings. Except for species with very small seeds, fertilizer is not needed if seeds are to be germinated in pots and pricked off into flats at about the time the first true leaves are developing. Sand or perlite is often mixed with peat or vermiculite in equal portions. I am most consistently successful with sand and peat, but other people find the other mixes more satisfactory. A soil mix or an artificial mix with fertilizer should be used if seedlings are to be grown to transplant size without being pricked off or if species like petunia or impatiens, with very tiny seed, are being germinated. The germination medium for small-seeded species should be sifted through a screen to provide a fine seedbed.

Media for Growing Transplants and Potting. A good potting soil can be made by mixing one part organic matter, one part sand, and one to two parts garden soil. Use a higher proportion of soil if the soil is sandy and a lower proportion if it is mostly clay. The organic matter can be peat moss, well-rotted manure, or well-decomposed compost.

Many experts advise pasteurizing all nonsterile potting mixes to prevent the fungal decay of seedling stems at ground level, called damping-off (see Table 14-26). This may be advisable in many areas, especially if seedlings are to be grown to transplant size. When I use soil from uncultivated areas or from fields cropped to grains or forage and clean all containers and potting equipment, I find pasteurization to be unnecessary or even detrimental. Because there is little microbial competition in pasteurized soil, if root pathogens become established, they can spread and quickly destroy all plants in a container having pasteurized soil. For this reason it is doubly important to sterilize all equipment and containers when using a sterile medium.

Small amounts of soil can be pasteurized in shallow pans in an oven. If the soil layer is no thicker than 1½ inches (4 cm), most decay-causing organisms and most weed seeds should be destroyed when the soil has been baked for one hour with the oven set at 220°F (105°C). If a wooden flat is being used, do not turn the oven higher than 250°F (120°C). The flat, as well as organic matter, can char and burn.

The growing medium should be moistened before it is used. Overwatering is not usually a problem with artificial mixes. Mixes using garden soil should be moistened and mixed by hand or with a spade to the point that a ball of earth sticks together when squeezed but crumbles apart when dropped.

TESTING SEED GERMINABILITY

Vegetable and flower seed that has been stored from past seasons, has been subjected to unfavorable environmental conditions, or for any other reason has doubtful viability should be tested for its germination ability. This usually amounts to determining the percentage of seed that will germinate. Two simple home germination tests are illustrated in Figures 14-2 and 14-3. Several different kinds of small seed can be tested simultaneously on different parts of the dinner plate. The "rag doll" test is best suited for large seed. Germination times vary for different seeds. Radish seeds begin to germinate in two days, and a majority of other vegetables and annual flowers in three to five, but peppers, New Zealand spinach, and asparagus may require several weeks.

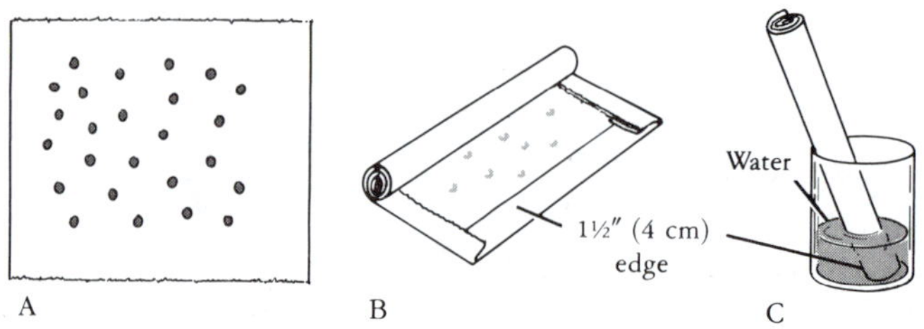

FIGURE 14-2 • The "rag-doll" germination test: (A) Fifteen to twenty-five seeds are counted onto a moistened paper towel. At least ¼ inch (2 cm) should be left free of seed on three edges for folding and 1½ inches (4 cm) or more on the other edge. (B) A second moistened towel is laid over the first. All four edges are folded over and creased, and the towel is rolled so that the wider edge is at one end of the roll. (C) The rolled "doll" is placed in a container with about 1 inch (2½ cm) of water, and the container is kept in a 70° to 80°F (21° to 27 C) room. The towel acts as a wick to keep the seeds moist but aerated. If the atmosphere is dry, additional water may be needed each day. The water should never reach above the level of the lowest seeds.

ESTIMATING PLANTING DATE

When to Seed Transplants Indoors for Early Production

In order to produce a crop as early as possible, growers of transplants in temperate-zone climates need to know the length of time required to grow the transplant and the date of the last killing frost.

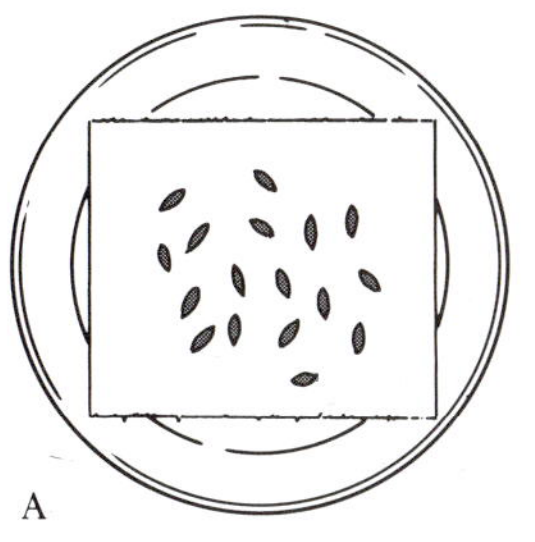

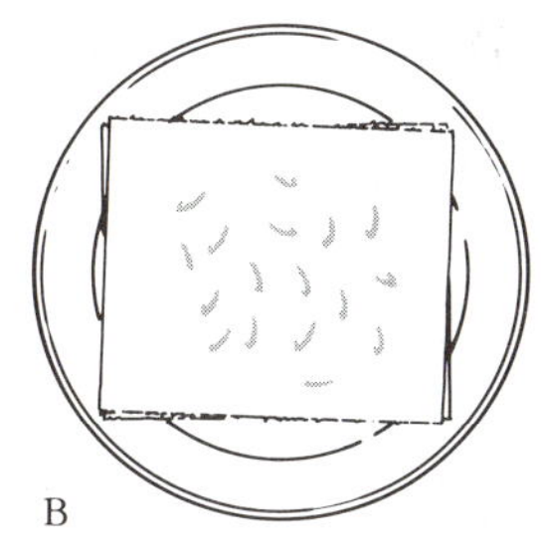

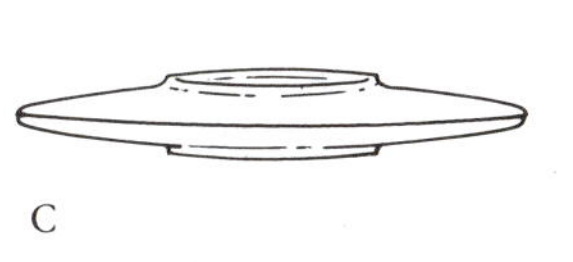

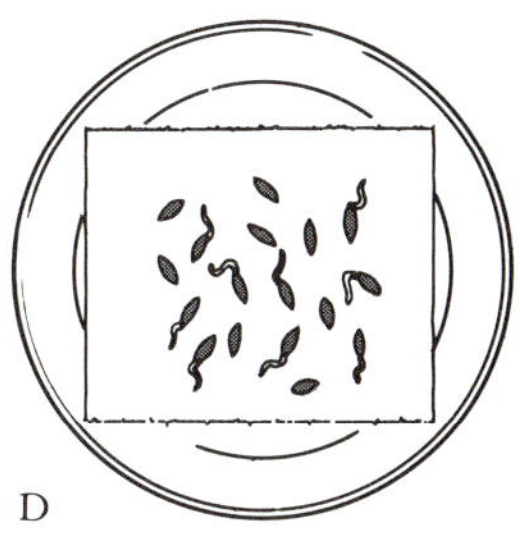

FIGURE 14-3 • The "dinner plate" germination test. In this test of the germinability of garden seeds, absorbent paper or cotton cloth is moistened and placed on a plate. An appropriate number of seeds are counted onto it (A). The seeds are covered with another piece of cloth or paper (B), and a second plate is inverted over the first (C). The germinator should be kept warm (between 70° and 80°F [21° to 27°C] is ideal) and moist but not too wet. The seeds should not rest in water. Germinated seeds (D) should be counted daily and discarded. After a week (or more, depending on the type of seed), you can calculate the percentage of germinated seeds by dividing the number of seeds that germinated by the total number of seeds originally on the plate.

Transplants of warm-season crops, those that need warm soil and most of those that germinate best at temperatures of 70°F (21°C) or above, should not be planted into the garden until at least a week after the average last killing frost. For example, in Peoria, Illinois, the average date of last spring frost is April 22 (see Table 14-27). Tomatoes require about six weeks to grow to transplant size (Table 14-2). Counting back from one week after the average last killing frost, a grower finds that tomatoes should be seeded indoors about March 18.

Most annual flowers require six to eight weeks plus the time they need to germinate to grow to transplant size; the small-seeded kinds usually require the longer time. A grower finds that in Caribou, Maine, where the last average frost is May 19, petunias, which have very small seeds and germinate best at 70°F (Table 14-3), can be seeded indoors by about March 28. Cool-season vegetables and flowers, those that tolerate cool soil and most of those that germinate best at temperatures of 65°F (18°C) or below, can be started indoors and transplanted into the garden two to four weeks earlier.

Dates for Spring and Fall Planting Outdoors

Vegetables that require or tolerate cool soil and most flowers that germinate at 65°F or below (see Tables 14-2 and 14-3) can be seeded outdoors in most areas as soon as the soil has dried and warmed sufficiently so that it can be worked. The exception might be in an arid region with sandy soil where soil can be worked whenever it is not frozen. The soil temperature should have reached at least 45°F (7°C). Vegetables that require warm soil and most flowers that germinate best at 70°F or above should not be seeded outdoors until danger of frost is over (see Table 14-27).

The latest date for summer or fall planting so that the crop will mature before cold weather stops its growth can be calculated from Table 14-4, Table 14-27, and other climatic data found later in this chapter.

TABLE 14-2 • *Suggestions for successfully propagating common vegetables from seed*

	Seeds		Distance				Soil Temperature for Seed[a]				
Vegetable	Depth to Plant (in)	No. to Sow (per ft)	Between Plants (in)	Between Rows (in)	Days to Germinate	Needs Light to Germinate	Needs Cool Soil	Tolerates Cool Soil	Needs Warm Soil	Weeks to Grow to Transplant Size[b]	Days to Maturity[c]
Asparagus	1½		18	36	7–21			X		1 year	3 years
Beans:											
Snap bush	1½–2	6–8	2–3	18–30	6–14				X		45–65
Snap pole	1½–2	4–6	4–6	36–48	6–14				X		60–70
Lima bush	1½–2	5–8	3–6	24–30	7–12				X		60–80
Lima pole	1½–2	4–5	6–10	30–36	7–12				X		85–90
Fava (broad bean or Windsor bean)	2½	5–8	3–4	18–24	7–14			X			80–90
Garbanzo (chick-pea)	1½–2	5–8	3–4	24–30	6–12				X		105
Scarlet runner	1½–2	4–6	4–6	36–48	6–14				X		60–70
Soybean	1½–2	6–8	2–3	24–30	6–14				X		95–100
Beet	½–1	10–15	2	12–18	7–10			X			55–65
Black-eyed cowpea (southern pea)	½–1	5–8	3–4	24–30	7–10				X		65–80
Yardlong bean (asparagus bean)	½–1	2–4	12–24	24–36	6–13				X		65–80
Broccoli, sprouting	½	10–15	18–24	24–30	3–10			X		5–7[d]	60–80T[e]
Brussels sprouts	½	10–15	18–24	24–30	3–10			X		4–6[d]	80–90T[e]
Cabbage	½	8–10	14–24	24–30	4–10			X		5–7[d]	65–95T[e]
Cabbage, Chinese	½	8–16	10–12	18–24	4–10			X		4–6	80–90
Cardoon	½	4–6	18	36	8–14			X		8	120–150
Carrot	¼	15–20	1–2	14–24	10–17			X			60–80
Cauliflower	½	8–10	18	30–36	4–10		X			5–7[d]	55–65T[e]
Celeriac	⅛	8–12	8	24–30	9–21		X			10–12[d]	90–120T[e]
Celery	⅛	8–12	8	24–30	9–21	X	X			10–12[d]	90–120T[e]
Celtuce (asparagus lettuce)	½	8–10	12	18	4–10			X		4–6	80
Chard, Swiss	1	6–10	4–8	18–24	7–10			X			55–65
Chicory, witloof (French or Belgian endive)	¼	8–10	4–8	18–24	5–12	X		X			90–120
Chive	½	8–10	8	10–16	8–12			X			80–90
Chop suey green (shungiku)	½	6	2–3	10–12	5–14			X			42
Collard	¼	10–12	10–15	24–30	4–10			X		4–6[d]	65–85T[e]
Corn, sweet	2	4–6	10–14	30–36	6–10				X		60–90
Cornsalad	½	8–10	4–6	12–16	7–10			X			45–55
Cress, garden	¼	10–12	2–3	12–16	4–10	X		X			25–45
Cucumber	1	3–5	12	48–72	6–10				X	4	55–65
Dandelion	½	6–10	8–10	12–16	7–14	X		X			70–90
Eggplant	¼–½	8–12	18	36	7–14				X	6–9[d]	75–95T[e]
Endive	½	4–6	9–12	12–24	5–9			X		4–6	60–90
Fennel, Florence	½	8–12	6	18–24	6–17			X			120
Garlic (from sets)	1		2–4	12–18	6–10			X			90
Ground cherry husk tomato	½	6	24	36	6–13				X	6[d]	90–100T[e]

(continued)

TABLE 14-2 • *(Continued)*

	Seeds		Distance				Soil Temperature for Seed[a]				
Vegetable	Depth to Plant (in)	No. to Sow (per ft)	Between Plants (in)	Between Rows (in)	Days to Germinate	Needs Light to Germinate	Needs Cool Soil	Tolerates Cool Soil	Needs Warm Soil	Weeks to Grow to Transplant Size[b]	Days to Maturity[c]
Horseradish (root divisions)	3		10–18	24				X			180–220
Jerusalem artichoke (tubers)	4		15–24	30–60				X			100–105
Kale	½	8–12	14–24	24–30	3–10			X		4–6	55–80
Kohlrabi	½	8–12	3–4	18–24	3–10			X		4–6	60–70
Leeks	½–1	8–12	2–4	12–18	7–12			X		10–12	80–90T[e]
Lettuce:											
Head	¼–½	4–8	12–14	18–24	4–10	X	X			3–5	55–80
Leaf	¼–½	8–12	4–6	12–18	4–10	X	X			3–5	45–60
Muskmelon	1	3–6	18	48–72	4–8				X	3–4	75–100
Mustard	½	8–10	2–6	12–18	3–10	X		X			40–60
Nasturtium	½–1	4–8	4–10	18–36				X			50–60
Onion (sets)	1–2		2–3	12–24			X				95–120
(plants)	2–3		2–3	12–24			X			8	95–120T[e]
(seed)	½	10–15	2–3	12–24	7–12		X				100–165
Parsley	¼–½	10–15	3–6	12–20	14–28			X		8	85–90
Parsnip	½	8–12	3–4	16–24	15–25			X			100–120
Pea	2	6–7	2–3	18–30	6–15		X				65–85
Peanut	1½	2–3	6–10	30					X		110–120
Pepper	¼	6–8	18–24	24–36	10–20				X	6–8	60–80T[e]
Potato (tubers)	4	1	12	24–36	8–16			X			90–105
Pumpkin	1–1½	2	30	72–120	6–10				X		70–110
Radish	½	14–16	1–2	6–12	3–10		X				20–50
Rutabaga	½	4–6	8–12	18–24	3–10			X			80–90
Salsify	½	8–12	2–3	16–18			X				110–150
Salsify, black	½	8–12	2–3	16–18			X				110–150
Shallot (bulb)	1		2–4	12–18				X			60–75
Spinach	½	10–12	2–4	12–14	6–14		X				40–65
Malabar	½	4–6	12	12	10			X			70
New Zealand	1½	4–6	18	24	5–10			X			70–80
Tampala	¼–½	6–10	4–6	24–30				X			21–42
Squash (summer)	1	4–6	16–24	36–60	3–12				X		50–60
Squash (winter)	1	1–2	24–48	72–120	6–10				X		85–120
Sunflower	1	2–3	16–24	36–48	7–12				X		80–90
Sweet Potato (plants)			12–18	36–48					X		120T[e]
Tomato	½		18–36	36–60	6–14				X	5–7	55–90T[e]
Turnip	½		1–3	15–18	3–10		X				45–60
Watermelon	1	14–16	24–48	72	3–12				X	3–4	80–100

Adapted and reprinted with permission from the Ortho book, *All About Vegetables*. Copyright 1973, Chevron Chemical Co. Information on light from Dr. Henry M. Cathey.

[a]Seeds that "need cool soil" do best in a temperature range of 50–65°F; those that "tolerate cool soil" in a 50–85°F range; those that "need warm soil" in a 65–85°F range.

[b]The variation of 4–6, 5–7, 10–12 weeks allows for hot-bed, greenhouse, window sill, and under grow-lamp conditions. Generally the warmer the growing conditions, the shorter the time to grow transplants. However, there must be allowance for a change from indoor to outdoor environment.

[c]The *relative* length of time needed to grow a crop from seed or transplant to table use. The time will vary by variety and season.

[d]Transplants preferred over seed.

[e]T = Number of days from setting out transplants; all others are from seeding.

TABLE 14-3 • *Guidelines for the germination of annual, pot plant, and ornamental herb seeds*

Common Name and Cultivar	Group[a]	Temp. for Best Germination (°F)	Contin. Light or Dark	Germination (days)
Ageratum 'Blue Mink'	VI	70	L	5
Ageratum 'Golden'	I	70	D	5
Alyssum 'Carpet of Snow'	I	70	DL	5
Amaranthus 'Molten Fire'	III	70	DL	10
Anise	IV	70	DL	10
Aster 'Ball White'	I	70	DL	8
Balsam 'Scarlet'	III	70	DL	8
Basil 'Dark Opal'	III	70	DL	10
Basil 'Lettuce Leaves'	III	70	DL	10
Begonia, fibrous-rooted 'Scandinavian Pink'	V	70	L	15
Begonia, tuberous-rooted 'Double Mix'	VI	65	L	15
Borage	VIII	70	D	8
Browallia 'Blue Bells' and 'Silver Bells'	VI	70	L	15
Browallia 'Sapphire'	V	70	L	15
Calceolaria multiflora nana	VI	70	L	15
Calendula 'Orange Coronet'	VIII	70	D	10
Campanula 'Annual Mix'	III	70	DL	20
Candytuft 'Giant White'	I	70	DL	8
Carnation 'Chaband's Giant' and 'Imp. Cardinal Red'	IV	70	DL	20
Celosia 'Toreador'	III	70	DL	10
Centaurea 'Blue Boy'	VIII	65	D	10
Centaurea 'Dusty Miller'	VIII	65	D	10
Centaurea, yellow	VIII	70	D	10
Chives (grass onion)	IV	60	DL	10
Christmas cherry 'Masterpiece'	III	70	DL	20
Cineraria 'Maritima Diamond'	VII	75	L	10
Cineraria 'Vivid'	III	70	DL	10
Clarkia 'Florist Mixture'	I	70	DL	5
Cobaea (cup-and-saucer vine), purple	I	70	DL	15
Coleus 'Red Rainbow'	VII	65	L	10
Coriander, annual	VIII	70	D	10
Cosmos 'Radiance'	II	70	DL	5
Cuphea 'Firefly'	VI	70	L	8
Cyclamen 'Pure White'	IX	60	D	50
Cynoglossum 'Firmament'	IV	60	D	5
Dahlia 'Unwins Dwarf Mix'	I	70	DL	5
Dianthus 'Bravo'	I	70	DL	5
Didiscus 'Blue Lace'	IV	65	D	15
Dill	IV	60	L	10
Dimorphotheca 'Orange Improved'	II	70	DL	10
Euphorbia, annual poinsettia	I	70	DL	15

(continued)

TABLE 14-3 • *(Continued)*

Common Name and Cultivar	Group[a]	Temp. for Best Germination (°F)	Contin. Light or Dark	Germination (days)
Exacum 'Tiddly-Winks'	V	70	L	15
Fennel, sweet	IV	65	D	10
Feverdew 'Ball Double White Improved'	VII	70	L	15
Freesia 'White Giant'	IV	65	DL	25
Gaillardia 'Tetra Red Giant'	III	70	DL	20
Gazania 'Mix'	IV	60	D	8
Gloxinia 'Emperor Wilhelm'	V	65	L	15
Gomphrena 'Rubra'	III	65	D	15
Grevillea (Australian silk oak)	VI	80	L	20
Gypsophila 'Covent Garden'	I	70	DL	10
Helichrysum (everlasting)	VII	70	L	5
Heliotrope 'Marine'	IV	70	DL	25
Hollyhock 'Powderpuffs Mix'	IV	60	DL	10
Hunnemannia (bush escholtzia) 'Sunlite'	III	70	DL	15
Impatiens 'Holstii Scarlet'	VI	70	L	15
Kalanchoe 'Vulcan'	V	70	L	10
Kochia 'Bright green'	I	70	DL	15
Larkspur 'White Supreme'	IX	55	D	20
Lobelia 'Crystal Palace'	III	70	DL	20
Lupine 'Giant King' and 'Oxford Blue'	IV	55	DL	20
Marigold 'Doubloon'	I	70	DL	5
Marigold 'Spry'	I	70	DL	5
Marjoram, sweet	II	70	DL	8
Mesembryanthemum criniflorum	IX	65	D	15
Migonette 'Early White'	I	70	DL	5
Mimosa (sensitive plant)	VIII	80	D	8
Morning glory 'Heavenly Blue'	III	65	DL	5
Myosotis 'Ball Early'	IV	55	D	8
Naegelia 'Art Shades'	V	70	L	15
Nasturtium 'Golden Giant'	IV	65	D	8
Nemesia 'Fire King'	IX	65	D	5
Nicotiana 'Crimson Bedder'	VII	70	L	20
Nierembergia 'Purple Robe'	III	70	DL	15
Pansy 'Lake of Thun'	IX	65	D	10
Parsley 'Extra Triple Curled'	IX	75	D	15
Penstemon 'Sensation Mixture'	VIII	65	D	10
Perilla 'Burgundy'	VI	65	L	15
Petunia 'Maytime'	VI	70	L	10
Phlox 'Glamour'	VIII	65	D	10

(continued)

TABLE 14-3 • *Guidelines for the germination of annual, pot plant, and ornamental herb seeds (Continued)*

Common Name and Cultivar	Group[a]	Temp. for Best Germination (°F)	Contin. Light or Dark	Germination (days)
Plumbago, blue	IV	75	DL	25
Poppy nudicaule 'Iceland'	I	70	D	10
Portulaca, yellow	IV	70	D	10
Primula 'Chinese Giant Fringed'	VIII	70	D	25
Primula malacoides 'White Giant'	VI	70	L	25
Primula 'Fasbender's Red'	VI	70	L	25
Rosemary, perennial	IV	60	DL	15
Rudbeckia, single 'Gloriosa Daisy'	III	70	DL	20
Sage, perennial	VIII	70	D	15
Saintpaulia 'Blue Fairy Tale'	V	70	L	25
Salpiglossis 'Emperor Mix'	III	70	D	15
Salvia (St. John's Fire)	VI	70	L	15
Savory, 'Bohnenkraut'	VI	65	L	15
Scabiosa 'Giant Blue'	III	70	DL	10
Schizanthus ball 'Giant Mix'	VIII	60	D	20
Shamrock 'True Irish'	IX	65	D	10
Smilax	VIII	75	D	30
Snapdragon 'Orchid Rocket'	VII	65	L	10
Statice 'Iceberg'	I	70	DL	15
Statice suworowii 'Russian'	VIII	70	D	15
Stock 'Lavender Column'	I	70	DL	10
Streptocarpus	V	70	L	15
Sweetpea 'Ruth Cuthbertson'	IV	55	D	15
Thunbergia gibsoni	III	70	DL	10
Thyme, perennial	IV	75	DL	10
Tithonia 'Torch'	VIII	70	D	20
Torenia	III	70	DL	15
Verbena 'Torrid'	VIII	65	D	20
Viola 'Blue Elf'	IX	65	D	10
Vinca, periwinkle (alba aculata)	VIII	70	D	15
Wallflower 'Golden Standard'	I	70	DL	5
Zinnia 'Isabellina'	III	70	DL	5

Adapted from "Guidelines for Germination of Annual, Pot Plants, and Ornamental Herb Seeds," *Florists Review* 144:26–29, 1975–1977. By permission of Dr. Henry M. Cathey.

[a]Annuals divided into groups on basis of response to temperature and light:

Group I—Germination over a wide temperature range without a light requirement.
Group II—Germination only at cool temperatures without a light requirement.
Group III—Germination only at warm temperatures without a light requirement.
Group IV—Germination at a restricted range of temperatures without a light requirement.
Group V—Germination over a wide range of temperatures when exposed to light.
Group VI—Germination enhanced over a wide temperature range when exposed to light.
Group VII—Germination over a wide temperature range and enhanced at warm temperatures when exposed to light.
Group VIII—Germination over a wide temperature range when held in the dark.
Group IX—Germination over a wide temperature range and enhanced at warm temperatures when held in the dark.

PROPAGATING PLANTS FROM SEED*

◆ ◆ ◆

Starting Plants Indoors for Later Outdoor Planting

For time of planting, see the previous section. Containers and media are described at the beginning of Chapter 4 and in the "Soil Preparation" section of this chapter. Preplanted trays of some crops are available at grocery and garden stores. All that is necessary to start plant growth in these trays is to punch holes in the top, water, place them in the proper environment, and wait.

Sowing Seeds. Place the germination mix in the selected container. Firm with the fingers at the container edges and corners, level even with the container top, and press down the entire surface lightly but firmly to provide a uniform flat surface.

*Adapted from *Propagating Plants from Seed*, by F. E. Larsen. Pacific Northwest Cooperative Extension Publication 170. Extension Services of Washington State University, Oregon State University, and University of Idaho. Pullman, Wash. Revised periodically.

For very small seeds, at least the top ¼ inch (½ cm) should be of the fine-screened mix (Figure 14-4).

For medium and large seeds, make furrows about 1 inch (2½ cm) apart across the surface of the container. Individually space the large seeds. For medium-sized seeds, open the seed packet, hold in one hand, and lightly tap the packet with the index finger as you move the packet down the furrow; this will distribute the seeds fairly evenly. Do not plant too thickly, as the seedlings will be crowded and spindly if they lack growing space. Cover the seeds lightly with the screened growing mix. A suitable planting depth is usually equal to about twice the diameter of the seed.

Broadcast small seed like petunias or begonias over the surface of the germinating medium rather than in rows or furrows. Do not cover with the growing mix.

If you use peat pots, strips, cell packs, or other individual plant containers (Figure 14-5), they must be filled with planting mix and firmed, as with larger containers. Before seeds are sown in them, the pellets must be expanded with water. Plant the seeds in the center of each small con-

A

B

C

FIGURE 14-4 • Preparing the seeding mix. (A) Screening the mix. (B) Leveling the mix in the flat. (C) Making furrows for the larger seed. (Courtesy of Washington State University)

TABLE 14-4 • *Latest dates, and range of dates, for safe fall planting of vegetables in the open (average dates of first fall frost shown in Table 14-27)*

Crop	Planting Dates for Localities in Which Average Date of First Freeze Is—					
	Aug. 30	Sept. 10	Sept. 20	Sept. 30	Oct. 10	Oct. 20
Asparagus[a]	—	[b]	[b]	[b]	Oct. 20–Nov. 15	Nov. 1–Dec. 15
Bean, lima	—	—	—	June 1–15	June 1–15	June 15–30
Bean, snap	—	May 15–June 15	June 1–July 1	June 1–July 10	June 15–July 20	July 1–Aug. 1
Beet	May 15–June 15	May 15–June 15	June 1–July 1	June 1–July 10	June 15–July 25	July 1–Aug. 5
Broccoli, sprouting	May 1–June 1	May 1–June 1	May 1–June 15	June 1–30	June 15–July 15	July 1–Aug. 1
Brussels sprouts	May 1–June 1	May 1–June 1	May 1–June 15	June 1–30	June 15–July 15	July 1–Aug. 1
Cabbage[a]	May 1–June 1	May 1–June 1	May 1–June 15	June 1–July 10	June 1–July 15	July 1–20
Cabbage, Chinese	May 15–June 15	May 15–June 15	June 1–July 1	June 1–July 15	June 15–Aug. 1	July 15–Aug. 15
Carrot	May 15–June 15	May 15–June 15	June 1–July 1	June 1–July 10	June 1–July 20	June 15–Aug. 1
Cauliflower[a]	May 1–June 1	May 1–July 1	May 1–July 1	May 10–July 15	June 1–July 25	July 1–Aug. 5
Celery[a] and celeriac	May 1–June 1	May 15–June 15	May 15–July 1	June 1–July 5	June 1–July 15	June 1–Aug. 1
Chard	May 15–June 15	May 15–July 1	June 1–July 1	June 1–July 5	June 1–July 20	June 1–Aug. 1
Chervil and chive	May 10–June 10	May 1–June 15	May 15–June 15	[b]	[b]	[b]
Chicory, witloof	May 15–June 15	May 15–June 15	May 15–June 15	June 1–July 1	June 1–July 1	June 15–July 15
Collard[a]	May 15–June 15	May 15–June 15	May 15–June 15	June 15–July 15	July 1–Aug. 1	July 15–Aug. 15
Cornsalad	May 15–June 15	May 15–July 1	June 15–Aug. 1	July 15–Sept. 1	Aug. 15–Sept. 15	Sept. 1–Oct. 15
Corn, sweet	—	May 15–June 1	June 1–July 1	June 1–July 1	June 1–July 10	June 1–July 20
Cress, upland	May 15–June 15	May 15–July 1	June 15–Aug. 1	July 15–Sept. 1	Aug. 15–Sept. 15	Sept. 1–Oct. 15
Cucumber	—	—	June 1–15	June 1–July 1	June 1–July 1	June 1–July 15
Dandelion	June 1–15	June 1–July 1	June 1–July 1	June 1–Aug. 1	July 15–Sept. 1	Aug. 1–Sept. 15
Eggplant[a]	—	—	—	May 20–June 10	May 15–June 15	June 1–July 1
Endive	June 1–July 1	June 1–July 1	June 15–July 15	June 15–Aug.1	July 1–Aug. 15	July 15–Sept. 1
Fennel, Florence	May 15–June 15	May 15–July 15	June 1–July 1	June 1–July 1	June 15–July 15	June 15–Aug. 1
Garlic	[b]	[b]	[b]	[b]	[b]	[b]
Horseradish[a]	[b]	[b]	[b]	[b]	[b]	[b]
Kale	May 15–June 15	May 15–June 15	June 1–July 1	June 15–July 15	July 1–Aug. 1	July 15–Aug. 15
Kohlrabi	May 15–June 15	June 1–July 1	June 1–July 15	June 15–July 15	July 1–Aug. 1	July 15–Aug. 15
Leek	May 1–June 1	May 1–June 1	[b]	[b]	[b]	[b]
Lettuce, head[a]	May 15–July 1	May 15–July 1	June 1–July 15	June 15–Aug. 1	July 15–Aug. 15	Aug. 1–30
Lettuce, leaf	May 15–July 15	May 15–July 15	June 1–Aug. 1	June 1–Aug. 1	July 15–Sept. 1	July 15–Sept. 1
Muskmelon	—	—	May 1–June 15	May 15–June 1	June 1–June 15	June 15–July 20

(*continued*)

tainer or cell. For medium and large seeds, punch a small hole in the center of the growing mix of each container or cell, place two or three seeds in each hole, and cover the seeds as with large containers. Place small seeds on the surface.

Watering. After you sow the seed, wet the planting mix. Place the containers in a pan, tray, or tub of water that has about one inch of water in the bottom. When the water has seeped upward through the container to the surface, remove the container and set aside to drain for an hour or two. Then slip the container into a clear plastic bag and tie it shut. A pane of glass can also be used to cover the containers to hold in moisture.

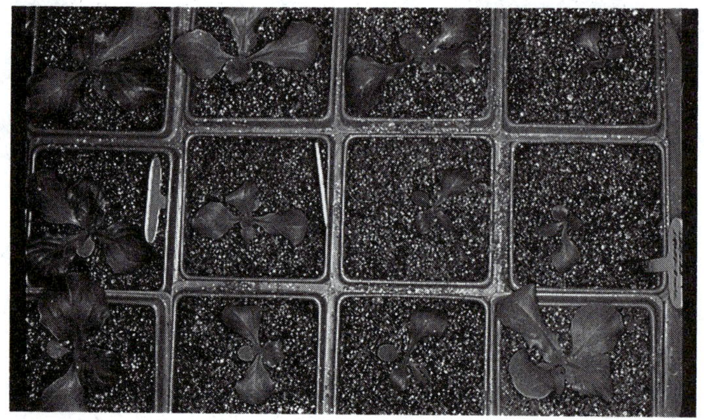

FIGURE 14-5 • Lettuce seeded into individual containers. (Courtesy of Arthur R. Hill/Visuals Unlimited)

Planting Dates for Localities in Which Average Date of First Freeze Is—					
Oct. 30	Nov. 10	Nov. 20	Nov. 30	Dec. 10	Dec. 20
Nov. 15–Jan. 1	Dec. 1–Jan. 1	—	—	—	—
July 1–Aug. 1	July 1–Aug. 15	July 15–Sept. 1	Aug. 1–Sept. 15	Sept. 1–30	Sept. 1–Oct. 1
July 1–Aug. 15	July 1–Sept. 1	July 1–Sept. 10	Aug. 15–Sept. 20	Sept. 1–30	Sept. 1–Nov. 1
Aug. 1–Sept. 1	Aug. 1–Oct. 1	Sept. 1–Dec. 1	Sept. 1–Dec. 15	Sept. 1–Dec. 31	Sept. 1–Dec. 31
July 1–Aug. 15	Aug. 1–Sept. 1	Aug. 1–Sept. 15	Aug. 1–Oct. 1	Aug. 1–Nov. 1	Sept. 1–Dec. 31
July 1–Aug. 15	Aug. 1–Sept. 1	Aug. 1–Sept. 15	Aug. 1–Oct. 1	Aug. 1–Nov. 1	Sept. 1–Dec. 31
Aug. 1–Sept. 1	Sept. 1–15	Sept. 1–Dec. 1	Sept. 1–Dec. 31	Sept. 1–Dec. 31	Sept. 1–Dec. 31
Aug. 1–Sept. 15	Aug. 15–Oct. 1	Sept. 1–Oct. 15	Sept. 1–Nov. 1	Sept. 1–Nov. 15	Sept. 1–Dec. 1
July 1–Aug. 15	Aug. 1–Sept. 1	Sept. 1–Nov. 1	Sept. 15–Dec. 1	Sept. 15–Dec. 1	Sept. 15–Dec. 1
July 15–Aug. 15	Aug. 1–Sept. 1	Aug. 1–Sept. 15	Aug. 15–Oct. 10	Sept. 1–Oct. 20	Sept. 15–Nov. 1
June 15–Aug. 15	July 1–Aug. 15	July 15–Sept. 1	Aug. 1–Dec. 1	Sept. 1–Dec. 31	Oct. 1–Dec. 31
June 1–Sept. 10	June 1–Sept. 15	June 1–Oct. 1	June 1–Nov. 1	June 1–Dec. 1	June 1–Dec. 31
[b]	[b]	Nov. 1–Dec. 31	Nov. 1–Dec. 31	Nov. 1–Dec. 31	Nov. 1–Dec. 31
July 1–Aug. 10	July 10–Aug. 20	July 20–Sept. 1	Aug. 15–Sept. 30	Aug. 15–Oct. 15	Aug. 15–Oct. 15
Aug. 1–Sept. 15	Aug. 15–Oct. 1	Aug. 25–Nov. 1	Sept. 1–Dec. 1	Sept. 1–Dec. 31	Sept. 1–Dec. 31
Sept. 15–Nov. 1	Oct. 1–Dec. 1	Oct. 1–Dec. 1	Oct. 1–Dec. 31	Oct. 1–Dec. 31	Oct. 1–Dec. 31
June 1–Aug. 1	June 1–Aug. 15	June 1–Sept. 1	—	—	—
Sept. 15–Nov. 1	Oct. 1–Dec. 1	Oct. 1–Dec. 1	Oct. 1–Dec. 31	Oct. 1–Dec. 31	Oct. 1–Dec. 31
June 1–Aug. 1	June 1–Aug. 15	June 1–Aug. 15	July 15–Sept. 15	Aug. 15–Oct. 1	Aug. 15–Oct. 1
Aug. 15–Oct. 1	Sept. 1–Oct. 15	Sept. 1–Nov. 1	Sept. 15–Dec. 15	Oct. 1–Dec. 31	Oct. 1–Dec. 31
June 1–July 1	June 1–July 15	June 1–Aug. 1	July 1–Sept. 1	Aug. 1–Sept. 30	Aug. 1–Sept. 30
July 15–Aug. 15	Aug. 1–Sept. 1	Sept. 1–Oct. 1	Sept. 1–Nov. 15	Sept. 1–Dec. 31	Sept. 1–Dec. 31
July 1–Aug. 1	July 15–Aug. 15	Aug. 15–Sept. 15	Sept. 1–Nov. 15	Sept. 1–Dec. 1	Sept. 1–Dec. 1
[b]	Aug. 1–Oct. 1	Aug. 15–Oct. 1	Sept. 1–Nov. 15	Sept. 15–Nov. 15	Sept. 15–Nov. 15
[b]	[b]	[b]	[b]	[b]	[b]
July 15–Sept. 1	Aug. 1–Sept. 15	Aug. 15–Oct. 15	Sept. 1–Dec. 1	Sept. 1–Dec. 31	Sept. 1–Dec. 31
Aug. 1–Sept. 1	Aug. 15–Sept. 15	Sept. 1–Oct. 15	Sept. 1–Dec. 1	Sept. 15–Dec. 31	Sept. 1–Dec. 31
[b]	[b]	Sept. 1–Nov. 1	Sept. 1–Nov. 1	Sept. 1–Nov. 1	Sept. 15–Nov. 1
Aug. 1–Sept. 15	Aug. 15–Oct. 15	Sept. 1–Nov. 1	Sept. 1–Dec. 1	Sept. 15–Dec. 31	Sept. 15–Dec. 31
Aug. 15–Oct. 1	Aug. 25–Oct. 1	Sept. 1–Nov. 1	Sept. 1–Dec. 1	Sept. 15–Dec. 31	Sept. 15–Dec. 31
July 1–July 15	July 15–July 30	—	—	—	—

(*continued*)

Place the containers in a warm or cool place as required (see the discussion on temperature), but not in direct sunlight. Some types of seed must be placed in the dark (see the discussion on lighting). Check each day to be sure the mix is still moist and to watch for emerging plants. When plants are emerging, remove the plastic or glass covering and place in full natural or artificial light (if placed in sunlight, be sure that it does not get too hot). Continue to check the moisture level of the mix. If water is needed, apply as previously described for small-seeded plants or add to the top of the container with medium- and large-seeded plants. Be careful not to overwater or wash out the plants.

Lighting. The germination of some seed is retarded by light; some require light for germination; and many germinate in either light or dark. Of the common garden vegetable crops, only a few are affected significantly by light. Consult Tables 14-2 and 14-3 for light requirements for seed germination.

When the seeds have germinated, they will need adequate lighting for good growth. A window that is well lighted through the day will usually provide enough light. Because the plants will bend toward the window, turn the containers daily to prevent permanent curves in the stems and to allow sturdier plants to develop.

TABLE 14-4 • *Latest dates, and range of dates, for safe fall planting of vegetables in the open (average dates of first fall frost shown in Table 14-27) (Continued)*

Crop	Planting Dates for Localities in Which Average Date of First Freeze Is—					
	Aug. 30	Sept. 10	Sept. 20	Sept. 30	Oct. 10	Oct. 20
Mustard	May 15–July 15	May 15–July 15	June 1–Aug. 1	June 15–Aug. 1	July 15–Aug. 15	Aug. 1–Sept. 1
Okra	—	—	June 1–20	June 1–July 1	June 1–July 15	June 1–Aug. 1
Onion[a]	May 1–June 10	May 1–June 10	[b]	[b]	[b]	[b]
Onion, seed	May 1–June 1	May 1–June 10	[b]	[b]	[b]	[b]
Onion, sets	May 1–June 1	May 1–June 10	[b]	[b]	[b]	[b]
Parsley	May 15–June 15	May 1–June 15	June 1–July 1	June 1–July 15	June 15–Aug. 1	July 15–Aug. 15
Parsnip	May 15–June 1	May 1–June 15	May 15–June 15	June 1–July 1	June 1–July 10	[b]
Pea, garden	May 10–June 15	May 1–July 1	June 1–July 15	June 1–Aug. 1	[b]	[b]
Pea, black-eye	—	—	—	—	June 1–July 1	June 1–July 1
Pepper[a]	—	—	June 1–June 20	June 1–July 1	June 1–July 1	June 1–July 10
Potato	May 15–June 1	May 1–June 15	May 1–June 15	May 1–June 15	May 15–June 15	June 15–July 15
Radish	May 1–July 15	May 1–Aug. 1	June 1–Aug. 15	July 1–Sept. 1	July 15–Sept. 15	Aug. 1–Oct. 1
Rhubarb[a]	Sept. 1–Oct. 1	Sept. 15–Oct. 15	Sept. 15–Nov. 1	Oct. 1–Nov. 1	Oct. 15–Nov. 15	Oct. 15–Dec. 1
Rutabaga	May 15–June 15	May 1–June 15	June 1–July 1	June 1–July 1	June 15–July 15	July 10–20
Salsify	May 15–June 1	May 10–June 10	May 20–June 20	June 1–20	June 1–July 1	June 1–July 1
Shallot	[b]	[b]	[b]	[b]	[b]	[b]
Sorrel	May 15–June 15	May 1–June 15	June 1–July 1	June 1–July 15	July 1–Aug. 1	July 15–Aug. 15
Soybean	—	—	—	May 25–June 10	June 1–25	June 1–July 5
Spinach	May 15–July 1	June 1–July 15	June 1–Aug. 1	July 1–Aug. 15	Aug. 1–Sept. 1	Aug. 20–Sept. 10
Spinach, New Zealand	—	—	—	May 15–July 1	June 1–July 15	June 1–Aug. 1
Squash, summer	June 10–20	June 1–20	May 15–July 1	June 1–July 1	June 1–July 15	June 1–July 20
Squash, winter	—	—	May 20–June 10	June 1–15	June 1–July 1	June 1–July 1
Sweet potato	—	—	—	—	May 20–June 10	June 1–15
Tomato	June 20–30	June 10–20	June 1–20	June 1–20	June 1–20	June 1–July 1
Turnip	May 15–June 15	June 1–July 1	June 1–July 15	June 1–Aug. 1	July 1–Aug. 1	July 15–Aug. 15
Watermelon	—	—	May 1–June 15	May 15–June 1	June 1–June 15	June 15–July 20

Adapted from *Suburban and Farm Vegetable Gardens*, USDA Home and Garden Bulletin 9. U.S. Government Printing Office, Washington, DC. Revised periodically.
[a]Plants.
[b]Generally planted in the spring.

If a place with good natural light is not available, artificial light must be provided. Even where good natural light is available, it is usually beneficial to supplement it with artificial light to extend the day length and increase the intensity.

A fluorescent fixture with 40-watt cool or warm light or gro-type tubes provides a good source of light. Suspend the fixture about 4 to 6 inches (10 to 15 cm) above the small plants. Provide light 16 to 18 hours per day. The light can be turned on and off automatically by commercially available timing devices.

Transplants can, of course, be grown in hotbeds or greenhouses where there is ample natural light.

Temperature. Most flower and vegetable seeds rapidly germinate at 75° to 80°F (24° to 27°C). At temperatures of 60°F (16°C) or lower, germination is slow, and damage from damping-off diseases can be a major problem. There are some plants, however, that germinate better at 50° to 65°F (10° to 18°C). See Tables 14-2 and 14-3 for favorable germination temperatures of a variety of garden plants.

Planting Dates for Localities in Which Average Date of First Freeze Is—					
Oct. 30	Nov. 10	Nov. 20	Nov. 30	Dec. 10	Dec. 20
Aug. 15–Oct. 15	Aug. 15–Nov. 1	Sept. 1–Dec. 1	Sept. 1–Dec. 1	Sept. 1–Dec. 1	Sept. 15–Dec. 1
June 1–Aug. 10	June 1–Aug. 20	June 1–Sept. 10	June 1–Sept. 20	Aug. 1–Oct. 1	Aug. 1–Oct. 1
b	Sept. 1–Oct. 15	Oct. 1–Dec. 31	Oct. 1–Dec. 31	Oct. 1–Dec. 31	Oct. 1–Dec. 31
b	b	Sept. 1–Nov. 1	Sept. 1–Nov. 1	Sept. 1–Nov. 1	Sept. 15–Nov. 1
b	Oct. 1–Dec. 1	Nov. 1–Dec. 31	Nov. 1–Dec. 31	Nov. 1–Dec. 31	Nov. 1–Dec. 31
Aug. 1–Sept. 15	Sept. 1–Nov. 15	Sept. 1–Dec. 31	Sept. 1–Dec. 31	Sept. 15–Dec. 31	Sept. 1–Dec. 31
b	b	Aug. 1–Sept. 1	Sept. 1–Nov. 15	Sept. 1–Dec. 1	Sept. 1–Dec. 1
Aug. 1–Sept. 15	Sept. 1–Nov. 1	Oct. 1–Dec. 1	Oct. 1–Dec. 31	Oct. 1–Dec. 31	Oct. 1–Dec. 31
June 1–Aug. 1	June 15–Aug. 15	July 1–Sept. 1	July 1–Sept. 10	July 1–Sept. 20	July 1–Sept. 20
June 1–July 20	June 1–Aug. 1	June 1–Aug. 15	June 15–Sept. 1	Aug. 15–Oct. 1	Aug. 15–Oct. 1
July 20–Aug. 10	July 25–Aug. 20	Aug. 10–Sept. 15	Aug. 1–Sept. 15	Aug. 1–Sept. 15	Aug. 1–Sept. 15
Aug. 15–Oct. 15	Sept. 1–Nov. 15	Sept. 1–Dec. 1	Sept. 1–Dec. 31	Aug. 1–Sept. 15	Oct. 1–Dec. 31
Nov. 1–Dec. 1	—	—	—	—	—
July 15–Aug. 1	July 15–Aug. 15	Aug. 1–Sept. 1	Sept. 1–Nov. 15	Oct. 1–Nov. 15	Oct. 15–Nov. 15
June 1–July 10	June 15–July 20	July 15–Aug. 15	Aug. 15–Sept. 30	Aug. 15–Oct. 15	Sept. 1–Oct. 31
b	Aug. 1–Oct. 1	Aug. 15–Oct. 1	Aug. 15–Oct. 15	Sept. 15–Nov. 1	Sept. 15–Nov. 1
Aug. 1–Sept. 15	Aug. 15–Oct. 1	Aug. 15–Oct. 15	Sept. 1–Nov. 15	Sept. 1–Dec. 15	Sept. 1–Dec. 31
June 1–July 15	June 1–July 25	June 1–July 30	June 1–July 30	June 1–July 30	June 1–July 30
Sept. 1–Oct. 1	Sept. 15–Nov. 1	Oct. 1–Dec. 1	Oct. 1–Dec. 31	Oct. 1–Dec. 31	Oct. 1–Dec. 31
June 1–Aug. 1	June 1–Aug. 15	June 1–Aug. 15	—	—	—
June 1–Aug. 1	June 1–Aug. 10	June 1–Aug. 20	June 1–Sept. 1	June 1–Sept. 15	June 1–Oct. 1
June 10–July 10	June 20–July 20	July 1–Aug. 1	July 15–Aug. 15	Aug. 1–Sept. 1	Aug. 1–Sept. 1
June 1–15	June 1–July 1	June 1–July 1	June 1–July 1	June 1–July 1	June 1–July 1
June 1–July 1	June 1–July 15	June 1–Aug. 1	Aug. 1–Sept. 1	Aug. 15–Oct. 1	Sept. 1–Nov. 1
Aug. 1–Sept. 15	Sept. 1–Oct. 15	Sept. 1–Nov. 15	Sept. 1–Nov. 15	Oct. 1–Dec. 1	Oct. 1–Dec. 31
July 1–July 15	July 15–July 30	—	—	—	—

The temperature variations within a home can often be taken advantage of to locate the spot with the best temperature conditions for seed germination. Temperatures can be more precisely controlled by placing the containers in a cool area on top of thermostatically controlled heating cables to raise the temperature of the germinating medium.

Pricking Off. If plants have not been seeded in individual containers, they must be transplanted soon after they germinate to give greater growing space and to allow proper plant development; this is called **pricking off**. Transplant them when the plants develop their first true leaves. Do not confuse the cotyledons (seed leaves) with true leaves, which have quite a different appearance. Failure to transplant on time results in hardened, spindly, or overdeveloped plants that seldom grow properly.

Fill growing containers as described for germinating seeds. In flats, mark rows about 2 inches (5 cm) apart. Using a sharpened pencil, make holes about 2 inches apart along the row for individual plants.

Several approaches can be used to extract plants from their germinating containers. First water the seedlings. If they were germinated in a very loose mix, you can usually lift them out gently with the tip of a pencil with little loss of roots. However, if the mix contains sand and garden soil, it will be more compact. In this case cut the mix in a flat into sections as if you were cutting a cake. Lift out one section at a time. If pots were used, remove the entire contents at once.

Gently break up each section by separating the plant roots, and remove one plant at a time. If there is a heavy intertwining root mass, place the sections in water in a clean bucket and gently agitate the mass. The soil will be washed away, and you can separate the plants with no loss of roots. Place the plants on moist newspaper while transplanting to prevent damage from drying roots. Discard spindly or poorly developed plants.

Hold each separated plant carefully by the top and tuck the roots in the holes previously prepared in flats or pots. Attempt to keep the roots pointed downward. Do not jam the roots in the hole in a ball or use a hole that is too shallow, so that the roots form a "U" going down into the soil and back out. Plant the seedlings slightly deeper than they were in the germinating containers. Place soil around each plant as you set it in place and gently firm the soil around the stem and roots with your fingers. Figures 14-6 and 14-7 illustrate pricking off.

After transplanting, water the plants as described for seedlings or gently water from the top, taking care not to wash out or flatten the plants with the water.

For a few days after transplanting, give plants special care to help them overcome transplanting shock. Syringing tops with water or covering the plants with a plastic bag to maintain high humidity helps prevent wilting. Keep them away from drafts or high temperatures.

Growing Transplants or Plants Started in Individual Containers. Plants started in individual containers must be thinned. Remove all but the most vigorous, healthy plants in each container or cell. After transplanting, or with plants of the same age started in individual containers, keep the plants growing at a steady, rapid rate so that they will be in good condition for outdoor planting.

A

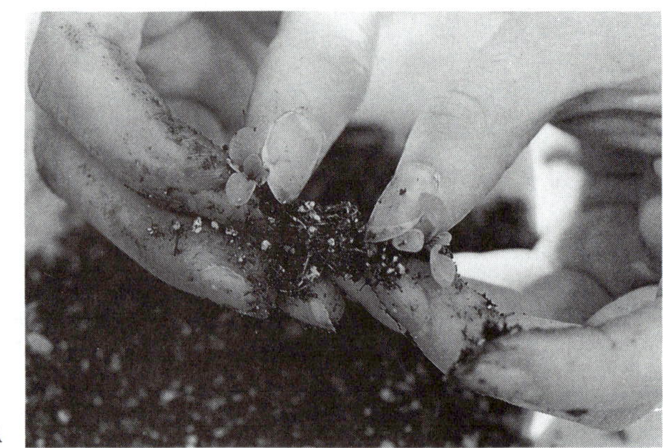

B

C

FIGURE 14-6 • Pricking off into a flat. (A) Separate plants grown in a loose mix. (B) Punch holes for transplants. (C) Firm planting medium around the roots. (Courtesy of Washington State University)

A

B

FIGURE 14-7 • Pricking off into individual containers. (A) Separate entwined roots by agitating in water; (B) position plant in container, fill with mix, and firm around the roots. (Courtesy of Washington State University)

Adequate light ensures adequate plant development. Poor lighting results in spindly, weak plants. If natural light is used, be sure it is bright throughout the day. Artificial lighting, as described earlier, usually helps provide adequate light intensity and day length. For most plants, 14 to 16 hours of light daily is adequate. Keep the lights 4 to 6 inches above the plants.

The information in Tables 14-2 and 14-3 provide a general guide to growing temperatures for various plants. However, optimal growing temperatures may differ from optimal seed germination temperatures. In general, most plants grow best between 60° and 80°F. Day temperatures should usually be between 70° and 80°F and night temperatures between 60° and 70°F. Do not subject the plants to cold drafts.

At each watering, apply enough water to wet the entire volume of growing mix so that some drains through the bottom. Apply water early enough in the day so that plant leaves dry before nightfall. This prevents damping-off diseases. Apply the water carefully to avoid washing the plants out or splashing soil on the leaves. Keep the soil slightly moist to the touch but not waterlogged.

If the plants are pale green or otherwise discolored, apply a water-soluble houseplant fertilizer at half strength. They should not need fertilizer more than once or twice before they are ready to plant outdoors.

Hardening Plants for Moving Outdoors. For best results, do not abruptly transfer seedlings from indoors to the uncertain outdoor climate. Gradually harden or toughen plants for about two weeks before you plant them in the garden. Do this by slowing down their rate of growth to prepare them to withstand such conditions as cold, drying winds, water shortage, or high temperatures. Reducing water and lowering the temperature are methods usually used to harden plants.

A suitable way to harden plants is to place them outdoors in the daytime in partial shade.

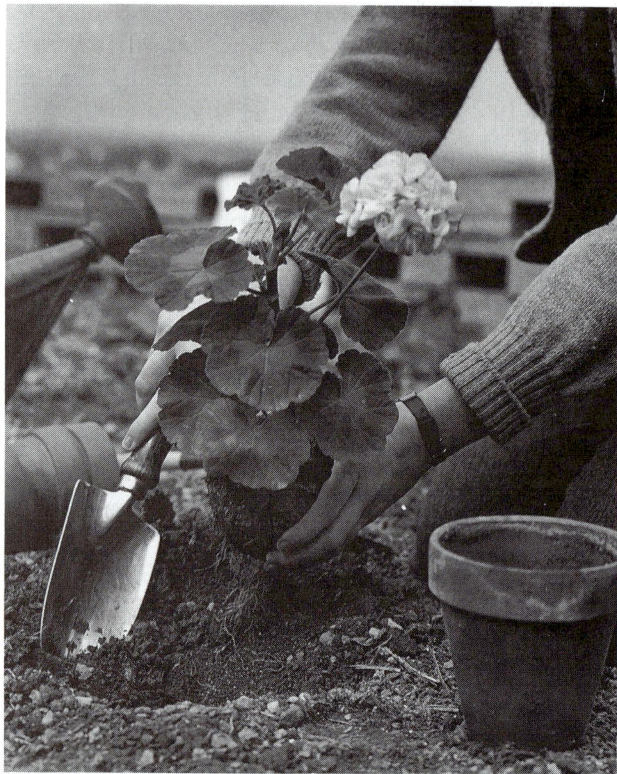

FIGURE 14-8 • Transplanting geraniums. (Courtesy of Grant Heilman)

Over a period of a few days, gradually move them into direct sunlight. One or two days before planting outdoors, leave them outside during the night on the sidewalk or steps but not directly on the ground. During the hardening period, water them less, but do not allow them to wilt. Transplants can be hardened in a cold frame.

Transplanting to the Garden. Prepare the planting area. If plants are in flats, cut the mix into cubes as if cutting a cake. The plants can then be lifted out individually. If individual plastic or clay pots are used, place one hand on top of the pot with your fingers around the plant. Tip the pot upside down, and tap the edge of the pot on a table edge. The contents of the pot should fall out intact in your hand.

When setting the plants in the garden soil, use the same procedures and the precautions for root placement described earlier for indoor transplanting (Figure 14-8). Set plants slightly deeper in the soil than they were previously growing. You can place containers such as peat pots, expanded pellets, and cubes directly in the garden soil. Be sure to plant these containers deep enough to cover the upper edges and surfaces with soil. If exposed, these surfaces sometimes act as a wick, resulting in a rapid loss of moisture from around the plant's roots.

After the plant is set, leave a slight dish-shaped depression around the stem. Fill this with water or starter solution (see "Fertilizing Garden Crops" in this chapter).

Choose a cloudy day for transplanting, or wait until evening. Avoid windy or very cold days. The more moderate the conditions, the more likely plant survival will be. If conditions the day following transplanting are very hot or windy, protect plants with shingles pushed into the soil on the sunny or windy side of each.

You can plant outdoors one or two weeks earlier with some plants by covering them with waxed-paper HotKaps, or with plastic beverage or milk jugs with their bottoms removed, after transplanting. Plastic tunnels supported by wire frames can be used to cover entire rows.

HotKaps and plastic tunnels trap heat from the soil to protect against light frosts. Check them carefully during warm days to be sure that inside temperatures are not too high. Venting slots may be cut on the side of the HotKaps or tents away from the sun or caps can be removed from the plastic jugs to reduce this problem.

The transplanting sequence is illustrated in Figure 14-9.

FIGURE 14-9 • Transplanting to the garden. (A) Place plant slightly deeper than it was indoors; (B) firm soil around the roots. (C) water generously; (D) apply Hot-Kap for earlier outdoor planting; and (E) anchor Hot-Kap with soil.

Planting Seeds Outdoors

Directions for seedbed preparation were given earlier in this chapter. For suggestions regarding the timing, irrigation, and depth of planting, see Chapter 4 and Tables 14-2 and 14-3.

Seeds are planted outdoors after the soil has warmed sufficiently and the seedbed is raked smooth. Measure the correct between-row distance and mark the ends of the rows with small stakes. Using either a string attached to stakes or a straight board as the row guide, dig a shallow trench for the seeds with the corner of a hoe. Straight rows make cultivation easier. Place the seeds in the furrow, cover to the proper depth, and tamp the soil firmly with the hoe or a rake (Figure 14-10). Packing with a rake is recommended with heavy soil that tends to crust after rain or sprinkling if the surface is left smooth. Planting a few more seeds than are necessary to ensure adequate stand in case of poor germination is all right if the plants are thinned soon after seedlings emerge. Generally, however, amateurs tend to plant far too many seeds, resulting in crowding and stunted growth.

Crops that require wide between-plant spacing—squash, watermelon, muskmelon, cucumbers, pole beans, sweet corn—can be planted in hills (Figure 14-11) and thinned to two or three plants per hill. The total number of plants remaining after thinning should be the same as the number that would remain if the planting were thinned to the suggested between-plant distance in Table 14-2.

Where crusting is a problem, it can be prevented with a narrow, shallow mulch of peat moss, vermiculite, barkdust, or sawdust over the row.

If the garden is to be furrow irrigated or if drainage after heavy rains is required, it is necessary to furrow the garden area and plant the garden in beds. Large gardens can be furrowed with power equipment, but smaller areas can be furrowed with the corner of a hoe as the garden is being planted. Crops should be seeded near the furrow rather than in the center of the bed so that irrigation water can soak to the planting. Furrows should slope gradually so that water can flow slowly from top to bottom. On a sloping site this may mean planting on the contour. Beds are seldom less than 2½ feet (about ¾ m) wide from center to center, and closely spaced crops are planted two rows per bed (Figure 14-12).

Begin thinning as soon as germination is complete. Do not thin all at once, but go over the rows several times. The first plants thinned out, if carefully removed, can be transplanted to areas where germination was poor or can be used to plant other areas. Edible plants removed later can be eaten. Consult Table 14-2 or follow the directions on the seed packets for thinning.

Starting Woody Plants from Seed

Because most woody plants are heterozygous, those grown from seed usually differ somewhat from the parent plant and from one another. Many are inferior to the parent plant in horticultural qualities.

Treating the Seed. Seed from woody plants is frequently affected by one or more types of dormancy, which must be overcome before it can germinate. Scarification and stratification to overcome seed dormancy are described in Chapter 4. Seeds should be planted immediately after they are treated.

Planting the Seed. After dormancy has been overcome, the seeds can be grown as described for vegetables and herbaceous ornamentals. They can be started indoors for later transplanting outside, or they can be planted outdoors at the proper time. Table 14-5 lists suggestions for handling the seeds of selected woody plants.

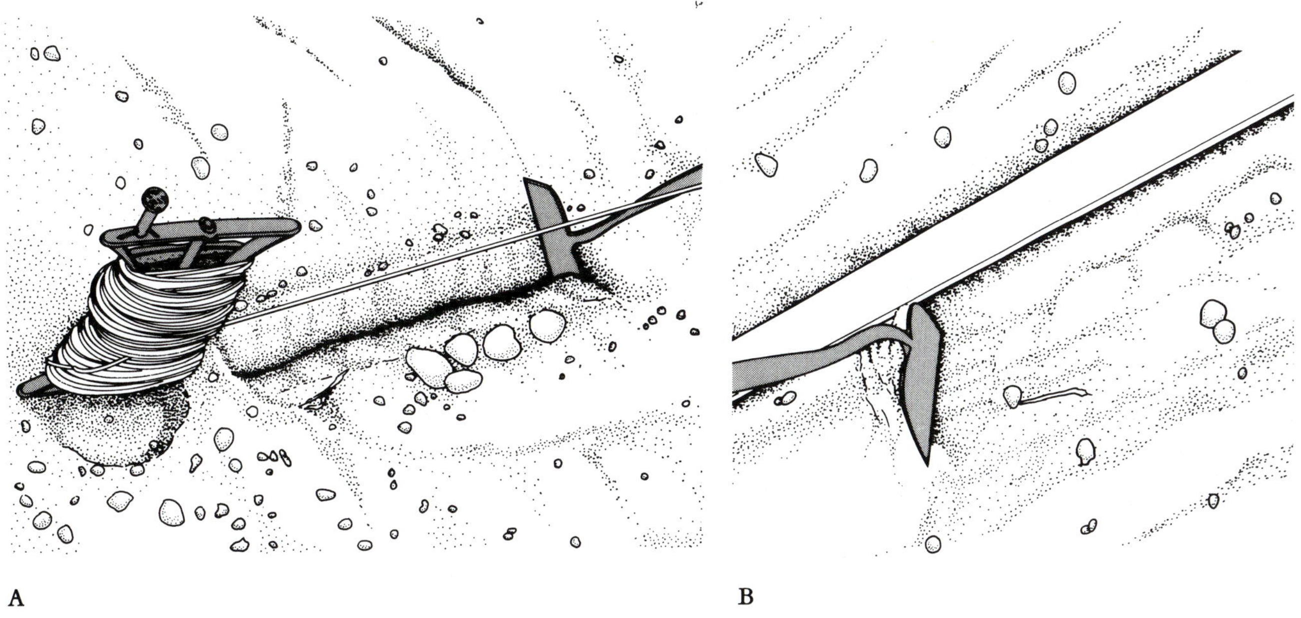

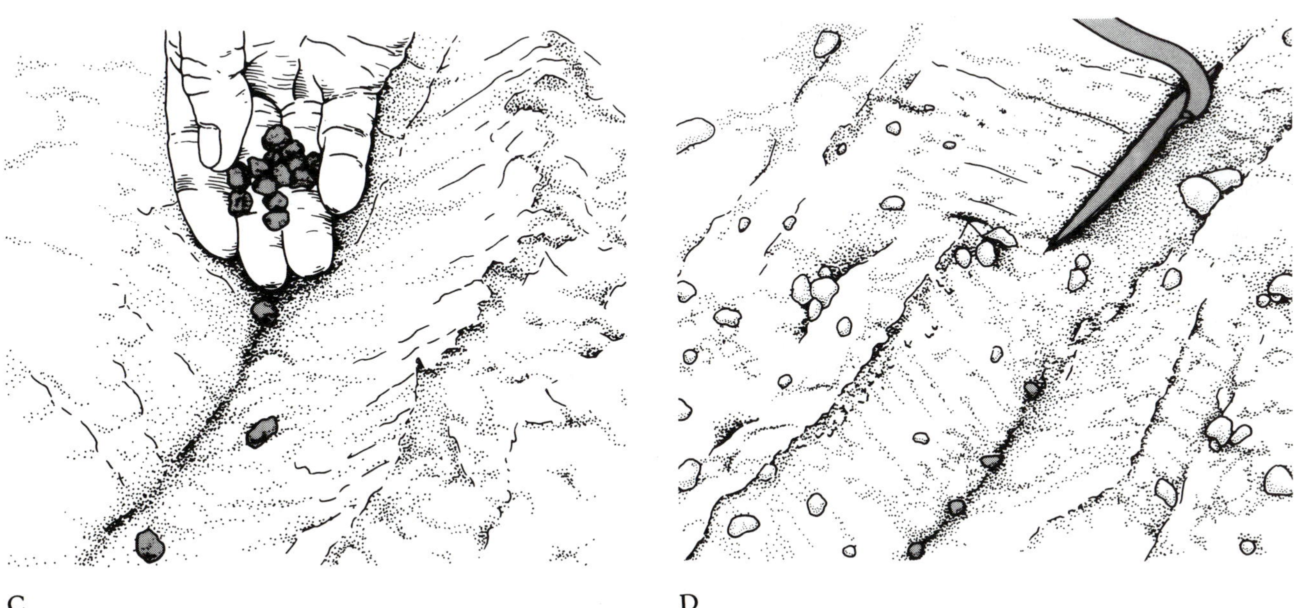

FIGURE 14-10 • Direct seeding without furrow irrigation. (A) Marking planting furrows using a string for a guide; (B) marking planting furrows with a straight-edge guide; (C) placing seed in a furrow; and (D) packing soil firmly over the seeds.

A

B

FIGURE 14-11 • Planting (A) and covering (B) a hill of seed. (Courtesy Washington State University)

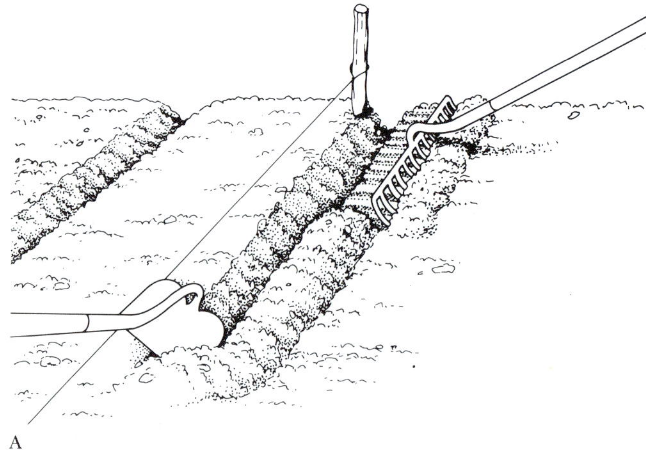

A

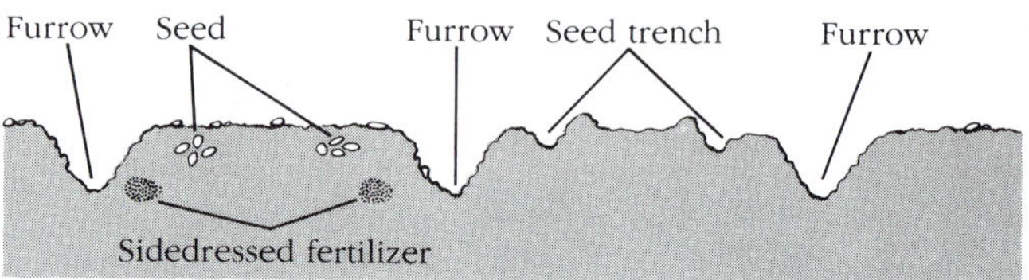

B

FIGURE 14-12 • Direct seeding with furrow irrigation. (A) Making furrows. With a taut string as a guide, use the corner of a hoe to dig a furrow 3 to 4 inches (8 to 10 cm) deep. The soil from the furrow should be pulled away from the completed bed and piled. Then rake the pile of soil over the area of the next bed, and at the same time level any humps and fill in any depressions. (B) Cross section of furrowed garden. Shallow trenches for planting the seed are dug a few inches from the furrow. Seed should be distributed and covered immediately after the seed furrow is dug, in order to limit drying of the soil in the seed trench. Fertilizer sidedressing, if needed, is most effective if the fertilizer is placed slightly below and on the furrow side of the seed or seedling.

TABLE 14-5 • *Treatments necessary to stimulate seed germination of selected woody plants*

Plant	Outdoor Planting Time	Stratification Conditions Necessary
Apple	Fall	None
	Spring	30–90 days; 32–50°F; sand or peat
Arborvitae	Fall	None
	Spring	30–60 days; 32–50°F; sand or peat
Ash	Fall	None
	Spring	60–90 days; 35–41°F; sand or peat
Barberry	Fall	None
	Spring	15–40 days; 32–41°F; sand or peat
Birch	Fall	None
	Spring	30–60 days; 32–50°F; sand or peat
Blackberry	Plant immediately from the berry	None
Cherry	Fall	None
	Spring	60–170 days; 35–45°F; sand or peat
Chestnut (American)	Fall	None
	Spring	90–120 days; 41°F; sand or peat
Cotoneaster[a]	Fall	None
	Spring	90–120 days at 60–75°F followed by 90–120 days at 41°F; sand or peat
Dogwood[b]	Fall	None
	Spring	60 days at 70–85°F followed by 90–100 days at 41°F; sand or peat
Elm	Fall	None
	Spring	60–90 days; 41°F; sand or peat
Euonymus	Fall	None
	Spring	90–120 days; 32–50°F; sand or peat
Filbert	Fall	None
	Spring	90 days; 41°F; sand
Fir	Fall	None
	Spring	30–90 days; 41°F; sand or peat
Hickory	Fall	None
	Spring	90–150 days; 32–45°F; sand or peat
Holly	Fall	None (may require 2 years or more for complete germination)
	Spring	60 days at 68–86°F followed by 60 days at 41°F; sand or peat
Honeylocust[c]	Spring	None
Horse chestnut	Fall	None
	Spring	120 days; 41°F; sand
Lilac	Fall	None
	Spring	30–90 days; 41°F; sand
Maple	Fall	None
	Spring	60–120 days; 41°F; sand or peat
Mountain ash	Fall	None
	Spring	60–150 days; 41–50°F; sand or peat
Pear	Fall	None
	Spring	60–90 days; 32–45°F; sand or peat
Pine	Fall	None
	Spring	30–90 days; 32–41°F; sand or peat
Plum	Fall	None
	Spring	60–120 days; 41°F; sand or peat
Poplar	Spring	No treatment necessary
Raspberry	Plant immediately from the berry	
Rose	Plant immediately from rose hip	
Spruce	Fall	None
	Spring	Some may require 30–90 days; 41°F; sand or peat
Walnut	Fall	None
	Spring	90–120 days; 34–41°F; sand or peat
Willow	Sow immediately after collection	
Yew	Fall	None (may require 2 years for complete germination)
	Spring	90–270 days; 37–41°F; sand or peat

Adapted from *Propagating Plants from Seed*, by F. E. Larsen. Pacific Northwest Cooperative Extension Publication 170. Extension Services of Washington State University, Oregon State University, and University of Idaho. Pullman, Wash. Revised periodically.

[a] Requires scarification treatment: 1½ hours in concentrated sulfuric acid.

[b] Requires mechanical scarification or 1–3 hours in concentrated sulfuric acid.

[c] Requires scarification treatment: 1–2 hours in concentrated sulfuric acid.

PROPAGATING WITH CUTTINGS*

◆ ◆ ◆

Cuttings are detached vegetative plant parts that develop into complete new plants by reproducing their missing parts. In accordance with what is likely to work best for each plant, cuttings can be taken from stems, roots, or leaves (Figure 14-13).

Types of Woody Plant Cuttings

Cuttings of deciduous plants are usually taken from stem sections or tips one year or less in age, evergreens usually just from stem tips. The basal part of a cutting is sometimes older wood.

Tip cuttings are probably the most common type for use with deciduous plants during the growing season; they generally do not give the best results at any other part of the year. The tip section of a shoot is more vulnerable to winter-cold damage, may have flower buds rather than shoot buds, and may not have the proper internal nutritional and hormonal balance for good rooting during the dormant season. Simple or straight cuttings, starting 8 to 10 inches (20 to 25 cm) from the shoot tip, are usually more satisfactory for dormant cuttings.

For evergreen plants, tip cuttings are the most common type and generally give satisfactory results. They are cut about 4 to 10 inches long from the stem tips, using stems one year or less in age. Tip cuttings can be made from the main shoot or long side branches. Large cuttings produce a usable plant in shorter time than do small cuttings but may require more care while rooting.

Simple or **straight cuttings** are made from long, one-year-old shoots that can be cut into sections. This is the most common type of cutting for propagating dormant cuttings of deciduous plants and may occasionally be used for broad-leaved evergreens.

Heel cuttings are made from side shoots produced on stems two or more years in age. To make the cuttings, pull the side shoots from the main stem. Pull directly away from the tip end of the main stem. This usually leaves a "heel" of older, main-stem tissue attached to the basal end of the side shoot. The heel cutting can also be made by cutting the heel portion from the main stem with a knife.

Mallet cuttings are similar to heel cuttings, but they include a complete cross section of the older, main stem at the base of the side shoot. This requires using a knife or, better yet, a pair of small pruning shears.

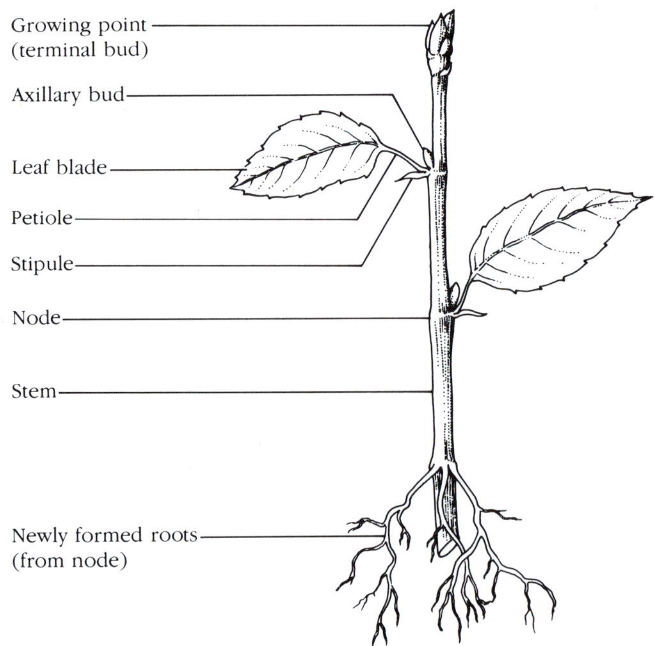

FIGURE 14-13 • Rooted stem cutting. Both leaves and new roots normally arise from the nodes (enlarged areas on the stem). (Courtesy of Washington State University)

---

*Adapted from *Herbaceous Plants from Cuttings*, by W. E. Guse and F. E. Larsen. Pacific Northwest Cooperative Extension Publication 151; and from *Propagating Deciduous and Evergreen Shrubs, Trees and Vines with Stem Cuttings*, by F. E. Larsen and W. E. Guse. Pacific Northwest Cooperative Extension Publication 152. Extension Services of Washington State University, Oregon State University, and the University of Idaho. Pullman, Wash. Revised periodically.

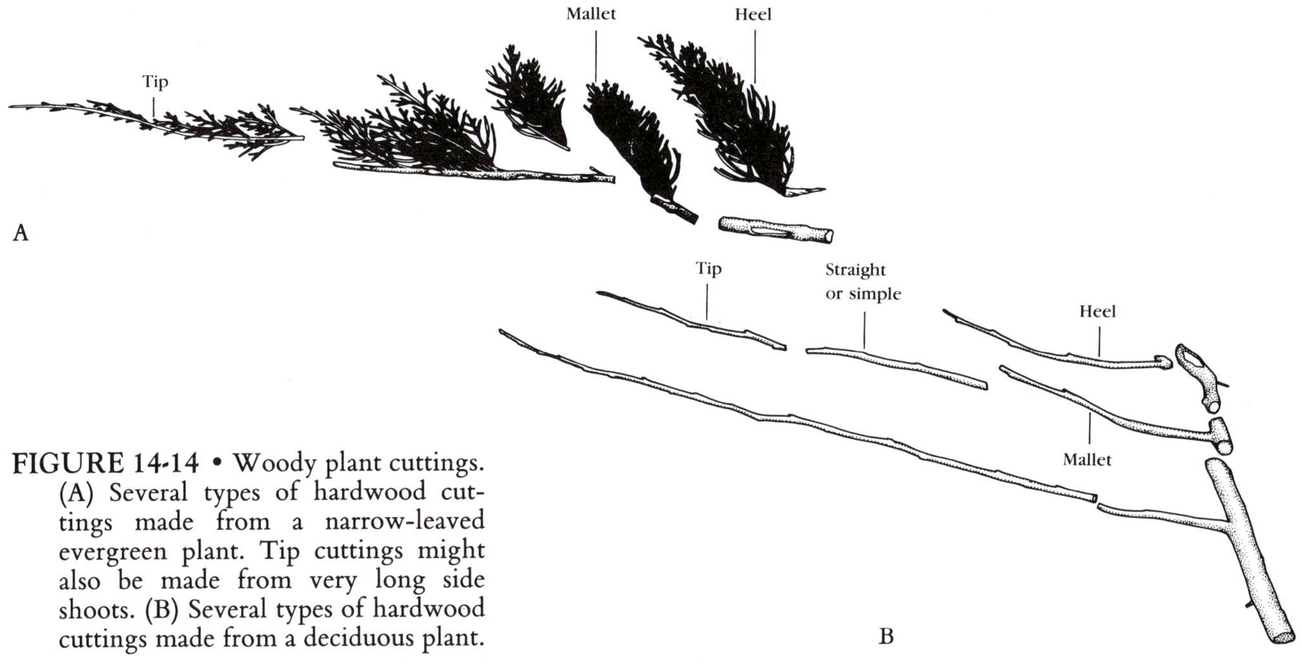

FIGURE 14-14 • Woody plant cuttings. (A) Several types of hardwood cuttings made from a narrow-leaved evergreen plant. Tip cuttings might also be made from very long side shoots. (B) Several types of hardwood cuttings made from a deciduous plant.

Some evergreens may root better from heel or mallet cuttings because these plants normally develop root **primordia** (specialized cells that can develop into roots) in older stems. These root primordia remain dormant until the stem bends naturally to the moist soil or until the stem is cut from the plant and placed in a rooting medium. Some deciduous plants also produce root primordia. Figure 14-14 illustrates woody plant cuttings.

Types of Herbaceous Plant Cuttings

Stem cuttings are the most frequently used type of cutting for herbaceous plants. Leaves or parts of leaves are also used to propagate herbaceous plants. Leaves of some plants form roots but do not produce new shoots. To propagate these, you must use a leaf-bud cutting, which includes the leaf plus an axillary bud and a portion of the stem; the shoots of the new plant will then form from the axillary bud.

Factors Affecting Rooting

The *time of year* that cuttings are taken may affect the rooting of woody plants. For many deciduous plants the best results can be expected from cuttings that are taken from late fall to early winter before there has been enough cold weather to complete the rest requirements of the leaf buds. This allows the cutting to be rooted under warm conditions without its developing leaves. After the rooting has started, however, the cuttings must be subjected to cold temperatures according to the individual plant's requirements. Some deciduous plants can be rooted only from leafy softwood or semihardwood cuttings taken during the growing season. Others root readily almost any time of the year.

For many narrow-leaved evergreens the best results can be expected of cuttings that are taken from late fall to late winter. Exposure of the parent or stock plant to cold temperatures before the cuttings are taken stimulates rooting. But cuttings of broad-leaved evergreen plants usually root best if taken during the growing season after a flush of growth, when the wood is partially matured. Some plants root readily at almost any time of the year.

Softwood cuttings are taken during the growing season from new growth that has not matured or hardened significantly. When the wood is partially matured, they are called **semihardwood** cuttings. Those taken during the subsequent dormant season when the wood is mature and hardened or from wood older than one year are called **hardwood cuttings**.

Herbaceous plants are most easily propagated in the spring when there is a natural increase in the rate of growth. They can, however, be propagated successfully throughout the year as long as succulent plant tissue is available and proper environmental conditions are provided.

The *age of the stock plant* may be important with hard-to-root plants. Cuttings from young seedling plants may root better than those from older plants. The chances of rooting cuttings from large old trees or shrubs may not be very good unless they are easy-to-root types.

Wounding the basal end of the cutting often stimulates rooting of such evergreen plants as rhododendrons and junipers, especially if the cutting has older wood at its base. Slight wounding is done by using the tip of a sharp knife to make a 1- to 2-inch (2½ to 5 cm) vertical cut down each side of the base of the cutting. Stripping off the lower side branches of the cutting during its preparation can also be considered as a slight wounding (Figure 14-15). For more severe wounding on difficult-to-root types or larger diameter cuttings, make several vertical cuts. Wounding can also be done by removing a thin slice of bark down one or both sides of the base of the cutting. Expose the cambium but avoid cutting very deeply into the wood.

Wounding may stimulate rooting by promoting cell division and more absorption of water or applied root-promoting chemicals, or it may remove tough tissue that is a barrier to outward root growth from the cutting. Wounding is most often done on evergreen plants, but it may at times be useful on deciduous plants.

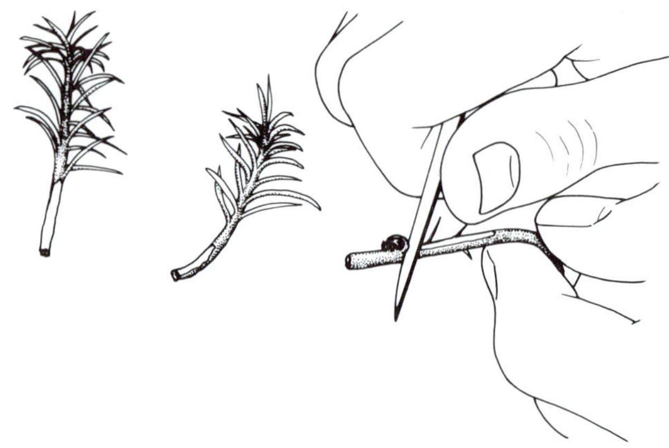

FIGURE 14-15 • Wounding. A narrow-leaved evergreen cutting can sometimes be induced to root more easily when a thin layer of bark is sliced or scraped from its base.

The *physical condition of the stock* affects the rooting of cuttings. Cuttings taken during the growing season often root poorly if they are from rapidly growing, succulent shoots. Instead, take them after growth has stopped and the wood has begun to harden; otherwise, many may rot. Shoots that have grown very little also root poorly. Neither type of shoot has the optimal physical condition and nutritional balance for the best rooting.

Too much or too little fertilizer on the stock plants may hinder the rooting ability of the cuttings because of its effect on growth and internal nutritional balance. Because of better physical condition and nutritional balance, lateral shoots may root better than do terminal shoots from the same plant. Similarly, when a very long shoot can be made into several cuttings, sections from the central part of the shoot may root better than do those from either end.

Shoots with flower buds or flowers may not root as well as do shoots that are strictly vegetative in some hard-to-root plants. In such plants removing the flower buds sometimes helps rooting. Take both woody and herbaceous cuttings only from healthy plants that are free of insects, disease, and nutritional disorders.

The *plant species* may influence rooting. Many deciduous and evergreen plants are propagated from hardwood cuttings, but they vary considerably in ease of rooting. Honeysuckle, currant, grape, and willow root readily. Apple and pear are more difficult, and cherry and lilac are usually very difficult to root using hardwood cuttings.

Among evergreen plants, false cypress, arborvitae, and low-growing juniper generally root readily. Yew roots fairly well. The upright junipers, spruces, and hemlocks are difficult to root. Cuttings of firs and pines are usually very difficult to root.

There is also considerable variation among species within these groups. Even genetic variability from plant to plant may affect ease of rooting. Environmental conditions, number of leaves remaining on the cutting, internal nutritional and chemical factors, and synthetic hormones all affect rooting (see Chapter 4).

Procedures for Making and Handling Cuttings

Cuttings of Woody Evergreen and Leafy Deciduous Plants. Remove from the parent plant a portion of stem 4 to 8 inches (10 to 20 cm) long with the leaves attached. For most deciduous plants, a tip, simple, or straight cutting is sufficient. For most evergreen plants, use tip or heel cuttings. Snip off leaves (or needles) that would be in contact with the rooting medium (the bottom 1½ to 2 inches of stem) to prevent these leaves' rotting. The remaining leaves will continue to produce substances that aid in forming roots on the cutting. If hardwood cuttings of evergreen plants are used, wound the base of the cutting by one of the methods described. Use the more severe methods of wounding for hard-to-root types.

Spread a small amount of auxin compound on waxed paper or in a clean dish. Dip the base (cut end) of the cutting in the powder so that some adheres to the cut surface and wounded areas. Discard any leftover powder to prevent contamination. Talc preparations lose their effectiveness after about eight months, even if kept in a closed container and refrigerated.

Make a hole in the rooting medium so that the powder is not scraped off when you insert the cutting. Insert the base of the cutting into the prepared hole in the rooting medium. If bottom heat is used, insert the base of the cutting nearly to the bottom of the container so that it is close to the heat source. Firm the rooting medium around the base of each cutting. After all cuttings are inserted and firmed in place, apply enough water to the rooting medium to settle it around the cuttings. This "watering-in" procedure leaves the rooting medium in close contact with the base of each cutting.

Place the cover over the propagation box (Figure 14-16) or container and keep it in a moderately warm room. Most leafy cuttings do best at temperatures of 60° to 70°F (16° to 21°C). Inspect the cuttings daily and remove any leaves that have fallen. Syringe the tops of the cuttings and keep the rooting medium moist. When the cuttings resist a slight tug and begin to feel anchored, they

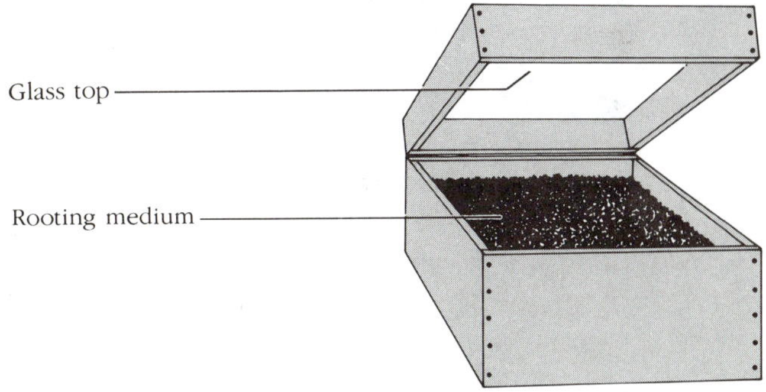

FIGURE 14-16 • Propagation chamber. A simple propagation chamber can be made from two boxes. The top box has a glass cover to admit light (the cover could also be made of plexiglass). When closed, the interior of box becomes humid, creating an environment similar to that of a mist chamber. Provide drainage in the bottom box to prevent waterlogging. For a few cuttings, the same effect can be obtained by putting a plastic bag over a flowerpot. (Courtesy of Washington State University)

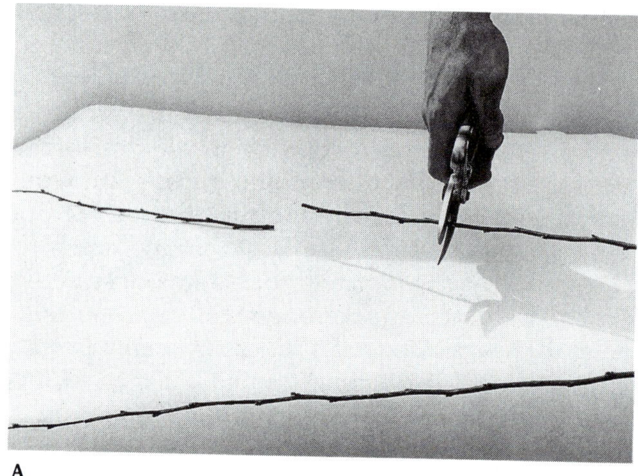

A

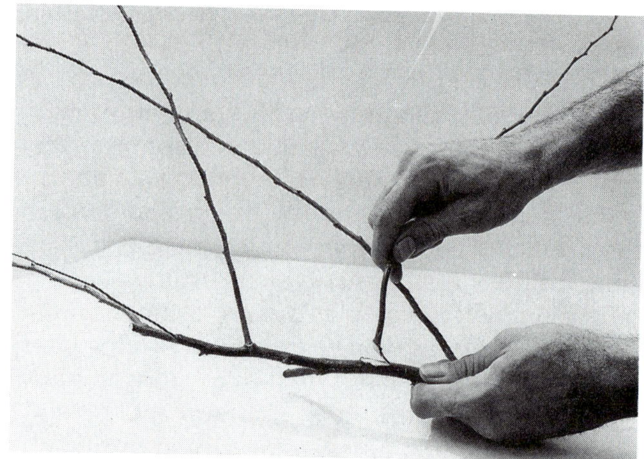

B

C

D

E

FIGURE 14-17 • Procedures for making and handling hardwood cuttings. (A) Making tip and straight cuttings from a one-year whip of a deciduous plant. (B) Making heel cuttings from a deciduous plant. (C) Treating the basal end of a simple or straight cutting with a root-promoting chemical. (D) Inserting a cutting into the rooting medium. (E) Rooted hardwood cuttings of deciduous plants. Both shoots and roots developed while the cutting was in the rooting medium. (Courtesy of Washington State University) are beginning to root. Some types may require two to three months or more to form sufficient roots to allow removal from the rooting medium.

When the cuttings have two or three roots about one-half inch long, place them in pots about four inches in diameter. Use a good potting soil. Because the cuttings have been accustomed to the humid atmosphere of the propagating box (or mist, if used), accustom them to the "outside" atmosphere by gradually aerating the propagation box (or reducing the mist) before potting. Another way is to cover the potted cutting with perforated plastic film for about a week after potting; this is another example of hardening off.

After potting, do not expose the cuttings to direct sunlight or temperature extremes until they have had several weeks to become accustomed to outdoor conditions.

Hardwood Cuttings of Deciduous Plants. Many of the techniques for rooting hardwood cuttings (Figure 14-17) are similar to those just described for rooting leafy deciduous and evergreen cuttings. However, these cuttings may not need a covered propagation box or mist unless they require a long time to root, during which leaves develop from dormant buds. Easy-to-root types can be taken in the fall and rooted outdoors in the soil in mild climates, or they can be taken in the spring if winters are cold. Take difficult-to-root types in late fall. They require treatment in a moist, warm (60° to 70°F) rooting medium until rooting begins. This is followed by holding in cool (40° to 45°F; 4° to 7°C) moist storage until spring weather allows outdoor planting. Wounding and treatment with root-promoting chemicals may be helpful.

A

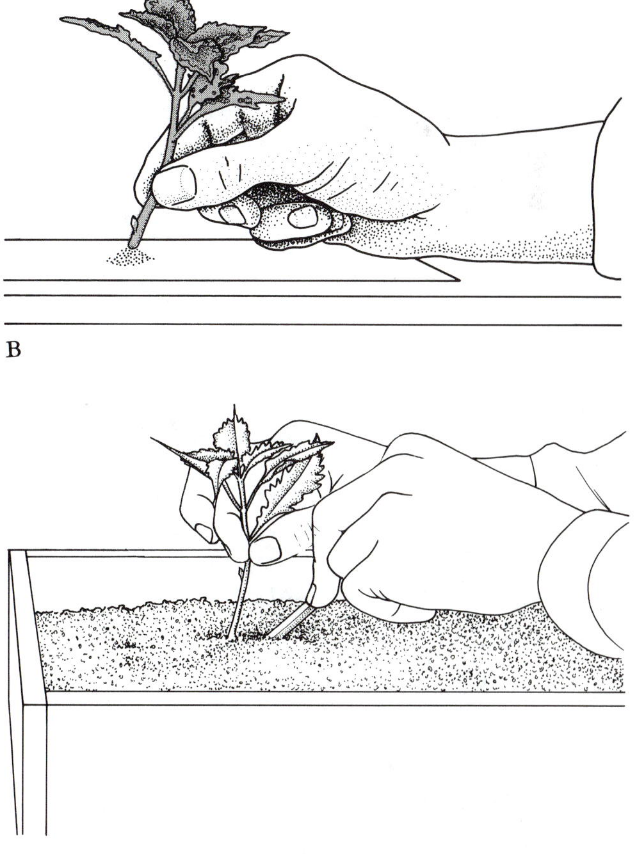

FIGURE 14-18 • Making a herbaceous stem cutting. (A) Cuttings are taken below a node from a healthy, vigorous plant. (B) A small amount of rooting hormone such as Rootone or Hormodin is applied to the cut surface of the cutting. Excessive amounts of hormone may inhibit rooting. (C) A furrow or hole is made in the rooting medium, and the cutting is inserted. The medium is then pressed firmly around the cutting.

Cuttings handled in this way are often tied in bundles with the basal ends all in the same direction. The bundle is plunged into the rooting or storage medium. When the root initiation and storage period are over, the bundles are untied, and the cuttings are individually planted, usually outside in a closely spaced nursery row.

Herbaceous Plant Cuttings. Remove from the parent plant a portion of stem 3 to 5 inches (8 to 13 cm) long with the leaves attached. Make a clean cut or break just below a node of the donor plant; the nodes contain actively dividing cells and are the areas where roots are likely to form most readily.

Snip off leaves and stipules from the bottom 1½ inches of stem, so they will not be in contact with the rooting medium and rot. The remaining leaves will continue to produce substances that aid in forming roots on the cutting.

Apply rooting hormone to the base of the cutting. Then place the base of the cutting in firm contact with a moist, warm rooting medium (Figure 14-18). After roots form, transplant the cutting to a permanent pot (Figure 14-19).

Cuttings of plants that exude a sticky sap—such as geraniums and cacti—will do better if the cut ends are allowed to dry for a few hours before being placed in the rooting medium. This helps prevent the entrance of disease organisms.

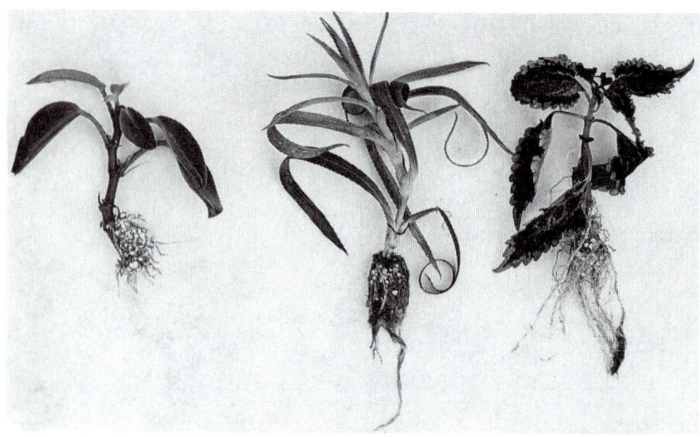

FIGURE 14-19 • Rooted cuttings ready for transplanting (left to right): peperomia, carnation, coleus.

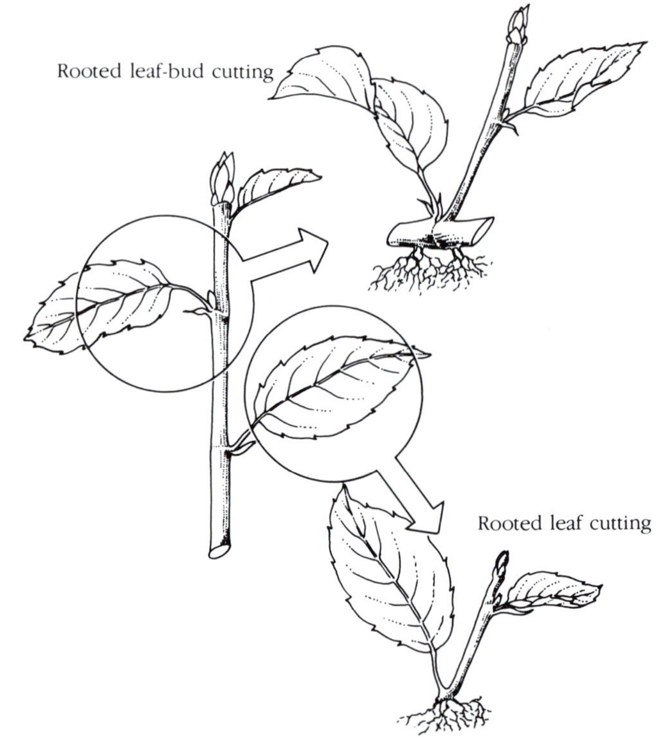

FIGURE 14-20 • Propagation from leaf cuttings. A single leaf is used for leaf cuttings. A leaf-bud cutting includes a portion of the stem and an axillary bud; the new shoots will arise from this bud. (Courtesy of Washington State University)

Some plants can be propagated from a single leaf (Figure 14-20). Generally, you can place the petiole of the leaf into the rooting medium just as you do the stem of a stem cutting. Roots and shoots form at the base of the petiole.

Leaves of such plants as begonia, bryophyllum, and jade plant are laid flat with their lower surface in firm contact with the rooting medium. Roots and shoots form from the leaf, which eventually decays.

The swordlike leaves of sansevieria can be cut into cross sections. Place the base of each section in the rooting medium. In a similar way the leaves of many begonias can be cut into pie-shaped sections. Shoots and roots form from the basal end of the cutting. Figure 14-21 shows some leaf cuttings. Tables 14-6, 14-7, and 14-8 list selected plants that can be propagated from cuttings.

A

B

FIGURE 14-21 • Leaf cuttings. (A, left to right) Peperomia leaf with roots formed from the petiole; bryophyllum leaf with new plants forming in the notches of the leaf edge; unrooted jade leaf. (B) Whole-leaf cutting of begonia showing root formation from both the petiole and at cuts through the large veins on the underside. (A, courtesy of Washington State University)

LAYERING TO RENEW OR MULTIPLY PLANTS*

Layering, or layerage, is the process of forming roots on a stem that is still attached to a plant. Some plants reproduce themselves naturally by layering.

Many plants can be propagated in limited numbers by layering. Layering does not require the skilled techniques necessary for grafting or the close attention to environment necessary for rooting cuttings. It is an ideal method for the home gardener to renew an old plant or to produce a limited number of new plants from an existing one. A layer (the stem on which roots are formed) is supported by the parent plant, from which it draws water and nutrients during root formation.

Tip Layering

Tip layering is not adapted to as many kinds of plants as are some other methods of layering. It is used primarily for black and purple raspberries and some blackberries that are commercially propagated and may reproduce naturally by tip layering.

In early summer when new canes are 24 to 30 inches (60 to 75 cm) high, remove the cane (shoot) tips. This stimulates the growth of lateral shoots from the main shoot. The laterals are used for tip layering when they are long enough to reach the ground (about late July or early August) and the tips have small, curled leaves, giving them a rat-tailed appearance.

Insert the lateral shoot tips vertically upside down into a 4- to 6-inch (10 to 15 cm) hole in the soil next to the parent plant. Firm the soil around the tip. Keep the soil moist (Figure 14-22).

---

*Adapted from *Layering to Renew or Multiply Plants*, by F. E. Larsen. Pacific Northwest Cooperative Extension Publication 165. Extension Services of Washington State University, Oregon State University, and University of Idaho. Pullman, Wash. Revised periodically.

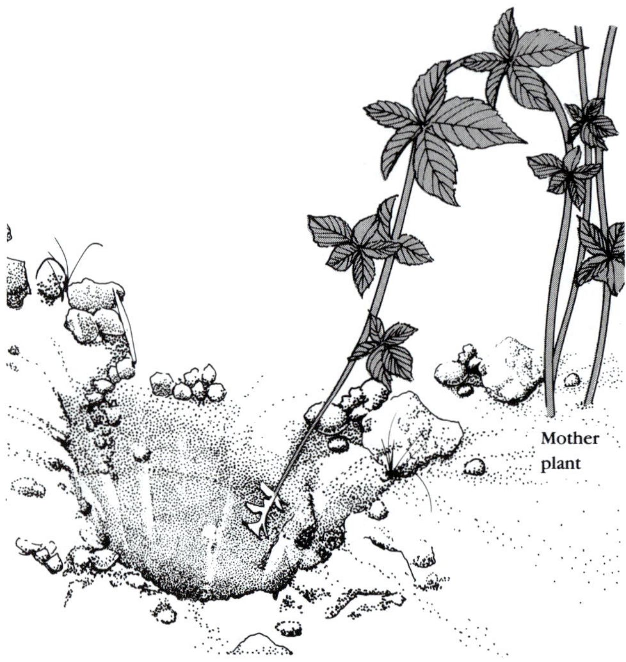

FIGURE 14-22 • Tip layering. Some raspberries and blackberries can be tip layered by inserting the stem tip into a hole 6 or 8 inches (15 or 20 cm) deep. The stem should be cut about 6 inches above the ground when the tip is rooted.

By fall the tips will form a good root system. Cut the lateral cane from the parent plant 6 to 8 inches (15 to 20 cm) above the soil where the tip was buried. The rooted tip can be dug and replanted the same fall or the following spring. The new plant is composed of the rooted tip with a terminal shoot bud, a good root system, and the section of cane from the parent plant. When the layer resumes growing, the terminal bud or another bud turns up, pushes out of the soil, and produces a new shoot oriented in the proper direction.

Simple Layering

Simple layering can be done with many deciduous and evergreen plants. With deciduous plants, simple layering is usually accomplished in the spring, using long, low branches that were produced during the previous growing season; however, layering later in the season with current-season shoots is also possible.

One-year-old branches or shoots can also be used to layer broad-leaved evergreen plants such as magnolia or rhododendron. Layering broad-leaved plants is more often done during the growing season, using shoots of current-season growth when they are long enough and after they have matured to the point that they will break when bent sharply. Low-growing, narrow-leaved evergreens such as yew and juniper can also be propagated by simple layering.

To layer deciduous and broad-leaved evergreen plants, bend a branch to the ground into a hole or trench about 6 inches deep. Bend the branch up sharply about 12 inches (30 cm) from the tip and cover the bent portion with soil, leaving about 6 inches of the top exposed. Remove any leaves that will be covered with soil. In some cases, you will need to place a wire loop or wooden peg over the lowest point of the bend to hold the branch in the soil. You may have to stake the protruding shoot tip to hold it upright (Figure 14-23).

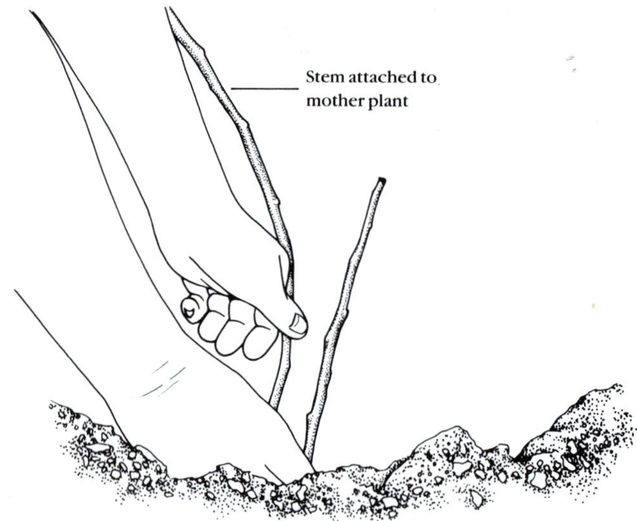

FIGURE 14-23 • Simple layer. Simple layering is done by bending a long stem (still attached to the parent plant) in a U-shape in the bottom of a hole. Use a wire loop or forked wooden stake to secure the bent stem to the ground.

TABLE 14-6 • *Selected woody evergreen plants that might be propagated from stem cuttings*[a]

Plant		Favorable Time to Take Cuttings	Kind of Cutting[b]	Rooting Success Expected
Common Name	Scientific Name			
Arborvitae	*Thuja occidentalis* (American)	Summer	Semihardwood	High
		Winter	Hardwood	
	Thuja orientalis (Oriental)	Late spring	Softwood	Low
Azalea	*Rhododendron* spp.	Summer	Semihardwood	Moderate to high
Barberry	*Berberis* spp.	Summer	Softwood	Moderate to high
		Fall	Hardwood	
Boxwood	*Buxus* spp.	Spring, summer, fall	Softwood or semihardwood	High
Camellia	*Camellia* spp.	Summer	Semihardwood	Moderate to high
Cedar	*Cedrus* spp.	Late summer or fall	Semihardwood	Low
Chamaecyparis (false-cypress)	*Chamaecyparis* spp.	Late fall or winter	Hardwood	Moderate to high
Cryptomeria	*Cryptomeria japonica*	Summer	Semihardwood	Slow to root
Daphne	*Daphne* spp.	Summer	Semihardwood	Moderate
Euonymus	*Euonymus* spp.	Summer	Semihardwood	High
Fir	*Abies* spp.	Winter	Hardwood	Low
Heath	*Erica* spp.	Summer	Semihardwood	High
		Winter	Hardwood	
Heather	*Calluna vulgaris*	Summer	Semihardwood	High
		Winter	Hardwood	
Hemlock	*Tsuga* spp.	Fall	Semihardwood	Low
		Winter	Hardwood	
Holly	*Ilex* spp.	Summer	Semihardwood	Moderate to high
		Winter	Hardwood	
Ivy	*Hedera helix*	Summer	Semihardwood	High
Juniper	*Juniperus* spp.	Summer	Semihardwood	Upright types may root poorly
		Winter	Hardwood	
Laurel (cherry)	*Prunus laurocerasus*	Summer	Semihardwood	High
		Winter	Hardwood	
Laurel (mountain)	*Kalmia latifolia*	Winter	Hardwood	Low
Madrone (Pacific)	*Arbutus menziesii*	Fall	Semihardwood	Moderate
Magnolia	*Magnolia* spp.	Summer	Softwood or semihardwood	Moderate to high
Oleander	*Nerium oleander*	Summer	Semihardwood	High
Oregon grape	*Mahonia aquifolium*	Summer	Semihardwood	Moderate to high
Pachistima	*Pachistima canbyi*	Summer	Softwood	Moderate to high
Pachysandra (spurge)	*Pachysandra terminalis*	Summer	Semihardwood	High
Pieris	*Pieris* spp.	Summer	Semihardwood	Moderate to high
Pine	*Pinus* spp.	Winter	Hardwood	Low
Privet	*Ligustrum* spp.	Summer	Softwood	Low to high
		Winter	Hardwood	
Pyracantha	*Pyracantha* spp.	Summer	Semihardwood	High
Rhododendron	*Rhododendron* spp.	Summer	Softwood or semihardwood	Low to high
Spruce	*Picea* spp.	Winter	Hardwood	Low
Viburnum	*Viburnum* spp.	Summer	Semihardwood	Moderate to high
Yew	*Taxus* spp.	Fall	Semihardwood	Moderate
		Winter	Hardwood	

Adapted from *Propagating Deciduous and Evergreen Shrubs, Trees and Vines with Stem Cuttings*, by F. E. Larsen and W. E. Guse. Pacific Northwest Cooperative Extension Publication 152. Extension Services of Washington State University, Oregon State University, and University of Idaho, Pullman, Wash. Revised periodically.

[a]Some plants listed also have closely related deciduous types that might be handled differently.

[b]Good results can usually be obtained with tip cuttings of most evergreen plants. The use of heel or mallet cuttings might be desirable with juniper and yew.

TABLE 14-7 • *Selected woody deciduous plants that might be propagated from stem cuttings*[a]

Plant		Favorable Time to Take Cuttings	Kind of Cutting[b]	Genera in Which Some Species Are Difficult to Root
Common Name	Scientific Name			
Alder	*Alnus* spp.	Winter	Hardwood	
Azalea	*Rhododendron* spp.	Summer	Softwood	X
Barberry	*Berberis* spp.	Summer	Softwood or semihardwood	
		Winter	Hardwood	
Bittersweet	*Celastrus* spp.	Summer	Softwood or semihardwood	
		Winter	Hardwood	
Blueberry	*Vaccinium* spp.	Summer	Softwood	
		Winter	Hardwood	
Boston ivy	*Parthenocissus tricuspidata*	Summer	Softwood	
		Winter	Hardwood	
Bottlebrush	*Callistemon* spp.	Summer	Semihardwood	
Boxwood	*Buxus* spp.	Summer	Softwood or semihardwood	
		Winter	Hardwood	
Broom	*Cytisus* spp.	Summer	Semihardwood	
		Winter	Hardwood	
Butterfly bush	*Buddleia* spp.	Summer	Softwood or semihardwood	
Catalpa	*Catalpa* spp.	Summer	Softwood	
Ceanothus	*Ceanothus* spp.	Summer	Softwood or semihardwood	
		Winter	Hardwood	
Cherry	*Prunus* spp.	Summer	Softwood or semihardwood	X
Clematis	*Clematis* spp.	Summer	Softwood or semihardwood	
Cotoneaster	*Cotoneaster* spp.	Summer	Softwood or semihardwood	
Crabapple	*Malus* spp.	Summer	Softwood or semihardwood	X
		Late fall	Hardwood	
Currant	*Ribes* spp.	Summer	Softwood	
		Winter	Hardwood	
Deutzia	*Deutzia* spp.	Summer	Softwood	
		Winter	Hardwood	
Dogwood	*Cornus* spp.	Summer	Softwood or semihardwood	X
Elderberry	*Sambucus* spp.	Summer	Softwood	
Elm	*Ulmus* spp.	Summer	Softwood	
Euonymus (spindle tree)	*Euonymus* spp.	Winter	Hardwood	
Forsythia	*Forsythia* spp.	Summer	Softwood	
		Winter	Hardwood	
Fringe tree	*Chionanthus* spp.	Summer	Softwood	X
Ginkgo (maidenhair)	*Ginkgo biloba*	Summer	Softwood	
Goldenrain tree	*Koelreuteria* spp.	Summer	Softwood	
Grape	*Vitis* spp.	Summer	Softwood	
		Winter	Hardwood	
Hawthorn	*Crataegus* spp.	Summer	Softwood	
		Winter	Hardwood	
Hibiscus (rose mallow)	*Hibiscus* spp.	Summer	Softwood or semihardwood	
		Winter	Hardwood	
Honeylocust	*Gleditsia triacanthos*	Winter	Hardwood	
Honeysuckle	*Lonicera* spp.	Summer	Softwood	
		Winter	Hardwood	
Hydrangea	*Hydrangea* spp.	Summer	Softwood	
		Winter	Hardwood	

(*continued*)

TABLE 14-7 • *(Continued)*

Plant		Favorable Time to Take Cuttings	Kind of Cutting[b]	Genera in Which Some Species Are Difficult to Root
Common Name	Scientific Name			
Jasmine	*Jasminum* spp.	Summer	Semihardwood	
		Winter	Hardwood	
Lilac	*Syringa vulgaris*	Summer	Softwood	X
Locust (black)	*Robinia pseudoacacia*	Summer	Semihardwood	
Maple	*Acer* spp.	Summer	Softwood	X
Mock orange	*Philadelphus* spp.	Summer	Softwood	
		Winter	Hardwood	
Magnolia	*Magnolia* spp.	Summer	Softwood or semihardwood	
Mulberry	*Morus alba*	Summer	Softwood	
Peach	*Prunus* spp.	Summer	Softwood or semihardwood	
Pear	*Pyrus* spp.	Late fall	Hardwood	X
Plum	*Prunus* spp.	Summer	Softwood or semihardwood	
Poplar	*Populus* spp.	Summer	Softwood	
		Winter	Hardwood	
Quince (flowering)	*Chaenomeles* spp.	Summer	Semihardwood	
		Winter	Hardwood	
Redbud	*Cercis* spp.	Summer	Softwood	X
Rose	*Rosa* spp.	Summer	Softwood or semihardwood	
		Winter	Hardwood	
Russian olive	*Elaeagnus angustifolia*	Winter	Hardwood	
St.-John's-wort	*Hypericum* spp.	Summer	Semihardwood	
Serviceberry	*Amelanchier alnifolia*	Summer	Softwood	
Smoke tree	*Cotinus coggygria*	Summer	Softwood	
Snowberry	*Symphoricarpos* spp.	Summer	Softwood	
		Winter	Hardwood	
Spiraea	*Spiraea* spp.	Summer	Softwood or semihardwood	X
		Winter	Hardwood	
Sumac	*Rhus* spp.	Summer	Softwood	X
Sweetgum	*Liquidambar* spp.	Summer	Softwood	
Tulip tree	*Liriodendron tulipifera*	Summer	Softwood	
Viburnum	*Viburnum* spp.	Summer	Softwood or semihardwood	X
		Winter	Hardwood	
Virginia creeper	*Parthenocissus quinquefolia*	Summer	Softwood	
		Winter	Hardwood	
Weigela	*Weigela* spp.	Summer	Softwood or semihardwood	
		Winter	Hardwood	
Willow	*Salix* spp.	Summer	Softwood or semihardwood	
		Winter	Hardwood	
Wisteria	*Wisteria* spp.	Summer	Semihardwood	
		Winter	Hardwood	

Adapted from *Propagating Deciduous and Evergreen Shrubs, Trees and Vines with Stem Cuttings*, by F. E. Larsen and W. E. Guse. Pacific Northwest Cooperative Extension Publication 152. Extension Services of Washington State University, Oregon State University, and University of Idaho. Pullman, Wash. Revised periodically.

[a]Some plants listed also have closely related evergreen types that may be handled differently.

[b]In general, use tip cuttings for those taken during the growing season (softwood or semihardwood) and simple (straight) cuttings for the leafless dormant type of cutting. Heel or mallet cuttings might be used for quince, which may have preformed root initials in 2-year-old wood.

TABLE 14-8 • *Selected herbaceous plants that can be propagated from cuttings*

Plant		Type of Cutting	Approximate Time to Root (weeks)[a]
Common Name	Scientific Name		
African violet	*Saintpaulia* spp.	Leaf	3–4
Aluminum plant	*Pilea* spp.	Stem	2–3
Aloe	*Aloe* spp.	Leaf	4–6
Aphelandra	*Aphelandra* sp.	Stem	2–3
Arrowhead plant	*Syngonium albolineatum*	Stem	2–3
Begonia	*Begonia* spp.	Stem (fibrous rooted); whole leaf or leaf section (Rex)	4–5
Cactus	*Cephalocereus senilis*	Stem	3–4
	Opuntia microdasys	Stem	3–4
Chrysanthemum	*Chrysanthemum* spp.	Stem	1–2
Carnation	*Dianthus* spp.	Stem	2–3
Coleus	*Coleus blumei*	Stem	1–2
Crown of thorns	*Euphoria splendens*	Stem	4–5
Dahlia	*Dahlia* spp.	Stem or leaf-bud	3–4
Dieffenbachia (dumbcane)	*Dieffenbachia* spp.	Stem	4–6
Dracaena	*Dracaena* spp.	Stem	3–4
Echeveria	*Echeveria* spp.	Leaf or stem	4–6
Euphorbia	*Euphorbia* spp.	Stem	4–6
Fittonia	*Fittonia* spp.	Stem	2–3
Fuchsia	*Fuchsia* spp. (also hybrids)	Stem	1–2
Geranium	*Pelargonium* spp.	Stem	1–2
Hoya	*Hoya* spp.	Stem	3–4
Hydrangea	*Hydrangea* spp.	Stem	2–3
Impatiens	*Impatiens* spp.	Stem	2–3
Ivy	Several genera and species	Stem	2–3
Jade	*Crassula* spp.	Stem or leaf	4–5
Kalanchoe (bryophyllum)	*Kalanchoe* spp.	Stem or leaf	4–5
Lantana	*Lantana* sp.	Stem	3–4
Monstera (split-leaf philodendron)	*Monstera deliciosa*	Stem	4–5
Mint	*Mentha* spp.	Stem	2–3
Peperomia	*Peperomia* spp.	Leaf, leaf–bud, or stem	4–6
	P. obtusifolia	Leaf–bud or stem works best	4–6
	P. obtusifolia variegata	Leaf–bud or stem works best	4–6
Periwinkle (myrtle)	*Vinca* spp.	Stem	3–4
Petunia	Petunia hybrids	Stem	2–3
Philodendron	*Philodendron* spp.	Stem	2–4
Piggyback plant	*Tolmiea menziesii*	Leaf with plantlet	3–4
Pothos	*Scindapsus aureus*	Stem	2–3
Poinsettia	*Euphorbia pulcherrima*	Stem	2–3
Sansevieria (snake plant)	*Sansevieria* spp.	Leaf, leaf section	4–6
Velvet plant	*Gynura* spp.	Stem	1–2
Wandering Jew	*Tradescantia* spp. *Zebrina* spp.	Stem	2–3

Adapted from *Herbaceous Plants from Cuttings*, by W. E. Guse and F. E. Larsen. Pacific Northwest Cooperative Extension Publication 151. Extension Services of Washington State University, Oregon State University, and University of Idaho. Pullman, Wash. Revised periodically.

[a]The indicated time for rooting is only approximate and may be longer under some conditions. When new shoots must develop in addition to roots, the time required for shoot development is often longer.

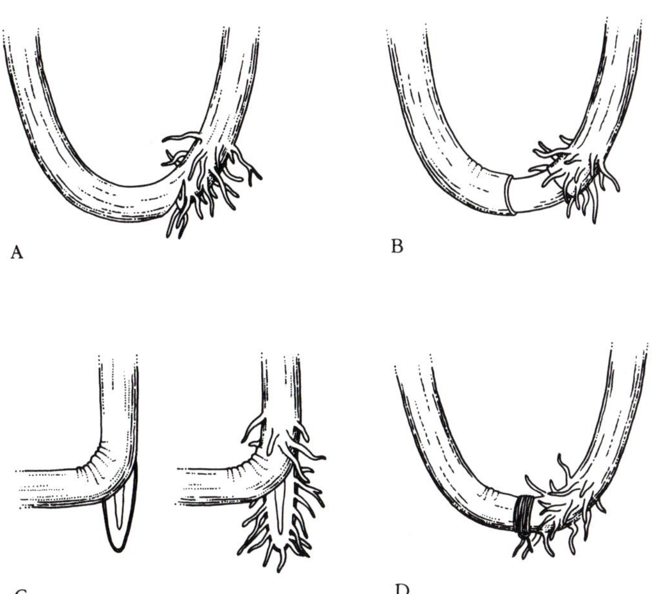

FIGURE 14-24 • Ways to stimulate rooting. (A) Stem cut on underside, (B) stem girdled by bark removal, (C) stem cut and twisted, (D) stem girdled by tight wire. (Courtesy of Washington State University)

Rooting may be stimulated by a shallow cut or notch in the underside of the shoot at the point of the bend. This also makes bending very stiff stems much easier. A root-promoting chemical such as Rootone may be applied to the cut. Rooting may also be improved by twisting the stem in the region of the bend to loosen the bark slightly or by placing a tight wire around the stem just behind the bend, between the bend and the parent plant. Rooting is also encouraged by keeping the soil moist where the stem is covered (Figure 14-24).

You can often layer low-growing, narrow-leaved evergreens by covering a branch with 3 or 4 inches (8 to 10 cm) of soil about 10 to 12 inches (25 to 30 cm) back from the tip. Some, such as 'Tam' juniper, often layer themselves.

Branches that were layered in the spring should be well rooted by fall. You can sever them from the parent plant after they are dormant. They can be transplanted either that fall or next spring before growth begins. Do not dig up those layered during the summer until the following spring.

If the top of the new plant (layer) is large in proportion to the root system, prune the top to reduce its size so that the water demands of the top can be met by the roots. Dig evergreen layers with a ball of soil (about 6 inches in diameter) attached to the roots. Broad-leaved evergreens will do best if you pot them after digging and hold them for three or four weeks in a shaded area before planting in a permanent location.

Compound (Serpentine, Multiple) Layering

Compound layering is used on plants with long, flexible vine-type stems, such as grape, clematis, and thornless, trailing blackberries that would otherwise reproduce from thorny root suckers (see "Gene Mutations and Bud Sports" in Chapter 3). The techniques are similar to simple layering except that the long, flexible stems of these plants allow alternate coverage and exposure along their length.

Treatments such as notching and chemical root promoters applied at the lowest point of each buried part of the stem may aid rooting. See that each exposed part of the stem has one or more leaves attached, to ensure that a bud will be present to form a shoot for the new plant.

The stem should root at each buried location. After it has rooted, cut the stem into sections so that each portion contains roots and a node (point of leaf attachment) with a shoot bud (Figure 14-25). The time of layering, digging, and methods of handling are the same as for simple layers.

Mound (Stool) Layering

Many well-established, vigorous shrubs and plants that have stiff branches that do not bend easily to the soil can be propagated by mound layering. This method is used commercially to produce rootstocks for fruit and nut trees. It is also used to propagate trees that produce suckers at their base.

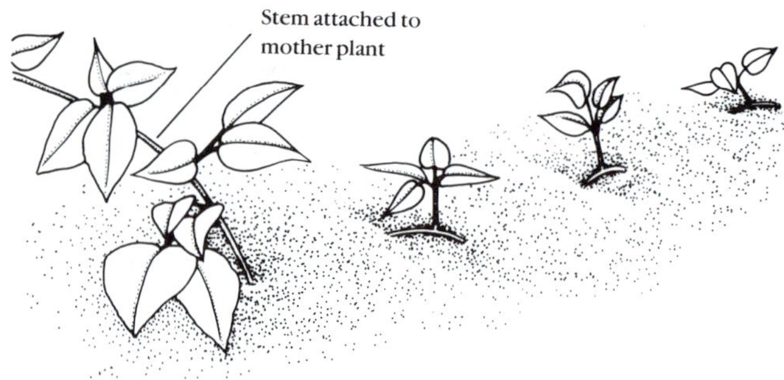

FIGURE 14-25 • Compound layering. This long flexible stem to be compound layered is alternately covered and exposed. When roots develop, several new plants can be obtained by cutting the stem into sections. (Courtesy of Washington State University)

If a well-established shrub can be sacrificed for a year, many new plants can be propagated from it by mound layerage. The entire plant is cut to within 2 to 3 inches (5 to 8 cm) of the ground in early spring before growth starts. When growth does begin, the remaining branch stubs of the plant will produce numerous shoots.

When the new shoots are 3 or 4 inches long, mound soil, compost, or shavings around the plant so that the bases of the new shoots are covered to about one-half their length. Add soil two or three more times throughout the growing season as the shoots grow. The final depth of soil should be 8 to 10 inches.

Shoots will be rooted at their base by fall and can be removed and replanted in the fall or the following spring (Figure 14-26). If the shoots are removed in the fall, the original plant should be recovered with soil until spring, to protect it from winter damage. More plants can be produced each year for several years after the mounding process is started.

An alternative method for plants that root poorly is to cover completely the cut stubs of the plant in the spring before growth starts so that the stub ends are buried one-half inch deep. The new shoots will be forced to grow through the soil;

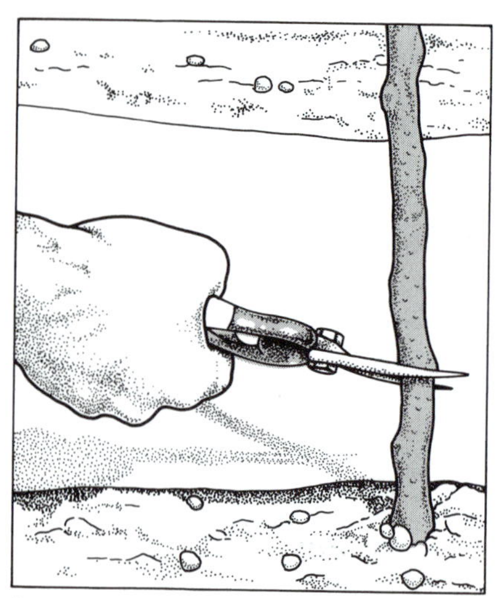
A

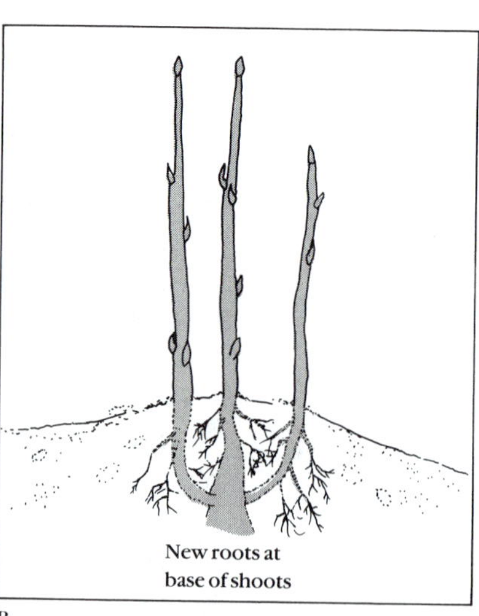

B

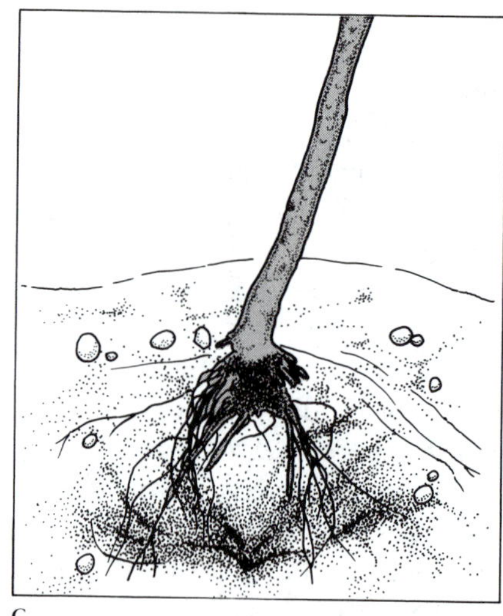
C

FIGURE 14-26 • Mound layering. For mound layering, a rooted plant is allowed to grow in place for a year and then is headed back close to the ground (A). The stub is covered with moist soil, shavings, or similar material. Shoots develop from mound-layered plants, and rooting at the base of the shoots results (B). The rooted shoots can be removed and planted (C).

gradually add soil to the base of the shoots as they grow. The final depth is the same as indicated above. By using this method, the base of the shoots will never develop a green color (chlorophyll), and the stem tissue will produce roots more easily.

Girdling with wire at the base of the new shoots about 1½ to 2 months after they begin to grow may stimulate the rooting of hard-to-root types. Notching or partial cutting of the stem or removal of a ring of bark may also aid rooting (see Figure 14-24).

If established plants are not available to mound-layer, a new plant can be planted, allowed to grow for a year, and then handled as just described. Even if the plant initially has only one stem, usually it will produce a half-dozen or more shoots that can be layered.

Soil to be used for this type of layering should be porous and well drained; sawdust or wood shavings instead of soil are sometimes used for mounding. The mound must be kept moist, as drying slows rooting or destroys any roots already formed. Do not waterlog the area, however.

Trench Layering

Trench layering is another method often used by nurseries to propagate rootstocks for fruit and nut trees.

With this method, rooted cuttings or liners are planted at an angle of about 30° from horizontal and allowed to grow for one year. The spring following planting, before growth starts, a 2-inch-deep trench is opened in the direction the plant is leaning. The plant is bent into the bottom of the trench and held against the soil with wire loops or wooden pegs. Weak, thin branches are removed or cut back severely.

Before the buds begin to grow, cover the plant with about 1 inch (2½ cm) of soil, sawdust, or wood shavings. New shoots from buds on the plant will push up through the covering. Add more covering as the shoots elongate. The process from this point is like that for mound layering (Figure 14-27).

FIGURE 14-27 • Trench layering. To trench layer, set plant at an angle in a shallow trench. Remove small, weak branches, and head back the others. Wire hoops can be used to hold the plant close to the ground. Branch stubs are mounded with a moist medium. New rooted shoots will develop from the stubs.

A similar method, called *continuous layering*, is often used for ornamental shrubs or other plants with long stems that can be bent to the ground. In this case the long stem is placed in the trench and covered over its entire length except for the tip, which is left exposed. New shoots will develop from the buds along the stem. They should usually be mounded to develop a greater area for root formation at the stem bases.

Air Layering

Air layering is used for plants with stiff or large stems that cannot be bent to the soil or for plants that do not readily produce shoots at their base. It is a good method to use on such ornamental houseplants as figs, rubber plants, or dieffenbachia, but it is adapted to many other plants as well.

The layer should usually be made on a portion of a branch that is one year old. This means that the layer will be made within about one foot of the end of a branch.

TABLE 14-9 • *Selected plants that might be propagated by layering*

Plant			
Common Name	Scientific Name	Type of Layerage	Timing
Apple	*Malus* spp.	Mound or trench	Spring
Ash	*Fraxinus* spp.	Simple	Spring, summer
Azalea	*Rhododendron* spp.	Simple, mound	Spring, summer
Barberry	*Berberis* spp.	Simple, mound	Spring
Blueberry	*Vaccinium* spp.	Mound	Spring
Blackberry	*Rubus* spp.	Tip	Summer
Beech	*Fagus* spp.	Simple	Spring
Buckthorn	*Rhamnus* spp.	Simple	Spring
Birch	*Betula* spp.	Simple	Spring, summer
Bittersweet	*Celastrus* spp.	Simple	Spring, summer
Boxwood	*Buxus* spp.	Simple	Summer
Camellia	*Camellia* spp.	Simple	Spring
Ceanothus	*Ceanothus* spp.	Simple	Spring, summer
Chestnut	*Castanea* spp.	Simple	Spring, summer
Clematis	*Clematis* spp.	Simple, compound	Spring, summer
Cotoneaster	*Cotoneaster* spp.	Simple	Summer
Currant	*Ribes* spp.	Mound, simple	Spring
Daphne	*Daphne cneorum*	Simple	Spring, summer
Dogwood	*Cornus* spp.	Simple, continuous	Spring, summer
Dumbcane	*Dieffenbachia* spp.	Air	Anytime
Dracaena	*Dracaena* spp.	Air	Anytime
Euonymus	*Euonymus* spp.	Simple	Spring, summer
Elder	*Sambucus* spp.	Simple	Spring

(*continued*)

FIGURE 14-28 • Completed air layer on a rubber plant. (Courtesy of Washington State University)

First, either girdle the stem at this point by removing a ½-inch-wide ring of bark, or make a slanting cut about halfway through the stem on the bottom side. Apply a root-promoting chemical to the girdled area, or force the root promoter into the knife cut. It may also help to force a toothpick into the knife cut to hold it open and prevent the cut's healing.

The final step is to place a handful of moist (not saturated) sphagnum or peat moss around the treated area. Hold this in place by a wrap or two of clear polyethylene film. Tie the polyethylene to the stem above and below the treated area. Add moisture periodically as needed at the top of the film after loosening the tie. Do not overwater, as excess moisture promotes decay (Figure 14-28).

With some plants under some conditions producing a good root system on an air layer may require as long as a year, although usually it is quicker. When you see a mass of roots through the

TABLE 14-9 • *(Continued)*

Plant			
Common Name	Scientific Name	Type of Layerage	Timing
Fiddle-leaf fig	*Ficus lyrata*	Air	Anytime
Filbert	*Corylus* spp.	Simple	Summer
Forsythia	*Forsythia* spp.	Tip, simple	Summer
Grape	*Vitis* spp.	Simple, compound	Spring
Gooseberry	*Ribes* spp.	Mound	Spring
Heather	*Calluna vulgaris*	Simple	Summer
Hemlock	*Tsuga* spp.	Simple	Spring
Hibiscus, Chinese	*Hibiscus rosa-sinensis*	Air	Spring, summer
Holly	*Ilex* spp.	Air, simple	Summer, fall
Honeysuckle	*Lonicera* spp.	Simple	Spring, summer
Horse chestnut	*Aesculus* spp.	Simple	Spring
Hydrangea	*Hydrangea* spp.	Mound	Spring, summer
Ivy	*Hedera helix*	Simple	Spring
Juniper	*Juniperus* spp.	Simple	Summer
Jasmine	*Jasminium* spp.	Simple	Spring
Laburnum	*Laburnum* spp.	Simple	Summer
Laurel (mountain)	*Kalmia latifolia*	Simple	Summer
Laurel (sweet bay)	*Lauris nobilis*	Air	Anytime
Lilac	*Syringa vulgaris*	Air	Spring
Linden	*Tilia americana*	Simple, mound (suckers)	Spring
Magnolia	*Magnolia* spp.	Simple	Spring
Oleander	*Nerium oleander*	Simple	Spring, summer
Philodendron	*Philodendron* spp.	Air	Anytime
Pittosporum	*Pittosporum tobira*	Air	Anytime
Quince	*Chaenomeles* spp.	Mound	Spring
Rhododendron	*Rhododendron* spp.	Trench, simple	Spring, summer
Raspberry, black, purple	*Rubus* spp.	Tip	Summer
Redbud	*Cercis* spp.	Simple, mound	Spring
Rose	*Rosa* spp.	Simple, tip	Spring, summer
Rubber plant	*Ficus elastica decora*	Air	Anytime
Split-leaf philodendron	*Monstera deliciosa*	Air	Anytime
Tree ivy	*Fatshedera lizei*	Air	Anytime
Trumpet creeper	*Campris* spp.	Simple	Summer
Viburnum	*Viburnum* spp.	Simple	Spring, summer
Virginia creeper	*Parthenocissus quinquefolia*	Compound	Summer
Weeping fig	*Ficus benjamina*	Air	Anytime
Weigela	*Weigela* sp.	Simple	Spring
Willow	*Salix* sp.	Simple	Spring
Wisteria	*Wisteria* sp.	Simple	Spring

Adapted from *Layering to Renew or Multiply Plants*, by F. E. Larsen. Pacific Northwest Cooperative Extension Publication 165. Extension Services of Washington State University, Oregon State University, and University of Idaho. Pullman, Wash. Revised periodically.

polyethylene film, remove the ties and film. The stem can be cut off below the rooted area (Figure 14-29). If possible, do this when the plant is not actively growing.

Pot the new plant immediately. Handle it carefully, because there is usually a large top in relation to the size of the root system. When possible, prune the top to balance more evenly its size

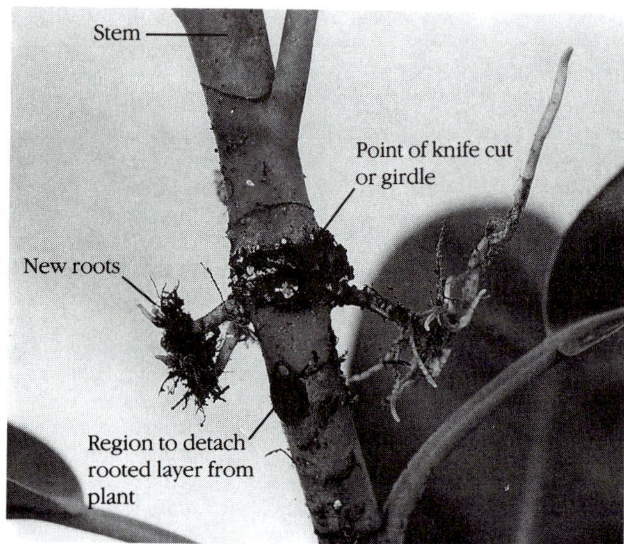

FIGURE 14-29 • Uncovered air layer, showing several large roots that developed from the wounded area. (Courtesy of Washington State University)

with that of the roots. Where this is not possible—particularly with leafy foliage plants—place the newly potted plant in a cool, shaded, humid area until it has had time to recover and establish a larger root system. Frequent syringing or misting, or covering with a plastic bag (left open at the bottom), helps it recover. Table 14-9 lists selected plants that can be propagated by layering.

PROPAGATING FROM FLESHY STORAGE ORGANS*

◆ ◆ ◆

Tunicate Bulbs

There are a number of ways in which tunicate bulbs (defined in Chapter 2) can be used for propagation.

Offsets. The simplest way to produce more plants from tunicate bulbs is by using **offsets**, small bulbs that form naturally from the parent bulb (Figure 14-30). When the bulb is dug these can be separated and planted to produce a new plant. Small offsets usually produce only leaves the first year and do not flower until the second year or later.

In some plants, such as hyacinths, offsets do not readily form, and new bulbs must be artificially induced by such methods as scooping, scoring, coring, and sectioning (Figure 14-31).

Scooping. Scooping removes the entire basal plate. When properly done, this removes the main shoot and flower bud at the center of the bulb and exposes the bases of the rings of leaves (bulb scales). Small bulblets then form at the base of these modified leaves.

Dip the bulb in a fungicide after cutting to protect the cut surface. Keep the bulbs in a warm (about 70°F; 21°C), dark place for about two weeks to dry and form wound tissue on the cut surface. Bulbs are usually kept in a shallow box with a wire mesh bottom.

A

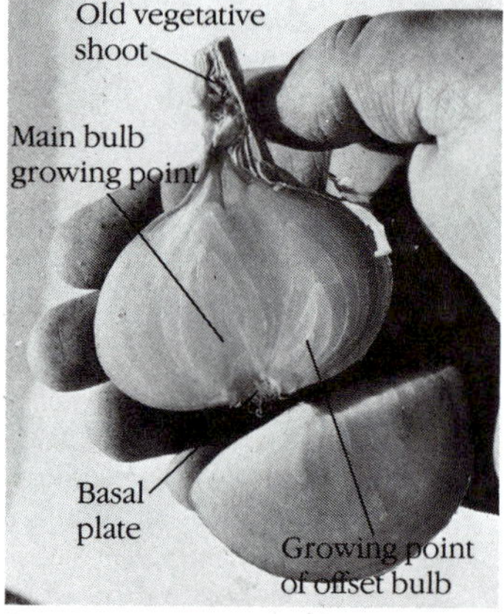

B

FIGURE 14-30 • Propagation of tunicate bulbs. (A) The tunicate-type onion bulb has formed an offset. (B) A longitudinal section of an onion bulb, showing an early stage in the formation of an offset. (Courtesy of Washington State University)

---

*Adapted from *Propagation from Bulbs, Corms, Tubers, Rhizomes, and Tuberous Roots and Stems,* by F. E. Larsen. Pacific Northwest Cooperative Extension Publication 164. Extension Services of Washington State University, Oregon State University, and University of Idaho. Pullman, Wash. Revised periodically.

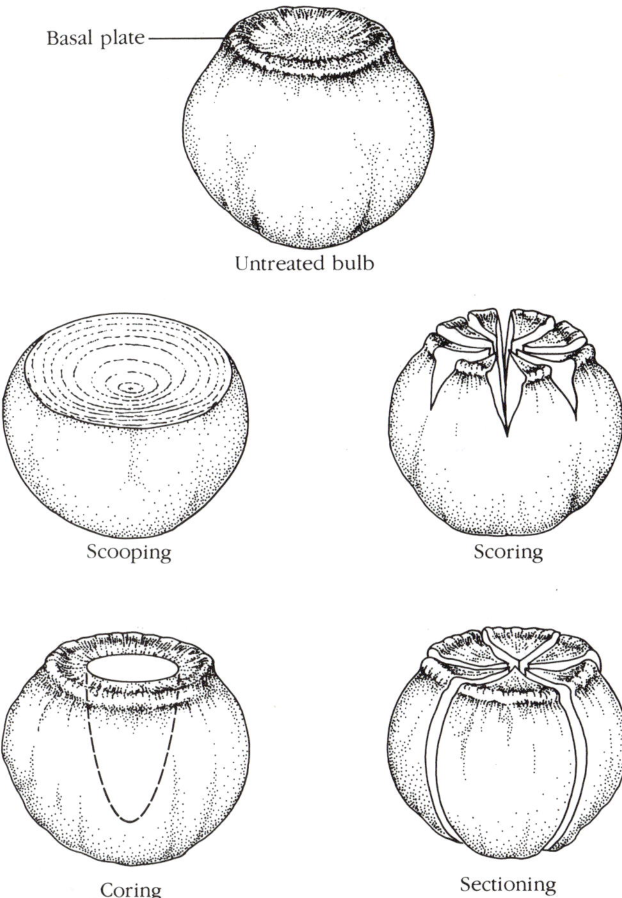

FIGURE 14-31 • Several methods for propagating hyacinth bulbs. (Courtesy of Washington State University)

When the scales begin to swell (by the third week), raise the temperature from 70°F to about 85°F (30°C) and hold the relative humidity at about 85 percent. The bulblets are ready for planting when new roots begin to form.

Plant the bulblets still attached to the parent bulb, in loose soil with the tip of the parent bulb about 1 inch (2½ cm) deep. The bulblets will produce only foliage the first year. When the foliage is yellow and dry, they can be dug and separated. Although scooping produces twenty-five to fifty bulblets per parent bulb, these will be small and may require four or five years of growth before they will flower.

Scoring. In scoring, three V-shaped cuts are made through the basal plate of the bulb so that there are six pie-shaped sections. Make cuts deep enough to destroy the main growing shoot and reach to just below the widest point of the bulb. Bury the cut bulbs upside down in clean, dry sand about 2 inches (5 cm) below the surface. After wound tissue has formed in the cuts, remove the bulbs from the sand, and treat them the same as scooped bulbs. Scoring produces about half as many bulbs as scooping does, but they will be larger and should flower in three or four years.

Coring. Coring removes the center portion of the basal plate and the main growing point of the bulb. Cored bulbs are treated like scored bulbs. They produce still fewer bulblets, but these will be larger and should flower in two or three years.

Sectioning. Some bulbs can be cut into sections with a portion of the basal plate attached to each section. Bulblets then form from the basal plate of each cutting. The bulb is cut into five to ten pie-shaped vertical sections. These sections can be further divided by slipping a knife down between each third or fourth pair of leaf-scale rings and cutting through the basal plate. Each bulb section should include a portion of basal plate with segments of three or four leaf scales attached. The length of time required for bulblets formed from sections to flower depends on the size of the sections and may vary from two to four or five years.

Scaly Bulbs

Offsets. Like tunicate bulbs, scaly bulbs are most easily propagated by offsets. Offset production is often too slow for commercial purposes.

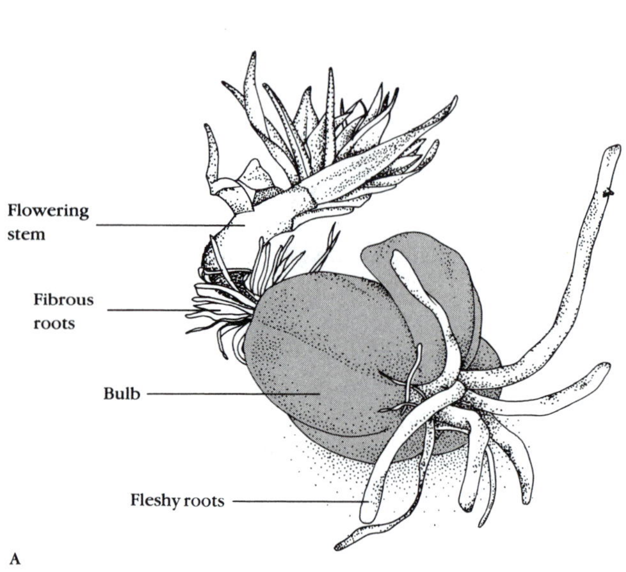

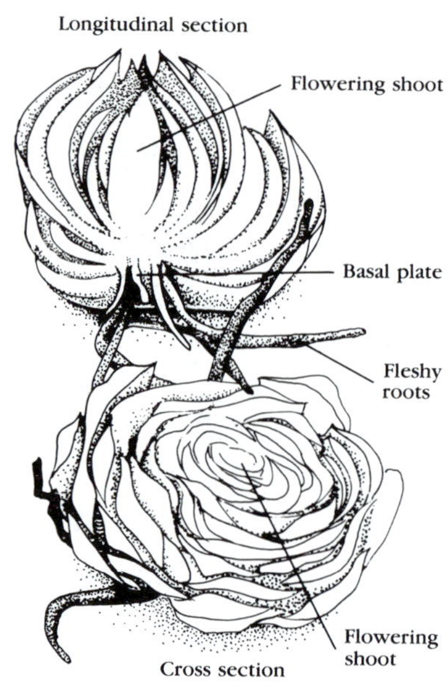

FIGURE 14-32 • Scaly bulbs. (A) A lily bulb in the early stage of growing a flowering shoot. (B) Longitudinal and cross sections of a lily bulb.

Scaling. Scaly bulbs are often propagated by removing the outer scales from the bulb and planting them one-half their length in a rooting medium. Bulbs for this purpose are best dug after flowering. Plant the scales about 1 inch apart in rows 6 inches (15 cm) apart. New bulblets will form at the base of the scales by fall, when they can be planted. The parent bulb can be replanted and will regenerate to provide more scales in one or two years. If the bulbs are not dug until fall, the scales can be stored in moist sand until spring and then planted.

Aerial Bulbs (Bulbils). Some lilies produce tiny aerial bulbs called *bulbils* where the leaves join the stem. These can be used to produce new plants by separating and growing them for two or three years to flowering size. Aerial bulbs can be induced to form more readily by removing flower buds from the plant.

Underground Stem Bulblets. Bulbs also form below ground on the flower stalks of some lilies. These can sometimes be induced by pulling the stalk from the plant after it flowers and covering the basal portion with the moist rooting medium. Bulbs formed in this way can be separated and planted to form new plants. They require one to two years to reach flowering size. Figures 14-32 and 14-33 illustrate methods of scaly bulb propagation.

Corms

Natural Corm Production. Plants that grow from corms produce a new corm at the base of each shoot every year. The old corm is used in producing the plant, and the plant then produces a new corm. More than one flowering shoot may grow from a large corm. As a result, two (not usually more) corms of smaller size form from the original corm (Figure 14-34).

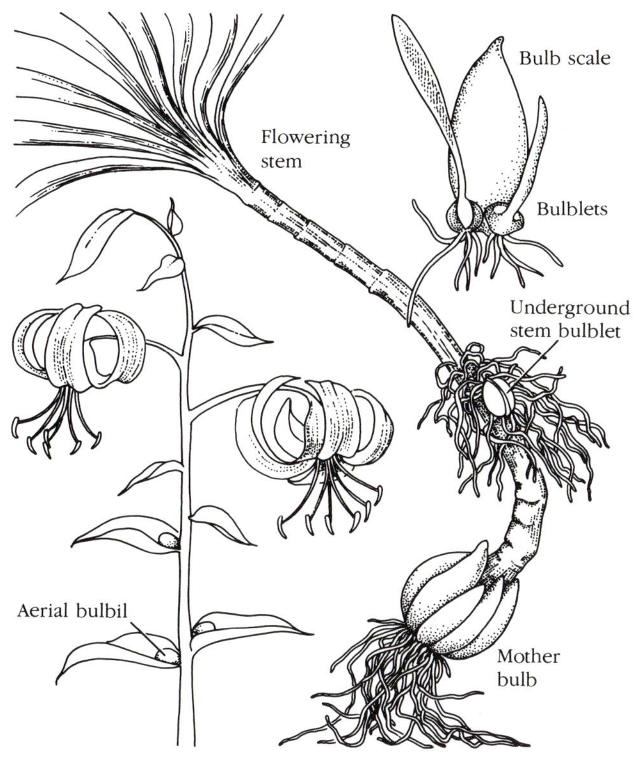

FIGURE 14-33 • Several methods of lily propagation. (Courtesy of Washington State University)

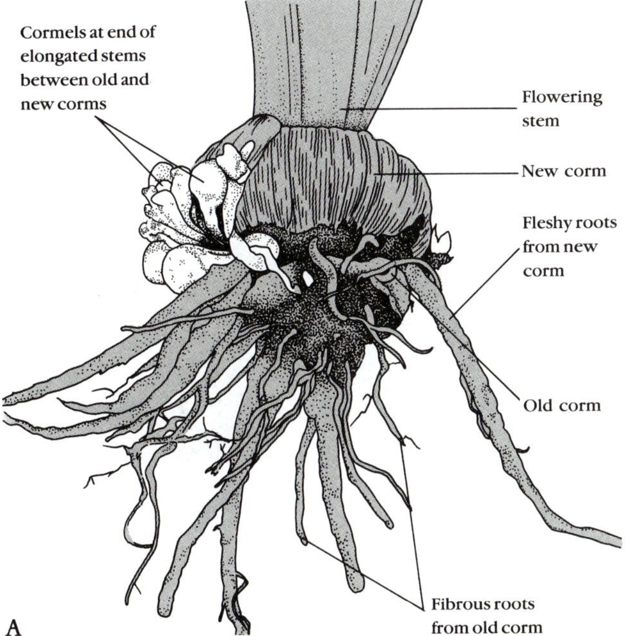

Cormels. Small corms called *cormels* are formed at the base of the new corm. Shallow planting of corms encourages their formation. These can be separated and planted and will flower in one to three years. Plant cormels only about 1 inch deep because of their small size.

Corms are dug in the fall while the leaves are still somewhat green or after a light frost. They may be dried either outdoors or indoors, but rapid drying is best. Only after the corms and leaves have thoroughly dried should the corms be cleaned and the cormels separated. Treat with a fungicide for disease control and insecticide to control thrips. Store with adequate ventilation and at temperatures below 60°F (16°C) and about 70 percent relative humidity. If corm diseases are a problem, store them below 40°F (4°C).

Hardy corms, such as spring-flowering crocus, should be planted in the fall. Tender corms, such as gladioli, are usually planted in the spring.

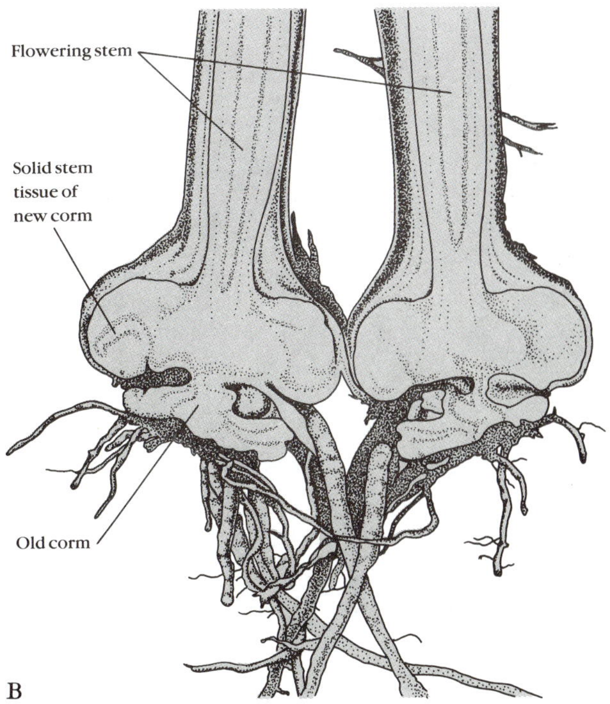

FIGURE 14-34 • Structure of a gladiolus corm.

Tubers, Tuberous Roots, and Tuberous Stems

Tuberous plants can be propagated by cutting the tuber into sections so that each section has a bud. Allow the cut surface to dry. Treatment with a fungicide helps prevent the section from decaying before a new plant forms.

Tuberous roots are sometimes confused with tubers. However, tuberous roots are actually root tissue and do not have "eyes" or buds on them as tubers do. When propagating with tuberous roots, it is usually necessary to include a section of the crown or stem with a bud on it to produce the shoots of the new plant. Tuberous roots, such as dahlias, are usually divided so that each root contains one bud from the crown of the plant (Figure 14-35). Divide the clumps before the buds begin to grow, usually in February or March just before planting.

Sweet potatoes do not need a section of crown with a shoot bud for propagation. Instead, they produce shoots directly from the tuberous root, and these shoots then form roots. These young plants, called *slips*, can then be separated and planted.

Tuberous roots dug in the fall can be stored on shelves in a cellar where temperatures range from 40° to 50°F (4° to 10°C). If the storage area is rather dry, the roots can be packed in dry peat or dry sand. When the loss from drying is severe, the roots can be dipped in melted paraffin wax that is floated on hot water.

Some plants, such as tuberous begonias and gloxinias, have enlarged stems located between the regular stem and the roots. These stems, called *tuberous stems*, enlarge each year. The plants can be propagated by cutting the tuberous stem into sections so that each section includes a bud (Figure 14-36). Apply fungicide to the cut surface to combat decay, and dry each section for several days after cutting before you plant it. These plants are often propagated more readily by using stem, leaf, or leaf-bud cuttings.

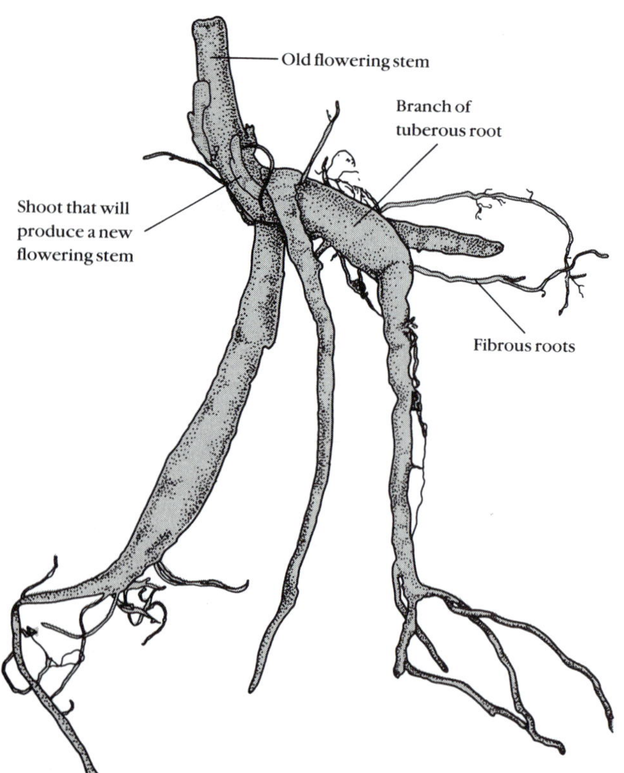

FIGURE 14-35 • Dahlia tuberous root.

FIGURE 14-36 • Tuberous stem of tuberous begonia. (Courtesy of Washington State University)

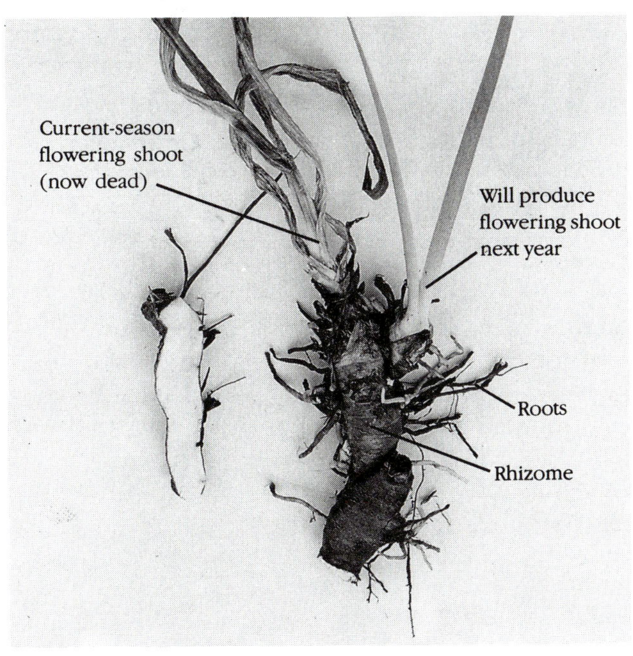

FIGURE 14-37 • Iris rhizome. (Courtesy of Washington State University)

Rhizomes

A rhizome is a modified stem that runs horizontally just under or partially under the ground. Rhizomes contain shoot buds and can be propagated by being cut into sections so that each section contains at least one bud (Figure 14-37). Plant the sections horizontally, the same as the parent plant. Lily of the valley and German (bearded) iris are well-known examples of this type of plant.

Pseudobulbs

Orchids produce both rhizomes and another type of modified stem called a *pseudobulb.* The exact structure of these organs varies among different species of orchids. Rhizome cuttings of new growth that include four or five nodes can be used to propagate orchids. The pseudobulb itself can sometimes be used, a new shoot forming at the base. Either back bulbs (those without leaves) or green bulbs (those with leaves) can be used to propagate the species *Cymbidium.*

FIGURE 14-38 • Pseudobulb of orchid.

Treating pseudobulbs with the rooting hormone IBA (indolebutyric acid) helps. Place the pseudobulbs in a rooting medium to about half the depth of the "bulb." When one new shoot is formed, separate it with its roots from the pseudobulb. Additional shoots usually are produced from the pseudobulb (Figure 14-38). Table 14-10 lists common flowering plants that are propagated from fleshy storage organs.

GRAFTING AND BUDDING*

◆ ◆ ◆

Graftage refers to any process of inserting a part of one plant into or on another in such a way that the two will unite and continue growth as a single unit. The term includes two similar processes, grafting and budding. Specific methods are described in the following sections, and see also Chapter 4.

---

*Adapted from *Grafting and Budding to Propagate, Topwork, Repair,* by F. E. Larsen. Washington State Extension Bulletin 683. Extension Service, Washington State University. Pullman, Wash. Revised periodically.

TABLE 14-10 • *Common flowering plants grown from specialized structures*

HARDY Fall Planted, Spring Flowering	SEMIHARDY Fall Planted, Summer and Fall Flowering	TENDER Spring Planted, Summer and Fall Flowering; Dug and Stored in Winter	TENDER Greenhouse or Houseplants
		BULBS	
Glory of the snow (*Chionodoxa*) Snowdrop (*Galanthus*) Hyacinth (*Hyacinthus*) Bulbous iris (*Iris*) Grape hyacinth (*Muscari*) Daffodil (*Narcissus*) Squill (*Scilla*) Tulip (*Tulipa*)	Lily (*Lilium*) Hardy amaryllis (*Lycoris*)	Tuberose (*Polianthes*) Summer hyacinth (*Galtonia*) *Amaryllis belladonna*	Amaryllis (*Hippeastrum*) Oxalis (bulbous) Amazon lily (*Eucharis grandiflora*)
		CORMS	
Crocus (*Crocus*)	Autumn crocus (*Colchicum*) Crocus (some species)	Freesia (*Freesia*) Gladiolus (*Gladiolus*)	

(*continued*)

Factors That Influence Grafting and Budding Success

Time of Year. Grafting is usually done during the dormant season, whereas budding is done during the growing season or just as growth is beginning in the spring (spring budding). Budding done in early summer in areas with long growing seasons (e.g., parts of California and the South) is called *June budding*. Budding done in August or early September is called *fall budding*.

Growth Condition of Plant Parts. Scions for grafting should be dormant. Spring budding requires dormant budsticks (shoots from which buds are taken). For other budding, buds are taken from actively growing shoots. For budding (except chip budding) and bark grafting, the cambium of the stock must be actively growing, allowing the bark to "slip" (separate) readily from the wood. Grafting potted evergreens requires actively growing stock. For other forms of budding and grafting, the stock is usually dormant or just beginning to grow.

Age of Plant Parts. Budsticks are usually one year or less in age. Scions for grafting are usually one or not more than two years old. Rootstocks for producing new plants are usually two years or less in age.

Temperature. Grafting is usually done during the dormant season when temperatures are cool. The graft union depends on the uniting of new cells formed from the cambium of stock and scion. These new cells, which are not differentiated into

TABLE 14-10 • (*Continued*)

HARDY Fall Planted, Spring Flowering	SEMIHARDY Fall Planted, Summer and Fall Flowering	TENDER Spring Planted, Summer and Fall Flowering; Dug and Stored in Winter	TENDER Greenhouse or Houseplants
		TUBERS	
	Aerial begonia (*Begonia evansiana*)	Caladium (*Caladium*)	Caladium (*Caladium*)
		TUBEROUS ROOTS AND STEMS	
Wind flower (*Anemone*) Jack in the pulpit (*Arisaema*) Bleeding heart (*Dicentra*)		Tuberous begonia (*Begonia*) Dahlia (*Dahlia*) Gloriosa (*Gloriosa*)	Elephant's ear (*Colocasia*) Cyclamen (*Cyclamen*) Ranunculus (*Ranunculus*) Black calla (*Arum*) Gloxinia (*Sinningia*)
		RHIZOMES	
Lily of the valley (*Convallaria*) Bearded iris (*Iris*)		Canna (*Canna*)	Calla (*Zantedeschia*) Achimenes (*Achimenes*)

Adapted from *Plant Propagation: Principles and Practices*, 3rd ed., by Dale E. Kester and Hudson T. Hartmann. Englewood Cliffs, N.J.: Prentice-Hall, 1975. With permission of the publisher.

a specific plant tissue, are called *callus*. Callus formation is slow at 40°F (4°C) or lower. However, if warm temperatures arrive too soon after grafting, shoot buds may grow and produce a leaf surface that depletes moisture reserves in the scion before a graft union is formed. For this reason temperatures should not exceed 60°F (16°C) for two to three weeks following grafting unless the scion buds are still in their rest period.

Union formation following summer budding is favored by temperatures around 70°F (21°C) because callus forms rapidly at this temperature. Temperatures above 90°F (32°C) slow or stop callus formation.

Protective Measures. The surfaces of stock and scion where the union is to form must be protected from drying. This is usually done by covering the exposed surfaces, after the scion and stock are fitted together, with grafting wax or other protective materials. Any material that can prevent tissue drying without itself causing tissue damage or excessive oxygen reduction is satisfactory. Following bench grafting, completed grafts are often protected from drying by covering them with moist peat moss. In the field, grafts can sometimes be protected by mounding them with moist soil. For some kinds of budding, no special protective measures except tying are necessary.

Compatibility. Only plant parts with relatively close botanical relationships can be joined by graftage. Unrelated plants have chemical and physiological differences that prevent a union. Viruses may also cause incompatibility.

Scion Orientation. Scions (or stocks) for grafting can form a permanently successful union only if they are oriented as they normally grow. Those fitted together upside down will not grow properly. Budding scions often can grow normally regardless of orientation.

Soil Moisture. For maximum cambial activity, the soil moisture must be ample, particularly during summer budding. Rootstocks must be kept actively growing during the summer by keeping the soil moisture high before budding and for a time afterward.

Applied Pressure. Graft and bud unions are promoted by a good, snug fit and intimate contact of stock and scion. In some cases this is provided by the nature of the graft itself; in others it is promoted by using tying materials.

Follow-up Attention. Grafts may require rewaxing, tying for support, or light pruning to direct the growth after shoots begin growing. (Waxing is explained later.)

Tools and Materials (Figure 14-39). Although one type of knife can be used for budding and grafting, there are special knives best suited for each operation. They differ primarily in blade shape. Grafting knives have a straight blade, whereas budding knife blades curve upward at the end. Some budding knives also have an attachment on the handle opposite the blade for opening the bark on the stock so that the bud can be inserted. A cutting blade with high-quality steel that will take and hold a good edge is desirable.

A good-quality, fine-grained sharpening stone is important for developing a good edge on your knife. A sharp knife is essential to make smooth, straight grafting and budding cuts. Good cuts are essential for a high degree of success.

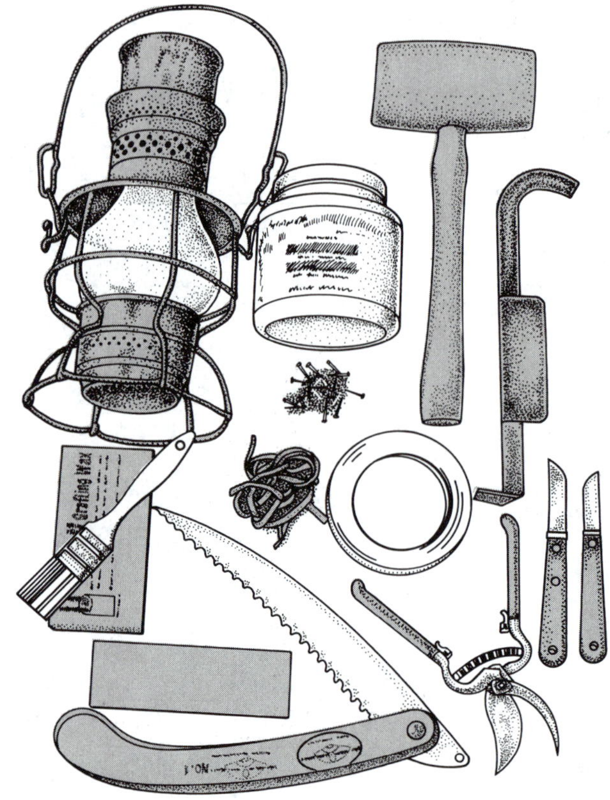

FIGURE 14-39 • Tools and materials used in grafting and budding. Clockwise from top center: latex-base grafting compound, wooden mallet, cleft graft tool, grafting knife (left), budding knife (right), hand clippers, pruning saw, sharpening stone, brush (for applying grafting wax or compound), grafting wax, lantern (for keeping grafting wax liquid). Center: nails (for fastening bark graft), tape (for fastening cleft and splice grafts), budding rubbers.

Several kinds of protective and tying materials can be used. Waxes are the most common material to protect grafts from drying. Some must be heated and applied with a brush; others are soft and pliable enough to be applied cold by hand. Cold liquid wax emulsions and latex-base materials to be brushed on also are available.

Adhesive cloth or masking-type paper tape are frequently used to protect grafts. If applied under tension, tapes will hold the joined parts snugly and promote union formation. If tapes are properly applied, waxes or similar coverings are not needed. However, tapes are not readily adapted for application to all types of grafts. Waxed string or rubber budding strips are sometimes used to tie grafts; they must be covered with a layer of wax to protect the graft adequately.

For budding, strips of thin rubber about 3/16 inch (2/3 cm) wide are most commonly used to tie buds securely to the stock. String, tape, and strips of plastic may be used.

Other tools are sometimes needed. For cleft grafting, a wooden mallet and clefting tool are useful. The clefting tool is used to split the stock and hold it open for insertion of the scions. Pruning shears and saws are also handy.

Handling the Scion Wood

If freezing damage is likely, collect grafting scion wood in the fall after normal leaf drop but before severe winter temperatures. Otherwise, wait until late winter to collect it. Store the wood in a plastic bag. Enclose a moist cloth, but allow no free water in the bag. Store the wood in a refrigerator between 35° and 40°F (2° to 4°C). If refrigeration is not available, store the wood outdoors in moist sand in a well-drained, protected location where the soil will not freeze.

For spring budding, use the same scion wood that is used for grafting. For budding during the growing season, new shoots of the current season's growth with mature, plump buds can be used. The leaves are removed by snipping through the petiole (the stalk of the leaf) and leaving a petiole stub of about ½ inch (2/3 cm) attached to the budstick. Store scion wood budsticks in a refrigerator as you would grafting wood. It does not keep as long as does dormant wood and should be used in a few days. It is best if it can be collected and used immediately.

For either budding or grafting, select only healthy wood free of insect, disease, and winter damage from plants of known quality or performance. For fruit trees, collect wood only from those in production, to be sure that the kind and quality of fruit will be what you expect. The terminal ends of long shoots collected for scion wood should be discarded, because the buds and wood are usually poorly developed. Extreme basal buds may also be undesirable.

Kinds of Grafts

Splice Grafting. The simplest way to join stock and scion is by splice grafting. This method is best suited to herbaceous plants in a protected location. The stock and scion should be less than 1 inch (2½ cm) in diameter and of equal thickness. Make long, diagonal cuts of equal length on the stock and scion. Fit together the cut surfaces of the stock and scion, and use tape or other tying materials to hold them together. Additional protection with wax or similar materials is usually advisable.

Whip-and-Tongue Grafting (Whip Grafting). Whip-and-tongue is one of the most commonly used and useful grafts for woody plants (Figure 14-40). It is used for topworking and producing new plants, primarily deciduous trees. It works best with stock and scion of equal diameter and less than 1 inch (preferably ¼ to ½ inch; 2/3 to 1¼ cm) thick.

Two identical cuts are made on stock and scion. The first is a diagonal cut like that of a splice graft. The length of the cuts varies with the diameter of the stock and scion, increasing in length with the greater diameter. In general, the length of the cut should be four to five times the diameter of the stock or scion. Make this cut with a single knife stroke. Wavy cuts may prevent a satisfactory union. Make the second, or tongue, cut on stock and scion by placing the knife on the surface of the first cut about half the distance between the pith (the center core of stem) and the outer bark, or epidermis, on the upper part of the cut. Bring the knife down through the pith until it is opposite the base of the first cut. This cut should not follow the grain of the wood but should parallel the first cut.

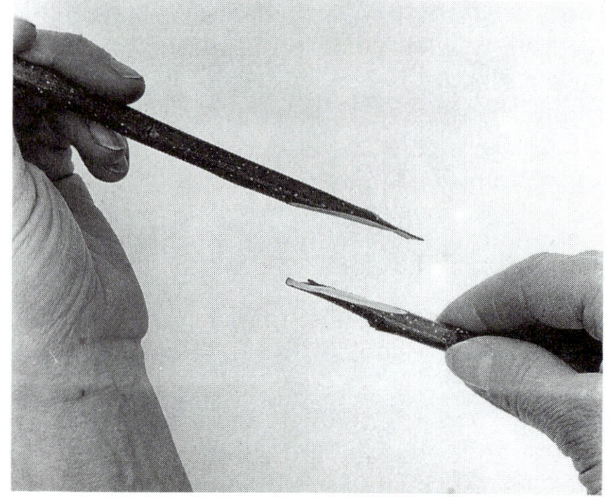

A

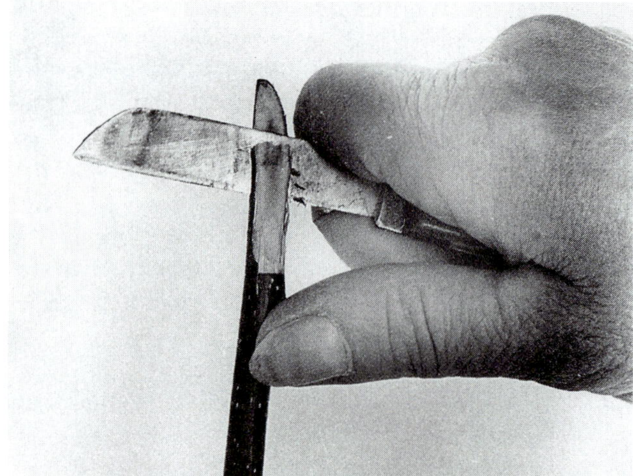

B

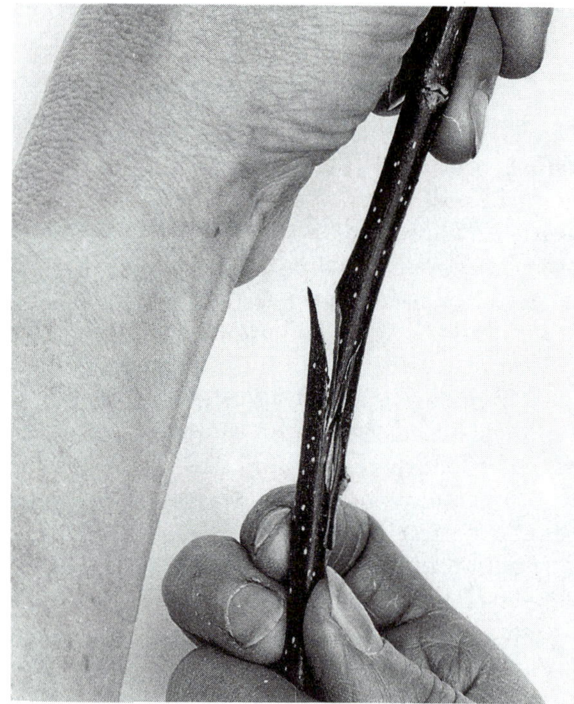

C

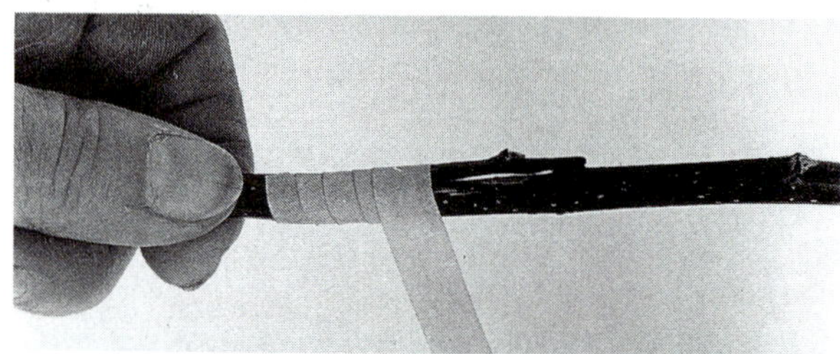

D

E

FIGURE 14-40 • The whip-and-tongue graft. (A) Splice graft, or initial cut for whip graft, (B) final cut on whip graft, (C) fitting scion and stock together, (D) wrapping the whip graft, (E) established whip graft. (E, courtesy of Washington State University)

When the tongues are cut, insert them into each other until they are interlocked. Then secure the parts by wrapping them tightly with tape or other tying materials. If tape is properly applied, additional protection with wax may not be necessary.

If the scion is smaller than the stock, fit the tongues together so that the outside surfaces of stock and scion are aligned on one side only.

Cleft Grafting. Cleft grafting is used for topworking and should be done before the stock begins active growth. Scions are usually about ¼ inch in diameter and two to three buds long. Stocks should be 1 to 4 inches (2½ to 10 cm) in diameter and straight grained. Saw off the stock at a right angle in relation to its main axis. Make the cut so there are 4 to 6 inches (10 to 15 cm) below, with no knots or side branches. Use a clefting tool or heavy knife to split down the center for 2 to 3 inches (5 to 8 cm). Drive in the tool with a wooden mallet. Remove the cutting edge of the clefting tool, and drive the wedge part of the tool in the center of the stock to open the split to receive the scions.

Prepare two scions. Cut the basal end of each into about a 2-inch-long tapered wedge. One side of the wedge should be slightly thicker. These long cuts on the scion should be smooth and each made with a single sweep of the knife. The wedge should be long and if the wedge is short, the stock-scion contact will be at only one point.

Insert the cut wedge of the scions, one on each side of the stock, with the narrow part of the wedge toward the center of the stock. Align the cambium layers of stock and scion without regard to the outside surfaces. Remove the metal wedge of the clefting tool from the stock, leaving the scions held snugly in place. Completely cover the cut surfaces and the splits down the side of the stock with wax. Also cover the tip of the scion.

If both scions grow, the healing of the large stock stub will be more rapid than if only one scion grows. However, eventually one scion must be removed. From the beginning one scion should be dominant; keep the other small by pruning. After two or three years, prune out the smaller scion (Figure 14-41).

Bark Grafting. Bark grafting is used for topworking (Figure 14-42). It can be used with larger stocks (up to 12 inches [30 cm] in diameter) than for cleft grafting, but the scions are similar in size. Several scions can be inserted around the stock. The stock is cut off as for cleft grafting, except that it is not split through the center. It must be done when cell division in the stock has begun in early spring, allowing the bark to separate readily from the wood.

Cut the base of the scion on one side with a long, smooth, sloping cut about 1½ inches (4 cm) long, going completely through the scion so that it comes to a point at the base. Make a vertical cut about 1½ inches long through the bark in the stub of the stock. Slightly loosen the bark at the top of the cut, and insert the wood surface of the scion base next to the wood of the stock. Push the scion down in behind the bark to the extent of the cut on the scion base. Secure it in place by driving one or two wire brads through the base of the scion into the stock. Cover all cuts and exposed surfaces with grafting wax. Because the union with this type of graft is weak for a year or two, the scions may need to be tied up for support after growth begins.

For topworking place scions every 2 to 4 inches around the stock stub. As is true for cleft grafting, the intent is usually for only one to eventually remain. Train and prune as for cleft grafting.

Side Grafting. Side grafting can be used for topworking or producing new plants. Several forms of side grafting are used. The stub-side graft is used primarily for topworking fruit trees with branches too small for cleft or bark grafting and too large for whip grafting. The other forms are used mostly for producing new evergreen plants by grafting on small seedling stocks.

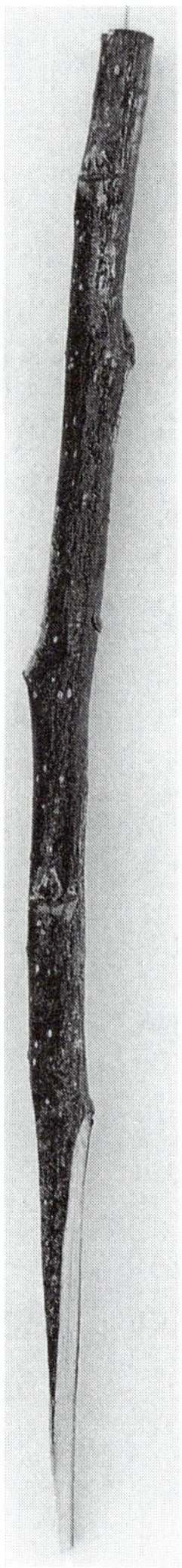

B

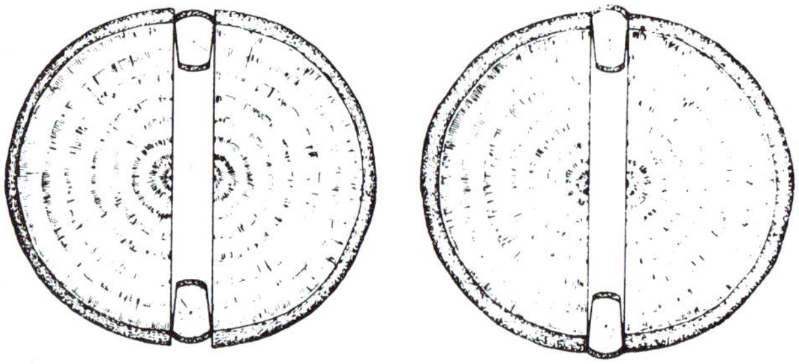

C

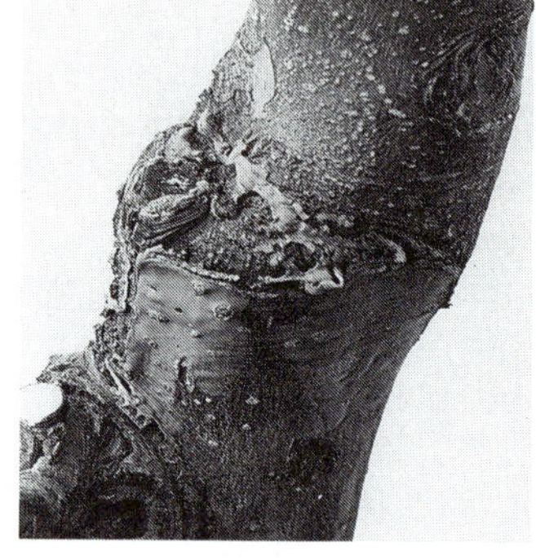

F

A D E

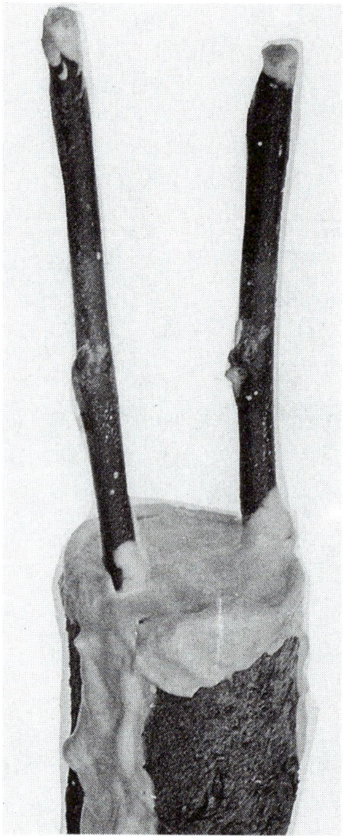

FIGURE 14-41 • The cleft graft. (A) Cleft graft scion. The wedge is cut so that the bottom bud is on the thick side. (B) Positioning scions for cleft graft—cambiums must touch where stock is against scion; left-hand drawing is correct, and right-hand drawing is wrong. (C through E) Thick side of scion is inserted on outside. Final step in cleft graft is to wax all cut surfaces. (F) Advanced cleft graft. (B and F, courtesy of Washington State University)

Make **stub-side grafts** on stock branches that are between ½ and 1 inch in diameter. Make a cut in the stock at a 45° angle going about halfway through the stock. Cut the scion as for a cleft graft except with a shorter wedge. Open the cut in the stock by pulling down on the stock branch beyond the cut. Insert the scion into the stock cut with the thick side of the wedge out. Little or no cut surface should show on the scion wedge. Let the stock branch spring back into place. The natural tension of the branch will hold the scion in place. Cut the stock off about 6 inches beyond the graft. Cover the graft area, stock stub, and end of the scion with a protective compound (Figure 14-43).

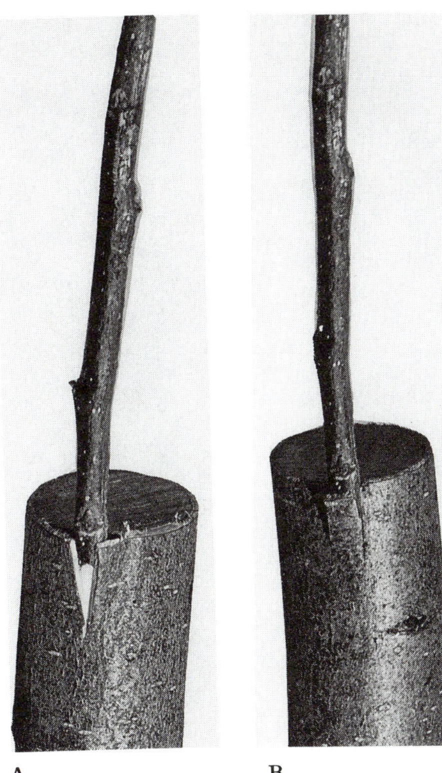

A B

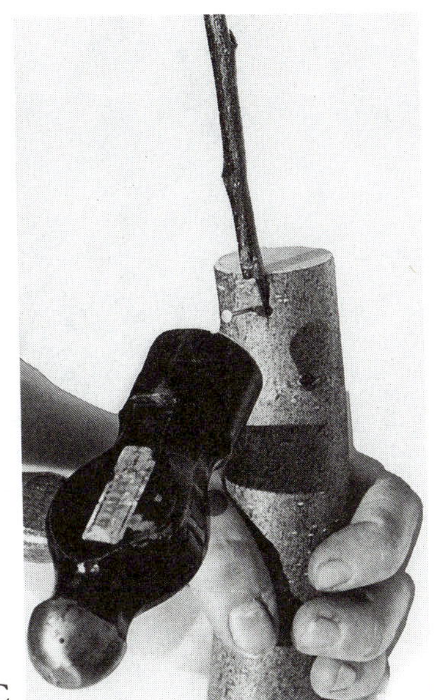

C

D

FIGURE 14-42 • The bark graft. (A) The bark graft scion is inserted after a short slit is made in the bark. (B) The bark graft scion can also be inserted after cutting a bark flap on stock the width of the scion. (C) The bark graft scion is held in place with nails. The final step is to wax all cut surfaces. (D) Bark grafts after becoming established. (D, courtesy of Washington State University)

For **side-veneer** grafting, make a rather shallow cut about 1½ inches long at the base of the stock, cutting slightly inward as the cut is made. At the base of this cut, make a short inward, downward cut to intersect the first cut, thus allowing the removal of a piece of wood and bark. Prepare the scion with a long cut the same length and width as that of the first cut on the stock. Make a short cut on the opposite side of the base of the scion.

Insert the scion in the stock with the long cut of the stock next to the long cut on the scion. Secure the scion by wrapping it with tape or rubber budding strips. Cover the graft region with a protective material. When the graft union forms, cut off the stock just above the union (Figure 14-44).

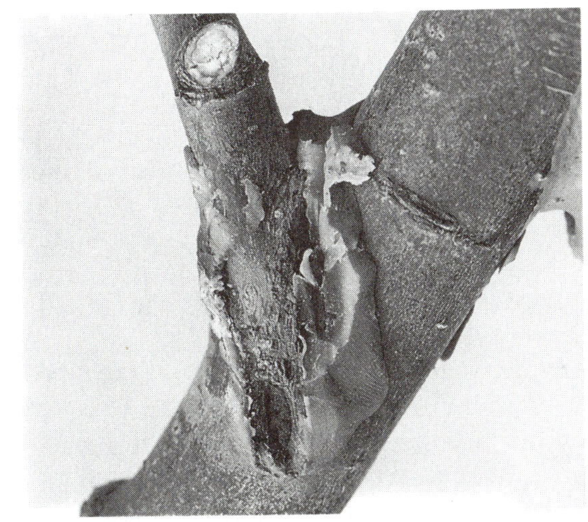

FIGURE 14-43 • Established stub-side graft. (Courtesy of Washington State University)

A

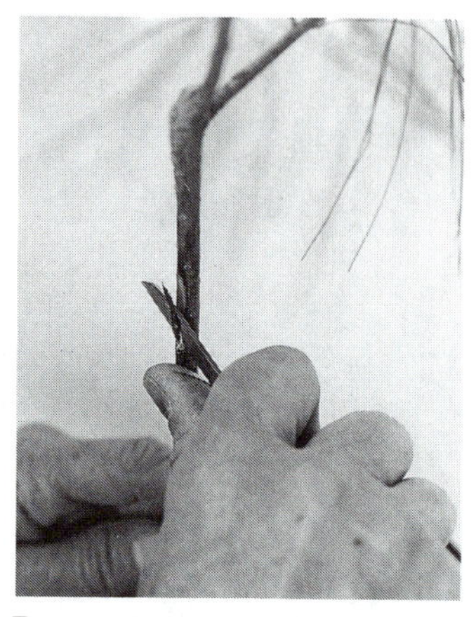
B

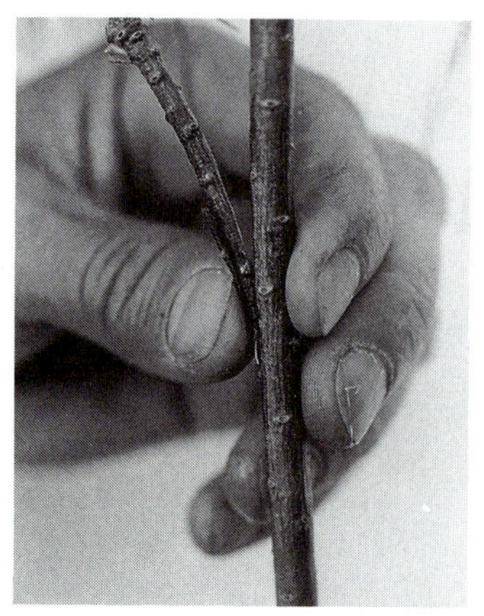
C

D

FIGURE 14-44 • A side-veneer graft. (A) Preparing stock, (B) cutting scion, (C) placing scion on stock, (D) wrapped and waxed side-veneer graft. (Courtesy of Washington State University)

For **side-tongue grafting**, cut the scion as for whip grafting. On a smooth place on the stock remove a thin slice of wood and bark about 1 to 2 inches long. Make a tongue cut by starting about one-third of the distance from the top of the first cut and progressing to the base of the first cut. Fit the tongues of stock and scion together; wrap the graft with tape or other tying material; and add a protective covering to the graft region. Cut off the stock above the graft after union has formed (Figure 14-45).

Bridge Grafting. Bridge grafting is used to repair damaged bark areas at the base of a tree. Bark damage caused by cold, rodents, or implements may kill a tree if it is severe enough. If the trunk is not completely girdled, the tree can usually be saved by bridge grafting.

Bridge grafting must be done when the bark "slips," which usually happens just as active growth is becoming apparent in the spring. Select dormant 1-year-old scion wood long enough to bridge the damaged area. Make cuts like those for bark grafting on both ends of the scions, being sure that both cuts are in the same plane. Make a flap cut the width of the scion through the bark of the stock below the injured area. Pull the end of the bark flap loose from the wood, insert the base of the scion under the flap, and push the scion under the flap until the cut surface on the base of the scion is covered. Drive nails through the base of the scion as for bark grafting. In a similar fashion, attach the top of the scion to the stock above the injured area.

Attach scions to the stock about 3 inches apart across the injured area. If the tree is young enough to allow the trunk to bend in a strong wind, the scions must retain an outward bow after completing the graft. This allows the trunk to bend without pulling the ends of the scions loose from the trunk. Cover all cut surfaces with protective waxes, being sure to seal the areas where the scion is inserted into the stock, particularly under the scion. Remove shoots that grow from scion buds (Figure 14-46).

If trunk damage extends below ground level, the lower graft must be made on a large root. Uncover the root and proceed as if you were working on the trunk. Recover the root with soil.

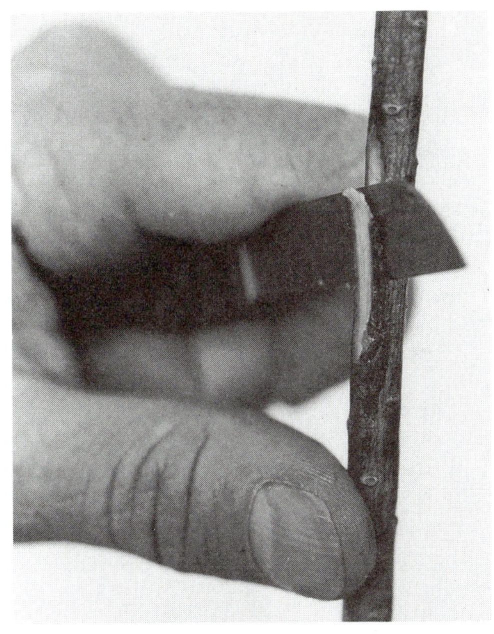

A

B

FIGURE 14-45 • The side-tongue graft. (A) Making the second cut on stock for the side-tongue graft. The first cut is similar to the cut made for the side-veneer graft. (B) Inserting the scion (cut as for a whip graft) on stock. (Courtesy of Washington State University)

A

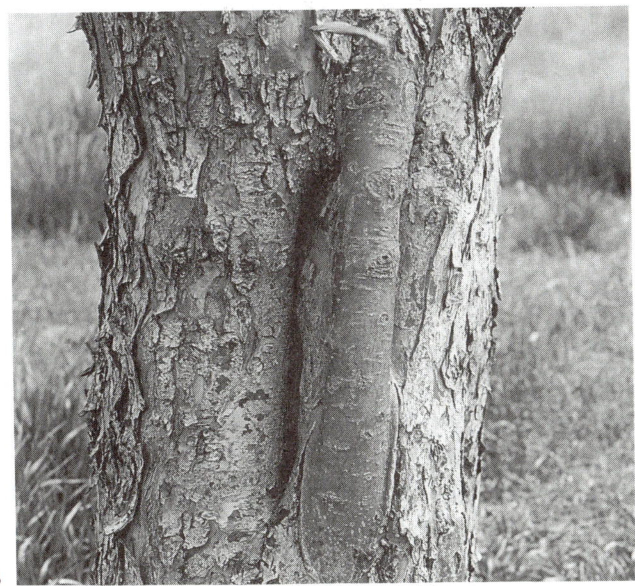

B

FIGURE 14-46 • The bridge graft. (A) A single bridge graft scion held in place with nails. The exposed areas are coated with wax or other protective material. (B) An established bridge graft. (B, courtesy of Washington State University)

FIGURE 14-47 • Inarching. The trunk of this flowering crabapple was completely girdled just under the soil line by mice during a winter of deep snow two years before this photo was taken. This kind of damage stimulates the production of root suckers. Carbohydrates manufactured in the leaves of the suckers and transported downward throughout the phloem of the stem kept the roots alive. Water and mineral elements absorbed through the roots and transported upward through the still-intact xylem has allowed the girdled tree to survive until the suckers have become large enough to be bark grafted above the girdle. Note the part of the top growth of the suckers that has been allowed to remain to continue carbohydrate manufacture. After the graft union has become well established, the tops of the suckers will be removed. Eventually the suckers will enlarge to replace the lower trunk.

Inarching. Inarching is a repair technique similar to bridge grafting except that suckers growing at convenient locations next to the injured area or seedlings planted next to the damaged trunk are used as scions. These are bark grafted into the trunk above the injured area. Cover the graft area with a protective material (Figure 14-47).

Remove shoots that develop on the inarches. If the tree is on a size-controlling rootstock, the inarch should be of the same variety as the rootstock, as otherwise the size-controlling benefits of the original rootstock will be reduced or eliminated.

Approach Grafting. The approach graft method is used to support a weak crotch in a tree or to graft together two plants while both remain on their own roots. To give support, two adjacent branches are joined together. For two plants on their own roots the main stems are joined together, because the objective is eventually to remove one top and the opposite root system. This method has the advantage of an uninterrupted flow of water to the scion from its own roots until the union is formed and its roots are removed. Similarly, the rootstock receives manufactured food from its top during the healing process.

Stock and scion or adjacent branches within a tree may be joined by the **spliced method**, which uses single, long, smooth cuts on adjacent surfaces. Bring the cut together and use wrapping material to hold it tightly in place. Cover the area with a protective material. If opposing tongues are cut on the face of the splice cuts of stock and scion as for side-tongue grafting, this method is referred to as a **tongued-approach graft**. In this case the tongues are splipped together for added stability while healing. The other procedures are the same as for the spliced approach (Figure 14-48).

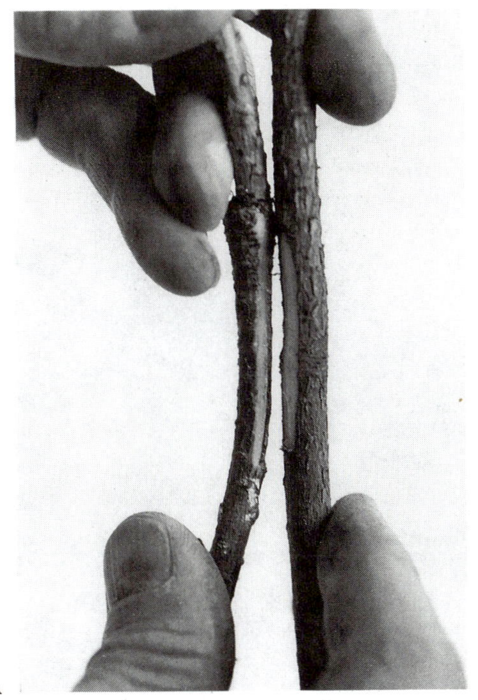
A

B

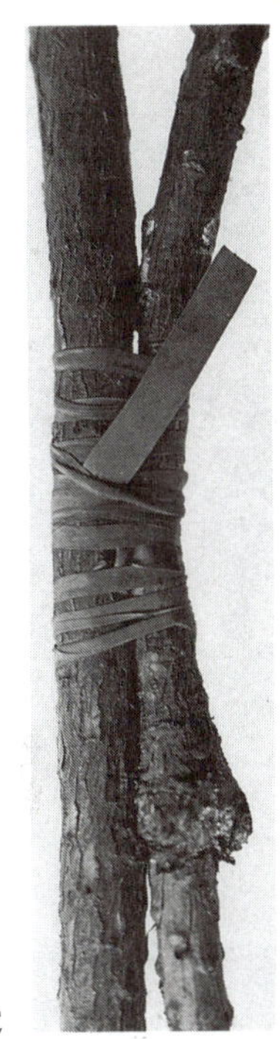
C

FIGURE 14-48 • A spliced-approach graft. The first step in making a spliced-approach graft is to remove thin slices of bark from adjacent surfaces of both stock and scion (A). The cut surfaces are then brought together and wrapped (B and C), and all surfaces are covered with grafting wax. (Courtesy of Washington State University)

Budding Methods

T- or Shield Budding. The T-budding method is used to topwork or produce new plants. It is the most common budding method for producing fruit and ornamental plants. It works best on rootstocks of ¼ to 1 inch (⅔ to 2½ cm) in diameter with thin bark. It must be done when the bark slips.

Prepare the stock by removing side branches to provide a smooth area of at least 6 inches (15 cm) in which to work. For summer and fall budding, this preparation begins with the early-season removal of shoots while they are still soft and succulent. Scions are selected from dormant 1-year-old wood for spring budding and current-season growing shoots for summer budding.

To begin the budding process, select a smooth, branch-free area on the stock to insert the bud. If you are topworking, this area should be on the side of a lateral branch, 12 to 18 inches (30 to 45 cm) from the main stem or trunk. If you are budding on seedlings to produce new plants, select an area about 6 inches from the ground. On clonal rootstocks the buds are often inserted 12 to 18 inches from the ground.

Make an upward vertical cut through the bark for about 1½ inches (4 cm) on the selected area. Next, make a horizontal cut to form a "T" with

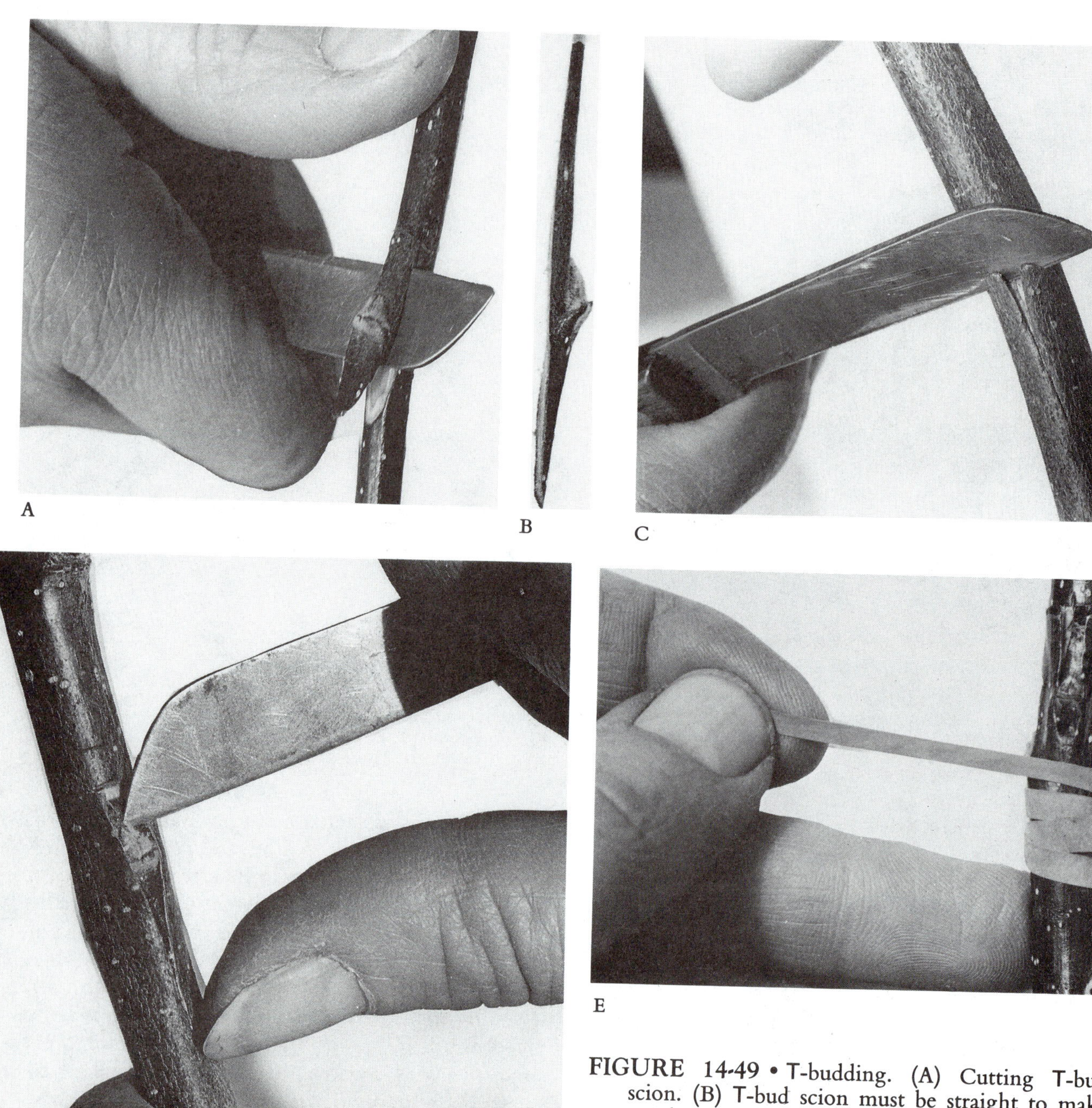

FIGURE 14-49 • T-budding. (A) Cutting T-bud scion. (B) T-bud scion must be straight to make good contact with stock. (C) Cutting stock for T-bud. Note the angle of the knife. (D) Pushing bud-shield scion of T-bud under bark flaps of stock. (E) Securing scion to stock with rubber strips.

the vertical cut. As the last cut is made, hold the knife at an acute angle in relation to the upper part of the rootstock. This technique opens the bark to allow an easy start of the scion bud.

Remove scion buds from the budstick in one smooth stroke. Start the cut about ½ to ¾ inch (1¼ to 2 cm) below the bud; pass just under the bud, taking a sliver of wood with the bud; and extend it about the same distance above the bud. As the cut is completed, pinch the bud shield against the knife blade to force the knife through the bark. This positions the bud in your hand so it can be immediately inserted into the stock.

To insert the bud, place the lower tip of the bud shield in the opening at the top of the T-cut. When the opening is properly made when cutting the top of the T, there should be no difficulty in starting the bud. When the bud is started, push it down into the opening with the tip of the budding knife inserted in the shield above the bud. Slide the bud down so that the top of the shield is even with the top of the T in the stock.

Wrap the bud in place with rubber budding strips by starting a self-binding loop just below the lower end of the bud shield. While stretching the rubber strip, make three or four loops below and above the bud, being sure to cover the top of the T. Insert the end of the rubber strip under the last wrap and pull it tight (Figure 14-49).

Cut off the top of the rootstock at a point just about even with the top of the T-cut. For fall budding this is not done until the following spring, just as growth starts. For spring budding it is done two to four weeks after budding. With June budding it is done in two steps starting 4 to 5 days after budding. Cut 5 or 6 inches (13 to 15 cm) above the bud, allowing at least one leaf of the rootstock to remain above the scion bud. About two weeks later, when the scion bud has started, cut the rootstock just above the scion shoot.

After its top has been removed, the rootstock may produce a number of shoots around and below the bud. Break these off as soon as they appear, except in June budding, when these shoots should remain until the scion shoot is 10 or 12 inches (25 to 30 cm) long.

Patch Budding and Related Forms. Patch budding is usually done in the summer and includes several related forms used on plants with thick bark that give poor results with T-budding. The scions used with these methods include a bud on a patch of bark varying from about 1 × 1½ inches to a complete ring of bark removed from the budstick. The scion contains no wood behind the bark patch. Budsticks and stocks should be approximately equal in diameter; the best size is between ½ and 1 inch. The bark of both stock and budstick must slip readily.

The scion patch is best removed from the budstick with a special four-bladed cutting tool with the blades fixed in a square or rectangle. With this tool an exact duplicate of the scion patch can be removed from the stock, and the fit will be perfect. Another common approach is to use a double-bladed knife to make the horizontal cuts on budsticks and stock while using a single-bladed knife to make the vertical cuts. It is especially important that the scion-stock fit be perfect at the horizontal cuts.

When removing the scion patch from the budstick, lift only the edges; remove the remainder of the patch by sliding sideways to break the woody connection between the bud and the budstick (Figure 14-50). If the entire patch is lifted off, this connection will be torn from the bud, and the bud will fail to unite properly with the stock.

Fit the scion bud patch into the prepared area of the stock, and wrap the patch in place. If the stock bark is thicker than the scion, this bark around the edge of the patch may require trimming so that the patch can be held snugly in place. Wrap the bud in place with tape, being careful to seal all cuts, but do not cover the bud. If you wrap

FIGURE 14-50 • Removing scion for patch budding. (Courtesy of Washington State University)

it carefully, no other protection may be necessary. An added precaution, however, is to use wax or other protective materials. Cut the stock back as for T-budding.

Chip Budding. Chip budding does not require bark that slips on either stock or budstick. It is usually done in the spring just as growth begins. However, it may be done in the summer at the same time as other techniques. Stocks and budsticks are usually ½ to 1 inch in diameter.

The chip from the rootstock is removed by making two cuts. The first is a downward cut at a

A

B

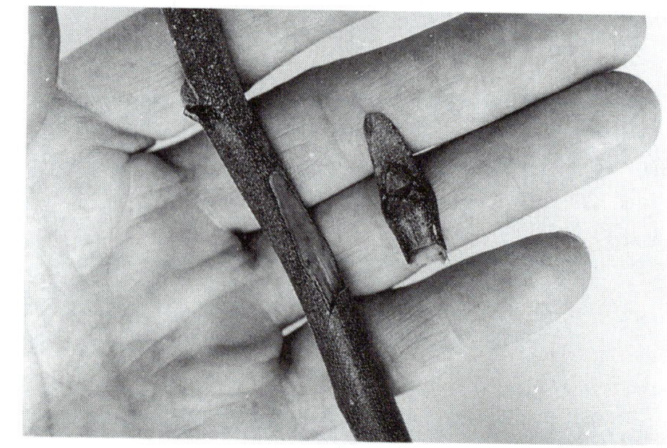

C

FIGURE 14-51 • Cutting chip bud scion. (A) Making the first cut. (B) Making the second cut. (C) Scion of chip bud ready to be inserted into prepared cut on stock. (Courtesy of Washington State University)

TABLE 14-11 • *Selected plants that can be propagated by budding or grafting and common methods and rootstocks for each*

Plant	Method[a]	Time[b]	Rootstock
Almond	T	S, Su, F	Almond, peach
Apple	T	S, F	Apple
	Whip	W	
Apricot	T	S, Su, F	Apricot, peach
Arborvitae	Side	W	Arborvitae
Avocado	T	S, Su, F	Avocado
	Whip, side	W	
Azalea	Side	F	Azalea
Beech	Whip, side	W	Beech
Birch	T	F	Birch
	Side	W	
Butternut	Bark	S	Black walnut
Camellia	Side	W	Camellia
Carob	T	S	Carob
Cedar	Side	W	Cedar
Cherry	T	S, F	Cherry
Chestnut	Whip	W	Chestnut
Citrus species	T	S, F	Citrus
Clematis	Side	W	Clematis
Dogwood	T	F	Dogwood
	Whip	W	
Fir	Side	W	Fir
Fringe tree	T	F	Fringe tree
	Side	W	
Ginkgo	Patch	F	Ginkgo
	Side	W	
Grape	Chip	Su, F	Grape
	Whip	W	
Hackberry	Chip	S	Hackberry
	Side	S	
Hawthorn	T	F	Hawthorn
	Whip, side	W	
Hibiscus	T	F	Hibiscus
	Whip, side	W	
Hickory	Patch	F	Hickory
	Side	W	
Holly	T	F	Holly
	Whip, side	W	
Honeylocust	T	F	Honeylocust
	Whip, side	W	
Horsechestnut	T	F	Horsechestnut
	Whip, side	W	
Juniper	Side	W	Juniper
Kiwi	T	F	Kiwi
	Whip	W	
Larch	Side	W	Larch
Lilac	T	F	Lilac, privet, ash
	Whip, side	W	
Magnolia	Side	W	Magnolia
Maple	T	F	Maple
	Side	W	
Mountain ash	T	F	Mountain ash
	Whip	W	
Mulberry	T	F	Mulberry
	Whip, side	W	
Nectarine	T	Su, F	Peach, apricot, some plums
Oak	Bark, side, whip	W	Oak
Olive	T, patch	F	Olive
	Whip, side	W	
Pawpaw	Side	W	Pawpaw
Peach	T	Su, F	Peach, apricot, some plums
Pear	T	F	Pear, quince
	Whip	W	
Persimmon	T	F	Persimmon
	Whip	W	
Pine	Side	W	Pine
Pistache	T	F	Pistache
Plum, prune	T	F	Plum, peach, apricot, almond
Quince	T	F	Quince
Redbud	T	Su	Redbud
Rhododendron	Side	W	Rhododendron
Rose	T	F	Rose
Spruce	Side	W	Spruce
Viburnum	Side	W	Viburnum
Walnut	Patch	F	Walnut
	Whip	W	
Wisteria	Whip, side	W	Wisteria
Witch hazel	Whip	W	Witch hazel
Yew	Side	W	Yew

Adapted from *Grafting and Budding to Propagate, Topwork, Repair*, by F. E. Larsen. Washington State Extension Bulletin 683. Extension Service, Washington State University. Pullman, Wash. Revised periodically.

[a]The grafting and budding methods indicated are primarily for producing new plants. For topworking other methods might be used.

[b]S = spring, Su = summer, F = fall, W = winter.

45° angle going about one-fourth through the stem. The second starts about 1 inch higher than the first, going downward and inward until it connects with the first cut. A similar cut is made on the budstick to remove the scion (Figure 14-51). The first cut starts about ¼ inch below the bud, the second about ½ inch above the bud. Fit the scion to the stock so that the cambium layers of stock and scion match on at least one side, but preferably on both. Wrap the bud in place with tape to cover all cut edges but not the bud. An added precaution is to cover the area with grafting wax. Cut the stock back as for T-budding. Table 14-11 lists selected plants that can be propagated by budding or grafting.

FIGURE 14-52 • Flowering crabapple topworked to a fruit-producing apple variety. (Courtesy of Washington State University)

Topworking and Repair

Topworking can be done by a variety of grafting or budding techniques. Trees younger than 3 or 4 years old can be topworked rapidly by T-budding or whip grafting. The branches should be less than ½ inch in diameter. For larger branches side, cleft, or bark grafts must be used.

Graft or bud scions should usually be placed within about 18 inches (45 cm) of the main trunk of a tree. This means that large cuts are required on older trees. Insert the buds on the side of a horizontal branch and the outside of a vertical branch to encourage outward growth.

When the buds or grafts begin to grow, they may require support or pruning.

Shoots will develop from the old or original parts of the tree (Figure 14-52). Unless you wish to have more than one variety on the tree, all these shoots must eventually be removed. They should not be removed all at one time, but gradually during the first year. Some shoots will continue to appear for two to three years.

Trees are repaired by bridge grafting, inarching, or possibly by approach grafting. See the descriptions of these specific methods.

GROWING GARDEN SEED AT HOME

◆ ◆ ◆

Caution: *Do not save or attempt to grow seed of F_1 hybrid cultivars* (see Chapter 3).

Isolation and Pollination

Except for the few self-pollinated species (Table 14-12), garden plants must be isolated from other cultivars of the same species if they are to produce seed true to type. Commercial seed producers are required to plant seed fields from ¼ to 1 mile (about ½ to ⅔ km) from the nearest planting of a different cultivar of the same species. Although an occasional stray pollen grain may reach the planting, seed satisfactory for home gardening usually

TABLE 14-12 • *Classification of garden plants according to reproduction*

Asexually Propagated Garden Plants				
Fruits and Nuts (almost all)			Ornamental Shrubs and Trees	Vegetables
Almond	Currant	Peach	Almost all	Garlic
Apple	Date	Pear		Globe artichoke
Apricot	Fig	Pecan		Horseradish
Avocado	Gooseberry	Pineapple		Jerusalem artichoke
Banana	Grape	Plum		Potato
Blackberry	Grapefruit	Raspberry		Rhubarb
Blueberry	Lemon	Strawberry		Sweet potato
Cherry	Lime	Walnut		
Cranberry	Orange			

Sexually Propagated Garden Plants (including some normally propagated asexually that can be propagated sexually)		
Naturally Self-Pollinated Crops		
Vegetables		Flowers
Bean	Pea	Larkspur
Eggplant	Pepper	Nicotiana
Lettuce	Potato	Sweet pea
Lima bean	Tomato	

Cross-Pollinated Crops			
Vegetables			Other Plants
Asparagus	Cucumber	Pumpkin	Hops
Beet	Endive	Radish	Sugar beets
Broccoli	Jerusalem artichoke	Rhubarb	Sunflowers
Brussels sprouts	Leek	Rutabaga	Most flowers
Cabbage	Muskmelon	Spinach	Most forest trees
Carrot	New Zealand spinach	Squash	Most ornamental trees and shrubs
Cauliflower	Okra	Sweet corn	
Celery	Onion	Sweet potato	
Chard	Parsley	Turnip	
Cress	Parsnip	Watermelon	

can be produced with an isolation of 200 yards (about 180 m). When this kind of distance is not feasible, individual plants can be isolated with a screened cage, and individual florets with a piece of cheesecloth. They must be isolated before the flowers from which seed is to be saved have opened.

Nature usually takes care of pollinating uncaged plants. Caged flowers should be hand pollinated when they become receptive, which for most species is shortly after they open. Pollen from another plant of the same cultivar should be used to ensure fertilization in case the species is self-incompatible. Pollen is generally most viable shortly after it matures and begins to be shed from the anthers. Pollen can be transferred by brushing the pollen-shedding stamens onto the stigma or by touching the stigma with the point of a knife blade containing a bit of pollen scraped from an anther (Figure 14-53).

FIGURE 14-53 • Artificial pollination of a squash flower. One day before it opens, a bud of a female cucubit flower is fastened shut with a piece of paper and a paper clip (A). Next morning the petals of a pollen-shedding male flower that has just opened are stripped away from the anther cone. The clip and paper are removed from the female flower, and the anther cone is brushed against the stigma (B) to pollinate that flower. The pollinated flower is again fastened shut to prevent stray pollen from reaching its stigma. The paper and clip can be removed one day later when the flower will remain closed naturally.

Collecting the Seed

The seed of most plants that produce a dry fruit or pod should be allowed to mature fully and dry on the plant. Seedpods of species that burst and scatter their seed before they are fully dry need to be gathered and dried artificially before they burst. Because gardeners usually produce only small quantities of seed of any one cultivar, chaff and other extraneous material can be blown away by pouring the seed from one container to another in a slight breeze or the airstream from a small fan.

Seed produced in a moist fruit like tomato or muskmelon should be squeezed or scraped care-

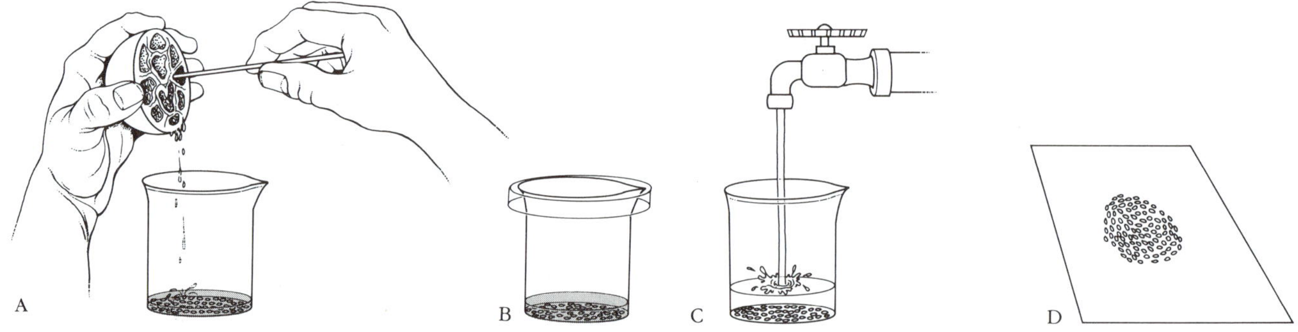

FIGURE 14-54 • Extracting seed from a tomato. (A) The fruit is cut open, and the seed, with as little pulp as possible, is scraped and squeezed into a container. A loose cover is placed over the container (B) and the pulp and juice are allowed to ferment for four to seven days. The seed is rinsed several times (C) and allowed to dry on a paper towel (D).

fully into a container with as little extraneous pulp as possible. If the liquid extracted with the seed is not adequate to keep the seed from drying out, a small amount of water should be added. A loose cover is placed over the container and the mixture is allowed to ferment for four to seven days; it is then rinsed several times with water to remove the fermented liquid and pulp. The seed is then placed on paper towels or other absorbent material and allowed to dry thoroughly (Figure 14-54).

Seed Production of Biennial Crops

Biennial crops must be subjected to a cool rest period after their first season of growth before they will grow a seed stalk. This cold period can be provided by allowing them to winter over in the garden. Where freezing damage is likely, root and bulb crops can be protected with a heavy loose mulch of straw or leaves. Root and bulb crops and cabbage also can be dug and wintered over in a cool, moist root cellar or pit (see "Storing Horticultural Products" in this chapter).

TRANSPLANTING WOODY PLANTS

◆ ◆ ◆

The technique required for successfully transplanting woody plants depends on the kind of plant; its age and size; whether it is dormant or actively growing; its nutritional status; whether it is nursery grown, growing around a home, or a native plant; and the weather conditions and climate of the area.

Securing and Planting Nursery-Grown Woody Plants

Woody plants are sold in three ways: bare-root, balled and burlapped, and in containers.

Sources. Nursery stock can be purchased from local nurseries and garden stores, mail-order nurseries, and supermarkets and department stores. Good buys on trees and shrubs are often available from department stores and supermarkets, and stores of this kind that have plant and garden departments managed by plant specialists are reliable sources of nursery stock. Those that sell plants seasonally as an adjunct to produce or hobby departments may be a less reliable source as they may not have facilities or personnel trained to care properly for plant materials. Occasionally plants not salable elsewhere are sold at bargain prices to these outlets. Mail-order nurseries are a good source of bare-root planting stock, especially of uncommon and unusual trees and shrubs, during the dormant season. A local nursery or garden store is usually the most reliable, albeit the most expensive, year-round source of woody plants, and sometimes the only source during the summer.

Method of Planting. Select a well-drained site that provides the environment required by the tree or shrub—sunny, shady, wind free, and so on. Dig a hole that allows plenty of room for root growth—a minimum of 3 to 4 feet (about 1 m) in diameter and 2 feet (⅔ m) deep for a tree and 2 feet in diameter and 1½ feet (½ m) deep for shrubs. If the soil dug from the hole is not good topsoil, it should be mixed with 20 to 25 percent well-decomposed organic matter (peat moss, compost, aged manure). Do not place unmixed organic matter in the bottom of the hole where it will be in contact with roots.

Prune away at least 50 percent of the leaf-bearing surface of bare-root plants and about 20 to 25 percent of balled and burlapped plants. Because leaves are borne primarily on smaller twigs, the pruning does not need to reduce the size extensively. Overpruning is preferable to underpruning. Leaving too many leaves to dissipate the limited moisture absorbed by the drastically reduced root system is the most common cause of death due to transplanting. Damaged and excessively long roots also should be removed. Container-grown plants generally do not need pruning. However, before concluding that a woody transplant from a container does not need pruning, you should confirm that the plant in question was established in the container and is not a bare-root transplant that has been recently potted, a common practice in most nurseries.

Roots of bare-root transplants should be spread around the hole. The string around the trunk or crown of balled and burlapped stock should be cut after the plant has been properly placed in the hole. The burlap should be pulled back from the top of the ball so that it will be covered with soil, but it need not be removed from the plant. Container-grown plants can often be knocked from wider-mouthed pots by tipping the container upside down and tapping it lightly. The sides of metal cans should be cut from top to bottom in three places and pulled back so that the plant with its ball of earth can be removed without disturbing the root system (Figure 14-55). The planting of a tree and a shrub is shown in Figures 14-56 and 14-57.

Transplanted trees and shrubs require a steady supply of water until roots are regenerated. Do not overwater; more transplants are killed by overwatering than by underwatering. In most areas a thorough soaking each ten to fourteen days is enough. It is a good idea to dig down 4 to 6 inches

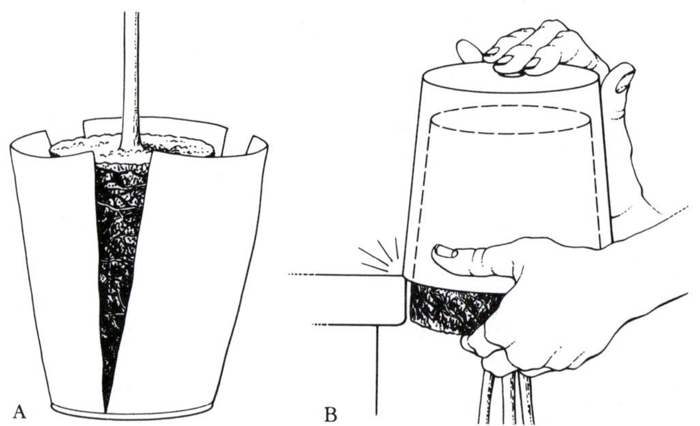

FIGURE 14-55 • Removing a nursery plant from its container. The sides of a metal straight-sided can should be cut from top to bottom in three places (A). A tapered container with an opening wider than its base can be turned upside down and tapped against the edge of a table or bench (B).

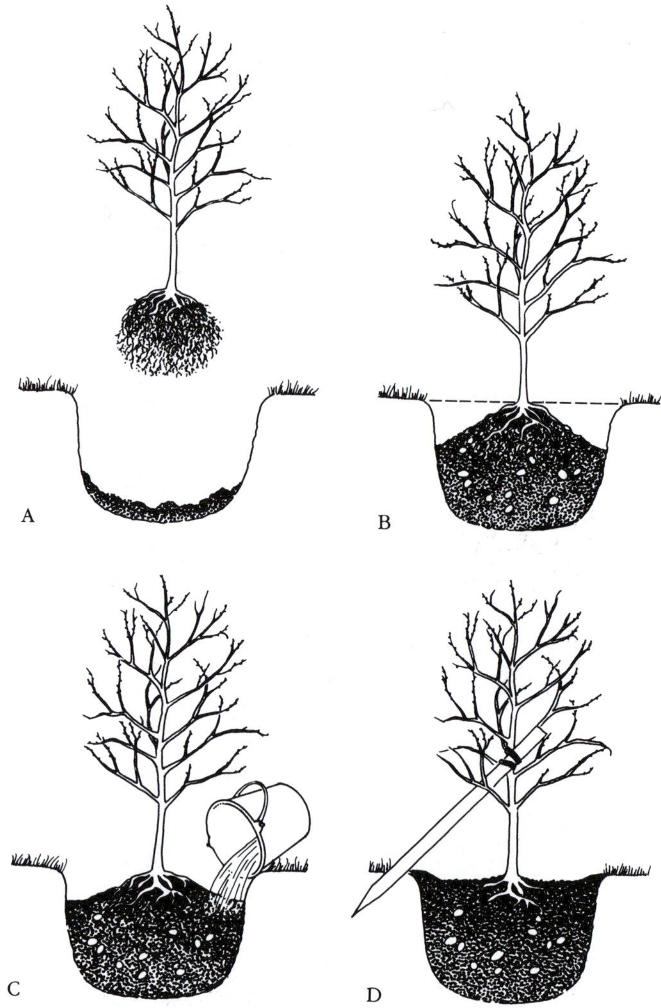

FIGURE 14-56 • Planting a tree. (A) Dig a hole a foot deeper than height of roots and twice as wide as the root span or rootball. Loosen several inches of soil at bottom of hole to aid drainage. (B) Add soil to the hole, and build it up in a mound beneath and among the roots so the plant is at the same ground level as it was before it was moved. (C) Fill three-fourths of hole with soil, and then water it. Finish filling the hole with soil and then water again. In arid regions, leaving a slight depression around the tree aids irrigation during the first summer. (D) Drive a stake into the soil at a 45° angle to brace small trees. Pad stake at the point of intersection, and secure the tree with soft cord or rag strips. (From B. Adams, *Transplanting Woody Plants.* Washington State University Extension Bulletin 675. Pullman, Wash., revised periodically)

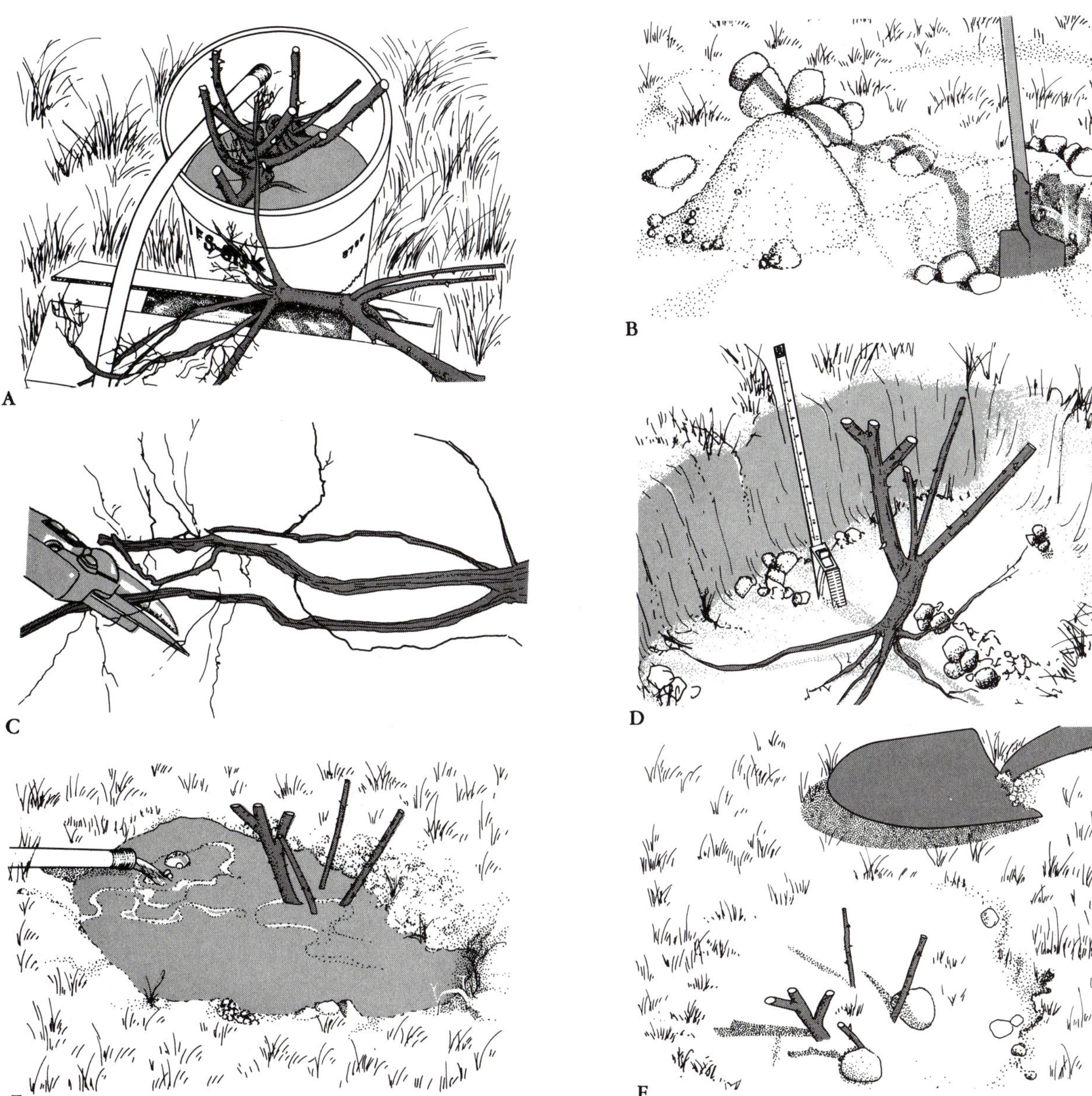

FIGURE 14-57 • Planting a rosebush. As soon as the bush arrives, it should be placed in a container and covered with water for several, but no more than twenty-four, hours (A). Holes are dug large enough to accommodate the depth and spread of the root system and any additional material that is to be added to the bottom of the hole (B). Damaged and excessively long roots are cut away (C). A small quantity of well-rotted compost or manure or other nitrogen-containing fertilizer (no more than the equivalent of 2 tablespoons [60 ml] of ammonium nitrate) can be added to the bottom of the planting hole. Where drought is likely, about 2 inches (5 cm) of peat moss in the bottom of the hole will retain moisture in the root zone. Fertilizer and organic matter should then be covered with at least 2 inches (5 cm) of soil. The bush is then placed in the hole and its roots spread. In areas where winter damage is likely, the bush should be planted to a depth so that its graft union (about an inch below the point of branching on this bush) is covered with soil (D). The hole is filled about halfway with soil and then is filled to the top with water (E). When the water has soaked into the soil, the remainder of the hole should be filled (F). Stems should be pruned back so that there are no more than two buds on each stem.

TABLE 14-13 • *Season and method of transplanting that will give reasonable success for most woody plants*

Class of Plants	Season	Balled and Burlapped	Containerized	Bare Root
Evergreens under 3 years	Dormant	X	X	X
Evergreens over 3 years	Dormant	X	X	
Evergreens over 3 years	Summer		X	
Deciduous	Dormant	X	X	X
Deciduous	Summer		X	

(10 to 15 cm) near the plant occasionally to check soil moisture.

Do not permit fertilizer to come in contact with the root system. If the plant needs fertilizer, it can be watered with a gallon or two of nutrient solution (see "Fertilizing Garden Crops" in this chapter).

Transplanting Established Plants

The main difference between nursery-grown plants and native or cultivated plants that need to be moved from their present location is that the nursery plants have been root pruned to confine and concentrate their roots. Digging around a plant to cut wide-spreading roots six months and/or a year before it is to be transplanted greatly increases the chances of its being successfully moved.

As was mentioned in Chapter 2, plants with fibrous roots are easier to move with a ball of earth intact than are those with taproots. Determining which plants can be easily moved is mostly trial and error; I know of no reliable root-system classification. For instance, when moving trees in the woods, I have had no problem keeping a good ball of earth around the roots of Douglas fir (*Pseudotsuga menziesii*) and Engelmann spruce (*Picea engelmannii*), but a great deal of difficulty keeping any soil whatsoever on the less-concentrated root system of Grand fir (*Abies grandis*) and most pines.

Size and Transplantability. Smaller plants are obviously easier to move, and the smaller the plant is, the greater the probability of successful reestablishment. However, with some experience, two strong people can move (tug or drag may be more appropriate terms) shrubs and coniferous trees up to 6 to 8 feet (2 to 2½ m) with a ball of earth that can be encased in a 3 × 5 foot (1 × 1½ m) piece of burlap.

Method of Transplanting. If the plant cannot be transplanted with bare roots, several options may be possible (Table 14-13). Often, especially when the plants are small, the roots are fibrous, and the soil is heavy, the ball of earth will adhere without being encased. In some cold-winter areas it is a common practice to move larger shrubs and trees with their roots in a frozen ball of earth. Before the ground freezes, a trench is dug around and under the root system just as for balling and burlapping. The planting hole is also prepared. After the ball is frozen, it is broken from the soil below with a digging bar and moved to its new location. The roots should be protected from extreme cold and dehydration with straw, peat moss, or similar material until the ground thaws enough to complete the planting.

Balling and Burlapping. The standard method of moving medium-sized and large trees and shrubs without exposing their root system is balling and burlapping, as illustrated in Figure 14-58.

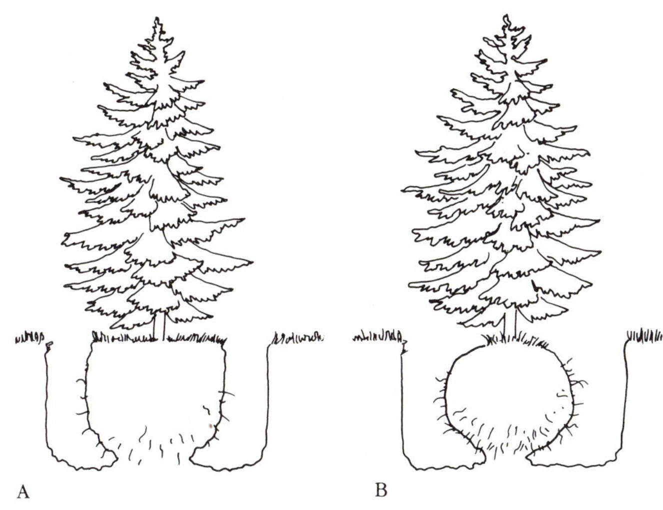

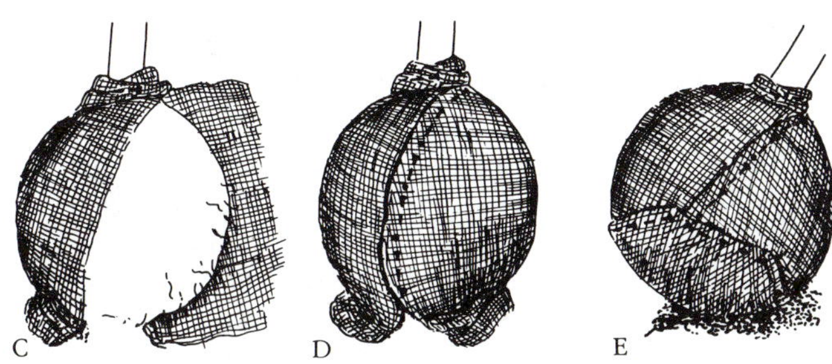

FIGURE 14-58 • Balling and burlapping. (A) Using a sharpened, straight-handled, round-mouth spade, dig a trench about half as deep as the plant is high all the way around the tree or shrub at about the outer perimeter of the leaf canopy. The diameter of the ball relative to the canopy spread and height of the plant varies somewhat for cultivars of unusual shape. The initial cuts should be made with the back of the spade toward the tree so that the ball of earth is kept intact. (B) Round off the ball of earth, and dig under it until only a small part of it remains attached to the soil beneath. Roots that protrude should be clipped off with a pair of sharp shears as close to the soil ball as possible. (C) Wrap one corner of a piece of burlap of adequate size around the trunk or crown. Fasten it using a 6- or 8-penny nail as a pin. (D) After the sack is securely fastened around the trunk or crown, it can be pulled tightly around the earth ball and pinned with nails. With some kinds of soil, nails will hold (and a tighter fit is possible) if they are pushed straight into the soil ball through both overlapping layers of burlap. The excess burlap should be positioned at one side of the base of the ball. (E) With its upper soil tightly bound by the burlap, the ball can be cut from the soil supporting its base and rolled onto one side against the edge of the hole. The loose end of the unpinned burlap is pulled under the pinned to enclose the basal soil and complete the operation.

REPOTTING

◆ ◆ ◆

As houseplants and other potted plants increase in size, they will eventually need to be moved into larger containers.

There are several conditions that suggest that a plant needs to be repotted:

1. The plant looks overgrown for the size of its pot. The balance between plant and container is no longer aesthetically pleasing.
2. The top part of the plant has become so large that its container tends to be unstable and tips easily.
3. The plant has become root bound—the roots are either compacted along the top and sides of the container or are growing through the drainhole.
4. The soil in the container dries rapidly. The plant has to be watered more frequently than do the other plants in the home.
5. The plant is doing poorly, and there is no other readily discernible cause.

Figure 14-59 explains the method of repotting a houseplant.

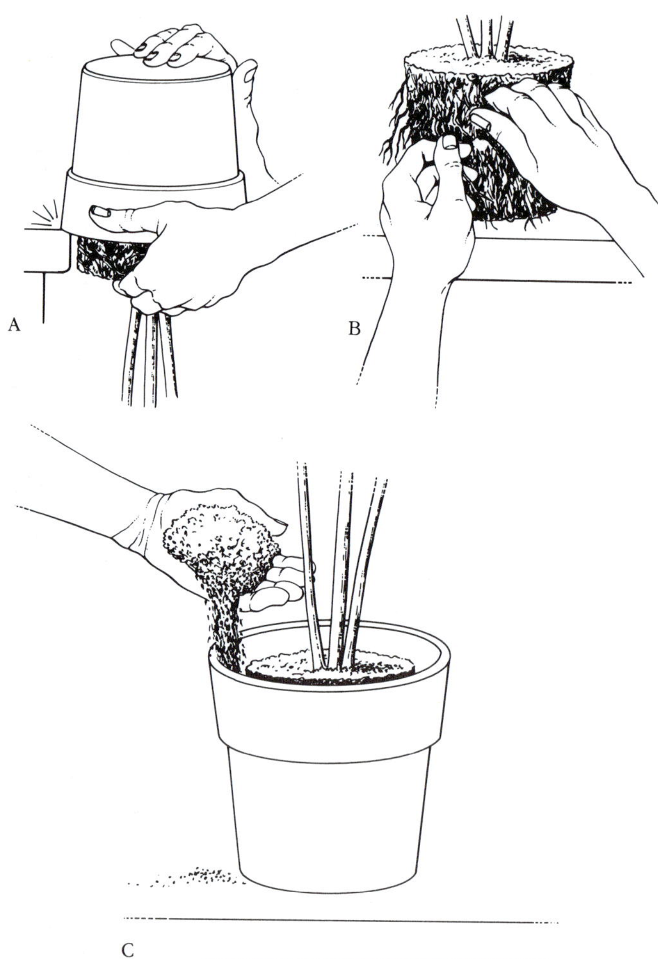

FIGURE 14-59 • Repotting a houseplant. (A) Remove the roots and rooting medium from the pot by carefully tipping the plant upside down and tapping the container lightly against the edge of a bench or table. (B) Use your fingers to thin out and spread the roots matted around the edge and base of the pot. Heavily matted roots may be clipped off with a pair of shears. (C) Place a piece of broken clay pot or other loose-fitting material over the drain hole of the new pot. Add ½ to 1 inch (about 2 cm) of fine gravel to the bottom for drainage and enough potting medium so that the plant and its old soil ball are at the desired level. (Setting the plant somewhat deeper than it originally was to hide a stemmy base will not usually be detrimental.) Finally, fill the remaining space in the pot with the potting medium and water.

FIGURE 14-60 • (*Facing page*) Covering a small garden bed with plastic mulch. (A) With the corner of a hoe dig a furrow at least 6 inches (15 cm) deep on each side of the bed that is to be mulched, and a furrow 10 inches (25 cm) deep at one end, leaving the soil mounded beside the furrows. The completed bed should be 1 foot (30 cm) narrower than the width of the plastic. (B) Begin unrolling the roll of plastic by placing its end across the end furrow and tucking it in all the way to the bottom. While holding the plastic in place, fill the trench with soil and tamp it to secure the end of the plastic. If two people are working together, they should place a hoe or rake handle through the roll of plastic and, keeping the mulch stretched tightly, unroll it over the bed. One person can unroll a roll as wide as 4 feet (1¼ m) by holding it upright over his open hands. With the tips of his fingers at the point that the sheet is leaving the roll, he can cause the roll to turn over his wrists by walking backward along the center of the bed. (Don't attempt to lay plastic mulch by yourself if the wind is blowing.) (C) After you have unrolled about 50 feet (15 m) of plastic sheet, hold its edges in place in the furrow by scraping a small quantity of soil onto them. Do this each 5 to 6 feet (about 2 m) on both sides of the bed. Then bury both edges by shoveling soil into the furrow. Make certain that the mulch is stretched tightly across the bed. The weight of soil will usually do this, but some manipulation by hand occasionally may be necessary. Tamp the soil well to seal down the edges of the mulch. (D) Using the corner of the hoe or a small garden trowel, cut through the plastic at intervals to set transplants or plant hills of seed at their proper spacing. If the plot is to be furrow-irrigated, plant near one edge of the bed. Moisture will soak under the edge of the mulch. If the plot is to be sprinkler-irrigated, punch holes in the plastic over a few low places in the bed. It is necessary to cover only a part of the plot for a wide-spaced crop like melons or cantaloupe, e.g., 3 feet of their 9-foot bed. If the plastic used is polyethylene, its exposed part will deteriorate by the end of the growing season, but the soil-covered strips along the edge will remain intact and will have to be removed before the soil can be reworked.

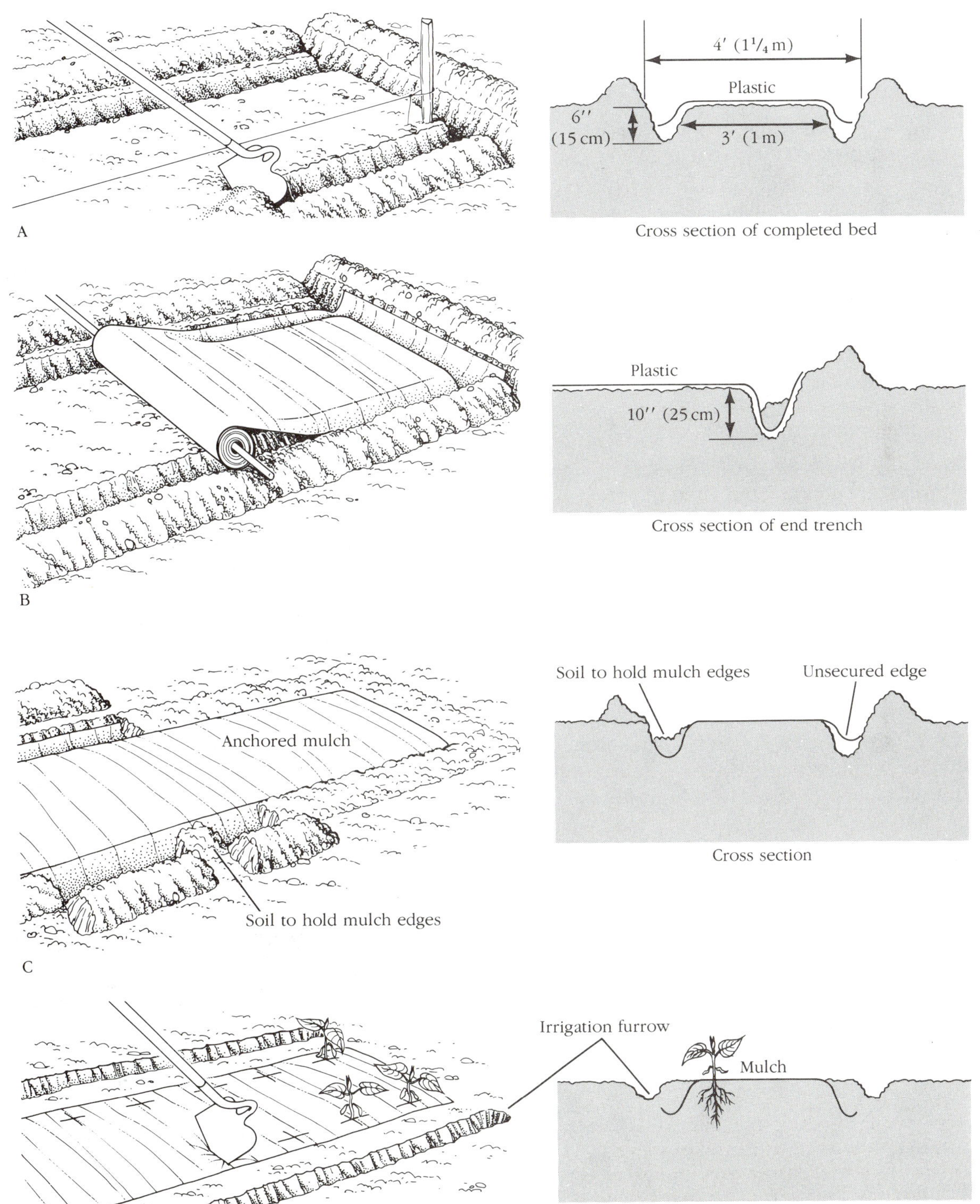
A
4′ (1¼ m)
Plastic
6″
(15 cm)
3′ (1 m)
Cross section of completed bed
B
Plastic
10″ (25 cm)
Cross section of end trench
Anchored mulch
Soil to hold mulch edges
C
Soil to hold mulch edges
Unsecured edge
Cross section
D
Irrigation furrow
Mulch
Cross section

MULCHING WITH SHEET MATERIALS

◆ ◆ ◆

The benefits of mulching and the relative merits of polyethylene and landscape fabric were discussed in Chapter 5. Polyethylene or other kinds of plastic packaged in rolls 3 to 5 feet (1.3 to 1.6 m) wide can be conveniently used as mulch for row crops that are normally spaced a foot or more apart and either transplanted or direct seeded into hills (Figure 14-60). As has been mentioned, polyethylene breaks down in a few months when subjected to the sun's ultraviolet rays, so it is especially well suited to using on annual crops. Wider sheets of polyethylene can be used as semipermanent mulching materials for level or very slightly sloping areas if holes are punched at intervals no farther apart than 2 feet (60 cm), to permit water to penetrate, and if the sheet is completely covered with loose mulching material so that the sun's ultraviolet rays do not destroy it.

Landscape fabric is usually a more satisfactory, albeit more expensive, ground cover when an area, rather than a row, is to be protected. Landscape fabric overlain with chicken wire is by far the best choice for a moderate to steeply sloping area where water would soon wash away loose mulching material placed over plastic (Figure 14-61).

COMPOSTING

◆ ◆ ◆

Materials to Use

Straw	Sawdust	Leaves	Manure

Vegetable and fruit peelings, tops, cores

Garden refuse	Lawn clippings	Immature weeds

Materials Not to Use

Woody branches	Bones	Diseased plant material

Weeds that have formed seed

Weeds or garden refuse that has been killed with herbicides or have been recently treated with other pesticides

The Composting Structure

Organic matter can be composted by piling it in a corner, but generally the composting process is more rapid and satisfactory in an enclosure. The enclosure can be a pit or a plastic bag, but more commonly it is built with mesh wire, wood, or another structural material. A common composting bin has three enclosed sides, each 4 to 6 feet (about 1¼ to 2 m) long (a size convenient for handling) and 4 or 5 feet high. (Aeration is reduced by compaction, resulting in slowed decomposition if the pile is over 6 feet high.) One side is often open to permit easy mixing of the compost.

The compost pile is made by alternating layers of 6 to 8 inches (15 to 20 cm) of organic matter with about an inch of garden soil (Figure 14-62). One-fourth pound (112 g) of nitrogen should be mixed with each cubic foot or bushel of composted dry matter (about half that amount if the compost is mainly kitchen wastes, lawn clippings,

FIGURE 14-61 • (*Facing page*) Installing landscape fabric around a shrub planting on a sloping site. After the soil has been prepared and raked smooth and the shrubs planted, the fabric is rolled over the surface (A). X-shaped slits are cut over each shrub; the branches are carefully pulled through; and the fabric is fitted around the shrub bases. The fabric edges are secured with long wire staples. Wooden laths are placed at intervals on the fabric and woven chicken wire is rolled over the fabric, laths, and shrubs. As the wire is cut, it is secured with staples (B). The laths are oriented so that their wide dimension is vertical, and they are fastened in place with staples (C). The lath keeps the wire above the fabric, and the wire prevents the loose-covering mulch from sliding downhill. The wire is cut and fitted around the shrubs and all edges are secured with staples (D). Shredded bark mulch is hauled to the site and raked smooth over the area around the shrubs (E). Wire is not needed on level sites not subject to heavy wind.

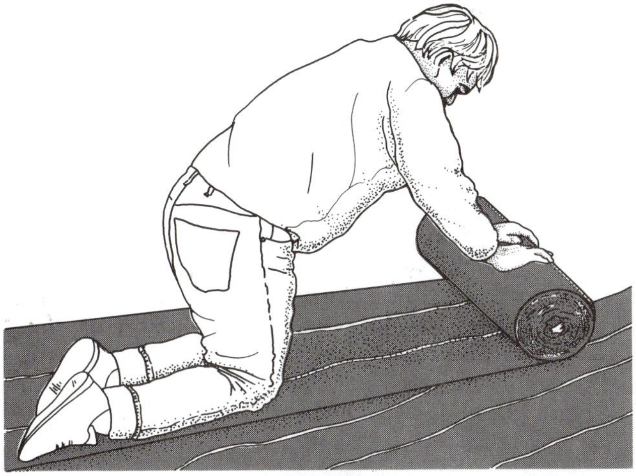

A

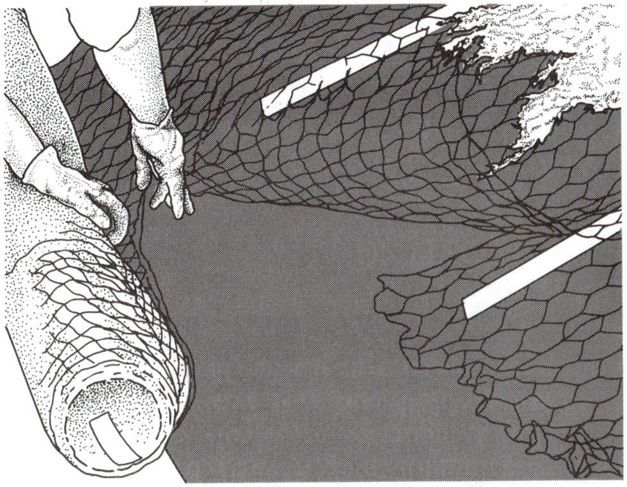

B

C

D

E

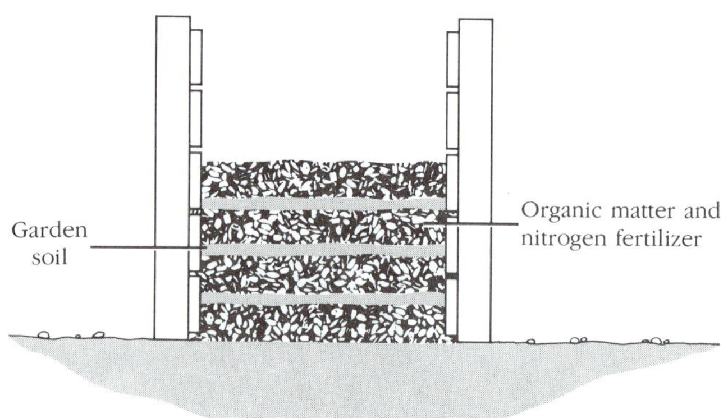

FIGURE 14-62 • The compost pile. Organic waste can also be composted by digging it into the soil of an unused part of the garden.

or other material containing some nitrogen; see Table 14-14). The pile should be maintained at about 60 to 70 percent moisture. During dry weather the pile should be checked each week (or each time it is turned), and water should be added if the material feels dry. It should not remain wet enough so that water can be squeezed from it. The process of decomposition keeps the composting material warm, and it should be turned a few times during the summer (or every three to four days for rapid decomposition). Decomposition rates vary and can be as short as three weeks. It requires less effort to let the process proceed for most of one growing season. The volume of the pile will decrease as it decomposes, but it is generally more convenient to start a new pile each year and to spread the compost from the previous season around the garden as the need arises.

Composting by Digging Organic Wastes into the Garden

Where there is space that has not been planted, the simplest way to compost organic wastes from the kitchen and elsewhere is to bury them in the garden. At one end of an area where vegetables have been harvested or where annual flowers have completed their blooming, dig a trench, piling the soil on the edge away from the garden. When a container of biodegradable kitchen scraps or other organic matter has accumulated, it can be spread on the bottom of the trench. The amount of nitrogen needed to decompose organic matter can be added to the trench, which is then covered and a new trench formed by digging the adjacent 8 or 10 inches of soil onto it. If scraps are added every few days as they accumulate, by spring even a sizable garden will have been spaded and "manured" and be ready to plant. During periods when there is no empty space in the vegetable or annual flower gardens, scraps can be buried between rosebushes or other shrubs. Meat scraps should not be buried shallowly where roaming dogs are likely to smell and dig for them.

TABLE 14-14 • *The nitrogen, phosphorus, and potassium content, as a percentage of fresh weight, of several soil-improving crops and organic wastes used frequently in gardening*

Crop or Product	N (%)	P_2O_5 (%)	K_2O (%)
Alfalfa, vetch	2.5	0.5	2.0
Clovers	2.0	0.5	1.5
Bean and pea vines	0.5	0.1	0.5
Small grains, grass clippings	0.4	0.1	0.3
Dairy manure (medium amount bedding)	0.7	0.3	0.7
Sawdust, shavings	0.2	0.1	0.2
Grain straw	0.6	0.2	0.1
Peat moss (woody or sedge)	0.2	<0.1	<0.1
Peat moss (sphagnum)	0.1	<0.1	<0.1
Vegetable and fruit peelings	0.4	0.1	0.5
Dry leaves	0.8	0.2	0.6

Information for compiling this table came from various sources, including *Western Fertilizer Handbook*, 5th ed. Calif. Fertilizer Assoc., Sacramento. Copyright © 1975. *Composts for the Garden*, by A. A. Duncan. Fact Sheet 134. Extension Service, Oregon State University, Corvalis, Ore. 1971. *Soil*, USDA Yearbook of Agriculture, 1957. U.S. Government Printing Office, Washington, D.C., 1957.

TABLE 14-15 • *Approximate amounts of finely ground limestone needed to raise the pH of a 7-inch layer of soil as indicated*[a]

Soil Regions and Textural Classes	Limestone Requirements: From pH 3.5 to pH 4.5 (tons per acre)[c]	From pH 4.5 to pH 5.5 (tons per acre)[c]	From pH 5.5 to pH 6.5 (tons per acre)[c]
Soils of warm-temperate and tropical regions			
Sand and loamy sand	0.3	0.3	0.4
Sandy loam	—	0.5	0.7
Loam	—	0.8	1.0
Silt loam	—	1.2	1.4
Clay loam	—	1.5	2.0
Muck	2.5[b]	3.3	3.8
Soil of cool-temperate and temperate regions			
Sand and loamy sand	0.4	0.5	0.6
Sandy loam	—	0.8	1.3
Loam	—	1.2	1.7
Silt loam	—	1.5	2.0
Clay loam	—	1.9	2.3
Muck	2.9[b]	3.8	4.3

Adapted from *Soil Survey Manual*, USDA Agricultural Handbook 18. U.S. Government Printing Office, Washington, D.C., 1951.

[a]All limestone goes through a 2-mm mesh screen and at least half through a 0.15-mm mesh screen. With coarser materials, applications need to be greater. For burned lime, about half the amounts given are used; for hydrated lime, about three-quarters.

[b]The suggestions for muck soils are for those essentially free of sand and clay. For those containing much sand or clay the amounts should be reduced to values midway between those given for muck and the correponding class of mineral soil. If the mineral soils are unusually low in organic matter, the recommendations should be reduced about 25%; if unusually high, increased by about 25% or even more.

[c]Multiply the tons per acre required by 4.6 to obtain pounds per 100 square feet. Multiply tons per acre by 2.24 to obtain metric tons per hectare.

FERTILIZING GARDEN CROPS

◆ ◆ ◆

Determining the Amount of Fertilizer

Fertilization of the garden should be based on the following:

1. Your own or neighbor's experience during previous seasons.
2. Soil test from your state university soil-testing laboratory (see Table 14-1), from a reliable private soil-testing laboratory, or, as a rough guide, from a do-it-yourself soil-test kit.
3. If better estimates are not available, use Tables 14-16 and 14-17 as a general guide.
4. In humid areas the soil pH often is too low for most garden crops to grow well. Quick pH test kits, available at garden stores, can be used if a more accurate determination of pH from an official soil test is not available. If the soil has a pH below 6.2, lime should be added. The amount initially required to bring soil pH to the desired level between 6.2 and 6.8 varies (Table 14-15). After the pH has been raised to the desired level, an application of 60 to 80 pounds (30 to 40 kg) per acre of ground limestone, or its equivalent, each four to five years usually keeps the pH at the optimum level. Blueberries, rhododendrons, azaleas, heathers, and heaths require a low pH and should not be limed.
5. An additional ⅛ to ¼ pound (75 to 125 g) of nitrogen should be added for each 100 pounds (45 kg) of organic mulch or crop residue that has less than 1 percent nitrogen (Table 14-14).

Fertilizing Vegetables and Flowers

See Tables 14-16, 14-17, and 14-18. Most fertilizer for vegetables and annual flowers should be applied in the spring. If manure is available, it should be incorporated when the soil is worked, preferably by digging or plowing it under. In areas where phosphorus is deficient, the manure should be supplemented with a fertilizer high in phosphorus. Tomatoes, the cucurbits, carrots, peas, beans, and some of the short-season vegetables do not require as much fertilizer as do most other annual vegetables. The amount required by these crops can be broadcast onto the garden before the soil is dug in the spring. More fertilizer can be **banded**—applied in a narrow band parallel to the crop row—at planting time for those crops requiring it. Ideally, fertilizer should be banded 2 inches (5 cm) to the side and 1 inch (2½ cm) below the seed, especially if the planting is to be furrow irrigated or if rain is not anticipated. The band should be between the plant row and the irrigation furrow so that moisture can dissolve and carry the fertilizer to the plant roots. Soluble nitrate-nitrogen fertilizer can be banded on the surface if the plot is watered by sprinkler or rainfall.

For short-season vegetables and flowers and on soils with high organic matter content and high cation-exchange capacity, a spring application of fertilizer may be all that is required. For long-season crops growing on soils low in organic matter, one or more additional fertilizer applications may be needed. Fertilizer applications banded after the crop is growing are called **sidedressings**. These later applications are usually banded a few inches from the plant six to ten weeks after it is planted.

Perennial flowers and perennial vegetables, except asparagus, are usually fertilized in the early spring. Asparagus responds best to being fertilized right after the cutting season. The fertilizer for perennial flowers and vegetables can be either sidedressed or spread in a circle a few inches away from the crown of each plant.

Fertilizing Woody Plants

General directions for fertilizing most woody plants are given in Tables 14-16 and 14-17. The amount of fertilizer for plants like grapes, when the location of branches may not be directly above the root system, can be calculated on the basis of normal spacing of the plant (Chapter 13 and Table 14-28). Fertilizer should be spread around the trunk over the soil area allotted to the plant.

General Precautions for Fertilizing Woody Plants

1. Use less N if vegetative growth is excessive and/or if flowering and fruit set are not adequate.
2. With plants and at locations where winter damage is common, do not fertilize after midsummer.
3. Do not place large amounts of fertilizer close to the crown of a plant.
4. When fertilizer is broadcast on low-growing shrubs, be sure it is washed from their leaves and soaked into the soil.

Recommendations for Some Specific Plants

1. Grapes growing on medium and high organic-matter soils require about ⅕ lb (90 g) elemental nitrogen per plant per year. Currants, gooseberries, and blueberries require about a tablespoon or ½ oz (14 g) per plant.
2. Another common method of calculating fertilizer requirements for apple and pear trees is

$$\frac{\text{trunk diameter}}{9} = \text{pounds of N required per tree}$$

3. In arid regions, both tree-fruit and bush-fruit plants often exhibit a yellow interveinal chlorosis as a result of calcium-induced iron deficiency. Applications of a chelated iron is usually the best way of overcoming this problem

TABLE 14-16 • *Average pounds of N, P, and K needed for 1,000 square feet of garden crops in humid and subhumid areas*[a,b,h] *(divide by 2 to determine kg/100 m²; multiply by 40 to determine pounds/acre)*

		Low Organic Matter Sandy Soil				High Organic Matter Clay Soil			
Unit	Method of Application[c]	When[c,d]	N	P	K	When[c,d]	N	P	K
Temp.-zone tree fruits, nuts	B[e]	E. Sp & Su	3 & 1	3	3	E. Sp	2	2	2
Citrus fruits	B[e]	Sept., Jan.	3 & 2	3	3	Sept., Jan.	2,2	2	2
Strawberries	B	E. Sp	2	4	0	E. Sp	1½	3	0
Grapes	B & Si[e]	E. Sp & Su	3 & 1	3	3	E. Sp	2	0	2
Bushberries	Si	E. Sp	3	6	3	E. Sp	2	4	2
Asparagus	Si	E. Sp & Su	1 & 1	3	4	Su	1½	2	3
Other perennial vegetables	Si	E. Sp & Su	1 & 1	3	4	E. Sp	1½	2	3
Lettuce, radishes, spinach, turnips[f]	B & Si	PT	3	3	3	PT	2½	2½	2½
Peas, beans, lima beans	B	PT	1	2	2	PT	1	2	2
Carrots, cucurbits, tomatoes, herbs	B & Si	PT & Su	2 & 1	4	2	PT	1½	3	1½
Other long-season vegetables	B & Si	PT & Su	3 & 2	6	3	PT & Su	2½ & 1½	5	2½
Bulbs and corms	B	E. Sp	2½	5	2½	E. Sp	2	4	2
Annual flowers	B & Si	PT & Su	2½ & 2	5	2½	E. Sp & E. Su	2 & 1½	4	2
Perennial flowers, spring and summer blooming	B	E. Sp	3	6	3	E. Sp	2	4	2
Perennial flowers, fall blooming	B & Si	Sp & Su	3 & 1½	6	3	Sp & Su	2 & 1	4	2
Roses	B	E. Sp & Su	2 & 2	4	2	E. Sp & Su	1½ & 1½	3	1½
Other shrubs and lianas	B[e]	E. Sp & Su	2 & 1	4	2	E. Sp	2	4	2
Spreading trees	B[e]	E. Sp & Su	2 & 1	4	2	E. Sp	2	4	2
Tall trees	B[e]	E. Sp & Su	3 & 1½	2	2	E. Sp	3	2	2
Turf[g]	B	March, June, August	2,2,2	2	2	March, June, August	1½,1½,1½	1½	1½

[a]Humid and subhumid areas are those areas east of a line drawn from Winnipeg, Manitoba, to Corpus Christi, Texas; plus coastal Alaska and British Columbia, Oregon, and Washington west of the Cascades and California north of San Francisco and north and west of the Central Valley.

[b]Where annual rainfall is over 60 inches, the growing season is more than 200 days, and the fertilizer used is not slow-release, N, P, and K additional to the one or two applications recommended in the table should be applied during mid-summer in an amount equal to half the initial spring recommendation.

[c]B = broadcast; Si = sidedressed; E. Sp = early spring; Su = summer; E. Su = early summer; PT = planting time.

[d]If the main source of fertilizer is slow-release, a small amount of sidedressed, fast-release N and P will often enhance growth of early-planted crops. With slow-release fertilizers the later summer application may not be necessary.

[e]The area to be fertilized around a tree or shrub is a square or rectangle just beyond the periphery of the canopy. If there is no cover crop or if the cover is sparse, the fertilizer can be broadcast on the soil surface. If the woody plant is growing in a lawn, fertilizer should be placed in holes punched to a depth of 14 to 18 inches and spaced 2½ feet each way across the entire area. Turf growing under a tree or shrub should also receive its allotted broadcast of fertilizer. Other suggestions for woody plant fertilization are found in the text.

[f]Broadcast 1 or 2 pounds of N, and other elements if required, on each 1,000 square feet of vegetable garden before the soil is worked. Apply the extra amount as a sidedressing at planting time to those vegetables that require more.

[g]Lawns composed of Bermuda grass will need more N, 5–10 pounds of actual N per 1,000 sq ft per year applied three to five times during the growing season.

[h]Lime is needed periodically on many soils in humid areas. See Item 4 under "Determining the Amount of Fertilizer" in the text; also Table 14-15.

TABLE 14-17 • *Average pounds of N, P, and K needed for 1,000 square feet of garden crops in arid and semiarid areas*[a] *(divide by 2 to determine kg/100 m²; multiply by 40 to determine pounds/acre)*

Unit	Method of Application[c]	Low Organic Matter Sandy Soil				High Organic Matter Clay Soil			
		When[c,d]	N	P	K	When[b,c]	N	P	K
Temp.-zone tree fruits	B[d]	E. Sp	3	3	0	E. Sp	2	0	0
Citrus trees	B[d]	Sept., Jan.	3,2	3	0	Sept., Jan.	2,2	0	0
Strawberries	B	E. Sp	2	2	0	E. Sp	1½	0	0
Grapes	B[d]	E. Sp	3	2	2	E. Sp	2	0	0
Bushberries	Si	E. Sp	2½	2½	0	E. Sp	2	0	0
Asparagus	Si	E. Sp	2	2	0	Su	2	0	0
Other perennial vegetables	Si	Su	2	2	0	E. Sp	2	0	0
Lettuce, radishes, spinach, turnips[e]	B & Si	PT	3	3	0	PT	2	0	0
Peas, beans, lima beans	B	PT	1	1	0	PT	1	0	0
Carrots, cucurbits, tomatoes, herbs	B	PT	2	2	0	PT	1½	0	0
Other long-season vegetables	B & Si	PT & Su	3 & 2	3	0	PT	3	0	0
Bulbs and corms	B	E. Sp	2½	2	0	E. Sp	2	0	0
Annual flowers	B & Si	PT & Su	2 & 1	2	0	PT	2	0	0
Perennial flowers, spring and summer blooming,	B	E. Sp	3	3	0	E. Sp	2	0	0
fall blooming	B & Si	Sp & Su	3 & 1½	3	0	Sp	2	0	0
Roses	B	E. Sp & Su	2 & 1½	2	0	E. Sp	2	0	0
Other shrubs and lianas	B[d]	E. Sp	2	2	0	E. Sp	2	0	0
Spreading trees	B[d]	E. Sp	2½	2½	0	E. Sp	2	0	0
Tall trees	B[d]	E. Sp & Su	3½ & 3½	3½	0	E. Sp	3	0	0
Turf[f]	B	March, June, August	1½, 1½, 1½	1½	0	March, June, August	1½,1½,1½	0	0

[a]Arid and semiarid areas would include the region west of a line drawn from Winnipeg, Manitoba, to Corpus Christi, Texas, except for the area west of the Cascades in Washington and Oregon, the coastal valleys of northern California, coastal British Columbia, and coastal Alaska.
[b]B = broadcast; Si = sidedressed; E. Sp = early spring; Su = summer; PT = planting time.
[c]See footnote [d], Table 14-16.
[d]See footnote [e], Table 14-16.
[e]See footnote [f], Table 14-16.
[f]See footnote [g], Table 14-16.

TABLE 14-18 • *Approximate number of pounds of various analyses of fertilizer to apply if recommendation is given in pounds of actual N, P, or K per 1,000 square feet or per acre (divide by 2 to determine kg/100m²)*

RECOMMENDATION[a] →	40 LB/ACRE EQUIVALENT TO 1 LB/1,000 SQ FT		60 LB/ACRE EQUIVALENT TO 1½ LB/1,000 SQ FT		80 LB/ACRE EQUIVALENT TO 2 LB/1,000 SQ FT		100 LB/ACRE EQUIVALENT TO 2½ LB/1,000 SQ FT		120 LB/ACRE EQUIVALENT TO 3 LB/1,000 SQ FT	
	POUNDS REQUIRED		POUNDS REQUIRED		POUNDS REQUIRED		POUNDS REQUIRED		POUNDS REQUIRED	
ANALYSIS	100 SQ FT	1 ACRE	100 SQ FT	1 ACRE	100 SQ FT	1 ACRE	100 SQ FT	1 ACRE	100 SQ FT	1 ACRE
0.3	35.0	14,000	50.0	20,000	70.0	26,000	80.0	35,000	100.0	42,000
0.5	20.0	8,000	30.0	12,000	40.0	16,000	50.0	20,000	60.0	24,000
0.7	15.0	6,000	22.5	9,000	30.0	12,000	37.0	15,000	45.0	18,000
1.0	10.0	4,000	15.0	6,000	20.0	8,000	25.0	10,000	30.0	12,000
1.5	6.7	2,700	10.0	4,000	13.3	5,300	16.7	6,700	20.0	8,000
2	5.0	2,000	7.5	3,000	10.0	4,000	12.5	5,000	15.0	6,000
3	3.3	1,300	5.0	2,000	6.7	2,700	8.3	3,300	10.0	4,000
5	2.0	800	3.0	1,200	4.0	1,600	5.0	2,000	6.0	2,400
7–8	1.3	500	1.9	750	1.5	1,000	3.3	1,250	3.7	1,500
9–10	1.0	400	1.5	600	2.0	800	2.5	1,000	3.0	1,200
11–12	0.8	330	1.3	500	1.7	670	2.1	830	2.7	1,000
15–16	0.6	240	0.9	360	1.2	480	1.5	600	1.8	720
18–20	0.5	200	0.75	300	1.0	400	1.2	500	1.5	600
25–27	0.4	160	0.60	240	0.8	320	1.0	400	1.2	480
33–36	0.3	120	0.45	180	0.6	240	0.8	330	0.9	360
46–50	0.2	80	0.30	120	0.4	160	0.5	200	0.6	240

[a]For higher application rates—160, 200, or 240 lb/acre or 4, 5, or 6 lb/1,000 sq ft—apply twice the amount recommended for 80, 100, or 120 lb/acre, respectively. For lower application rates, 20 or 30 lb/acre or ½ or ¾ lb/1,000 sq ft, apply half the amount recommended for 40 or 60 lb/acre.

Fertilizing Lawns

In areas where they stay green year-round, lawns should be fertilized approximately every three months. In northern areas they should generally receive an application in March, June, and August. Fertilizer requirements vary, and recommendations for specific locations are available from the county agent or state experiment stations. For lawns composed entirely of grass, from 1 to 1½ lb of elemental nitrogen are required for every 1,000 sq ft (500 to 700 g/100 m²) every three months (Tables 14-16 and 14-17).

It is important that fertilizer be spread uniformly over the lawn area. This can be done with a fertilizer spreader, which can be purchased or rented from a local hardware or garden store. Directions for calibrating should be followed carefully, and fertilizer should be spread over the entire area. Often an operator allows too little overlap to fertilize wheel tracks, which results in strips of light green grass. Fertilizer can also be spread by hand broadcasting. When this is done, the amount needed should be divided into two equal portions so that the area can be covered twice, the second application being at right angles to the first.

Fertilizing Houseplants

Houseplants should be fertilized approximately once each month. Various houseplant fertilizer formulations are available at nurseries and garden stores. For the gardener who already has commercial fertilizer on hand, approximately 3 tablespoons (1½ oz or 40 g) of 10:10:10 analysis fertilizer mixed in a gallon of water provide about the right nutrient concentration and can be used in place of a usual watering once every three or four weeks. A tablespoon of treble superphosphate, a tablespoon of ammonium nitrate, and a tablespoon of potassium sulfate in a gallon of water also provide about the same balance.

Examples Illustrating the Use of Fertilizer Tables

In each example, if the fertilizer recommendation is not given, it must be determined using either Table 14-16 or Table 14-17. Find the plant and its soil type in the appropriate table to determine the amount of N, P, and K needed per 1,000 sq ft. Then refer to Table 14-18 to find how many pounds of fertilizer to apply, given the analysis of the fertilizer you wish to apply. If the fertilizer analysis is not given, check Table 14-19, which lists the analysis of many common fertilizers. In Table 14-18, select either "100 sq ft" or "1 acre," depending on the size of the area to be fertilized. This "pounds required" figure from Table 14-18 must then be multiplied by (square footage to be fertilized/100) or by the number of acres to be fertilized. Table 14-19 gives weight/volume equivalents for various units of measure, to convert pounds to the appropriate unit for dispensing the fertilizer. This final number is the amount (in desired units) of a fertilizer with given analysis to be broadcast or sidedressed over a given area. Tables 14-16 and 14-17 give the method and times for application.

I. A 40 × 50 ft lawn growing in a silt loam soil in the Upper Midwest; no soil test; the fertilizer available is ammonium nitrate and 10-10-10.

1. The required fertilizer for this soil and climate are 1½ lb of N, 1½ lb of P_2O_5, and 1½ lb of K_2O for each 1,000 square feet for the March application; and 1½ lb of N in June and August (Table 14-16).
2. From Table 14-18: 1½ lb of a fertilizer with an analysis of 10 are required for each 100 sq ft. Because this lawn (2,000 sq ft) is twenty times as large, it requires 20 × 1½ or 30 lb of 10-10-10 fertilizer.
3. The 30 pounds can be weighed out and spread on the lawn, or it can be measured. Table 14-19 shows that 1 pound of 10-10-10 fertilizer equals approximately 1 pint, so 30 pints (15 quarts or 3¾ gal) are needed.
4. In June, 0.45 × 20 = 9 lb of ammonium nitrate (analysis 33-0-0) are required, and the same amount is needed in August (Tables 14-18 and 14-19).

II. An apple tree growing in a yard at Greeley, Colorado, in a relatively light sandy soil. An abundance of manure is available from cattle-feeding operations nearby.

1. Measure a square just beyond the outer spread of branches (Table 14-16, note e). For this medium-sized tree the area is 18 × 18 = 324 sq ft. An apple tree requires about 3 lb each of N and P_2O_5/1,000 sq ft in this climate and soil (Table 14-17).
2. Manure from a feedlot has an N analysis of about 2 (Table 14-19), and about 15 lb of this analysis are required to supply N for each 100 sq ft (Table 14-18). The 325 sq ft under this tree require 3¼ × 15 = 49 lb of manure. Because a bushel of feedlot manure weighs 30 lb (Table 14-19), about 1⅔ bushels are needed.
3. The manure supplies about one-fourth of the needed P and should be supplemented with about 2¼ lb of P_2O_5 from a phosphate-containing fertilizer. There is considerable latitude in the amount of all elements except N, so the extra K supplied by manure usually does not cause a problem. If manure is used year after year for many years, potassium and some other salts can accumulate in arid soil to a point that they could be detrimental.

III. A 5 × 10 ft bed of annual flowers growing in sandy soil along the Virginia coastal plain.

1. From Table 14-16: Annuals in this soil require a complete fertilizer with 2½ lb N, 5 lb P_2O_5, and 2½ lb K/1,000 sq ft (fertilizer with 1:2:1 ratio). This suggests that a fertilizer of an analysis 5-10-5 might be used.
2. Table 14-18 shows that this application rate requires 5 lb of a fertilizer with an analysis of 5 for each 100 sq ft. The 50 sq ft garden needs half that much, or 2½ lb, to supply all three major fertilizer elements.

TABLE 14-19 • *Composition, effect on soil pH, and weight/volume equivalent of common fertilizers*

Formula	Analysis	Effect on Soil pH[a]	Pounds	Cu Ft or Bushels	Pints	Tbsp	Kg	Liters
Ammonium nitrate	33-0-0	A						
Ammonium sulfate	20-0-0	A						
Potassium chloride	0-0-55	N						
Sodium nitrate	16-0-0	B						
Ammonium phosphate sulfate	16-20-0	A	1	1/60	1	32	0.45	0.45
Mixed lower analysis	5-10-5	A	60	1	60		27	27
fertilizers, including	10-10-10	A	2.2	1/27	2.2		1	1
	10-6-4	A						
Mixed higher analysis	19-9-0	A						
fertilizers, including	27-12-0	A						
Treble superphosphate	0-48-0	N						
Potassium sulfate	0-0-50	N						
Ground limestone	(Ca)	B						
Ground dolomitic limestone	(Ca & Mg)	B						
			1	1/70	0.8	27	0.45	0.4
Superphosphate	0-18-0	N	1.2	1/60	1	32	0.55	0.45
Ammonium nitrate (high density)	33-0-0	A	70	1	60		32	27
Mixed fertilizers,	12-12-12	A	2.2	1/32	1.8		1	0.8
including	16-16-16	A						
	11-48-0	A						
	15-5-25	A						
	18-46-0	A						
Bonemeal (steamed)	0-20-0	N						
Urea	48-0-0	A						
Borax	(B)	N						
Digested sewage sludge[b]	2-3-0	N	1	1/45	1.3	42	0.45	
Activated sewage sludge[b]	6-3-0.5	N	3/4	1/60	1	32	0.34	0.45
Urea-form[b]	36-0-0	A	45	1	60		20	27
Dairy manure[b]	0.7-0.3-0.7	N	2.2	1/20	2.9		1	1.3
Hog manure[b]	1-0.7-0.7	N						
Poultry droppings[b]	4-3-2	N						
Poultry manure[b]	1.5-1-1	N						
Sulfur	(S)	A						
Cottonseed meal[b]	6-3-1.5	N						
Tankage (dry)[b]	8-9-1.5	N						
Fish scraps (dry)[b]	8-6-1	N	1	1/30	2	64	0.45	0.9
Cattle feedlot manure[b]	2-0.5-2	N	1/2	1/60	1	32	0.22	0.45
Horse manure[b]	0.7-0.3-0.5	N	30	1	60		13	27
Sheep manure[b]	2-1-2	N	2.2	1/14	4.4		1	2
Rabbit manure[b]	2-1-1	N						
Goat manure[b]	3-1.5-3	N						
Compact wood ashes	0-2-5	B						

[a] A = acid, B = basic, N = neutral.

[b] Slow-release fertilizers to which plants will usually not show a response for at least 14 days after application. Other fertilizers are quick- to moderate-release, and plants will respond to them in 3–14 days.

IV. A soil analysis shows your garden soil to have a pH of 5.2, to be low in organic matter and potassium, and to be slightly low in phosphorus. It recommends 1,200 lb of ground limestone, 160 lb of nitrogen, and 160 lb of potassium per acre. You want to fertilize a 6-foot wide 50-foot row of black raspberries with a pile of rabbit manure that your neighbor wants to get rid of.

1. According to Table 14-19, rabbit manure has an analysis of 2-1-1. Table 14-18 does not list 160 lb/acre, but it does show 10 lb of 2 percent fertilizer/each 100 sq ft for a rate of 80 lb/acre. For 160 lb/acre, apply double the 80 lb rate, or 20 lb for each 100 sq ft. This would be 60 lb to supply the N for the 300 sq ft of raspberries. Each bushel of rabbit manure weighs 30 lb, so you need about 2 bushels.
2. The 2 bushels of manure supply only half the potassium required. The remainder (80 lb/acre) could come from potassium chloride. According to Table 14-18, 0.4 lb of a 46 to 50 percent fertilizer would supply 100 sq ft. Because potassium chloride has an analysis of 55, you will need a little less than $3 \times 0.4 = 1.2$ lb. About 1 lb would supply the additional potassium.
3. None of the tables lists values as high as 1,200 lb/acre, the amount of limestone required; however, Table 14-18 shows that 120 lb/acre is approximately equivalent to 3 lb/1,000 sq ft. That means that 1,200 lb/acre would be equivalent to 30 lb/1,000 sq ft, or 3 lb/100 sq ft. The raspberries need about 9 lb or (from Table 14-19) $9 \times 0.8 =$ about 7 pints.
4. Because rabbit manure is organic and thus a slow-release kind of fertilizer, the total required amount could probably be applied at one time during the early spring. Applying 160 lb of N in a rapid-release form, for example, ammonium nitrate or ammonium sulfate, could be injurious; if these forms are used, a split application, 80 to 100 lb during the early spring and 60 to 80 lb 6 weeks later, would be desirable.

V. The fertilizer recommendation is 1,200 lb of 5-10-5 for your acre of garden, but you have ammonium nitrate (33-0-0), treble superphosphate (0-48-0), and potassium sulfate (0-0-50) available.

1. Multiply 1,200 by the concentration of each element (0.05 N, 0.10 P, and 0.05 K) to find that you need 60 lb of N, 120 lb of P_2O_5, and 60 lb of K_2O.
2. Table 14-18 shows that you need 180 lb of 33-0-0, 240 lb of 0-48-0, and 120 lb of 0-0-50 to supply the N, P, and K for your acre.

VI. Estimate the amount of horse manure to supply enough nitrogen to decompose 3 cu ft of dry leaf compost. According to Table 14-19, horse manure has about .7 percent, or 0.007 N. Directions in the "Composting" section of this chapter recommend ¼ (0.25) lb nitrogen for each cu ft, which would be 0.75 for 3 cu ft. Manure needed would be 0.75/0.007 or 750/7, or a little over 100 lb!

IRRIGATING GARDEN CROPS

◆ ◆ ◆

Irrigating Vegetables, Flowers, and Strawberries

If the soil is dry at seeding time, it is better to irrigate before annual crops are seeded and then, if possible, not to water them again until after seedlings have emerged. If rain does not fall, annual garden plants should be frequently and lightly watered while they are becoming established in the early spring. Because small plants use and transpire less moisture than do large ones, irrigation can be reduced as soon as plants have become well established but should be increased gradually as plants grow larger and the season becomes warmer and drier. Most garden soils hold 1 to 2 inches (2½–5 cm) of available moisture in their upper 2 feet (60 cm) (see Table 6-1), and despite the variation in water requirements from crop to crop, most garden plants during the warmer part of the season use, on the average, 1 inch of water per week (up to 1½ inches [4 cm] in some desert areas). Thus an average irrigation recommendation for annual crops is 1 inch per rainless week. There are some exceptions. Celery and onions, for example, need frequent lighter irrigation. In its native environment, celery is a swamp plant with a very small root system. The root system of onions also is restricted. The plants of both crops can quickly deplete the small amount of moisture available in their limited root zones. Although onions should be watered frequently early in the season, their moisture must be limited later, or the bulbs will not mature properly.

Deep-rooted crops, such as melons, cucumbers, tomatoes, and hollyhocks, are quite drought tolerant and even in semiarid climates can often be grown with very little added water. Sweet corn tolerates drought until the period just before it starts to silk. At that time it must have moisture, or it will not produce a crop.

The frequency of irrigation of herbaceous crops is somewhat dependent on the type of soil and the amount of moisture it can hold. Light, sandy soils may need their inch each five to seven days, whereas heavy soils and those high in organic matter may be better supplied with 1½ to 2 inches every ten to fourteen days.

The amount and frequency of water for these crops should be reduced as the weather becomes cooler and the crop matures.

Perennial flowers, vegetables, and strawberries need a good supply of water until after they have bloomed or the crop is harvested. After bloom or harvest they can be irrigated less frequently but they still require enough water to keep them producing vegetative growth and manufacturing carbohydrates for the following season's crop. Some, like rhubarb, peonies, and bearded iris, become semidormant during late summer. Extreme care is required in watering dormant plants during hot weather. Because dormant plants do not transpire, they remove very little water from the soil. Under these conditions heavy irrigation can result in prolonged soil saturation, reducing the oxygen supply essential to root and crown respiration and resulting in severe injury or death of the root system.

Irrigating Woody Plants

Trees and shrubs require an average of about an inch of water each week during the growing season. It is important that their entire rooting area be moistened, so irrigations should be heavier and less frequent than for herbaceous crops, as much as 3 or 4 inches (8 to 10 cm) and as infrequent as each three to four weeks for large trees in soil with good moisture retention.

Peaches are somewhat more drought tolerant than are other tree fruits, so peaches, apricots, plums, and cherries are grafted onto peach rootstock when drought-resistant fruit trees are needed. Orchard or forest management also determines the amount of water required. A tree grown with clean cultivation needs less water than does one grown with grass or another cover crop, because enough water must be applied to the latter to supply the tree as well as the cover crop. Fruit trees require more water when their fruit is expanding rapidly.

The most common mistake in irrigating home plantings of shrubs, including shrubby small fruits, is applying too little water too often. A thorough irrigation every two weeks supplies the moisture required by most flowering shrubs, although roses and berries may need water each week while they are flowering or fruiting.

In most situations woody plants can be either surface or sprinkler irrigated unless height and foliage interfere with the sprinkler pattern. Roses, however, are subject to leaf diseases and generally should not be sprinkled. Juniper and arborvitae are subject to damage by mites, which are partially controlled by sprinkling. In dry locations and along unpaved roadways sprinkling may be necessary to remove dust that not only detracts from appearance but also impedes photosynthesis and growth.

Irrigation of woody plants growing in areas where they could be winter damaged needs to be carefully controlled as winter approaches. The soil in which the plants are growing should be permitted to become relatively dry in September and early October in order to allow the plants to enter their rest period. After the plants become dormant but before the soil freezes soil moisture should be brought to field capacity, by either autumn rains or irrigation.

Irrigating Potted Plants

Houseplants should not be watered too frequently and should receive a good soaking when they are watered. They may need to be watered more often during winter than during summer, because the atmosphere of a heated home is often very dry. Those growing in porous containers require more frequent irrigation than do those growing in nonporous containers, and different kinds of plants require different amounts of water. Thus the temptation to water all plants at once with equal amounts should be avoided. Each plant should be watered according to its individual needs, which can be determined by feeling the soil in each container with a finger two or three times each week. Water should not be added to any container in which the soil feels moist. It is essential that the soil below peat moss or other mulch be tested, as materials used to mulch the surface of houseplant containers can remain dry even when floating on water.

Cacti and some succulents should not be watered until after they have been dry for seven to ten days, but most other plants should be watered well as soon as the soil in their containers feels dry. Because most houseplants are tropical, lukewarm water should be used. Generally the water is poured into the container from the top, but it can also be added from the bottom, a practice advisable for plants such as African violets and gloxinias that develop dead spots wherever cold water touches their leaves. The containers of plants to be watered from the bottom are usually kept in a flat pan or dish into which the water is poured as the plant requires it. Sometimes a cloth or fiber wick is used to conduct water from the drainhole up into the soil medium, but this is usually not necessary, as water is conducted through most potting media almost as well as along a wick. Newly potted plants should be carefully watched the first few days to make certain that no obstruction is preventing water from being conducted up through the pot.

Bottom watering is also desirable for ferns, because the pan of water supplies needed humidity as well as irrigation. During the winter when humidity is low, spraying foliage each week benefits ferns and other humidity-loving plants.

Irrigating Lawns

A lawn will use more water per unit area than does any other part of the garden if it is to be kept growing vigorously. Most well-established grass lawns will, however, survive prolonged dry periods if irrigation is impossible.

An area in which a new lawn is seeded must be kept wet until the seedlings have germinated and become firmly rooted. This may require two or three irrigations every day if the weather is warm and dry. The frequency of irrigation can be gradually reduced as the seedling roots penetrate the soil.

Established lawns should be irrigated thoroughly and no oftener than necessary. **Pan evaporation** is sometimes used to determine the frequency of lawn irrigation and the amount of water needed. This procedure involves placing a pan under the sprinkler at the time of lawn irrigation. When the pan has approximately ¾ inch of water in it, dig along one edge of the lawn to see how far down the water has soaked. Most soils require from about ¾ to 1¼ inches (2 to 4 cm) of moisture to bring the top foot (30 cm) of soil to field capacity (Table 6-1), and as grass roots do not extend much below a foot, there is no need to soak the soil below this depth. If the top foot of soil is wet, stop irrigating; if not, continue until that depth is reached. Leave the pan containing the amount of water required to soak 1 foot in the yard; when the water has nearly all evaporated, it is time to irrigate again. For example, if you live in an area where 1 inch of water evaporates from a pan each week, and it takes 1 inch to soak the soil to 1 foot, the recommended irrigation for your lawn during the warmer part of the season would be 1 inch of water each week. After observing the amount that evaporates each week for a few weeks, you can usually judge when and how much to water.

PRUNING AND TRAINING

◆ ◆ ◆

Pruning Tools

Strong, well-sharpened tools are essential to good pruning. Purchasing cheap, poorly constructed pruning tools not only wastes money but, more important, may waste considerable time and be harmful to plants. A home gardener needs three basic tools: a pair of loppers, a pair of one-hand pruning shears, and a pruning saw. Many kinds of pruning saws are available. Some gardeners attempt to use a carpenter's handsaw or a bowsaw, but most handsaws are not designed with either the type of teeth or the set (the pattern of outward bending of the teeth that aids in the removal of sawdust and determines the width of the cut) to cut green, wet wood. A bowsaw is difficult to manipulate among branches and to guide through a large cut. I prefer a nonfolding curved speed saw with raker teeth because it cuts rapidly and is easy to grasp.

Depending on the amount and the type of planting being trimmed, a gardener may also need a pair of hand or power hedge clippers, grass clippers, a pole saw (for reaching limbs to about 12 feet [4 m] from the ground), a pole pruner, and/or a small chain saw (Figure 14-63).

Pruning equipment will last for many years if it is properly cared for. Plant sap should be washed from the equipment and the cutting blades, and the assembly joint should be oiled lightly after the tool has been used. Dull or slightly nicked loppers and shears with a simple nut and bolt assembly can be disassembled and sharpened with a mill file or oil stone. The sharpening of all saws and of shears badly nicked or with complicated assembly mechanisms requires special tools; they should be taken to experts who have the proper equipment to repair them.

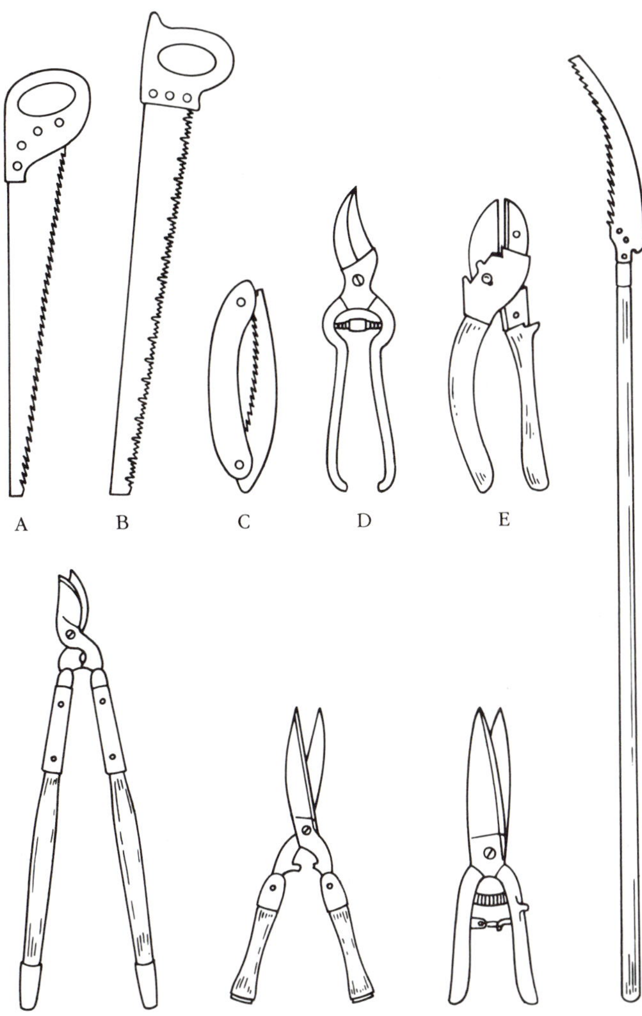

FIGURE 14-63 • Pruning tools. (A) Speed saw with lance teeth. (B) Speed saw with raker teeth. (C) Folding saw. (D) One-hand hook and blade shears. (E) One-hand anvil shears. (F) Hook-and-blade lopping shears. (G) Hedge shears. (H) Grass clippers. (I) Pole saw.

How to Make a Pruning Cut

Canes or branches originating at soil level that are to be completely removed should be cut as near the soil as possible to eliminate unsightly stubs that interfere with new growth and the future management of the planting. For thinning-out cuts of trees and branching shrubs, the wound will heal most rapidly and completely if the cut is made flush with, but leaving intact, the collar or enlarged ridge of tissue that forms at the base of branches of many kinds of trees (see Chapter 8). Although the drawings in this and other texts show trees with collars, many branches in the garden do not have a distinct ridge at their base, so the pruner has to judge where to cut. It is important not to leave a stub that is unsightly, can interfere with new growth, can be subject to injury, and can be an entrance site for decay organisms.

With smaller branches, less damaging cuts are possible if the sharp blade of the loppers or shears is placed next to the trunk away from the branch being removed. The cut should be made with the grain of the wood (Figure 14-64). Figure 14-65 shows the correct method for removing larger branches. There is some disagreement on using sealant for pruning wounds. Many texts recommend that cuts larger than 1½ inches (4 cm) be sealed with tree paint. I personally have not noticed much difference in the healing of pruning cuts on which I have used a sealant compared with those on which I have not. Ordinary paint should not be used, as it may contain additives harmful to the plant.

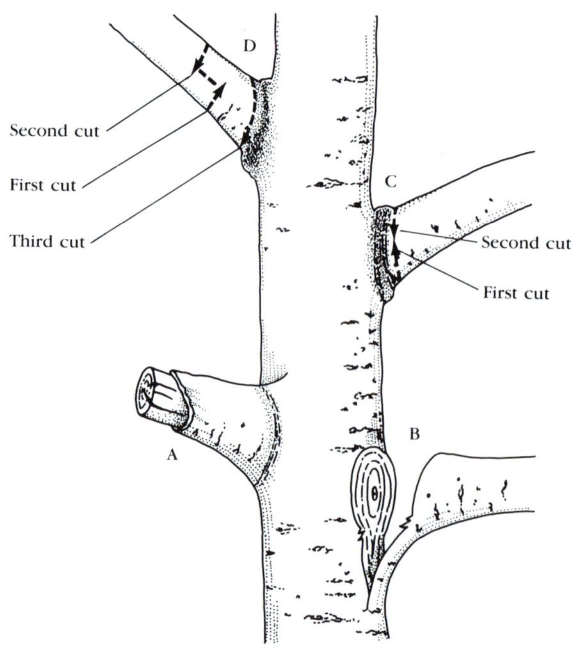

FIGURE 14-65 • Pruning larger branches. When a large limb is pruned, the main concerns are that the cut be made so that it does not leave a stub (A) that will die back and serve as an entrance point for decay organisms and that it does not tear the bark (B), leaving a larger wound than necessary. There are several correct ways of removing a large limb. I prefer (C) because it requires a minimum of cutting. If it is difficult to make the upper and lower cuts meet, three cuts can be made (D). Note that the cuts are being made just beyond the collar, not flush with the trunk.

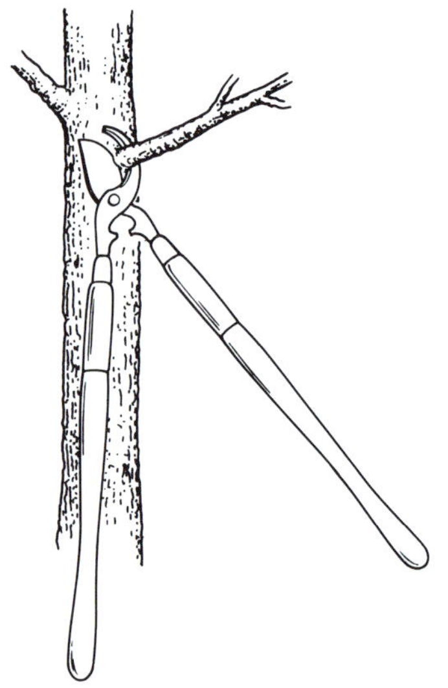

FIGURE 14-64 • Pruning a small branch. When a branch is being pruned from a larger limb or trunk, the sharp blade of the loppers or shears should be held as close to the larger limb or trunk as possible so that a stub will not remain. Even more important, the blade should be positioned so that it cuts with the grain, which usually means cutting from the lower side. This lessens splitting and the development of small cracks that permit entry of pathogenic organisms.

Training and Pruning Small Fruits

The following general principles apply to pruning small fruits:

1. Unless the number of fruit buds is reduced by pruning, small fruit plants will set more fruit than they can mature to optimal size and quality.
2. The best fruit is produced on young wood.
3. The best fruit is produced on the most vigorous branches.

Grapes. Grapevines should be pruned while dormant. If they are pruned during the growing season, plants may "bleed" or lose sap. Bleeding does not, however, cause serious damage.

Grapes should be pruned so that only enough previous-season wood to contain forty to eighty buds remains. These buds can be distributed on numerous short canes (Figure 14-66) or on a few long canes (Figure 14-67). When the grape plant is trained to cover an arbor, the new wood may be at the end of fairly long, older branches, or it may consist of a few buds on each of a number of shortened canes. In the East growers leave a minimum of forty buds on a moderately growing plant. In the West, where plants generally grow larger —perhaps because of the greater light intensity— sixty buds may be left. If the plant is vigorous, it will support ten to twenty additional buds.

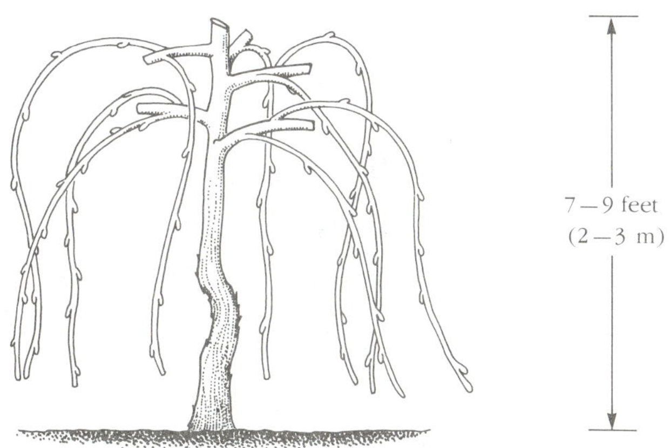

FIGURE 14-66 • Grape plant trained on a self-supporting trunk. Canes that have fruited are pruned away each spring, and canes that grew the previous year, with forty to eighty buds, are left to replace them. Clematis can be trained in the same manner.

Because it can be used with almost all cultivars in almost all areas, the four-cane Kniffen is a popular home garden system of pruning grapes (see Figure 14-67). The principles described for this system can be used as a pruning guide no matter how the grapevine is to be trained. For the Kniffen system the trellis to support the vines is two wires, one 5 to 6 feet (about 2 m) and the other 2 to 3 feet (about 1 m) from the ground, with supporting posts.

Brambles. The training and pruning of bramble fruits are based on their biennial-bearing habit. After the canes have fruited, they should be removed; this should be done promptly in areas where fungus diseases of the cane are prevalent. In areas free of disease and having heavy winter snow the old canes should remain until the following spring, as they afford a degree of protection from breaking by wind and snow.

Red raspberries send up canes from buds initiated on the roots, and these canes may be handled in a number of ways. In the **hedgerow system**, the canes are allowed to develop freely, but the row is restricted to a width of from 1½ to 3 feet (½ to 1 m). Generally, the taller canes are more productive than are the shorter ones so the tall canes should be cut back only a short distance and the short ones should be removed. If wire supports are used, longer canes may be left. The distances between canes also should be controlled. A suggested guide to cane spacing is to thin the canes in the row so that they stand from 5 to 7 inches (13 to 18 cm) apart each way, leaving only vigorous, well-matured canes. If the canes are left in hills or clumps, there should be about seven to fourteen

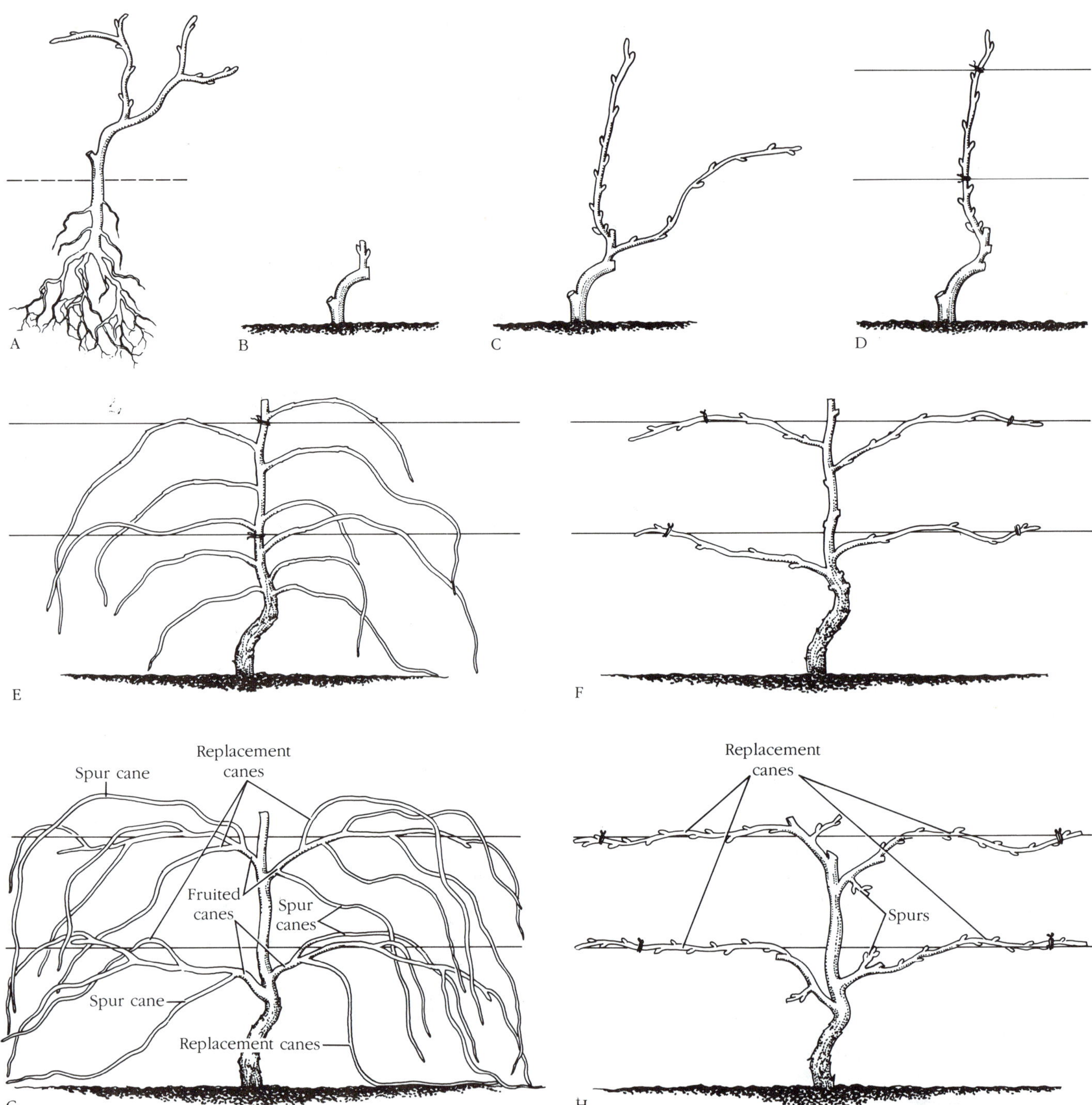
A
B
C
D
E
F
Replacement canes
Spur cane
Fruited canes
Spur canes
Spur cane
Replacement canes
G
Replacement canes
Spurs
H

FIGURE 14-67 • (*Facing page*) The four-cane Kniffen system. The newly planted grape plant (A) is cut back to two or three buds (B). At the end of the first growing season (C), one branch is selected for a permanent trunk and tied to the supporting wires (D); the other growth is pruned away. At the end of the second or third and each succeeding season (E), four canes of wood grown that season are tied to wires to produce the crop the following summer (F). After the third or fourth season, pruning grapes is a replacement operation. The canes that have fruited are replaced by four canes from the past season's growth. In addition, four to six spurs each containing one or two buds are left near the trunk to produce new canes for the following year. A mature grape plant before (G) and after (H) it is pruned.

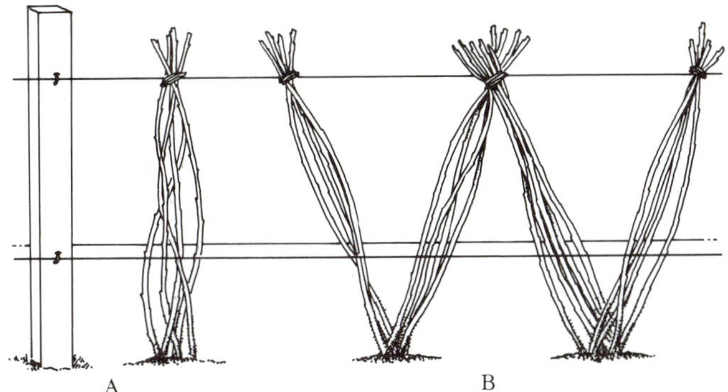

FIGURE 14-69 • A three-wire trellis for longer raspberry canes. Wires are fastened directly to posts. The single top wire is stapled to the posts, and the two bottom wires are attached on hooks or bent nails so they can be lifted and swung out over new canes to pull them in. Hills with up to six or seven canes can be brought up and tied in a single bundle (A). Split hills are possible for more canes (B), with part going halfway to the next plant in the row. (Courtesy of Washington State University)

per hill, depending on the vigor of the plant—more for a plant that produces numerous large canes (Figures 14-68 and 14-69).

Black and purple raspberries grow from a single-stem base or crown, so they always are grown as individual plants. As the new canes develop, they are pinched back to a height of 18 to 30 inches (about 45 to 75 cm) to force the development of fruiting lateral branches (these are the laterals used for layerage). In the spring before growth starts, these laterals are headed back to eight to twelve buds each (Figure 14-70).

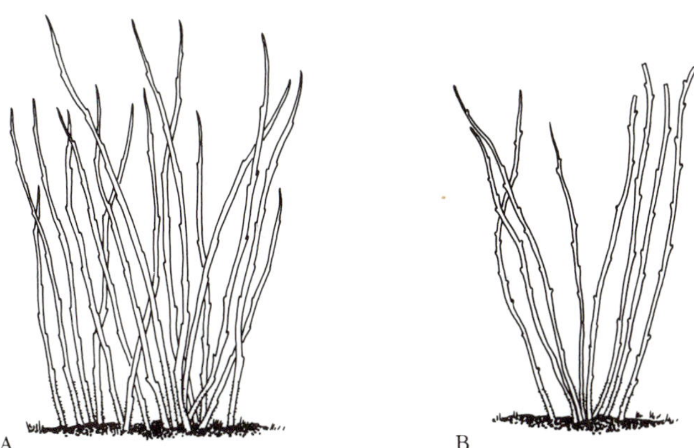

FIGURE 14-68 • Pruning bramble fruits. (A) A red raspberry plant before pruning. (B) The same plant after pruning. (After U.S. Department of Agriculture)

With blackberries, annual pruning and the frequent removal of suckers are essential to prevent a few plants from becoming an impenetrable briar patch. Upright blackberries are pruned in the same manner as black raspberries, except that the canes are headed from 30 to 48 inches (about 75 to 120 cm) from the ground, and in the spring the lateral branches are cut back to 10 to 24 inches (25 to 60 cm). Different cultivars of blackberries fruit on different sections of the lateral branches, and so the severity of heading back depends on the fruiting habit of the cultivar in question.

Trailing blackberries such as boysenberries or loganberries are lianas and must be given support. Most of their fruit is produced near the base of vigorous canes and on spurs 15 inches (40 cm) or more in length, so canes of moderate length are sufficient. Boysenberry, youngberry, and loganberry canes may be left from 9 to 15 feet (3 to 5 m) long. Training systems vary considerably. Most

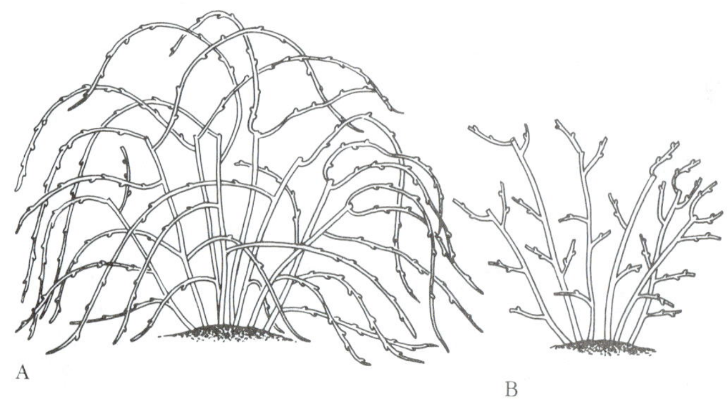

FIGURE 14-70 • A mature black raspberry plant before and after pruning. New shoots were headed during the growing season by pinching out the tips. (A) Before dormant pruning. Old fruited-out canes and some of the weaker ones have been removed. Note the length of laterals resulting from heading. (B) After pruning. Weak canes (less than ⅓ inch [¾ cm] in diameter at 1 foot above ground) were removed. Laterals were cut five to eight buds long. The stronger the cane is, the lighter the pruning will need to be. (After U.S. Department of Agriculture)

often these fruits are trained to a single-wire or two-wire trellis, a horizontal trellis, or stakes. During the summer the new canes are grown on the ground in the line of the row or on the lower wire of two-wire trellis. Later, after the old canes have fruited and have been removed, the young canes are raised to the upper wires where they are to fruit.

Training and Pruning the Home Orchard

Fruit trees may be pruned at any time during the dormant season in areas with mild winters, but should not be pruned until February or early March in areas where winter damage is possible.

Apple and Pear Trees. The modified central leader system of training (Chapter 8) is the most satisfactory for both dwarf and standard apple and pear trees.

First year. When a tree is planted, it will ordinarily have been growing for one season after having been grafted. It is usually unbranched and is referred to as a *whip*. The whip is headed back to about 30 inches and little more is necessary the first year (Figure 14-71).

Second and third years. Three or four well-spaced scaffold branches are selected during the second and third years. If possible, the lowest scaffold should be about 18 inches from the ground. In northern areas where winter sun is intense and winds are from the southwest, it is best to have the lowest scaffold on the southwest side of the tree. This helps reduce winter damage, which frequently results from dehydration of the southwest side of the trunk. The other laterals should be spaced 6 to 10 inches (15 to 25 cm) vertical distance apart and should also be evenly spaced around the tree on all sides. The central leader is usually allowed to grow during these years because its growth causes the laterals to produce wider, stronger crotch angles (Figure 14-72). The extra laterals are stubbed back rather than being cut off completely. They produce leaves for food manufacture and afford some competition, which seems to aid in developing wider crotch angles and a stronger framework.

Fourth through seventh years. During the fourth through seventh years the tree should be pruned as little as possible, because pruning delays production. The central leader can be headed back somewhat; with standard and semidwarf trees it may be entirely removed during the sixth or seventh year. It is usually not necessary to remove the central leader of fully dwarf trees. The brushy interior caused by the growth of the stubbed laterals must be kept in bounds, and this extra wood should be removed during the fifth to seventh years.

Fruiting period. With apples and pears only light pruning is necessary during the fruiting period. Weak, unfruitful, and dead branches are removed, and some heading back of wood that tends to become too high may be necessary. As the trees reach twenty-five to thirty years of age, somewhat heavier pruning to stimulate more vigorous shoot growth may be desirable.

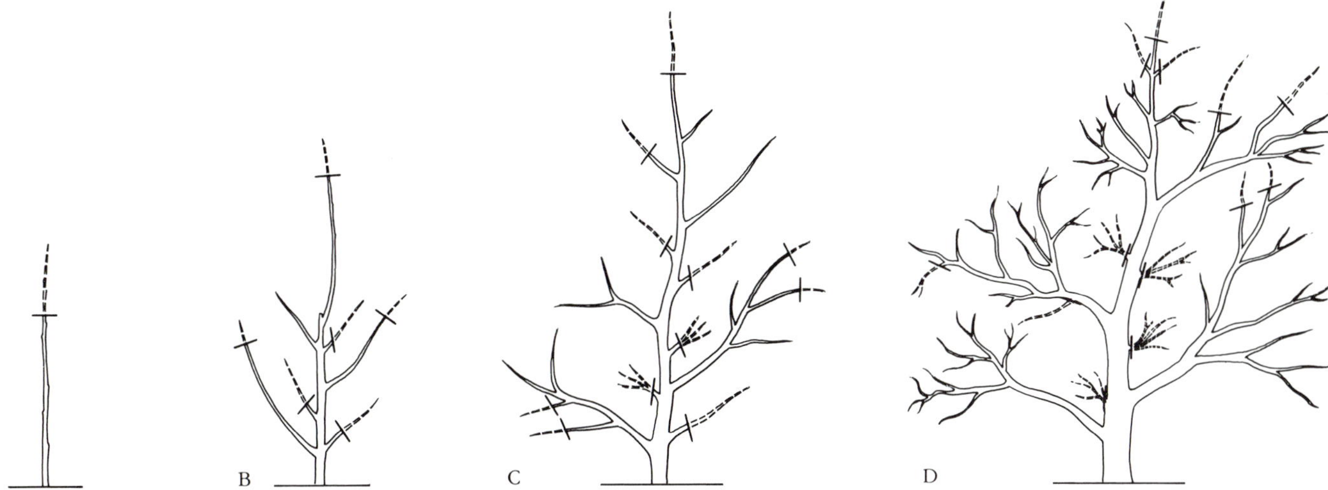

FIGURE 14-71 • Training pome fruits. To train trees to a modified central leader, cut the newly planted whip (A) back to about 30 inches (75 cm). During the first two years, three or four main scaffold branches are selected. Other branches from the main trunk are cut back but not entirely removed, and the central leader and other secondary branches on the scaffolds tending to grow out of bounds are headed back slightly (B and C). The central leader and extra side branches are removed after the fruit load starts to spread the tree, in four to seven years (D).

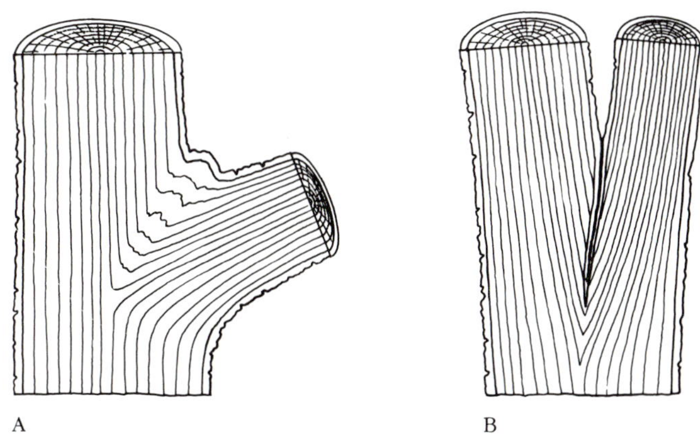

FIGURE 14-72 • Crotch angles. A wide crotch angle (A) strengthens the framework of a tree. A narrow crotch angle (B) is weak and often splits as the branches become larger and heavier or when they are loaded with fruit.

Apples, pears, citrus, and many shrubs can be trained flat against a wall or on wires (similar to the Kniffen system of training grapes). The two-dimensional plant produced by this system is called an espalier. The advantage of the espalier for homeowners is a saving of space and the assurance that sunlight reaches all parts of the plant. The most popular form of espalier for fruit trees is a vertical stem with horizontal branches (Figure 14-73), although the branches can be angled, curved into a crescent, turned upward halfway to the tip to form an L, or trained to other forms or combinations of forms.

The pillar system of training common in commercial European orchards also has possibilities around a home where space is limited. Dwarf or semidwarf trees are permitted to grow with their central leader intact. Stiff upright side branches are removed as they begin to develop, which encour-

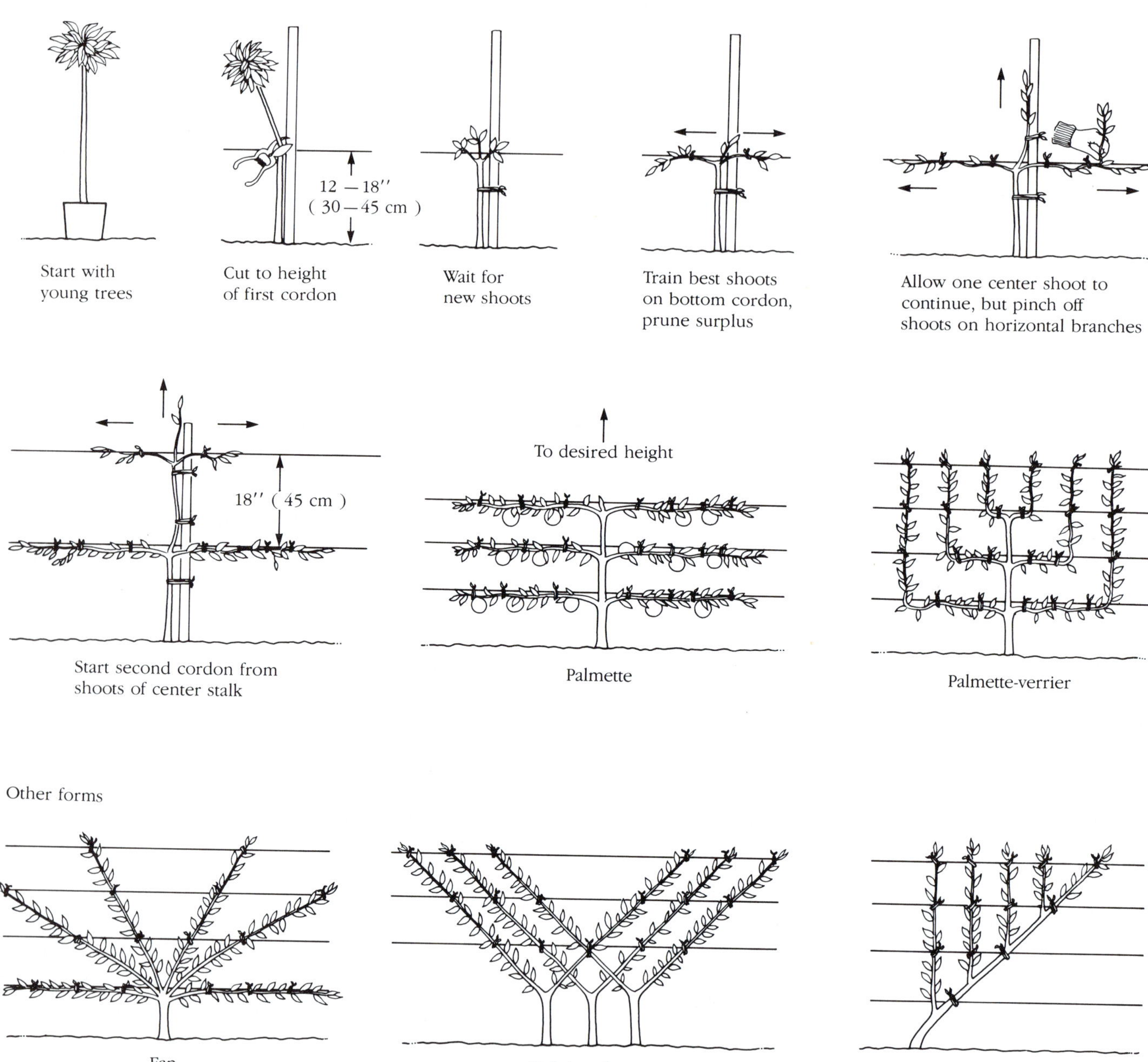

12 — 18″
(30 — 45 cm)
Start with young trees
Cut to height of first cordon
Wait for new shoots
Train best shoots on bottom cordon, prune surplus
Allow one center shoot to continue, but pinch off shoots on horizontal branches
18″ (45 cm)
Start second cordon from shoots of center stalk
To desired height
Palmette
Palmette-verrier
Other forms
Fan
Belgium fence
Oblique

FIGURE 14-73 • The creation of an espalier. (From Jules Janick, *Horticultural Science*, 4th ed., W. H. Freeman and Company, New York, copyright © 1985)

ages the growth of more horizontal willowy laterals. Bearing trees are pruned in the late winter or early spring. All laterals that have produced fruit are completely removed or cut back to a single bud. Buds originating on branches near the trunk or on the trunk are left to produce wood for future crops. Excess bushy growth from the trunk and the past season's growth on laterals beyond the fruiting spurs are also removed (Figure 14-74). With this system, trees can be planted 5 feet apart and still have adequate light for quality fruit.

Stone Fruits. Peach trees grow rapidly and normally are branched when they come from the nursery. Often it is possible to cut back the top when the peach tree is first planted, leaving only the three or four laterals that will become the scaffolds as the tree begins to grow. Ideally the scaffolds should originate about 20 to 24 inches (50 to 60 cm) above the ground. Stubbing back but not entirely removing the central leader helps

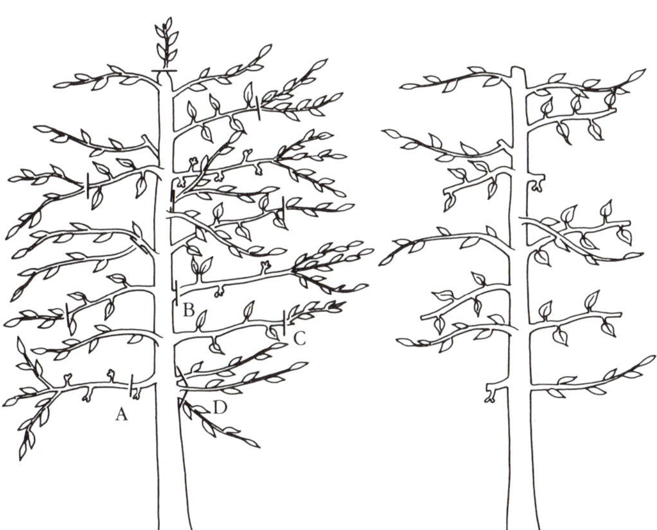

FIGURE 14-74 • Diagrammatic sketch of a pillar-trained tree before (left) and after (right) pruning. Laterals that have fruited are stubbed back to a single bud (A) or are entirely removed (B). The past season's growth on laterals beyond fruiting spurs (C) and excess brushy growth from the trunk (D) are removed.

spread the scaffolds. Little pruning is necessary during the next two or three years. At the end of the third year the central leader is removed to give an open tree for ease of spraying and to allow sunlight to reach the fruit (Figure 14-75).

After the third year when the tree begins to bear, pruning must be moderately heavy to keep the new fruiting wood near the central axis of the tree and to stimulate new wood production. Because the peach tree tends to produce many more fruits than it can support, pruning becomes a way of thinning the crop. Enough wood is removed to eliminate at least 50 percent of the bloom. Moderately vigorous branches with a high proportion of buds in groups of three produce the best fruit, so pruning should remove both the weak, slow-growing and the extremely vigorous shoots.

Because the fruiting habits and rates of growth of plums, sour cherries, and apricots are intermediate between those of apple and peach, their training and pruning are also intermediate. They are usually trained to the modified central leader system as described for apples and pears. Mature trees should be pruned somewhat more heavily than are apples or pears but somewhat less so than are peaches. If it is necessary because of space limitations, the stone fruits can be pruned heavily, as they do not tend toward alternate bearing.

Sweet cherry trees grow slowly, and pruning practices are similar to those described for apple.

Citrus Trees. With the exception of lemons, citrus trees do not require much pruning. They produce fruit buds at the terminals of the current-season wood, and most kinds grow slowly. Pruning at any time of year is possible. At planting time young trees should be headed back to about 3 feet (1 m). During the first two years, four to six strong laterals are selected for scaffolds, and the remaining branches are pinched back somewhat but not removed. The lower branches and surplus twiggy interior growth are removed gradually during the third and fourth years to obtain a clean trunk to the desired height. The gardener should attempt to develop a tree with a strong framework

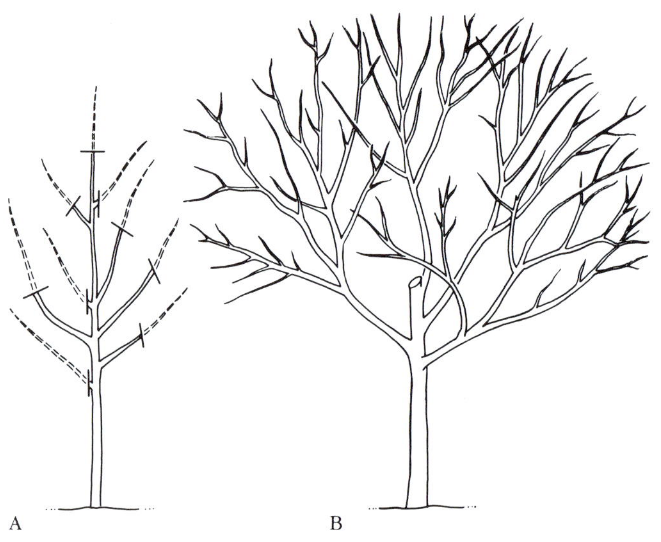

FIGURE 14-75 • Training stone fruits. To be trained to an open center, a peach tree should be cut back to three or four selected scaffolds at the time of planting (if it has enough branches then) or at the end of the first growing season (A). Only minimal further pruning will be required until the tree begins to bear fruit two growing seasons later. The central leader should be headed back each spring and entirely removed after two years (B). Even with proper training, peach trees may need to be propped or braced to prevent their being broken down by a heavy load of fruit (C).

of upright branches because the weight of foliage and fruit will bend the branches downward. Shade is not so detrimental to citrus as to stone and pome fruits, so gardeners usually cut back branches that start to grow out of bounds in order to develop a pleasingly compact tree that is ornamental as well as fruit producing. If the terminals of unwanted growth are pinched back several times a year, almost no actual pruning will be required.

The lemon tree has a more vigorous and unpredictable growth habit. It should be headed back to 36 inches (90 cm) at planting time, and the three to four laterals selected for scaffolds should be headed quite severely. Several more scaffolds should be selected high up the trunk from second-year growth. If there are gaps in the tree, new scaffolds can be formed later by gradually arching one or more upright suckers toward the ground. If the sucker is of the right age, it will stay in the arched position; if it is too old, it may require tying. There usually is considerable sucker growth each year on lemon trees, and this should be removed along with the ends of long pendulous branches that often grow beyond the remainder of the tree.

Citrus can also be trained as espaliers (see Figure 14-73), and sour oranges are often clipped to form a hedge.

Training and Pruning Woody Ornamentals

When to Prune. Ornamentals can be lightly pruned whenever they require cutting back; however, there is often a season when a plant is physiologically and structurally best conditioned for major pruning, and this season varies depending on the type of ornamental. General guidelines for some woody ornamentals follow:

1. Spring-flowering shrubs: right after they bloom.
2. Pines: spring, when the new growth is succulent (at the "candle" stage) and can be broken off easily.
3. Rhododendrons and azaleas: midspring, as the blooms fade and while the new growth is succulent enough to be pinched back.
4. Formal hedges: whenever they begin to look ragged or to grow out of bounds, several times a growing season.
5. Birches, walnuts, maples: late fall or winter. They will "bleed" profusely if pruned in the spring.
6. Most other trees, lianas, and shrubs: late winter and very early spring.

Deciduous Trees. If the homeowner has been careful to select trees to fit the location, there will be little need to prune shade trees. Some trees such as American elms or Norway maples have no definite leaders like those found in conifers, birches, most oaks, and poplars; however, a tree's natural growth habit usually produces its most desirable form and is certainly easiest to maintain. Except for removing crossing and dead or broken branches, cutting back side branches that occasionally tend to outgrow the central leader, and eliminating balanced crotches, young shade trees need very little pruning. Balanced crotches, formed when two branches of the same size form a crotch, are always narrow and weak (see Figures 8-10 and 14-72) and usually split when the tree becomes older. A balanced crotch is especially undesirable when it produces two central leaders of equal size. When shade trees have reached a height of 15 to 19 feet (5 to 6 m), lower branches should be removed to give a basal clearance of 7 to 10 feet (2 to 3 m).

Drastic pruning to rejuvenate or reduce the size of an older tree should be gradual, with a few large limbs and some smaller ones removed or headed back each year over a period of three to six years until the desired size and shape are developed. The common practice of stubbing back a mature tree to its basic scaffolds is deleterious to its health and beauty and frequently causes the decline and death of the tree.

Pruning Deciduous and Broad-leaved Evergreen Shrubs

Some shrubs are slow growing and produce most of their growth at the tips of canes or branches each year. If they have plenty of room for full development, they will need pruning or pinching back only to maintain good form and shape. These shrubs include azalea, many of the viburnums, flowering dogwood (*Cornus florida*), redbud (*Cercis canadensis*), mountain laurel (*Kalmia latifolia*), and rhododendron. Another group can be left alone to grow naturally into large shrubs or can be kept smaller by heavy pruning. These include bush arbutus (*Abelia grandiflora*), beauty bush (*Kolkwitzia amabilis*), African tamarisk (*Tamarix africana*), winged euonymus (*Euonymus alata*), English laurel (*Prunus laurocerasus*), Oregon grape (*Mahonia aquifolium*), and pyracantha (*Pyracantha* spp.)

Other shrubs send up new unbranched canes each year. These canes branch in the second and third years but do not grow from the tip. A few of these kinds of shrubs that are late blooming produce better flowers or fruits if the whole shrub is cut back to within 6 to 12 inches of the ground each spring. These include rose of sharon (*Hibiscus syriacus*), beautyberry (*Callicarpa dichotoma, C. japonica*), butterfly bush (*Buddleia* spp.), hydrangea, hills of snow (*Hydrangea arboresens* 'Grandiflora'), various kinds of summer flowering *Spiraea*, umbrella catalpa (*Catalpa bignonioides*), and the tamarisk species that bloom on current-season wood. Older unthrifty or overgrown shrubs of kinds like mock orange (*Philadelphus*), lilac (*Syringa*), many *Prunus* species, and rhododendron can also be cut back severely to rejuvenate them. Like the trees mentioned earlier, these shrubs respond better if a few old canes are removed each year over a period of 2 to 4 years rather than all at once.

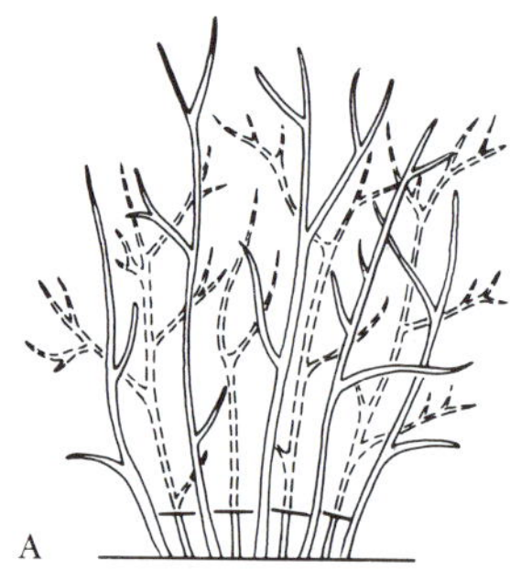

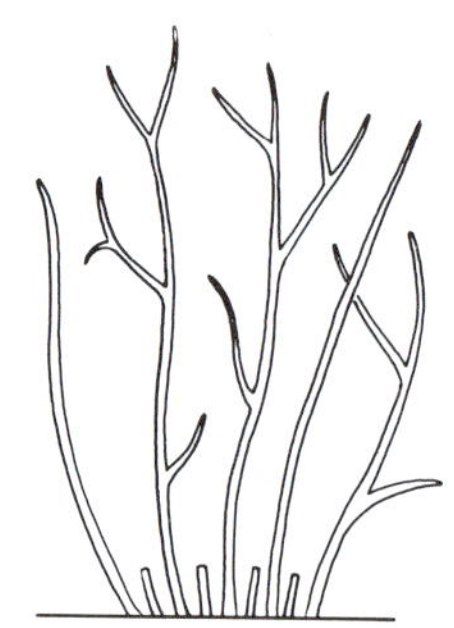

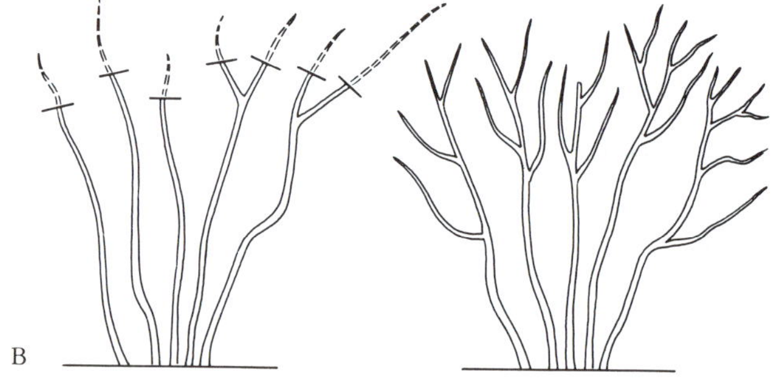

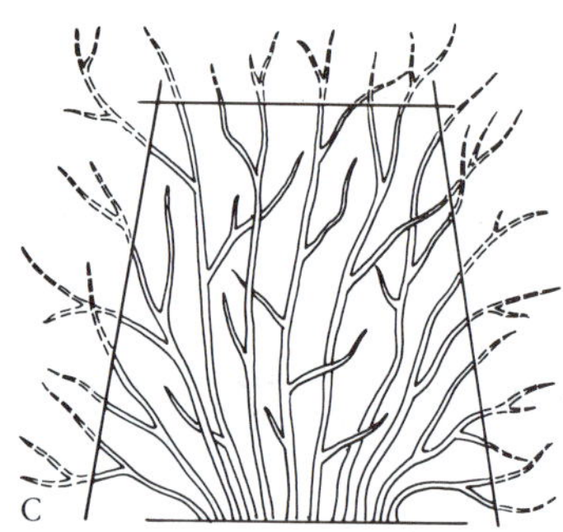

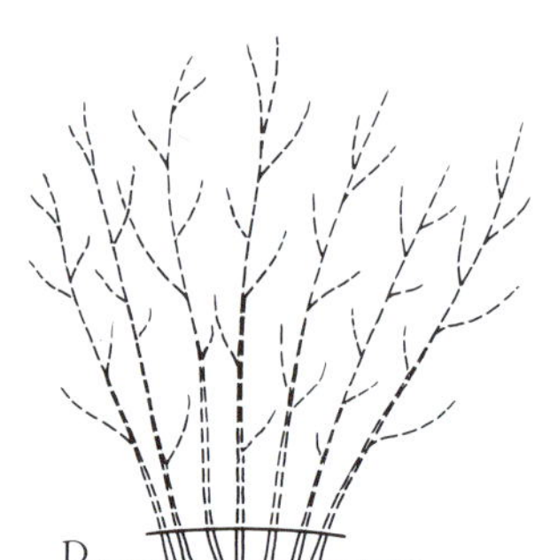

FIGURE 14-76 • Pruning shrubs. (A) Thinning, before and after. Thinning removes old, twiggy, weak, crossing, or excess branches and produces a softer texture and more desirable flowers on plants that bloom. (B) Heading, before and after a season's growth. Heading produces a more compact and symmetrically shaped shrub. (C) Shearing or clipping shapes shrubs to regular predetermined lines. It is used mainly for formal hedges. (D) Rejuvenation is used to reinvigorate shrubs. Some of the canes can be cut back each season for two or three years.

Many common flowering shrubs respond best to a moderate amount of annual pruning. Removal of 10 to 30 percent of their wood is enough to stimulate them to produce a supply of young vigorous wood. The first step is to cut out dead wood and then remove weak and dead flowers and seedpods. With most of these kinds of shrubs all branches more than three years old should be removed. Those, like forsythia, that grow rapidly and tend to become leggy may have to be pruned several times each year to keep them within their allotted confines.

Various methods of pruning shrubs are illustrated in Figure 14-76.

Hedges. Informal hedges or background plantings require no more pruning than do the same plants growing under other circumstances, but a hedge that is to be trained to a specific form must be given attention periodically. Formal hedges should be clipped one or more times per year according to their growth habit, to keep the hedge thick, neat, and under control.

The base of a hedge should be wider than the top. This permits growth to remain dense and leaf covered to the ground, because light can reach all parts of the hedge. There also will be less injury from snow to a hedge with a base wider than the top (Figure 14-77).

FIGURE 14-77 • Good shapes and a poorly shaped formal hedge (end views).

Roses. Prune rosebushes according to the type of plant and the blooms desired. Roses in the hybrid perpetual, the hybrid tea, and the grandiflora groups should be pruned toward the end of the dormant season but before the buds break in the spring. All broken, winter-damaged borer-infested, weak, and crossing canes should be removed. If the plant is to produce exhibition-quality blooms, pruning must be severe. Only two or three buds on three or four of the strongest canes should be left. If more blooms are desired for general garden growing, more buds should be left. The more vigorously growing cultivars can be cut back to five or six buds on the four to seven heaviest canes. On less vigorous plants, three to five buds per cane should be left (Figure 14-78). Wherever possible the upper bud left should face outward so that the new growth will be away from the center, keeping the plant open.

Polyantha, old-fashioned, hybrid perpetual, shrub, and miniature roses require little pruning other than removing dead wood and a few old branches each spring. Old branched canes and weak new canes should be removed from climbing and trailing roses when the plants have finished blooming in the fall or early spring. Four to six of the strongest unbranched canes should be tied to a trellis or other support. Long unwieldy branches can be cut back. Vigorous older branches will bloom, but if they are left, their lateral side shoots should be shortened to spurs of two to four buds (Figure 14-79).

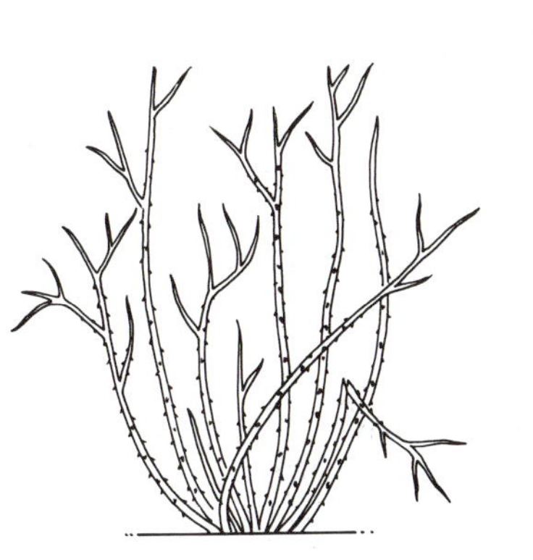

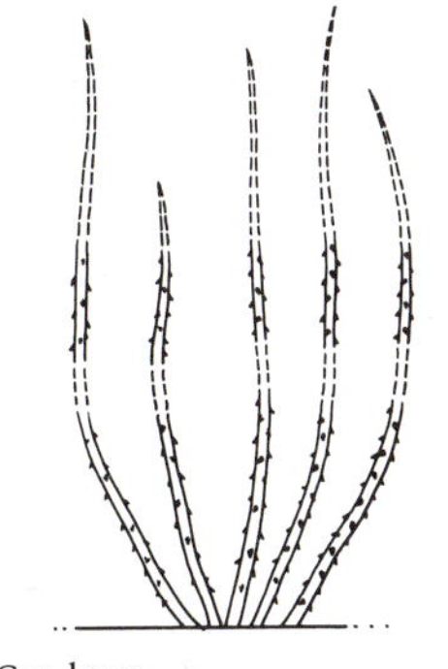
Cut high.
Leave 5 or 6 buds/stem
for many smaller blooms
Cut low.
Leave 2—3 buds/stem
for fewer large blooms

FIGURE 14-78 • Pruning hybrid tea and other similar rosebushes.

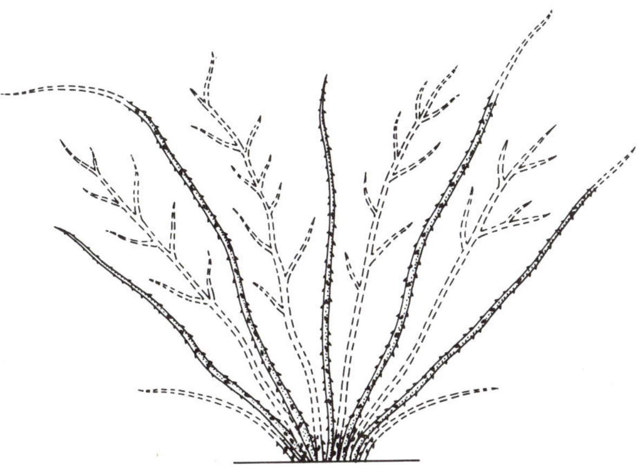

FIGURE 14-79 • Pruning climbing roses. Four to six of the youngest, strongest canes are left to produce the blooms.

Conifers. Prune conifers according to their type and use. Pines produce new growth, referred to as candles, only at the terminal end of branches and are best pruned by pinching back the candles in the spring after they have grown to about their full length but before the wood has hardened. Allowing the candles to grow to full length before they are pinched back permits the pruner to know precisely how much to remove. Pinching back most of the new growth each year keeps 'Mugho'—or other pines to be grown as shrubs—dwarf and compact for many years. Leaving about 12 inches (30 cm) of new terminal growth each year, along with some pinching of candles on the lateral branches, causes young pine trees to develop a relatively close branched, pleasing growth habit without becoming too squatty (Figure 14-80). As long as the candle of a pine is still soft when pinched, it will form new buds at its terminal. If a pine terminal is broken or cut accidentally or

A

B

FIGURE 14-80 • Pruning conifers. The growth of pine can be regulated by the amount of "candle" removed. Removing part of the candle (A) results in moderate growth. Removing the entire candle (B) results in branched compact growth.

otherwise after the wood is hardened, it usually will not produce new growth.

Because fir and spruce form buds more or less along the entire branch, these species are usually pruned by clipping back the tips of branches to give them a more compact growth habit. They can be pruned at any time of the year. Young fir and spruce usually will develop the most attractive shape if the terminal is allowed to grow no more than a foot (30 cm) per year. When a terminal of these species must be shortened, it is best to leave 2 or 3 inches (5 to 8 cm) of disbudded wood above the bud that is to grow the new terminal. This provides some protection for the new terminal from birds, which tend to perch on the highest point of a conifer and frequently break off the fragile new shoot that forms from the top bud. If the leader of pine, spruce, or fir is lost, it is wise to form a new one by using a stick to tie a branch from the terminal branch whorl into an upright position (Figure 14-81). Otherwise the tree is likely to form a number of leaders simultaneously.

Yew, arborvitae, cypress, and juniper can form new growth from any part of the plant and consequently can be pruned in almost any way the owner desires. When restricting the growth of spreading evergreens, pruners should cut the branches back so that unsightly stubs are hidden by other branches. Cutting out complete branches produces a more naturally shaped spreading evergreen than does heading back or shearing. Because they are so tolerant of various pruning practices,

FIGURE 14-81 • Renewing the leader on a conifer.

these conifers, along with various species of boxwood (*Buxus*), were used for the ornate topiary of the formal gardens of earlier years.

Vines and Lianas. Some pruning is needed to train a vine to climb or cover an object. The method of handling depends on the way the plant "climbs" or attaches itself to its support. English ivy climbs by aerial roots that penetrate small cracks. Woodbine and Boston ivy have adhesion disks; clematis and grapes have twining petioles; and bittersweet has a twining stem growth.

Most vines and lianas require little pruning. Dead or injured wood and growth that has developed where it is not wanted should be cut off. Lianas grown for their bloom, such as clematis and wisteria, require more extensive pruning. Clematis types that bloom only during summer are blooming on current-season wood. They should be pruned back to within 2 feet (60 cm) from the ground during each dormant season. Those that bloom during both spring and summer need light corrective pruning during the dormant season plus heavy pruning of spring-blooming portions immediately after they have bloomed.

Wisteria can be trained as a tree, a shrub, or a liana. During the first and second years it is trained to its desired form by staking, tying, and pinching back unwanted growth. During subsequent years, long streamers are pinched back, and unwanted growth is removed to keep it in bounds (Figure 14-82). Rampantly growing older wisteria plants that fail to bloom can often be made more reproductive by digging vertically with a sharp spade to prune the roots.

Pruning Herbaceous Plants

Most herbaceous plants do not require pruning, but a few are benefited by pinching back, disbudding, and/or staking (Figures 14-83 to 14-85).

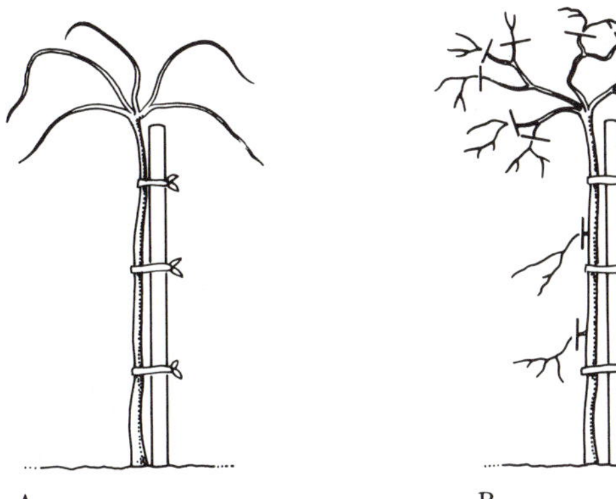

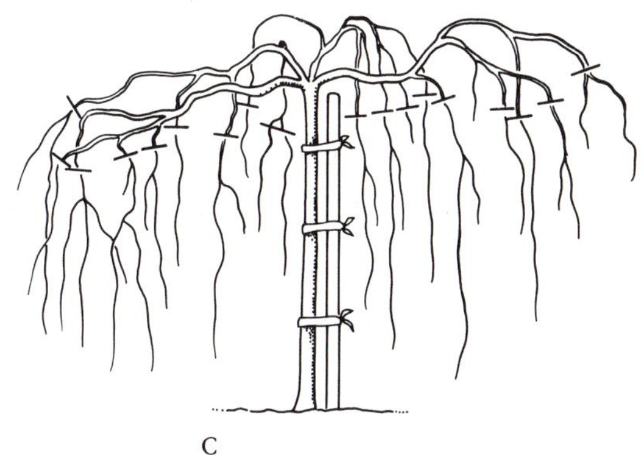

FIGURE 14-82 • Training a wisteria to tree form. The first year the plant is staked and tied, and the top is pinched back at the height it is to head (A). The second year the suckers are removed and the branches are shortened (B). The third and subsequent years the streamers are pinched or cut back to shape the head and to keep the plant in bounds.

FIGURE 14-83 • Pruning peonies. Most peony cultivars produce flower stems with a larger center bud and two small side buds (A). The main flower will be stronger if the side buds are removed (B).

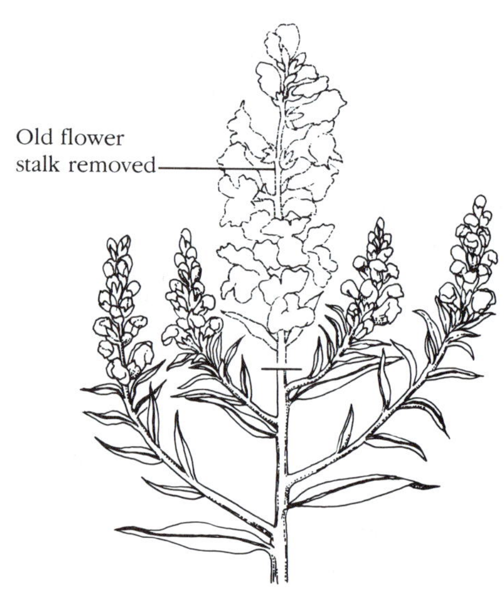

FIGURE 14-84 • Pruning faded flowers. Removing the flower stalk from snapdragons as the florets fade forces new flower shoots to elongate from the flower leaf axils and eventually flower. Removing the spent flower stalk from delphinium produces the same response. Pansies and violas will continue to bloom only if the flowers are picked before they form seed. In fact, most annual and many perennial flowering plants will bloom longer and more profusely if faded blooms are removed promptly.

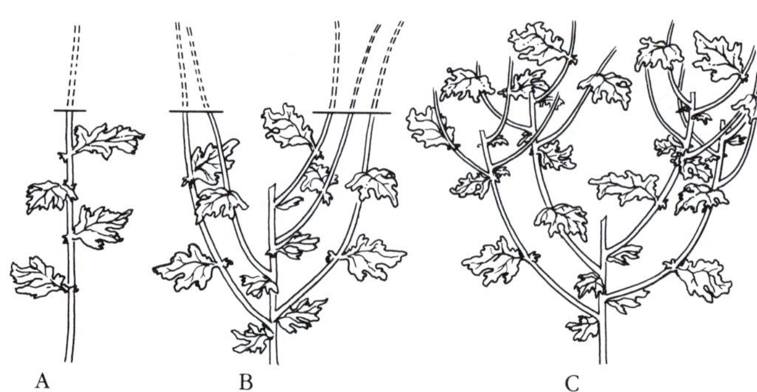

FIGURE 14-85 • Pruning for a compact growth habit. Chrysanthemum plants will produce more flowers and become more bushy and compact if their new growth is pinched back. From a few inches to about one-third of the growth should be removed in early to mid-July (A). This forces new branches from the leaf axils, which, in turn, can be pinched back in early August (B) in time for new growth, on which flower buds are initiated and blooms are produced in September and October (C). Similarly, rooted cuttings of many houseplants, including coleus, bergenia, and velvet plant, need to be pinched back for a compact growth habit.

LANDSCAPE CONSTRUCTION

◆ ◆ ◆

Landscape construction is a complex profession including such disciplines as geology, engineering, architecture, and landscape architecture. Even if most gardeners do not actually do this kind of construction themselves, the following information should provide some idea of what is involved in some common landscape construction projects.

Legal Considerations

Most incorporated municipalities have ordinances that specify minimum standards for sidewalks, curbs, gutters, and driveways. The specifications vary depending on the climate and soil of the region as well as on municipal traditions. Although these ordinances often apply only to the sidewalks and portions of drives that are along the street and used by the public, they require standards that ensure reasonable endurance of the structures in the local environment. The following is a brief summary of the essential points of a representative sidewalk standards code for a small city (the full text of the code would take six printed pages).

1. Sidewalks shall be constructed adjacent to the curb.
2. They shall be 4.5 feet wide, exclusive of curbs.
3. Side slope shall be ¼ inch to 1 foot of sidewalk width.
4. Sidewalk slab shall be not less than 3⅝ inches thick except at driveway crossing sections, where thickness shall be not less than 5.5 inches.
5. Sidewalks containing curbs and gutters shall be made of Portland cement concrete mix, not less than six bags of Portland cement per cubic yard, and shall have ultimate strength of 3,600 psi, minimum, at 28 days after mixing.
6. Expansion joints shall be not less than 20 or more than 25 feet apart.

Construction of Walks, Drives, Patios

Gravel, Cinders, Bark, and Turf. Gravel, cinders, bark, and turf are inexpensive to purchase and easy to lay. Bark or turf paths have appeal in naturalistic gardens. However, they also have disadvantages. Gravel and cinder paths and drives can become dusty in areas with a dry climate. Turf paths cannot withstand heavy traffic. Bark breaks up and must be renewed frequently. Gravel tends to get scattered into lawn areas, where it can be a hazard for rotary mowers.

Drives, walks, and patios made of these materials need considerable upkeep. Turf must be trimmed, and weeds and grass tend to come through the other materials. A layer of 4 mil perforated polyethylene or a thorough treatment with a nonselective, persistent herbicide applied before the gravel, cinders, or bark are laid helps control weeds.

Loose Bricks, Cement Blocks, Fieldstone, Cedar Rounds. When loose bricks, cement blocks, fieldstone, and cedar rounds are laid singly as stepping stones, they should be centered at about 28 to 32 inches (70 to 80 cm) apart, the distance of a normal step. They should be anchored well, with the surface about ¼ inch (⅔ cm) above the surrounding turf so that they do not teeter when walked upon and do not collect moisture when it rains.

In the South and along the Pacific Coast, where frost seldom penetrates the soil, walks and patios can be made with loose blocks laid close together in well-settled soil from which the plant cover has been removed. Herbicides and/or perforated polyethylene can be used to limit weeds. Wooden 2 × 4s or 2 × 6s treated to resist decay should be used as a border to keep bricks or smaller stones from working their way out of place. In colder locations, where freezing and thawing of soil water tends to displace individual blocks, walks and patios must be laid on a well-drained foundation or else be mortared into a unified structure (Figure 14-86).

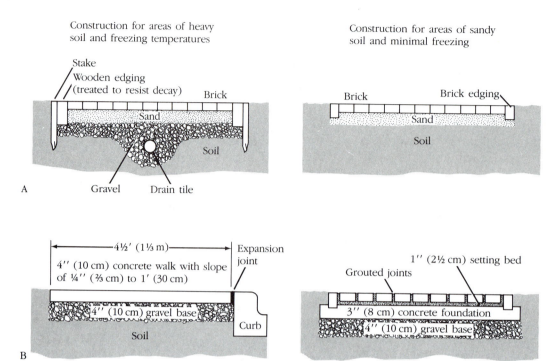

Construction for areas of heavy soil and freezing temperatures

Stake
Wooden edging (treated to resist decay)
Brick
Sand
Soil
Gravel
Drain tile

A

Construction for areas of sandy soil and minimal freezing

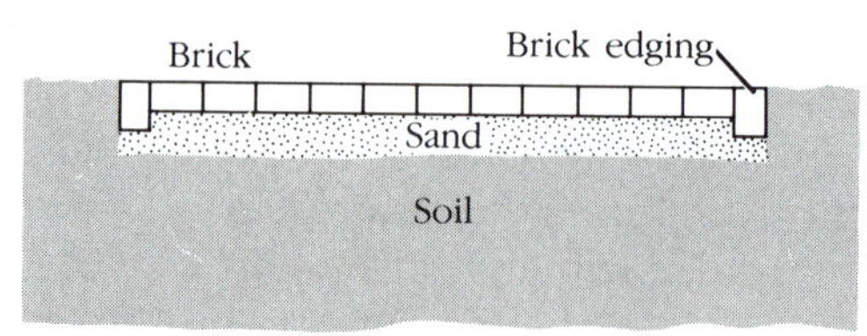

4½′ (1⅓ m)
4″ (10 cm) concrete walk with slope of ¼″ (⅔ cm) to 1′ (30 cm)
Expansion joint
4″ (10 cm) gravel base
Curb
Soil

B

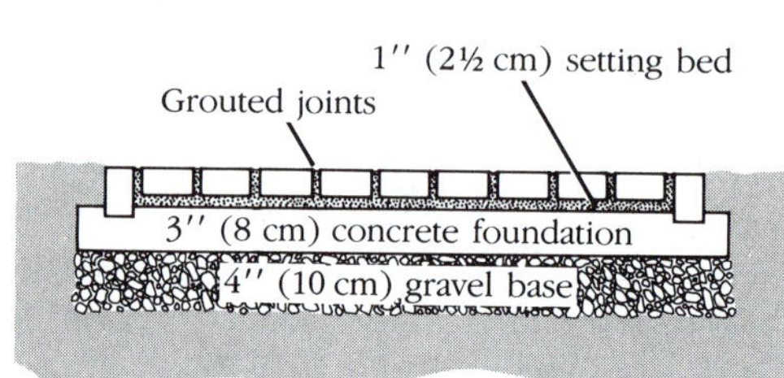

FIGURE 14-86 • Construction detail of unmortared brick walks (A) and of cement and mortared brick walks (B). The same construction principles apply to flagstone walks and patios. Even with adequate drainage, loose bricks or stones are likely to be displaced by frequent freezing and thawing so require leveling every few years (see A, left).

Concrete or Masonry. Where soil is porous and well drained, concrete or solid masonry walks, drives, and patios can be placed directly on a well-packed soil surface. If drainage is less adequate, several inches of gravel should be spread before the structure is laid.

Walks should be at least 2 feet (60 cm) wide for each person who is to walk abreast. Walks and patios should be constructed slightly higher than the surrounding area and tilted so that water drains from them. They should be at least 4 inches (10 cm) thick.

Drives should be at least 8 feet (about 2⅓ m) wide for each automobile, have a minimum thickness of 6 inches (15 cm) of concrete reinforced with steel, and be constructed so that water drains from them. Monolith drives and patios should have expansion joints every 8 to 12 feet (2⅓ to 4 m) in each direction. Expansion joints are ½- to ¾-inch (1¼ to 2 cm) spaces filled with asphalt or other material to allow the concrete to shrink and expand with changes in temperature.

Concrete walks, drives, and patios are constructed by placing forms around the excavated area they are to occupy. Metal forms can be rented, or unwarped 2 × 4 or 2 × 6 planks can be used as forms for straight segments. Thinner bendable boards or metal can be used as forms for curved sections. After the forms are adjusted to the correct position and firmly fixed in place with stakes and soil, the excavation is filled with concrete that has been mixed with correct proportions of sand, gravel, Portland cement, and water. Today concrete already mixed is usually purchased from and

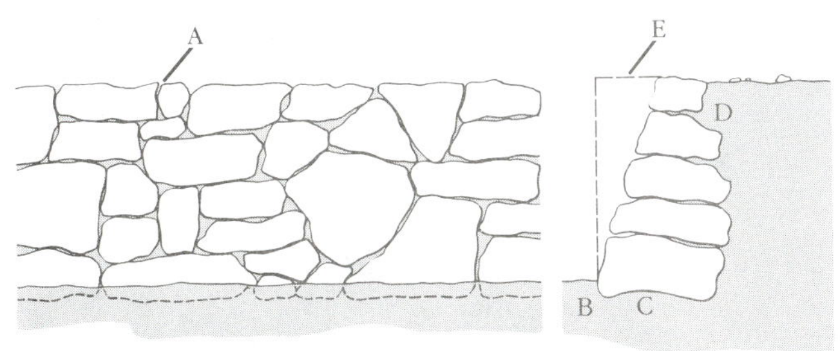

FIGURE 14-87 • Dry wall. A retaining wall made of loose stones with no mortar (dry wall) should have the stones fit together as well as possible (A), should have a solid base (B), should have the longest dimension of the stones fit back into the retained soil (C), should have soil packed solidly into the area behind and crevices between the stones (D), and should slope strongly toward the soil it is to retain (E).

delivered by a premix plant. After the concrete is poured, the slab is leveled with a plank that is pushed back and forth to force excess cement into areas not yet filled. The poured mixture should be worked with a shovel and trowel so that air pockets are eliminated and coarse aggregates are worked beneath the surface, but not to the point that the surface becomes completely smooth. A smooth surface is slippery when wet. The surface can be brushed lightly with a broom after it has begun to set but before it has hardened, to provide better traction. Concrete that is to be the base for a brick or flagstone and masonry patio walk should receive a minimum of troweling so that its surface will remain rough, thereby permitting the masonry to bond more tightly.

Newly finished concrete should be protected from rain until it has hardened. After hardening, concrete must undergo a series of chemical and physical changes, called curing, that require four to five days and are essential to durability. It must be protected from freezing temperatures and not be allowed to dry out until it is cured. During hot dry weather, concrete that is curing may need to be sprinkled as many as eight or ten times each day.

Patios and walks of brick or flagstone with mortared joints are not difficult to construct (see Figure 14-86). The area should be excavated to a depth of 10 inches (25 cm). A 4-inch layer of fine gravel is placed in the bottom, wet thoroughly, and rolled or tamped. A 3-inch (8 cm) base layer of concrete is spread over the gravel and leveled. After the concrete foundation has set for twenty-four hours, the brick or stones are laid in the desired pattern on a thin layer of mortar. When the mortar has set, the joints should be filled. If the joints are over ¼ inch wide, they can be filled carefully with a mixture of wet mortar. If joints are less than ¼ inch wide, a dry mixture of one part cement to three parts sand can be dusted onto the surface and swept into the joints. When the joints are filled and the stones or bricks have been swept clean, the surface can be watered with a fine gentle mist until the mortar in the joints has become thoroughly wet.

Construction of Retaining Walls

The construction of retaining walls made of loose stone (dry wall) is illustrated in Figure 14-87. They are subject to movement from frost and ero-

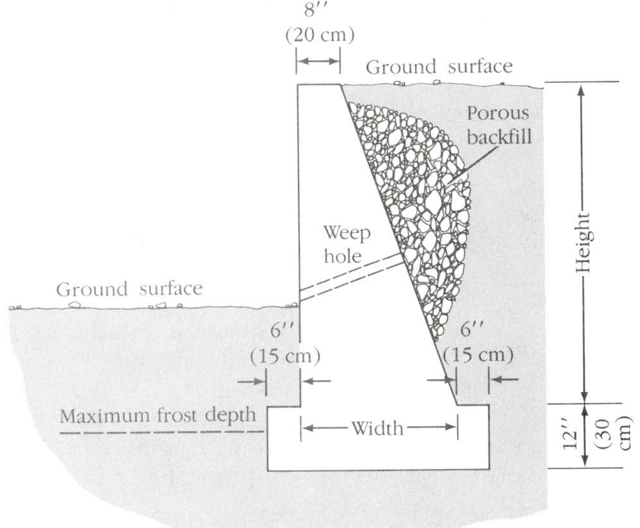

FIGURE 14-88 • Solid concrete gravity-type retaining wall. The base width should be a minimum of half the height; the top should be at least 8 inches (20 cm) wide; and the footing should extend below the maximum frost penetration for the area. Other minimum specifications are shown in the diagram.

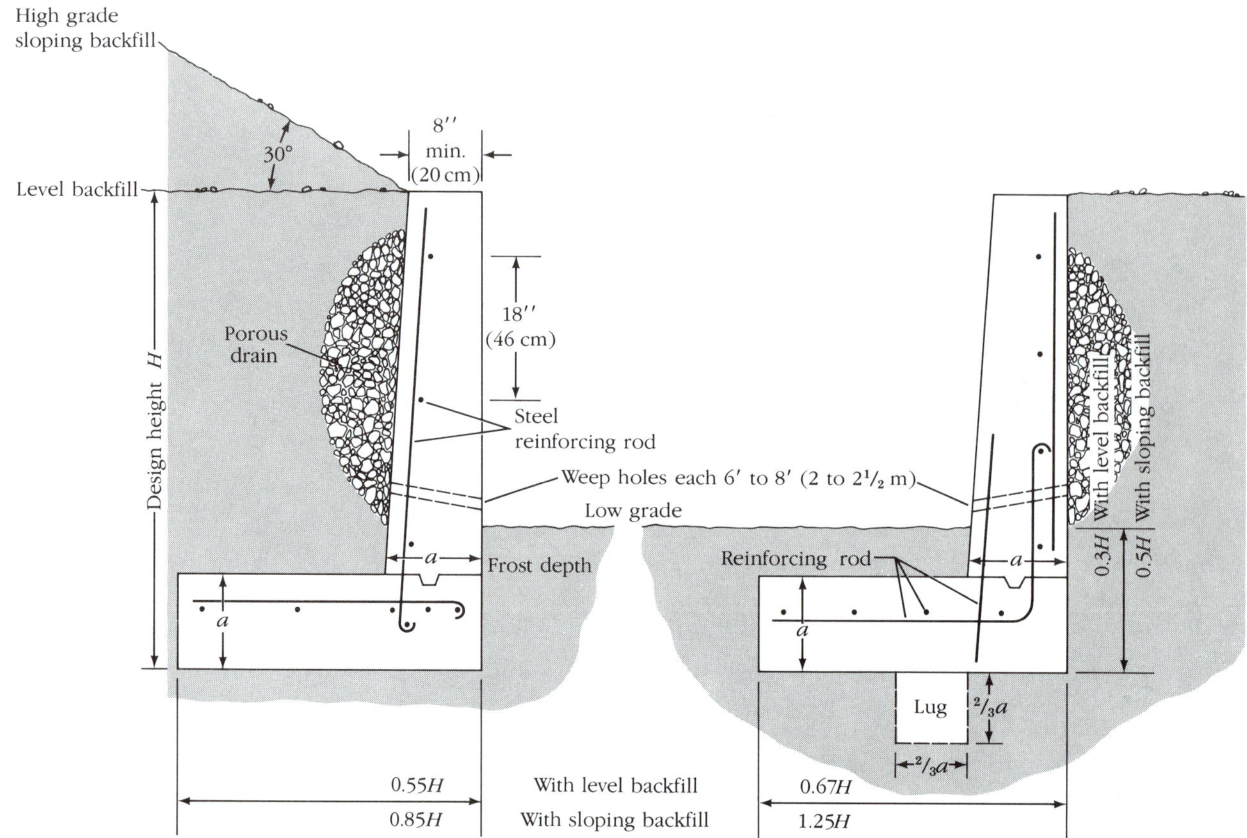

FIGURE 14-89 • L-type reinforced concrete cantilever retaining wall. Reinforcing rods should be 18 inches (46 cm) apart each way and near to, but at least 2 inches (5 cm) from, the "fill" side of the wall. The thickness of the wall base and the footing or toe, *a*, is 11 inches (28 cm) for a wall 3 feet (1 m) high. Add ½ inch (1¼ cm) to the thickness of *a* for each foot of added wall height (*H*) if the backfill is level, and 1 inch (1½ cm) for each added foot of *H* if the backfill slopes 30 degrees. A lug (lower right) helps prevent the sliding of walls built on moist clay. The specifications of a T-type wall are the same as for the L-type, with the toe extending in the direction of the backfill (left), provided that no more than one-third of the T-type footing extends toward the low-grade side of the wall. An engineer should design walls over 10 feet (3 m) high or 25 feet (8 m) long. Solid brick or stone masonry walls up to 6 feet (2 m) high can be constructed with similar specifications. They should be at least 9 inches (23 cm) wide with a masonry cap 2 inches thick. The fill side of a masonry wall should be waterproofed before the wall is backfilled, to prevent discoloration from moisture and salts.

sion and, especially in areas that have heavy or poorly drained soil, require some maintenance and repair each spring.

Solid retaining walls are of two types: the mass concrete or gravity type, which relies on the weight of the wall to prevent movement (Figure 14-88), and the cantilever type, which is prevented from sliding by the weight of the soil on a toe or footing (Figure 14-89). Figure 14-90 shows the average depth of frost penetration in the United States. (The specifications in Figures 14-88 and 14-89 come from *Architectural Graphic Standards*, 6th ed., by C. G. Ramsey and H. R. Sleeper, Wiley, New York, 1970; *Time Saver Standards for Architectural Design Data*, 5th ed., ed. J. H. Callender, McGraw-Hill, New York, 1974; and *Use of Concrete on the Farm*, Farmer's Bulletin 2203, U.S. Department of Agriculture, U.S. Government Printing Office, Washington, D.C. 1970.)

Grading Around a Tree

Woody plants already partly grown are an asset to a building lot and should be protected. Before any construction begins, the owner should establish a written agreement with construction contractors concerning the value of plant materials that are to be saved. Placing barriers around trees or shrubs during excavation helps prevent damage to the trunks. Figure 14-91 illustrates ways of protecting trees from various grading procedures.

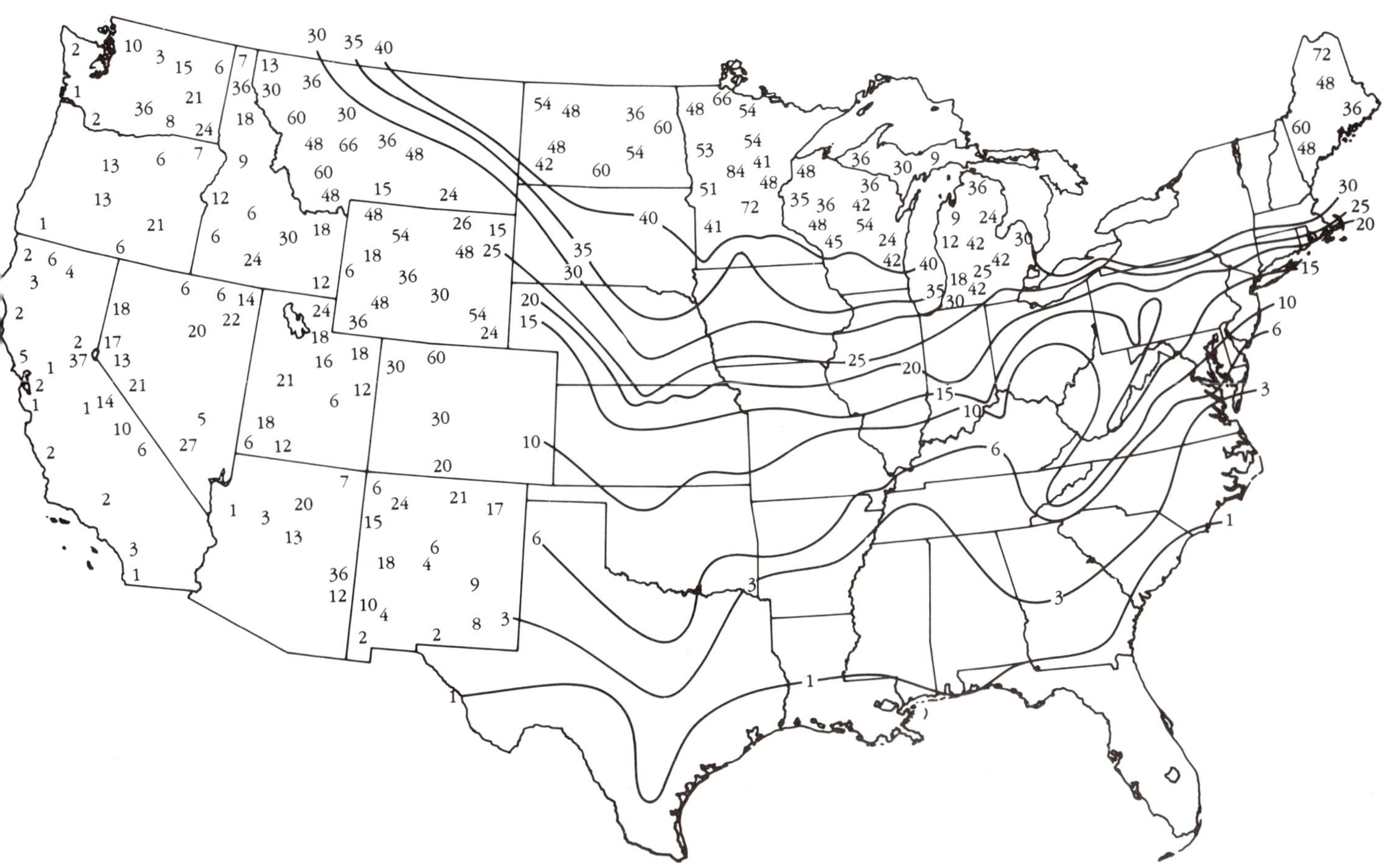

FIGURE 14-90 • Average depth of frost penetration, in inches.
(U.S. Department of Commerce)

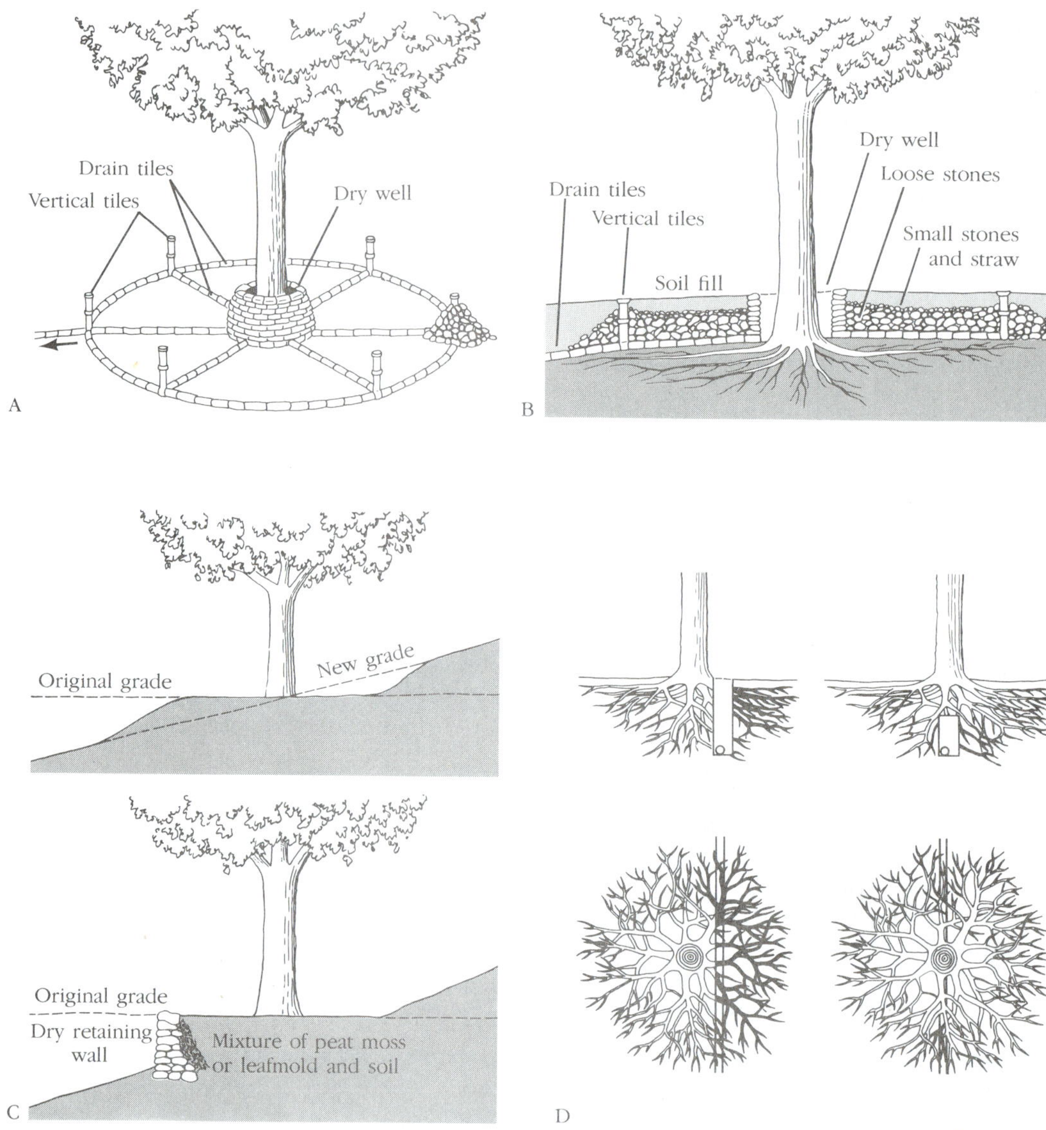

FIGURE 14-91 • Grading around a tree. When the yard is graded or trenched, special precautions are necessary to protect and provide aeration for tree roots. A tile system protects a tree from a raised grade. (A) The tile is laid out on the original grade, leading from a dry well around the tree trunk. (B) The tile system is covered with small stones to allow air to circulate over the root area. (C) A retaining wall protects a tree from a lowered grade. (D) Tunnel beneath root systems; do not trench through them. Left: These trenches will probably kill the tree. Right: Tunneling under the tree will preserve many of the important feeder roots. (From *Protecting Shade Trees During Home Construction*, USDA Home and Garden Bulletin 104. U.S. Government Printing Office, Washington, D.C. Revised periodically)

HARVESTING

◆ ◆ ◆

As mentioned in previous chapters, the quality of perishable vegetables and fruits deteriorates rapidly once they are harvested. Wherever possible, crops such as strawberries, peas, and sweet corn should be harvested when the temperature is cool, and the harvested product should be prepared for the table, processed, or placed in storage immediately. Carelessness during the harvest operation can cause serious problems. Spurs and branches broken from fruit trees and berry plants will not produce fruit in succeeding years. Throwing or dropping fruit, roots, bulbs, tubers, or even dry seed, or other careless handling greatly reduces quality and storage life. All horticultural products are easily bruised, and the damage from careless handling at harvest may not be obvious at the time the damage occurs. Even so, deterioration and disease, which get their start on bruised or damaged tissue, can in a short time spread not only through the damaged fruit or vegetable but also through other items stored in the same container or area.

Stage of Maturity and Method of Harvest

Cutting Flowers. Cut flowers for arranging should be gathered before the florets have fully expanded, to ensure the longest possible life. Roses are best cut when they are in the bud stage. Gladioli, snapdragons, and other spiked flowers should be harvested soon after the lowest florets have opened. Mums, zinnias, marigolds, daisies, and other composites should be cut when the outer petals are fully colored but before the inner parts of the flower have matured or shed pollen.

Wilted flowers will not last, so cutting beds should be kept well watered, and flowers should be cut during late afternoon or early morning when the temperature is cool. If possible, take a bucket of lukewarm water to the garden and immerse the stems immediately after they are cut. The cut ends of flowers such as dahlias and poppies that give off a milky exudate should be seared by immersion in boiling water, by burning in a flame for a few seconds, or by immersion in very hot tap water for ten minutes. Some woody-stemmed flowers such as lilac are better able to take up water if the ends of their cut stems have been crushed with a hammer. The flowers, with their container of warm water, should be kept in a cool environment for at least three hours and preferably overnight.

All containers, vases, frogs, and other material used for gathering and arranging flowers should be sterilized with heat or chemicals after they have held or been in contact with cut flowers. Shredded styrofoam, floral blocks, and other disposable material used to support flower arrangements should be discarded or sterilized in boiling water before being used a second time.

Harvesting Vegetables and Fruits. The timing of fruit and vegetable harvest, especially of those crops produced for their fruit or immature seed, is critical. Timing is usually less important for crops for which leaf, stem, root, or petiole is the edible portion. The times and methods of harvesting selected fruits and vegetables are summarized in Table 14-20.

STORING HORTICULTURAL PRODUCTS

◆ ◆ ◆

In most parts of the United States the season during which a horticultural product is available directly from the garden is rather short. But proper storage and/or processing can prolong the season during which the table is supplied from the garden.

Causes of Deterioration

You will recall from Chapter 2 that as long as a plant is living, respiration continues to use carbohydrates and oxygen to produce plant energy, releasing carbon dioxide, water, and heat energy as by-products. Most living products also continue to transpire and thus gradually lose moisture.

In addition to using up sugars and moisture as a result of respiration and transpiration, many plant products undergo gradual chemical changes

TABLE 14-20 • *Time and method of harvesting vegetables and fruits*

Vegetable	Stage for Harvest	Methods of Harvest
Artichoke (globe)	When bud is fully expanded but still tight.	Cut ¾ in (2 cm) below bud.
Asparagus	When spears are 6–10 in (15–25 cm) long; harvest all spears for 8–10 weeks in spring; do not harvest after June 20; do not harvest first year after transplanting.	Cut below soil surface or grasp the tip and bend; all of the spear harvested can be used with the latter method.
Rhubarb	As soon as petioles are of sufficient size; never harvest more than half the petioles from a plant at one time; do not harvest after July 1; do not harvest first year after transplanting.	Pull petiole from stalk, do not cut it off; pull and discard seed stalks.
Radish	As soon as roots have expanded to sufficient size but before seed stalks form or roots become pithy.	Pull roots; first harvest can thin plants so nearby roots can enlarge.
Spinach, chard	As soon as plants reach sufficient size; before spinach bolts. Early harvest can thin plants to provide more room for those that remain.	Cut chard above crown so regrowth can occur. Spinach can be cut above or below crown.
Lettuce	Thinnings can be used for early salad; heads of iceberg should be solid but not overmature; butterhead and cos can be harvested as soon as heads form, leaf lettuce, anytime before it bolts.	Pull or cut at ground level.
Celery	When fully grown; usually requires the full season.	Cut below crown.
Cabbage	When head is solid but before it cracks. Twisting the mature head part way around to sever half the roots permits cabbage to remain in the garden longer.	Cut below the head.
Cauliflower	Tie leaves above the head to shade it when head reaches golf ball size; cut head 4–6 days later depending on temperature but before curd starts to separate.	Cut below first whorl of wrapper leaves.
Broccoli	Cut center head before buds begin to separate; continue to cut side shoots as they form.	Cut 3 in (8 cm) below the flower buds.
Brussels sprouts	Remove lower leaves as sprouts start to enlarge. Harvest sprouts as they become solid; the lowest mature first.	Break sprouts from stalk.
Beets, carrots, turnips, rutabagas	As soon as roots are large enough to use. Early harvests can thin to provide more room for plants remaining. Small beets with tops can be used for greens; harvest for storage before they become woody.	Pull and cut off tops *above* the crown. Cutting below the crown creates an entrance wound for decay organisms.
Onions	Thinnings can be used as green onions or scallions. For storage, bulbs should be pulled when two-thirds of the tops have fallen over.	Pull and allow to cure in the field 5–10 days. Remove tops and place in containers where air can circulate.

(*continued*)

TABLE 14-20 • *(Continued)*

Vegetable	Stage for Harvest	Methods of Harvest
Potatoes	For immediate use, dig as soon as tubers are large enough to use; small tubers will have formed about two weeks after bloom. For storage dig a few days after vines have died, been frozen, or artificially killed.	Dig carefully with a spading fork or for larger quantities with a garden plow or digger.
Peas and edible-podded peas	When pods are nearly full but before pods begin to wrinkle; edible podded peas should be harvested while pods are still flat.	Pick from vine during cool part of the day.
Snap beans	When pods are 3 in (8 cm) long but before seed is much larger in diameter than a pencil lead.	Pick from vine each 3–4 days (disturbing wet vines spreads rust and other diseases).
Lima beans	When pods are fully expanded but before pods turn yellow or seeds white.	Pick from vines and shell.
Sweet corn	When liquid squeezed from a kernel with the thumb nail is milky (watery, immature; creamy or solid, overmature); when individual kernels can be felt through the husk.	Pull cob from stalk with a quick downward motion.
Sweet potatoes	Whenever "potatoes" are large enough; before soil temperature drops below 50°F (10°C).	Dig carefully; injured roots rot.
Tomatoes	After red color first shows, they ripen to high quality indoors. For fall storage, pick all green fruit that is nearly full size.	Pick from vine and remove stem if it stays with tomato.
Eggplant	After fruit reaches egg size but before it matures; quality of young fruit is better than that of older fruit.	Cut stem of fruit from plant. Leave some stem with the fruit.
Peppers	Anytime after they are large enough to use.	Break stem from plant.
Summer squash and cucumbers	As soon as fruits have reached desired size but before cucumbers turn yellow or summer squash form hard seeds or rinds.	Break fruit from vine; leave a piece of stem with the fruit.
Winter squash	When fully mature, rind is hard.	Leave stem on fruit.
Pumpkins	When they turn gold in color.	Leave stem on fruit.
Muskmelon	When a crack forms around the area where fruit attaches to stem; at this time melon will slip easily from the vine.	Pull to detach stem from fruit.
Watermelon	When vine tendril next to fruit yellows and dries; when thumping with fingers causes a dull rather than a ringing sound. If melon is to be used immediately it can be tested by applying pressure with the palm of hand; a splitting sound indicates a ripe melon, but pressure causes an inside crack.	Cut to leave some stem with the fruit. Pulling the stem from the fruit may damage the fruit.

(continued)

TABLE 14-20 • *Time and method of harvesting vegetables and fruits (Continued)*

Fruit	Stage for Harvest	Methods of Harvest
Apples—summer and fall	'Yellow Transparent' and 'Lodi' can be picked whenever they have reached size desired; with others, ground color (color between stripes or where they are not red) turns from green to light green or yellow; flesh softens somewhat.	Turn fruits back on stem so that stem but not spur remains with fruit.
Apples—winter	Ground color turns green to yellow; seeds turn brown; flesh softens slightly.	Same as above.
Pears	Picked when full size but still hard; pears are of low quality if ripened on trees. Commercially they are picked according to pressure required to push a plunger into their flesh.	Same as apple.
Sweet and sour cherries	For home use when fully ripe if birds will permit them to ripen. Dark sweet cherries should be sweet and almost black; pie cherries will be bright or dark red depending on variety.	Pick with stems on fruit unless they are to be canned or otherwise preserved immediately.
Apricots	When fully grown and orange colored but before they soften. Some varieties may require picking the same tree several times in order to harvest fruit at the right stage.	Twist carefully to prevent damage to nearby spurs or the fruit.
Peaches	When fully grown but at least 2 days before they become soft; peaches are better quality, especially for canning, if they are allowed to ripen after being picked.	Same as above.
Plums	When mature but before they begin to shrivel.	Same as above.
Gooseberries	Gooseberries full size but still firm and green in color are best for jam and pies; can be ripe or green for jelly.	Pick with stem and blossom; remove stem and blossom for jam or pie but not for jelly.
Currants	For the best jelly currants should be picked when 90% are ripe and 10% are still green. Green ones supply more pectin.	Pick entire cluster with stem; stem need not be removed for jelly. Pick all fruit from each cane before moving to the next.
Raspberries and blackberries	Pick when berries slip easily from stem.	Pick berries without stem.
Blueberries	When fully ripe.	Harvest individual berries without stem.
Strawberries	When red but still firm.	Harvest with cap and stem.
Citrus	When fully mature and sweet; citrus can be left on the tree for some time after it is mature without deteriorating. In certain weather conditions fully ripe oranges may be green in color.	Twist to avoid tree or fruit injury.
Nuts	When they drop to the ground in the fall.	Shake from the tree and gather before the squirrels do. Filberts must be separated from husks. Black walnut husks are allowed to decay for removal.

in storage. Most fruits, for example, give off ethylene, a growth-regulating substance that may have profound effects on other products stored nearby. Stored carrots turn bitter, and potatoes may fail to sprout and may undergo other changes if there is ethylene in the atmosphere where they are stored. Fruits are likely to absorb an earthy flavor if they remain very long in close contact with root crops.

Another major cause of fruit and vegetable deterioration in storage is decay or spoilage due to the action of microorganisms. A horticultural product usually is quite resistant to microorganism attack unless the product has been damaged by rough handling or is beginning to deteriorate as a result of age or improper or too-lengthy storage. Spoilage microorganisms generally enter through wounds or through dead or dying cells.

The length of time a plant product can be stored depends partly on the nature of the product. The relation of low respiration rate to ability to store was mentioned in earlier chapters. Physical structure and chemical composition are related to storage life and quality of the stored product. A waxy epidermis or thick periderm provides protective coverings that prevent the entry of microorganisms and retard moisture loss, enabling products like apples and potatoes to be stored for relatively long periods. Products high in acids or sugars are resistant to many kinds of microorganisms that cause spoilage.

The optimal storage temperature and humidity vary depending on the product being stored. The majority of fruits, vegetables, and flowers that originated in the temperate and subtropical zones store best at 32°F (0°C) and 90 to 100 percent relative humidity. Crops of tropical origin, such as tomatoes, bananas, eggplants, and avocados, will physically deteriorate if stored in temperatures lower than about 40°F (4°C). Optimal storage environments for a number of fruits and vegetables are given in Table 14-21.

How to Store

Short-term Storage. For those with a large garden, a used refrigerator that can be reserved entirely for fruit and vegetable storage and can be placed in some out-of-the-way corner of the basement is a wise investment. Lettuce, spinach, cauliflower, broccoli, radishes, chard, summer squash, and a host of fruits can be kept from one to three weeks in this kind of storage. One precaution—if fruits and vegetables are to be kept in the same refrigerator, be sure that one or the other is in a tightly closed container.

Winter pears and cultivars of late-fall apples, such as 'Red' and 'Golden Delicious', 'Jonagold', 'Yellow Newtown', 'Winesap', 'Idared', and 'York Imperial', can be kept during the fall almost until Christmas in an unheated garage or shed in many areas where the temperature during this period remains between 20° and 40°F (−7° and +4°C). A heavy quilt or other cover for insulation on colder nights, a thermometer to measure the temperature of the area around the fruit, and a careful watch of weather so that the stored produce can be moved inside or be otherwise protected during excessively cold periods are necessary if fruit is to be stored this way. The respiration of the fruit will provide considerable heat if the containers are insulated. Plastic box liners perforated with ten to twelve ¼-inch holes help keep apples of cultivars such as 'Golden Delicious' and 'Yellow Newtown' from shriveling in this kind of storage.

Root vegetables in light plastic bags can be stored in the same way, although in many areas they can be left in the garden during the fall. In fact, parsnips and salsify can be stored all winter where they are growing, because they are not damaged by freezing. In some areas, beets, carrots, turnips, gladioli corms, and the storage organs of other flowers normally dug in the fall and kept indoors through the winter can also be left all winter where they are growing. After the first light frost but before heavy freezes, a thick cover of straw is raked over the row of plants. Leaves can be used to cover flowers, but many kinds of leaves impart an undesirable flavor to root vegetables.

Winter Storage in a Cellar. A number of horticultural products can be stored through the winter

TABLE 14-21 • *Freezing points, recommended storage conditions, and length of storage period of vegetables and fruits*

Commodity	Freezing Point (°F)	Place to Store	Storage Conditions		Length of Storage Period
			Temperature (°F)	Humidity	
Vegetables:					
Dry beans and peas		Any cool, dry place	32° to 40°	Dry	As long as desired
Late cabbage	30.4	Pit, trench, or outdoor cellar	Near 32° as possible	Moderately moist	Through late fall and winter
Cauliflower	30.3	Storage cellar	Near 32° as possible	Moderately moist	6 to 8 weeks
Late celery	31.6	Pit or trench; roots in soil in storage cellar	Near 32° as possible	Moderately moist	Through late fall and winter
Endive	31.9	Roots in soil in storage cellar	Near 32° as possible	Moderately moist	2 to 3 months
Onions	30.6	Any cool, dry place	Near 32° as possible	Dry	Through fall and winter
Parsnips	30.4	Where they grew, or in storage cellar	Near 32° as possible	Moist	Through fall and winter
Peppers	30.7	Unheated basement or room	45° to 50°	Moderately moist	2 to 3 weeks
Potatoes	30.9	Pit or in storage cellar	35° to 40°	Moderately moist	Through fall and winter
Pumpkins and squashes	30.5	Home cellar or basement	55°	Moderately dry	Through fall and winter
Root crops (miscellaneous)		Pit or in storage cellar	Near 32° as possible	Moist	Through fall and winter
Sweet potatoes	29.7	Home cellar or basement	55° to 60°	Moderately dry	Through fall and winter
Tomatoes (mature green)	31.0	Home cellar or basement	55° to 70°	Moderately dry	4 to 6 weeks
Fruits:					
Apples	29.0	Fruit storage cellar	Near 32° as possible	Moderately moist	Through fall and winter
Grapefruit	29.8	Fruit storage cellar	Near 32° as possible	Moderately moist	4 to 6 weeks
Grapes	28.1	Fruit storage cellar	Near 32° as possible	Moderately moist	1 to 2 months
Oranges	30.5	Fruit storage cellar	Near 32° as possible	Moderately moist	4 to 6 weeks
Pears	29.2	Fruit storage cellar	Near 32° as possible	Moderately moist	See text

Adapted from *Storing Vegetables and Fruits in Basements, Cellars, Outbuildings and Pits,* USDA Home and Garden Bulletin 119. U.S. Government Printing Office, Washington, D.C. Revised periodically.

in the proper conditions. A refrigerated storage, in which temperature and humidity are automatically controlled, is ideal; however, it is not economically practical for most homeowners. A version of the old cellar storage works well in areas where winters are cold and may be practical for the homeowner who grows a large garden and has the right location. This kind of structure is most easily constructed by digging into a sloping site. The walls can be constructed of concrete, cinder block, or mortared stone and can be insulated by soil piled against their outside. If the storage is dug into a slope, the floor and sometimes the back wall are exposed soil, which can be watered down oc-

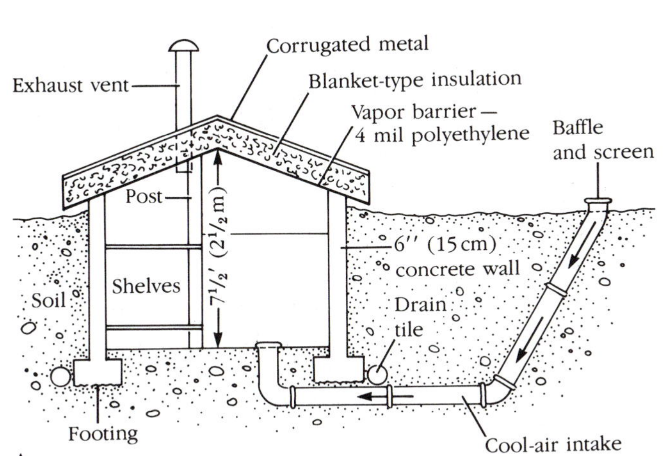

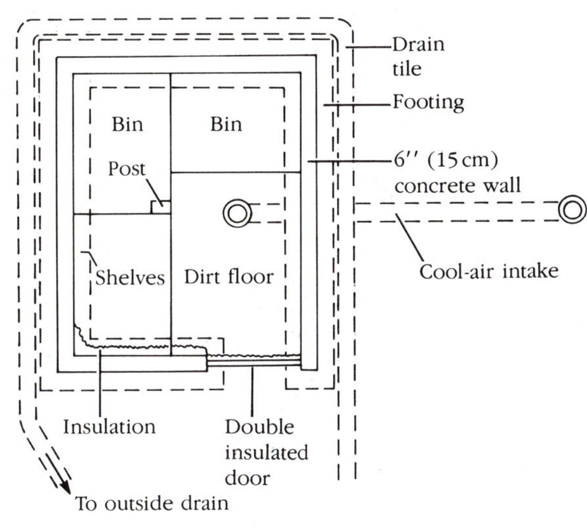

FIGURE 14-92 • Vertical cross section (A) and floor plan (B) of a below-ground storage cellar with three sides of undisturbed earth and an open front. Vents that can be opened and closed are necessary to permit heavier cold air to enter at the bottom and warm air to escape through the roof. At least 6 inches (15 cm) of rock wool batting or similar insulation are required to keep up the temperature during cold weather and to prevent condensation on the roof. The exposed front also must be insulated and drainage provided. Underground storage can be made with roofs of reinforced concrete covered by soil for insulation. Some cellars are still being built with supports made entirely with timbers. These usually have three sides of undisturbed earth with a roof supported by upright posts set in concrete. The roof poles are covered with brush and baled straw topped with a layer of fine soil low in organic matter.

casionally to increase humidity in case the natural moisture is insufficient. Only the front and roof are exposed (Figure 14-92). The U.S. and Canadian Departments of Agriculture have publications and working plans of storages. These are available at many county extension offices for a small fee or from the two national departments.

An unheated basement with a dirt floor under a home may be an ideal storage location, or sometimes an unheated area of a concrete basement can be insulated from the rest of the home for storage. The basement storage area should have a window that can be opened for ventilation. Where basement humidity is lower than 90 percent, root crops can be kept from dehydrating by being covered with sand that is kept moist.

Storage Pits. I usually store root vegetables, gladioli corms, and dahlia tubers in a pit that provides about the same storage environment as the cellar storage. I dig a hole in a well-drained location and line it with straw and a section of a hollow cedar log. A barrel or wooden box would do as well. A solid liner is convenient but not essential. Vegetables are washed and placed in gallon-sized perforated plastic bags, and other products are cleaned and placed in bags. The bags are placed in the pit. The pit is covered with a wooden

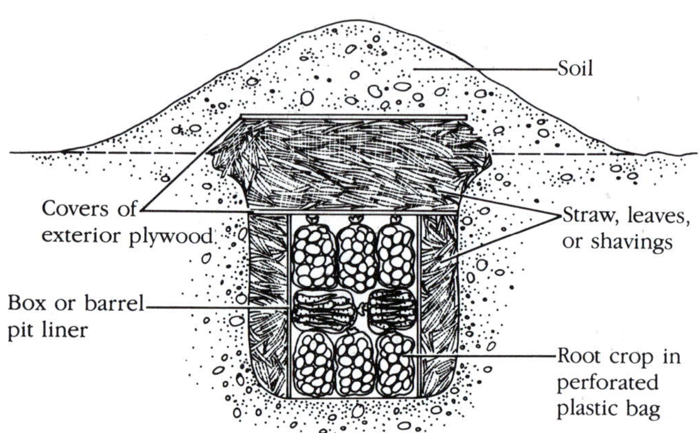

FIGURE 14-93 • Cross section of a below-ground storage pit.

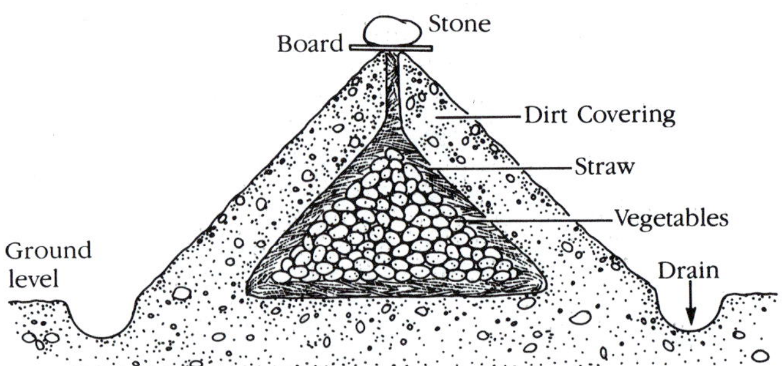

FIGURE 14-94 • Cross section of an above-ground storage pit for areas with a moderate climate or drainage problems. (From *Storing Vegetables and Fruits*, USDA Home and Garden Bulletin 119. U.S. Government Printing Office, Washington, D.C. Revised periodically)

lid and a layer of straw or leaves; soil is piled on the straw so that water drains away from the pit. The straw provides enough insulation to protect the pit from freezing. Throughout most of the winter it is possible to reach down through the straw and pull out a bag of carrots that are ready to be popped into the refrigerator. In areas where soil temperatures remain below 45°F (7°C) most of the winter, carrots can be kept until May in this kind of pit (Figure 14-93).

Where the temperature does not get too cold or where enough insulation is used, a barrel or above-ground pit storage is feasible (Figure 14-94). Cabbage and celery also can be stored in outdoor pits (Figure 14-95). Apples and pears can be stored in a pit but are likely to pick up an earthy flavor.

Washing Products to Be Stored. Generally home storage instructions advise against washing vegetables before they are stored, because washing increases the likelihood of decay. My own experience with carrots and beets has been that washing and then spreading the roots to permit most liquid moisture to evaporate from them before they are placed in storage does not increase the incidence of decay; in fact, it may actually reduce it. There are undoubtedly situations where this would not be true. Potatoes to be stored and fruits and vegetables that grow above ground should ordinarily not be washed before they are stored.

Storage Requirements for Specific Crops. If very much fruit is to be stored through the winter, a special storage should be built for it. Storage temperature for temperate-zone fruits and citrus should be as near 31°F (−1°C) as possible. Winter pears are harvested while still green and held at 32°F (0°C). A week or two before they are to be

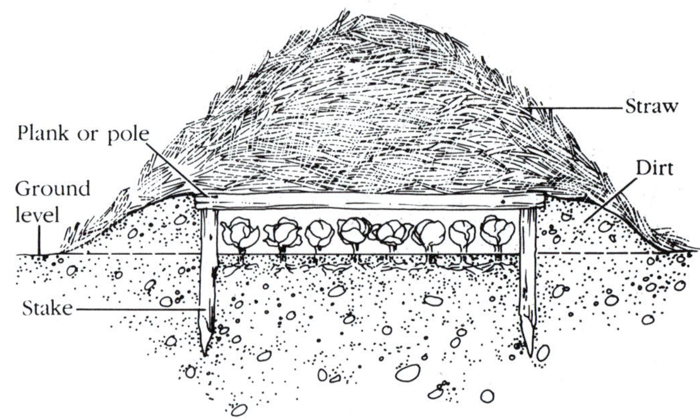

FIGURE 14-95 • Cross section of a cabbage storage pit made of stakes and poles covered with straw. (From *Storing Vegetables and Fruits*, USDA Home and Garden Bulletin 119. U.S. Government Printing Office, Washington, D.C., revised periodically)

used, winter pears should be transferred to a room where the temperature is 60° to 65°F (16° to 18°C), which will allow them to ripen.

Potatoes require a high humidity for storage, and once their rest period is broken, usually in December or January, they will sprout if temperatures rise much higher than 40°F (4°C). Moreover, the starch in potato tubers rapidly changes to sugar at temperatures below 38°F (3°C). As a result, the ideal temperature range for potato storage, at least during the spring, is 38° to 40°F, with 90 to 100 percent humidity.

If potatoes have been stored at too low a temperature, the resulting undesirable sweetness can be eliminated by keeping them where the temperature is above 55°F (13°C) for a week or ten days. The potato storage should be kept dark as potato tubers develop green chlorophyll and associated bitter alkaloids when exposed simultaneously to light and temperatures higher than 40°F.

If possible, after they are dug and before they are stored, onions should be left outdoors in the sun for a week to ten days until the top and scales are completely dry. If the weather is rainy or cloudy, they can be cured indoors in a warm, dry location. Dirt and loose scales should be removed before they are stored. Onions with large necks or decay around the neck should not be stored. Onions store best at 32°F with a relatively low humidity and can be kept on a shelf in a corner of the root cellar. Onions and well-matured pumpkins and squash can keep for several months in a cool, dry basement or on a shelf in an unheated bedroom where temperatures are 55°F or lower.

Because tomatoes are subject to freezing and are injured by long-term exposure to temperatures below 45°F (7°C), mature green fruits should be harvested before frost or before daytime temperatures start to remain in the low 40s. They can be spread on a shelf after harvest and ripened in a room where the temperature is 55° to 65°F. I have kept tomatoes harvested in early October ripening from then until Thanksgiving both in New York and Washington states.

After being harvested, sweet potatoes should be cured in a warm moist atmosphere for from ten days at 85°F (29°C) to two to three weeks at 65° to 75°F (18° to 24°C). They should then be moved to a dry 55° to 65°F (13° to 18°C) area. They are subject to cold-temperature injury at temperatures below 50°F (10°C). A summary of storage requirements for various vegetables and fruits is given in Table 14-21.

HOME PROCESSING

◆ ◆ ◆

Processing fruits and vegetables subjects them to treatments that preserve their edibility for from one to several years. Changes that bring about spoilage of fruits and vegetables can be attributed to three factors: (1) the continuation of life processes, including respiration and transpiration; (2) enzymatic changes; and (3) the action of microorganisms, either by their direct feeding or from their chemical by-products. Thus stopping life processes, inactivating enzymes, and preventing the multiplication of microorganisms are necessary to preserve fruits and vegetables.

Canning

When foods are processed by canning, their life processes and enzymes are inactivated, and any microorganisms associated with them are killed by heat. The microorganisms are prevented from reentering when the product is sealed in a container impervious to them.

Botulism. One problem associated with home canning that has received considerable publicity is poisoning by botulism, a frequently fatal condition caused by the ingestion of even minute quantities of a toxin produced by the spore-forming bacteria *Clostridium botulinum*. These bacteria are ubiquitous, although they are poor competitors and cannot multiply in the presence of other microorganisms. The heat-tolerant spores they produce are a problem in canned products because other microorganisms are destroyed with less heat, leaving the spores of *C. botulinum* free to multiply without competition. Fortunately, *C. botulinum* cannot grow in an acid medium, and so there is no danger in eating home-canned fruits or pickles. But non-acid vegetable and meat products should be canned at home only in a pressure cooker that has been recently tested to see that it is operating properly. In addition, as a further precaution, home-canned meats and vegetables should be boiled for ten minutes before they are eaten.

Because of the strict adherence to quality control by commercial processing companies, there is almost no danger of botulism from products canned commercially in North America.

Canning Fruits and Juices. Most home-canned fruits are packed in screw-cap Mason jars. The jars should be washed with soap and water and scalded or washed in an electric dishwasher. The metal rings can be reused, but used caps should be discarded. The manufacturer's directions for heating the caps and placing them on the filled jars should be followed.

In preparation for canning, peaches and tomatoes are peeled by dipping the fruit in hot water for a few seconds, just long enough to loosen the skin. Pears and apples are peeled and cored with a knife or small hand peeler made specifically for that purpose. Peeled peaches, pears, and apples can be kept from browning if they are peeled into a solution of 1 tablespoon (15 g) salt and 1 tablespoon (15 ml) vinegar dissolved in a gallon (4 liters) of water. We (canning is a family enterprise at my house) seldom use the salt/vinegar solution with peaches and pears, preferring to pack the peeled fruit directly into jars so that it can be processed as quickly as possible.

Plums should have their skins pricked with a fork if they are to be canned whole. Rhubarb is cut into very small (about ½-inch) pieces. Apricots (which usually are not peeled), peaches, and sometimes plums are halved to remove the stone. Most berries and sweet cherries are canned whole. Sour cherries are often pitted before they are processed, especially if they are to be used for pies. If raspberries and blackberries have been grown without pesticides in an insect- and dust-free, unpolluted atmosphere, and if hands and picking containers are scrupulously clean, they may not require washing. Washing can crumble ripe berries. All purchased fruit should, of course, be washed.

Fruit may be canned by either the cold- or the hot-pack method. Cold packing involves fewer operations, so we usually prefer that method for all fruits but apples and a few plum cultivars. These two fruits contain air. That air is replaced by liquid during processing, and cold-packed apples and certain plums often have a solid mass of fruit floating on liquid in jars that are one-third empty. When the fruit is exposed to air in the top of the jar, it is likely to turn brown unless the jars are stored upside down for part of the time. For cold-pack canning, the prepared fruit is packed in a jar and covered with hot water or a syrup to within ½ inch (1¼ cm) of the jar top. A light syrup is made by heating two parts sugar with four parts water until sugar is dissolved. A medium syrup is three parts sugar and four parts water, and heavy syrup is equal measures of sugar and water (all volume measures). Canning fruit can also be sweetened with corn syrup or honey. A sweetener is not needed to prevent spoilage, so the fruit can be covered with water if that is preferred. For most tree-ripened fruit, a light syrup provides ample sweetening. The liquid used to cover the fruit should be hot, to lessen the likelihood that the jars will break when they are lowered into the hot-water bath. As a further precaution the stove unit should be turned off while the canner is being unloaded and reloaded, so as to allow the water bath to cool slightly. After the jars are filled, the lids are screwed on tightly, and the jars are completely submerged in a hot-water bath.

Almost any container deep enough to allow the jars to be completely submerged can be used for the water bath. A low perforated platform should be placed in the bottom of the water-bath container to keep the jars from close contact with the heat unit of the stove, and a loose-fitting lid should be provided. When we have a single jar to be processed, we have occasionally used an empty and thoroughly cleaned 1-gallon (4 liter) latex-base paint can with a piece of folded and flattened chicken wire in the bottom and the lid from a kitchen saucepan. A commercially made home canner, however, is more convenient. These are available in various sizes, the most common being an enameled kettle that holds seven quart (or pint) jars. A lid and a wire rack with handles for lowering and raising the jars into and from the water bath are included.

When being canned by the hot-pack method, the fruit (other than apples), along with the desired amounts of sweetener and water, is heated to boiling before it is packed into jars. Apples should be boiled for about 5 minutes to eliminate gases. After the jars are filled, the lids are screwed on tightly, and the jars are processed in a water bath.

Canning guides do not entirely agree on processing times. We have processed thousands of quart jars of cold-packed fruit for a standard 20 minutes after the water bath starts to boil (15 minutes for pints, 30 minutes for half-gallons) and have never had a problem with spoilage. Slightly longer times—22, 16, and 33 minutes—are required for liter, half-liter, and 2-liter containers, respectively. Hot-packed fruit is processed for 15 minutes for quarts and for 10 minutes for pints. The processing time should be increased 5 percent for each 1,000 foot (300 m) rise in elevation.

To can fruit juices, tomato juice, and purees, including apple sauce, the raw product is washed, and any blemishes are removed. The calyx, but not the core or seeds, of apples is removed. Fruit for purees and tomatoes for juice are strained through a colander or sieve with holes small enough to keep out the seeds. Fruit for juice is filtered through a cloth bag. The strained product can be sweetened if desired (1 teaspoon of salt/quart is added to tomato juice), poured into hot jars to within ½ inch of the top, and processed in a water bath for 10 minutes (20 minutes for tomato juice).

Peeled tomatoes are packed in jars and pushed down with a spoon or fork to eliminate air pockets and allow them to become covered by their own juice. A teaspoon of salt per quart is added, and they are processed in a water bath for 35 minutes.

Canning Vegetables. Many home-canned vegetables become mushy during the heating necessary to ensure their being free of *Clostridium botulinum*. For this reason and because freezing is a much more convenient method of processing them, vegetables are usually processed by freezing if a home freezer or rented locker is available.

Vegetables, except tomatoes and pickles, should be canned only in a steam-pressure canner. Pressure canning raises temperatures high enough to eliminate the danger of botulism. A pressure saucepan with a weighted gauge for accurately controlling pressure at 10 lb (510 mm) (240°F; 115°C) is satisfactory for processing pint jars, but 20 minutes should be added to the processing times listed in Table 14-22 if such a container is used. Pressure canners of various sizes with racks for holding jars are more convenient, and one should be bought if more than a few jars of vegetables are to be canned. The gauge should be thoroughly cleaned. The gauge on a pressure canner should be checked after the first year of use and every few years thereafter to determine its accuracy; consult the manufacturer or the county extension office to see where this can be done.

Most vegetables can be packed by either the raw-pack or the hot-pack method. Exceptions are spinach and other greens that have to be cooked for a few minutes in order to concentrate their bulk, and beets, which are usually cooked for a few minutes to loosen their peeling. Vegetables for canning are prepared as they would be for the table and packed lightly into jars. One teaspoon of salt is added for each quart, and boiling water is added to fill the jar to ½ inch from the top.

For processing, the jars are placed on a rack in the canner containing 2 or 3 inches (5 to 8 cm) of water. The canner cover should be fastened securely so that steam can escape only through the petcock or vent opening. After the steam has been coming through the opening for 10 minutes or more, the air will have been driven from the canner, and then the petcock can be closed or the weighted gauge placed on the opening. The processing time should be counted as soon as the pressure has risen to 10 pounds. When processing time is up, the canner should be removed from the heat. With glass jars the canner should be left

TABLE 14-22 • *Canning directions and processing times at 240°F (115°C) recommended for common vegetables*

Vegetable	Directions[a]	Minutes of Processing Time, 10 lb (510 mm) Pressure	
		Pints	Quarts
Asparagus	Break tender portions into 1-inch lengths.	25	30
Beans, fresh lima	Leaves 1½-inch space at top of quart jar and 1 inch at top of pints for expansion.	40	50
Beans, snap	Trim ends and cut into 1-inch lengths.	20	25
Beets	Cook with 1 inch of stem and entire root attached. Peel and pack.	30	35
Carrots	Slice, dice, or pack small carrots whole.	25	30
Corn (cream style)	Cut from cob at center of kernel and scrape cob.	90	—
Corn (whole kernel)	Cut at about ⅔ depth of kernel.	55	85
Mushrooms	Steam 4 minutes or heat gently for 15 minutes. Pack hot.	30	—
Okra	Pack only young pods. Cook for 1 minute. Pack hot.	25	35
Peas (blackeye)	Shell. Leave 1½ inch at top of quarts and 1 inch at top of pints.	35	40
Peas (fresh green)	Pack to 1 inch of top.	30	35
Potatoes	Cook cubes or small tubers for 2 minutes. Pack hot.	35	40
Spinach	Steam for 10 minutes. Pack loosely and hot.	70	90
Squash, summer	Cut into ½-inch slices.	25	30
Squash, winter	Cube and bring to boil. Pack hot.	55	90
Sweet potatoes	Boil 20 to 30 minutes. Remove skin. Pack with or without liquid.	65	90

Prepared from information in *Home Canning of Fruits and Vegetables*, USDA Home and Garden Bulletin 8. U.S. Government Printing Office, Washington, D.C. Revised periodically.

[a]Except where otherwise noted, all vegetables can be packed cold or brought to a boil and packed hot. Jars should be filled and covered with liquid to ½ inch from the top.

undisturbed until the pressure returns to zero. Then the petcock can be slowly opened or the weighted gauge removed, and after a couple more minutes the lid can be taken off and the jars removed. Table 14-22 lists the processing directions for common vegetables.

Freezing

When products are processed by freezing, the growth of microorganisms and most chemical changes are prevented by the lack of heat. Certain enzymes that cause undesirable flavors in vegetables are inactivated by blanching. Blanching is heating in steam or boiling water for a short period. Once the desired amount of heat has been applied, the product is immediately cooled, in ice water if available, to stop the softening action of high temperatures. Enzymatic activity can be stopped in some fruits by adding sugar or an acid, usually ascorbic acid.

Products processed by freezing should be sealed in containers so that they are not exposed to air, which causes freezer burn, and so that escaping volatiles do not flavor other products in the freezer. Never fill a freezing jar to more than 85 percent capacity, especially if the product is packed in liquid, as some head space is necessary to allow for the expansion of freezing. Newly packaged containers should be separated so that they will freeze more rapidly. After they are frozen, vegetables packaged in plastic bags without a rigid cover should be placed together in a box or heavy bag. Loose packages not protected are often punctured during the daily use of the freezer. The temperature of the freezer should be kept at 0°F (−18°C) or lower.

The general recommendation for freezing cherries, berries, and most other fruits is to pack them with dry sugar or in a light syrup. Peaches, fruit cocktail, and sliced strawberries keep best in a light syrup, but my own experience suggests that most other fruit and berries do not juice out as much if packed without sugar. If desired, sugar can be added when they are consumed.

Blanching is done with a blancher, which has a blanching basket and lid, or with a large covered kettle and wire basket. At least 1 gallon of water is used for each pound of produce, and blanching time should start as soon as the vegetables are plunged into the boiling water. Vegetables can also be blanched in a microwave oven. Blanching times in boiling water for vegetables are given in Table 14-23, and the directions for microwave blanching are shown in Table 14-24.

Dehydrating

Because of the ready availability of supplies and equipment for home canning and freezing and because of the lengthy cooking time required to reconstitute most home-dried products, the home drying of fruits and vegetables has not been as popular as home canning or freezing. Moreover, it is difficult to remove enough moisture so that the product will store for many months without spoiling. In parts of the West where the humidity is low and summer rainfall is infrequent it is possible to spread fruit on trays covered with a screen in direct sun for a week to ten days. Some kinds of fruits and vegetables can be dehydrated satisfactorily by cutting them into thin strips and spreading them on a rack in a partly open oven turned to the lowest heat possible. A small fan to circulate out the air humidified by the moisture from the fruit speeds oven drying. The oven can be used in conjunction with sun drying in cases of unexpected wet weather. If completely dried, fruits and vegetables will keep indefinitely. Fruit that is dried just to the rubbery stage will keep without refrigeration for several weeks and, if stored in a home freezer, is an excellent supplement for backpack trips.

TABLE 14-23 • *Blanching time in hot water for selected vegetables*

Vegetable	Blanching Time (minutes)	Vegetable	Blanching Time (minutes)
Asparagus	3	Corn, frozen on cob	9
Beans, lima	3	Kohlrabi, whole	3
Beans, green shell	1	Kohlrabi, cubed	1
Beans, snap	3	Okra	3
Broccoli	3	Parsnips, cubed	2
Brussels sprouts	4	Peas, blackeye	2
Cabbage, shredded	1½	Peas, green	1½
Carrots, whole	5	Peppers	No blanching
Carrots, diced	2	Pumpkin, squash, sweet potato	Cook until tender
Cauliflower	3	Rutabagas and turnips, cubed	2
Celery	3	Spinach, chard, kale, collards, and New Zealand spinach	2
Corn, sweet, whole kernel (blanch on cob)	4	Beet greens and mustard greens	2

Prepared from information in *Home Freezing of Fruits and Vegetables*, USDA Home and Garden Bulletin 10, revised. U.S. Government Printing Office, Washington, D.C., 1971.

TABLE 14-24 • *Microwave blanching of vegetables*

Vegetable	Amount of Vegetable	Casserole Size	Amount of Water	Blanching Time on Full Power
Asparagus	1 lb	2 qt	¼ c	3 min
Beans, snap	1 lb or 3 c	1½ qt	⅓ c	4 to 5 min
Broccoli	1 lb	2 qt	⅓ c	4 min
Carrots	1 lb	1½ qt	¼ c	4 min
Cauliflower	1 head	2 qt	⅓ c	4 to 5 min
Corn on the cob	4 ears	2 qt	none	4 min
Corn, whole kernel	4 cups	1½ qt	none	4 min
Peas	4 cups	1½ qt	¼ c	4 to 5 min
Spinach	½ lb	2 qt	none	1½ to 2 min
Squash, summer and zucchini	1 lb	1½ qt	¼ c	2 to 3 min

Today, the renewed interest in almost-forgotten rural arts has encouraged several companies to manufacture small home fruit and vegetable driers, and plans are available for driers that can be built at home with materials as common as a light bulb, a small fan, and plywood. Check with your county extension office, a local natural food store, or some of the "back-to-the-earth" movement books if you are interested in home dehydrating.

Other Methods of Processing

Some of the oldest known methods of preserving foods are pickling; fermenting; and preserving with sugar, salt, and/or some other chemical. These techniques all involve a change in the chemistry of the food and are sometimes classed in a group as chemistry alteration. Often chemistry alteration is not permitted to continue to the point that the product will keep without further treatment, and so such foods as chili sauce, catsup, and even some pickles are canned to prevent spoilage.

Vinegar pickles are made by soaking the product in acetic acid and combinations of sugars, herbs, and spices. Cucumbers are the most common pickled product, but such items as crabapples, apple slices, beets, peppers, cauliflower, and carrots also are sometimes pickled.

Common table salt in precise but not too concentrated amounts is added to cucumbers and cabbage to cause lactic acid fermentation and produce "fermented" pickles and sauerkraut. Yeast acting on sugars or starches of various kinds produces ethyl alcohol, which is the basis of beer and wine making.

Jelly and jam are made by combining fruit juice, high concentrations of sugar, and pectin. Pectin is found naturally in many fruits. Boiling the juice or puree of those fruits for a long period of time evaporates enough moisture to concentrate the pectin and cause the product to "set" into jelly or jam. Jelly making used to be a real art; today commercially manufactured pectin, available everywhere, greatly simplifies the making of jelly and jam. Recipes for making jelly, jam, and conserves from most kinds of fruit are found on each package or bottle of pectin.

NUTRITIONAL VALUES OF HORTICULTURAL FOODS

Almost every week the news media report the results of a research project that has uncovered new health benefits of fruits and vegetables in the diet. Some of those benefits are mentioned in Chapter 1, and Table 14-25 lists the nutritional components of various fruit and vegetable products.

CONTROLLING GENERAL GARDEN PESTS

Wherever feasible, the control of major insect and disease pests of individual crops has been included with the discussion of those crops in the text. It would be impossible, however, to cover all the thousands of ornamental and vegetable crops that might be grown by North American gardeners. Moreover, many pests are general feeders on many kinds of plants. Others produce symptoms and respond to control measures in ways that permit them to be grouped, as in Table 14-26.

Table 14-26 should help gardeners diagnose several pest problems and find methods of preventing or overcoming them. Other sources should be consulted when identification and control measures for specific pests are required.

(text continues on p. 491)

TABLE 14-25 • *Nutrients in common foods in terms of household measures*

Food	Water (%)	Food Energy (calories)	Protein (g)	Fat (g)	Total Carbohydrate (g)	Calcium (mg)	Iron (mg)	Vitamin A Value (International Units)	Thiamine (mg)	Riboflavin (mg)	Niacin (mg)	Ascorbic Acid (mg)
Mature beans and peas; nuts												
Almonds, shelled; 1 cup	5	850	26	77	28	332	6.7	0	.34	1.31	5.0	Trace
Beans, dry seed:												
Common varieties, as Great Northern, navy, and others, canned; 1 cup:												
Red	76	230	15	1	42	74	4.6	0	.13	.13	1.5	Trace
White, with tomato or molasses:												
With pork	69	330	16	7	54	172	4.4	140	.13	.10	1.3	5
Without pork	69	315	16	1	60	183	5.2	140	.13	.10	1.3	5
Lima, cooked; 1 cup	64	260	16	1	48	56	5.6	Trace	.26	.12	1.3	Trace
Brazil nuts, broken pieces; 1 cup	5	905	20	92	15	260	4.8	Trace	1.21	0	0	0
Cashew nuts, roasted; 1 cup	5	770	25	65	35	51	5.1	0	.49	.46	1.9	0
Coconut; 1 cup:												
Fresh, shredded	50	330	3	31	13	15	1.7	0	.06	.03	.5	4
Dried, shredded (sweetened)	3	345	2	24	33	13	1.6	0	.04	.02	.4	0
Cowpeas or black-eyed peas, dry, cooked; 1 cup	80	190	13	1	34	42	3.2	20	.41	.11	1.1	Trace
Peanuts roasted, shelled; 1 cup	2	840	39	71	28	104	3.2	0	.47	.19	24.6	0
Peanut butter; 1 tablespoon	2	90	4	8	3	12	.4	0	.02	.02	2.8	0
Peas, split, dry, cooked; 1 cup	70	290	20	1	52	28	4.2	120	.36	.22	2.2	Trace
Pecans, halves; 1 cup	3	740	10	77	16	79	2.6	140	.93	.14	1.0	2
Walnuts, shelled; 1 cup:												
Black or native, chopped	3	790	26	75	19	Trace	7.6	380	.28	.14	.9	0
English or Persian, halves	4	650	15	64	16	99	3.1	30	.33	.13	.9	3
Vegetables												
Asparagus:												
Cooked; 1 cup	92	35	4	Trace	6	33	1.8	1,820	.23	.30	2.1	40
Canned; 6 medium-size spears:												
Green	92	20	2	Trace	3	18	1.8	770	.06	.08	.9	17
Bleached	92	20	2	Trace	4	15	1.0	70	.05	.07	.8	17
Beans:												
Lima, immature, cooked; 1 cup	75	150	8	1	29	46	2.7	460	.22	.14	1.8	24
Snap green:												
Cooked; 1 cup:												
In small amount of water, short time	92	25	2	Trace	6	45	.9	830	.09	.12	.6	18
In large amount of water, long time	92	25	2	Trace	6	45	.9	830	.06	.11	.5	12
Canned:												
Solids and liquid; 1 cup	94	45	2	Trace	10	65	3.3	990	.08	.10	.7	9
Strained or chopped; 1 ounce	93	5	Trace	Trace	1	10	.3	120	.01	.02	.1	1
Beets, cooked, diced; 1 cup	88	70	2	Trace	16	35	1.2	30	.03	.07	.5	11
Broccoli, cooked, flower stalks; 1 cup	90	45	5	Trace	8	195	2.0	5,100	.10	.22	1.2	111
Brussels sprouts, cooked; 1 cup	85	60	6	1	12	44	1.7	520	.05	.16	.6	61

(continued)

TABLE 14-25 • *(Continued)*

Food	Water (%)	Food Energy (calories)	Protein (g)	Fat (g)	Total Carbohydrate (g)	Calcium (mg)	Iron (mg)	Vitamin A Value (International Units)	Thiamine (mg)	Riboflavin (mg)	Niacin (mg)	Ascorbic Acid (mg)
Cabbage; 1 cup:												
Raw, finely shredded	92	25	1	Trace	5	46	.5	80	.06	.05	.3	50
Raw, coleslaw	84	100	2	7	9	47	.5	80	.06	.05	.3	50
Cooked:												
In small amount of water, short time	92	40	2	Trace	9	78	.8	150	.08	.08	.5	53
In large amount of water, long time	92	40	2	Trace	9	78	.8	150	.05	.05	.3	32
Cabbage, celery or Chinese; 1 cup:												
Raw, leaves and stem (1-inch pieces)	95	15	1	Trace	2	43	.9	260	.03	.04	.4	31
Cooked	95	25	2	1	5	82	1.7	490	.04	.06	.6	42
Carrots:												
Raw; 1 carrot (5½ × 1 inch) or 25 thin strips	88	20	1	Trace	5	20	.4	6,000	.03	.03	.3	3
Raw, grated; 1 cup	88	45	1	Trace	10	43	.9	13,200	.06	.06	.7	7
Cooked, diced; 1 cup	92	45	1	1	9	38	.9	18,130	.07	.07	.7	6
Canned, strained or chopped; 1 ounce	92	5	Trace	0	2	7	.2	3,400	.01	.01	.1	1
Cauliflower, cooked, flower buds; 1 cup	92	30	3	Trace	6	26	1.3	110	.07	.10	.6	34
Celery, raw:												
Large stalk, 8 inches long	94	5	1	Trace	1	20	.2	0	.02	.02	.2	3
Diced; 1 cup	94	20	1	Trace	4	50	.5	0	.05	.04	.4	7
Collards, cooked; 1 cup	87	75	7	1	14	473	3.0	14,500	.15	.46	3.2	84
Corn, sweet:												
Cooked; 1 ear, 5 inches long	76	65	2	1	16	4	.5	[a]300	.09	.08	1.1	6
Canned, solids and liquid; 1 cup	80	170	5	1	41	10	1.3	[a]520	.07	.13	2.4	14
Cowpeas, immature seeds, cooked; 1 cup	75	150	11	1	25	59	4.0	620	.46	.13	1.3	32
Cucumbers, raw, pared; 6 slices (⅛ inch thick, center section)	96	5	Trace	Trace	1	5	.2	0	.02	.02	.1	4
Dandelion greens, cooked; 1 cup	86	80	5	1	16	337	5.6	27,310	.23	.22	1.3	29
Endive, curly (including escarole); 2 ounces	93	10	1	Trace	2	45	1.0	1,700	.04	.07	.2	6
Kale, cooked; 1 cup	87	45	4	1	8	248	2.4	9,220	.08	.25	1.9	56
Lettuce, headed, raw:												
2 large or 4 small leaves	95	5	1	Trace	1	11	.2	270	.02	.04	.1	4
1 compact head (4¾-inch diam.)	95	70	5	1	13	100	2.3	2,470	.20	.38	.9	35
Mushrooms, canned, solids and liquid; 1 cup	93	30	3	Trace	9	17	2.0	0	.04	.60	4.8	0
Mustard greens, cooked; 1 cup	92	30	3	Trace	6	308	4.1	10,050	.08	.25	1.0	63
Okra, cooked; 8 pods (3 inches long, ⅝-inch diam.)	90	30	2	Trace	6	70	.6	630	.05	.05	.7	17
Onions:												
Mature:												
Raw; 1 onion (2½-inch diam.)	88	50	2	Trace	11	35	.6	60	.04	.04	.2	10
Cooked; 1 cup	90	80	2	Trace	18	67	1.0	110	.04	.06	.4	13
Young green; 6 small, without tops	88	25	Trace	Trace	5	68	.4	30	.02	.02	.1	12
Parsley, raw; 1 tablespoon chopped	84	1	Trace	Trace	Trace	7	.2	290	Trace	.01	.1	7
Parsnips, cooked; 1 cup	84	95	2	1	22	88	1.1	0	.09	.16	.3	19
Peas, green; 1 cup:												
Cooked	82	110	8	1	19	35	3.0	1,150	.40	.22	3.7	24

(continued)

TABLE 14-25 • *Nutrients in common foods in terms of household measures (Continued)*

Food	Water (%)	Food Energy (calories)	Protein (g)	Fat (g)	Total Carbohydrate (g)	Calcium (mg)	Iron (mg)	Vitamin A Value (International Units)	Thiamine (mg)	Riboflavin (mg)	Niacin (mg)	Ascorbic Acid (mg)
Canned, solids and liquid	82	170	8	1	32	62	4.5	1,350	.28	.15	2.6	21
Canned, strained; 1 ounce	86	10	1	Trace	2	5	.3	160	.03	.02	.3	2
Peppers, sweet:												
Green, raw; 1 medium	93	15	1	Trace	3	6	.4	260	.05	.05	.3	79
Red, raw; 1 medium	91	20	1	Trace	4	8	.4	2,670	.05	.05	.3	122
Pimientos, canned; 1 medium	92	10	Trace	Trace	2	3	.6	870	.01	.02	.1	36
Peppers, hot, red, without seeds, dried, ground (chili powder); 1 tablespoon	13	50	2	1	9	20	1.2	11,520	.03	.20	1.6	2
Potatoes:												
Baked or boiled; 1 medium, 2½-inch diam. (weight raw, about 5 ounces):												
Baked in jacket	75	90	3	Trace	21	9	.7	Trace	.10	.04	1.7	20
Boiled; peeled before boiling	80	90	3	Trace	21	9	.7	Trace	.11	.04	1.4	20
Chips; 10 medium (2-inch diam.)	3	110	1	7	10	6	.4	Trace	.04	.02	.6	2
French fried:												
Frozen, ready to be heated for serving; 10 pieces (2 × ½ × ½ inch)	64	95	2	4	15	4	.8	Trace	.08	.01	1.2	10
Ready-to-eat, deep fat for entire process; 10 pieces (2 × ½ × ½ inch)	45	155	2	7	20	9	.7	Trace	.06	.04	1.8	8
Mashed; 1 cup:												
Milk added	80	145	4	1	30	47	1.0	50	.17	.11	.2	17
Milk and butter added	76	230	4	12	28	45	1.0	470	.16	.10	1.6	16
Pumpkin, canned; 1 cup	90	75	2	1	18	46	1.6	7,750	.04	.14	1.2	0
Radishes, raw; 4 small	94	10	Trace	Trace	2	15	.4	10	.01	.01	.1	10
Sauerkraut, canned, drained solids; 1 cup	91	30	2	Trace	7	54	.8	60	.05	.10	.2	24
Spinach:												
Cooked: 1 cup	91	45	6	1	6	223	3.6	21,200	.14	.36	1.1	54
Canned, creamed, strained; 1 ounce	90	10	1	Trace	2	19	.3	750	.01	.03	.1	1
Squash:												
Cooked, 1 cup:												
Summer, diced	95	35	1	Trace	8	32	.8	550	.08	.15	1.3	23
Winter, baked, mashed	86	95	4	1	23	49	1.6	12,690	.10	.31	1.2	14
Canned, strained or chopped; 1 ounce	92	10	Trace	Trace	2	7	.1	510	.01	.01	.1	1
Sweet potatoes:												
Baked or boiled; 1 medium, 5 × 2 inches (weight raw, about 6 ounces):												
Baked in jacket	64	155	2	1	36	44	1.0	[b] 8,970	.10	.07	.7	24
Boiled in jacket	71	170	2	1	39	47	1.0	[b]11,610	.13	.09	.9	25
Candied; 1 small, 3½ × 2 inches	60	295	2	6	60	65	1.6	[b]11,030	.10	.08	.8	17
Canned, vacuum or solid pack; 1 cup	72	235	4	Trace	54	54	1.7	17,110	.12	.09	1.1	30
Tomatoes:												
Raw; 1 medium (2 × 2½ inches), about ⅓ pound	94	30	2	Trace	6	16	.9	1,640	.08	.06	.8	35
Canned or cooked; 1 cup	94	45	2	Trace	9	27	1.5	2,540	.14	.08	1.7	40
Tomato juice, canned; 1 cup	94	50	2	Trace	10	17	1.0	2,540	.12	.07	1.8	38
Tomato catsup; 1 tablespoon	70	15	Trace	Trace	4	2	.1	320	.02	.01	.4	2
Turnips, cooked, diced; 1 cup	92	40	1	Trace	9	62	.8	Trace	.06	.09	.6	28
Fruits												
Turnip greens, cooked; 1 cup	90	45	4	1	8	376	3.5	15,370	.09	.59	1.0	87
Apples, raw; 1 medium (2½-inch diam.), about ⅓ pound	85	70	Trace	Trace	18	8	.4	50	.04	.02	.1	3
Apple betty; 1 cup	64	350	4	8	69	41	1.4	270	.13	.10	.9	Trace
Apple juice, fresh or canned; 1 cup	86	125	Trace	0	34	15	1.2	90	.05	.07	Trace	2
Applesauce, canned:												
Sweetened; 1 cup	80	185	Trace	Trace	50	10	1.0	80	.05	.03	.1	3

(continued)

TABLE 14-25 • *(Continued)*

Food	Water (%)	Food Energy (calories)	Protein (g)	Fat (g)	Total Carbohydrate (g)	Calcium (mg)	Iron (mg)	Vitamin A Value (International Units)	Thiamine (mg)	Riboflavin (mg)	Niacin (mg)	Ascorbic Acid (mg)
Unsweetened; 1 cup	88	100	Trace	Trace	26	10	1.0	70	.05	.02	.1	3
Apricots, raw; 3 apricots (about ¼ pound)	85	55	1	Trace	14	18	.5	2,890	.03	.04	.7	10
Apricots, canned:												
Heavy sirup pack, halves and sirup; 1 cup	78	200	1	Trace	54	34	1.0	4,070	.05	.07	1.1	10
Water pack, halves and liquid; 1 cup	90	80	1	Trace	21	27	.7	3,320	.04	.05	.9	8
Apricots, dried:												
Uncooked; 1 cup (40 halves, small)	25	390	8	1	100	100	8.2	16,390	.02	.24	4.9	19
Cooked unsweetened, fruit and liquid; 1 cup	76	240	5	1	62	63	5.1	10,130	.01	.13	2.8	8
Apricots and applesauce, canned, strained or chopped; 1 ounce	80	20	Trace	Trace	5	3	.2	440	.01	.01	.1	Trace
Apricot nectar; 1 cup	85	135	1	Trace	36	22	.5	2,380	.02	.02	.5	7
Avocados, raw, California varieties (mainly Fuerte): 1 cup (½-inch cubes)	74	260	3	26	9	15	.9	430	.16	.30	2.4	21
Avocados, raw, California varieties (mainly Fuerte): ½ of a 10-ounce avocado (3½ × 3¼ inches)	74	185	2	18	6	11	.6	310	.12	.21	1.7	15
Avocados, raw, Florida varieties:												
1 cup (½-inch cubes)	78	195	2	17	13	15	.9	430	.16	.30	2.4	21
½ of a 13-ounce avocado (4 × 3 inches)	78	160	2	14	11	12	.7	350	.13	.24	2.0	17
Bananas, raw; 1 medium (6 × 1½ inches), about ⅓ pound	76	85	1	Trace	23	10	.7	170	.05	.06	.7	10
Blackberries, raw; 1 cup	85	80	2	1	18	46	1.3	280	.05	.06	.5	30
Blueberries, raw; 1 cup	83	85	1	1	21	22	1.1	400	.04	.03	.4	23
Cantaloupes, raw; ½ melon (5-inch diam.)	94	40	1	Trace	9	33	.8	[c]6,590	.09	.07	1.0	63
Cherries, sour, sweet, and hybrid, raw; 1 cup	83	65	1	1	15	19	.4	650	.05	.06	.4	9
Cherries, canned:												
Red sour, pitted; 1 cup	87	120	2	1	30	28	.8	1,840	.07	.04	.4	14
Cranberry juice cocktail, canned; 1 cup	85	135	Trace	Trace	36	10	.5	20	.02	.02	.1	5
Cranberry sauce, sweetened; 1 cup	48	550	Trace	1	142	22	.8	80	.06	.06	.3	5
Dates, "fresh" and dried, pitted and cut; 1 cup	20	505	4	1	134	103	5.3	170	.16	.17	3.9	0
Figs:												
Raw; 3 small (1½-inch diam.), about ¼ pound	78	90	2	Trace	22	62	.7	90	.06	.06	.6	2
Dried; 1 large (2 × 1 inch)	23	60	1	Trace	15	43	.3	20	.02	.02	.2	0
Fruit cocktail, canned in heavy sirup, solids and liquid, 1 cup	81	175	1	Trace	47	23	1.0	360	.04	.03	1.1	5
Grapefruit:												
Raw; ½ medium (4¼-inch diam., No. 64s):												
White	89	50	1	Trace	14	21	.5	10	.05	.02	.2	50
Pink or red	89	55	1	Trace	14	21	.5	590	.05	.02	.2	48
Raw, sections, white; 1 cup	89	75	1	Trace	20	31	.8	20	.07	.03	.3	72
Canned:												
Sirup pack, solids and liquid; 1 cup	81	165	1	Trace	44	32	.7	20	.07	.04	.5	75
Water pack, solids and liquid; 1 cup	91	70	1	Trace	18	31	.7	20	.07	.04	.5	72
Grapefruit juice:												
Raw, 1 cup	90	85	1	Trace	23	22	.5	[d]20	.09	.04	.4	92
Canned:												
Unsweetened; 1 cup	89	95	1	Trace	24	20	1.0	20	.07	.04	.4	84
Sweetened; 1 cup	86	120	1	Trace	32	20	1.0	20	.07	.04	.4	78
Frozen concentrate, unsweetened:												
Undiluted; 1 can (6 fluid ounces)	62	280	4	1	72	70	.8	60	.29	.12	1.4	286
Diluted, ready-to-serve; 1 cup	89	95	1	Trace	24	25	.2	20	.10	.04	.5	96
Frozen concentrate, sweetened:												
Undiluted; 1 can (6 fluid ounces)	57	320	3	1	85	59	.6	50	.24	.11	1.2	245
Diluted, ready-to-serve; 1 cup	88	105	1	Trace	28	20	.2	20	.08	.03	.4	82

(continued)

TABLE 14-25 • *Nutrients in common foods in terms of household measures (Continued)*

Food	Water (%)	Food Energy (calories)	Protein (g)	Fat (g)	Total Carbohydrate (g)	Calcium (mg)	Iron (mg)	Vitamin A Value (International Units)	Thiamine (mg)	Riboflavin (mg)	Niacin (mg)	Ascorbic Acid (mg)
Grapefruit juice (*continued*):												
Dehydrated:												
Crystals; 1 can (net weight 4 ounces)	1	400	5	1	103	99	1.1	90	.41	.18	2.0	399
With water added, ready-to-serve; 1 cup	90	90	1	Trace	24	22	.2	20	.10	.05	.5	92
Grapes, raw; 1 cup:												
American type (slip skin)	82	70	1	1	16	13	.4	100	.05	.03	.3	4
European type (adherent skin)	81	100	1	Trace	26	18	.6	150	.08	.04	.4	7
Grape juice, bottled; 1 cup	82	165	1	1	42	25	.8	0	.11	.06	.7	Trace
Lemon juice:												
Raw; 1 cup	91	60	1	Trace	20	27	.5	Trace	.08	.03	.3	129
Canned; 1 cup	91	60	1	Trace	20	27	.5	Trace	.07	.03	.3	102
Lemonade concentrate, frozen, sweetened:												
Undiluted; 1 can (6 fluid ounces)	48	305	1	Trace	113	9	.4	Trace	.05	.06	.7	67
Diluted, ready-to-serve; 1 cup	88	75	Trace	Trace	28	2	.1	Trace	.01	.01	.2	17
Lime juice:												
Raw; 1 cup	90	65	1	Trace	22	22	1.5	Trace	.03	.04	.4	80
Canned; 1 cup	90	65	1	Trace	22	22	1.5	Trace	.02	.04	.4	52
Limeade concentrate, frozen, sweetened:												
Undiluted; 1 can (6 fluid ounces)	50	295	Trace	Trace	109	11	.7	Trace	.01	.02	.2	262
Diluted, ready-to-serve; 1 cup	90	75	Trace	Trace	27	2	.2	Trace	Trace	.01	.1	6
Oranges, raw; 1 large orange (3-inch diam.):												
Navel	86	70	2	Trace	17	48	.3	270	.11	.03	.4	83
Other varieties	86	70	1	Trace	18	63	.3	290	.12	.03	.4	66
Orange juice:												
Raw; 1 cup:												
California (Valencias)	88	105	2	Trace	26	37	.5	500	.20	.05	.6	126
Florida varieties:												
Early and midseason	90	90	1	Trace	23	25	.5	490	.20	.05	.6	127
Late season (Valencias)	88	105	1	Trace	26	25	.5	500	.20	.05	.6	92
Canned, unsweetened; 1 cup	87	110	2	Trace	28	25	1.0	500	.17	.05	.6	100
Frozen concentrate:												
Undiluted; 1 can (6 fluid ounces)	58	305	5	Trace	80	69	.8	1,490	.63	.10	2.4	332
Diluted, ready-to-serve; 1 cup	88	105	2	Trace	27	22	.2	500	.21	.03	.8	112
Dehydrated:												
Crystals; 1 can (net weight 4 ounces)	1	395	6	2	100	95	1.9	1,900	.76	.19	2.5	406
With water added, ready-to-serve; 1 cup	88	105	1	Trace	27	25	.5	500	.20	.05	.6	108
Orange and grapefruit juice, frozen concentrate:												
Undiluted; 1 can (6 fluid ounces)	59	300	4	1	78	61	.8	790	.47	.06	2.3	301
Diluted, ready-to-serve; 1 cup	88	100	1	Trace	26	20	.2	270	.16	.02	.8	102
Peaches:												
Raw:												
1 medium (2½ × 2-inch diam.), about ¼ pound	89	35	1	Trace	10	9	.5	[c]1,320	.02	.05	1.0	7
1 cup, sliced	89	65	1	Trace	16	15	.8	[c]2,230	.03	.08	1.6	12
Peaches:												
Canned (yellow-fleshed) solids and liquid:												
Heavy-sirup pack; 1 cup	80	185	1	Trace	49	13	.8	1,000	.02	.06	1.3	8
Water pack; 1 cup	92	65	1	Trace	17	15	.7	1,100	.02	.07	1.4	9
Strained; 1 ounce	82	20	Trace	Trace	5	2	.2	150	Trace	.01	.2	Trace
Dried:												
Uncooked; 1 cup	25	420	5	1	109	80	9.6	6,330	.02	.32	8.4	32
Cooked, unsweetened; 1 cup (10–12 halves and 6 tablespoons liquid)	77	220	3	1	58	43	5.1	3,350	.01	.16	4.1	6

(continued)

TABLE 14-25 • *(Continued)*

Food	Water (%)	Food Energy (calories)	Protein (g)	Fat (g)	Total Carbohydrate (g)	Calcium (mg)	Iron (mg)	Vitamin A Value (International Units)	Thiamine (mg)	Riboflavin (mg)	Niacin (mg)	Ascorbic Acid (mg)
Frozen:												
1 12-ounce carton	79	265	1	Trace	69	20	1.4	1,770	.04	.10	1.8	[f] 99
1 16-ounce can	79	355	2	Trace	92	27	1.8	2,360	.05	.14	2.4	[f]132
Peach nectar, canned; 1 cup	87	115	Trace	Trace	31	10	.5	1,070	.02	.05	1.0	1
Pears:												
Raw; 1 pear (3- × 2½-inch diam.)	83	100	1	1	25	13	.5	30	.04	.07	.2	7
Canned, solids and liquid:												
Heavy-sirup pack; 1 cup	81	175	1	Trace	47	18	1.3	10	.02	.05	.4	3
Strained; 1 ounce	84	15	Trace	Trace	4	3	.1	Trace	Trace	.01	.1	Trace
Pear nectar, canned; 1 cup	86	125	1	Trace	33	8	.2	10	.01	.05	Trace	1
Pineapple:												
Raw, diced; 1 cup	85	75	1	Trace	19	22	.4	180	.12	.04	.3	33
Canned:												
Sirup pack, solids and liquid:												
Crushed; 1 cup	78	205	1	Trace	55	75	1.6	210	.20	.04	.4	23
Sliced, 2 small or 1 large slice and 2 tablespoons juice	78	95	Trace	Trace	26	35	.7	100	.09	.02	.2	11
Pineapple juice, canned; 1 cup	86	120	1	Trace	32	37	1.2	200	.13	.04	.4	22
Plums:												
Raw; 1 plum (2-inch diam.), about 2 ounces	86	30	Trace	Trace	7	10	.3	200	.04	.02	.3	3
Canned (Italian prunes):												
Sirup pack, solids and liquids; 1 cup	79	185	1	Trace	50	20	2.7	560	.07	.06	.9	3
Prunes, dried:												
Uncooked; 4 medium prunes	24	70	1	Trace	19	14	1.0	430	.02	.05	.5	1
Cooked, unsweetened; 1 cup (17–18 prunes and ⅓ cup liquid)	65	295	3	1	78	57	4.3	1,780	.08	.18	1.7	3
Canned, strained; 1 ounce	73	25	Trace	Trace	7	8	.4	170	.01	.01	.2	1
Prune juice, canned; 1 cup	80	170	1	Trace	45	36	10.6	0	.01	.03	1.1	4
Raisins, dried; 1 cup	18	460	4	Trace	124	99	6.2	30	.13	.12	.7	2
Raspberries, red:												
Raw; 1 cup	84	70	1	Trace	17	49	1.1	160	.03	.08	.4	29
Frozen; 10-ounce carton	74	280	2	1	70	79	1.7	220	.03	.12	.5	45
Rhubarb, cooked, sugar added; 1 cup	63	385	1	Trace	98	112	1.1	70	.02	0	.2	17
Strawberries:												
Raw; 1 cup	90	55	1	1	12	42	1.2	90	.04	.10	.4	89
Frozen; 10-ounce carton	72	300	2	1	75	62	1.7	120	.05	.14	.5	116
Frozen; 16-ounce can	72	485	3	2	121	100	2.7	190	.08	.23	.8	186
Tangerines; 1 medium (2½-inch diam.), about ¼ pound	87	40	1	Trace	10	34	.3	360	.05	.01	.1	26
Tangerine juice:												
Canned; 1 cup	89	100	1	Trace	25	45	.5	1,050	.14	.04	.3	56
Frozen concentrate:												
Undiluted; 1 can (6 fluid ounces)	58	315	4	1	80	130	1.5	3,070	.43	.12	.9	202
Diluted, ready-to-serve; 1 cup	88	105	1	Trace	27	45	.5	1,020	.14	.04	.3	67
Watermelon; 1 wedge (4 × 8 inches), about 2 pounds (weighed with rind)	92	120	2	1	29	30	.9	2,530	.20	.22	.7	26

From USDA *Yearbook of Agriculture*, 1959.

[a]Vitamin A based on yellow corn; white corn contains only a trace.

[b]Average vitamin A value for important commercial varieties. Varieties with pale flesh contain very small amounts; those with deep orange-colored flesh have much higher contents than the value shown in the table.

[c]Vitamin A based on deeply colored varieties.

[d]Vitamin A value for juice from white grapefruit. The vitamin A value per cup of juice from pink or red grapefruit is 1,080 I.U.

[e]Vitamin A value of yellow-fleshed varieties; the value is negligible in white-fleshed varieties.

[f]Content of frozen peaches with added ascorbic acid; when not added the content is 14 milligrams per 12-ounce carton and 18 milligrams per 16-ounce can.

TABLE 14-26 • *General garden pests*

Pest	Description and Damage	Control
	Chordates	
Mice and rats	Consume and contaminate stored products. Mice girdle woody plants by chewing away bark.	Poison baits placed where other animals cannot reach. Traps. Areas around the crowns of trees and shrubs should be kept free of grass and loose mulches where mouse damage is a problem.
Rabbits	Chew off bark and young twigs of woody plants during winter and consume leafy plants during summer.	Fine mesh screen around lower trunk; tightly woven fences well-anchored to the ground; repellents painted on trunks and lower branches.
Moles, voles, gophers	Burrow through ground, feeding on root crops and roots of garden plants.	Poison baits, fumigant-type pellets, or traps placed in their runs. Control is usually easiest in early spring or fall when activity is evidenced by fresh mounds.
Ground squirrels, chucks	Voracious feeding on leafy succulent plants during spring and summer.	Traps or poisoned baits (strychnine baits can be dangerous to pets that feed on dead rodents).
Dogs	Males urinate and kill parts of leafy plants, especially conifers; females urinating may cause small dead patches in a lawn; leave feces on lawns or flower beds.	Fences. Repellents are partially successful.
Cats	Can severely damage bark on young trees where they sharpen their claws. House cats are the number-1 enemy of song birds in the garden.	Screens around base of young trees. Keep cats' claws clipped.
Deer	Damage woody plants by browsing.	Fence 7 to 10 ft (2 to 2½ m) high. Repellents are partially successful.
Birds	Consume and destroy fruit and seed crops like sunflowers. Especially fond of strawberries and sweet cherries. Starlings, because of their prolific numbers and flocking habit, are usually most damaging, but robins and others can be pests.	Cheesecloth or other mesh material can be draped over trees susceptible to bird damage. Screen or cloth can be placed over strawberries and other small fruits. Commercially designed noisemakers are partially effective but not very popular in populated areas.
	Insects and Insectlike Pests	
Ants	Nurture aphids, scale, mealybugs on plants; nuisance in garden and home. Plants are killed around nests of some kinds.	Insecticides when control is required.
Aphids	Green, black, pink, or yellow soft-bodied, small sucking insects that feed in colonies. May be extremely numerous. Cause unthrifty plants and transmit many virus diseases. Some excrete honeydew.	Encourage predators (wasps, ladybird beetles) by using insecticides only where absolutely necessary. Insecticide where needed.
Borers	Larvae of various beetles and moths bore into stems of plants, causing feeding damage and breakage.	Cut off and destroy infested parts. Spray with insecticide before eggs hatch to kill larvae as they enter the stem.

(*continued*)

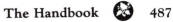

TABLE 14-26 • *(Continued)*

Pest	Description and Damage	Control
Insects and Insectlike Pests		
Cabbage loopers	Green larvae of the white cabbage butterfly. Center part of body "loops" as the insect moves. Feeds on leaves of vegetables and flowers of Cruciferae (mustard) family.	Weekly or biweekly insecticidal sprays are usually necessary to protect cabbage and related plants from this insect. B.T., an insecticide approved for organic growing, is effective.
Corn earworms	Large striped tan or green worms. Cause wormy corn. Also feed on tomatoes, gladiolus, and other vegetables and flowers.	Mineral oil or an insecticide on developing corn silks. Spray other infected plants.
Cucumber beetles	Medium-sized spotted and closely related striped beetles that feed on cucurbits and many other vegetables and flowering plants. Larvae feed on roots.	Apply insecticide as soon as damage is noticed and repeat as directed on the label.
Cutworms	Hairless caterpillars of moths. Feed on leaves and young stems, usually at night. Most damage is from cutting off new seedlings or transplants at base.	Spray plant and/or soil (follow directions on label) with insecticide. Use metaldehyde bait. Most prevalent in soil plowed from old sod.
Earwigs	Insects with long pincers at their rear. Feed on leaves, flowers, fruit, and roots. Become extremely numerous and can infest a home; hide in dark corners and crevices.	Soil treatment with a suitable insecticide. Destroy hiding places by getting rid of trash.
Flea beetles	Small, black jumping insects that chew small holes in leaves. Can destroy newly emerged seedlings in a few hours.	Spray emerging seedlings with a recommended insecticide at the first sign of the insect or its damage.
Grasshoppers	Late summer pests that consume large amounts of material from many kinds of plants. Eggs laid in soil in fall hatch the following spring.	Apply insecticide to plant leaves and stems as damage is noticed. Baits are available for heavy infestations.
Grubs	Root-feeding larvae of various beetles and weevils. Cause dead patches in lawns and reduce vigor or kill other plants. May feed on above-ground organs at night.	Treat soil with an appropriate insecticide.
Japanese beetles	Large, metallic green beetles. Extremely destructive to many kinds of plants, especially their flowers and fruit, from early July to September. Not yet a pest west of the Rockies.	Foliage can be protected by coating it with insecticide. It is much more difficult to protect flower buds.
Leafhoppers	Small hopping green or brown insects. Their feeding on the underside of leaves causes whitish spots on upper leaf surface. Winter over on and transmit virus diseases from desert plants.	Apply insecticide when pest becomes damaging. Because of their erratic feeding and long-distance movement, spraying will not usually control curly top and other virus diseases spread by this insect.
Leaf miners	Tiny larvae that burrow and feed beneath the leaf epidermis, causing unsightly serpentine feeding tunnels.	Spray insecticide to kill adults before they lay eggs or larvae before they enter leaves. Sprays cannot reach larvae after they enter leaves.

(*continued*)

TABLE 14-26 • *General garden pests (Continued)*

Pest	Description and Damage	Control
Insects and Insectlike Pests		
Mealybugs	Small white "scale" insects usually identified by the waxy white secretion with which they surround themselves. Sap the plant by sucking juices; some also feed on roots.	When only a few are present on houseplants, they can be controlled by touching each with a cloth dipped in alcohol. Systemic insecticides give best control for larger infestations.
Scale	Small insects that attach themselves to and suck juices from stems and leaves. They become covered with a protective shell. May secrete honeydew that attracts ants.	Treat infested woody plants with an oil spray during the dormant season. Treat with an insecticide (a systemic where one can be used) when damage is noted.
Snails and slugs	Not an insect but can be very damaging to plant parts near ground. Feed at night and on cloudy or rainy days, leaving slimy trails. Hide in soil when sun shines.	Wherever damage has occurred during previous years, slug bait should be put out during early spring and as required later in the growing season.
Spider mites	Also not true insects but one of the worst summer pests in areas with warm, dry climates. Leaves of infested plants are finely stippled on top, with webs on underside. Many kinds are too small to see without magnification.	Frequent light sprinkling to thoroughly wet foliage may help control mite infestation. Miticide sprays may need to be repeated several times as many don't destroy eggs. Encourage mite predators by avoiding unnecessary pesticide application in the yard.
Thrips	Tiny, slim insects that damage by rasping and distorting leaves. Often distort and/or prevent flower buds from opening. Gladiolus and onions seem especially susceptible.	Encourage predators by avoiding unnecessary pesticide applications. Spray with insecticide when damage is noted and repeat as recommended on label or as needed.
Weevils	Long-snouted insects with hard protective wing covers. Adults feed on leaves and fruit during night. Larvae destroy roots or hatch in grain products. Pea and bean weevils lay eggs in blossoms. Larvae grow and reach adulthood in seed.	Treat soil with insecticide before planting or treat after and water in. Use insecticide for adults when damage is noted. Spray peas and beans during bloom where dried seed is being grown in areas where weevils are a problem.
Whiteflies	Small, pure white adults flutter erratically when disturbed. Scalelike young attach to and feed on underside of leaves. Common on house and greenhouse plants as well as outdoors.	Apply insecticide when you see the pest and repeat to destroy those newly hatched. Difficult to control. A systemic can be effective with ornamentals.
Wireworms	Larvae of "click" beetle. Wavy yellow hard grubs from ½ to 2 in (1¼ to 5 cm) long. Kill roots, burrow into bulbs, fleshy roots, tubers. Attack germinating seed.	Treat soil with recommended insecticide before planting or treat after planting and water in.

(*continued*)

TABLE 14-26 • *(Continued)*

Pest	Description and Damage	Control
	Diseases	
Root knot nematodes	Nematodes are microscopic wormlike entities. In a field of susceptible plants infection starts with circular patches of dead or unthrifty plants that enlarge each year until the entire field is affected. Root symptoms are swellings of various shapes and sizes on major roots, causing death of feeder roots and areas for entry of other pathogenic organisms.	Prevent garden infestation by planting only nematode-free stock from a reliable nursery. Clean thoroughly garden tools that have been borrowed or used in another location. Fumigate infested areas before planting susceptible crops. Grow grasses, grains, and sweet corn, which are resistant, for several years to reduce the nematode population. Plant other monocots, most of which are highly tolerant or resistant.
Other nematodes	Cause unthrifty plants. Many affect only one or two kinds of plants. Some cause root lesions, and nematodes and organisms for which they provide points of entry may cause decay.	Same control as for root knot nematodes except that resistant species of garden plants will be different for each nematode.
Root diseases	Unthrifty plants that wilt readily. Infection by some pathogens result in sudden death. Roots will often be rotted. A longitudinal cut will often reveal a discolored vascular system.	Same sanitation, rotation, and fumigation practices as for nematodes. Do not plant stone fruits where potatoes or tomatoes have recently grown. Dig onions before cold, wet weather. Treatment with fungicide will often control seed-borne organisms. Dig and burn infected plants; do not use them for compost. Do not overwater.
Damping-off	A number of organisms kill plants by destroying their stems at ground level. This is called damping-off. Young seedlings are especially susceptible.	Treat seed with fungicide. Germinate seed and prick off seedlings into a pasteurized growing medium if damping-off has been a problem. Make certain that all containers for growing seedlings are free of soil and thoroughly clean. A light dusting of sulfur or other fungicide helps control these diseases.
Rots and decays	These are caused by both bacteria and fungi or sometimes a combination of pathogens. Rotting organisms usually enter through a break in the protective layer. Breaks are usually caused by rough handling or insects or other pathogens.	Keep plants and plant parts from becoming crowded, which prevents free circulation of air. Do not permit free moisture to remain on plant parts for long periods. Don't allow fruits and vegetables to become overmature. Harvest and handle all perishable products carefully to avoid bruising. Provide optimum storage conditions (Table 14-21), and cool products as quickly as possible. Sort out and destroy plants, plant parts, or stored products that have begun to decay.

(continued)

TABLE 14-26 • *General garden pests (Continued)*

Pest	Description and Damage	Control
Diseases		
Leaf-spot diseases	Leaf spots in center or along margins of leaves. Spots may spread and leaves yellow and fall. Usually more serious after heavy rains or sprinkler irrigation.	Avoid frequent light sprinkling where leaf diseases are a problem. Water during early morning so leaves can dry before evening. Sulfur and other fungicidal dusts will prevent some leaf diseases.
Mildews	Weblike or powdery white fungal growth (mycelium), usually beginning on underside of leaves or lower crowded stems, often spreading to remainder of plant. Mildewed plants may be attacked by other decay-causing organisms.	Same as for leaf-spot diseases. Avoid crowding plants.
Sclerotinia	Sclerotinia is almost ubiquitous in garden soils. Affects flowers, fruits, stems, and leaves that are in contact with soil, usually during cool weather of fall. Infection results in water-soaked areas that soon begin to rot and in white cottony mycelial growth often containing hard black fruiting bodies.	Avoid overwatering. Stake tomato plants. Pumpkins and melons can be placed on platforms before they mature. Do not leave fruit in contact with soil after it is mature. Give plenty of space to fall flowers and keep blooms from touching the soil.
Virus diseases	Virus diseases are difficult to diagnose because symptoms are so variable. A combination of two or more of the following usually suggests a virus: stunted growth or year-by-year decline of perennials; yellowed or markedly light colored leaves; cupping up or down of leaves; brittle leaves, that is, leaves that break with a crackling sound when crushed; areas of light and dark green (mosaic pattern) in leaves and stems; dead spots on leaves or around leaf margins; dark colored or dead streaks in leaves and/or on petioles and stems, flowers having streaks of two colors; dark streaks in the vascular system; pitting of stems, leaves, or fruit; dying back of new shoots; distorted flowers, leaves, or other plant parts; excessive branching; growth habit different from that of other plants of the species.	Once a plant is infected with a virus, it is impractical to attempt a cure. Plant a resistant cultivar. Use certified virus-free planting stock whenever available. Rogue out and destroy plants that become infected. Wash hands and pruning tools frequently and avoid use of tobacco products when handling plants; especially potato, tomato, pepper, eggplant, petunia, and nicotiana. Keep plants free of aphids and leafhoppers. Keep plants vigorously growing and healthy.

CLIMATE, HARDINESS, AND MATURITY

◆ ◆ ◆

The mean temperature, hardiness zones, record temperatures, precipitation, and degree days listed in Table 14-27 and the USDA Plant Hardiness Zone Map (Figure 14-96), coupled with the hardiness zones for various plants shown in Table 14-28, should help gardeners determine which kinds of plants are likely to mature or survive and do well in the climate where they live. Spring and fall frosts are listed, wherever available, to help determine planting date and length of growing season. Precipitation amounts suggest whether or not irrigation is likely to be needed. Remember that many kinds of cool-season plants do not do well where temperatures are hot. Thus the range of zones to which each plant is adapted is given in Table 14-28 as a rough guide to both cold hardiness and heat tolerance.

Cold Hardiness

Traditionally, woody plants for North American gardens have been classified into winter-hardiness categories based on the lowest temperature they are likely to survive. The classification having the widest use is the one established by the USDA, which classifies into ten hardiness groups based on 10°F increments, from those that can survive 40° to 30°F (4° to −1°C) (hardiness group 10) to those that can survive temperatures below −50°F (−46°C) (hardiness group 1). North America has been divided into ten zones based on the average minimum winter temperature. This zone map was revised a short time ago to reflect more recent and longer-term weather information.

To decide whether or not a particular plant will survive, look at the map to find the zones in which you live and then at the hardiness zone listed for the plant in Table 14-28. As a further check, I have listed the hardiness zones for a few weather station locations in each state and province (see Table 14-27). Those people living in the vicinity of these weather stations usually know whether their gardens are in a warmer or colder location.

The minimum temperature recorded for each location listed in Table 14-27 enables growers to decide which kinds of plants may require occasional winter protection in their climate.

Weather stations are sometimes located where conditions differ from the average of the surrounding areas and, as was stated in Chapter 7, many factors affect cold-temperature survival. Consequently, although the plant hardiness zone designation is useful as a rough guide of winter survival, plants listed as hardy in a specific zone cannot always be counted on to do well there. As is true with so many facets of gardening, the experience of local growers is likely to be the most accurate predictor of plant winter survival.

Predicting Maturity

The ability of warm-season crops to mature in cold-climate areas depends largely on the amount of heat energy accumulated during the frost-free period. The accumulation of heat is usually measured in heat units, also called degree days, as described in Chapter 7.

The utilization of degree days is based on the fact that most cool-season crops do not grow until the temperature is above about 40°F (5°C) and that most warm-season crops do not grow until the temperature reaches 50°F (10°C). Also, within the growing range, the rapidity of growth increases as the temperature rises. The number of degree days for any one day is calculated by subtracting the base temperature (40° or 50°F) from the mean temperature for that day. Thus if on June 15 the maximum temperature is 80°F and the minimum is 60°F, the mean will be 70°F and the number of degree days for June 15 will be 70 minus 50 or 20 for warm-season crops and 70 minus 40 or 30 for cool-season crops.

The long-term average number of degree days likely to accumulate on any one day is calculated by subtracting the base temperature from the long-term mean temperature for that day. The average number of annual degree days for a geographic location (Table 14-27) is determined by adding together the average number of degree days for each day of the growing season.

(*text continues on p. 502*)

TABLE 14-27 • *Climatic data for selected municipalities in the United States and Canada*

City and State	Temperature (mean) (Fahrenheit) January	July	Average Annual	Killing Frost Spring	Fall
ALABAMA					
Birmingham	45.5	80.0	63.2	3-19	11-14
Mobile	51.7	81.8	67.5	2-17	12-12
Montgomery	49.2	81.2	65.4	2-27	12-3
ALASKA					
Anchorage	11.4	57.6	34.7	5-18	9-13
Fairbanks	−12.0	60.4	25.6	5-24	8-29
Juneau	22.8	55.5	39.9	4-27	10-19
ARIZONA					
Flagstaff	27.8	65.7	45.5	6-8	10-2
Phoenix	51.6	90.7	70.2	1-27	12-11
Tucson	50.3	86.1	67.4	3-6	12-23
ARKANSAS					
Little Rock	41.7	81.3	62.2	3-16	11-15
CALIFORNIA					
Bakersfield	47.4	84.3	65.1	2-14	11-28
Los Angeles	55.9	71.3	63.6	b	b
Red Bluff	45.5	83.8	63.5	2-25	11-29
Sacramento	44.5	75.9	60.5	1-24	12-11
San Diego	55.0	68.3	61.9	b	b
San Francisco	50.2	58.8	56.5	b	b
COLORADO					
Colorado Springs	29.5	70.7	48.7	5-7	10-8
Denver	30.2	72.7	50.2	5-2	10-14
Grand Junction	26.0	78.3	52.6	4-20	10-22
CONNECTICUT					
Hartford	27.0	73.0	50.0	4-22	10-19
New Haven	29.1	71.2	49.7	4-15	10-27
DELAWARE					
Dover	36.8	77.2	56.3	4-15	10-26
DISTRICT OF COLUMBIA	35.6	78.4	57.1	4-10	10-28
FLORIDA					
Jacksonville	55.9	82.6	69.5	2-6	12-16
Miami	66.9	82.2	75.3	b	b
Orlando	60.5	82.3	72.4	1-31	12-17
Tallahassee	53.9	81.3	68.0	2-26	12-3
Tampa	60.9	81.8	72.2	1-10	12-26
GEORGIA					
Atlanta	43.3	78.5	61.5	3-20	11-19
Columbus	47.8	81.1	64.4	3-10	11-20
Savannah	51.7	81.5	66.8	2-21	12-9
HAWAII					
Hilo	71.0	75.1	73.2	Never	
Honolulu	72.4	78.8	76.0	Never	
IDAHO					
Boise	29.9	74.5	51.3	4-29	12-16
Lewiston	32.7	73.8	51.6	4-21	10-17
Pocatello	22.3	72.4	47.0	5-8	9-30

Hardiness Zone[a]	Record Temperatures (Fahrenheit) High	Low	Precipitation Average Annual (inches)	Degree Days Average Annual (Base 50°F)	(Base 40°F)
7	107	-10	53.25	5,191	8,509
9	104	-1	63.11	6,412	10,062
8	107	-5	53.66	5,694	9,301
4	86	-38	14.83	532	1,863
2	99	-66	11.57	783	2,004
6	89	-21	54.18	391	1,832
5	96	-30	20.16	937	3,238
8	118	16	7.41	7,412	11,062
8	112	6	11.22	6,382	10,032
7	110	-13	47.87	5,067	8,125
9	118	13	6.36	5,644	9,176
10	110	28	14.87	4,953	8,603
7	115	17	22.05	5,200	8,612
9	115	17	17.32	4,180	7,499
10	111	25	9.76	4,359	8,009
10	101	27	21.51	2,391	6,041
5	100	-32	14.81	2,200	4,208
5	105	-30	14.47	2,500	4,565
5	105	-23	8.51	3,391	5,611
6	102	-26	42.38	2,684	4,824
7	101	-15	44.99	2,463	4,573
7	104	-11	46.40	3,724	6,231
7	106	-15	39.54	4,013	6,564
9	105	12	53.36	7,141	10,791
10	100	28	60.19	9,255	12,905
9	103	20	50.90	8,186	11,836
9	100	10	58.86	6,597	10,247
10	98	18	49.30	8,128	11,778
8	103	-9	48.40	4,714	7,872
8	104	3	48.67	5,439	8,941
9	105	8	48.47	6,164	9,814
>10	94	51	133.27	8,467	12,117
>10	92	54	24.30	9,506	13,156
6	112	-28	11.97	2,613	4,833
6	117	-23	13.24	2,606	4,827
5	105	-31	10.85	2,169	4,116

(*continued*)

TABLE 14-27 • *Climatic data for selected municipalities in the United States and Canada (Continued)*

City and State	Temperature (mean) (Fahrenheit)		Average Annual	Killing Frost	
	January	July		Spring	Fall
ILLINOIS					
Chicago	24.7	73.7	49.9	4-19	10-28
Peoria	24.4	75.6	51.2	4-22	10-16
Springfield	27.3	77.3	53.3	4-8	10-30
INDIANA					
Evansville	34.7	78.2	56.9	4-2	11-4
Ft. Wayne	26.3	73.5	49.9	4-24	10-20
Indianapolis	28.4	75.7	52.6	4-17	10-27
South Bend	24.5	73.1	49.4	5-3	10-16
IOWA					
Burlington	24.4	76.6	51.2	4-22	10-17
Des Moines	20.8	76.0	49.9	4-20	10-19
Sioux City	18.7	77.4	49.1	4-28	10-12
Waterloo	17.9	73.8	47.2	4-28	10-4
KANSAS					
Dodge City	30.3	79.9	55.0	4-22	10-24
Topeka	28.6	79.0	54.8	4-9	10-26
Wichita	31.7	80.2	56.6	4-5	11-1
KENTUCKY					
Lexington	33.5	76.2	55.1	4-13	10-28
Louisville	34.6	78.4	56.8	4-1	11-7
LOUISIANA					
Baton Rouge	52.4	81.1	67.5	2-22	12-1
New Orleans	54.0	82.4	69.0	2-13	12-12
Shreveport	47.4	83.2	66.0	3-1	11-27
MAINE					
Caribou	10.5	64.9	38.7	5-19	9-21
Portland	22.4	68.2	45.5	4-29	10-15
MARYLAND					
Baltimore	32.5	76.8	54.9	4-28	11-17
MASSACHUSETTS					
Boston	38.7	72.5	50.3	4-16	10-25
Worcester	23.8	69.9	47.0	5-7	10-2
MICHIGAN					
Detroit	25.2	73.0	49.1	4-25	10-23
Grand Rapids	24.4	72.8	48.5	4-25	10-27
Marquette	17.4	65.8	41.7	5-14	10-17
MINNESOTA					
Duluth	8.6	65.1	38.6	5-22	9-24
Minneapolis	13.2	73.0	44.9	4-30	10-13
MISSISSIPPI					
Jackson	48.2	81.8	65.5	3-10	11-13
Meridian	47.5	80.9	64.5	3-13	11-14
MISSOURI					
Kansas City	29.8	79.5	55.6	4-5	10-31
St. Louis	31.7	79.4	56.2	4-2	11-8
Springfield	33.6	78.8	56.5	4-10	10-31

Hardiness Zone[a]	Record Temperatures (Fahrenheit) High	Low	Precipitation Average Annual (inches)	Degree Days Average Annual (Base 50°F)	(Base 40°F)
6	105	-23	33.23	2,840	4,926
5	113	-27	34.80	3,204	5,356
6	112	-24	25.33	3,598	5,828
6	105	-23	41.37	4,024	6,239
5	103	-17	34.21	2,778	4,852
6	107	-25	39.90	3,310	5,507
5	109	-22	35.19	2,778	4,858
5	111	-27	34.60	3,287	5,427
5	110	-30	31.24	3,128	5,268
4	111	-37	24.77	3,212	5,319
4	112	-34	31.48	2,760	3,946
5	109	-26	20.58	3,874	6,176
6	114	-25	33.18	3,901	6,227
6	114	-22	29.99	4,210	6,651
6	108	-21	43.14	3,640	6,036
6	107	-20	42.60	4,025	6,525
9	103	19	59.13	6,407	10,057
9	102	7	57.49	6,953	10,603
8	110	-5	44.33	5,975	9,523
3	103	-41	35.76	1,251	2,887
6	103	-39	41.89	1,841	3,756
7	107	-7	40.61	3,585	5,965
6	104	-18	41.40	2,635	4,781
5	102	-24	45.09	2,157	4,150
6	105	-24	31.52	2,680	4,721
5	108	-24	33.02	2,610	4,651
5	108	-27	31.66	1,446	3,178
4	106	-41	28.19	1,310	2,949
4	108	-34	26.72	2,482	4,499
8	107	-5	50.46	5,754	9,333
8	105	-7	55.07	5,449	8,965
6	113	-22	36.47	4,054	6,437
6	115	-23	36.65	4,084	6,513
6	113	-29	41.08	4,017	6,431

(*continued*)

TABLE 14-27 • *Climatic data for selected municipalities in the United States and Canada (Continued)*

City and State	Temperature (Mean) (Fahrenheit)		Average	Killing Frost	
	January	July	Annual	Spring	Fall
MONTANA					
Billings	23.2	74.7	47.5	5-15	9-24
Great Falls	22.1	69.4	44.7	5-14	9-26
Kalispell	19.8	65.7	42.8	5-12	9-23
Miles City	16.5	75.3	45.8	5-5	10-3
NEBRASKA					
North Platte	23.7	74.8	49.3	4-30	10-7
Omaha	22.0	77.4	51.1	4-14	10-20
NEVADA					
Las Vegas	44.0	89.4	65.8	3-13	11-13
Reno	31.2	69.6	49.4	5-14	10-2
NEW HAMPSHIRE					
Concord	21.3	70.1	46.0	5-11	9-30
NEW JERSEY					
Atlantic City	30.8	74.4	53.0	3-31	11-11
Newark	31.6	76.2	53.7	4-3	11-8
NEW MEXICO					
Albuquerque	34.6	77.1	55.7	4-16	10-29
Clayton	33.2	74.5	53.1	5-2	10-15
Roswell	37.9	78.6	58.5	4-9	10-2
NEW YORK					
Albany	22.9	72.5	48.1	4-27	10-13
Buffalo	25.0	70.2	47.3	4-30	10-25
New York	32.1	76.1	54.0	4-7	11-12
Syracuse	24.1	71.1	47.7	4-30	10-15
Watertown	20.4	70.5	46.3	5-7	10-4
NORTH CAROLINA					
Asheville	34.9	72.6	54.6	4-12	10-24
Charlotte	42.7	79.2	60.8	3-21	11-15
Raleigh	41.6	78.3	60.0	3-24	11-16
Wilmington	47.9	80.0	63.8	3-8	11-24
NORTH DAKOTA					
Bismarck	9.2	72.1	41.7	5-11	9-24
Fargo	5.0	69.9	40.1	5-13	9-27
Williston	10.0	70.9	41.3	5-14	9-23
OHIO					
Cincinnati	31.7	76.3	54.6	4-15	10-25
Cleveland	27.4	72.2	49.9	4-21	11-2
Columbus	29.3	74.8	52.3	4-17	10-30
Toledo	26.0	73.3	49.8	4-24	10-25
Youngstown	27.5	72.3	49.8	4-23	10-20
OKLAHOMA					
Oklahoma City	37.3	81.5	60.1	3-28	11-7
Tulsa	37.3	82.5	60.7	3-31	11-2
OREGON					
Burns	23.9	69.8	46.8	5-20	9-21
Eugene	38.2	66.6	52.4	4-9	10-31
Medford	37.2	71.8	54.5	4-25	10-20
Pendleton	32.5	73.3	52.4	4-27	10-8
Portland	38.4	65.3	52.3	2-25	12- 1

Hardiness Zone[a]	Record Temperatures (Fahrenheit) High	Low	Precipitation Average Annual (inches)	Degree Days Average Annual (Base 50°F)	(Base 40°F)
5	112	-49	13.23	2,420	4,425
5	107	-49	14.07	1,734	3,605
5	105	-38	15.42	1,360	3,122
4	111	-49	12.17	2,512	4,492
5	112	-35	18.61	2,767	4,868
5	114	-32	28.44	3,391	5,531
8	117	8	3.85	6,161	9,455
6	104	-16	6.96	1,993	4,089
5	102	-37	38.08	2,093	4,046
7	106	-9	41.27	3,121	5,438
7	105	-14	41.32	3,342	5,666
6	104	-17	8.42	3,652	6,101
5	105	-21	14.51	3,057	5,276
6	110	-29	11.62	4,222	6,893
5	104	-28	36.29	2,555	4,590
6	99	-21	35.09	2,226	4,165
7	106	-15	43.00	3,388	5,745
5	102	-26	35.63	2,368	4,373
5	99	-39	38.85	2,279	4,254
7	99	-7	45.39	3,165	5,619
8	104	-5	43.38	4,598	7,627
8	105	-2	45.23	4,348	7,321
8	105	5	51.29	5,209	8,701
3	114	-45	15.40	2,116	3,916
3	114	-48	21.00	1,996	3,768
3	110	-50	14.66	1,958	3,745
6	109	-17	39.40	3,576	5,938
6	103	-19	33.82	2,680	4,778
6	106	-20	36.79	3,167	5,373
6	105	-17	31.43	2,763	4,843
5	100	-12	41.33	2,683	4,757
7	113	-17	31.47	4,738	7,486
7	115	-16	37.37	4,854	7,658
5	103	-25	10.25	1,838	3,789
8	105	-4	37.51	1,986	4,587
8	115	-10	18.15	2,687	5,249
6	119	-28	12.97	2,633	4,970
8	107	-3	37.72	1,964	4,564

(*continued*)

TABLE 14-27 • *Climatic data for selected municipalities in the United States and Canada (Continued)*

City and State	Temperature (mean) (Fahrenheit)		Average Annual	Killing Frost	
	January	July		Spring	Fall
PENNSYLVANIA					
Harrisburg	30.3	75.2	52.6	4-10	10-28
Philadelphia	33.0	76.6	54.6	3-30	10-17
Pittsburgh	30.6	74.6	52.7	4-20	10-23
Scranton	27.1	72.2	49.6	4-24	10-14
RHODE ISLAND					
Providence	20.2	72.7	50.5	4-13	10-27
SOUTH CAROLINA					
Charleston	50.0	81.1	65.8	2-19	12-10
Columbia	46.9	81.6	64.0	3-14	11-21
SOUTH DAKOTA					
Rapid City	21.1	72.3	46.1	5-7	10-4
Sioux Falls	15.2	74.1	46.3	5-5	10-3
TENNESSEE					
Knoxville	39.3	77.7	58.9	3-31	11-6
Memphis	41.2	81.2	61.9	3-20	11-12
Nashville	38.9	79.4	59.5	3-28	11-7
TEXAS					
Amarillo	36.6	77.9	57.2	4-20	10-28
Corpus Christi	57.4	84.1	71.8	2-9	12-12
Dallas	45.5	85.0	65.9	3-18	11-22
El Paso	42.9	81.9	63.3	3-14	11-12
Houston	51.7	83.2	68.0	2-5	12-11
Midland	44.0	82.9	64.3	4-3	11-6
San Antonio	52.1	84.0	69.1	3-3	11-26
UTAH					
Milford	23.8	74.0	49.0	5-21	9-26
Salt Lake City	28.1	77.2	51.7	4-12	11-1
St. George	38.7	83.5	60.8	4-3	10-30
Vernal	15.4	69.5	44.3	5-29	9-25
VERMONT					
Burlington	17.9	69.6	44.5	5-8	10-3
VIRGINIA					
Norfolk	41.4	78.6	59.8	3-18	11-27
Richmond	37.7	77.7	57.6	4-2	11-8
Roanoke	36.3	76.2	56.4	4-20	10-24
WASHINGTON					
Aberdeen	39.7	60.1	50.3	4-16	10-30
Seattle	38.2	64.2	50.9	2-23	12-1
Spokane	26.9	70.2	48.2	4-20	10-12
Walla Walla	33.2	76.0	54.2	3-28	11-1
Yakima	27.5	71.0	49.8	4-19	10-15
WEST VIRGINIA					
Charleston	36.5	76.1	56.4	4-18	10-28
Parkersburgh	34.4	75.7	54.9	4-16	10-21
WISCONSIN					
Green Bay	16.1	69.9	43.6	5-6	10-13
La Crosse	15.7	74.0	46.2	5-1	10-8
Madison	17.3	71.3	46.0	4-26	10-19
Milwaukee	20.9	70.7	46.5	4-20	10-25

Hardiness Zone[a]	Record Temperatures (Fahrenheit) High	Low	Precipitation Average Annual (inches)	Degree Days Average Annual (Base 50°F)	(Base 40°F)
6	107	-14	37.38	3,177	5,425
7	106	-11	40.97	3,498	5,873
6	103	-20	35.99	3,170	5,406
5	103	-19	36.33	2,595	4,705
6	102	-17	40.30	2,645	4,809
9	104	7	48.51	5,786	9,436
8	107	-2	46.82	5,374	8,772
4	109	-33	17.10	2,211	4,158
4	110	-42	25.29	2,632	4,685
7	104	-16	47.68	4,186	6,926
7	106	-13	48.23	4,999	8,010
7	107	-15	46.12	4,434	7,191
6	108	-16	20.54	3,946	6,498
9	105	-11	28.34	7,973	11,623
8	111	-3	35.00	6,063	9,498
7	109	-8	7.89	5,312	8,533
8	108	5	46.42	6,603	10,253
7	107	-11	14.24	5,618	8,907
9	107	0	27.14	6,995	10,645
5	104	-34	8.44	2,483	4,557
5	107	-30	15.58	2,974	5,121
6	116	-11	8.22	4,825	7,648
4	106	-38	8.22	1,919	3,871
5	98	-27	32.30	2,037	3,924
8	105	2	15.13	4,333	7,259
7	107	-12	43.11	3,973	6,573
7	105	-12	39.09	3,719	6,218
9	105	6	84.54	1,302	3,795
8	100	0	40.15	1,665	4,053
5	108	-30	16.17	2,049	4,083
7	113	-16	15.50	3,153	5,548
6	111	-25	7.86	2,296	4,495
6	108	-17	43.35	3,737	6,264
6	106	-27	39.11	3,511	5,913
5	104	-36	26.51	2,052	3,897
4	108	-43	28.92	2,638	4,676
5	107	-37	30.13	2,359	4,388
5	105	-25	30.04	2,243	4,220

(continued)

TABLE 14-27 • *Climatic data for selected municipalities in the United States and Canada (Continued)*

City and State	Temperature (mean) (Fahrenheit) January	July	Average Annual	Killing Frost Spring	Fall
WYOMING					
Casper	22.3	71.1	45.1	5-18	9-25
Cheyenne	26.2	67.8	45.1	5-20	9-27
Lander	16.8	70.4	43.2	5-15	9-20
Sheridan	20.1	70.6	44.5	5-21	9-21

City and Province	Temperature (mean) (Celsius) January	July	Average Annual	Killing Frost Spring	Fall
ALBERTA					
Calgary	−9.9	16.7	3.6	5-26	9-10
Edmonton	−14.1	17.3	2.7	5-15	9-17
Lethbridge	−8.2	18.9	5.4	5-21	9-17
BRITISH COLUMBIA					
Pr. George	−11.3	14.9	3.3	6-10	8-28
Pr. Rupert	1.8	13.4	7.6	4-28	10-28
Vancouver	2.9	17.7	10.2	3-22	11-11
MANITOBA					
Churchill	−27.5	12.0	−7.2	6-25	9-11
The Pas	−21.7	18.2	−0.4	5-27	9-19
Winnipeg	−17.7	20.2	2.5	5-25	9-21
NEW BRUNSWICK					
St. John	−6.9	17.2	5.4	5-10	10-12
NEWFOUNDLAND					
Goose	−16.6	16.3	0.2	6-6	9-17
St. John's	−4.3	15.4	4.7	6-2	10-3
NORTHWEST TERRITORIES					
Ft. Smith	−24.5	16.2	−3.2	6-15	8-19
Frobisher Bay	−26.5	7.9	−8.9	6-30	8-29
NOVA SCOTIA					
Halifax	−3.3	18.5	7.4	5-8	10-23
ONTARIO					
Kapuskasing	−17.8	17.3	0.8	6-13	9-5
Moosonee	−20.6	15.6	−1.1	6-21	9-1
North Bay	−12.2	18.7	3.8	5-18	9-23
Ottawa	−10.8	20.7	5.7	5-8	10-4
Toronto	−3.9	21.9	8.7	5-7	10-14
QUEBEC					
Ft. Chimo	−23.9	11.8	−5.2	6-27	8-30
Montreal	−8.7	21.6	6.9	5-4	10-12
Quebec	−11.5	19.3	4.4	5-12	10-6
SASKATCHEWAN					
Regina	−16.9	19.3	2.2	6-1	9-10
Saskatoon	−17.6	19.3	2.0	5-27	9-15
YUKON					
White Horse	−18.1	14.2	−0.7	6-5	9-1

[a]See Figure 14-96.
[b]Occurs less than 1 year in 10.

Hardiness Zone[a]	Record Temperatures (Fahrenheit) High	Record Temperatures (Fahrenheit) Low	Precipitation Average Annual (inches)	Degree Days Average Annual (Base 50°F)	Degree Days Average Annual (Base 40°F)
5	104	-40	14.09	1,939	3,758
5	100	-38	14.55	1,640	3,411
4	102	-40	14.18	1,847	3,583
4	106	-41	16.75	1,884	3,724

Hardiness Zone[a]	Record Temperatures (Celsius) High	Record Temperatures (Celsius) Low	Precipitation Average Annual (mm)	Degree Days Average Annual (Base 10°C)	Degree Days Average Annual (Base 5°C)
3	36	-43	444	483	1,254
3	37	-48	473	590	1,358
4	39	-43	439	765	1,616
2	34	-50	626	357	1,112
6	32	-19	2,399	340	1,250
8	33	-18	1,044	870	1,987
2	33	-45	407	112	467
2	37	-45	451	588	1,313
3	42	-47	517	911	1,714
5	34	-33	1,362	662	1,511
5	38	-39	837	401	1,014
6	30	-23	1,551	404	1,085
1	34	-54	337	409	1,037
1	24	-45	380	0	149
5	34	-25	1,384	843	1,769
2	36	-42	858	556	1,256
2	36	-47	789	386	1,002
3	33	-40	1,034	782	1,596
4	38	-36	850	1,100	1,973
6	41	-30	776	1,299	2,279
2	32	-46	417	71	468
5	36	-34	1,048	1,232	2,169
5	36	-36	1,058	858	1,682
3	41	-46	394	783	1,551
3	40	-46	352	861	1,626
1	33	-52	257	283	907

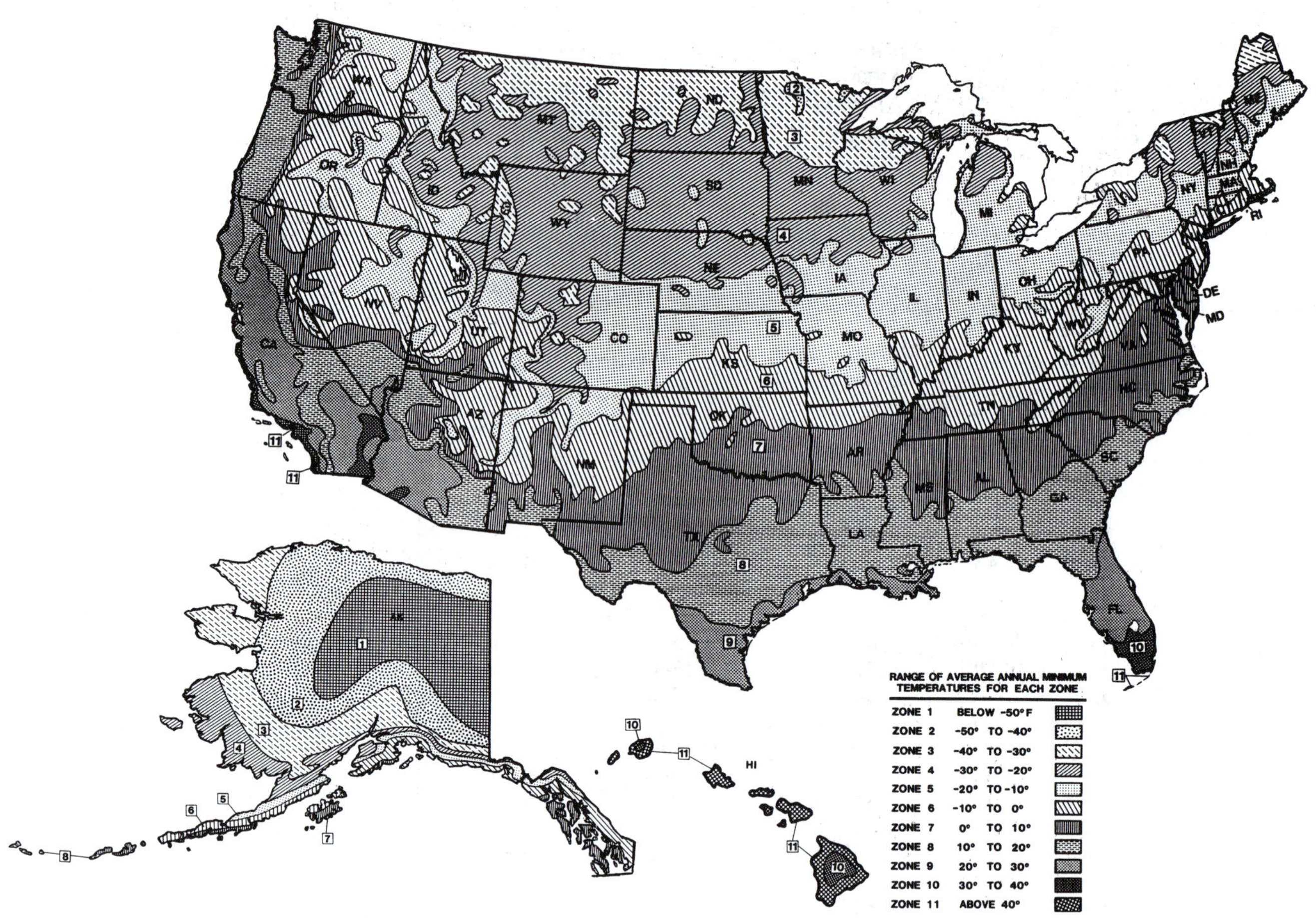

FIGURE 14-96 • The zones of plant hardiness. (Courtesy of U.S. Department of Agriculture)

The degree days (base 50°F) required for various grape cultivars are listed in Table 13-1. The 'Red Delicious' apple and 'Red Haven' peach cultivars require about 4,000 degree days (base 40°F) to mature, and so earlier-maturing cultivars should be planted in locations where there are lower heat accumulations. Mid-season sweet corn and early pepper and tomato cultivars require 1,900 to 2,100 degree days, and the standard mid-season watermelon and muskmelon cultivars cannot mature in fewer than 2,500 to 2,700 degree days (base 50°F).

PLANTS FOR THE LANDSCAPE

The characteristics of many of the woody plants most popular for the beautification of home grounds are included in Table 14-28. Selected flowers, turf plants, rock garden plants, cacti and related plants, ferns, vines, and roses are briefly described in the tables in Chapter 11. These lists are not meant to be complete, and they do not include many fine and popular ornamentals.

TABLE 14-28 • *Selected woody plants for the landscape*

Name	Hardiness Zone[a]	Growth Habit	Height (feet)	Soil and Exposure[b]	Remarks
		Trees — Conifers			
Abies balsamea Balsam fir	3–(9)	Columnar	60	B	Grows best in cool humid areas. Native to eastern N.A.
Abies concolor White fir	3–8	Columnar	75	A	Better specimens are bluish-green and very symmetrical.
Abies fraseri Fraser fir	4–9	Columnar	70	B	Performs better in eastern N.A. than most firs.
Abies nordmanniana Nordmaun fir	4–9	Dense; pyramidal	40	A	Native to Midwest; widely adapted.
Abies pinsapo Spanish fir	7–10	Pyramidal	30	A	Slow growing; rigid needles make this an interesting specimen.
Araucaria araucana Monkey puzzle tree	8–10	Oval	50	A	Twisted, ropelike branches; a unique specimen.
Calocedrus decurrens Incense cedar	5–10	Columnar	80	A	Widely adapted; good as background.
Cedrus atlantica Atlantic cedar	7–9	Pyramidal	60	B	Blue-green needles; spreading to 30 ft.
Cedrus deodara Deodar cedar	6–9	Pyramidal	80	A	Fast growing; spreading to 40 ft; many variations.
Cedrus libani Cedar of Lebanon	3–9	Dense; pyramidal	60	A	Slow growing, scarce; wide, flat crown at maturity.
Chamaecyparis lawsoniana Lawson false-cypress	6–8	Variable	to 100	A	200 forms known from small shrubs to large trees.
Chamaecyparis nootkatensis Alaska yellow cedar	4–8	Pyramidal	60	A	Slow growing with striking coarse, pendulous branches.
Cupressus glabra Arizona cypress	7–10	Broadly pyramidal	40	D	Adapted to hot interior climates; drought tolerant; fast growing.
Cupressus sempervirens Italian cypress	7–9	Narrow; columnar	60	A	Normally only the narrow upright varieties are sold.

(*continued*)

TABLE 14-28 • *Selected woody plants for the landscape (Continued)*

Name	Hardiness Zone[a]	Growth Habit	Height (feet)	Soil and Exposure[b]	Remarks
		Trees — Conifers			
Juniperus spp. Junipers	3–10	Variable	to 40	A	Many species and types; most are extremely adaptable.
Larix decidua European larch	3–9	Pyramidal	75	A	Larch are deciduous conifers. Lacy foliage; pendulous branches.
Larix occidentalis Western larch	4–9	Narrow columnar	100	A	Rapid growth for a conifer.
Metasequoia glyptostroboides Dawn redwood	5–9	Pyramidal	80	A	Can grow 60 ft in 20 years; deciduous; good reddish-brown autumn color.
Picea abies Norway spruce	2–9	Pyramidal	100	A	Fast growing; extremely hardy and wind resistant.
Picea glauca White spruce	2–7	Pyramidal	60	A	Tolerates extreme cold. Alberta spruce is a slow growing, compact form.
Picea pungens Colorado blue spruce	3–9	Pyramidal	90	A	Foliage varies from green to blue; one of the most popular conifers.
Pinus cembra Swiss stone pine	3–9	Dense; pyramidal	30	A	Slow growing; very hardy.
Pinus contorta latifolia Lodgepole pine	4–9	Bushy	40	A	Tolerant of adverse environment; variety of shore pine.
Pinus densiflora Japanese red pine	5–9	Irregular	50	A	Damaged by cold winds and desert heat; good informal effect.
Pinus mugo Swiss mountain pine	3–9	Irregular; variable	(20) Variable	A	Hardy; damaged by desert heat; bushy, twisted, open.
Pinus nigra Austrian pine	4–9	Pyramidal	40	A	Attractive rough bark; dense when young; open when old.
Pinus ponderosa Ponderosa pine	5–9	Oval	100	A	Fast-growing western native; long needles; drought tolerant.

(continued)

TABLE 14-28 • *(Continued)*

Name	Hardiness Zone[a]	Growth Habit	Height (feet)	Soil and Exposure[b]	Remarks
		Trees — Conifers			
Pinus strobus Eastern white pine	3–9	Oval	100	A	Fine-textured, handsome; subject to blister rust.
Pinus sylvestris Scotch pine	2–8	Pyramidal	70	A	Regular and compact when young; irregular and open when older.
Pinus thunbergianna Japanese black pine	(5)–9	Irregular	80	A	Widely adapted where hardy; excellent for bonsai.
Platycladus orientalis Oriental arborvitae	5–9	Varied	to 25	A	Mostly used in its various shrubby forms.
Pseudotsuga menziesii Douglas fir	4–9	Pyramidal	100	A	In cold areas the hardy form 'Glauca' should be grown.
Taxodium distichum Bald-cypress	5–10	Pyramidal; columnar	80	C	Deciduous; feathery foliage and attractive shredding bark; native to southern swamps.
Sequoia sempervirens Coastal redwood	7–10	Columnar	100	B	World's tallest growing tree in nature. Fast growing, pest free.
Sequoiadendron giganteum Giant-sequoia	6–10	Wide columnar	90	A	World's biggest tree. More hardy than Coastal redwood.
Thuja occidentalis American arborvitae	3–9	Pyramidal	60	A	Tolerant of most environments; many types.
Thuja plicata Western red cedar	4–9	Pyramidal	100	A	Fast-growing massive tree; can be pruned to hedge.
Tsuga canadensis Canadian hemlock	4–9	Pyramidal	90	B	Graceful dense tree; tolerant of shade.
		Trees — Palms			
Jubaea chilensis Chilean wine palm	(9)–10	Feather leaves	60	A	Slow growing; hardy to 20°F.
Phoenix spp. Date palms	10	Feather leaves	80	D	Tall, stately; grow and fruit best in arid regions.

(continued)

TABLE 14-28 • *Selected woody plants for the landscape (Continued)*

Name	Hardiness Zone[a]	Growth Habit	Height (feet)	Soil and Exposure[b]	Remarks
			Trees — Palms		
Roystonea spp. Royal palms	10	Feather leaves	80	A	Magnificent palms of the more rainy tropics.
Sabal mexicana Mexican palmetto	9–10	Fan leaves	40	A	Sabals are some of the hardiest of palmlike plants.
Sabal palmetto Cabbage palm	9–10	Fan leaves	40	A	Dense globular head with big green leaves.
Washingtonia filifera California fan palm	(9)–10	Fan leaves	60	A/D	Fast growing; old leaves bend to form thatch; open crown.
Washingtonia robusta Mexican fan palm	(9)–10	Fan leaves	100	A/D	More slender and more compact crown than *W. filifera*.
			Trees — Broadleaved Deciduous (Planted for Foliage)		
Acer circinatum Vine maple	5–(9)	Irregular	12	B	Orange fall color; maples don't grow well in warmer areas of zones 8–10.
Acer ginnala Amur maple	2–(9)	Shrubby tree	18	A	Fragrant flowers; attractive winged fruit; red fall color.
Acer griseum Paper-bark maple	5–(9)	Broadly pyramidal	25	A	Attractive peeling bark; brilliant red fall color.
Acer palmatum Japanese maple	5–(9)	V-shaped	20	A	Refined, deeply cut foliage; several cultivars; red fall color; slow growing.
Acer platanoides Norway maple	3–(9)	Round; dense	90	A	Casts heavy shade; many types; lacks fall color; seedy; honeydew from aphids.
Acer rubrum Red maple	3–(9)	Round	100	A	Rapid growth; attractive spring flowers; early autumn color.
Acer saccharinum Silver maple	3–(9)	Oval	80	A	Rapid growth; fairly open form; subject to breakage and aphids.

(*continued*)

TABLE 14-28 • *(Continued)*

Name	Hardiness Zone[a]	Growth Habit	Height (feet)	Soil and Exposure[b]	Remarks
Trees — Broadleaved Deciduous (Planted for Foliage)					
Betula papyrifera Paper birch	2–8	Pyramidal	60	A	Cold tolerant; open habit; white bark.
Betula verrucosa European white birch	3–8	Oval; weeping	40	A	Several forms; dramatic in effect; lacy and open.
Carpinus betulus European hornbeam	5–(9)	Round	70	A	Dark grey bark; medium growth rate; easily grown.
Carya illinoensis Pecan	6–9	Oval	120	A	Massive and beautiful; no nuts in cool areas; won't tolerate alkalinity.
Celtis occidentalis Common hackberry	4–9	Oval	50	A	Similar to elm; deep rooted; doesn't heave sidewalks.
Cercidiphyllum japonicum Katsura tree	4–9	Spreading	45	B	Multiple trunks; clean appearance; protect from hot sun, dry wind.
Elaeagnus angustifolia Russian olive	3–9	Irregular	20	D	Hardy and adaptable; fine grey foliage is landscape contrast.
Fagus sylvatica European beech	5–9	Oval	80	A	Many forms; pest free, handsome large tree.
Fraxinus americana White ash	3–8	Oval	80	A	Rapid growing, cold-climate tree; twigs litter; use male form.
Fraxinus pennsylvanica Green ash	3–8	Oval	50	A	Good for Plains states; choose male or seedless form.
Ginkgo biloba Maidenhair tree	4–9	Pyramidal or V-shaped	40	A	Plant only male type; graceful; yellow fall color; slow growing; pest free.
Gleditsia triacanthos inermis Thornless honeylocust	4–9	Round	50	A	Rapid growing; open habit makes this a good lawn tree.

(continued)

TABLE 14-28 • *Selected woody plants for the landscape (Continued)*

Name	Hardiness Zone[a]	Growth Habit	Height (feet)	Soil and Exposure[b]	Remarks
		Trees — Broadleaved Deciduous (Planted for Foliage)			
Gymnocladus dioica Kentucky coffee tree	4–9	Contorted	50	A	Winter form is effective in landscape; tolerant of poor soil.
Juglans nigra Black walnut	4–9	V-shaped; open	100	A	Big, hardy shade tree; inhibits growth of nearby plants.
Juglans regia English walnut	7–9	V-shaped	60	A	Many forms; messy as a shade tree.
Liquidambar styraciflua American sweet gum	5–9	Narrow oval	80	B	Nice fall color and winter branch pattern; shows iron chlorosis in alkaline soils.
Morus alba White mulberry	4–9	Round	35	D	Birds are attracted to fruit; fruitless form good for desert and polluted areas.
Nyssa sylvatica Sour gum	4–9	Pyramidal; irregular	40	A	Slow growth; dependable fall color even in warm climates.
Phyllodendron amurense Amur cork tree	4–9	Spreading	35	A	Fast growing; imposing winter silhouette.
Platanus acerifolia London plane tree	5–9	Round	80	A	Colorful bark; withstands smog; subject to anthracnose.
Platanus occidentalis Sycamore	5–9	Round	100	A	Massive tree, large leaves; not as adaptable as *P. acerifolia*.
Populus nigra 'Italica' Lombardy poplar	4–9	Narrow; columnar	80	A	Graceful upright sentinel; fast growing but short lived.
Populus tremuloides Quaking aspen	1–9	Oval	40	A	Widely adapted; bark white; leaves flutter; good for naturalizing.
Quercus alba White oak	5–9	Oval	80	A	Stately; slow growing, long lived; red fall color; nice winter effect.

(*continued*)

TABLE 14-28 • *(Continued)*

Name	Hardiness Zone[a]	Growth Habit	Height (feet)	Soil and Exposure[b]	Remarks
Trees — Broadleaved Deciduous (Planted for Foliage)					
Quercus coccinea Scarlet oak	5–9	Oval	70	A	Superb fall color; difficult to transplant.
Quercus palustris Pin oak	4–9	Pyramidal	70	A	Branches drooping; autumn color variable; needs ample water.
Quercus rubra Red oak	4–9	Pyramidal	90	A	Needs deep irrigation and fertile soil; fast growing; red fall color.
Quercus robur English oak	4–9	Massively spreading	80	A	Picturesque silhouette; small leaves; poor fall color.
Salix alba 'Tristis' Golden weeping willow	2–7	Weeping	60	C	The most colorful weeping willow; fast growth; willows drop litter.
Tilia americana American linden	3–9	Oval	50	A	Straight trunk; narrow crown; slow growth; long lived.
Tilia cordata Littleleaf linden	3–9	Pyramidal	40	A	Good lawn tree; pest free; July flowers attract bees.
Ulmus americana American elm	2–9	Vase	120	A	Subject to Dutch elm disease; not recommended for East.
Ulmus parvifolia Chinese elm	6–9	Round	60	A	Resistant to Dutch elm disease; fast growing; best elm where hardy.
Trees — Broadleaved Evergreen					
Arbutus menziesii Pacific madrone	(7)–10	Round	60	B	Large spring flowers, red berries; exacting in requirements.
Ceratonia siliqua Carob	10	Round or shrubby	30	A	Rapid growing; subject to root rot if watered heavily.
Cinnamomum camphora Camphor tree	9–10	Oval	50	A	Needs hot summers; roots competitive.

(continued)

TABLE 14-28 • *Selected woody plants for the landscape (Continued)*

Name	Hardiness Zone[a]	Growth Habit	Height (feet)	Soil and Exposure[b]	Remarks
		Trees — Broadleaved Evergreen			
Citrus spp. various kinds	9–10	Round	20	A	Good fruit and ornamental trees in warm climates; potted plants elsewhere.
Eucalyptus camalduensis Red gum	8–10	Vase	80	A	Many species available; rapid growth; pest free.
Ficus macrophylla Moreton Bay fig	10	Massive; spreading	80	A	Large leathery leaves; massive trunk.
Ficus retusa India laurel fig	(9)–10	Pendulous	30	A	New rose-colored leaves produce two-toned effect.
Ilex aquifolium English holly	7–10	Columnar	25	B	Dioecious; male and female plants necessary for berries.
Ilex opaca American holly	7–10	Columnar	25	B	Better than English holly for the East.
Jacaranda acutifolia Jacaranda	9–10	Round	35	A	Lavender flowers; may lose leaves in February.
Magnolia grandiflora Southern magnolia	(7)–10	Round	80	A	Large blooms through summer.
Myrica californica Pacific wax myrtle	(7)–10	Round	20	B	Tolerant of infertile soil; neat appearing.
Olea europaea Olive	8–10	Round	30	A	Grey narrow-leaved foliage; tolerant of drought.
Prunus caroliniana Carolina laurel cherry	7–10	Round	35	A	Single or multistemmed tree; drought tolerant.
Prunus laurocerasus English laurel cherry	7–10	Shrubby	25	A	Grows rapidly; can be trained to small tree or hedge.
Quercus agrifolia Coast live oak	8–10	Round	50	A	Rapid-growing, handsome shade tree.
Quercus ilex Holly oak	9–10	Round	60	A	Moderate growth rate; pest tolerant; less graceful than Coast oak.
Quercus virginiana Southern live oak	7–10	Spreading crown	60	A	Better than other live oaks for hot interior climates.
Spathodea campanulata African tulip tree	10	Round	50	A	Fiery-red flowers year round.

(*continued*)

TABLE 14-28 • *(Continued)*

Name	Hardiness Zone[a]	Growth Habit	Height (feet)	Soil and Exposure[b]	Remarks
			Trees — Flowering		
Aesculus carnea Ruby horsechestnut	4–9	Oval	40	A	Bright-red flowers, May; popular for street plantings; fall color.
Aesculus hippocastanum Common horsechestnut	4–9	Oval	60	A	Larger and coarser than *A. carnea*; showy white blooms.
Albizia julibrissin Silk tree	6–(10)	Round	25	A	Fluffy pincushion flowers, July; rapid, open growth.
Amelanchier canadensis Serviceberry	3–9	Columnar	25	A	White flowers, April; tree or shrub; attractive all year.
Cassia spp. Senna	9–10	Flat; round	20	A	Pea-type flowers over a long season; many types.
Castanea mollissima Chinese chestnut	5–9	Round	60	B	Long white catkins, June; plant two trees if nuts are desired.
Catalpa speciosa Catalpa	4–10	Pyramidal	80	A	Very adaptable, but large and coarse; white panicles, June.
Cercis canadensis Eastern redbud	4–9	Round	25	A	Cultivars with several flower colors; not well adapted to Northeast or coast.
Cornus florida Flowering dogwood	(6)–9	Oval	25	A	Several varieties; white or pink flowers before leaves; widely adapted.
Cornus nuttallii Pacific dogwood	(6)–9	Oval	30	A	Grown mostly in West; white flowers before leaves.
Crataegus oxyacantha English hawthorn	4–9	Round	15	A	Dense foliage; white or pink flowers, May; red berries; several varieties.
Crataegus phanenopyrum Washington hawthorn	4–9	Round	20	A	White flowers, May; red berries; autumn foliage color.

(continued)

TABLE 14-28 • *Selected woody plants for the landscape (Continued)*

Name	Hardiness Zone[a]	Growth Habit	Height (feet)	Soil and Exposure[b]	Remarks
		Trees — Flowering			
Franklinia alatamaba Franklinia	5–9	Oval	25	B	Large white flowers, August, September; leaves turn scarlet, fall.
Koelreuteria paniculata Goldenrain tree	5–9	Oval	30	A	Yellow flowers, July; pods, late summer; good winter form.
Laburnum watereri Goldenchain tree	5–9	Oval	20	A	Yellow flowers, mid-May; needs neutral pH.
Liriodendron tulipifera Tulip tree	4–9	Pyramidal	100	A	Yellow cup-shaped blooms, late spring; yellow leaves, fall.
Magnolia grandiflora Southern magnolia	8–10	Round	80	A	Evergreen; many types; huge white flowers, summer through fall.
Magnolia kobus Kobus magnolia	6–9	Oval	40	A	Creamy-white flowers, April; several types.
Magnolia soulangiana Saucer magnolia	5–9	Oval	20	A	Many forms; large rose or white flowers before leaves.
Malus spp. Flowering crabapples	2–9	Various	10–30	A	Many types; beautiful year round; white to pink flowers, May; some have colorful fruit and leaves.
Oxydendrum arboreum Sourwood	4–9	Narrow; oval	35	B	White panicles, July; attractive seed pods; fall color.
Prunus persica 'Alboplena' Double white-flowering peach	6–9	Rounded; flat	15	A	White flowers, mid-April; also pink- and white-flowered forms.
Prunus serrulata Japanese flowering cherry	6–9	Rounded; upright	15–30	A	Year-round interest; white to pink flowers, April; many types.

(continued)

TABLE 14-28 • *(Continued)*

Name	Hardiness Zone[a]	Growth Habit	Height (feet)	Soil and Exposure[b]	Remarks
Trees — Flowering					
Prunus subhirtella 'Pendula' Weeping higan cherry	6–9	Weeping	30	A	Several forms; pink flowers, April.
Pyrus calleryana 'Bradford' Bradford pear	4–9	Pyramidal	40	A	White flowers, spring; red foliage, fall; resistant to fireblight.
Sophora japonica Pagoda tree	4–9	V-shaped	40	A	Shape resembles American elm; pods are messy; flowers, mid-summer.
Sorbus aucuparia European mountain ash	3–9	Round	35	A	White flowers, spring; clustered red berries, fall.
Styrax japonica Japanese snowdrop	5–9	Rounded	30	A	Pendulous bell-shaped flowers, late spring; dainty, refined.

Name	Hardiness Zone[a]	Growth Habit	Flowers	Soil and Exposure[b]	Remarks
Tall Shrubs and Shrubby Trees — 8–20 Feet High					
Caragana arborescens Siberian peashrub	3–9	V-shaped or oval	Yellow, March–May	A	Deciduous; hedge, screen or windbreak; cut back for dense form.
Ceanothus thyrsiflorus Blueblossom ceanothus	7–9	Oval	Blue, May–July	A	Broadleaved evergreen native of West; to 15 ft.
Ceanothus velutinus Snowbrush ceanothus	6–9	Rounded	White, June–July	A	Glossy green broadleaved evergreen native of West; to 15 ft.
Corylus avrellana Hazelnut	6–9	Rounded	Catkins, late winter	A	Grown for nuts and as an ornamental.
Cotinus coggygria Common smoketree	(5)–9	Rounded	See remarks; June–August	A	Deciduous; yellowish flowers; large plumes of smoky-appearing flower parts.

(continued)

TABLE 14-28 • *Selected woody plants for the landscape (Continued)*

Name	Hardiness Zone[a]	Growth Habit	Flowers	Soil and Exposure[b]	Remarks
Tall Shrubs and Shrubby Trees — 8–20 Feet High					
Hibiscus syriacus Rose of Sharon	5–9	V-shaped or oval	See remarks; August–September		Deciduous shrub; tolerant of urban settings; white, red, or purple to violet flowers.
Holodiscus discolor Creambush rockspirea (Oceanspray)	4–9	Oval	Creamy white, June–July	A	Deciduous; to 12 ft; panicles of flowers; flowerlike seed pods persistent.
Ilex crenata Japanese holly	7–9	Rounded	Unimportant	B	A fine-textured broadleaved evergreen foliage plant; useful as screen.
Juniperus chinensis 'Reeves' Reeves Chinese juniper	4–9	Pyramidal	Unimportant	A	Vigorous conifer; light blue-green color.
Ligustrum amurense Amur privet	4–9	Oval	Unimportant	A	Hardiest of privets; screen or hedge plant.
Ligustrum ovalifolium California privet	6–9	Oval	White, July	A	Deciduous or half-evergreen hedge plant; to 15 ft.
Lonicera tatarica Tatarian honeysuckle	3–9	Rounded	Pink to white, April–May	A	Deciduous; to about 10 ft; pink or white flowers.
Magnolia stellata Star magnolia	6–9	Oval to round	White, March–April	B	Deciduous shrub; to 10 or 12 ft.
Photinia serrulata Chinese photinia	7–9	Oval	White, April–May	A	Broadleaved evergreen; 20 ft; leaves reddish when young, turning glossy green; red berries.
Prunus laurocerasus Common laurel cherry	7–9	Round	White, June–July	A	Vigorous, coarse-textured broadleaved evergreen.
Prunus triloba Flowering almond	4–9	Oval	Pink, April–May	A	Deciduous; magnificent show of double flowers.
Pyracantha coccinea lalandi Laland firethorn	6–9	Irregular	White, May–June	A	Hardy broadleaved evergreen; to 20 ft; orange-red berries.

(*continued*)

TABLE 14-28 • *(Continued)*

Name	Hardiness Zone[a]	Growth Habit	Flowers	Soil and Exposure[b]	Remarks
Tall Shrubs and Shrubby Trees — 8–20 Feet High					
Rhododendron marcrophyllum Coast rhododendron	7–9	Round	Rosy-pink, May–June	B	Broadleaved evergreen; West Coast native; to 12 ft.
Rhododendron vaseyi Pinkshell azalea	6–9	Oval; irregular	Light rose, April–May	B	Deciduous; to 10 or 15 ft.
Rhus typhina Staghorn sumac	4–9	Round or irregular	Greenish, June–July	D	Deciduous; to 20 ft; greenish flowers, crimson fruiting bodies; fall color bright red.
Salix discolor Pussy willow	2–8	Irregular	Catkins, late winter	C	Vigorous shrub; moist or well-drained soil.
Sambucus canadensis American elder	3–9	Loose	White, June	C	Coarse-leaved suckering plant; black edible berries.
Syringa chinensis Chinese lilac	4–9	Rounded	Purplish-rose, May	A	Free-flowering lilac; grows to 15 ft; similar to Persian lilac.
Syringa vulgaris varieties Common lilac	3–9	Oval to rounded	Various, April–May	A	Many cultivars with blooms from white, pink, blue to purple in single- or double-flower forms.
Tamarix tetrandra Spring-flowering tamarisk	4–9	Upright; irregular	Pink, April–May	D	Deciduous; 15 ft; tolerant of alkaline soil and drought.
Tamarix pentandra Salt cedar	3–9	Oval to round	Rosy-pink, August–September	D	Deciduous to 25 ft; tolerant; heavy pruning encourages bloom.
Thuja occidentalis 'Pyramidal' Pyramidal eastern arborvitae	4–9	Narrowly columnar	Cones	A	Slender conifer useful as narrow hedge; to 25 ft ultimately.
Thuja occidentalis 'Ware Gold' Ware Gold eastern arborvitae	4–9	Narrowly pyramidal	Cones	A	Conifer with golden-yellow foliage; to 25 ft.
Viburnum lantana Wayfaring tree viburnum	4–9	Rounded	White, April–May	A	Deciduous shrub; to 15 ft; fruit red in July, black later.

(continued)

TABLE 14-28 • *Selected woody plants for the landscape (Continued)*

Name	Hardiness Zone[a]	Growth Habit	Flowers	Soil and Exposure[b]	Remarks
Tall Shrubs and Shrubby Trees — 8–20 Feet High					
Viburnum opulus European cranberrybush viburnum	4–9	Round	White, May–June	A	Deciduous plant to 12 ft; red fall color and red berries.
Viburnum rhytidophyllum Leatherleaf viburnum	(7)–9	Oval	Light-yellow, May–June	A	Broadleaved evergreen; to 15 ft; large, leathery leaves; coarse.
Large Shrubs — 5–8 Feet High					
Abelia gaucheri Gaucher abelia	7–9	Round	Lavender-pink, June–November	A	Evergreen with bronzy foliage in winter.
Abelia grandiflora Glossy abelia	7–9	Round; dense	Flushed-pink, June–November	A	Broadleaved evergreen; glossy foliage; shorter in North.
Aucuba japonica Japanese aucuba	7–9	Round; dense	Purplish-green, March–April	B	Broadleaved evergreen; red berries, winter; needs pollenizer.
Berberis darwini Darwin barberry	7–9	Oval; dense	Golden-yellow, April	A	Broadleaved evergreen plant; most useful at 4–5 ft, has been known to grow 8 ft; foliage small, hollylike, and dark green.
Berberis julianae Wintergreen barberry	6–9	Oval	Yellow, May	A	Broadleaved evergreen; makes a dense, spiny hedge.
Berberis mentorensis Mentor barberry	6–9	Round	Yellow, May	A	Dense thorny shrub with leaves persistant into winter.
Buddleia davidii Orange-eye butterfly bush	5–9	Lanky	Various, summer	A	Long flower spikes; cut back to ground each winter in North.
Buxus sempervirens Common box	6–9	Round	Unimportant	A	Broadleaved evergreen hedge or specimen; grows slowly to 10 ft.
Calycanthus floridus Common sweetshrub	5–9	Round	Reddish-brown, June–July	A	Deciduous shrub with dark-green leaves; dark reddish-brown fragrant flowers.

(*continued*)

TABLE 14-28 • *(Continued)*

Name	Hardiness Zone[a]	Growth Habit	Flowers	Soil and Exposure[b]	Remarks
		Large Shrubs — 5–8 Feet High			
Camellia japonica Common camellia	7–9	Oval	Various	B	Many varieties of this broadleaved evergreen shrub available.
Camellia sasanqua Sasanqua camellia	7–9	Oval	Various	B	Many varieties of this broadleaved evergreen shrub available.
Ceanothus impressus Santa Barbara ceanothus	(7)–9	Irregular; arching	Dark-blue, April–May	A	Fine-textured broadleaved evergreen. *Ceanothus* spp. do best in West.
Chaenomeles Flowering quince	4–9	Round	White to red, early spring	A	Deciduous; scarlet or white to dark-red flowers, depending on variety.
Chamaecyparis obtusa 'Nana gracilis' Dwarf ninoki cypress	6–9	Conical	Unimportant	A	Very slow growth to 7 ft.
Cornus sericea (stolonifera) Red-osier dogwood	2–9	Round	White, May	A	White berries, summer; red twigs, winter; hardy.
Cortaderia selloana Pampas grass	7–9	Round	Silvery-yellow, September	A	Giant ornamental grass; arching, razor-sharp blades.
Cotoneaster divaricata Spreading cotoneaster	5–9	Vase; arching	Pink, profuse	A	Refined shrub; small leaves; red berries.
Cotoneaster franchetii Franchet cotoneaster	(7)–9	Round	Pinkish-white, June	A	A broadleaved evergreen; slender arching stems; grey leaves, orange-red fruit.
Elaeagnus umbellata Autumn elaeagnus	4–9	Tall; spreading	—	A	Silver foliage; brown berries turn red in fall.
Enkianthus perulatus White enkianthus	(5,6)–9	Erect; oval	White, May	B	Deciduous shrub; fall color scarlet.
Escallonia 'Appleblossom' Appleblossom escallonia	7–9	Round; arching	Pinkish-white, summer	A	Broadleaved evergreen; arching branches; many cultivars.
Euonymus alata Winged euonymus	4–9	Rounded	Unimportant	A	Deciduous; to 10 ft; crimson to scarlet fall color.

(continued)

TABLE 14-28 • *Selected woody plants for the landscape (Continued)*

Name	Hardiness Zone[a]	Growth Habit	Flowers	Soil and Exposure[b]	Remarks
		Large Shrubs — 5–8 Feet High			
Euonymus japonica Evergreen euonymus	7–9	Oval	Unimportant	A	Broadleaved evergreen hedge plant; tolerates pruning.
Exochorda racemosa Common pearlbush	5–9	Round	White, April–May	A	Deciduous shrub to 10 ft; flowers pearl-like in bud.
Fatsia japonica Japan fatsia	8–9	Oval to round	White, October–January	B	Bold tropical-appearing broadleaved evergreen; leaves to 16 in across; flowers and fruit, October to January.
Forsythia intermedia Showy forsythia	5–9	Round; upright	Yellow, early	A	Several named cultivars; the most showy forsythia.
Forsythia viridissima Greenstem forsythia	6–9	Round	Yellow, March–April	A	This forsythia develops a purple-green fall color.
Hydrangea arborescens Smooth hydrangea	4–9	Round to oval	White, June–July	B	Deciduous; appears to grow best in zones 6, 5, and 4.
Hydrangea macrophylla Bigleaf hydrangea	6–9	Round	Blue or pink, June–July	B	Coarse-textured, vigorous; several varieties available.
Hydrangea paniculata 'Grandiflora' Peegee hydrangea	4–9	V-shaped or round	White, purplish, August-September	B	Deciduous; to 10 ft; huge flower clusters.
Ilex crenata 'Convexa' Box-leaf holly	5–9	Round; dense	Inconspicuous	A	Broadleaved evergreen; widely adapted; several forms of *I. crenata*.
Juniperus chinensis 'Hetz' Hetz Chinese juniper	5–9	Oval; ascending	Unimportant	A	Broad conifer; fountain effect with age.
Juniperus squamata meyeri Meyer singleseed juniper	5–9	V-shaped; irregular	Unimportant	A	Unique-shaped conifer; blue color.
Kalmia latifolia Mountain laurel	5–9	Round	White, pink, May–June	B	Dense evergreen; moist acid soil; same care as rhododendron.

(*continued*)

TABLE 14-28 • *(Continued)*

Name	Hardiness Zone[a]	Growth Habit	Flowers	Soil and Exposure[b]	Remarks
Large Shrubs — 5–8 Feet High					
Kerria japonica 'Pleniflora' Double Japanese kerria	4–9	V-shaped to oval	Yellow, April–May	A	Green stems in winter; may spread if not confined.
Kolkwitzia amabilis Beautybush	4–9	Round	Pinkish-lavender, May–June	A	Vigorous deciduous shrub; grows in infertile soil with minimum moisture.
Lagerstroemia indica Crape myrtle	7–10	Oval	Red to white, summer	A	Deciduous to 10 ft; beautiful in flower in summer; numerous cultivars.
Ligustrum obtusifolium regelianum Regel privet	5–9	Round	White, July	A	Reliable screen plant; horizontal character; deciduous.
Lonicera morrowi Morrow honeysuckle	4–9	Round	White, April–May	A	Hardy old-timer; most frequently seen in zones 5 and 4.
Magnolia liliflora Lily magnolia	6–9	Oval	Purple, white, March–April	A	Deciduous shrub; grows to 10 or 12 ft; petals deep-purple outside, white inside.
Myrica pensylvanica Northern bayberry	2–8	Oval	Inconspicuous	A	Deciduous; aromatic leaves, silver berries; likes sandy soil.
Nandina domestica Nandina	7–9	Oval	White, June–July	A	Broadleaved evergreen; erect habit gives distinction; grows in most soils.
Osmanthus heterophyllus Holly osmanthus	7–9	Round	White, September–October	A	Broadleaved evergreen with hollylike leaves; good screen.
Philadelphus coronarius Common mock-orange	4–9	Rounded; upright	White, June	A	Traditional fragrant favorite; some newer types have large flowers & no scent.

(continued)

TABLE 14-28 • *Selected woody plants for the landscape (Continued)*

Name	Hardiness Zone[a]	Growth Habit	Flowers	Soil and Exposure[b]	Remarks
Large Shrubs — 5–8 Feet High					
Pieris japonica Japanese pieris	(5)–9	Oval	White, April–May	B	Refined evergreen to 9 ft; clusters of bell-shaped flowers.
Pinus aristata Bristlecone pine	5–9	Irregular	Unimportant	A	Slow-growing shrub in East to small tree in West.
Pinus mugo mughus Mugho Swiss mountain pine	3–8	Round; irregular	Unimportant	A	Hardy conifer; compact habit; useful as foundation plant.
Prunus laurocerasus schipkaensis Schipka laurel cherry	5–9	Round	Yellowish-white, May	A	Hardiest of laurels; compact; lustrous dark-green leaves.
Prunus tomentosa Nanking cherry	3–8	Rounded; upright	White, April	A	Hardy; attractive edible red fruit.
Pyracantha 'Government Red' Government red firethorn	7–9	Rounded; irregular	White, May–June	A	Bright-red fruit; broadleaved evergreen; some winter injury in zone 7.
Pyracantha 'Rosedale' Rosedale firethorn	7–9	Rounded; irregular	White, May–June	A	Glossy evergreen foliage; bright-red berries; screen; espalier, or hedge.
Rhododendron calendulaceum Flame azalea	5–9	Oval	Yellow-orange to scarlet, May–June	B	Deciduous; several brilliant color variations.
Rhododendron nudiflorum Pinxterbloom azalea	(4)–9	Oval	Light-pink, white, April–May	B	Deciduous; very hardy.
Rhododendron occidentalle Western azalea	5–9	Upright to round	Pinkish with yellow, May–June	B	Flowers fragrant; deciduous.
Rhododendron schlippenbachii Royal azalea	(4)–9	Oval to round	Pink, April–May	B	Deciduous azalea with clear-pink blossom.
Rhododendron named hybrids	7–9	Round; upright	Various	B	Dozens of named hybrids, 5–8 ft; evergreen and deciduous, are available.
Rhus typhina 'Laciniata' Cutleaf staghorn sumac	3–9	Irregular	Greenish, June–July	A	Foliage crimson in fall; suckers freely; attractive seed head.
Salix purpurea Purple osier willow	4–9	Rounded	Unimportant	A	Deciduous hedge plant; grey-green foliage.

(continued)

TABLE 14-28 • *(Continued)*

Name	Hardiness Zone[a]	Growth Habit	Flowers	Soil and Exposure[b]	Remarks
			Large Shrubs — 5–8 Feet High		
Sorbaria sorbifolia Ural false-spirea	2–8	Oval	Cream, June–July	A	Deciduous screen plant; ultimate height 6 ft; suckers freely.
Spiraea prunifolia Bridalwreath spirea	5–9	Round	White, April–May	A	Brilliant red and yellow fall color.
Spiraea vanhouttei Vanhoutte spirea	4–9	Round	White, May	A	Arching white cascades of bloom.
Syringa persica Persian lilac	4–9	Rounded	Pale lilac, May	A	Hardy, free-flowering lilac.
Viburnum burkwoodii Burkwood viburnum	(5)–9	Rounded	Pinkish-white, March–April	A	Semievergreen; vigorous; fragrant flowers; dark-green foliage.
Viburnum odoratissimum Sweet viburnum	7–9	Oval	White, May–June	B	Large glossy leaves; to 10 ft; fragrant flowers.
Viburnum plicatum Japanese Snowball viburnum	(5)–9	Rounded	White, May–June	A	Similar to 'Doublefile' except sterile and flowers in round clusters.
Viburnum plicatum tomentosum Doublefile viburnum	(5)–9	Rounded	White, May–June	A	Deciduous; grows to about 10 ft; bright-red fall color. Flat flower clusters.
Viburnum tinus Laurestinus viburnum	(7)–9	Rounded	White, March–April	A	Broadleaved evergreen; useful as screen.
Weigela florida Old-fashioned weigela	(4)–9	Rounded	Various, May–June	A	Deciduous plant; several color forms, white, pink, or rose.
			Shrubs — 3–5 Feet High		
Berberis darwinii Darwin barberry	7–9	Oval; dense	Yellow, early spring	A	Broadleaved evergreen; foliage small, hollylike, and dark-green.
Berberis thunbergii Japanese barberry	4–9	Rounded; dense	Yellow, April	A	Spiny, deciduous shrub; brilliant scarlet and yellow fall color; red berries.

(continued)

TABLE 14-28 • *Selected woody plants for the landscape (Continued)*

Name	Hardiness Zone[a]	Growth Habit	Flowers	Soil and Exposure[b]	Remarks
		Shrubs — 3–5 Feet High			
Berberis thunbergii 'Atropurpurea' Redleaf Japanese barberry	4–9	Rounded; dense	Yellow, early spring	A	Same as above; leaves dark reddish-purple, spring and summer.
Berberis verruculosa Warty barberry	4–9	Round; dense	Yellow, April	A	Spiny broadleaved evergreen; fine texture, dark-green leaves.
Buxus sempervirens Common box	6–9	Round	Unimportant	A	Broadleaved evergreen hedge or specimen; grows slowly to height of 10 ft or more, can be kept lower with pruning; occasionally seen in zone 5.
Chamaecyparis pisifera 'Filifera Nana' Dwarfthread false-cypress	6–9	Round; ascending	Unimportant	A	This conifer forms a dense, rounded mass with weeping effect.
Chamaecyparis pisifera 'Nana Aurea' Yellowdwarf false-cypress	6–9	Round; ascending	Unimportant	A	Same as above except for golden-yellow color of foliage.
Corylopsis pauciflora Winter-hazel	6–9	Round	Yellow, March	B	Dense shrub, bell-shaped flowers.
Cotoneaster microphylla Small-leaf cotoneaster	7–9	Spreading	White, early spring	A	Spreads quickly to 3–4 ft.
Cytisus praecox Warminister broom	6–9	Round; dense	Cream, April	A	Green branches; useful in sunny, dry locations or poor soil.
Daphne mezereum February daphne	5–9	Erect; oval	Rosy-purple, February–March	A	Early flowering; deciduous; flowers fragrant.
Daphne odora Winter daphne	7–9	Dense mound	White, rose, March–April	B	Broadleaved evergreen; dark-green in partial shade, yellowish in full sun.
Erica stricta Corsican heath	7–9	Round; ascending	Purple, late summer	A	Can be kept low by pruning; attractive brown seed capsules.

(continued)

TABLE 14-28 • *(Continued)*

Name	Hardiness Zone[a]	Growth Habit	Flowers	Soil and Exposure[b]	Remarks
		Shrubs — 3–5 Feet High			
Euonymus fortunei 'Vegeta' Bigleaf wintercreeper	6–9	Viny or shrubby	Unimportant	A	Broadleaved evergreen; can be trained to shrub, liana, espalier.
Hydrangea arborescens Smooth hydrangea	4–9	Erect; oval	White, July–fall	A	Deciduous; flowers, large snowballs.
Hydrangea quercifolia Oakleaf hydrangea	5–9	Loose; spreading	White, early summer	A	Coarse-textured; deciduous; dark-green summer, red fall color.
Hypericum prolificum Shrubby St.-John's-wort	5–9	Dense	Bright-yellow, July	A	Brown stems; should be pruned to the ground in spring.
Juniperus chinensis 'Pfitzeriana' Pfitzer juniper	4–9	Spreading	Unimportant	A	Conifer; tolerant of dry soil.
Leucothoe fontanesiana Drooping leucothoe	6–9	Round; arching	White, late spring	B	Broadleaved evergreen; leaves bronze in winter.
Ligustrum vicaryi Vicary golden privet	5–9	Round	Unimportant	A	Golden foliage; likes full sun; deciduous.
Ligustrum vulgare 'Lodense' Lodense privet	4–9	Mound; dense	Unimportant	A	Suitable for untrimmed hedge.
Mahonia aquifolium Oregon grape	5–9	Open	Golden, spring	A	Evergreen leaves resemble holly; variable in type.
Philadelphus 'Miniature snowflake'	4–9	Round	White, June	A	Compact form of this fragrant blooming species.
Picea glauca 'Conica' Dwarf Alberta spruce	3–9	Pyramidal; dense	Unimportant	A	Grows slowly; very formal and full.
Pieris floribunda Mountain pieris	5–9	Round	White, early spring	B	Broadleaved evergreen; several planted 4 ft apart will form a single mass.
Pieris japonica 'compacta' Japanese pieris	(5)–9	Oval	White, early spring	B	Broadleaved evergreen.
Pinus mugo mughus Swiss mountain pine	3–9	Round to spreading	Unimportant	A	Hardy conifer; compact growth; climatic adaptability.
Pinus strobus 'Nana' Dwarf white pine	3–9	Round	Unimportant	A	Bluish coniferous shrub.

(continued)

TABLE 14-28 • *Selected woody plants for the landscape (Continued)*

Name	Hardiness Zone[a]	Growth Habit	Flowers	Soil and Exposure[b]	Remarks
			Shrubs—3–5 Feet High		
Prunus glandulosa 'Siensis' Dwarf pink flowering almond	(5)–9	Rounded	Pink, spring	A	Profuse display of double flowers; foliage somewhat coarse.
Prunus laurocerasus zabeliana Zabel laurel cherry	7–9	Rounded to round	White, spring	A	Broadleaved evergreen; broader than high; foundation plant or hedge.
Punica granatum 'Dwarf' Dwarf pomegranate	(7)–9	Round; ascending	Orange-red, June–September	A	Deciduous shrub; rich soil required; protect from cold winds.
Raphiolepis umbellata ovata Yeddo hawthorn	8–10	Round	White, May–June	A	Broadleaved evergreen plant; grows slowly; mainly for South and West.
Rhododendron (Azalea mollis hybrids) Mollis azalea	(5)–9	Oval	Various, April–May	B	Loosely classified group of azaleas of good garden quality.
Rhododendron mucronulatum Korean rhododendron	(4)–9	Oval	Rosy-purple, March–April	B	Deciduous; grows to 7 ft; fall color yellow and crimson.
Rhododendron 'Blue Diamond'	6–9	Oval to round	Lavender-blue, April	B	Broadleaved evergreen; fertilizer not beneficial.
Rhododendron 'Bowbells'	6–9	Rounded; compact	Shell-pink, May	B	Broadleaved evergreen; 3 or 4 ft tall; small, coinlike bronzed leaves.
Rhododendron 'Bric-a-Brac'	6–9	Round	White with pink, February–March	B	Broadleaved evergreen; grows to about 30 in.
Rhododendron 'Brittania'	6–9	Round	Crimson-red, June		Broadleaved evergreen; to 5 ft or slightly higher; compact, broad mass; flowers excellent.
Rhododendron 'Broughtoni Aureum'	6–9	Oval	Yellow, May	B	Cross between deciduous and broadleaved evergreen; persistent leaves.

(*continued*)

TABLE 14-28 • *(Continued)*

Name	Hardiness Zone[a]	Growth Habit	Flowers	Soil and Exposure[b]	Remarks
			Shrubs — 3–5 Feet High		
Rhododendron 'Gomer Waterer'	(7)–9	Rounded; compact	Apple-blossom pink, June	B	Broadleaved evergreen; to about 4 ft.
Rhododendron 'Mars'	(6)–9	Rounded; compact	Blood-red, May–June	B	Broadleaved evergreen plant; hardy.
Rhododendron PJM-hybrids	(5)–9	Round; compact	Lavender, April	B	Tight mound; small bronze-tipped leaves.
Rhododendron 'Unique'	6–9	Round; compact	Pale-yellow, April–May	B	Broadleaved evergreen; flowers pink in bud, pale yellow in full bloom.
Ribes alpinum Alpine currant	(2)–7	Round; compact	Greenish, April	A	Maplelike leaves; hedge for cold climates; red autumn foliage.
Rosa rugosa	3–9	Round	Magenta, white, late May		Red fruit; orange fall color; many hybrids.
Senecio greyii Grey's groundsel	8–9	Rounded	Yellow, summer	D	Broadleaved evergreen; 3 ft high; grey foliage.
Skimmia japonica Japanese skimmia	7–9	Rounded	Light-yellow, April–May	B	Evergreen with bright-red fruit in winter; male plant needed for fruit.
Spiraea bumalda 'Froebel' Froebel spirea	5–9	Rounded	Crimson, July	A	Deciduous; similar to Anthony Waterer spirea but somewhat taller with darker foliage.
Spiraea thunbergii Thunberg spirea	5–9	Round	White, February–May	A	Deciduous shrub with light-green leaves; good fall color.
Symphoricarpos orbiculatus Indiancurrant coralberry	3–9	Oval to round	Yellow, August	A	Deciduous; purplish-red fruit ornamental during winter.
Taxus cuspidata 'Densiformis' Dwarf Japanese yew	4–8	Cushion	Unimportant	A	Slow growing conifer; 4 ft high, 8 ft broad.

(continued)

TABLE 14-28 • *Selected woody plants for the landscape (Continued)*

Name	Hardiness Zone[a]	Growth Habit	Flowers	Soil and Exposure[b]	Remarks
Shrubs—3–5 Feet High					
Thuja orientalis 'Berckmanns' Berckmanns Oriental arborvitae	6–9	Oval	Unimportant	A	Slow growing, golden-foliaged conifer.
Vaccinium ovatum Box blueberry	7–9	Rounded; stems ascending	Light-pink, April–May	B	West Coast broadleaved evergreen native; bronze in spring and darker bronze in winter; edible fruit.
Viburnum carlesii Korean spice viburnum	5–9	Oval; spreading branches	Light-pink, April–May	A	Fragrant-flowered, deciduous viburnum.
Shrubs—18 Inches to 3 Feet					
Abies balsamea 'Nana' Dwarf balsam fir	3–8	Round	Unimportant	A	Hardy dwarf conifer; good for cold locations.
Berberis thunbergii 'Crimson pygmy' Crimson pygmy barberry	4–9	Round	Unimportant	A	Red-leaved barberry that doesn't grow over 2 ft high.
Buxus microphylla koreana Korean box	5–9	Spreading	Unimportant	A	Evergreen; loose-growing; selected types are more compact.
Calluna vulgaris Scotch heather	(6)–9	Spreading	White-pink, summer–fall	B	Many types; all low-growing evergreens.
Chamaecyparis obtusa 'Nana' Dwarf false cypress	5–9	Mound	Unimportant	B	Dwarf conifer; squat habit; dark green foliage.
Cotoneaster horizontalis Rock cotoneaster	6–9	Spreading	Pale-pink, late spring	A	Bright-red berries; good bank cover; can espalier.
Cotoneaster microphylla Rockspray cotoneaster	7–9	Spreading	White, late spring	A	Broadleaved evergreen; red berries.
Cryptomeria japonica 'Dwarf' Dwarf Japanese cryptomeria	6–9	Dense; round	Unimportant	A	Dwarf conifer; green in summer, reddish in winter.
Cycas revoluta Sago palm	9–10	Spreading	Unimportant	A	Primitive plant; looks like dwarf palm; taller with age.
Deutzia gracilis Slender deutzia	5–9	Round; stems ascending	White, spring	A	Needs pruning after bloom.

(*continued*)

TABLE 14-28 • *(Continued)*

Name	Hardiness Zone[a]	Growth Habit	Flowers	Soil and Exposure[b]	Remarks
Shrubs — 18 Inches to 3 Feet					
Euonymous fortunei	5–9	Varies	Unimportant	A	Evergreen with broad waxy leaves; many kinds with varied growth.
Gaultheria shallon Salal	7–9	Spreading; stems ascending	Light-pink, late spring	B	Broadleaved evergreen.
Ilex crenata 'Hetzii' Hetz Japanese holly	(6)–9	Round; dense	Unimportant	B	Evergreen; other dwarf hollies with various forms.
Juniperus chinensis sargentii Sargent juniper	4–9	Spreading	Unimportant	A	More dense and slower growing than most low junipers.
Juniperus sabina 'Tamariscifolia' Tamarix juniper	5–9	Spreading	Unimportant	A	A most useful form; does not exceed height of 2 ft.
Lavandula officinalis True lavender	6–9	Round; stems ascending	Lavender, late summer	D	Tolerant of dry, alkaline soil; flowers fragrant.
Lonicera pileata Privet honeysuckle	6–9	Spreading horizontal	White, spring	A	Semievergreen; 2 to 3 ft tall with 6-ft spread.
Mahonia nervosa Cascades mahonia	7–9	Spreading; stems ascending	Yellow, spring	A	A 2- to 3-ft broadleaved evergreen; western native; similar to Oregon grape but much smaller.
Nandina domestica 'Nana' Dwarf nandina	7–9	Round; stems ascending	White, summer	B	Resembles a diminutive bamboo; thrives in moist soil.
Pachystima myrsinites Oregon boxwood	4–9	Dense round	Unimportant	A	Similar to boxwood, but hardier and more tolerant.
Picea abies 'Nidiformis' Nest spruce	3–9	Spreading	Unimportant	A	Slow-growing conifer; to 18 in high; spreads to 3 ft.
Potentilla fruticosa Bush cinquefoil	2–8	Round; stems ascending	Yellow, white, all summer	A	Deciduous; several varieties; tolerant of wet, dry, acid, or alkaline soil.

(continued)

TABLE 14-28 • *Selected woody plants for the landscape (Continued)*

Name	Hardiness Zone[a]	Growth Habit	Flowers	Soil and Exposure[b]	Remarks
		Shrubs — 18 Inches to 3 Feet			
Raphiolepis indica 'Rosea' Pink India raphiolepis	7–9	Spreading loose	Pink, late spring	A	Broadleaved evergreen; may reach 4 or 5 ft when old.
Rhododendron 'Bluetit' Bluetit rhododendron	6–9	Round; compact	Blue, early spring	B	2 to 3 ft high.
Rhododendron impeditum	5–9	Compact mound	Lavender, early spring	B	Small scaly evergreen leaves; 18 in high.
Rhododendron 'Macrantha' Macrantha azalea	6–9	Spreading	Deep-rose, early summer	A	Double flowers; broadleaved evergreen; 24 to 30 in high.
Rhododendron mucronatum Snow azalea	6–9	Spreading; stems ascending	White, spring	A	Large white flowers and dull-green leaves.
Rhododendron 'Ramapo'	5–9	Compact mound	Violet, spring	A	2-ft evergreen mound; light blue-green foliage.
Salix purpurea 'Gracilis' Dwarf Arctic willow	2–(9)	Compact	Unimportant	A	Grey foliage; dwarf hedges.
Skimmia japonica Dwarf skimmia	7–9	Round	White, spring	B	A compact broadleaved evergreen shrub for a shady place; bright-red berries.
Spiraea bumalda 'Anthony Waterer' Anthony Waterer spirea	3–9	Stems ascending	Lavender, late summer	A	Deciduous shrub to about 3 ft; desirable for summer color.
Symphoricarpos albus Common snowberry	3–9	Round	Pink, all summer	A	Deciduous; 3 ft high; tolerant of most conditions; white berries.
Taxus baccata 'Repandens' Weeping English yew	5–9	Weeping	Unimportant	A	Dwarf slow-growing conifer; tolerates shade.
Thuja occidentalis 'Hetz Midget' Hetz midget arborvitae	3–9	Globe	Unimportant	A	Slow growing; to 2½ ft.
Viburnum davidi David viburnum	7–9	Spreading; dense	White, June	A	Broad, dark-green evergreen leaves; 2 to 3 ft high; spreads 5 to 6 ft.
Viburnum opulus 'Nanum' Dwarf European cranberry bush	4–9	Round; compact	Unimportant	A	Slow growing; deciduous; ornamental foliage.
Yucca filamentosa Adam's needle yucca	4–9	Round; ascending	Cream, late summer	D	Hardy desert plant; flower spikes 3 to 5 ft; leaves spear-shaped.

(*continued*)

TABLE 14-28 • *(Continued)*

Name	Hardiness Zone[a]	Growth Habit	Flowers	Soil and Exposure[b]	Remarks
Small Shrubs to 18 Inches High (See Also Table 11-9)					
Andromeda polifolia Dwarf Bog-rosemary	2–9	Dense mound	Pink, May	C	Narrow, grey-green evergreen leaves.
Berberis buxifolia 'Nana' Dwarf Magellan barberry	6–10	Dense mound	Unimportant	A	Evergreen; small leaves.
Buxus sempervirens 'Suffruticosa' Truedwarf common box	6–9	Round; dense	Inconspicuous	A	Slow-growing broadleaved evergreen; to 3 ft high, usually 6 to 18 in.
Calluna vulgaris 'Aurea' Goldleaf Scotch heather	6–9	Mound; stems ascending	Pink, July–September	B	Golden leaves in summer; red in winter.
Calluna vulgaris 'County Wicklow' County Wicklow Scotch heather	7–9	Spreading; ascending	Shell-pink, August–September	B	Double-flowered form; ground cover.
Ceanothus gloriosus Point Reyes ceanothus	7–9	Spreading	Blue, April	A	Broadleaved evergreen plant; to about 12 in with spread of 3 to 4 ft.
Daboecia cantabrica 'Alba' White bell Irishheath	7–9	Spreading; ascending	White, May–November	B	Broadleaved evergreen; heathlike; masses well.
Daboecia cantabrica 'Atropurpurea' Purple bell Irishheath	7–9	Spreading; ascending	Purple, June–November	B	Same comment as above; space 2 ft.
Erica spp. Heath	7–9	Spreading; ascending	Various, summer	B	Colorful spreading ground covers.
Euonymous fortunei Purple leaf wintercreeper	4–9	Spreading	Unimportant	A	Broadleaved evergreen; winter protection in zones 4 and 5.
Hedera canariensis Algerian ivy	7–9	Spreading or climbing	Unimportant	A	Vigorous ground cover or climbing vine; tolerates dense shade.
Hedera helix English ivy	6–9	Spreading or climbing	Unimportant	A	See above; plant ivy 4 ft apart.
Helianthemum nummularium Sunrose	5–9	Spreading	Various, May–June	D	To 12 in; drought tolerant; red, white, yellow.
Hypericum calycinum Aaron's beard St.-John's-wort	6–9	Spreading; stoloniferous	Yellow, July–September	A	Vigorous and invasive ground cover; keep in bounds.
Hypericum moserianum St.-John's-wort	7–9	Spreading; stems ascending	Gold, July–September	A	Same as above.
Juniperus horizontalis 'Bar Harbor' Bar Harbor creeping juniper	4–9	Spreading	Unimportant	A	Red foliage in winter; too low to discourage weeds.

(*continued*)

TABLE 14-28 • *Selected woody plants for the landscape (Continued)*

Name	Hardiness Zone[a]	Growth Habit	Flowers	Soil and Exposure[b]	Remarks
Small Shrubs to 18 Inches High (See Also Table 11-9)					
Juniperus horizontalis 'Douglasii' Waukegan creeping juniper	4–9	Trailing	Unimportant	A	Prostrate conifer 12 to 18 in; 4- to 5-ft spread.
Rhododendron impeditum Cloudland rhododendron	7–9	Rounded; ascending	Bluish-purple, April	B	Broadleaved evergreen to 20 in; foliage slightly grey.
Lianas and Perennial Vines					
Actinidia polygama Silver vine	6–9	15 ft; spreading	White, early summer	A	Green fruit in September; sun or shade; needs support.
Akebia quinata Fireleaf akebia	5–9	15 ft; spreading	Purple, spring	A	Sun or shade; flowers not showy; dainty five-parted leaves.
Campsis radicans Common trumpet creeper	5–10	30 ft; ascending	Orange, July–September	A	Clings to walls or trees; bright foliage; spectacular flowers.
Celastrus scandens American bittersweet	4–9	15 ft; spreading	White, June	A	Brilliant orange-red berries persist all winter; need male and female plants for fruit.
Clematis spp.	5–9	15 ft; trailing	Various	A	Large blooms, profuse; cultivars of many colors.

(*continued*)

TABLE 14-28 • *(Continued)*

Name	Hardiness Zone[a]	Growth Habit	Height (feet)	Soil and Exposure[b]	Remarks
Lianas and Perennial Vines					
Euonymus fortunei radicans Evergreen euonymus	5–9	20 ft; ascending	Greenish-white, June	A	One of the hardiest evergreen lianas; sun to full shade; bank or wall cover.
Hedera (see "Small shrubs," above)					
Lonicera henryi	5–9	20 ft; spreading	Red-yellow, June–August	A	Semievergreen; showy flowers; purple berries.
Lonicera japonica 'Halliana' Hall's honeysuckle	5–9	30 ft; spreading	White, June–September	A	Evergreen; rampant growth; can be a weed.
Lonicera sempervirens Trumpet honeysuckle	5–9	30 ft; spreading	Orange, May–August	A	Evergreen; very showy flowers.
Parthenocissus quinquefolia Virginia creeper	5–9	50 ft; ascending	Unimportant	A	Rapid-growing wall or bank cover; sun to shade.
Parthenocissus tricuspidata Boston ivy	5–9	75 ft; ascending	Unimportant	A	Wall or bank cover; only on north or east walls in warm climates.
Wisteria spp.	(5)–9	20 ft; spreading	White-violet, June	A	Deciduous; many types; can be trained as tree, shrub, vine; showy flowers.

[a]See Figure 14-96. Parentheses around a zone number indicate marginal tolerance in that zone.
[b]A—General garden loam; sun to light shade tolerant.
B—Needs acid, well-drained soil; usually shade tolerant.
C—Tolerates wet marshy situations.
D—Needs perfect drainage, full sun; usually alkaline tolerant.

Questions for Review and Discussion

CHAPTER 1

◆ ◆ ◆

1. Describe how the components necessary for prolonged crop cultivation (i.e., temperature, light, fertility, water, and transportation) were supplied in the Egyptian and Aztec farming systems.

2. What were the major staple crops of the ancient Middle East, Aztec, and Peruvian civilizations?

3. Why do we refer to the present as a time of agricultural revolution?

4. Discuss the technological and sociological developments that permit 2.5 percent of the North American labor force to produce the food and fiber for the whole population, plus a considerable surplus for export. What are the advantages and disadvantages of having such a small percentage of the labor force engaged in farming?

5. Define and explain the differences between horticulture and agronomy. What other disciplines are closely related to horticulture?

6. It is often said that the U.S. and Canadian food supply depends on the introduction of new plants. Why?

7. What factors influence the increase or decrease in consumption of different kinds of horticultural products? By analyzing the changes in life-style of North Americans, predict which horticultural crops will increase and which will decrease in consumption during the next few years and explain why.

8. Botanically the tomato is a perennial, yet in North America we generally think of it as an annual. Explain the reason for this. Why don't carrots generally produce seed when grown in home gardens?

9. List at least five annual, five biennial, and five perennial horticultural crops with which you are familiar.

10. What are the differences among a vegetable, an ornamental, and a fruit? Give some examples of plants that are difficult to classify according to this horticultural system of classification.

11. What is the binomial system of plant classification and who originated it? Why is it considered so useful?

12. Define or explain the meaning of kind, cultivar, forma, and variety. The scientific name for cabbage is *Brassica oleraceae* var. *capitata*. Name the kingdom, division, class, family, genus, and species to which cabbage belongs.

13. 'Thompson Seedless' grapes are known by their scientific name, *Vitis vinifera*; the scientific name of 'Concord' grapes is *Vitis labruska*. Would you expect these two species of grape to cross-pollinate? Would you expect to be able to intergraft them?

14. Using Table 14-25, name five horticultural foods with a high vitamin C content and five with a high vitamin A content. What are the major contributions of fruits and vegetables to the human diet?

CHAPTER 2

◆ ◆ ◆

1. Rhubarb is grown as a forcing crop in Michigan, Ontario, and Washington State. Crown divisions are planted and grown for two seasons. During the winter after the second growing season, the crowns are dug and placed in a warm dark enclosure, which results in the growth of light pink petioles that command a high price as a gourmet food product. Forced rhubarb would sell well at Christmas time but is seldom available then. Why not?

2. Provide a chronological time schedule for the growth and dormant phases of the following:

Plant	Dormancy	Rest	Vegetative Growth	Reproductive Growth
Apple tree				
Radish				
Carrot				

3. What is the function of each of the following cell components: chloroplasts, cell walls, chromosomes, mitochondria, plasmodesmata, and ribosomes?

4. Which two cell components expand the most when cells enlarge?

5. Why is grass better adapted to mowing than is a herbaceous dicot?

6. A palm tree is a monocot. Does it have annual rings? Does its stem expand in diameter year by year? Under what conditions would a woody dicot plant growing in the tropics be likely to have annual rings?

7. What is the major function of a leaf? What is a stoma, and what factors cause it to open and close? Why do plant growers attempt to keep stomata open for as much of the daylight period as possible, even though plants with open stomata lose moisture?

8. What are the environmental conditions needed for photosynthesis? Why is this plant function necessary for life on this planet? Why can't an albino plant survive beyond the seedling stage of growth?

9. Explain briefly how nutrients are absorbed and translocated throughout a plant.

10. Recently, when one of my friends bumped her head on a low-growing oak tree branch hanging over a corner of her garden, she commented, "I'll

be glad when that branch grows higher." How long will she have to wait? Would the length of her wait be different if she had bumped her head on a palm frond?

11. Trees transplanted during the growing season, without a ball of growing medium around their roots almost invariably wilt and die, even though most of their roots remain intact; but transplanted with bare roots during their dormant period, they usually survive. Why is there a difference in survival rate?

12. Contrast photosynthesis and respiration from the point of view of (a) the part of the plant in which each occurs; (b) the time of day during which each occurs; (c) the effect of each on weight of the plant; (d) the effect of each on the temperature, humidity, and carbon dioxide content of the atmosphere if the plant is grown in a closed room or container.

13. What is the difference between a corm and a bulb; a tuber, a rhizome, and a stolon; separation and division; a node and a spur?

CHAPTER 3

◆ ◆ ◆

1. Name the four major parts of a complete flower, and describe the function of each. Also, define or explain the following: complete flower, staminate, monoecious, perfect flower (hermaphrodytic), pistillate, dioecious.

2. Describe pollination and fertilization, and compare the two terms as they relate to seed production. Discuss the mechanisms by which nature ensures cross-pollination in many plant species.

3. Why does the method by which a plant species is pollinated determine whether the species is self- or cross-pollinated? Why is knowing whether a plant species is self- or cross-pollinated important to horticulturists? Explain what is meant by the statement, Self-pollination leads to homozygosity, and cross-pollination perpetuates heterozygosity.

4. Explain why self-incompatibility aids the evolutionary survival of plant species and also is frequently a problem for horticulturists. What can growers do to ensure that self-incompatibility will not be a problem in their fruit planting?

5. Which temperate-zone fruits require pollinators, and what are the characteristics of a good pollinator? Cabbage is a self-incompatible crop, yet commercial cabbage growers are not concerned about this. Why not?

6. Define or explain microspore, megaspore, embryo sac, pollen grain, generative nucleus, pollen tube, embryo, endosperm, polar body, gene, gene mutation, gene segregation, dominant and recessive genes, bud sport, quantitative character, qualitative character, diploid, haploid, and F_1 hybrid.

7. What is F_1 hybrid seed? Why is hybrid seed popular with gardeners? What are the advantages and disadvantages of hybrid cultivars? Why should seed from hybrid cultivars not be saved for replanting?

8. How does the seed of monocots like wheat or corn differ anatomically from the seed of dicots like beans or squash?

9. Which parts of a seed and fruit are composed only of tissue from the female parent and, therefore, will be like the mother plant? Which are composed of tissue that results from the fusion of the male and female nuclei?

10. Based on your answer to the preceding question, do you think that planting cucumbers next to cantaloupe can cause the cantaloupe to taste like cucumbers?

11. How are seedless watermelons propagated? Why is it easier to propagate seedless grapes than seedless watermelons?

12. Name some crops for which the botanical and horticultural definitions of their fruit or seed differ. How do multiple and aggregate fruits differ from simple fruits? What are some species that produce multiple fruits? Aggregate fruits?

13. Alternate bearing can be a serious problem for orchardists. It can also occur on flowering shrubs or trees such as lilac, mountain ash, and flowering crabapple. What causes it, and how can it be prevented or remedied?

14. Under what conditions is it feasible to save seed from the garden for replanting the following year?

CHAPTER 4

◆ ◆ ◆

1. What is the difference between physical and physiological dormancy in seeds? Define or explain what is meant by stratification and by scarification. Which kind of seed dormancy is overcome by scarification, and which is overcome by stratification?

2. How does seed dormancy enable a species to survive? Would you expect tropical plant seeds to display dormancy? Why or why not?

3. What characteristics should growers look for in the seeds they buy? How can they ensure that these seeds will have these characteristics?

4. What conditions are necessary for seeds to germinate? What is the difference between the viability and the germinability of seeds?

5. Would you expect seeds stored in the natural environment to remain viable for a longer period in Miami, Florida, or in Spokane, Washington? Why? The National Seed Storage Laboratory is located at Ft. Collins, Colorado. Environmentally why is this a good location for this facility?

6. How can gardeners determine whether seeds that have been stored for several years have retained good germinability?

7. Why is it usually unwise to seed all of a vegetable garden at the same time?

8. Explain what you should look for in transplants you wish to buy. In an area where the date of last frost is May 1, about when would you seed the following for growing transplants: pansies, petunias, peppers, tomatoes, celery, cabbage, zinnias, snapdragons?

9. Explain how sexual and asexual propagation differ. Cite at least five reasons for using asexual propagation and five general methods of asexual propagation.

10. How does an apomictic seed differ from an ordinary sexually produced seed? Name two horticultural crops that reproduce by apomixes.

11. By what means does grass spread from the lawn into flower beds? Why are tubers considered to be stem, rather than root, modifications?

12. Cuttings of some species root with ease at any time of year; cuttings of others root with difficulty only during a particular season and under ideal conditions; and cuttings of still others never form roots even under the best of circumstances. What factors are responsible for this extreme variation in ease of rooting? What precautions would you take to ensure that a cutting has the best possible chance to form roots?

13. What are the characteristics of a good rooting medium? Mist chambers, bottom heat, and hormones are often used to enhance the rooting of cuttings. From a physiological standpoint, how does each promote rooting? Why should the leaf area of herbaceous cuttings not be reduced if wilting can be otherwise avoided?

14. Why do cuttings generally root better at nodes than at internodes? Why are vegetative shoots usually easier to root or use for graftage than are reproductive ones?

15. Why is layerage a good method of propagation for homeowners? For what crops is mound layerage an important commercial propagation technique?

16. What three conditions are required for graftage to be successful? Graftage is more difficult and expensive than are most other kinds of propaga-

tion. Why is it used so extensively? Distinguish between grafting and budding.

17. What is tissue culture? Cell culture? Under what conditions are these techniques used to propagate plants?

CHAPTER 5

◆ ◆ ◆

1. Which of the environmental ingredients essential for photosynthesis and plant growth come from the soil?

2. Why is soil said to be a nation's most valuable natural resource?

3. What is meant by soil texture? Why is organic matter beneficial to both heavy-textured and light-textured soils?

4. Describe the most common methods by which organic matter can be added to and maintained in soils, and discuss the relative merits of each.

5. Describe the serious consequences of past and current soil erosion, and discuss practices by which erosion can be reduced or eliminated.

6. What is pH? How can growers change the pH of their soil? What conditions might make growers want to change the pH of their soil?

7. Which soil components are responsible for high cation-exchange capacity? Why is a high cation-exchange capacity valuable for growing crops?

8. What is the difference among fertilizer analysis, ratio, and formula? Under what conditions would the application of a low-analysis fertilizer be more effective than that of a high-analysis fertilizer?

9. Why are deficiency symptoms not always a good criterion of the kind, time, and amount of fertilizer application?

10. Why are deficiencies of minor elements more common today than they were fifty years ago? How can such deficiencies be corrected?

11. Why do plants often show a deficiency of nitrogen when large amounts of organic matter have been added to the soil? How can this kind of deficiency be prevented?

12. Describe cropping systems that provide gardens with needed mineral elements without the use of commercial fertilizers.

13. Why is crop rotation important to both gardens and commercial agriculture? Under what circumstances would succession planting and intercropping be justified in home gardens?

14. Using Tables 14-16 to 14-19, calculate the amount of ammonium nitrate, treble superphosphate, and potassium chloride you would need each season to fertilize three spreading shade trees, each having a canopy spread of 20×20 feet, growing in a central Atlantic coast state. How much dairy manure would be required to supply the nitrogen that these trees need?

15. What are the benefits of using landscape fabric, polyethylene, and other sheet mulches alone or in combination with bark or other loose mulching materials? What are some of the problems with using mulches?

CHAPTER 6

◆ ◆ ◆

1. Describe the moisture cycle of the earth. Explain why conserving the quality and quantity of water is vital to America today. How do such human activities as the indiscriminate destruction of forests and plant cover and the release of pollutants into the atmosphere affect the moisture cycle?

2. Discuss the relationship between "available" and "unavailable" soil moisture and soil texture, structure, and organic matter.

3. What are the functions of water in a plant, and how does the plant respond to a lack of, and to an excess of, moisture?

4. Describe four general methods of irrigation, and explain briefly the advantages and disadvantages of each. Why is drip irrigation receiving so much attention from commercial horticulturists today?

5. In Chapter 5, soil erosion was targeted as a major contributing factor to the loss of productivity and eventual abandonment of many long-cultivated lands. How have faulty irrigation practices contributed to this loss of productivity and abandonment?

6. Explain how an excess or deficiency of water affects blossom-end rot and the cracking of tomatoes; the quality of potatoes and other vegetables and fruits; the cracking of cherries, carrots, and cabbage; the quality of flowers; foliage diseases of beans; and the disfiguration of leaves of African violets and similar tropical houseplants.

7. Discuss ways of deciding when to irrigate around the home. Describe the pan evaporation method of determining the timing and amount of water required for lawn irrigation.

8. What is the summer-fallowing system of agriculture? Discuss the feasibility of using variations of this system in the water-short home garden. Describe other methods of gardening with a limited water supply.

9. Explain the importance of drainage from the standpoint of plant growth, soil pH and surface salt accumulation, insect control, and other factors that might affect gardening and a pleasant outdoor and indoor environment. How can good drainage of the yard be ensured?

CHAPTER 7

◆ ◆ ◆

1. Discuss the factors that determine climate of an area. The climate of North America is somewhat cooler and more variable from region to region than is the climate of areas of the same latitude in Europe. What are the reasons for this variation?

2. How does a maritime climate differ from a continental climate? Why is the production of perennial horticultural crops usually more extensive in maritime climates?

3. What are some of the factors that a gardener might consider when choosing a building site for a house — factors that would enhance the prospects for growing a variety of landscape and garden plants during as long a season as possible?

4. When harvesting and handling sweet corn and peas for processing, what precautions should you take to ensure the highest-quality processed product? Why is the bulk of processed sweet corn not grown in the "corn belt." Give at least two reasons.

5. Explain what is meant by temperature inversion. Why are so many orchards located on hillsides although conversely, commercial vegetable production in the same region is usually on relatively flat land?

6. Why are fruit orchards often located near large bodies of water? Why are apples not grown extensively in southern California and Florida?

7. What is meant by heaving, and how can straw mulch protect perennial flower or strawberry plantings from heaving?

8. Will trees that have produced a relatively heavy or a relatively light crop be more vulnerable to cold-winter damage? Why? Describe cultural practices that might lessen the chance of winter damage to cold-susceptible woody plants.

9. In a climate marginal for their survival, where in the yard would you plant grapes? rhododendrons? Holly, rhododendrons, and other broad-leaved evergreen trees and shrubs often suffer winter damage in exposed areas of climatic zones of the Rocky Mountains and Midwest to which they should be adapted. Why? How is this kind of damage related to the "catfacing" that results on the southwest side of trees in cold-winter regions? How can damage due to dehydration be lessened?

10. Why is spinach grown as an early-spring or early-fall crop in most areas of the United States and Canada? How would spinach respond if planted in late May in the north?

11. What is meant by light intensity? Light quality? Photoperiodism?

12. Why do leaves appear green? What percentage of the total energy delivered by the Sun to the Earth is used in photosynthesis? What happens to the rest?

13. Why are apples often red on only one side? How does color of apples relate to pruning practices?

14. In regard to light, what should a homeowner do to create an environment conducive to the blooming of a Christmas cactus or a poinsettia kept for a second season?

15. What kind of growth would 'Bermuda' onion adapted to growing in Texas display if planted in a garden in Minnesota at the usual April–May planting period for that region? What kind of growth would a 'Yellow Globe' onion adapted to growing in the northern United States or southern Canada display if planted in Texas in February?

16. Describe the effects of moisture, temperature, and light on the storage quality of horticulture products.

17. A high percentage of plant species grown in the interiors of homes and offices are native to tropical jungles. Why are these kinds of plants adapted to the indoor environment?

CHAPTER 8

◆ ◆ ◆

1. Why does pruning a tree reduce its growth? Explain from a physiological point of view why top pruning promotes vegetative rather than reproductive growth. What effect does root pruning have on a tree's growth? Under what conditions and for what purposes might root pruning be a good idea?

2. Discuss the role of auxin and apical dominance in training fruit trees. How does a "thinning-out" cut differ from a "heading-back" cut? How does growth of a woody plant pruned with "thinning-out" cuts differ from growth of a similar plant pruned with "heading-back" cuts?

3. What is meant by each of the following terms as they are used in relation to pruning?

central leader system	hedgerow system	vase system
training	pruning	scaffold branch
four-cane kniffin	vegetative wood	fruiting spur
blossom bud	mixed bud	espalier
thin-wood pruning	delayed heading	topiary

4. Describe the fruiting habits of major deciduous fruit trees, and explain how its fruiting habit, rapidity of growth, years of juvenility, and tendency for apical dominance affect the way a tree should be pruned.

5. An apple fruit spur bears fruit in alternate years, whereas a properly managed apple tree bears fruit annually. Explain.

6. Describe the fruiting habits and pruning of brambleberry bushes, and discuss the relationship between the fruiting habits of blueberries and currants and the best pruning practices for them. What determines how many buds one should leave on a grapevine in order to have the best quality and yield of fruit?

7. At what time or times of year should most orchard-tree and small-fruit pruning be done? Most pruning of roses? Of ornamentals that bloom early in the spring? Of ornamentals that bloom later in the summer? Of pines and rhododendrons?

8. Under what circumstances would a gardener want to prune vegetables and flowers?

9. Growth regulators bring about varied responses in plants, resulting from the basic function of the regulator at the cellular level. Briefly describe the cellular effect of each of the following: auxins,

gibberellins, cytokinins, and ABA. What is the major effect of ethylene on the biology of plants?

10. Name several commercial and home garden uses for each of the plant growth regulators. What are some of their unwanted effects on horticultural products?

11. Name three methods of modifying a plant's growth besides pruning and treating it with growth regulators, and explain how each of these can be directly or indirectly useful to home gardeners.

CHAPTER 9

◆ ◆ ◆

1. Why is it important for gardeners to be familiar with pests and various kinds of pest control, even if they do not contemplate using pesticides?

2. Why is it important that the entire pesticide label be studied? How should gardeners dispose of empty pesticide containers and unused pesticide? Under what circumstances do gardeners need a pesticide applicator's license, and how can they obtain it?

3. What are weeds, and how do they damage crops and gardens? What characteristics make weeds so persistent?

4. Why are herbicides not often used in home gardens? Considerable research is being conducted on biological control for rangeland weeds. Is biological control likely to become important to home gardens? Why or why not?

5. Why is it so desirable from the perspective of both the hours required and the quality of a crop to cultivate frequently? Discuss the control of weeds by means of mulching.

6. Define or explain the following terms as they relate to chemical weed control:

preemergence	nonselective
translocated herbicide	phenoxy herbicides
volatility	drift

7. Why are herbicides usually not as toxic to humans and animals as are insecticides? Describe the dangers and benefits to the environment of using herbicides.

8. Distinguish among virus, bacteria, fungus, and nematodes, and explain the general similarities and differences in control measures used for these classes of pathogens.

9. Describe the "disease cycle" and the insect life cycle. Why is it necessary that these life cycles be understood if pests are to be effectively controlled?

10. Discuss the dangers and benefits to society of using chemical pesticides for disease and insect control. Why are chemicals becoming less and less of a solution to controlling garden pests?

11. Why is it necessary for all citizens to cooperate if legal control is to be effective in preventing the spread of plant diseases and insects?

12. Distinguish among the physical, cultural, and biological control of insects and diseases, and suggest how each of these control measures may be used around the home.

13. How can plant breeding control plant pests? What role might genetic engineering play in the future control of insects and diseases?

14. Discuss the pros and cons of "organic growing." Suggest ways of growing lawns, vegetables, fruits, and ornamentals without pesticides.

CHAPTER 10

◆ ◆ ◆

1. Name the three environmental factors that are most limiting to indoor plant growing, and explain what can be done to lessen their impact.

2. In many locations, plants grow quite well in outdoor gardens having 1 or 2 percent organic matter and a high percentage of either clay or sand; however, it is essential that the growing medium for container-grown plants have at least

25 percent organic content and a balance of fine and coarse soil particles. Why are the growing media requirements so much more exacting for container-grown plants?

3. What kinds of pests are most likely to be troublesome to houseplants? Why are chemicals not a common pest-control measure for indoor plants? What are the various means by which the diseases and insects most common to houseplants can be controlled?

4. What special conditions are likely to be required for the indoor growing of the following: cacti and succulents; plants from bulbs or corms; vegetables; fruits; and herbs? Describe how you would plant and grow a terrarium? A bottle garden?

5. Describe how you would gather, condition, and care for flowers from the garden that are used in an arrangement.

6. Explain the difference between a hotbed and a cold frame. Under what conditions and with what kinds of plants are translucent plant covers likely to be beneficial?

7. What are the advantages and disadvantages of polyethylene, as compared with glass, for a greenhouse cover? Describe the heating and cooling of greenhouses.

8. What are the advantages of fluorescent light tubes, as compared with incandescent bulbs, for indoor plant growing? What are Gro-Lux fluorescent tubes, and what are their claimed advantages? (see also "Kind or Quality of Light," Chapter 7).

9. Bedding plants, roses, carnations, chrysanthemums, and snapdragons, and various kinds of foliage houseplants are the ornamentals most often produced in commercial greenhouses. Tomatoes are the only vegetable produced in quantity anymore. Explain the popularity of these kinds of crops for greenhouse growing.

CHAPTER 11

◆ ◆ ◆

1. What is the purpose of a home landscape? Name as many mistakes as you can that you would want to avoid when landscaping your home.

2. When selecting the site for a new home, what are some of the factors that an ardent gardener should consider? What are some of the factors that need attention during the planning, excavation, and construction of a new home that will make the installation and maintenance of the landscape easier and enhance the later enjoyment of the outdoor environment around the home?

3. In planning the landscape, into what areas should the lot be divided? What is the major function of each area, and how should each be landscaped?

4. How would the landscaping of a small city lot differ from the landscaping of a large country homesite? What is meant by "formal" and "informal" styles of landscaping, and in what situations would each be most suitable?

5. Why is it essential to develop a landscape plan before beginning any landscape construction or planting? What should be included in a landscape plan?

6. Why is it important for homeowners to become acquainted with city codes before they begin any landscape construction? With what elements of the landscape are city codes likely to be concerned?

7. What are the minimum standards and guidelines that should be followed when constructing walks? Driveways? Retaining walls?

8. What are the main uses of trees in the landscape? Of shrubs? Of lianas? A landscape architect can picture a plant ideally adapted for each location. What characteristics should that plant possess? Why is it sometimes necessary to compromise this ideal when choosing a tree or shrub?

What can homeowners do to avoid pest problems in their landscape plantings?

9. Why are roses among the most popular flowers? Explain how and when you would purchase, plant, prune, and otherwise care for hybrid tea and floribunda roses?

10. How does the time and method of planting bulbs and the later care of spring-flowering bulbous flowers differ from the planting and care of summer-flowering bulbous plants?

11. How does the use in the landscape, planting, and care of herbaceous perennials differ from the use, planting, and care of annual flowering plants? What are the most important considerations of color, height, texture, and time of bloom when planning a bed of several kinds of flowering herbaceous plants?

12. Regarding the growing of a lawn, comment on the following:

a. Time of planting
b. Irrigating
c. Kind of grass
d. Weed control
e. Grass substitutes
f. Fertilization

13. Construct a table that includes the common name, genus and species, and use in the landscape of two plants adapted to the climate of your home town, from each of the following categories:

a. Tall deciduous trees
b. Tall conifers or palms
c. Flowering deciduous trees
d. Tall shrubs or shrubby trees
e. Shrubs 5′ to 8′ high
f. Shrubs 3′ to 5′ high
g. Shrubs under 3′ tall
h. Lianas, ground covers

14. Where could you obtain information regarding pest control for home plantings? How does the fertilization and irrigation of a tree or shrub growing in a lawn differ from the fertilization and irrigation of one growing in a cultivated bed?

15. There is considerable sentiment in North America for eliminating lawns from the public areas of homes, the rationale being the claim that lawns are wasteful of scarce resources and that the pesticides and fertilizers used on them pollute the environment. What are some alternative treatments for public areas? Discuss the pros and cons of eliminating lawns.

CHAPTER 12

◆ ◆ ◆

1. In this day of abundance in supermarkets, what are some reasons for having a home vegetable garden?

2. What practices might a grower consider if space for a garden is limited? Which vegetables might be included in and excluded from a small garden?

3. Give examples of cool-season and warm-season vegetables. How can home gardeners who live in hot-summer areas grow cool-season crops? How might growers who live in cool-season areas increase their chances of maturing warm-season vegetables?

4. How can poor soil be improved so that it can grow a good garden? What crops can you grow if you have a heavy clay soil in your garden plot?

5. What precautions should gardeners take, and what kinds of vegetables should they grow if moisture is limiting?

6. Which vegetables can be transplanted? When should each be started for transplanting?

7. Discuss practices that would ensure a household fresh vegetables from the garden for the longest season possible? What are some ways to have unprocessed vegetables from the garden during the winter (see also "Storing Horticultural Products," Chapter 14)?

8. Describe how you would grow asparagus and rhubarb in a home garden. How could globe artichokes be grown in an area where the winter temperature might be expected to drop as low as 10° F (−12° C)?

9. Draw a vegetable garden plan for a location in your home town. If possible, the plot should be an actual location. If you are not able to use an actual location, draw the plan for a 30 × 30 ft (9 × 9 m) plot. Show the location of nearby large trees or buildings, and list the approximate frost-free period (see Figure 14-97 and Table 14-27). List the kind, cultivar, and spacing of the vegetables you wish to include. Cultivar names and descriptions can come from seed catalogs. List family likes and dislikes or any other reasons for your choices.

10. Draw a plan for a small ornamental herb garden that includes at least six herbs. Show their spacing, and explain why you chose each. Remember that only two or three herb plants of any one kind will supply a family.

11. What temperature (degrees F or C) and what humidity (high or low) are best for storing each of the following vegetables: asparagus, cabbage, carrots, sweet corn, lettuce, onions, potatoes, squash and pumpkins, tomatoes, and sweet potatoes?

CHAPTER 13

◆ ◆ ◆

1. How do American, European, and muscadine grapes differ in the genus and species to which each belongs, in anatomical characteristics, in cultural and pest-control requirements, in climatic adaptation, in the products for which they are used, and in areas of North America where they are produced?

2. How would you protect strawberry plants from freezing damage during the winter? From information learned in previous chapters, explain what would happen if June-bearing strawberries were planted under a bright yard light.

3. How are bramble fruits propagated? Why are most thornless trailing blackberries propagated by layering rather than from root suckers?

4. Why are strawberries and bramble fruits so expensive to buy? Why is it risky to propagate small fruits, or, for that matter, any perennial from a neighbor's garden, especially from a yard where you have not seen the parent plants growing?

5. Distinguish among highbush, lowbush, and rabbiteye blueberry types. Why are blueberries not grown extensively in the Great Plains, the Southwest, or the arid valleys of the Rocky Mountains?

6. Rank the major kinds of temperate-zone tree fruits according to their ability to survive cold-winter temperatures. Which kinds of tree fruits have the best chance of producing a normal crop in the northern Great Plains or other areas in Cold Hardiness Zone 3? Under what conditions might peaches be used as a rootstock for plums?

7. How have the plant breeding and training-related research of the past fifty years made it easier to grow tree fruits on a small lot? Explain how you would espalier and care for one or more pear trees planted at the base of a south-facing wall, making certain that all of the factors necessary for them to produce a crop were present.

8. Because they bloom so early, apricots are the temperate-zone fruit trees most likely to have their blossoms killed by early-spring frost. Explain what kind of site you would choose for planting an apricot tree and how you would care for it in order to give it the best possible chance to produce a crop year after year.

9. Which kinds of fruits and nuts studied in this chapter need pollinators? What characteristics should a good pollinator have?

10. Citrus trees come true from apomictic seed, or they can be propagated from cuttings. Why are they usually propagated by budding or grafting? How does the harvest and storage of citrus differ from the harvest and storage of temperate-zone tree fruits?

11. Name five subtropical fruits (not including citrus), and explain briefly where and how each is produced. What is the most unusual aspect of the production of each?

12. Nut trees are often planted as dual-purpose ornamental and food trees. As nearly as you can, rank the four mentioned in your text according to size and cold hardiness. Which are native to the Americas?

13. Explain how you would decide when to harvest each of the major fruit and nut crops discussed in this chapter. How do storage requirements differ for the major temperate-zone tree fruits? (See "Harvesting" and "Storing Horticultural Products" in Chapter 14.)

14. What are the major nutrients contributed to the human diet by each of the temperate-zone tree fruits and nuts? How does the vitamin C content of citrus fruits compare with that of various temperate-zone fruits? With that of vegetables like peppers, tomatoes, and broccoli (see Table 14-25)?

Glossary

Abscission Dropping off of a leaf, fruit, or flower; shedding.

Adventitious organ Plant organ, such as a bud, shoot, or root, produced in an abnormal position or at an unusual time of development.

Adenosine triphosphate (ATP) The energy storage molecule resulting from the breakdown of glucose; the molecule from which energy in the quantity needed for cell life processes can be almost instantly released. When energy is released to the cell ATP changes to adenosine diphosphate (ADP).

Aeration (soil) Air in the spaces around soil particles.

Aerial Bulb See Bulbil.

Aggregate fruit Fruit developed from a flower having a number of pistils, all of which ripen together and are more or less cohesive at maturity.

Aggregates (soil) Masses or clusters of soil particles variable in shape, size, and degree of coherence; as granules, nuciform aggregates, clods, prisms.

Agronomy Science of soil management and production of crops grown on large acreages.

Air layering Method of propagation by which plant parts are rooted while they remain attached to the mother plant.

Allele One of the contrasting genes that may exist at a particular location on a pair of chromosomes. The gene that produces pink flower color in sweet peas is an allele of the one that produces white flowers and also of the one that produces lavender flowers.

Allelopathy Detrimental influence of one plant on another due to chemical interactions.

Alternate bearing Bearing of heavier and lighter crops of flowers or fruits, or both, in successive years.

Alternate buds Leaf buds (or leaves) that occur singly at a node.

Analysis plan Preliminary drawing of an area to be landscaped, showing the environmental, topographical, and construction features that must be considered in designing the landscape.

Angiosperms Flowering plants; plants having their seeds enclosed in an ovary (the most advanced class of plants).

Annual Plant in which the entire life cycle is completed in a single growing season.

Anther Upper portion of a stamen, containing the pollen grains.

Anthocyanin Pigment in sap responsible for scarlet to purple or blue coloration in plants.

Apical dominance Influence exerted by a terminal bud in suppressing the growth of lateral buds.

Apical meristem Meristematic cells of the apex of the root and shoot.

Apomictic seed Seed developed from an unfertilized egg or other ovarian cell without sexual fusion.

Approach grafting Method of grafting by which two branches are joined while each remains attached to its own root system.

Arthropods Phylum or division of the animal kingdom that includes insects, spiders, and Crustacea; characterized by a coating that serves as an external skeleton and by legs with distinct movable segments or joints.

Asexual (or vegetative) propagation Propagation by utilizing a part of the body tissue of the mother plant as opposed to sexual union.

Auxin Organic compound active at low concentrations that promotes plant growth by cell enlargement and affects other aspects of plant development. Sometimes used loosely as synonymous with growth substance.

Available moisture Amount of water in soil that can be absorbed by the roots of plants. Technically, it is the difference in the weight of moisture held in a soil at field capacity and that held at the wilting point.

Axil Angle on upper side between leaf and stem.

Bacteria Microscopic, one-celled organisms that lack chlorophyll, multiply by fission, and do not form noticeable fungus threads. May be parasites on other plants or animals, or may live saprophytically on nonliving, organic matter.

Bactericide Substance that destroys bacteria; germicide.

Balanced crotch An undesirable situation that occurs when two branches grow from the same point on a tree at the same rate. Balanced crotches tend to split easily.

Balled and burlapped plant Plant with a compact mass of earth, covered with sacking, left on the roots for transplanting.

Banding Fertilizing close to a row of seed or seedlings.

Bare-root transplanting Method of transplanting in which plants are taken from the ground with little soil left on the roots.

Bark grafting Method of joining plants in which the scion is inserted between the bark and the xylem of the stock.

Bark inversion Type of phloem disruption in which a strip of bark is removed, turned upside down, and tacked back to the area from which it was removed. Used as a means of hastening reproduction of a nonfruiting tree or shrub.

Basal Pertaining to the base or lowest part of an organ or part.

Basal plate Short, fleshy stem axis within a bulb.

Bedding plants Flowers appropriate for growing in flower beds for massed decorative effect.

Berry Simple fleshy fruit, as a grape or tomato.

Biennial Plant that normally requires two growing seasons to complete the life cycle. Only vegetative growth occurs the first year; flowering and fruiting occur the second year.

Biennial bearing Bearing fruit once every two years.

Binomial system of nomenclature System in which the scientific name for any plant is composed of two Latin terms that designate genus and species.

Biological pest control (biocontrol) Destruction or suppression of undesirable insects, plants, or animals by the introduction or propagation and dissemination of predators, parasites, and diseases.

Blanching 1. Bleaching or whitening a vegetable as it is growing by wrapping the stalk and leaves with paper or outer leaves, or by throwing soil around the portion to be whitened, as celery is blanched. Also called etiolating. 2. Heating vegetables in water, live steam, or dry heat, to inactivate enzymes preparatory to processing.

Blastula Hollow sphere formed during tissue development that is reminiscent of certain stages of lower life forms; also one of the stages of animal embryonic development.

Blossom-end rot Disorder of tomato fruits in which a sunken dry rot develops on the distal end; associated with calcium deficiency and water stress.

Bolting Premature flower and seedstalk formation; usually refers to seed formation in biennial crops during their first year of growth.

Bonsai Culture of miniature potted trees that have been dwarfed by pruning and controlled nutrition.

Border masses Masses of shrubs and trees grown as plant walls.

Bract Modified and reduced leaflike structure.

Bramble Any plant of the genus *Rubus*, family Rosaceae; as the blackberry, raspberry, and dewberry.

Bridge grafting Method of preserving trees that have suffered bark damage of the lower trunk. The damaged area is bridged by long suckerlike scions grafted into healthy bark above and below the wound.

Bud Protuberance on a plant stem, leaf, or root that gives rise to vegetative shoots, flowers, and/or leaves.

Budding Grafting by inserting a single bud under the bark.

Bud mutation Genetic change in a bud that causes it to develop a shoot, flower, or fruit different from other shoots, flowers, or fruits of that plant.

Bud shield Bud with attached segment of bark and wood cut in the shape of a shield. (See T-budding.)

Bud sport Cultivar originating from bud mutation.

Budstick Shoot from which buds are removed for propagation.

Bulb Subterranean budlike storage organ produced by some plants; has a short stem surrounded by overlapping, fleshy leaf bases, as in onions and tulips.

Bulbil (aerial bulb, brood bulb, bulbel) Small bulb produced above the ground, among the flowers, or in the axil of a leaf.

Bulblet Small bulb borne in the axil of a bulb scale.

Bulb scale Fleshy sheathing leaf base of a bulb.

Bundle sheath Group of cells surrounding or associated with the vascular bundles in stems and leaves of some plants.

Callus Protective covering that forms over a wounded plant surface.

Calyx Outer or lowest of the four series of floral parts composed of the sepals. Usually green and leaflike, but may be colored like the petals.

Cambium Zone or cylinder of meristematic cells, lateral in position, which gives rise to secondary xylem and secondary phloem. Derived from provascular tissues and located between the xylem and phloem.

Cane 1. Woody stem of any small fruits, such as grape or raspberry. 2. Stem of reeds and large grasses, such as bamboos and sorghums. Also sometimes applied to the stem of rosebushes and some small palms.

Capillary moisture Water held by the soil against the force of gravity and available for plant absorption. The amount of water a soil will hold between wilting point and field capacity.

Carbohydrate/nitrogen balance Relative proportion of accumulated carbohydrates and nitrogen in stems and leaves of plants, important because it influences flower bud initiation and fruit set.

Catface Healing or healed wound on the trunk of a tree, frequently occurring on the southwest side of trees growing in cold winter areas and caused by physiological drought.

Cation Ion carrying a positive charge of electricity.

Cation exchange Interchange between a cation in solution and another cation on the surface of a colloidal or other surface-active material such as a clay or organic matter particle.

Cation exchange capacity Measure of a soil's ability to retain fertility, the sum total of exchangeable cations absorbed by a soil, expressed in milliequivalents per 100 g of soil equivalent to the milligrams of H^+ that will combine with 100 g of dry soil.

Cell Structural unit composing the bodies of plants and animals; an organized unit of protoplasm, in plants usually surrounded by a cell wall. Also the individual unit of a larger container as "the cell of a plug transplant container."

Cell culture The growing of new plants from single somatic (body or nonreproductive) cells, a technique widely used today for clonal propagation and biological research.

Cell membrane Structure inside the cell wall that appears to have the function of regulating the flow of nutrients and other materials into and out of the cell.

Cellulose A carbohydrate, the chief component of the cell wall in most plants.

Cell wall Membranous covering of a cell secreted by the cytoplasm in growing plants; consists largely of cellulose but may contain chitin in some fungi and silica in some algae.

Central leader System of tree training in which the trunk is encouraged to form a central axis with branches distributed laterally around it.

Certified seed or **certified plants** Propagating material that has been grown under grower-authorized government supervision and is certified to be true to cultivar name, free of contaminants, and relatively free of disease and insect pests.

Chelate Metal ion bonded to an organic molecule from which it can be released. For example, iron, only slightly available to plants growing in calcarious soils in its usual ferric hydroxide form, is readily absorbed when applied as chelate sequestrene 138 Fe.

Chemical pest control Use of chemical pesticides to control diseases, weeds, insects, and other pests that reduce crop yields.

Chemistry alteration Methods of preserving foods that involve a change in the chemistry of the food, including pickling; fermenting; and preserving with sugar, salt, and/or some other chemical.

Chlorophyll Green pigment located in plastids; necessary to the process of photosynthesis.

Chloroplast Specialized body in the cytoplasm that contains chlorophyll.

Chlorosis Interveinal yellowing of foliage that results from chlorophyll deficiency.

Chromosome Threadlike structural unit in the nucleus that preserves its individuality from one cell generation to the next and is the site of the hereditary determiners, the genes.

Class Taxonomic grouping of plants more comprehensive than an order and more specialized than a division (phylum).

Clay 1. Soil particle less than 0.002 mm in diameter. 2. Textural class of soil; one that contains 40 percent or more of particles of clay size.

Clean cultivation Intensive cultivation of a field so as to remove all plant growth except the crop.

Cleft grafting Method of grafting in which large trees are used for stock. The branch is sawed squarely across and split lengthwise, and two scions are inserted into the cleft.

Climacteric peak (climacteric) Maximum point of the respiration rate of mature fruit. The respiration rate rises dramatically just prior to reaching the climacteric.

Clone Group of plants derived by asexual propagation from a single mother plant.

Colchicine Poisonous alkaloid extracted from the common autumn crocus and used in plant breeding to block anaphase separation during cellular division, thereby producing polyploidy and doubling the number of chromosomes.

Cold frame Bottomless box with a removable glazed top; used to protect, propagate, or harden off plants. No heating device is used.

Cole crop Any plant of the genus *Brassica*, family Cruciferae (e.g., cabbage, cauliflower, broccoli).

Coleoptile Sheathlike pointed structure covering the shoot of grass seedlings; commonly interpreted as the first leaf of the plant above the cotyledon.

Collar On woody plants, the enlarged ring of tissue at the base of a branch where it attaches to a trunk or larger branch.

Colloid 1. Insoluble substance consisting of particles small enough to remain suspended indefinitely in a medium. 2. Mineral particle less than 0.002 mm in diameter. 3. Substance that does not form a true solution in water and does not diffuse readily through animal or vegetable membranes. Its presence does not affect the freezing point or vapor tension of the solution.

Companion cropping Form of intercropping in which specific kinds of plants are supposed to be mutually benefited by close association in the garden.

Complete flower Flower having all four series of floral parts—stamen, pistil, corolla, calyx.

Compost Material formed when organic residues, such as peat, manure, or discarded plant material, are aerobically decomposed.

Compound (serpentine) layering Propagation, usually of vines, in which several portions of a branch are covered with soil and intervening portions left above the soil until rooting takes place.

Contact herbicide Herbicide that kills a plant primarily by contact with tissue rather than by internal absorption.

Cool-season crop Crop that thrives best in cool weather; as apple, dahlia, and radish.

Core 1. Innermost part of pome and certain other fruits that contains the seeds. 2. Receptacle in certain plants, as the raspberry.

Cork cambium Lateral meristem producing cork in woody and some herbaceous plants.

Corm Short, thickened underground storage organ formed usually by enlargement of the base of the main plant stem.

Cormel Small corm, usually produced from a bud of the parent or major corm.

Corolla Second (beginning from below) of the series of floral organs composed of petals.

Cortex Outer primary tissues of the stem or root, extending from the primary phloem (or endodermis, if present) to the epidermis composed chiefly of parenchyma cells.

Cotyledon Leaves (seed leaves) of the embryo, one or more in number.

Cover crop Crop grown to add organic matter to soil and/or protect against erosion.

Cross-compatible (cross-fruitful) Condition in which each of two cultivars is capable of fertilizing and/or inducing fruit set on the other.

Cross-incompatible (cross-unfruitful) Condition based on genetic factors in which two different cultivars cannot fertilize or induce fruit set on each other.

Cross-pollination Transfer of pollen from the anther of one plant to the stigma of another plant.

Crown 1. Upper part of a tree, which bears branches and leaves. 2. Place at which the stem and root join in a seed plant; top of the root.

Crown division Method of reproduction of perennial plants, in which the crown is divided to form several separate plants.

Crumb (soil) A natural structure in soil; small, spheroidal, very porous, easily crushed aggregate.

Cucurbit Any plant of the family Cucurbitaceae, as cucumber, squash, watermelon.

Cultivar Official name for all cultivated variants of plants; also called horticultural or agricultural varieties, but distinguished from the botanical use of the term variety.

Cultivation 1. Planting, tending, and harvesting of plants. 2. Tillage of the soil to promote crop growth after the plant has germinated and appeared above ground. 3. Loosening of the soil and removal of weeds from among desirable plants.

Cultural (pest) control Control of pests through cultural practices; e.g., cultivating to destroy pests, planting at a time when pests are not likely to be destructive, regulating irrigation.

Cuticle Thin layer of cutin that covers the epidermis of above-ground plant parts.

Cuttage Method of propagation by which stem, leaf, or root tissue is removed from the plant and caused to form new roots and shoots.

Cutting Any part that can be severed from a plant and be capable of regeneration.

Cytoplasm Protoplasm of the cell exclusive of the nucleus.

Damping-off Rotting of seedlings and cuttings caused by any of several fungi. Usually refers to fungal attack near the soil line that results in falling over and death of cuttings or emerged seedlings, although preemergence damping-off is the killing of seedlings after germination but before the seedlings appear above soil.

Day-neutral plant Plant in which the flowering period or some other process is not influenced by length of daily exposure to light.

Deciduous 1. Parts of a plant that fall at the end of the growing period, such as leaves in autumn or fruits or flower parts at maturity. 2. Broadleaved trees or shrubs that drop their leaves at the end of each growing season; contrasted with evergreen plants.

Delayed dormant spray Pesticide applied to fruit trees when the fruit buds show green leaf tips about ¼ in (½ cm) long.

Deoxyribonucleic acid (DNA) Hereditary material of the cell; molecules composed of a double helix of sugar-phosphate linkages (forming the sides of a twisted ladder) with purine and pyrimidine bases joined across (to form the rungs).

Design elements One of the three areas of consideration in planning the landscape, including cubic space, topography, plants, rock, water, and building materials.

Determinant A type of growth habit that eventually terminates in a flower cluster and the end of shoot elongation.

Dicot Plant in which the embryo has two cotyledons or seed leaves.

Dioecious Bearing staminate and pistillate flowers (or pollen and seed cones of conifers) on different individuals of the same species.

Diploid Having two sets of chromosomes; the $2n$ number characteristic of the sporophyte generation.

Disbudding Removal of flower buds and/or shoot buds from a plant.

Diurnal Plant whose blossoms open during the day and close at night. Occurring daily.

Division 1. See Crown division. 2. The highest category of classification of plants according to rules of nomenclature; an aggregation of classes; synonymous with phylum as used by zoologists.

Dormancy Period of inactivity in bulbs, buds, seeds, and other plant organs.

Dormant spray Pesticide applied to a plant during its period of physiological inactivity.

Double working Rebudding or regrafting on a previously established graft on a plant. This system is used when two varieties or species of stock and scion do not unite except through an intermediary.

Drainage The drawing off of excessive moisture, usually the moisture in excess of field capacity.

Drupe Simple fleshy fruit in which the inner part of the ovary wall develops into a hard stony or woody endocarp, as in the peach.

Drupelet A small drupe, often one of many in a cluster or group; e.g., the pulpy grain of bramble fruits.

Dwarf Plant, especially one that has been grafted, that is much smaller when mature than others of its species.

Ecosystem Interacting system of one to many living organisms and their nonliving environment.

Egg cell Female reproductive cell of animals and plants.

Embryo Rudimentary plant formed in a seed resulting from fusion of the egg cell with a sperm.

Embryo sac (ovule) Female gametophyte of angiosperms, containing at maturity typically eight cells, three of which, the egg and two polar nuclei, are important in the formation of the embryo and endosperm tissue of the seed.

Endocarp Inner leathery, woody, or stony part of the wall of a fruit, as in a drupe (peach) or pome (apple).

Endodermis One-celled layer of specialized cells, frequently absent in stems but usually present in young roots, which separates the pericycle from the cortex. Often acts as a barrier to loss of moisture from vascular system of older roots.

Endogenous Growing from within or developing internally.

Endoplasmic reticulum Much-folded submicroscopic, double-layered membranes found in the cytoplasm; associated with the major biosynthesis of the cell.

Endosperm Nutritive portion of seeds formed by fusion of the two polar bodies of the embryo sac with a sperm. In many plants the endosperm is absorbed as food by the embryo before the seed matures, but in some, such as cereal grains, a large part of the mature seed is endosperm tissue.

Enology Art and science of wine making.

Epicotyl Part of a seedling stem above the cotyledons but below the first foliage leaves.

Epidermis Outermost layer of cells of the leaf and of young stems and roots.

Espalier system Method of training a woody plant in which the tree is planted against a wall or by a fence and the main branches trained in a plane parallel to the wall or fence in a geometric design.

Ethylene C_2H_4, a colorless, flammable, unsaturated hydrocarbon gas manufactured at several locations in the plant and considered a growth regulator. Ripening fruit and damaged tissues give off large quantities. Used artificially for many purposes, including ripening and coloring fruit.

Everbearing (everblooming) Producing fruit or bloom throughout most of the season.

Evergreen Plant that retains its leaves or needles longer than one growing season so that leaves are present throughout the year.

Exocarp Outermost layer of the pericarp or fruit wall; often the skin of the fruit.

F_1 Hybrid First generation following cross-pollination; F_2 and F_3 are the second and third generations.

Family Taxonomic grouping of plants more comprehensive than a genus and more specialized than an order; composed of one or (usually) a number of genera.

Fasciation Flattening and enlargement of a branch as if several stems were fused, often accompanied by curving. Believed to be caused by injury to the cells of the bud or by multiple terminal buds arranged in a single plane.

Fertilizer analysis Statement, usually on the label of a fertilizer container, of the percentages of nitrogen, phosphoric acid, and potash contained.

Fertilizer formula Quantity and grade of crude stock materials used in making a fertilizer mixture.

Fibrous root Root system in which the roots branch near the crown and become finely divided.

Field capacity Amount of water held in the soil after the excess of gravitational water has drained away.

Filament Stalk of the stamen, supporting the anther.

Flat Shallow box containing soil in which seeds are sown or to which seedlings are transplanted from the seedbed.

Floret Single individual flower that is a part of a flower head.

Flower Reproductive structure of the angiosperms.

Foliar analysis Detailed laboratory procedure that analyzes leaf tissue to furnish information on the minerals or other compounds within the plant.

Foot-candle Density of light striking the inner surface of a sphere with all surface area being one foot away from a one candle-power source.

Forma Group of individuals within a population that differs from the rest of the population in a regular but trivial way. Usually there is less difference between two forma of a population than between two varieties or subspecies. In horticulture the term is often used with ornamentals to distinguish groups with different growth characteristics not reproducible with seed.

Friable soil Soil with aggregates that can be readily ruptured and crushed with application of moderate force; one easily pulverized or reduced to crumb or granular structure.

Fruit 1. (botanical) Matured ovary of a flower and its contents, including any external part that is an integral portion of it. 2. (horticultural) Fleshy, ripened ovary of a woody plant, tree, shrub, or vine, used as a cooked or raw food.

Full slip In harvesting of melons, the easy separation of the fruit from the vine.

Fungi (kingdom fungi) A lower order of plant organisms, excluding bacteria, that contain no chlorophyll, have no vascular system, and are not differentiated into roots, stems, or leaves. Many cause diseases of horticultural crops; others, the mushrooms, are grown as food.

Fungicide Chemical that kills or inhibits fungi.

Furrow Depression in the ground surface dug along a prescribed line for planting seed, irrigating, controlling surface water, or reducing soil loss.

Gamete Reproductive body capable of fusion with another; most frequently refers to the sperm from the pollen grain and the egg from the ovule.

Gametophyte Plant during the haploid part of its life cycle. In higher plants, the sperm and egg and the haploid cells from which they develop.

Gene Unit of inheritance; located on chromosomes.

Generative nucleus One of the two nuclei of the pollen grain, responsible for fertilization of the ovule.

Genetic resistance Ability of an organism, because of its genetic makeup, to tolerate a condition (e.g., pesticide application, insect, disease) that would ordinarily kill other members of the same species.

Genus Group of closely related species clearly differentiated from other groups.

Germination Resumption of growth of an embryo or spore, including pollen grain on a stigma; the sprouting of a seed.

Germ plasm Hereditary materials (chromosomes, genes, and any other self-propagating particles) transmitted to the offspring through the reproductive cells; often used to denote the total genetic resources available in the entire population of a crop or species.

Girdling Encircling a living plant with a wound involving tissues as deep or deeper than the cambium layer; often done to reduce the downward flow of carbohydrates through the phloem in order to encourage reproduction.

Graftage (grafting) Process of inserting a part of one plant into or on another in a way that the two will unite and continue growth as a single unit.

Graft-compatibility Ability of parts of two different plants, when grafted together, to produce a successful union, and of the resulting single plant to develop satisfactorily. This condition is usually met when scion and stock are relatively closely related botanically.

Graft-incompatibility Inability of parts of two different plants, when grafted together, to produce a successful union, and of the resulting single plant to develop satisfactorily.

Graft union Healed wound, with an additional, foreign, piece of tissue (scion) incorporated into it. The union is accomplished entirely by cells that develop after the actual grafting operation has been made.

Granule 1. Rounded or subangular, relatively dense soil aggregate. 2. Particle containing volatile forms of a pesticide designed to be scattered among plants.

Gravel Rounded or angular particles of rocks or minerals greater in size than coarse sand and up to 75 mm in diameter.

Gravitational water Water that moves through soil under the influence of gravity; the source of spring and well water.

Green manure Crop plowed under when green for its beneficial effect on the soil.

Ground cover 1. Any vegetation that grows close to the ground, producing protection for the soil. 2. Any of many different plants, usually perennials, that grow well on sites on which grass does not thrive. Often used as a substitute for grass.

Groundwater Water contained in reservoirs in the soil.

Growth substance (plant growth regulator, plant hormone) Organic chemical that circulates in the plant in minute quantities and is a primary regulator of growth and other plant activities.

Guard cells Specialized crescent-shaped epidermal cells surrounding a stomate.

Gymnosperms Seed plants having ovules borne on open scales; mostly the needle evergreens, like pine, fir, and cedar.

Half-slip In harvesting of melons, a stage of ripeness in which, as the fruit is pulled from the vine, only a portion of the stem separates easily from the base of the fruit.

Hardening Treating plants to make them more resistant to adverse environmental conditions, usually by increasing their cold resistance.

Hard seed Seed that is unable to take in water because of an impervious seed coat.

Hardwood stem cutting Mature shoot of the last season's growth that is removed from the plant after the leaves have fallen to be used in propagating new plants.

Heading back Pruning the end of a branch or stem by cutting back to a bud or side branch.

Heaving Upward movement of soil caused by freezing and thawing of free water in the soil, thus involving expansion and contraction. Damage, and sometimes destruction, of plants may result from the lifting action.

Hedgerow 1. Method of training strawberries by definite placement in the row of the runners from each mother plant. 2. Widened row used for some bramble fruits in which sucker plants are permitted to grow between the mother plants in the row. 3. Close within-row planting of dwarf fruit trees so that they resemble a hedge.

Heel cutting Basal end of a plant stem cutting along with a piece of the older stem.

Herb 1. A plant used primarily for flavoring foods. 2. The flavoring product of that plant. Herbs mainly come from herbaceous plants or small shrubs grown in the temperate zones of the Earth as contrasted to spices which come primarily from trees, shrubs, lianas, and, occasionally, herbaceous plants grown in the tropics.

Herbaceous Plant or portion of a plant that lacks a pronounced woody structure.

Herbicide Plant killer; chemical used for weed control. A nonresidual herbicide kills only at the time of application, whereas a residual herbicide remains active in the soil for a few days to a number of years. A nonselective herbicide kills all vegetation to which it is applied, whereas a selective herbicide kills weeds without injuring the surrounding plants.

Hermaphroditic Bearing both male and female sex organs, e.g., a flower having anthers and ovaries.

Hesperidium A berry fruit, primarily from citrus, in which the exocarp and mesocarp are the rind and the endocarp is fleshy.

Heterozygous Condition in which the genes for a given character on the homologous chromosomes are unlike.

High-analysis fertilizer Fertilizer containing more than 30 pounds total N, P, K per 100-pound bag.

Homologous chromosomes Chromosomes that associate in pairs in the first stage of meiosis; one member of the pair is derived from a male and the other from the female parent.

Homozygous Condition in which the genes for a given character on homologous chromosomes are alike.

Horizon Stratum of the soil. Horizons start with "A" at the surface and usually end with "C," which is the parent material from which the soil formed.

Horticulture 1. Department of the science of agriculture that relates to intensively cultivated crops. 2. Cultivation of gardens or orchards, including the growing of vegetables, fruits, flowers, and ornamental shrubs and trees.

Host Any animal or plant upon or in which another organism lives as a parasite.

Host range Various kinds of plants that may be affected by a given pathogen.

Hotbed Small enclosed garden bed, having a transparent covering, in which the soil is heated.

Hybrid Progeny of a cross between two individuals differing in one or more genes.

Hybridization Process of crossing two individuals that differ in genetic makeup.

Hygroscopic (unavailable) water Moisture a soil contains after it has dried or been depleted to the wilting point. Such water does not move in the soil and cannot be used by plants.

Hypocotyl Part of the stem of an embryo or seedling below the cotyledons and above the radicle or embryonic root.

Imperfect flower Flower containing either stamens or pistils but not both.

Inarching Method of propagation in which a plant, still attached to its own roots, is grafted to another; frequently done with root suckers or seedling trees to bridge lower trunk damage of fruit trees.

Inbred line Homozygous line of plants or animals produced by inbreeding and selection.

Inbreeding Breeding of closely related plants or animals; in plants it is usually brought about by self-pollination.

Incomplete flower Flower lacking one or more of the four kinds of floral organs: sepals, petals, stamens, or pistil.

Indeterminant Growth habit that can continue indefinitely.

Indole-3-acetic acid (IAA) Plant hormone that causes elongation of cells when it is present in suitable concentrations; usually considered the natural plant auxin.

Indole-3-butyric acid (IBA) Synthetic auxinlike hormone used to stimulate root formation and other plant growth responses.

Inorganic Not made up of or derived from plant or animal materials.

Insecticide Substance that kills insects by chemical action.

Integrated (pest) control Type of pest control in which the pest-host relationship is monitored carefully, and every conceivable control measure, including cultural practices, environmental manipulation, and the use of natural predators, is utilized to control the pest. Chemicals are used mainly as the last resort and then with as low a concentration and as minimal a coverage as possible.

Intercropping Growing two or more crops simultaneously, as in alternate rows in the same field or single tract of land.

Intermittent mist Propagating system in which water sprays over the rooting bed at intervals to prevent the cuttings from dehydrating while roots are being initiated.

Internode Region of the stem between any two nodes.

Interspecific cross Cross between two different species.

Interstock Intermediate stock grafted between a rootstock and a scion.

Ion Atom or group of atoms carrying an electrical charge, which may be positive (cation) or negative (anion). Usually formed when salts, acids, or bases are dissolved in water.

June drop Shedding of tree fruits during the early summer; believed to be caused most frequently by, or associated with, embryo abortion.

Juvenile Type of growth in young plants that is not found in older plants of the same kinds.

Kingdom One of the five main areas of biological classification now recognized by most biologists. The five kingdoms include the traditional Kingdom Animalia; Kingdom Monera, or the bacteria, including blue-green algae; Kingdom Protista, or the algae and slime molds; Kingdom Fungi; and Kingdom Plantae.

Kniffen system Method of training grape vines, in which one or more trunks are carried to wires of a trellis along which fruiting canes are renewed and tied annually.

Landscape 1. In soil geography the total natural and human-made characteristics that distinguish a certain area of the Earth's surface from other areas; as soil types, vegetation, rock formations, hills, valleys, streams, cultivated fields, roads, and buildings. 2. To beautify terrain, as with plantings or ornamental features.

Landscape fabric Fabric used as a soil cover, pervious to moisture but impervious to light and, thus, to weed growth; usually used in conjunction with a bark or fiber mulch cover.

Larvicide Chemical used to kill the larval or preadult stages of insects.

Lateral bud Bud attached to the side of a branch or spur.

Layering Method of propagating woody plants by covering portions of their stems or branches with moist soil or sphagnum moss so that they take root while still attached to the parent plant.

Leaching 1. Removing alkali and/or salt from soil by abundant irrigation combined with drainage. 2. Removing soluble materials in downward percolating water.

Leaf More or less flattened outgrowth from a plant stem, varying in size and shape and usually green in color, that is concerned primarily with the manufacture of carbohydrates by photosynthesis.

Leaf bud cutting Method of propagation in which parts of a stem are split lengthwise so that each cutting has one leaf and its axillary bud. The bud is then buried under a shallow covering of rooting medium to root.

Legal (pest) control Exclusion of pests from an area by prohibiting importation of plant materials from areas where the pest is endemic.

Legume Plant of the family Leguminosae, as alfalfa, clovers, peas, beans, and others; characterized botanically by a fruit called a legume or pod that opens along two sutures when ripe.

Lenticel Opening through the bark or outer covering of fruits, etc., that permits exchange of gases from the inner tissues with the surrounding air.

Liana Woody climbing plant.

Lignification Process in which plant cells become woody by conversion of certain constituents of the cell wall into lignin; generally considered to include the hardening, strengthening, and cementing of the cell walls in the formation of wood.

Lignin Principal noncellulosic constituent of wood. Tends to harden and preserve the cellulose.

Loam Soil not definitely sandy or claylike; one not strongly coherent, mellow, and well supplied with organic matter. Technically, a soil that contains 7 to 27 percent clay, 28 to 50 percent silt, and less than 52 percent sand.

Locus Position on a chromosome occupied by a particular gene.

Lodging Pertaining to plants that break, bend over, or lie flat on the ground, sometimes forming a tangle.

Long-day plant Plant in which the flowering period or other process is accelerated by daily exposure to light longer than a certain minimum number of hours.

Low-analysis fertilizer Fertilizer containing less than 30 pounds of total N, P, K per 100-pound bag.

Macroclimate Long-term weather pattern of a fairly broad geographical area.

Macronutrient Mineral required in relatively large amounts for the healthy growth of plants.

Megaspore Large spore that germinates to form a female gametophyte.

Megaspore mother cell Cell that undergoes two meiotic divisions to produce four megaspores.

Meiosis Process of two divisions during which the chromosomes are reduced from the diploid to the haploid number. In higher plants it occurs only in the reproductive cells.

Meristem Undifferentiated, thin-walled tissue of a plant from which, as development proceeds, the permanent tissues are produced.

Mesocarp Middle layer (usually fleshy) of the fruit wall of a drupe or other fruit.

Metabolism Total of the chemical processes in the plant body.

Microclimate Purely local variations from the general or regional climate due to slight differences in elevation, direction of slope exposure, soil, density of vegetation, etc.

Micronutrient Nutrient essential to plants in only very small amounts.

Micropylar end Part of the embryo sac that is attached to the remainder of the ovary. Has a thin wall from which there is living cellular tissue leading to the main stylar tissue of the flower.

Microspore Small spore that germinates to form the male gametophyte.

Microspore mother cell Cell that divides to produce microspores.

Middle lamella (intercellular layer) The wall layer common to two adjoining cells and lying between the primary walls.

Mineral soil Common soil of land surfaces, consisting of broken-down minerals and rocks. The solid matter is preponderantly inorganic (as contrasted to organic soil).

"Mini-til" (minimum tillage) Method of cultivation utilizing the least amount of tillage possible. Usually residue from the previous crop remains between the rows until the current crop is established.

Miticide Any chemical mixture or compound used to kill mites.

Mitochondria Minute protoplasmic bodies in the cytoplasm, believed to be the site of the enzymes responsible for the oxygen-requiring steps in respiration.

Mitosis Process during which the chromosomes become doubled longitudinally, the daughter chromosomes then separating to form two genetically identical daughter nuclei. Mitosis is usually accompanied by cell division, in which each daughter cell has the same number of chromosomes as the mother cell.

Mixed bud Bud that produces both leaves and flowers.

Modified central leader system A training system extensively utilized with apples, pears, and some stone fruits, in which the central leader is headed back slightly but not completely removed until after the tree is five or six years old and has borne a crop of fruit, at which time the main framework will have been established.

Moisture cycle Circulation of the earth's moisture, involving evaporation from oceans; falling to earth in rain, snow, or hail; various pathways through the soil and in streams back to the ocean; and evaporation from soil and transpiration from plants back to the atmosphere.

Mold and hold system System of training in which trees are permitted to grow to any convenient size desired and are then kept at that size by heavy pruning. The downward orientation of side branches overcomes the inhibition of fruiting that would otherwise occur as a result of the heavy pruning.

Monocot Plant in which the embryo has a single cotyledon.

Monocropping (monoculture) Cultivation of a single crop, such as wheat or cotton, to the exclusion of other possible uses of the land.

Monoecious Bearing both staminate and pistillate flowers (or pollen and seed cones of conifers) at different locations on the same plant.

Morphology Form, structure, and development of plants.

Mound layering Rooting of branches of woody plants or shrubs by leaving the branches upright and mounding soil about the basal portions of the stems.

Muck Organic soil derived mainly from plant matter that is more highly decomposed than in peat and has lost its botanical identity. May be granular or amorphous but is humified and blackish.

Mulch 1. Soil, straw, peat, plastic, or any other loose or sheet material placed on the ground to conserve soil moisture, promote early maturity, or prevent undesirable plant growth or soil erosion. 2. Material, such as straw, placed over plants or plant parts to protect them from cold or heat.

Multiple cropping Growing of two or more crops consecutively on the same field in a single year.

Multiple fruit Fruit composed of a number of closely associated ovaries derived from different flowers that, with the fleshy tissue surrounding them, forms one body at maturity; as a pineapple.

Mutation Change in a gene that results in a change in descendents produced from the cell containing that gene.

Mycelium Hyphae or filaments (plant body) of a fungus.

α-Naphthalene-acetic acid (NAA) One of the synthetic organic acids of hormone mixtures used to stimulate root development and other plant responses.

Natural target pruning A system of pruning espoused by forester Alex Shigo in which the branch is removed where it narrows just to the exterior of the collar, instead of flush with the trunk or larger branch to which it is attached.

Necrosis Death of a cell or group of cells, usually while a part of the plant is still living.

Nematocide Agent that kills nematodes.

Nematode Any of the round, threadlike, unsegmented animal worms of the phylum Nematoda, ranging in size from microscopic to one meter long. May be saprophytes or parasites of plants and animals. Responsible for important animal and plant diseases resulting in much economic loss.

Nitrogen-fixing bacteria Species of the genus *Rhizobium*, family Rhizobiaceae, which live symbiotically in the root nodules of leguminous plants, upon which they are dependent. They are capable of extracting nitrogen from the air and converting it to a form that can be used by the plant.

Node Region of the stem where one or more leaves are attached. Buds are commonly borne at the node, in the axils of the leaves.

Nucleus Specialized body within the protoplasm that contains the chromosomes.

Nut Hard, dry, one-seeded fruit.

Obligate parasite Any parasite that cannot exist independently of its living host.

Offset Short, prostrate, many-noded branch growing from the crown of a plant and having a somewhat fleshy, scaly bud or a rosette of leaves located terminally. Offsets often form roots and are used to propagate some kinds of plants.

Offshoot Lateral shoot or branch that rises from one of the main stems of a plant; often used for propagation.

Olericulture Vegetable culture.

Open-pollinated Cultivars of cross-pollinated crops, seed of which is produced by allowing plants in seed fields to intercross freely; contrasted to inbred, F_1 hybrid, and other cultivars in which pollination is controlled.

Opposite buds Buds (and leaves) occurring in pairs at a node.

Order Category of classification more comprehensive than a family and more specialized than a class; composed of one or more families.

Organelle Part of the protoplasm of a cell having a particular function.

Organic 1. Of plant or animal origin. 2. More inclusively, chemical compounds that contain carbon.

Organic soil Any soil in which the solid part is predominantly organic matter, as contrasted to mineral soil; muck or peat.

Ornamental horticulture Production and utilization of flowers, shrubs, and trees.

Osmosis Flow of a fluid through a semipermeable membrane separating two solutions that permits passage of the solvent but not of the dissolved substance. The liquid will flow from a weaker to a more concentrated solution, thus tending to equalize concentrations.

Ovary Swollen basal portion of a pistil; the part containing the ovules or seeds.

Ovicide Substance that kills parasites in the egg stage.

Ovule (embryo sac) Part of the ovary containing one female gametophyte. Following fertilization, the ovule develops into the seed.

Palisade layer Cells of the mesophyll lying next to the upper epidermis of leaves. The process of food manufacture, or photosynthesis, is most active in these cells.

Parasite Organism that lives at least for a time on or in and at the expense of living animals or plants.

Parenchyma Unspecialized, simple cell or tissue, usually thin-walled, living at maturity and retaining a capacity for renewal of cell division.

Parthenocarpic fruit Fruit produced without fertilization.

Peat Geologic deposit, consisting predominantly of plant remains only very slightly decomposed, that accumulates in lakes, marshes, and some swamps. Various kinds are recognized according to origin, texture, and plant composition.

Peat pellet Type of seedling container made of compressed peat moss surrounded by coarse netting. Usually contains fertilizer and expands to several times its size when soaked in water.

Pectin Any of the fruit juice substances that form a colloidal solution with water and are derived from pectose (protopectin) in ripening processes or other forms of hydrolysis. Pectin is derived from citrus fruits and apple wastes and is used in jelly making to firm the body of the product.

Pepo Fleshy or succulent fruit, often of large size, formed from an inferior syncarpous ovary, and containing many seeds.

Perennial Woody or herbaceous plant living from year to year not dying after flowering once.

Perfect flower Flower containing both stamens and pistil; also called a bisexual flower.

Pericycle Cylinder of vascular tissue, three to six cells thick, lying immediately inside the endodermis of a root from which branch roots are initiated.

Periderm Secondary protective tissue formed in secondarily thickened stems and roots. It consists of the cork cambium, cork, and secondary cortex.

Perlite White and very porous volcanic mineral that is sometimes used as a medium for rooting cuttings.

Pest cycle Sequential changes and interactions that occur in the host/pathogen relationship through their respective life cycles.

Pesticide Any substance that kills pests. Today the term usually refers to synthetic chemicals used to control weeds (herbicides), insects (insecticides), and fungal diseases (fungicides).

Petal One of the units of the corolla of a flower.

Petiole Thin stem supporting the blade of a leaf.

pH Index designating relatively weak acidity and alkalinity, as encountered in soils and biological systems. A pH of 7.0 indicates neutrality; higher values indicate alkalinity, lower values, acidity.

Pheromone A chemical substance secreted by an insect that elicits a response, most often a sexual response, in other insects of the same species.

Phloem Vascular tissue that conducts synthesized foods in vascular plants. Characterized by the presence of sieve tubes and in some plants companion cells, fibers, and parenchyma.

Phloem disruption (as growth regulator) Disruption of phloem by scoring, girdling, or bark inversion for the purpose of hastening the reproduction of a nonfruiting tree or shrub.

Photoperiodism Reaction of plants to periods of daily exposure to light; generally expressed in formation of blossoms, tubers, fleshy roots, runners, etc.

Photosynthesis Production of carbohydrate from carbon dioxide and water in the presence of chlorophyll, using light energy and releasing oxygen.

Phototropism Response of a plant to the stimulus of sunlight, in which parts of the plant receiving the direct rays grow more slowly and the plant appears to turn toward the light.

Phylum Major division of the plant or animal kingdom. The term division is used more frequently in the plant kingdom.

Physical (pest) control Control of pests through physical force; e.g., physical removal of infested and infesting entities, barriers against infestation.

Physical seed dormancy Failure of a seed to germinate for a physical reason, such as a hard seed coat that is impervious to water.

Physiological drought Inability of a plant to obtain water from soil although the water may be present in it, as when a soil is frozen or by reason of weak osmotic force of plant roots.

Physiological seed dormancy Failure of a seed to germinate for physiological reasons, such as an immature embryo when the seed is otherwise ready to harvest, or chemical inhibitors within or outside the seed.

Physiological self-incompatibility Condition in which self-pollination frequently occurs but self-fertilization does not. Pollen may fail to germinate on the stigma, or the pollen tube may grow only part way through the style.

Pillar system A system of training in which a permanent trunk is developed and new side branches are permitted to grow each year. The following year's crop comes from newer side branches. Side branches oriented downward are kept to encourage fruiting

Pistil Central or female organ of the flower, composed of one or more carpels and enclosing the ovules.

Pistillate Designating a flower that has a pistil or pistils but lacks stamens; an imperfect flower.

Pith Tissue occupying the center of the stem within the vascular cylinder. Usually consists of parenchyma, but other types of cells may also occur.

Plant band Short strip of heavy paper that may be folded or rolled into a potlike unit to replace clay pots for growing young plants, which are later transplanted directly to the field without removal of the plant band.

Plant pathology Branch of botanical science that deals with the diseases and disorders of plants.

Plant protector Any device used to protect plants from nuisances such as rabbits and birds or from excessive sunlight, winter injury, or cold temperatures.

Plant volatile Aromatic substance emitted by plants in gaseous form. Some repel pests; for example, a cedar closet repels moths.

Plasmodesmata Streams of protoplasm that extend through pores in the cell wall and connect the protoplasts of adjacent living cells.

Plug, plug transplants 1. A seedling plant with its root surrounded by the tightly packed fibrous medium in which it was grown; may be transplant size ready to sell as a bedding plant or 2- or 3-true-leaf size grown with plug culture. 2. A unit of compressed medium, as the plug of grass used for plug sodding, or a wedge cut from something, as a plug from a melon to test its ripeness.

Plug culture A highly mechanized system for growing seedlings to the 2- or 3-true-leaf stage. Seeds are planted individually into growing media in closely spaced cells, germinated and grown in a controlled environment, and used or sold while still very small for further growing into transplants or potted flowering plants.

Plug sodding Method of planting a new lawn with grasses that reproduce asexually, in which plugs of the grass are set at specified intervals and allowed to spread.

Plumule Bud of the embryo. May consist of a shoot apex alone or of the apex and one or more embryonic leaves. Also applied to the primary bud of a seedling.

Polar bodies Two of the eight cells of the embryo sac. They stay in the approximate center of the embryo sac, and during fertilization they fuse with one of the nuclei of the pollen grain to form the initial endosperm cell.

Pollen (grain) Mature, usually two-nucleated, microspore of seed plants.

Pollen tube Tube formed in the style following germination of the pollen grain.

Pollination Transfer of pollen from the anther to the stigma of the same or another flower.

Pollinator Cultivar grown primarily as a source of pollen for other cultivars.

Pome Fleshy fruit with a leathery endocarp, as produced by apple, pear, and quince.

Pomology Art and science of growing and handling fruits, especially tree fruits.

Pore In plant and animal membranous tissue, minute opening for absorption and transpiration of matter.

Postbloom drop Period of time right after petals fall from the blooms of a fruit tree when small fruits are normally lost.

Postemergence herbicide Herbicide that is applied after the crop has emerged.

Potherb Greens; any plant yielding foliage that is edible when cooked, such as spinach, kale, chard.

Predator Any animal, including insects, that preys upon and devours other animals. Distinguished from a parasite, which lives on only one host at a time and usually does not destroy the host.

Preemergence herbicide Herbicide that is applied after the crop has been seeded but before it comes through the ground.

Prepink spray Spray applied to apples in the stage just before the flower buds turn pink.

Preplant herbicide Herbicide that is applied before the crop is seeded.

Pricking off Lifting very small seedling plants from seed beds and transferring them to transplant flats.

Primordia Organ of a plant in its earliest condition.

Propagating Causing to generate or to multiply by sexual or asexual means.

Propagule Newly propagated plant.

Protectant Chemical containing heavy metals, sulfur, or organic compounds used as sprays, dusts, or dips on seeds, stems, leaves, or wounds of living plants to prevent entrance of fungi or bacteria.

Protoplasm Living material of a cell.

Pruning Removal of live or dead branches, roots, and other parts from trees, shrubs, vines, etc., for purposes of improvement.

Pseudobulb Swollen, stemlike base of many orchids, or an elongated above-ground, fleshy plant stem in which food and moisture are held.

Pteridophytes Vascular plants that reproduce by spores; ferns.

Qualitative characteristics Plant characteristics in which differences of expression, such as color, leaf form, presence of hairs, can be easily distinguished.

Quantitative characteristics Characteristics in which differences of expression, such as size, shape, yield, and quality, intergrade. Usually under the control of large numbers of genes, each of which adds to or modifies the characteristic.

Radicle Basal end of the embryonic axis, which grows into the primary root.

Random segregation Capacity of members of each pair of alleles to randomly separate into different sex cells or gametes and thence into different offspring.

Receptacle Part of the axis of a flower stalk that surrounds the floral organs.

Region of cell division Area of the root tip between the root cap and the region of cell elongation.

Region of cell elongation Area just behind the region of cell division at the tip of stems or roots or at nodes of plants having growth in the nodal area.

Repellent Substance obnoxious to insects (or chordates) that prevents them from injuring their hosts or laying eggs.

Reproductive phase Stage in the growth of a plant when it changes from purely vegetative growth to production of flowers, fruit, and seeds.

Respiration Intracellular process by which energy is released from the breakdown of food. Most respiration in higher plants is aerobic (oxygen requiring). Anaerobic respiration (without oxygen) occurs in some bacteria and yeasts.

Rest period Stage during which a plant is physiologically unable to initiate growth, even though environmental conditions may be favorable.

Rhizome Underground stem, usually horizontal in position. Distinguished from a root by the presence of nodes and internodes and sometimes buds and scalelike leaves at the nodes.

Ribonucleic acid (RNA) Nucleic acid found in some nuclei and in the cytoplasm. Believed to carry a copy of the genetic information contained in the genes and to apply it in the synthesis of specific protein molecules.

Ribosome Submicroscopic granule in the protoplasm that contains RNA and protein and is associated with protein formulation.

Rill Furrow.

Roguing Removing and destroying undesirable plants.

Root Lower portion of a plant that usually develops underground and anchors the plant in the soil; bears the root hairs, which absorb water and mineral nutrients.

Root cap Thimble-shape mass of parenchyma cells over the root apex, protecting it from mechanical injury.

Root hair zone Area of the root tip behind the region of cell elongation. In the root hair zone and younger root tissue the endodermis is permeable enough to permit passage of water and nutrients.

Root primordia Specialized cells that will develop into roots.

Rootstock Underground stock upon which a desirable variety may be grafted.

Root sucker Sprout that rises from a root.

Rotation Growing of two or more crops on the same piece of land in different years in sequence and according to a definite plan.

Runner Horizontal shoot or branch forming roots at the tip or nodes; stolon.

Russeting Brownish, roughened areas on the skins of fruit, tubers of potatoes, etc., resulting from abnormal production of cork tissue. May be caused by disease, insects, or injury; or may be a natural varietal characteristic.

Salad crop Food plant grown primarily for its edible leaves, stalk, or other vegetative parts used in salads.

Samara Single-seeded, dry fruit having a winglike extension of the pericarp.

Sand Group of textural classes of soil in which the particles are finer than gravel but coarser than silt, ranging in size from 2.00 to 0.5 mm in diameter. Class of any soil that contains 85 percent or more sand and not more than 10 percent clay.

Scaling Method for propagating scaly bulbs, in which individual bulb scales are separated from the mother bulb and placed in growing conditions so that adventitious bulblets form at the base of each scale.

Scaly bulb Bulb, such as lily, with fleshy overlapping leaves resembling scales.

Scarification Abrasion, scratching, or modification of a surface for increasing water absorption; as scarification of an impervious seed coat.

Scion Branch or portion of a branch having one or more buds. Detached from a woody plant, it is then used in grafting or budding.

Sclerenchyma fiber Elongated cells with tapering ends and thick secondary walls; usually nonliving at maturity; supporting tissue.

Scooping Method of basal cuttage in which the entire basal plate of a bulb is scooped out. Adventitious bulblets develop from the base of the exposed bulb scales.

Scoring 1. Method of bulb propagation in which three straight knife cuts are made across the base of a bulb, each deep enough to go through the basal plate and the growing point. Growing points in the axils of the bulb scales grow into bulblets. 2. Type of phloem disruption that consists of running a knife blade around the tree or branch to cut through the phloem.

Sectioning Method of propagation in which a bulb is cut into sections with a portion of the basal plate attached to each section. Bulblets then form from the basal plate of each cutting.

Seed Organ formed by seed plants following fertilization. Embryonic plant with food supply and protective covering.

Seed coat Hard outer layer of a seed; the protective covering, or integument.

Self-compatible (self-fruitful) Able to fertilize and/or mature fruit without the aid of pollen from another cultivar.

Self-incompatible (self-unfruitful) Unable to set viable seed and/or fruit from self-pollination although pollen and ovules may be normal; may result from the arrest of pollen tube growth in the style.

Self-pollination Transfer of pollen from the anther to the stigma of the same flower or of another flower on the same plant or within a clone.

Senescence Stage in the life of an individual plant or plant part when the rate of metabolic activities declines and there is a change in the physiology prior to death.

Sepal One of the units of the calyx.

Serpentine layering See Compound layering.

Set Small propagative part—a bulb, shoot, tuber, etc.—suitable for setting out or planting.

Sexual (seed) propagation Propagation utilizing the fusion of male and female gametes, or their nuclei, to form a zygote, which develops into a new individual.

Sheath Leaf base when it forms a tubular casing around the stem.

Short-day plant Plant in which flowering period or some other process is accelerated by daily exposure to light shorter than a specified maximum.

Short-season crop Crop that reaches maturity in a short period of time.

Sidedressing Applying fertilizer to the soil at the side of a plant row, usually after the crop has started to grow.

Side graft A type of graft used for topworking or for producing new plants. The scion is inserted into the side of the stock, which is generally larger in diameter than the scion.

Silt 1. Small, mineral soil particles ranging from 0.05 to 0.002 mm in diameter. 2. Textural class of soils that contains 80 percent or more silt and less than 12 percent clay.

Simple fruit Fruit derived from a single pistil, simple or compound; ovary superior or inferior.

Slip Softwood or herbaceous cutting from a plant, used for propagation or grafting.

Sludge Residual solids after sewage treatment; solids deposited by sedimentation in sewage treatment. Often used as an organic fertilizer.

Sodding Removing sod from one area and placing it on a bare soil area in another location.

Softwood Immature, succulent stem of a woody plant.

Soil profile Vertical section of a soil. The section, or face of an exposure made by a cut, may exhibit with depth a succession of separate layers, although these may not be separated by sharp lines of demarcation.

Solanaceous crop Crop that is a member of the family Solanaceae, including potato, tomato, pepper, eggplant.

Species Taxonomic grouping of plants more specialized than genus. Species is the basic unit in which each plant is classified, even though some species may be further divided into subspecies, varieties, or other groupings. Plants within a species will usually intercross.

Sperm Mature male germ cell.

Spermatophytes Vascular plants that reproduce by seed such as cycads, ginkgos, conifers, and angiosperms.

Spheroidal aggregate Soil aggregate that is built around a central core and has rounded or irregular surfaces; the most desirable structural form of soil aggregate.

Spine Stiff pointed protuberance from a plant, especially one that is a modified leaf or leaf part.

Spongy parenchyma Leaf tissue composed of loosely arranged chloroplast-bearing cells; also called spongy tissue. Found usually toward the lower side of the leaf.

Sporophyte Plant during the diploid part of its life cycle. In higher plants, all parts of the cycle but egg and sperm and the cells from which they develop.

Sprigging Method of planting a lawn with grasses that reproduce asexually, in which individual plants, cuttings, or stolons are planted at spaced intervals. Sprigs are obtained by tearing apart established lawns.

Spur Short, stubby shoot, as in some fruit trees.

Spur-type tree Fruit tree (primarily apple and cherry) that has shortened internodes and consequently buds and spurs much closer together; about two-thirds the height of normal trees.

Stamen Male organ of the flower producing the pollen; usually composed of anther and filament.

Staminate Designating a flower that has stamens but no pistil and hence is imperfect.

Stem Axis of a plant bearing leaves with buds in their axils. It may be above or below ground, and the leaves may be functional or scales.

Stem cutting Any part of a stem used for plant propagation by cuttage.

Stem tuber The enlarged base of the main plant stem of such plants as tuberous-rooted begonia and gloxinia; they differ from corms in lacking scaly leaves and enlarging rather than being renewed each year.

Stigma Summit of the pistil; receives the pollen grains.

Stipule Basal appendage of a leaf or petiole. May photosynthesize or be scales, and may protect the axillary buds.

Stock Plant or plant part upon which a scion is inserted in propagation by graftage.

Stolon Trailing and rooting shoot (in higher plants); also called runner.

Stolonizing Method of planting a lawn with grasses that reproduce asexually. Shredded stolons are spread on the soil surface and raked lightly to firm them into the soil.

Stoma (Stomate) Opening or pore, mainly in leaves, through which CO_2 for photosynthesis is absorbed and transpired moisture lost.

Stone fruit Fruit with the seed or kernel surrounded by a hard endocarp (or stone) within the pulp or flesh; as a plum, peach, or cherry.

Storage organ Any plant part in which elaborated food materials are stored.

Strain Group of plants of common lineage that, although not taxonomically distinct from others of the species or variety, are distinguishable on the basis of ecological or physiological characteristics.

Stratification Method of storing seeds at a temperature between 35° and 45° F (2° and 7° C) in alternate layers or mixed in moist sand, peat moss, or other medium, as a means of overcoming physiological dormancy.

Strip sodding Laying of sod in strips separated by unsodded spaces.

Structural incompatibility Evolutionary adaptation to insure cross-pollination, in which the stigma and anthers of a plant are located in such a way that self-pollination does not occur.

Structure Natural arrangement of individual particles in soil into separate aggregates, various in form and size.

Style Part of the pistil that connects the ovary and stigma, through which the pollen tube grows to the ovule.

Suberization Healing of wounded plant tissue by formation of a corky layer.

Subspecies Group of individuals within a species, distinguished by certain common geographical or varietal characters.

Subtropical crop Crop that will take some freezing temperatures but will not survive in areas with a cold winter climate.

Succession cropping Growing of two or more crops, one after the other on the same land, in one growing season.

Succulent Juicy; plant having a high percentage of water.

Sucker Secondary shoot that develops from the root, crown, or stem of a plant; a rapid-growing upright vegetative shoot.

Summer fallowing System of farming where a crop is produced every other year; used primarily in dry regions where the moisture that falls on the soil during two seasons is needed to produce one crop.

Supercooling Phenomenon by which water kept absolutely motionless does not form ice crystals until the temperature falls several degrees below the freezing point.

Tap-root Stout, tapering main root from which arise smaller, lateral branch roots.

T (shield) budding Bud grafting by insertion of a bud of a specified variety, with an attached segment of bark and wood in the shape of a shield, into an opening in the bark of a stem or branch of a different stock. The opening in the bark of the stem is a T-shaped cut.

Taxon (Taxa) Categories in a plant classification system.

Temperate zone crop Crop able to adapt so that it survives temperatures considerably below the freezing point.

Temperature-induced hardiness Cold hardiness of plants native to the temperate zones that develops only if the plant is subjected to below-freezing temperatures.

Temperature inversion Condition in the atmosphere in which the temperature rises with increased elevation.

Terminal bud Bud that develops at the end of a branch or stem.

Terracing Construction of a raised, level area of earth supported on one side by a wall, bank, etc.; as a terraced yard.

Terrarium Tightly fitted, glass-enclosed, indoor garden, resembling an aquarium, in which plants are grown in rooting medium.

Tetraploid Organism whose cells contain four haploid (monoploid) sets of chromosomes.

Texture Relative proportion in a soil of the various size groups of individual soil grains. The coarseness or fineness of the soil depends on the predominance of one or the other of these groups, which are silt, clay, and sand.

Thatch Dry layer of organic matter at the soil surface in a lawn.

Thinning out Removal of an entire shoot or branch.

Tilling Cultivating land.

Tissue Group of organized plant cells that perform a specific function.

Tissue culture Growing detached pieces of tissue in nutrient solutions under sterile conditions; an important research tool and method of propagation for some plants.

Topiary Shrubs that have been clipped and trained into ornamental but unnatural shapes.

Topworking Top grafting; changing the cultivar of an old tree by graftage.

Tracheophyta Division of the plant kingdom containing plants with vascular (xylem and phloem) tissue, such as ferns and seed plants.

Training Directing the growth of a plant to a desired shape by pruning while young or fastening the stem and branches to a support.

Translocation Movement of a substance, such as water or an herbicide, from one part of a plant to another.

Transpiration Loss of water from plant tissues in the form of vapor.

Trashy fallowing Soil management procedure in which the soil is stirred but dried weeds, stubble, and other debris are left as a mulch to protect fine soil particles from erosion.

Trickle irrigation System of irrigation in which a constant drip of water is supplied.

Triple fusion Union in the embryo sac of the two polar nuclei and a male nucleus; the starting point for the development of the endosperm.

Triploid Having three times the haploid number of chromosomes.

Tropical crop Crop that originated in tropical areas of the Earth; subject to cold injury at temperatures considerably above the freezing point.

Tube nucleus The nongenerative nucleus in a pollen-tube; probably plays a part in regulating the development and behavior of that organ.

Tuber Enlarged, fleshy, usually terminal portion of a rhizome, bearing "eyes" or buds.

Tuberous root Enlarged root that tapers toward both ends, as in dahlia and sweet potato.

Tuberous stem Enlarged stem located between the regular stem and the roots; enlarges each year.

Tunica Dry, protective cover surrounding a tunicate bulb.

Tunicate bulb Bulb in which the fleshy scales are in continuous, concentric layers. Has a dry and membranous outer covering that protects the bulb. Examples are onion and tulip bulbs.

Ultraviolet Portion of the spectrum composed of light waves just shorter than violet light. It is used in irradiation, disinfection, and sterilization.

Unavailable (hygroscopic) water Water held by the soil below the wilting point.

Vacuole Cavity within the protoplasm containing a solution of sugars, salts, pigments, etc., together with colloidal materials.

Variety Subdivision of a species. Horticultural variety is synonymous with cultivar.

Vascular bundle Strandlike portion of the vascular tissue of a plant, composed of xylem and phloem.

Vase (open center) system System of training in which the central leader is cut off 18 to 30 inches (45 to 75 cm) from the ground, and two or three side branches become the scaffolds and spread to form the framework of the tree.

Vegetable 1. Crop plant that produces food which requires little refinement before being consumed (in contrast to agronomic crops), and which is generally eaten with the entree or as a salad rather than as a dessert (in contrast to fruits). 2. The food produced by such a crop.

Vegetative Growth, tissues, or processes concerned with maintenance of the plant body; contrasted with tissues or activities involved in sexual reproduction.

Vegetative phase Stage in the growth of a plant when food resources are directed primarily to the growth of leaves, stems, and roots.

Vegetative (asexual) propagation Reproduction by plant parts other than seed of the parent plant.

Vein Vascular bundle forming a part of the framework of the conducting and supporting tissue of a leaf or other expanded organ.

Vermiculite Mineral or minerals, classified with the micas, which, with treatment at high temperatures, expand into wormlike scales and become a loose, absorbent mass. Commercial vermiculite is used as a mulch for seed beds, as a medium for rooting plant cuttings, and in potting plants.

Viable Able to live. In plant science the term *viability* is frequently used in conjunction with seed and connotes survivability and vigor of the seedling, as well as the ability to germinate.

Vine crop Plant of the family Cucurbitaceae, such as cucumber, squash, pumpkin.

Virus Self-reproducing agent that is considerably smaller than a bacterium and can multiply only within the living cells of a suitable host. Often severely damages or kills the host.

Viticulture Art and science of growing grapes.

Warm-season crop Crop, usually of tropical origin, that is killed as soon as temperatures drop slightly below freezing.

Water stress Physiological disorder of plants (usually manifested by wilting) due to a lack of water.

Whorl 1. Three or more leaves or branches at a node. 2. Circle of floral organs, such as a whorl of sepals or stamens.

Wilted Lacking turgidity, drooping, or shriveling of plant tissue usually due to a deficiency of water.

Wilting point Stage in soil moisture depletion where a plant is unable to take additional moisture from the soil and, as a consequence, becomes wilted.

Windbreak Object that serves as an obstacle to free movement of surface winds; most frequently refers to rows of trees that serve that purpose.

Wounding Practice of making wounds in the basal end of a cutting to stimulate rooting.

Xeriscape Landscapes for arid regions planted to drought tolerant plants that require little or no irrigation.

Xylem One of the two component tissues of vascular tissue; primarily responsible for transporting water and mineral nutrients from the roots.

Conversion Tables

Temperature

Fahrenheit (°F)	to Celsius (°C)	Celsius (°C)	to Fahrenheit (°F)
−40	−40	−40	−40
−35	−37	−35	−31
−30	−34	−30	−22
−25	−32	−25	−13
−20	−29	−20	− 4
−15	−26	−15	5
−10	−23	−10	14
− 5	−21	− 5	23
0	−18	0	32
5	−15	5	41
10	−12	10	50
15	− 9	15	59
20	− 7	20	68
25	− 4	25	77
30	− 1	30	86
32	0	35	95
35	2	40	104
40	4	50	122
45	7	60	140
50	10	70	158
55	13	80	176
60	16	90	194
65	18	100	212
68	20		
70	21		
75	24		
80	27		
85	29		
90	32		
95	35		
100	38		
120	49		
140	60		
160	71		
180	82		
200	93		
212	100		

Conversion formulas:
$C° = 5/9\,(F° - 32)$
$F° = (9/5\,C°) + 32$

Length

1 micrometer (micron)	=	0.001 millimeter
1 millimeter	=	0.001 meter
	=	0.0394 inch
1 centimeter	=	10 millimeters
	=	0.3937 inch
	=	0.01 meter
1 meter	=	39.37 inches
	=	3.281 feet
	=	1,000 millimeters
	=	100 centimeters
1 kilometer	=	3,281 feet
	=	1,094 yards
	=	0.621 mile
	=	1,000 meters
1 inch	=	25.4 millimeters
	=	2.54 centimeters
1 foot	=	30.48 centimeters
	=	0.3048 meter
	=	12 inches
1 yard	=	0.9144 meter
	=	91.44 centimeters
	=	3 feet
1 mile	=	1,609.347 meters
	=	1.609 kilometers
	=	5,280 feet
	=	1,760 yards

Area

1 square centimeter	=	0.155 sq inch
	=	100 sq millimeters
1 square meter	=	1,550 sq inches
	=	10.764 sq feet
	=	1.196 sq yards
	=	10,000 sq centimeters
1 square kilometer	=	0.3861 sq mile
	=	1,000,000 sq meters
1 hectare	=	2.471 acres
	=	10,000 sq meters
1 square inch	=	6.452 sq centimeters
	=	1/144 sq foot
	=	1/1296 sq yard
1 square foot	=	929.088 sq centimeters
	=	0.0929 sq meter
1 square yard	=	8,361.3 sq centimeters
	=	0.8361 sq meter
	=	1,296 sq inches
	=	9 sq feet
1 square mile	=	2.59 sq kilometers
	=	640 acres
1 acre	=	0.4047 hectare
	=	43,560 sq feet
	=	4,840 sq yards
	=	4,046.87 sq meters

Weight

1 milligram	=	0.001 gram
	=	0.0154 grain
1 centigram	=	0.01 gram
	=	0.1543 grain
1 gram	=	0.0353 avoirdupois ounce
	=	15.4324 grains
1 kilogram	=	1,000 grams
	=	353 avoirdupois ounces
	=	2.2046 avoirdupois pounds
1 metric ton	=	1,000 kilograms
	=	2,204.6 pounds
	=	1.102 short tons (U.S.)
	=	0.984 long ton (British)
1 grain	=	1/7000 avoirdupois pound
	=	0.064799 gram
1 ounce (avoirdupois)	=	28.3496 grams
	=	437.5 grains
	=	1/16 pound
1 pound (avoirdupois)	=	453.593 grams
	=	0.45369 kilograms
	=	16 ounces
1 short on	=	907.184 kilograms
	=	0.9072 metric ton
	=	2,000 pounds

Yield

1 kilogram per 100 sq meters	=	2.05 pounds per 1,000 sq ft
1 kilogram per hectare	=	0.89 pound per acre
1 cubic meter per hectare	=	14.2916 cubic feet per acre
1 pound per 1,000 sq ft	=	0.488 kilograms per 100 sq meters
1 pound per acre	=	1.121 kilograms per hectare
1 ton (2,000 lb) per acre	=	2.242 metric tons per hectare
1 cubic foot per acre	=	0.0699 cubic meter per hectare
1 bushel (60 lb) per acre	=	67.26 kilograms per hectare

Volume

1 liter	=	1.057 U.S. quarts liquid	1 quart dry	=	1.1012 liters
	=	0.9081 quart, dry		=	67.20 cubic inches
	=	0.2642 U.S. gallon		=	2 pints (dry)
	=	0.221 Imperial gallon		=	0.125 peck
	=	1,000 milliliters or cc		=	1/32 bushel
	=	0.0353 cubic foot	1 cubic inch	=	16.387 cubic centimeters
	=	61.02 cubic inches			
	=	0.001 cubic meter	1 cubic foot	=	28,317 cubic centimeters
				=	0.0283 cubic meter
1 cubic meter	=	61,023.38 cubic inches		=	28.316 liters
	=	35.314 cubic feet		=	7.481 U.S. gallons
	=	1.308 cubic yards		=	1.728 cubic inches
	=	264.17 U.S. gallons			
	=	1,000 liters	1 U.S. gallon	=	16 cups
	=	28.38 U.S. bushels		=	3.785 liters
	=	1,000,000 cu centimeters		=	231 cubic inches
	=	1,000,000,000 cu millimeters		=	4 U.S. quarts liquid
				=	8 U.S. pints liquid
1 fluid ounce	=	6 teaspoons		=	8.3453 pounds of water
	=	2 tablespoons		=	128 fluid ounces
	=	1/128 gallon		=	0.8327 British Imperial gallon
	=	29.57 cubic centimeters			
	=	29.562 milliliters	1 British Imperial gallon	=	4.546 liters
	=	1.805 cubic inches		=	1.201 U.S. gallons
	=	0.0625 U.S. pint (liquid)		=	277.42 cubic inches
1 U.S. quart liquid	=	946.3 milliliters			
	=	57.75 cubic inches	1 U.S. bushel	=	35.24 liters
	=	32 fluid ounces		=	2,150.42 cubic inches
	=	4 cups		=	1.2444 cubic feet
	=	1/4 gallon		=	0.03524 cubic meter
	=	2 U.S. pints (liquid)		=	2 pecks
	=	0.946 liter		=	32 quarts (dry)
				=	64 pints (dry)

(From Janick, J., Schery, R. W., Woods, F. W., and Ruttan, V. W. *Plant Science*, 2nd ed. W. H. Freeman and Company, San Francisco. Copyright © 1974.)

Index

See tables (t) indexed under fruits, ornamentals, and vegetables for further information on specific crops and for a tabular description of plants not listed in the index. References to illustrations are designated (f).